Interpreting Canada's Past

J.M. Bumsted

Interpreting Canada's Past

Volume One
Pre~Confederation

Second Edition

Toronto

OXFORD UNIVERSITY PRESS

1993

Oxford University Press, 70 Wynford Drive, Don Mills, Ontario M3C 1J9

Toronto   Oxford   New York
Delhi   Bombay   Calcutta   Madras   Karachi   Kuala Lumpur
Singapore   Hong Kong   Tokyo   Nairobi   Dar es Salaam
Cape Town   Melbourne   Auckland   Madrid

and associated companies in
Berlin   Ibadan

This book is printed on permanent (acid-free) paper ⊖.

Canadian Cataloguing in Publication Data

Main entry under title:

Interpreting Canada's past

2nd ed.
Includes bibliographical references.
Contents: v. 1. Before confederation. — v. 2. After
confederation.
ISBN 0-19-540946-9 (v. 1) ISBN 0-19-540947-7 (v. 2.)

1. Canada — History. 2. Canada — Social conditions.
I. Bumsted, J. M., 1938–

FC170.I58 1993   971   C93-093566-7
F1026.I57 1993

Maps on pages 5, 16, 112, 115, 368, 552 by Visutronx
Copyright © Oxford University Press Canada, 1993
OXFORD is a trademark of Oxford University Press
1 2 3 4 – 96 95 94 93
Printed in Canada

Contents

~~~~

Acknowledgements

R. ARTHUR BOWLER. 'Propaganda in Upper Canada in the War of 1812', *American Review of Canadian Studies*, 18:1 (1988). Reprinted by permission of the American Review of Canadian Studies.

J.M. BUMSTED and WENDY OWEN. 'The Victorian Family in Canada in Historical Perspective: The Ross Family of Red River and the Jarvis Family of Prince Edward Island', *Manitoba History* 13 (Spring 1987). Reprinted by permission of the Manitoba Historical Society.

BÉATRICE CRAIG. 'Agriculture and the Lumberman's Frontier in the Upper St. John Valley, 1800–1870', *Journal of Forest History* 32 (July 1988), 125–37. Reprinted by permission of the Forest History Society, Inc.

IAN E. DAVEY. 'The Rhythm of Work and the Rhythm of School' in Neil McDonald and Alf Chaiton, eds, *Egerton Ryerson and His Times: Essays in the History of Education* (Macmillan, 1979).

W.J. ECCLES. 'The Fur Trade and Eighteenth-Century Imperialism', *William and Mary Quarterly* 40 (1983). Reprinted by permission of the author.

JUDITH FINGARD. 'The Relief of the Unemployed Poor in Saint John, Halifax, and St. John's, 1815–1860', *Acadiensis* V,1 (1975). Reprinted by permission of *Acadiensis* and the author.

ROBIN FISHER. 'British Columbia and the Indians: The Transitional Years, 1849–1888', *Contact and Conflict: Indian-European Relations in British Columbia, 1744–1890* (1970). Reprinted by permission of the University of British Columbia Press.

TIMOTHY FOOTE. 'Europe in the Age of "Discovery", 1450–1500' [originally entitled 'Where Columbus was Coming From'], *Smithsonian Magazine* (Dec. 1991). Used by permission of the author.

ALLAN GREER. 'Mutiny at Louisbourg, December 1744', *Histoire Sociale/Social History* 10 (1977), 305–36. Reprinted by permission of *Histoire Sociale/Social History*.

R. COLE HARRIS. 'The French Background of Immigrants to Canada Before 1700'. Reprinted by permission of the author.

ELIZABETH HOPKINS. 'A Prison-House for Prosperity: The Immigrant Experience of the Nineteenth-Century Upper-Class British Woman', from Jean Burnet, ed., *Looking Into My Sister's Eyes: An Exploration in Women's History*, Toronto: Multicultural History Society of Ontario, 1986. Reprinted by permission of the publisher.

CORNELIUS J. JAENEN. 'Characteristics of French-Amerindian Contact in New France' in Stanley H. Palmer and Dennis Reinhartz, eds, *Essays on the History of North American Discovery and Exploration* (1988). Used by permission of the Walter Prescott Webb Memorial Lectures Committee, The University of Texas at Arlington.

GWYN JONES. 'The First Europeans in America', *The Beaver* 295 (Winter 1964). Used by permission of the author.

STEVEN LANGDON. 'The Emergence of the Canadian Working-Class Movement, 1845–1867', *Journal of Canadian Studies* vol. 8, no. 2. Reprinted by permission of the *Journal of Canadian Studies*.

J.I. LITTLE. 'The Social and Economic Development of Settlers in Two Quebec Townships, 1851–1870', *Canadian Papers in Rural History* i, 89–101. Reprinted by permission of Canadian Papers in Rural History.

DOUGLAS MCCALLA. 'The Wheat Staple and Upper Canadian Development', *Canadian Historical Association Historical Papers*, 1978. Reprinted by permission of the author and the Canadian Historical Association.

PHILLIP MCCANN 'Culture, State Formation and the Invention of Tradition: Newfoundland 1832–1855', *Journal of Canadian Studies* 23 (Spring/Summer 1980). Reprinted by permission of the *Journal of Canadian Studies*.

ROBERT MCGHEE. 'The Vinland Map: Hoax or History?', *The Beaver* 67,2 (April–May 1987). Reprinted by permission of the author.

CALVIN MARTIN. 'The European Impact on the Culture of a Northeastern Algonquian Tribe: An Ecological Interpretation'. This article first appeared in *William and Mary Quarterly*. Reprinted by permission of the author.

GED MARTIN. 'Painting the Other Picture: The Case Against Canadian Confederation'. Reprinted by permission of the author.

W. THOMAS MATTHEWS. 'The Myth of the Peaceable Kingdom: Upper Canadian Society During the Early Victorian Period', *Queen's Quarterly* 94,2 (Summer 1987). Reprinted by permission of *Queen's Quarterly* and the author.

PETER N. MOOGK. 'Les Petits Sauvages: The Children of Eighteenth-Century New France' from *Childhood and Family in Canadian History* by Joy Parr. Used by permission of the Canadian Publishers, McClelland & Stewart, Toronto.

W.L. MORTON. 'British North America and a Continent in Dissolution, 1861–1871', *History* XLVIII (1962). Reprinted by permission of The Historical Association.

MARY BETH NORTON. 'Eighteenth-Century American Women in Peace and War: The Case of the Loyalists', *William and Mary Quarterly* 33 (1976). Reprinted by permission of the author.

FERNAND OUELLET. 'The 1837/8 Rebellion in Lower Canada as a Social Phenomenon', *Histoire Sociale/Social History* 2 (1968). Reprinted by permission of *Histoire Sociale/Social History*.

MICHAEL PAYNE and GREGORY THOMAS. 'Literacy, Literature and Libraries in the Fur Trade', *The Beaver* 63 (Spring 1983). Reprinted by permission of the author.

JAMES S. PRITCHARD. 'The Voyage of the *Fier*: An Analysis of a Shipping and Trading Venture to New France, 1724–1728', *Histoire Sociale/Social History* (April 1973). Used by permission of *Histoire Sociale/Social History*.

JOHN G. REID. 'The 1600s: Decade of Colonization' from *Six Crucial Decades: Times of Change in the History of the Maritimes* (Nimbus Publishing, 1987). Reprinted by permission of the publisher.

IAN ROSS ROBERTSON. 'Highlanders, Irishmen, and the Land Question in Nineteenth-Century Prince Edward Island'. Reprinted by permission of the author.

ARTHUR I. SILVER. 'Conferation and Quebec' from *The French-Canadian Idea of Confederation 1864–1900* by A.I. Silver. Reprinted by permission of the University of Toronto Press.

DONALD B. SMITH. 'The Dispossession of the Mississauga Indians: A Missing Chapter in the Early History of Upper Canada', *Ontario History* 73,2 (1981), 67–87. Reprinted by permission of The Ontario Historical Society.

PETER J. SMITH. 'The Ideological Origins of Canadian Confederation', *Canadian Journal of Political Science* 20,1 (March 1987). Reprinted by permission of the author and The Canadian Political Science Association.

DAVID RICARDO WILLIAMS. 'The Administration of Criminal and Civil Justice in the Mining Camps and Frontier Communities of British Columbia'. Reprinted by permission of the author.

GRAEME WYNN. 'A Region of Scattered Settlements and Bounded Possibilities: Northeastern America 1775–1800', *The Canadian Geographer* 31, 4 (1987). Reprinted by permission of The Canadian Association of Geographers.

Preface

The past few years have seen some profound changes in the writing and interpretation of Canadian history, in both the subjects being explored and the methodologies and conceptualizations used to illuminate them. Canadian historians have been asking new questions and investigating new subjects and at the same time examining old themes, such as the fur trade and political development, from new perspectives. While it is most stimulating, the new history often does not fit easily into the traditional patterns of Canadian historical scholarship. Teachers of Canadian history who wish to introduce the new history to undergraduate students find that much of the best scholarship is inaccessible both physically and intellectually to neophyte historians. This collection of readings, concentrating on early Canada up to and including the period of Confederation, represents one attempt to address this problem.

While Canadian historians have not on the whole been given to explicit theorizing, it is plain that new developments and a new methodology inform much of the scholarship of the past decade. Conceptually one direction has been towards the recognition of the complexities of economic and social structures within Canada. A generation ago the study of social class was regarded as one of the greatly neglected areas of Canadian historical scholarship. Today nearly all Canadian historical analysis owes some debt to Marxism, although not all historians would agree on the results. Along with studies of economic and social structure has come a corresponding emphasis on previously neglected elements of the population, such as women and native peoples. Also important over the past few years has been the influence of the international trend toward cultural studies, in which cultural matters are explored in ways that go well beyond the traditional query, 'Is there a Canadian Culture?'.

The study of society and its cultural manifestations requires the generation of evidence drawn not only from literary sources (letters, diaries, etc.) but from such non-literary sources as legal records, vital statistics, and census data. Cultural studies have encouraged the use of various theories of language and textual analysis in dealing with artifacts previously not regarded as important. As scholarship has turned increasingly to a study of those people once thought to be on the margin of Canadian society, and often relatively inarticulate, the importance of new sorts of evidence and of new ways of examining old evidence became apparent. The computer has made possible the collection of much new data, but quantification has not been the only new technique employed, and many of the essays in this collection testify to the possibility of non-quantitative production of new evidence, often by reading the old with fresh eyes.

Not surprisingly, many of the new practitioners in the Canadian historical enterprise are associated with disciplines outside traditional history. Indeed the expansion of historical scholarship, as well as the teaching of history outside departments of history, have been major developments in recent years. At almost any Canadian university, courses in Canadian history—albeit with a specialized focus—are taught in departments of economics, geography, law, and women's studies, among other locations. I hope this collection proves of value in such courses as well as in the standard Canadian history surveys normally offered in history departments.

As well as expanding historical horizons with new questions and new empirical techniques, recent Canadian scholarship has greatly extended the geographical scope of investigation. Much of the best and most innovative work of the past few years has focused on regions and localities peripheral to the central Canadian heartland, and no compilation that ignores the resurgence of local and regional historiography, or the excellent work being done on these regions, can satisfactorily reflect the present state of scholarship. Studies of both the Atlantic region and the West are well represented within these pages, not as any concession to regional sensibilities but because, to a considerable extent, they have been on the frontiers of current scholarship.

One basic assumption underlying this book is that teachers of courses in Canadian history are already providing for their students a broad chronological and interpretative framework and covering adequately familiar ground. Introductory courses, almost by definition, must consider the traditional issues that have concerned scholars for generations, and each instructor has no doubt worked out an acceptable approach to these standard historiographical questions. The predecessor of this collection received some notoriety on the editorial page of one of Canada's leading newspapers not very long ago, when it was attacked for not providing adequate coverage of the battles of World War II. The critic, who was an academic, ought to have known better. But it is worth emphasizing here that this collection is not a survey text, but a supplementary collection of recent writings in Canadian history—most of them either implicitly or explicitly revisionist—that will introduce students to insightful discussions about traditional and current scholarly issues. The selections range widely, and however unexpected some of them may be, all have been selected for their potential utility in a typical introductory course in Canadian history, and in some cases also for the provocative arguments they raise.

In preparing this volume one other criterion for selection has been absolutely critical. One of the ironies of modern Canadian history is that research intended to get beyond traditional male élites engaged in traditional male élite activities—chiefly politics and war—to topics appropriate for all Canadians has lost contact with its audience. Historians have become increasingly specialized in vocabulary and narrow in focus, filling the pages of learned journals with articles for fellow specialists, not the average Canadian reader. I have thus attempted to select only work that addresses the larger audience of informed Canadians, of which students in our introductory courses are representative.

Obviously no two people would choose the same set of selections. I hope that the one I have made here will prove not only broadly representative of the best (and mainly recent) scholarship on early Canada, but illuminating and accessible as well.

J.M. BUMSTED
St John's College
University of Manitoba

I

European Intrusions,

Aboriginal Peoples,

Early Settlements

1

The First Europeans in America

Gwyn Jones

While historians have come to appreciate that the very notion of 'discovering' America is profoundly Eurocentric—for the American continents had long been inhabited by native peoples who had no particular need to be 'discovered'—the debate over the achievements of various early European explorers and voyagers continues, particularly for the period before Christopher Columbus and John Cabot. Much of the discussion now attempts to understand how much impact pre-Columbian visitors may have had in the Americas and how much knowledge Europeans had of the vast region before the explosion of western voyages in the late fifteenth century.

Of all the pre-Columbian candidates, the strongest case can be made out for the Vikings, those great Scandinavian warriors and mariners of the Middle Ages. The Vikings indisputably settled Iceland and Greenland in the North Atlantic before 1000 A.D., and evidence from a variety of sources, including Viking literary remains and recent archaeological excavations in Newfoundland, support Viking claims to further settlement in a new land west of Greenland. The following selections explore the problem of Viking impact in two different areas.

In 'The First Europeans in America', Gwyn Jones contrasts the substantial record of Viking voyaging in the North Atlantic with the evidence for a controversial theory that the Norse settlements of Greenland and further west blended with the native population to produce the Thule Eskimo culture. As with most scholarship dealing with the pre-Columbian period, Jones must attempt to distinguish fact from legend, no easy matter in a world of confused and often contradictory information. What sorts of assumptions does he make about the nature of the evidence? Why does he put 'the verities of Vinland' in a different category from the 'half-glimpsed possibilities of Norse activity north of latitude 64°N.'?

In his article on the so-called Vinland Map, Robert McGhee explores its authenticity and its meaning. The problem of forged documents substantiating revisionist theories is a common one in scholarship, and the peregrinations of the Vinland Map from authentic document to forgery back to respecta-bility are most illuminating about the process of authentification. Why has the Vinland Map been so controversial? Are McGhee's claims for the value of the 'Vinland configuration' convincing?

Finally, what conclusions would you reach about European activity in America in the years before Columbus and Cabot?

This article first appeared in *The Beaver* outfit 295 (Winter 1964), 37–44.

The Reconnaissance

The first European to sight the coast of North America, live to tell the tale, and have his story recorded for posterity, was a young Icelander named Bjarni Herjolfsson. But there were brave men before Agamemnon, and storm-driven mariners before Bjarni; and maybe in trireme or dromond, curach or knorr, some unremembered crew made an unrecorded voyage to New England or Newfoundland or the outer verges of Hudson Bay fifty, a hundred, or even a thousand years before Bjarni found America while looking for Greenland in the summer of 985 or 986. Since at least 2500 B.C. men had been sailing the western waterways of Europe. The megalith builders, Phoenicians and Greeks, Celts, Carthaginians and Romans, and the religious of Ireland and Brittany, Cornwall, Wales and Strathclyde, were all busy sailors for whom great claims have rightly been made. But if any of them made an Atlantic crossing posterity knows nothing of it. The Irish are the likeliest candidates, but all the patriotism and ingenuity of the world have not reduced to credibility the whirling fantasies of Whitemen's Land or Ireland the Great, six days out in the ocean from Hibernia of the saints and princes; while as for the Welsh (a Welshman myself) I willingly leave Prince Madoc and the Welsh Indians, along with King Arthur's visitation of Greenland in A.D. 530 (when its inhabitants were 23 feet tall), to the misty dubiety from which they should never have emerged.

So our story opens with Bjarni Herjolfsson towards the end of the tenth century. Opens, that is, with the Norsemen. Starting from their continental homelands the Norwegians and Danes were by the end of the eighth century exploiting the possibilities of profit in the lands that lay west of them. In the 790s they were plundering in England and Wales, Scotland and Ireland. By 820 (to confine ourselves to their movement west) the Norwegians were occupying the Faeroes. In the 870s they reached Ireland and had settled the habitable parts of that country by 930. By 930 too they had sighted the east coast of Greenland, somewhere near Angmagssalik; and in 982 Eirik the Red went looking for habitable land there. He was of Norwegian stock, from Jaeren, but he and his father had been forced to leave Norway because of some killings. So they settled in the north of Iceland, at Drangar, a poorish, demanding farm, lying south of Hornbjarg, the North Cape. Eirik was always an awkward and ambitious neighbour, and after some further killings he was banished from Iceland for three years in 982. Once more he left his country for his country's good, sailed west on the 65th parallel, and having reached the inhospitable east Greenland coast headed south in search of prospects more genial. But it was only after he had cleared Cape Farewell and headed in a northerly direction up the western coast that he discovered what he was looking for. Between Herjolfsnes (Ikigait) and Eiriksfjord (Tunugdliarfik) he found himself traversing a noble archipelago with deep, life-teeming fiords to starboard, and inside these fiords when he entered them he saw long stretches of grass enamelling the rocky hillsides. For three years he explored the fiords and coastline of the southwest without nature's let or human hindrance, and when he returned to Iceland in 985 he called the country Greenland or the Green Land, believing that an attractive name and his private persuasion would be enough to lure land-hungry men to colonize it.

What happened now was of first importance for the Norse entry into the American continent. All the voyages of discovery and colonization to America of which the sagas have preserved any record were mounted from the Greenland settlements, and if there was any Norse penetration of the Canadian Arctic the starting point for this too must have been Greenland.

Before the year 1000, Norse settlers were strongly established in two places in Greenland. There was the so-called Eastern Settlement (Eystribyggd) in what is now the Julianehaab region, and the Western Settlement, around the modern Godthaab. The Eastern Settlement was the larger, numbering eventually 190 farms, 12 parish churches, a cathedral at Gardar (the modern Igaliko), an Augustine monastery and Benedictine nunnery. In the Western Settlement would be 90 farms and 4 churches; and the 20 farms, with no church, round Ivigtut are sometimes described as a Middle Settlement, sometimes as a northern offshoot of the Eastern. The population of the Greenland settlements, a determining factor for their future expansion north or west, is hard to calculate, but is unlikely to have exceeded 3,000.

The question is sometimes asked: Why did the Norsemen settle in Greenland? Why did they ever go to such a place? But there is no puzzle. They went because they wanted land, and more especially grassland. They were animal-husbandmen, stock-farmers, in need of new pastures, such as were to be found in fair abundance inside the fiords of the southwest. No one today can sail up Eiriksfjord or past Julianehaab to the church at Hvalsey (Kakortoq) without understanding how strong a pull their often grassy slopes

Norse voyages to the West

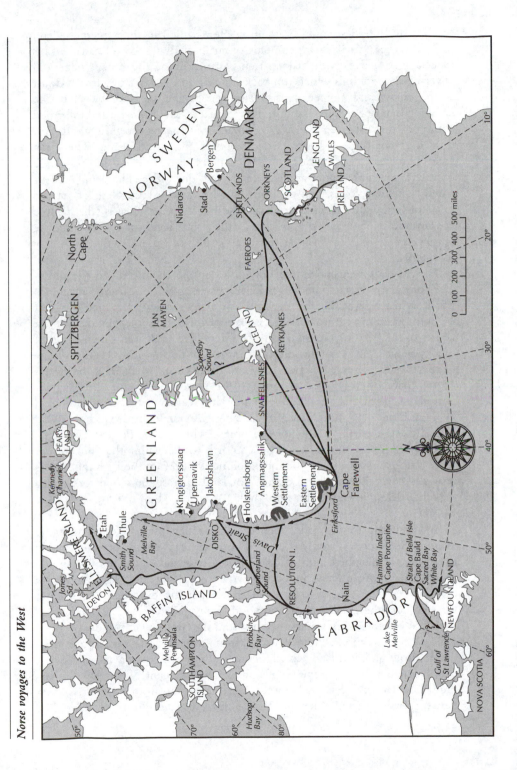

and verdant hillsides would exert upon men baffled in their quest for land back in Iceland. Eirik's own complex of farms at Brattahlid (Qagssiarssuk) is especially attractive, with its long rich pastures lining the water's edge and covering the low hills which run back mile upon mile, spattered with dwarf birch, willow, and juniper, dark streams and bright lakes, right over to the icy splendour of Sermilik-Isafjord. 'It is reported,' says the wise and informed author of the 13th century *King's Mirror*, 'that the pasturage is good, and that there are large and fine farms in Greenland.' And again, 'The earth yields good and fragrant grass. . . . The farmers raise cattle and sheep in large numbers, and make butter and cheese in great quantities. The people subsist chiefly on these foods, and on beef; but they also eat the flesh of various kinds of game, such as reindeer, whales, seals, and bears. That is what people live on in that country.' And, of course, the fish that fill the fiords. After the bitter famine of 976 such abundance would prove irresistible to many Icelanders.

The Norse Greenlanders did not long confine themselves to the grassy oases of the southwest. The fast-gathering wave of Norse seaborne adventure was now reaching its height, and in so far as its movement was to the west it could not in the nature of things slacken or die before it lapped the farthest verges of the Atlantic Ocean. From the Greenland settlements men could in theory progress in every direction but it did not take long for them to learn of the barrier presented eastwards by the Inland Ice. 'Men,' says the *King's Mirror*, 'have often tried to go up into the country and climb the highest mountains in various places to look about and learn whether any land could be found that was ice-free and inhabitable. But nowhere have they found such a place, except what is now occupied, which is a little strip along the water's edge.' So first they would press north to determine the limits of the 'little strip', and then they would be looking west. From the high mountains near the coast they could discern if not land at least the cloud formations they had learnt to associate with land. Out west, they quickly knew, lay *something*.

But first, the route north. That the Norsemen pressed far beyond the Western Settlement is amply attested. The evidence is mainly but not entirely documentary. The best hunting grounds in Greenland lay north of the modern Holsteinsborg as far as the Nugussuaq peninsula beyond Disko, and these the Greenlanders quickly discovered and steadfastly exploited, for fishing, hunting, and the collection of driftwood. They called them the *Nordrsetr* or *-seta*, the Northern Encampment(s) or Hunting Ground(s). The discovery in 1824 by the Eskimo Pelimut of a small stone inscribed with runes in one of three cairns on the island Kingigtorssuaq, just north of Upernavik, shows that Norsemen, i.e., Europeans of Scandinavian descent, were close to latitude 73°N. in the year 1333. In 1267 an expedition from the Eastern Settlement had reached Melville Bay, almost at the 76th parallel. 'The

Greenlanders,' it is recorded in the *Graenlandsannall* of Bjorn Jonsson, which we believe to be based on old and trustworthy sources, 'must constantly sail north to the uninhabited areas at the northern land's end or peninsula, both for wood and for procuring game. The regions there are called Greipar and Kroksfjardarheidi. It is a long and arduous course, as the saga of Skald-Helgi clearly shows. The following lines are composed about these voyages: 'Heroes went to Greipar, which is the end of the settlement of Greenland.' And at Greipar (probably north of Holsteinsborg), Kroksfjardarheidi (near Disko), Upernavik and Melville Bay, we may for the moment leave them, while we shift our gaze westward across Davis Strait and Baffin Bay to the islands and peninsulas of arctic Canada.

The Norsemen in the Canadian Arctic

The theory that the Norsemen, their blood and culture, are part of the medieval history of arctic Canada is a two-pronged one. Both prongs depend on what we know, or imagine, to be the facts of the rise and fall of the Norse settlements in Greenland, especially in relationship to the non-European peoples they encountered. Ari Thorgilsson, the most respected and reliable of twelfth-century Icelandic historians, tells us that when the Norsemen entered Greenland towards the end of the tenth century they found there traces of an earlier and, as they judged, non-European occupation. 'Both east and west in the country [i.e., presumably at both the Eastern and Western Settlements] they found the habitations of men, fragments of boats [? *keiplabrot*], and stone artifacts, from which it may be seen that the same kind of people had passed that way as those that inhabited Vinland, whom the Greenlanders call Skraelings' (*Islendingabok, c.* 1125). But the Skraelings themselves they did not find. 'Skraeling' was the name applied by the Norsemen to everyone of non-European race encountered west of Iceland. It stood for both Indian and Eskimo, whatever their kind and culture. The Skraelings whose traces were found in the southwest are thought to be Eskimos of the Dorset Culture, who had long since disappeared from the area. Documentary evidence attests that the Norse Greenlanders were again in contact with Skraelings about the middle of the 13th century, somewhere north of Disko, and these we call Eskimos of the Thule Culture. By the 1340s we hear on the authority of Ivar Bardarson that 'the Skraelings hold the entire Western Settlement,' and while the reasons for the Settlement's disappearance or extermination have been much debated the fact itself is incontestable. In its turn the Eastern Settlement came to an end *c.* 1500, but here too we have neither a clear nor a detailed picture of what happened.

One view is that the Norse settlements in Greenland remained white, Norse, European and Christian to the end, and that their end came about for a complex of reasons, among which the encroaching Eskimos, climatic change, and the difficulty of maintaining communication with Europe were the most important. First the Western and then the Eastern Settlement ceased to be viable and failed to survive. Another view is that the Norse Green-landers became so blended with the native population of Skraelings that they ceased to be white, Norse, European and Christian, and their disappearance from the Western Settlement in about 1340 and from the Eastern Settlement some 160 years later is because they migrated westwards to the adjacent parts of Canada. Both views have lent themselves to variation and refinement and to prolonged discussion. The importance of the second in the context of the present article is that it stakes a claim for a Norse or rather Eskimo-Norse entry into Canada by the mid-14th century, and offers a pre-emptive expla-nation for all such highly debatable phenomena as rectangular houses, bear-traps, cairns, eider-duck walls, boat-houses, iron nails and knives, cor-respondences of vocabulary, tall or blond Eskimos, whenever and wherever found in the Canadian Arctic. But even if we accept it, and buttress it with the often-quoted but in its religious assertions demonstrably inaccurate entry for 1342 in the Icelandic Annals of Bishop Gisli Oddsson (written in Latin *c.* 1637), that 'The inhabitants of Greenland of their own will abandoned the true faith and the Christian religion, having already forsaken all good ways and true virtues, and went over to the people of America (*ad Americae populos se converterunt*)'—even if we do this, and beg the entire question of what the Bishop meant by 'the people of America' (whether for example, he meant like Ari before him *skraelingas*), we are left at best with a curiously inconclusive parenthesis in the history of the Canadian Arctic, and an unnat-ural dying fall to the history of Norse expansion west.

Which brings us to the second prong of the theory concerning the Norse entry into Canada, as it is advanced by Jon Duason in his *Landkonnun og Landnam Islendinga i Vesturheimi* (Reykjavik, 1941–47, dealing with the pre-Columbian explorations and settlements of the Icelanders in the western hemisphere), and by Tryggvi Oleson in the first volume of the Canadian Centenary Series, *Early Voyages and Northern Approaches, 1000–1632* (Toronto, 1963).

Their argument, briefly (and I draw it from Professor Oleson's book as the one immediately available to English-language readers), is that as soon as the Icelanders were settled in the southwestern districts of Greenland they began to make voyages farther afield: to the east coast, which need not concern us; northwards as far as Inglefield Land and Kennedy Channel; and west to Ellesmere, Devon and Baffin Islands; also by way of Hudson Strait to the region round Melville Peninsula and Southampton Island, and possibly still farther into Hudson Bay. 'All these regions, although more particularly north Greenland, were known as Nordrseta. Labrador may have been included as voyages were frequently made there for timber' (p. 36). That the Norsemen made voyages to Baffin Island and Labrador we know from reliable Icelandic sources, both sagas and annals. That they voyaged to the other named Canadian territories is possible but hardly to be proved from the documents. A cautious reading of the literary and historical material would not place the 'northern land's end' of Greenland at Etah, but considerably farther south; and particularly when one considers the nomenclature and compass-bearings of the *Eastern* and *Western* Settlements it is hard to believe that Hudson Bay could be part of any *northern* camping grounds. For Labrador the objection is stronger still. Indeed Labrador (Markland, i.e., Wood Land) and Baffin Island (Helluland, Flatstone Land) seem specifically excluded both by name and definition from that area. It would, of course, be folly to argue that no Norse Greenlander (Oleson's term Icelander is unacceptable for the European inhabitants of Greenland after the immediate period of settlement: it is like calling Icelanders of the same period Norwegians) ever set foot on Devon Island or nosed his way into Foxe Basin. But unless the documents are interpreted with determined ingenuity they yield no evidence of it. Unlike the journeys north from the settlements to Holsteinsborg and Disko, to Upernavik and (once) to Melville Bay, and unlike the voyages west and thereafter south to Baffin Island, Labrador, Newfoundland, and possibly New England, the Norse entries into the waters and islands of northeastern Canada were too unrewarding, ill-fated, or generally unsustained to force themselves into the literary record. That courage, curiosity, greed, ambition, accident and plain misfortune carried Greenlanders over the water to Canada may be assumed; that the two cairns discovered in Jones Sound in latitude 76° 35′ N., and a further two on Washington Irving Island in latitude 79°, are proof of this, is a fair deduction; but that the explorers were few and their journeyings inconclusive in terms of settlement or trade seems all too clear. Norse wanderings north or west of Melville Bay, gallant and arduous though they must have been, provide meagre illumination today for the medieval history and geography of the North.

It is a feature of the Duason-Oleson thesis that it lays little or no stress on climatic conditions during the period 1000–1500. Yet this would seem central to the whole subject of the Norse Atlantic voyages and Norse acquaintance with the North American continent. For unless we accept some theory of climatic change, postulating a comparatively warm period around the year 1000, and a progressive deterioration after 1200, much of what all scholars regard as credible and authenticated in the vital Icelandic documents is not to be believed. Thus in modern conditions of ice (by no means the worst on record) Eirik the Red's voyages of exploration and settlement to Greenland, and those of Leif and Karlsefni to the Canadian coast, could just not have taken place at the time of year and in the directions in which we are told they did take place; while the evidence for worsening conditions of cold and drift ice after 1200 is both plentiful and picturesque in the mid-13th century *King's Mirror*, in Ivar Bardarson's celebrated mid-14th century

Description of Greenland, and in Abbot Arngrim Brandsson's description of Iceland and her surrounding waters of roughly the same date. Indeed to speak of a 'theory' of climatic change seems now out-of-date; the deterioration of the climate after 1200 would appear to be a fact; and the bearing of this on the Norsemen's exploitation of the Canadian Arctic, conservative as they were in their food, habits and clothing, needs no stressing, allied as it must be with the known circumstance of the loss or degeneration of their sea-going vessels.

Exploitation of the Arctic, that is, as Norsemen of the Viking Age. For it is the contention of Duason and Oleson that they made a striking contribution of yet another kind to arctic and sub-arctic history. In a sentence, that by intermixture with people of the Dorset Culture, with whom they found themselves in contact in the 11th and 12th centuries in Canada and Greenland, they were the direct ancestors of the Thule Eskimos. The idea is a startling one and contradictory of the generally held view of the Thule Eskimos as yet another Eskimo people who made their way from Alaska across the far north of Canada, and with Ellesmere Island as their final stepping stone crossed into the Thule region of Greenland shortly before the year 1200. It was the descendants of these Eskimos who, as the Inugsuk folk, proceeded in the centuries that followed to occupy the habitable portions of Greenland, including those held by the Norsemen. The Dorset Eskimos were a much older people, whose origins go back to the first millennium B.C. and who still existed at a date well after the Norse settlement of Greenland and the Vinland voyages of *c.* 1000. Their remains have been found in Newfoundland and Labrador and in many parts of the Canadian archipelago, including Melville Peninsula, in the Thule and Disko districts of Greenland, including the all-important dating site at Sermermiut near Jakobshavn, and in Peary Land and northeastern Greenland too. In a still remoter past they had been preceded by the Sarqaq Culture people. A fuller picture of Eskimo habitation in Greenland is possible, from Independence I. to Inugsuk (see Jens Rosing's convenient summary in *Bogen om Gronland*, Copenhagen, 1962, pp. 29–45), but is not here relevant, whereas a third name most decidedly is. Integral to the Duason-Oleson theory is the identity of the Tunit (Tunnit, Tornit). These have been identified as pre-Thule Eskimos, and more specifically as people of the Dorset Culture, as the creations of Eskimo folklore, and (Duason-Oleson) as 'Icelanders [read Norse Greenlanders] who for one reason or another found it more congenial or advisable to leave the farming districts and to adopt what we know as an Eskimo way of life, bringing to it, however, many of the features of the material culture of Scandinavia in the Middle Ages.'

Such information as we possess about the Tunit is often confused, not rarely contradictory, and always capable of different glosses and explanations. It offers at present only a shaky foundation for any theory of race and origin, and if a generally acceptable explanation emerges in the future it must come not from written sources but from archaeology and its ancillary sciences. At the moment the likeliest explanation of the Tunit is that they were the Dorset Eskimo, though the facts concerning them have become mingled with folktale and, at a late stage, with reminiscence of the Norse Greenlanders.

It is these same sciences, archaeology, anthropology, ethnology, which must effectually pronounce sentence on the theory that the fair gigantic Greenlanders and the dark dwarfish Skraeling (for the Duason–Oleson theory is a highly dramatic one, and some of its elements not unlike folktale itself) achieved so harmonious a miscegenation as to produce the Thule Eskimo, who therefore are to be considered not as a new wave of Eskimos moving across Canada from Alaska into Greenland but as Norse-Dorset hybrids moving east to west. Meantime a student of the literature ventures three observations. First, there is nothing in Scandinavian written or runic sources which lends unambiguous support to the Duason–Oleson theory, and much which contradicts it. Every reference to the apostasy of the Greenlanders and their 'going-over' to another way of life is capable of a different explanation, and one more in accord with what we know of late Greenlandic history. Second, from everything we know of the Scandinavians in Iceland and Greenland they were uncompromisingly tenacious of their family genealogies and their status as Europeans. Third, it would require the most compelling and incontrovertible evidence to make one believe that within a period of less than two centuries a fair proportion of Norse Greenlanders could depart the settlements, produce a hybrid race, and that this race could subsequently inherit the colonies of the fellow-countrymen of these same Norse Greenlanders, with apparently no one on either side aware of their blood-tie and family relationship. But as reference to the literature of the subject shows, the evidence, whether archaeological, anthropological, or linguistic, far from being incontrovertible, has been and still is the subject of keen debate and sharp division. One wonders too where the Norse women came into all this. In the present state of knowledge the mildest verdict possible upon the Duason-Oleson thesis is 'Not Proven'.

The Vinland Voyages

From these half-glimpsed possibilities of Norse activity north of latitude 64°N. we turn to the verities of Vinland. That men from Greenland and from Iceland by way of Greenland made voyages that brought them to southern Baffin Island, to Labrador and Newfoundland, and maybe farther south is a plain matter of record. These voyages are well documented and accord with everything we know of Norse maritime and colonial practice during the great age of Viking expansion west. The two main documents are Icelandic, *The Greenlanders' Saga (Groenlendinga Saga)* and *Eirik the Red's Saga (Eiriks Saga Rauda)*, and we begin by determining their authority.

The Greenlanders' Saga (GS) was probably first written down about 1200, and *Eirik the Red's Saga (ESR)* some seventy years later. *ESR* exists in two versions, which tell the same story with the same order of events, but with frequent and sometimes considerable differences of wording. Both *GS* and *ESR* contain varying amounts of matter which can be described as fictional, whether its origins lie in legend, folklore, ecclesiastical propaganda, pseudo-learning and the like, or in the saga writer's desire to give shape to his material; but in their essentials, even so, they are repositories of genuine tradition and reputable history. In the light of everything learnt during the last thirty-five years about the art and practice of saga-writing, our ability to distinguish history, tradition, legend, folktale, one from the other has become much increased, and our awareness of the processes of deviation, accretion, sources and influences, reinterpretation, misunderstanding and change of emphasis much sharpened. In particular we are better informed as to the historicity of individual sagas. In the case of *GS* and *ESR* there are features and circumstances still unclear; but it requires a violent eccentricity to deny that voyages to Vinland took place and that we have gone a long way towards identifying many of the places reached.

Which brings us again to Bjarni Herjolfsson and the late tenth century. For according to *GS* it was this young man who, seeking Greenland in 985–86, was first swept off course, then beset by wind and fog, till after many days' uncertainty his crew beheld the hitherto unknown eastern coast of Canada. *ESR*, however, says nothing of Bjarni, but in a section notable for confusion, irrelevance, and clumsiness, ascribes the honour of the discovery to Leif Eiriksson, the eldest son of Eirik the Red, founder of the Greenland settlements. To Leif *GS* assigns the credit of the first landings in the New World and the first sojourn in Vinland.

In all *GS* makes mention of six voyages to the North American coast, made by 1, Bjarni Herjolfsson; 2, Leif Eiriksson; 3, Thorvald Eiriksson; 4, Thorstein Eiriksson; 5, Thorfinn Karlsefni; 6, Freydis Eiriksdottir. *ESR* makes mention of three of these only: 1, Leif Eiriksson; 2, Thorstein Eiriksson; 3, Thorfinn Karlsefni. According to both sources Thorstein's voyage was a failure: he never even sighted America. According to both, the one real attempt at establishing a colony in America was made by Thorfinn Karlsefni. Thorvald Eiriksson's voyage (*GS* 3) has been incorporated in part, and not without substantial change, in *ESR*'s account of Karlsefni's expedition.

On examination the following pattern emerges. *GS* is much less concerned with Iceland and Icelanders than is *ESR*. *GS* is mainly interested in the family of Eirik the Red, *ESR* in the Icelander Karlsefni and his wife Gudrid. Nevertheless it is *GS* which records the voyage of Bjarni Herjolfsson, and since this may be held to detract from the achievement of Eirik's son Leif, we must accept it as a convincing concession to truth. Further, it is entirely natural that *GS* and *ESR* should sometimes handle separate material, like the murderous voyage to Vinland of Freydis, Eirik the Red's daughter, in the one, and the heroic death at sea of Bjarni Grimolfsson the Icelander in the other. Nor will any student of the sagas be surprised that they sometimes produce differing and yet reconcilable versions of the same event, like Thorstein's abortive voyage and his death by plague, or Thorvald's death by an arrow on a voyage somewhere north of the main area of Vinland settlement. When in addition we remove from both sagas the more obvious encrustations of fantasy and misunderstanding, we are left at a wary estimate with the following facts:

1. Bjarni Herjolfsson made a sea-voyage from Iceland to Greenland in 985 or '86 and sighted the American-Canadian coastline.

2. Leif Eiriksson made a voyage from Greenland soon after and went ashore at various points of the newly discovered land.

3. Thorfinn Karlsefni attempted not many years later to establish a colony there, but had soon to abandon it.

4. Thorvald Eiriksson made a voyage to the new land, either with his own crew before Karlsefni, or in Karlsefni's company, and was killed there.

5. These voyages were over and done with by 1020 or earlier.

There are trustworthy and important references to Vinland in Adam of Bremen, *c.* 1075, in the Icelandic Annals for 1121, and in Ari's *Islendingabok, c.* 1125; an unsatisfactory one preserved in connection with the no longer extant Honen runic inscription found in Ringerike, Norway, and possibly of the period *c.* 1050; a number of casual ones in Icelandic histories and sagas of the 13th century; and what appear to be derivative mentions in some Icelandic geographical treatises of the 14th century. To conclude, Norse knowledge of a region of the North American (Canadian) coast, and recognition of it as the goal of Norse voyages of exploration is handsomely attested, and this being so, we turn to the narrower problem of geographical identification.

The place to start is where the sagas start, with Bjarni Herjolfsson. He had been in Norway for the winter of 985–86, and when he returned to Eyrar (the present Eyrarbakki) in the south of Iceland the following summer was much taken aback to find that his father had sold up and left for Greenland with Eirik the Red. However, he determined to follow him. *GS* recounts:

> They put out the moment they were ready, and sailed for three days before losing sight of land. Then their following wind died down, and north winds and fogs overtook them, so that they had no idea which way they were going. This continued over many days, but eventually they saw the sun and could then get their bearings [or determine the quarters of the heavens]. They now hoisted sail, and sailed that day before sighting land, and debated among themselves what land this could be. To his way of thinking, said Bjarni, it could not be Greenland. They asked him whether he proposed to sail to this land or not.

'My intention', he replied, 'is to sail close in to the land.' Which they did, and could soon see that the land was not mountainous and was covered with forest, with low hills there, so they left the land to port of them and let their sheet turn towards the land.

After this they sailed for two days before sighting another land. They asked whether Bjarni thought this in its turn was Greenland. In his opinion, he said, this was no more Greenland than the first place—'For there are very big glaciers reported to be in Greenland.' They soon drew near to this land, and could see that it was flat country and covered with woods. Then their following wind died on them. The crew talked things over and said they thought it common sense to put ashore there; but this Bjarni would not allow. They reckoned they were in need of both wood and water. 'You lack for neither,' said Bjarni and got some hard words for this from his crew.

He gave orders to hoist sail, which was done; they turned their prow from the land and sailed out to sea three days with a southwest wind, and then they saw the third land, and this land was high, mountainous, and glaciered. They asked whether Bjarni would put ashore there, but no, he said, he had no wish to. 'For to me this land looks good for nothing.' So without so much as lowering their sail they held on along the land, and came to see that it was an island.

Once more they turned their prow from the land and held out to sea with the same following wind. Soon the wind freshened, so Bjarni ordered them to reef, and not crowd more sail than was safe for their ship and tackle. This time they sailed for four days, and then saw the fourth land. They asked Bjarni whether he thought this was Greenland or not. 'This is very like what I am told about Greenland,' replied Bjarni, 'and here we will make for the land.'

And Greenland it was. What then were the three other lands sighted and described? A growing consensus of opinion would settle for Newfoundland or, better, southeastern Labrador as the first, somewhere farther north in Labrador as the second, and Baffin Island as the third. When Leif Eiriksson sailed the same coasts in reverse order he gave to Baffin Island the name Helluland, 'Flatstone Land'; Labrador he named Markland, 'Wood Land'; and the place still further south where he built booths and a house he named Vinland, 'Wineland', because his crew found grapes there. There was an island lying north of this third land, and 'they sailed into the sound which lay between the island and the cape projecting north from the land itself. They made headway west round the cape.' The other voyages recorded in *GS* followed Leif's course exactly, and all the voyagers arrived by the same route at the same place, Leifsbudir, 'Leif's Booths'.

ESR, we have noticed, has nothing to say of Bjarni, and nothing very illuminating to say of Leif, while its two versions present us with somewhat different sailing directions for Karlsefni. What follows is part of *ESR* 557 (the earlier version of *ESR*):

They had a hundred and sixty men on board their ships. They then sailed away for the Western Settlement and for Bjarneyjar, Bear Isles. From Bjarneyjar they sailed with a north wind, were at sea two days, and then found land. They rowed ashore in boats and explored the country, finding many flat stones there, so big that a pair of men could easily clap sole to sole on them. There were many arctic foxes there. They gave the land a name, calling it Helluland, Flat-stone Land. Then they sailed with a north wind for two days, when land lay ahead of them, with a great forest and many wild animals. Off the land to the south-east lay an island, where they found a bear, so called it Bjarney, Bear Island. But the land where the forest was they called Markland, Wood Land.

Then when two days were past they sighted land, and sailed to the land. Where they arrived there was a cape. They beat along the coast and left the land to starboard; it was an open harbourless coast there, with long beaches and sands. They put ashore in boats, came across the keel from a ship, so called the place Kjarlarnes, Keelness. Likewise they gave a name to the beaches, calling them Furdustrandir, Marvelstrands, it was such a long business sailing past them. Then the land became bay-indented, and towards these bays they headed their ships.

There follows an account of how Karlsefni put the two scouts Haki and Hekja ashore south of Furdustrandir to spy out the land and how they returned, the man with grapes in his hand and the woman with wild wheat.

They took them on board ship and went their ways until the land was indented by a fjord. They laid the ships' course up into this fjord, off whose mouth there lay an island, and surrounding the island strong currents. This island they called Straumsey [Straumey]. There were so many birds there that a man could hardly set foot down between the eggs. They held on into the fjord, and called it Straumsfjord [Straumfjord], and here they carried their goods off the ships and made their preparations. They had brought all kinds of live-stock with them.

Karlsefni seems to have followed what may be called the 'classic' route to Vinland, sailing from the Eastern Settlement up the coast of Greenland to somewhere north of the Western Settlement, though whether to the modern Holsteinsborg or Disko we cannot say. From there he dropped across Davis Strait to the southern part of Baffin Island, kept sailing south to below the northern tree-line of Labrador (below Nain), and then south again to a place called Straumfjord which either is, or has in large measure been confused in saga tradition with, Leifsbudir. Here he made his bid for a permanent settle-ment, but after three years was forced to withdraw by the native population. Meantime he had for a while sailed further south, to a wheat and vine-blest district whose main feature was a landlocked bay, again somewhat reminis-cent of Leifsbudir. This he called Hop, after the Icelandic word for such a topographical feature, and this too he found untenable by reason of native hostility.

The situation and extent of Vinland in general, and the sites of Leifsbudir, Straumfjord and Hop in particular, are still the subject of debate, and will no doubt long remain so. Straumfjord, for example, has been sought and

Markland and Vinland

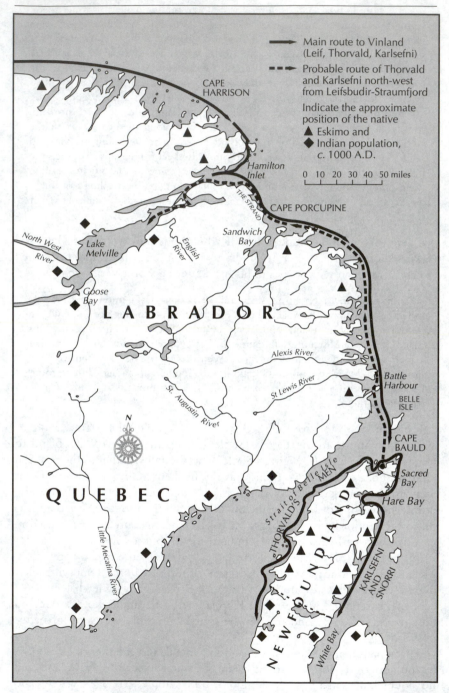

Main route to Vinland
(Leif, Thorvald, Karlsefni)

Probable route of Thorvald
and Karlsefni north-west
from Leifsbudir-Straumfjord

Indicate the approximate
position of the native

▲ Eskimo and
◆ Indian population,
  c. 1000 A.D.

0 10 20 30 40 50 miles

CAPE HARRISON

Hamilton Inlet

THE STRAND

CAPE PORCUPINE

Sandwich Bay

North West River

Lake Melville

English River

Goose Bay

L A B R A D O R

Alexis River

St. Augustin River

St Lewis River

Battle Harbour

BELLE ISLE

CAPE BAULD

Q U E B E C

N

Sacred Bay

Hare Bay

Strait of Belle Isle

THORVALD'S MEN

Little Mecatina River

N E W F O U N D L A N D

KARLSEFNI AND SNORRI

White Bay

found at well over a dozen points on the Canadian and American coasts between Hudson Bay and Florida. The continent has been prodigal of weapons, runes, round towers, fireplaces, houses and mooring-holes, which have proved at once the jest and despair of sober scholarship. How then shall we most profitably proceed?

Cautiously, as ever. For it is too early as yet to elucidate the entire Vinland problem. What can now be done, with assurance, is to define the northern limits of Vinland in northern Newfoundland and the region of Belle Isle Strait.

This does not mean, and is not intended to mean, that there were no Norse voyages to regions farther south, to Massachusetts, Rhode Island, New York, or even to Maryland. But for the present these are incapable of proof, and must wait on archaeological discovery, whereas the case for northern Newfoundland as the Promontorium Winlandiae of Norse geographical tradition grows stronger each year. The decisive recent stages have been Vaino Tanner's monumental survey of the eastern part of the Labrador Peninsula in the late 1930s, Jorgen Meldgaard's travels from Hamilton Inlet to the Strait of Belle Isle in 1956, and the prolonged explorations of Helge Ingstad along the coasts of Labrador, Newfoundland and Quebec in the summers of the 1960s, culminating in his and Anne Stine Ingstad's discovery of what they claim to be early Norse ruins in Epaves Bay, just south of L'Anse-aux-Meadows in the Sacred Bay area of northern Newfoundland.

To argue the full case of Northern Newfoundland as the Promontorium Winlandiae would be a long undertaking, and since it has already been argued elsewhere, I confine myself to presenting its main features:

1. Northern Newfoundland falls within the normal belt of latitude of the Norsemen's western voyages.

2. It accords with what we hear of the voyages and landfalls of Bjarni, Leif and Karlsefni.

3. To whatever destination the Norsemen were to sail on the course Greenland-Baffin Island-Labrador and farther south, they could not miss Belle Isle Strait and Northern Newfoundland.

4. It accords with what the sagas tell us about such topographical features as Straumfjord (Belle Isle Strait), Straumey (Belle Isle or Sacred Isle), Kjalarnes (Cape Porcupine), Furdustrandir (the Strand).

5. The area has the right configuration of sound *or* fiord, island, and cape projecting north (but admittedly is not alone in this).

6. It accords with the Promontorium Winlandiae of the Stefansson and Resen maps, and with Capt. Solver's reconstruction of the former 'in proper proportion to degrees of longitude and on Mercator's principles'.

7. It accords with what is known of the distribution of the local Indian and Eskimo populations *c.* A.D. 1000.

8. It accords with saga accounts of the death of Thorvald Eiriksson by an (Indian) arrow on a voyage which had taken him north then west from his

base in Vinland. He would, by this identification, be killed at the mouth of English River, where it flows into the south shore of Lake Melville inside Hamilton Inlet, Labrador.

9. It accords with what we are told of the projected but abortive voyage of Thorhall the Hunter in search of Vinland.

10. The right of announcing a scientific confirmation of his L'Anse-aux-Meadows discoveries belongs to Helge Ingstad.[1] But it is permissible to point out that the Epaves Bay site has attracted human habitation over a long period of time, and that it would offer the Norsemen a simple sailing direction, an unmistakable landfall, fresh water in abundance, a good anchorage, workable iron ore, timber and grass, fishing and hunting, and a desirable mobility by sea.

It will be seen that no comment has been passed on two of the most debated clues to the situation of Vinland. One is the statement of *GS* that at Leifsbudir, 'The sun had there *eyktarstadr* and *dagmalastadr* on the shortest days *or* days (*um skammdegi*)', which is presumably intended to convey that the sun was visible at certain points on the horizon somewhere about 3 p.m. and 9 a.m. during the depth of winter, but whose precise significance in terms of latitude has done little save provide a headache for its calculators. The other is the name Vinland itself, whether it should mean, as it undoubtedly meant to Adam of Bremen and the sagamen, 'Wineland,' from *vin-* with a long vowel, or 'Grassland', from *-vin* with a short vowel. The evidence is in favour of Wineland, but whether in the warmer climatic conditions of about A.D. 1000 the Norsemen found vines in northern Newfoundland, or whether grape-clusters found their way into saga-tradition after voyages pressed farther south, who shall say?

A final word. More than two hundred years were to elapse between the known voyages to Vinland and their recording by the authors of *GS* and *ESR*, who had no first-hand knowledge of the places they wrote about. It is not surprising then that the saga narratives show signs of confusion, faulty memory and garbled report in what they have to say about Leifsbudir, Straumfjord, and Hop. There is a very strong case for Norse contact with northern Newfoundland, a reasonable case for finding either Leifsbudir or Straumfjord or conceivably both on the one site there, but no weighable case for putting Hop on the map. Beyond these modest claims lies little save conjecture.

The period of settlement was a brief one, and while the memory of Vinland persisted in northern tradition it almost disappears from the written historical record. Suddenly in 1121 the Icelandic Annals announce that 'Bishop Eirik of Greenland went in search of Vinland', to what end and with what result we do not know. Then, in 1347, out of a prodigious silence comes news if not of Vinland at least of its neighbour Markland. 'There came also a ship from Greenland, smaller in size than the small Icelandic boats; she came into the outer Straumfjord [near Budir, in Iceland] and had no anchor. There were seventeen [var. eighteen] men on board. They had made a voyage to Markland, but were afterwards storm-driven here.' This entry in the Annals is of great interest for the concluding days of the Norsemen in Canada. Presumably they had been to Labrador for timber, and maybe for furs too, and only the accident of their being storm-driven to Iceland (as it were Bjarni Herjolfsson, the first discoverer, in reverse) allows us to know of their venture. How many other such voyages were made, we wonder, in the preceding three centuries, and could any such be undertaken again after the loss of the Western Settlement and the Greenland Nordseta in the middle of the fourteenth century? Mastery of any part of the Canadian coast, and of Vinland in particular, depended on a strong base in Greenland, superior weapons and steady reinforcement, and assured lines of communication. These the Norsemen no longer had, as the Greenlanders came to feel the remorseless pressures of geography and history, and Iceland and Norway ceased to be ocean-going nations. Wise after the event we now see that the Norsemen had over-extended themselves in the North Atlantic, and that compared with the enduring nation of Iceland and the 500-year colony in Greenland, the Norse entries into Newfoundland, Labrador, and Baffin Island, and, such as they were, into the islands and peninsulas farther north, were not of much importance in their own day, though to posterity they left a proud story, a high challenge, and a long enduring puzzle.

Suggestions for Further Reading

Gwyn Jones, *The Norse Atlantic Saga* (London, 1963).
T.J. Oleson, *Early Voyages and Northern Approaches, 1000–1632* (Toronto, 1963).
R.A. Skelton *et al.*, *The Vinland Map and the Tartar Relation* (New Haven: 1965).

Notes

[1] Ingstad's article on the Vinland site appeared in the *National Geographic*, November 1964. Ed.

2

The Vinland Map: Hoax or History?

Robert McGhee

The library of Yale University holds, but rarely exhibits, a map which may be a key to better understanding early European exploration across the Atlantic. The map was supposedly drawn around A.D. 1440, 50 years before Christopher Columbus' discovery of the New World, yet it shows a land that can be interpreted as the east coast of Canada from northern Baffin Island to the south coast of Newfoundland. If it is genuine, this is the earliest known representation of Canada on European maps. More importantly, it also suggests that knowledge of Canada had existed in Europe for the preceding 500 years, and probably influenced the European explorations into the western Atlantic which began in 1492. The story of the 'Vinland Map', as it has come to be known, provides a fascinating insight into the processes of modern historical scholarship.

Eleventh October 1965 was the eve of Columbus Day, the great Italian-American celebration of the Genoese navigator who 'discovered' America. This was the day on which Yale University chose to announce that they were in possession of a map which was drawn half a century before Columbus' voyage, and which showed North America. Headlines in the *Chicago Tribune* called it 'The Map that Spoiled Columbus Day'.

The map had been given to Yale seven days earlier by an anonymous donor. This donor had purchased it, almost certainly at the instigation of the Yale Library, from an American bookdealer. He, in turn, had recently purchased it from a European dealer who claimed not to be at liberty to reveal the source from which it had been obtained.

Because of its scholarly importance, and its shadowy pedigree, the map was subjected to intense study. When purchased, it had been bound into a large manuscript volume called *The Tartar Relation*, a record of an expedition sent by the Pope in 1245–47 to negotiate with and spy upon the Khan of the Mongols, the nephew of Genghis Khan and the major rival of the Pope

Map based on the 1570 chart of Sigurdur Stefansson, identifying place names by latitude markings.

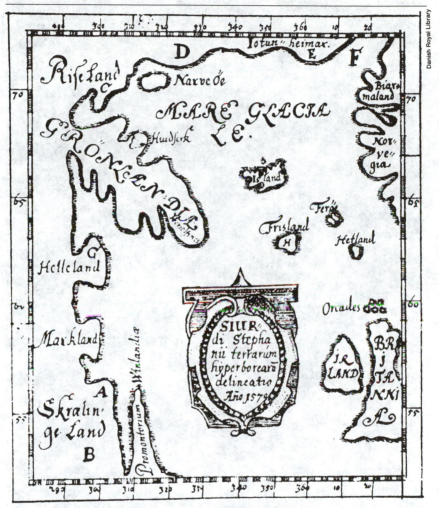

for political control of Europe. Records of this expedition were well known from other sources, but *The Tartar Relation* added much new information. The map had apparently been drawn in order to illustrate the Relation, and its representation of the Old World was consistent with other known European maps of the period. It also shared with contemporaneous European maps a penchant for placing islands in the Atlantic Ocean, islands such as Brasil and St Brendan's Isle, which we now know to be non-existent. It differed from other maps, however, in including two large named islands in the western Atlantic.

Part of the controversial Vinland map.

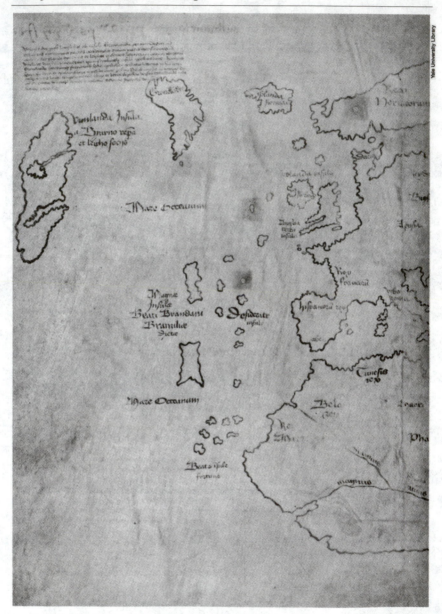

The more northerly of these islands is labelled *Gronelada*, and is immediately recognizable as Greenland. This caused grave suspicions among the scholars who studied the map; although Greenland was known to European geographers of the period, it was never portrayed as an island, but as a peninsula descending from a large polar continent extending westward from northern Norway. This map not only showed Greenland as an island, but as an island with a general outline which closely resembles that which appears on modern maps.

The second configuration, lying to the south and west of Greenland, is another large island with a roughly semi-circular form, the western boundary very vague while the eastern coast is marked by two deep inlets. A label identifies this island as *Vinilanda Insula* (Island of Vinland). This caused the scholars even greater concern. Although Vinland, the land discovered by the mediaeval Greenlandic Norse around A.D. 1000, was generally considered to be eastern North America, and although its name appears in European geographies dating from the eleventh century and later, it had never appeared on a map dating from the period before Columbus' voyages.

Knowing that the map might represent a major advance in knowledge of mediaeval European geography, but also that they would be judged extremely gullible if the map proved to be a forgery, the Yale scholars set to work to authenticate their find. To begin, they satisfied themselves that the *Tartar Relation* manuscript was a genuine document dating from the early fifteenth century. This was fairly easily accomplished, and its authenticity has not been doubted by most critics. Next, they compared the Old World portions of the Vinland Map with other known maps of the period, and were satisfied that it fit nearly into the period from which it was purported to come; the only unexpected elements were the Greenland and Vinland configurations and their accompanying notes.

They analyzed the handwriting of both the *Tartar Relation* and the Vinland Map, which appeared to be in the same hand and in a style which was characteristic of the Upper Rhineland during the early fifteenth century. Next, they checked the watermarks of the paper on which the Relation was written; the paper came from a small paper-mill in southern Germany or Switzerland, and also dated to the early fifteenth century. The map itself, however, was drawn on parchment and therefore could not be so easily dated.

There was one simple means, however, of checking whether the questionable map and the apparently genuine Relation belonged together. Both documents contained a few holes made by book worms which, at some point in its history, had tunnelled through the volume. Unfortunately, the worm holes in the map did not align with the worm holes in the Relation manuscript, suggesting that the two documents had only recently been bound together, and throwing further doubt on the authenticity of the map. Then something very curious happened. It had been 1957 when Yale had first been approached by the American bookdealer who owned the volume containing the Vinland Map and *Tartar Relation*. In 1958, one of the Yale scholars who had shown polite interest in the volume, happened to look through an English bookdealer's catalogue. He saw a copy of a fairly common late-mediaeval manuscript, the *Speculum Historiale* of Vincent de Beauvais, selling for a low price, and ordered it by mail for his own collection. When it arrived, he lent it to the American dealer who had originally approached him. That evening, the scholar received a telephone call from the dealer, who had compared the Beauvais manuscript with the *Tartar Relation*: the handwriting was the same, the paper was the same, and when the Beauvais volume was placed between the Map and the Relation, the worm holes all aligned! It seemed that all three manuscripts had originally been bound together for a long time, and only relatively recently had they been separated. The supposition was that both volumes came onto the market at about the same time from the same private library, where they had become separated at some time over the past century when the original bindings had worn out and new ones had been added to the Map and Relation. The original bindings remained with the Beauvais manuscript, and were in a style which was consistent with the handwriting and the paper of the Relation: southern Germany in the fifteenth century. Thus, after an apparently amazing coincidence and several years of study, the Yale scholars finally concluded that the Vinland Map was a genuine fifteenth-century map of the world which showed a portion of North America. They even suggested that it may have been drawn at the Council of Basle (1431–49), an important church event which attracted scholars from throughout Europe, and could have served as a centre for the exchange of geographical and historical knowledge.

Not everyone was convinced by the Yale scholarship. The critics, who continued to suggest that the map was most probably a recent forgery inserted into an old manuscript, were especially suspicious of the representation of Greenland. The true outline of Greenland was not known to European scholarship before the early decades of the twentieth century, and this supposedly fifteenth-century representation was simply too accurate. Others found apparent problems in the Latin used in written legends on the map, as well as in the *Tartar Relation*. Scientists at the British Museum briefly examined the map in 1967 and, although their results were not conclusive, suggested that there were signs that the parchment on which the map was drawn may have been chemically treated, perhaps in order to remove an older document and substitute a recently drawn map. The Vinland Map hung in a sort of scholarly limbo for a decade, never becoming sufficiently accepted that it could be used as a convincing argument that Europe had geographical knowledge of North America half a century before the voyages of Columbus.

The blow finally fell in 1974, when a Chicago laboratory specializing in the analysis of very small samples was allowed to remove several tiny scraps of ink from the map and subject them to chemical and microscopic tests. Their tests showed that the ink contained an average of 30% of a form of titanium dioxide, a major constituent of twentieth-century inks but one which had not been available before about 1920. The critics of the Vinland Map were triumphant, its supporters were chastened by the demonstration that fine scholarship could be gulled by a clever forger, and the large and impressive book which Yale University had produced on the subject was remaindered at a loss. Through a series of vague inferences, the forgery began to be attributed to an obscure Yugoslavian church scholar, an enthusiast of mediaeval missionaries, who would have had access to the necessary knowledge and materials before his death in 1924.

Little was heard of the Vinland Map over the following decade. Most of the scholarly works which made any reference to it did so only to remark it as an obvious fraud. Yet some scholars continued to be troubled by two questions, both of essentially a psychological nature. First, the alleged forger must have gone to great trouble to find an ancient parchment which could be associated by worm holes with genuine fifteenth-century documents, and had been extremely careful in matching the handwriting and contents of the map with the associated documents. Would such a forger then have used a patently twentieth-century ink, when a perfectly good mediaeval ink could have been easily manufactured at home from such ingredients as acorns or soot? Second, why would a twentieth-century forger of such a map draw a modern likeness of Greenland? Surely this would be a certain give-away, and any competent forger would represent Greenland either as a vague blob in the northwestern Atlantic, or as a peninsula depending from a polar continent, as it was represented on other fifteenth-century maps.

In early 1986 the fortunes of the Vinland Map changed once again. Physicists at the University of California at Davis had developed non-destructive techniques for studying the chemical characteristics of ancient documents. Sub-atomic particles, accelerated to immense speeds in a cyclotron, were aimed at a document in their path, and the resulting scatter of X-rays measured in order to determine the number and amounts of chemicals in ancient paper and ink. They had already tested the Dead Sea Scrolls and other documents, and were confident that their techniques gave accurate readings. This was a technique which was much more sophisticated than the earlier Chicago tests on the ink of the Vinland Map. The only tests then available had required the destruction of the sample, so they were based on only tiny samples of ink and the results extrapolated to the entire map. The accelerator tests were non-destructive, gave more accurate readings, and could be applied to the entire document. The Davis physicists announced that not only did they detect only trace amounts of titanium in the ink of the map, but that both the ink and the parchment were entirely characteristic of a fifteenth-century origin. Suddenly the Vinland Map was once more respectable.

If the Vinland Map does prove to be a genuine fifteenth-century document, how can we explain its Greenland and Vinland configurations? The manner in which Greenland is represented is perhaps not as surprising as was thought when the map first came to light. The Greenland configuration is not nearly as accurate as it appears at first sight; the island is much too small in relation to the remainder of the map, and its north coast is much further south than it should be. The coast has many apparently random indentations, which cannot be matched with known bays and fiords. The only two features which obviously coincide with modern maps are the convergent shape of the southern tip of the island, and a long straight section of the northwestern coast which appears to represent Melville Bay. During the early years of Norse settlement in Greenland, the climate was somewhat warmer than at present and the amount of sea ice somewhat less. The standard sailing route from Iceland took ships directly west to a point on the East Greenland coast, then south to round Cape Farewell and north along the west coast to the settlements; approximately the southern quarter of the east coast was therefore well known. Archaeological finds testify to the fact that Norse hunting expeditions penetrated as far north as the present Upernavik District, well over half-way up the western coast of the island and at the southern edge of Melville Bay. In the 1960s, when the map was first studied, it was generally thought that the Greenlandic Norse had had few if any contacts with the Eskimos who arrived in Greenland at about the same time, and that such contacts would have been limited to hostilities. It has since become apparent that the relationships between the two groups must have been considerably more complex, and existed over a period of several centuries. Finds of Norse material in Eskimo villages in far northwestern Greenland and adjacent Ellesmere Island indicate that the Norse were in some form of contact with the Eskimos as early as the twelfth century. The remains of an Eskimo umiak, a large skin-covered boat, has been found on the north coast of Greenland, an area of almost permanent sea-ice under present conditions. Radiocarbon dates indicate that this boat voyage was made during the time of the Norse settlements, and indeed parts of the wooden frame of the boat were of oak, almost certainly derived from the Norse. The Eskimos circled Greenland and were in a position to assure the Norse that it was an island. This is essentially all that the Vinland map shows: that Greenland is an island with a convergent southern tip and a straight northwestern coast, where the inland ice-cap abuts directly and very impressively on the iceberg-strewn waters of Melville Bay.

If the Greenland configuration can be explained, what of the Vinland configuration, and what does the map tell us of mediaeval European knowledge of Canada? First, it tells us very little that we didn't already know from the Icelandic sagas and other sources regarding Greenlandic Norse explorations of the New World. The two map labels referring to Vinland are somewhat at variance with other sources. The shorter one says simply 'Island of

Vinland, discovered by Bjarni and Leif in company'. This appears to be a conflation of two accounts in the Greenlanders' Saga, which states that the new lands were first sighted by Bjarni Herjulfsson (about A.D. 986) and later explored by Leif Eiriksson (about A.D. 1000). The longer text repeats the story of Bjarni and Leif, describes Vinland as a fertile country, and states that Bishop Henricus (Eirik) travelled there in A.D. 1117, stayed there for some time in both summer and winter, and then returned to Greenland and Europe. The Icelandic Annals report that in the year A.D. 1121 Bishop Eirik Gnupsson voyaged in search of Vinland, but says nothing about his finding it. The two accounts disagree regarding the year of the bishop's explorations, and whether or not he actually found Vinland and spent time there, yet the one account seems as likely as the other, and there is little to choose between them.

It seems generally agreed that the Vinland configuration on the map does not derive from actual Norse charts. Rather, it probably derives from the same sort of oral traditions which we know from the sagas, and which the mapmaker interpreted as best he could on parchment. For example, the sagas refer to three New World 'lands' ranging from north to south: Helluland, Markland and Vinland. The two major inlets on the east coast of the map's Vinland configuration, dividing the coast into three sections, may simply be an arbitrary interpretation of this reference. Yet a comparison of the latitudes of these three sections of the Vinland configuration with those of Greenland and Europe, as they are shown on the Vinland Map, suggests the possibility that the mapmaker may have had more precise knowledge than that which we can obtain from study of the surviving Icelandic accounts and traditions. Before making such a comparison, two facts should be noted. First, the Vinland configuration on the map is almost as distant from Greenland as Greenland is from Europe, indicating that we are not dealing with an accurate navigational chart of the northwestern Atlantic; we should remember, however, that in Norse times and until well after the fifteenth century, longitudes could be only vaguely estimated by sailing times and speeds, while latitudes could be easily determined and compared by the altitude of the noon sun or the Pole Star. Secondly, the label *Vinilanda Insula* is placed adjacent to the northern tip of the configuration, and appears to refer to the entire large island.

The most northerly of the three sections of *Vinilanda Insula* lies between roughly the same latitudes as the west coast of Greenland from Melville Bay to just north of the southern tip; these latitudes correspond well with those of Baffin Island, which was probably the barren and mountainous Helluland (flat stone land) of the Icelandic sagas. It is separated from the section to the south by a long and narrow channel ending in a large lake; the latitude of this channel is just north of the southern tip of Greenland, at approximately the same latitude as Hudson Strait. The next section spans the distance from about the southern tip of Greenland, south to about the latitude of the south coast of Ireland; this approximates the latitudes of Labrador, which is probably the Markland (forest land) of the sagas. This area is separated from that to the south by a deep indentation running southwesterly into the land mass, setting off a long peninsular piece of land reminiscent of the Great Northern Peninsula of Newfoundland; the latitude of the northern tip is approximately equal to that of the south coast of Ireland, the southern coast equal to the northern Bay of Biscay; these are approximately the latitudes of the northern tip and southern coast of Newfoundland. The peninsular configuration is reminiscent of that on the Sigurdur Stefansson map, a late sixteenth-century Icelandic chart which labels a similar configuration the *Promontorium Winlandiae*, and which has been used as evidence to assign a Newfoundland location to the Vinland of the sagas.

If the map is genuine, and if the latitudes of the Vinland configuration are actually the product of more than mere guesswork on the part of the mapmaker, the latitudes of the three sections of coast tend to confirm current identifications of the three 'lands' mentioned in the sagas: Helluland with Baffin Island, Markland with Labrador, and Vinland with Newfoundland, the location of the probable mediaeval Norse occupation site at L'Anse au Meadows. It is perhaps worth mentioning that these identifications were not current in the 1920s, when the suspected forgery of the Vinland Map occurred; at that time, Vinland was generally considered to refer to a region south of the Gulf of Saint Lawrence, probably on the Atlantic coast of the United States.

If we assume that the Vinland configuration on the map is actually a graphical representation of the east coast of Canada surviving from Greenlandic Norse tradition, does it suggest that knowledge of Canada was current in Europe at the time of the transatlantic explorations of the late fifteenth century? As has been pointed out by sceptics, the Vinland Map is unique, and was outside the general European cartographical traditions of the fifteenth century. As far as is known, its Greenland and Vinland configurations were not copied by any other mapmakers prior to the age of exploration, which has been taken as evidence that it could not have contributed to European knowledge of the period.

However, something resembling the Vinland configuration does appear on several southern European maps dating from the first years of the 1500s. These maps (the Cantino chart of 1502, the Caneiro chart which was also probably drawn in 1502, and the King chart of 1500–1503) were produced following the explorations of Cabot (1497) and Cortereal (1501). Each shows a semicircular island with a vague western coast and deeply indented eastern coast, lying to the southwest of Greenland. This configuration is variously titled *Terra cortereal* or *Terra del Rey du Portuguall* (the land of the King of Portugal), and represents Newfoundland and the adjacent coast of Labrador,

Map based on the Cantino chart of c. 1502, representing Newfoundland as 'Terra del Rey du Portuguall'.

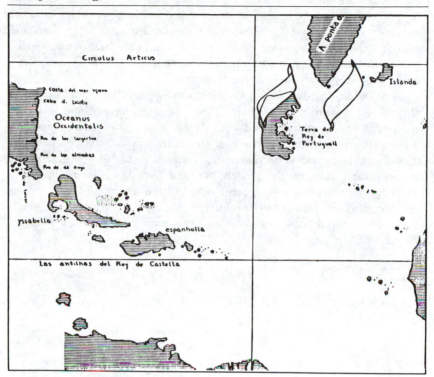

which were explored by the Portuguese sailor Manuel Cortereal. This is the same portion of North America which was explored 500 years earlier by the Greenlandic Norse, and almost certainly the area which they knew as Vinland. The island which the Portuguese placed on their maps illustrating these discoveries is very like the Vinland configuration on the Vinland Map, supposedly drawn 80 years previously. This suggests that southern European cartographers may indeed have been familiar with this mapmaking tradition, and that they correctly identified the newly found *Terra del Rey du Portuguall* with the ancient *Vinilanda Insula*.

Did Christopher Columbus know about Vinland when he set out across the Atlantic? Some scholars have proposed, on the basis of very shaky evidence, that Columbus had made a previous visit to Iceland where he may have learned of the land in the west discovered some 500 years earlier. If the Vinland map is genuine, and if its knowledge had some currency in southern Europe during the late fifteenth century, Columbus might have learned of it much closer to home. There is one piece of evidence which strongly suggests that, however he came by the knowledge, he did know of the eastern coast of Canada. Fifteenth-century explorers knew, as well as do the navigators of modern polar flights from Europe to North America, that the shortest way from east to west is in the higher latitudes. Why, then, did Columbus choose to sail straight west from Spain, rather than work his way north along the European coast to perhaps Ireland, and then make a relatively short passage westward to the Orient?

The most likely answer is that Columbus knew what he would find if he followed such a course: a rockbound coast guarding a land of spruce forests, with perhaps some grazing land and maybe even some wild grapes. No spices, no gold, no slaves, nor any of the other magical attractions of the Orient could be expected on this route. It is perhaps not an exaggeration to conclude that Columbus deliberately bypassed Canada. That he did so, in turn suggests that the knowledge embodied in the Vinland Map may have been common in the seaports of Europe during the fifteenth century, a poorly documented legacy of the first Europeans to explore the western Atlantic half a millenium before.

Notes

This article first appeared in *The Beaver* 67, 2 (April/May 1987), 37–44.

3

~~✒~~

Europe in the Age of 'Discovery', 1450–15\

Timothy Foote

While the history of Canada is usually seen as being quite independent
of that of other regions—and normally is studied that way—it is
really quite impossible to understand the European voyages of
'exploration and discovery' without
examining the Europe that spawned
them. At first glance, Europe was in
the midst of a flowering of achievement usually labelled 'the Renaissance', described more than a
century ago by one of its chroniclers
as 'the discovery of the world and
of man'. Renaissance Europe's
accomplishments were many: unified (and sovereign) nation states, a
new spirit of capitalistic enterprise,
a fresh emphasis upon individualist
humankind usually called humanism, and a new sense of aesthetic
values. In some complicated way,
this outburst of transforming energy
was related to the Reformation
within Christianity begun by Martin
Luther, and to the Catholic
Counter-Reformation of the sixteenth century. Whether such

achievements entitled Europeans to
treat the inhabitants of North
America as though they were savage
barbarians whose lives did not
matter—the typical European conceit of the time and long
afterwards—is quite another matter.

In the following article, American scholar Timothy Foote attempts
to put Renaissance Europe into perspective. The same age that gave us
such enduring monuments as Michelangelo's sublime Sistine Chapel
also produced considerable urban
squalor and such popular entertain-
ments as bearbaiting and public executions. There was a general
European acceptance of—even a
fascination with—death, violence,
and torture. While Foote does not
seek to deny Renaissance Europe's
real achievements, he does suggest
that they had serious social limitations, particularly among the under-
classes of European society.

On balance, do the negative
aspects of European society in the
fifteenth and sixteenth centuries

31

outweigh the accomplishments? Would you have wished to have lived in such a society? If so, in what guise? Perhaps more importantly, could such a society regard itself as the arbiter of the world, superior in many respects to the native peoples upon whom it had stumbled?

This article, titled 'Where Columbus Was Coming From', first appeared in *The Smithsonian Magazine* (December 1991), 28–41.

There they all are, just as they were in the dingy engravings of our schoolbooks. The welcoming aborigines clad mainly in innocence. The handful of Spaniards with swords, their heads scrunched into pointy helmets. The Great Discoverer himself, roasting in dark doublet and hose, usually on his knees in the sand, head raised to heaven. And beside them the shape of a great cross which, in perspective, looms higher than the distant masts of the three delicate little ships offshore.

In the long context of history, some shock is in order. If we are surprised, though, it may be because, apart from a Borgia orgy or two, we tend to think of the period that launched Columbus to the New World as a golden age. Bold thrusts across uncharted seas. Forays back in time to revive the lost learning of Rome and Greece. And that sunburst of artistic genius never since equalled. In *Everything You Always Wanted To Know About Sex (But Were Afraid To Ask)*, Woody Allen urges a girl to hurry up and make love because 'before you know it, the Renaissance will be here and we'll all be painting.'

Showtime for humanism; in short, the end of the Middle Ages and the dawn of Western science; the dazzling moment when modern man was born.

Modern man was a long way off, however, and human nature, then as now, was notoriously unreliable. Despite all the splendid expenditure of intellectual energy and egg tempera, Western Europe from 1450 to 1506, roughly Columbus' lifetime, was a time breathtakingly different from ours. Among other things, and this we tend to forget, it was a time when men believed so deeply that the body is but a sleeve of flesh containing an immortal soul, that in good faith they could see other men tortured to save their souls. It was a time so precarious that any rise in population was taken as a sign of prosperity. It was also a time much given to terror, war, pestilence, famine, slavery and religious persecution, most emphatically *not* one to encourage gentleness or ecological concern.

During Columbus' lifetime, his eventual sponsors, Ferdinand and Isabella, united the kingdoms of Aragon (his) and Castile (hers), and with startling religious and secular ferocity turned Spain, with a population of under ten million, into a nation. The great event of the year 1492 was not Columbus' sailing but their victory in Granada, bringing back to Spain the last portion of Spanish soil in Moorish hands. That same year the Spanish Inquisition issued an ultimatum to all Spanish Jews: convert to Christianity or quit the country in four months. A major exodus to North Africa occurred in August 1492, the very month the *Niña*, the *Pinta* and the *Santa Maria* hoisted sail and headed west into the stream of history.

The long boot of Italy, where the Renaissance was born, consisted of five principal parts: the kingdom of Naples, the republic of Florence (richly dominated by the Medicis), the dukedom of Milan, the Papal States, which waxed and waned according to churchly ambition, and Venice. Only Venice was a great power, a sprawling city-state that stretched for miles westward and north from the Adriatic. The parts of Italy were constantly fighting with one another, and later being fought over by Spain and France in combinations and alliances that shifted, sometimes from month to month, making carnage fairly constant. 'And all this time,' Swiss historian Jacob Burckhardt wrote of the end of the 15th century and after, 'the monarchs of the West year by year became more and more accustomed to a colossal political card game in which the stakes were this or that province of Italy.'

Other Italian cities, nominally republics, had given themselves into the hands of despots, benevolent and otherwise, to insure a defense against roving bands of soldiers, and to maintain some kind of order within their gates. Venice alone remained a real republic, run by an austere and farsighted oligarchy, with overseas possessions like the island of Cyprus. The city served as a trading center for the Mediterranean world, as far as the Black Sea, and her fleet was a bulwark against the encroaching Ottoman Turks. Venice was renowned for her courtesans. She had a retirement fund and a pension system for domestic servants. She created the world's most skilled diplomatic corps. Her espionage service, like that of Israel today, was the envy of the world. 'It can find out what the fish are doing and also about the fleet which Spain is preparing in her ports,' one sultan wrote an agent in Seville.

In 1453, when Columbus was not yet two years old, the armies of the Ottoman sultan, Muhammad II, sent a shudder through Venice and all Christendom by taking Constantinople, center of the Eastern Orthodox Church and Byzantine Empire. In those days, if a city resisted, it was official policy, often not followed, to kill the men and sell the women and children into slavery. They killed Emperor Constantine in battle and converted the basilica of Santa Sophia into a mosque. Two years later they took Athens and converted the Acropolis into a mosque. The threat from Islam did not end until 1683, outside the gates of Vienna.

Like the city-states of Italy, the courts of 15th-century Europe, famous for splendor and squalor, were more medieval than modern. Think of nobles and ladies arrayed in gorgeous, particolored costumes that trailed in the mud, or swept among the rushes on the floor of the great hall where bones and leavings were gnawed by dogs. Baths were rare by modern standards, perfume prevalent. You brought your own knife to table, used it to cut off what you would eat, which was deposited on a slab of hardtack bread, known as a trencher. Whence the expression 'a good trencherman'. Basically you ate with your hands. (Even in the 16th century people ate with their hands. The great essayist Michel de Montaigne noted glumly that in his haste at meals he sometimes bit his fingers.)

There were new codes of manners (don't scratch yourself or pick your teeth at table) and how-to books (how to give a joust). Mêlées—mock war between mounted knights—caused so many injuries that the practice would soon be phased out. War never went out of style, but it was changing with the advent of guns and explosives. Meanwhile, one measure of how wide a road had to be was the length of a knight's lance if he rode with it sideways across his saddle.

Kingdoms were becoming nation-states or absolute monarchies, enlisting or extorting financial help from rich cities and merchants, raising forces to make war on rival countries and also to strengthen the crown by putting down brigandage and local disorders. The cumulative effect of violence on the common people, who suffered most from war, can hardly be imagined. Much of the fighting was done by groups of undisciplined men who fought for hire or for booty. In Italy they were led by *condottieri*, freelance commanders who also were pretty much a law unto themselves. One of the most feared, Bartolomeo Colleoni, still throws a chill into tourists who run across his grim likeness, a huge equestrian statue by Verrocchio that stands in a piazza in Venice.

If passing troops did not rape and burn and pillage, they lived off the land, stripping it so thoroughly that military commanders understood an army could never retreat along the same path it had advanced over. People huddled together, praying to be passed by, or ran for the nearest walled town. As guns and explosives were perfected, even walled towns were no guarantee of safety. And when the fighting eased off, bands of ex-soldiers roamed the countryside, robbing and killing, sometimes taking possession of whole towns.

Even so, it was a time of trade and pilgrimages to holy sites with saints' relics, and if a careful count could show that some saints must have had two heads and four arms, few of the faithful complained. In peace or war you tried not to travel except in a large group, and it was unwise to talk too openly about what route you planned to take. Even in the city no one went out at night. At dark all doors were locked and double-barred. Tallow candles cost a lot and smelled, so people slept from dark till dawn. City gates were locked at nightfall. If a tired traveler arrived a minute or so too late, he was out of luck—and in danger—until morning, unless he could find a spot in one of the inns that grew up outside the city walls.

Violence and the threat of violence bred terror. Punishments were terrible, yet people eagerly flocked to see them. Few ages, except our own—and we screen it through the medium of film—had more morbid fascination with torment, killing and death, or more art and action to satisfy it. A patron saint of those who suffered from the Black Death, which had killed off a third of Europe's population the century before, was the martyred Sebastian, painted again and again and again as a fleshly pincushion shot full of arrows. Skeleton-filled woodcuts were plentiful, variously depicting the Triumph of Death, the Dance of Death or the Art of Dying.

If executioners wanted to be especially humane, they strangled a man before hanging or burning him. Such leniency did not always please the crowd. Records show that spectators would sometimes buy a thief who was to be quickly executed and arrange to see him being drawn and quartered instead. Flaying and burial alive, head down, were also used. Cruelty permeated many pastimes. Bear-baiting, dog-fighting and the worrying of badgers were common. In the Low Countries, crowds at fairs enjoyed watching blind men with clubs being penned up in a small enclosure and coerced into trying to beat each other's brains out.

Religion and art, culture and learning, all profoundly intermingled, produced profoundly shocking and contrary effects. Pure, radiant faith and raw repression, philosophy and savage propaganda, incipient science and ingrained superstition. We know best and love most the art and architecture: timeless, stately piety (and geometric glimpses of Tuscan countryside) in the paintings by Piero della Francesca, who died in 1492, Leonardo Da Vinci's *Last Supper* and, as the 1500s dawned, the Michelangelo ceiling of the Sistine Chapel. Painters were more and more visibly enthralled by the visual beauty of the world, and even by ravishing pagan subjects (overlaid, of course, with Christian symbolism), like Sandro Botticelli's *The Birth of Venus.*

Whatever a painting's subject, most were painted 'for the Greater Glory of God'. These days, however, we rarely tend to connect the religious spirit that infuses such paintings with the tormenting faith that helped produce figures like Torquemada, Queen Isabella's state inquisitor, or the auto-da-fé, an institution with which he tortured Spain. But they had a common source. If Christians spilled one another's blood copiously over the form of religion in the 15th century and after, it was partly because they never doubted that the world was a divine creation.

The civil war in the human heart, between the claims of this world and the next, ran right through the Renaissance. Worldliness among merchants and bankers, who gloried in activity and threw off the medieval notion that being rich was a spiritual liability, paid for civic improvements and history's greatest art boom. Worldliness in thought and inquiry led to humanism, which ultimately would threaten both the simple faith that allowed people to bear up under adversity, and the secular power of the Roman church. Worldliness and corruption among the leaders of that church all but destroyed it. (The term 'nepotism' is linked to the proclivity that officially celibate popes had for favoring their 'nephews'—sometimes bastard sons—

for high office.) Throughout, unworldly purity within the church tried to reform it and failed, though thousands of the selfless religious took care of lepers and ran the hospitals, almshouses and orphanages.

Savonarola's 'Bonfires of the Vanities'

Some of the early apostles of purity were gentle, like Saint Francis. Some were savage. In 1494, after the death of Lorenzo the Magnificent and the expulsion of his son Piero, the preacher-priest Savonarola took control of the city of Florence. He expanded the city's constitution to give more people the right to vote, but his main target was worldly excess, not only in the Florentine citizenry but in the papacy. He banned books and challenged the authority of the pope. At his fiery preachment, people gave up swearing for a time, and gaming. At huge public gatherings to expunge lechery and luxury, known as 'bonfires of the vanities', they outdid one another in zeal, tossing into the flames rich clothes, perfumes, jewelry, wigs, toiletries, veils, dice, playing cards, musical instruments and paintings of beautiful women. After four years of this, history's most notorious pope, Alexander VI, a Borgia who had his murderous son Cesare made a cardinal at age 17, accused Savonarola of heresy and had him hanged from, and burned on, a gibbet placed on a special causeway built out into the city's main square.

We think of the Western world's first movable type and the Gutenberg Bible in 1455, and concentrate on the upbeat news, of the general spread of learning through printed books—some 20 million volumes in Europe by the time Columbus sailed in 1492. Among those titles, though, was a best-seller called *The Hammer of Witches*. Written by a pair of Dominican scholars and made public in 1486, with a little help from a papal bull against the heresy of witchcraft it helped set off two centuries of torturing, hanging, burning and drowning. The book describes how witches consort with the Devil and how they can be identified. It helpfully provided the formula for preparing the magic salve they rubbed on themselves so they could fly: first, feed stolen, consecrated wafters to toads; then burn the toads and mix with powder from the bones of hanged men and the blood of newborn infants.

Moveable type was also used to mass-produce indulgences for remission of the penalties of sin, which a succession of popes sold pretty much like war bonds to finance ambitious projects. This was one of many outrages about to split the Christian world from within, setting off the Reformation and a train of religious wars that devastated much of Europe off and on for more than a hundred years. By 1506, the year Columbus died in Spain, bitter and forgotten, a man named John Tetzel, who had acquired a papal indulgence concession in Germany, was auctioning indulgences at mass meetings to the highest bidder, the very thing that was soon to outrage young Martin Luther.

Advances in the fields of engineering, design and science proceeded by fits and starts. More universities were founded. Arabic numerals began replacing Roman numerals in the pagination of books. Arabic and Greek learning in the fields of geometry, algebra, astronomy, geography and medicine were introduced into study. But people's notions of the Universe and of the human body remained hopelessly inaccurate. Even with the new type, word often didn't get around.

Take, for example, the designs of Leonardo, the man who, more than any other, today symbolizes the artistic genius and omnivorous curiosity of Renaissance humanism. We know now about his practical 'inventions': all those marvelous things—drawn with almost machine-shop detail—like chain links, the spinning wheel, the rope ladder, the parachute. But Leonardo kept his designs to himself, except for warlike devices, including some exploding cannonballs that he offered to Lodovico Sforza, the Duke of Milan, to get a job as Sforza's military engineer. The duke did not use them. And the rest of the more than 100 devices that prefigure the modern world of machinery were not rediscovered for centuries.

Millers Were Highly Suspect

Cookstoves had just been invented. Three years before Columbus set out on his third voyage, in 1498, the first drydock was built in England. But machinery was rare in Renaissance Europe, and most of it dated back to the Middle Ages or before. The big piece of machinery that a country person was most likely to see in his lifetime was a water mill, a great, clanking thing whose mysteries were known only to the miller. For centuries millers were hated characters (more even than lawyers today) because farmers suspected they took more than a proper share of the grain brought to the mill for grinding. It was widely thought that returned flour was bulked out with a little fine sand. There were strict punishments. Cheating was hard to prove, though, so people went on feeling cheated. The comic cuckolding of the miller in Chaucer's *Canterbury Tales* was the equivalent of a modern anti-lawyer joke.

High school history teachers inspiringly tell us that in the inexorable march of progress, Nicolaus Copernicus, born during Columbus' lifetime, made the world understand that Earth orbited the Sun. (This theory had been explored by Arab astronomers two centuries before, but Western scholars were unaware.) Copernicus' reason was that if the Sun moved around Earth, the eccentric movements of planets and the more distant stars didn't make mathematical sense.

Copernicus was largely right. But his outrageous claim made little impression. If Earth revolved around the Sun, scoffers pointed out, it would have to be spinning pretty fast. Wouldn't birds be left behind? If you dropped a stone from a tower, wouldn't it hit the ground yards away? For more than a century, even learned folk went on believing that the Sun and the planets moved around Earth on powered belts called spheres, which resembled the rings of Saturn and were driven by the outermost sphere, known as the prime mover.

Copernicus could not prove this theory because there was no telescope for accurate study of celestial bodies. Moreover, the church set about making it heresy to say that Earth orbited the Sun. It wasn't until 1610 that Galileo perfected a telescope good enough to see the moons of Jupiter and to observe that Venus had phases like our moon, which meant that it circled the Sun, virtually proving Copernicus right. By then, however, the struggle between science and religion had hardened enough so that Galileo was forced to recant his findings.

Sometimes a great leap forward produced by the revival of ancient science was actively pursued, but with limited results, not because of church disapproval, but because the new humanist scholars had a tendency to regard any scientific observations by the ancients as sacrosanct. Example: the rediscovery of medical writings by Hippocrates, and especially by the great second-century anatomist Galen, which encouraged further study and practice.

The church had been against the dismemberment of bodies ever since the Crusades, when dying crusaders sometimes got friends to promise to boil them down or cut them up, the better to transport them home. But after his rediscovery, Galen was recognized as the father of the science of anatomy, and approvals were given, especially to celebrated physicians and painters, to dissect human cadavers.

The work was mostly done in winter and in haste (there being no refrigeration), and performed on the bodies of convicted thieves and murderers who, presumably, had less chance at bodily resurrection than virtuous folk. At such events, the exalted physician did no cutting. He stood on a high pulpit reading from Galen, while below, the poor barber-surgeon did his best to prove that the cadaver matched Galen's description. Pictures of these scenes show crowds of students and plain rubberneckers pressing in around the corpse—also, sometimes, a small dog waiting for any choice bits that may come his way.

Galen had used Barbary apes in his experiments, and there were some dramatic anatomical discrepancies. But since Galen could not be wrong, these were usually blamed on the ineptitude of the surgeon. Even Andreas Vesalius, one of the great anatomists of all time, born just eight years after the death of Columbus, deferred to Galen's errors. Yet he finally incurred the wrath of professors at the University of Paris because many of his findings, based on dozens of personal dissections of human bodies, disagreed with Galen's. What physicians could quote from Galen's text was, in a sense, their meal ticket in the profession; they did not want it jeopardized by anything so mere as accuracy.

A great hindrance to medicine was ignorance of physiology. Galen never understood that the heart is a muscle; he thought blood was moved back and forth, like the tide, impelled by some mysterious heavenly spirit. It was not until the 17th century that William Harvey unlocked the secrets of the circulatory system. In Columbus' time and for several hundred years after, doctors thought health and temperament were determined by the mix of the famous four humors (i.e., fluids) of the body: blood, phlegm, choler (yellow bile) and melancholy (black bile). The ideal was balance. Whatever mix you received from the gene pool determined your disposition, then known as your 'complexion'. A choleric man was likely to be yellow-faced, lean, proud, ambitious, shrewd and quick to anger. A sanguine man, having much blood, was likely to be cheerful and optimistic. Doctors mostly sought to change a patient's body-fluid balance, the old standbys being puking, purging and bleeding.

Clearly the early Renaissance was no time to be sick. Public faith in the medical profession had fallen because doctors had proved so helpless during the plague years, earnestly suggesting such cures as inhaling the smell of billy goats. Besides, even after its worst period of killing, the plague did not go away either, and there was still no cure and almost no prevention. As late as 1484, when the 33-year-old Columbus had just asked for backing from King John II of Portugal and been rebuffed, the plague killed 50,000 people in Milan.

Diagnosis was like blindman's buff. Indiana University professor Ann Carmichael, author of *Plague and the Poor in Renaissance Florence* and doctor of medicine turned medical historian, has been studying computerized medical and death records from 100,000 cases recorded in Florence and Milan *circa* 1450 and after. She notes that people did not really expect cures. Doctors were simply expected to provide some care and easing of pain.

Except for the bleeding and puking, Carmichael feels, much of the care was good. Doctors kept patients quiet, saw that wounds were cleaned and bandaged, and used effective herbs and salves, many of them left over from the medically underrated Middle Ages. Though Renaissance barber-surgeons were looked down upon by lordly physicians who spouted mock science and took high fees, they could set bones and cut off legs. (To ease the pain, the patient was given things like mandrake root, henbane or opium in wine. As late as the 18th century, however, it sometimes took five people to extract a tooth—four to hold down and one to pull.) Surgery and bone setting were expensive. If you fractured a wrist or dislocated a shoulder and hadn't the means, chances were you'd get an enduring bone infection or be left to heal gradually—more or less crooked and crippled for the rest of your life.

There were no antibiotics. Pus was taken as a sign of healing (whence, until late in the 19th century, the term 'laudable pus'). Babies died in the thousands of gastrointestinal diseases. Even today, Carmichael notes, in the

Third World, 'diarrhea can turn a baby into a prune in less than four days.' In the 15th century three out of five children failed to reach age five; fully half the children born did not make it to age 20.

The plague had taught people some things. As a great maritime power, Venice established the quarantining of sailors off arriving ships, initially for a period of 30 days. To cut down possible sources of contagion when plague threatened, many cities banned the resale of old clothes (which were burned instead). Communal public baths were banned, too.

Florence had a city ordinance forbidding citizens to throw dead cats into the river Arno. But there, as elsewhere, people were regularly buried in city churchyards that leached into nearby streams. In some places garbage was burned or collected to be tossed over the city walls. (In Paris as late as 1512, the pile outside the walls was so high that the king had it removed because he thought invaders might climb up the garbage and scale the city's defenses.) In Italian cities piazzas were kept clean, but in the backstreets, refuse often simply lay around to be churned to a kind of black muck after rains. Farm animals living inside the cities added to the mess, but when cities, with a view to cleanliness, banned their presence inside the walls, things got worse. It turned out that city pigs had been performing a major cleanup service.

Occasionally the revival of ancient learning was swiftly absorbed, extended and applied to a real problem, changing Man's conception of the world. By far the happiest example, especially for Columbus' quincentennial year, lay in the field of sailing, after Portugal's Henry the Navigator set up a center for sharing knowledge. One notable event was the recovery of *Geography*, a treatise written by Claudius Ptolemy in the second century A.D. and lost to Western Europe for hundreds of years.

In the 1400s, a European man in the street may possibly have figured the world was flat. But church scholars, as well as other learned men, had long regarded it as a globe. Nevertheless, they thought that its lower half was uninhabitable except for weird creatures, such as giants with a single huge foot. Around the Equator lay a 'torrid zone', where the sea was boiling hot. For purposes of spiritual orientation, on most 'world maps' of the time, Jerusalem was presented as the center of the world. On others, more realistic in intent, only the Mediterranean, Europe, the Middle East and the top part of the bulge of Africa had any detail. The Indian Ocean was a vague inland sea. The nether regions of the globe were as firmly closed as outer space to the questing imagination.

Ptolemy's *Geography*, printed up in book form in the late 1470s, helped change all that because it used information garnered from longtime Islamic experience, as well as from the far-flung records of the Roman Empire and the conquests of Alexander the Great. Ptolemy's maps projected the surface of the globe onto a flat surface, pretty much as we do today, and showed some detail about the East African coast and the Indian Ocean. Perhaps more important, Ptolemy had divided the complete circle of the globe into 360 degree units of longitude, estimating each degree as about 57 miles long at the Equator, considerably less than the 69 miles we now know to be the case.

'Maps,' as J.R. Hale puts it, 'are diagrams of the possible.' To sail anywhere, risking your life, you must at least imagine where you are going. With Ptolemy's *Geography*, and others, in hand, Portuguese sailors who had been following the coast of Africa farther and farther south could imagine sailing around the tip of Africa to India and the Spice Islands, instead of paying Arab middlemen a whopping price for dear items like pepper and cloves. In 1487 Portuguese captain Vasco da Gama did just that, dramatically expanding Europe's vision of the world.

Columbus Cooked His Figures

Then came Columbus. Using Ptolemy's distances, in addition to the observations of another scholar, Pierre d'Ailly, who reasoned that between Spain and the Indies there were only 135 degrees of open sea, Columbus cooked his figures to reduce the number of sea or land miles in each degree of longitude. By his reckoning, Japan lay only 2,760 miles from Spain, or roughly a quarter of what it is. Wild for financial backing, he once noted, 'The end of Spain and the beginning of India are not far apart . . . and it is known that this sea is navigable in a few days' time with favoring wind.' History has much derided the Spanish experts who were leary of Columbus' estimates. They were right. But Ferdinand and Isabella were right to back him anyway. By risking the equivalent of $7,200 and the use of two ships (he had to charter the third) they got title to much of the New World.

Within 30 years, trading ships were shuttling back and forth where, shortly before, hardly a man had dreamed of going. The Western Hemisphere was being explored, the Pacific had been crossed and, with Magellan's voyage of 1519, Europeans had made it around the world. All this eventually meant a flood of silver, gold, land and sugarcane profits, as Spain became the most powerful country in Europe, with a far-flung, enduring empire. It also brought an appalling expansion of slavery.

There was little in Columbus' background to make him feel glum about any of the above. He was very much a man of his time in his courage and in his faith that God wanted all this to happen, as well as in his passion for trade and his desire to exploit the physical world. His Europe was a smallish peninsula sticking out from the landmass of Asia, with much seacoast north and south reachable from inland, many harbors for shipping and rivers for waterpower and trade. Europe's way to the gold and spices of the East had been slow and expensive, since it was controlled by the Arab world and lay through the Middle East, until navigators solved the problem. As historian Fernand Braudel notes, 15th-century Europe needed to expand into the New World.

Columbus needed to make his trip pay. When it turned out there wasn't much gold where he landed, he naturally turned to the enslavement of the poor people of the Indies. Hadn't Aristotle, a fount of Renaissance learning and the father of scientific classification, decreed that mankind is divided into two classes, the few (and smart) destined to be masters, the many to be properly classified as slaves?

Slavery existed everywhere—including the New World (though no one in Europe knew that yet) and Africa. The Turkish sultan's whole army and many of his administrators were his personal slaves. William Phillips, author of the recent study *Slavery from Roman Times*, draws on data showing that by 1400, Arab traders working West Africa had brought back four million slaves for the Middle East alone.

The cruelty and expansion of slavery in the New World seems more reprehensible, however, precisely because in 15th-century Europe slavery was relatively rare and getting rarer. This was partly because Christianity taught that manumission of slaves was pleasing to God, partly because peasants were more efficient than slaves in handling European agriculture.

Many Families Had a Slave or Two

Christians were not allowed to enslave other Christians, but many city families in 15th-century Europe had a domestic slave or two. Mostly young, white and female, they lived with the family and found it relatively easy to marry or work their way to freedom. They were acquired as pagans, usually in Eastern Europe or Circassia, and baptized to save their souls only after they were in service. (As early as the 12th century, the word for 'slave' in Italian, German, Spanish, French and English derived from the word 'Slav.')

From the start, there was anguished complaint by a few Spaniards about Spanish mistreatment of native people in New Spain—and about slavery. By 1542, with slaves being brought in from Africa, the church and the Spanish government had banned enslavement of 'Indians' in the New World, but for some groups in the Caribbean it was too late. They were all but extinct.

It is the fresh awareness of such things (often overlooked in previous, upbeat histories of the period), as well as the new environmental passion, that have led to condemnations of Columbus and what followed him. The European 'discovery' of the New World, as one outraged chronicler recently put it, defiled the Garden of Eden, corrupted paradise, and brought little with it but 'deforestation, extermination, cruelty, destruction and despoliation.')

Such a view may be forgiven, perhaps, as distorted overstatement in a virtuous cause. It is hardly necessary, though, to start a list of hard-won and useful things that eventually resulted from Europeanized thought and action after the Old World arrived in the New: trial by jury, freedom of religion, medicine to cure or prevent almost all manner of plagues, painless dental drills, attempts at universal education, the Bill of Rights and rights for women, the seeds of parliamentary democracy, hope at last for a united United Nations, not to mention the whole rich complexity of Hispanic America today.

The real foolishness of such judgments lies in the utopian delusion that there ever was a paradise here, and a hopelessly skewed perspective that seems to want us to believe that the globe has been going downhill since the Paleolithic period when, granted, few human beings were defiling it. The New World in 1492 was sparsely populated and largely underdeveloped. But war and slavery existed. So did slashing and burning for agriculture, and imperial exploitation. And those who ceremonially split a virgin's heart each day to please their deity, or sacrificed babies for rainfall (the more tears, the more rainfall, it was thought) can hardly be seen as denizens of a Garden of Eden, free of violence and greed, wholeheartedly dedicated to benevolence and ecological harmony.

If the biblical story of the Garden of Eden has any application here, in fact, it is only as a figurative reminder that humans are not angels. They seem, instead, creatures doomed by providence or evolution to a prolonged, perhaps endless, struggle with greed, lust, violence and ignorance. Anyone who doubts it has only to glance at the daily papers.

Medieval Europeans knew this, but blamed Man's sinfulness for much that happens in the world, figuring that the issue mostly would be settled between the Devil (in those days he was 'as real as a sore tooth') and the Deity. From the Renaissance on, men felt more prideful about mankind. This remarkable creation, cruel and greedy, yet capable of selflessness and heroism, located somewhere between the beasts and the angels in the great chain of being, had one unique and distinguishing skill and virtue—the compulsion and the capacity to learn and experiment—and so might yet prove able to change history for the better.

Since Charles Darwin's *Origin of Species* we've understood that it will be a slow business at best, a matter of trial and error. Little use in blaming this race or that government. In any Garden of Eden drama, Man will always be the serpent—and Adam and Eve as well. James Madison said it all at the Constitutional Convention: 'If men were angels no government would be necessary.' Columbus, and the land that launched him, simply helped another act begin.

Suggestions for Further Reading

Fernand Braudel, *Civilization and Capitalism, 15th-18th Century* 3 vols (New York, 1982–4).

George Huppert, *After the Black Death: A Social History of Early Modern Europe* (Bloomington, Ind., 1986).

S.J. Watts, *A Social History of Western Europe, 1450–1720: Tensions and Solidarities among Rural People* (London, 1984).

4

The 1600s: French Settlement in Acadia

John G. Reid

By the end of the sixteenth century, Europe had developed a sufficient body of information about the northern Atlantic coast of North America to realize that neither the Northwest Passage nor fabled kingdoms like the Saguenay could any longer be pursued. The Northwest Passage would continue to lure mariners and adventurers into the high Arctic and the interior of the continent for several centuries, and rich mineral wealth was always a possibility; the arctic adventurer Martin Frobisher had brought back tons of supposedly gold-bearing rock from his expedition to Baffin Island in 1578. But European nations were forced to recognize that the wealth of the northeast Atlantic coast would have to be exploited in a different way, perhaps through trade with the native peoples but also through settlement and colonization by the Europeans themselves.

In the following article, John Reid discusses the background and development of the first French settlements in the Atlantic region in the first decade of the seventeenth century. His story is one of continual European blundering amidst constant evidence of native goodwill and assistance.

What motivated the French to attempt a settlement in Acadia? Why did they have so much difficulty in establishing a decent foothold in the region? Why were the native peoples so helpful? Was friendship with the Europeans in the best interests of the natives?

This article first appeared in John G. Reid, *Six Crucial Decades: Times of Change in the History of the Maritimes* (Nimbus, 1987), 3–26.

The 1600s: Decade of Colonization

During the decade from 1600 to 1610, the Maritime provinces of Canada had not yet been invented. Had events turned out differently in this decade, they might never have been invented, and undoubtedly the entire course of the history of the region would have been altered. Already by the year 1600, the human history of the territory now comprising the Maritime provinces was in an era of rapid change. People had been living there continuously for more than 10,000 years and the direct ancestors of the Micmac and Maliseet-Passamaquoddy Indian peoples had been established since about 1000 B.C.[1] Since then their culture had altered and evolved. Among the periods of most significant change was the century following the first European contacts in or about the year 1500.[2]

The visits of European explorers and fishermen did not lead immediately to any permanent European presence, and yet they left their mark on native culture. By trading furs, the Indian peoples acquired European artifacts such as metal knives and copper kettles, which could be used to make hunting and domestic tasks easier. The purpose of the trade, for them, was not to change radically their existing way of life but rather to strengthen it.

Trade, however, brought more to native people than the artifacts they wanted. It also brought European disease. Never before exposed to diseases such as smallpox and influenza, Indian people had little or no immunity. Together with changes in diet caused by eating dried European foods acquired in trade, and in some cases problems of alcoholism, disease brought about massive changes in the size of the Indian population. In 1600 the Micmac people probably numbered about 3,500. A hundred years before, they may have been as many as 35,000.[3]

The depletion of native population before 1600 was a human tragedy on a scale that later generations can only guess at. A few years after, an old Micmac chief told a French priest that in his youth he had seen his people 'as thickly planted . . . as the hairs on his head'. Now, the priest reported back to France, the Micmac 'are astonished and often complain that, since the French mingle with and carry on trade with them, they are dying fast, and the population is thinning out'.[4]

There were also other changes. The fur trade caused Indian peoples to change the yearly cycle of their lives. Instead of harvesting diverse food resources—river and coastal fisheries, inland hunting grounds, and gathering of nuts and berries were among the most important—in long-established patterns that varied from place to place, native bands now increasingly centered their attention on the summer trade with European ships. Inland bands would spend more time at the coast, and there was a tendency for the time and energy devoted to hunting beaver to detract from more traditional pursuits. Disruption of food supplies, and eventual dependence on European trade goods, were among the subtle and far-reaching effects of European contact on native society and culture. In the long term the opportunity for trading profits would also tend to make native society less coherent, as individuals asserted their claims to own fur-trapping lands, as opposed to the more traditional collective ownership.[5]

Yet it would be entirely wrong to think of the Micmac and Maliseet in 1600 as societies falling apart. They were societies in the grip of massive changes that had already had tragic consequences for many individuals and families. They were societies under strain. The decade of the 1600s would show that they were societies which had not broken under that strain. The native peoples of the region still retained a resilience that showed in their response to the onset of European colonization.

The story of the early French colonization of Acadia has often been told, and needs only brief outlining here. The colony of Acadia was formally created in 1603, when King Henry IV of France granted a charter to Pierre Du Gua, Sieur de Monts, to authorize de Monts to settle and govern Acadia. De Monts was also granted a ten-year monopoly of the fur trade in the colony. In return for these grants, he undertook to send at least 60 settlers to Acadia each year, and to sponsor efforts to convert native people to Christianity.[6]

The Sieur de Monts was a former military officer who had already had experience in North America. His first visit to the hemisphere had probably been in the year 1600 when he was one of the participants in an unsuccessful French colonizing attempt at Tadoussac, on the St Lawrence River. The boundaries of Acadia, as defined in 1603, indicated a more southerly area of interest. Extending from the 40th to the 46th line of latitude, the colony included the entire eastern seaboard from present-day New Jersey to Cape Breton Island.

In March 1604, de Monts set sail from the French port of Le Havre. His fleet of three ships carried some 80 colonists who would spend the following winter in Acadia. Of most of them, no exact record has survived. It may be that some were criminals and vagrants who had been conscripted for the venture. Among the few whose names and biographies are known was Samuel de Champlain, a writer and cartographer who had made a voyage up the St Lawrence River the previous summer. Champlain carried no official title in 1604, but took charge of the process of finding a site for colonization, and emerged as one of the leaders of the colony.

Champlain's choice of the first settlement site proved disastrously mistaken. St Croix Island (later known as Dochet's Island) was located in the St Croix River, half a mile from shore and not far from present-day St Andrews, New Brunswick. It was a tiny island, and its chief attraction was strategic: no any ship could pass it without coming within cannon-range. It also had some disadvantages, in that there was no fresh water supply and, after trees had been cut down to build housing for the colonists, no source of firewood either. For these necessities, and for hunting, the settlers would have to make the crossing to the river bank. In summer, that was merely inconvenient; in winter, it was difficult and dangerous.

To be fair, Champlain and his colleagues were understandably ill-informed about the Acadian climate. Prevailing European geographical theories held that climate was determined solely by north-south latitude. By that standard Acadia should have had weather very similar to that of the south of France. The influence of the continental land mass of North America, and of ocean currents, ensured in fact that this was not so.[7] 'There are six months of winter in this country,' Champlain tersely observed in a later account of the episode.[8]

The results for the colonists were devastating. At least 35 of the 80 died of scurvy, caused by lack of fresh fruit and vegetables, and only ten were unaffected by the disease. The winter was exceptionally severe that year, with the first snow falling in early October. Confined on their island, residents of the small 'habitation' lived on salt meat, and melted snow for water. Only in March 1605 did they successfully establish contact with Passamaquoddy Indian people and trade with them for additional food supplies.[9]

In the spring de Monts and Champlain began to look in earnest for a site further south. They searched in vain. Despite coasting down as far as the Cape Cod peninsula, the small expedition could not identify any location that had the required combination of a good harbour, potentially fertile land, and cooperative native people. Ironically, the rejected territories would soon support the populous New England colonies that would play a leading role in the later British conquest of Acadia.

As it was, de Monts had to make a difficult decision. What alternative could be found to the unsuccessful St Croix site? As a temporary measure, until further explorations could be made, the choice was made to move across the Bay of Fundy to a location first visited by the colonizing fleet in June 1604: Port Royal, near today's Annapolis Royal, Nova Scotia. Port Royal had the advantage of offering a mainland location on a safe harbour. Also important was the receptive attitude of the local Micmac band, headed by its chief, Membertou. Reputedly over 100 years old, Membertou was a strong leader who also had the power of a shaman, or medicine-man. For the remainder of his life—he died in 1611—he was a consistent supporter of the French presence at Port Royal.[10]

Membertou established a close personal friendship with one of de Monts' senior lieutenants, Jean de Biencourt de Poutrincourt. Poutrincourt, a noble-man and military officer, had been impressed by the scenic beauty of Port Royal, and in the summer of 1604 de Monts had promised him a land gr[...] in the area.[11] The grant was confirmed by Henry IV in early 1606, an[...]

when Poutrincourt returned to Acadia later that year after spending the winter in France, he had a new personal stake in the colony.[12]

By 1606, the French colony of Acadia was in better condition than it had been during the previous two years. The winter of 1605–06 had been relatively mild, and only a few colonists had died of scurvy. Among them, ironically, were the Catholic priest and the Protestant minister. This early colonizing effort, unlike later ones in Acadia, included both Catholic and Protestant participants. Tradition holds, probably correctly, that the two clergymen were buried in the same grave: 'to see', in a contemporary's sardonic phrase, 'whether they could rest in peace together in death, since they were unable to reach agreement in life.'[13]

The winter of 1606–07 was the most successful yet enjoyed by the colonists in Acadia. There were no food shortages, and although scurvy was not eliminated entirely, the French writer Marc Lescarbot recorded that only four deaths had resulted.[14] Lescarbot, a friend of Poutrincourt, spent the winter in the colony and in a later *History of New France* he presented a favourable picture of what his friend had achieved in Acadia. Champlain recalled similarly that 'we passed this winter very pleasantly, and had good fare . . .'[15] It was during this time that Lescarbot's famous *Theatre of Neptune* was first produced, and also founded was Champlain's 'Order of Good Cheer', an informal dining club in which the colonists took their turn in hunting to provide food for the table.

The good cheer did not last long. Between 1604 and 1607, the price of beaver furs rose in France by 150 per cent.[16] Superficially, that seemed to be a healthy trend for the Acadian colonists, who could sell their furs at a good profit. In reality, two serious dangers were arising. One was that there would be competition from rival merchants who would take advantage of the many secluded harbours on the Acadian coastline to land a crew and trade illegally for furs, thus breaking into the monopoly of de Monts. There had always been such competition, but rising prices would inevitably intensify the problem. Secondly, there were merchants who, for similar reasons, were actively pressing the French government to revoke the monopoly altogether and declare free access to the furs of the region.

De Monts took this latter danger seriously. He could hardly do otherwise, as the Duc de Sully, chief minister of Henry IV, was known to believe that attempts at colonization of the northern parts of North America were unlikely to prove successful, and that the fur trade monopoly in Acadia was a useless restriction. De Monts had returned to France in the fall of 1605 to counter the threat. In the spring of 1607 he sent word to Port Royal that he had been unsuccessful, and that the monopoly had been cancelled. Confronted by large losses, arising from the expenses of colonization, de Monts instructed Poutrincourt, Champlain, and the other colonists to abandon Port Royal and return to France.[17]

The first major French colonizing effort in Acadia had thus ended in failure. High hopes of finding precious metals, of conquering great native empires, or of finding a sea passage to the lucrative trading markets of Asia, had quickly proved unrealistic. Even the more modest idea of basing colonization on fur-trading profits had also proved unworkable. De Monts was not yet finished with North America, but from 1608 his efforts (and those of Champlain) were focused on the potentially more productive fur-trading territories of the St Lawrence Valley. One individual who was not disillusioned with Acadia was Poutrincourt. For the moment, though, he lacked the financial support that would be needed if the colony were to be reestablished.

From all appearances, it must have seemed that French colonization in Acadia was a dead issue in 1607, and yet the significance of this series of events can only be fully assessed when put in a European context. Just why did this first French effort in Acadia take place in the decade of the 1600s rather than sooner or later? Was the timing coincidental? The answer is that coincidence had little or nothing to do with it. Strong economic and political forces were at work in Europe, reaching a peak in this decade. It was already a hundred years since European fishermen and explorers had made contact with the coast of today's Maritime provinces. Norse voyagers may in fact have landed some five centuries before that—certainly they were in Newfoundland. The Norse presence in North America was fleeting, however, and European contact was re-established within a few years before or after the year 1500.

As to exactly who was the first European of that era to set foot in the Maritime region, we do not know. It may have been the explorer John Cabot in 1497, or the later explorer Gaspar Corte-Real in 1501. More likely it was a fisherman whose name has never appeared on any written record. What is clear is that fishing vessels of various European nationalities—French, English, Spanish, Portuguese, Basque—continued to visit these coasts. They came to take on fresh water, to build temporary stages for drying fish, to do some fur-trading on the side. They might stay for a few hours, or for a summer fishing season, but never year-round. Only in the 1600s was this pattern conclusively changed in the region. A forerunner of the change was an ill-fated attempt by another would-be colonial promoter, the Marquis de la Roche, to found a colony on Sable Island in 1598. Forty convicts and about ten armed guards lived there for five years before the venture collapsed in violent conflict.[18] It would be left to the de Monts expedition to make the real beginning of French settlement.

Why, then, was the pattern of a hundred years broken in the 1600s? One reason was economic. The demand for North American furs, and especially beaver furs, developed on a large scale in Europe only in the latter part of the previous century. Small shipments of furs brought back by fishermen had stimulated the demand and led to the emergence of the beaver-fur hat as a major fashion item for men. This had two implications for North American colonization: first, that it provided a possible source of revenue to fund the high costs of founding colonies, and secondly, that (unlike the fisheries) the fur trade required extended contacts with native peoples and thus there was more incentive to make year-round settlements.[19]

There was also a political reason for the colonization of the 1600s. Spain and Portugal had long been colonial powers in central and South America. Their empires had quickly aroused the admiration of other European nations, which looked enviously at the gold and silver drawn especially from New Spain, and at the feats of conquest by which large native empires had been destroyed. The nations of northern Europe had made some efforts to follow the Spanish example, but never with any success. The disastrous attempt by Jacques Cartier and the Sieur de Roberval from 1541 to 1543 to establish a French colony, near the present site of Quebec City, was one example.[20] After that time, France became preoccupied with internal political disputes, until in the 1590s the country emerged from the series of civil wars known as the Wars of Religion. Only then was the government of France able to turn its attention once again to the Americas as a possible source of wealth, power and prestige.

When de Monts was granted his charter in 1603, his merchant investors hoped the colony of Acadia would be a productive investment of capital in the new and flourishing fur trade. From the point of view of the royal government, the colony was to be a start in the process of developing an overseas empire to rival those of Spain and Portugal. De Monts, like other European colonial promoters of the time, was faced with the difficult task of trying to satisfy both of these aspirations at the same time. The task was made more difficult by other complications. For one thing, merchant communities were divided by competitive rivalries. This was true even within particular port towns, such as La Rochelle or St Malo, where de Monts obtained much of his capital. The result was seen in the damaging attacks on his monopoly that de Monts encountered from the start. Furthermore, the royal government was not unanimously convinced of the merits of colonization. Although Henry IV himself was sympathetic, his chief minister Sully was sceptical. To be a colonial promoter in these circumstances was no easy task.

Thus, although there were strong, long-term economic and political forces operating to favour colonization in the 1600s, there were also practical difficulties that stood in the way. Add to these the difficulties of adaptation to the North American environment that would face the colonists on arrival, and the failure of the Acadian colony in 1607 becomes readily understandable. It becomes even more explicable in the context that the experience of the de Monts colony was not just a French experience, but a northern European one.

France was not the only country to feel the effects of long-term forces leading towards North American colonization. The possible profits to be made from fur-trading were obvious to others, such as English and Dutch merchants. Both England and the Netherlands were emerging in the decade of the 1600s from a long period of political and military preoccupation with European affairs. Both had been at war with Spain for several decades. England concluded its peace treaty with Spain in 1604, while the Dutch republic signed a 12-year truce with Spain in 1609.

From those countries too came an outflow of economic and political energy into colonization in the decade of the 1600s. England had already made its claim to ownership of Newfoundland, and now in 1606 it proclaimed the existence of two other North American colonies: North and South Virginia. South Virginia was to be a southern colony, centred in the area still known as Virginia. North Virginia was defined as extending from the 38th to the 45th lines of latitude, and thus went far enough northwards to include a major part of the Nova Scotian peninsula. To complicate matters further, the Netherlands would act just a few years later, in 1614, to claim the territory from the 40th to the 45th parallels for its New Netherlands Company.[21]

In the decade of the 1600s, however, France and England were the two northern European nations most active in North American colonization. Potentially, their interests were in conflict. In practical terms, each was able to found colonies only on a limited basis. The English colonies in this decade included the South Virginia settlement at Jamestown, and its North Virginia equivalent at Sagadahoc, in present-day Maine. Both were founded in 1607, and three years later came the settlement of John Guy at Cupids Cove, in Newfoundland.

All of these colonies proved fragile. The Jamestown settlement survived, but only narrowly. Up until 1612, when the Virginia Company began successfully to develop a tobacco-based economy, the tiny colony struggled to cope with food shortages, internal disputes, and conflicts with native peoples. The Cupids settlement suffered from some of the same problems. It too survived, but only after disputes between Guy and the English-based Newfoundland Company had seriously threatened its existence in 1614. The Sagadahoc venture failed entirely. A severe winter in 1607–08, disputes with Abenaki Indian people, and the failure to find mines of gold and silver— 'the mayne intended benefit' of the colony, wrote one discouraged participant—all combined to bring about the abandonment of the settlement in the fall of 1608.[22]

When the de Monts colony in Acadia is examined in a comparative context, therefore, two major points become clear. First, that the enterprise of de Monts was no isolated event. It proceeded from the same economic and political forces that were stimulating other northern European colonial attempts in this decade. Secondly, that despite these strong forces, such ventures could easily result in failure. Problems in adjusting to the climate and environment, and financial problems arising from the difficulties encountered in trying to develop an economic base, were common to all North American colonial ventures at the time. So too was the crucial importance of developing a close relationship with native people. For the early colonizers reaching North America was in many cases just the beginning of their troubles, as they quickly discovered the difficulties of settlement.

The evacuation of Port Royal by the French colonists in 1607 could reasonably have been expected to mark the end of French efforts at colonization in this part of North America. Just as the Sagadahoc failure a year later was described by its chief promoter as 'a wonderful discouragement' to future English colonial schemes, so the abandonment of Port Royal could only confirm the cynicism of de Monts' critics.[23] Furthermore, when de Monts and Champlain turned their attention in 1608 to the St Lawrence Valley, it seemed clear that Acadia was to be by-passed from now on. Had this turned out in fact to be true, it is hard to estimate what the consequences would have been. Would Acadia (under some other name) have been colonized by another European nationality, such as English, Dutch, or Scots? Would Acadia have been spared all colonizing attempts for the time being? Both of these would have been possibilities. What is certain is that the history of the region would have been different from the form which it has since taken.

That Acadia was not permanently abandoned by French colonization was owed in part to the actions of a single individual. To be sure, those actions were heavily influenced by the same economic and political forces which had influenced de Monts. Yet the personal determination of the Baron de Poutrincourt to return to Port Royal was an important factor also. In early 1608, de Monts formally turned over to Poutrincourt the ownership of the building that had housed the colony, and planning began for a new expedition.

Poutrincourt faced major difficulties. First and foremost was the problem of finance. After the failure of de Monts' attempt in Acadia, merchant investors were not likely to come forward unless they could be convinced that the new venture would be more successful. Poutrincourt had no such evidence to offer, and accordingly commercial support did not materialize. Poutrincourt, however, had one advantage that de Monts had lacked. De Monts was a Protestant. Poutrincourt was a Catholic and could readily appeal for support to wealthy French Catholic sponsors on the ground that he intended to bring about the religious conversion of native people. From the beginning Poutrincourt used this as an argument in efforts to find private financing. Even so, the process was not easy.

In the summer of 1608, Poutrincourt believed that he had found a sponsor in the Bishop of Verdun, who was a powerful and wealthy aristocrat as well as being bishop. On the strength of this support, Poutrincourt bought and equipped a ship. Only then did he find out that a misunderstanding had somehow arisen: the bishop refused outright to pay the large bill presented by the outfitter of the ship. Without a source of support, and deep in debt, Poutrincourt did not even get as far as leaving the shores of France.[24]

After spending more than a year putting his finances back in order, Poutrincourt decided on a new strategy. He would invest heavily from his own resources, would send a ship to Acadia in early 1610, and would hope for success in both fur-trading and religious conversion. Using that success as an argument, he would then try again to obtain financial support.

Accordingly, Poutrincourt left the French port of Dieppe in February 1610. With him was his oldest son Charles de Biencourt, the priest Jessé Flesché, and about twenty other potential colonists. As in the case of the earlier settlement of de Monts, all were male. They included Claude and Charles de la Tour, a father and son who were later to play prominent roles in the evolution of Acadia. Following a long voyage, the Acadian coast was reached, and after a number of stops the ship arrived at Port Royal in June.

The habitation was intact. Guarded by Membertou and his Micmac band, it needed little more than repairs to the roof. The structure and the furnishings were exactly as Poutrincourt had left them in 1607. A new well had to be dug, and nearby land cleared for cultivation; then the settlement was apparently ready to take up where the previous colonists had left off three years before.

Yet matters were not quite so simple. Still to be resolved was the long-term financial position of the colony. Poutrincourt and his son, Biencourt, quickly set about implementing their strategy. As well as trading with native people for furs, they also prompted the religious conversion of Membertou and his family. Just three weeks after the arrival of the French expedition, Membertou and some twenty other Micmacs were baptized by Flesché. Shortly afterwards Biencourt departed for France with a shipload of furs and, as Champlain later recorded, 'to carry the good news of the baptism of the savages'.[25] The haste with which the whole series of events had taken place was no accident. It represented a deliberate effort to create quickly an impression of achievement both in trade and in religious conversion.[26]

The effort was partly successful. Biencourt arrived in France in the late summer of 1610 with two immediate objectives. One was to secure a monopoly of the fur trade on a similar basis to that of de Monts years before. The other, supported by the baptismal register brought from Port Royal, was to appeal for financial support from wealthy individuals in the cause of religious conversion. In this regard, Biencourt recruited Marc Lescarbot, the writer who had visited Acadia in 1606–07, to write an elaborate account of

Lescarbot

the baptism of Membertou and his family. Lescarbot accomplished the task within weeks. 'The poor [native] people,' he wrote, 'groan for religious instruction'; he went on to threaten God's vengeance against those who 'could help them to become Christians, and do not'.[27] Obviously, the best way to avoid that vengeance was to contribute to Poutrincourt's treasury.

In his first purpose, Biencourt failed completely. To expect to be given a trade monopoly so soon after the cancellation of the similar privilege of de Monts was unrealistic. The support for religious conversion was more easily available, although not in the exact form Biencourt would have liked. When Biencourt arrived in France, King Henry IV had recently been assassinated by a religious opponent. He was succeeded by his nine-year-old son, Louis XIII, but real power was held for the time being by Henry's queen, Marie de Medici. The queen, who met with Biencourt in early October 1610, had close connections with the powerful Jesuit religious order. The result was that Biencourt was put in contact with a potential sponsor in the person of the Marquise de Guercheville, a noblewoman who was also strongly pro-Jesuit. Agreement was reached in January 1611 that Guercheville would provide support on condition that Jesuit missionaries would take over the work of religious conversion in Acadia. Six days later, on 26 January 1611, Biencourt left Dieppe with 36 new colonists and the Jesuit missionaries Pierre Biard and Enemond Massé.[28]

The events following the arrival of Biencourt and his fellow voyagers at Port Royal in May 1611 obviously fall outside the decade of the 1600s. Acadia as a French colony had many remaining years of difficulty. Quarrels between Biencourt and the Jesuits would even lead to the splitting of the settlement into two in 1613, when the Jesuits left Port Royal to establish a mission near Mount Desert Island, on the coast of present-day Maine. Both that settlement and Port Royal were burned shortly afterwards by an English raiding party from Virginia. For many subsequent years, Biencourt, Charles de la Tour, and other colonists lived a tenuous life in Acadia, living on meagre profits from the fur trade and fishery.[29]

Yet the re-establishment of Acadian settlement by Poutrincourt in 1610, and Biencourt's efforts later in the year to obtain support in France, had marked a genuine turning-point. From 1610 onwards the French presence in the Maritime region was continuous. To be sure, Biencourt's sojourn in France was not completely successful. Not only did he fail in his quest for a trade monopoly, which might have brought benefits in the form of capital investment by merchants, but the intricate negotiations with Guercheville and the Jesuits delayed his intended departure for Port Royal from November 1610 to the following January. By the time he finally arrived back, Poutrincourt was on the point of abandoning the colony for lack of necessary supplies. Also, the presence of the Jesuits had only reluctantly been accepted by Biencourt. The Jesuits' first priority in Acadia was religious conversion rather than commercial profit, and in this they differed from Biencourt and his father. Their close connection with Guercheville gave the Jesuits a position of power, and this too would quickly become a divisive issue.[30]

Nevertheless, the arrival of the Jesuits had been a necessary price to pay for the survival of the colony. In the long term, the presence of religious missionaries in Acadia would prove to be an effective way of establishing cultural links with the native people whose support was essential to the survival of the colony. In the short term, the financial support obtained by Biencourt—and he ultimately managed to drive a good bargain with Guercheville and the Jesuits, involving a series of interest-free loans—made the difference between the survival or abandonment of the French colony in Acadia.

The colony in Acadia, however, could not survive only through the efforts of its French promoters. While the bare outline of events can be written— and all too often has been written—with the French at the centre and native people relegated to the fringes, this approach is not enough in itself to bring out one of the basic realities of the whole process. That reality is the power and influence of native people. Traditional histories of the Maritime region have allowed Indian people the role of assisting the colonists in times of difficulty. More recent research in Indian history reveals that their importance was much greater than that. Simply put, native people had the power in the decade of the 1600s to say 'yes' or 'no' to French colonization.

By the beginning of the decade, native peoples of the region, whether Micmac or Maliseet-Passamaquoddy, were continuing to struggle with the disastrous population decline that had so recently taken place. These native societies were still vital and coherent, and their resilience was seen clearly in their response to colonizing Europeans. The missionary Pierre Biard looked at Indian people with the biases that were characteristic of Europeans of his day, but he was too honest an observer to report the Indians' own attitudes in anything but a truthful way. Those attitudes surprised him. 'You will see these poor barbarians . . .,' he wrote on the basis of his experiences in Acadia, 'holding their heads so high that they greatly underrate us, regarding themselves as our superiors.' On another occasion, Biard wrote with some exasperation that 'they think they are better, more valiant and ingenious than the French; and, what is difficult to believe, richer than we are.'[31]

What Biard was finding out was that Indian people were not overwhelmingly impressed by the Europeans they met, including the French in Acadia. They did value some of the trappings of European society, especially goods such as metal tools, or glass beads that could be used for decorative purposes. The Europeans themselves, however, were seen as weak and sometimes foolish, especially in their stumbling efforts to cope with the North American environment. Their appearance, especially those who had beards, was regarded as interesting but unattractive. Their materialism, as reflected in the lust for fur-trading profits, seemed vulgar to the native people, and so at times did their personal morality. Biard reported that native women were 'very modest' and that once when 'a certain madcap took some liberties', a Micmac delegation 'came and told our Captain that he should look out for his men, informing him that any one who attempted to do that again could not stand much of a chance, that they would kill him on the spot.'[32]

Native people in Acadia, therefore, were fully able to appraise the French presence critically, and to assert the superiority of their own values when necessary. They also had considerable military force. To be sure, that force was not unified throughout the region, in that the Micmac and Maliseet-Passamaquoddy were separate peoples, and in that Micmac political and military organization was decentralized. Yet the Micmac held regular councils of chiefs, at which issues of war and peace were discussed. They were traditional allies of the Maliseet-Passamaquoddy. Furthermore, individual chiefs could themselves build impressive military power in their own localities. Membertou, for example, was known to be a formidable warrior. Given the small numbers of French present in the region, the fact was that they were there only as long as native people chose to tolerate them. They could just as easily have been killed or driven out, or simply left alone to struggle unsuccessfully with the North American climate and environment.[33]

There was also another side to the French dependence on native people. Aside from immediate questions of survival, the longer-term success of the colonial enterprise depended squarely on the colonists' ability to forge cooperative relationships with Indian people. Indians were the suppliers of the furs which were crucial to the commercial success of the colony. Trading relationships with the Micmac had obvious importance. Trade was also carried on on the opposite side of the Bay of Fundy from Port Royal, with the Maliseet. For this reason alone, the friendship of native people was necessarily courted by the French.

In the matter of religious conversion, the French also had a compelling need for Indian cooperation, especially during Poutrincourt's efforts to re-establish Acadian settlement in 1610. The need to demonstrate success in making Indian converts was central to the financial health of the colony. There could be no question, however, of making conversions by force or deception. As in all other areas of interaction between Indians and colonists, native people approached the religious question from a position of strength. It was unlikely that any significant numbers would be found who would be willing to give up their own traditional beliefs for the doubtful benefits of a new religion preached by recently arrived aliens.

Nevertheless, certain factors made religious conversion possible. One was the breadth of native religious beliefs. Native spirituality did not involve any one exclusive faith, but rather implied a belief in the power of a large number of spiritual forces. It was quite possible in that context to accept Christianity as one aspect of religious truth, while not abandoning more traditional beliefs. Also, religious conversion was often seen by native people as a means of symbolizing friendship or of cementing an alliance.[34]

The conversion of Membertou and his family in 1610 can best be seen in this context. Baptized only some three weeks after the arrival of the priest Flesché—who did not speak the Micmac language—these converts had not been given any elaborate course of instruction in the Christian religion. Pierre Biard later remarked specifically on the failure of Flesché to prepare potential converts thoroughly enough for baptism, and reported that Flesché himself had been glad to hand over his tasks to the Jesuits.[35] Be that as it may, the conversions of 1610 had served their purpose as far as Membertou and Poutrincourt were concerned: for Membertou, a sign of alliance and friendship renewed, as well as a means of access to a new aspect of the spiritual world; for Poutrincourt, also a symbol of alliance, as well as being a vital piece of evidence that the colony was serving a genuine religious purpose.

The importance of Membertou in sustaining the French presence in Acadia was profound. That importance has often been interpreted as stemming from Membertou's role as the amiable helper of the French. The truth was that Membertou's real significance for the French colonists was that he was an ally much more powerful than themselves. From the first arrival of the de Monts group at Port Royal in 1605, Membertou's support had offered a military guarantee as well as access to the necessary technology of survival in this part of North America. During the three years of French absence from Port Royal, it had been Membertou's Micmac band which had preserved the buildings of the settlement. When the French returned in 1610, it was the same chief and the same band who supplied the need for alliance and support, symbolized in religious conversion.

For the Micmac, the French presence was valued for very specific reasons. While native traditions of hospitality, and the personal friendship of Poutrincourt and Membertou, cannot be discounted as influential factors, the native interest in the French colony was not altruistic. European trade goods had an immediate economic and military value. As long as they were obtained only from short-term European visitors, the supply was not assured. When trade was conducted with a permanently established habitation, this disadvantage no longer existed. The benefits of trade would apply especially to the Indian band in the immediate locality of the settlement. A chief such as Membertou would not only enjoy easy access to trade goods, but would also have the possibility of acting as an intermediary in trading those goods to other Indian people. For Membertou, as a powerful but aging leader, this was a strong attraction.

Had the Micmac had the power to see into the future, their decision might have been different. In the long term the fur trade had destructive effects on native society, which compounded the results of disease and the population decline that had already taken place. Yet in the context of the 1600s, the decision of the Micmac, and specifically that of Membertou, to accept the French presence was a rational response to prevailing circumstances. European trade goods could reasonably be seen at that time as strengthening native society rather than weakening it. Long experience in trading with visiting Europeans had given native people a shrewd appreciation of the value of their furs in terms of European products. Lescarbot later reported that the price of beaver in terms of such trade goods as knives had increased rapidly during the very years when the price of furs on the European market had also risen.[36] The Micmac had good reason to be self-confident in their ability to trade productively with the French.

Furthermore, a small settlement such as the one at Port Royal posed no evident threat of any kind to native people. On the contrary, it was so small and militarily so weak, that it needed the protection of native allies. Later events would show that even this small settlement was part of a much larger invasion of North America which would have disastrous results for native people. Although it would take another century and a half, the Micmacs themselves would ultimately be reduced to the status of a powerless minority. In the decade of the 1600s, however, it was clear that the French needed the Micmac more than the Micmac needed the French. Since there was no apparent reason to suppose that this would change, the toleration of French settlement—and even its encouragement, as by Membertou and his band—was neither rash nor foolish.

The decade of the 1600s represented a major turning-point in the human history of what is now the Maritime region. At the beginning of the decade, this was overwhelmingly the territory of native people. It was true that French and other European traders were arriving in increasing numbers for seasonal visits, and that the small and doomed French occupation of Sable Island had recently begun. Yet on the mainland, no non-native people lived in the region. By 1610, this was no longer true. To be sure, the impact of the Port Royal settlement should not be exaggerated. It too was very small, and as yet its French inhabitants were exclusively male. This in itself would emerge as a further element of the French-Micmac interaction, for stable family relationships could and did develop between the settlers and native women. Charles de la Tour and his Micmac wife, for example, had three daughters in the 1620s and early 1630s.[37] The immigration to Acadia of exclusively French family groups can be dated to the 1630s, and thus lay well in the future during the decade of the 1600s.

Yet the French presence in Acadia was continuous from 1610 onwards. The origin of that presence lay in the economic and political developments in France which had impelled de Monts to undertake Acadian settlement in 1604. Although the actual attempt of de Monts ended in failure in 1607, the effort of Poutrincourt to re-establish the colony was the direct descendant of that original venture. The later establishment of the Acadian people on the Bay of Fundy marshlands was, in turn, a development made possible by the persistence of the small colonial community established by Poutrincourt. Not only did the presence of Biencourt, La Tour, and others keep alive the economic interest of French merchants in this part of North America, but it was also one of the main arguments used by the French government to defend the French claim to ownership of Acadia against other competing European claims.[38] Had it not been for Poutrincourt's venture, the future of Acadia as a French colony would have been doubtful indeed.

What has all too often been overlooked by historians is the essential role played by native people in this entire process. In the decade of the 1600s, it was the native people of the region who held the real power. European colonizing attempts up and down the coasts of North America were small and fragile. They might succeed, but they often failed. Everywhere, the consequences of European success or failure were important to the subsequent course of history. Just as elsewhere, that was true in Acadia. The native peoples of the region, and especially the Micmac, could easily have eliminated the French colonial presence if they had chosen to do so. Some might argue in hindsight that they made a tragic mistake in tolerating any European settlement. Others would contend that, in the context of the massive European invasion of North America, it was to the Indians' benefit to support a form of colonization that was at least seemingly compatible with their own way of life.

What is certain is that, while the French and their leaders—de Monts, Champlain, Poutrincourt, and the others—were important participants in the events that took place, they were not in a position to determine the outcome. Native people, on the other hand, were in such a position. That they chose to offer toleration and support, particularly through the response of Membertou to the French presence at Port Royal, was essential to the persistence of French colonization. That choice was a crucial determining factor in a crucially important decade in the history of the region.

Suggestions for Further Reading

Andrew Hill Clark, *Acadia: The Geography of Early Nova Scotia to 1760* (Madison, Wis., 1968).

H.F. McGee, Jr, ed., *The Native Peoples of Atlantic Canada* (Ottawa, 1983).

John G. Reid, *Acadia, Maine, and New Scotland: Marginal Colonies in the Seventeenth Century* (Toronto, 1981).

Notes

[1] See Robert E. Funk, 'Post-Pleistocene Adaptations', in Bruce G. Trigger, ed., *Handbook of North American Indians, vol. 15, Northeast* (Washington, 1978), 16–17; James A. Tuck, 'Regional Cultural Development 3000 to 300 B.C.', *ibid.*, 34.

[2] T.J. Brasser, 'Early European Contacts', *ibid.*, 78–80; on changes prior to European contact, see James A. Tuck, *Maritime Provinces Prehistory* (Ottawa, 1984).

[3] See Virginia Miller, 'Aboriginal Micmac Population: A Review of the Evidence', *Ethnohistory* 23 (1976), 117–27.

[4] *The Jesuit Relations and Allied Documents: Travels and Explorations of the Jesuit Missionaries in New France, 1610–1791*, ed. Reuben Gold Thwaites (73 vols; Cleveland, 1896–1901), I, 177; III, 105.

[5] See John G. Reid, *Acadia, Maine, and New Scotland: Marginal Colonies in the Seventeenth Century* (Toronto, 1981), 4–5; for recent research findings, see David Sanger, 'An Introduction in the Prehistory of the Passamaquoddy Bay Region', *American Review of Canadian Studies* 16 (1986), 139–59.

[6] Reid, *Acadia, Maine, and New Scotland*, 14–15; Marcel Trudel, *The Beginnings of New France, 1524–1663* (Toronto, 1973), 83–4.

[7] See Karen Ordahl Kupperman, 'The Puzzle of the American Climate in the Early Colonial Period', *American Historical Review* 87 (1982), 1262–89.

[8] Henry Percival Biggar, ed., *The Works of Samuel de Champlain* (6 vols; Toronto, 1922–36), I, 307.

[9] Trudel, *Beginnings*, 86–7; George MacBeath, 'Pierre Du Gua de Monts', *Dictionary of Canadian Biography* (hereafter DCB), (12 vols to date; Toronto, 1966–   ), I, 292–3.

[10] See Lucien Campeau, 'Henri Membertou', DCB, I, 500–1.

[11] See Huia Ryder *et al.*, 'Jean de Biencourt de Poutrincourt et de Saint-Just', DCB, I, 96–9.

[12] *Ibid.*

[13] Gabriel Sagard, quoted in Marcel Trudel, *The Beginnings of New France, 1524–1663* (Toronto, 1973), 88; on the probable accuracy of the story, see Elizabeth Jones, *Gentlemen and Jesuits: Quests for Glory and Adventure in the Early Days of New France* (Toronto, 1986), 68.

[14] Marc Lescarbot, *The History of New France . . .*, ed. W.L. Grant (3 vols; Toronto, 1907–14), II, 344.

[15] Biggar, *Works of Champlain*, I, 447.

[16] Robert Le Blant, 'Le commerce compliquée des fourrures canadiennes au début du XVIIᵉ siècle', *Revue d'histoire de l'Amérique française* 26 (1972–3), 56–7.

[17] Reid, *Acadia, Maine and New Scotland*, 15–18; MacBeath, 'De Monts', DCB, I, 293.

[18] Gustave Lanctot, 'Troilus de la Roche de Mesgouez', DCB, I, 421–2.

[19] See Reid, *Acadia, Maine, and New Scotland*, 6–7.

[20] Trudel, *Beginnings*, 34–53.

[21] See John G. Reid, 'The Scots Crown and the Restitution of Port Royal, 1629–1632', *Acadiensis* 6, 2 (Spring 1977), 39–40.

[22] William Strachey, 'History of travaile into Virginia', in Henry O. Thayer, ed., *The Sagadahoc Colony* (Portland, Me., 1892), 85; David B. Quinn, *North America from Earliest Discovery to First Settlements: The Norse Voyages to 1612* (New York, 1977),

439–64; Gillian T. Cell, *English Enterprise in Newfoundland, 1577–1660* (Toronto, 1969), 53–80; Reid, *Acadia, Maine, and New Scotland*, 15–18.

[23]Sir Ferdinando Gorges, 'Brief Relation', in Henry Sweetser Burrage, ed., *Gorges and the Grant of the Province of Maine* (Portland, Me., 1923), 142.

[24]Lucien Campeau, ed., *Monumentae Novae Franciae, vol. I: la première mission d'Acadie* (Quebec and Rome, 1967), Introduction, 191–3.

[25]Biggar, *Works of Champlain*, IV, 4.

[26]Trudel, *Beginnings*, 107–8; Campeau, 'Membertou', DCB, I, 500–1.

[27]Translated from Marc Lescarbot, 'La Conversion des Sauvages', in Campeau, *Première mission*, 86.

[28]Trudel, *Beginnings*, 108–11; Campeau, *Première mission*, Introduction, 195–210.

[29]See Reid, *Acadia, Maine, and New Scotland*, 19.

[30]Trudel, *Beginnings*, 111–14.

[31]*Jesuit Relations*, I, 173; III, 75.

[32]*Jesuit Relations*, III, 103–5.

[33]Philip K. Bock, 'Micmac', Trigger, *Handbook, vol. 15*, 116; Campeau, 'Membertou', DCB, I, 500.

[34]Reid, *Acadia, Maine, and New Scotland*, 74–5.

[35]Campeau, 'Membertou', DCB, I, 500–1; Campeau, *Première mission*, 139–40.

[36]See Cornelius J. Jaenen, 'Amerindian Views of French Culture in the Seventeenth Century', *Canadian Historical Review* 55 (1976), 267.

[37]George MacBeath, 'Charles de Saint-Etienne de la Tour', DCB, I, 595; M.A. MacDonald, *Fortune and La Tour; The Civil War in Acadia* (Toronto, 1983), 13, 43.

[38]See Reid, 'Scots Crown and the Restitution of Port Royal', 39–63.

5

French and Native Peoples in New France

Cornelius J. Jaenen

The matter of the nature of the relationship between European and native peoples remains at the heart of the origins of the Canadian peoples—and the Canadian nation. While it was once possible to deal with the history of Canada as if the native people were part of the landscape—like the flora and fauna or the Canadian Shield—rather than independent actors in the drama, most modern scholarship now recognizes the importance of the native inhabitants before and after the intrusion of Europeans.

If the dynamic of the interaction between native peoples and Europeans has become a critical component of early Canadian history, identifying its exact nature has not been easy. In the past, two general interpretations dominated. One, still common, views the interaction as a conflict between superior and primitive civilizations, although as suggested by Foote in Reading 3, European superiority was less certain than has often been conceived.

In this view, Europe would inexorably triumph. An alternative approach, more critical of Europe, sees the dynamic in equally stark terms, insisting that the natives were inevitably doomed once they were exposed to imported disease, technology, and immorality. Such a 'fatal-impact' theory stresses the victimization of the natives by forces essentially beyond their comprehension and control.

In the following discussion, Cornelius Jaenen re-examines the French-Amerindian contact from the perspective of recent scholarship. What does Jaenen see as the principal characteristics of the French-Amerindian experience? To what extent and on what grounds does he defend the French from charges of bad faith and worse treatment? What is his evidence for the assertion that circumstance rather than national origin accounts for Indian policy? On balance, is Jaenen more sympathetic to Europe or to the Amerindians?

This article first appeared in Stanley H. Palmer and Dennis Reinhartz, eds., *Essays on the History of North American Discovery and Exploration* (Texas A & M University Press, 1988), 79–101.

The French experience with the native peoples of New France, collectively known as Amerindians, seems to have been unique in the annals of colonial history in a number of respects.[1] It differed substantially from the Anglo-American, the British, and the subsequent American and Canadian national contacts. It differed even from the French experience in Louisiana, the Antilles, and Guiana. While acknowledging that Western Europeans shared some common attitudes and traditions, or a cultural baggage based on Classical and medieval Christian concepts, and acknowledging that French relations with native peoples were not wholly consistent when considered spatially or temporally, we maintain basically the views expressed in *Friend and Foe*, that the French experience was different from the Iberian and Britannic contacts. The *sauvages*, a generally nonpejorative term employed to designate the native peoples, were undoubtedly regarded as inferior beings not on racial grounds but on sociocultural grounds. Yet they were deemed capable of acquiring European *civility* and partaking of divine grace. *Francisation*, that virtually unattainable objective of total assimilation, would make of them the Frenchman's equal. Our conviction remains, therefore, that Gary Nash's thesis (i.e., that the circumstances of colonization rather than nationalistic or religious differences accounted for the different policies pursued in the Americas by the various European powers) fits New France.[2]

The belief that the French relationship was unique, or at least notably different from the Anglo-American approach, was well established in French, British, and even Amerindian minds during the colonial period. In France, this conviction was canonized eventually in the *génie colonial* thesis—the assertion that the French possessed a peculiar ability for getting along with native peoples, a national trait of compatibility. In view of this supposedly inherent Gallic quality, France seemed destined to assume a *mission civilisatrice* abroad. This interpretation also stressed the heavy-handed nature of Dutch and English colonization, and the cruelties of the Portuguese and Spaniards. In the eighteenth century the French had rediscovered Las Casas and his indictment of the *conquistadores*, and had revived their sixteenth-century Black Legend charging the Spaniards with genocide, the systematic extermination of fifteen million to twenty million people. Even Voltaire recalled the first-hand description of Amerindians hunted down by fierce dogs and of natives hanged publicly in groups of thirteen. These nationalistic views, stressing the benign French approach to native peoples, were propagated by writers as diverse in background as the naturalist Buffon, the polemicist de Pauw, and the soldier Duret.[3]

In North America, Governor Vaudreuil opined that the s(
'prefer the French to all other nations'. The missionary Cl
wrote a six-volume history of the colony in the 1740s, added
was 'the only one which has had the secret of winning the an
American natives'. The trader Jérémie, who intruded into the regi(
claimed by the Hudson's Bay Company, found that the native hunting bands
received the French as 'brothers', but, said he, 'they do not have the same
attachment for the English.' He was restating an affirmation made a generation earlier in Louisiana, where an officer remarked of the Amerindians that
although the English of Carolina 'appear richer and more liberal to them,
yet they do not find their intercourse as pleasant as that of the French.'[4]
These sentiments confirm the sentiments of the native prophet who aroused
Pontiac's supporters in 1763 against the Anglo-Americans, 'these dogs
dressed in red, who have come to rob you of your hunting grounds, and
drive away the game.' The Great Lakes tribes were asked to 'take up the
hatchet' against them, to 'wipe them from the face of the earth', adding that
'the children of your great father, the King of France, are not like the English', that they 'love the red men', and even more improbable, 'they understand the true mode of worshipping me', which referred to a revitalization
movement. Another example is the Saulteaux chief who told the trader Alexander Henry in the autumn of 1761 that he knew that 'our father, the king
of France, is old and infirm' and tired of making war, so he had fallen asleep
and consequently Canada had been conquered. But, he warned, 'this slumber
is drawing to a close. Already I hear our father waking up and asking about
the fate of his children, the Indians.'[5]

English commentaries at the time do not seem to have been in disagreement with these views. An observer in 1755 conceded that 'the French have
always had a great advantage over the English in treating with them.' An
anonymous pamphleteer specified that 'according to their superior dexterity
in address and civility of usage, they are more successful than we, in procuring and retaining their friendship.' The clearest statement remains Thomas
Mante's judgment in his *History of the Late War in North America* (1772):

> . . . and it must be owned, that the general behaviour of the French to the
> Indians was so very different from that of the English, as to give all the weight
> the French could wish to those lessons; the effects of which, accordingly,
> became every day more and more visible. We mention these particulars, not
> only to recommend the manner in which the French treat the Indians as highly
> deserving to be imitated by us: but to wear out the minds of such of our deluded
> countrymen as are not entirely destitute of good sense and humanity, the prej-
> udice conceived against an innocent, much abused, and once happy people,
> who with all their simplicity, are no strangers to the first principles of morality;
> and, accordingly, entertain as deep a sense of the justice, benevolence, and
> condescension of their former friends, the French, as they do of the injustice,

cruelty, and insolence, with which they have been used by their present fellow-subjects, the English.[6]

His appraisal attributed the French colonizing genius to an espousal of the myth of the *bon sauvage*, the Noble Savage of primitivist and Romantic literature, but also to an absence of the racism which marked the Anglo-Saxon contact.

The school of French imperial historians defined, canonized, and gave great prominence to this myth after 1870. Georges Hardy wrote that his countrymen 'have been delivered more quickly of primitive expansionism and we have from the beginning incorporated with our needs of colonial domination the scruples of civilized peoples and the concern of educators.' André Julien added that the 'French had without argument a gift for conciliating the aborigines that no other people possessed to the same degree.' Hubert Deschamps, in describing French colonial doctrines since the sixteenth century, stated that 'their gift of sympathy [for the Amerindians], their facility of assimilation, their absence of racism were there from the beginning.'[7]

The English-speaking world since Edmund Burke has generally adopted the same interpretation. No historian expressed the thesis more elegantly and succinctly than did the 'Boston brahmin' Francis Parkman in the late nineteenth century: 'Spanish civilization crushed the Indian; English civilization scorned and neglected him; French civilization embraced and cherished him.' Philip Means, writing in the 1930s, commended the 'singularly sympathetic and conciliating spirit which Frenchmen have always displayed toward races distinct from their own.' Mason Wade, dean of Canadian studies in the United States, concluded that the French exemplified 'a peculiar ability to conciliate aboriginal peoples' and win their confidence.[8]

Was this presumably felicitous relationship accompanied by positive, optimistic, and constructive assessments of native character and culture? Very early in the French contact experience a wide range of views emerged, among them contradictory evaluations even within the writings of a single author. Writers throughout Western Europe, including the few who had firsthand experience in the New World, portrayed Amerindians according to the traditional philosophical concepts and intellectual constructs that were part of their cultural baggage and bias. There were optimistic assessments couched in the frameworks of the Golden Age, the Earthly Paradise, the Millennial Kingdom, the Lost Tribes of Israel, and Christian Utopianism; there were also pessimistic ones couched in the frameworks of the Chain of Being, the Monstrous World, Wild Men, and Satanic domination.[9] The emergence of positive themes such as the Noble Savage myth, the Four States theory, and the idea of inevitable progress and human perfectibility requires balancing with the emergence of negative themes such as colonial degeneration, the Vanishing Red Man thesis, figurism, and the infancy of the New World.

The Renaissance writers—Rabelais, Ronsard, and Montaigne—on the basis of travelers' tales, the gossip of fishermen in the port taverns, and glimpses of sometimes exotically bedecked Amerindian captives exhibited on public and religious occasions, set the pattern for an optimistic and romantic interpretation which passed into literature and history as the myth of the Noble Savage. Montaigne wrote: 'Those people are wild, just as we call wild the fruits that Nature has produced by herself and in her normal course; whereas really it is those that we have changed artificially and led astray from the common order that we should rather call wild.'[10] Montaigne initiated not only the concept of the natural man, unspoiled by social artificiality, but also indicated an effective and safe method of employing the New World and its cultures to criticize both church and state and both European man and European institutions.

Of equal antiquity and tenacity was the view of the Amerindian as a cruel, ferocious, subhuman, treacherous brute, and a cannibalistic savage. The savagery-civility dichotomy, which became implicit in so much of anthropological and historical writing, was explicitly and unashamedly present in many French assessments from the foundations of New France. In 1558 André Thévet described Amerindians as 'a marvelously strange, wild and brutish people, without faith, without law, without religion and without any civilities' and 'living like unreasoning beasts as nature had produced them, eating roots, men as well as women remaining ever naked, until perhaps such time as they will be frequented by Christians, from whom they will little by little learn to put off this brutishness to put on more civil and humane ways.'[11] Savagery was defined as the absence of certain qualities and institutions. *Sauvages* were people devoid of civility, those possessing *ni foi, ni roi, ni loi*, as the popular expression phrased it. They were often seen as bestial, *homines sylvestris*, or the wild, hairy, naked, lustful, and dangerous beings who lived in the forests beyond the pale of organized life, fulfilling their animalistic instincts, while largely ignorant of God and morality. Jacques Cartier described them as 'savage peoples living without a knowledge of God and the use of reason', and later Samuel de Champlain wrote of hostile tribes as 'brute beasts having neither faith nor law, living without God and religion'.[12]

Toward the end of the French régime in the Age of the Enlightenment the stereotype persisted. The great naturalist, the Comte de Buffon, gave the scientific assessment of America's native peoples as creatures that were barely human because they were still mired in *animalité*, subject to most natural phenomena, and were passive beings, almost inert peoples in static cultures in terms of dominating their environment. In his *Epoques de la Nature*, he generalized from the northern nomadic hunting bands for all Amerindians:

'. . . having never brought into submission either the animals or the elements, having neither conquered the seas nor directed the course of rivers, nor cultivated the soil, he was in himself only an animal of the first order, and existed merely as a being of little consequence, a kind of powerless automaton incapable of reforming or reinforcing nature.'[13] Although Buffon believed, as did most of his contemporaries, that human nature was the same everywhere, he related racial or national differences to such factors as climate and environment, and consequently, to his consternation, he was cited as an authority on colonial degeneration.[14]

The theory of colonial degeneration received its clearest, most virulent and doctrinaire expression in the writings of Cornelius de Pauw. He argued that plants, animals, humans and possibly institutions inevitably degenerated when transplanted in the unfavorable American environment. Only snakes, insects, and harmful animals prospered. Amerindians were its natural inhabitants; consequently, they were idiot children, incurably lazy, and incapable of any mental progress. De Pauw argued that physical degeneration was accompanied by moral and intellectual decline:

> . . . degeneration had attacked their senses and their organs: their soul had lost proportionately to the decline of their body. Nature having taken everything from one hemisphere of this globe in order to give it to the other, had placed in America only children, of whom it as yet had been unable to make men. When Europeans first reached the West Indies, in the fifteenth century, there was not a single American who could read or write: in our day there is still no American who can think.[15]

He undermined his own thesis somewhat through exaggeration, for even the most gullible French readers found it difficult to believe some Amerindians had pyramidal or conical craniums, and that many animals lost their tails and dogs their bark in America.

The abbé Raynal combined the degeneracy thesis with the figurist views of many of the Jesuit missionaries to arrive at his own interpretation. He relied heavily on the testimony of the missionary Joseph François Lafitau who saw the religion of the Iroquois among whom he labored as an imperfect survivor of an earlier universal revelation which God had given to primitive peoples and which was the foundation of a universal cultural unity. He wrote: 'Everything points to some sickness from which the human race still suffers. The ruin of his world is still imprinted on the faces of its inhabitants; a race of men degraded and degenerate in their physical constitution, in their build, in their way of life, and in their minds which show so little aptitude for all the arts of civilization. . . .'[16] It was on the basis of such views that the religious in New France had concluded that the native peoples required tutors and executors because they were incapable of administering their own affairs.

The existence of eighteenth-century philosophical pessimism has often been obscured by the emphasis placed upon Enlightenment perfectibility, progress, cosmopolitanism, and rationalism. There has also been a widespread misunderstanding of Father Lafitau's and J.J. Rousseau's contributions to the myth of the noble savage. No single intellectual construct dominated the field and none was able to encompass the great diversity of views or to reflect the spectrum of interpretations. The discovery of America and the contact with 'new men', according to some *philosophes*, may have been not only the most important event in European history but also the most disastrous. Many remained pessimistic about the value of colonial ventures and held very negative views about the virtue of colonized peoples.

The French relationship with the native peoples of New France was characterized, first of all, by a consistent, unitary, and centralized policy after Louis XIV assumed personal direction of his government in the metropole (1661) and in the colony (1663). It has sometimes been argued that New France was subject to arbitrary and despotic government, stifling metropolitan mercantilist economic controls, and burdensome clerical and seigneurial interference with personal liberty and innovation. Francis Parkman still casts a long shadow over the history of the French regime in North America. Yet, it can be demonstrated that a colonial government, located at the relatively isolated outpost of Quebec and functioning through correspondence with the Ministry of Marine, was more paternalistic than despotic. The Canadian colony held few attractions for settlers, little interest for investors, and limited opportunities for economic expansion. Of necessity, there was sensitivity to colonial and Amerindian interests as bureaucrats proceeded through consultations with local notables who were sensitive to regional and strategic issues. It can be argued that a traditional hierarchical society transplanted in the colony provided stability and order.[17]

Perhaps what is indicated as being a particular strength of the French relationship with the Amerindians is merely the reverse of the Anglo-American ineffectiveness, chaotic disunity, and inconsistency in dealing with the native peoples. Each British colony had its own particular policy, seldom in agreement with that of its neighbors, often at odds with trading partners, legislative assemblies, and land speculators, and nearly always in disagreement with imperial policies. Even after the defeat of Dieskau in 1755, Thomas Mante acknowledged the superiority of the French relationship: 'These (Marine) troops, with the Canadians, who were as well, if not better qualified for service in the country, than the French regulars, joined to the numerous tribes of Indians in the French interest, being conducted by one chief, formed an infinitely more formidable power than the regular and provincial troops of the English, who could not unit their strength on account of the jarring interests of the different provinces.'[18]

Amerindian affairs were within the jurisdiction of the governor-general in New France, who was also the chief military officer and the king's representative. Onontio (as the Amerindians called this man) spoke with authority, often commanded respect from friendly and unfriendly tribes alike, was careful to observe the protocol and even vocabulary associated with gift exchanges, formalization of alliances, and distribution of prisoners and booty; he represented a line of conduct applicable from Micmac and Abenakis country in the east to the Sioux and Cree country in the west. Generally, the tribes knew where they stood in their trade and warfare arrangements, and when there were shifts in French tactics and local practice, Canadian officers who commanded the scattered posts were instructed to explain how long-term strategy and alliances remained unchanged.[19] Missionaries were often influential in maintaining the 'allied tribes' faithful to the French cause. Little distinction was made between the interests of the kingdom of France and those of the kingdom of God.

An important aspect of the consistent French policy was the avoidance of authoritarian overbearing and of pretension to rule the tribes of the upper country. A perspective British observer reported in 1755 on the 'secret', as he called it, of French influence among the Amerindians in comparison to the lack of British success: 'They know too well the Spirit of the Indian Politics to affect a Superiority of Government over the Indians; Yet they have in Reality & Truth, of more solid Effect an Influence an Ascendency in all the Councils of all the Indians on the Continent and lead and direct their Measures, Not even Our Own Allies the Six Nations excepted.'[20] Just as Versailles through its officials in the colony was sensitized to the limitations on the exercise of its authority and to the Canadian love of liberty, so the officials at Quebec, through the network of posts and mission stations manned by Marine soldiers, *congé* holders, and missionaries, were sensitized to the needs of the native peoples and the limitations on the exercise of French sovereignty. France exercised her sovereignty in North America through the independent Amerindian 'nations': native self-government was the instrument of French power.

Another important characteristic of the French contact was the exploitation of the continent without extensive European occupation of the vast hinterland. Unlike the situation in the Anglo-American colonies, there was no westward-moving frontier of white settlement necessitating dispossession of the native peoples. New France was a collection of small seaboard colonies —Acadia, Isle Royale, and Louisiana—and the valley of the Saint Lawrence. The latter had been uninhabited when first visited by Cartier in the sixteenth century, but it had become a no-man's-land by the time Champlain built his *habitation* at Quebec in 1608 and the religious zealots founded Ville-Marie, that Christian utopian community on the strategic island of Montreal, in 1642. No natives were displaced to make room for French settlement in Canada, just as no Micmacs were displaced to make way for the implantation of Acadia.

There were posts in the interior with a small nucleus of French soldiers, Canadian farmers, and traders, at Detroit, Michilimackinac, and Kaskaskia, for example. But in 1664 the government forbade agricultural settlement up-country from Montreal and in 1716 refused to grant seigneuries in the region. There were two distinct regions, so to speak, in Canada: a riverine colony of French settlement where Amerindians were welcomed on designated seigneuries granted to missionaries and styled *réserves* or *réductions*, and the upper country or *pays d'en haut* comprising Amerindian ancestral lands where scattered missionaries, garrison troops, traders, and a few cultivators of corn, wheat, and tobacco benefited from natives' hospitality and sharing of land. The matters of discussion with the Amerindians revolved about fur trade issues, intertribal wars, the brandy traffic, and missionary activities and not, as in the cause of English contacts, about land cession, settlement, and treatment of captives.[21]

In recent historiography, it has become fashionable to portray the Amerindians as victims of European exploitation and as pawns in imperial rivalries and wars. This is a depiction which does little justice to Amerindian independence, initiative, and ability to exploit European involvement in the continent to native advantages. The French were unique perhaps in the sense that their experience in the hinterland or upper Canada quickly taught them that they were obliged in matters both of war and of trade to keep constantly in mind the Amerindian interests. Le Maire's memorandum of 1717 defined the situation succinctly:

> The Trade with the Indians is a necessary commerce; and even if the colonists were able to manage without it, the State is virtually forced to maintain it, if it wishes to maintain Peace, unless one wished to follow the cruel resolution of destroying all the Indians, which is contrary at once to both nature and Religion. There is no middle course; one must have the natives either as friend or foe; and whoever wants him as a friend, must furnish him with his necessities at conditions which allow him to procure them.[22]

The Intendant Raudot said that it was impossible to force French military or commercial policy on them: 'We can only solicit them not to deal with the English and we can in no way prevent them from doing so.' There was no question of coercion or threat in dealing with native peoples.

Nevertheless, it is true that Amerindians became increasingly dependent on European trade goods and services. Similarly, Frenchmen became dependent on Amerindian hospitality, support, and services. Neither party was able to extricate itself from this relationship, although there is evidence to indicate that there were times when each party would have welcomed such a course of action. A memorandum prepared for the Ministry of the Marine in 1730 reminded French bureaucrats of this North American reality: 'It is agreed and it is a fact that generally all the natives like and fear the French, mistrust the English and believe all our goods to be superior; and they recognize that they cannot get along without our powder, without our white blankets, our cloth for over-clothing, our vermillion, cutlery, trinkets—so there are only yard-goods and kettles which they obtain more reasonable from the English and which are two items to which our attention must be turned. . . .'[23] The assertion made by Harold Innis in the *Fur Trade in Canada* (1930) and widely repeated, that English trade goods were of superior quality and more cheaply priced than French goods, seems questionable. It does not seem to have been the case along Hudson Bay, for example, because a factor of the Hudson's Bay Company wrote in 1728: 'Never was any man so upbraided with our powder, kettles and hatchets, than we have been this summer by all the natives, especially by those that borders near the French.'[24] This was by no means an isolated comment in the honorable London company's correspondence. There is abundant evidence that the Amerindians were astute traders who determined both the quality and quantity of goods they found acceptable. There are no reliable figures for the value of goods bartered in the upper country, but it is clear that the French enjoyed a preferred status throughout most of the period.

Thirdly, the French experience with aboriginal rights and title was quite different from the Anglo-American approach. It is often stated that the French never recognized any native entitlement. On the other hand, W.J. Eccles has contradicted this view and asserted that the French did recognize native sovereignty and never forced their dominion over the Amerindians.[25] The documentation would seem to indicate a position somewhere between these two extreme views. France did not formulate an explicit theory of aboriginal rights; she never treated with indigenous peoples for the surrender of their rights in the land; she never imposed her laws, never exacted tribute or taxes, and never imposed military obligations on the native peoples she considered to be under her protection and rule. But she did assert her sovereignty through the usual symbolic acts of taking possession of *terra nullius*, or lands not claimed and settled by another Christian prince. French dominion was proclaimed through the recognition of the independence of the 'allied nations' who identified with the French in military, commercial, and missionary encounters.

Native concepts of property and of territory, whether horticultural plots or hunting territories, did not coincide with European legal concepts. Property was conceived by Europeans as being the basis of the social order; yet, during the Enlightenment, some theorists attacked its accumulation through inheritance and rank and regarded it as the basis for inequities. The abbé Pierre Dolivier, for example, went so far as to assert that 'the earth belongs to all in common, and to no one in particular.' Morelly, in his *Codes de la Nature* (1755), ranked in first place the precept that 'nothing shall belong to anyone individually as his sole property, except such things as he puts to his personal use, whether for his needs, his pleasure, or his daily work.'[26] These were views most Amerindians would have supported. They saw land as being no more the absolute possession of any individual than the air one breathed or the water on which one traveled.

That is not to say that Amerindians had no concept of possessory rights. The English traders had to obtain Iroquois permission to cross their territories to reach the Western tribes. The Montagnais granted right of passage across band territory, sometimes exacting a toll, in what anthropologists have called the hunting range system. The Montagnais were fearful that this right might not be respected when the five Postes du Roi passed to the British in 1760. They therefore instructed their missionary to appeal to the commander of the British occupation forces: 'Our father, we learn that our lands are to be given away not only to trade thereon but also to give them in full title to various individuals. . . . We have always been a free nation, and now we will become slaves, which would be very difficult to accept after having enjoyed our liberty for so long.'[27] The implication in this statement is that under French rule, even in the territory around Tadoussac, which had been reserved as the Postes du Roi and closed to colonization, the native peoples were free and independent.

In New France there was no alienation of Amerindian lands. Governor Courcelles' instructions in 1665 were that 'all his adult subjects treat the Indians with kindness, justice and equity, never resorting to violence against them, nor will anyone take the lands on which they are living under the pretext that it would be better and more suitable if they were French.'[28] There was no displacement of native population to make way for white European settlement; there was no advancing and threatening frontier of colonization. Instead, there were native peoples settled voluntarily within the French seigneurial tract in the Saint Lawrence valley on *réserves* administered by the missionary clergy, and there were also small islands of French settlement scattered at strategic commercial and military locations in the Amerindian hinterlands. The French, like other European powers, claimed sovereignty over the lands they 'discovered' and employed symbolic acts such as planting crosses, nailing the king's coat of arms on trees, or burying inscribed lead plates to establish this claim against the claims of European rivals. La Vérendrye's son, for example, took possession of the lands west of the Mandans in March, 1743 by secretly burying a lead plate and then erecting a stone cairn, saying to the local inhabitants that he was doing so 'in memory of our coming to their lands'.[29]

It would seem that under French sovereignty, Amerindian nations were *nations* because these people were conceived of as an ethnic group specific to a particular geographical location; they were not *états* because they were not believed to be organized under sovereign governments possessing coercive powers, and therefore they were not among the diplomatically recognized international 'family of nations'.

The missionary Charlevoix said that, although they made war in the manner of barbarians, 'it must however be allowed that in treaties of peace, and generally in all negotiations, they display such dexterity, address and elevation of soul, as would bring honour to the most civilized nations.' Although they looked upon themselves 'as the lords and sovereigns of the soil', they were 'not so jealous of their property as to find fault with newcomers who settle on it, provided they do not attempt to molest them.'[30] Hospitality and peaceful coexistence appeared to characterize the relationship, so long as dominance, coercion, and authoritarianism were avoided by the French.

The case of the Iroquois is an especially illuminating one because after 1713, by the terms of the Treaty of Utrecht, they theoretically came under British sovereignty. The French claimed that the Iroquois had made a formal submission to them in 1666, a fact reaffirmed by numerous *prises de possession*, but all the Five Nations themselves would concede was that they had extended hospitality and had promised that the French 'would always be assured of a lodge among them' and that the missionary 'would always find his mat to welcome him'.[31] A memorandum on missions in 1712 stated:

> It must seem that the Iroquois recognize no masters. And although the French have posted the coat of arms of France among them before and after the English posted those of England, they nevertheless recognize no domination. That is what they reiterated and tried to establish twice during two assemblies which they held in Montreal during the summer of the present year. To leave in perpetuity marks of their independence from both the English and the French, they had an act drawn up in proper form to which they put their signs and native hieroglyphs.[32]

The French exploited such sentiments against the British. The Ministry of Marine expressed great satisfaction with La Galissonnière's tactics in this respect: 'These Indians claim to be and in effect are independent of all nations, and their lands incontestably belong to them.' A military report on the boundaries of the colony, dated 1755, expressed the official French view: 'The Savages in question are free and independent and there are none who may be termed subjects of one crown or the other. The declaration of the Treaty of Utrecht in this respect is erroneous and cannot alter the nature of things. . . . These native nations are governed only by themselves. . . .'[33]

The Micmacs were quite emphatic in their assertions to the French governor at Louisbourg when they challenged France's right to cede their lands to Britain by the Treaty of Utrecht (1713): 'But learn from us that we are on this ground which you trod under foot and upon which you walk as the trees which you see have started to come forth from it. It is ours and nothing will ever be able to take it away from us or make us abandon it.'[34] Governor St Ovide replied that he knew well that 'the lands on which I tread, you possess them from all time', and then added that 'the King of France your Father never had the intention of taking them from you' but had ceded only his own rights to the British Crown. This was a fine distinction between French sovereignty and Amerindian possession and rights of usufruct.

The French position was based in good measure on their peculiar military relationship with the Amerindians. The Abenakis, for example, were essential to the defense of Canada, serving as a buffer between the two European areas of settlement. A memorandum to Versailles explained the situation in these terms:

1. that this nation is the sole bulwark against the English or Iroquois.
2. that if we do not agree or do not pretend to agree to their rights over the country which they occupy, never will we be able to engage them in any war for the defence of this same country which is the first line of defence of Canada.[35]

The French claim to the Great Lakes region, and to the loyalty of its tribes, was founded on the same distinction between French sovereignty and Amerindian possession and independence. A memorandum of 1755 explained the situation as follows. 'In 1671, all the Peoples of the North, of the West and the South adopted the King of France as their Father and their Sovereign, and declared themselves to be his faithful subjects. M. de St Lusson, sub-délégué general at Montreal, went to visit their coasts, received their homage and took once more solemn possession of their country.'[36] The French might interpret this as a quasi-feudal submission, but the Amerindians would see it as a formal declaration that they voluntarily became His Most Christian Majesty's children inasmuch as their traditional rights were being respected.

European powers by the eighteenth century had created two different treaty systems: a European treaty system, in which the powers dealt with each other as members of the 'family of nations', and an extended treaty system, in which the imperialistic powers dealt with the rest of the world, particularly aboriginal peoples. The French in dealing with their European rivals did not operate on the same diplomatic level or sphere as when dealing with the Iroquois, Abenakis, or Ottawa.[37] Sovereignty and spheres of influence were emphasized in interactions with other nation-states, whereas native independence and self-rule were stressed in the context of North American coexistence. The genius of French policy was that there was no inherent contradiction perceived between these two positions. So long as French seigneurial grants were limited to the Laurentian lowlands and so long as post commandants in the interior were circumspect in their statements and actions when dealing with the 'allied nations', France could assume responsibility under international law for both her colonists and the aboriginal people. Native nationhood was protected by French sovereignty; French sovereignty was exercised through native nationhood and self-determination.

Fourthly, the French system of reserves, as has already been suggested, was an important aspect of interracial relations. The reserves as originally perceived in 1637 were designed to assist in the integration of Amerindian and French populations. The objective was to attract nomadic hunting and food-gathering tribes to designated seigneuries administered by the missionaries with proximity to French colonists in order to introduce the Amerindians to a sedentary, disciplined, agricultural, and Catholic community life. At the outset the reserves were intertribal and included traditionalists as well as Catholic converts. The Jesuits operated the Sillery reserve near Quebec and Prairie de la Madeleine reserve near Montreal, while the Sulpician secular priests had a reserve near Ville-Marie called La Montagne. The lack of assimilation into French society, the slow pace of conversion, the evil influences of the nearby French settlements, and especially the ravages of the brandy traffic imposed some fundamental changes on the reserve system. The reserves tended to move away from close contact with French settlers and the chief towns; thus, Lorette replaced Sillery, Sault au Récollet and eventually Lac des Deux Montagnes replaced La Montagne, while Sault Saint Louis or Kahnawaké replaced Prairie de la Madeleine. Later reserves, such as the Abenakis reserves at Bécancour and Saint François and the Mississiquoi, la Présentation, and Saint Régis reserves were even farther removed from the centers of French population and acted as buffers along the frontier with the English colonies. The reserve became an institution of segregation, or at least of gradual acculturation in relative isolation from the towns and seigneuries of Canada.

The uniqueness of the French reserves is demonstrated in the motives various natives had for settling there or remaining on them when return to ancestral homelands was a viable alternative. The Hurons at Lorette were remnants of the four Huron nations that had once lived in the Georgian Bay region where the Récollets and Jesuits had started their utopian interior mission. They were originally refugees from the Iroquois invasion of Huronia. Similarly, some of the Abenakis who settled on reserves south of Trois-Rivières were refugees from New England expansion into their lands. Others, notably Iroquois converts, came to Sault Saint Louis or Lac des Deux Montagnes as refugees from persecution and discrimination in their traditionalist villages.

The Iroquois council at Sault Saint Louis told the governor in 1722: 'The first and sole motive which made us quit our country and our families was Religion. We sought a place to make it secure among us and in imitation of our Missionaries we found no better place than near the French.'[38] There were some, on the other hand, who fled to the safety of the reserve because they had been accused of witchcraft in their village; the missionaries received them willingly, saying that 'the devil unwillingly becomes the occasion of the salvation of these wretched fugitives by making it less difficult for them to embrace Christianity.'[39]

The reserves also augmented their members through adoption of prisoners. These might even include New Englanders, especially women and children, who not infrequently would refuse to return to their relatives when the French arranged prisoner-of-war exchanges and offered to redeem them from adoptive families on the reserve. A missionary at Kahnawaké reported as follows in 1741: 'Our Indians are always at war with the Chicachas, and from time to time they bring in a good number of slaves; but instead of retaliating by burning them at the stake, they adopt them in the village, instruct them in the mysteries of religion, and by holy baptism place them in a way of reaching heaven.'[40]

The reserves were not without economic attraction to some enterprising individuals and families. Gifts of food, clothing, and arms were regularly distributed on the reserves, and when the services of canoe-men, guides, and interpreters were needed, the French turned first to the reserves for assistance, which was well remunerated. At Sault Saint Louis and Lac des Deux Montagnes the illicit fur trade that developed between Montreal and Albany merchants, and which may have siphoned off about one-third of the peltries of New France between 1710 and the 1750s, was an important source of employment for the 'domiciled savages'.[41] The legal situation was that Amerindians could be stopped only from carrying furs to Albany and luxury and trade goods back from northern New York in the interest of Montreal merchants; the natives were free to trade in their own interest with anyone. The mission Iroquois were the principal intermediaries in this substantial Albany trade, and their missionaries were widely believed to support their initiative. Toward the end of the French regime the Montagnais and Hurons at Lorette turned to selling moccasins, snowshoes, sashes, fur caps and mittens, collars of porcupine quills, bows and arrows, and paddles at the Quebec market.

Satisfactory economic rewards tended to make loyal military allies. The domiciled tribes, as they were called, made up an important contingent in all of the chief French military expeditions. They participated not only in frontier raiding on English settlements but also in long-range expeditions such as the war against the Chickasaws in the Carolinas. During such campaigns, wives and families of warriors were fed and clothed by the French. The reserves became veritable military bases, which served as a buffer to protect the French and their domiciled Amerindians from surprise attacks from the south and also as liaison posts to maintain the neutrality of the neighboring tribes under British rule. The French found themselves obliged to maintain the reserves, at considerable and increasing costs, even after it became apparent that the initial objective of assimilation into a French life-style was proceeding very slowly.[42]

The reserves never made French-style peasants of the Amerindians. At Lac des Deux Montagnes, for example, the Nipissings and Algonkins, who were nomadic hunters, left their village to hunt each winter and they were soon joined by the Iroquois of the same reserve, who, though originally semi-sedentary horticulturalists, showed little more interest in farming. The proximity of the forest of the Laurentides was reassuring to the Lorette families who, although their raising of cows, wheat, and rye in addition to traditional maize, beans, pumpkins, and sunflowers had brought some progress in agricultural skills, they nevertheless still sold the produce of their hunting, trapping, and fishing at Quebec. The reserves, in short, were successful in that they permitted some continuation of the traditional occupations and skills.[43]

Finally, the French contact was important for the degree to which it promoted or accelerated evaluation and criticism of metropolitan French society. This critique culminated, in a sense, in the French Revolution. The Baron de Lahontan, who gave a soldier's view of the New World, had a fictional chieftain named Adario satirize the illogic of Catholic beliefs and the vices of European society. Similarly, Claude Buffier concocted a dialogue in which the artificiality and boredom of civilized life were stressed, while at the same time native life was portrayed as being free and happy. Maubert de Gouvest also, in his *Lettres Iroquoises*, had his fictitious Igli write from France to Alha in Iroquois country urging a critical reconsideration of the earlier favorable impression of the French. Alha was asked to consider whether 'these men are worthy of the sublime idea which our illustrious Iroquois had formed of them' and was advised to assure the Iroquois that 'they are themselves the Sages of the Earth'.[44]

Jean-Jacques Rousseau has been associated widely, and somewhat erroneously, with the myth of the Noble Savage. Rousseau never suggested that Frenchmen should or could return to the Iroquois level of human society. Nevertheless, he gave one of the clearest statements of the thesis that self-perfection in the individual led to all manner of evil in the human species. He concluded: 'The more one thinks about it, the more one finds that this state was the best for man. . . . The example of the savages, who have almost all been found at this point, seems to confirm that the human race was made to remain in it always; that this state is the veritable prime of the world; and that all subsequent progress has been in appearance so many steps toward the perfection of the individual and in fact toward the decrepitude of the species.'[45] Grasset de Saint-Sauveur, on the basis of similar assessments, doubted very much that Frenchmen should persist in attempting to civilize the native peoples: 'Such are the mores of a people too often calumniated by travelers; in the depths of his wilderness, the Amerindian is adroit, laborious, intelligent, virtuous, a faithful friend, good husband and good father. What would he be were philosophy to discipline his soul and manners? . . . Perhaps he might stand to lose: he would become disciplined (*policé*) but corrupted.'[46] Even the missionary-traveler, Father P.F.X. de Charlevoix, conceded that the liberty which the Amerindians enjoyed compensated sufficiently for the deprivations and inconveniences that characterized their life-style. These were as much reflections on a Europe burdened with its own complexities, controls, and class divisions as they were statements that primitive peoples exhibited naturally many of the virtues civilized men sought to cultivate.

In refuting de Pauw's thesis of colonial degeneracy, Pierre Poivre attempted in 1772 to assess the predominant French impression of Amerindian societies. He wrote:

> It follows from all that I have said above, that the soil and terrain of America, far from being degenerated, are virgin and generally better than those of our hemisphere; that the natural and exotic products are good and abundant; that the prodigious quantity of animals and plants have kept men there for a longer period in a savage way of life, through the facility they have enjoyed in clothing and feeding themselves: that the savages are certainly inferior in intellect and in learning to Europeans; but that they possess no less good sense, or reason than they; and that they are generally as robust, as brave, and much happier.[47]

Such a statement is valuable to the historian in indicating both the understanding and the prejudice, the sympathy and the ignorance, of a well-informed man of the Age of the Enlightenment.

The purpose of this essay has been to set out some characteristics of the French contact with the Amerindian peoples in the period from first recorded contact to the end of French rule in North America, with special emphasis placed on the eighteenth-century experiences. It does not come as a surprise that this experience played a role in the emergence of a theoretical framework for the social sciences concerned with native peoples, the concept of civilization, and the evolution of societies in a pattern sometimes called progress. It was in part out of the reported nature of North American native societies that Turgot conceived and formulated his Four Stages theory of progression from hunting and collecting economies through pastoralism to agricultural societies, and eventually to sophisticated commercial and industrial societies. Turgot's lectures in the late 1740s at the Sorbonne developed the thesis that human societies progressed through successive stages according to their mode of subsistence, not according to different modes of political organization or some other kind of 'life cycle'.[48] Algonkin society, accordingly, could be regarded as a living model of human society in the first stage of its development, while Iroquoian society was already more 'progressive', an assessment with which the missionary Joseph François Lafitau would have agreed. This hypothesis that all mankind progressed through the four successive stages of development, with the 'sauvage' being the most primitive, was adopted eventually by Lewis H. Morgan in his *Ancient Society*. Both Friedrich Engels and Karl Marx relied heavily on Morgan's assumption that social evolution was universal, unilinear, automatic, and progressive. This theory of social evolution, according to which no country can skip any important phase in its industrial development, was important in the formulation of the Marxist 'mode of production' concept.

Our chief concern, however, is not to establish some direct linkage between contemporary social theory and the interpretations of early French contact with native peoples. One cannot help notice, nevertheless, the overwhelming Europocentric view of history and of the world that Frenchmen had. They placed themselves at the center of the universal stage and judged other societies by the measure of their own. Be that as it may, in the French experience in America one catches sight of another spirit as well, that of cosmopolitanism and humanitarianism. This spirit manifested itself eventually in the Declaration of the Rights of Man and in such acts as the abolition of slavery. The French seem to have believed in their *génie colonial*, although it may have been more imagined than real, and in doing so they espoused a benevolent universalism.

What also emerges from this overview is the dynamism and vitality of Amerindian cultures at the time of contact. The Amerindians were free and independent peoples, willing to adjust to new circumstances, and sufficiently dynamic to deflect certain intruding elements of European civility to their own advantage. European and Amerindian societies were very different, each having some positive things to learn from the other. Neither saw the other as its ideal; yet neither saw the other as worthless.

The French contact experience has relevance today. Aboriginal rights need to be understood in native terms as well as European juridical terms. Sovereignty can be conceived in national, regional, and local spheres, and native self-government is once more perceived as feasible. There are other more general characteristics that we have singled out which are equally relevant to our times. There remains a need for clear and consistent policies. More attention needs to be given to peaceful coexistence and to historic rights. There is still need for greater self-criticism and the acknowledgment that we are not at the apex of human development, but that we ourselves are, in the words of the early writers, only in the 'infancy of the world'.

Suggestions for Further Reading

A.G. Bailey, *The Conflict of European and Eastern Algonkian Cultures, 1504–1700: A Study in Canadian Civilization* 2nd ed. (Toronto, 1969).

C.J. Jaenen, *Friend and Foe: Aspects of French-Amerindian Cultural Contact in the Six-teenth and Seventeenth Centuries* (Toronto, 1976).

Bruce G. Trigger, *Natives and Newcomers: Canada's 'Heroic Age' Reconsidered* (Montreal, 1985).

Notes

This essay is a revised version of public lectures given at the University of Delhi in December 1983, Columbia University in February 1984, and the University of Texas at Arlington in April 1986.

[1] The term *Amerindian* is an unambiguous and practical appellation, used in the same sense as one would use *European* or *African*, to refer to peoples of many different cultures, languages, and traditions who historically share a continent and are perceived by 'outsiders' as sharing some common social, political, and intellectual attributes. *Native peoples* is the politically accepted term in Canada at the present time.

[2] Cornelius J. Jaenen, *Friend and Foe: Aspects of French-Amerindian Cultural Contact in the Sixteenth and Seventeenth Centuries* (Toronto: McClelland and Stewart, 1976), 190–7; Gary B. Nash, *Red, White and Black: The Peoples of Early America* (Englewood Cliffs, N.J.: Prentice-Hall, 1974), 66–88.

[3] Michèle Duchet, *Anthropologie et histoire au siècle des lumières* (Paris: François Maspero, 1971), 194–9, 279: Cornelius de Pauw, *Recherches philosophiques sur les Américains* (Berlin: F.J. Decker, 1768), I, 55–6, 61–3; Sieur Duret, *Voyage de Marseille à Lima et dans les autres lieux des Indes Occidentales* (Paris: J.B. Coignard, 1720), 261–2; Pierre Chaunu, 'La lègende noire antihispanique', *Revue de Psychologie des Peuples* (1969) 188–223. The tradition had been established in France as early as 1667 by the Dominican missionary Jean-Baptiste du Tertre, author of *Histoire générale des Antilles habitées par les Français*, 4 vols. (Paris: Thomas Jolly, 1667–71).

[4] Huntington Library, Vaudreuil Papers. Letterbook 1, Vaudreuil to Maurepas, 1 June 1744, 260; P.F.X. de Charlevoix, *Histoire et description générale de la Nouvelle-France, avec le Journal historique, d'un voyage* (Paris: O.F. Griffart, 1744), vii; Public Archives of Canada (hereafter cited as PAC), MG 18, H-27, Félix Martin Papers, Description of Hudson Bay and Strait by Jérémie, 196; J.F. Bernard, *Relation de la Louisiane, et du Fleuve Mississippi* (Amsterdam: J.F. Bernard, 1720), 10.

[5] Citations from Francis Parkman, *The Conspiracy of Pontiac* (New York: Macmillan, 1962), 169; Sylvie Vincent and Bernard Arcand, *L'Image de l'Amerindian dans les manuels scolaires du Québec* (Montreal: H.M.H., 1979), 188.

[6] Anonymous, *The Expediency of Securing Our American Colonies* (Edinburgh: n.p., 1763), 57; Thomas Mante, *The History of the Late War in North America and the Islands of the West-Indies* (London: Strahan and Cadell, 1772), 479. Professor Herman Merivale's lectures at Oxford on colonization in 1839–41, published in 1861, contained the following assessment of the French contact: 'No other Europeans have ever displayed equal talents for conciliating savages, or, it must be added, for approximating to their usages and modes of life.'

[7] Georges Hardy, *Histoire de la colonisation française* (Paris: Payot, 1931), vii; André Julien, *Les voyages de découverts et des premiers établissements* (Paris: Presses universitaires

de France, 1948), 182; Hubert Deschamps, *Les méthodes et les doctrines coloniales de la France* (Paris: Armand Colin, 1953), 16.

[8]Francis Parkman, *The Jesuits in North America in the Seventeenth Century* (Toronto: George Morang, 1899), I, 131: Philip Means, *The Spanish Main: Focus of Envy, 1492–1700* (Reprint, New York, 1965), 197; Mason Wade, 'The French and the Indians', in H. Peckham and C. Gibson, eds, *Attitudes of Colonial Powers toward the American Indian* (Salt Lake City: University of Utah Press, 1969), 61–79.

[9]Cornelius J. Jaenen, 'L'image de l'Amérique', in Fernand Braudel, ed., *Le monde de Jacques Cartier* (Paris: Berger-Levrault, 1984), 201–16: 'Conceptual Frameworks for French Views of America and Amerindians', *French Colonial Studies*, no. 2 (1978), 1–22; and 'L'Amérique vue par les Français aux XVIe et XVIIe siècles', *Rapports, XVe Congrès International des Sciences historiques* (Bucharest, 1980), II, 272–8. See also, Lewis Hanke, *Aristotle and the American Indians* (Bloomington: Indiana University Press, 1970), 44–73, and *The Spanish Struggle for Justice in the Conquest of America* (Boston: Little, Brown, 1966), 111–31.

[10]Donald M. Frame, ed., *Montaigne's Essays and Selected Writings* (New York, 1963), 89.

[11]André Thévet, *Les singularitéz de la France antarctique, autrement nommée Amérique* (Paris: n.p., 1557), 51.

[12]Olive P. Dickason, 'The Concept of *l'homme sauvage* and Early French Colonialism in the Americas', *Revue Française d'Histoire d'Outre-Mer* 63, 234 (1977), 5–32; Archives Municipales de Saint-Malo, Série HH, Carton I, MS 1: Samuel de Champlain, *Voyages et découvertes faites en la Nouvelle-France* (Paris: 1620), 1.

[13]Cited in Michèle Duchet, *Anthropologie et histoire au siècle des lumières* (Paris: François Maspero, 1971), 246. The translation is mine.

[14]Georges-Louis Leclerc, Comte de Buffon, *Oeuvres complètes* (Paris: Imprimerie Royale, 1767), XV, 445–6.

[15]Cornelius de Pauw, *Recherches philosophiques sur les Américains* (Berlin: F.J. Decker, 1774), I, 35, 221; II, 102, 153–4.

[16]Guillaume-Thomas-François Raynal, *Histoire philosophique et politique des établissements des Européens dans les deux Indes* (Paris: Amable, Coste, 1820–21), IX, 25. Cf. Arnold H. Rowbotham, 'Jesuit Figurists and Eighteenth Century Religion', *Journal of the History of Ideas* 17, 4 (October, 1956), 482–3.

[17]Guy Frégault, *La civilisation de la Nouvelle-France* (Montreal: Pascal, 1944), 126, 134–6.

[18]Mante, *History of the Late War in North America*, 56. For a full treatment of the subject, consult Harry M. Ward, *Unite or Die: Intercolony Relations, 1690–1763* (Port Washington, N.Y.: National University Publications, 1971).

[19]La Chauvignerie to Saint-Pierre, 10 February 1754, in Fernand Grenier, ed., *Papiers Contrecoeur et autres documents* (Quebec: Presses universitaires Laval, 1952), 100–1, gives a good account of such an occasion.

[20]Stanley Pargellis, ed., *Military Affairs in North America, 1748–1765* (New York: Archon Books, 1969), Thomas Pownall's Consideration of 1755, 165.

[21]Cornelius J. Jaenen, *The French Relationship with the Native Peoples of New France* (Ottawa: Indian and Northern Affairs, 1985), *passim*.

[22]PAC, MG 7, A-2, I, Fond français, MS. 12105, Mémoire de Le Maire (1717), 83.

[23]PAC, MG 4, C-2, III, Mémoire sur l'état présent du Canada (1730), 12.

[24]Archives des Colonies (hereafter, AC) (Paris), Série C¹¹D, VI, Subercase to Minister, December 20, 1708, fols. 166–66v; H.G. Davies, ed., *Letters from Hudson Bay, 1703–40* (London: Hudson Bay Record Society, 1965), 136. For the recent debate on the views expressed by Harold A. Innis in *The Fur Trade in Canada: An Introduction to Canadian Economic History* (New Haven, Conn.: Yale University Press, 1930), see W.J. Eccles, 'A Belated Review of Harold Adam Innis, *The Fur Trade in Canada*', *Canadian Historical Review* 60, 4 (1979), 419–41; Hugh M. Grant, 'One Step Forward, Two Steps Back: Innis, Eccles, and the Canadian Fur Trade', *Canadian Historical Review* 62, 2 (1981), 304–22: W.J. Eccles, 'A Response to Hugh M. Grant on Innis', *Canadian Historical Review* 62, 3 (1981), 323–9.

[25]Robert J. Surtees, *The Original People* (Toronto: Holt, Rinehart, and Winston, 1974), 60. Bruce G. Trigger, *Natives and Newcomers* (Montreal and Kingston: McGill-Queen's University Press, 1985), 330–1; Peter A. Cumming and Neil H. Mickenburg, *Native Rights in Canada* (Toronto: Indian-Eskimo Association of Canada, 1972), 14–16; W.J. Eccles, 'Sovereignty-Association, 1500–1783', *Canadian Historical Review* 65, 4 (1984), 475, 478, 505, 510.

[26]Pierre Dolivier, *Essai sur la justice primitive* (Paris: 1972), 17; Morelly, cited in Paul Hazard, *European Thought in the Eighteenth Century* (Cleveland: World Publishing Company, 1967), 177.

[27]Coquart to General Murray, 12 March 1765, in Lorenzo Angers, *Chicoutimi, Poste de Traite (1676–1856)* (Montreal: Editions Leméac, 1971), 60.

[28]Cited in Cumming and Mickenburg, *Native Rights in Canada*, 79. It should be noted that most of the ideas about native land tenure are based on comparatively recent ethnographic studies, not on the original historical sources of the sixteenth to eighteenth centuries. See Ralph Linton, 'Land Tenure in Aboriginal America', in O. Lafarge, ed., *The Changing Indian* (Norman: University of Oklahoma Press, 1943), 53–4.

[29]Pierre Margry, ed., *Découvertes et établissements des Français dans l'ouest et dans le sud de l'Amérique septentrionale*, vol. VI, *Journal de la Vérendrye* (1743) (Paris: Maisonneauve, 1888), 609.

[30]P.F.X. de Charlevoix, *Journal of a Voyage to North-America* (Reprint, Ann Arbor, Mich.: University Microfilms, 1966), I, 380.

[31]PAC, MG 1, Série C¹¹A, I, Extracts from Diverse Relations (1646–84), 427.

[32]PAC, MG 1, Série C¹¹E, II, Memorandum on Establishment of Missions among the Iroquois (12 Nov. 1712), 27–28.

[33]AC (Paris), Série B, LXXXIX, Rouillé to La Jonquière, 4 May 1749, fol. 67; PAC, MG 5, B-1 XXIV, Discussions on Limits of Canada (9 May 1755), 354.

[34]PAC, MG 18, E-29, Discourse of Saint Ovide, n.d., n.p.

[35]PAC, MG 18, H-27, Félix Martin Papers, Memorandum on Acadia and the Abenakis, 235.

[36]PAC, MG 4, C-1, I, article 14, I, no. 5, Rights of French Crown in Canada (1755), 33.

[37]Dorothy V. Jones, *License for Empire* (Chicago: University of Chicago Press, 1982), 5–20; Brian Slattery, 'The Land Rights of Indigenous Canadian Peoples as Affected by the Crown's Acquisition of Their Territories', D. Phil. thesis, Oxford University, 1979, 91–2.

[38]PAC, MG 1, Série C¹¹A, CVI, Memorandum of the Missionaries of Sault Saint Louis (12 May 1722), 113.

[39]Nau to Bonin, 2 October 1735, in Arthur E. Jones, ed., *The Aulneau Collection, 1734–1745* (Montreal: St. Mary's College, 1893), 64.

[40]*Ibid.*, Nau to Mme. Aulneau, 3 October 1741, 140.

[41]PAC, MG 1, Série C¹¹A, XXXIII, Vaudreuil and Bégon to Minister (12 Nov. 1712), 56; PAC, MG 1, Série F-3, X, pt. 1, King to Vaudreuil and Bégon (8 June 1721), 168–9.

[42]PAC, MG 1, Série C¹¹A, XXXV, Bégon to Minister (25 September 1715), 273–5.

[43]PAC, MG 18, K-5, Franquet Papers, II, Voyage from Quebec (1752), 61–4.

[44]Baron de Lahontan, *Conversations de l'auteur de ces voyages avec Adario sauvage distingué* (Montreal: Editions Elysée, 1974), *passim*; Claude Buffier, *Cours des sciences sur des principes nouveaux pour former le langage et le coeur dans l'usage ordinaire de la vie* (Paris: Imprimerie Royale, 1732), 954–7; J.H. Maubert de Gouvest, *Les lettres iroquoises* (Reprint, Paris, 1962), 84.

[45]Jean-Jacques Rousseau, *Second Discours* (Reprint, New York, 1964), pt. 2, 151.

[46]Jacques Grasset de Saint-Sauveur, *Moeurs, loix et coutumes des sauvages du Canada* (Paris: Auteur, 1788), 8.

[47]Pierre Poivre, *De l'Amérique et des Américains, observations curieuses du philosophe La Douceur* (Berlin: Samuel Pitra, 1772), 114.

[48]G. Schelle, ed., *Oeuvres de Turgot* (Reprint, Paris, 1913), I, 255–74.

6

The European Impact on Native Peoples

Calvin Martin

Although the fur trade is commonly associated with western Canada, the great fur-trading companies (the North West Company, the Hudson's Bay Company), and a later period than that of first settlement, it served as one of the basic economic activities of Europe from the beginning of European intrusion into North America. Intrusion was indeed the operational word. Long before most native peoples had even seen a European, they had been infected—and their numbers often decimated—by the spread of disease, carried to America by the newcomers, for which the First Nations had no immunity. European technology replaced native ingenuity, creating a demand for kettles, knives, and firearms. Along with the introduction of new disease and new technology went the introduction of new value systems, including Christianity.

In the following highly controversial article, Calvin Martin explores the meaning of the European impact on the Micmac of the extreme eastern tip of Canada. Martin's argument has three parts. The first, which insists that in the pre-European native world, humankind and the natural environment were precariously but continuously balanced in a mutually reciprocal 'ecosystem', is in general accepted by most specialists in this period. The second part, which maintains that the Micmac ecosystem—like that involving all native peoples—was reflected and reinforced in the cultural worldview of the natives, is not particularly controversial until Martin insists on a particular relationship between the game hunted and the spiritual or cultural worldview. Criticism of Martin's position here by many anthropologists and ethnohistorians carries over into the third (and most hotly contested) part of his argument: that the interference of European missionaries with the traditional Indian worldview so disoriented the natives that they overhunted the game upon which they had previously depended.

Even if one rejects the most extreme aspects of his thesis, Martin's revisionist argument is extremely thought-provoking. Is it necessary to agree wholeheartedly with an argument to find it stimu-lating? Why does the concept of an aboriginal ecosystem so appeal to modern Canadians? What sort of view of native culture does Martin hold? Is it the same view as Jaenen's in Reading 5?

This article first appeared, titled 'The European Impact on the Culture of a North-eastern Algonquian Tribe: An Ecological Interpretation', in *The William and Mary Quarterly* 3rd ser., XXXI (1974), 3-26.

As the drive for furs, known prosaically as the fur trade, expanded and became more intense in seventeenth-century Canada, complaints of beaver extermination became more frequent and alarming. By 1635, for example, the Huron had reduced their stock of beaver to the point where the Jesuit Father Paul Le Jeune could declare that they had none.[1] In 1684 Baron Lahontan recorded a speech made before the French governor-general by an Iroquois spokesman, who explained that his people had made war on the Illinois and Miami because these Algonquians had trespassed on Iroquois territory and overkilled their beaver, 'and contrary to the Custom of all the Savages, have carried off whole Stocks, both Male and Female'.[2] This exploi-tation of beaver and other furbearers seems to have been most intense in the vicinity of major trading posts and among the native tribes most affected by the trade (the Montagnais, Huron, League Iroquois, Micmac, and others[3]), while those tribes which remained beyond European influence and the trade, such as the Bersimis of northeastern Quebec, enjoyed an abundance of beaver in their territories.[4]

Even before the establishment of trading posts, the Micmac of the extreme eastern tip of Canada were engaged in lively trade with European fishermen. Thus areas that were important in the fishing industry, such as Prince Edward Island, the Gaspé Peninsula, and Cape Breton Island, were cleaned out of moose and other furbearers by the mid-seventeenth century.[5] Reviewing this grim situation, Nicolas Denys observed that game was less abundant in his time than formerly; as for the beaver, 'few in a house are saved; they [the Micmac] would take all. The disposition of the Indians is not to spare the little ones any more than the big ones. They killed all of each kind of animal that there was when they could capture it.'[6]

In short, the game which by all accounts had been so plentiful was now being systematically overkilled by the Indians themselves. A traditional expla-nation for this ecological catastrophe is neatly summarized by Peter Farb, who conceives of it in mechanistic terms: 'If the Northern Athabaskan and Northern Algonkian Indians husbanded the land and its wildlife in primeval times, it was only because they lacked both the technology to kill very many animals and the market for so many furs. But once white traders entered the picture, supplying the Indians with efficient guns and an apparently limitless market for furs beyond the seas, the Indians went on an orgy of destruction.' The Indian, in other words, was 'economically seduced' to exploit the wild-life requisite to the fur trade.[7]

Such a cavalier dismissal of northeastern Algonquian culture, especially its spiritual component, renders this explanation superficial and inadequate. One can argue that economic determinism was crucial to the course of Algon-quian cultural development (including religious perception) over a long period of time. Yet from this perspective European contact was but a moment in the cultural history of the Indians, and it is difficult to imagine that ideals and a life-style that had taken centuries to evolve would have been so easily and quickly discarded merely for the sake of improved technological con-venience. As we shall see, the entire Indian-land relationship was suffused with religious considerations which profoundly influenced the economic (subsistence) activities and beliefs of these people. The subsistence cycle was regulated by centuries of spiritual tradition which, if it had been in a healthy state, would have countered the revolutionizing impact of European influ-ence. Tradition would doubtless have succumbed eventually, but why did the end come so soon? Why did the traditional safeguards of the northeastern Algonquian economic system offer such weak resistance to its replacement by the exploitive, European-induced regime?

When the problem is posed in these more comprehensive terms, the usual economic explanation seems misdirected, for which reason the present article will seek to offer an alternative interpretation. The methodology of cultural ecology will be brought to bear on the protohistoric and early contact phases of Micmac cultural history in order to examine the Indian-land relationship under aboriginal and postcontact conditions and to probe for an explanation to the problem of wildlife overkill.[8]

Cultural ecology seeks to explain the interaction of environment and cul-ture, taking the ecosystem and the local human population as the basic units of analysis.[9] An ecosystem is a discrete community of plants and animals, together with the nonliving environment, occupying a certain space and time, having a flow-through of energy and raw materials in its operation, and composed of subsystems.[10] For convenience of analysis, an ecosystem can be separated into its physical and biological components, although one should bear in mind that in nature the two are completely intermeshed in complex interactions. And from the standpoint of cultural ecology, there is a third component: the metaphysical or spiritual.

The ecosystem model of plant and animal ecologists is somewhat strained when applied to a human population, although, as Roy A. Rappaport has demonstrated in his *Pigs for the Ancestors*, the attempt can be very useful.[11] The difficulties encountered include the assignment of definite territorial limits to the area under consideration (resulting in a fairly arbitrary delimitation of an ecosystem), the quantification of the system's energy budget and the carrying capacity of the land, and the identification of subsystem interrelations. Assigning values to variables becomes, in many instances, quite impossible.

The transposition of the ecosystem approach from cultural anthropology to historical inquiry complicates these problems even further, for the relationships between a human population and its environment are seldom amenable to rigorous quantitative analysis using historical documents as sources. Yet this is certainly not always so. In the case of the fur trade, for example, one may in fact be able to measure some of its effects on the environment from merchants' records—showing numbers of pelts obtained from a region over a certain time period—and also from lists of goods given to the Indians at trading posts and by treaties. Even when available, such records are too incomplete to satisfy the rigorous demands of the ecologist, but to say that they are of limited value is not to say that they are useless.

Few historians have used the ecological model in their work.[12] Recognizing the need for the environmental perspective in historiography, Wilbur R. Jacobs recently observed that 'those who hope to write about such significant historical events [as the despoiling of the American west] . . . will need a sort of knowledge not ordinarily possessed by historians. To study the impact of the fur trade upon America and her native people, for instance, there must be more than a beginning acquaintance with ethnology, plant and animal ecology, paleoecology, and indeed much of the physical sciences.'[13]

In the case of the northeastern Algonquian, and the Micmac in particular, the fur trade was but one factor—albeit an important one—in the process of acculturation. Long before they felt the lure of European technology, these littorial Indians must have been infected with Old World diseases carried by European fishermen, with catastrophic effects. Later, the Christian missionaries exerted a disintegrative influence on the Indians' view of and relation to their environment. All three of these factors—disease, Christianity, and technology—which may be labeled 'trigger' factors, must be assessed in terms of their impact on the Indians' ecosystem.[14]

Among the first North American Indians to be encountered by Europeans were the Micmacs who occupied present-day Nova Scotia, northern New Brunswick and the Gaspé Peninsula, Prince Edward Island, and Cape Breton Island. According to the Sieur de Dièreville, they also lived along the lower St John River with the Malecites, who outnumbered them.[15] For our present purposes, the Micmac territory will be considered an ecosystem, and the Micmac occupying it will be regarded as a local population. These designations are not entirely arbitrary, for the Micmac occupied and exploited the area in a systematic way; they had a certain psychological unity or similarity in their ideas about the cosmos; they spoke a language distinct from those of their neighbors; and they generally married within their own population. There were, as might be expected, many external factors impinging on the ecosystem which should also be evaluated, although space permits them only to be mentioned here. Some of these 'supralocal' relations involved trade and hostilities with other tribes; the exchange of genetic material and personnel with neighboring tribes through intermarriage and adoption; the exchange of folklore and customs; and the movements of such migratory game as moose and woodland caribou. The Micmac ecosystem thus participated in a regional system, and the Micmac population was part of a regional population.[16]

The hunting, gathering, and fishing Micmac who lived within this Acadian forest, especially along its rivers and by the sea, were omnivores (so to speak) in the trophic system of the community. At the first trophic level, the plants eaten were wild potato tubers, wild fruits and berries, acorns and nuts, and the like. Trees and shrubs provided a wealth of materials used in the fashioning of tools, utensils, and other equipment.[17] At the time of contact, none of the Indians living north of the Saco River cultivated food crops. Although legend credits the Micmac with having grown maize and tobacco 'for the space of several years',[18] these cultigens, as well as beans, pumpkins, and wampum (which they greatly prized), were obtained from the New England Algonquians of the Saco River area (Abnakis) and perhaps from other tribes to the south.[19]

Herbivores and carnivores occupy the second and third trophic levels respectively, with top carnivores in the fourth level. The Micmac hunter tapped all three levels in his seasonal hunting and fishing activities, and these sources of food were 'to them like fixed rations assigned to every moon'.[20] In January, seals were hunted when they bred on islands off the coast; the fat was reduced to oil for food and body grease, and the women made clothing from the fur.[21] The principal hunting season lasted from February till mid-March, since there were enough marine resources, especially fish and mollusks, available during the other three seasons to satisfy most of the Micmacs' dietary needs. For a month and a half, then, the Indians withdrew from the seashore to the banks of rivers and lakes and into the woods to hunt the caribou, moose, black bear, and small furbearers. At no other time of the year were they so dependent on the caprice of the weather: a feast was as likely as a famine. A heavy rain could ruin the beaver and caribou hunt, and a deep, crustless snow would doom the moose hunt.[22]

Since beaver were easier to hunt on the ice than in the water, and since their fur was better during the winter, this was the chief season for taking them.[23] Hunters would work in teams or groups, demolishing the lodge or cutting the dam with stone axes. Dogs were sometimes used to track the beaver which took refuge in air pockets along the edge of the pond, or the beaver might be harpooned at air holes. In the summer hunt, beaver were shot with the bow or trapped in deadfalls using poplar as bait, but the commonest way to take them was to cut the dam in the middle and drain the pond, killing the animals with bows and spears.[24]

Next to fish, moose was the most important item in the Micmac diet, and it was their staple during the winter months when these large mammals were hunted with dogs on the hard-crusted snow. In the summer and spring, moose were tracked, stalked, and shot with the bow; in the fall, during the rutting season, the bull was enticed by a clever imitation of the sound of a female urinating. Another technique was to ensnare the animal with a noose.[25]

Moose was the Micmacs' favorite meat. The entrails, which were considered a great delicacy, and the 'most delicious fat' were carried by the triumphant hunter to the campsite, and the women were sent after the carcass. The mistress of the wigwam decided what was to be done with each portion of the body, every part of which was used. Grease was boiled out of the bones and either drunk pure (with 'much gusto') or stored as loaves of moose-butter;[26] the leg and thigh bones were crushed and the marrow eaten; the hides were used for robes, leggings, moccasins, and tent coverings;[27] tools, ornaments, and game pieces were made from antlers, teeth, and toe bones, respectively.[28] According to contemporary French observers, the Micmac usually consumed the moose meat immediately, without storing any, although the fact that some of the meat was preserved rather effectively by smoking it on racks, so that it would even last the year, demonstrates that Micmac existence was not as hand-to-mouth as is commonly believed of the northeastern Algonquian.[29] Black bear were also taken during the season from February till mid-March, but such hunting was merely coincidental. If a hunter stumbled upon a hibernating bear, he could count himself lucky.[30]

As the lean months of winter passed into the abundance of spring, the fish began to spawn, swimming up rivers and streams in such numbers that 'everything swarms with them'.[31] In mid-March came the smelt, and at the end of April the herring. Soon there were sturgeon and salmon, and numerous waterfowl made nests out on the islands—which meant there were eggs to be gathered. Mute evidence from seashore middens and early written testimony reveal that these Indians also relied heavily on various mollusks, which they harvested in great quantity.[32] Fish was a staple for the Micmac, who knew the spawning habits of each type of fish and where it was to be found. Weirs were erected across streams to trap the fish on their way downstream on a falling tide, while larger fish, such as sturgeon and salmon, might be speared or trapped.[33]

The salmon run marked the beginning of summer, when the wild geese shed their plumage. Most wildfowl were hunted at their island rookeries; waterfowl were often hunted by canoe and struck down as they took to flight; others, such as the Canada geese which grazed in the meadows, were shot with the bow.[34]

In autumn, when the waterfowl migrated southward, the eels spawned up the many small rivers along the coast. From mid-September to October the Micmac left the ocean and followed the eels, 'of which they lay in a supply; they are good and fat.' Caribou and beaver were hunted during October and November, and with December came the 'tom cod' (which were said to have spawned under the ice) and turtles bearing their young.[35] In January the subsistence cycle began again with the seal hunt.

As he surveyed the seasonal cycle of these Indians, Father Pierre Biard was impressed by nature's bounty and Micmac resourcefulness: 'These then, but in a still greater number, are the revenues and incomes of our Savages; such, their table and living, all prepared and assigned, everything to its proper place and quarter.'[36] Although we have omitted mention of many other types of forest, marine, and aquatic life which were also exploited by the Micmac, those listed above were certainly the most significant in the Micmacs' food quest and ecosystem.[37]

Frank G. Speck, perhaps the foremost student of northeastern Algonquian culture, has emphasized that hunting to the Micmacs was not a 'war upon the animals, not a slaughter for food or profit'.[38] Denys's observations confirm Speck's point: 'Their greatest task was to feed well and to go a hunting. They did not lack animals, which they killed only in proportion as they had need of them.'[39] From this, and the above description of their effective hunting techniques, it would appear that the Micmac were not limited by their hunting technology in the taking of game. As Denys pointed out, 'the hunting by the Indians in old times was easy for them. . . . When they were tired of eating one sort, they killed some of another. If they did not wish longer to eat meat, they caught some fish. They never had an accumulation of skins of Moose, Beaver, Otter, or others, but only so far as they needed them for personal use. They left the remainder [of the carcass] where the animals had been killed, not taking the trouble to bring them to their camps.'[40] Need, not technology, was the ruling factor, and need was determined by the great primal necessities of life and regulated by spiritual considerations. Hunting, as Speck remarks, was 'a *holy occupation*'; [41] it was conducted and controlled by spiritual rules.

The bond which united these physical and biological components of the Micmac ecosystem, and indeed gave them definition and comprehensibility, was the world view of the Indian. The foregoing discussion has dealt mainly with the empirical, objective, physical ('operational') environmental model of the observer; what it lacks is the 'cognized' model of the Micmac.[42]

Anthropologists regard the pre-Columbian North American Indian as a sensitive member of his environment, who merged sympathetically with its living and nonliving components.[43] The Indian's world was filled with super-human and magical powers which controlled man's destiny and nature's course of events.[44] Murray Wax explains:

> To those who inhabit it, the magical world is a "society", not a "mechanism", that is, it is composed of "beings" rather than "objects". Whether human or nonhuman, these beings are associated with and related to one another socially and sociably, that is, in the same ways as human beings to one another. These patterns of association and relationship may be structured in terms of kinship, empathy, sympathy, reciprocity, sexuality, dependency, or any other of the ways that human beings interact with and affect or afflict one another. Plants, animals, rocks, and stars are thus seen not as "objects" governed by laws of nature, but as "fellows" with whom the individual or band may have a more or less advan-tageous relationship.[45]

For the Micmac, together with all the other eastern subarctic Algonquians, the power of these mysterious forces was apprehended as 'manitou'—trans-lated 'magic power'—much in the same way that we might use the slang word 'vibrations' to register the emotional feelings emanating (so we say) from an object, person, or situation.[46]

The world of the Micmac was thus filled with superhuman forces and beings (such as dwarfs, giants, and magicians), and animals that could talk to man and had spirits akin to his own, and the magic of mystical and medicinal herbs—a world where even inanimate objects possessed spirits.[47] Micmac subsistence activities were inextricably bound up within this spiritual matrix, which, we are suggesting, acted as a kind of control mechanism on Micmac land-use, maintaining the environment within an optimum range of conditions.

In order to understand the role of the Micmac in the fur trading enterprise of the colonial period, it is useful to investigate the role of the Micmac hunter in the spiritual world of precontact times. Hunting was governed by spiritual rules and considerations which were manifest to the early French observers in the form of seemingly innumerable taboos. These taboos connoted a sense of cautious reverence for a conscious fellow-member of the same ecosystem who, in the view of the Indian, allowed itself to be taken for food and clothing. The Indian felt that 'both he and his victim understood the roles which they played in the hunt; the animal was resigned to its fate.'[48]

That such a resignation on the part of the game was not to be interpreted as an unlimited license to kill should be evident from an examination of some of the more prominent taboos. Beaver, for example, were greatly admired by the Micmac for their industry and 'abounding genius'; for them, the beaver had 'sense' and formed a 'separate nation'.[49] Hence there were various regulations associated with the disposal of their remains: trapped beaver were drawn in public and made into soup, extreme care being taken to prevent the soup from spilling into the fire; beaver bones were carefully preserved, never being given to the dogs—lest they lose their sense of smell for the animal—or thrown into the fire—lest misfortune come upon 'all the nation'—or thrown into rivers—'because the Indians fear lest the spirit of the bones . . . would promptly carry the news to the other beavers, which would desert the country in order to escape the same misfortune.' Likewise, menstruating women were forbidden to eat beaver, 'for the Indians are convinced, they say, that the beaver, which has sense, would no longer allow itself to be taken by the Indians if it had been eaten by their unclean daughters.' The fetus of the beaver, as well as that of the bear, moose, otter, and porcupine, was reserved for the old men, since it was believed that a youth who ate such food would experience intense foot pains while hunting.[50]

Taboos similarly governed the disposal of the remains of the moose—what few there were. The bones of a moose fawn (and of the marten) were never given to the dogs nor were they burned, 'for they [the Micmac] would not be able any longer to capture any of these animals in hunting if the spirits of the martens and of the fawns of the moose were to inform their own kind of the bad treatment they had received among the Indians.'[51] Fear of such reprisal also prohibited menstruating women from drinking out of the common kettles or bark dishes.[52] Such regulations imply cautious respect for the animal hunted. The moose not only provided food and clothing, but was firmly tied up with the Micmac spirit-world—as were the other game animals.

Bear ceremonialism was also practiced by the Micmac. Esteem for the bear is in fact common among boreal hunting peoples of northern Eurasia and North America, and has the following characteristics: the beast is typically hunted in the early spring, while still in hibernation. It is addressed, when either dead or alive, with honorific names; a conciliatory speech is made to the animal, either before or after killing it, by which the hunter apologizes for his act and perhaps explains why it is necessary; and the carcass is respectfully treated, those parts not used (especially the skull) being ceremonially disposed of and the flesh consumed in accordance with taboos. Such rituals are intended to propitiate the spiritual controller of the bears so that he will continue to furnish game to the hunter.[53] Among the Micmac the bear's heart was not eaten by young men lest they get out of breath while traveling and lose courage in danger. The bear carcass could be brought into the wigwam only through a special door made specifically for that purpose, either in the left or right side of the structure. This ritual was based on the Micmac belief that their women did not 'deserve' to enter the wigwam through the same door as the animal. In fact, we are told that childless women actually left the wigwam at the approach of the body and did not return until it had been entirely consumed.[54] By means of such rituals the hunter satisfied the soul-spirit of the slain animal. Of the present-day Mistassini (Montagnais) hunter, Speck writes that 'should he fail to observe these formalities an unfavorable reaction would also ensue with his own soul-spirit, his "great man" . . . as it is called. In such a case the "great man" would fail to advise him when and where he would find his game. Incidentally the hunter resorts to drinking bear's grease to nourish his "great man".'[55] Perhaps it was for a similar reason that the Micmac customarily forced newborn infants to swallow bear or seal oil before eating anything else.[56]

If taboo was associated with fishing, we have little record of it; the only explicit evidence is a prohibition against the roasting of eels, which if violated, would prevent the Indians from catching others. From this and from the fact that the Restigouche division of the Micmac wore the figure of a salmon as a totem around their neck, we may surmise that fish, too, shared in the sacred and symbolic world of the Indian.[57]

Control over these supernatural forces and communication with them were the principal functions of the shaman, who served in Micmac society as an intermediary between the spirit realm and the physical. The lives and destinies of the natives were profoundly affected by the ability of the shaman to supplicate, cajole, and otherwise manipulate the magical beings and powers. The seventeenth-century French, who typically labeled the shamans (or *buowin*) frauds and jugglers in league with the devil, were repeatedly amazed at the respect accorded them by the natives.[58] By working himself into a dreamlike state, the shaman would invoke the manitou of his animal helper and so predict future events.[59] He also healed by means of conjuring. The Micmac availed themselves of a rather large pharmacopoeia of roots and herbs and other plant parts, but when these failed they would summon the healing arts of the most noted shaman in the district. The illness was often diagnosed by the *buowin* as a failure on the patient's part to perform a prescribed ritual; hence an offended supernatural power had visited the offender with sickness. At such times the shaman functioned as a psychotherapist, diagnosing the illness and symbolically (at least) removing its immediate cause from the patient's body.[60]

It is important to understand that an ecosystem is holocoenotic in nature: there are no 'walls' between the components of the system, for 'the ecosystem reacts as a whole.'[61] Such was the case in the Micmac ecosystem of precontact times, where the spiritual served as a link connecting man with all the various subsystems of the environment. Largely through the mediation of the shaman, these spiritual obligations and restrictions acted as a kind of control device to maintain the ecosystem in a well-balanced condition.[62] Under these circumstances the exploitation of game for subsistence appears to have been regulated by the hunter's respect for the continued welfare of his prey—both living and dead—as is evident from the numerous taboos associated with the proper disposal of animal remains. Violation of taboo desecrated the remains of the slain animal and offended its soul-spirit. The offended spirit would then retaliate in either of several ways, depending on the nature of the broken taboo: it could render the guilty hunter's (or the entire band's) means of hunting ineffective, or it could encourage its living fellows to remove themselves from the vicinity. In both cases the end result was the same—the hunt was rendered unsuccessful—and in both it was mediated by the same power—the spirit of the slain animal. Either of these catastrophes could usually be reversed through the magical arts of the shaman. In the Micmac cosmology, the overkill of wildlife would have been resented by the animal kingdom as an act comparable to genocide, and would have been resisted by means of the sanctions outlined above. The threat of retaliation thus had the effect of placing an upper limit on the number of animals slain, while the practical result was the conservation of wildlife.

The injection of European civilization into this balanced system initiated a series of chain reactions which, within a little over a century, resulted in the replacement of the aboriginal ecosystem by another. From at least the beginning of the sixteenth century, and perhaps well before that date, fishing fleets from England, France, and Portugal visited the Grand Banks off Newfoundland every spring for the cod, and hunted whale and walrus in the Gulf of St Lawrence.[63] Year after year, while other, more flamboyant men were advancing the geopolitical ambitions of their emerging dynastic states as they searched for precious minerals or a passage to the Orient, these unassuming fishermen visited Canada's east coast and made the first effective European contact with the Indians there. For the natives' furs they bartered knives, beads, brass kettles, assorted ship fittings, and the like,[64] thus initiating the subversion and replacement of Micmac material culture by European technology. Far more important, the fishermen unwittingly infected the Indians with European diseases, against which the natives had no immunity. Commenting on what may be called the microbial phase of European conquest, John Witthoft has written:

All of the microscopic parasites of humans, which had been collected together from all parts of the known world into Europe, were brought to these [American] shores, and new diseases stalked faster than man could walk into the interior of the continent. Typhoid, diphtheria, colds, influenza, measles, chicken pox, whooping cough, tuberculosis, yellow fever, scarlet fever, and other strep infections, gonorrhea, pox (syphilis), and smallpox were diseases that had never been in the New World before. They were new among populations which had no immunity to them. . . . Great epidemics and pandemics of these diseases are believed to have destroyed whole communities, depopulated whole regions, and vastly decreased the native population everywhere in the yet unexplored interior of the continent. The early pandemics are believed to have run their course prior to 1600 A.D.[65]

Disease did more than decimate the native population; it effectively prepared the way for subsequent phases of European contact by breaking native morale and, perhaps even more significantly, by cracking their spiritual edifice. It is reasonable to suggest that European disease rendered the Indian's (particularly the shaman's) ability to control and otherwise influence the supernatural realm dysfunctional—because his magic and other traditional cures were now ineffective—thereby causing the Indian to apostatize (in effect), which in turn subverted the 'retaliation' principle of taboo and opened the way to a corruption of the Indian-land relationship under the influence of the fur trade.

Much of this microbial phase was of course protohistoric, although it continued well into and no doubt beyond the seventeenth century—the time period covered by the earliest French sources. Recognizing the limitations of tradition as it conveys historical fact, it may nevertheless be instructive to examine a myth concerning the Cross-bearing Micmac of the Miramichi River which, as recorded by Father Chrestien Le Clercq, seems to illustrate the demoralizing effect of disease. According to tradition, there was once a time when these Indians were gravely threatened by a severe sickness; as was their custom, they looked to the sun for help. In their extreme need a 'beautiful' man, holding a cross, appeared before several of them in a dream. He instructed them to make similar crosses, for, as he told them, in this symbol lay their protection. For a time thereafter these Indians, who believed in dreams 'even to the extent of superstition', were very religious and devoted in their veneration of this symbol. Later, however, they apostatized:

> Since the Gaspesian [Micmac] nation of the Cross-bearers has been almost wholly destroyed, as much by the war which they have waged with the Iroquois as by the maladies which have infected this land, and which, in three or four visitations, have caused the deaths of a very great number, these Indians have gradually relapsed from this first devotion of their ancestors. So true is it, that even the holiest and most religious practices, by a certain fatality attending human affairs, suffer always much alteration if they are not animated and conserved by the same spirit which gave them birth. In brief, when I went into their country to commence my mission, I found some persons who had preserved only the shadow of the customs of their ancestors.[66]

Their rituals had failed to save these Indians when threatened by European diseases and intergroup hostilities; hence their old religious practices were abandoned, no doubt because of their ineffectiveness.

Several other observers also commented on the new diseases that afflicted the Micmac. In precontact times, declared Denys, 'they were not subject to diseases, and knew nothing of fevers'.[67] By about 1700, however, Dièreville noted that the Micmac population was in sharp decline.[68] The Indians themselves frequently complained to Father Biard and other Frenchmen that, since contact with the French, they had been dying off in great numbers. 'For they assert that, before this association and intercourse [with the French], all their countries were very populous, and they tell how one by one the different coasts, according as they have begun to traffic with us, have been more reduced by disease.' The Indians accused the French of trying to poison them or charged that the food supplied by the French was somehow adulterated. Whatever the reasons for the catastrophe, warned Biard, the Indians were very angry about it and 'upon the point of breaking with us, and making war upon us'.[69]

To the Jesuit fathers, the solution to this sorry state of affairs lay in the civilizing power of the Gospel. To Biard, his mission was clear:

> For, if our Souriquois [Micmac] are few, they may become numerous; if they are savages, it is to domesticate and civilize them that we have come here; if they are rude, that is no reason that we should be idle; if they have until now profited little, it is no wonder, if it would be too much to expect fruit from this grafting, and to demand reason and maturity from a child.
>
> In conclusion, we hope in time to make them susceptible of receiving the doctrines of the faith and of the christian and catholic religion, and later, to penetrate further into the regions beyond.[70]

The message was simple and straightforward: the black-robes would enlighten the Indians by ridiculing their animism and related taboos, discrediting their shamans, and urging them to accept the Christian gospel. But to their chagrin the Indians proved stubborn in their ancient ways, no matter how unsuited to changing circumstances.[71]

Since the advent of European diseases and the consequent disillusionment with native spiritual beliefs and customs, some Indians appear to have repudiated their traditional world view altogether, while others clung desperately to what had become a moribund body of ritual. We would suppose that the Christian message was more readily accepted by the former, while the latter group, which included the shamans and those too old to change, would have fought bitterly against the missionary teachings.[72] But they resisted in vain for, with time, old people died and shamans whose magic was less potent than that of the missionaries were discredited.[73] The missionary was successful only to the degree that his power exceeded that of the shaman. The non-literate Indian, for example, was awed by the magic of handwriting as a means of communication.[74] Even more significant was the fact that Christianity was the religion of the white man, who, with his superior technology and greater success at manipulating life to his advantage, was believed to have recourse to a greater power (manitou) than did the Indian. Material goods, such as the trading articles offered the Indians by the French, were believed by the native to have a spirit within, in accord with their belief that all animate and inanimate objects housed such a spirit or power.[75] Furthermore, there were degrees of power in such objects, which were determined and calibrated in the Indian mind by the degree of functionalism associated with a particular object.[76] For example, the Micmac believed that there was a spirit of his canoe, of his snowshoes, of his bow, and so on. It was for this reason that a man's material goods were either buried with him or burned, so that their spirits would accompany his to the spirit world, where he would have need of them. Just as he had hunted game in this physical world, so his spirit would again hunt the game spirits with the spirits of his weapons in the land of the dead.[77] Denys described an incident which emphasized the fact that even European trading goods had spirits, when he related how the brass kettle was known to have lost its spirit (or died) when it no longer rang when tapped.[78] Thus Christianity, which to the Indians was the ritual harnessing all of this power, was a potent force among them. Nevertheless, the priests who worked among the Indians frequently complained of their relapsing into paganism, largely because the Micmac came to associate Christianity and civilization in general with their numerous misfortunes, together with the fact that they never clearly understood the Christian message anyway, but always saw it in terms of their own cosmology.[79]

As all religious systems reflect their cultural milieux, so did seventeenth-century Christianity. Polygamy was condemned by the French missionaries as immoral, the consultation of shamans was discouraged, the custom of interring material goods was criticized, eat-all feasts were denounced as gluttonous and shortsighted, and the Indians were disabused of many of their so-called superstitions (taboos).[80] The priests attacked the Micmac culture with a marvelous fervor and some success.[81] Although they could not have appreciated it, they were aided in this endeavor by an obsolescent system of taboo and spiritual awareness; Christianity merely delivered the coup de grace.

The result of this Christian onslaught on a decaying Micmac cosmology was, of course, the despiritualization of the material world. Commenting on the process of despiritualization, Denys (who was a spectator to this transformation in the mid-seventeenth century) remarked that it was accomplished with 'much difficulty'; for some of the Indians it was achieved by religious means, while others were influenced by the French customs, but nearly all were affected 'by the need for the things which come from us, the use of which has become to them an indispensable necessity. They have abandoned all their own utensils, whether because of the trouble they had as well to make as to use them, or because of the facility of obtaining from us, in exchange for skins which cost them almost nothing, the things which seemed to them invaluable, not so much for their novelty as for the convenience they derived therefrom.'[82]

In the early years of the fur trade, before the establishment of permanent posts among the natives, trading was done with the coast-wise fishermen from May to early fall.[83] In return for skins of beaver, otter, marten, moose, and other furbearers, the Indians received a variety of fairly cheap commodities, principally tobacco, liquor, powder and shot (in later years), biscuit, peas, beans, flour, assorted clothing, wampum, kettles, and hunting tools.[84] The success of this trade in economic terms must be attributed to pressure exerted on a relatively simple society by a complex civilization and, perhaps even more importantly, by the tremendous pull of this simple social organization on the resources of Europe.[85] To the Micmac, who like other Indians measured the worth of a tool or object by the ease of its construction and use, the technology of Europe became indispensable. But as has already been shown, this was not simply an economic issue for the Indian; the Indian was more than just 'economically seduced' by the European's trading goods.[86] One must also consider the metaphysical implications of Indian acceptance of the European material culture.

European technology of the sixteenth and seventeenth centuries was largely incompatible with the spiritual beliefs of the eastern woodland Indians, despite the observation made above that the Micmacs readily invested trading goods with spiritual power akin to that possessed by their own implements. As Denys pointed out, the trade goods which the Micmac so eagerly accepted were accompanied by Christian religious teachings and French custom, both of which gave definition to these alien objects. In accepting the European material culture, the natives were impelled to accept the European abstract culture, especially religion, and so, in effect, their own spiritual beliefs were subverted as they abandoned their implements for those of the white man. Native religion lost not only its practical effectiveness, in part owing to the replacement of the traditional magical and animistic view of nature by the exploitive European view, but it was no longer necessary as a source of definition and theoretical support for the new Europe-derived material culture. Western technology made more 'sense' if it was accompanied by Western religion.

Under these circumstances in the early contact period, the Micmac's role within his ecosystem changed radically. No longer was he the sensitive fellow-member of a symbolic world; under pressure from disease, European trade, and Christianity, he had apostatized—he had repudiated his role within the ecosystem. Former attitudes were replaced by a kind of mongrel outlook which combined some native traditions and beliefs with a European rationale and motivation. Our concern here is less to document this transformation than to assess its impact on the Indian-land relationship. In these terms, then, what effect did the trade have on the Micmac ecosystem?

The most obvious change was the unrestrained slaughter of certain game. Lured by European commodities, equipped with European technology, urged by European traders,[87] deprived of a sense of responsibility and accountability for the land, and no longer inhibited by taboo, the Micmac began to overkill systematically those very wildlife which had now become so profitable and even indispensable to his new way of life. The pathos of this transformation of attitude and behavior is illustrated by an incident recorded by Le Clercq. The Indians, who still believed that the beaver had 'sense' and formed a 'separate nation', maintained that they 'would cease to make war upon these animals if these would speak, howsoever little, in order that they might learn whether the Beavers are among their friends or their enemies'.[88] Unfortunately for the beaver, they never communicated their friendliness. The natural world of the Indian was becoming inarticulate.

It is interesting to note that Dièreville, who observed the Micmac culture at the beginning of the eighteenth century, was the only witness to record the native superstition which compelled them to tear out the eyes of all slain animals. Somehow, perhaps by some sort of symbolic transference, the spirits of surviving animals of the same species were thereby blinded to the irreverent treatment accorded the victim; otherwise, through the mediation of the outraged spirits, the living would no longer have allowed themselves to be taken by the Indians.[89] The failure of the earlier writers to mention this particular superstition suggests that it was of fairly recent origin, a result of the overexploitation of game for the trade. To the Micmac mind, haunted by memories of a former time, the practice may have been intended to hide his guilt and insure his continued success.

Together with this depletion of wildlife went a reduction of dependency on the resources of the local ecosystem. The use of improved hunting equipment, such as fishing line and hooks, axes, knives, muskets, and iron-tipped arrows, spears, and harpoons,[90] exerted heavier pressure on the resources of the area, while the availability of French foodstuffs shifted the position of the Micmac in the trophic system, somewhat reducing his dependency on local food sources as it placed him partly outside of the system. To be sure, a decreasing native population relieved this pressure to a degree, but, according to evidence cited above, not enough to prevent the abuse of the land.

Other less obvious results of the fur trade were the increased incidence of feuding and the modification of the Micmac settlement patterns to meet the demands of the trade. Liquor, in particular brandy, was a favorite item of the trade—one for which the Indians 'would go a long way'.[91] Its effects were devastating. Both Jean Saint-Vallier (François Laval's successor as bishop of Quebec) and Biard blamed liquor as a cause for the increased death rate of the natives. Moreover, it was observed that drunkenness resulted in social disintegration as the Indians became debauched and violent among themselves, and, at times, spilled over into the French community which they would rob, ravage, and burn. Drunkenness also provided a legitimate excuse to commit crimes, such as murdering their enemies, for which they would otherwise be held accountable.[92]

European contact should thus be viewed as a trigger factor, that is, something which was not present in the Micmac ecosystem before and which

initiated a concatenation of reactions leading to the replacement of the aboriginal ecosystem by another.[93] European disease, Christianity, and the fur
trade with its accompanying technology—the three often intermeshed—
were responsible for the corruption of the Indian-land relationship, in which
the native had merged sympathetically with his environment. By a lockstep
process European disease rendered the Indian's control over the supernatural
and spiritual realm inoperative, and the disillusioned Micmac apostatized,
debilitating taboo and preparing the way for the destruction of wildlife which
was soon to occur under the stimulation of the fur trade. For those who
believed in it, Christianity furnished a new, dualistic world view, which
placed man above nature, as well as spiritual support for the fur trade, and
as a result the Micmac became dependent on the European marketplace both
spiritually and economically. Within his ecosystem the Indian changed from
conservator to exploiter. All of this resulted in the intense exploitation of
some game animals and the virtual extermination of others. Unfortunately
for the Indian and the land, this grim tale was to be repeated many times
along the moving Indian-white frontier. Life for the Micmac had indeed
become more convenient, but convenience cost dearly in much material and
abstract culture loss or modification.

The historiography of Indian-white relations is rendered more comprehensible when the Indian and the land are considered together: 'So intimately
is all of Indian life tied up with the land and its utilization that to think of
Indians is to think of land. The two are inseparable.'[94] American Indian
history can be seen, then, as a type of environmental history, and perhaps it
is from this perspective that the early period of Indian-white relations can
best be understood.

Suggestions for Further Reading

Shepard Krech III, ed., *Indians, Animals, and the Fur Trade: A Critique of Keepers of the
Game* (Athens, Ga., 1981).

Conrad Heidenreich and Arthur J. Ray, *The Early Fur Trades: A Study in Cultural
Interaction* (Toronto, 1976).

Calvin Martin, *Keepers of the Game: Indian-Animal Relationships and the Fur Trade*
(Berkeley, 1978).

Notes

Mr. Martin would like to thank Professors Wilbur R. Jacobs, Roderick Nash, and
Albert C. Spaulding for their helpful comments and criticisms of this article.

[1]Reuben Gold Thwaites, ed., *The Jesuit Relations and Allied Documents: Travels and
Explorations of the Jesuit Missionaries in New France, 1610–1791* (New York, 1959
[orig. publ. Cleveland, Ohio, 1896–1901]), VIII, 57.

²Baron Lahontan, *New Voyages to North-America . . . An Account of the Several Nations of that vast Continent . . .* , ed. Reuben Gold Thwaites (Chicago, 1905), I, 82.

³Thwaites, ed., *Jesuit Relations*, V, 25; VI, 297–9; VIII, 57; XL, 151; LXVIII, 47, 109–11; LXIX, 95, 99–113.

⁴*Ibid.*, VIII, 41.

⁵Nicolas Denys, *The Description and Natural History of the Coasts of North America (Acadia)*, ed. and trans. William F. Ganong, II (Toronto, 1908), I, 187, 199, 209, 219–20, hereafter cited as Denys, *Description of North America*.

⁶*Ibid.*, 432, 450.

⁷Peter Farb, *Man's Rise to Civilization as Shown by the Indians of North America from Primeval Times to the Coming of the Industrial State* (New York, 1968), 82–3.

⁸See Wilson D. Wallis and Ruth Sawtell Wallis, *The Micmac Indians of Eastern Canada* (Minneapolis, Minn., 1955), for a thorough ethnographic study of the Micmac, Jacques and Maryvonne Crevel, *Honguedo ou l'Histoire des Premiers Gaspesiens* (Quebec, 1970), give a fairly good general history of the Micmac during the 17th century, together with a description of the fishing industry.

⁹Julian H. Steward, 'The Concept and Method of Cultural Ecology', in his *Theory of Culture Change: The Methodology of Multilinear Evolution* (Urbana, Ill., 1955), 30–42, and Andrew P. Vayda and Roy A. Rappaport, 'Ecology, Cultural and Noncultural', in James A. Clifton, ed., *Introduction to Cultural Anthropology: Essays in the Scope and Methods of the Science of Man* (Boston, 1968), 494.

¹⁰W.D. Billings, *Plants, Man, and the Ecosystem*, 2d ed. (Belmont, Calif., 1970), 4.

¹¹Roy A. Rappaport, *Pigs for the Ancestors: Ritual in the Ecology of a New Guinea People* (New Haven, Conn., 1968).

¹²Among the few who have are William Christie MacLeod, 'Conservation Among Primitive Hunting Peoples', *Scientific Monthly* XLIII (1936), 562–6, and Alfred Goldsworthy Bailey in his little-known book, *The Conflict of European and Eastern Algonkian Cultures, 1504–1700*, 2d ed. (Toronto, 1969).

¹³Wilbur R. Jacobs, *Dispossessing the American Indian: Indians and Whites on the Colonial Frontier* (New York, 1972), 25.

¹⁴Billings, *Plants, Man, Ecosystem*, 37–8.

¹⁵Sieur de Dièreville, *Relation of the Voyage to Port Royal in Acadia or New France*, trans. Mrs Clarence Webster and ed. John Clarence Webster (Toronto, 1933), 184, hereafter cited as Dièreville, *Voyage to Port Royal*. According to the editor, 216, the Malecites later replaced the Micmacs living along the St John, the latter withdrawing to Nova Scotia. See also Diamond Jenness, *The Indians of Canada*, 3d ed. (Ottawa, 1955), 267.

¹⁶See Rappaport, *Pigs for the Ancestors*, 225–6. If the present article were intended as a more rigorous analysis of the Micmac ecosystem, we would report on the topography of this region, on the soil types, the hydrological characteristics, the climate, the influence of the ocean, and the effects of fires caused by lightning. But since neither the Micmac nor the first Europeans had any appreciable effect on these physical variables—except perhaps that of water relations—we shall pass over the physical environment and go on to the biological. Suffice it to say that the water of numerous rivers and streams was regulated in its flow by beaver dams throughout

much of this region, and Indian beaver hunting and trapping certainly upset this control.

[17]For a thorough discussion of Micmac plant and animal use see Frank G. Speck and Ralph W. Dexter, 'Utilization of Animals and Plants by the Micmac Indians of New Brunswick', *Journal of the Washington Academy of Sciences* XLI (1951), 250–9.

[18]Father Chrestien Le Clercq, *New Relation of Gaspesia, with the Customs and Religion of the Gaspesian Indians*, ed. and trans. William F. Ganong (Toronto, 1910), 212–13, hereafter cited as Le Clercq, *Relation of Gaspesia*. Thwaites, ed., *Jesuit Relations*, III, 77; Marc Lescarbot, *The History of New France*, trans. W.L. Grant (Toronto, 1907), III, 93, 194–5, hereafter cited as Lescarbot, *History of New France*. Lescarbot asserts that the Micmac definitely grew tobacco, most likely the so-called wild tobacco (*Nicotiana rustica*): *ibid.*, 252–3.

[19]Lescarbot, *History of New France*, II, 323–5; III, 158.

[20]Thwaites, ed., *Jesuit Relations*, III, 77–83.

[21]*Ibid.*; Denys, *Description of North America*, II, 403; Lescarbot, *History of New France*, III, 80; Le Clercq, *Relation of Gaspesia*, 88–9, 93; Dièreville, *Voyage to Port Royal*, 146.

[22]Lescarbot, *History of New France*, III, 219–20, and Thwaites, ed., *Jesuit Relations*, III, 77–9.

[23]Lescarbot, *History of New France*, III, 222–4. See Horace T. Martin, *Castorologia, or the History and Traditions of the Canadian Beaver* (Montreal, 1892), for a good treatise on the beaver.

[24]Le Clercq, *Relation of Gaspesia*, 276–80; Dièreville, *Voyage to Port Royal*, 133–4; Denys, *Description of North America*, II, 429–33; Lescarbot, *History of New France*, III, 222–4.

[25]Lescarbot, *History of New France*, III, 220–2; Denys, *Description of North America*, II, 426–9; Le Clercq, *Relation of Gaspesia*, 274–6. Speck and Dexter place caribou before moose in order of importance, but they cite no evidence for such ranking. Speck and Dexter, 'Utilization of Animals and Plants by Micmacs', *Jour. Wash. Acad. Sci.* XLI (1951), 255.

[26]Le Clercq, *Relation of Gaspesia*, 118–19.

[27]*Ibid.*, 93–4; Denys, *Description of North America*, II, 412; Lescarbot, *History of New France*, III, 133; Speck and Dexter, 'Utilization of Animals and Plants by Micmacs'; *Jour. Wash. Acad. Sci.* XLI (1951), 255.

[28]Speck and Dexter, 'Utilization of Animals and Plants by Micmacs', *Jour. Wash. Acad. Sci.* XLI (1951), 255.

[29]Le Clercq, *Relation of Gaspesia*, 116, 119; Dièreville, *Voyage to Port Royal*, 131; Thwaites, ed., *Jesuit Relations*, III, 107–9.

[30]Denys, *Description of North America*, II, 433–4.

[31]Thwaites, ed., *Jesuit Relations*, III, 79.

[32]*Ibid.*, 81, and Speck and Dexter, "Utilization of Animals and Plants by Micmacs,' *Jour. Wash. Acad. Sci.* XLI (1951), 251–4.

[33]Lescarbot, *History of New France*, III, 236–7, and Denys, *Description of North America*, II, 436–7.

[34]Le Clercq, *Relation of Gaspesia*, 92, 137; Lescarbot, *History of New France*, III, 230–1; Denys, *Description of North America*, II, 435–6.

[35]Thwaites, ed., *Jesuit Relations*, III, 83.

[36]*Ibid.*

[37]Le Clercq, *Relation of Gaspesia*, 109–10, 283, and Denys, *Description of North America*, II, 389, 434.

[38]Frank G. Speck, 'Aboriginal Conservators', *Audubon Magazine* XL (1938), 260.

[39]Denys, *Description of North America*, II, 492–3.

[40]*Ibid.*, 426.

[41]Speck, 'Aboriginal Conservators', 260. Italics in original.

[42]Rappaport, *Pigs for the Ancestors*, 237–8, and Vayda and Rappaport, 'Ecology, Cultural and Noncultural', in Clifton, ed., *Cultural Anthropology*, 491.

[43]See, for example, the writings of Speck, esp. 'Aboriginal Conservators', *Audubon Magazine* XL (1938), 258–61; John Witthoft, 'The American Indian as Hunter', *Pennsylvania Game News* XXIX (Feb.-Apr. 1953); George S. Snyderman, 'Concepts of Land Ownership among the Iroquois and their Neighbors', *Bureau of American Ethnology Bulletin* 149, ed. William N. Fenton (Washington, D.C., 1951), 15–34. Robert F. Heizer, 'Primitive Man as an Ecological Factor', *Kroeber Anthropological Society, Papers*, XIII (1955), 1–31. See also William A. Ritchie, 'The Indian and His Environment', *Conservationist* (Dec.-Jan. 1955–1956), 23–7; Gordon Day, 'The Indian as an Ecological Factor in the Northeastern Forest', *Ecology* XXIV (1953), 329–46; MacLeod, 'Conservation', *Scientific Monthly* XLIII (1936), 562–6.

[44]Witthoft, 'American Indian', *Pa. Game News* (Mar. 1953), 17.

[45]Murray Wax, 'Religion and Magic', in Clifton, ed., *Cultural Anthropology*, 235.

[46]See William Jones, 'The Algonkin Manitou', *Journal of American Folk-Lore* XVIII (1905), 183–90, and Frederick Johnson, 'Notes on Micmac Shamanism', *Primitive Man* XVI (1943), 58–9.

[47]See Stansbury Hagar, 'Micmac Magic and Medicine', *Jour. Am. Folk-Lore* IX (1896), 170–7, and Johnson, 'Shamanism', *Primitive Man* XVI (1943), 54, 56–7, who report that such beliefs in the supernatural and spiritual survive even in modern times, although in suppressed and attenuated form. Le Clercq, *Relation of Gaspesia*, 187, 209, 212–14, and Denys, *Description of North America*, II, 117, 442.

[48]Witthoft, 'American Indian', *Pa. Game News* (Feb. 1953), 16.

[49]Dièreville, *Voyage to Port Royal*, 139, and Le Clercq, *Relation of Gaspesia, 225–9, 276–7.*

[50]Le Clercq, *Relation of Gaspesia*, 225–9.

[51]*Ibid.*, 226.

[52]*Ibid.*, 227–9.

[53]Witthoft, 'American Indian', *Pa. Game News* (Mar. 1953), 16–22; A. Irving Hallowell, 'Bear Ceremonialism in the Northern Hemisphere', *American Anthropologist* N.S., XXVIII (1926), 1–175.

[54]Le Clercq, *Relation of Gaspesia*, 227.

[55]Frank G. Speck, 'Mistassini Hunting Territories in the Labrador Peninsula', *Am. Anthropologist* XXV (1923), 464. Johnson, 'Shamanism', *Primitive Man* XVI (1943), 70–2, distinguishes between the Montagnais, Wabanaki, and Micmac ideas of the 'soul'.

[56]Le Clercq, *Relation of Gaspesia*, 88–9; Dièreville, *Voyage to Port Royal*, 146; Lescarbot, *History of New France*, III, 80.

[57]Denys, *Description of North America*, II, 430, 442, and Le Clercq, *Relation of Gaspesia*, 192–3.

[58]Denys, *Description of North America*, II, 417–18, and Le Clercq, *Relation of Gaspesia*, 215–18.

[59]Thwaites, ed., *Jesuit Relations*, II, 75; Le Clercq, *Relation of Gaspesia*, 215–16; George H. Daugherty, Jr, 'Reflections of Environment in North American Indian Literature' (PhD diss., University of Chicago, 1925), 31; Johnson, 'Shamanism', *Primitive Man* XVI (1943), 71–2.

[60]Le Clercq, *Relation of Gaspesia*, 215–18, 296–9; Denys, *Description of North America*, II, 415, 417–18; Hagar, 'Micmac Magic', *Jour. Am. Folk-Lore* IX (1896), 170–7. Denys, *Description of North America*, II, 418, observed that most of these ailments were (what we would call today) psychosomatic in origin.

[61]Billings, *Plants, Man, Ecosystem*, 36.

[62]Thwaites, ed., *Jesuit Relations*, II, 75.

[63]H.P. Biggar, *The Early Trading Companies of New France: A Contribution to the History of Commerce and Discovery in North America* (New York, 1965 [orig. publ. Toronto, 1901]), 18–37.

[64]John Witthoft, 'Archaeology as a Key to the Colonial Fur Trade', *Minnesota History* XL (1966), 204–5.

[65]John Witthoft, *Indian Prehistory of Pennsylvania* (Harrisburg, Pa., 1965), 26–9.

[66]Le Clercq, *Relation of Gaspesia*, 146–52. The Recollet fathers, especially Father Emanuel Jumeau, were able to cause a renaissance of the old traditional religion by encouraging these people to look to the cross once more for their salvation, although, of course, this time it was the Christian cross. We should bear in mind that the cross was an art motif common among non-Christian people, and of independent origin from that of the Christian cross. Whether the cross mentioned in this particular tradition was of Christian or aboriginal origin should make little difference, for the story still serves to illustrate the process of apostatization.

[67]Denys, *Description of North America*, II, 415. Estimates of the aboriginal population of North America at the time of European contact are constantly being revised upward. Henry F. Dobyns, 'Estimating Aboriginal American Population: An Appraisal of Techniques with a New Hemispheric Estimate', *Current Anthropology* VII (1966), 395–416, has recently placed the figure at a controversial and fantastically high total of 9,800,000 natives.

[68]Dièreville, *Voyage to Port Royal*, 116. See Thwaites, ed., *Jesuit Relations*, I, 177–9.

[69]Thwaites, ed., *Jesuit Relations*, III, 105–7.

[70]*Ibid.*, I, 183.

[71]*Ibid.*, II, 75–7; III, 123; and Le Clercq, *Relation of Gaspesia*, 193, 220, 224–5, 227, 239, 253. See also Denys, *Description of North America*, II, 117, 430, 442.

[72]Notice that when a custom in any society becomes a mere formality and loses its practical meaning, it is easily discarded when challenged by detractors, who may or may not replace it with something more meaningful. See Le Clercq, *Relation of Gaspesia*, 206, 227, and Lescarbot, *History of New France*, III, 94–5.

[73]Jean Baptiste de la Croix Chevrières de Saint-Vallier, *Estat Présent de l'Eglise et de la Colonie Françoise dans la Nouvelle France, par M. l'Evêque de Québec* (Paris, 1688), 36–7, and Thwaites, ed., *Jesuit Relations*, II, 75–7. See Le Clercq, *Relation of Gaspesia*, 220–1, where he speaks of converting a noted shaman to Christianity. André Vachon, 'L'Eau-de-Vie dans la Société Indienne', Canadian Historical Association, *Report of the Annual Meeting* (1960), 22–32, has observed that the priest replaced the shaman and sorcerer in Indian society by virtue of his superior powers. By

discrediting his Indian counterparts (and rivals), the priest became the shaman-sorcerer (i.e., a source of both good and evil power).

[74]Lescarbot, *History of New France*, III, 128, and Le Clercq, *Relation of Gaspesia*, 133–5.

[75]Le Clercq, *Relation of Gaspesia*, 209, 213–14, and Bailey, *Conflict of Cultures*, 47.

[76]Denys, *Description of North America*, II, 439.

[77]Le Clercq, *Relation of Gaspesia*, 187, 209, 212–14, 238–9, 303; Lescarbot, *History of New France*, III, 279, 285; Thwaites, ed., *Jesuit Relations*, I, 169; Denys, *Description of North America*, II, 437–9; Dièreville, *Voyage to Port Royal*, 161.

[78]Denys, *Description of North America*, II, 439–41.

[79]Le Clercq, *Relation of Gaspesia*, 125, 193, and Thwaites, ed., *Jesuit Relations*, I, 165. See *ibid.*, II, 89, where baptism was understood by the Micmac (of Port Royal, at least) 'as a sort of sacred pledge of friendship and alliance with the French'.

[80]Lescarbot, *History of New France*, III, 53–4; Denys, *Description of North America*, II, 117, 430, 442; Le Clercq, *Relation of Gaspesia*, 116; Dièreville, *Voyage to Port Royal*, 161; Thwaites, ed., *Jesuit Relations*, III, 131–5. See *ibid.*, II, 75–7, where the shamans complain of having lost much of their power since the coming of the French.

[81]Le Clercq observed that since the introduction of Christianity and especially baptism the manitou had not afflicted them to the degree that he did formerly. See Le Clercq, *Relation of Gaspesia*, 225. See also *ibid.*, 229–33, where cases are recorded of native men and women who seemed to feel a divine call and ordination, representing themselves as priests among their fellows.

[82]Denys, *Description of North America*, II, 440–1.

[83]Samuel de Champlain, *The Voyages of the Sieur de Champlain of Saintoge . . .* in H.P. Biggar, ed. and trans., *The Works of Samuel de Champlain*, I (Toronto, 1922), *passim*, and Thwaites, ed., *Jesuit Relations*, III, 81.

[84]Lescarbot, *History of New France*, II, 281–2, 323–4; III, 158, 168, 250; Thwaites, ed., *Jesuit Relations*, III, 75–7; Le Clercq, *Relation of Gaspesia*, 93–4, 109; Dièreville, *Voyage to Port Royal*, 132–3, 130–41.

[85]Harold A. Innis, *The Fur Trade in Canada: An Introduction to Canadian Economic History*, rev. ed. (Toronto, 1956), 15–17.

[86]Farb, *Man's Rise to Civilization*, 82–3.

[87]See Thwaites, ed., *Jesuit Relations*, I, 175–7, and Denys, *Description of North America*, II, 439, for mention of the French lust for furs.

[88]Le Clercq, *Relation of Gaspesia*, 276–7. See also Dièreville, *Voyage to Port Royal*, 139.

[89]Dièreville, *Voyage to Port Royal*, 161.

[90]Lescarbot, *History of New France*, III, 191–2, and Denys, *Description of North America*, II, 399, 442–3.

[91]Dièreville, *Voyage to Port Royal*, 174, and Denys, *Description of North America*, II, 172, 443–52. If we are to believe Craig MacAndrew and Robert B. Edgerton, *Drunken Comportment: A Social Explanation* (Chicago, 1969), III, the Micmac encountered by Jacques Cartier along the shores of Chaleur Bay in 1534 were the first historically documented North American tribe to receive European liquor.

[92]Saint-Vallier, *Estat Présent*, 36–7, 42; Thwaites, ed., *Jesuit Relations*, III, 105–9; Denys, *Description of North America*, II, 443–52; Dièreville, *Voyage to Port Royal*, 166; Le Clercq, *Relation of Gaspesia*, 244–5, 254–7. The subject of North American Indian drinking patterns and problems has been the topic of much debate from the

17th century to the present. The best current scholarship on the subject, which has by no means been exhausted, is contained in MacAndrew and Edgerton, *Drunken Comportment*; Vachon, 'L'Eau-de-Vie', Can. Hist. Assn., *Report* (1960), 22–32; Nancy Oestreich Lurie, 'The World's Oldest On-Going Protest Demonstration: North American Indian Drinking Patterns', *Pacific Historical Review* XL (1971), 311–32.

[93]Billings, *Plants, Man, Ecosystem*, 37–8.

[94]See John Collier's report on Indian affairs, 1938, in the *Annual Report of the Secretary of the Interior* (Washington, D.C., 1938), 209–11, as quoted by Wilcomb Washburn, ed., *The Indian and the White Man* (Garden City, N.Y., 1964), 394.

7

The Colonists of Seventeenth-Century Canada

R. Cole Harris

One of the principal factors in the gradual European transformation of North America was, of course, settlement. The isolated activities of explorers, missionaries, and business entrepreneurs would have had considerably less impact had not other people also begun to arrive, and in fairly substantial numbers. The settlement of Canada was begun in earnest in the first years of the seventeenth century by both the British and the French, although the latter were the first to achieve any measure of success. Later in the seventeenth century thousands of individuals in Britain and France uprooted themselves, risking the dangers of a lengthy transatlantic voyage and unknown wilderness conditions to establish new homes in North America. We are accustomed to thinking about immigration as a much later phenomenon, forgetting that even the first European settlers were immigrants who shared many of the same problems and patterns as their successors in

the nineteenth and twentieth centuries. The early immigrants were like those who followed them in bringing with them their European heritage and being forced to adapt to new conditions. Moreover, as 'founding peoples' their background influenced the society they would help to create in the New World.

The first immigration to Canada is often not well understood, partly because historians have tended to focus on the immigrants as settlers only after their arrival, finding it difficult to document their background. As Cole Harris points out in the following article, the problems involved in researching the origins of 10,000 individual immigrants are formidable. His solution is to analyse research done for genealogical purposes, thus adapting for historical investigation material that many people would regard as beyond (or beneath) their purview. The reader may well question whether Harris has satisfactorily dealt with the methodological difficulties his evidence produces.

Beyond methodology, however, are the conclusions and their implications. Harris attempts to deal with a number of aspects relating to the early immigrants: their geographical origins, both in terms of region and whether urban or rural; their occupations; and their family status as immigrants. All of these factors are obviously important, and are among the first questions any historian of immigration attempts to answer. Harris notes in his conclusions some of the implications of his findings; but if his data are correct, they suggest much about the way in which French Canada would develop. How does this evidence fit into our understanding of early Canada? Is it different from what one would expect? Is the background of the early immigrants a major factor in influencing the direction of development in New France? In what ways do Harris's findings confirm our overall impressions about New France? In what ways do they suggest the need for new questions and frameworks of analysis?

This article first appeared, titled 'The French Background of Immigrants to Canada before 1700', in *Cahiers de Géographie de Québec* XVI (1972), 312–24.

Any appreciation of the human landscape and society of Canada during the French régime depends on some understanding of changes in the immigrants' way of life after their Atlantic crossing. Presumably there was change—it is hard to conceive of such displacement without it—but the nature and scale of change as well as the reasons for it are still subjects for a good deal of conjecture. To a great extent this uncertainty reflects our ignorance of the French roots of immigrants to Canada for, other than in the most general terms, we have not been able to say where immigrants had come from in France, whether their backgrounds had been rural or urban, what social and economic strata of French society they represented and in what proportion, and in what social and economic condition they arrived in Canada. Without such data, any discussion of social change is exceedingly difficult. Certainly, information about French origins is elusive. The contract drawn up when a man signed on as an *engagé* or as a soldier seldom gives his place of origin in France, his occupation, or his father's. When information is obtained about a few individuals, its representative value is always in question. The only way to obtain the quantitative data that are needed may be to search, immigrant by immigrant, through the relevant notarial records on both sides of the Atlantic. If a contract of indenture drawn up in La Rochelle indicates the approximate data at which an emigrant embarked for Canada and the period and wages for which he had contracted to work, a Canadian marriage contract a few years later may give his place of birth, and perhaps also his father's occupation. But to search in this way through the records pertinent to the some 10,000 immigrants to Canada during the French régime could well take a lifetime.

In an attempt to correct the many inaccuracies in Mgr Cyprien Tanguay's *Dictionnaire généalogique des familles canadiennes*,[1] Father Archange Godbout, OFM, began such a study. The published results of Father Godbout's work appear in five volumes of the *Rapport de l'Archiviste de la Province de Québec*,[2] and cover immigrants with surnames beginning with A or BA through BOU who arrived in Canada before 1700, in all 454 people.[3] Drawing on the nominal censuses, parish records, cadastral maps, and local histories and biographies, but principally on the notarial deeds, Father Godbout has outlined, where possible, the salient events in the life of each immigrant. In some cases his outline is extremely sketchy—perhaps he has found only that a given settler was in Canada by 1694, a date for which there is a notarial deed that refers to him—but Father Godbout has found some mention of the place of birth or of residence in France of the great majority of immigrants he has studied. From these data the regional distribution in France of immigrants to Canada may be mapped and the percentage of immigrants from rural or urban backgrounds ascertained. In some cases there is information about the occupation in France of the immigrant or of his father. Usually it is possible to determine whether the immigrant came alone or with relatives. This short paper assembles these data in quantitative or cartographic form and, in conclusion, suggests some of their implications for an understanding of early Canada.

Father Godbout's list of 454 people comprises approximately 8 per cent of the immigrants to Canada before 1700.[4] Were it a random sample, information derived from it could be accepted with a small margin of error, but immigrants with surnames beginning with A or B cannot be considered to be a random sample if the proportion of A and B surnames varied regionally in seventeenth-century France. Some indication that this was not the case is the fact that there is not a significant difference between the distribution of A surnames on the one hand and of B surnames on the other. If this is a biased sample, A and B surnames have the same bias, which seems unlikely. A check of contemporary telephone books does not reveal an unusual percentage of A and B surnames in those parts of France from which most immigrants came.[5] In short, there is no evidence of bias in Father Godbout's sample.

The Place of Origin

All but ten of the 454 immigrants were born in France. Of those who were not, three were Indians (see note 3), three were English, two were Swiss, one was German, and one Flemish. There is information about the place of origin within France of 414 of the 444 French born. Usually this information is very specific—an urban parish or a village that, with the aid of a gazetteer and the contemporary topographic sheets, can be located exactly—but in some cases Father Godbout has determined only that the immigrant came from 'the diocese of Poitiers' or, perhaps, only that he came from Poitou. In most cases this information is based on a parish record of baptism, or on an immigrant's recollection before some Canadian notary that he was born in such and such a place of such and such parents. Sometimes there is information about the immigrant's place of residence in France (which may or may not be his place of birth) and about his port of embarkation. In the figures that follow, the port of embarkation has been disregarded unless there is good evidence that it was also the emigrant's residence. Whenever there is information only about place of birth or about place of residence then this location, whichever it is, is assumed to be the place of origin. In a few cases it can be established that an immigrant lived for some time immediately prior to his departure in a place that was not his place of birth. In these cases the place of origin is considered to be the place of residence. However, the most common information is about place of birth, and for some three quarters of the immigrants for whom a place of origin can be assigned it is, in fact, their place of birth.

These data are mapped by departments on Figure 1. Just over half of the immigrants came from south of the Loire River with easily the greatest concentration of them from around the port of La Rochelle in the old provinces of Aunis, Poitou, and Saintonge. A good many came from the valley of the lower Seine between Paris and Le Havre, some others from central Normandy and Maine (now the departments of Calvados, Orne, and Sarthe). The rest were scattered through west-central France. Very few came from Brittany or the Massif Central, even fewer from the far south, and none from east of the Rhône.

Figure 2 shows the distribution of immigrants who arrived in Canada before the introduction of royal government (1663), and Figure 3 shows those who came thereafter. The colonists sent by the Crown (Figure 3) were drawn from a much wider area of France than were those who came out during the years in which Canada was administered by the Company of New France. Paris, which contributed few settlers before 1663, and the southwest which, in this sample, contributed none, both show up as important sources of immigrants after 1663. Norman immigrants before 1663 were likely to have come from the present departments of Calvados and Orne, but after 1663 to have come from the lower Seine (especially from the department of Seine-Inférieure). Some of these differences between the regional pattern of French emigration to Canada before and after 1663 are explained by Figure 4, which shows the place of origin of soldiers and of single women, both substantial components of the immigrant stream after 1663. Most of the single women came from poor houses in Paris, and many were Parisians

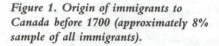

Figure 1. Origin of immigrants to Canada before 1700 (approximately 8% sample of all immigrants).

Figure 2. Origin of immigrants to Canada before 1663 (approximately 8% sample of all immigrants).

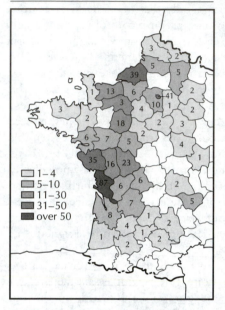

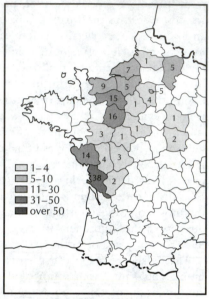

Figure 3. Origin of immigrants to Canada from 1663 to 1700 (approximately 8% sample of all immigrants).

Figure 4. Migration of soldiers and single women after 1662.

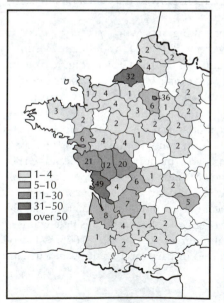

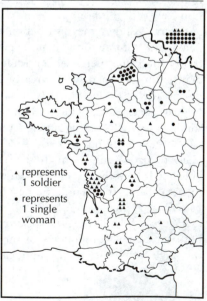

by birth. Clearly, the soldiers who settled in Canada were drawn from a much wider part of France than were the *engagés* who contracted to work in the colony.

In all but sixty-five cases, the rural or urban origin of immigrants also can be determined. When an immigrant came from a sizeable city—Paris, Bordeaux, or Tours, for example—there is no question about his urban background. Similarly a place that is today a village almost certainly was not more than a village late in the seventeenth century, whereas places that are today towns or small cities may have been either rural or urban three hundred years ago. In these latter cases Robert de Hesseln's *Dictionnaire Universel de la France*[6] has been used to distinguish between the two. If de Hesseln describes a place as a city (ville) it is so considered in this study; if he describes it as a village (a bourg) or does not mention it, it is considered to be rural.

Table 1 gives the number and percentage of urban and rural immigrants in several groups of settlers. In each group the proportion of immigrants from an urban background is far higher than the urban proportion of the French population at the time (under 10 per cent). Although the number of immigrants whose origins are unknown leaves the matter somewhat in doubt, it is likely that considerably more than half of the immigrants had come from towns. As might be expected, the urban proportion was particularly high among female immigrants, and partly for this reason the strength of urban over rural migration was most pronounced in the early years of royal government when several contingents of women were sent to the colony.

Figure 5 shows the exact point of origin in west-central France of more than three quarters of the immigrants in Father Godbout's list. More than 20 per cent of all immigrants had come from three cities, Paris (41), La Rochelle (35), and Rouen (20), but all the other cities indicated on Figure 5 had contributed to this sample. Generally, urban immigrants were likely to come from north and rural immigrants from south of the Loire. Many rural immigrants came from villages within a few miles of La Rochelle, but the concentration of rural migration that focused on La Rochelle also extended well to the east and north of the port.

Table 1. Urban-Rural Background

Immigrants	urban		rural		unknown	
	no.	%	no.	%	no.	%
Total	206	45.6	180	40.0	65	14.4
Arriving before 1663	63	45.3	63	45.3	13	9.4
Arriving after 1662	143	45.8	117	37.5	52	16.7
Male	136	40.4	150	44.5	51	15.1
Female	70	61.4	30	26.3	14	12.3

Economic and Social Background

Father Godbout's list contains almost no information about the economic background of the women who came to Canada, but there is such information about approximately one third of the men. In some cases Father Godbout has found the occupation of the immigrant's father, in others the occupation in France of the immigrant himself, and in a few cases the occupations of both father and immigrant. When there is no direct information about an immigrant's occupation in France it may occasionally be inferred from his activities in Canada. If, for example, a man is described within a year or two of his coming to Canada as a *maître charpentier* he had undoubtedly learned his trade in France. On the other hand, a man described at Québec as a domestic or as a day labourer may or may not have been so employed in France. Still, by combining several sources of information, data can be obtained on the occupational background of 112 male immigrants. This is a small sample, some 3 per cent of the male immigrants to Canada in the seventeenth century; it is probably not a random sample of the 330 male immigrants described by Father Godbout, and findings based on it should be treated cautiously.

Table 2 groups the 112 immigrants by occupational category, and compares their occupational background with that of a much larger sample of troops in the French army in 1737.[7] There is reason to assume that male immigrants to Canada and recruits to the ranks of the French army were drawn from much the same occupational strata: many immigrants were sol-

Table 2. Occupational Background of Immigrants and Soldiers

Occupation	Immigrants to Canada		Troops in French Army, 1737	
			Soldier	Father of soldier
	no.	%	%	%
military[8]	1	0.9	—	1.2
noble	2	1.8	1.3	3.8
royal officers and agents	4	3.6	.6	3.6
intellectuals	—	—	1.0	.7
medicine	4	3.6	3.0	1.7
commerce	18	16.1	7.6	13.0
artisans	59	52.5	50.7	35.9
agriculture	18	16.1	34.6	39.2
servants	—	—	1.0	.7
other	6	5.4	.2	.2

Figure 5. Rural and urban origins of immigrants to Canada before 1770 (approximately 8% sample of all immigrants).

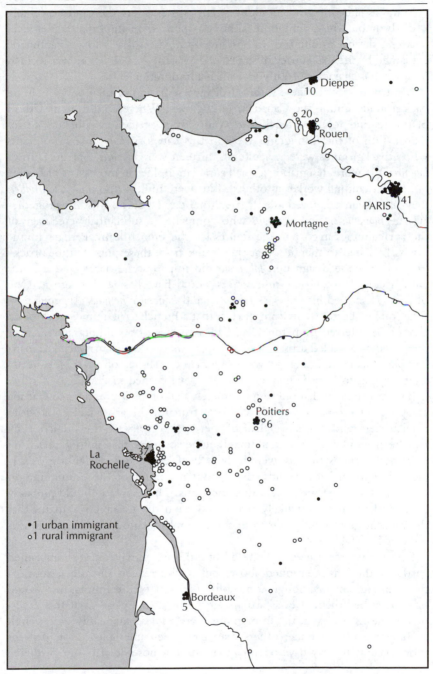

Dieppe
10

20
Rouen
8
8

PARIS 41
Mortagne
9

8

Poitiers
6

La
Rochelle 37

8

•1 urban immigrant
○1 rural immigrant

Bordeaux
5

diers, and the larger number who came as *engagés* may have been recruited in much the same way as soldiers, and may have viewed the army or the colonies as almost equivalent choices. In a general way the figures in Table 2 do bear out this assumption, although there were important differences between the backgrounds of troops and immigrants that perhaps cannot be explained by the inadequacy of the Canadian sample, and that appear to shed light on the character of early Canadian immigration.

Most important of these is the small representation of men of agricultural backgrounds among the Canadian immigrants. Whereas more than a third of the recruits for the French army came from agricultural pursuits, fewer than a fifth of the immigrants were in this category. Of those immigrants whose backgrounds were agricultural, thirteen were *laboureurs* or the sons of *laboureurs* (a word designating a small rural landholder in most parts of France but an agricultural worker in others), four were millers, and one, a *journalier*, may have been employed as an agricultural day labourer. Missing altogether are the *manouvriers* and *vignerons* who comprised a substantial percentage of the agricultural category in the figures for the French army. Perhaps immigrants hesitated to mention that they came from these unpretentious backgrounds, but the designation *laboureur* did impart some status, and if status were a consideration, few immigrants would have hesitated to use it. One of them described his father as *laboureur* and *honorable homme*. Another possible source of error stems from the fact that a French agricultural background cannot be inferred from the Canadian activities of an immigrant. A man described as a skilled artisan within a year or two of his arrival in Canada had been an artisan in France, whereas a man established on a farm lot shortly after coming to Canada may or may not have farmed in France.

The fact remains that only approximately half of the immigrants to Canada as opposed to some two-thirds of the recruits for the army had come from rural backgrounds.[9] Just over half of the rural recruits for the French army had been employed in agriculture. If it be assumed that immigrants from rural backgrounds were as likely to have been engaged in agriculture as soldiers from rural backgrounds, then about a quarter of the immigrants to Canada had come from agricultural vocations. This estimate should probably be considered the most likely figure, although the possibility remains that the percentage of immigrants from agricultural backgrounds was as low as is indicated in Table 2.

The high percentage of artisans among the immigrants may be explained partly by the bias mentioned above, but it also reflects the urban roots of many immigrants. Although some fifty per cent of the immigrants would have described themselves as artisans, it is not always clear what this designation means. Many of the immigrants were adolescents hardly old enough to have practised a trade, others may have been unemployed or, perhaps more accurately, may have been day labourers whose descriptions of themselves as carpenters or masons were decidedly optimistic. The considerable block of immigrants from commercial backgrounds fits into two groups: most appear to have been the sons of shopkeepers, but six were the sons of *bourgeois* who appear to have been involved in commerce at a considerably larger scale. Most of the sons of these men, judging by Father Godbout's sample, came to Canada as army officers.

Table 2 indicates that most broad categories of French society were represented among seventeenth-century immigrants to Canada. But a man whose background was in trade or in agriculture, in the nobility or the bourgeoisie, may have been comfortably off or destitute when he arrived in Canada. Emigration may have been an adventure, an economic opportunity or necessity, or an escape from a deteriorating social situation. It may have involved people whom force of circumstances—a father's early death, for example—had already dislocated from their economic or social strata in France. If this were the case, the immigrants' common economic and social vulnerability may have been more important than their different occupational backgrounds, but this case remains to be demonstrated. Father Godbout's material does little to clarify the matter. Many of the girls sent out to marry brought dowries of one to three hundred livres.[10] A few men came out to investigate the colony before sending for their families, a practice not unknown in early New England,[11] and some immigrants crossed the Atlantic three times.

The Condition of Crossing

There is no indication in Father Godbout's materials that extended families or kin groups emigrated to Canada, but there are many indications of the migration of nuclear families. Migration is considered to be of this latter type if at least one member of the immigrant's immediate family—a spouse, child, parent, or sibling—crossed the Atlantic with him, or if an immigrant joined or was subsequently joined by such a relative in Canada. Such immigrants were not destitute, but there is no way of determining the extent to which they were representative. Five women in the sample had come to Canada as widows. The fathers of at least seventy-four immigrants (16 per cent of the sample) appear to have died when their children were young.[12]

In general, most immigrants to Canada before 1700 came alone (see Table 3), although there was a striking difference in this respect between those coming before and after the beginning of royal government. Although the Company of New France did not bring nearly as many settlers as stipulated in its contract, and lost its charter for this failure, the settlers it did bring appear to have been of superior quality. Most arrived in families and it was in these early years that some men crossed the Atlantic to scout out the colony before sending for or returning to fetch their wives and children.

Company of N.F.

Table 3. Individual and Family Immigration

	Immigrants arriving alone		Immigrants arriving with family		unknown	
	no.	%	no.	%	no	%
Immigrants before 1663	48	34.8	83	60.1	7	5.1
Immigrants after 1662	258	82.4	39	12.5	16	5.1
Total	306	67.8	122	27.1	23	5.1

Migration during the proprietary years was not of indigent people, but primarily of artisans with a little capital and solid skills. The immigrants sent to Canada after 1662 usually came alone, and almost never returned to France. They reflected an official decision to colonize and a broadside approach to colonization that brought out a larger percentage of immigrants who were destitute, unskilled, and of little immediate use to the colony.[13]

There is indication that some unrelated immigrants had known each other before they crossed the Atlantic. Settlers who came from near Mortagne, for example, appear to have been drawn to Canada by the Boucher family. The many soldiers in the Carignan-Salières regiment who came from the Dordogne suggest that recruitment for this regiment was of the seigneurial type,[14] with officers drawing men from their own region or seigneurie. Then too, it can be assumed that some colonists, especially some of those who came from villages around La Rochelle, decided to emigrate because they knew people from their own village who were established in Canada.

Conclusion

The principal results of this examination of Father Godbout's geneaological material may be briefly summarized:

(1) More than half of the immigrants to Canada in the seventeenth century came from south of the Loire River, particularly from the old provinces of Aunis and Poitou.

(2) Approximately half of the immigrants came from cities, particularly from cities north of the Loire.

(3) About half of the immigrants were artisans, whereas agricultural people probably were not more than one quarter and may have been less than one fifth of the total.

(4) As a rule, immigrants before 1663 came in families, while those arriving thereafter came without relatives.

Some implications of these findings for an understanding of the geography of French settlement in early Canada may be briefly stated. If Acadians and Canadians came from similar parts of France,[15] then antecedents for the dykes that enclosed the marshes of the Bay of Fundy may well lie in the ill-drained coastal plain of Aunis and Poitou. Similarly, the roots of the vernacular house of the lower St Lawrence may lie less in Normandy, as has usually been supposed, than in the hinterland of La Rochelle. The high rate of land sale among settlers in Canada is almost certainly associated with their lack of agricultural experience; immigrants who had never wielded an axe or worked the land settled down to farm only as a last resort. The absence in Canada of open-field agriculture and the rarity of collective agricultural practices and of villages may have to do with the weakness of the immigrants' agricultural tradition. The importance of the towns throughout the French regime may be seen partly as an outgrowth of the heavily urban character of Canadian immigration. These and other implications of Father Godbout's material will need to be explored in any synthesis of early Canadian landscape and society.

Suggestions for Further Reading

W.J. Eccles, *The Canadian Frontier, 1534–1760* (New York, 1960).
Marcel Trudel, *Introduction to New France* (Montreal, 1968).
Marcel Trudel, *La population du Canada en 1663* (Montreal, 1973).

Notes

[1] 7 vols, Montréal, Eusèbe Sénécal, 1870.

[2] 1951–1952 and 1952–1953, 449–544; 1953–1954 and 1954–1955, 445–536; 1955–1956 and 1956–1957, 379–489; 1957–1958 and 1958–1959, 383–440; 1959–1960, 277–354.

[3] More precisely, Father Godbout's material contains information about people who founded Canadian families. Therefore, a man who spent several years in the colony and returned to France without leaving Canadian offspring is not considered, whereas three Indian women who married French-speaking men and settled in the colony are included. His list also contains a good deal of information about first- and, in some cases, about second-generation Canadian descendants of immigrants, but these people are not treated in my analysis. The total of 454 people comprises 451 people who crossed the Atlantic to Canada (whether as adults or as children) plus three Indian women.

[4] Approximately 10,000 immigrants are thought to have come to Canada during the French régime, between 5,000 and 6,000 of them probably arriving before 1700. The surnames of more than 8 per cent of contemporary Frenchmen or French Canadians begin A or BA through BOU, which may indicate that Father Godbout missed some immigrants, or that fewer immigrants came to Canada than is commonly supposed.

[5]Listings were checked for Amiens, Bordeaux, Caen, Dieppe, La Rochelle, Lyon, Marseille, Paris, Poitiers, Rouen, and Tours. Except in the case of Marseille where 16 per cent and of Tours and Rouen where 11 per cent of the listings came before the end of the BOUs, all were in the 13–14 per cent range.

[6]6 vols, Paris, 1771. This is an early and somewhat discursive form of gazetteer, giving a good deal of information about all but the smallest centres in France. Even more useful in this regard might have been l'Abbé d'Expilly, *Dictionnaire géographique, historique, et politique des Gaules et de la France*, Paris, 1762–70; or Marin Saugrain et des Thuileries, *Dictionnaire universel de la France ancienne et moderne et de la nouvelle France*, Paris, 1726; but neither was available. I am confident, however, that in all but perhaps one or two cases a designation of rural or urban based on de Hesseln is not misleading.

[7]André Corvisier (1964), *L'Armée française de la fin du XVIIe siècle au ministère de Choiseul*. Paris: Presses Universitaires de France, vol. 1, 468–9.

[8]The occupational background of an immigrant who came to Canada as a soldier is not considered to have been military unless there is evidence that his father was a soldier before him.

[9]Corvisier, *ibid.*, 387–410.

[10]The king also contributed a dowry of 50 livres, but there is evidence in Father Godbout's materials that at least a third of the girls who came with the intention of marrying in Canada brought a larger sum with them.

[11]For example, see C.S. Powell, *Puritan Village, The Formation of a New England Town*, Chapter 1.

[12]Perhaps there were more, but Father Godbout's material is incomplete in this respect. Frequently it is impossible to determine how long before the immigrant's voyage to Canada his father had died.

[13]In Canada intendants frequently complained about the quality of immigrants sent by the crown, describing them as young, sickly, and unskilled, and occasionally suggesting that Swiss immigrants should be sent instead.

[14]Corvisier, *ibid.*, 159–78.

[15]See A.H. Clark, *Acadia*, Madison: University of Wisconsin Press, 397–400, for a discussion of the background of the Acadians. Clark notes that Geneviève Massignon in *Les Parlers français d'Acadie* (enquête linguistique), 2 vols. Paris, 1962, argues that a substantial percentage of the Acadians came from northeastern Poitou, a conclusion which accords generally with the results of this analysis of Father Godbout's genealogical data.

II

Conflict

and Readjustment

in the Eighteenth

Century

8

Childhood in New France

Peter N. Moogk

One of the principal demographic characteristics of developing societies (of which Canada was one until the twentieth century) was a very high birth rate, which invariably meant the presence of great numbers of children. Despite the fact that throughout most of its history about half of Canada's population has been at any point in time under the age of 15 or 16, these children have traditionally been part of the great invisible substrata of Canadian society, virtually unrecorded by historians. Children did not hold public office, were ineligible to vote, and did not serve in the military; they did not fit into the standard historical paradigms. Moreover, recovering their history required research in different places than those sources for the politically active, including the rubbish heaps of the past, as well as placement in the context of a different unit—the family, rather than the state.

Peter N. Moogk offers a revealing look at children in eighteenth-cen-

tury New France. He points out that despite the appellation of 'petit sauvage', the child in New France was carefully controlled and circumscribed. Although childhood appears in some ways to have lasted longer along the banks of the St Lawrence than it did in the mother country, rural children were always expected to work. Urban children received more formal education than rural ones. Foreign observers, using language similar to that employed to describe their American counterparts, agreed that French-Canadian children were precocious.

What was the age of childhood in New France? To the extent that it varied from one context to another, was that very different from the situation in our own times? Using our own time as a guide, were practical or legal restrictions more important? Moogk finds an important written chronicle of childhood in the journals of a young girl in Montreal. Are there reasons for questioning whether the experiences here recorded would be typical? Why does Moogk argue that young *Canadiens* were 'truly children of the New World'?

This article first appeared in Joy Parr, ed., *Childhood and Family in Canadian History* (McClelland & Stewart, 1982), 17–43, 192–5.

In French Canada today little children are sometimes called *les petits sauvages*. This characterization of Canadian children as little Indians or savages would have been accepted by the administrators of New France. In their corre- spondence French officials described the youth of the North American col- ony in the blackest terms. Young *Canadiens* were rarely mentioned and then only with adjectives that expressed censure and disapproval. The boys of the colony were reproached with being lawless and disobedient; the girls were portrayed as vain and lazy. Even Father Charlevoix, a Jesuit teacher who knew the *Canadiens* well and excused many of their faults, ventured his own criticism of their children. The healthful climate and fertility of New France ought to have retained the native Canadians, he wrote, 'but inconstancy, aversion to assiduous and regular work, and a spirit of independence have always caused a large number of young people to leave the colony.'[1]

In the late seventeenth century the governors and intendants of Canada blamed involvement in the fur trade, wandering in the woods, and associa- tion with the Amerindians for the insubordination of the young males. In 1685 Governor Brisay de Denonville wrote that 'the great liberty of long standing which the parents and Governors have given to the youth, permit- ting them to dally in the woods under the pretext of hunting or trading . . . has reached such an excess that from the time children are able to carry a gun, fathers are not able to restrain them and dare not anger them.'[2]

In the eighteenth century, when the fur trade involved only a small minor- ity of male *Canadiens*, French observers shifted the blame for the rebellious- ness of the colony's youth to the Canadian home. Charlevoix mentioned the *dissipation* in which young colonials were brought up. In 1707 Intendant Jacques Raudot was more specific: 'the residents of this country have never had a proper education because of the over-indulgence (*la foiblesse*) resulting from a foolish tenderness shown to them by their mothers and fathers during their infancy. In this they imitate the Amerindians. It prevents them from disciplining the children and forming their character.' According to the intendant, the children of the colony developed 'a hard and ferocious char- acter' and they showed no respect for their parents 'as well as toward their superiors and parish priests'.[3] Another writer claimed that the children would abandon their mothers and fathers whenever it suited them.[4] Even Father Charlevoix chided the young *Canadiens* for 'the small amount of kindness many show to their parents who, for their part, have an ungoverned fondness for their children.'

To restrain the licence of Canadian youngsters, Jacques Raudot proposed that resident school masters be established in each parish. Other French writers suggested a variety of disciplinary measures: more schools, more parish priests, confinement to the settled parts of the colony, fines and punishment for the parents of delinquents, military justice, and an increase in the garrison troops. Intendant Michel Bégon proposed the most bizarre remedy. He favoured the introduction of more Negro slaves into New France because, among other things, the slaves would free infirm parents from dependence on their fickle and ungrateful children.[5]

As we trace the sequence of life in Canada before the end of French rule in 1760, we shall see that child-rearing was not so permissive nor were the children so unruly as these writers claimed. Conditions in early Canada encouraged self-reliance and assertiveness while reducing the social distance between ranks. French observers exaggerated, rather than falsified, the facts. Their conception of a good and orderly society required the clear subordination of children to their parents, even after the child had reached adulthood. By our standards, the life of the young might even appear hard and circumscribed. The following narrative explores the reality that underlay the characterization of the children of eighteenth-century New France as *les petits sauvages*.

Defining Childhood

The French word *enfant* refers more to a social relationship than to a stage of life. The 1728 edition of Antoine Furetière's *Dictionnaire Universel* defined *enfant* as 'a son or daughter who owes his or her birth to someone, in relationship to a father or mother'. Thus, an adult might properly be described as the *enfant* of a certain person, although the terms *fils de* (son of) or *fille de* (daughter of) were preferred. Secondarily, according to Furetière, '*Enfant* is used for a boy or girl when they were under 12 or 15 years of age, without reference to the father and the mother.' A 1787 edition of the French Academy's dictionary repeated Furetière's primary definition. In the secondary sense, however, it stated that '*Enfant* is still used for a very young boy or girl, and until the age of ten or twelve years.' These definitions were an extension of the older legal definition of *enfance* as a stage ending at the age of seven. The older explanation was retained by Claude-Joseph de Ferrière in his *Dictionnaire de Droit et de Pratique*, first published in 1734. De Ferrière used *impuberes* (pre-pubescents) for both infants and sexually immature children above the age of seven. Canonical and Roman law placed the age of puberty at twelve for girls and fourteen for boys. *Impuberes* could be guilty of, but not physically punished for, a crime. Since both of the literary dictionaries placed the end of *enfance* or early childhood at the age of twelve or, possibly, fifteen, that word seems to have acquired a more extensive, secular meaning in the eighteenth century.

Despite the tendency to identify *enfance* with the period of life before puberty, sexual maturity rarely brought an end to the dependence of childhood. In theory, a person who had reached puberty could be married and marriage was an attribute of grownups. Contemporary summaries of population censuses in the French regime separated married or widowed persons from another group made up of children and unmarried persons. Marriage emancipated one from the legal disabilities of being a minor, yet the social and legal benefits of matrimony did not encourage early marriages in eighteenth-century New France. The demographer Jacques Henripin has noted that 'for the marriages celebrated in Canada during the period 1700–30, the mean age was 22.4 for spinsters and 26.9 for bachelors.'[6] Legal emancipation was automatic at the age of majority and, under the civil laws of the colony, majority was attained at the age of twenty-five. This was the standard age throughout most of France.

It seems clear that a person was still not an adult at puberty. It was also apparent that, socially, one could assume adult responsibilities before the legal age of majority, twenty-five. Between these two poles, where did the transformation from child to adult occur? The fifteenth or sixteenth year of life seems to have been a critical point. After 1688 population censuses classified single males and females as being under fifteen or as being fifteen and older. By the late seventeenth century New France was a society dominated by youth: just over 70 per cent of the colonists were under the age of thirty-one. The following table shows the percentage of the European stock population in the St Lawrence Valley that was under the age of fifteen. On average, this group accounted for 44 per cent of the populace.

In Acadia in 1698 just over half of the population of 789 persons was under the age of sixteen. In New France boys were enrolled in the militia at sixteen and, on average, craft apprentices were indentured between the ages of sixteen and seventeen. The apprentices were expected to be masters of their trade within three years.[7] Preparation for manhood began in earnest at the

Table 1. European Population in the St Lawrence Valley, 1698–1734

Year	Total Population	% Under Fifteen
1698	15,355	41.7
1706	16,417	47.2
1719	22,530	44.3
1734	37,716	43.6

age of fifteen or sixteen. Even at this age, farm children would be already well-versed in agriculture and the care of livestock. Yet, the link with childhood was not severed.

The fact that, after the age of fifteen, one could still be considered a child is evident from censuses that divided the population into the married, the widowed, and *enfants*. The percentage of 'children' always exceeded the 42 per cent to 44 per cent who were under the age of fifteen. In peninsular Acadia in 1714 the *enfants* accounted for 66.5 per cent of the population. In 1733 they were 64 per cent of the people on the St John River. In the St Lawrence settlement 'boys' and 'girls' were 68.5 per cent of the population in 1714 and 64.5 per cent in 1737. In the last census of this region before the British conquest, the enumeration of 1754, the category of 'children of all ages and servants' comprised 70 per cent of the population of 55,009. It therefore appears that the use of *enfant* was not confined by the contemporary definitions of *enfance*; people above the age of fifteen and as old as twenty could be classified as children. The word *adolescent*, though known to the educated, was not used. It is likely that, for all practical purposes and the civil law notwithstanding, one became an adult at around twenty. Most craft apprentices would be ready to earn their living at nineteen or twenty, and orphans, paupers, and foundlings were indentured to foster parents until their eighteenth or twentieth year. In practice, then, the people of New France recognized a 'functional' adulthood that was attained by the age of twenty.

The Patriarchal Family

Birth brought the young person into a network of legally reinforced family relationships. In rural New France the nuclear family was strengthened by the dispersal of private dwellings and the confined living conditions of each family. A farmhouse was customarily a one-storey structure measuring, in English feet, about twenty-three by nineteen. Inside there was a common area for cooking and eating, and this also served as a living room. Bedrooms were separated from this area by wooden partitions, and an overflow of children would sleep in the attic. The young, however, had the advantage of numbers. Adult *Canadiens*, with an average of six living children per family and plenty of work to do, would be hard pressed to give their progeny the strict and continuous supervision recommended by French observers.

For the legislators and magistrates of New France, the patriarchal family was the ideal social unit. The *Coûtume de Paris* subjected the wife and children to the fatherly authority or *puissance paternelle* of the adult male. He was the overlord or *seigneur* of the couple's joint property and his consent was required for all property transactions and legal acts by his dependents. Remember than an unmarried child was legally dependent until the age of twenty-five. The corollary of subordination was that the law protected the material interests of the wife and children from an imprudent or unjust husband and father. Children were equal as heirs and the immovable properties that they were to inherit from a dead parent could not be disposed of by the surviving spouse. Disinheritance out of pure malice was also frowned upon. At the age of seventeen, Marie-Jeanne Renaud Desmeloizes was betrothed by her grandfather and guardian to a man that she did not wish to marry. When she resisted the marriage, her infuriated grandfather gave a large portion of her estate to the intended groom. In 1716 Marie-Jeanne's brother-in-law protested this action and the Crown Attorney of Quebec's lower court agreed that she had been unjustly disinherited.[8] These safeguards protected only the rights of legitimate children; illegitimate children had no claim on the estate of their natural parents.

After the British conquest of New France in 1760, the *Canadiens* in what became the Province of Quebec opposed changes in the civil laws inherited from the French regime. Those laws maintained French Canada's identity and they perpetuated the *Canadiens'* distinctive social values. When the civil usages of the Province of Quebec were modernized and codified in 1866, they retained that compassion for the weak and the submission demanded from inferiors which characterized institutions in New France. On the subject of children, the articles of the Civil Code of Quebec stated:

166. Children are bound to maintain their father, mother and other ascendants [e.g., grandparents] who are in want, . . .

242. A child, whatever may be his age, owes honour and respect to his father and mother.

243. He remains subject to their authority until his majority or his emancipation, but the father alone exercises this authority during marriage, . . .

244. An unemancipated minor cannot leave his father's house without his permission.

245. The father and, in his default, the mother of an unemancipated minor have over him a right of reasonable and moderate correction, which may be delegated to . . . those to whom his education has been entrusted.

In the terms of the Civil Code, 'reasonable and moderate correction' meant physical punishment without injury or danger to life. Society in New France was tolerant of the male who occasionally did beat his wife and children. Since the courts were reluctant to intervene in family disputes, the violence used by a man against his dependents had to be extreme and notorious before it received judicial attention. Without grievous injury or death, domestic violence was a civil matter that required a private complaint. A wife could ask for legal separation from a brutal, insane, or profligate husband; he might even be deprived of his paternal authority by interdiction. An abused child, however, could not make a legal complaint by himself. Like Marie-Jeanne Renaud Desmeloizes, he needed the assistance of a grownup kinsman.

The continuing subordination of an unmarried child to his parents, even after the attainment of majority, is evident from legal documents called *sommations respectueuses* or respectful requisitions. Because marriage entitled one to the aid and support of in-laws, parents had the right to approve the choice of their child's marriage partner. During the child's minority this was an absolute right; after the age of twenty-five it was a social, but not a legal, right. Parental disapproval might entail the withholding of a dowry or a contribution to the newlyweds' estate. It was also believed that a parent could disinherit a child of any age who married against his or her elders' wishes. To avert this possibility, adults who had been refused parental approval registered three respectful requisitions begging their father and mother for their consent. Once this was done, the future couple could obtain the opinion of a magistrate or of other relatives that there was no lawful impediment to the marriage and then proceed with the wedding. In the 1730s, when twenty-one-year-old Jean-Claude Louet *fils* vowed to marry an English shoemaker's daughter, whom he had made pregnant, his father, who was a royal notary, opposed the match. 'Could it be possible,' asked Jean-Claude in his second respectful summons, 'that the great tenderness that you formerly showed to your child might be changed into perpetual disgrace? I beg you most humbly, my dear father, to once again look upon me as your own child.'[9]

Infancy

In Antoine Furetière's words, *enfance* was 'the first and most tender age of man, until he has attained the use of reason.' Life began in the mother's bed at home. The birth was assisted by a *sage femme* whose knowledge of midwifery was acquired by experience. In the first months of life, infants were tightly bound in swaddling clothes which, it was believed, would help to straighten the legs and back of the newborn child. A swaddled baby also tended to be more tranquil than an unbound infant. There was no awareness of the need for hygiene. For example, in the absence of mother's milk or a wet nurse, infants were given raw cow's milk diluted with river or well water. As a result of this and other unsanitary measures, many children died in infancy. Jacques Henripin's demographic studies of the early eighteenth century show that one child in four died in the first year of life. 'We may also assume—on the basis of less reliable information—,' wrote Henripin, 'that almost 45 per cent died before the age of ten years, and 50 per cent before the age of twenty.'[10] This mortality rate, which was close to that in France, was countered by a phenomenal birth rate. After the birth of the first child and until the age of thirty-five, a married *Canadienne* bore one child every two years. Such fecundity amazed European visitors, who noted the prodigies of reproductive valour. Jacques Henripin's figures are less astounding. When both partners survived to the age of fifty, they would have, on average, 5.65 living children.

In early French Canada chronological age was a vague thing that became less certain as a person grew older. In documents it is common to find adolescents described as being of so many years of age *ou environ* (or thereabout), or as being of one age or another. An exact figure in years and months is exceptional. The anniversary of the birthdate does not seem to have been remembered or celebrated. A person's *fête* was the feast day of that individual's patron saint, and the saint's day did not have to be related to the person's date of birth.

Birthday or no birthday, the *Canadiens* favoured certain saints in the choice of names. The child's namesake was usually his or her patron saint. The favourites in New France were the Virgin Mary, Mary Magdelene, Joan of Arc (*Jeanne*), and the male saints Joseph, John, Peter, and Francis (*François*). Many parents shrewdly laid claim to the favour of two saints by giving their children such double-barrelled names as *Joseph-Marie* or *Marie-Anne. Marie*, alone or in combination, was the most popular name in Canada.

Christian names are given at baptism and, in New France, baptism was required within three or four days of birth. The clergy preferred to administer this sacrament themselves and they were annoyed by some *Canadiens* who used the distance and difficulty of travel in winter to justify lay baptism at home. The approved procedure was to have the parents present the newborn infant to the nearest priest for baptism. The parents were accompanied by the child's godfather and godmother who gave surety for the young person's religious education. The spiritual relationship between a godparent and child was almost as binding as blood kinship. A godparent would be expected to favour the child in later life with influence or assistance. In the eighteenth century godparents were customarily drawn from the parents' own social and occupational group.

In the parish register of Notre-Dame de Montréal Church is found the following sample entry for a baptism:

> Wednesday, the Seventh of March, One Thousand seven hundred and thirty-one, was baptised Marie Marguerite, born at half past two in the evening (i.e., morning) of the same day, daughter of Samuel Payne, silversmith, and of Marguerite Garreau, his wife. The Godfather was M. Pierre Guy, merchant, and the Godmother was Marie Catherine Le Gras, wife of M. Chaumont. The father being present, they all signed (the register) with us (the priest).

Children were frequently the namesake of the godparent of the same sex; in this instance the girl's name was a combination of the first names of her mother and godmother.

In the first year or two of life, the infant slept in a wooden cradle. The cradles of early French Canada were open pine troughs on rockers. They were also fitted with turned birchwood posts that could be grasped to rock the child. At night a cord could be attached to one of these posts to enable the mother to rock a fretful infant without leaving her bed. The incidence of births suggests that children were weaned at around fourteen months of age. The infant who had learned to use its hands was given a rattle to play with. The rattles that appear in inventories of the French regime were made of wood, bone, and silver. Surviving examples in France and Canada consist of a short staff girdled with bells, with either a ring or teething bar at one end.

Guardianship and Foster Parentage

Death was no stranger to the people of New France. The population was ravaged by smallpox epidemics, by war, and, in the seaports, by shipborne infections. Nearly half of the adolescents in the colony had lost one parent. When the father died, there was a well-established procedure to ensure continuity in the maintenance and upbringing of the minor children. A council of paternal and maternal relations was convened to determine the future of the orphans. Contributions for their upkeep might be apportioned among the kin who elected a tutor and 'subrogate tutor' to record and then manage each child's inheritance as well as oversee the child's upbringing. The widow was eligible to be one of the tutors, but she was not considered to be competent enough to be her children's sole guardian. She would be given the assistance of an adult male, usually an uncle of the children and sometimes her own grownup son. When she remarried, which was very likely, her role as tutor passed to her new husband.

Without kin in the colony, which would be the case with poor immigrants, food and shelter were obtained for orphaned and destitute children on hard terms. A single mother had no bargaining power. In 1736 an abandoned wife at Quebec described herself as 'incapable of feeding and maintaining' her eight-year-old son. She was forced to bind him to a merchant as 'a domestic servant until . . . the full age of twenty years.' A Louisbourg widow likewise indentured her son to someone who could provide his upkeep, 'not being in a situation to do it (herself) without help.'[11] Children under the age of twelve were disdained as apprentices by craftsmen; they were only acceptable as servants. Thus the children of the poor and other young unfortunates without family support were customarily hired out to work without pay until the age of eighteen or even twenty-one. These paupers and orphans were typically indentured at five or six years of age and they were destined for a dozen or more years of servitude for the sake of food, clothing, and shelter.[12] Mature and able-bodied Canadiens scorned the servant's life and it appears that indentured children provided nearly two-thirds of the household servants in New France. This explains why the 1754 census treated 'children of all ages and servants' as one category; most of the servants were children!

Far from regretting this private system for settling young paupers and orphans, the colonial administration enforced children's indentures and copied them in dealing with foundlings and bastard children. Illegitimate births were an increasing problem in eighteenth-century New France and the royal officials were slow to react. Pregnancies out of wedlock were indicative of the breakdown of communal social restraints in the rural parishes where, according to Intendant Michel Bégon, 'this disorder is becoming extremely common.'[13] From 1701 to 1760 the church registers in what is now the Province of Quebec recorded the baptism of 1,112 illegitimate children. At the beginning of this period bastards accounted for two out of every thousand births; in the last decades of the French regime they represented 12.2 out of every thousand.[14] Because the rate fell after the conquest, wartime conditions and the presence of thousands of French regular troops must have contributed to the growing number of illegitimate births in the 1740s and 1750s. These figures are incomplete because, in spite of laws requiring the disclosure of illicit pregnancies, illegitimate children born to *Canadiennes* were frequently given to the Amerindians in preference to letting the infants die of exposure. Infanticide was a capital crime. In the villages of the Christian Amerindians, Louis Franquet observed numerous illegitimate children of the French colonists as well as white children abducted from the English colonies. The youngsters were adopted by the native peoples and they fully accepted the aborigines' way of life.

For most of the French regime the settlement of foundlings depended on private sponsors and religious institutions. Foster parents expected some payment for accepting an infant who was not yet capable of earning his keep and there was no regular source of funds for these payments. In the late seventeenth century the short-lived Poor Boards of Quebec and Montreal placed foundlings with families or delivered the children to the Quebec *Hôpital-Général* and the Montreal hospice of the Charon Brethren. Craft apprenticeship was not used, as it was in the English colonies, for the settlement of paupers; very few foster parents promised to teach the child a trade or skill.

In France royal court officials were made responsible for the care of foundlings by an edict in November, 1706. The first Canadian *enfant du Roi*, as the foundlings were called, was placed at Montreal in 1709. The local King's Attorney paid the receiving couple eighty *livres* and they promised to raise the boy until the age of eighteen. When the putative father of a bastard could be found, he was charged the full cost of the child's upbringing. The Crown was still reluctant to bear all of the expenses of settlement. An intendant's ordinance issued in February, 1722, authorized payments from the revenues of the tax farm and other sources to wet nurses caring for the *enfants du Roi*. The same ordinance set severe penalties for concealed pregnancies and for giving illegitimate children to the Amerindians. An ordinance of June, 1736, complained about the cost of maintaining the growing number of foundlings; it therefore reduced the amounts paid to wet nurses and called upon the King's Attorneys 'to indenture the said children as soon as they are four years old, and sooner if possible.'[15]

In 1748 Intendant Gilles Hocquart sanctioned an increase in the forty-five *livres* 'ordinarily agreed to and paid' to foster parents in order to dispose of the foundlings still being supported by the Crown. In the Montreal region there were twenty *enfants du Roi* above the age of three for whom no homes had been found.[16] At Quebec the King's Attorney paid as much as 240 *livres* to the foster parent of an abandoned boy.[17]

The evident reluctance of the *Canadiens* to accept the *enfants du Roi* when they would receive young paupers or orphans as unpaid servants might be explained by two things. The first is the extreme youth of the foundlings. They were unable to perform profitable labour for a few more years. Moreover, as sponsors, the royal officials were in a stronger position than any widowed or single parent to compel the foster parents to live up to their obligations. The King's Attorneys were able to obtain favourable terms for their wards. Witness this foundling's contract concluded in the house of the King's Attorney at Quebec in November, 1729:

> Before the Royal Notaries in the Prévôté of Quebec here resident and under-signed were present Joseph Demers, habitant of Saint-Nicolas, Côte de Lauzon, who has acknowledged and stated that, with the approval and consent of Monseigneur the King's Attorney, he has taken by contract a child born of an unknown father, named Jean-Baptiste and aged five years, two months or thereabout. The boy is to serve him in all that will be commanded of him, provided it be licit and decent and proportionate to his strength as he grows older . . . , until the full age of eighteen years. The said Demers binds himself to raise him (Jean-Baptiste) in the Catholic, Apostolic and Roman religion, to feed and maintain him, and to take care of him as one of his own children. At the end of the said term he will give the boy four shirts of Meslis cloth; a hooded coat, vest, and breeches of Mazamet cloth; a pair of Saint-Maixent stockings, a pair of French shoes, and a hat—all new and in addition to the other clothes that Jean-Baptiste will have received by then. Moreover, he will give the boy (at the end of service) twenty-five *livres* in the currency of this land, for thus has been agreed . . .[18]

The King's Attorneys were empowered in 1748 to bind the foundlings out until the age of eighteen or twenty; Jean-Baptiste's term was the shorter of the two. The gift outfit of new clothing was not unusual; the bonus payment was, however, exceptional. Both served to encourage the boy to serve out his full term and not to run away.

Tender Youth

Tendre jeunesse was an expression used to describe that stage of life that took a young person from the end of infancy to the beginning of puberty. Though clothing did not signal the transformation from child to adult, it did mark the passage from infancy to youth. Swaddling was characteristic of the first months of life; afterward the infant was wrapped naked in a cloth. Once the child was able to crawl or walk, it was dressed in a shift or long shirt. The shift may have been longer for girls, but both sexes wore the same costume. We see the infant's attire in a painting of the Guardian Angel executed in about 1707 and now in the Quebec hospital. The little girl sheltered by the angel wears a lined cap tied under the chin, and a long, loose gown with a sash at the waist.

Seven had been the conventional age for the end of infancy. In New France the costume of infancy was abandoned at the age of four or earlier. This is apparent from the votive painting of Angélique Gaulthier, Madame Riverin, and her four children. She was the wife of a French-born magistrate, landowner, and company director. This work was painted in 1703 to testify to their survival from a shipwreck through the intercession of St Anne, to whom the Riverins had addressed their prayers. At the time the children were aged three, four, five, and six. They were all infants and yet they are all dressed as miniature adults. Five-year-old Denis-François wears a flared *justaucorps* with a ruff, just like a man. The girls' clothing copies that of their mother: a high headdress of lace and ribbons *à la Fontanges*, a pearl necklace, and a velvet or silk gown trimmed with lace. Soon after his arrival in the colony, Bishop Saint-Vallier had deplored the fact that in New France 'at an early age . . . little girls, even those of lowly birth, are dressed and adorned like dolls and appear with bare shoulders and necks.'[19] The only distinction between little Marie-Clémence and Marie-Madeleine Riverin and their mother and older sister is that the youngest girls have round collars rather than a low-cut front. It would not be surprising if there were also ribbons or leading strings attached to the back of the three-year-old's dress. Leading strings, familiarly called *tatas*, were used to assist a toddler who was still learning how to walk. The Riverin portrait was ostensibly a religious painting; it was also an opportunity for a family of the colony's ruling class to parade its wealth and rank. The clothing portrayed is not representative of the everyday attire of lower-class colonists.

It has been suggested that because West Europeans of the seventeenth and early eighteenth centuries dressed their children as miniature adults, they did not have a conception of childhood and adolescence as stages of life that were separate from adulthood. Ross W. Beales has shown that this is a false assumption, when applied to colonial New England.[20] In New France, though young and old shared many activities, there was that period of 'tender youth' between the ages of four and twelve and an adolescence in which the young gradually assumed the duties and prerogatives of adulthood. The characteristics of *tendre jeunesse* were expressed in the adjectives applied to children of this age: small, weak, innocent, foolish, and unreasonable. French writers, such as Bossuet and Molière, used the child as a metaphor for someone who believed in fantasies, prattled about trivial things, or lived only for the present.

The journals kept by Marie-Elisabeth Rocbert, Madame Bégon, from 1748 to 1750 are a rare, perhaps unique, chronicle of childhood in early French Canada. Her world was that of the privileged élite. Widow Bégon raised her late daughter's two children at Montreal. She left an affectionate and indulgent portrait of her granddaughter, Marie-Catherine-Elisabeth, in words. Marie-Catherine was nine in 1748. The girl is called *notre chère petite*, *chère innocente*, and *chère mignonne*. The grandmother delighted in the girl's childish traits. Like most *Canadiennes*, Marie-Catherine loved to have her hair curled and to be dressed up for formal occasions. She would hop for joy when invited out to a grownups' supper or when she was told that the governor of the colony would be visiting them. Marie-Catherine recited fables and verses for the governor and, at the dinner table, her chirpy conversation delighted the adults. According to Madame Bégon, Marie-Catherine 'is devoted to mischievousness; she believes in phantoms, but never in tranquility.'[21] Marie-Catherine played April Fool's jokes and could be short-tempered and disobedient. Her grandmother did not punish her and accepted the promise of future good conduct. Madame Bégon frequently referred to the girl's 'mutinous' temper. She described this humour as a family trait and looked upon it as unalterable.

While Madame Bégon took pleasure in Marie-Catherine's childish behaviour, she was also proud of her granddaughter's precocity. Although the girl disliked confession, she was very solemn about religious matters. The two recited prayers and went to Mass together. When Marie-Catherine bowed her head in prayer at mealtime, the governor teasingly called her 'madame l'abbesse'. Most Canadians simply crossed themselves before eating. Marie-Catherine was truly Canadian in not letting her religious scruples extend into submission to the moral dictates of the clergy. When a priest said that he would permit her to read *Don Quixote*, the nine-year-old replied, 'I need only the permission of *maman* (grandmother) who, I believe, is capable of judging if I might read a book or not.'[22] Madame Bégon was inwardly pleased by her granddaughter's bold assertions and by the girl's ability to uphold her own views in discussions with adults. On the anniversary of Monsieur Bégon's death, she proudly wrote that Marie-Catherine had consoled her 'like a twenty-year-old girl'.

The world of play is inseparable from childhood. Marie-Catherine once received a doll, played with other little girls, and amused herself in the garden. Her grandmother did not mention other toys nor did she describe the games that must have been a part of Marie-Catherine's life. Documents surviving from the French regime do not provide much information on the amusements of youth. The notarized estate inventories that facilitate the reconstruction of material life in New France were made for adults with heirs. Toys, however, belonged to children and, because they were often homemade, they were of little value. On those rare occasions when the things of infancy and childhood appear in the inventories, the description is a cursory phrase such as 'four new napkins for children'. Robert-Lionel Séguin, a folklorist who has mined the notarial records of the Montreal region, found only a dozen references to babies' rattles, toy carts, dolls and their clothing, marbles, sleighs, and skates.[23] The skates and sleighs could have belonged to grownups. The estate inventories made at Louisbourg mention furniture especially made for the young.

The most extensive collection of children's toys from the French regime is to be found in the archaeological finds from the site of the Fortress of Louisbourg on Cape Breton Island. The playthings confirm the existence of childhood as a recognized stage in life while revealing where the world of children overlapped with adult life. Things that unquestionably belong to the young are the stone and clay marbles, a jack, and a miniature plate and bowl suitable for a girl. For boys there is a wooden sailboat that was found in a pond, a lead anchor for another toy boat, a small bronze cannon, and a six-inch wooden sword. This rough-hewn weapon is probably not the 'little child's sword' mentioned in a merchant's inventory of 1756.[24] Other Louisbourg toys were homemade: there were round counters chipped from pottery fragments and whizzers fashioned from broken roof slates or salvaged lead. A looped string would be passed through the two holes in the centre of the circular whizzer and, by alternating the tension on the string, a child could make the disk spin and produce a whirring sound with its rough or serrated edge.

As parents well know, children enjoy making noise. The collection from Louisbourg contains bone and metal whistles, a small flute, and several jew's harps. Were the modern reader able to visit eighteenth-century New France, he might also see children pounding drums and playing with tops and cup-and-ball—a mania for all ages in seventeenth-century France. The absence of these things among the archaeological finds does not mean that they never existed; paper, leather, and wood are simply more perishable than bone, pottery, and metal.

Jacques Stella's illustrated book, *Les jeux et plaisirs de l'enfance* (Paris, 1657), provides the context for the toys of New France. This book shows children rolling dice for money, using toy swords in duels and mock wars, firing cannons improvised from hollow keys, and rolling marbles at holes in a game called *fossette*. Marbles were also thrown at pyramids or 'castles' of an opponent's marbles in an attempt to knock them down. Widespread children's games that would leave no material evidence of their existence were blind man's buff, king of the castle, and hot cockles, in which a child with face hidden and a bared hand behind his back tried to guess who had slapped his palm.

It was the games of the naughtiest of the *petits sauvages* that received the attention of legislators in New France. At Quebec children bowled over water barrels and threw stones from the battery overlooking Sault-au-Matelot in the Lower Town.[25] In 1741 and 1753, with very little evidence of success, a pompous French magistrate in Montreal called Guiton de Monrepos tried to outlaw the throwing of snowballs in the town's streets.[26] In winter grown-ups and the young slid down the streets of Quebec on skates, sleighs, or whatever came to hand. Intendant François Bigot described the sliders as a menace to passers-by because of 'the speed with which they fall upon them, not giving them the time to move aside to avoid the sliders.' As in the case of stone-throwers, the fine against violators was ten *livres*, and Bigot threatened to hold the delinquent children in prison until their parents had paid the fine.[27]

The recognition of childhood as a distinct phase of life did not mean that childhood was divorced from adult life; children, without ceasing to be juveniles, probably had more in common with their elders than children today. In *Centuries of Childhood* (1962), Philippe Ariès observed that among the lower classes of France, children and adults continued to dress alike and to find diversion in the same pastimes during the eighteenth century. In New France the blending of age groups was evident on the icy streets of Quebec and from the fact that the jew's harps, bowling ball, ivory dice, and gaming counters found at Louisbourg could have been used by persons of all ages. Gambling was a passion among the colonists which was countenanced among the young. Even the toy sailing boat, the miniature crockery, the cannon, and the sword uncovered at the fortress reflected the activities of grownups in that fortified seaport. In a way, these toys prepared childen for adult life.

At home, and especially on the farms, children were introduced to productive labour before adolescence. Beyond the age of infancy, youngsters became valued contributors to the family's welfare. In the countryside the littlest boys and girls helped by scaring birds away from the ripening crops and by herding cows. They could assist their mother by amusing the baby and, with a firm grip on the leading strings, taking toddlers for a walk. Service indentures reveal that children in New France dug in the vegetable gardens, sifted flour, helped in sowing seeds, and gathered firewood. Adolescents were strong enough to cut cordwood and to thresh and winnow grain. At harvest-time every member of the family was expected to lend a hand: the boys at mowing and cutting and the girls at raking hay and stooking wheat. With the exception of Louisbourg and Quebec, there was no sharp division between rural and urban life. Within their palisades or walls, most towns were open villages with large gardens and paddocks separating the houses. There were stables to be cleaned, livestock and gardens to be tended. Whether in town or in country, the young of families without servants were up at dawn to bring in firewood and to light the hearth fire. During the day, they would be employed in scraping dirty boots, emptying chamber pots into the outside privy, and sweeping floors. Running errands and fetching water from the river for cooking and washing were commonplace duties of the young. At Quebec in 1749 the Swedish-speaking botanist Peter Kalm watched boys take barrel-laden carts drawn by dogs down to the river to fill the water barrel. The young ladies of Quebec, he noted, left the household work to their mothers. By contrast, the girls of Montreal—a town more influenced by the North American frontier—were 'not quite so flighty, and more industrious': working in the kitchen with the servants, doing needlework, and going to the market to buy food.[28] Kalm's picture of feminine activities was likely drawn from observations in the homes of the educated and prosperous colonists; the life of most young *Canadiennes* would have been less genteel.

Adolescence and Formal Education

The lack of education among Canadian children that was noted by French writers needs to be precisely defined. For these observers, education meant training in self-discipline as well as formal schooling. On the first point there was unanimity: young *Canadiens* were undisciplined and their parents were to blame. 'You will be surprised,' wrote Antoine-Denis Raudot in 1709, 'to learn that fathers keep their children busy only when they are able to do so (by persuasion),—they love their children too much to compel them to do something against their will.'[29] On the matter of schooling, we must distinguish between religious instruction, occupational training, and academic education. In each area there was a great variation in the level of instruction.

Father Charlevoix, who was a trustworthy witness, praised the Canadians for their knowledge of the Christian faith. 'What, above all, ought to make our colonials respected is their great capacity for piety and devotion, and there is no deficiency in their religious education.'[30] Instruction in catechism was one form of institutional education that was provided to all children in the colony. Catechism prepared the young for the first communion which itself was a major step toward adulthood. A catechumen who had been examined and confirmed became, theoretically, a full member of the church. As intended, catechism conveyed the creed and moral standards of the Roman Catholic Church. In the absence of a competing ideology, the church defined community standards of behaviour. These standards were often violated, but they were not supplanted.

In his *Catéchisme du Diocèse de Québec* (1702), Bishop Saint-Vallier did not specify the age at which one should receive formal religious instruction. There is secondary evidence that children attended catechism classes soon after puberty. The evidence comes from servants' and apprentices' indentures made in the 1730s and after. For children under the age of sixteen, a clause was inserted that gave the ward leave to attend catechism until he had made his first communion. Farm families hesitated to surrender their children for prolonged instruction and the religious training of rural children was, perforce, cursory. In the 1720s one country parish scheduled catechetical instruction for one Sunday of each month.[31] During Bishop Dosquet's episcopate (1729–1739), such classes were to be held, at the very least, in the three weeks preceding confirmation ceremonies and the children's first communion.[32] Bishop Saint-Vallier foresaw the limitations of time available and of a child's comprehension, because his large catechism contains an abridged *Petit Catéchisme* of twenty-five pages for 'very young children or coarse persons (*personnes grossières*)'.

Catechism classes involved the memorization of set answers and prayers; they introduced the child to abstract ideas without demanding independent inquiry. Here are a few of the preliminary questions and responses from Saint-Vallier's large catechism:

What is Catechism?
It is simple instruction at which one learns Christian truths, how to serve God, and to save oneself. . . .

Are all sorts of persons obliged to attend Catechism?
Yes, if they are ignorant of things concerning their salvation, as are ordinarily children, craftsmen, male and female servants.

Who must see that children and servants attend Catechism?
Fathers and Mothers, Masters and Mistresses will answer for it before God, unless they instruct them (these dependents) themselves at home. . . .

How many parts are there to this Catechism?
There are three parts.

What are they?
Sacred History (the Bible story), the Christian Doctrine, the explanation of holy days, of the sacred rituals and ceremonies of the church.

The idea that children should also receive free education in reading, writing, arithmetic and, perhaps, Latin did have currency in New France. The reality fell short of the ideal. Writers blamed the colonials for their lack of an elementary and academic education. As early as 1664 Pierre Boucher claimed that the children of the colony were 'a bit dissolute, that is to say, it is difficult to captivate them with studies.'[33] Over fifty years later Charlevoix noted that 'many people are persuaded that they (the *Canadiens*) are unsuited for the sciences that require great application and methodical study. I am unable to say if this prejudice is well founded but, we have not yet seen a Canadian who has attempted to disprove it. It is due, perhaps, to the carelessness (*la dissipation*) of their upbringing.'[34] The truth is that, apart from catechism, poor boys without a religious vocation had little chance of obtaining a free elementary or secondary education in New France.

Boys and girls were educated separately and there was a shortage of schoolmasters for the boys. The French Crown upheld the prerogatives of the Roman Catholic Church as the principal educator: an intendant's ordinance in 1727 decreed that lay schoolteachers would have to be licensed by the Bishop of Quebec. In the early eighteenth century the Charon Brethren of Montreal sponsored teachers of proven virtue in the countryside. Virtue was not a sufficient qualification because, in 1730, the Crown ended its subsidy of the brothers' schools after receiving reports of their financial mismanagement and ineffectiveness.

The main burden of providing boys with a free elementary education fell on the overworked parish and missionary priests of the colony. The clergy were not only responsible for their customary ecclesiastical duties, but they also kept parish records and acted as notaries and scribes. In 1740 there were seventy-six diocesan priests as well as sixty-nine Franciscans and Sulpicians capable of acting as diocesan priests for a scattered population of 43,400 in the St Lawrence Valley. Some of the resident clerics were able to establish *petites écoles* in which they instructed boys in catechism and other subjects. At St Joachim, Peter Kalm found 'two priests, and a number of young boys, whom they instruct in reading, writing and Latin. Most of these boys are designed (destined) for the priesthood.'[35] It is not surprising that rural illiteracy, always widespread, increased in the eighteenth century. Even in the towns, which were well-endowed with schools, illiteracy was common. Of 506 Montreal householders surveyed in 1741, nearly 60 per cent declared that they did not know how to write their names.[36]

Sexual segregation in the schools of New France benefited lower-class girls, especially those in the countryside, because the problems that beset the elementary education of boys had less effect on the instruction of girls. Female education belonged to nuns and sisters as well as to priests and schoolmasters. Unlike the Charon Brethren, the female religious orders were vigorous and well-organized. This was particularly true of the Sisters of the *Congrégation de Notre-Dame*, whose community had been founded in seventeenth-century Canada. The sisters took simple vows, were not cloistered, and were devoted to education. In the 1750s, with about eighty members, theirs was the largest female religious community in the colony. Their schools spread throughout the towns and countryside. 'In many places in the country,' wrote Kalm, 'there are two or more of them (sisters).' He added, 'their business is to instruct young girls in the Christian religion, to teach them reading, writing, needlework and other feminine accomplishments.'[37] Most of the girls attended these schools for one or two years as day-students. Thanks to the Sisters of Notre-Dame, many country girls were better education than their brothers.

Louis Franquet, a military engineer, was horrified by the sisters' success as educators. In 1752 he wrote that their 'usefulness would seem to be demonstrated, but the evil that results from them is like a slow-acting poison that depopulates the countryside, since an educated girl is a gentlewoman; she is finicky, she wants to settle in the town, she requires a merchant (for a husband), and she looks down upon the state in which she was born as beneath her.' His advice was to curtail the work of the sisters and 'thereby oblige children to be satisfied with their curate's religious instruction, and not to acquire any principles that divert them from their father's occupation.'[38] Franquet did not comment on the nuns of the Quebec *Hôpital Général*, who also taught little girls the rudiments of religion and domestic skills; nor did he censure the Ursuline nuns' schools at Trois-Rivières and Quebec. These schools educated the daughters of the colony's notable families and they did not disturb the social order.

The administrative, judicial, and military élite of New France was concentrated in the towns and had access to lucrative offices; it had no trouble obtaining elementary and secondary education for its children. Secondary education, however, was reserved for males. Elementary education in reading and writing seems to have coincided with catechetical instruction and for most children it took no more than one year. The *Petit Séminaire* of Quebec trained boys in Latin, rhetoric, philosophy, and theology; in the late seventeenth century, youths between the ages of nine and fifteen and with some knowledge of reading and writing were admitted to this school.[39] At Quebec older boys and seminarians attended the Jesuit College, which followed the *ratio studiorum* of classical studies. There was a seminary at Montreal that was comparable to the Quebec *Grand Séminaire*. The French Crown also sponsored occasional courses for young men in hydrography, pilotage, surveying, and the law.

Education does not require an institutional framework and in early French Canada parents, tutors, and master craftsmen taught more children than were instructed in schools. From the 1670s there are contracts in which private tutors promised to teach their employers' children at home how to read and write within one year.[40] Notaries of the colony sometimes acted as schoolmasters and as tutors. In the mid-eighteenth century a Montreal notary taught a child of the Panet family how to write; the boy's writing exercises have survived because they were written on the blank pages and empty spaces in the notary's index of documents. The boy was told how to hold his pen and, after the notary had written a model text, the child copied it ten or more times underneath. Young Antoine Méru Panet reproduced legal phrases, commercial bills and receipts, and such philosophic reflections as 'God consoles the afflicted in their afflictions; he is with us in our persecution, he bears us up in moments of weakness.'[41]

Manual trades and the professions of notary, surgeon, and merchant were usually learned in adolescence by association with a skilled practitioner. In most cases the practitioner was the pupil's father or another close relative. When the instructor was not kin, a formal apprenticeship was in order. Some agreements were verbal, some were by unregistered contract, and others were made before a notary who filed the indenture. Considering that the last category represented a fraction of all the apprenticeships made, and that a sixth of the notarial files have been lost, it is remarkable that there are still in existence some 1,200 notarized apprenticeships from this underpopulated French colony. This flourishing and widespread form of instruction reveals the importance of non-institutional education in New France. As a means of learning a manual trade, private apprenticeship, whether formal or casual, had no rival; not from the short-lived hospice of the Charon Brethren in Montreal, where orphans learned joinery, metalwork, and the manufacture of stockings; nor from the Quebec Seminary and its farms, where unsuccessful students and peasant children learned farming and handicrafts.

The conventional formula of contracts summed up the apprentice's motives by describing him as 'desiring to make his fortune and establishment and to earn his living'. Personal inclinations and the economic prospects of a trade determined the choice of most apprentices. The absence of craft guilds and the near disappearance of the master's fee in New France gave apprentices access to a wide range of occupations. Though the Canadian apprentices might have selected any skill, from wigmaking to saddlery, they preferred blacksmithing, shoemaking, cooperage, and joinery—crafts whose products were in demand.

The boys of the colony benefited most from craft apprenticeship. Scarcely one apprentice in a hundred was a female and the girls were all destined to become seamstresses. If a young woman did not intend to join a religious community, she was expected to make marriage her career. The *Canadiennes*, 'especially the girls', whom Peter Kalm characterized as vain and flirtatious, 'commonly sing songs in which the words *amour* and *coeur* are very frequent' while working indoors. Much has been made of a few female entrepreneurs in New France, but unless a woman had evaded marriage until the age of twenty-five or became a widow while still wealthy and energetic, she had little hope of being self-employed.

For one Quebec seamstress, apprenticeship in a trade was a last resort and it had failed her. At the age of twenty-seven, she stated that 'in her childhood (*enfance*), having no family estate to allow her to live (independently), she had been obliged to learn the craft of seamstress. Since that time she had worked for the public and had great difficulty in feeding herself, having received no help from her parents, who were incapable of assisting her,' nor from her godfather, a notary. A farmer had offered to marry her, yet her parents disapproved of the match. She therefore petitioned a magistrate, at the age of twenty-seven, for permission to issue a respectful summons to her parents. For the seamstress, marriage was an escape from her 'sorry situation'.[42]

The characterization of Canadian children as unruly savages has been over-drawn. It is true that the youth of New France had little formal schooling. By the standards of the mother country, they were shockingly presumptuous and precocious. Among 'the common people', Peter Kalm saw 'boys of ten or twelve years of age' who 'run about with a pipe in their mouth'.[43] Young *Canadiens* drank brandy, refused to doff their hats in the presence of ladies while indoors, and rode about on their own horses of which they were inordinately proud. The fact that in New France young peasants rode horses and country girls dressed in the finery of gentlewomen did not accord with the outsiders' sense of propriety.

The official culture of France glorified submission to authority, both sec-ular and clerical. The family, the church, and the state were organized as hierarchies in which authority descended from the top. An orderly society was one in which people accepted their hereditary social rank and obeyed their superiors without question. Small wonder, then, that the ambitious, wilful, and proud *Canadiens* offended senior administrators from France.

Were the children of early French Canada any worse than their parents? The weakening of communal restraints in New France had opened the door to anti-social behaviour by children. Institutions such as municipal corpo-rations and jointly administered common lands had disappeared from the colony. Thanks to dispersed settlement in the countryside, villages, which had provided the framework for French rural life, were slow to develop in Canada. Only nine communities in the St Lawrence Valley were worthy of being called towns or villages. The increase in births out of wedlock was evidence of the relaxation of social restraints. According to Louis Franquet, rural children stole produce from their parents in order to buy trifles from country merchants. In the intendants' ordinances compelling the heirs and in-laws of aged and destitute persons to provide assistance, we see evidence of a callousness that would not have been acceptable in a closely knit society.

In the rural areas of New France, where over three-quarters of the pop-ulation resided, the enforcement of social discipline belonged, initially, to the family. Colonial society had fragmented into autonomous family groups. Within the nuclear family there was a conflict between the customary obli-gation to maintain paternal authority and the need to win the consent of the subordinates. The large number of children also undermined parental authority. Children under fifteen constituted at least 42 per cent of the pop-ulation. Like a mild but persistent acid, little children can eat away at their elders' rigid standards for youthful behaviour. It was also difficult to maintain social differences, while living together in close proximity.

Lower-class *Canadiens* were dependent on their children and this dependence was a good reason for considering the opinions of the young. Parents did protect themselves from the caprice of their children by giving one adult son or heir the family farm or workshop in return for providing their needs until death. Yet all of the children were morally bound to support their aged and infirm parents. Sons and daughters were not only necessary for a secure retirement; they also contributed to the success of the family as an economic unit in their youth. The proverb 'children are the riches of the poor' rang true because a family was required to run a farm or manage a shop. In New France hired labour was scarce and costly and, as we have seen, the young could be usefully employed. Colonial children were economic partners as well as social subordinates. Just as the dependence of the French colonists on the Amerindians as trading partners and military allies made the *Canadiens* more respectful toward the native peoples, so the dependence of adults on their children forced grownups to consider the wishes of the young. Thus the expression '*les petits sauvages*' provides an insight into the changing relationship of parents and children in early French Canada.

A good reason for regarding this characterization of children in New France as more indicative of French attitudes rather than of Canadian reality is the fact that British travellers who visited the United States from 1845 to 1935 described American children in similar terms. The travellers agreed that children in the United States were detestable, hard, and precocious. 'Precocity', wrote Richard L. Rapson, 'politely expressed the British feeling that American children were pert, impertinent, disrespectful, arrogant brats.'[44] Like the French visitors to New France, the British writers attributed the deficiencies of the children to indulgent and negligent parents. In a favourable interpretation of these observations, Richard Rapson presented the independence and self-reliance of the young as the products of an egalitarian and companionate family structure that was suited to republican and democratic values. The parallels with monarchical and undemocratic New France, however, suggest the existence of a more widespread phenomenon: a North American departure from the European perception of the ideal child and from Old World standards for raising the young. In Canada the levelling process did not reach the extremes observed in the United States. The limited sources from the French regime only permit an impressionistic picture of the world of youth. This picture reveals that, if young *Canadiens* were not *petits sauvages*, they were truly children of the New World.

Suggestions for Further Reading

Philippe Aries, *Centuries of Childhood: A Social History of Family Life* (New York, 1962).

Raymond Douville and Jacques Casanova, *Daily Life in Early Canada* (London, 1968).
Joy Parr, ed., *Childhood and Family in Canadian History* (Toronto, 1982).

Notes

The author thanks Jean (Carlson) Barman, doctoral candidate, and Neil Sutherland, professor in the Faculty of Education, University of British Columbia, for their helpful comments on early drafts of this article. The emphasis on little girls is due, in part, to my newborn daughter, Anna.

1 Pierre François-Xavier de Charlevoix, *Histoire et description générale de la Nouvelle-France*, 6 vols (Paris: Nyon fils, 1744), III, 253.

2 Governor de Denonville to M. de Seignelay, 12 November 1685, quoted in J.H. Stewart Reid *et al.* (eds), *A Source-Book of Canadian History* (Toronto: Longman Canada, 1976), 34.

3 Public Archives of Canada (hereafter PAC), C11A Series transcript, Vol. 26, 28–30, Intendant Raudot to the Minister of the Navy, 10 November 1707.

4 Antoine Silvy [actually Antoine-Denis Raudot], *Relation par Letters de l'Amérique Septentrionale* (Paris: Letouzey & Ane, 1904), 4.

5 Archives nationales de France, Archives des Colonies (hereafter ANF, AC), C11A Series, Vol. 43, 80-1 ff., Intendant Bégon to the Minister of the Navy, 26 October 1720.

6 Jacques Henripin, 'From Acceptance of Nature to Control: The Demography of the French Canadians', in Michiel Horn and Ronald Sabourin (eds), *Studies in Canadian Social History* (Toronto: McClelland and Stewart, 1974), 76; see also Henripin's *La Population canadienne au début du xviiie siècle* (Paris: Presses universitaires de France, 1954), which served as a source of data.

7 Peter N. Moogk, 'Manual Education and Economic Life in New France', *Studies on Voltaire and the Eighteenth Century*, Vol. 167 (Oxford: Voltaire Foundation, 1977), 125–68.

8 Archives du Québec (hereafter AQ), Collection de Pièces judiciares et notariales, No. 551 3/4, 23 juillet 1716.

9 AQ, Pièces detachées de la Prévôté de Québec, No. 929, 23 janvier 1733. This document is transcribed in Pierre-Georges Roy, 'Les "Sommations respectueuses" autrefois', *Rapport de l'Archiviste de la Province de Québec* (hereafter RAPQ), 1921–22, 59–78.

10 Henripin, 'From Acceptance of Nature', 75.

11 AQ, GNRF, Jacques Barbel, 30 mars 1736; ANF, AC, Outremer, G3 Series, Vol. 2058, pièce 22, 11 avril 1725. This last reference comes from Kenneth Donovan, 'Rearing Children in Louisbourg—A Colonial Seaport and Garrison Town 1713–1758', paper presented at the Atlantic Society for Eighteenth Century Studies meeting, April, 1979.

12 Edouard-Zotique Massicotte, 'Le travail des enfants à Montréal, au XVIIe siècle,' *Bulletin des Recherches historiques* (hereafter BRH) 22 (1916), 57; 'Comment on disposait des Enfants du Roi', BRH 37 (1931), 49–54. Volumes 18 (1956) and 19 (1960) of the *Inventaires des Greffes des Notaires* series published by the Quebec

Provincial Archives provide synopses of private paupers' and orphans' indentures passed by the notary Louis Chambalon.

[13]Quoted in Fortier De la Broquerie, 'Les "Enfants Trouvés" sous le régime français', *Trois Siècles de Médecine québécoise* (Québec: Société historique de Québec, 1973), 113–26.

[14]Cyprien Tanguay, *Dictionnaire généalogique des familles canadiennes*, 7 vols (Montreal: Eusèbe Sénécal, 1871–90), Vol. 4, 607–8.

[15]Yves-François Zoltvany (ed.), *The French Tradition in North America* (New York: Harper & Row, 1969), 75.

[16]*Arrêts et Réglements du Conseil supérieur de Québec et Ordonnances et Jugements des Intendants du Canada* (Québec: E.R. Fréchette, 1855), 395–6. Synopses of indentures of *enfants du Roi* from the files of Joseph-Charles Raimbault can be found in Volume 21 (1964) of the *Inventaires des Greffes des Notaires* series noted above. Unpublished indentures from the Quebec region are to be found in AQ, GNRF, Jean-Etienne Dubreuil, and Henri Hiché, *passim*.

[17]AQ, GNRF, Henri Hiché, 20 septembre 1735.

[18]AQ, GNRF, Henri Hiché, 28 novembre 1729.

[19]Zoltvany, *The French Tradition*, 83.

[20]Ross W. Beales, 'In Search of the Historical Child: Miniature Adulthood and Youth in Colonial New England', *American Quarterly* XXVII, 4 (October, 1975), 379–98.

[21]'La Correspondance de Madame Bégon, 1748–1753', *RAPQ*, 1934–35, 51.

[22]'La Correspondance de Madame Bégon', 22.

[23]Robert-Lionel Séguin, *Les Jouets anciens du Québec* (Ottawa: Editions Lemeac, 1976), 117.

[24]ANF, AC, Série G2, Vol. 203, dossier 380, pièce 3—Estate inventory of Jean Castaing, 6 June 1756, and noted in Donovan, 'Rearing Children in Louisbourg'.

[25]PAC, C11A transcript, Vol. XXV, 32-de Louvigny to the Minister, 21 October 1706; Pierre-Georges Roy (ed.), *Inventaire des Ordonnances des Intendants de la Nouvelle-France*, 4 vols. (Beauceville: L'Eclaireur, 1919), I, 218.

[26]Edouard-Zotique Massicotte, *Répertoire des Arrêts, Edits, Mandements, Ordonnances et Réglements conservés dans les archives du Palais de justice de Montréal, 1640–1760* (Montréal: G. Ducharme, 1919), 120; *BRH* 24 (1928), 526.

[27]*Arrêts et Réglements*, 398.

[28]Adolph B. Benson (ed.), *Peter Kalm's Travels in North America*, 2 vols. (New York: Dover Publications, 1966), Vol. II, 526.

[29]Silvy, *Relation par Lettres*, 4.

[30]Charlevoix, *Histoire et description générale*, Vol. III, 257.

[31]Roy, *Inventaire des ordonnances*, Vol. I 237.

[32]Cornelius Jaenen, *The Role of the Church in New France* (Toronto: McGraw Hill-Ryerson, 1976), 27.

[33]Pierre Boucher, *Histoire Véritable et Naturelle des moeurs et productions du pays de La Nouvelle France* (Paris: Florentin Lambert, 1664), 139.

[34]Charlevoix, *Histoire et descrébcion générale*, Vol. III, 255.

[35]Benson, *Peter Kalm's Travels*, Vol. II, 481.

[36]Edouard-Zotique Massicotte, 'Un recensement inédit de Montréal, en 1741', *Mémoires de la Société Royale du Canada*, Serie III, Vol. XV (mai, 1921), 6.

[37]Benson, *Peter Kalm's Travels*, Vol. II, 538.

[38]Louis Franquet, *Voyages et Mémoires sur le Canada* (Québec: Institut Canadien de Québec, 1889), 31–2.

[39]Archives du Séminaire de Québec, Manuscrit 2, Annales du Petit Séminaire de Québec, 1668–*c.*1780; Manuscrit 6, a variant of the Annales.

[40]AQ, GNRF, Gilles Rageot, 18 avril 1674; AQ (Montréal), GNRF, Bénigne Basset, 18 août 1677.

[41]AQ (Montréal), GNRF, François LePallieur, index for 1733–1739. The internal evidence suggests that these writing exercises were done in 1771.

[42]Petition of Catherine Frontigny to the *lieutenant-général* at Quebec, 9 September 1745, in *RAPQ*, 1921–22, 66–7.

[43]Benson, *Peter Kalm's Travels*, Vol. II, 510.

[44]Richard L. Rapson, 'The American Child as Seen by British Travelers, 1845–1935', *American Quarterly* XVII, 3 (Fall, 1965), 520–34.

9

The Overseas Trade of Eighteenth-Century New France

James S. Pritchard

In New France, a colony dominated by subsistence agriculture, war or threat of war was probably the most important single consistent economic element. Yet in the peaceful years between the Treaty of Utrecht (1713) and the outbreak of a new round of European war in the early 1740s some of the colony's economic and commercial possibilities were actually realized. During this period an Atlantic trading community and a French overseas trade involving New France emerged, although it was statistically much smaller than that of the American colonies to the south, and arguably different in other ways besides size. Whether New France could be usefully compared to the American colonies collectively, or perhaps to one of the least well developed, is another matter. What is important is that the colony was not totally self-sufficient, and that it did by the eighteenth century have an expanding set of relationships with the outside world.

In a fascinating case study, James Pritchard explores what the surviving records of one shipping and trading venture to New France can tell us about the patterns of overseas trade. 'Waste-book' details enable Pritchard to discuss the extent to which this venture was typical, as well as to compare some of its principal aspects to similar ventures in the English-speaking American colonies. He suggests that it was fairly typical, particularly in its relative ineffiency and absence of substantial profitability, and offers a number of illustrations of both attributes. He concludes that such ventures were risky businesses, raising the question of why, given the small returns, owners invested in them.

What does the *Fier* tell us about the overseas trade of New France? Why were expenses so high for a voyage of this kind? How could costs have been trimmed? Why did people invest in this sort of enterprise, given the low return on investment? Pritchard suggests that absence of alternatives may have been one explanation. Can you think of others? Given the general conditions surrounding the *Fier*, was this sort of overseas venture likely to expand and flourish?

This article first appeared, titled 'The Voyage of the *Fier*: An Analysis of a Shipping and Trading Venture to New France, 1724–1728', in *Histoire Sociale/Social History* VI, 2 (April 1973), 75–97.

Historians have drawn attention to the emergence of an Atlantic trading community during the seventeenth and eighteenth centuries and pointed to the underlying importance of the primary means of communication—ocean shipping. Studies have appeared in Europe and the United States devoted to the general growth and development of maritime activity and to the ways and means of measuring and comparing its several elements: profitability, changes in productivity, freight rates, and capital costs.[1] No one has yet extended his examination to include French maritime activity to New France in any but the most general manner. This study is an attempt to add to an already large body of literature on ocean shipping, and to indicate some of the differences between the conclusions that have been drawn concerning the British American colonies and similar developments in New France. It appears that there were important variations. The evidence for such a study is meagre and, in the absence of data, does not lend itself to quantitative measurement. It may therefore be useful to present the information about one voyage for which there is sufficient information to draw some conclusions about the state and conditions under which maritime traffic was carried on in France's northern colony.[2]

Several documents recently discovered among supplementary volumes of the *jurisdiction consulaire* in the departmental archives of the Charente-Maritime at La Rochelle were collated with a waste-book in the same records to provide the information for the present study.[3] The *brouillard* or 'waste-book' was used by merchants to keep rough preliminary entries of commercial transactions. In this instance it consists of forty-seven closely written pages of chronologically recorded purchases and other expenses made from 1724 to 1728 to refit and furnish a merchant vessel for a voyage to and from Quebec.

The record is important for the period it covers: in no decade during the *ancien régime* are the port records so scanty as that prior to 1725. At La Rochelle they are virtually non-existent; at Quebec, the years following the death of Louis XIV were very poorly covered by ministerial records, for during the regency the old secretariats were abolished in favour of less efficient councils.

The notebook contains several lists including one of the crew, another of the cargo put on board by the owners, a record of its sale at Quebec, another of cargo laded at La Rochelle for other metropolitan merchants, and also accounts of cargo purchased in the colony for the return voyage and its later sale at La Rochelle. A great deal can be found wanting in the notebook. The careless manner in which entries were sometimes made and withdrawn, the use of the backs of folio pages to record later accounts of expenditures after the initial departure and the errors in arithmetic have all made for confusion. They point to it as a running draft and not a final record. Consequently, seven given totals and sub-totals are useless for analytical purposes. Only the raw data in this and other documents have been used in the paper.

Despite its flaws, the source has great significance. Among the French colonial records concerning New France it is perhaps unique in its wealth of detail. It reveals some of the intricacies of ship ownership, the tasks of an outfitter, the nature and cost of materials and labour employed, as well as the size, composition and wages of a French crew. It also provides information about the manner in which cargo shipped to Quebec was estimated, consigned and loaded; and finally, it allows us to examine the relations of these many elements and to indicate to some degree their effect upon the ship's ability to earn profits.

The ship, the *Fier*, of 140 tons burden, was typical. There seems no reason to believe that her voyage to New France was in any way out of the ordinary or that the picture that emerges from the record does not reflect the normal procedures in commercial shipping between La Rochelle and Quebec. In every respect the record seems to concern the business activities of typical Rochelais merchants engaged in the most common sort of Canadian colonial activity involving an ordinary ship, crew and cargo.

The owners of *Fier* were engaged in trading on their own account as well as in shipping. In the Quebec colonial trade this was the most common procedure. Canada produced no bulk cargoes to warrant the use of charter-parties, wherein merchants hired ships from their owners for the delivery or collection of a cargo. In later years numerous ships arrived in the colony under charter, but almost always to the government or its agents for transporting troops, munitions and supplies. Before the outbreak of the Anglo-French wars in the middle of the eighteenth century such passengers and cargoes were most often carried to New France by the single naval transport which called annually. The vast majority of merchantmen sailed under the same circumstances as did the *Fier*. The record, then, reflects the common experience of both colony and metropolitan ports in the years before and after 1725. Unfortunately, the interrelationship between the owners' shipping and trading activities makes it difficult to draw conclusions solely about maritime operations. This itself, however, is an important conclusion about colonial shipping to New France.

The men who outfitted the *Fier* were no strangers to ocean shipping, the colonial trade, or New France. André Estournel, the author of the waste-book, had been sending goods to Quebec at least since 1711. At that time his nephew and later co-owner of the *Fier*, Jean-Jacques Catignon, son of a former stores-keeper at Quebec, resided in the colony, receiving trade goods from France and sending back bills of exchange in return.[4] Four years later Catignon was in partnership with a Sieur Guillet, a colonial merchant.[5] In 1718 Estournel purchased a one-third interest in a merchantman. During the next few years the ship sailed regularly to New France carrying cargo for the owners and other merchants. In the fall of 1723 after departing Quebec, the ship gave out and was forced to return and winter in the colony.[6] Probably the news of this moved Estournel to purchase a new hull. In March, 1724, he paid 4,600 *livres* to M. de Maulusson, an agent of a *fermier-général*, for a *patache* that had been used on the Île de Ré,[7] and subsequently named it the *Fier*.

Estournel met most of the costs, but the same day that he purchased the ship, Catignon made over to him a bill of exchange worth 2,820 *livres* 10 *sols*, and a year later transferred several accounts to meet some of the mounting costs. Before the ship left La Rochelle, Catignon had paid his associate a little less than one-quarter of the total capital outlay to that date. The third and major interest holder was a somewhat enigmatic M. de Courcy who may have been a naval officer. In 1718 a Chevalier Pothier de Courcy had commanded His Most Christian Majesty's frigate, *Mutine*, on a voyage to Quebec. There had been insufficient funds in the marine treasury that year and the ship had been outfitted by a private merchant from La Rochelle.[8] This experience may have convinced Courcy of the profits to be made from similar ventures and led him six years later to invest in the refit and voyage of the *Fier*.

Like Catignon, Courcy also put up some cash soon after the original purchase in order to meet the current expenses of the refit. Throughout the year he continued to pay for various materials used and before the ship sailed he had contributed almost one-third of the total investment. Estournel, himself, contributed the remainder. The total of 24,816 *livres* 3 *sols* does not represent any final figure but illustrates the approximate investment required to get a ship of 140 tons burden ready for sea, and the flexibility of the financial arrangements needed. A more accurate and useful presentation of the capital outlay is presented in Tables 1 to 3.

The sums contributed in the initial venture by each of the owners over the fourteen months following the purchase represented both the investment in the ship and a portion of its cargo. Although it is well known that individuals most often owned only portions of different vessels in order to spread the risk of financial loss and to limit the liability of their total investments, it is apparent that no shares in the vessel were sold. Estournel made the initial purchase of the hull but that did not prevent Catignon from paying for the construction of the ship's longboat, twenty empty barrels, several more of nails, tallow and a set of blocks and pulleys. The three men owned the ship jointly.

No declaration of ownership has been found, but a single entry in the waste-book and the discovery of two current accounts drawn up later between Estournel and his partners' widows provide the key to ownership. Initially Estournel and Catignon each held one-quarter interest in the ship while Courcy and a Richard Gauthier held five-twelfths and a one-twelfth interest respectively. Before sailing, however, Gauthier dropped out, and the three partners split his holdings equally between them.[9]

The details of ownership noted part of the total investment in the venture, but it is important to see what this total amount consisted of in order to obtain an estimate of shipping production costs. The generalized and imprecise nature of some of the amounts given in the waste-book are a hindrance to accurate calculation and several accounts for work done and materials bought were not paid for until after the ship had departed La Rochelle thereby adding to the total capital outlay. Nevertheless a list of items including more than three hundred entries has been drawn and arranged in several categories to attempt to reveal the fixed and replacement costs which, along with the investment in cargo, made up the total capital outlay in the venture to New France.

The *Fier* did not undergo a normal armament for the colonial trade. Before she was purchased by Estournel she had been moored in the harbour on the Île de Ré. Much of her hull timber was unfit for the high seas. The ship had to undergo a major refit which took more than a year to complete. One may discern the ship's original condition in the list enumerating beams, knees and futtocks, the thousands of running feet of deck and hull planking, a new bowsprit, a mainmast and three new topmasts. More than 2,135 man-days of labour were expended on her, 1,469 man-days by carpenters alone. The ship was practically rebuilt.

The capital expended represented considerably more than a normal armament which would have entailed only victualling, advances to the crew and replacement of worn-out material: sails, rigging, running gear and planking where necessary. The totals in Tables 1 to 3 represent the capital invested in a nearly new ship of one hundred and forty tons burden.[10] A portion of this amount was considered along with the crew's wages, victuals and incidental contingency expenses as a replacement cost rather than as part of the fixed cost of the total capital outlay. It is difficult, however, to determine what portion of this total is replacement cost. By subtracting the sum of the replaceable items in the expenditures: rigging, running gear, rope, cordage, sails, artisan labour and other miscellaneous expenses, one may reduce the fixed element in the total capital outlay to 15,789 *livres* 5 *sols* 6 *deniers*. This final sum is an estimate of the cost of building a ship as opposed to making it ready for sea. Equally important it represents the amount of capital investment, minus the depreciation that remained to the owners after the ship returned from her voyage to Quebec.

In 1725 the cost of a relatively new merchantman of 140 tons burden amounted to approximately 15,790 *livres*, or 113 *livres* per ton. Using an approximate currency equivalent of one *livre* to one shilling sterling, this amount compares very favourably with the estimated peacetime price of 6½ pounds sterling per ton for an English ship of similar size, considering only the fixed element in the price.[11] The two figures would be even more comparable if the true replacement cost were known.

It is all too easy to forget just how much of a wooden ship needed replacing after a single trans-ocean voyage. Suits of sails, rope, blocks and spars were in need of replacement. Rope alone for the *Fier* represented nearly eight per cent of the capital outlay necessary to ready the ship for sea and twenty per cent of the total replacement expenditure. Following the ship's return to La Rochelle Estournel sold 2,736 *livres weight*, or between one-quarter and one-fifth of the rope used during the voyage, to oakum pickers but this act represented only a small return on a large investment. Similarly, all of the ship's running gear had to be replaced, but probably at less frequent intervals than after every voyage.

Which of the many expenditures ought to be classified as fixed or replacement? It is obvious that the above subtraction of the total cost of items which needed replacement errs on the side of excess. Using the English figure given above, a ship of 140 tons burden had a fixed cost of 18,200 *livres*. The fixed cost of the *Fier* was probably somewhat higher than the 15,789 *livres* determined.

The total replacement cost, however, consisted of more than the replaceable items in the ship. The crew had to be paid and victuals provided. It is from the sum of the fixed cost and the total replacement cost that the ship's earnings were determined, but in the case of the *Fier* the owners also purchased a cargo worth 9,781 *livres* 2 *sols* 8 *deniers* and loaded it onboard for the voyage. A statement of their total capital outlay appears in Table 4.

Two features of these totals and sub-totals are not altogether obvious. First, the replacement cost per ton is much less than the fixed cost per ton. The *Fier*'s replacement cost amounted to approximately 66 *livres* per ton (see Table 4) which again is somewhat less than the equivalent figure of 4½ pounds sterling for a similar English vessel.[12] Second, taking the round figure of 25,000 *livres* as the cost of making the ship ready for sea, one finds a ratio of 3:2 between fixed costs and replacement costs. In other words, a French colonial merchantman of median tonnage required about 179 *livres* per ton of capital investment when undertaking a voyage to New France.[13] This figure probably holds good only for the period of peace and growing financial stability following 1725.

The accuracy of the figure for Total Capital Outlay (Table 4) is, of course, open to question but it is remarkably close to the given total of 35,173 *livres* 4 *sols* 8 *deniers* which appeared in Estournel's waste-book as the total amount involved in the purchase, refit, armament and cargo on which he levied a commission of two percent for services rendered to the association.[14] The difference between the two totals is 1.1 per cent. Even if the figures are not strictly accurate, however, the general principle they illustrate remains valid, and they lead to some suggested conclusions about colonial shipping using very limited amounts of data.

On 25 May 1725 the *Fier* departed the roads at La Palisse for Quebec where she arrived on 22 August after a normal crossing of ninety days.[15] As usual she carried a greater complement than either English or Dutch ships of a similar size. The *Fier's* inefficiency can be seen by comparing the ton-man ratio of 6.1 with those for unarmed English merchantmen of similar size that sailed from England to Jamaica in 1729–31 and to Charleston in 1735–39, which are 8.8 and 11.9 respectively.[16] The larger French crew may be explained by different and less efficient hull and rig design, but more likely by regulation from the era of Colbert and his successors. The Ordonnance de la Marine required commercial vessels to ship various inexperienced personnel as trainees.[17] The case of the *Fier* proved to be no exception. Besides the captain there was a second in command, six petty officers, a surgeon, ten seamen, two boys, a cook and a pilot in training for a total complement of twenty-three. All, with the exception of the *pilottin*, were paid a monthly wage and even he received a bonus at the end of the voyage adding to the already large expense for food and wages that such a crew required.

The salary scale varied widely. The two ship's officers each received one hundred and ninety *livres* per month, which set them well above the remainder of the crew. The pilot, boatswain's mate and ship's carpenter were each paid forty-five *livres*. The other petty officers, the bosun, coxswain and steward were paid between thirty and thirty-four *livres* monthly while the surgeon with twenty-eight *livres* was ranked very low. His replacement on the return voyage—for the first one deserted at Quebec—received an even lower wage.

The surgeon was one of the crew members required by law on all French ships, but he seems to have been treated almost as though he were superfluous. Others, too, were so treated, if one may judge from the disparity between the wages and special treatment given to three seamen and the remainder. At the beginning of the voyage the three highest paid sailors received a bonus of one week's wage for signing on and at the conclusion they were paid off at a higher rate than the one originally set. There were no formal distinctions in France between able and ordinary seamen but the wide range in rates of pay among the deck hands does reflect the degree of skill among them. Ordinary seamen earned monthly rates of pay between sixteen and twenty-two *livres*. Two others earned two *livres* more per month while the senior crewmen had their rate of pay increased to twenty-seven *livres* for each of the last four months of the voyage. These men were paid for the complete voyage almost three times the rate for boys in training. Along with the boatswain, who received the highest wage of those serving on deck, they provided the backbone of the crew.

The crew were paid for the full time away from La Rochelle, and the long lay-over spent by most ships at Quebec ate into the ship's earning capacity. The long delays often encountered in the St Lawrence River where captains were forced to wait for the proper winds before moving upstream also served to increase sailing time. These two factors combined to make the New France run more costly than others in the French colonial network, especially as the increased cost of the large crew's wages and victuals was a part of the replacement cost of capital outlay or was charged against earnings before profit could be taken. One month's wage for this oversized crew represented almost two percent of the owner's total capital outlay (see Table 12).

The absence of any commission or bonus paid to the captain who sold the owners' cargo at Quebec is surprising. Usually such activity entitled a captain to a percentage of the gross sales but there is no record of it in this case. This appears to have been the captain's first voyage for the owners and they may have placed him on salary for that reason. Certainly their instructions to him suggest that he lacked experience: several persons at Quebec were recommended to him in case he needed advice.[18]

Before leaving La Rochelle the crew received two months' advance on their wages; when signing-on bonuses were added, this amounted to 1,416 *livres*. On the ship's return nearly seven months later the remaining wages were paid and the crew dismissed. The whole amount of their wages came to 4,735 *livres* 10 *sols* and with the cost of their victuals was deducted from the ship's earnings. These figures show how the expense of large crews might reduce the earning power of French ships. The owners endeavoured to increase their earnings by other means such as, for example, the practice of returning from Quebec with specie and coin as a result of trading activity. It was used to pay off the crew at La Rochelle and thereby avoided the necessity for the merchants to tie up any more capital for that purpose than what had been required for the initial outlay.

The *Fier* carried approximately one hundred and thirty tons of cargo and more than ten tons of victuals for her crew. In France, and on this voyage, the various bales, packets, bundles and barrels of merchandise were estimated by the shipper into standard volumes of *barriques*, *tierçons*, *quarts*, *ancres* and *demi-ancres*, representing a quarter, sixth, eighth, sixteenth and thirty-second of a *tonneau de mer* respectively. For instance, one consignment of two *ballots*, two *caissons*, four *pacquets* and one *baril* was estimated as four *barriques*, two *tierçons*, one *quart* and a *demi-ancre*, or one and forty-seven ninety-sixths tons of freight.

These freight-tons were the units recorded by port officials on the arrival and departure of ships of the period. The totals of these figures reveal the amount of cargo imported and exported, not the tonnage of shipping entering the port. On her arrival at Quebec in 1725 and again four years later the *Fier* was reported carrying one hundred and thirty and one hundred and twenty tons respectively.[19] The historian cannot, then, assume that the ship always carried full ladings and he must consider the differences between potential and real load when relating the requirements for capital outlay to the earnings to be made based on freight and cargo carried. Fortunately in the present case the cargo space appears to have been filled so that no additional calculations concerning real and potential earnings needed to be made.

The owners' cargo was largely wine and brandy but also included salt, vinegar and household wares (see Table 5). It filled less than seventy tons of cargo space. Estournel hired out a bit more than sixty tons of remaining space at one hundred *livres* per ton to other merchants who wished to consign goods to agents and merchants at Quebec. Eleven metropolitan merchants dispatched to thirty different merchants at Quebec forty-seven loads varying in size from one small bale of general merchandise to ten bales and two *barriques* of general wares, two *quarts* and one *ancre* of nails, one packet of steel, one case of muskets and ten barrels of lead. At each end of the maritime link both large and small commercial houses were represented. Undoubtedly there were even some consignments sent not to merchants but to clients in the colony for their own consumption. Fully one-half the space was taken by one of the owners, Jean-Jacques Catignon, whose major consignment went to Jean Crespin, already *colonel de la milice* at Quebec and soon to become a councillor on the Superior Council.[20]

The captain sold the owners' cargo for slightly more than twice its original value (see Table 6). Nearly half the amount was received in colonial goods and the remainder in specie and bills of exchange drawn on commercial houses and institutions in France. Almost one-third of their cargo was purchased by Mme Soumande, widow of a prominent local merchant. In return for 200 *minots* of salt, 50 *barriques* of wine and 362½ *velts* of brandy valued at 6,987 *livres* 10 *sols*, she exchanged 23 packets of moose and deer hides, two bales of lynx and bearskins all valued at 5,537 *livres* 10 *sols*. Mme Soumande made up the difference with a bill of exchange and 753 livres in cash.[21] This was a typical exchange between colonial and metropolitan merchants in that Mme Soumande needed to make over ten per cent of her payment in cash. For in general the colonists were unable to supply colonial goods for the full equivalent of French goods delivered to them. Captain Chiron took more than 3,000 *livres* in coin out of the colony as a result of his single trading operation, which provides a good illustration of the constant difficulty the Canadian colonists had in paying for their manufactures (see Table 8). In view of this flow of specie eastward across the Atlantic we shall not be surprised to learn that the specie was devalued on arrival in France.

Almost four thousand *livres* from the sale of goods remained in New France in the form of duties levied on wine and brandy, loading and lightering costs, and expenditures for revictualling (see Table 7). In all, the captain returned with goods, coin and bills which eventually realized 17,955 *livres* 1 *sol* 6 *deniers* in La Rochelle. When added to the amounts earned from carrying freight in both directions the total gross earnings of the ship amounted to 25,556 *livres* 14 *sols* (see Table 10). This figure represents earnings from both trading and shipping.

The proportion of one type of earning from the other is significant. Only 29.3 per cent of the total earnings were derived from freight. Slightly more than seventy per cent of the earnings came from selling about 54 per cent of the total cargo carried. To have earned a similar amount on freight alone the *Fier* would have had to carry 256 tons of cargo, or in other words had a full lading while sailing to and from New France (see Table 12). There was little or no hope of earning sufficient profits from shipping activity alone. It was probably a characteristic that shippers customarily owned a large portion of the cargo being carried on ships sailing to New France, that trading activity was an integral part of the growth of maritime activity in the colony, and that the shipper-traders from France occupied a paramount position.

In order to obtain a complete picture of the commercial venture under discussion see Tables 5 to 10. The value of the figures in the tables is that they show the earnings of the outbound cargo, the reduction in the quantity of items sold at Quebec from that loaded at La Rochelle, the devaluation of specie and the failure of the return cargo to earn any profit. The striking feature is the difference between the earnings of the French and Canadian cargos. Purchased at La Rochelle for 9,781 *livres* 2 *sols* 8 *deniers*, the cargo sold at Quebec for 21,482 *livres* 2 *sols* (Colonial value), an increase of ninety-three per cent after the currency equivalent is taken into account. By comparison, the cargo purchased at Quebec for 17,538 *livres* 6 *sols* 10 *deniers* (Colonial) sold at La Rochelle for 17,596 *livres* 13 *sols* 1 *denier* (tournois), an increase of only fifteen per cent. As in the case of freight the merchant had to count on the earnings of the outbound run to provide his profits.[22]

It may be objected that in 1725 specie no longer circulated in the French colonies at higher fixed rates than in France. But nevertheless Estournel made a devaluation of 12.5 per cent on the coins after they arrived in La Rochelle, and this illustrates another feature of the finances of the period which, together with the refusal by the central government to permit card money to circulate, led to the demoralization and decline of trade in the colony. According to letters patent issued and put into effect by order of the *Conseil de Marine* in April, 1717 all different rates at which specie circulated in the empire were abolished. Henceforth the coin of the realm was to circulate equally within the empire. Economic circumstances, however, dictated otherwise. Owing to the failure of the Crown to meet its financial obligations and to the collapse of John Law's 'System', the government pushed through a bewildering series of specie devaluations during the next decade. Financial stability was not achieved in France until June, 1726, when Cardinal Fleury, who then became chief minister, insisted that the devaluations cease. The rate set then did not change until 1785.

Until 1726, then, the devaluations always placed the colonial merchants at a disadvantage in their dealings with their metropolitan counterparts. Currency was always over-valued in New France.[23] In the case of the trading which originated from the voyage of the *Fier*, the colonists followed the rates set for specie in an *arrêt* of September, 1724, which had established the *Louis d'or* at 16 *livres*. By the time the *Fier* had returned to La Rochelle another *arrêt* of September, 1725, had further reduced the *Louis d'or* to 14 *livres*.[24] Estournel devalued the specie accordingly.[25]

A second significant feature, made all the more important by the profit-earning role of the outbound voyage, was the decline in the size of the cargo sold relative to the cargo initially laded in France. For instance, of the forty-five *barriques* of Saintonge wine carried, only twenty-seven were sold. Every other item in the cargo was in a similar case. A statement of the 'coullage' [sic], or leakage, reveals that an eighteenth-century merchant expected to absorb fairly high losses through spoilage, leakage and breakage; in the case just mentioned, this amounted to forty per cent.[26] The type of commodity seems to have little bearing upon the degree of loss, for while the Saintonge registered the highest rate, the Bordeaux registered the lowest, which was not more than three percent. On an average, eleven per cent of the wine was lost, and ten per cent brandy and drinking glasses. The earthenware suffered heavily, with losses amounting to twenty-two per cent of the total while, not unexpectedly, the relatively indestructible ironware experienced losses of only three per cent. These losses show how the historian may easily be misled if he only compares the per unit prices in France with those in the colony without taking into consideration the losses which the merchant trader was expected to absorb and (before 1726) the specie devaluations in the calculation of his selling price.[27]

Wine and brandy carried an additional burden of entry duties. These had been set in the seventeenth century at ten per cent of their sale value at Quebec but in the present instance were levied at a fixed rate of nine *livres* per *barrique* of wine and twenty-two and a half *livres* for a similar quantity of brandy. In this venture 2,195 *livres* 3 *sols* 4 *deniers* were paid into the coffers of the *Domaine d'Occident* at Quebec. When the duty is compared to the price received after the sale of the wine and brady, the duty appears to represent nearly twelve per cent of the amount received. This suggests that the prices obtained were not as high as might have been expected.[28]

Before the net profit to the owners of the wine and brandy can be determined, the carriage charges must be added. These were hidden in the outfitting costs, but rather than attempt to fix a portion of those costs against the cargo, it seems reasonable to use the prevailing freight rates. Wine and brandy occupied 50 $^{7}/_{12}$ tons of cargo space. At one hundred *livres* per ton a charge of 5,058 *livres* 6 *sols* 8 *deniers* must be put against the earnings from the sale at Quebec. By subtracting the sum of the original cost and the carriage charges from the sale price less the duties levied, and taking into consideration the difference between current metropolitan and colonial currency values, we establish that the merchants were left with a net profit from the sale of wine and brandy of ten per cent.

The remainder of the outbound cargo of salt, vinegar and household wares, amounting to approximately fifteen tons, was worth 1,372 *livres* 12 *sols* 8 *deniers* and earned 2,587 *livres* 14 *sols* in equivalent *livres tournois*.[29] After freight charges were deducted this portion of the cargo resulted in a net *loss* of ten per cent to the owners. Certainly these figures are only approximate. The amount of space occupied by these items remains unknown except for the drinking glasses. They were packed in four *quarts*, or half a ton, and the proceeds from their sale resulted in a net *loss* of twenty-three and a half per cent. The most profitable item was the iron pots. We do not know their bulk but they were transported for other merchants at a flat rate of thirty *livres* for forty and forty-eight units respectively. Even allowing for the currency equivalent it is possible that the owners realized a net profit of slightly more than thirty per cent. The thirty-four *muids* of salt occupied 11$^{1}/_{3}$ tons of cargo space, but as only about one quarter of the total was sold the remainder may have been carried as ballast and would not have had a charge levied against it. In that case the freight charge of 1,500 *livres* determined for the additional cargo is far too high and the loss exaggerated. Nevertheless the case of the glassware must be considered against such a view.

Turning to the return cargo (see Tables 8 and 9) the results reveal the third major feature of the trading portion of the venture. The total cargo obtained in New France was disbursed at La Rochelle for about fifteen per cent more than was paid for it at Quebec. This figure included not only colonial products, but also specie and bills of exchange. When exchange commodities are considered alone the picture is enlightening. Codfish, wood products, furs and hides purchased for 10,764 *livres* 14 *sols* (9,420.1 *livres tournois*) sold in France for 11,226 *livres*, an increase of nineteen per cent. The greater the amount of colonial products laded, the better the financial picture. But this gross figure could not begin to pay for the operational costs of the ship let alone yield significant profit. The largest item of the return cargo, cod, occupied less than ten tons of cargo space. The earnings on the return freight amounted to no more than 1,455 *livres*. Even if the return rates were lower than those for the outbound voyage, it is doubtful whether the freight totaled to more than eighteen or twenty tons. The ship probably carried no more than forty tons of cargo across the Atlantic; and it is not surprising that at least one street in La Rochelle is paved with ballast stones from Canada.

Although the *Fier*'s return cargo consisted of Canadian products that 'helped to provide France with the raw materials which she needed', it would be completely erroneous to see in this traffic, as one student has done, an opportunity to 'double profits' compared to those being earned for a single crossing of the Atlantic.[30] These Canadian products bore no resemblance to sugar or tobacco which were valuable enough to bear high freight rates and to pay for outbound as well as inbound voyages. Furs could carry high freight rates, but even during the most prosperous years of the *ancien régime* all the furs exported from the colony in any one year could be carried in one good-sized merchantman.[31] It seems doubtful, indeed, whether furs can really be considered a staple in the same sense as tobacco or sugar.

Tobacco and sugar were bulky valuable cargoes which could earn large profits. When a ship was under charter to carry bulk cargoes homeward, it presumably provided the owners with their main earnings, but there was nothing to prevent them from shipping their own cargoes on the outward run like the owners of the *Fier*. In other colonies shippers could expect to earn profits from transporting in two directions.

In Europe it was not unusual for a shipper to earn a profit by transporting a cargo in only one direction. But it may well have been the exception in colonial shipping where distances were greater, navigation less certain and the risk generally increased. The triangular trade routes which developed between several colonies might best be viewed as attempts to improve the earning power of ships by moving cargo for a profit along two sides of a triangle rather than as the outgrowth of a desire to exchange mutually beneficial commodities between temperate and tropical colonies. It is notable for instance, that New England, with an economy somewhat similar to that of New France, developed triangular trade routes with the West Indies, whereas Virginia, with a bulk cargo export commodity, provided shippers with the opportunity to earn profits by moving goods in both directions directly between the colony and England, no time being wasted moving along an unprofitable route.

In New France, on the other hand, shippers and owners had to forego such expectations. The return cargo for most was not a means to increase earnings, but a necessary result of the barter system employed wherein one commodity was exchanged for another. Despite the existence of about a hundred tons of empty cargo capacity on the voyage home, the owners made no attempt to fill it. Profits were earned by transporting goods from the mother country to the colony and selling them to the inhabitants. There was little profit to be had from carrying Canadian products to France.

Several questions arise from this examination of the owners' cargo. In view of the great difference between profit and loss on certain items, were the earnings on non-luxury goods sufficient to justify their carriage to New France at all? The answer seems to be a qualified yes, but only provided that luxury items made up the bulk of a cargo and that no other goods were available to a shipper. It was certainly better to carry something if only to reduce the carriage costs of the luxury goods.

This in no way implies that manufactures of daily use were not carried to the colony. Historians have recently found evidence that during the *ancien régime* large quantities of French manufactured goods, especially clothes, were present in New France, among the common people.[32] The failure of return cargoes to earn profit in the traffic with New France poses the additional question not just whether the colonial merchants ever dominated the trade, but whether they ever could have dominated the maritime trade and traffic between New France and the mother country given additional adverse factors of climate and geography. Does not the picture portrayed suggest a reason for the little enthusiasm shown by merchants in New France to accept molasses from the Antilles in exchange for local products? Can there be any wonder at the vigorous reactions displayed on any occasion when the suppression of liquor in the fur trade was discussed? Did the low profit margins on household goods—iron pots excepted—lead to their being imported by colonial merchants rather than metropolitan merchants? Unfortunately on this point we have perhaps carried our speculation beyond what the evidence will bear. Certainly profits were sufficient to encourage merchants to venture into the colonial trade of New France, but the margin was narrow enough to bring about many failures. The Canadian trade was not a gateway to instant riches. Knowledge, experience and not a little luck were keys to commercial success on the route to New France.

It has been useful thus far to divide the total capital outlay into three parts; the fixed cost, the replacement cost and the amount invested in the cargo. The returns from this last portion of the outlay we have considered in some detail for they lead to conclusions regarding trade to New France. It remains now to examine the earning of the maritime and trading portions of the venture considered as a whole and to determine net earnings. But this cannot be done without first making three final calculations of factors in the fixed cost element of the ship's capital. They are the depreciation of the ship, the insurance risk against loss or peril of the sea and the interest on the capital investment represented in the fixed cost.

It was in order to arrive at some approximate idea of these elements that I attempted earlier to distinguish between building a ship and making it ready for sea. The division of capital into two parts arose from the great difference in the longevity of the portions thus split, and hence in determining the rate of depreciation of the two parts of the investment. Only the first portion depreciated very slowly. A wooden ship that had been properly maintained and which sailed in northern waters might last beyond the quarter century mark, even to the half century although this was unlikely. Nevertheless the fixed portion of the outlay had to be depreciated at between two and four percent annually. This figure naturally increased when, as in the case of the *Fier*, the ship did not sail to New France every year and was laid up in her home port, continually losing value without earning any profits. The *Fier* did not sail again from La Rochelle until the spring of 1729.

The other portion of the outlay in the ship was not depreciated at all but was considered along with victuals and advances as replacement expenditure. Not all of the replacements were made every year, but at frequent intervals. Also, the ratio between the two kinds of outlay, fixed:replacement, was 3:2. In attempting to find a rate of depreciation for the whole amount needed to get the ship ready for sea the figure of four per cent seems to be on the high side.[33] Applying this rate to the *Fier*, the depreciation charge would have amounted to 1,000 *livres*.

The element of risk is even more difficult to estimate. One could well imagine that special rates existed on voyages to New France where long periods of close navigation were involved in the confines of the Saint Law-rence River and where delayed departures increased the danger from ice and snow, but no such development seems to have occurred. Like the differences between old and new ships, other factors served to balance the risks on any particular trade route in peacetime. Nevertheless French marine insurance rates were high, higher than in either England or the Netherlands, and this prevented the owners from insuring their whole investment. The high rates were due to the failure of any central clearing house to develop and to the control of Parisian underwriters who were notorious for their delays and their failure to pay claims. In the third decade of the eighteenth century the merchants of La Rochelle depended largely on their own and other merchant communities to insure their vessels and were naturally unable to deal in low rates. The owners of the *Fier* insured their venture at the rate of ten per cent of the coverage, which was high even for France. Consequently they only took out protection for 16,000 *livres* on both the ship and the cargo. It is probably no accident that this amount covered the fixed cost value of the ship.

The reduction in coverage may have been made in order to bring the risk into closer agreement with the rate of loss in French shipping which was considerably lower than ten per cent and to give a more accurate reflection of reality. In determining the English rate of loss, five per cent has been suggested as a reasonable, if largely approximate figure.[34] There seems no reason not to use the same rough figure in the French instance. Also, 16,000 *livres* represents forty-six per cent of the total gross capital outlay, on the ship and cargo. By covering this percentage of their investment at the high rate of ten per cent, the French owners may have been estimating the real risk at a loss rate of approximately 4.6 per cent and compensating for it, thereby refusing to overinsure their venture.

The third element, the interest on the capital invested in fixed cost, is the sum of the insurance, 4.6 per cent of the total investment or 1,600 *livres* (1,600 *livres* was the actual premium paid), and the depreciation of the fixed cost, 645.6 *livres* in the first year of operation. In the years to come the owners would diminish the accumulated depreciation charge by a similar amount after each voyage. The total from this addition had to be earned each year, more if the voyages took place at greater intervals, before there was any return on the investment. In the case of the *Fier*, approximately 6.5 per cent of the total capital outlay, or 2,245 *livres* went toward depreciation and provision for sea risks before any interest or profit became available to the owners. It is significant in this respect that the *Fier*'s insurance premium was not paid until four months after the ship's return from Quebec.[35]

The foregoing estimates cannot pretend to a high degree of accuracy, but the main point of the exercise has been to show that the amount involved was considerable and must not be ignored. No record of such calculations has been discovered but this was to be expected in a period when fixed assets in commercial enterprises were a novelty. Nevertheless in the eighteenth century merchants must have begun making such calculations in order to consider the feasibility of commercial ventures of the kind undertaken by the *Fier*, which included fixed assets.

The total earnings from the *Fier*'s voyage to Quebec amounted to 25,556 *livres* 14 *sols*. After all the deductions are made (see Table 11) net earnings of 4,640 *livres* 3 *sols* 6 *deniers* were obtained from a capital outlay of 34,777 *livres* 9 *sols* 8 *deniers*, or a return of approximately 13.3 per cent was realized on the owners' investment. By this time, however, the initial investment had been reduced to the fixed cost element of the ship, or by less than fifty per cent of the total. The question remains why the owners, or anyone else, were willing to accept such small returns for such risky investment as ocean shipping; compared with *rentes* yielding between three and five per cent annually, the profits from this venture were not enormous. When the risks of the two kinds of investment are compared, the question only increases in significance.

Several reasons have been suggested which indicate why the shipping industry attracted capital and grew in France throughout the eighteenth century. At that time merchants did not depreciate their fixed assets, and therefore they might consider a ship's earnings to be larger than was the case, but in the example of the *Fier*, the failure to determine depreciation would raise net earnings on investment only slightly to 15.2 per cent of the total outlay. Nevertheless, as in the case of the *Fier*, the combination of trading with shipping gave the forwarder greater control and security over his goods while *en route* to their destination and permitted him to set departure and arrival dates with greater accuracy so as to avoid tying up large amounts of capital in unprofitable waiting periods. Convenience might well encourage merchant traders to own their own ships especially in the New France trade where margins appeared so narrow. It has already been suggested that it was nearly impossible to earn a profit through shipping alone. Also, the position of the co-owner who outfitted the *Fier* is revealing. Although the capital outlay was equally owned by three men, André Estournel alone outfitted the ship. He charged himself and his co-owners a commission of two per cent on 35,173 *livres* for his services. Thus, in addition to his share of one-third of the net earnings (1,860 *livres*), he also received 702 *livres* for outfitting the venture.[36] Finally the figures in Table 12 reveal the manner in which shippers *could* obtain significant returns. *Fier*'s voyage took approximately 6.75 months to complete during which time 13.1 per cent profit was realized on the investment. The estimated annual rate of return, however, was nearly double that figure. Thus, the ship owner made significant returns when he was able to re-invest his capital as rapidly as possible. Every delay, however, cut into his ability to profit from his venture. As the *Fier* did not sail again until 1729, the annual rate of return might be said to have dropped to a mere 3.4 per cent when spread over four years. Nevertheless, ship owning could be quite attractive to individuals who were willing to pay attention to their ventures and exploit every available opportunity.

Perhaps the nature of shipowning also provides a partial explanation. Ships became a source for the investment of surplus capital. Shares in ships, unlike ordinary commercial partnerships, were freely transferable and there was a considerable market for them.[37] The dangers of non-limited partnerships generally were not as great on the continent as they were in England, but the limited amount of the total capital outlay was attractive everywhere. Shipowning represented a limited liability operation in two senses. First, unlike ordinary commercial partnerships shipping ventures were for relatively short terms and had a specific object in view. Second, a ship represented in its fixed cost a tangible asset, a piece of property with a low rate of depreciation. The only liability to be registered against it would be wages which would hardly exceed the value of the ship. In the case of cargo liability it could be assumed that were the ship to be lost the liability would be covered by insurance. In practice, then, shipowning was a form of limited liability in a period when such a form of investment was almost unheard of, and attractive to surplus capital despite possible low rates of return.

Finally, unlike most commercial partnerships of the period in which capital outlay was tied up in goods to be exchanged, the ship represented a very large lump sum investment which held out possibilities, given the right combination of circumstances, of great gains through fluctuating freight rates.

This was a distinct advantage over the normal commercial partnership that had very little xed element. In the ordinary course of events most of the capital went into exchangeable commodities with a consequent higher rate of risk on return.

It has recently been argued that the distinctive feature of eighteenth century French capitalism was its lack of xed assets and that maritime voyages were viewed as joint ventures at the end of which the ship was sold and the loss or pro t from this transaction entered into the total statement of the voyage.[38] This was undoubtedly the normal case and because of the absence of xed assets eighteenth century books of account contain no evidence of the concept of depreciation. But it must by now be clear that the *Fier* was not a short term asset to its owners. The ownership of the *Fier* represents something new in the development of capitalism. May not it and shipowning generally represent an intermediary step in the development from commercial to industrial capital investment? If so, we have yet another reason why investors or merchants were not deterred from entering shipping activities. Even so the case of *Fier* illustrates the need for these individuals to pursue their activities with great care in order to avoid losses.

TABLES OF EXPENDITURE AND REVENUE
RELATING TO THE VOYAGE OF THE *FIER* TO QUEBEC IN 1725
(all gures are in French *livres, sols* and *deniers*)

Table 1. Total Cost of Material

Wood[1]	3,414	17/6
Pitch, Tar and Oakum	510	18
Masts and Spars	529	
Nails, Ironware and Fixtures	1,913	12
Miscellaneous xed expenditures	276	19
Rigging and Running gear	1,270	
Rope and Cordage	2,090	14
Sails	940	15
Miscellaneous replacement expenditure[2]	966	8/4
Total	11,913	3/10

[1]This sum includes 1,112 *livres* for oak planks *and* some pitch and tar.
[2]This represents an arbitrary attempt to separate those items which last for only one or two voyages from more permanent xtures of construction.

Table 2. Total Cost of Labour

Sailors, 557¹/₆ days @ 30 *sols* each	761	5
Carpenters,³ 1,469⁵/₆ days @ 30 *sols* each	2,395	
Soldiers (unskilled), 89 days @ 20 *sols* each	94	
Gardien during re t	73	18/6
Artisans (xed cost)	488	8/6
Artisans (replacement cost)	276	
Towing, Haulage and Transportation	165	16
Total	4,454	8

³Ship s carpenters wages in New France were considerably higher than those in La Rochelle. In 1735 master shipbuilders were paid between sixty and seventy *livres* per month, or 2¹/₂ *livres* per day; at the same time unskilled labour earned 30 *sols* per day. AN, Col., C11A, CXIV, f. 9.

Table 3. Total Capital Outlay

Hull (purchase price)	4,600	
Materials	11,916	3/10
Labour	4,454	8
Miscellaneous⁴	365	11
Total	21,333	2/10

⁴Includes rent of a berth and expenditure made while away from La Rochelle in search of materials.

Table 4. Total Capital Outlay of the Owners

Fixed cost of the *Fier*			15,789	5/6
Replacement cost of the *Fier*	5,543	17/4		
Ship s victuals⁵	2,247	4/2		
Advances to the crew	1,416			
Total Replacement cost			9,207	1/6
Cost of Cargo onboard			9,781	2/8
Total			34,778	9/8

⁵The cost of revictualling the ship at Quebec, 1,534 *livres* 18 *sols* 10 *deniers*, is not included as part of the capital outlay but as a charge against earnings. This only arose, however, because the owners loaded their own cargo. In another instance the owners would have had to give the captain this amount to purchase supplies for the return voyage and thus increase their investment.

Table 5. Value of the Ship's Cargo Purchased at La Rochelle

34 *Muids* salt @ 8#5s/*muid*	280	10
40 Tonneaux Bordeaux @ 135#/tx	5,400	
11¼ Tonneaux Saintonge @ 110#/tx	1,237	10
8 *grosses barriques* and 28 *quarts* brandy @ 66#/barrique of 27 *velts*	1,771	
8 Quarts vinegar	90	
60 Dozen pieces of Earthenware	144	
55 Dozen drinking glasses in 4 *quarts*	82	10
296 Cooking pots and 300 each covers and handles	775	10/8
Total	9,781	2/8

Table 6. Value of the Owners' Cargo Sold at Quebec

443 *Minots* salt @ 45s & 50s/*minot*	1,001	10
155 *Barriques* Bordeaux @ 80#/barrique	12,400	
27 *Barriques* Saintonge @ 50# & 60#/*barrique*	1,590	
640¼ *Velts* Brandy @ 7# & 8#/*velt*	4,534	15
6½ *Quarts* Vinegar @ 30#/*quart*	195	
47 Dozen pieces of Earthenware @ 4#10s and 4#5s/dozen	218	15
49½ Dozen drinking glasses @ 36s, 40s, 45s and 50s/dozen	107	2
287 Cooking pots, covers and handles @ 5# each	1,435	—
Total	21,482	2

Table 7. Total Expenditures Made at Quebec

Value of cargo purchased at Quebec	17,438	6/10
Duties paid on Wine and Brandy	2,195	3/4
Revictualling charges	1,534	18/10
Lightering and Lading costs	204	13
Total	21,473	2

Table 8. Value of Owners' Cargo Purchased at Quebec

188 Quintals of Dry Cod @ 14#/quintal	2,632	
Planks, Staves and Caskwood	1,480	19
3 Bales of Mixed Furs	903	15
23 Packets and 2 Parcels of Hides	5,748	
64 *Louis d'or*, 550 *Ecus* & *monnaye*	3,224	9/10
10 Bills of Exchange	3,549	3
Total	17,538	6/10

Table 9. *Value of Owners' Cargo Sold at La Rochelle*

180 *Quintals* of Dry Cod[6] @ 15#, 16# & 21#/*quintal*	3,394	2
Planks, Staves and Caskwood	2,188	12
3 Bales of Mixed Furs	1,248	5
Moose and Deer Hides	4,395	1/3
64 *Louis d'or* and 550 *Ecus* diminished by ⅛th of their value in France	2,821	9/10
10 Bills of Exchange	3,549	3
Total	17,596	13/1

[6]The discrepancy between the two amounts is explained by the five percent normally deducted for "bon poid et trait," the figure given includes 380 *livres* weight of scraps sold to a street vender in the port at 8#/quintal.

Table 10. *Gross Earnings from the Voyage*

Total Value of Owners' cargo sold at La Rochelle	17,596	13/1
Additional amounts realized from other sales[7]	358	8/5
Freight earned outbound	6,146	12/6
Freight earned inbound[8]	1,455	
Total	25,556	14

[7]This amount includes prices received for one of the ship's pumps, a broken mast sold for use elsewhere as a bowsprit, and 2,736 *livres* weight of used rope sold to oakum pickers.

[8]Freight inbound was earned on the carriage of mixed furs worth 21,362 *livres* 10 *sols* laded at Quebec for other merchants. (See waste-book, f. 28.) Cargo is noted in ACM, Série B, 4202, 'Estat des pelleteries chargees a fret dans le navire Le Fier cap[ne] Chiron venant de Quebec.'

Table 11. *Net Earnings from the Voyage*

Gross Earnings			25,556	14
Deductions: Cost of Original Cargo	9,781	2/8		
Provisions for depreciation and Sea Risk	2,245			
Replacement costs (victuals and crew's advance)	6,982	14/2		
Post-voyage expenses[9]	1,825	10/10		
Duties and Charges at La Rochelle	82	2/10		
			20,916	10/6
Total			4,640	3/6

[9]It may seem unreasonable to include this amount but most of these expenses occurred immediately after the ship's return and include fresh food for the crew, lightering costs, disarmament and storage charges.

Table 12. Estimated Annual Rate of Return

Length of Voyage		6.75 months
Total Capital Outlay		34,778.5 livres
Total Capital Outlay, less owners' cargo		24,996.3 livres
Gross Earnings		25,556.7 livres
Net Earnings		4,640.2 livres
Monthly Costs: Wages	701.6 livres	
Victuals	322.9 livres	
Ship Replacement	339.5 livres	
Ship Fixed	2339.0 livres	
		3703.0 livres
Monthly Gross Earnings		3786.2 livres
Monthly Net Earnings		687.4 livres
Monthly rate of return on investment		2.0 per cent
Estimated Annual Rate of Return		24.0 per cent

Suggestions for Further Reading

J.F. Bosher, *The Canada Merchants, 1713–1763* (Oxford, 1987).

Dale Miquelon, *Dugard of Rouen: French Trade to Canada and the West Indies, 1729–1770* (Montreal, 1978).

Dale Miquelon, *New France, 1701–1744: A Supplement to Europe* (Toronto, 1987).

Notes

[1] Among recent studies are the monumental work of P. and H. Chaunu, *Séville et l'Atlantique (1504–1650)*, 12 vols. (Paris; 1955–60); B. and L. Bailyn, *Massachusetts Shipping, 1697–1714: A Statistical Study* (Cambridge, Mass.; 1959); J.M. Hemphill II, 'Freight Rates in the Maryland Tobacco Trade, 1705–62', *Maryland Historical Magazine* LIV (1959), 36–58 and 153–87; R. Davis, *The Rise of the English Shipping Industry in the Seventeenth and Eighteenth Centuries* (London: 1962); P. Dardel, *Navires et Marchandises dans les ports de Rouen et du Havre au XVIIIe siècle* (Paris: 1963); J. Delumeau, *Le Mouvement du port de Saint-Malo 1681–1720, bilan statistique* (Paris: 1966); more recently J.F. Shepherd and G.M. Walton, *Shipping, Maritime Trade and the Economic Development of Colonial North America* (Cambridge: University Press, 1972), have used a theoretical framework in their explanation, as have G. Paquet and J.P. Wallot in several recent articles in the *Revue d'Histoire de l'Amérique française*.

[2] The Admiralty archives for the port of Quebec were returned to France after 1760 and subsequently lost. See 'Introduction' to L.G. Verrier's 'Procès-verbal de l'état des registres des greffes du siège de l'Amirauté de Québec', in *Rapport de l'archiviste de la province de Québec, 1920–21*, 106–31. Jean Meyer has noted that "L'examen d'une campagne maritime isolée est fallacieuse: alors que les bénéfices assurés par les 'retours' courent, le capital, aussitôt reinvesti, est deja redevenu productif. C'est le phenomene cumulatif par excellence qui, pour etre vraiment superieur aux place-

ments traditionnels, doit s'effectuer dans les delais les plus courts possibles'; see *L'Armement nantais dans la deuxième moitié du XVIIIe siècle* (Paris: 1969), 222. But despite this warning the rarity of data relating to New France, and the commonly held view that enormous profits were made in maritime trade to New France continues to justify this attempt to analyse the results of a shipping venture to Quebec.

[3] Archives départementales de la Charente-Maritime [hereafter ACM], Série B, volume 355, is the designation of the *brouillard*; fourteen other documents were found in the same series, bundles no. 4202 and 4203; these consisted of captain's instructions, receipts, lading bills and current accounts which all served to confirm and clarify many of the entries written in the waste-book.

[4] ACM, B 4202, Balance sheet of Catignon's account with Estournel from 25 July 1711 to 17 July 1712; also, he was probably the same Jean-Jacques Catignon who rented a room in lower town Quebec in 1713, *Inventaire des greffes des notaires du régime français*, ed. A. Roy, tomes XVIII and XIX, Louis Chamballon (Quebec: 1960–64), XIX, 425–6; see also A. Godbout, 'Familles venues de la Rochelle en Canada', in *Rapport des Archives nationales du Québec*, tome 48, 1970, 170, for information that through marriage in 1714 Catignon became a brother-in-law of the Montreal merchant, Pierre Charly.

[5] ACM, B 4202, Bill of Lading, 11 May 1714; and B 4203, invoice, 17 April 1717.

[6] ACM, B 5715, no. 29, 'declaration de presence,' 14 June 1718; B 4202, crew rolls for 1721 and 1723. While in Quebec during the winter of 1723 the captain became involved in a law suit regarding the payment of the crew's wages, *Inventaire des jugements et délibérations du conseil supérieur de la Nouvelle-France de 1717 à 1760*, par P.G. Roy, 7 volumes (Quebec, 1932–35), I 191, 201; also Archives nationales [hereafter, AN], Colonies, C11A, XLVII, f. 144 and F3, f. 418 also contain references to this ship.

[7] *Encyclopédie, ou dictionnaire raisonné des sciences, des arts et des métiers*, 17 vols. (Paris, 1755–74), vol. XII, 159, defines *patache* as a stationary ship used as lodgings and offices by clerks of the *fermier-général* charged with visiting, entering and departing ships for purposes of collecting duties and examining passports.

[8] AN Col. C11A, CXXIV, *pièce* no. 74, Decision du Conseil de Marine, 3 May 1718; and *ibid.*, XXXIX, f. 3, Vaudreuil and Bégon to the minister, Quebec, 4 October 1718, for a report of the ship's arrival at Quebec.

[9] On page 18 of the waste-book appears the following, '*Les 5 douzieme a Mr. de Courcy est de 11,854 8/9; 2,370 17/9 p[ou]r la 12e de M. Gautier que nous avons pris par tiers.*' These figures indicate that the *Fier* was valued at 28,450 *livres* 13 *sols*. Thus, Gautier removed himself before the outfit was completed.

[10] ACM, B 4202, The burden of the *Fier* is noted on a lading bill signed by the captain for the owners' cargo, 22 May 1725. Nothing is more difficult to unravel than the units of measurement used during the *ancien régime*. Historians have confounded the problem by confusing displacement, tonnage and weight. Tons burden, dead-weight tonnage and capacity are synonymous terms. They are the units used in this paper where tons refers to *tonneaux de mer* of 2,000 French pounds. In 1681 the Ordonnance de la Marine fixed the volume equivalent of this unit at forty-two French cubic feet although a ton weight of wine does not fill quite twenty-eight cubic feet. One explanation assumes that a ship's load was two thirds its capacity to carry it; hence forty-two cubic feet of interior space was needed for each ton

of weight carried. For further details see the very good articles by Paul Gille, 'La jauge au XVIIIe siècle', in M. Mollat, éd., *Les Sources d'histoire maritime en Europe* (Paris: 1952), 465–70; and F.C. Lane, 'Tonnages, Modern and Medieval', *The Economic History Review*, 2nd Series, XVII (1964), 213–33.

[11]R. Davis, 'Earnings of Capital in the English Shipping Industry, 1670–1730', *Journal of Economic History* XVII (1957), 410. This essay has been a constant guide in the preparation of this paper.

[12]*Ibid.*, 410.

[13]A similar calculation for a 160-ton merchantman, bought and outfitted at Bordeaux in 1725 for 28,805 *livres* 10 *sols* would give the same *livres*-ton ratio, 179 *livres* 9 *sols*. In this case, however, the ratio of purchased price to outfitting costs was closer to 4:1 (see J. Cavignac, *Jean Pellet commerçant de gros 1694–1772: contribution a l'étude du négoce bordelais du XVIIIe siècle* (Paris: 1967), 48).

[14]*Brouillard*, f. 22. This differs slightly from the figure of 34,597 *livres* 5/8 that appears on f. 18 of the same.

[15]AN, Col. C11A, XLVII, f. 308v for date of arrival.

[16]See Shepherd and Walton, *Shipping, Maritime Trade and the Economic Development*, 201–3. *Fier*'s ton-man ratio is low even when compared to those for five ships of similar size that sailed to Quebec from La Rochelle between 1676 and 1687! (See ACM, Série B, 5675:210; 5679:381; 5682:391; 235:107 and 137.) During the later portion of the eighteenth century ships of similar tonnage entering Quebec from England were much more efficient. See G. Paquet and J.P. Wallot, 'International Circumstances of Lower Canada, 1786–1810: Prolegomenon', *Canadian Historical Review* LIII (1972), 396–9. Table V, 'Tons per Man on Ships in and out of Quebec by Ship's Size and Origin or Destination, 1786–1810.'

[17]P.W. Bamford, *Forests and French Sea Power, 1660–1769* (Toronto: 1956), 166.

[18]ACM, B 4203. 'Ordre pour le capitaine Chiron lorsque Dieu lui aura conduit a Quebec', 24 May 1725.

[19]AN Col. C11A, XLVII, f. 308v; ACM, B 247, f. 115v; and *Ministère de la France d'outre mer*, Série G 1, 464, no. 1.

[20]*Rapport de l'archiviste de la province de Quebec, 1949–1951*, 285, 'notice biographique'. Crespin's close relations with the owners is revealed in the captain's instructions to seek him out for advice when confronted by any business problems.

[21]ACM B 4202, '*Madame Soumande, son compte courant avec Capitaine Chiron de la Rochelle.*"

[22]By considering the equivalent, the profits from the outbound voyage were reduced, but those from the homebound trip were increased, over the apparent rates.

[23]A. Shortt, ed., *Documents relating the Canadian currency, exchange and finance during the French regime*, 2 vols. (Ottawa: 1925), I:375–93 for the letters patent; some of the devaluation arrêts are also included.

[24]*Ibid.*, I:529 and 551, n. 1.

[25]*Brouillard*, page 29. The owners had to make this currency calculation only for the specie brought back to France. Due to the usual commercial practice of keeping accounts in local currencies no other reduction was required. Cargo was sold and purchased at Quebec at the prevailing rate. In attempting to determine profit on the items traded, rather than on the whole venture, however, it was necessary to

use a common rate and so reduce the prices in New France to *livres tournois*. If this was not done the profit rates would have appeared to be 12.5 per cent higher than those given.

[26]ACM, The previously cited '*Estat de la vente de la cargaison . . .*' included a statement of *coulage*. It reveals that cargo could sometimes be used by the crew for victuals, as was the case for an *ancre* of vinegar, or could disappear completely as did a *barrique* of Bordeaux which was found to be empty on arrival at Quebec.

[27]Salt was measured in *muids*, *boisseaux* and *minots* which themselves varied according to the items being measured. The *Fier* carried thirty-four *muids* or 1632 *minots* of which only 443 were sold. There are several possible explanations of this fact any one of which is probable, but the lack of any indication has forced an exclusion of this disrepancy of seventy-three per cent from these calculations. Cf. *Encyclopédie*, x:558 'muid'.

[28]ACM, B 4202, '*Acquit de payment du Bureau de Quebec*', 15 Oct. 1725. The duties on one *barrique* that was not sold, but was presented to the governor, have been subtracted from the above calculation.

[29]The actual price received at Quebec was 2,957 *livres* 7 *sols*.

[30]A.G. Reid, 'Intercolonial Trade during the French Regime', *Canadian Historical Review* XXXII (1951), 236, 248.

[31]A.J.E. Lunn, 'Economic Development in New France, 1713–1760' (Unpublished Ph.D. thesis, McGill University, 1942), 456 for estimates of annual fur exports after 1716.

[32]See R.-L. Séguin, *Le costume civil en Nouvelle-France*, Musée national du Canada, Bulletin 215, Ottawa, 1968.

[33]R. Davis, 'Earning of capital . . .', 411.

[34]R. Davis, 'Earning of capital . . .', 411.

[35]*Brouillard*, fol. 45.

[36]See Meyer, *L'Armement nantais*, 154–7, for a discussion of the significant profits earned by *armateurs* above those of other co-owners.

[37]Davis, 'Earnings of capital . . .', 424, refers to England, but Meyer, *L'Armement nantais*, provides many French examples.

[38]G.V. Taylor, 'Types of Capitalism in Eighteenth Century France', *English Historical Review* LXXIV (1964), 478–501, see especially 483. Taylor continues his discussion in 'Non-capitalist wealth and the Origins of the French Revolution', *American Historical Review* LXXIII (1967), 469–96.

10

The Military in Eighteenth-Century French America

Allan Greer

Fortified garrisons manned by regular troops, often mercenaries, were part of the standard military landscape in Europe, and a fortress designer named Sebastien le Prestre de Vauban was probably the most famous French military figure in the age of Louis XIV. Most mercenaries were recruited from among the transient elements of society, not always from among one's own nationals. They were not necessarily loyal to the death, and besieging or defending fortified places was less risky than fighting on open fields. The theory of fortresses, left over from the mediaeval period, was that they could dominate the surrounding countryside, and thus had to be captured—usually by expensive and time-consuming sieges—before armies could advance.

In 1713 the French surrendered most of their northeastern territory (much of the country known as Acadia) to the British, retaining Isle Royale and Isle Saint Jean. On the former they soon constructed a major fortress garrison and colony capital, Louisbourg. In 1745 Louisbourg was attacked by a combined navy/army expedition of Britons and American colonials, and it surprisingly surrendered to the invaders after only a brief resistance. In the ill-starred Treaty of Aix-la-Chapelle (1748) it was returned to the French in return for the city of Madras, in India.

One of many weaknesses of Louisbourg was garrison morale, poisoned by a mutiny which had occurred in the garrison over the winter of 1744/45. Allan Greer's article explores this mutiny and its implications in detail. As might have been expected, the mutiny was centred among the mercenary troops, although soldiers from all parts of the garrison had a number of grievances, basically about material losses. The French found in the mutiny a convenient scapegoat for the loss of Louisbourg to the New Englanders. Greer attempts to put the grievances of the troops in the context of garrison life in Louisbourg, and in the process tells us a good deal about military assumptions and expectations in the eighteenth century. What strikes the modern reader is the frequent confusion between civil and military, a feature of life everywhere in the period, which made the mutiny of 1744 more like a strike than an organized rebellion against military authority. In what ways were civilian and military roles mixed together at Louisbourg? Was the action of the troops really a mutiny? What does the rebellion tell us about life in this garrison town? How was the eighteenth-century military different from that of our own time?

This article first appeared, titled 'Mutiny at Louisbourg, December 1744', in *Histoire Sociale/Social History* 10 (1977), 305–36.

Late in December 1744, a mutiny erupted in the fortress of Louisbourg, capital of the French colony of Isle Royale. With only a few exceptions, the soldiers in the garrison turned on their officers, threatening to kill them and ransack the town. Faced with such complete rebellion, the local authorities could only give into the insurgents' demands. As a result, no blood was spilled and the openly violent confrontation was short-lived. Nevertheless, this episode seems to be a noteworthy event in the military history of the eighteenth-century French empire. Unlike other contemporary mutinies, it occurred in wartime and involved the nearly unanimous participation of the soldiery. Certainly the French authorities in the Marine ministry considered it a serious matter and, as a result, some mutineers were severely punished at Rochefort where the garrison was quartered after Louisbourg surrendered to the English in June 1745. The purpose of this essay will be, first of all, to reconstruct the events of the mutiny, not a simple task since the only usable sources, court-martial transcripts and the reports of officers and colonial officials, are all the special pleas of men anxious to save their lives or their careers. Secondly, an attempt will be made to outline the long-term and immediate causes of the revolt. This involves an examination of some of the peculiar characteristics of military life in Louisbourg in the decades preceding the outbreak.

The colony of Isle Royale was established in 1713, although Louisbourg had only been its capital for 25 years by 1744. Administrative hub and centre of the fisheries that were the mainstay of the island's economy, Louisbourg was also a military stronghold. Its massive stone fortifications were designed to protect the colony and guard the maritime approaches to Canada. In the year of the mutiny, the Isle Royale garrison was made up of nine companies of *Troupes de la Marine*, or *Compagnies franches de la Marine*, one of them a special artillery company, together with 150 men from the Swiss Karrer regiment. There were about 600–650 men in all and the majority (perhaps 525–575) were concentrated in the capital, leaving 75 soldiers to man the colony's isolated outposts. Soldiers—that is, military personnel excluding officers—made up about one quarter of Louisbourg's population when a census was taken in 1737. The most important organizational unit in the garrison was the company. Each *compagnie franche* was commanded and administered by a captain who was fairly autonomous, although subordinate to the *état-major*. This body included the town major and his assistants and the commanding officer, who also generally acted as governor of the colony.

The Swiss contingent with its peculiar organization and special privileges was a complicating element in the garrison. It apparently operated as a large company with three subaltern officers and almost 150 men all under the command of a *capitaine-lieutenant*. The latter, usually referred to as the 'Swiss commandant', owed allegiance to his colonel who resided at the regiment's base in France, but he was also subject to the control of the colonial *état-major*. Colonel Karrer was bound by contract to maintain his regiment in the service of the Marine ministry in return for a monthly payment of 16 *livres* per man.[1] In principle, he was responsible for recruiting, equipping, and paying his officers and men. However, in practice, part of the 16 *livres* per man-month owed to Karrer was remitted directly to his officers stationed at Isle Royale for distribution as wages to the troops. The French authorities at Louisbourg gave rations to the Swiss soldiers like those issued to the men of the *troupes de la Marine*. The cost of this food was retained in the colonial treasury. In effect, the Swiss soldiers paid for their rations through wage deductions exactly as the French did, even though Colonel Karrer was theoretically responsible for their upkeep and pay. Karrer's contract guaranteed his regiment certain special privileges, notably judicial autonomy. Most of these were common to all Swiss regiments in the French service. The special status of the Karrer contingent at Louisbourg was often a source of annoyance to the military and civilian administrators of the colony. Bitter disputes occasionally arose when the Swiss officers felt their rights were threatened.[2]

Isle Royale had been at peace with its neighbours during the two decades and more that the fortifications of Louisbourg were under construction but, in the spring of 1744, war broke out between France and England. In the North American possessions of the two belligerents, privateers were soon equipped to prey on enemy shipping and consequently one of the first effects that the war produced in Louisbourg was a shortage of provisions and other supplies. The colony was heavily dependent on imported commodities but French traders hesitated to send their ships across the Atlantic where they might be captured. In Canada, another major supplier of foodstuffs, harvests were poor. To make matters worse in Louisbourg, hundreds of British prisoners captured by the colony's raiders had to be fed in the summer and autumn. More than most other groups however, the soldiers of the garrison, both French and Swiss, were sheltered from the effects of shortages of this kind. In return for a constant deduction from their pay that was unaffected by market fluctuations, the men received rations from the large stocks of flour, salt pork and other staples that the government maintained for their consumption. Occasionally, in times of food shortages, they would be given reduced rations or biscuit instead of bread so that the authorities could distribute supplies from the king's storehouse to needy civilians. Often the problem was one of food quality rather than quantity and soldiers frequently complained when their bread was made of rotten flour mixed with good.[3] Thus, it was not an unprecedented development when late in 1744 the *commissaire-ordonnateur* François Bigot, the colony's highest ranking civilian official, ordered the public sale of foodstuffs from the government storehouse and the soldiers, whose rations were still not reduced, received inferior provisions as a result.

The event that pushed the garrison to revolt occurred about one week before Christmas when the troops received their fortnightly issue of 'vegetables'. These were the dried peas and beans which were the major ingredient of the soup that formed the soldiers' evening meal. In this case, they were rotten and completely inedible. Some men apparently became ill from eating them but those who simply did without and ate only their bread ration and their spruce beer were in no danger of starving.[4] What infuriated the troops was the knowledge that there were good vegetables in the storehouse but that these were being sold to the townspeople; meanwhile, they received swills which they were obliged to pay for through wage deductions. A deputation of Swiss soldiers therefore attempted to return the bad vegetables in exchange for good ones but was rebuffed by the keeper of the royal storehouse.[5] Complaints were made to the commander of the Karrer detachment, Gabriel Schönherr, but they were unavailing.[6]

About 22 or 23 December, a petition addressed to Louis Dupont Duchambon, the acting garrison commanding officer, was drawn up. Some Swiss soldiers visited the barrack-rooms of the *troupes de la Marine* and secured the support of some of the French troops.[7] Thus the petition read, 'A large number of French and Swiss soldiers very respectfully beg you . . . ,' although it seems that only the Swiss, and especially Abraham Dupâquier, Joseph Renard and Laurent Soly, played an active role at this stage. Soly, of unknown nationality, had previously served in the Spanish army and elsewhere. He was killed or captured early in the siege of 1745 and therefore was never brought to trial.[8] Renard was 33 years old, a Catholic and was born in German Lorraine.[9] Most active of the three, it seems, was Dupâquier, a 25-year-old native of Neuchâtel. His family's social standing cannot have been humble as his father was previously lieutenant-colonel in a Swiss regiment in the service of the king of Sardinia.[10] It was apparently he who was chiefly responsible for composing the petition. Fortunately a copy has been preserved and a reading of it makes it evident that rotten vegetables was not the only issue that annoyed the soldiers. In a deferential yet somewhat menacing tone, this document begins with complaints about the vegetables and then proceeds to allude to a number of other grievances after the general observation. ' . . . *vous sçavez Monsieur que l'Injustice regne a touttes mains en ce pays.*'[11]

This petition was not handed over to the commandant immediately, no doubt because the soldiers did not expect it would have any more effect than the complaints to Schönherr if it were submitted in the regular way. Instead, plans were made for a peaceful assembly where it would be presented and the authorities forced to take notice. Joseph Renard testified at his court-martial that there was no question of assembling at the time the petition was drawn up and he and Dupâquier insisted that the idea of bringing the troops out in a mass only occurred to them on the evening before the mutiny. Their testimony seems suspect however. They had every reason to portray their actions as a relatively sudden outburst (all the less culpable since they had been drinking the night of the twenty-sixth) rather than as a premeditated plot. However, the Swiss sergeant Christophe Jout admitted that Soly and Renard had spoken to him the day before Christmas of plans for a peaceful protest gathering.[12] The judges who later tried these men did not, in fact, consider it necessary to establish the existence of a plot before 26 December in order to convict them and showed no interest in pursuing this question. The sources therefore give no indication as to how elaborate the plot was in the day or two before and after Christmas, how many soldiers were privy to it, whether the French were involved or whether a decision was made to bear arms at the projected assembly.

Whenever the plot was hatched, it was the evening of 26 December that Soly, Renard and Dupâquier went from room to room in the Swiss section of the barracks asking the men to join them, *'pour s'assembler le landemain afin de demander a leurs off.ʳˢ de leur procurer Justice sur les Vivres qui leurs Etoient dus . . .'*[13] Some of the men were sleeping but Renard made a list of the names of those who agreed to participate. Afterwards, Renard and Dupâquier were nominated to go to speak with the French soldiers who occupied adjoining rooms.[14] Dupâquier was sent because he 'knew the French', apparently a rare quality for a member of the Karrer detachment. He admitted to having communicated with only a few men in two of the eight French companies and he claims that he merely informed them of the Swiss plans for an assembly. The three leaders then returned to their room and remained awake for the rest of the night.

Next morning, the twenty-seventh, at about six o'clock, the Swiss began assembling behind the barracks building in the courtyard enclosed by the King's Bastion. Although this gathering was completely unauthorized and illegal, it was effected through the use of normal military procedures and routine discipline. The sergeants did not appear as most of them had their own dwellings in the town. However, a corporal named du Croix, who had apparently not been involved in the plans, took charge and arranged the men in their ranks, ordered the drummers to beat out the signal for the assembly and returned to the barracks to order those who had not yet appeared to fall in.[15] He even overruled one of the leading organizers, Joseph Renard, and ordered him to return to his place when the latter began to take some initiative. Dupâquier and Renard later declared at the court-martial that they had not intended to carry arms but had changed their minds when all the others went for their guns after a voice in the crowd had urged them to 'give more weight to their just demands'. They may well have been lying. In any case, the officer who was eventually fetched by the first sergeant found himself facing almost the entire Karrer detachment, armed and in battle formation.

Schönherr was sick at the time and it was Ensign Rasser, the second Swiss officer, who first met the rebellious troops.[16] When the drumming ceased Rasser asked for an explanation and was handed a note which outlined the men's grievances.[17] He examined this and then spoke with a few individual soldiers, one by one, about their complaints. When the ensign recalled the scene eight months later, he remembered the troops' orderly and respectful behaviour and their assurances that they had no intention of committing violent actions or of neglecting their duties to their superiors; they wished only '*de Reclamer leur Justice des Vexations qu'on leur Faisoit Journellement . . .*'[18] Rasser mentioned three specific grievances in this affidavit and prominent among them was the problem of the rotten vegetables. There was also a complaint about work the soldiers were forced to perform without wages for the king's service and for private individuals. Lastly, the men asked for compensation for work they had done on an expedition against Canso earlier in the year and for the pillage they had been promised but had never received.[19]

The complaint about unpaid labour was not a new one for the Swiss. In 1727 they had contested the custom of *piquoit* duty by which the *état-major* made soldiers coming off guard duty spend a few hours cleaning the barracks or doing chores in the government storehouse.[20] The practice persisted however and Joseph Renard complained of having to fetch wood and clean the governor's latrine.[21] Men were often obliged to work without remuneration for their own officers as well.[22] Both Renard and Dupâquier declared at their court-martials that such *ouvrages extraordinaires* were a major source of dissatisfaction.

The treatment of the soldiers who took part in the Canso raid was a specific case that aroused the anger of both French and Swiss troops. Soon after war broke out in March 1744, plans had been made to capture this nearby English fishing post. In its aims and its organization, the Canso expedition bore more resemblance to a privateering venture than to a normal military campaign.[23] It was largely financed by merchants and government officials and was composed of soldiers from the Louisbourg garrison as well as over 200 sailors all under the command of Dupont Duvivier, an influential officer of the *troupes de la Marine.* Duquesnel, the colony's governor, convinced 80 French soldiers and 37 Swiss to volunteer for the mission with the promise that they would have a share of the booty.[24] A small fleet left Louisbourg 20 May and quickly captured Canso and a British naval sloop after a short exchange of cannon fire.[25] The soldiers saw no action until they landed and were ordered to load quantities of codfish, government stores and the private effects of the British inhabitants into the boats. When some hesitated they were roughly treated by their officers. '*Le moindre des Miserables seroit mieux traitté parmi des barbares,*' wrote the men who served on board one of the boats.[26] As soon as the victorious party returned to Louisbourg, the ships' officers and sailors and the garrison officers who had accompanied them made off with most of the plunder before anything was turned over to the courts to be distributed as lawful prize. In the end, the soldiers received nothing for their trouble. Governor Duquesnel, who had guaranteed them a share of the spoils, died on 9 October and, although one group of soldiers addressed a petition to the *ordonnateur* in November, they received no satisfaction.[27]

Rasser listened to these grievances in the courtyard of the citadel. He promised only to communicate them to his superior, Schönherr. Then, warning the men not to repeat their demonstration, he made them present arms and ordered them to return to the barracks and stay there. This done, the ensign rushed to Schönherr's bedside and reported the disturbance. The senior officer told Rasser to ask de la Perelle, the town major, to order the replacement of the bad vegetables. But already it was too late. As he emerged from Schönherr's house, the drums were beating again. This time it was the French sounding the general alarm. After their officer had left, it seems, some Swiss soldiers had gone to the other side of the barracks and reproached the French as cowards for not joining in the demonstration. The men of the *troupes de la Marine* may have been slow to act but once they took up the challenge they were far less restrained than the others. With their intervention the relatively mild protest was transformed into a serious revolt.

Soldiers, both French and Swiss, poured out into the courtyard equipped for battle. The drummers continued to beat the *générale* and, as their comrades assembled, they marched out of the citadel[28] surrounded by an escort with bayonets fixed. As this body passed through the streets of the town, the garrison officers, who for the most part lived in private houses, were roused by what must have sounded like a signal that the fortress was under attack. Coming to the citadel to investigate, they found themselves facing the muskets of men who threatened to 'blow their heads off' if they entered the enclosure.[29] These were the ten soldiers, French and Swiss, who had spent the night on routine guard duty at the entrance to the citadel under the command of the Swiss sergeant, Christophe Jout. Soly and Renard had spoken with him three days earlier about their plans for a demonstration and, the morning of the mutiny, Jout ordered his sentries not to allow any officers or civilians to pass. As the party of drummers marched by the guard post, he was heard to say, '*Les françois commencent à s'animer et ils font mieux les choses que les notres Etant armés Bayonnette au Bout fusil.*'[30]

Eventually a number of officers managed to elude the sentries and gain entry to the courtyard. Among them was Ensign Rasser who described the scene inside as one of tumult and disorder. The soldiers talked openly of killing all the officers and burning the town. The officers present tried desperately with bravado and cajoling to regain control of their companies. According to Rasser, he brought the Karrer contingent to obedience first while the French were still pointing guns at their officers and threatening to shoot if their demands were not met.[31] Meanwhile, Major de la Perelle was following the drummers and their escort through the town vainly ordering them to halt. At one point, he attempted to stand in their path but he was picked up roughly and carried thirty paces.[32] Giving up at length, he went to the citadel where by now the atmosphere had cooled somewhat. The officers had apparently agreed to accept all the rebels' demands and the men showed their willingness to recognize de la Perelle's authority by following, more or less, his parade-ground commands.

Before the major's arrival, acting Governor Duchambon, the supreme military authority in the colony, had appeared at the citadel and surrendered to the troops' demands. Duchambon had no alternative but capitulation. His garrison, almost to a man, was in open revolt.[33] At the best of times, help from France or Canada would take months to arrive but, given the war and British command of the seas, the colony was particularly isolated in 1744. Moreover, there was no alternative force within the colony that could dream of opposing the rebels, as the Isle Royale militia, unlike its Canadian counterpart, was small and ineffective. The promise to redress all grievances quelled the violence, but the soldiers remained uneasy. Duchambon and Bigot, writing to the Minister of Marine four days later, declared that the complaints of the French and the Swiss were identical but the specific demands they mentioned as having come from the French troops were not the same as those presented to Rasser by the Swiss. The situation was confused and a great variety of demands were apparently put forward. The governor and *ordonnateur* recorded three of them: (1) an increase in the issue of firewood and the return to the soldiers of five cords of wood confiscated for theft; (2) the immediate distribution of the rations that some of the men had missed because they were away participating in the Canso attack and in a later expedition against Port Royal, and (3) the reimbursement of the clothing deduction that had been taken from the wages of more than 100 French recruits who had arrived in 1741 but never received the uniforms it was supposed to have paid for.[34]

The second demand in Duchambon's and Bigot's list was not repeated in any other document. It is possible that, in reporting to the minister, they may have misinterpreted or misrepresented much more serious complaints about the treatment of volunteers during and after the Canso raid. At any rate, the only contemporary account of the mutiny not written by an observer directly involved in the events considered injustices committed against the Canso volunteers to be the major grievance of all the soldiers.[35] The complaint about the missing uniforms was a uniquely French affair but it had much in common with the rotten vegetables problem which aroused the anger of both French and Swiss troops. The soldiers had often endured with patience delays and shortages in the issue of military supplies and allowances but they were annoyed that wage deductions were not adjusted when items they paid for were not delivered.

The soldiers' demand for more firewood cannot have come as a surprise to the local authorities as they had long been aware that fuel supplies were inadequate. Within a few years of the founding of Louisbourg the scrubby spruce forest had been stripped from all the country within three miles. The minister in France was eventually persuaded to allow wood to be purchased for the garrison but only at the rate of one half cord per man even though about twice that quantity was required to last through the long Cape Breton winter.[36] The men were therefore obliged to cut and transport half their fuel and each year several of them contracted frostbite and injured themselves scrambling over the brush and stumps in order to fetch a few logs of what was in fact inferior firewood. The exceptionally cold winter that had arrived earlier than usual in 1744 must have made the mutineers' demand for an adequate fuel supply especially emphatic.[37] As for the confiscation before Christmas of five cords of 'stolen' wood, the soldiers' petition to Duchambon alluded to this event in rather different terms. It seems that a group of soldiers returning to the town with a load of firewood were met by some officers claiming to own the land where it had been cut. The officers ordered them to turn over the wood and then broke the sledge they had used to carry it.[38]

Military discipline and punishment, wages, the routine hardships of service and the dangers of war do not seem to have been issues for the mutinous soldiers. Instead, their objectives were extremely modest. They showed no desire in their words or actions to modify the military system or to subvert the hierarchical structure of the garrison except as a temporary emergency measure. All the recorded grievances that were brought up by the French and the Swiss were essentially complaints about material losses and the redress the men sought was monetary compensation.

Consequently, one of the rebels' first acts was to make use of the established sentry posts in the town to secure control of the government storehouses and the house of François Bigot, the man in charge of finances and guardian of the colonial treasury.[39] The governor and the officers had promised to give in to the soldiers' demands but it was up to Bigot to make the actual payments. Of course, had they wished, the mutineers could simply have seized what they wanted but, despite repeated threats to do so, they never undertook such bold action. Apparently interpreting Duchambon's surrender as implicit recognition that their demands were justified, the soldiers ended their complete and open defiance of the officers and proceeded to secure what they felt was legitimately theirs in a fairly orderly fashion.

A deputation went to call on Bigot to arrange for the fulfillment of the officers' promises and presented the *commissaire-ordonnateur* with accounts of sums due to all the men for injustices committed over the past few years. It is not clear how long the negotiations lasted but the deputies apparently returned on several occasions over a period of months. Bigot later bragged of how he stalled and prevaricated with the representatives, '*les amusant de belles promesses*' and avoiding payment for as long as possible until frightened into submission by veiled threats against his life.[40] His own accounts indicate that only 3000 *livres* were given to the men. This would have amounted to an average of about six *livres*, the price of three or four bottles of wine, for each man in the garrison.[41]

Although there were no further dramatic confrontations like the one that took place on the morning of 27 December, Louisbourg remained in a state of alarm in the days that followed. The civilian population was terrified as groups of soldiers spoke openly of massacres and destruction and engaged in a form of *taxation populaire*, threatening merchants with swords and forcing them to sell them goods at what they considered a 'just price'.[42] Bigot and Duchambon described this situation when they first reported their predicament to the minister on 31 December. Their letter had a tone of urgency that verged on panic: '*Nous sommes ici leurs Esclaves, ils font tout le mal qu'ils veulent.*'[43] Bigot outlined the elaborate precautions he took to keep this communication and its destination a secret. He was convinced that the troops would sack the town and turn it over to the English if they knew he was requesting that an armed force be sent from France to punish the rebels. And yet the fact that no one was killed or even injured, the absence in the records of complaints from merchants who actually sustained losses and, most of all, the soldiers' subsequent conduct during the siege, all lead to the conclusion that these men were remarkably restrained in the use of every weapon except their mouths. Certainly the soldiers were extremely angry. The situation was an explosive one that could easily have erupted into open violence but the mutineers seemed well aware that their bravado and threats frightened the authorities and had the effect of advancing their own interests. Moreover, it was no accident that the mutiny occurred at a time when the state of war and rumours of impending British attack strengthened the soldiers' position by making the officers and colonial officials feel all the more vulnerable.

Unfortunately, it is impossible to discover exactly what happened in the early months of 1745 since the best sources, the courts-martial and Ensign Rasser's deposition, concentrate exclusively on the period up to and including the morning of the assembly. For the courts of military justice, it was this act of defying and threatening officers that constituted the crime of mutiny and they showed no interest in its aftermath. However, according to François Bigot, the only informant for the later period, the revolt lasted five months. '*Tout l'hiver se passa dans cette émotion*', he wrote, stating elsewhere that the troops '*n'avoient pour ainsi dire reconnu aucune autorité*' from December to May 1745.[44] Bigot of course is not the most trustworthy of witnesses and he had an obvious interest in exaggerating the duration of the mutiny and his own role in handling it. It would be more accurate to describe this period as one of latent rather than open revolt. The men had recognized the officers' authority after their capitulation in the courtyard, but the latter must have exercised that authority with the greatest of caution. Unwilling to overturn the established hierarchy, the soldiers were nevertheless in a position of unaccustomed power at this time and they used the threat of violence to ensure that those in command treated them fairly according to their own standards. The officers and civilian officials did not dare oppose them and even avoided using *le ton de leurs places*.[45] This was hardly a normal situation and, in Bigot's eyes, it constituted continued revolt.

Nor do we know how the soldiers organized themselves at this stage, how they chose their representatives or how they managed the business of compiling their demands for compensation and distributing the proceeds. Bigot mentions in passing that the men elected their own officers and he describes the deputies who negotiated with him simply as *les plus séditieux*.[46] He felt that most of the rebel leaders were Swiss and that Abraham Dupâquier was most prominent among them. Bigot noted no dissension between the men of the *troupes de la Marine* and those of the Karrer regiment and, in fact, he gives the impression that they co-operated more fully in the period of negotiations than they had earlier. In any case, whatever the state of relations within the garrison may have been, the entire situation changed drastically with the intervention of an outside force six months after the outbreak of revolt.

When the New Englanders landed to lay siege to Louisbourg 11 May 1745, Duchambon assembled the garrison and urged the troops to forget the past and unite with the officers and townspeople in facing the enemy. The men demurred at first and asked for a guarantee that no one would be punished for taking part in the mutiny. Naturally the governor consented and, together with Bigot, solemnly promised a complete pardon in the name of the king.[47] In the subsequent fifty-day siege the troops according to all reports acquitted themselves well.[48] At no time had they ever questioned or attempted to evade what they considered to be their duty as soldiers. Still, when they were called upon to repair the fortifications that were damaged by cannon fire, they would only work for double the normal labourer's wage and with immediate payment in cash.[49] Perhaps twenty or thirty soldiers were killed before the town surrendered at the end of June,[50] and among the first casualties was Laurent Soly, one of the principal Swiss instigators of the mutiny.

After the surrender of Louisbourg the garrison was evacuated and most of its members arrived at the French port of Rochefort in August 1745. The French companies were later sent back to Isle Royale in 1749 when the colony returned to French rule, but a great many, perhaps the majority, of the men who had experienced the mutiny and siege died or deserted before the garrison was re-established.[51] No detachment from the Karrer regiment ever went back to Isle Royale as Duchambon and Bigot convinced Maurepas, the Minister of Marine, that it was the Swiss who had not only initiated the mutiny but also led the French soldiers in the days that followed the first outbreak.[52]

Although aware that the garrison had fought well, Maurepas felt that news of the soldiers' discontent had determined the English to attack Louisbourg and he tended to blame the mutiny for the fall of the fortress.[53] Perhaps a certain desire to identify a scapegoat for the loss of Isle Royale accounts for the minister's insistence on the need for severe punishment to restore discipline among the colonial troops. In August 1745 he instructed de Barrailh, the governor of Rochefort, to make discreet inquiries on the subject of the Louisbourg mutiny and to arrest those identified as ring-leaders by the colonial commander and *ordonnateur*. When courts-martial were organized late in the fall, Maurepas ordered them to look into the soldiers' complaints against their officers.[54] There was no excuse for rebellion but Maurepas, who was well aware that irregularities had long been common in the Isle Royale garrison, intended to take some disciplinary action against those officers whose unfair treatment of the men had been particularly flagrant. The records give no indication that any officer was ever actually punished.

In view of the special status of the Karrer regiment, the Swiss mutineers could only be tried by courts-martial composed of their own officers. These were held in the second half of November 1745. A number of those accused were released but five men were convicted and sentenced to death.[55] Of these, one died in prison and another, Abraham Dupâquier, escaped. François Bigot was furious when he learned that the *premier chef* of the rebels had escaped the noose. '*Si celuy de qui dependoit sa sûreté eut été pendant six mois à la discrétion de ce misérable, comme je l'ay été,*' he wrote, '*il seroit encore en prison.*'[56] Maurepas was also displeased, all the more so as there were hints that Colonel Karrer and his officers may have intentionally provided the Lieutenant-Colonel's son with an opportunity to flee.[57] Some of Dupâquier's comrades were not so fortunate. Joseph Renard and Corporal du Croix were hanged on 7 December and their bodies were left on the gallows at Rochefort all day, *afin de servir d'exemple a un chacun.*[58] Two days later, Christophe Jout was decapitated hours after appearing before the court-martial where he expressed the hope that he too would be an example to others.

. . . il savoit bien qu'il alloit perdre la Vie . . . mais que son Exemple devoit
apprendre aux off. command. pour le Roy de tenir la main a ce que le soldat ne fut
point Vexé et que Luy fut distribué bons conformem. a l'intention de sa majesté les
Vivres payés sur leur solde . . . [59]

The courts-martial of the French mutineers were delayed for a time when
the accused brought up the pardon they had been promised by Duchambon
and Bigot. Maurepas quickly intervened however, declaring that the king
could not be bound by the promise since he had had no knowledge of it and
insisting that examples be made of some of the men of the *troupes de la Marine.*
We have no accounts of the French courts-martial but other records indicate
that at least eight men were condemned. Five of these were hanged in January
1746, one died in prison and two were sentenced to life terms as galley slaves.[60]
In all, eight men were executed as a result of the Louisbourg mutiny, making
it a more severely punished event than any of the revolts André Corvisier
mentions in his study of the French army from 1700 to 1763.[61]

Because of the limitations of the historical sources, our knowledge of the
mutiny is far from complete. Still, it seems sufficient to support a few conclusions about the basic nature of the event which should be reviewed as a
preliminary to an analysis of the mutiny's origins. Occurring at a time when
the state of war provided the soldiers with a favourable opportunity for
successful action and touched off by an issue of spoiled vegetables, the revolt
was essentially an armed assembly of protest intended to achieve some limited
objectives. Almost all the men in the garrison were involved and they
demanded material compensation for certain specific grievances. They did
not attempt to depose their superiors but rather frightened them into com-
plying with their wishes. If the mutineers' behaviour was restrained considering the circumstances, it must not be supposed that they acted with cool
detachment in the pursuit of rationally defined goals. In fact, they were
extremely angry. Simply by disobeying and threatening the officers, they
committed an offense punishable by death. They would not likely have done
so if their resentment was not deeply rooted and if they did not have more
at stake than a few *livres.* Some of the rebels' spleen was vented against the
merchants of the town and against François Bigot but the primary target of
their ire was the officers. Whereas actions against Louisbourg's civilians were
sporadic and relatively mild, only the officers had to face the assembled
muskets and staunch hostility of their men.

In attempting to explain the Louisbourg mutiny, historians have tended to
emphasize two causal factors, the officers' exploitation of the men and the
soldiers' miserable living conditions.[62] The mutineers certainly felt they had
been cheated by their officers but nowhere in the documents concerned
with the mutiny is there any hint (beyond the reference to a demand for
more firewood) that they revolted because they were 'disgusted with their

living conditions'.[63] It is true that the material conditions of life were very hard for the men of the Louisbourg garrison but generally they were no worse, and in many respects they were better, than those to which other eighteenth-century soldiers were subjected. A Louisbourg soldier did not always receive his rations in the prescribed amounts or qualities but he could easily supplement his diet by hunting and scrounging and never went hungry as his counterparts in France often did when they were in the field or in peacetime when sudden rises in food prices would occasionally make them unable to subsist on their fixed money allowance.[64] His annual issue of cloth-ing was often defective and sometimes was not delivered for years in a row. Still, he was no worse off than soldiers in the French infantry and he could consider himself blessed in comparison to the men of the Albany garrison in 1700 who were, according to the governor of New York, in a 'shameful and miserable condition for the want of cloaths that the like was never seen in so much that those parts of 'em which modesty forbids me to name, are expos'd to view.'[65] He was not given an adequate supply of firewood and, although this did not make him unique among soldiers of the period, he may have suffered more from it than men who served in France because of the severe climate of Isle Royale. As for the 'squalid and oppressive barrack conditions' that supposedly 'led to the mutiny',[66] the Louisbourg barracks were certainly not luxurious accommodation but they were probably more comfortable than the stuffy and disease-ridden barracks at Aix and less crowded than those in Marseilles where 30 or 40 men lived in a room with seven beds, 'comme du bétail dans une écurie'.[67] In fact, the soldiers' rooms were repaired and the bedding improved in the early 1740s so that they would likely have been more comfortable in 1744 than they had been in earlier periods.[68] In general, the notion that the men of the Louisbourg garrison were particularly wretched by contemporary standards is difficult to accept in view of their exceptionally low mortality rates.

Misery and hardship were the common characteristics of all soldiers in the eighteenth century, and of a great many civilians as well. Their presence alone accounts for neither the turbulence of the Louisbourg soldiers nor the loyalty of other, more wretched troops. Neither does it help to explain the timing of the mutiny which occurred when the men of the colonial garrison were, in some respects, better off than they had ever been in the past. The revolt should therefore not be dismissed simply as an *émeute de misère*; instead, it should be understood as the reaction of a group of men with a certain set of material interests and attitudes faced with a particular combination of circumstances. The main motive for the soldiers' uprising was the economic exploitation to which their officers subjected them. Var-iations in the intensity of this exploitation along with the mens' evaluation of the prospects for successful violent action help to explain the timing of the event.

More important however are the 'structural causes' of the mutiny. These are the enduring characteristics of the soldier's position in the Louisbourg garrison which generally encouraged the formation of group habits of thought and action among the soldiers and kept them at odds with the officers. Obviously, the first pre-condition of concerted group action is the existence of a group with some common interest and awareness of itself. The structure of military life in Louisbourg from about 1720 to 1744 formed such a group of the soldiers and enabled them to react collectively to the situation that arose in 1744. Besides the positive factors promoting unity among the men, there were negative factors which intensified solidarity through common hostility to the officers. The colony's system of recruitment emphasized the division between soldiers and officers and was one of the most important of these negative factors.

Of course, officers and soldiers occupied very different positions in the social hierarchy of the eighteenth century. In the Isle Royale garrison, however, the gulf between the two groups was exaggerated, partly because of the very different backgrounds of their members. The officers of the *troupes de la Marine* had very strong roots in the Louisbourg community. Most of those serving in 1744 had been born in the colony or had come from elsewhere in North America at an early age. They had extensive ties of kinship and marriage with their fellow-officers and with the Louisbourg merchants who were often their business partners as well. Their men, on the other hand, were almost all born in France and came to Isle Royale as isolated individuals. Parish and judicial records provide the places of birth in France of 67 men of the French companies between 1720 and 1745. Of these, 31 (46 per cent) were born in towns and cities (12 in Paris alone), a disproportionate urban representation in a country where about 5/6 of the population was born in the country.[69] The backgrounds of members of the Karrer detachment were extremely diverse but they did not distinguish officers from soldiers in any clear way. However, the impersonal recruitment practices of both the French and Swiss elements of the Isle Royale garrison reinforced the alienation of soldiers and officers.

In the regular army, each captain was responsible for recruiting men to fill the vacancies in his company. Ideally he solicited recruits from the same region year after year and would have some knowledge of the populace and they of him.[70] In many cases, the family estate provided a captain with a steady supply of replacements and this 'feudal recruitment' was, according to the most eminent historian of the French army, an important factor promoting cohesion in many companies where the officers and some of the men would be linked in a paternalistic relationship that often predated their entry into the military.[71] In actual practice however, much of the manpower needs of the eighteenth-century army were supplied by professional recruiters whose only interest was in collecting the cash payment they earned for each body they delivered and whose unscrupulous methods for extracting signatures from young men earned them the pejorative title of *racoleurs*. The impersonal practice of *racolage* divorced the act of recruitment from the responsibilities of command. While it was not uncommon in the regular army, it was all but universal in the colonial *troupes de la Marine* and in the Karrer regiment.[72]

The men who eventually came to Louisbourg, then, did not enlist in a particular company under a particular officer. In fact, few of them could have been certain when they signed their names that they would be sent to Isle Royale and not another colony. Until the 1720s, recruits for all the French colonies were gathered together at the Ile d'Oleron near Rochefort, and then embarked on ships bound for Canada, Isle Royale or the Caribbean with no regard for the wishes of the men involved.[73] In later years, a certain number of troops were raised each year specifically for the Isle Royale garrison but there was always a certain amount of shuffling and mixing of recruits at Rochefort so that a man destined for service in one colony could easily end up in another.[74]

In the *troupes de la Marine*, recruitment was not only impersonal, it was also frequently involuntary. A few recruits sent to Louisbourg were victims of *lettres de cachet*;[75] others were taken straight from the prisons of La Rochelle,[76] and of these a substantial number were army deserters whose lives were spared on condition that they serve in the colonies.[77] A great many ostensibly voluntary enlistments were doubtless the result of the tricks and pressure tactics of *racoleurs*. It would be a mistake, however, to conclude that such *soldats malgré eux* were ever a majority in the Isle Royale garrison. Some men joined the colonial troops to escape from legal or other difficulties in France.[78] Most probably enlisted out of a desire for adventure, a need for security and an assured subsistence or a sincere military vocation. They would likely have received a more substantial enlistment bounty from an infantry regiment, but they ended up in the *troupes de la Marine* because, in many cases, their health, size or age would have made them unacceptable to any other branch of the French armed forces.[79] The number of soldiers appearing in the Isle Royale records who were under the official minimum height of 5 *pieds* 1 *pouce* or below the minimum age of 18 years, is proof of the laxity of recruitment standards in the colonial troops.[80]

Obviously, recruitment standards were not effectively enforced simply because sufficient numbers of volunteers could not be found otherwise. The colonial forces did not enjoy a good reputation in France and it was not so much because of their niggardly recruitment bounties or because service overseas was considered particularly hard. Men hesitated to join the *troupes de la Marine* because they did not expect ever to return home once they had left Europe.[81] This popular 'prejudice', although exaggerated, was not without foundation. While men joining the regular French army or the Karrer regiment were committed to serving a limited term (usually six years), most recruits for the colonial *troupes de la Marine* signed *engagements perpétuels* which effectively bound them to remain soldiers until the king saw fit to release them.[82]

The sources do not allow any precise calculation of the duration of military service at Isle Royale. However, circumstantial evidence and the testimony of contemporaries make it clear that soldiers in the colony, *troupes de la Marine* much more than Swiss, generally served for unusually long periods. Swiss and French had little hope of terminating their military careers except with an official discharge and the French *troupes de la Marine* usually obtained one only after a great many years. In France and in the colonies, most men left the service through death, desertion or discharge and the following table shows the respective importance of each compared with similar statistics for a typical regiment of the French infantry.

Soldiers Leaving the Isle Royale Garrison, 1721–1742[83]

	total	death	desertion	discharge	other
IR troupes de la Marine, 1721–42	670	130	43	470	27
	100%	19%	6%	70%	4%
IR detachment, Karrer regt., 1723–24;	153	37	2	112*	2
1730–42	100%	24%	1%	73%	1%
Vivarais-Infanterie regt., 1716–49	3842	1374	1046	1290	132
	100%	36%	27%	34%	3%

*The officials at Louisbourg could not discharge men from the Karrer regiment but only record their return to France where presumably they were discharged.

These figures clearly demonstrate the preponderance of discharges as the end-point of soldiers' careers in the colonial garrison. This contrasts strongly with the situation which prevailed in the regular army where—paradoxically, in view of the predominance of limited periods of enlistment there—only one-third of the men left with discharges while roughly equal numbers died or deserted. The relative importance of discharges does not mean that the Isle Royale authorities were more generous in this regard than their counterparts in France; instead it is the result of comparatively low rates of death and desertion in the Isle Royale garrison.

Between 1730 and 1740 inclusive, the average annual rate of mortality among the Isle Royale soldiers, French and Swiss, was slightly less than 20 per thousand.[84] The annual average in the Vivarais-Infanterie regiment was over 80 per thousand during the same period (34 per thousand if wartime years are excluded).[85] The men of the colonial garrison were of course spared the rigours and dangers of campaigning, but they also lived in a healthy climate and seem to have suffered much less than the infantry soldiers from epidemics and food shortages. The statistics are also affected by the artificial selection process that resulted from the government's policy of discharging the sickly and the lame.

Desertion from the French army was quite common in the eighteenth century. Soldiers who were dissatisfied with the service, and those who were momentarily annoyed with an officer or in danger of being punished for a crime could generally escape and disappear into the surrounding population with only a minimum of planning and luck.[86] Deserters from the Isle Royale garrison, on the other hand, found themselves in a wilderness that was an extremely hostile environment for Europeans with a few settlements that were far too small for a fugitive to avoid detection. In most of the 45 recorded cases therefore, men, usually in groups of two or more, attempted to reach the Acadian settlements at Beaubassin, some 250 miles from Louisbourg in the British colony of Nova Scotia. The journey was difficult and perilous and the destination unattractive. It must be assumed that these deserters had extremely pressing motives for leaving the garrison—in fact, a few of them were fleeing justice after committing a theft—or else an immoderate degree of determination or foolhardiness.[87] Of the 45, nineteen were apprehended and ten of these executed, a very high rate of capture by contemporary standards even if one assumes that only half the actual desertions were recorded. Moreover, the majority of the colony's desertions occurred at the outposts of Port Toulouse and Isle St Jean which were much closer than Louisbourg to the mainland. Desertion, then, was hardly a practical option for Louisbourg soldiers who were unhappy with their lot.

The official policy on discharges was frequently repeated in the minister's despatches to Isle Royale governors:

> *l'Intention de sa majeste est que les congez ne soient donnés qu'aux Invalides et a ceux qui voudront se faire habitans, Je vous recommande de ne point en congedier d'autres sans des ordres exprès.*[88]

At least 24 men left the colony's *troupes de la Marine* between 1721 and 1742 with *congés de grace* which their families had obtained by petitioning the minister and paying 150 *livres* to the Marine treasury.[89] A few other soldiers, Swiss and French, obtained discharges that were conditional on their remaining in the colony. The metropolitan authorities hoped to establish at Isle Royale a system which had contributed greatly to the development and population of Canada where soldiers had often been encouraged to marry and settle on the land with offers of discharges and material assistance.[90] Because of the inferior quality of Cape Breton soils however and because of the absence of established agricultural communities, the military settlement program was a failure. As the colonial administrators were unwilling to lose good soldiers in what they considered a vain scheme, only a handful received discharges or permission to marry. The most important result of this for our purposes was that the Isle Royale soldiers were denied an exit route by which many men stationed in Canada were able to escape from a service that was not to their liking.

Most of the discharges at Isle Royale were given to men described as 'disabled'. When the documents occasionally give more details about individual cases, the most striking feature of the lists is the large number of soldiers who were sent home crippled from injuries received in accidents during the construction of the fortifications of Louisbourg.[91] Another form of discharge, the *congé d'ancienneté*, though not mentioned in the minister's instructions cited above, was awarded to old soldiers who had served as long as forty years.[92] Depending upon the number of recruits available and the vacancies created by deaths, desertions and discharges of other sorts in a given year, as many as ten or twelve of these veterans might be released or none at all. Men on six-year enlistments had priority but even they were not always sent home as soon as their terms had expired.[93] There is no way of determining the length of time that the majority who had unlimited enlistments served but it seems that in most cases it was considerable. Unless he were particularly lucky, a man in the *troupes de la Marine* of Isle Royale could expect to serve for decades or until he was the victim of a crippling injury. Still, the Louisbourg official who referred to service of this sort as *un Espece d'esclavage* was exaggerating.[94] There were a number of escape hatches such as the *congés de grace*, the settler's discharges and perhaps a few fictitious invalid's discharges.[95] However, these opportunities for departure were rare and unreliable. For most of the colony's French soldiers, the prospect of leaving the service must have appeared remote and uncertain in the extreme. The situation was temporarily worsened after 1743 when, because of the threat of war, the awarding of discharges was entirely suspended in both the *troupes de la Marine* and the Karrer regiment.[96]

It would certainly be a mistake, however, to assume that every soldier wanted to escape the Isle Royale garrison. There is actually one case of a sickly young man who cried and begged his captain not to discharge him as an invalid.[97] The point is that, insofar as there was discontent and resentment in the garrison, it had few outlets. Contemporaries frequently remarked that the prevalence of unlimited terms of enlistment in the *troupes de la Marine* was productive of low morale.[98] The prospects for promotion into the officer corps, which were nil, could not have improved matters.[99] Admittedly, six-year terms were the rule in the Karrer detachment which initiated the revolt. However, since all the Swiss in the colony were stationed at Louisbourg, desertion was even rarer among them than among the French. They were also less likely to benefit from settlers' discharges. If he were angry with his officers, homesick or dissatisfied with military life, the Isle Royale soldier, Swiss at least as much as French, was discouraged from responding in an individualistic fashion. More than a continental French soldier who could desert with little chance of being punished, and more than a man attached to the Canadian troops who could exchange the military musket for the colonist's axe with relative ease, he had a permanent stake in his position as a soldier. Individual evasion of the military being more difficult at Isle Royale than elsewhere, collective action within the system was proportionately more likely.

Several characteristics of military life in Louisbourg operated in a more positive and direct way to encourage cooperative habits and a group spirit among the soldiers. To begin with, almost all of them were housed in one large barracks building. In the first half of the century, barracks were still a novelty and, in many French garrison towns and throughout Canada, troops were dispersed and billeted in the homes of civilians.[100] In Louisbourg, by contrast, every man was in close contact with his comrades and especially with the fifteen or twenty who shared his room and who together formed a group called a *chambrée*. Besides sharing common living and sleeping quarters, the men of a *chambrée* ate together and cooked common meals in one large pot. They also tended to spend a great deal of their leisure time together and the barracks room was a favourite spot for drinking, conversation and lounging. Not only was the *chambrée* an important unit in a soldier's life—Renard, Soly and Dupâquier, the three principal instigators of the mutiny, were apparently of the same room— but the barracks environment, where officers seldom entered, was well suited for the discussion of grievances and for conspiracies and plans for concerted action. The frequency of mutinies among naval forces has often been explained in terms of the solidarity bred by life in the fo'c's'le.[101] Similarly, the Louisbourg revolt can be seen partly as a result of the barracks situation which helped to foster a sense of community and also provided an environment favourable to secret organized action. The accounts of the mutiny show that the leaders took good advantage of its potential.

Outside the barracks, the men of the Louisbourg garrison, like soldiers everywhere, were in constant contact with their fellows while engaged in such activities as guard-duty and drills. What makes them unique however is the fact that so many of them devoted very little time to these military pursuits as they worked six months of every year, building Louisbourg's fortifications. The construction of a European-style fortress in North America was an ambitious project and one which was never completed. Since civilian workers could not be persuaded to come to the colony, all the unskilled labour was performed by the troops of the garrison.[102] Not all the soldiers were employed in this way. Many were not strong enough for the heavy work involved and a number were always required for duty in the outposts and guardrooms. In the 1720s when many of the massive excavations were completed, more than half of the colony's soldiers worked on the fortifications.[103] By the years around 1740, the proportion of working soldiers may have been somewhat smaller but most of the men must have had some experience as construction workers. Canada also had a labour shortage and many men in the *troupes de la Marine* stationed there were allowed to take jobs in the community. However, the soldiers from Canada were generally employed by private individuals, and so their work, like their system of lodging, had the effect of dispersing them.[104] Some Isle Royale soldiers also found employment with civilian parties but generally the voracious labour demands of state-financed construction at Louisbourg tended to concentrate them at one place under one employer.

If there were factors promoting a certain group feeling among Louisbourg's soldiers, there were nevertheless some divisions within the garrison that precluded the formation of a completely unified outlook. First of all, non-commissioned officers wielded considerable authority over the men in their daily affairs and received higher wages. The thirty members of the élite artillery company were also better paid than the other French soldiers. Because of their specialized duties, the cannoneers did not work on the fortifications and they were further set off from the others by their special barracks rooms and distinctive uniforms.[105] Most importantly, both the cannoneers and the French sergeants owed their special positions to the officers' appreciation of their superior merit (corporals were chosen on the basis of seniority alone).[106] Not surprisingly, they stayed aloof from the mutiny.

The most significant complicating factor in the Louisbourg garrison however was the division between Swiss and French. The men of the Karrer regiment with its special privileges, traditions and procedures were separated from the others in many of the external formalities of military life, such as uniforms and drum signals, and also in some more essential matters, such as pay. Many of them were Protestants and most spoke German as a first language. The few glimpses of the soldiers' daily life afforded by judicial records give the impression that socializing between French and Swiss was not common. A Swiss or a French soldier would have had more extensive dealings with others of his own group, and especially those who were in his company and *chambrée*. In the 22 years the Karrer regiment was represented in the garrison, however, its members would have had considerable contact with the men of the *troupes de la Marine* as they worked together on the fortifications, served together in mixed guard details and were housed in the same building and treated in the same hospital. There is even evidence of a high degree of mutual trust between individual French and Swiss in the two recorded desertions from the Karrer detachment. In both cases, a Swiss soldier fled with a group of French deserters.[107] Generally, the two major components of the Louisbourg garrison lived separately but enjoyed harmonious relations. Certainly, there is no evidence of hostility of the sort that led to fist-fights and duels between the men of two infantry regiments that were stationed at Louisbourg in the 1750s. In the early stages of the mutiny, the French and the Swiss acted independently but their differing tactics were aimed at achieving essentially, though not exactly, identical objectives.

Although the men of the Louisbourg garrison did not form a completely cohesive group, they shared a common awareness of their distinct identity as soldiers that, along with the factors mentioned earlier, helps to explain the solidarity they manifested during the mutiny. The judicial records occasionally give indications of the importance they attached to the external signs of the warrior's profession. In one case, two men were convicted of breaking into a house and stealing a few items of little value. One of their prizes was a piece of ribbon which they had a tavern keeper's wife fashion into fifteen *cocardes* so that they and their comrades could wear these specifically military adornments in their hats.[108] Another incident resulted from a dispute between a butcher named Dupré and a Swiss soldier who wished to sell some partridges he had shot. At one point, the soldier threatened to hit his opponent with the butt of his musket but the butcher managed to wrestle the weapon away from him. Hurling insults behind him, the vanquished soldier retreated towards the barracks but returned later, accompanied by two Swiss armed with sticks, and demanded the return of his gun. When Dupré refused, the three attacked him, calling him *bougre* and shouting, '*Tu desarme un soldat.*' They beat him savagely, stabbed him in the chest and finally left him in the street, unconscious and gravely wounded.[109] The accounts of the victim and other witnesses give no hint that any national or religious animosity was involved in this incident. Instead, the brutal actions of the Swiss can best be interpreted as revenge against what they considered to be a serious offence on the part of a civilian who deprived a soldier of his weapon, the distinguishing mark of the military estate.[110] Similarly, anger over the treatment of the volunteers who participated in the Canso expedition—anger which helped produce the outbreak in December 1744—should be seen as a product of the traditional notion that a victorious warrior ought to receive a share of the fruits of conquest.

Behind the actions of the mutineers seems to be the general belief that a soldier is an armed man who receives the king's money and his bread, as well as plunder on appropriate occasions, in order to fight his master's enemies and protect his possessions. When the men were given bad rations without what they considered legitimate reason, they felt not only deprived but insulted. Being made to work at unsoldierlike tasks without remuneration was also galling. The cannoneers received high wages for their special duties and skills, but the other soldiers felt they were entitled to their subsistence pay by virtue of performing strictly military service such as guard-duty.[111] Work in itself was not unacceptable as long as it was considered quite independent of a man's duties and status as a soldier and was paid for as such. What incensed the mutineers was having their officers treat them as mere labourers rather than as men-at-arms who occasionally worked for extra money. At his court-martial, Joseph Renard was asked if he had any complaints against his officers. He replied, *qu'il avoit grievem', lieu de se plaindre des Torts a luy arrivés par la mauvaise qualité des Vivres qui faisoient partie de sa solde ainsy que de tous les ouvrages qu'on l'avoit forcé de faire a la descente de la garde et cela sans salaire quoique ces ouvrages Etoient Indépendans de son Service et de son devoir . . .*[112]

The authorities shared the soldiers' attitude to a large degree and they never questioned the proposition that men who worked on the fortifications should be given a supplement to their normal wages. The way in which this extra pay was remitted however was not always to the soldier-workers' satisfaction and the economic history of Louisbourg's military labour force sheds a great deal of light on the origins of the soldiers' hostility towards their officers which characterized the mutiny.

The construction of Louisbourg's fortifications was not administered directly by the crown but rather farmed out to a private contractor who was responsible, among other things, for paying the soldier-workers. The state nevertheless took an active role in the project, partly through the chief engineer, a military officer independent of the colony's military command, who superintended the works and was in charge of the discipline of the work force. The engineer and the contractor usually cooperated closely but the governor also had some authority over the works and he and the other staff and company officers also exercised authority over the men.[113] Thus the administration was complicated and, in the 1720s when the soldier-workers still received their wages directly from the contractor, they were often able to take advantage of the fact that the engineer together with the contractor was often at odds with the governor and the officers, and neither party was able to claim their undivided obedience.

Although theoretically free agents in the labour market, physically fit soldiers who were not required for duty in the outposts and guardrooms were often obliged to work. One of their primary tasks was excavating and moving earth for the massive ramparts and ditches and they worked as day labourers or, more frequently, on a piece-work basis in gangs led by a *'chef d'attelier'* who was himself presumably a soldier.[114] The workers were allowed to negotiate pay scales collectively with the contractors and, in the early years, they occasionally staged demonstrations and refused to work in order to force their employer to raise the rates.[115] The governor could intervene in case of deadlock. He was not directly interested in keeping down construction costs but was more concerned about morale and about the difficulties of keeping the soldiers at the fortifications at a time when a boom in private construction provided them with an alternative source of employment. Therefore, he often settled disputes in favour of the men.[116] As the only substantial work force in the 1720s when public works in the colony were particularly extensive, the soldiers were in a relatively strong position and one that was in some ways strengthened by their military status, which meant that their subsistence was secure and their physical welfare the responsibility of the company captains. It is difficult to determine how much money the soldier-workers earned as a result but the minister of Marine concluded from the reports of 'strikes' and *émeutes* that they were becoming rich and consequently insubordinate.[117] It was one thing to establish pay rates, however, and another to collect the actual wages. Owing to delays in forwarding funds, the contractor frequently found himself unable to pay the men in cash and resorted to the expedients of distributing notes which could only be redeemed at a discount, or paying in goods, especially wine. When funds were available, the workers were paid every two weeks, after which, according to the authorities, the majority went straight to the taverns and did not reappear for several days.[118]

As a wage earner the soldier-worker was well-placed, but as a consumer he was extremely vulnerable. Since soldiers were not allowed to buy from merchants on credit, the custom was established from the earliest years of the colony's existence of giving each captain a monopoly on sales to the men of his company.[119] This commerce was considered a duty as well as a privilege as it consisted mainly of essential items such as shoes and stockings—the standard military issues of these articles were never sufficient—as well as tobacco, liquor and extra food.[120] The officers provided these *fournitures* at greatly inflated prices and, in order to collect their debts, simply had the 30 *sols* per month that remained of their men's military wages after deductions paid directly into their hands. This monopoly was not complete, however, and in the 1720s the captains frequently complained of the contractor's practice of increasing his profits by advancing goods to the workers in lieu of wages.[121] Furthermore, these officers claimed the soldier-workers consumed much more merchandise than their military pay would afford and, although they had to be given clothing to protect them from the winter, they quickly squandered any cash they received from the contractor in the summer and neglected to repay their officers.[122] Thus, captains and contractors struggled for a greater share of the soldier-worker's earnings.

In the early years, the contractor had the advantage of being supported by the Marine ministry but the captains had the backing of the colonial governor. The officers scored their first victory in 1721 when they obtained permission for a sergeant to be present at paydays in order to compel workers in need of new clothing to purchase it on the spot.[123] The contractor successfully resisted these pretensions however, and in 1727 the French officers complained that their men were being paid mostly in merchandise and in advance. They asked that the wages soldiers earned working on the fortifications, like their military wages, be turned over from the contractor to the company captains who could deduct the value of each man's debts and pay him the balance in cash.[124] This was already the practice in the Swiss contingent but it was not until some time in the 1730–1735 period that the officers of the *troupes de la Marine* gained such complete control over the fruits of their men's labour. How or why they defeated their opponent is not clear but it is certain that, from that time until 1744, the captains derived a substantial portion of their total incomes from the profits they made from their soldier-workers. They were not negligent in searching for ways to increase these.

The administration of the Isle Royale garrison was never very orderly before 1745 and there is no indication that the captains were obliged to keep close accounts or to report to anyone on how they disposed of the workers' wages with which they were entrusted. They soon began paying the men their cash balances only once a year at the end of the construction season, thereby all but eliminating the possibility that any of them could stay out of debt.[125] In view of the limited demand for shirts and shoes, they expanded their merchandising facilities, concentrating on an institution called the canteen. In the 1730s and forties, each captain operated a canteen where his men could drink wine and spirits on credit and at exorbitant prices. Complaints about the canteens and their effects on drunkenness and absenteeism multiplied around 1740 when there were even allegations that officers forced working soldiers to spend their earnings on drink.[126] When the newly appointed governor Duquesnel arrived in the colony, he reported that the soldier-workers generally received no money whatsoever and he identified the situation as *un viel mal.*

> *Il faut attaquer les fournitures qu'on fait aux soldats et les Cantines, qui font que quelque travail que fasse un travailleur, il ne voit jamais un sol on luy fait tout Consommer, de la livrongnerie et le degout pour le travail, auquel ils ne vont que forcés.*[127]

In the late 1730s and early 1740s, the minister of Marine in France manifested a concern over abuses in the Louisbourg garrison that indicates he thought matters were more serious there than in Canada where the officers' routine appropriation of the military pay of working soldiers had been tolerated for years.[128] He had received reports about the confiscation of soldier-workers' pay and about other forms of exploitation, such as the captains' practice of taking the uniforms from the bodies of dead soldiers and 'selling' them to new recruits.[129] Two new governors were appointed from outside the colony, de Forant in 1739 and Duquesnel in 1740, and instructed to remedy the situation. The officers were threatened with exemplary punishment unless they began treating their men more fairly and Maurepas actually went so far as to suspend the awarding of the *Croix de St Louis* in the garrison in 1742.[130] Neither the minister nor the governors however could effectively oppose the firmly entrenched interests of the officers. The latter convinced them that their salaries were not sufficient to support a family in a difficult and expensive colony like Isle Royale. Consequently, no fundamental change was made in the system of exploitation which left a captain free to dispose of his men and their earnings as he saw fit.[131] Still, the governors exercised some restraining influence over the officers. However, when Duquesnel died in October 1744 and the command was assumed by Duchambon, a veteran of the Isle Royale officer corps, there is reason to suspect that the inhibitions that limited officers' profiteering at the soldiers' expense were abandoned.

The gap in outlook, background and material interests between the Louisbourg soldiers and their officers was considerable. The impersonal recruiting practices of the Karrer regiment and the *troupes de la Marine* were not of a sort to reinforce the soldier's deferential attitude to his superiors nor his attachment to his company commander. Neither did the divided loyalties that accompanied the soldiers' employment under the fortifications contractor enhance the officers' authority. More important though was the unexampled economic tyranny which the officers, as paymasters, creditors and monopoly retailers, exercised over their men. As they gained exclusive control over the soldiers' earnings, they used their power for increasingly blatant exploitation which probably had a severe effect on their men's material prosperity. Whether it impoverished them or not however, it certainly appeared unjust to its victims and, more than anything else, it accounts for the discontent that eventually led to violence.

The company officers at Isle Royale showed more concern for their own profits than for their men's morale but they had little incentive to do otherwise. In the regular French army, by contrast, captains who wished to minimize the considerable trouble and expense of recruitment had a selfish interest in preventing desertion and encouraging re-enlistment by keeping their men as contented as possible.[132] Colonial officers of the Karrer regiment as well as the *troupes de la Marine*, on the other hand, had no regular recruitment responsibilities and those resident at Louisbourg were in relatively little danger of losing men through desertion and military settlement programs, regardless of the level of morale.

As it was so difficult for soldiers, especially those who served in the *troupes de la Marine*, to leave the colonial garrison, Louisbourg was very much a 'pressure-cooker'. As the officers' exploitation became more intense, there was no real 'safety valve' of desertion which otherwise might have rid the community of its most disaffected elements. Instead, the likelihood of a major explosion increased. This is not to say that the relationship between stimulus and response was mechanical in any literal sense. Rather, the objective circumstances of the soldier's position in Louisbourg were such that aggressive group action was a relatively feasible reaction to severe discontent. Individual evasion was not a practical alternative as it was for many of the French troops stationed in France and in Canada. Moreover, factors such as the systems of work and lodging gave the men experience that enabled them to think and act collectively.

Already, in the 1720s, the soldier-workers had been involved in confrontations resembling modern strikes. Their opponent however was generally the fortifications contractor. When the company captains gained control of their wages in the following decade, the men were much less bold in dealing with such powerful and prestigious adversaries who had at their disposal the military system of discipline and punishment. As a result, there were no reported *émeutes* from the late 1720s until 1744. In the end, the soldiers only overcame their fear and deference when the exploitation they suffered became particularly severe and when the state of war temporarily strengthened their hand.

Nevertheless, although these structural and short-term factors that produced both unity and discontent among the soldiers made a confrontation likely in 1744, they do not entirely account for the outbreak of mutiny by themselves. Soldiers in the eighteenth century simply were not accustomed to defying their officers. Like other contemporary groups from among the popular classes, they only opposed their superiors openly when they were convinced that their cause was a righteous one. The 'justifying ideology' that sanctioned the revolt and determined the form it took can, to some extent, be inferred from the mutineers' words and actions. Certainly the men felt their actions were legitimate. They showed no desire to command in the place of their officers, but only to force the latter to rule in a proper fashion. Therefore the mutiny as an open revolt ended quickly and the men returned to nominal subordination as soon as assurances were given that their grievances would be redressed. Throughout the period that followed, the leaders drew up accounts and negotiated payments in an orderly fashion without ever challenging the authority of the *commissaire-ordonnateur*. The soldiers had only resorted to force after milder forms of protest were ignored. This type of action was, of course, extremely destructive of military subordination, but it was intended only as a temporary emergency measure that would compel the authorities to correct the situation in which wages and other benefits were unlawfully withheld. The men seemed quite confident that their aims were not a threat to the hierarchical system since they merely demanded that actual practice in the garrison be consistent with official policy.

What the soldiers sought in 1744 was 'justice' and the word itself occurs frequently in the courts-martial and other records of the mutiny. On the surface, the justice they demanded was in the form of monetary compensation for material losses to cheating officers. On another level, they were asking to be treated with the respect due to a soldier. A soldier, these men apparently felt, earned plunder and subsistence wages by fighting and guarding. He might agree to perform other, unrelated duties in return for pay but he should not be used as a beast of burden or as a milk-cow by those who exercised military authority over him. From the mutineers' point of view, it was the officers who had subverted the military system over the years, and the soldiers who were obliged to restore a proper balance. Their procedures, as they assembled behind the barracks to the beat of drums and under the supervision of corporals, were eminently soldier-like and consistent with their limited objectives.

Was the mutiny a success? In the short term, the men's limited objectives were apparently achieved. They were given compensation for unfair wage deductions—admittedly, the sources do not make it clear whether the soldiers were ever completely satisfied on this point—and the officers and government officials treated them with respect. Trusting the authorities' promises of amnesty, however, they were defeated in the end. It is possible that matters might have ended differently had the garrison not had the bad luck to be conquered six months after the first uprising and sent to France where the soldiers' power relation with the officers was reversed. A few men might have been saved from the hangman in this case and the officers might have been more restrained in their profiteering as long as their memory of the mutiny remained vivid, but the economic and power position of the soldiers would not have changed in any fundamental or enduring way. Since they had no intention of effecting any institutional or structural changes in the garrison, it is difficult to imagine their revolt resulting in anything more than a temporary modification of the existing order.

The mutiny was not without lasting results, however. The minister of Marine had attempted to reform the abuses in the Isle Royale garrison from as early as 1739 but, when the colony was re-established as a French possession in 1749, the recollection of the violence of 1744 must have added some urgency to his campaign to reform the military administration. As a result, the garrison was run in a much more regular fashion in the second period. There was still exploitation but it was controlled and systematized so that Captains were limited to profits of 25 per cent on purchases made by their men.[133] Perhaps the soldiers found this parasitic system less annoying than the more blatant one that prevailed earlier. In any case, no further incidents of organized resistance at Louisbourg were recorded. However, most of the 'structural causes' of the mutiny remained after 1749. The fundamental characteristics of military life in the colony were always of a sort that insurrection was possible, since they promoted solidarity among the soldiers and alienated them from the officers. Accordingly, in 1750 the engineer Franguet still observed among the soldier-workers '*un Esprit de Sedition et de revolte*'.[134]

Suggestions for Further Reading

Raymond F. Baker, *A Campaign of Amateurs: The Siege of Louisbourg, 1745* (Ottawa, 1978).

Reginald Blomfield, *Sebastien Le Prestre de Vauban, 1633–1707* (London, 1938).

Christopher Moore, *Louisbourg Portraits: Life in an Eighteenth-Century Garrison Town* (Toronto, 1982).

George A. Rawlyk, *Yankees at Louisbourg* (Orono, Maine, 1967).

Notes

[1] Archives Nationales, Archives de la Marine (hereafter cited as AM), A1, Art. 69, pièce 33, *Capitulation du Regiment Suisse de Karrer*, 25 Sept. 1731.

[2]See, for example, Archives Nationales, Archives des Colonies (hereafter cited as AC), C11B, Vol. 23, fols. 60–64, Duquesnel to Minister, 19 Oct. 1741.

[3]See, for example, *ibid*., Vol. 20, fols. 104–5, de Bourville to Minister, 24 Dec. 1738.

[4]Three years earlier, they had gone without vegetables for an extended period although their bread ration was reduced at the same time. *Ibid*., Vol. 24, fols. 87–89v, Bigot to Minister, 18 June 1742.

[5]Archives de la Guerre, Archives du Service Historique de l'Armée (hereafter cited as ASHA), XI *Deposition juridique reçue par ordre de Monsier de Karrer . . . de Mrs. les officiers des detachements de la compagnie colonelle . . . en garnison cy devant à Louisbourg . . . à l'occasion de l'émeute à l'Isle Royale au mois de decembre 1744*, 29 Aug. 1745 (hereafter cited as 'Rasser deposition'). The French may also have participated; the document is not precise on this point.

[6]*Ibid*.

[7]AC, C7, 272, dossier Joseph Renard, transcript of the court-martial of Joseph Renard, 7 Dec. 1745 (hereafter cited as 'Renard court-martial'); *ibid*., copy of the petition of a number of soldiers addressed to Duchambon, [22–23?] Dec. 1744 (hereafter cited as 'Soldiers' Petition').

[8]Renard court-martial.

[9]*Ibid*.

[10]AC, E, 157, dossier Abraham Dupâquier, transcript of the court-martial of Abraham Dupâquier, 9 Dec. 1745 (hereafter cited as 'Dupâquier court-martial').

[11]Soldiers' Petition.

[12]AC, E, 233, dossier Christophe Jout, transcript of the court-martial of Christophe Jout, 9 Dec. 1745 (hereafter cited as 'Jout court-martial').

[13]Renard court-martial.

[14]Dupâquier court-martial.

[15]AC, E, 145, dossier Jean-Baptiste du Croix, transcript of the court-martial of Jean-Baptiste du Croix, 7 Dec. 1745 (hereafter cited as 'du Croix court-martial').

[16]Rasser deposition.

[17]Renard court-martial; Dupâquier court-martial. The testimony does not make it clear whether this was the same petition to Duchambon that was written several days earlier. Dupâquier testified that he wrote a note outlining grievances the morning of the demonstration. He may have been lying in order to be consistent with his story that there was no plot before 26 December. Since the specific complaints that Rasser recalled were not the same as those listed in the petition to Duchambon, it is quite possible that Dupâquier drew up a second petition shortly before the mutiny began.

[18]Rasser deposition.

[19]These are the same three complaints that Renard and Dupâquier later mentioned at their court-martials.

[20]AC, C11B, Vol. 9, fols. 72–78v, St-Ovide to Minister, 21 Nov. 1727.

[21]Renard court-martial.

[22]Antony Steur seems to have been in this case when he passed the winter of 1739 at Spanish Bay hunting partridges for the benefit of Cailly, the Swiss commander. AC, Outremer, G2, Vol. 185, fols. 379–424, trial of Jean Larue dit le Gascon, accused of murder, 16 Mar.–30 Apr. 1739. For evidence of similar illicit practices

in the French companies, see AC, C11B, Vol. 11, fols. 61–68, de Mézy to Minister, 4 Dec. 1730.

23George Juan de Ulloa and Antonio de Ulloa, *A Voyage to South America* (trans. J. Hopkins) vol. II (London: 1806), 380.

24AC, F3, Vol. 50, fol. 415, an account of the Canso expedition, n.s., n.d. [1744].

25G.A. Rawlyk, *Yankees at Louisbourg* (Orono, Maine: 1967), 3–5.

26AC, Outremer, G2, Vol. 188, fols. 304–05, Requette à M. Bigot de Marin Halest et *25 autres volontaires*, 8 Nov. 1744.

27*Ibid.*

28The King's Bastion and the barracks building formed an enclosed citadel usually referred to in French as '*le fort*'. The 'fortress', on the other hand, was the town together with the entire system of fortifications.

29Rasser deposition.

30Jout court-martial.

31Rasser deposition.

32AC, C11B, Vol. 26, fols. 231–34, '*Copie de la Lettre ecritte à Mr. le Comte de Maurepas par Mrs. Duchambon et Bigot à Louisbourg le 3ʳᵉ Xᵇʳᵉ 1744*', [31 Dec. 1744] (hereafter cited as 'Duchambon's and Bigot's letter').

33Duchambon and Bigot reported that only the French sergeants and the thirty men of the elite artillery company refused to join in the mutiny. *Ibid.*

34*Ibid.*

35Anon., *Lettre d'un Habitant de Louisbourg* (trans., ed., G.M. Wrong) (Toronto: 1897), 34.

36AC, C11B, Vol. 23, fols. 13–14v, Duquesnel and Bigot to Minister, 10 Oct. 1741.

37De Ulloa, *op. cit.*, 375.

38Soldiers' Petition.

39Anon., *Mémoire pour Messire François Bigot, ci-devant Intendant de Justice, Police, Finance & Marine en Canada, Accusé: contre Monsieur le Procureur-General du Roi en la Commission, Accusateur*, vol. 1 (Paris: 1763), 7–9.

40*Ibid.*, 8.

41AC, C11C, Vol. 12, fol. 167, '*Bordereaux de la recette de dépense faitte à l'Isle Royale pendant l'année [1744]*', 2 Apr. 1746.

42Price-setting of this sort was a common feature of eighteenth-century insurrections, especially bread riots in England and France. See, George Rude, *The Crowd in History; a Study of Popular Disturbances in France and England* (New York: 1964), especially 19–32; E.P. Thompson, 'The Moral Economy of the English Crowd in the Eighteenth Century', *Past and Present*, 50 (Feb. 1971), 76–136. Only one account of the mutiny (Duchambon's and Bigot's letter) reports any manifestation of this type of behaviour. The other documents mention vague threats to sack the town but they give no evidence of hostility on the part of the soldiers directed specifically against the merchants.

43Duchambon's and Bigot's letter.

44Anon., *Memoire pour Messire François Bigot . . .* , I, 8; AC, Dépôt des Fortifications des Colonies, Am. Sept., no. d'ordre 218, Bigot, '*Relation du siege de Louisbourg*,' 15 Aug. 1745.

45Anon., *Mémoire pour Messire François Bigot . . .* , I, 8.

46*Ibid.*

[47]*Ibid.*, 9.

[48]*Ibid.*; AC, C11C, Duchambon to Minister, 23 Sept. 1745. Two Swiss deserted and one French soldier was executed for treason during the siege but this is not a sign of excessive disaffection by eighteenth century standards.

[49]AC, F³, Vol. 50, fol. 378v, Bigot, 'Sur la prise de Louisbourg', Aug. 1745.

[50]One list of casualties reported a total of 50 deaths on the French side but this includes civilians as well as soldiers. AC, F3, Vol. 50, fol. 407, n.d., n.s.

[51]AC, D²C, Vol. 48, 'Liste des Soldats des Troupes servant ci devant a l'Isle Royale désertés à Rochefort', [n.d.], [n.s.]; AC, B, Vol. 84-2, fol. 289, Maurepas to de Serigny, 10 Feb. 1746.

[52]Duchambon's and Bigot's letter; AC, B, Vol. 82-2, fol. 377, Maurepas to Karrer, 14 Sept. 1745.

[53]AC, B, Vol. 82-2, fol. 369, Maurepas to de Barrailh, 20 Aug. 1745; *ibid.*, fol. 377, Maurepas to Karrer, 14 Sept. 1745. In fact, news of the mutiny could not have reached New England in time to affect the plan to attack Louisbourg. Reports in the summer and fall of 1744 of low morale in the garrison however did encourage the New Englanders to attempt the invasion. Rawlyk, *op. cit.*, 27–57.

[54]AC, B, Vol. 82-2, fol. 403, Maurepas to de Barrailh, 23 Nov. 1745.

[55]AC, C11C, Vol. 9, fols. 118-21, Bigot to Maurepas, 11 Dec. 1745.

[56]*Collection de Manuscrits contenant lettres, mémoires, et autres documents historiques relatifs à la Nouvelle-France* vol. III (Québec: 1884), 271 (Bigot to Minister, 2 Dec. 1745).

[57]AC, B, Vol. 82-2, fol. 412, Maurepas to Karrer, 10 Dec. 1745; *ibid.*, fol. 415, Minister to de Barrailh, 15 Dec. 1745.

[58]Du Croix court-martial.

[59]Jout court-martial.

[60]AC, D²C, Vol. 53, 'Isle Royale, Rolle général des Troupes françoises commencé en 1739,' n.d., n.s.; Archives Maritimes, Port de Rochefort (hereafter cited as Port de Rochefort), IE, 141, Maurepas to Ricouart, 18 Jan. 1746.

[61]André Corvisier, *L'Armée Française de la fin du XVIIᵉ siècle au ministère de Choiseul; le Soldat* (Paris: 1964), 883.

[62]Guy Frégault, *François Bigot, Administrateur français* (Montréal: 1948), I, 207; Rawlyk, *op. cit.*, 71–2; Robert J. Morgan and Terrence D. MacLean, 'Social Structure and Life in Louisbourg', *Canada, an Historical Magazine* 1 (June 1974), 66.

[63]Rawlyk, *op. cit.*, 71.

[64]Corvisier, *op. cit.*, 834–6.

[65]Quoted in W.J. Eccles, 'The Social, Economic, and Political Significance of the Military Establishment in New France', *Canadian Historical Review* LII (March 1971), 6.

[66]Morgan and MacLean, *loc. cit.* Cf. Frégault, *loc. cit.*

[67]Quoted in Albert Babeau, *La Vie militaire sous l'Ancien Régime*, Vol. I, *Les Soldats* (Paris: 1889), 85–8.

[68]For example, new sheets and mattresses replaced the vermin-infested straw in the barracks rooms in 1740. AC, C11B, Vol. 22, fols. 40–40v, de Bourville and Bigot to Minister, 20 Oct. 1740.

[69]This sample is too small to be statistically valid, but it does suggest that the proportion of urban recruits was much greater in the *troupes de la Marine* than in the regular French army where about 30% of the men were born in towns. Corvisier, *op. cit.*, 390, 394.

[70]De Guignard, *L'École de Mars* tome I (Paris: 1725), 682; Corvisier, *op. cit.*, 163–78.

[71]Corvisier, *op. cit.*, 355–6.

[72]On 'racolage', see *ibid.*, 179–95; Georges Girard, *Racolage et Milice; Le service militaire en France à la fin du règne de Louis XIV* (Paris: 1922), 75–161. Occasionally officers from the Isle Royale *troupes de la Marine* on leave in France would raise some recruits for the colonies, but they did so to fill vacancies not in their companies but in their purses. There was an exception in 1730 when two companies were added to the garrison. The newly appointed captains, de Gannes and Dailleboust, were sent to France to recruit some of the men they would later lead. These officers were born in Acadia and Canada respectively and it is unlikely that they engaged in the traditional sort of recruitment that required a certain degree of mutual confidence. Still, they at least had some long-term interest in the men they enlisted. AC, B, Vol. 54-2, fol. 520, '*Ordre du Roy au sr. de Gannes pour levée de Soldats*', 7 Mar. 1730. The recruitment of Swiss soldiers for service at Isle Royale was also impersonal. Karrer officers enlisted men for the regiment as a whole and not for particular companies. The officers stationed at Louisbourg had no recruitment responsibilities as long as they stayed in the colony. AC, F2C, Art, 3, fols 323–26v, Décisions de la Marine, 29 June 1722.

[73]See, for example, Port de Rochefort, IE, Vol. 86, fols. 241–46, Pontchartrain, 27 Feb. 1715.

[74]*Ibid.*, Vol. 116, fol. 404, Maurepas, 10 June 1732.

[75]These were special orders of the king that, in these specific cases, were granted at the request of parents who wished to have troublesome sons exiled. See, for example, AC, C11B, Vol. 8, fols 55–64v, St. Ovide to Minister, 20 Nov. 1726.

[76]Port de Rochefort, IE, Vol. 101, fols. 617, 621–22, de Morville, 31 May 1723.

[77]*Ibid.*, Vol. 87, fols. 645–51, Council, 28 May 1716. Cf. Corvisier, *op. cit.*, 720.

[78]Thomas Beranger dit La Rosée, for example, injured a peasant in a drunken brawl. When criminal proceedings were initiated, he fled to Rochefort and immediately joined the *troupes de la Marine*. AC, Outremer, G2, Vol. 182, fol. 215. '*Conseil Supérieure, Procedure criminelle . . . a l'encontre du nommé Nicolas LeBegue dt, Brulevillage et Thomas Beranger dt La Rosée soldats acusés de vol*,' 3 Mar.–2 June 1733.

[79]Isle Royale recruiters generally received only 30 *livres* per man. This sum was supposed to cover their expenses (including enlistment bounties) and provide them with a profit. See, for example, Port de Rochefort, IE, Vol. 116, fols. 360–61, Maurepas, 20 May 1732. Even if the entire amount were turned over to the recruits it would have compared unfavourably with the more substantial bounties offered by the recruiters who supplied the other branches of the French armed forces. Corvisier, *op. cit.*, 328–39.

[80]Of 21 men whose heights were recorded because they deserted or appeared in court between 1720 and 1745, four were under the minimum height. In the regular army, such short men were extremely rare. Corvisier, *op. cit.*, 640–1. Underage recruits were accepted even more readily, again in contrast with the more selective infantry. One governor remarked with satisfaction that the majority of the 40 soldiers arriving at Louisbourg in 1726 were 15 and 16 years old. AC, C11B, Vol. 8, fols. 55–64v, St Ovide to Minister, 20 Nov. 1726, Cf., Corvisier, *op. cit.*, tables between 476 and 477.

[81]AC, C11B, Vol. 33, fols. 89–91v, de Raymond to Minister, 12 Oct. 1753.

[82]See AC, B, Vol. 69, fol. 68, Maurepas to Duval, 22 Feb. 1739. The only systematic listing of terms of enlistment is a muster roll which dates from 1752. It indicates that, of 1067 men in the Isle Royale garrison at that time, only 59 (5.5%) had six-year *engagements limités*. Archives du Séminaire de Québec, Papiers Surlaville, 55–8, *Signallement general des trouppes de l'Isle Royale*, [13 Mar. 1752]. The proportion may have been slightly higher before 1744.

[83]These figures were pieced together from a variety of sources. All of them, whether ration lists, reviews or isolated references in the governor's correspondence, were apparently based on the official headcounts prepared by a civilian bureaucrat and updated with information supplied by the major. The most consistent and useful source is the accounts of the keepers of the government storehouse. AC, C11B, Vols. 11–25, *passim.*, '*Etat de la recette et consommation des vivres faittes dans les magasins du Roy à l'isle Royale . . . subsistance des troupes . . .* '. They are complete for the 1730–41 period and they show the number of men supplied with rations in each company and in the Swiss contingent along with the date at which the number changed because of a death, desertion, discharge or the arrival of a recruit. These statistics are not completely reliable. Desertion in particular may have been somewhat under-recorded, but data on the regular army were subject to similar distortions. Figures on the Vivarais-Infanterie are from Corvisier, *op. cit.*, 585 (cf. 583–8).

[84]Calculated on the basis of information derived from the ration accounts (see note 83).

[85]Corvisier, *op. cit.*, 684–5.

[86]*Ibid.*, 700–3. Under similar conditions, groups of French and Swiss recruits destined for Isle Royale were often decimated by desertion before they left France. Port de Rochefort, IE, Vol. 103, fol. 319, Maurepas, 6 June 1724; AC, B, Vol. 58, fols. 167v–68, Maurepas to de la Croix, 13 July 1733.

[87]For an account of the difficulties encountered by one deserter who was eventually apprehended on the Nova Scotia mainland, see AC, C11B, Vol. 7, fols. 78–93, '*Procedure criminelle extraordinaire instruite à l'Encontre du nommé michel Laugier d^t alexandre accusé de desertion*', 18 Oct. 1724.

[88]AC, B, Vol. 53, fols. 584–84v, Maurepas to St Ovide and de Mézy, 22 May 1729.

[89]For example, *ibid.*, Vol. 65, fol. 442v, Maurepas to St Ovide and LeNormant, 26 Feb. 1737. The governor and *commissaire-ordonnateur* were not allowed to accept money payments directly from soldiers anxious to purchase their freedom. The minister reserved to himself the right to order discharges '*par des considerations particuliers*'. AC, B, Vol. 74, fol. 563v, Maurepas to Bigot, 6 June 1742.

[90]AC, F3, Vol. 50, fols. 161–62v, ordonnance, 26 June 1725. Cf., Louise Dechêne, *Habitants et Marchands de Montreal au XVIIe siècle* (Paris and Montréal: 1974), 80–8.

[91]AC, D2C, Vol. 47, *passim*. Many of these 'invalids' would have been unable to earn a living but only a small minority could ever hope to draw a pension.

[92]AC, C11B, Vol. 7, fol. 19, St Ovide to Minister, 16 Nov. 1724; *ibid.*, Vol. 20, fols. 317–17v, '*troupe*' (unsigned, undated mémoire), [1738].

[93]AC, B, Vol. 70, fols. 389–89v, Maurepas to de Forant, 7 May 1740.

[94]AC, C11B, Vol. 7, fols. 267–71, de Mézy to Minister, 7 Dec. 1725.

[95]For one example of a healthy man discharged as an invalid, see AC, B, Vol. 53, fols. 583v–87, Maurepas to St Ovide and de Mézy, 22 May 1729.

[96]*Ibid.*, Vol. 76, fols. 50–50v, '*Ordonnance du Roy qui suspend la deliverance des congés aux Soldats des Troupes des Colonies jusqu'au premier Janvier 1745,*' 20 Mar. 1743.

[97]' . . . *étant toujours attaqué de l'escorbut son capitaine voulu le congedier, mais le Repondant qui pour lors n'avait qu'environ seize a dix sept ans se mit a pleurer, disant que s'il était congédié il ne scaurait que faire pour gagner sa vie . . .*' This soldier adds that his reluctance to leave the island produced a great deal of consternation among his comrades. AC, C11B, Vol. 17, fols 296–315v, court-martial of Joseph Lagand dit Picard, charged with desertion, 24 Oct. 1736.

[98]*Ibid.*, Vol. 33, fols. 89–91v, de Raymond to Minister, 12 Oct. 1753.

[99]Only one man from the ranks, Jean Loppinot, received a commission in the colony's *troupes de la marine* before 1745. AC, D2C, Vol. 47, *Isle Royale— Officiers de guerre*, 8 May 1730. Loppinot was an exceptional case, having come with many of the original officers of the Isle Royale garrison from Acadia where his family was politically prominent. R.J. Morgan, 'A History of Block 16, Louisbourg; 1713–1768' (typed manuscript, Fortress of Louisbourg project, Louisbourg, 1975), 59.

[100]Corvisier, *op. cit.*, 94; W.J. Eccles, *Frontenac, the Courtier Governor* (Toronto: 1968), 220.

[101]T.H. Wintringham, *Mutiny; Being a Survey of Mutinies from Spartacus to Invergordon* (London: 1936), 256.

[102]F.J. Thorpe, 'The Politics of French Public Construction in the islands of the Gulf of St. Lawrence, 1695–1758' (unpubl. Ph. D. diss., University of Ottawa, 1973), 232–62.

[103]In September 1724, for example, when the strength of the colonial garrison was no more than 430, there were 236 soldiers (along with 17 civilians) employed in the construction of the fortifications. AC, C11B, Vol. 7, fols. 156–56v, de Verville, '*Etat des ouvriers . . . ,*' [Sept. 1724].

[104]Eccles, *Frontenac, the Courtier Governor*, 215–18; C.J. Russ, 'Les Troupes de la Marine, 1683–1713' (unpubl. M.A. thesis, McGill, 1971), 95–8.

[105]AC, C11B, Vol. 26, fols. 236–38, ordonnance, 20 June 1743.

[106]*Ibid.*, Vol. 21, fol. 55v, de Forant to Minister, 2 Oct. 1739.

[107]*Ibid.*, Vol. 18, fols. 85–87, LeNormant to Minister, 6 July 1736; *ibid.*, Vol. 23, fols. 60–64, Duquesnel to Minister, 19 Oct. 1741.

[108]AC, Outremer, G2, Vol. 182, fols. 148–357, '*Conseil Superieur Procedure criminelle . . . à l'encontre du nommé Nicolas LeBegue dit Brulevillage, et Thomas Berranger dit La Rosée soldats acusés de vol.*' 3 Mar.–2 June 1733.

[109]*Ibid.*, Vol. 179, fols. 462–502, '*Conseil Superieur-Procedure Criminelle a l'Encontre de Reintender Sergent Suisse et deux autres Complices accuses de vol.* [sic],' 11 Sept.–20 Oct. 1727.

[110]Babeau, *op. cit.*, I, 240.

[111]This attitude was also manifested, for example, among the French dragoons who, in the time of Louis XIV, refused to help collect taxes. '*Nous nous sommes engagés pour dragons, et non pour sergeants et porteurs de contraintes.*' *Ibid.*, I, 235.

[112]Renard court-martial.

[113]Thorpe, *op. cit.*, 251.

[114]The sources shed little light on the organization and function of these gangs and only mention the '*chefs d'atteliers*' occasionally and incidentally. AC, B, Vol. 99, fols. 245–49, '*Instructions pour le S^r. franquet D^{eur} des fortiffications de la N^{lle}, france sur les ouvrages que le Roy veut être executées à l'isle Royale,*' 12 May 1754.

[115]The engineer and contractor reported these '*contestations tumultueuses*' and '*émeutes*' without providing details. AC, C11B, Vol. 5, fols. 235–37, de Verville to Council, 19 June 1720; *ibid.*, Vol. 6, fols. 127–30, Isabeau to Council, 30 Nov. 1722.

[116]*Ibid.*, Vol. 7, fols. 142–50, de Verville, mémoire [1724].

[117]' . . . *les travaux que l'on fait dans cette isle donnant l'occasion au soldat de gagner de l'argent l'aysance qu'elle leur* [sic] *procure le rend delicat et difficile.*' AC, B, Vol. 52-2v, fols. 574v–77, Maurepas to St Ovide, 18 June 1728. In 1719, the engineer estimated that a man could earn five *livres* per day and 465 *livres* in a season. AC, C11B, Vol. 4, fols. 66–68, de Verville to Council, 24 Jan. 1719.

[118]AC, C11B, Vol. 5, fol. 136v, St Ovide and de Mézy to Minister, 10 Nov. 1720.

[119]*Ibid.*, Vol. I, fols. 73–76v, l'Hermitte to Council, 3 Nov. 1714; AC, B, Vol. 88-1, fols. 175–75v, Maurepas to Guillet, 15 Oct. 1748.

[120]AC, C11B, Vol. 12, fol. 252, St Ovide to Minister, 11 Nov. 1732.

[121]*Ibid.*, Vol. 5, fols. 386–88v, St Ovide to Minister, 30 Nov. 1721.

[122]*Ibid.*, Vol. 4, fols. 285–85v, Petition of de Rouville to the Comte de Toulouse, 1719.

[123]AC, B, Vol. 44-2, fol. 569v, Council to St Ovide, 1 July 1721.

[124]AC, C11B, Vol. 9, fols. 72–78v, St Ovide to Minister, 21 Nov. 1727.

[125]*Ibid.*, Vol. 23, fols. 88–90v, Bigot to Minister, 15 Oct. 1741; *ibid.*, Vol. 29, fols. 306–15, Franquet to Minister, 13 Oct. 1750.

[126]See, for example, AC, B, Vol. 68, fols. 347–48v, Maurepas to de Forant and Bigot, 26 May 1739.

[127]AC, C11B, Vol. 22, fol. 93v, Duquesnel to Minister, 1 Dec. 1740.

[128]Russ, *op. cit.*, 181–3. In Canada, even this relatively mild form of exploitation aroused the indignation and opposition of the bishop and clergy. If Canadian officers were more restrained in this regard than were their Isle Royale counterparts, the difference can be explained partly in terms of the more complex public élite of the St Lawrence colony which was not so completely dominated by the military. However, the greater ease with which Canadian soldiers could leave the service, and the officers' consequent concern about morale, may have been more important.

[129]AC, B, Vol. 68, fols. 347–48v, Maurepas to de Forant and Bigot, 26 May 1739.

[130]*Ibid.*, Vol. 74, fols. 592–92v, Maurepas to Duquesnel, 15 June 1742.

[131]Although Duquesnel claimed that he abolished the canteens in 1741 (AC, C11B, Vol. 23, fols. 24–29, Duquesnel and Bigot to Minister, 20 Oct. 1741), subsequent correspondence shows that he did no more than limit their operation. *Ibid.*, Vol. 24, fols. 52–52v, Duquesnel to Minister, 7 Oct. 1742.

[132]Babeau, *op. cit.*, I, 176–80.

[133]AC, C11B, Vol. 28, fols. 44v–46, Desherbiers and Prévost to Minister, 21 Oct. 1749.

[134]*Ibid.*, Vol. 29, fols. 313v–14, Franquet to Minister, 13 Oct. 1750.

11

The French Fur Trade in the Eighteenth Century

William J. Eccles

An all-encompassing aspect of life in New France was the fur trade. The trade, the principal 'cash crop' of the colony from its foundation, greatly influenced French relations with the native peoples, served as the motivation for the great inland explorations of the seventeenth and eighteenth centuries, and employed several thousand men, who shifted back and forth between the colony and the wilderness on a regular basis. Inevitably the trade had developed an imperial dimension, so that by the end of the seventeenth century it had become a principal bone of contention between the French and the English. During the eighteenth century the French need to preserve the fur trade became virtually indistinguishable from the need to maintain a French presence in the interior to frustrate the English. Defending the fur trade frontier was not only expensive, but continually brought New France into conflict with English America.

W.J. Eccles explores the imperial dimension of the fur trade in a wide-ranging article which covers more than a century and much of the continent. He argues that throughout the eighteenth century, the French fur trade in North America was less a commercial enterprise than a political instrument. Despite the political motivation, Eccles insists, the French never lost their commercial advantage over the English, the Indians consistently preferring French goods—and attitude—to British. In the end, the political nature of the fur trade would cost the Canadians dearly. Because of the imperial dimension to the rivalry between the French and the English colonies, the colony on the St Lawrence—which had no real reason to confront the Anglo-Americans—would be conquered by the enemy.

What evidence does Eccles advance for the politicization of the fur trade at the end of the seventeenth century? What place did the Indians play in the imperial rivalry?

Were the native peoples merely pawns in a larger European game, or did they play an active role? What, according to Eccles, was their tragedy? What is the basis for the assertion that the Canadians had no real quarrel with the English colonies? Can commercial and political policy ever be as neatly separated as Eccles attempts in this article?

This article first appeared, titled 'The Fur Trade and Eighteenth-Century Imperialism', in The William & Mary Quarterly, 3rd ser., 40 (1983), 341–61.

The North American fur trade of the seventeenth and eighteenth centuries has usually been viewed, until recently, as merely another commercial enterprise governed by the premise 'buy cheap, sell dear' in order to reap the maximum profit. Of late, the Canadian end of the trade has come to be regarded as having been more a means to a non-commercial end than a pursuit conducted solely for economic gain. As European penetration and dominance of the continent progressed, the trade, which had begun as an adjunct of the Atlantic shore fishery, became a commercial pursuit in its own right. After 1600, when the first Roman Catholic missionaries were sent to New France, it became a means to finance and further that tragic drive to convert the Indian nations to Christianity. This attempt continued until mid-century, when the Jesuit mission in Huronia was destroyed, along with the Hurons as a nation, by the Iroquois Confederacy.[1] For the rest of the century the fur trade of New France went through vexed and troubled times.[2]

Stability was temporarily restored to the trade in 1663, when the Crown took over the colony from the Company of One Hundred Associates. Near the end of the century a huge glut of beaver fur completely disrupted the market in Europe and caused Louis Phélypeaux de Pontchartrain, the minister of marine responsible for the colonies, to try to force the Canadian fur traders to withdraw from the West completely. For political reasons this could not be done. Despite its economic unviability, the French, in order to maintain good relations with the Indian nations, were forced to continue the trade in furs. Then, in 1700, on the eve of a new war in Europe, Louis XIV embarked on an expansionist policy in North America to hem in the English colonies on the Atlantic seaboard. From that point forward, the fur trade was used mainly as a political instrument to further the imperial aims of France.

In the 1650s, after the Iroquois had virtually destroyed the Huron nation and scattered the Algonkian nations allied with it far to the west, French traders began to push into the interior of the continent, where they established direct trade relations with the hunting nations that had previously supplied furs to the Huron middlemen. These traders, a mere handful at first, voyaged through the Great Lakes and beyond, then down into the Mississippi Valley. This French thrust into the West occurred just as the Five Nations Iroquois Confederacy, having subdued the tribes surrounding them and being well supplied with firearms by the Dutch and English merchants of Albany, embarked on an imperialistic drive to conquer and control the Ohio Valley, a region almost as vast as the kingdom of France.[3] Their first incursion into the region in 1678 was repelled by the Illinois nation. The following year Robert Cavelier de La Salle began establishing fur-trade posts on the Illinois River and thereby claimed suzerainty for the French Crown over the lands of both the Illinois and the Miami nations.[4]

In 1680 the inevitable clash came between these rival imperial powers. La Salle's lieutenant, Henri de Tonty, attempted to mediate when an Iroquois army invaded the Illinois country. He received a nasty wound for his pains but managed to escape to Michilimackinac with his men.[5] The French presence in the West was now seriously threatened. An attempt to cow the Iroquois by military force failed miserably. Instead, the Iroquois dictated humiliating peace terms to the governor-general of New France, Le Febvre de La Barre, and stated their determination to destroy the Illinois, whom the French claimed to be under the protection of Louis XIV. When La Barre protested this arrogant Iroquois declaration, the great Onondaga chief and orator, Hotreouati, brusquely retorted, 'They deserve to die, they have shed our blood.'[6] To that La Barre could make no response. When Louis XIV was informed of what had transpired, La Barre was summarily dismissed from his post and recalled to France in disgrace.[7]

The long-range aim of the Confederacy appears to have been to bring under subjection all the Indian nations south of the Great Lakes as far as the Mississippi, and at the same time to divert the western fur trade from Montreal to Albany, with the Confederacy controlling it. Because the Iroquois failed to provide a written record of their aims, their motives cannot be determined with certainty, yet their actions and the policies they pursued during the ensuing decades indicate clearly enough that what they sought was power—dominance over this vast region—rather than mere commercial advantage.

A few years after this Franco-Iroquois struggle in the interior of North America was joined, events occurred in Europe that were to affect it profoundly. The Revolution of 1689 ousted James II and brought William of Orange, bitter enemy of Louis XIV, to the throne of England. This ushered in hostilities between England and France that were to occupy nineteen of the ensuing twenty-four years. The Iroquois, now confident of English military aid, pressed their attacks against the French in the West and at their settlements in the St Lawrence Valley, inflicting heavy casualties. The settlers, aided by some 1,500 *Troupes de la Marine*, regular troops sent from France, managed to beat back these attacks and in the process became, of necessity, highly skilled at guerrilla warfare. The alliance with the Indian nations who had long feared the Iroquois was strengthened and the war was carried to the enemy. Iroquois casualties mounted, and the frontier settlements of their ineffectual English allies were ravaged by Canadian war parties. Both the Iroquois and the English colonials were relieved when, in 1697, the war ended in Europe. The Iroquois, now bereft of English logistical support, their fighting strength reduced by casualties and disease to half what it had been, were forced to sue for peace.[8]

This proud people had not been brought so low, however, that they would accept any terms that the French cared to impose. Consequently the negotiations dragged on for four years. Moreover, the twenty-eight tribes allied with the French had to be party to the peace treaty that was eventually drawn up at Montreal in 1701. The principal factor that now made possible an enduring peace between the French and the Iroquois, thereby ending a war that had lasted for nearly a century, was that the French negotiators recognized the Iroquois presence to be an essential buffer between their Indian allies in the Northwest and the English colonies. Moreover, the Iroquois had learned to their cost that they could not rely on the English for military support. Rather they perceived that the English had always sought to make use of them merely to serve English ends. There was no longer any question of the French seeking to destroy the Iroquois; in fact just the reverse had become the case. The Iroquois had now to abandon all hope of ever driving the French out of Canada or from the posts in the West. The French presence had become essential to them to balance that of the English and to allow them to play one off against the other. Thus the French negotiators were able to insert a clause into the peace treaty declaring that in any future war between England and France, the Iroquois would remain neutral. At one stroke the greatest military threat to New France and the main defence of New York had been eliminated; and this occurred just as England and France were preparing for a renewal of hostilities that were to last for more than a decade.[9]

On the French side the preceding wars had been fought for a specific Canadian aim, control of the western fur trade, and France had provided the military aid needed to achieve that end. The ensuing wars were to be fought solely for French imperial aims. In 1701, with the War of the Spanish Succession about to erupt, Louis XIV declared that the English colonies must be hemmed in between the Atlantic and the Appalachians. On no account were the English to be allowed to flood over that mountain range to occupy the region between it and the Mississippi. Were they to do so, Louis feared, their numbers would swell immeasurably and England's wealth and power would increase proportionately. In all likelihood they would then push southwest to conquer Mexico with its silver mines. With Louis XIV's grandson now on the throne of Spain, France had to defend the Spanish colonies as though they were her own.[10] Louis XIV feared that English domination of North America would upset the balance of power in Europe. The French in America, with their Indian allies, were to be the means of containing the English colonies.[11] In the implementation of this imperial policy the fur trade had a vital role to play, of an importance far in excess of its economic value.

In 1701 Louis XIV gave orders for the creation of the new colony of Louisiana, in the Mississippi Valley, to forestall the English, who, it was reported, planned to establish a settlement at the mouth of that great river.[12] Another French settlement was ordered to be placed at the narrows between Lake Erie and Lake Huron. This new colony, to be named Detroit, was intended to bar English access to the Northwest and maintain French control of the western Great Lakes.[13] It is not without significance that the Canadian merchants and the royal officials at Quebec were bitterly opposed to both these settlements, declaring that they would be the ruin of Canada—Detroit, because it would bring the Indian nations allied with the French into close proximity to the Iroquois, who might grant them access to the Albany traders; Louisiana, because the fur traders who obtained their trade goods on credit from Montreal merchants would be tempted to defraud their creditors by shipping their furs to France from the port to be established on the Gulf of Mexico.[14]

French imperial policy now required that the Indian nations of the West and of Acadia be welded into a close commercial alliance and that all contact between them and the English colonists be prevented by one means or another. The main instruments of this policy, it was envisaged, would be missionaries and fur traders. The great age of French proselytization that had produced the Jesuit martyrs was, however, a thing of the past. The clergy were eager enough to serve, but some of them were ill suited for the task and too often their efforts were hampered by squabbling among rival groups—secular priests with Jesuits, Capuchins with both. For several years the bishop of New France was an absentee, unable to restore order and discipline from his residence in Paris.[15] Thus the implementation of this new policy was left to two groups: the Canadian fur traders and the officers and men of the colonial regulars, the *Troupes de la Marine*, who garrisoned the re-established posts.

The fur trade was now definitely subordinated to a political end. It was required to pay a large share of the costs of maintaining a French presence in the interior to bar the English from it. The West was divided into regions, each with a central post commanded by an officer of the colonial regulars. For some years these officers were not permitted to engage in the trade, the sole right to which in each region was auctioned off to merchants on a three-year lease.[16] When it was found that this led to exploitation of the Indians by merchants whose only aim was to make as great a profit as possible during their lease, the trade was turned over to the commandants, who could, it was thought, be kept under tighter control by the senior officials at Quebec.[17] Complaints against them by the Indians could bring instant recall and might jeopardize promotion or the granting of commissions to sons.

The post commandants usually formed companies in partnership with Montreal merchants who provided the trade goods, hired the *voyageurs*, and marketed the furs, and with professional traders who took charge of the actual trading with the Indians. The *modus operandi* was thus very simple: the companies usually comprised three men for a three-year term, at the end of which the merchant who had supplied the goods withdrew their cost, and whatever profit or loss remained was shared by the partners.[18] At the main bases of Michilimackinac and Detroit the trade was open to all who obtained a permit from the governor-general and paid the base commandant his 500-*livre* fee. From these fees the commandants had to pay the costs of maintaining the posts, thereby sparing the Crown the expense.[19]

Louis XIV, in order to end the war that was reducing his government to bankruptcy, agreed to make sweeping concessions on the Atlantic frontier of New France to avoid having to make them in Europe. He therefore agreed to cede Newfoundland and Acadia, the latter 'within its ancient limits', to England. A joint commission was appointed to determine those limits; but, predictably, no agreement could be reached and France retained Cape Breton, where it proceeded to construct the fortress of Louisbourg as a naval base for the protection of French maritime interests in the North Atlantic. The British continued to claim title to all the land up to the St Lawrence River, and it was upon the Indian nations of the region—the Abenaki, Micmacs, and Malecites—that the French relied to hold the English back from the vital St Lawrence waterway.[20] The governor-general at Quebec made sure that those nations were well supplied with all the European goods they needed, and that a continual state of hostility existed between them and the expanding population of New England.[21]

In the implementation of this policy the French received unwitting aid from the New England settlers. What the latter coveted most was land for settlement, the very lands that the Indians required to maintain their hunting economy and that they believed had been granted them by God for that very purpose. The Indians denied that they were or ever had been subjects of either the French or the English Crown. They asserted vehemently that the French could not have ceded their land by treaty as the Massachusetts authorities claimed, since no one could cede what had never been his.[22] Although the French, with their meagre population, did not covet any of that land, they were determined to deny it to the English. In 1727 the king stated in a *mémoire* to the governor-general and intendant at Quebec that he had learned with pleasure that the Abenaki of Saint-François and Bécancourt intended to continue the war against the English and not entertain proposals for peace until the English had razed the forts they had built on Abenaki lands. 'This is so important for Canada', the *mémoire* went on, 'that the Sieur de Beauharnois could not take measures more just than such as would foment that war and prevent any accommodation.'[23]

To the north, where France had relinquished its claims to Hudson Bay, a dispute arose over the interpretation of the covering clause in the Treaty of Utrecht. The British claimed that they had thereby gained title to all the lands whose waters drained into Hudson Bay—almost a quarter of the continent. They themselves, however, negated their claim by insisting that the operative clause in the treaty state that France *restored* rather than *ceded* to Great Britain the lands claimed by the latter—this in order to establish that Britain had always had the prior claim. France agreed but riposted by declaring that only the lands that Britain had formerly occupied could be restored to her: by definition, restoration could not be made of lands that had never been conquered, purchased, or occupied.[24] In fact, merely an infinitesimal fraction of that vast territory had ever been seen by a British subject. The argument was really an academic one, since the Hudson's Bay Company made no attempt to challenge French control of the interior. As long as enough furs reached its posts to produce a dividend for its shareholders, the company's servants were content to remain in a 'sleep by the frozen sea'.[25]

The French now established fur-trade posts on the rivers that ran down to the Bay and thereby controlled the flow of furs to the English. They kept the choicest furs for themselves and allowed the Indians to trade only their poorer quality pelts at the Bay Company's posts.[26] Had it not been that the Indians were astute enough to maintain trade relations with both the English and the Canadians in order to reap the advantages of competition, Britain's hold on Hudson Bay would early have been severed.[27]

From the signing of the Treaty of Utrecht in 1713 to the conquest of New France, the French maintained their presence among the nations of the West, penetrating steadily farther into the interior until they eventually reached the barrier of the Rocky Mountains.[28] Only at Detroit, Kaskaskia, and Cahokia in the Illinois country, and on the lower Mississippi, were they able to establish small agricultural settlements.[29] Elsewhere they merely maintained fur-trade posts consisting of three or four log buildings surrounded by a palisade. Always these posts were placed in an area that no Indian nation claimed as its own—Detroit, for example—or were established with the express permission of the dominant nation of the region. Some of the posts had been maintained during the Iroquois war, ostensibly as bases and places of refuge for the nations allied with the French against the Iroquois Confederacy. Experience had proven that posts on the fringe of Iroquois-controlled territory were more prisons than forts. Their garrisons did not dare venture beyond musket range of the palisades, and too many of the men—deprived of fresh meat or fish, reduced to hard rations of stale salt pork and sea biscuit—succumbed to scurvy.[30]

After the Iroquois wars of the seventeenth century, and with the proclamation of Louis XIV's containment policy in North America, fur-trade posts had to be sustained among all the nations that could conceivably have contact, direct or indirect, with the English colonials or the Hudson's Bay Company. With the exception of the Sioux nation, who always kept the French at arm's length, most of the nations were glad to have these posts on their territory. Although the French maintained that the posts gave them title to the land, their claims were made to exclude the English, not to deny the Indians' title, something they did not dare do. The French were certainly not sovereign in the West, for sovereignty implies the right to impose and collect taxes, and to enforce laws—and they were never able to do either. The Indians never considered themselves to be French subjects, and the French were never able to treat them as such.[31] Moreover, the Canadian *voyageurs* who transported trade goods and supplies to the western posts and took the furs back to Montreal always had to travel in convoy for protection against the Indians through whose lands they passed. One or two canoes alone were an invitation to extortionate demands or outright pillage.[32] The Indians allowed the French only the right of passage to the posts, since this assured them a ready supply of European goods close at hand. The land on which the trade posts stood they considered still to be theirs, the French occupants being mere tenants during the Indians' pleasure.

Another significant factor in this imperial rivalry was the superiority of most French trade goods. In only one item, woollen cloth, did the English have an advantage, and even this is open to question. The factors at the Hudson's Bay Company's posts were continually pleading with their superiors in London to provide them with goods of the same quality as those traded by the French.[33] In one of the more important trade items, liquor, the French had a distinct advantage. Showing commendable good taste, the Indians greatly preferred French brandy to the rot-gut rum and gin supplied by the British and Americans. The Hudson's Bay Company produced imitation brandy made from cheap gin, adulterated to give it the colour and something resembling the taste of cognac, but it never replaced the real thing in the Indians' opinion.[34] Alcohol was crucial in the fur trade for two reasons. First, the Indians craved it more than anything else; even though they knew that it could destroy them, they could not resist it, and they would go to any lengths to obtain all that was available.[35] Second, from the purely economic aspect of the trade, alcohol was the ideal exchange item. Of other goods—cloth, wearing apparel, pots, knives, axes, muskets—the Indians had a limited need. It is now coming to be recognized that they were by no means as dependent on European goods as has been claimed.[36] A musket would last many years, as would other metal goods. A few items of clothing each year per family did not result in large entries in the Montreal merchants' ledgers. An Indian hunter could garner enough pelts in a couple of months' good hunting to provide for his family's needs, but the appetite for *eau de vie* was virtually insatiable, driving the Indians to produce furs in ever larger quantities. In the 1790s a Nor'wester, Duncan McGillivray, remarked, 'When a nation becomes addicted to drinking it affords a strong presumption that they will soon become excellent hunters.'[37]

The French traders who lived among the Indians were only too well aware of the terrible effects that liquor had on their customers. Frequently they paid for it with their lives when Indians, in their cups, went berserk and set about them with knife or *casse tête*.[38] Some of the senior French officials who were involved in the fur trade for personal gain tried to make light of these dread effects. Governor-General Louis de Buade, comte de Frontenac, for example, contended vociferously that the Indians did not get any more drunk, or behave any worse when in their cups, than did the average Englishman or Netherlander.[39] The French missionaries, in particular the Jesuits who resided in the Indian villages, knew better. They fought to have liquor barred completely from the trade and threatened excommunication for any traders who persisted in its use.[40] Governor-General Philippe de Rigaud de Vaudreuil and his successor, Charles de la Boische, marquis de Beauharnois, both recognized the horrors caused by the liquor trade, but for political reasons they had to condone it, while at the same time striving to restrict its use to prevent the worst abuses. As they and others pointed out to Jean-Fréderic Phélypeaux, comte de Maurepas, appointed minister of marine in 1723, were they to refuse to trade alcohol the Indians would go the Anglo-American traders, who had no scruples whatsoever, despite frequent pleas from tribal chieftains to keep the rum pedlars out of their villages.[41] Thus in the imperial contest liquor was a powerful but pernicious weapon.

Throughout the eighteenth century the Montreal fur traders took the lion's share of the North American fur trade. The customs figures for fur imports at London, La Rochelle, and Rouen make this plain.[42] Moreover, the Albany merchants who dominated the Anglo-American fur trade admitted that they obtained the bulk of their furs clandestinely from the Canadians.[43] It could hardly have been otherwise, since they did not have access to the Northwest, which produced the fine-quality furs. The minister of marine, Maurepas, and after 1749 his successor, Antoine-Louis Rouillé, comte de Jouy, continually demanded that the smuggling of Canadian furs to Albany be stopped, but to no avail.[44] They simple-mindedly believed that if the English desired something, then France must strive to deny it to them. The senior officials at Quebec well understood the complexity of the situation. They declared vociferously that they were doing everything possible to curb this clandestine trade, but the evidence indicates that their unenthusiastic efforts were less than efficacious. They tolerated the existence of an agent of the Albany traders at Montreal and frequent visits of the merchants themselves. Similarly, Montreal traders called at Albany from time to time, and credit arrangements between the merchants of the two centres were extensive.[45] One suspects that the governor-general and the intendant despaired of bringing first Maurepas, then Rouillé, ministers of marine, to grasp how closely intertwined were the economics and politics of the situation. Certainly they did not make a determined attempt to explain the subtleties of the issue.

The main agents of this clandestine trade were the Christian Indians of Sault St Louis and Lake of Two Mountains missions, both close by Montreal.[46] The Canadian officials claimed that they dared not forbid these Indians to trade at Albany whenever they pleased lest they become disaffected and quit Canada. Since their services were vital in time of war, and in peacetime as intelligence agents, they had to be indulged. Thus they quite openly transported Canadian furs to Albany, along with fine French cloth, wines, and spirits, on behalf of Canadian merchants.[47] In fact Governor-General Beauharnois declared that the Mission Iroquois of Sault St Louis constituted virtually an independent republic over which he had no authority.[48]

Although the Canadian fur traders undoubtedly reaped considerable benefits from this clandestine trade, a far more significant consequence was that it removed any incentive the Albany merchants might have had to contest the hold of the French over the western nations.[49] This issue was of great concern to the Crown officials of New York, who took an imperial view of the situation, but the Albany merchants were interested only in preserving their well-established Canadian trade. When furs were shipped to their doors by the Canadians at prices that afforded them a good profit, they saw no reason to incur the great risks, capital outlay, and trouble that would be involved in trying to compete with the Canadians on their ground, the Indian country of the Northwest. Moreover, they lacked the birch-bark canoes, the *voyageurs* to man them, and the prime requisite, the willingness to accept the Indians on their own terms—in short, all the special skills needed for this particular trade.[50] In November 1765 Sir William Johnson commented sadly on this phenomenon to the Lords of Trade:

> I have frequently observed to Your Lordships, that His Majesty's subjects in this Country seem very ill calculated to Cultivate a good understanding with the Indians; and this is a notorious proof of it, for notwithstanding the Expence of transporting Goods from New Orleans to the Illinois is greater than by the Lakes and Consequently French goods are in general Dearer than Ours, yet such is the Conduct of all persons under the Crown of France, whether Officers, Agents, Traders, that the Indians will go much farther to buy their Goods, and pay a much higher price for them. This all persons acquainted with the nature of the Commerce to the Westward can fully evidence.[51]

Nor was the trade all one way. The Iroquois made annual trips to Canada to confer with the French authorities. The Crown officials of New York were deeply worried by the influence that the French gained over the Iroquois during these visits. The French entertained the Iroquois delegates lavishly, after a fashion that the British officials could not or would not match.[52] In October 1715 the Albany Indian commissioners stated: 'Trade between Albany & Canada is of fatal Consequence to the Indian Interest of this Colony, that of our Indians who are employed in it many stay at Canada & others return so Attached to the French Interest & so Debauched from ours that it puzzels them how to preserve amongst them that Respect & Regard to this Gov't so necessary to the Public Good and Tranquility.'[53]

By 1720 the French had gained a secure hold on the Great Lakes basin by ringing it with garrisoned fur-trade posts. Although the mercantile interests of New York were not perturbed by this development, the Crown officials were, and they sought to counter it. In 1719 the governor-general of New France, Vaudreuil, heard reports that New York intended to establish a fort at Niagara, which would have given the English access to the West, including the Mississippi Valley. Vaudreuil very adroitly forestalled them by obtaining the permission of the Senecas to establish a post on their land at the mouth of the Niagara River. Ostensibly the post was to serve their needs; in reality it barred the West to the English.[54] The following year another post was established at the Toronto portage, barring that route from Lake Ontario to Lake Huron.[55]

Although the Iroquois had given the French permission to establish the post at Niagara and bluntly told the protesting Albany authorities that they had 'given the French liberty of free Passage thru Lake Ontario',[56] they had no desire to see the French become overpowerful in the region. To balance their position they therefore granted New York permission to build a trading post at Oswego on the south shore of Lake Ontario across from Fort Frontenac. At the same time deputies from the Iroquois Confederacy met with the Albany Indian commissioners, who reported that the Indians 'exhort us to live in Peace and Quiet with the French and carry on our Trade without Molesting each other'.[57] The Quebec authorities responded by claiming that the south shore of the Great Lakes belonged to France by right of prior discovery and conquest.[58] Governor-General Beauharnois began making preparations for a campaign to take and destroy Oswego, but he was restrained by the government in France, which at the time enjoyed good relations with Great Britain, this being the era of the *entente cordiale* established by Cardinal André-Hercule de Fleury and Robert Walpole.[59] Nevertheless the Canadian authorities replaced the trading post at Niagara with a solid stone edifice that would have required heavy cannon to demolish, greatly to the dismay of the Albany authorities.[60]

Events were to demonstrate that Oswego posed no serious threat to French control of the Great Lakes. The fear was that it would seduce the western nations out of the French alliance by undercutting the French prices for furs and, more particularly, by the unrestricted sale of liquor. But here again, as at Albany, the New York traders were their own worst enemies. They did indeed supply all the cheap liquor the Indians desired, but the latter, when under its influence, were unmercifully cheated and their womenfolk debauched.[61] This bred bitter resentment.

Oswego posed an additional problem for the authorities at Quebec. Some of the less-scrupulous Canadian traders found it convenient to obtain large supplies of cheap rum there, as well as English woollens, which they traded at the distant Indian villages.[62] In an attempt to keep both the allied Indians and the renegade Canadians away from the English post, the French government retained the trade at forts Frontenac, Niagara, and Toronto as Crown monopolies so that prices could be kept competitive with those at Oswego by selling at a reduced profit or even a loss if necessary. The commandants at these posts had to see to it that nothing transpired that could upset the Indians and endanger their alliance with the French.[63]

The French thus managed to maintain a tenuous hold over the interior of North America west of the Appalachians, and in the vast region north and west of the Great Lakes as far as the Rocky Mountains. This tremendous feat was, moreover, accomplished at very little cost to the French Crown and by a mere handful of men. In 1754, when this military fur-trade empire was nearing its greatest extent, the cost to the Crown for maintaining the garrisoned posts was but 183,427 *livres*.[64] The number of officers and enlisted men in these garrisons in 1750 was only 261,[65] but in addition there were the men engaged directly in the trade with the Indians—the *voyageurs*, traders, clerks, and merchants—whose number cannot be calculated with any great degree of accuracy. All that can be offered here is an educated guess that the number directly employed in the western fur trade for the period 1719 to 1750 would have ranged from about 200 for the earlier years to some 600 at most by mid-century.[66] This means that with fewer than 1,000 men France maintained its claim to more than half the continent.

Had the French been content to confine their activities to the fur trade they might well have retained their control, in alliance with the Indian nations, over the northern half of the continent—that is, over the area that today forms the Dominion of Canada. However, the interests of the Canadian fur traders and French imperial policy began to diverge at mid-century, immediately after the War of the Austrian Succession. Fur traders from Pennsylvania and Virginia, serving as advance agents of land-speculation companies, had begun to penetrate the Ohio Valley by way of the Cumberland Gap with pack-horse trains.[67] To win the allegiance of the Indian nations they flooded the region with cheap trade goods, liquor, and expensive presents for the chiefs. A Canadian officer later declared, 'The presents that they receive are so considerable that one sees nothing but the most magnificent gold, silver, and scarlet braid.'[68] The Canadian fur traders had no interest in the furs of that region, which were of poor quality.[69] They preferred to confine their activities to the Northwest, where the furs were the best obtainable, river communications far easier than they were south of the Great Lakes, and the Cree tongue was a lingua franca in the entire region.

Marquis Roland-Michel Barrin de la Galissonière, governor-general of New France, in opposition to the prevailing and strongly held Canadian sentiment, advocated that the Ohio Valley be occupied by the French and that forts be built and garrisoned, merely to deny the region to the English. He freely admitted that it would be of no economic benefit to France in the foreseeable future, but he feared that were the English to succeed in occupying and settling the valley they would become extremely powerful and dangerous. They would eventually sever communications along the Mississippi between Canada and Louisiana and then go on to conquer Mexico with its silver mines.[70]

The minister of marine, Rouillé, newly appointed to the post and without previous experience in colonial affairs, accepted this policy. Despite the strong opposition of the senior Canadian officials in the colonial administration,[71] and at immense cost in funds and Canadian lives,[72] the French drove the American traders out of the region. They established a chain of forts and supply depots from Lake Erie to the forks of the Ohio, thereby overawing the local tribes, who quickly abandoned their commercial alliance with the Anglo-Americans and pledged their support to the French.[73] This was accomplished by *force majeure* pure and simple, and the Indian nations remained in this uneasy alliance only as long as it appeared to them to suit their interests and, as events were to show, not a day longer.

Previously when the French had extended their fur-trade empire into new territory they had always done so at the invitation, or at least with the tacit consent, of the Indians. In the Ohio Valley, however, Galissonière's successor, Ange de Menneville, marquis Duquesne, made it plain to the Iroquois, who claimed sovereignty over the region, that he would brook no interference, that he regarded the valley as belonging to the French Crown, and that if they chose to oppose him he would crush them.[74] Some of his Canadian officers, long accustomed to dealing with the Iroquois, were more diplomatic. They pointed out that the French did not covet the land but merely wished to prevent the English from seizing it, and that the Indians could hunt right up to the walls of the French forts, whereas wherever the English went the forest was destroyed and the animals driven out, the Indians with them.[75]

Here also the Anglo-Americans were the agents of their own defeat. They had treated two nations on the frontiers of Pennsylvania and Virginia, the Shawnee and the Delaware, so ruthlessly, seizing their land by dint of fraudulent title deeds, debauching them with liquor, murdering them with impunity, that it did not require a great deal of persuasion by the French to bring these Indians into a close military alliance once hostilities broke out.[76] This rejection of the Anglo-Americans was immeasurably strengthened by the

initial French victories, first over Major George Washington's motley provincial force at Fort Necessity, where Washington accepted humiliating terms
and fled back over the mountains; then, a year later when Major-General
Edward Braddock's army of 2,200 British regulars and American provincials
was destroyed near Fort Duquesne by 250-odd Canadian regulars and militia
and some 600 Indians.[77]

The French were now able to arm and send out Indian war parties,
accompanied by a few Canadian regulars or militia, to ravage the frontiers
of the English colonies from New York to Georgia, thereby retaining the
initiative and tying down large British and provincial forces. Successful
though it was, this strategy posed massive problems in logistics that the minister of marine, Jean-Baptiste de Machault d'Arnouville, and his staff at Versailles were never able to comprehend. Appalled by the Canadian accounts
for 1753, he warned Governor-General Duquesne that unless the excessive
costs of the western posts were reduced, the king would abandon the colony.[78] He thereby blandly overlooked the fact that the expenditures had been
incurred in consequence of his ministry's policy and direct orders. To implement this policy all the needs of the Indian allies had to be supplied.[79] This
required the transport of vast amounts of goods from Montreal to Forts
Niagara and Duquesne by canoe, barque, horse, and pirogue. The wastage
at the Niagara portage alone was appalling. In 1753 Duquesne complained
to Captain Paul Marin de la Malgue, commander of the Ohio expedition,
that he had learned that forty-eight canoe loads of supplies had been stolen
or spoiled by being left uncovered in the rain. He voiced the suspicion that
the Canadians, who were bitterly opposed to the Ohio adventure, were
destroying the supplies deliberately to force its abandonment.[80]

For many years the western Iroquois had demanded and received the right
to carry all fur-trade and military supplies over the portage, which they
regarded as their territory. This was a cost that the Crown officials at Quebec
had been quite willing to see imposed on the fur traders in order to maintain
good relations with the Iroquois Confederacy. Governor-General Duquesne,
however, considered excessive the 40,000 *livres* a year that it was now costing
the Crown to have military supplies transported around Niagara Falls by the
Senecas. At the grave risk of alienating them and the other Iroquois nations,
he had horses shipped from Montreal and dispensed with the Senecas' services. Many of the horses then mysteriously vanished.[81]

For the Canadian officers charged with the implementation of these
orders, the task at times seemed insuperable. A lack of rain meant low water
in the shallow rivers that linked Lake Erie, with a fifteen-mile portage, to
the Ohio. The supply boats and pirogues then had to be manhandled along
the river beds, driving both officers and men to despair.[82] To make matters
worse, the Indian allies were extremely demanding and wasteful. Their loyalty could be counted on only as long as their demands for goods and services

were met, and frequently not even then. In 1756 Vaudreuil ruefully explained to the minister of marine:

> I am not in the least surprised that expenses have risen so high, the Indians are the cause of immense expenditures, forming the largest part of those charged to the Crown in the colony. One has to see to believe what they consume and how troublesome they are. I deny and reduce their demands as much as I can at Montreal, but despite it they succeed in having themselves equipped several times in the same campaign. They continually come and go between the army or the posts and Montreal, and one is forced to supply them with food for every trip which they justify by claiming that they have been refused things by the army, or that having been on a raid they must now return home, or they dreamt that they ought to do so. Every time that one wants to send them to support the army one cannot avoid supplying them. When they go on a war party they are given 10, 12, or 15 days rations . . . at the end of two days they return without food or equipment and say they have lost it all, so they have to be provided afresh. They consume an astonishing quantity of brandy and a Commandant would be in grave difficulties were he to refuse them, and so it is with all their requests.[83]

One important factor, all too often overlooked, was that these Indian nations fought alongside the French purely to serve their own needs. They were allies, not mercenaries. In fact they regarded the French as little more than an auxiliary force aiding them in their struggle to preserve their hunting grounds from further encroachment by the Anglo-Americans and to oblige the latter to treat them with respect.[84] This was compellingly illustrated when, in May 1757, the American colonial authorities entered into negotiations with Iroquois, Shawnee, and Delaware tribes to end the fighting that had destroyed their frontier settlements to a depth of over a hundred miles. For once the Indian negotiators refused to be put off with vague promises; in the past they had been hoodwinked all too often. Eventually a Moravian missionary, Frederick Post, who sympathized deeply with the Indians, went to the villages of the Shawnee and Delaware. There, within sight of Fort Duquesne, with frustrated French officers in attendance, the proposed terms of the Easton Treaty were promulgated.[85]

The Indian nations south of the Great Lakes then ceased to support the French. When Brigadier-General John Forbes, marching on Fort Duquesne with an army of some 7,000 British regulars and American provincial troops, suffered heavy and humiliating losses at the hands of the Canadians and Indians in one brisk battle, he deliberately slowed his advance until he received word that the Indians had signed a separate peace, the Easton Treaty. That defection left the French no choice but to abandon Fort Duquesne and, with it, control of the Ohio Valley. Colonel Henry Bouquet commented: 'After God the success of this Expedition is intirely due to the General, who by bringing about the Treaty of Easton, has struck the blow which has knocked the French in the head . . . in securing all his posts, and giving nothing to chance.'[86]

The following year, 1759, Quebec and Niagara fell. Despite a valiant last attempt by the French and Canadians under François de Lévis to retake Quebec in the spring of 1760, six months later they were compelled to surrender to the armies of Major-General Jeffery Amherst at Montreal. This spelled the end of French power on the mainland of North America.

The fate of that empire had been decided by the incompetence of its government at home and that of the headquarters staff—with the exception of the Chevalier de Lévis—of the army sent to defend Canada. During the course of the war there had been four controllers-general of finance, four of foreign affairs, four of war, and five of the marine.[87] In the fateful year, 1759, the minister of marine was Nicolas-René Berryer. Before his appointment to that post in November 1758 he had been *lieutenant de police* for Paris.[88] As for the army sent to Canada, its morale and efficiency steadily deteriorated under the command of the incompetent, defeatist Louis-Joseph, marquis de Montcalm. It was not a shortage of supplies or overwhelming enemy superiority or corruption that brought on the British conquest of Canada. The West was lost when the Indian allies defected. Louisbourg fell because it lacked a fleet to protect it. Canada fell after the loss of Quebec in a battle that should have been won crushingly by the French but was lost owing to the stupidity and panic of Montcalm.[89] Even then Quebec might well have been retaken by Lévis had the minister of marine dispatched in time the reinforcements that Lévis had requested.[90] Etienne-François, duc de Choiseul, who was given charge of the ministries of war, foreign affairs, and marine, then decided that it would serve the interests of France better were England to acquire Canada since, with the menace of French power removed from mainland America, England's colonies could be counted on to strike for independence in the not-too-distant future. France's loss of Canada, Choiseul decided, would be as nothing compared to England's loss of her American colonies.[91]

If the Canadians had had control of French policy in North America, neither the decisive battle at Quebec nor, for that matter, the war itself would likely have taken place, for the Canadians had no real quarrel with the English colonies. In war the Anglo-Americans had demonstrated time and again that they were no match for the Canadians and their Indian allies. Their record in the Seven Years' War indicated clearly enough their lack of enthusiasm for the conflict.[92] The Canadians knew that they had little to fear from that quarter, nor did they have any illusions that they could conquer the English colonies. In commerce there was no real conflict between them. The fur trade was of vital economic importance to the Canadians but certainly not to France, and of little, and that declining, importance to the Anglo-Americans. Among the latter, a group of well-placed rapacious land speculators and a barbarian horde of would-be settlers coveted the lands of the Indian nations on their frontier, a region that the Canadians had made plain was of no interest to them. The Albany merchants who dominated the Anglo-American fur trade chose not to compete with the Canadians; instead they entered into a cosy commercial partnership. They had not exhibited any eagerness to dispute the French hold on the West. As for the Hudson's Bay Company, its steadily declining returns indicated its inability to compete with the Canadians; moreover, it no longer had the same influence that it once had wielded in government circles. It was a monopoly, and all trade monopolies were then being looked at askance in Britain.[93] Only the shareholders would have wept had the Hudson's Bay Company been driven to the wall by the Canadians.

For over half a century the fur trade was used by France as an instrument of its foreign policy and, owing to the peculiar skills of the Canadians, with considerable success. By means of it, most of the Indian nations supported the French cause in the colonial wars, but they did so only as long as it appeared to them to serve their immediate interests. The French were acutely aware of the Indians' true feeling towards them. Governor-General Beauharnois remarked that they had their policies just as had the French. 'In general', he stated, 'they greatly fear us, they have no affection for us whatsoever, and the attitudes they manifest are never sincere.'[94] A certain Monsieur Le Maire put the French position very succinctly, explaining that there was no middle course: one had to have the Indians either as friends or as foes, and whoever desired them as friends had to furnish them with their necessities, on terms they could afford.[95] The policy of the Indian nations was always to play the French off against the English, using the fur trade as an instrument of their own foreign policy.[96] Their tragedy was not to have foreseen the consequences were the French to be eliminated from the equation.

Suggestions for Further Reading

William J. Eccles, *The Canadian Frontier: 1534–1760* (Hinsdale, Illinois, 1969).

Harold Innis, *The Fur Trade in Canada: An Introduction to Canadian Economic History*, rev. ed., (Toronto, 1970).

Francis Parkman, *A Half Century of Conflict* (Toronto, 1898).

Notes

[1]On the Huron-Iroquois conflict see Bruce G. Trigger, *The Children of Aataentsic: A History of the Huron People to 1660*, 2 vols (Montreal, 1976), and John A. Dickinson, 'Annaotaha et Dollard vus de l'autre côté de la palissade', *Revue d'histoire de l'Amérique française* XXXV (1981), 163–78.

[2]The best study of this early period is Marcel Trudel, *The Beginnings of New France, 1524–1663*, trans. Patricia Claxton (Toronto, 1973). The period of 1663–1701 is covered in W.J. Eccles, *Canada under Louis XIV, 1663–1701* (Toronto, 1964). The latter work is now somewhat dated.

[3]In order of conquest or dispersal these tribes were the Mahicans, 1628; Hurons, 1649; Neutrals, 1651; Eries, 1653–7; and Susquehannocs, 1676.

[4]Mémoire de Henri Tonty, Nouvelles Acquisitions, vol. 7485, f. 103, Bibliothèque Nationale, Paris; Duchesneau au ministre, 13 nov. 1680, C11A, vol. 5, ff. 39–40, Archives Nationales, Colonies, Paris.

[5]W.J. Eccles, *Frontenac: The Courtier Governor* (Toronto, 1959), 82–4, 107–10; François Vachon de Belmont, *Histoire du Canada, D'après un manuscrit à la Bibliothèque du Roi à Paris* (Québec, 1840), 14.

[6]Belmont, *Histoire du Canada*, 15–16; Eccles, *Frontenac*, 167–71; Presens des Onontaguez à Onontio à la Famine le Cinq Septembre 1684, Le febvre de la barre, C11A vol. 6, ff. 299–300.

[7]Le roy au Sr. de Meules, 10 mars 1685, B, vol. II, f. 96, Archs. Nationales.

[8]Eccles, *Frontenac*, 157–97, 244–72.

[9]*Ibid.*, 328–33.

[10]*Ibid.*, 334–7; Marcel Giraud, *Histoire de la Louisiane française I: Le règne de Louis XIV (1698–1715)* (Paris, 1953), 13–23.

[11]M. Tremblay à M. Glandelet, 28 mai 1701, Lettres, Carton O, no. 34, Archives du Séminaire de Québec.

[12]Giraud, *Histoire de la Louisiane*, I, 39–43.

[13]Yves F. Zoltvany, *Philippe de Rigaud de Vaudreuil: Governor of New France, 1703–1725* (Toronto, 1974), 39–41.

[14]*Ibid.*, 40, 86–7; Champigny au ministre, 8 août 1688, C11A, vol. 10, ff. 123–4; Callières et Champigny au ministre, 5 oct. 1701, *ibid.*, vol. 19, ff. 6–7. That this fear was soon to be realized is made clear in d'Iberville's journal for 1702 where he mentions his accepting furs from Canadian *coureurs de bois* for shipment to France. See Richebourg Gaillard McWilliams, trans. and ed., *Iberville's Gulf Journals* (University, Ala., 1981), 165, 178.

[15]Charles Edwards O'Neill, *Church and State in French Colonial Louisiana: Policy and Politics to 1732* (New Haven, Conn., 1966), *passim*.

[16]Rapport de l'Archiviste de la Province de Québec 1938–9 (hereinafter RAPQ), 69, Ministre à Vaudreuil, Versailles, 17 juin 1705.

[17]Beauharnois et d'Aigremont au ministre, 1 Oct. 1728, C11A, vol. 50, ff. 31–3; minister to La Jonquière and Bigot, 4 May 1749, State Historical Society of Wisconsin, *Collections*, XVII (1908), 25–6; Beauharnois to the minister, 18 Oct. 1737, Michigan Pioneer and Historical Society, *Historical Collections*, XXXIV (1905), 146–7.

[18]For a revealing commentary on the working of a typical fur-trade company of the period see Meuvret au Lt Joseph Marin de la Malgue [Commandant, la Baie des Puants], 15 mai 1752, Fonds Verreau, Boite 5, no. 38 1/2, Archs. Sém. Québec. See also Acte de Société, 23 mai 1726, Jean Le Mire Marsolet de Lignery, Guillaume Cartier, Greffe J-B, Adhemar, no. 1854, Archives Nationales du Québec à Montréal.

[19]Pierre-Jacques Chavoy de Noyan to the minister, 18 Oct. 1738, Mich. Pioneer Hist. Soc., *Hist. Colls.* XXXIV (1905), 158–9; Le Conseil de Marine à MM de

Vaudreuil et Bégon, 20 oct. 1717, C11A, vol. 37, ff. 378–9; Beauharnois et Hocquart au ministre, 5 oct. 1736, *ibid.*, vol. 65, ff. 57–8; Greffe J., David, 28 avril 1723, Archs. Québec (Mtl.), is but one of hundreds of permits that specify the obligations to the crown of those allowed to trade in the west. See also *ibid.*, Greffe J-B, Adhemar, no. 1257, 23 mai 1724, and no. 1211, 8 mai 1724; Beauharnois et d'Aigremont au ministre, 1 oct. 1728, C11A, vol. 50, ff. 31–3; Wilbur R. Jacobs, *Dispossessing the American Indian: Indians and Whites on the Colonial Frontier* (New York, 1972), 194, n. 38; and Zoltvany, *Vaudreuil*, 174–5.

[20] Zoltvany, *Vaudreuil*, 166–8, 196–209.

[21] Canada. Conseil. MM de Vaudreuil et Bégon, 26 oct. 1720, C11A, vol. 41, ff. 390–1.

[22] Parole de toute la Nation Abenaquise et de toute les autres nations sauvages ses alliés au gouverneur de Baston au sujet de la Terre des Abenaquise dont les Anglois s'Emparent depuis la Paix . . . fait à Kenaskis[?] au bas de la Rivière de Kenibeki Le 28 juillet 1721, F3 Moreau de St. Méry, vol 2, ff. 413–16, Archs. Nationales.

[23] Mémoire du Roy à MM de Beauharnois et Dupuy, 29 avril 1727, *Nouvelle-France, Documents historiques. Correspondance échangée entre les autorités française et les gouverneurs et intendants*, I (Québec, 1893), 64.

[24] E.E. Rich, *The History of the Hudson's Bay Company, 1670–1870, I: 1670–1763* (London, 1958), 423–5, 482–6; 'Memorial of the Governor and Company of Adventurers of England Trading into Hudson's Bay to the Council of Trade and Plantations', in W. Noel Sainsbury *et al.*, eds, *Calendar of State Papers, Colonial Series, America and the West Indies* (London, 1860–), XXXI, no. 360; Mr. Delafaye to the Council of Trade and Plantations, 4 Nov. 1719, *ibid.*, no. 443; Observations et réflexions servant de réponses aux propositions de Messieurs les Commissaires anglais au sujet des limites a régler pour la Baie d'Hudson, RAPQ 1922–3, 95–6.

[25] Rich, *Hudson's Bay Company*, I, 554, 434, 556, 575, and *The Fur Trade and the Northwest to 1857* (Toronto, 1967), 118.

[26] Lawrence J. Burpee, ed., 'The Journal of Anthony Hendry, 1754–55', Royal Society of Canada, *Proceedings and Transactions*, 2d Ser., XIII, Pt. ii (1907), 352–3.

[27] Rich, *Hudson's Bay Company*, I, 482, 526, 529; Arthur J. Ray, 'Indians as Consumers in the Eighteenth Century', in Carol M. Judd and Arthur J. Ray, eds, *Old Trails and New Directions: Papers of the Third North American Fur Trade Conference* (Toronto, 1980), 255–71; W.J. Eccles, 'A Belated Review of Harold Adams Innis, *The Fur Trade in Canada*', *Canadian Historical Review* LX (1979), 427–34.

[28] Mémoire ou Extrait du Journal Sommaire du Voyage de Jacques Legardeur Ecuyer Sr de St Pierre . . . chargé de la Descouverte de la Mer de l'Ouest, Fonds Verreau, Boite 5, no. 54, Archs. Sém. Québec.

[29] The population figures for these settlements are revealing: Detroit in 1750, 483; Illinois in 1752, 1,536; lower Louisiana in 1746, 4,100.

[30] Denonville et Champigny au ministre, 6 nov. 1688, C11A, vol. 10, f. 8, et le ministre à Denonville, 8 jan. 1688, B, vol. 15, f. 20, Archs. Nationales.

[31] Similarly the Iroquois specifically rejected British claims that they were subjects of the British crown. See Acte authentique des six nations iroquoises sur leur indépendance (2 nov. 1748), *Rapport de l'Archiviste*, 1921–2, unnum. plate following 108.

[32] D'Iberville au ministre, 26 fév. 1700, C13A, vol. I, f. 236, Archs. Nationales; Pièces détachés judiciares 1720: Archs. Québec (Mtl.), Vaudreuil à Beauharnois, 9 nov.

1745, Loudon Collection, Henry E. Huntington Library, San Marino, Calif.: Ordonnance de Beauharnois, 8 juin 1743, Fonds Verreau, Boite 8, no. 96, Archs. Sém. Québec, Duquesne à Contrecoeur, 12 juin 1753, *ibid.*, Boite 1, no. 19; Duquesne à Contrecoeur, 24 juin 1754, Fernand Grenier, ed., *Papiers Contrecoeur et autres documents concernant le conflit anglo-français sur l'Ohio de 1745 à 1756* (Québec, 1952), 193.

[33]On this controversial issue see Ray, 'Indians as Consumers', in Judd and Ray, eds, *Old Trails and New Directions*, 255–71, and Eccles, 'Belated Review of Innis', *Canadian Hist. Rev.* LX (1979), 419–41.

[34]Rich, *Hudson's Bay Company*, I, 545.

[35]Calvin Martin, *Keepers of the Game: Indian-Animal Relationships and the Fur Trade* (Berkeley, Calif., 1978), 63–4; André Vachon, 'L'eau de vie dans la société indienne', Canadian Historical Association, *Report* (1960), 22–32.

[36]Ray, 'Indians as Consumers', in Judd and Ray, eds, *Old Trails and New Directions*, 255–71.

[37]Arthur S. Morton, eds, *The Journal of Duncan M'Gillivray of the North West Company at Fort George on the Saskatchewan, 1794–5* (Toronto, 1929), 47.

[38]Beauharnois et Hocquart au ministre, 12 oct. 1736, C11A, vol. 65, ff. 49–51; Observation de la Conseil de la Marine, 1 juin 1718, *ibid.*, vol. 39, ff. 242–6. See also Reuben Gold Thwaites, ed., *The Jesuit Relations and Allied Documents: Travels and Explorations of the Jesuit Missionaries in New France, 1610–1791* (Cleveland, Ohio, 1896–1901), *passim.*

[39]Eccles, *Frontenac*, 66.

[40]For a brief overview of this contentious issue see *ibid.*, 61–8.

[41]Peter Schuyler to Gov. Donagan, 2 Sept. 1687, E.B. O'Callaghan *et al.*, eds. *Documents Relative to the Colonial History of the State of New-York . . .* (Albany, N.Y., 1856–57), III, 479, hereafter cited as *N.-Y. Col. Docs.*; Propositions made by four of the Chief Sachems of the 5 Nations to his Excell. Benjamin Fletcher . . . in Albany, 26 Feb. 1692/3, *ibid.*, IV, 24; 27 Dec. 1698, Peter Wraxall, *An Abridgement of the Indian Affairs . . . Transacted in the Colony of New York, from the Year 1678 to the Year 1751*, ed. Charles Howard McIlwain (Cambridge, Mass., 1915), 31; Relation de ce qui s'est passé de plus remarquable en Canada . . . 1695, F3 Moreau de St Méry, vol. 7, ff. 370–2, Archs. Nationales; Vaudreuil au ministre, 25 oct. 1710, *Rapport de l'Archiviste*, 1946–7, 385; Vaudreuil et Bégon au ministre, 20 sept. 1714, *ibid.*, 1947–8, 275–6; Beauharnois et Hocquart au ministre, 12 oct. 1736, C11A, vol. 65, ff. 44–6.

[42]Eccles, 'Belated Review of Innis', *Canadian Hist. Rev.* LX (1979), 434.

[43]Thomas Elliot Norton, *The Fur Trade in Colonial New York, 1686–1776* (Madison, Wis., 1974), 100–3, 122, 124.

[44]Jean Lunn, 'The Illegal Fur Trade out of New France, 1713–1760', Canadian Hist. Assn., *Report* (1939), 61–76; Wraxall, *New York Indian Records*, ed. McIlwain, *passim.*

[45]Le Ch[er] Dailleboust à Madame d'Argenteuil, 5 jan. 1715, Collection Baby, g 1/12, Université de Montréal, Montréal, Que.; Ordonnance de Gilles Hocquart, 25 avril 1738, C11A, vol. 69, ff. 180–3; Pierre-Georges Roy, ed., *Inventaire des Ordonnances des Intendants de la Nouvelle-France, conservées aux Archives provinciales de Québec.* I (Beauceville, Que., 1919), 160–1, 222; J.W. De Peyster à Jean Lidius, 23 sept. 1729,

NF 13–17, Procédures Judiciares, III, ff. 389–93, Archs. Québec (Mtl.); Myndert Schuyler à Jean Lidius, 15 oct. 1729, *ibid.*; Extrait des Registres du Conseil Supérieur de Québec, 28 sept. 1730, *ibid.*, ff. 385–8.

[46]Lunn, 'Illegal Fur Trade', Canadian Hist. Assn., *Report* (1939), 61–76.

[47]Vaudreuil et Bégon au ministre, 12 nov. 1712, *Rapport de l'Archiviste*, 1947–8, 183–4; Mémoire du Roy pour servir d'instructions au Sieur marquis de Beauharnois, gouverneur et lieutenant-général de la Nouvelle-France, 7 mai 1726, *Nouvelle-France, Documents historiques*, I, 57; Report of Messrs. Schuyler and Dellius' Negotiations in Canada, 2 July 1698, *N.-Y. Col. Docs.*, IV, 347; Bellomont to Council of Trade and Plantations, 24 Aug. 1699, Sainsbury *et al.*, eds, *Calendar of State Papers Colonial, America and West Indies* XVII, 406.

[48]Beauharnois to Maurepas, 21 Sept. 1741, *N.-Y. Col. Docs.*, IX, 1071.

[49]Arthur H. Buffinton, 'The Policy of Albany and English Westward Expansion', *Mississippi Valley Historical Review* VIII (1922), 327–66.

[50]For contemporary British comment on the superior skills of the Canadian traders see *American Gazetteer . . .* (London, 1762), II, S.V. 'Montreal': 'The French have found some secret of conciliating with the affections of the savages, which our traders seem stranger to, or at least take no care to put it in practice.' See also Burpee, ed., 'Journal of Anthony Hendry', Royal Soc. Canada, *Procs. and Trans.*, 2d Ser., XIII, Pt. ii (1907), 307.

[51]Johnson to the Lords of Trade, 16 Nov. 1765, C.O. 5/66, f. 296, Public Record Office. I am indebted to Dr Francis P. Jennings for providing me with this piece of evidence.

[52]For a specific instance of this see the entry for Teganissorens in David M. Hayne, ed., *Dictionary of Canadian Biography*, II (Toronto, 1969), 619–23.

[53]Wraxall, *New York Indian Records*, ed. McIlwain, III.

[54]Zoltvany, *Vaudreuil*, 168–9; Wraxall, *New York Indian Records*, ed. McIlwain, 132–5.

[55]Percy J. Robinson, *Toronto during the French Régime: A History of the Toronto Region from Brulé to Simcoe, 1615–1793*, 2d ed. (Toronto, 1965), 66.

[56]Wraxall, *New York Indian Records*, ed. McIlwain, 161.

[57]*Ibid.*

[58]Mémoire touchant du droit françois sur les Nations Iroquoises, 12 nov. 1712, C11A, vol. 33, f. 284. The Iroquois admitted to the Albany commissioners that the French had five posts on the south side of Lake Ontario, from Niagara to Cayouhage, east of Oswego. See 10 Sept. 1720, Wraxall, *New York Indian Records*, ed. McIlwain, 130–1.

[59]On Anglo-French relations at this time see Paul Vaucher, *Robert Walpole et la politique de Fleury (1713–1742)* (Paris, 1924).

[60]Zoltvany, *Vaudreuil*, 199.

[61]Wraxall, *New York Indian Records*, ed. McIlwain, 113, Charles Thomson, *An Enquiry into the Causes of the Alienation of the Delaware and Shawanese Indians from the British Interest . . .* (London, 1759), 56, 76, 114, 118–22; Wilbur R. Jacobs, ed., *The Appalachian Indian Frontier: The Edmond Atkin Report and Plan of 1755* (Columbia, S.C., 1954), *passim*.

[62]Duquesne à Contrecoeur, 30 avril 1753, Fonds Verreau, Boite 1, no. 13, Archs. Sém. Québec.

[63]14 mars 1721, 25 avril 1726, Roy, ed., *Inventaire des Ordonnances des Intendants*, I, 196, 282; Hocquart au ministre, 25 oct. 1729, C11A, vol. 51, f. 264; Vaudreuil, Beauharnois, et Raudot au ministre, 19 oct. 1705, *Rapport de l'Archiviste*, 1938–9, 87–8.

[64]Mémoire sur les postes de Canada . . . en 1754 . . . , *Rapport de l'Archiviste*, 1927–8, 353.

[65]Extrait Général des Revenues des Compagnies Entretenues en la Nouvelle-France . . . 1750, D2C, vol. 48, f. 130, Archs. Nationales.

[66]Many of the *voyageurs* hired to serve in the west had notarized contracts, a copy of which had to be preserved in an official register by the notary. Unfortunately, many *voyageurs* were instead hired *sous seing privé*, that is, with a written contract not drawn up by a notary. A few of the latter type of contract have survived by accident or because they were submitted as evidence in legal proceedings. Many men may well have been hired with a mere verbal understanding of the terms of service. Statistical studies based on the notarized contracts alone therefore cannot help but be misleading since there is no way of knowing what proportion of the total number of *voyageurs* employed in any given year the contracts represent. See Gratien Allaire, 'Les engagements pour la traite des fourrures, évaluation de la documentation', *Revue d'histoire de l'Amérique française* XXXIV (1980), 3–26.

[67]W.J. Eccles, *France in America* (New York, 1972), 178–9.

[68]La Chauvignery à [Contrecoeur], 10 fév. 1754, Fonds Verreau, Boite 1, no. 77, Archs. Sém. Québec.

[69]As early as 1708 François Clairambault d'Aigremont, sent to investigate conditions in the west, stated in a momentous report to the minister that the French could not take enough precautions to conserve the trade north of Lake Superior, since the furs at Detroit and those of the region to the south were not worth much. The reluctance of the Canadian fur traders to engage in trade in the Ohio country is made plain in Gov.-Gen. Duquesne's correspondence with Claude-Pierre Pécaudy du Contrecoeur, commandant at Fort Duquesne. Le Sr d'Aigremont au Ministre Pontchartrain, 14 nov. 1708, C11A, vol. 29, f. 175; Grenier, ed., *Papiers Contrecoeur*, 126, 128, 209, 224, 248–9, 253.

[70]Galissonière au ministre, 1 sept. 1748, C11A, vol. 91, ff. 116–22.

[71]Donald H. Kent, *The French Invasion of Western Pennsylvania, 1753* (Harrisburg, Pa., 1954), 12; Sylvester K. Stevens and Donald H. Kent, eds, *Wilderness Chronicles of Northwestern Pennsylvania* . . . (Harrisburg, Pa., 1941), 56; Duquesne à Contrecoeur, 8 sept. 1754, Grenier, ed., *Papiers Contrecoeur*, 250; Duquesne à Rouillé, 31 (sic) nov. 1753, C11A, vol. 99, ff. 139–43; Duquesne à Rouillé, 29 sept. 1754, *ibid.*, ff. 242–3; Duquesne à Rouillé, 7 nov. 1754, *ibid.*, f. 259.

[72]By Oct. 1753, of over 2,000 men who had left Montreal the previous spring and summer only 880 were fit for service. Duquesne à Marin, 16 nov. 1753, Grenier, ed., *Papiers Contrecoeur*, 81; Ministre à Duquesne 31 mai 1754, B, vol. 99, f. 199, Archs. Nationales; Kent, *French Invasion*, 64.

[73]Duquesne à Contrecoeur, 1 juillet 1754, Grenier, ed., *Papiers Contrecoeur*, 207–8.

[74]In Apr. 1754 Capitaine de Contrecoeur warned the Indians who were trading with the English at their post on the Ohio that he intended to drive the English out. If the Indians chose to support the enemy, they too would be crushed; it was up to them to decide whether or not they wished to be destroyed. Paroles de Contrecoeur aux Sauvages, Grenier, ed., *Papiers Contrecoeur*, 116–17. See also Duquesne à Contrecoeur, 15 avril 1754, *ibid.*, 113–16.

[75]Duquesne à Contrecoeur, 14 Aug. 1754, *ibid.*, 248; Duquesne to the minister, 31 Oct. 1754, *N.Y. Col. Docs.*, X, 269; Thomas Pownall, cited in Louis De Vorsey, Jr., *The Indian Boundary in the Southern Colonies, 1763–1775* (Chapel Hill, N.C., 1961), 56–7.

[76]Thomson, *Enquiry into the Causes, passim*; Journal de Chaussegros de Léry, *Rapport de l'Archiviste*, 1927–8, 409–10.

[77]For French and British casualties see Grenier, ed., *Papiers Contrecoeur*, 390–1.

[78]Ministre à Duquesne, 31 mai 1754, B, vol. 99, f. 199, Archs. Nationales.

[79]Vaudreuil au ministre, 13 oct. 1756, C11A, vol. 101, ff. 117–19.

[80]Duquesne à Marin, 20 juin, 10 juillet 1753, Fonds Verreau, Boite 5, nos. 62, 66:6, Archs. Sém. Québec; Duquesne à Contrecoeur, 22 juillet, 6 août 1753, *ibid.*, Boite 1, nos. 27, 28; Varin à Contrecoeur, 18 août 1753, *ibid.*, Boite 5, no. 311.

[81]Mémoire sur les sauvages du Canada jusqu'à la Rivière de mississippi . . . Donné par M. de Sabrevois en 1718, C11A, vol. 39, f. 354; Varin à Contrecoeur, 17 mai, 1 juin, 26 juillet, 1753, Fonds Verreau, Boite 4, nos. 501, 502, 307, Archs. Sém. Québec; Varin à de la Perrière, 21 oct. 1754, *ibid.*, Boite 8, no. 78; Contrecoeur à Douville, 14 avril 1755, Grenier, ed., *Papiers Contrecoeur*, 310–11.

[82]Duplessis Faber à Lavalterie, 16 avril 1756, Baby, no. 137; Péan à Contrecoeur, 15 juin 1754, Fonds Verreau, Boite 1, no. 80, Archs. Sém. Québec; Varin à Contrecoeur, 4 fév. 1753, *ibid.*, no. 294; Varin à (?), 10 mai 1753, *ibid.*, no. 300; Contrecoeur à Douville, 14 avril 1755, Grenier, ed., *Papiers Contrecoeur*, 310; La Perrière à Contrecoeur, 20 avril 1755, *ibid.*, 321; Benoist à Contrecoeur, 30 juin 1755, *ibid.*, 370–3; Saint-Blin à Contrecoeur, au for [sic] de la riviere au bœuf [sic] le 3 juiletts [sic] 1755, *ibid.*, 374–5; Journal de Joseph-Gaspard Chaussegros de Léry, 1754–5, *Rapport de l'Archiviste, 1927–1928*, 385.

[83]Vaudreuil au ministre, 13 oct. 1756, C11A, vol. 101, ff. 117–19.

[84]Thomson, *Enquiry into the Causes*, 108–14.

[85]*Ibid.*, 138–60.

[86]Niles Anderson, 'The General Chooses a Road', *Western Pennsylvania Historical Magazine* XLII (1959), 138, 249, quotation on 396.

[87]Lee Kennett, *The French Armies in the Seven Years' War: A Study in Military Organization and Administration* (Durham, N.C., 1967), 3–13.

[88]H. Carré acidly remarked, in describing the chaos that reigned in the Ministry of Marine, 'enfin le lieutenant de police Berryer, sous l'administration duquel s'effondra la marine. A la fin, il suspendit les travaux des ports et vendit à des particuliers le matériel des arsenaux. Choiseul, son successeur, relèvera la marine, mais trop tard pour le succès de la guerre engagée' (*La Règne de Louis XV (1715–1774)*, in Ernest Lavisse, ed., *Histoire de France* . . . , VIII, Pt. ii [Paris, 1909], 272).

[89]W.J. Eccles, 'The Battle of Quebec: A Reappraisal', French Colonial Historical Society, *Proceedings of the Third Annual Meeting* (Athens, Ga., 1978), 70–81.

[90]28 Dec. 1758, C11A, vol. 103, ff. 453–5; Guy Frégault, *La guerre de la conquête* (Montréal, 1955), 365–72.

[91]Mémoire du duc de Choiseul, déc. 1759, Manuscrits français, Nouvelles Acquisitions, vol. 1041, ff. 44–63, Bib. Nationale.

[92]One interesting aspect of this attitude, as manifested in New England, is discussed by F.W. Anderson, 'Why Did Colonial New Englanders Make Bad Soldiers? Contractual Principles and Military Conduct during the Seven Years' War', *William and Mary Quarterly* 3d Ser., XXXVIII (1981), 395–417.

[93]Rich, *Fur Trade and the Northwest*, 115, and *Hudson's Bay Company*, I, 554, 572, 575–86.

[94]Beauharnois au ministre, 17 oct. 1736, C11A, vol. 65, f. 143.

[95]MG7, I, A–Z, Fonds français, MS 12105, Mémoire de Le Maire 1717, f. 83, Public Archives of Canada.

[96]Conférence avec les Onondagués et Onneiouts, 28 juillet 1756, et Conférence, 21 déc. 1756, C11A, vol. 101, ff. 55–61, 263.

12

The Loyalists

Mary Beth Norton

Most historical writing about the Loyalists has a fascinating split personality, for the Loyalists represent two quite different movements on either side of the Canadian-American border. For the Americans, the Loyalists are the inhabitants of the thirteen colonies who lost the great civil war usually called the American Revolution. They are of interest to the American story only until they depart into exile, at which point they are picked up by Canadian scholars, who deal with them as a pioneering population important to the development of nineteenth-century British North America. Scholars on either side of the border have come in recent years to appreciate that the Loyalists were a far more complex group of people than had previously been assumed. There was no such person as the 'typical' Loyalist, and a substantial proportion of the exiled newcomers to the various provinces of British North America were native peoples, blacks (both slave and free), various non-English peoples (German sectarians and mercenaries, Gaelic-speaking Highland Scots), and women.

In the following article, Mary Beth Norton explores the meaning of Loyalism in one of its subgroups —women—employing a particularly detailed set of documents collected by the British government for processing claims of losses during the revolutionary years. From this material she is able to tease out all sorts of fascinating information about the role of women in both American society and the revolution itself. Women Loyalists seemed particularly vague about family finances outside their own household concerns, and they often fared badly in exile, using a different language than men to describe their suffering.

Despite Norton's assurances that the claims she analysed included women from all walks of life and strata of society, what obvious biases are likely to be present in a set of written claims presented for reimbursement to government? Are there explanations other than the one Norton presents for the relative financial ignorance of the female claimants? Does it follow that because Loyalist women knew their household finances best they were constrained into household roles? And does the language of helplessness automatically imply a lack of positive identity? Might women present themselves as helpless claimants to deal more effectively with impersonal government?

This article first appeared, titled 'Eighteenth-Century American Women in Peace and War: The Case of the Loyalists', in *The William and Mary Quarterly* 3rd ser., 33 (1976), 386–409.

In recent years historians have come to recognize the central role of the family in the shaping of American society. Especially in the eighteenth century, when 'household' and 'family' were synonymous terms, and when household manufactures constituted a major contribution to the economy, the person who ran the household—the wife and mother—occupied a position of crucial significance. Yet those who have studied eighteenth-century women have usually chosen to focus on a few outstanding, perhaps unrepresentative individuals, such as Eliza Lucas Pinckney, Abigail Smith Adams, and Mercy Otis Warren. They have also emphasized the activities of women outside the home and have concentrated on the prescriptive literature of the day. Little has been done to examine in depth the lives actually led by the majority of colonial women or to assess the impact of the Revolution upon them.[1]

Such a study can illuminate a number of important topics. Demographic scholars are beginning to discover the dimensions of eighteenth-century households, but a knowledge of size alone means little without a delineation of roles filled by husband and wife within those households.[2] Historians of nineteenth-century American women have analyzed the ideology which has been termed the 'cult of true womanhood' or the 'cult of domesticity', but the relationship of these ideas to the lives of women in the preceding century remains largely unexplored.[3] And although some historians of the Revolution now view the war as a socially disruptive phenomenon, they have not yet applied that insight specifically to the study of the family.[4]

Fortunately, at least one set of documents contains material relevant to an investigation of all these aspects of late eighteenth-century American family life: the 281 volumes of the loyalist claims, housed at the Public Record Office in London. Although these manuscripts have been used extensively for political and economic studies of loyalism, they have only once before been utilized for an examination of colonial society.[5] What makes the loyalist claims uniquely useful is the fact that they contain information not only about the personal wartime experiences of thousands of Americans but also about the modes of life the war disrupted.

Among the 3,225 loyalists who presented claims to the British government after the war were 468 American refugee women. The analysis that follows is based upon an examination of the documents—formal memorials, loss schedules, and private letters—submitted by these women to the loyalist claims commission, and on the commission's nearly verbatim records of the women's personal appearances before them.[6] These women cannot be said to compose a statistically reliable sample of American womanhood. It is entirely possible that loyalist families differed demographically and economically, as well as politically, from their revolutionary neighbors, and it is highly probable that the refugee claimants did not accurately represent even the loyalist population, much less that of the colonies as a whole.[7] Nonetheless, the 468 claimants included white women of all descriptions, from every colony and all social and economic levels: they were educated and illiterate; married, widowed, single, and deserted; rural and urban; wealthy, middling, and poverty-stricken. Accordingly, used with care, the loyalist claims can tell us much about the varieties of female experience in America in the third quarter of the eighteenth century.[8]

One aspect of prewar family life that is systematically revealed in the claims documents is the economic relationship of husband and wife within the household. All claimants, male and female alike, had to supply the commission with detailed estimates of property losses. Given the circumstances of the war, documentary evidence such as deeds, bills of sale, and wills was rarely available in complete form, and the commission therefore relied extensively upon the sworn testimony of the claimants and their witnesses in assessing losses. The claimants had nothing to gain by withholding information, because the amount of compensation they received depended in large part on their ability to describe their losses. Consequently, it may be assumed that what the loyalists told the commission, both orally and in writing, represented the full extent of their knowledge of their families' income and property.[9] The women's claims thus make it possible to determine the nature of their participation in the financial affairs of their households.

Strikingly, although male loyalists consistently supplied detailed assessments of the worth of their holdings, many women were unable to place precise valuations on the property for which they claimed compensation. Time after time similar phrases appear in the records of oral testimony before the commission: 'She cant say what the Houses cost or what they would have sold for' (the widow of a Norfolk merchant); 'Says she is much a Stranger to the state of Her Husband's Concerns' (the widow of a storekeeper from Ninety-Six, South Carolina); 'It was meadow Land, she cannot speak of the Value' (a New Jersey farmer's widow); 'Her husband was a Trader and had many Debts owing to him She does not know how much they amounted to' (a widow from Ninety-Six); 'She can't speak to the Value of the Stock in Trade' (a Rhode Island merchant's widow); 'It was a good Tract but does not know how to value it' (the widow of a Crown Point farmer).[10]

Even when women submitted detailed loss schedules in writing, they frequently revealed at their oral examinations that they had relied on male relatives or friends, or even on vaguely recalled statements made by their dead husbands, in arriving at the apparently knowledgeable estimates they had initially given to the commission. For example, a New Jersey woman, questioned about her husband's annual income, referred the commissioners to her father and other male witnesses, admitting that she did not know the amount he had earned. Similarly, the widow of a Charleston saddler told the commissioners that 'she does not know the Amount of Her husband's Property, but she remembers to have heard him say in the year 1777 that he was worth £2,000 sterling clear of all Debts.' Such statements abound in the claims records: 'She is unable to speak to the value of the Plantn herself, but refers to Mr. Cassills'; 'Says she cannot speak to the Value—the Valuatn was made by Capt McDonald and Major Munro'; 'Says her Son in Law Capt Douglas is better acquainted with the particulars of her property than herself and she refers to him for an Account thereof.'[11]

Although many female claimants thus lacked specific knowledge of their families' finances, there were substantial variations within the general pattern. The very wealthiest women—like Isabella Logan of Virginia (who could say only that she and her husband had lived in 'a new Elegant, large double Brick House with two wings all finish'd in the best taste with Articles from London') and Mrs. Egerton Leigh of South Carolina (who gave it as her opinion that her husband had 'a considerable real Estate as well as personal property . . . worth more than £10,000 . . . tho' she cannot herself speak to it with accuracy')—also tended to be the ones most incapable of describing their husbands' business affairs.[12] Yet some wealthy, well-educated women were conversant with nearly every detail of the family finances. For the most part, this latter group was composed of women who had brought the property they described to their husbands at marriage or who had been widowed before the war and had served as executrixes of the estates in question for some time. A case in point is that of Sarah Gould Troutbeck, daughter, executrix, and primary heir of John Gould, a prosperous Boston merchant. Her husband John, an Anglican clergyman, died in 1778, and so she carried the full burden of presenting the family's claim to the commission. Although she deprecatingly described herself to the board as 'a poor weak Woman unused to business', she supplied the commissioners with detailed evidence of her losses and unrelentingly pursued her debtors. 'Your not hearing from me for so long a time may induce you to think I have relinquishd my claim to the intrest due on your note,' she informed one man in 1788. 'If you realy entertain any such thoughts I must beg leave to undeceive you.' In addition, she did what few loyalists of either sex had the courage to attempt—return to the United States to try to recover her property. When she arrived in 1785, she found her estates 'in the greatest confusion' but nevertheless managed within several months to repossess one house and to collect some debts. In the end she apparently won restoration of most of her holdings.[13]

Yet not all the female loyalists who had inherited property in their own right were as familiar with it as was Sarah Troutbeck. Another Massachusetts woman admitted to the commissioners that she did not know the value of the 550 acres left her by a relative, or even how much of the land was cultivated. 'Her Brother managed everything for her and gave her what Money she wanted,' she explained. In the same vein, a New Yorker was aware that her father had left her some property in his will, but 'she does not know what property.' A Charleston resident who had owned a house jointly with her brother commented that 'it was a good House,' but the commission noted, 'she does not know the Value of it.' And twice-widowed Jane Gibbes, claiming for the farms owned by her back-country South Carolina husbands, told the commission that she had relied on neighbors to assess the worth of the property, for 'she can't speak positively to the value of her Lands herself.'[14]

But if Jane Gibbes could not precisely evaluate the farms she had lived on, she still knew a good deal about them. She described the total acreage, the amount of land under cultivation, the crops planted, and the livestock that had been lost. In this she was representative of most rural female loyalists with claims that were not complicated by the existence of mortgages or outstanding debts. Although they did not always know the exact value of the land for which they requested reimbursement, they could supply the commission with many important details about the family property: the number of cattle, horses, sheep, and hogs; the types of tools used; the acreage planted, and with what crops; the amounts of grain and other foodstuffs stored for the winter; and the value of such unusual possessions as beehives or a 'Covering Horse'. It was when they were asked about property on which they had not lived, about debts owed by their husbands, or about details of wills or mortgages that they most often admitted ignorance.[15]

A good example is Mary McAlpin, who had settled with her husband on a farm near Saratoga, New York, in 1767. She did not know what her husband had paid for some unimproved lands, or the acreage of another farm he had purchased, but she was well acquainted with the property on which they had lived. The farm, she told the commissioners, 'had been wholly cleared and Improved and was in the most perfect State of Cultivation.' There were two 'Log Houses plaistered and floored', one for them and one for their hired laborers, and sufficient materials on hand to build 'a large and Commodious Brick House'. Her husband had planted wheat, rye, peas, oats, barley, corn, turnips, potatoes, and melons; and 'the Meadows had been laid down or sown with Clover and Timothy Grass, the two kind of Grass Seeds most Valued in that Country.' The McAlpins had had a kitchen garden that produced 'in great abundance every Vegitable usually cultivated in that part of America'. Moreover, the farm was 'well Provided' with such utensils as 'a Team waggon, Carts sledges Carwls [*sic*] Wheels for Waggons, Wheels for Carts, Wheelbarrows, drags for Timber Ploughs, Harrows Hay Sythes Brush Sythes Grubbling Harrows, and all sorts of Carpenters Tools Shoemakers Tools Shovels, Spades, Axes Iron Crow Barrs etc.'

After offering all these details, however, Mrs. McAlpin proved unable to assess the value of the property accurately. She gave the commission a total claim of £6,000, clearly an estimate, and when asked to break down a particular item on her schedule into its component parts she could not do so, saying that 'She valued the Whole in the Lump in that Sum.' Moreover, she proved ignorant of the terms of her husband's will, confusedly telling the commissioners that he had 'left his real personal Estate to his Son—This she supposes was his Lands' (the board's secretary noted carefully, 'This is her own Expression'), when in fact she had been left a life interest in the real estate plus half the personal estate.[16] In short, Mary McAlpin typifies the rural female claimant, though her husband's property was substantially larger than average. She knew what he had owned, but she did not know exactly how much it was worth. She was well acquainted with the day-to-day operations of the farm but understood very little about the general family finances. And she knew nothing at all about legal or business terminology.

The pattern for urban dwellers was more varied. In the first place, included in their numbers were most of the wealthy women mentioned earlier, both those who knew little or nothing about their husbands' estates and those who, like Sarah Troutbeck, were conversant with the family holdings. Secondly, a higher percentage of urban women engaged directly in business. Among the 468 female claimants there were forty-three who declared either that they had earned money on their own or that they had assisted their husbands in some way. Only three of these forty-three can be described as rural: a tavernkeeper's wife from Ticonderoga, a small shopkeeper from Niagara, and the housekeeper for the family of Col. Guy Johnson. All the other working women came from cities such as Boston, Philadelphia, Charleston, and New York, or from smaller but substantial towns like Williamsburg, Wilmington, N.C., and Baltimore. The urban women's occupations were as varied as the urban centers in which they resided. There were ten who took lodgers, eighteen shopkeepers and merchants of various sorts, five tavernkeepers, four milliners, two mantua makers, a seamstress, a midwife, an owner of a coffeehouse, a schoolteacher, a printer, one who did not specify an occupation, and two prostitutes who described themselves as owners of a small shop and declared that their house had been 'always open' to British officers needing 'aid and attention'.[17]

As might be expected, the women who had managed businesses or assisted their husbands (one wrote that she was 'truly his Partner' in a 'steady Course of painfull Industry') were best informed about the value of their property. Those who had been grocers or milliners could usually list in detail the stock they had lost; the midwife had witnesses to support her claim to a high annual income from her profession; the boardinghouse keepers knew what they had spent for furniture and supplies; and the printer could readily value her shop's equipment.[18] But even these working women could not give a full report on all aspects of their husbands' holdings: the widow of a Boston storekeeper, for example, could accurately list their stock in trade but admitted ignorance of the value of the property her husband had inherited from his father, and although the widow of another Boston merchant had carried on the business after her husband was wounded at Bunker Hill, she was not familiar with the overall value of their property.[19]

It is therefore not surprising that women claimants on the average received a smaller return on their claims than did their male counterparts. Since the commissioners reimbursed only for fully proven losses, the amounts awarded are a crude indicator of the relative ability of individual refugees to describe their losses and to muster written and oral evidence on their own behalf. If women had known as much as their husbands about the family estates, there would have been little or no difference between the average amounts granted to each sex. But of the claims heard in England for which complete information is available, 660 loyalist men received an average return of 39.5 per cent, while for 71 women the figure was 34.1 per cent. And this calculation does not take into account the large number of women's claims, including some submitted by businesswomen, which were entirely disallowed for lack of proof.[20]

In the absence of data for other time periods and populations, it is difficult to assess the significance of the figures that show that slightly less than 10 per cent (9.2 per cent, to be exact) of the loyalist refugee women worked outside the home. Historians have tended to stress the widespread participation of colonial women in economic enterprise, usually as a means of distinguishing them from their reputedly more confined nineteenth-century counterparts.[21] The claims documents demonstrate that some women engaged in business, either alone or with their husbands, but 9.2 per cent may be either a large or a small proportion of the total female population, depending on how one looks at it. The figures themselves must remain somewhat ambiguous, at least until additional data are obtained.[22] What is not at all ambiguous, however, is the distinctive pattern of the female claimants' knowledge.

For regardless of whether they came from rural or urban areas, and regardless of their background or degree of participation in business, the loyalist women testified almost exclusively on the basis of their knowledge of those parts of the family property with which their own lives brought them into regular contact. What they uniformly lacked were those pieces of information about business matters that could have been supplied only by their husbands. Evidently, late eighteenth-century American men, at least those who became loyalists, did not systematically discuss matters of family finances with their wives. From that fact it may be inferred that the men—and their wives as well, perhaps—accepted the dictum that woman's place was in the home. After all, that was where more than 90 per cent of the loyalist women stayed, and their ignorance of the broader aspects of their families' economic circumstances indicates that their interest in such affairs was either minimal or else deliberately thwarted by their husbands.[23]

It would therefore appear that the 9 per cent figure for working women is evidence not of a climate favorable to feminine enterprise but rather of the opposite: women were expected to remain largely within the home unless forced by necessity, such as the illness or death of their husbands, to do otherwise. The fact that fewer than one-half (seventeen, to be precise) of the working women enumerated earlier had healthy, living husbands at the time they engaged in business leads toward the same conclusion. The implication is that in mid-eighteenth-century America woman's sphere was rigidly defined at all levels of society, not merely in the wealthy households in which this phenomenon has been recognized.[24]

This tentative conclusion is supported by evidence drawn from another aspect of the claims, for a concomitant of the contention that colonial women often engaged in business endeavors has been the assertion that colonial men, as the theoretical and legal heads of household, frequently assumed a large share of domestic responsibilities.[25] Yet if men had been deeply involved in running their households—in keeping accounts and making purchases, even if not in doing day-to-day chores—they should have described household furnishings in much the same detail as their wives used. But just as female claimants were unable to delineate their husbands' business dealings accurately, so men separated from their wives—regardless of their social status—failed to submit specific lists of lost household items like furniture, dishes, or kitchen utensils. One such refugee observed to the commission in 1788, 'As Household Furniture consists of a Variety of Articles, at this distance of time I cannot sufficiently recollect them so as to fix a Value on them to the Satisfaction of my mind'.[26] It is impossible to imagine a loyalist woman making a comparable statement. For her, what to a man was simply 'a Variety of Articles' resolved itself into such familiar and cherished objects as '1 Compleat set blue and white Tea and Table China', 'a Large new Goose feather Bed, bolster Pillows and Bedstead', 'a Small painted Book Case and Desk', 1 Japan Tea Board', '2 smoothing Irons', and '1 old brass Coffee Pott'. Moreover, although men usually noted losses of clothing in a general way, by listing a single undifferentiated sum, women frequently claimed for specific articles of jewelry and apparel. For example, Mary Swords of Saratoga disclosed that she had lost to rebel plunderers a 'Long Scarlet Cloak' and a

'Velvet Muff and Tippett', in addition to 'One pair of Ear Rings French paste set in Gold', 'One small pair of Ear Rings Garnets', and 'one Gold Broatch with a small diamond Top'.[27]

The significance of such lists lies not only in the fact that they indicate what kinds of property the claimants knew well enough to describe accurately and in detail, but also in the insight they provide into the possessions which claimants thought were sufficiently important to mention individually. For example, a rural New York woman left no doubt about her pride in 'a fine large new stove'; a resident of Manhattan carefully noted that one of her lost beds was covered in 'Red Damask'; and a Rhode Islander called attention to the closets in her 'large new dwelling house'.[28] The differentiated contents of men's and women's claims thus take on more importance, since the contrasting lists not only suggest the extent of the claimants' knowledge but also reveal their assessments of the relative importance of their possessions. To men, furniture, dishes, and clothing could easily be lumped together under general headings; to women, such possessions had to be carefully enumerated and described.

In the end, all of the evidence that can be drawn from the loyalist claims points to the conclusion that the lives of the vast majority of women in the Revolutionary era revolved around their immediate households to a notable degree. The economic function of those households in relation to the family property largely determined the extent of their knowledge of that property. In rural areas, where women's household chores included caring for the stock and perhaps occasionally working in the fields, women were conversant with a greater proportion of the family estates than were urban women, whose knowledge was for the most part confined to the furnishings of the houses in which they lived, unless they had been widowed before the war or had worked outside the home. The wealth of the family was thus a less significant determinant of the woman's role than was the nature of the household. To be sure, at the extreme ends of the economic scale, wealth and education, or the lack of them, affected a woman's comprehension of her family's property, but what the women displayed were relative degrees of ignorance. If the loyalist claimants are at all representative, very few married colonial women were familiar with the broader aspects of their families' financial affairs. Regardless of where they lived, they were largely insulated from the agricultural and business worlds in which their husbands engaged daily. As a result, the Revolutionary War, which deprived female loyalists of the households in which they had lived and worked, and which at the same time forced them to confront directly the wider worlds of which they had little previous knowledge, was for them an undeniably traumatic experience.

At the outbreak of the war, loyalist women expected that 'their Sex and the Humanity of a civilized People' would protect them from 'disrespectfull Indignities'. Most of them soon learned otherwise. Rebel men may have paid lip service to the ideal that women and children should be treated as noncombatants, but in practice they consigned female loyalists to much the same fate as their male relatives. Left behind by their fleeing husbands (either because of the anticipated difficulties of a journey to the British lines or in the hope that the family property might thereby be preserved), loyalist wives, with their children, frequently found themselves 'stripped of every Thing' by American troops who, as one woman put it, 'not contented with possessing themselves of her property were disposed to visit severity upon her person and Those of her friends'.[29] Female loyalists were often verbally abused, imprisoned, and threatened with bodily harm even when they had not taken an active role in opposing the rebel cause.[30]

When they had assisted the British—and many aided prisoners or gathered intelligence—their fate was far worse. For example, the New Yorker Lorenda Holmes, who carried letters through the lines in 1776, was stripped by an angry band of committeemen and dragged 'to the Drawing Room Window . . . exposing her to many Thousands of People Naked'. On this occasion Mrs. Holmes admitted that she 'received no wounds or bruises from them only shame and horror of the Mind', but a few months later, after she had shown some refugees the way to the British camp, an American officer came to her house and held her 'right foot upon the Coals until he had burnt it in a most shocking manner', telling her 'he would learn her to carry off Loyalists to the British Army.'[31]

As can readily be imagined, the women did not come through such experiences emotionally unscathed. One Massachusetts mother reported that her twelve-year-old daughter suffered from 'nervous Fits' as a result of 'the usage she met with from the Mobs'; and another New England woman, the wife of a merchant who was an early target of the local committee because he resisted the nonimportation movement, described to a female friend her reaction to a threatening letter they had received: 'I have never injoyed one hours real Sattisfaction since the receipt of that Dreadfull Letter my mind is in continual agitation and the very rustling of the Trees alarms me.' Some time later the same woman was unfortunate enough to be abused by a rebel militiaman. After that incident, she reported, 'I did not recover from my fright for several days. The sound of drum or the sight of a gun put me into such a tremor that I could not command myself.'[32] It was only natural for these women to look forward with longing to the day when they could escape to Canada or, better still, to England, 'a land of peace, liberty and plenty'. It seemed to them that their troubles would end when they finally left America. But, as one wrote later with the benefit of hindsight, their 'severest trials were just begun'.[33]

Male and female refugees alike confronted difficult problems in England and Canada—finding housing, obtaining financial support, settling into a new environment. For women, especially widows with families, the difficulties were compounded. The Bostonian Hannah Winslow found the right words: it was a 'cruell' truth, she told her sister-in-law, that 'when a woman with a family, and Particularly a large one, looses her Husband and Protector People are afraid to keep up the Acquaintance least they may ask favrs.'[34] Many of the men quickly reestablished their American friendship networks through the coffeehouses and refugee organizations; the women were deprived not only of the companionship such associations provided but also of the information about pensions and claims that was transmitted along the male networks. As a result, a higher proportion of female than male loyalists made errors in their applications for government assistance, by directing the memorials to the wrong officials and failing to meet deadlines, often because they learned too late about compensation programs. Their standard excuses —that they 'had nobody to advise with' and that they 'did not know how to do it'—were greeted with skepticism by the claims commission, but they were undoubtedly true.[35]

On the whole, female loyalists appear to have fared worse in England than their male counterparts, and for two major reasons. In the first place, the commissioners usually gave women annual pensions that were from £10 to £20 lower than those received by men, apparently because they believed that the women had fewer expenses, but also because in most cases the women could not claim the extra merit of having actively served the royal cause.[36] Second, fewer women than men found work to supplement the sums they received from the government. To the wealthier female refugees work seemed so automatically foreclosed as an option that only a small number thought it necessary to explain to the commission why they could not con- tribute to their own support. Mary Serjeant, the widow of a Massachusetts clergyman, even regarded her former affluence as a sufficient reason in itself for her failure to seek employment. In 1782 she told the commissioners, 'Educated as a Gentlewoman myself and brought up to no business I submit it to your [torn], Gentlemen, how very scanty must be the Subsistence which my Own Industry [can] procure us.' Those who did try to earn additional income (many of whom had also worked outside the home in America) usually took in needlework or hired out as servants or housekeepers, but even they had trouble making ends meet. One orphaned young woman reported, 'I can support myself with my needle: but not my two Sisters and infant Brother'; and another, who had learned the trade of mantua making, commented, 'I now got Work for my self [sic]—but being obliged to give long credit and haveing no Money of my one [sic] to go on with, I lived Cheifly upon tea which with night working brought me almost into the last stadge of a Consumtion so that when I rec'd my Money for work it went almost [all] to dockters.'[37]

Many of the loyalist women displayed a good deal of resilience. Some managed to support themselves, among them the Wells sisters of Charleston, who in 1789 opened a London boardinghouse for young ladies whose parents wished them to have a 'suitable' introduction to society. Others survived what might seem an overwhelming series of setbacks—for example, Susannah Marshall of Maryland, who, after running taverns in Baltimore and Head of Elk and trying but failing to join Lord Dunmore off Norfolk in 1776, finally left the United States by sea the following year, only to have her chartered ship captured first by the Americans and then by the British. In the process she lost all the goods she had managed to salvage from her earlier moves, and when she arrived in England she not only learned of her husband's death but was unsuccessful in her application for a subsistence pension. Refusing to give up, she went to work as a nurse to support her children, and although she described herself to the commission in 1785 as 'very Old and feeble', she lived long enough to be granted a permanent annual allowance of £20 in 1789.[38]

Susannah Marshall, though, had years of experience as a tavernkeeper behind her and was thus more capable of coping with her myriad difficulties than were women whose prewar experience had been restricted to their households. Such women recognized that they were 'less able than many who never knew happier days to bear hardships and struggle with adversity'. These women, especially those who had been, as one of them put it, *'born to better expectations'* in America, spoke despairingly of encounters with 'difficultys of which she had no experience in her former life', of 'Adversities which not many years before she scarcely thought it possible, that in any situation, she should ever experience'.[39]

For women like these, exile in England or Canada was one long nightmare. Their relief requests have a desperate, supplicating tone that is largely absent from those submitted by men. One bewailed the impending birth of her third child, asking, 'What can I do in my Condishtion deprived of helth with out Friends or mony with a helpless family to suffer with me?' Another begged the commission's secretary for assistance 'with all humility' because 'the merciless man I lodge with, threatens to sell the two or three trifling articles I have and put a Padlock on the Room unless I pay him the Rent amounting to near a Pound.' By contrast, when a man prepared a memorial for the exceptionally distressed Mrs. Sarah Baker, he coolly told the commissioners that they should assist her because her children 'as Soldiers or Sailors in his Majesty's Service may in future compensate the present Expence of saving them'.[40]

The straits to which some of the female refugees were driven were dramatically illustrated in early 1783 when a South Carolina woman appeared before the commission 'in Rags', explaining that she had been 'obliged to pawn her Goods'. It was but the first incident of many. Time and again women revealed that they had sold or pawned their clothes—which were usually their most valuable possessions—to buy food for themselves and their children. One was literally 'reduced to the last shift' when she testified before the commission; another, the New Yorker Alicia Young, pawned so much that 'the want of our apparel made our situation very deplorable' until friends helped her to redeem some of her possessions. Strikingly, no man ever told the commission stories like these. Either male refugees were able to find alternatives to pawning their clothes, or, if they did not, they were too ashamed to admit it.[41]

Such hardships took a terrible mental as well as physical toll. Evidence of extreme mental stress permeates the female loyalists' petitions and letters, while it is largely absent from the memorials of male exiles. The women speak constantly of their 'Fear, Fatigue and Anxiety of Mind', their 'lowness of Spirit', their 'inexpressable' distress, their 'accumulated anguish'. They repeatedly describe themselves as 'desolate and distressed', as 'disconsolate, Distressed and helpless . . . with a broken Spirit Ruined health and Constitution', as 'Oppressed in body and distressed in mind'.[42] 'I am overwhelm'd with misfortunes,' wrote one. Poverty 'distracts and terrifies me', said another; and a third begged 'that she may not be left a Prey to Poverty, and her constant companons [*sic*], Calamity and Sorrow.' 'My pen is unable to describe the horrors of My Mind—or the deploreable Situation of Myself and Infant family,' Alicia Young told a member of the commission. 'Judge then Dr Sir what is to become of me, or what we are to exist upon—I have no kind of resource. . . . oh Sir the horrors of my Situation is almost too much for me to bear.' Most revealing of all was the wife of a Connecticut refugee: 'Nature it self languishes,' Mary Taylor wrote,

> the hours that I should rest, I awake in such an aggitation of mind, as though I had to suffer for sins, that I neaver committed, I allmost shudder when I approache the Doone [doom?]—as every thing appears to be conspired against me, the Baker, and Bucher, seams to be weary of serving me oh porvity what is its Crime, may some have Compassion on those who feeals its power—for I can doo nothing—but baith my infant with my tears—while seeing my Husbands sinking under the waight of his misfortuens, unable to afford me any release.[43]

Even taking into account the likelihood that it was more socially acceptable for women to reveal their emotions, the divergence between men's and women's memorials is too marked to be explained by that factor alone. It is necessary to probe more deeply and to examine men's and women's varying uses of language in order to delineate the full dimensions of the difference.[44] As C. Wright Mills pointed out in an influential article some years ago, actions or motives and the vocabularies utilized to describe them cannot be wholly separated, and commonly used adjectives can therefore reveal the limitations placed on one's actions by one's social role. Mills asserted that 'the "Real Attitude or Motive" is not something different in kind from the verbalization or the "opinion",' and that 'the long acting out of a role, with its appropriate motives, will often induce a man [or, one is compelled to add, a woman] to become what at first he merely sought to appear.' Furthermore, Mills noted, people perceive situations in terms of specific, 'delimited' vocabularies, and thus adjectives can themselves promote or deter certain actions. When adjectives are 'typical and relatively unquestioned accompaniments of typal situations,' he concluded, 'such words often function as directives and incentives by virtue of their being the judgements of others as anticipated by the actor.'[45]

In this theoretical context the specific words used by female loyalists may be analyzed as a means of understanding the ways in which they perceived themselves and their circumstances. Their very phraseology—and the manner in which it differs from that of their male counterparts—can provide insights into the matrix of attitudes that helped to shape the way they thought and acted. If Mills is correct, the question whether the women were deliberately telling the commission what they thought it wanted to hear becomes irrelevant: it is enough to say that they were acting in accordance with a prescribed role, and that that role helped to determine how they acted.[46]

With these observations in mind, the fact that the women refugees displayed an intense awareness of their own femininity assumes a crucial significance. The phrases permeate the pages of the petitions from rich and poor alike: 'Though a Woman'; 'perhaps no Woman in America in equal Circumstances'; 'being done by a Woman'; 'being a poor lame and infirm Woman'. In short, in the female loyalists' minds their actions and abilities were to a certain extent defined by their sex. Femininity was the constant point of reference in measuring their achievements and making their self-assessments. Moreover, the fact of their womanhood was used in a deprecating sense. In their own eyes, they gained merit by not acting like women. Her services were 'allmost Matchless, (being done by a Woman)', wrote one; 'tho' a Woman, she was the first that went out of the Gates to welcome the Royal Army,' declared another. Femininity also provided a ready and plausible excuse for failures of action or of knowledge. A South Carolinian said she had not signed the address to the king in Charleston in 1780 because 'it was not posable for a woman to come near the office.' A Pennsylvanian apologized for any errors in her loss estimate with the comment, 'as far as a Woman can know, she believes the contents to be true.' A Nova Scotian said she had not submitted a claim by the deadline because of 'being a lone Woman in her Husband's Absence and not having any person to Advise with'. A Vermonter made the ultimate argument: 'had she been a man, Instead, of a poor helpless woman—should not have faild of being in the British Servace.'[47]

The pervasive implication is one of perceived inferiority, and this implication is enhanced by the word women used most often to describe themselves: 'helpless', 'Being a Poor helpless Widow'; 'she is left a helpless Widow'; 'a helpless woman advanced in life'; 'being a helpless woman': such phrases appear again and again in the claims memorials.[48] Male loyalists might term themselves 'very unhappy', 'wretched', 'extremely distressed', or 'exceedingly embarrassed', but *never* were they 'helpless'. For them, the most characteristic self-description was 'unfortunate', a word that carried entirely different, even contrary, connotations.[49] Male loyalists can be said to have seen their circumstances as not of their own making, as even being reversible with luck. The condition of women, however, was inherent in themselves; nothing they could do could change their circumstances. By definition, indeed, they were incapable of helping themselves.

It should be stressed here that, although women commonly described themselves as 'helpless', their use of that word did not necessarily mean that they were in fact helpless. It indicates rather that they perceived themselves thus, and that that perception in turn perhaps affected the way they acted (for example, in seeking charitable support instead of looking for work). Similarly, the fact that men failed to utilize the adjective 'helpless' to refer to themselves does not mean that they were not helpless, for some of them surely were; it merely shows that—however incorrectly—they did think that they could change their circumstances. These two words, with all their connotations, encapsulate much of the divergence between male and female self-perceptions in late eighteenth-century America, even if they do not necessarily indicate much about the realities of male-female relationships in the colonies.[50]

There was, of course, more to the difference in sex roles than the sex-related ways in which colonial Americans looked at themselves. The claims documents also suggest that women and men placed varying emphases on familial ties. For women, such relationships seemed to take on a special order of magnitude. Specifically, men never said, as several women did, that after their spouses' deaths they were so 'inconsolable' that they were unable to function. One woman declared that after her husband's execution by the rebels she was 'bereft of her reason for near three months', and another described herself as 'rendred almost totally incapable of Even writing my own Name or any assistance in any Shape that Could have the least Tendency to getting my Bread'.[51] Furthermore, although loyalist men expressed concern over the plight of the children they could not support adequately, women were much more emotionally involved in the fate of their offspring. 'Your goodness will easily conceive, what I must feel for My *Children*,' Alicia Young told a claims commissioner; 'for myself—I care not—Misfortunes and distress have long since made me totally indifferent to everything in the World but *Them*—they have no provision—no provider—no protector—but God—and me.' Women noted that their 'Sorrows' were increased by the knowledge that their children were 'Partners in this Scene of Indigence'. Margaret Draper, widow of a Boston printer, explained that although she

had been ill and suffering from a 'disordered Mind', 'what adds to my afflic-
tion is, my fears for my Daughter, who may soon be left a Stranger and
friendless.' In the same vein, a New Jersey woman commented that she had
'the inexpressible mortification of seeing my Children in want of many necessaries and conveniencies. . . . and what still more distresses me, is to think
that I am obliged by partaking of it, to lessen even the small portion they
have.'[52]

The women's emphasis on their families is entirely compatible with the
earlier observation concerning the importance of their households in their
lives. If their menfolk were preoccupied with the monetary consequences of
adhering to the crown, the women were more aware of the human tragedy
brought about by the war. They saw their plight and that of their children
in much more personal terms than did their husbands. Likewise, they personalized the fact of their exile in a way that male loyalists did not, by almost
invariably commenting that they were 'left friendless in a strange Country'.
Refugee men, though they might call themselves 'strangers', rarely noted a
lack of friends, perhaps because of the coffeehouse networks. To women, by
contrast, the fact that they were not surrounded by friends and neighbors
seemed calamitous. 'I am without Friends or Money,' declared one; I am 'a
friendless, forlorn Woman . . . a Stranger to this Country, and surrounded
by evils,' said another. She is 'far from her native Country, and numerous
Friends and Relations where she formerly lived, much respected,' wrote a
third of her own condition.[53]

When the female refugees talked of settling elsewhere or of returning to
the United States, they spoke chiefly of the friends and relatives they would
find at their intended destinations. Indeed, it appears from the claims that at
least six women went into exile solely because their friends and relatives did.
A loyalist woman who remained in the United States after the war explained
that she did so because she chose 'to reside near my relations [rather] than
to carry my family to a strange Country where in case of my death they
would be at the mercy of strangers.' And Mary Serjeant's description of her
situation in America as it would have been had her husband not been a
loyalist carried the implication that she wished she too had stayed at home:
'His poor Children and disconsolate Widow would now have had a House
of their own and some Land adjoining to it And instead of being almost
destitute in a Land of Strangers would have remained among some
Relatives.'[54]

In sum, evidence drawn from the loyalist claims strongly suggests that late-
eighteenth-century women had fully internalized the roles laid out for them
in the polite literature of the day. Their experience was largely confined to
their households, either because they chose that course or because they were
forced into it. They perceived themselves as 'helpless'—even if at times their

actions showed that they were not—and they strongly valued ties with family and friends. When the Revolution tore them from the familiar patterns of their lives in America, they felt abandoned and adrift, far more so than did their male relatives, for whom the human contacts cherished by the women seemed to mean less or at least were more easily replaced by those friendships that persisted into exile.

The picture of the late-eighteenth-century woman that emerges from the loyalist claims, therefore, is of one who was almost wholly domestic, in the sense that word would be used in the nineteenth-century United States. But at the same time the colonial woman's image of herself lacked the positive attributes with which her nineteenth-century counterpart could presumably console herself. The eighteenth-century American woman was primarily a wife and a mother, but America had not yet developed an ideology that would proclaim the social value of motherhood. That was to come with republicanism—and loyalist women, by a final irony, were excluded by their political allegiance from that republican assurance.[55]

Suggestions for Further Reading

Wallace Brown and Hereward Senior, *Victorious in Defeat: The Loyalists in Canada* (Toronto, 1984).

J.M. Bumsted, *Understanding the Loyalists* (Sackville, N.B., 1986).

Christopher Moore, *The Loyalists: Revolution, Exile, and Settlement* (Toronto, 1984).

Notes

Ms Norton wishes to thank Carol Berkin, Carl Kaestle, Pauline Maier, Robert Wells, and Peter Wood for their comments on an earlier version of this article. A portion of it was read at the Second Berkshire Conference on the History of Women, held at Radcliffe College, October 1974.

[1]See, for example, such works as Mary Summer Benson, *Women in Eighteenth-Century America: A Study of Opinion and Social Usage* (New York, 1935); Elisabeth Anthony Dexter, *Colonial Women of Affairs*, 2d ed. (New York, 1931); and Joan Hoff Wilson, 'Dancing Dogs of the Colonial Period: Women Scientists', *Early American Literature* VII (1973), 225–35. Notable exceptions are Julia Cherry Spruill, *Women's Life and Work in the Southern Colonies* (Chapel Hill, N.C., 1938), and Eugenie Andruss Leonard, *The Dear-Bought Heritage* (Philadelphia, 1965). On the importance of the early American family see David Rothman, 'A Note on the Study of the Colonial Family', *William and Mary Quarterly* (hereafter *WMQ*) 3d ser., XXIII (1966), 627–34.

[2]Two recent works that deal with family size, among other topics, are Robert V. Wells, 'Household Size and Composition in the British Colonies in America, 1675–1775', *Journal of Interdisciplinary History* IV (1974), 543–70, and Daniel Scott Smith, 'Population, Family and Society in Hingham, Massachusetts, 1635–1880' (PhD

diss., University of California, Berkeley, 1973). Internal household relationships in 17th-century New England have been analysed by Edmund S. Morgan, *The Puritan Family: Religion & Domestic Relations in Seventeenth-Century New England* (Boston, 1944), and John Demos, *A Little Commonwealth: Family Life in Plymouth Colony* (New York, 1970).

[3]Barbara Welter, 'The Cult of True Womanhood, 1820–1860', *American Quarterly* XVII (1966), 151–74, was the first to outline the dimensions of this ideology. For writings dealing with some of the implications of the 'cult of domesticity' see Carroll Smith-Rosenberg, 'The Hysterical Woman: Sex Roles and Role Conflict in 19th-Century America', *Social Research* XXXIX (1972), 652–78; Ann Douglas Wood, 'Mrs. Sigourney and the Sensibiilty of the Inner Space', *New England Quarterly* (hereafter *NEQ*) XLV (1972), 163–81; Kathryn Kish Sklar, *Catharine Beecher: A Study in American Domesticity* (New Haven, Conn., 1973); and Nancy Falik Cott, 'In the Bonds of Womanhood: Perspectives on Female Experience and Consciousness in New England, 1780–1830' (PhD diss., Brandeis University, 1974), esp. chap. 6. An explicit assertion that women were better off in 18th-century America than they were later is found in Dexter, *Colonial Women of Affairs*, viii, 189–92, and in Page Smith, *Daughters of the Promised Land* (Boston, 1970), 37–76. But two European historians have appropriately warned that it may be dangerous to assume the existence of a 'golden, preindustrial age' for women, noting that the 'goldenness is seem almost exclusively in terms of women's work and its presumed relationship to family power, not in terms of other vital aspects of their lives, including the physical burdens of work and child bearing.' Patricia Branca and Peter N. Stearns, 'On the History of Modern Women, a Research Note', *AHA Newsletter* XII (September 1974), 6.

[4]For example, John Shy, 'The American Revolution: The Military Conflict Considered as a Revolutionary War', in Stephen G. Kurtz and James H. Hutson, eds, *Essays on the American Revolution* (Chapel Hill, N.C., 1973), 121–56; John Shy, 'The Loyalist Problem in the Lower Hudson Valley: The British Perspective', in Robert A. East and Jacob Judd, eds, *The Loyalist Americans: A Focus on Greater New York* (Tarrytown, N.Y., 1975), 3–13; and Ronald Hoffman, *A Spirit of Dissension: Economics, Politics, and the Revolution in Maryland* (Baltimore, 1973), esp. chaps. 6, 8.

[5]Catherine S. Crary, 'The Humble Immigrant and the American Dream: Some Case Histories, 1746–1776', *Mississippi Valley Historical Review* XLVI (1959), 46–66.

[6]For a detailed examination of the claims process see Mary Beth Norton, *The British-Americans: The Loyalist Exiles in England, 1774–1789* (Boston, 1972), 185–222. More than 468 women appear in the claims documents; excluded from the sample selected for this article are all female children, all English women who never lived in America (but who were eligible for compensation as heirs of loyalists), and all American women who did not personally pursue a claim (that is, whose husbands took the entire responsibility for presenting the family's claims). In addition to those requesting reimbursement for property losses, the sample includes a number of women—mostly the very poor, who had lost only a small amount of property, if any—who applied soley for the subsistence pensions which were also awarded by the claims commissioners. On the allowance system see *ibid.*, 52–61, 111–21, and 225–9.

[7]On the statistical biases of the loyalist claims see Eugene Fingerhut, 'Uses and Abuses of the American Loyalists' Claims: A Critique of Quantitative Analyses', *WMQ*, 3d ser., xxv (1968), 245–58.

[8]This approach to women in the Revolutionary era differs from the traditional focus on their public contributions to the war effort. See, for example, Elizabeth F. Ellet, *The Women of the American Revolution* (New York, 1848–1850); Walter Hart Blumenthal, *Women Camp Followers of the American Revolution* (Philadelphia, 1952); Elizabeth Cometti, 'Women in the American Revolution', *NEQ* xx (1947), 329–46; and Linda Grant DePauw, *Four Traditions: Women of New York during the American Revolution* (Albany, 1974).

[9]Only if they intended to commit fraud could loyalists gain by withholding information from the commission; two refugees, for example, requested compensation for property they had already sold during the war. But the commissioners found deliberately fraudulent only 10 of the claims submitted to them, and although they disallowed others for 'gross prevarication', none of the claims falling into either category were submitted by women. See Norton, *British-Americans*, 217–19, on the incidence of fraud, and 203–5, 216–17, on the importance of accurate testimony.

[10]Joyce Dawson, testimony, 5 May 1787, A.O. 12/56, 330, Public Record Office; Isabella McLaurin, testimony, 27 November 1784, A.O. 12/47, 233; Margaret Hutchinson, testimony, 10 August 1786, A.O. 12/16, 34; Margaret Reynolds, testimony, 9 December 1783, A.O. 12/46, 168; case of Mrs. Bowers, 24 February 1783, A.O. 12/99, 48; Elizabeth Campbell, testimony, n.d., A.O. 12/26, 267. For other similar statements see A.O. 12/10, 254, A.O. 12/48, 233, A.O. 12/50, 390–1, and A.O. 13/68, pt. 1, 183.

[11]Frances Dongan, testimony, 6 December 1784, A.O. 12/13, 267–72; case of Charlotte Pollock, 27 June 1783, A.O. 12/99, 336; Mary Ann Balfour, testimony, 13 March 1786, A.O. 12/48, 242; Janet Murchison, testimony, 26 July 1786, A.O. 12/34, 405; Mary Kearsley, testimony, 28 April 1785, A.O. 12/38, 282. Cf. Mrs. Kearsley's testimony with her written memorial, A.O. 13/102, 324–9. And see, for other examples, A.O. 12/4, 220, A.O. 12/14, 265, A.O. 12/47, 239, A.O. 13/63, 342, and A.O. 13/94, 318–26.

[12]Isabella Logan, loss schedule, 17 February 1784, A.O. 13/32, 129; case of Lady Leigh, 1 July 1783, A.O. 12/99, 313. See also the claim of Mary Auchmuty, A.O. 12/24, 114–17, 264–6, and A.O. 13/63, 133–40.

[13]Sarah Troutbeck to commissioners, 5 June 1787, A.O. 13/49, pt. 2, 565; Troutbeck to Samuel Peters, May 22, 1788, Peters Papers, III, fol. 83 (microfilm), New-York Historical Society, New York City; Troutbeck to commissioners, 3 January 1785, A.O. 13/137, 609. Her total claim covers fols. 539–90 in A.O. 13/49, pt. 2, and fols. 726–40 in A.O. 13/74. On the recovery of her property see A.O. 12/81, 47. For other examples of well-to-do women with a good knowledge of the family property see A.O. 13/134, 571–4, and A.O. 12/54, 61–71 (Mary Rothery), A.O. 13/64, 81–99, and A.O. 13/97, 344–8 (Henrietta Colden), and A.O. 12/13, 311–14 (Mary Poynton). Mary Winslow knew her own property in detail but was not so familiar with her husband's (A.O. 13/79, 757–8).

[14]Case of Mrs. Dumaresq, 31 March 1783, A.O. 12/99, 134; case of Margaret Smithies, 13 November 1783, A.O. 12/100, 66; case of Barbara Mergath, 8 May 1783,

A.O. 12/99, 234; Jane Gibbes, testimony, 15 December 1783, A.O. 12/46, 245–7.

[15]Jane Gibbes, testimony, 16 December 1783, A.O. 12/46, 247–9; Widow Boyce, loss schedule, 16 October 1783, A.O. 13/90, 181; Elizabeth Hogal, loss schedule, n.d., A.O. 12/27, 37; Typical examples of claims submitted by rural women may be found in A.O. 13/56, 91–3, A.O. 13/138, 475, A.O. 12/4, 72–4, A.O. 12/20, 270–1, A.O. 12/26, 14–16, and A.O. 12/29, 79. Cf. claims from rural men in A.O. 13/79, 73–7, 211–16. For a claim involving property owned elsewhere see that of Elinor Maybee, A.O. 12/28, 343–6, and A.O. 12/64, 1; for one involving both a mortgage and a misread will see that of Margaret Hutchinson, A.O. 12/16, 33–7, and A.O. 12/63, 61.

[16]Mary McAlpin, loss schedule, n.d., A.O. 13/131, 10–11, and testimony, 14 November 1785, A.O. 12/21, 51–65.

[17]The list totals more than 40 because some women listed two enterprises. The women divided as follows: 10 each from New York City and Charleston, 7 each from Boston and Philadelphia, 2 from Baltimore, and 1 each from Savannah, Williamsburg, Wilmington, N.C., and St Augustine. Twenty-eight were long-time widows or single, or were married but operated businesses independently of their husbands; 8 assisted their husbands; and 7 took over businesses after the death or incapacitation of their husbands.

[18]The quotation is from Rachel Wetmore, claims memorial, 25 March 1786, A.O. 13/16, 271. For a milliner's claim see Margaret Hutchinson's, A.O. 13/96, 601–2; for a grocer and boardinghouse keeper's see Sarah Simpson's, A.O. 12/25, 25–8. The midwife, Janet Cumming, claimed to have made £400 sterling annually, and her witnesses confirmed that estimate (A.O. 12/50, 347–8). See also Margaret Draper's original and revised loss estimates, A.O. 13/44, 342–4, 387, and Mary Airey's schedule, A.O. 12/24, 79.

[19]Hannah Pollard, claims memorial and testimony, A.O. 13/49, pt. 1, 158–9, 166; testimony re: claim of Mary Campbell, 24 October 1786, A.O. 12/50, 103–5. The detailed schedule presented by the tavernkeeper Rachel Brain had been prepared by her husband before his death; see A.O. 12/26, 308–10.

[20]For a general discussion of claims receipts see Norton, *British-Americans*, 216–20. Property claims submitted by 10 of the businesswomen were disallowed, and at least another 10 of them apparently did not pursue a claim for lost property. (Because of the destruction and disappearance of some of the claims records it is impossible to be more precise.)

[21]This emphasis appears to have resulted from the influence of Dexter's *Colonial Women of Affairs*. Although she was careful to explain that she had searched only for examples of women who worked outside the home, and although she did not attempt to estimate the percentage of such women in the female population as a whole, historians who draw upon her book invariably stress the wide-ranging economic interests of colonial women. See, for example, Gerda Lerner, *The Woman in American History* (Reading, Mass., 1971), 15–19, and Carol Ruth Berkin, *Within the Conjuror's Circle: Women in Colonial America* (Morristown, N.J., 1974), 8–10.

[22]If anything, the loyalist claimants tended to be more urban than other loyalists and the rest of the American population, and therefore would presumably over-represent working women. See the analysis in Norton, *British-Americans*, 37–9, and Fingerhut, 'Uses and Abuses of Loyalists' Claims', *WMQ*, 3d ser., xxv (1968), 245–

58. Further, the method of choosing the sample—including only those women who themselves submitted claims and pension applications—would also tend to bias the result in favor of working women, since they would be the most likely to act on their own.

[23]The failure of 18th-century men to discuss finances with their wives is also revealed in such letters as that of Jane Robbins to her daughter Hannah Gilman, September 1799, Gilman Papers, Massachusetts Historical Society, Boston. Mrs. Robbins declared that, although her husband had made his will some years before, 'I never saw it till after his death.' Further, she informed her daughter, on his deathbed he told her, 'I should have many debts to pay that I knew nothing about.'

[24]Berkin, *Conjuror's Circle*, 12–14, and Nancy F. Cott, ed., *Root of Bitterness: Documents of the Social History of American Women* (New York, 1972), 8–10, link sex role differentiation specifically to the upper classes that were emerging in the process which has been called 'Europeanization' or 'Anglicization'.

[25]See, for example, Spruill, *Women's Life and Work*, 78–9.

[26]David Ingersoll to commissioners, 30 July 1788, A.O. 13/74, 288. For rare cases of men who did list household furnishings see A.O. 13/98, 431–2, and A.O. 13/73, 140–55.

[27]Martha Leslie, loss schedule, 25 March 1784, A.O. 13/91, 2–3; Frances Dongan, inventory, [1 November 1783], A.O. 13/109, 45; Catherine Bowles, loss schedule, 10 May 1783, A.O. 13/90, 175–6; Mary Swords, 'Things Plundered from me by the Rebels', n.d., A.O. 13/67, 311.

[28]Mary Gibbins, loss schedule, n.d., A.O. 13/80, 167; 'Estimate of Losses sustained at New York by Hannah Foy in the year 1775' [1782], A.O. 13/54, 431; Elizabeth Bowers, loss schedule, n.d., A.O. 13/68, pt. 1, 64.

[29]Sarah Stuart, memorial to Lords of Treasury, 22 January 1786, A.O. 13/135, 702; Elizabeth Phillips, affidavit, 9 October 1788, A.O. 13/67, 303; Phebe Stevens, claims memorial, 23 March 1784, A.O. 13/83, 580. For accounts of rebel looting see, for example, A.O. 12/56, 326–7, A.O. 13/73, 485, A.O. 13/91, 190, A.O. 13/93, 556, A.O. 13/102, 478, A.O. 13/109, 43, A.O. 13/121, 478, and A.O. 13/126, 589.

[30]See, for example, A.O. 12/21, 53–4, A.O. 13/110, 351, A.O. 13/112, 55, A.O. 13/123, 240–1, A.O. 13/128, 7, and A.O. 13/135, 698. Two women said they suffered miscarriages as a result of scuffles with Revolutionary troops (A.O. 13/81, 59, and A.O. 13/64, 76–7), and a third was raped by a rebel soldier. The latter incident is discussed in Thomas Goldthwait to his daughter Catherine, 20 August 1779, J.M. Robbins Papers, Mass. Hist. Soc.

[31]Lorenda Holmes, claims memorial, n.d., A.O. 13/65, 529–30. Similar though less graphic tales were recounted by other women whose assistance to the British was also discovered by the Revolutionaries. See A.O. 12/49, 56–8, A.O. 12/102, 80, A.O. 13/45, 530, A.O. 13/67, 192, A.O. 13/68, 125, A.O. 13/96, 263, and A.O. 13/102, 107.

[32]Mary Serjeant, loss schedule, 19 February 1783, A.O. 13/49, pt. 1, 285; Christian Barnes to Elizabeth Smith, July 13–28, 1770, Christian Barnes Letterbook, Library of Congress; Barnes to Elizabeth Smith Inman, April [2]9, [1775], in Nina Moore Tiffany, ed., *Letters of James Murray, Loyalist* (Boston, 1901), 187–8.

[33]Louisa Susannah Wells Aikman, *The Journal of a Voyage from Charlestown, S.C., to London undertaken during the American Revolution . . .* (New York, 1906), 52; Cath-

erine Goldthwait to Elizabeth [Inman], 27 March 1780, Robbins Papers, Mass. Hist. Soc. For a discussion of the loyalists' initial optimism and subsequent disillusionment see Mary Beth Norton, 'The Loyalists' Image of England: Ideal and Reality', *Albion* III (1971), 62–71.

[34]Hannah Winslow to [a sister-in-law], 27 June 1779, Winslow Papers, Mass. Hist. Soc. See also Rebecca Dolbeare to John Dolbeare, 30 August 1780, Dolbeare Papers, Mass. Hist. Soc.; Polly Dibblee to William Jarvis, November 1787, A.O. 13/41, 248. For a general discussion of the exiles' financial problems see Norton, *British-Americans*, 49–61. For another similar observation by a single woman see Louisa Oliver to Andrew Spooner, 1 March 1788, Hutchinson-Oliver Papers, Mass. Hist. Soc.

[35]The quotation is from the case of Mary Hind, February 1783, A.O. 12/99, 35. For examples of other women who claimed ignorance of proper forms and application procedures see A.O. 12/46, 165, A.O. 12/99, 238, A.O. 13/24, 284, A.O. 13/26, 63, 199, 282, 360, A.O. 13/113, 88, A.O. 13/131, 65, and A.O. 13/137, 150. Of course, a few men also made similar claims; see, for example, A.O. 12/43, 322–5, 328–31, and A.O. 12/46, 63. On the male networks see Norton, *British Americans*, 63–79, 162–4, 186–96, 206–16. The memorials submitted by women were not only more prone to error but also more informal, less likely to be written in the third person, less likely to contain the sorts of ritualistic phrases and arguments used by the men, and consequently more likely to be personally revealing.

[36]Norton, *British-Americans*, 52–61, 111–21, discusses the bases for pension decisions. It was standard practice for the commission to lower a family's allotment immediately after the death of the husband, regardless of the fact that the widow usually had to meet medical and funeral expenses at exactly that time. The pension records (A.O. 12/99–105, and T. 50/11ff, Public Record Office) show that women's pensions were normally smaller than men's. In addition, T. 50/11 reveals a clear case of discrimination: in 1789 the Charleston midwife Janet Cumming (see note 18 above) was, under the commission's rules, entitled to an annual pension of £200 for loss of profession (she was the only woman to qualify for one in her own right); instead, she was granted only a £50 widow's allowance.

[37]Mary Serjeant to John Wilmot and Daniel P. Coke, 1 December 1782, A.O. 13/49, pt. 1, 283; Ann Asby to commissioners, 14 April 1788, A.O. 13/43, 147; Susanna Sandys, memorial, n.d., A.O. 13/84, 613. (Sandys was English, though the daughter of a refugee, and is quoted here because of the detailed nature of her comments.) For a statement similar to Mrs. Serjeant's see Margaret Smythies to Lords of Treasury, 23 January 1782, A.O. 13/67, 230. For two women who did explain why they could not work see A.O. 13/75, 627, and A.O. 13/53, 193. Information about nearly all the loyalist women who worked in England may be located in the following documents: A.O. 12/30, 230, A.O. 12/99, 50, 244, 264, A.O. 12/101, 137, A.O. 12/102, 87, 136, 164, 165, 175, 187, A.O. 13/43, 661, A.O. 13/44, 427, A.O. 13/71, 156, and A.O. 13/131, 359.

[38]On the Wells sisters' enterprise see Steuart Papers, 5041, fol. 123, National Library of Scotland, Edinburgh; Ann Elmsley to James Parker [1789?], Parker Papers, Pt. IV, no. 15, Liverpool Record Office, England; and Aikman, *Journal of a Voyage*, 71.

Susannah Marshall's story may be traced in A.O. 13/62, 4, 7, A.O. 12/6, 257–63, and A.O. 12/99, 244.

[39]Harriet, Mary, Sarah, and Elizabeth Dawson and Ann Dawson Murray to commissioners, n.d., A.O. 13/113, 195; Mary Muirson to Lords of Treasury, 28 May 1784, A.O. 13/56, 342; Isabella Logan, claims memorial, 17 February 1784, A.O. 13/32, 126; Patience Johnston, claims memorial, 21 December 1785, A.O. 13/26, 196. For similar statements see A.O. 13/40, 93, A.O. 13/75, 354, 603. A.O. 13/132, 257, and A.O. 13/134, 504.

[40]Mary Lowry to [Samuel Remnant], n.d., A.O. 13/31, 202; Mary Curtain to Charles Monro, 7 July 1789, A.O. 13/137, 98; Samuel Peters to Daniel P. Coke, 20 November 1784, A.O. 13/43, 352. Cf. the statements in the text with those of men; for example, Samuel Porter to Lords of Treasury, 23 February 1776, T. 1/520, 27; Thomas Banks to Lords of Treasury, 9 February 1779, T. 1/552, 3; John Saunders to Lords of Treasury, 31 March 1785, F.O. 4/1, 248, Public Record Office.

[41]Case of Margaret Reynolds, 26 March 1783, A.O. 12/99, 116; Charlotte Mayne to—[August 1783], H.O. 42/3, Public Record Office; Alicia Young to Robert Mackenzie, 3 June 1789, A.O. 13/67, 641. Mrs. Young gave the commissioners a detailed list of the items she had pawned (A.O. 13/67, 646). For other similar accounts of women pawning or selling their goods see A.O. 12/99, 13, 56, 60, A.O. 12/101, 196, 364, A.O. 13/43, 350, A.O. 13/64, 76, and A.O. 13/135, 81, 426.

[42]'Mrs. Derbage's Narrative', March 1789, A.O. 13/34, 298; Penelope Nicoll, deposition, 6 July 1787, A.O. 13/68, 267; Mary Broadhead to commissioners, 12 November 1788, A.O. 13/125, 626; Margaret Draper to John Robinson, 27 June 1777, A.O. 13/44, 345; Rose Brailsford to Lords of Treasury, 29 December 1779, A.O. 13/125, 580; Joyce Dawson to Lord Dunmore, 24 July 1781, A.O. 13/28, 220; Charlotte Pollock to Lords of Treasury, n.d., A.O. 13/133, 442.

[43]Lucy Necks to Lady North, 14 August 1781, A.O. 13/32, 155; Elizabeth Barkesdale to commissioners, 24 November 1786, A.O. 13/125, 402; Lydia Doty to Lords of Treasury, 8 May 1782, A.O. 13/113, 328; Alicia Young to Robert Mackenzie, 6 June 1789, A.O. 13/67, 643; Mary Taylor to commissioners, 12 April 1783, A.O. 13/42, 590. In sharp contrast to such statements, Andrew Allen, a male refugee, wrote in February 1783, 'Notwithstanding what has happened I have the Satisfaction to feel my Spirits unbroken and my Mind prepared to look forwards without Despondency.' Allen to James Hamilton, 3 February 1783, Dreer Collection, Historical Society of Pennsylvania, Philadelphia.

[44]Recent articles by linguists raise provocative questions about sex differences in speech. Most of them are concerned with 20th-century oral expression, however, and it is difficult to determine how accurately they apply to 18th-century documents. Among the most interesting are Nancy Faires Conklin, 'Toward a Feminist Analysis of Linguistic Behaviour', *University of Michigan Papers in Women's Studies* I (1974), 51–73; Mary Ritchie Key, 'Linguistic Behaviour of Male and Female', *Linguistics: An International Review* LXXXVIII (1972), 15–31; Cheris Kramer, 'Women's Speech: Separate but Unequal?' *The Quarterly Journal of Speech* LX (1974), 14–

24; and Robin Lakoff, 'Language and Woman's Place', *Language in Society* II (1974), 45–79.

[45]C. Wright Mills, 'Situated Actions and Vocabularies of Motive', *American Sociological Review* V (1940), 904–13, esp. 906–9.

[46]The only woman claimant who appears to have manipulatively assumed a 'feminine' role was Sarah Troutbeck. It is also difficult to determine, first, what it was that the commission 'wanted' to hear from female loyalists and, second, how the women would know what the commission wanted, given their isolation from the male information networks. It could perhaps be argued that every 18th-century woman 'knew' what every 18th-century man expected of her, but the fact is that the women claimants had a great deal to gain by displaying a very 'unfeminine' knowledge of their husband's estates and by demonstrating their competence to the commission. See, for example, A.O. 12/101, 186, A.O. 12/40, 40–4, and A.O. 12/66, 6.

[47]The long quotations: Margaret Hutchinson, claims memorial, 23 February 1784, A.O. 13/96, 601; Eleanor Lestor, claims memorial, n.d., A.O. 12/48, 359; Elizabeth Thompson to John Forster, 21 December 1785, A.O. 13/136, 8; Mary Kearsley, testimony, 28 April 1785, A.O. 12/38, 282; Mary Williams, affidavit, 21 December 1785, A.O. 13/26, 535; Catherine Chilsom, claims memorial, 11 March 1786, A.O. 13/24, 90. The shorter phrases: A.O. 13/16, 271, A.O. 13/24, 357, A.O. 13/26, 357.

[48]A.O. 13/118, 488, A.O. 13/67, 234, A.O. 13/73, 586, A.O. 13/81, 59. Men also described women in the same terms; for examples see A.O. 13/28, 215, and A.O. 12/101, 235. The widows of Revolutionary soldiers also called themselves 'helpless'; see, for example, Papers of the Continental Congress, V, 16 (M-41), Roll 50, V, 37, 122 (M-42), Roll 55, National Archives.

[49]T. 1/612, 157, A.O. 13/53, 62, A.O. 13/137, 574, A.O. 12/8, 124. For a few 'unfortunate' men see A.O. 12/46, 104, A.O. 12/51, 208, A.O. 12/13, 188, and A.O. 12/42, 132.

[50]The women who were most definitely not helpless (for example, Susannah Marshall, Janet Cumming, and Sarah Troutbeck) did not use that word to describe themselves. Consequently, it appears that the term was not simply a formulaic one utilized by all women indiscriminately, but rather that it represented a real self-perception of those who did use it. At least one 18th-century woman recognized the sex-typed usage of the word 'helpless'. In her book of essays, Judith Sargent Murray noted that she hoped that 'the term, *helpless widow*, might be rendered as unfrequent and inapplicable as that of *helpless widower*.' See Judith Sargent Murray, *The Gleaner* III (Boston, 1789), 223.

[51]Isabella Logan, claims memorial, 17 February 1784, A.O. 13/32, 126; Jane Hilding, claims memorial, 30 July 1788, A.O. 13/46, 315; Joyce Dawson to Lord Dunmore, 24 July 1781, A.O. 13/28, 220. Also of interest is Jane Constable to Lords of Treasury, n.d., A.O. 13/73, 374.

[52]Alicia Young to Robert Mackenzie, 6 June 1789, A.O. 13/67, 643; Jane Roberts, claims memorial, 17 March 1784, A.O. 13/71, 245; Margaret Draper to Lord ——, 15 October 1782, A.O. 13/44, 349; Elizabeth Skinner to commissioners, 28 August 1786, A.O. 13/112, 61. Mrs. Draper lived to see her daughter well married (Mar-

garet Draper to the Misses Byles, 21 June 1784, Byles Papers, I, 134, Mass. Hist. Soc.). Cf. men's attitudes toward their children and other dependents in A.O. 13/75, 556, A.O. 12/105, 115, A.O. 13/131, 399, and A.O. 13/137, 2.

[53] Elizabeth Putnam to Thomas Dundas, 7 November 1789, A.O. 13/75, 309; Elizabeth Dumaresq to Lord Shelburne, 14 September 1782, A.O. 13/44, 429; Elizabeth Barkesdale to commissioners, 24 November 1786, A.O. 13/125, 402, Rachel Wetmore, claims memorial, 25 March 1786, A.O. 13/16, 272. Other comments on neighbors and relatives may be found in A.O. 12/3, 231, A.O. 12/56, 339, A.O. 13/25, 275, A.O. 13/32, 595, A.O. 13/44, 345, A.O. 13/75, 544, 641, and A.O. 13/107, 271. Mr. and Mrs. James Parker had an interesting exchange of letters on the subject of whether she would join him in England, in which her ties to her American friends figured strongly. 'Tho I would not hesitate one moment to go with you my Dearest friend to any place on earth, yet I cannot think of parting forever with my Dear and valuable friends on this side the atlantick, without many a heart felt sigh,' she wrote on 24 July 1783. His response (5 March 1784) recognized her concern: 'I realy sympathize with you on this trying scene of leaving of your Country and all our friends.' Parker Papers, Pt. VIII, nos. 26, 31, Liverpool Record Office.

[54] Elizabeth Macnair to John Hamilton, 27 December 1789, A.O. 13/131, 400; Mary Serjeant to John Wilmot and Daniel P. Coke, 1 December 1782, A.O. 13/49, pt. 1, 283. See also A.O. 13/34, 471, and A.O. 13/70B, 145, on resettlement. For women who followed friends and relatives into exile see A.O. 13/116, 468, A.O. 13/114, 662, A.O. 12/102, 24, and A.O. 13/37, 3.

[55] On the development of republican ideology pertaining to women see Linda K. Kerber, 'Daughters of Columbia: Educating Women for the Republic, 1787–1805', in Stanley Elkins and Eric McKitrick, eds, *The Hofstadter Aegis* (New York, 1974), 36–59.

13

The Maritime Provinces in the Late Eighteenth Century

Graeme Wynn

One of the most important new subfields of Canadian history is historical geography, and its enduring contribution is *The Historical Atlas of Canada*, a work with which every student of Canadian history should be familiar. As the *Historical Atlas* indicates, historical geography is concerned not only with maps and cartography, but also with all the changing geographical patterns (including those of human culture and settlement) of the political territory. There is in historical geography a distinctive emphasis upon the relationship between the physical landscape and what occurs upon it. While historical geographers are to be found around the world, they are arguably more numerous and influential in Canada than in most other places, perhaps because Canadians have always appreciated the crucial historical role of their landscape and climate.

In the following study in human geography, Graeme Wynn—who was chiefly responsible for the *His-torical Atlas* plate on 'Maritime Canada, Late 18th Century' (number 32)—expands and elaborates on the information on that plate. He discusses the arrival of the Loyalists and their impact on the economy, and concludes with an overview of the diversity of the four Maritime provinces (Nova Scotia, Cape Breton, New Brunswick, Prince Edward Island) of British North America around 1800. Maritime British North America in 1800, insists Wynn, was 'an unconsolidated amalgam of families and small communities' in which 'the reach of colonial institutions was limited'. Larger social patterns, in short, had not yet emerged.

What does Figure 1 (Origins and distribution of Loyalists) tell us about the process of Loyalist settlement in the Maritime provinces? What does Figure 3 (Settlement patterns and economic activity, 1800) indicate about the relationship between settlement and economic activity? How did the cultural land-

scape reflect the origins of the settlers? What was the ethnic composition of the population? How do

the patterns in 1800 prefigure the
later historical experience of the
region?

This article first appeared, titled 'A Region of Scattered Settlements and Bounded Possibilities: Northeastern America 1775–1800' in *The Canadian Geographer/Le Géographe canadien* 31, 4 (1987), 319–38.

With three-quarters of its population New Englanders, and numerous ties of trade and sentiment to the line of British colonies that ran from Newfoundland to the Bahamas, pre-Revolutionary Nova Scotia was part of a wider economic and cultural unit, only a fraction of which seceded from Britain between 1776 and 1783.[1] If in historian John Bartlett Brebner's vivid metaphor, the fires of rebellion burned less fiercely there than they did at the centre of the colonial arc, they glowed sporadically for all that. Nova Scotians protested the Stamp Act with their Boston cousins and celebrated with them its repeal in July 1776. Unexplained fires damaged the Halifax naval yard and destroyed hay consigned from the city to the British garrison in Massachusetts. And a few Nova Scotian merchants refused to handle East India Company tea.

But provincial opinion was far from unanimous. Halifax tea imports increased 26-fold and more in 1770, precisely at the time that non-importation agreements raised tea prices in New England. Large numbers of provincial vessels engaged in contraband trade with neighbouring colonies, but while some Nova Scotians were 'hearty in the Cause', others denounced the Revolutionary leaders as demagogues.[2] In the end, neither side mounted a decisive action. Beyond Halifax, where officials, the navy, and British coin demonstrated the reality and benefits of colonial dependence, most Nova Scotians were preoccupied with survival. Their settlements were isolated, they lacked capital, industry, and significant autonomous, merchant communities. Influenced by the revivalist preaching of Henry Alline, which flourished on the psychological unease of a migrant, still rootless people forced to recognize a new division between themselves and residents of their former homeland (and in which the war became God's retribution for the corruption of London and Boston), the 'weak and exposed' majority of Nova Scotians opted for neutrality.[3]

This was no shield from turmoil. American privateers raided almost every substantial settlement in the province except Halifax between 1776 and 1782. If bloodshed was rare, the spoils were often considerable. Ships, provisions, and valuables were carried away, 'neutral Yankees' were taunted, and some were drawn to the American side. Machias-based raiders disrupted the provision trade between Fundy settlements and British troops, and in 1775 they burned abandoned Fort Frederick at the mouth of the St John River. The next year a small force under Jonathan Eddy laid siege to Fort Cumberland in Chignecto.[4] Earlier, the principal officers of the island of St John had been removed by an unauthorized raiding party. To defend the Saint John valley, Fort Howe was built in 1778 on a cliff at the mouth of the river. In Halifax, the defences 'were extensive but hardly imposing'. Yet commerce there was, invigorated by the presence of wealthy exiles from the American colonies, military officers, and troops with money to spend.[5] The cargoes of condemned vessels were auctioned in the prize court. Prices rose, and suppliers and landlords benefited.[6] In contrast, many poorer citizens probably fared badly during the periodic shortages of food.[7]

Settlement, 1780–1800

By 1782 it was clear that substantial numbers of civilian refugees and disbanded soldiers (Provincials)—collectively Loyalists—who had taken the British side in the Revolution were to be settled in British North America. Prior to their arrival, negotiations with the Americans established the St Croix River (rather than the St John or Penobscot) as the western limit of Nova Scotia. From the source of the St Croix, the boundary was drawn through little-known territory northwards to the highlands separating the St Lawrence and Atlantic drainage basins. In the nineteenth century both the identity of the 'St Croix' and the precise meaning of this demarcation were to be debated in territorial disputes between New Brunswick and the United States and between New Brunswick and Quebec; but in the short term the boundary agreement secured the 'back part' of Nova Scotia for Loyalist occupation.[8]

To facilitate settlement of the Loyalists, almost 1.5 million acres of land, granted between 1752 and 1774 but still unoccupied, were escheated between 1783 and 1788. Added to the enormous area of Nova Scotian Crown land that remained beyond the handful of naval timber reserves established earlier in the 1770s, this made available a vast estate for distribution to the newcomers in free grants. Purchase fees (hitherto 10 shillings per 100 acres) and those for surveying and registering grants were waived to ensure that Loyalists received land without charge. Each family head was entitled to 100 acres, with a further 50 acres for each member of his household; those with the 'desire and ability to cultivate' more could apply for up to 1,000 acres of extra land; commissioned and non-commissioned officers received additional quantities according to their rank, ranging downwards from the 1,000 acres allowed field officers. Under these terms, approximately 4,750 Loyalist grants, amounting to an estimated 700,000 acres, were made in peninsular Nova Scotia during the 1780s; in New Brunswick, divided from the peninsula as a separate, largely Loyalist colony in 1784, some 476,000 acres passed into Loyalist hands before 1790.[9]

Quite how many Loyalists arrived in Nova Scotia and its neighbouring islands will never be known with certainty. Many departed without acquiring land or being enumerated in any of the several musters organized by harried authorities; more relocated—some twice or thrice—within the region; there were spurious applications for land; and the administrative challenge posed by so large a group of newcomers created its own confusions. By most estimates, the Loyalist influx amounted to some 35,000 persons. It transformed the geography of the region. Returns of those Loyalists entitled to government provisions in the late fall of 1785 recorded totals of almost 15,000 for Nova Scotia, almost 11,000 for New Brunswick, 420 for the Island of St John, and 121 for Cape Breton.[10] The number of Loyalists actually settled in these areas was certainly greater. In all, 6,220 Loyalists received Nova Scotian grants. Although slightly more than 700 of those were subsequently escheated, it is likely that the Loyalists added some 19,000 persons to the permanent population of the province. For New Brunswick, the equivalent figure is 15,000, some 85 per cent of whom are estimated to have 'remained in New Brunswick until the end of their lives'.[11] In broad terms, then, Loyalist migrations approximately doubled the population of the Nova Scotian peninsula and virtually quadrupled that of the 'mainland'. Some 500 Loyalists went to the Island of St John (Prince Edward Island after 1798), but many were transients, and probably no more than 200 remained in 1786. Cape Breton, created as a separate colony in 1785,[12] received a similar increment, but more stayed to play a significant role in its settlement, social development, and politics.

Drawn from all walks of life, and from each of the 13 former colonies, the Loyalists shared little but the experience of exile and the uncertainty of their prospects in British North America.[13] Before the Revolution, some had been persons of wealth and stature: Edward Winslow, who traced his American roots back to the *Mayflower*, was a graduate of Harvard, clerk of the General Sessions in Plymouth, and prominent Boston tory; John Saunders and Beverly Robinson were sons of rich and powerful Virginia families; an ordained Anglican minister and medical doctor, Jonathan Odell of New Jersey was outstanding among loyal satirists of the 1770s; Dr Azor Betts was 'a well known practitioner of physic in New York . . . noted for his success in inoculation' before he went to Nova Scotia; Mather Byles was the great-grandson of Increase Mather and minister of Christ Church, Boston; John Wentworth had succeeded his uncle as governor of New Hampshire and surveyor-general of the King's Woods in North America and held those offices for a decade before being proscribed by the Continental Congress.[14]

But for all their prominence in late-eighteenth-century Nova Scotia and New Brunswick, such individuals were the merest fraction of the Loyalist population. The overwhelming majority of their fellow migrants were men and women of modest circumstances, tradesmen, labourers, farmers, and their families, accustomed to hard work and simple comforts. Yeomen, carpenters, and cordwainers outnumbered gentlemen, esquires, and merchants four to one among the 530 persons given the freedom of Saint John at its incorporation in 1785, and the disproportion was almost certaintly greater in the New Brunswick countryside.[15]

Educated, relatively well-to-do Loyalists may have been drawn to established settlements such as Halifax and Annapolis, but these places also had large numbers of impoverished exiles. Public buildings sheltered scores of destitute newcomers through the Halifax winter of 1783; in the harbour a group, mainly women and children from the southern colonies, lived aboard a vessel 'crowded like a sheep-pen'; in the city as a whole, hundreds died and thousands survived on meagre rations of codfish, molasses, and hard biscuit.[16] In Annapolis, too, all available buildings were used to accommodate the newcomers, but many lacked shelter and several families had to make do with 'a single apartment built with sods, where men, women, children, pigs, fleas, bugs, mosquitoes and other domestic insects, mingle[d] in society'.[17]

Evidence assembled by the British Commission for Enquiry into the Losses, Services, and Claims of the American Loyalists confirms the essential elements of this picture. In all, 280 Nova Scotian and 308 New Brunswick claimants received awards; they averaged £552 and £364, respectively. Only 8 per cent of New Brunswick Loyalists (and a smaller proportion of those in Nova Scotia) sought restitution for their losses. On a per capita basis, they claimed at barely half the rate of all Loyalists. Their claims were also relatively modest. Sixty per cent sought less than £500, and fewer than 70 claimed more than £1,000, although the average value of all Loyalist claims exceeded £1,580.[18] Their submissions recounted their 'Low Sercumstances' and told of families 'in Great Poverty and Distress'.[19] Countless others who left little behind, who could not prove their losses, or who lacked the skill, time, and money to set down and pursue a claim were not heard from.

Information about Loyalist origins is most complete for New Brunswick (Figure 1).[20] Fully 90 per cent of those who settled in the new province were American born, and most were from families long established in the 13 colonies. Less than a quarter came from New England (Connecticut 12.9 per cent; Massachusetts 6.1 per cent; Rhode Island 1.9 per cent; and New Hampshire 1.2 per cent). Almost 70 per cent were from the middle colonies (New York 40 per cent; New Jersey 22 per cent; Pennsylvania 7.7 per cent). Maryland, Virginia, and Delaware counted 3.6 per cent, the Carolinas 3.1 per cent, and Georgia a bare 0.3 per cent. Surnames reflected something of the ethnic composition of the populations from which the migrants came and included at least 200 of Dutch derivation (from New York and New Jersey), 80 of Huguenot origin, and perhaps half as many German names, borne by Pennsylvania 'Dutch' families. Overall, peninsular Nova Scotia may have received a larger proportion of Massachusetts Loyalists than did New

Figure 1. Origins and distribution of Loyalists in Nova Scotia, New Brunswick, Cape Breton, and the Island of St John, 1785.

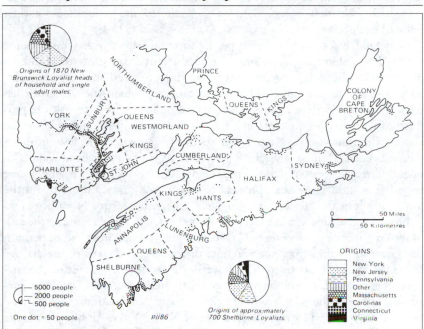

SOURCES: Public Archives of Canada, General Returns of Loyalists MC 23 D1(1) vol. 24; E.C. Wright, *The Loyalists of New Brunswick* (Moncton: Moncton Publishing, 1972); A.H. Clark, *Three Centuries and the Island* (Toronto: University of Toronto Press, 1959); R.J. Morgan, 'Orphan Outpost', PhD diss., University of Ottawa, 1973.

Brunswick and likely had fewer exiles from New Jersey. But an analysis of the origins of some 700 family heads among the Shelburne Loyalists confirms the dominance of the middle colonies as a source area. New Englanders were a less significant proportion of Shelburne than New Brunswick Loyalists, but both the Chesapeake and the Carolinas contributed an appreciable greater fraction to the population of the town than the province.[21]

Black Loyalists comprised fully a tenth of those who went to greater Nova Scotia.[22] Most were runaway slaves from Virginia and South Carolina, and, judging from the slim evidence of two lists enumerating 216 individuals, many (over 40 per cent) were skilled men; their numbers included blacksmiths, carpenters, coopers, and tailors. But rarely were their hopes of freedom and independence realized in British North America. For a few, skills learned in slavery or servitude were the foundations of later autonomy: Boston King was a carpenter in Shelburne; Willis caulked vessels in Simeon

Perkin's Liverpool shipyard; others were masons, coopers, blacksmiths, and blockmakers.[23] Often they toiled for less than white workers and—as in the 'Extraordinary . . . Riot' of 1784 in Shelburne, when disbanded soldiers 'Drove the Negroes out of the Town'—suffered the resentment of their fellow Loyalists.[24]

Generally, black Loyalists fared poorly in comparison with whites. Some survived by fishing to supplement the produce of small gardens. Hundreds became day-labourers, servants, or tenants. Many, realized one sensitive critic, were 'obliged to live upon White-mens property which the Governor has been liberal in distributing—and for cultivating it they receive half the produce so that they are in short in a state of Slavery.'[25] In the difficult climate and on the thin soils of Nova Scotia such arrangements held few prospects but indigence. Denied several of the privileges of white citizens, and frequently treated with cruel severity before the law, black Loyalists 'were regarded as little more than physical beings whose function was to fill the lowest levels of the labour force' in late-eighteenth-century Nova Scotia.[26]

Nova Scotian land-grant procedures were hopelessly inadequate to the task of settling so many newcomers. To secure a grant, individuals had to petition the governor, either for a specific tract or for an assignment of the acreage to which they were entitled. The governor referred the request to the surveyor-general, who conducted or commissioned a survey. Then the surveyor-general of the King's Woods had to certify that the timber on the land was neither required by nor reserved for the Royal Navy. All being well, the provincial secretary would prepare a draft grant for the signature of the attorney-general before the actual grant was drawn up. Once that had been signed by the governor and the applicant had sworn the oath of allegiance, the land was his. Although disbanded regiments were generally settled together under one petition and groups of civilian Loyalists could apply for land in conjunction, the system soon bogged down. Nor was that established in New Brunswick appreciably more efficient.

By 1784, a very small proportion, indeed, of the Loyalists were on their lands. 'Discontent and uneasiness' were reported in several settlements.[27] There were too many applicants, too few surveyors, too many administrative delays, and, in the climate of confusion, too many individuals jockeying for particular advantage, for the allocation of land to proceed without dispute and injustice. In Shelburne there was much strife over matters of property; in Annapolis County, Loyalists impatient at delays moved on to common and glebe land; black Loyalists in both locations waited longer than most to receive land, and those who eventually received it generally got smaller holdings; in 1791, a small group of Pictou Loyalists threatened to return to the United States if they did not soon receive their grants, and many Digby Loyalists waited until 1800 for clear title to their properties.[28]

By 1785, there were Loyalists in most parts of peninsular Nova Scotia. Generally they added little to the population of established agricultural districts, where free land was scarce. Horton and Cornwallis townships mustered fewer than 250 Loyalists, Windsor but a few dozen more; at most, 1,000 Loyalists settled about the fertile Minas Basin. Among the indented, rocky shore east of Halifax, and westward from Canso to Chignecto, by contrast, there were few pre-Loyalist settlers; provision musters enumerated over 3,000 newcomers in these areas. Halifax, according to Governor Parr, had approximately 1,200 Loyalists. Few of them received the royal bounty which, by contemporary account, was intended neither for the wealthy nor 'the vicious & indolent', but not all were merchants and placemen; some 200 of the city's Loyalists were sustained by charity. Beyond the capital there were four significant nodes of Loyalist settlement: a thousand and more clustered near the head of Chedabucto Bay; almost double that number settled in the Annapolis Valley, especially in the Granville, Wilmot, and Clements districts; Conway, renamed Digby in February 1784, had approximately 1,300 Loyalist settlers; and Shelburne, formerly Port Roseway, rose from insignificance to become, briefly, the fourth largest town in America, with some 10,000 residents. Within this matrix there developed three all-black settlements—Birchtown on the outskirts of Shelburne, with 1,500 inhabitants in 1784; Brindley Town near Digby (with perhaps 200 residents); and at Tracadie Harbour near Chedabucto. There were also significant concentrations of black Loyalists in Halifax (which had 422 blacks among its 1791 population of 4,897) and neighbouring Preston.[29]

Shelburne was the most spectacular achievement and greatest failure of the Loyalist resettlement. The town was built with astonishing rapidity. The survey of the site began in late April 1783. Two weeks later, the first Loyalists arrived. By late July the tent-town had a population of 7,600. In December, Governor Parr reported 800 houses built in Shelburne and 600 more 'in great forwardness'. Early in the new year residents celebrated Queen Charlotte's birthday with dancing, tea, and cards 'in a house which stood where six months ago there was an almost impenetrable swamp'. Within nine months of the first arrivals the town had 1,127 dwellings, 80 of them temporary, 231 framed, and the remainder of logs. According to the *London Chronicle* of 4–7 December 1784, 'the inhabitants vie[d] with each other in making fine appearances.'[30] But the pretensions of its citizens, the wharfs and stores of its waterfront, its three newspapers, and its fine harbour could not compensate for Shelburne's rocky, infertile hinterland, its failure to develop a firm economic foundation, and the fact, recognized by Governor Parr, that 'the generality of those who came [t]here, were not much burthened with Loyalty, a spacious name which they made use of.'[31] In 1785, the *Port Roseway Gazetteer and Shelburne Advertiser* offered substantial properties for sale: Peter Lynch thought his large, elegant two-storey house with 4 rooms per floor, cellar, adjoining kitchen, and large yard and garden 'in high cultivation' 'entirely proper for a merchant'. Others simply sought let, lease, or sale arrangements.[32] The majority of residents, observed a contemporary, were 'as poor as Rats in an empty house'. By 1790 upwards of two-thirds of the town was uninhabited; some 700 families (say 3,000 persons) made up the population of Shelburne and its vicinity. By 1818 the town had fewer than 500 occupants.[33]

Across the Bay of Fundy, Parrtown and neighbouring Carleton (incorporated as the city of Saint John in 1785) rivalled Shelburne in rapidity of development, if not size. Fewer than 425 persons (including a garrison of 118) occupied a site one Loyalist considered 'the roughest land . . . [she] ever saw' when the first exiles arrived in May 1783.[34] By July there were about 400 houses built, by September 700, almost all of them in Parrtown. By March 1784 the settlement comprised 'about fifteen hundred framed Houses, and about four hundred temporary ones constructed of hewn logs'. By 1788 it had 'near 2000 Houses' and had become, in Edward Winslow's judgment, 'one of the best cities in the new world'.[35] Functionally this new town was a funnel, a point of disembarkation through which Loyalists would move to lands in the interior. But with the finest harbour on the north side of the Bay of Fundy and the extensive, fertile St John valley its hinterland, it retained an importance that Shelburne did not. Although Fredericton was proclaimed the provincial capital, Saint John accounted for 2,000 of the near 11,000 New Brunswick Loyalists enumerated in the final provision muster of 1785 and was the largest urban centre in the province. Six years later a visitor described a 'well-planned' town 'of about five hundred houses, all of timber, well painted . . . and some of them even elegant'.[36]

By design intended to ensure colonization of the back country, civilian and military Loyalists were directed to different areas of New Brunswick. Loyalist regiments were assigned lands along the St John River above Fredericton; civilians were to settle in the lower St John and Passamaquoddy districts. But this plan was hardly realized. Several regiments refused their allocated blocks, and only a fraction of the officers and men in those regiments that accepted grants settled the designated lands. Most soldiers remained in the lower St John valley among the civilian refugees. In 1785, Fredericton had approximately 650 bounty claimants, the area up-river about 850; rather more than 5,000 were enumerated along the 90 miles of the St John river (and the lower reaches of its major tributaries) between Fredericton and Saint John. Passamaquoddy, the southwestern corner of the province, was the other important focus of settlement, with approximately 1,900 Loyalists; there were a few in the marshland district of Westmorland county and a handful on the lower Miramichi.[37]

For most Loyalists, strenuous exertion was necessary for survival in the wilderness of northeastern America. Hardship and privation were common. For some, such as Filer Dibblee, once a representative in the Connecticut Assembly who committed suicide in 1784, they were intolerable. For most they were burdens to be borne in hope of future comfort, but even 'the most industrious farmers', realized clergyman Jacob Bailey, faced several years of struggle before they could 'raise provisions sufficient for their families'.[38] After a year or two on their grants, most Loyalist families might have had a rough dwelling and 2 to 4 acres of cultivable land. With continuing effort, and good health and fortune, such a beginning might be turned into the comfortable property described in the mid-1780s by William Cobbett as comprising 'a large and well built log dwelling house . . . on the edge of a very good field of Indian corn, by the side of which was a piece of buckwheat just then mowed.'[39]

Several fared far worse than these New Brunswick settlers. Poor soils, inclement weather, and wheat blight dimmed the prospects of farmers in the late 1780s and early 1790s. Settlers of the Bear and Moose river districts of

---

Figure 2. Migration to and from the mid–St John valley, 1784–1800.

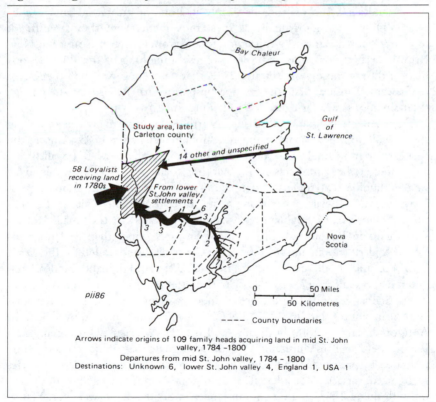

SOURCE: T.M.F. Kilbride, 'The Process of Growth and Change in Carleton County, 1783–1867', MA thesis, University of New Brunswick, 1969.

Nova Scotia described themselves as 'real objects of Charity' in their 'excessive distress'; in a petition for medical aid, Loyalists in Digby recounted their suffering from 'hard labor, incommodious Lodging open Huts Long Fastings and Unwholesome Provisions.' And clergyman Jonathan Wiswall drew a sorry picture of the disbanded soldier settlements of Aylesford and Wilmot in 1791: 'This part of the Province is very thinly settled by persons of all descriptions in general extremely poor & scattered over the country in all directions, they chiefly live in Hutts little if anything superior to the Cabins in Ireland—and can scarcely be said to have even the bare necessarys of life. They have been for so long a time habituated to what may be called a savage life, that it is extreme difficult to bring them off from it to a civilized state.'[40]

These were not the rewards of dreams. In Annapolis, Jacob Bailey found himself 'continually molested with the disappointments—the chagrin the complaints—the manners, the distresses of the loyalists.'[41] Disillusioned, many sought yet another new start on life by relocating either to join friends, relatives, or co-religionists, because of inadequacies in the initial hurried survey and allocation of land, or simply in hope of greater advantage elsewhere. Diffuse and idiosyncratic as these movements were, they are difficult to chart. Known patterns of migration to and from Carleton County in New Brunswick between 1786 and 1800 suggest something of the flux of population during those years (Figure 2). Perhaps as telling was the observation of Edward Winslow that 'the strange propensity [of Americans] to change their situations' was far exceeded in his province.[42]

Trans-Atlantic migration to British North America virtually ceased during the Revolution, but began again, in a sporadic way, after 1783. Among the first arrivals from England—several hundred in number—were Loyalists disappointed at their prospects in the Mother Country. They were joined by smaller numbers of traders and fortune seekers and, to the annoyance of Nova Scotian officials, at least one group of transported convicts.[43] But the major influx was of Highland Scots, who gravitated to the small Scottish settlements in Pictou and the Island of St John. More than 300 migrants from Moidart, Morar, and neighbouring Clanranald lands sailed for the island in 1790, and 1,300 emigrants from the Western Highlands and islands entered the Gulf in 1791. At least 650 of the latter group who landed in Nova Scotia depended upon government assistance to survive their first American winter, but in 1792 the Catholics among them moved east to Antigonish, and by 1800 both they and the Presbyterians who remained in Pictou were well established. Affluent enough to pay their passages, they migrated to preserve a traditional way of life and, as some contemporaries recognized, carried a considerable sum in goods and money across the Atlantic with them. Yet changing circumstances in Scotland and war with France slowed this migration to a trickle after 1793; in total it brought no more than 2,000 people—the vanguard of important nineteenth-century migrations—to the region between 1784 and 1800.[44]

These gains were more than offset by departures. According to some, whose dislike of the American republic was manifest, a large and deplorable exodus of Loyalists occurred once the government issue of provisions ceased; by these accounts several thousand returned to 'the Country of Traitors'. Whether they 'sold their Lotts . . . for a Gallon of New England rum and quit the Country without taking any residence', as many men in the Cumberland Regiment were alleged to have done, or went 'back to Egypt after living so long in idleness on the King's provisions', these migrants raised doubts in the minds of those who stayed.[45] But it is difficult to gauge their numbers with confidence. One observer put departures from Nova Scotia at 'Some Hundreds of Families in the 18 months before October 1787' and suggested that 'some Hundreds more' were 'preparing for removal'. A careful analysis of the New Brunswick record concludes that fewer than 600 of 6,000 families who remained in the province long enough to be identified there returned to the United States. Certainly the movement was substantial; equally it failed to 'un-people these provinces', as one critic feared it might.[46] More significant in its impact upon the demographic structure of Nova Scotia was the exodus, in January 1792, of almost 1,200 black Loyalists bound for Sierra Leone and the prospects of land, independence, and security that they had failed to achieve as marginal members of a predominantly white society.[47]

Across the region, however, population growth was sustained by early marriages, a high birth rate, and low mortality. If it was more extreme than characteristic, the experience of one New Brunswick missionary who married 48 couples, baptized 295 infants, and buried 17 persons between 1795 and 1800 suggests the dynamics that drove the population of Nova Scotia, New Brunswick, Cape Breton, and the island of St John (Prince Edward Island after 1798) upwards by some 35 per cent (a rate of approximately 2 per cent per annum) between 1785 and 1800.[48]

Economy

The impact of the Loyalist migrations on the Nova Scotian economy was dramatic. With the demand for housing, provisions, lumber, and other supplies overwhelming, price inflation was steep. According to one account, Nova Scotian prices for necessities doubled between 1775 and 1782, and they undoubtedly escalated further in the months that followed with 'the scarcity daily increasing by the daily increase of the number of the distressed starving Loyalists'. By 1783 costs in Annapolis were said to be three times those in New York. In Halifax, government officials complained at the rents demanded for 'very indifferent' accommodation, and one newcomer to the Fundy side of the province wondered how he might afford to build 'a small Hut, such as other unhappy fugitive Loyalists generally creep into'.[49]

Imports of foodstuffs and lumber from the United States eased immediate shortages, and fine flour and grains continued to come in from the south under vice-regal proclamation after 1786, but both demand and prices remained high and stimulated local production. From farms established on the Fundy borderlands in the 1760s and 1770s, livestock, butter, and cheese moved in unprecedented quantities to new urban and (at least for the first few years after 1783) rural markets in the region. Small sawmills cut lumber for local needs, and some soon found an export market for their product. In Nova Scotia, 25 sawmills were built between 1783 and 1785; in the two years that followed, when the government offered a bounty for mill construction, several more were erected. New Brunswick, with only a handful of mills in 1784, had 20 or more sawmills in Charlotte County alone by 1800. Shipbuilding also expanded.[50] Paying a bounty of 10 shillings per ton on new-built vessels of 40 tons or more, the Nova Scotian government disbursed approximately £1,000 in 1786 and 1787.[51] By 1793 some 160 sloops, schooners, and square-rigged vessels had been built in New Brunswick alone.[52]

Late in the 1780s, some Loyalist farms yielded their occupants 'bread enough & potatoes of their own raising & Hay sufficient to winter their small stock.'[53] Fish were taken from river and sea for local consumption and export. Settlements such as Sissiboo seemed to adumbrate the rapid progress and bountiful prospects of the region. There, reported Samuel Goldbury in 1785, Loyalists had found good lands and excellent timber. Four mills had been built, and more were under construction; 1,000 black cattle, as well as horses and sheep, grazed the fields; cod, taken from 'Log canoes and small Boats', had been consumed in 'considerable quantity' by the settlers and provided 1,200 quintals for export to the West Indies in the settlement's 120-ton sloop and 80-ton brig. Well might these 'generally Poor but industrious' individuals have contemplated regaining 'those agreeable Circumstances they sacrificed in consequence of the Late War'.[54]

But the foundations of such optimism were fragile. The fertility of new-cleared soils was soon exhausted; too few Loyalists were experienced fishermen or farmers; once the provision bounty ceased, the real difficulties of survival became apparent. Overland communication was difficult and costly. Loyalists from Remsheg mustered at Cumberland incurred costs of 5 shillings a hundredweight in transporting their provisions across the Chignecto Isthmus.[55] And despite considerable expenditure and effort on the opening of roads, little was achieved. Ways cut through forest soon grew back to scrub. Although communities were linked by water, connections were often circuitous and dangerous. Sawmills built near coastal settlements soon exhausted the good accessible timber of the spruce-fir forests in their immediate hinterlands, and several ceased operation as the costs of bringing trees from further afield became prohibitive. Recognizing that the rural economy was faltering, a group of prominent Haligonians formed the Society for Promoting Agriculture in Nova Scotia in 1789, and in 1791 both Nova Scotia and New Brunswick added lumber to the list of those articles allowed into the provinces from the United States for 'the supply of the Inhabitants'.[56]

External trade also fell short of expectations. With the Navigation Acts excluding American commodities from the British West Indies after 1783, Nova Scotian merchants hoped to assume an important place in trade with the islands.[57] Yet they were poorly equipped to do so: shipping was scarce, and local consumption left little for export in the first years of peace. By orders in council of 1783, American wood, livestock, and other provisions were allowed into the British West Indian islands in British ships; this left the fish and salt meat trade to the British North American colonies.

But the Nova Scotian fishery simply could not meet West Indian demands. American vessels continued to work northern waters in great numbers. In the summer of 1784, it was estimated that they would take at least 30,000 quintals along the Nova Scotian coast; larger vessels, some with 8 to 10 boats, fished the Gulf shore; and Nova Scotians cured the catch of New England fishermen as they had before the Revolution.[58] Several years later, Nova Scotian exports barely exceeded this American take from local waters. In 1787, the province exported 44,723 quintals of dried cod. In the same year, Cape Breton—more involved in the trans-Atlantic trade—shipped 36,736 quintals, and New Brunswick and the Island of St John together exported 2,203 quintals.[59] Dried cod exports from Newfoundland were almost nine times greater than those from the four provinces combined.

By the end of the decade, fish and other enumerated items were being admitted to the West Indies in American vessels. In fast-declining Shelburne, the leading citizens recognized the obvious when they acknowledged that American experience in the trade (and, they argued, the 'liberal indulgences' of the peace treaty) had 'hitherto precluded' them from rivalling their southern competitors in 'this valuable branch of Commerce'.[60] When Britain and France went to war in 1793, privateers disrupted such trade as there was between northeastern America and the British West Indies, and Jay's Treaty of 1794, which opened British Caribbean ports to American shipping, dealt it a further blow. In the 1790s observers found the trade of Annapolis 'very trifling' and reported that both the river and sea fisheries of Nova Scotia were in decline.[61]

In this context, payments from the British government to individual Loyalists were of enormous significance to fledgling British North American communities in the 1780s and 1790s. As compensation for losses sustained or as 'half-pay' pensions for military service, these remittances to Nova Scotia and New Brunswick Loyalists may have amounted to £475,000 between 1783 and 1800.[62] Not all of this money was spent in the colonies. After 1787, when military pensions were allowed to those resident beyond the empire, several recipients left for the United States; by one—likely high—contemporary estimate, £5,000 per annum crossed the border from New Brunswick in the early 1790s.[63] But whether consumed in the development of a country estate, invested in an inn or tavern, or filtered into the local economy month by month over the years, compensation and pension payments contributed a significant leaven to pioneer economies. If few Loyalists were willing to tenant farms, many depended, in the first years of settlement, upon the casual employment offered by Loyalist officers and gentlemen. The departure of such individuals, feared one observer, would have a catastrophic effect upon their communities: 'tis these Men's Pay we depend upon' he wrote, 'to keep our poor alive by finding Employment for labouring men. . . . If they go the poor must follow them or starve.'[64]

In Halifax, at least, the economic difficulties of the late 1780s and early 1790s were quickly dissipated by the war with France. A garrison of 600, the newly formed Royal Nova Scotia Regiment, the navy, and privateers bringing prizes into port put cash in circulation. When fears of French invasion heightened after the capture of St Pierre and Miquelon by men from the Halifax garrison, some 1,500 militiamen were embodied in the town. In 1796, a further 1,000 or so were called into the city from outlying districts. Five of ten batteries built to defend the harbour before the Revolution, but long in ruins, were reconstructed, and two new works were erected. In the next few years considerable sums were spent improving and strengthening these structures, and the stone Prince of Wales Tower was built on Point Pleasant to secure the rear of the defences.[65] The presence of Prince Edward, Duke of Kent, as commander of the British troops added to the social cachet of Halifax society, the upper echelons of which participated in a vigorous round of drinking, dining, and social calls.[66]

By 1801, Haligonians contemplated raising £100,000 to establish a bank, and the provincial legislature allocated funds for the paving of city streets. Despite the narrow blocks and small lots of the original survey, the élite concentrated in the centre of the city. Government House, St George's Church, and several substantial town houses were built in this area in the 1790s and reflected both its prestige and the expansive mood of these years.[67]

By this time, too, the benefits of prosperity in Halifax were percolating into other parts of the colony. Money from provincial coffers was being turned to road building. Bay of Fundy farmers received good prices for their surplus, and with militia obligations and the enlistment of provincials, a shortage of manpower raised the price of labour. Reflecting these developments, Loyalist storekeeper Henry Magee of Horton Corner (now Kentville) did a vigorous trade in the last years of the century. Although payment in kind was often recorded in his ledgers, some 80 per cent of his customers appear to have settled their accounts with cash. In 16 months of 1795–6 Magee took almost £3,000 in gold and silver, much of which he (literally) salted away, recording in his day book quantities of 'gold put by in the apel box', 'silver in the wheat', and 'gold in the salt'.[68]

New Brunswick, in contrast, was a backwater. With the war, troops were withdrawn to Halifax and the West Indies, and with them went their salaries and their contracts for fuel and provisions. The colony lacked the strategic importance of Nova Scotia, its annual revenue was barely a tenth of that colony's and the province was regarded, in official eyes, as a satellite of its neighbour.[69] Commercially, its chief importance lay in the rich pine forest brought under imperial jurisdiction early in the eighteenth century, but the quantities of New Brunswick wood entering trade were small. Masts were the most valuable of local commodities; annual shipments rarely exceeded 2,000 in number. In the 15 years to 1800, ton–timber and lumber shipments approximately doubled from their low 1785 levels of 2,000 tons and 2 million feet respectively.[70] Much of this material came from the southwestern corner of the province, where the American boundary was barely recognized by lumbermen and others who prosecuted a contraband trade in fish and gypsum (from the head of the Bay of Fundy) on 'the lines'. While the late 1790s brought prosperity to Nova Scotia, New Brunswick Loyalist Amos Botsford reported that the West Indies trade of his province 'ha[d] been reduced by frequent captures, shipbuilding ha[d] decreased, and exports of timber to the British market . . . [were] entirely decreased'.[71] By 1800 emigration from the province was discernible.

The islands of Saint John and Cape Breton also shared little in the prosperity of war. In 1797, when the former colony had a population of 4,300, a mere 36 families occupied 35 of its 67 townships. Half the population was Scottish, 15 per cent Acadian. In 1789 the island had neither school nor church, and the disruptive legacy of the preceding decade or so continued to stunt development into the nineteenth century. Although there were 18 grist and sawmills by the end of the century, there was little nucleated settlement.[72] Charlottetown was a muddy village of large lots, wide streets, and 70 dwellings. According to Lord Selkirk, Princetown and Georgetown were 'rotten boroughs' of three houses each.[73] Most settlers occupied small farms where arms of the sea ran deep into the island along the Malpeque-Bedeque and Hillsborough-St Peters axes. Herring and cod were taken along the north shore. Cattle were shipped to Newfoundland occasionally, and little vessels maintained frequent connection with Halifax, but the balance of trade in this underdeveloped colony was clearly inward.

Small as it was, Cape Breton held more economic importance. A centre of the migratory Jersey-based fishery that had expanded in the Gulf of St Lawrence since 1763, the island attracted approximately 100 Channel Islanders each summer.[74] At Arichat and Cheticamp they worked alongside resident Acadians to produce the prime merchantable fish for southern European markets that made up perhaps two-thirds of the colony's cod exports. Three-quarters of Cape Breton's population probably depended upon the resident fishery. Its product was generally inferior to that of the Jerseymen, and most of it went to West Indian markets through Halifax. Neither fishery returned very much to Cape Breton's inhabitants. Profits and wages from the Jersey enterprises accrued to Great Britain; resident fishermen—largely Acadian, with a few Irish from Newfoundland—depended on credit from local merchants, and, like their counterparts elsewhere in the fishery, many were deeply in debt. Coal from primitive mines on the north side of Sydney Harbour provided a second export commodity, but the costs of extraction and transport to markets in Halifax and St John's limited the trade: it never exceeded 10,000 tons per annum before 1800, and no more than 50 or 60 men worked in the mines. Farming supported 120 to 150 Cape Breton families. Most of them were Loyalists, few had more than 10 or 15 acres in cultivation, and the small surpluses they produced generated only a sporadic trade with Newfoundland. Sydney, never more than a shadow of the pretentious capital planned in 1785, supported a cluster of salaried officials and hangers-on amid the forest; by 1795 many of its wharfs and buildings were in ruins.[75]

Northeastern America in 1800

By 1800, the four maritime provinces of British North America were markedly diverse in economy, society, settlement patterns, and landscapes. Perhaps 75–80,000 people lived in the region. Halifax, with a fifth of Nova Scotia's population, and Saint John, with a tenth of New Brunswick's, were the only cities. Shelburne ranked third among the region's urban centres, but it was little bigger than Fredericton, a capital village of 120 to 150 houses, 'scattered,' according to the wife of a military officer, 'on a delightful common of the richest sheep pasture I ever saw.'[76] Despite their administrative functions, Charlottetown and Sydney were tiny places, and few other agglomerations were more than hamlets.

Along the rocky Atlantic shore of Nova Scotia and on the coast of Cape Breton (type 1 areas in Figure 3), kitchen gardens and fish provided a meagre subsistence for residents of isolated fishing settlements whose catch entered Atlantic commerce. In detail this was a complex trade. Liverpool fishermen took salmon in Newfoundland and Labrador and cod, mackerel, and herring along the Nova Scotian coast. Halifax merchants organized cargoes drawn from scattered outports. Pickled fish (salmon/herring) was exchanged for provisions and marine supplies in the mid-Atlantic states, and salt cod for salt, sugar, rum, and molasses in the West Indies. But life in the fishing settlements was simple; a scattered group of merchants apart, their residents had little contact with the world beyond. There was little geometric order to these places, the accretive growth of which was shaped by beach room,

Figure 3. Northeastern America: settlement patterns and economic activity, 1800.

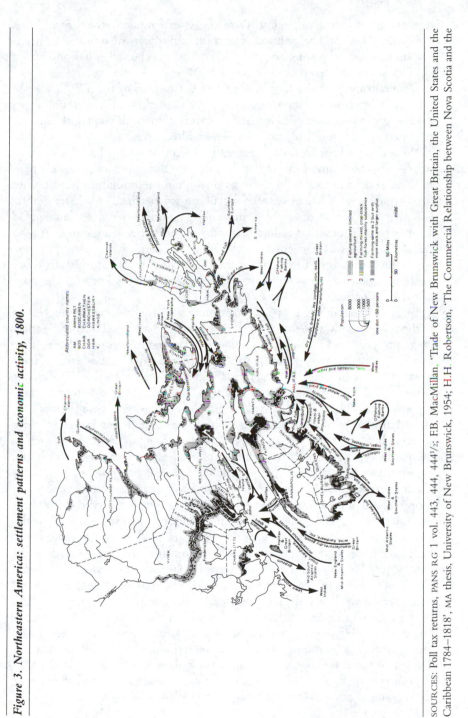

SOURCES: Poll tax returns, PANS RG 1 vol. 443, 444, 444½; F.B. MacMillan, 'Trade of New Brunswick with Great Britain, the United States and the Caribbean 1784–1818', MA thesis, University of New Brunswick, 1954; H.H Robertson, 'The Commercial Relationship between Nova Scotia and the

topography, and consanguinity. Dwellings were modest, their furnishings utilitarian. Sheds and flakes lined the strand; cabins were surrounded by irregular fences, encompassing the acre or two of rockbound soil from which families supplemented diets of fish.[77]

Generalizing from the fragmentary poll-tax returns of the 1790s, we can estimate that possibly three-quarters of the households in these communities owned cattle or horses.[78] Over half of those with cattle kept only one or two beasts; very few had more than five. Sheep were less numerous than cattle and were kept by fewer people, a handful of whom had flocks of 10 or more. Cattle numbers were less than double the numbers of taxable men in these communities, and most individuals paid the minimum head tax. In the Guysborough district over 80 per cent did so; mechanics made up slightly less than 10 per cent of taxables, and only 13 among 163 were enumerated as physicians, attorneys, vendors of goods, or recipients of annuities. Among the 300 taxables of Queens County, 70 per cent paid the basic poll tax. Mechanics made up 14 per cent of the total, vessel mates and masters 8 per cent, and merchants and shopkeepers 7 per cent. In Guysborough the ratio of cattle to taxables was 1.47, in Queens, 1.26.

Away from the fishing ports, mixed farming was characteristic. Through most of the region, farms were the means and purpose of existence. Potatoes, a variety of grains, peas, and turnips were grown. In those areas designated type 2 in Figure 3, surpluses were generally small and sporadic; when they entered trade it was, first and foremost, to sustain relatively high levels of local self-sufficiency. Again poll-tax returns indicate something of the economic structure of these communities. On a per capita basis, livestock holdings were clearly more substantial than in the fishing settlements. In broad terms, cattle and horses exceeded the number of taxables by a factor of three or four. In some areas, such as Windsor, with an unusual concentration of relatively well-to-do settlers, horses accounted for almost 25 per cent of this total; generally they were considerably less important. Several individuals kept 8 or more neat cattle (and some 25 or more). Sheep numbers were substantial and in some areas exceeded the number of cattle; flocks of 20 and 30 were not uncommon, but as in the fishing settlements fewer households kept sheep than cows. Here as in most farming settlements there was a considerable range of circumstances. By the standards of the day, 'Mount Pleasant' on the Kennebecasis River was a fine property, with 130 cleared acres (most of them intervale); it yielded 80–100 tons of hay each year.[79] More typical were two St John valley properties offered for sale near the turn of the century: one had '15 acres of interval and about 20 acres cleared ready for the plough'; the other—an 'agreeable' farm—'about 13 acres under improvements, a handsome two story Dwelling House . . . [and] an excellent Garden of about three-quarters of an acre, well enclosed with a pale fence.'[80] Yet others had a bare 5 or 6 acres under cultivation, and their occupants practised 'a crude catch-as-catch-can sort of agriculture'.[81]

Only a few parts of the region (designated 3 in Figure 3) contributed regularly to the regional trade in foodstuffs. From older-settled districts on the productive Fundy marshlands, livestock went to Halifax and Saint John. From Lunenburg, roots and other supplies accompanied shipments of firewood to the provincial capital, and hay, at least, moved downriver from the immediate hinterland of Saint John. In the Fundy settlements, farmers grew a variety of grains and other crops on marsh and upland, but American flour was stiff competition in the region's urban markets, and these were mainly for local consumption. Livestock offered better returns, and large areas of dyked and undyked marsh were turned to hay as economic connection prompted product specialization. Numbers of cattle and horses exceeded the number of taxables five- or six-fold in many parts of this district during the 1790s, and William Trueman surely followed a familiar line of trade when he made two trips from Chignecto to Halifax in the summer of 1802, the first with 30 oxen and the second with 24 cattle for sale.[82]

Landscapes revealed rather more of the social geography of the area. Contrasts and incongruities were many: a few large, well-established farms pointed up how little cleared land most settlers had; finely coifed ladies in 'pink and lilac high-heeled shoes' picked their ways over the 'rugged rocky paths' of Saint John; hard-scrabble fishing settlements bore little resemblance to the well-cultivated marshland fringes of the Bay of Fundy; the social world of the Halifax élite was a vast remove from the humble settings of countless provincial lives.[83] For every farm family comfortable upon the surplus of productive acres, there were many more squeezing a meagre subsistence from a rudimentary agriculture on thin, stump-strewn soils.

Through much of settled New Brunswick and southwestern Nova Scotia, building forms revealed the American origins of the settlers. The Cape Cod house—with its approximately square plan, low walls, tight eaves, large central chimney, one-and-a-half-storey height, and shingle-clad exterior—was an established form on the Atlantic coast of Nova Scotia, as it was along the Shores of Maine and Massachusetts (Figure 4).[84] A second recognizably American house type was also common by 1800 (Figure 5). Larger and more expensive, this symmetrical dwelling with central hall and two chimneys has generally been associated with Loyalist settlement in the region.[85] Houses of this type (modelled on American Georgian or 'Colonial' models that were widespread before the Revolution) and Cape Cod cottages were among those erected in Shelburne. They were also built in the Annapolis and Minas basins, in Passamaquoddy and the St John valley, and in other south shore towns. Clapboarded, they differed only slightly in appearance (albeit more in floor plan) from the houses of earlier New England settlers in the Fundy townships. Barns, where built, were generally of wood, free standing, and apparently of the English two-bay type, although the common northern New England practice of connecting dwelling, barn, and service buildings

Figure 4. The Cape Cod cottage of the Atlantic Coast.

Figure 5. The 'Loyalist House' of northeastern America.

Figure 6. Death head motif.
SOURCE: Lettice Doane gravemarker, Barrington, NS, 1766.

Figure 7. Cherubim motif.
SOURCE: Benajah Collins gravemarker, Liverpool, NS, 1788.

Figure 8. Trumpet of resurrection motif.
SOURCE: Middle Sackville, NB, 1794.

All sketches by the author.

Figure 9. The hall and parlour dwelling of northeastern America.

may have been followed in parts of New Brunswick before the nineteenth century.[86]

Gravestones were another indicator of cultural ties between New England and Nova Scotia. Traditional death head motifs, more fashionable in early than late-eighteenth-century Massachusetts, decorated gravemarkers shipped from Boston to the south shore communities between 1765 and the 1780s (Figure 6).[87] Angelheads, or cherubim, carved on late-eighteenth-century gravemarkers still stand in the graveyards of Liverpool, Cheboque, and Halifax; many have close stylistic counterparts in Salem and neighbouring Massachusetts towns (Figure 7). Death heads are absent from Connecticut-settled Horton and Cornwallis; the cherub on a stone shipped there from New London differs from those characteristic of the south shore, and here local carvers developed their own variants of the winged-head motif after 1783. Other symbols vied with cherubim in the 1790s. Angels sounding the trumpet of resurrection were perhaps most common in areas touched by evangelical Protestantism (Figure 8); urns—reflections of the neo-classical revival in the United States—appeared on imported and local stones by the turn of the century.

Elsewhere, distinctive cultural imprints on the landscape were less obvious. German inscriptions and simple floral designs distinguished the gravestones of Lunenburg. In Pictou, sandstone gravemarkers generally recorded the origins of the deceased but were rarely ornamented with more than a thistle or two. Yorkshiremen in Chignecto had begun to replicate in brick and stone, as well as wood, the Georgian and hipped roof forms of dwellings in their native county.[88] Through much of the Gulf shore, Prince Edward Island, and Cape Breton, however, the recency and economic marginality of settlement stamped a utilitarian similarity on the landscape. Crude cabins, hall and parlour dwellings, and simple log structures with two or three rooms were frequently home to returned Acadians and the first permanent shelters of immigrant families. Found throughout the region in 1800, and characteristic of settlement frontiers the length of eastern North America, they remained a persistent type in the lexicon of regional folk architecture (Figure 9).[89]

Yet the basic ethnic divisions that marked the region through the nineteenth century—an English/American south and west, a Scottish Gulf, Germans in Lunenburg, Irish in Halifax and the Cobequid area, and a cluster of Acadian enclaves in Madawaska, northeastern New Brunswick, western Prince Edward Island, southeastern Cape Breton, and St Mary's Bay—were already coming into focus at the end of the eighteenth century. So, too, were the associated patterns of religious differentiation.[90] And the essential and persistent patterns of economy and settlement in this overwhelmingly intractable region were clear: most people occupied modest farms or clustered in seagirt villages; their distribution was basically peripheral; fingers of population followed the region's major valleys inland.[91]

At the turn of the nineteenth century the Maritime colonies remained an unconsolidated amalgam of families and small communities. In most things, the reach of colonial institutions was limited. Although common backgrounds provided a measure of coherence among many groups of settlers, there had been little time for the settling of people into place. The flux of population continued. The considerable task of establishing, and maintaining, a subsistence threshold preoccupied the majority of the region's settlers. In these respects, as in the underdevelopment of manufacturing, the poor quality and slender articulation of overland transportation, the lack of an urban network, and the inchoate pattern of intellectual life, the Maritime colonies bore more resemblance to the back-country US south and the northern hill country of New England than they did to the older colonial hearths from which so many of their people had come and to which they remained connected by trade.[92]

In 1800, as in 1755, these four colonies accounted for an insignificant proportion of the wealth and population of America. Yet economic, social, and, above all, geographical changes in this corner of the continent during the last half of the eighteenth century reflected broader patterns of North American development. The migratory fishery of Cape Breton shared a great deal with the trade that shaped landscapes and settlements in Newfoundland and much of the Gulf of St Lawrence for better than three centuries. Essentially static in technology and organization, it turned 'surplus' European labour to the extraction of New World resources. Closely controlled by powerful merchants, and integrating the western Atlantic littoral into a complex international trading network, it made that area a distant work-place for several thousand young men from the farms and villages of Ireland, southern England, France, and the Channel Islands but returned little to local, North American economies.

The essential characteristics of the region's resident fishery—which was more widely dispersed and employed far more people than its migratory counterpart—were repeated the length of the coast, from Twillingate to Martha's Vineyard. Few prospered in this enterprise. In Nova Scotia, even more than in New England, the industry was 'delicately balanced between profit and loss'. Catches were variable, the cure was unreliable, and, as Ralph H. Brown recognized long ago, those engaged at all levels of the trade were caught up in 'a relentless battle on an economic front that included all countries of the North Atlantic basin'.[93] For the individual fisherman, the results were all too often debt and impoverishment. 'Who ever knew a Fisherman thrive?' asked New Brunswick Loyalist William Paine in 1788. 'I am persuaded that a coast calculated for fishing; is so far from being a benefit, that it really is a *curse* to the Inhabitants . . . [they] will ever be poor and *miserable* . . . At Salem, Marblehead and Cape Ann . . . [fishermen] are the most wretched of the community.'[94]

Although colonial rather than European merchants dominated the resident fishery, and although its connections to the West Indies were stronger than those of the Mediterranean-oriented migratory fishery, the commercial spheres of the two enterprises overlapped and interlocked. Together they sketched, in outline, the complex web that bound the North Atlantic into a triangle of trade. But with few forward, backward, or final demand linkages, neither migratory nor resident fishery was an effective motor of local economic growth in the Maritime colonies. Even the profits and multipliers generated for Nova Scotia by the resident fishery tended to concentrate in Halifax. Beyond, harsh toil on the rugged Atlantic coast yielded a meagre subsistence for scattered families.

In New Brunswick, Loyalist dreams of creating a stable, ordered, hierarchical society—an exclusive Elysium in the north—had faded through 15 years of settlement.[95] For all Edward Winslow's hope that his new province would be 'the most Gentlemanlike one on Earth' and the very 'envy of the American states', regardless of John Saunders's belief that education and rank should entitle young men to privilege and position, and despite the handful of extravagant estates financed by payments from the Loyalist Claims Commission, most colonists exhibited a sturdy independence while struggling to make their way in the new land.[96] Few, indeed, shared the social conceptions of the élite. For most New Brunswickers, pedigree was a thin claim to privilege, and tenancy was unpalatable. When 55 gentlemen petitioned for 5,000-acre grants on the basis of their 'most respectable Characters' and former status, 600 ordinary settlers refused to recognize the claimants' superiority in anything but 'deeper Art and keener Policy'. When Col. Kemble sought to rent properties on his 'Manor', he soon learned that 'no man . . . [would] become a tenant' and that 'even the best cultivated farms' could not be leased 'to any valuable purpose'. For Governor John Parr, such signs were evidence that many Loyalists had inherited 'a deal of that Liver, which disunited the [Thirteen] Colonies from their Mother Country'.[97] But prevailing attitudes were as much the product of conditions in New Brunswick as they were of convictions shaped in the old colonies.

In New Brunswick, as on countless New World frontiers, land had little intrinsic worth. Its value was created by the hard labour of forest clearance and cultivation. And where readily available land allowed men to work for themselves, they would rarely toil for others. Thus large land holdings brought few economic benefits. Gentlemen of education and refinement were obliged 'to undergo all the drudgery of farming'; servants were hard to come by; hirelings insisted on sharing their masters' tables; and British soldier William Cobbett, who had never thought of approaching a 'Squire without a most respectful bow' in England, found himself, 'in this New World', ordering many 'a Squire to bring me a glass of Grog and even to take care of my knapsack'.[98] Abhorred as they were by Loyalist leaders, the levelling democratic tendencies of North American settlement could not be excluded from New Brunswick. Around the indulgent islands of splendid houses, fine wines, and social pretensions sustained by military pensions and aristocratic conventions, most turn-of-the-century New Brunswickers inhabited an essentially egalitarian world. Recent and relatively remote, defined in opposition to the United States, and without a vigorous commercial outlet, their society bore a thin veneer of traditional English conservatism on its democratic New World core.[99]

Settlement in the four colonies had proceeded largely by chance. If, as Jacob Bailey adduced, many Loyalists were impelled by 'a passion for novelty and a love of rambling' rather than by 'any virtuous attachment to their royal masters', most other inhabitants of the area were there for equally capricious reasons: for many, the region had provided tolerable alternatives to unpromising or difficult circumstances in their former homelands; for some, it had offered prospects of real advantage; to few had it yielded substantial wealth or comfort. In 1800, as in the decades that followed, the eastern colonies of British North America formed a region of scattered settlements and bounded possibilities. Although much land remained to be taken up, although the economy would be invigorated by the early-nineteenth-century timber trade, and although the face of the country would be further transformed by ongoing settlement and development, the essential patterns of land and life in the Maritime provinces were clearly outlined in the half-century after 1755. Here and there across the region, newcomers might find, for a time, a modest niche for themselves and their families. Whether that niche were in narrow valley, along rocky shore, or on upland plateau, hard work, ingenuity, and versatility—to say nothing of good fortune—were generally required to take advantage of it and to survive. And within a generation or two (at most) the limits of local resources would be met. As contexts changed, so new adjustments were made. But always sons and daughters would move on, in the late eighteenth century to occupy new pockets of land and limited opportunity in the region, in the late nineteenth to find work in Boston, and in the late twentieth to seek their fortunes in Toronto and Alberta. Simply to recognize as much is to conceive the experience of settlement in these provinces as an important variant of a recurrent facet of life in the Canadian archipelago.[100]

Suggestions for Further Reading

R. Cole Harris, ed., *Historical Atlas of Canada: Volume I: From the Beginning to 1800* (Toronto, [1987]).

James R. Gibson, ed., *European Settlement and Development in North America: Essays on Geographical Change in Honour and Memory of Andrew Hill Clark* (Toronto, 1978).

W.S. MacNutt, *The Atlantic Provinces: The Emergence of Colonial Society 1712–1857* (Toronto, 1965).

Notes

[1]This point has been made recently in two important treatments of the colonial seaboard colonies: J.P. Greene and J.P. Pole, eds, *Colonial British America: Essays in the New History of the Early Modern Era* (Baltimore: Johns Hopkins University Press 1984) and J.J. McCusker and R.R. Menard, *The Economy of British America 1607–1789* (Chapel Hill, NC: University of North Carolina Press 1985).

[2]J.B. Brebner, *North Atlantic Triangle* (Toronto: McClelland and Stewart 1966) 56–7; D.C. Harvey, 'Machias and the invasion of Nova Scotia', Canadian Historical Association (hereafter CHA) *Report* (1932), 21; *Nova Scotia Gazette and the Weekly Chronicle* 10 September 1776, cited in G.A. Rawlyk, ed. *Revolution Rejected 1775–1776* (Scarborough, Ont: Prentice Hall 1968) 27; J.B. Brebner, *Neutral Yankees of Nova Scotia* (Toronto: McClelland and Stewart 1969), 264–5.

[3]J.M. Bumsted, *Henry Alline 1748–1784* (Toronto: University of Toronto Press, 1971); G. Stewart, 'Socio-economic factors in the Great Awakening: the case of Yarmouth, Nova Scotia', *Acadiensis* 3 (1973), 18–34; G. Stewart and G.A. Rawlyk, 'Nova Scotia's sense of mission', *Histoire Sociale/Social History* 2 (1968), 115–17; G. Stewart and G.A. Rawlyk, *A People Highly Favoured of God: The Nova Scotia Yankees and the American Revolution* (Toronto: Macmillan 1972); G.A. Rawlyk, *Ravished by the Spirit: Religious Revivals, Baptists and Henry Alline* (Montreal: McGill-Queen's University Press 1984); Brebner, *Neutral Yankees*, 275.

[4]J.D. Faibisy, 'Privateering and Piracy: The Effects of New England Raiding upon Nova Scotia during the American Revolution, 1775–1783', PhD thesis, University of Massachusetts, 1972. Considerable attention has focused on the reasons why Nova Scotia did not join the American Revolution. The debate is summarized in Rawlyk, *Revolution Rejected*. With a few exceptions the perceptive regional and biographical studies called for there have yet to appear.

[5]J. Greenough, 'The defence of Halifax 1783–1825', unpublished paper presented to the Canadian Historical Association, Halifax, 1982, 2.

[6]L.R. Fischer, 'Revolution without independence: the Halifax merchants and the American Revolution, 1749–1775', unpublished paper presented to the Canadian Historical Association, London, Ont, 1978, 28–31.

[7]P.M. Gouett, 'The Halifax Orphan House 1752–87', *Nova Scotia Historical Quarterly* 6 (1976), 281–91.

[8]N.L. Nicholson, *The Boundaries of the Canadian Confederation* (Toronto: Macmillan 1979), 27–30.

[9]M. Ells, 'Clearing the decks for the Loyalists', CHA *Report* (1939) 56–8; M. Gilroy, *Loyalists and Land Settlement in Nova Scotia*, Publication No. 4, Genealogical Committee of the Royal Nova Scotia Historical Society (1980). The Nova Scotian acreage estimate is based on a 5 per cent sample of grants. R. Fellows, 'The Loyalists and land settlement in New Brunswick, 1783–1790; a study in colonial administration', *Canadian Archivist* 2, 2 (1970–4) 5–15.

[10]Public Archives of Nova Scotia (PANS) RG1 Sec 4 Vol 107, Campbell to Sydney 30 November 1785; N. Mackinnon, 'The Loyalist Experience in Nova Scotia, 1783–1791', PhD thesis, Queen's University, 1975, 182–5; E.C. Wright, *The Loyalists of New Brunswick* (Moncton: Moncton Publishing 1972), 249–50; Public Archives of Canada (PAC) MG23 D1(1) Vol. 24, General Returns of Loyalists.

M. Ells, 'Settling the Loyalists in Nova Scotia', CHA *Report* (1935), 105–9; A.G. Condon, *The Envy of the American States: The Loyalist Dream for New Brunswick* (Fredericton: New Ireland Press, 1984), 2–3; A.H. Clark, *Three Centuries and the Island* (Toronto: University of Toronto Press, 1959), 58.

[12] W.S. MacNutt, 'Fanning's regime on Prince Edward Island', *Acadiensis* 1 (1971) 37–53; Clark, *Three Centuries*, 57–8. Still this period was of vital importance in shaping the pattern of eighteenth-century development in PEI. See J.M. Bumsted, 'The Patterson regime and the impact of the American Revolution on the Island of St. John 1775–1786', *Acadiensis* 13 (1983) 47–67; R.J. Morgan, 'The Loyalists of Cape Breton', *Dalhousie Review* 55 (1975) 5–22; R.J. Morgan, 'Orphan Outpost', PhD dissertation, University of Ottawa, 1973.

[13] Or, as Jacob Bailey described the Annapolis valley Loyalists: 'a collection of all nations, kindreds, complexions and tongues assembled from every quarter of the Globe and till lately equally strangers to me and each other,' cited in MacKinnon, 'The Loyalist Experience', 241. Additional recent work on Loyalists in the 'Maritime region' includes: H.C. Hazen, 'The Story of New Brunswick's black settlers 1700–1820', *Journal of New Brunswick Museum* (1979) 44–53; G.C.W. Troxler, 'The Migration of Carolina and Georgia Loyalists to Nova Scotia and New Brunswick', PhD dissertation, University of North Carolina at Chapel Hill, 1974; C. Troxler, ' "To get out of a troublesome neighbourhood": David Fanning in New Brunswick', *North Carolina Historical Review* 56 (1979) 343–65; W.S. MacNutt, 'The Loyalists: a sympathetic view', *Acadiensis* 6 (1976) 3–20; N. Mackinnon, 'The changing attitudes of the Nova Scotia Loyalists to the United States 1783–1791', *Acadiensis* 2 (1973) 34–54; N. Mackinnon, 'Nova Scotian Loyalists, 1783–1785', *Histoire sociale/Social History* 4 (1969) 25–38; J.W.St.G. Walker, 'Blacks as American Loyalists: the slaves' war for independence', *Historical Reflections* 2 (1975) 51–67; and R. Nason, 'Meritorious but Distressed Individuals: The Penobscot Loyalist Association and the Settlement of the Township of St. Andrews, New Brunswick, 1783–1821', MA thesis, University of New Brunswick, 1982. Two important books have appeared since this article went to press: J.M. Bumsted, *Land, Settlement, and Politics on Eighteenth Century Prince Edward Island* (Montreal: McGill-Queen's University Press 1987) and N. Mackinnon, *This Unfriendly Soil: The Loyalist Experience in Nova Scotia 1783–1791* (Montreal: McGill-Queen's University Press 1986).

[14] Condon, *The Envy, passim*; C. Moore, *The Loyalists: Revolution, Exile, Settlement* (Toronto: Macmillan 1984); Wallace Brown, 'Mather Byles' *Dictionary of Canadian Biography* v (1983) 127–8; A.G. Bailey, 'Jonathan Odell' *DCB* v 628–31; J. Fingard, 'Sir John Wentworth' *DCB* v 848–52; A.G. Condon, 'Edward Winslow' *DCB* v 865–9.

[15] Wright, *The Loyalists* 161.

[16] J.S. Macdonald, 'Memoir of Governor John Parr', Nova Scotia Historical Society *Collections 14* (1910) 54–6; Public Archives of Canada *Report* (1894) 412–8.

[17] C.W. Vernon, *Bicentenary Sketches and Early Days of the Church in Nova Scotia* (Halifax: Chronicle Printing 1910) 145. See also W.O. Raymond, ed. *The Winslow Papers, 1776–1826* (Saint John: Sun Printing 1901) 264.

[18] H. Temperley, 'Frontierism, capital and the American Loyalists in Canada', *Journal of American Studies* 13 (1979) 5–27; Wright, *The Loyalists* 165–6; J. Eardley Wilmot, *Historical View of the Commission of Enquiry . . .* (London 1815).

[19] Wright, *The Loyalists* 166.

[20]*Ibid.* 151–67.

[21]L. Sabine, *Biographical Sketches of Loyalists of the American Revolution* (Boston 1864). Sample of approximately 700 Shelburne family heads. Mackinnon, 'The Loyalist Experience' 252–3.

[22]J.W.St.G. Walker, *The Black Loyalists: The Search for a Promised Land in Nova Scotia and Sierra Leone, 1783–1860* (New York: Africana Publishing/Dalhousie University Press 1976) is the standard work on which much of this discussion depends.

[23]J.W.St.G. Walker, 'Boston King' *DCB* v 468–9.

[24]H.A. Innis, D.C. Harvey, C.B. Fergusson, eds. *The Diary of Simeon Perkins* (Toronto: Champlain Society 19) II 238; W.O. Raymond, 'The foundling of Shelburne and Earl Miramichi: Marston's Diary', New Brunswick Historical Society *Collections* III (1907) 265.

[25]John Clarkson, cited in Walker, *The Black Loyalists* 46.

[26]Walker, *The Black Loyalists* 57.

[27]PANS RG 1 Section II Vol 346, Province of Nova Scotia, Proclamations 1748–1807, Document 88, 22 January 1784; Col R. Morse, 'Report on Nova Scotia 1784', Canada Archives *Report* (1884) xli; Wright, *The Loyalists* 35; PAC MG II Vol 103, John Parr to Lord North Enclosure 21 October 1783.

[28]Raymond, 'The founding of Shelburne' 234; PANS RG 1 Vol 376, Muster Rolls of Loyalists and Military Settlers, Annapolis, Digby; Robinson to Winslow 16 September 1784; I.W. Wilson, *A Geography and History of the County of Digby Nova Scotia* (Halifax: 1950) 50–1.

[29]Gilroy, *Loyalists and Land Settlement;* Mackinnon, 'The Loyalist Experience' 183; Raymond, *Winslow Papers* 248; Walker, *The Black Loyalists* 21–32. Expansion of settlement pushed indigenous peoples of the region back to more remote territory and deprived them of land. In New Brunswick, at least, there were concerted efforts to anglicize and Protestantize the Indians. See J. Fingard, 'The New England Company and the New Brunswick Indians 1786–1826; a comment on the colonial perversion of British benevolence', *Acadiensis* 1 (1972) 29–42; L.F.S. Upton, *Micmacs and Colonists: Indian-White Relations in the Maritimes 1713–1867* (Vancouver: University of British Columbia Press 1979); W.D. Hamilton, 'Indian lands in New Brunswick: the case of the Little South West Reserve', *Acadiensis* 13 (1984) 3–28.

[30]M. Robertson, *Kings Bounty: A History of Early Shelburne* (Halifax: Nova Scotia Museum 1983); Raymond, 'The founding of Shelburne'; Mackinnon, 'The Loyalist Experience' 124, 154–6; Moore, *The Loyalists* 158–60.

[31]PANS Vert Mss file: Shelburne, Parr to Shelburne 9 October 1789 in tps.

[32]*Port Roseway Gazette and Shelburne Advertiser* (Shelburne) 7 February, 6 June 1785.

[33]PAC MG 23 D1(1) Vol. 1, S.S. Blowers to W. Chipman 13 May 1786; Parr to Shelburne 9 October 1789, PANS MG 1 Inglis Papers, Journal of Bishop Charles Inglis 1785–1810, Vol. 4, 2 August 1790; Inglis's estimate of 3,525 is too high because it takes no account of the single men (perhaps 15 per cent of the population) in applying a multiplier to the number of families. Raymond, 'The founding of Shelburne'. A parallel case is well recounted in T.H. Raddall, 'Tarleton's Legion' NSHS *Collections* 28 (1947) 1–50.

[34]W.O. Raymond, ed. *Kingston and the Loyalists of the Spring Fleet of AD 1783* (Saint John: Barnes 1889).

[35]D.G. Bell, *Early Loyalist Saint John: The Origin of New Brunswick Politics, 1783–1790* (Fredericton: New Ireland Press 1983) 48–9; Raymond *Winslow Papers*, 354.

[36]Wright, *The Loyalists* 249–50; P. Campbell, *Travels in the Interior Inhabitated Parts of North America in the Years 1791 and 1792* (Toronto: Champlain Society 1937 [1791]) 25.

[37]Wright, *The Loyalists* 177–83, 249–50; T.W. Acheson, 'A study of the historical demography of a Loyalist county' *Histoire sociale/Social History* 1 (1968) 53–65; Condon, *The Envy* 72–96.

[38]For Filer Dibblee and his family see W. Brown, *The Good Americans: The Loyalists in the American Revolution* (New York: W. Morrow 1969) 140–1, 206–7, Jacob Bailey, cited in Mackinnon, 'The Loyalist Experience' 211.

[39]G. Wynn, 'The Assault on the New Brunswick Forest 1780–1850', PhD dissertation, University of Toronto, 1974, 64–70; W. Cobbett, *Advice to Young Men and (Incidentally) to Young Women* (London: Anne Cobbett 1837) 137–9. Further detail about the patterns, achievements, and hardships of Loyalist settlement can be pieced together from a series of MA theses completed at the University of New Brunswick, including: T.W. Acheson, 'Denominationalism in a Loyalist County: A Social History of Charlotte, 1783–1940' (1964); T.M.F. Kilbride, 'The Process of Growth and Change in Carleton County, 1783–1867' (1969); W. Moore, 'Sunbury County, 1760–1830' (1977); B.D. Pilon, 'Settlement and Early Development of the Parish of Kingsclear, York County, New Brunswick, 1784–1840' (1966); C.A. Pincombe, 'The History of Moncton Township (ca. 1700–1875)' (1969); and W.A. Spray, 'Early Northumberland County 1765–1825: A Study in Local Government' (1963).

[40]Mackinnon, 'The Loyalist Experience' 462–4.

[41]PANS MG 1 Peters Papers 1–2 mfm, Jacob Bailey to Samuel Peters 7 November 1786.

[42]Raymond, *Winslow Papers* 468.

[43]Mackinnon, 'The Loyalist Experience' 193–4.

[44]J.M. Bumsted, *The People's Clearance: Highland Emigration to British North America, 1770–1815* (Edinburgh University Press 1982); D. Campbell and R.A. MacLean, *Beyond the Atlantic Roar: A Study of the Nova Scotia Scots* (Toronto: McClelland and Stewart 1974) 7–75.

[45]PANS RG 2 Vol 49, J. Wentworth to J. Parr 5 March 1788; Mackinnon, 'The Loyalist Experience' 500.

[46]PANS RG 2 Vol 4, Roger Viets to Samuel Peters 12 October 1787; Wright, *The Loyalists* 212; Mackinnon, 'The Loyalist Experience' 486.

[47]Walker, *The Black Loyalists* 115–44.

[48]Wright, *The Loyalists* 223.

[49]PAC MG 30 D62 Vol 15, Sir A. Hammond to—1782; Mackinnon, 'The Loyalist Experience' 120–1, 210.

[50]G. Wynn, 'Late eighteenth century agriculture on the Bay of Fundy Marshlands', *Acadiensis* 8 (1979) 80–9; PANS, Jacob Bailey to Dr. Maurice 28 October 1785 and 12 May 1786; MG1 mfm Bailey Papers Vol 14; CO 217 Vol 58, J. Parr to Sydney 31 December 1785; Mackinnon, 'The Loyalist Experience' 444; G. Wynn, *Timber Colony: A Historical Geography of Early Nineteenth Century New Brunswick* (Toronto: University of Toronto Press 1981) 20.

[51]This is a best estimate on the basis of conflicting evidence. Cf. Mackinnon, 'The Loyalist Experience' 444, 448.

[52]F.B. MacMillan, 'Trade of New Brunswick with Great Britain, the United States and the Caribbean 1784–1818', MA thesis, University of New Brunswick, 1954, 45–6.

[53]Mackinnon, 'The Loyalist Experience' 459.

[54]Samual Goldbury to Edward Winslow 1 March 1785 in Raymond, *Winslow Papers* 270–1.

[55]PAC MG 23 D1 Series 1 Vol 24, C. Stewart to Col. Winslow 29 September 1784, 148.

[56]Roads in this country 'covered with woods' and 'much intersected by waters' remained in very poor state a decade after the Loyalists' arrival; PANS RG 2 Vol 48 #120, Report of 20 Deember 1794, and material in RG 16. PAC MG 11 NBA 5 28–32, Carleton to Grenville 15 July 1791. A comparison with D. McCalla, 'The "Loyalist" Economy of Upper Canada 1784–1806', *Histoire sociale/Social History* 16 (1983) 279–304, the most useful survey of the Upper Canadian economy during these years, is revealing.

[57]D.A. Sutherland, 'Halifax merchants and the pursuit of development, 1783–1850', *Canadian Historical Review* 59 (1978) 1–17. See also Macmillan, 'The Trade of New Brunswick'. H.H. Robertson, 'The Commercial Relationship between Nova Scotia and the British West Indies, 1788–1828: The Twilight of Mercantilism in the British Empire', MA thesis, Dalhousie University, 1975.

[58]PAC MG 23 D1 Series I Vol 25, 251, William Shaw to Colonel Winslow, Canso, 15 June 1784.

[59]Wet cod shipments—of 13,363 barrels from Nova Scotia and 18,103 from the four colonies—increased the total quantity somewhat. Dry cod exports from Newfoundland in 1787 were 732,216 quintals (wet-cod shipments totalled 3,865 barrels). Mackinnon, 'The Loyalist Experience' 444–5.

[60]PANS RG 1 Vol 221, Memorial of Leading Citizens of Shelburne 20 June 1791.

[61]Mackinnon, 'The Loyalist Experience' 456–7, 403; W. Dyott, *Dyott's Diary 1781–1845; A Selection from the Journals of William Dyott, Sometime General in the British Army and Aide-de-camp to His Majesty King George III*, R.W. Jeffrey, ed. (London: A. Constable 1907) 68; G.S. Graham, *Sea Power and British North America 1783–1820: A Study in British Colonial Policy* (Cambridge, MA: Harvard University Press 1941); W.S. MacNutt, *New Brunswick: A History*, 1784–1867 (Toronto: Macmillan 1963) 70–2, 96–7.

[62]This is my own calculation based on data and statements in Temperley, 'Frontierism.' Compensation for losses sustained can be estimated at £266,000. A figure of £200–210,000 for half-pay receipts stems from assumptions that two-thirds of payments before 1813 were made before 1800, that the 'take-up' rate was 66 per cent, that slightly more than half of all payments went to North America, and that the 56 per cent of North American payments accounted for by Nova Scotia and New Brunswick in 1810 approximated the earlier distribution.

[63]PAC MG 11 NBA #6 30, Observations on the Province of New Brunswick, Enclosure in Daniel Lyman to Lord Hawkesbury 9 March 1793.

[64]P. Campbell, *Travels* 282–4; H. Temperley, ed. *Gubbins' New Brunswick Journals* (Fredericton: Kings Landing Corporation 1980); PANS MG 1 Vol 4 Peters Papers, Roger Viets to Samuel Peters 11 August 1789.

[65]Greenough, 'The defence of Halifax'.

[66]Dyott, *Dyott's Diary*. Such patterns were not unknown earlier, among wealthy Loyalists: *vide* Mackinnon, 'Nova Scotia Loyalists' and Raymond, *Winslow Papers* 141–2, 150, 252, 288.

[67]G.A. Stelter, 'The political economy of the city-building process: early Canadian urban development' in D. Fraser and A. Sutcliffe, eds. *The Pursuit of Urban History* (London: Edward Arnold 1983) 179; L.B. Jensen, *Vanishing Halifax* (Halifax: McCurdy Printing 1968) n.p.

[68]K.B. Wainwright, 'A comparative study in Nova Scotian rural economy 1788–1812; based on recently discovered books of account of old firms in Kings County, Nova Scotia', *Nova Scotia Historical Society Collections* 30 (1954) 78–119.

[69]In its economic vigour, Westmorland County, in Chignecto, was perhaps more akin to the Fundy settlements of Nova Scotia than to the rest of New Brunswick.

[70]Wynn, *Timber Colony* 11–25.

[71]PAC MG 11 NBA 5, 25, Amos Botsford to Provincial Agent 5 March 1796.

[72]Bumsted, 'The Patterson regime' 67; Clark, *Three Centuries* 58–65.

[73]P.C.T. White, *Lord Selkirk's Diary, 1803–4* (Toronto: Champlain Society 1958) 7–10.

[74]Cf. R. Ommer, 'All the fish of the post: property resource rights and development in a nineteenth century inshore fishery' *Acadiensis* 10, 2 (1981) 107–23 and R. Ommer, 'From Outpost to Outport: The Jersey Merchant Triangle in the Nineteenth Century', PhD thesis, McGill University, 1979. D. Lee, *The Robins in Gaspé* (Toronto: Fitzhenry and Whiteside 1986) is of general relevance.

[75]S. Hornsby, 'An Historical Geography of Cape Breton Island in the Nineteenth Century', PhD thesis, University of British Columbia, 1986, is a significant contribution to the geographical literature. I am grateful to Hornsby for considerably sharpening my understanding of the island in 1800. Other items of relevance include J.M. Bumsted, 'Scottish emigration to the Maritimes, 1770–1815: a new look at an old theme', *Acadiensis* 10 (1981) 65–85; Campbell and MacLean, *Beyond the Atlantic Roar*; B. Kincaid, 'Scottish Immigration to Cape Breton 1758–1838' MA thesis, Dalhousie University, 1964.

[76]PANB tps MYO/H/76, Mrs. Hunter to Elizabeth Bell 7 August 1804.

[77]For similar patterns see J.J. Mannion, *Point Lance in Transition* (Toronto: McClelland and Stewart 1976). F.P. Day, *Rockbound* (Toronto: University of Toronto Press 1973) is an evocative Nova Scotian source treating a later period (*c.* 1900–14).

[78]Poll tax returns are in PANS RG 1 vol 443, 333, 333 1/2, also available on microfilm. Some have been printed, viz. T.M. Punch, 'Assessment rolls of Halifax County 1792–93', *Genealogical Newsletter of the Nova Scotia Historical Society* 15 (1976) 14–23; T.M. Punch, 'Lunenburg County, Nova Scotia: poll taxes of the 1790s', *Canadian Genealogist* 1 (1979) 103–4. As with all following estimates from these returns, this is a very broad guess. Some 50–65 per cent of taxables had cattle and horses (an enumeration category—horses were scarce in these settlements), but extended family households and a proportion of taxable men living with their parents have to be allowed for.

[79]*Saint John Gazette* (Saint John) 6 April 1798.

[80]*Royal Gazette* (Saint John) 7 December 1803; *Saint John Gazette* 25 February 1791.

[81]Clark, *Three Centuries* 63.

[82]New Brunswick Museum (NBM) Jarvis Papes 1801–19, Stephen Jarvis to Munson Jarvis, 31 July 1805; Wynn, 'Eighteenth century agriculture'; Col R.E. Morse, 'Report on Nova Scotia 1784', Canadian Archives *Report* (1884) XXXVI; NBM Westmorland County Documents and Correspondence 1783–1859 70b F-30, J[ohn] K[eillor] to T. Millidge 9 November 1804; Mount Allison University Archives, Diary of William Trueman 5 May 1802–April 1809.

[83]Wynn, *Timber Colony* 24.

[84]P. Ennals and D. Holdsworth, 'Vernacular architecture and the cultural landscape of the Maritime provinces: a reconnaissance', *Acadiensis* 10 (1981) 86–106; P. Ennals, 'The Yankee origins of Bluenose vernacular architecture', *American Review of Canadian Studies* 12 (1982) 5–21.

[85]Ennals and Holdsworth, 'Vernacular architecture' 94–5; Ennals, 'Yankee origins' 10–12.

[86]Robinson and Rispin, *Journey through Nova Scotia Containing a Particular Account of the Country and Its Inhabitants* (York: C. Etherington 1774) 21; W. Zelinsky, 'New England connecting barns', *Geographical Review* 84 (1958) 540–53; Ennals, 'Yankee origins' 7.

[87]This discussion of the cultural landscape derives in large part from my own field observations. D. Trask, *Life How Short, Eternity How Long: Gravestone Carving and Carvers in Nova Scotia* (Halifax: Nova Scotia Museum 1978) is a useful first study of gravemarkers in the region, although the text is brief. For New England see A.I. Ludwig, *Graven Images* (Middletown, Conn: Wesleyan University Press 1966). E. Dethlefson and J. Deetz, 'Death's heads, cherubs and willow trees: experimental archeology in colonial cemeteries', *American Antiquity* 31 (1966) 502–10; J. Deetz and E. Dethlefson, 'Death's heads, cherub, urn and willow', *Natural History* 76 (1967) 28–37; P. Benes, *The Masks of Orthodoxy: Folk Gravestone Carving in Plymouth County, Massachusetts; 1689–1805* (Amherst: University of Massachusetts Press 1977).

[88]Trask, *Life How Short* 24–7; Ennals and Holdsworth, 'Vernacular architecture' 94; NBM F 30, Westmorland County, Documents and Correspondence, 1783–1859, Memorandum of 16 August 1790 between John Wheldon Esq. and Charles Cairns and Frederick McGuire (masons); NBM C 6, Westmorland County Petitions (Duplicates): Agreement between John Fawcett and John Harris, 7 April 1802.

[89]Ennals and Holdsworth, 'Vernacular architecture' 88–9; P.F. Lewis, 'Common houses, cultural spoor', *Landscape* 19 (1975) 1–22; H. Glassie, *Pattern in the Material Folk Culture of the Eastern United States* (Philadelphia: University of Pennsylvania Press 1968) 80–1.

[90]A.H. Clark, 'Old World origins and religious adherence in Nova Scotia', *Geographical Review* 50 (1960) 317–44; G. Wynn, 'The Maritimes: the geography of fragmentation and underdevelopment' in L.D. McCann, ed. Heartland and Hinterland: A Geography of Canada (Scarborough, Ont: Prentice-Hall 1982) 167–8; R.C. Harris and J. Warkentin, *Canada before Confederation* (Toronto: Oxford University Press 1974) 169–231. The religious patterns are reviewed in G.S. French, 'Religion and society in late eighteenth century Nova Scotia', *Acadiensis* 4 (1975) 102–11, which is in part a review of J. Fingard, *The Anglican Design in Loyalist Nova Scotia 1783–1816* (London: SPCK 1972). See also G. French, 'The papers of

Daniel Fidler, methodist missionary in Nova Scotia and New Brunswick 1792–1798', *The Bulletin: Records and Proceedings of the Committee on Archives of the United Church of Canada* 12 (1959) 3–18, 13 (1960) 28–46. See also J.M. Bumsted, 'Church and state in Maritime Canada 1749–1807', CHA *Report* (1967) 41–58.

[91]There are several published descriptions of parts of the region in the first years of the nineteenth century, among them: G.O. Bent, 'New Brunswick in 1802', *Acadiensis* 7 (1907) 128–48; D.A. Muise (intro.) 'A descriptive and statistical account of Nova Scotia and its dependencies in 1812', *Acadiensis* 2 (1972) 82–93; J.B. Gavin SJ (intro.) 'An extract from the memoirs of Alexander Drysdale', *Acadiensis* 5 (1975) 146–9; A.H. Clark, 'Titus Smith Junior and the geography of Nova Scotia in 1801 and 1802', *Annals of the Association of American Geographers* 44 (1954) 291–316; Temperley, *Gubbins*; Wynn, *Timber Colony* 11–25.

[92]Bumsted, 'Puritan and Yankee rediviva: recent writings on early New England of interest to Atlantic scholars', *Acadiensis* 2 (1972) 3–21 makes a similar point and touches on some of the links discussed below. P.S. Saxton, 'The Paragon of Localism in Nova Scotia 1760–1783', MA thesis, Saint Mary's University, 1975; R.R. Beeman, *The Evolution of the Southern Backcountry: A Case Study of Lunenberg County, Virginia 1746–1832* (Philadelphia: University of Pennsylvania Press 1984).

[93]R.H. Brown, *Historical Geography of the United States* (New York: Harcourt, Brace and World 1948) 111.

[94]PANS MG 1 Vol 940 Wentworth Papers, W. Paine to John Wentworth 1 March 1788.

[95]MacNutt, *New Brunswick* 11, 12, 42, 92; A.E. Morrison, 'New Brunswick: the Loyalists and the historians', *Journal of Canadian Studies* 3 (1968) 39–49; F. Cogswell, 'Literary activity in the maritime provinces, 1815–1880' in C.F. Klinck, ed. *Literary History of Canada* (Toronto: University of Toronto Press 1965) 103.

[96]Condon, *The Envy, passim*; Moore, *The Loyalists* 139–54.

[97]Wright, *Loyalists* 175–7; Condon, *The Envy* 42, 89–90, 108. Various items relating to Kemble's Manor are in the Ward Chipman correspondence, PAC MG 23 D1, CO 217 Vol 59 J. Parr to Nepean 3 September 1784. Similarly B. Marston spoke of the 'cursed republican town-meeting spirit' in Shelburne; Raymond, 'The Founding' 268.

[98]Temperley, *Gubbins*; W. Reitzel, ed. *The Autobiography of William Cobbett* (London: Faber and Faber 1933) 28.

[99]Broader theoretical statements of the interpretation offered here can be found in R.C. Harris, 'The simplification of Europe overseas', *Annals of the Association of American Geographers* 67 (1977) 469–83 and R.C. Harris, 'European beginnings in the northwest Atlantic: a comparative view' in D.G. Allen, *Seventeenth-Century New England* (Boston: Colonial Society of Massachusetts 1985) 119–52. A broadly similar argument about the development of New Brunswick, based on very different foundations, is in E.C. Wright, 'The settlement of New Brunswick: an advance toward democracy' CHA *Report* (1944) 60.

[100]Cf. J.M. Bumsted, 'Settlement by chance: Lord Selkirk and Prince Edward Island', *Canadian Historical Review* 59 (1978) 170–88. Bailey cited by Mackinnon, 'The Loyalist Experience' 242. D.A. McNabb, 'Land and Families in Horton Township, Nova Scotia', MA thesis, University of British Columbia 1986; A.A. Brookes, 'The

Golden Age and the Exodus: the case of Canning, Kings County', *Acadiensis* 11 (981) 57–82; R.C. Harris, 'Regionalism and the Canadian Archipelago' in McCann, *Heartland and Hinterland*, 458–84. In arguing thus I seek to illuminate one strand of regional experience rather than to deny (for example) the important struggles and achievements of Maritimers in the 1880–1930 period.

14

British Indian Policy in the Wake of the American Revolution

Donald B. Smith

After the departure of France from North America in 1763, the British government adopted a specific and benevolent (if paternalistic) Indian policy. By the Royal Proclamation of 1763, the British had attempted to protect the Indians beyond existing settlement by creating a vast Indian territory in the backcountry, and insisted on proper transfers of land from natives to the Crown before further settlement could proceed. That policy was completely shattered by the American Revolution. The American colonials regarded the prohibitions on western settlement as part of the arbitrary and tyrannical British imperial system against which they were ultimately to rebel, and during the consequent war the British incurred new obligations to many native tribes, particularly among the Iroquois. Nevertheless, as part of their terms for peace, the Americans insisted on ownership of the country south of the Lakes and east of the Mississippi and a British govern-

ment desperate to resolve the conflict with the United States agreed, however reluctantly. The transfer of the western Indian territory to the United States, which many native leaders argued was not within the sovereign possession of the British and hence could not be so surrendered, led to another lengthy period of native unrest in the West which eventually merged in the War of 1812. Nor were the British any less harried within territory they had not given away to the Americans.

One of the implications of the expansion of European settlement was a domino effect on the native inhabitants. As pioneers pushed natives further into the interior, those natives inevitably came into conflict with a group already in residence on that land. The American Revolution hastened the process of displacement, and, as Donald B. Smith demonstrates, had a significant impact upon the Mississauga Indians of the 'Golden Horseshoe' region, whose land title was 'extinguished' by the British for Loyalists —both European and native—in the post-revolutionary period. The pattern of misunderstanding over the meaning of land use and ownership in the treaties between natives and British was not new; only the particular circumstances were different.

What evidence does the author offer for his interpretation of Mississauga misunderstanding of the meaning of their land surrenders? Does this evidence seem convincing? How could the British have behaved differently, given their situation? Is the treatment of the Mississauga merely an unavoidable tragedy of misunderstanding? Does the continued persistence of the misunderstanding over the centuries make any difference in the answer to this question?

This article first appeared, titled 'The Dispossession of the Mississauga Indians: a Missing Chapter in the Early History of Upper Canada', in *Ontario History* 73, 2 (1981), 61–87.

Two centuries ago the Mississauga Indians alone controlled what is now the richest industrial area of Canada, the 'Golden Horseshoe', but today they no longer occupy any land along the shoreline of Lake Ontario. The Mississauga have been displaced to small reserves at New Credit (near Hagersville), Scugog (near Port Perry), Hiawatha and Alderville (on Rice Lake), and Curve Lake (immediately north of Peterborough). From Kingston to St Catharines five million newcomers live in their old hunting and fishing grounds. How did the Mississauga initially lose their mastery over the north shore of Lake Ontario? To describe and to explain their dispossession in the late eighteenth and early nineteenth centuries (to 1805) is the subject of this paper.

In 1763 the British Government, then involved in suppressing Pontiac's Rebellion, officially recognized the Great Lakes Indians' title to their lands. The Royal Proclamation of 1763 became the Magna Carta of Indian rights in British North America. It immediately ended the old system of unregulated land surrenders—before any further settlement could legally proceed Indian land must first be surrendered by the Indians to the Crown. Twenty years later, however, the former Thirteen Colonies renounced the Proclamation.[1] In the mid-1780s the new Republic argued that she had defeated Britain and her native allies, and that therefore, by the Treaty of Paris of 1783, she had gained political sovereignty as well as absolute ownership over all of the 'conquered' Indian territory south of the Great Lakes and east of the Mississippi.[2] In contrast, Britain continued to apply the Royal Proclamation on the lands remaining to her north of the Great Lakes. Britain was anxious to keep her Indian alliances intact in the event of another North American war.[3]

The Americans' attempt to enforce their 'Conquest Theory' led to another decade of border warfare throughout their new Northwest Territory, as land-hungry settlers continued to migrate down rivers and through mountain passes into the Ohio country. The Shawnee, Delaware, Miami, and Wyandots fought back against the invaders. It is estimated that 1500 Kentuckians lost their lives in the seven-year period from 1783 to 1790, and these losses were but the prologue for the Americans' greatest single tragedy. In early November 1791 the Indians defeated General St Clair, the Governor of the Northwestern Territory. The American force suffered over 900 casualties.[4] Only 'Mad Anthony' Wayne's decisive victory at Fallen Timbers on 20 August 1794, established American control in the Ohio country.

Canadian historians have noted with considerable satisfaction that Britain escaped similar Indian violence north of the Great Lakes. As Gerald Craig, the author of the well-respected *Upper Canada: The Formative Years*, has written: 'Unlike the nearby American states, Upper Canada never had an angry Indian frontier.'[5] The British kept to the letter of the Proclamation and did indeed avoid the bloody armed conflict of the American Northwest. But was the adjustment of Canada's native peoples to British rule really as harmonious as Canadian historians have assumed? A quick review of the experience of the Mississauga Indians under British domination strongly suggests a far more complex situation, in which, by the late 1790s, considerable discontent against British rule definitely existed.

Historians have made little reference to the Mississauga chiefly on account of the scarcity of available source materials. In contrast to the Hurons, whose past and present were so minutely described in the early seventeenth century by the Jesuit Fathers, white British North Americans in the late eighteenth century wrote very little about the Mississauga. Fortunately there is one hitherto ignored source of information. Shortly after the conversion to Christianity in the mid-1820s several Mississauga completed accounts of their people's recent past. Using these Indian sources, as well as the existing non-Indian materials, the story of the Mississauga's first years under British rule can be more fully told.

At the outset of white-Indian contact in the early seventeenth century, members of two large linguistic families occupied present-day southern Ontario: the Algonkians and the Iroquoians. The Algonkians, whose modern descendants include those peoples called Algonkins, Nipissings, Ojibwa and Ottawa, lived on the Georgian Bay, around Lake Nipissing and in the Ottawa Valley. Essentially nomadic peoples, the Algonkians relied almost exclusively on hunting and fishing. The Iroquoians, who included the Hurons and the Five Nations or Iroquois Confederacy, lived south of the Algonkians, the Hurons on the southern shore of the Georgian Bay and the Five Nations (Mohawk, Oneida, Onondaga, Cayuga, and Seneca) across Lake Ontario in what is now northern New York State.[6] Semi-sedentary peoples, the Iroquoians relied heavily on horticulture as well as on hunting and fishing for their survival.

Although they shared the same culture and spoke a similar tongue, the Hurons and the Iroquois at the moment of European contact were hostile to each other. Eventually the Five Nations or Iroquois obtained the upper hand and dispersed the Huron Confederacy in 1649–50, and then attacked the Hurons' allies, the Algonkian tribes.[7] For the next forty years the Five Nations held their territorial gains, until they were seriously weakened by disease and mounting casualties from their battles with the French. At this point the Ojibwa (or Chippewa as the Americans term the same tribe) took the offensive, migrating southward from Lake Superior and the north shore of Lake Huron and expelling the Iroquois from present-day southern Ontario.[8]

According to Kahkewaquonaby, or the Rev. Peter Jones, a native Mississauga missionary, the skirmishes between the two Indian groups in the late 1690s were so bloody that a century and a half after they took place, 'there has been, and still is, a smothered feeling of hatred and enmity between the two nations; so that when either of them comes within the haunts of the other they are in constant fear.'[9] Kahkewaquonaby pointed to the large mounds of human bones at the south and north ends of Burlington Beach as evidence of the intensity of the final battle. 'Besides these,' he added, 'there are traces of fortifications at short distances along the whole length of the beach, where holes had been dug into the sand and a breastwork thrown round them. They are about twenty or thirty feet in diameter, but were originally much larger.'[10]

By coming south the Ojibwa acquired new hunting and fishing grounds, and many obtained a new name. In 1640 the Jesuits first recorded the term Mississauga, or rather 'oumisagai', as the name of an Algonkian band near the Mississagi River on the northwestern shore of Lake Huron.[11] The French, and later the English, for unknown reasons applied this name to all the Ojibwa settling on the north shore of Lake Ontario. Only a tiny fraction of these Indians could have been members of the actual Mississauga band, but the name, once recorded in the Europeans' documents, has remained in use to this day.

The name 'Mississauga' puzzled the Ojibwa on the north shore of Lake Ontario. They continued to call themselves 'Anishinabe' (or 'Anishinabeg' to use the plural form) which meant 'human beings' or 'men'. The Indians had their own theories about how they had received their new name from the Europeans. In 1874 Wahsayahbunwashkung, or the Rev. Allan Salt, a Mississauga from the eastern end of Lake Ontario, explained how he believed it had originated. Many rivers such as the Moira, Trent, Rouge, Don, Humber, Etobicoke, and Credit, flowed into Lake Ontario. 'Those who settled at the Bay of Quinte and North Shore of Lake Ontario were called "Minzazahgeeg" (persons living where there are many mouths of rivers) now pronounced by the English Mississaga'.[12] At the western end of the lake a different theory prevailed. About one-quarter of the Credit River band belonged to the Eagle clan or totem, the name of which they pronounced in their dialect (which was slightly different than the Ojibwa spoken among the Mississauga to the east)[13], 'Ma-se-sau-gee'. According to Kahkewaquon-aby the Europeans' name for his people was derived from that of their dom-inant totem.[14]

One of the names the Mississauga gave a river in their new hunting ter-ritory betrays their northern origin. They termed the Humber 'Cobechenonk'—'leave the canoes and go back'—for this was the beginning of the Toronto Carrying Place.[15] Here they portaged their canoes northward to the Holland River, and paddled across Lake Simcoe. Then they took the Severn River to the Georgian Bay, crossed the huge lake named after their vanquished allies, then returned to their ancestral homeland, 'Ojibwa Kech-egame', 'the big water of the Ojibwas', or Lake Superior.

After the Iroquois left, a number of their Iroquois place names remained. Niagara, or 'Oo-noo-nah-gah-rah' as it was pronounced by the Mississauga, was one. On the east bank of the 'Oo-noo-nah-gah-rah' stood the large stone fort, originally built by the French in 1726. Here, twenty years after the departure of the French, the Mississauga agreed in the early 1780s to the first land surrenders with the British Crown. The great lake, on whose shores they had settled, retained its Iroquois name, Ontario, 'beautiful great lake' while the area around the foot of the important portage remained 'Toronto' an Iroquois word the Mississauga took to mean 'looming of trees'.

The Mississauga gave many new Ojibwa names to the landscape. To the west lay the 'Askuneseebe' or the 'Horn River' (or Thames), named from the river's resemblance in shape to the antlers of a deer. They termed Lake Erie 'Wahbeshkegoo Kechegame' ('the White Water Lake') from its colour which contrasted with the green and blue waters of the Upper Great Lakes.[16] Into Lake Erie flowed the 'Pesshinneguning Oeskinneguning' ('the one that washes the timber down and drives away the grass weeds') or Grand River. Here, where the annual flooding provided excellent weed control, they planted corn in the spring on the river flats. North of the Niagara River, called by the Mississauga the 'Whirlpool River', lay the creeks termed in Ojibwa 'Red Cedar', 'White Cedar Place', 'Eagles Nest Place', 'the salt lick where deer resort' (the forty-mile creek). They called the creek immediately south of Burlington Bay 'the place where small turtles lay their eggs'.

Immediately east of the large bay flowed two small creeks, the Bronte or Esquissink ('last creek') and the Sixteen Mile or Nesaugayonk ('having two outlets'). They named the next river to the east, Missinihe or Trusting Creek, for here the white traders came and gave them 'credit' for the following year.[17] They held the Credit River 'in reverential estimation as the favorite resort of their ancestors'.[18] The Mississauga at the western end of the lake were themselves known as the Credit River band.

Beyond the Credit lay the Adoopekog, 'Place of the black alder', a word still recognizable in 'Etobicoke'. Just past the Humber or 'leave the canoes and go back' River, one came to the long peninsula (now Toronto Islands) which formed a deep harbour. Here the Mississauga brought their sick to recover in its health–giving atmosphere.[19] Farther east one came to the 'Saugechewigewonk', 'strong waters rapids', the Trent.[20]

During the winter the Mississauga travelled to their hunting grounds (which reached from the lake to the heads of the watersheds of the rivers draining into the north shore of Lake Ontario). In the early spring they gathered at their maple sugar bushes to collect the sap needed to make maple sugar. During the summer they speared salmon at their river encampments by the river mouths. In the late summer the Indian women harvested the corn that they had planted on the river flats in the spring. When fall arrived the small villages broke up into family hunting groups who again returned by foot or by canoe to their inland ranges. The fortunate Mississauga between Toronto and the Trent River travelled first to Rice Lake where they harvested the abundant crop of wild rice.[21]

The Mississauga kept in contact with the Ojibwa to the north and their Algonkian relatives to the west.[22] Evidence exists that on occasion adventuresome warriors travelled as far as 1500 kilometers from the north shore of Lake Ontario (to join in raiding parties against the Cherokee living in the southern Alleghenies).[23] They also joined other Great Lakes tribes in aiding Britain in the American Revolution, participating in raiding parties against settlements in northern New York and Pennsylvania.[24]

When the armed conflict of the American Revolution broke out in 1775 the Mississauga immediately supported the Crown. From the Delaware, Shawnee and other neighbouring Algonkian tribes they knew of the American settlers' constant encroachments on Indian lands. They had always respected Sir William Johnson, the Northern Superintendent of Indian Affairs (1755–1774), who had attempted to control the westward onrush of the American settlers and who had supplied them with presents after his Councils with them.[25] They followed the advice of his two successors: his nephew Guy Johnson (to 1782) and then Sir William's son, Sir John Johnson (after 1782).

For seven years the British freely gave presents to attract as many warriors as possible to join their raiding parties into northern New York and Pennsylvania. The Indians appreciated the constant supply of iron axes with fine cutting edges, the new durable iron kettles, the wool clothing (which unlike leather did not shrink when wet), and most important of all, guns and ammunition for the hunt. During the American Revolution the Mississauga's dependency on European trade goods increased dramatically, and this same dependency contributed to their decision to agree to the first land purchases.

After the British Government's defeat by the American colonists, the Crown approached the Mississauga to make some of their lands available to the Loyalists. The Indians agreed for several reasons. First, they were most anxious that the flow of gifts from the British continue. As Nawahjegezh-egwabe, or Chief Joseph Sawyer, recalled in 1845 (he was then about sixty years old): 'our ancestors have always told us, that they surrendered a large and valuable territory of lands, in consideration of the presents, and that the British Government promised and covenanted to give clothing perpetually, as long as the sun shall shine, the waters flow, and grasses grow.'[26]

Another reason that the Indians readily accepted the land surrenders was their misunderstanding about their meaning. As anthropologist George Snyderman has pointed out in his excellent study, 'Concepts of Land Ownership Among the Iroquois and Their Neighbors', the Mississauga and other Eastern Woodlands groups initially experienced great difficulty in comprehending the European concept of the absolute ownership of land by individuals. The land belonged to the tribe—to its future yet-to-be-born members as well as to its present members. Moreover, Snyderman continued, the Indians felt that land itself was a gift from the 'Maker'. Like the rivers or the air above, it was not a commodity that could be bought or sold. From the standpoint of the Mississauga, who by the 1780s had been resident on the north shore of Lake Ontario for nearly a century, the initial purchases were simply 'grants to the use of land during good behavior'.[27] The agreements made no mention of the surrender of the Indians' rights over the rivers, lakes, and land under the water. The British assured them that they could 'encamp and fish where we pleased'.[28]

A third reason helps to explain the Mississauga's willingness to cede their interest in a large section of their lands. They were weakly organized, and had a small population. In the 1780s the Mississauga on the north shore of Lake Ontario numbered approximately two hundred warriors. They were organized in half a dozen or so small bands spread out along roughly 500 kilometers of lakefront. Although the 1,000 Mississauga[29] retained contact with their Ojibwa kinsmen on Lake Huron and to the immediate west on the Thames, they did not hold regular councils with them. Unlike the Iroquois Confederacy they lacked a League Council of Chiefs. Weakly organized, dependent on European trade goods, and seeing an advantage for themselves in the agreement (namely presents in perpetuity for the use of a portion of their land), the Mississauga agreed to the surrenders.

The first purchase took place during the American Revolution. On 9 May 1781, Guy Johnson summoned the leading Mississauga chiefs and warriors to Fort Niagara. Although the Seneca had previously ceded the west bank of the Niagara River in 1764 (some Mississauga had been present at this meeting in 1764, but they had not signed the agreement),[30] Guy Johnson now recognized the Mississauga as the rightful owners and corrected the indenture. In return for 'Three hundred suits of Clothing' he gained for the Crown a corridor of land four miles wide on the west bank of the Niagara River. Johnson reported to Governor Haldimand in Quebec that the Mississauga were 'well satisfied'.[31] Indeed they were, as game had been very scarce that previous winter and they needed help.[32]

The next surrender took place at the eastern end of the Lake. On 9 October 1783, Captain Crawford (a Loyalist officer who had accompanied the Mississauga on several raiding parties during the Revolutionary War) obtained all the lands from 'Toniata or Oniagara River [Toniata River, a tributary of the St Lawrence below Gananoque] to a River in the Bay of Quentie within Eight Leagues of the Bottom of Said Bay including all the Islands . . . ' The purchase (for which no deed survives) apparently extended back from Lake Ontario, 'as far as a man can Travel in a Day'. For this vast tract, with its loosely described northern boundary, the Indians asked for and obtained clothing for all of their families, guns for those without them, powder and ammunition for their winter's hunting, and 'as much coarse Red Cloth as will make about a Dozen Coats and as many Laced Hats. . . .'[33]

More purchases quickly followed, each of which confirms that the Mississauga had their own concept of the meaning of these agreements. Once the British promised them presents the Indians allowed them the use of as much land as they needed. Apparently at some point during the summer of 1784 (again no deed or indenture survives) the Mississauga at the eastern end of the lake made a second agreement with Captain Crawford, accepting, in the Government's understanding, to surrender the land on and above the Bay of Quinte to run 'Northerly as far as it may please Government to assign'.[34] The Government was left to set whatever boundary it desired. (The Mississauga apparently failed to point out to Captain Crawford that the Algonkins also had a claim to any land that the British might select in the Ottawa Valley.)[35]

In the first six to seven years of British settlement it appears as if both the Mississauga and the British felt that they gained from the agreement. For the use of their land the Mississauga believed that they had made a series of useful and profitable rental agreements. The British, in contrast, understood that they had extinguished the native title to the land. When the Credit band was approached in the spring of 1784 to make a huge transfer of their hunting grounds they consented. On May 22nd they yielded the Niagara Peninsula —roughly all the land from Burlington Bay to the headwaters of the Grand River to Long Point on Lake Erie.[36] In their desire to obtain the greatest number of gifts and presents, the Credit band apparently included some land that was not theirs. Later several Ojibwa of the Thames complained that the Mississauga had surrendered a portion of their hunting territory, the land west of the Grand River which (they claimed) belonged to them, not to the Credit band.[37]

To the east in 1787 and 1788 the Mississauga surrendered all of the central portion of their remaining lands on the north shore of Lake Ontario (from the Etobicoke Creek, just west of Toronto, to the Head of the Bay of Quinte).[38] These purchases, both very improperly prepared, opened up the land behind the lake, in the words of one white witness, 'as far back as a man could walk, or go on foot in a day'.[39] The Indians later believed that the area involved extended as far back as a gun-shot fired on the lakeshore could be heard in the interior, hence their description of the agreements as the 'Gunshot Treaties'.[40]

The British were also pleased. Governor-General Haldimand's directive that 'the utmost attention to Economy be paid'[41] in making the surrenders was closely followed. The purchase, for example, of the Niagara Peninsula, 3,000,000 acres of land, cost the Crown less than £1200 worth of gifts.[42] The agreements of 1787 and 1788 had simply meant the distribution of more supplies of guns, ammunition, clothing, tobacco and trinkets.[43]

Much of the initial good feeling between the two parties stemmed from the inaccurate translation of the agreements. At the surrender of the Niagara Peninsula in May 1784 the Iroquois interpreter, Nicholas Stevens, and an officer of the Indian Department, William Bowen,[44] acted as the official interpreters. They did an atrocious job, the proof of which is in the indenture itself which vaguely locates the northern border as a line drawn northwest from 'Waghquata' or 'Wequatelong' (Burlington Bay) to the headwaters of the Thames. If this had been properly explained to the Indians they would have realized that this was an impossibility—a line drawn northwest from the Bay will never reach the Thames, which lies to the southwest. The period of good relations quickly passed as the Indians learned the British government's interpretation of the surrenders.

The arrival of thousands of white settlers caused a tremendous upheaval on the north shore of Lake Ontario. The newcomers viewed the primeval forest as an enemy to be exterminated as quickly as possible. Throughout the 1780s and 1790s they cleared their bush lots, felling trees, burning the stumps, then harrowing and sowing the ground—actions which horrified the Indians. The Ojibwa had a feeling of reverence toward the land, the water, the plants, and the wildlife, believing as Kahkewaquonaby wrote in his *History of the Ojebway Indians* that they were 'endowed with immortal spirits, and that they possess supernatural power to punish any who may dare to despise or make any unnecessary waste of them'. They were so sensitive to their environment, he added, that they 'very seldom cut down green or living trees from the idea that it puts them to pain'.[45] They loved the earth as the mother of man for furnishing them with the plants and the animals which allowed them to survive.

In view of the Indians' conception of nature, one can be certain that they would have understood little of the white man's specialized legal jargon, regardless of the abilities of the two interpreters employed. The Mississauga lacked equivalents in the Ojibwa language for even the most basic terms and concepts of British law. As the British interpreter, James Givens, told Lord Selkirk in 1803, one could not even translate into Ojibwa the true meaning of the English word 'justice'.[46] Their understanding of English words like 'ownership' and 'sovereignty' would be equally confused. Similarly the British lacked any clear idea of the Mississauga's system of land use.

By the 1790s the Mississauga had begun to realize what the land surrenders really did mean to the British—the outright surrender of their land. While the British had recognized that the natives had certain tribal rights on the principle of prior occupancy, they believed that these rights were all extinguished by the agreements. Once the white farmers obtained patents they denied the Indians the right to cross over their farms. And on the tract that remained to the Credit River Mississauga on the northwest shore of Lake Ontario the white settlers encroached on their salmon fisheries.[47] As Quinipeno, the Chief of the Equissink (Bronte Creek) Mississauga, told the officers of the Indian Department in 1805:

> while Colonel Butler was our Father we were told our Father the King wanted some Land for his people it was some time before we sold it, but when we found it was wanted by the King to settle his people on it, whom we were told would be of great use to us, we granted it accordingly. Father—we have no[t] found this so, as the inhabitants drive us away instead of helping us, we want to know why we are served in that manner. . . . Colonel Butler told us the Farmers would help us, but instead of doing so when we encamp on the Land they drove us off and shoot our dogs and never give us any assistance as was promised to our old Chiefs.[48]

A generation after the surrenders the Mississauga remained bitterly resentful of them. When Kahkewaquonaby spoke in the 1820s and 1830s with the tribal elders he learned that when the white man came:

> Our fathers held out to them the hand of friendship. The strangers then asked for a small piece of land on which they might pitch their tents; the request was cheerfully granted. By and by they begged for more, and more was given them. In this way they have continued to ask, or have obtained by force or fraud, the fairest portions of our territory.[49]

Different interpretations of the Fort Niagara surrender of 1784 divided government officials and the tribal elders for the next century. After the agreement was signed the Mississauga held that the oral promises were as binding as those written down. They argued as late as 1860 that they had retained at Niagara in 1784 outright control of 'Burlington Beach and a portion of Burlington Heights and broken fronts along the shores of Lake Ontario between Burlington Beach and Niagara[;] these with considerable points jutting out into the Lake were always considered unsurrendered Indian land.' The Credit band claimed as well Long Point and Turkey Point on Lake Erie, a large island in the Grand River, and 'the peninsula forming Toronto Harbour' (now Toronto Island).[50]

Friction was at its peak during the mid-1790s. Several Mississauga of the Credit band dictated a protest to the Lieutenant-Governor in 1793, which David Ramsay, a white trader, wrote down.[51] In 1794 three Mississauga raided a farm thirty kilometers north of York, and took all of the farmer's servant's 'provision, and even the Shirt from off his back'.[52] Rumours circulated on the Bay of Quinte about a forthcoming attack on the settlement by the Rice Lake Mississauga during the summer of 1795. Fortunately for the settlers, once the Rice Lake Indians received their annual presents[53] the danger eased off and the anticipated attack was never made.

The most serious incident of all took place in late August 1796. Wabikinine was the Head Chief of all the Credit River band of Mississauga. He, like all Ojibwa chiefs, was first among equals, seeking consensus among his followers, rather than ruling with iron-clad authority. He was very good at it, and in the words of Peter Russell, the Administrator of the Government, he was 'greatly beloved' by the Indians.[54] As the foremost chief of the Mississauga at the western end of the lake, his name appeared in the land transfers of 1781, 1784 and 1787.[55] He was known as a firm friend of the British. His murder by a British soldier sent shock waves through the Ojibwa bands in southern Ontario.

Wabikinine and his band had come from the Credit River to York to sell salmon in exchange for the white settlers' rum. The Chief, his sister and his wife were camped on the waterfront opposite Berry's tavern, a short distance from the rest of the band on the peninsula. Having sold their fish they had begun drinking heavily.[56]

Early in the evening Charles McEwan, a soldier in the Queen's Rangers, had offered Wabikinine's sister a dollar and some rum to sleep with him. Just before midnight the soldier came with two white settlers to claim his prize. But Wabikinine's wife saw the white men pull his sister out from her resting spot under a canoe. Fearing that they would kill the woman, she roused her husband. Half asleep and half drunk the big, muscular Indian staggered from under his canoe and lunged at the white men.

In the scuffle in the darkness the soldier took a rock and knocked the Indian senseless, then kicked him in the chest and left him. When the rest of the Indians heard the wailing of the two women they rushed over from the peninsula. Hurriedly they took the women and the chief to their camping ground, and early the next morning by canoe back to the Credit River. He died that same day from his injuries. The chief's widow died a day or so after Wabikinine. Some of the Indians believed that she 'died in consequence of the ill treatment she had received from the Whites. . . .'[57]

Wabikinine's and his wife's deaths led to rumours of an Indian uprising. By chance, Isaac Weld, an Irish traveller, had been at West Niagara or Newark one day after a party of Mississauga had met with the commanding officer about the incident. In Weld's published account he recalled that only the presence of the English garrison had prevented the Indians from 'taking revenge openly on this occasion'.[58] The administrator, Peter Russell, himself sensed trouble. When he wrote Governor Simcoe on 31 December 1796, about McEwan's trial, and his acquittal for 'want of evidence' (the Indians although invited had not attended the trial to give evidence—yet another example of their lack of understanding of British law), he ominously added: 'something should be done to conciliate the affections of the tribes in the rear of York, who, for want of some such attention, may become unfriendly to the British name and harass the back settlements by their depredations.'[59]

The possibility of an Indian uprising had long terrified the British authorities. The fear was legitimate, as it appeared for several weeks in the late winter of 1796–97 as if the organization of the rebellion had begun. On 15 February 1797, Nimquasim, 'a Principal Chief lately from Lake Huron', 'one of the Chippaways, who they call their great Chief', met at Berry's tavern in York with several Mississauga. Rum had loosened the chief's tongue. He called Augustus Jones, an Ojibwa-speaking surveyor, over. As Jones reported the conversation to D.W. Smith, the Acting Surveyor General, Nimquasim was 'much displeased, at the murder of one of their Chiefs by the white people'. The powerful chief confessed 'that upon the whole it was his wish to open a war against the English to get satisfaction, for what had been done'.[60] Once the news reached Peter Russell, the administrator wrote Robert Prescott, the Governor General at Quebec, of the 'most inflamatory speech' by 'Nimqua-sim (who has great influence over the Warlike Tribes, bordering on Lakes Huron, Simcoe, &c.)'.[61]

The situation at York was serious. Only 240 settlers, men, women and children, lived at York, with another 435 in the neighbouring townships of York, Scarborough and Etobicoke. True, there were large white settlements in the Bay of Quinte and Niagara regions but York was cut off from them in winter. There was no road to the Bay of Quinte and that to Niagara was most unsatisfactory. York's garrison consisted of only 135 men, with another 25 or so at Newark.[62]

Lieutenant-Governor Simcoe had always considered the Indian as a potentially 'formidable' enemy as he 'is full of Martial Science and Spirit adapted to the nature of the Country'.[63] So did Administrator Russell. When he learned of Nimquasim or 'Cut Nose's' speech he wrote Aeneas Shaw, one of his Executive Councillors, then in York, that if the news was true and the citizens were alarmed that he should 'assemble the Inhabitants of the Town of York and advise them to provide themselves immediately with Arms and ammunition for their Mutual Defence, and take such other measures as may be likely to defeat the hostile Machinations of their Indian Neighbours'.[64] The following fall when John Elmsley, the Chief Justice of Upper

Canada, travelled by road to York from Niagara, Russell assigned him a military guard as he passed through the Mississauga Tract, the unsurrendered section between Burlington Bay and York.[65]

The rebellion never came. Credit for averting it can best be given to Joseph Brant of the Six Nations (the Five had become the Six Nations when the Tuscarora, a southern Iroquois group, joined around 1722). To understand Brant's influence some additional information is necessary. Over 2,000 Iroquois had come north after fighting for Britain in the American Revolution. Governor-General Haldimand had provided lands to the largest group under Captain Brant on the Grand River. From the land secured by Captain Crawford in 1784 the Government assigned the smaller Iroquois group under John Deseronto a reserve on the Bay of Quinte.[66]

When first asked to 'sell' their lands in July 1783 the Mississauga had voiced their immediate concern about the arrival of their hereditary enemies, the Iroquois. Sir John Johnson reported that the idea 'alarmed them greatly, as they apprehended it would be followed by disputes between them, and must terminate in One or the other leaving the Country. . .'[67] But when the Mississauga learned in early 1784 that large numbers of white farmers intended to settle on their hunting grounds, they reversed their position and welcomed the Iroquois.[68] At least the Iroquois, the old warriors reasoned, were fellow Indians with whom they might, if necessary, make common cause against the whites.

By the mid-1790s the Mississauga, now aware of the true meaning of the land surrenders, were anxious for a tight alliance with the Iroquois on the Grand River. The Six Nations, the Mississauga realized, had dealt with the British for over a century in New York and knew how to negotiate effectively with them. Early in 1798 the Mississauga formally elected Brant, the Indian who 'alone knows the value of the land',[69] as one of their chiefs. When they approached Brant to request military support he warned them against rebellion. Having visited England twice, the Iroquois war chief had an intimate knowledge of Britain's military strength. Locked himself in an argument with Russell and the Executive Council (Brant wanted the right to sell portions of the Six Nations Reserve on the Grand River—initially the Executive Council refused to allow it),[70] he knew the futility of armed resistance. Brant's cautionary advice helped to convince the Mississauga and their Ojibwa kinsmen to remain at peace.

Russell and his council, fully realizing the potential threat of a pan-Indian alliance in Upper Canada, acted immediately. Secretly Russell attempted to disrupt the understanding of the Iroquois with the Mississauga, notifying William Claus at Niagara and James Givens at York, 'to do everything in [their] power (without exposing the object of this Policy to Suspicion) to foment any existing Jealousy between the Chippewas & the Six Nations; and to prevent as far as possible any Junction or good understanding between those two Tribes'.[71] Then the Government sat back and waited for the link with the Six Nations to weaken, as their traditional hostility, dating back to the seventeenth century, appeared again.

By 1805 the Mississauga's close bond with the Six Nations had broken. In that year, without consulting Joseph Brant, they sold nearly 100,000 acres of land on the shoreline of Lake Ontario, the coastal section of the Mississauga Tract located between present-day Hamilton and Toronto. Animosity between the two groups, notwithstanding all the public protestations of good will, had never been very far beneath the surface. To the Iroquois the Ojibwa were 'a people they did not understand', a tribe 'they have a contemptible opinion of',[72] a group they scorned as 'stinking of fish' (the Mississauga greased their bodies with fish oil which gave off a rank smell).[73] The Ojibwa fully reciprocated in their dislike of the Iroquois. Memories of the fierce battles over a century before remained very much alive. Only in moments of extreme crisis could the Confederacy and the Mississauga unite, and then apparently only for a short period.

Another important explanation of the Mississauga's enfeebled response to Wabikinine's murder arises from their sharp decline in population. In 1798 the Credit band numbered three hundred and thirty persons, with three additional families at the Credit River. A decade earlier in 1787 there had been over five hundred band members.[74] A smallpox epidemic had swept the Indian communities of Lake Simcoe and the Niagara Peninsula in 1793. Three years later there were more outbreaks.[75] These epidemics carried away one-third of the Credit band's population. By 1827 their numbers would be reduced by another third, to just under two hundred persons.[76]

To the south of the Great Lakes lived thousands of potential allies for the Mississauga. During the early 1790s their fellow Algonkians—Shawnees, Miamis and Delawares—had defeated large American armies. Yet by 1796 these tribes were spent as military forces. After the Indians' defeat at the Battle of Fallen Timbers in August 1794 the Americans had destroyed corn fields and burnt villages. The next summer the hungry and tattered Indian delegations had ceded most of the present state of Ohio at the Treaty of Greenville,[77] and were not in a position to help any other Indian groups.

Alcohol abuse had also become a serious problem for the Indians. Since the departure of the French, scores of traders had come north from New York, men who have been described by one historian as the 'scum of the earth'.[78] Some brought only liquor to trade with the Indians. As they had no fermented beverage before the arrival of the Europeans they lacked social controls for it. A British officer commented as early as October 1783 that the Mississauga were 'absolutely devoted' to rum. By their own admission the Indians could not control their addiction. The settlers promoted alcohol abuse by trading rum for the Indians' fish and venison.[79] The alcoholism of many led to serious malnutrition, resulting in apathy, depression and an inability to hunt and fish.[80]

Finally, the Mississauga could not launch an effective uprising without the help of another European power. By the late 1790s they had become too dependent on manufactured goods and the services of European blacksmiths to repair their guns. The imported wares had become a large part of the Indians' culture. With Britain and America at peace in the late 1790s the Mississauga's only possible allies were the Spaniards, and the French agents, in Louisiana.[81] But the Spaniards in Louisiana—despite Russell's fears— never constituted a serious threat. Without substantial numbers of Indian allies, dependent for manufactured goods upon the British, weakened by disease and alcoholism, cautioned against rebellion by Brant, then separated from the Iroquois, the Mississauga could do little, and in the end accepted their fate. Active and passive resistance continued but the opportunity for a native rebellion passed.

Other hardships beset the Mississauga at this time. In late December 1797 the looting of Indian burial sites had reached such proportions that the authorities—to their credit—issued a proclamation to protect them.[82] Around the garrisons a number of British soldiers continued to molest native women. In 1801, for example, four soldiers descended on a small Mississauga encampment near Kingston. When the men tried to protect their women the soldiers 'beat the Indians' and only 'after having severely bruised some of them' did they leave.[83] Even the annual presents given by the Government to the Mississauga became a mixed blessing. The rum merchants plied the Indians with liquor in order to gain the goods that they had just received. John Cameron, an Indian Department official, commented in 1806 that many 'return to the Woods in much worse circumstances than when they left them'.[84]

The negative image that many Europeans held conditioned their actions toward the Mississauga. The settlers had little appreciation for a hunting and gathering society—if they could suffice on a few acres why did each Indian need many square miles to support himself? Mrs. Simcoe's opinion that they were an 'idle, drunken, dirty tribe' seems to have been the common one.[85] As Isaac Weld astutely noted, the English settlers 'cannot banish wholly from their minds as the French do, that the Indians are an inferior race to them'.[86]

From 1763 the British authorities upheld the Royal Proclamation. As Lieutenant-Governor Simcoe declared on 22 June 1793 to a group of Indians from the Western Great Lakes, 'no King of Great Britain ever claimed absolute power or Sovereignty over any of your Lands or Territories that were not fairly sold or bestowed by your ancestors at Public Treaties.'[87] To rectify the defective Niagara surrender of 1784 Simcoe, in 1792, secured a new indenture from the Mississauga in which the boundaries of the earlier purchase were adequately marked.[88] But despite the British officials' concern for legality, the end result for the Mississauga was the same—they lost their homeland. At least they were able to secure slightly better terms in 1805 than they had in 1781, 1784 and 1787/88.

The negotiations of 1805 mark a turning point in the Mississauga's relations with the British, the end of the period of blind trust. In the early agreements the Mississauga had allowed the British to set their own boundaries, but now they acted quite differently. When approached to surrender all of the Mississauga Tract the Indians declined the British offer. As Quinipeno, the Mississauga's speaker, explained:

> Now Father when Sir John Johnson came up to purchase the Toronto Lands [1787] we gave them without hesitation and we were told we should always be taken care of and we made no bargain for the Land but left it to himself.
>
> Now Father you want another piece of Land—we cannot say no: but we will explain ourselves before we say any more. . . . I speak for all the Chiefs and they wish to be under your protection as formerly But it is hard for us to give away more Land: The Young Men and Women have found fault with so much having been sold before, if it is true we are poor, and the Women say we will be worse if we part with any more; but we will tell you what we mean to do.[89]

Quinipeno went on to add that they would sell only the southern portion of the tract, retaining for themselves in the surrendered area small reserves at the mouths of the Twelve and Sixteen Mile Creeks and the Credit River, and the fisheries at the mouths of these rivers.

In 1806, after the purchase the previous year of the coastal section of the Mississauga Tract, the British Government formally gained control over nearly all of the northern shoreline of Lake Ontario.[90] The only substantial areas left to the Mississauga were the extensive tracts behind the lakeshore (these would be purchased in 1818/1819). Initially in the 1780s neither side had understood the other's concept of the land. By the early nineteenth century, however, the Mississauga realized the full implications of these 'surrenders'. In 1820 a Mississauga chief captured the feeling of his people when he told an English traveller, 'You came as wind blown across the great Lake. The wind wafted you to our shores. We rcd. [received] you—we planted you—we nursed you. We protected you till you became a mighty tree that spread thro our Hunting Land. With its branches you now lash us.'[91]

Suggestions for Further Reading

J.R. Miller, *Skyscrapers Hide the Heavens: A History of Indian-White Relations in Canada* rev. ed. (Toronto, 1991).

Robert Moore, *The Historical Development of the Indian Act* (Ottawa, 1978).

Donald B. Smith, *Sacred Feathers: The Reverend Peter Jones (Kahkewaquonaby) & the Mississauga Indians* (Toronto, 1987).

Notes

An earlier version of this paper was given at the conference on ethnohistory at Wilfrid Laurier University, 30 October–1 November 1980. My thanks to David McNab of Wilfrid Laurier for his helpful comments when I was preparing this revision.

[1] For a short overview of American policy see S. Lyman Tyler, *A History of American Indian Policy* (Washington: Department of the Interior, Bureau of Indian Affairs, 1973). A recent Canadian study is Robert Moore's *The Historical Development of the Indian Act* (Ottawa: Treaties and Historical Research Centre, Indian and Northern Affairs, 1978).

[2] Reginald Horsman, 'American Indian Policy in the Old Northwest, 1783–1812', *William and Mary Quarterly* 3rd series, 18 (1961), 39–40.

[3] Lieutenant-Governor John Graves Simcoe also (until 1794) favoured the creation of an Indian buffer state in the Indian lands immediately south of the Great Lakes. S.F. Wise, 'The Indian Diplomacy of John Graves Simcoe', *Canadian Historical Association Report, 1953*, 36–44. See also Robert F. Berkhofer, Jr., 'Barrier to Settlement: British Indian Policy in the Old Northwest, 1783–1794', in *The Frontier in American Development*, ed. David M. Ellis (Ithaca: Cornell University Press, 1969), 249–76.

[4] William T. Hagan, *American Indians* (Chicago: University of Chicago Press, 1961), 50–1.

[5] Gerald M. Craig, *Upper Canada: The Formative Years 1784–1841* (Toronto: McClelland & Stewart, 1963), 4. In a similar vein, A.L. Burt wrote in *The Old Province of Quebec*, 2 vols. (Toronto: Ryerson, 1933; Toronto: McClelland & Stewart, 1968), 2:88, that the Mississauga Indians of present-day southern Ontario 'welcomed the coming of white settlers'.

[6] The location of the Algonkian and Iroquoian groups is given in Conrad Heidenreich, 'Map 24. Indian Groups of Eastern Canada, ca. 1615–1640 A.D.', in *Huronia: A History and Geography of the Huron Indians 1600–1650* (Toronto: McClelland and Stewart, 1973).

[7] A brief sketch of this troubled period is provided in Bruce G. Trigger's *The Indians and the Heroic Age of New France* (Ottawa: Canadian Historical Association, 1977, booklet no. 30). For a full account see his *The Children of Aataentsic: A History of the Huron People to 1660*, 2 vols. (Montreal: McGill-Queen's Press, 1976).

[8] Donald B. Smith, 'Who are the Mississauga?' *Ontario History* 67 (1975), 215.

[9] Kahkewaquonaby (Peter Jones), *History of the Ojebway Indians; with especial reference to their conversion to Christianity* (London: A.W. Bennett, 1861), 114. Kahkewaquonaby, known in English as Peter Jones, was the son of Augustus Jones, one of Lieutenant-Governor Simcoe's surveyors, and a Mississauga woman. Until the age of fourteen Kahkewaquonaby was raised by his mother and her people.

[10] Kahkewaquonaby (Peter Jones), *History of the Ojebway*, 113.

[11] *Jesuit Relations*, ed. R.G. Thwaites, v. 18 (1640), 230; quoted in E.S. Rogers, 'Southeastern Ojibwa', in *Handbook of North American Indians*, v. 15, *The Northeast*, ed. Bruce G. Trigger (Washington: Smithsonian Institution, 1978), 769.

[12] Allan Salt, 'A Short History of Canada, according to the traditions of the Mississagues and Chippewas', Muncey, 1874, n.p. Notebook, 1872–1901, M 29 H 11, in PAC.

[13]For a reference to the two dialects of the Mississauga see David Sawyer's Journal, translated by John Jones, in the *Christian Guardian* 13 February 1833. The Journal describes a missionary tour by several Credit Indians to Sault Ste Marie. During the tour Thomas McGee, David Sawyer and James Young sent a note back to Peter Jones (the letter is now in the Peter Jones Collection, Victoria University Library): 'The Indians at Pahwitig [Sault Ste Marie] told us they could understand us more than they could them which were there last summer [John Sunday and two Mississauga from the Bay of Quinte]. Therefore the Credit dialect must be more genuine.'

[14]Kahkewaquonaby (Peter Jones), *History of the Ojebway*, 138, 164. For a fuller discussion of the name, Mississauga, see Donald B. Smith, 'Who are the Mississauga?' *Ontario History*, 67 (1975), 211–2.

[15]Augustus Jones, 'Names of the Rivers, and Creeks, as they are Called by the Mississagues . . . ,' dated 4 July 1796. Surveyors' Letters, 28 103–5, PAO.

[16]The Ojibwa names for Lake Superior, Lake Erie, and the Thames and Trent Rivers, the translation of Toronto, and the pronunciation of Niagara in Ojibwa are given in Kahkewaquonaby, *History of the Ojebway*, 40, 48, 163–4. In his *Valley of the Lower Thames* (3) Hamil comments further on the Ojibwa name of the Thames River. For the translation into English of the Iroquois word 'Ontario', consult Paul A.W. Wallace, *The White Roots of Peace* (Port Washington, Long Island, N.Y.: Ira J. Friedman, 1968; first published in 1946), 12.

[17]The English translations of the Ojibwa names for the Niagara River, the small creeks at the western end of Lake Ontario, the Bronte and Sixteen Mile Creeks, and the Credit River appear in Augustus Jones, 'Names of the Rivers . . . '.

[18]William Claus to Lieutenant-Governor Maitland, York, 1 May 1819, C.O. 42, 362:203, PAC.

[19]Mrs. John Graves Simcoe, *Diary*, ed. J. Ross Robertson (Toronto: William Briggs, 1911), 184.

[20]Augustus Jones, 'Names of the Rivers . . . '.

[21]For a short summary of the Algonkians' way of life in the eighteenth century before the arrival of the Loyalists consult E.S. Rogers, 'Southeastern Ojibwa', in *Handbook of North American Indians*, v. 15, *The Northeast*, 761–4.

[22]An early example appears in the Journal of George Croghan, entry for 21 November 1767, in *The Papers of Sir William Johnson*, 14 vols. (Albany: The University of the State of New York, 1921–1965), 13:440. The Mississauga around Toronto ('Tarunto') sent wampum belts to the Ojibwa of Saginaw Bay on Lake Huron. The Saginaw Ojibwa then forwarded them to the Shawnee and Delaware. The messages apparently originated with the Seneca (13:436).

[23]Pierre-François-Xavier de Charlevoix, *Histoire et description générale de la Nouvelle France* (Paris: Giffart, 1744), 3:207.

[24]Guy Carleton to Earl of Dartmouth, Secretary of State, Quebec, 14 August 1775, PAC, C.O. 42, 34:174; and references in the *Haldimand Papers* (henceforth cited as *HP*) in PAC, B107, 21767, 683, microfilm reel (henceforth cited as mfm) A-683; B111, 21771, 204, 207, mfm A-684; B127, 21787, 54, 56, 139, 243, mfm A-688.

[25]Claus Papers, Memoranda and Diary, 1771–1773, entry for 25 July 1772, MG 19, F 1, 3, PAC. 'The Interpr. St Jean observed to me that the Missiageys in that Quarter are in great Awe and have a great Respect for Sr. Wm. Johnson.'

[26]Joseph Sawyer in reply to T.G. Anderson, at the Indian Village, Credit, 25 October 1845, Paudash Papers, RG 10, 1011. Entry Book, 1831–1848, 128, PAC. Forty years earlier in 1805, Quinipeno, the Mississauga Chief at the Bronte Creek, recalled that in 1787 Sir John Johnson had promised that 'we should always be taken care of' (after they sold their lands). Quinipeno quoted at a meeting with the Mississauga at the River Credit, 1 August 1805, RG 10, 1:294, PAC.

[27]George S. Snyderman, 'Concepts of Land Ownership among the Iroquois and their Neighbors', in *Symposium on Local Diversity in Iroquois Culture*, ed. William N. Fenton, Smithsonian Institution Bureau of American Ethnology, Bulletin 149 (Washington: United States Government Printing Office, 1951), 15–34, particularly 28.

[28]Quinipeno quoted at a meeting with the Mississauga at the River Credit, 2 August 1805, RG 10, 1:299, PAC.

[29]Return of the Missesayey Nation of Indians, 23 September 1787, RG 10, 1834:197, PAC. The 'Distribution of Arms, Ammunition and Tobacco', 27 September 1787 lists seven bands. RG 10, 1834:195, PAC.

[30]Preliminary Articles of Peace . . . between the English and Seneca Indians by Sir William Johnson, 3 April 1764, RG 10, 15:22, mfm C-1224, PAC. Guy Johnson to Frederick Haldimand, Niagara, 20 August 1780, *HP*, B 107, 21767, 117, mfm A-683, PAC. In his letter to Governor Haldimand, Guy Johnson stated that he himself prepared the agreement of 1764; 'This cession was then made by the Senecas, and the Missisagas were not mentioned at all, neither were they partys in subscribing . . . '.

[31]Guy Johnson in Frederick Haldimand, Niagara, 9 May 1781, *HP*, B 107, 21767, 179, mfm A-683, PAC.

[32]Guy Johnson to Frederick Haldimand, Niagara, 20 April 1781, *HP*, B 107, 21767, 173, mfm A-683, PAC.

[33]Captain William R. Crawford to Sir John Johnson, Carleton Island, 9 October 1783, *HP*, B 128, 21818, 366, mfm A-746, PAC.

For references to Crawford as leader of Mississauga raiding parties in the Revolution see *HP*, B 127, 21787, 119, 139, 243, mfm A-688, PAC.

[34]Extract from the Minutes of the Land Committee held at the Council Chamber, Quebec, 30 April 1791 in Provincial Archives of Ontario *Report*, 1905, 454.

[35]John Small to D.W. Smith, Newark, 19 June 1794. Letters Received by the Surveyor-General, RG 1, A-I-1, v. 50, 476, PAO.

[36]Indenture, 22 May 1784, Simcoe Papers, Envelope 1, PAO.

[37]W. Chewitt to D.Wm. Smith, Newark, 4 September 1794, Simcoe Papers, Envelope 35, PAO.

[38]For the 'surrender' of 1787 see Dorchester to John Collins, Quebec, 19 July 1787 in Provincial Archives of Ontario *Report*, 1905, 379. Indenture 23 September 1787, in Canada, *Indian Treaties and Surrenders*, 3 vols. (Ottawa: Queen's Printer, 1891–1912), 1:32–33.

As so little information has survived the nature of Colonel Butler's agreement in 1788 is unclear. See John Butler to Sir John Johnson, Niagara, 28 August 1788, enclosed 'c' in Robert Prescott to Peter Russell, Quebec, 21 October 1797, RG 10, 15:413, mfm C-1224, PAC.

For a summary of the 1787 and 1788 agreements Percy J. Robinson's 'The Chevalier de Rocheblave and the Toronto Purchase,' *Transactions of the Royal Society of Canada*, 3rd series, 31 (1937), sect. 2, 138–146, is helpful.

[39]Letter of John Ferguson 1 August 1794, Letters Received by the Surveyor-General, RG 1, A-I-1, 50:520–521, PAO.

As the boundaries (like those of the Crawford Purchases of 1783 and 1784) were never accurately specified the cessions of 1787 and 1788 were eventually ruled invalid. The Toronto section was surrendered again and a proper deed secured in 1805. Only in 1923, however, did the Canadian Government obtain a proper deed for the section from Toronto to the Head of the Bay of Quinte (the two Crawford Purchases of 1783 and 1784 have still not been executed correctly).

[40]George Blaker's Declaration, 15 May 1903, and Thomas Marsden's Declaration, 12 May 1915.

Penetanguishene Agency-Papers. Affidavits and Sketches Regarding Mr. Sinclair's Report of the Claims of the Chippewas of Lakes Huron and Simcoe, RG 10, 2331, file 67, 071, Part 1, PAC.

[41]General Haldimand to Sir John Johnson, Quebec, 22 March 1784, *HP*, B 63, 21723, 44, mfm A-664, PAC.

[42]Memorandum by the Deputy Superintendent General of Indian Affairs upon the Controversy between the Six Nations of the Grand River and the Mississauga of the Credit, RG 10, v. 2357, file 72, 563, 4, PAC.

[43]Distribution of Arms, Ammunition and Tobacco made by Sir John Johnson to the Messagey Indians assembled at the Head of the Bay de Quinté, at which they made a formal Cession of Lands on the North Side of Lake Ontario to the Crown, RG 10, 15:195, mfm C-1224, PAC. See also list of additional presents to be given in 1788, 'for the Lands at Toronto and the Communications to Lake Huron', RG 10, 15:206.

[44]Proceedings of a Council held at Niagara, 22 May 1784, *HP*, B 175. Add. 21835, p. 231, mfm A-754, PAC. References to Stevens appear in RG 10, 15:106, 178, 183, mfm C-1224, PAC; and to Bowen in 'Grants of Crown Lands in Upper Canada, 1787–1791', in Provincial Archives of Ontario *Report*, 1928, 205.

[45]Kahkewaquonaby (Peter Jones), *History of the Ojebway*, 104.

[46]James Givens (or Givins) cited in Lord Selkirk, *Diary, 1803–1804*, ed. P.C.T. White (Toronto: The Champlain Society, 1968), 162.

[47]John Butler, Head of Lake Ontario, 16 October 1790, Simcoe Papers, Envelope 4, PAO; *Upper Canada Gazette*, 30 December 1797.

[48]Quinipeno quoted at a Meeting with the Messissagues at the River Credit, 1 August 1805, C.O. 42, 340:51, PAC. J.B. Rousseau was the interpreter.

[49]Kahkewaquonaby (Peter Jones), *History of the Ojebway Indians*, 27.

[50]Memorial to the Duke of Newcastle of the New Credit Band, 17 September 1860, C.O. 42, 623:458–460, PAC. They still claim the Toronto Islands. See 'Toronto islands their land, Indians tell Swadron inquiry', Toronto *Globe and Mail*, 18 September 1980.

Statement of the Mississauga Indians of the River Credit, 8 June 1847 in Letters, Minutes, New Credit Registry, 1847–1874. Woodland Indian Cultural Educational Centre, Brantford, Ontario.

Peter Jones to T.G. Anderson, dated Brantford, 30 March 1850 in Letters, Minutes, New Credit Registry.

51The Memorial of Differant famley of the Massesagoe Indeans to his Excellancy John Graves Simco, North side of Lake Onteareo the winter 1793, Simcoe Papers, Canada, Loose Documents, 1793, Envelope 17, PAO. Royston J. Packard, Forensic Consultant, Barrie, Ontario, has identified David Ramsay as the transcriber of this document; letter to D.B. Smith, 10 March 1979. For information on Ramsay see Donald B. Smith, 'The Mississauga and David Ramsay', *The Beaver*, outfit 305: 4 (Spring 1975), 4–8.

52W. Chewitt to D.Wm. Smith, Newark, 4 September 1794, Simcoe Papers, Envelope 35, PAO.

53David Van der Heyden's Affidavit re: Mississauga meeting, 1 May 1795, Simcoe Papers, Envelope 40, PAO.

David Van der Heyden was a métis who led the Mississauga in war parties against the Americans in the Revolutionary War. E.A. Cruikshank, 'The King's Royal Regiment of New York', *Ontario Historical Society Papers and Records*, 27 (1931): 267. For other references also see *HP*, B 127, 21787, 227, 231, mfm A-688, PAC. Simcoe felt that Van der Heyden 'labours under mental derangement,' and downplayed the rumour; see J.G. Simcoe to Lord Dorchester, Kingston, 3 May 1795, *The Correspondence of Lieut. Governor John Graves Simcoe*, ed. E.A. Cruikshank, 5 vols. (Toronto: Ontario Historical Society 1923–1931), 4:2.

The discontent was caused largely by the failure of the Indian Department to send the Rice Lake Indians their annual presents. Joseph Chew to Thomas Aston Coffin, Montreal, 18 May 1795, RG 8, 248:125, mfm C-2848, PAC. For three years the official responsible had not done so: Captain Porter to John Graves Simcoe, Kingston, 3 May 1794 in *Kingston Before the War of 1812*, ed. Richard A. Preston (Toronto: Champlain Society, 1959), 359.

54Peter Russell to J.G. Simcoe, Niagara, 28 September 1796, *The Correspondence of the Honourable Peter Russell*, ed. E.A. Cruikshank, 3 vols. (Toronto: Ontario Historical Society, 1932–1936), 150 (hereafter cited as *RP*).

55Canada, *Indian Treaties and Surrenders*, 3:196, 1:5, 1:34. The Credit band claimed as its hunting grounds the land from Long Point on Lake Erie along the northeastern shore of Lake Erie, to the west bank of the Niagara River, and then along the northwestern shoreline of Lake Ontario to the Rouge River (just east of Toronto). The grounds extended back from Lakes Erie and Ontario to the headwaters of the Thames, Grand, Credit, Humber and Rouge Rivers. See Peter Jones, 'Removal of the River Credit Indians', *Christian Guardian*, 12 January 1848.

56The details of Wabikinine's murder are taken from three sources: Russell to Simcoe, 28 September 1796, *RP*; 'State of Case, The King vs. Charles McCuen. For murder committed on the Body of Waipykanine an Indian Chief', RG 22, 7 Home, Volume 35, PAO; and the Council of the Mississauga at Navy Hall, 8 September 1796, RG 8, 249:369–373, PAC.

[57]Russell to Simcoe, 28 September 1796, *RP*. Russell fails to comment on whether or not this was true.

[58]Isaac Weld, *Travels through the States of North America and Provinces of Upper and Lower Canada during the years 1795, 1796, and 1797* (London: John Stockdale, 1799), 294–5.

[59]Peter Russell to J.G. Simcoe, Niagara, 31 December 1796, *RP*. 1:117.

[60]Augustus Jones to D.W. Smith, Saltfleet, 11 March 1797, Surveyors' Letters 28:137, PAO.

[61]Peter Russell to Robert Prescott, West Niagara, 18 April 1797, *RP*, 1:165.

[62]The population of York and surrounding area in 1797 appears in *The Town of York, 1793–1815*, ed. Edith Firth (Toronto: The Champlain Society, 1962), lxxvii.

The number of troops is listed in Peter Russell to the Duke of Portland, Niagara, 20 August 1796, Russell Papers, Letterbooks, 1796–1806, Baldwin Room, Toronto Public Library.

[63]J.G. Simcoe to H. Dundas, 26 August 1791, *The Correspondence of Lieut. Governor John Graves Simcoe*, ed. E.A. Cruikshank, 1:51.

[64]Peter Russell to Aeneas Shaw, West Niagara, 26 February 1797, Russell Papers, Miscellaneous No. 1, Baldwin Room, Toronto Public Library.

[65]Memoir by William Dummer Powell, Upper Canada, 1 November 1797, *RP*, 2:21.

[66]Canada, *Indian Treaties and Surrenders*, 1:251–252; 1:7–8.

[67]Proceedings with the Indians of the Six Nations Confederacy and Sir John Johnson, Niagara, July 1783, C.O. 42, 44:276, PAC. Johnson had met the Mississauga chiefs at Carleton Island at the Eastern end of Lake Ontario.

[68]Pokquan quoted at a meeting held at Niagara, 22 May 1784, with the Mississauga Indians accompanied by the Chiefs and Warriors of the Six Nations, Delawares, etc., C.O. 42, 46:224–225, PAC.

[69]William Dummer Powell to John Askin, Mount Dorchester, 7 May 1798, *The John Askin Papers*, ed. M.M. Quaiffe, 2 vols (Detroit: Detroit Library Commission, 1928–1931), 2:140.

[70]Charles M. Johnston, 'Introduction', *The Valley of the Six Nations* (Toronto: Champlain Society, 1964), xlviii–liv.

[71]Peter Russell to the Duke of Portland, York, 21 March 1798, *RP*, 2:122.

[72]Col. D. Claus to General Haldimand, Montreal, 15 December 1783, *HP*, B 114, 21774, 344, mfm A-685, PAC.

[73]Lord Selkirk, *Dairy*, 306.

[74]In 1787 Wabikinine was reported to command 'at the Head of the Lake 506, of which one hundred and forty two can make use of Arms'. Return of the Missessayey Nation of Indians assembled at the Head of the Bay de Quinté and Toronto, 23 September 1787, RG 10, 1834:197, PAC.

Quinipeno gave the population figures at a meeting with William Claus, [Burlington] Beach, 3 November 1798, *RP*, 2:306. Claus mentions that there were also three families at the Credit, *RP*, 2:304.

[75]Diary of Lieut. Governor Simcoe's Journey, entry for 1 October 1793, *The Correspondence of Lieut. Governor John Graves Simcoe*, 2:73.

William Osgoode to Ellen Copley, Niagara, 25 September 1793 in 'Three Letters of William Osgoode: First Chief Justice of Upper Canada', ed. A.R.M. Lower,

Ontario History, 57 (1965): 185.
    Extract of a letter from Nathaniel Lines, Interpreter for the Indian Department, Kingston, 17 October 1796, RG 8, 249:215, PAC. Augustus Jones to D.W. Smith, Saltfleet, March 1797, Surveyors' Letters, 28, 131, PAO.

76Return of the Indians who have received Presents in Upper and Lower Canada, during the year 1827, RG 10, 792:56, PAC.

77Hagan, *American Indians*, 52. My thanks to Franz Koennecke a graduate student at the University of Waterloo for this important point.

78C.H. McIlwain, 'Introduction', *An Abridgment of the Indian Affairs*, ed. Charles Howard McIlwain (Cambridge: Harvard University Press, 1915), xl.

79Major Ross to Capt. Mathews, Cataraqui, 2 October 1783, *HP*, B 124, 21784, 14, mfm A-688. The Indians admitted their addiction in their 'Memorial of Different famley of the Massesagoe Indeans', Winter 1793 (see note 51).

80For an excellent study of the effects of malnutrition consult 'Ecology and Nutritional Stress in Man', *American Anthropologist*, 64 (1963), 22–34.

81Reginald Horsman, *Matthew Elliott, British Indian Agent* (Detroit: Wayne State University Press, 1964), 123–4.

82'Proclamation to Protect the Fishing Places and the Burying Grounds of the Mississagas,' *Upper Canada Gazette*, 30 December 1797; also *RP* 2:41.

83Proceedings of a Garrison Court Martial Held by Order of Captain Mackenzie, 19 August 1801 in *Kingston before the War of 1812*, ed. R.A. Preston, 363.

84John Cameron to [unknown], York, 16 December 1806, MG 19, F 1, 9:155, PAC.

85Mrs. Simcoe, *Diary*, ed. J. Ross Robertson, 115.

86Weld, *Travels*, 361.

87Speech of Colonel Simcoe to the Western Indians, Navy Hall, 22 June 1793, *The Correspondence of Lieut. Governor John Graves Simcoe*, 1:364.

88Canada, *Indian Treaties and Surrenders*, 1:5–7.

89Quinipeno quoted at a meeting with the Mississauga at the River Credit, 1 August 1805, RG 10, 1:295–296, PAC.

90In 1818 (faced with continued population loss on account of disease) the Mississauga sold the interior section of the Mississauga Tract, and in 1820 the small reserves at the mouths of the Twelve and Sixteen Mile Creeks, and a large portion of their reserve at the Credit River. At the eastern end of Lake Ontario the Mississauga sold their inland territory in 1818 and 1819. The islands at the eastern end of Lake Ontario were surrendered in 1856.

91A Mississauga Chief quoted in William Graves, 'Diary', ed. Donald F. McOuat, *Ontario Historical Society Papers and Records*, 43 (1951): 10.

III

British

North America Before

Confederation

15

The War of 1812

R. Arthur Bowler

In the War of 1812, a conflict between Great Britain and the United States, the provinces of British North America, especially Upper Canada, became one of the major battlegrounds. The war had two distinctive sets of causes, one dealing with the rights of neutral shipping on the high seas and the other with jostling for advantage and expansion in the interior of the continent. It was fought as a maritime conflict on the ocean and on the Great Lakes, and as a struggle between armies in and around Upper Canada. Because of the number of Americans who had settled in Upper Canada and because of the extent to which the British government expected the local population to defend themselves (the war with the Americans was merely an incidental sideshow to the main event in Europe against Napoleon), the question of loyalty was a major one for the Upper Canadians. The War of 1812 saw the first serious outbreak of anti-Americanism in

British North America since the American Revolution. Both concepts—loyalty to Great Britain and hostility to Americans—survived the period of warfare intact.

The struggle for public opinion in Upper Canada was perhaps as important as the actual battlefield confrontations, as R. Arthur Bowler demonstrates. The Americans were able to do little to sway allegiance other than to issue proclamations; Anglo-Canadian activity was far more intensive and extensive. As was usually the case in such times, exaggeration and overstatement were the order of the day. Bowler finds that the propaganda had little effect at the time, but adds that it literally became the memory of the war in Upper Canada/Ontario for more than a century afterwards, thus shaping the self-image of the province (if not the nation).

What is 'propaganda'? Can it ever be reasoned and equitable? Are 'Big Lies' about the enemy justified during the heat of wartime? What steps did the Americans take to persuade people to support them? Why was a simple appeal to remain at home so insidious? To what extent did the propaganda of the Upper Canadian élite pass beyond wartime necessity? What was its longlasting effect?

This article first appeared, titled 'Propaganda in Upper Canada in the War of 1812', in *American Review of Canadian Studies* XVIII (1988), 11–32.

When in June 1812 the government of the United States declared war on Great Britain, it did so with the intention of waging that war against Britain's North American colonies, particularly Upper and Lower Canada. A number of reasons lay behind the choice of the Canadas as the war objective, the most important of which was the conviction of Madison and his administration that the Canadas had become a vital part of the British imperial system and that their loss would push Britain to negotiate her policies with respect to neutral trade.[1] But also important was the belief that the conquest of the Canadas would be relatively easy. The *National Intelligencer*, the informal voice of the Madison administration, appraised the situation in an article on 3 December 1812: the population of the Canadas was small, just over 300,000 (compared to the 7.5 million of the United States), and for its defense Britain, deeply engaged in Europe, could spare only a few thousand of her regular troops; in the event of war these troops would keep the fortress of Quebec and abandon all to the west. 'The distance of Great Britain— the ice of the St Lawrence—the difficulty of recruiting and supporting an army—the ease with which it might be outnumbered from the United States and the impossibility of retreat in case of disaster will prevent Great Britain from sending any considerable army into the interior.' And to make the task even easier, most of the people, it was believed, had no loyalty to Britain.

The French Canadians were described as 'disaffected . . . partly from an hereditary national antipathy; and partly from viewing her in the light of a conqueror'. As for the English Canadians, '20,000 or 30,000 may be considered as European or American Tories—the latter most incorrigible. The residue are a mixed multitude having few predilections, except those created by interest and consequently leaning on the side of America.'[2] There were many errors in this assessment of the Canadas but much also that was valid, especially as it pertained to Upper Canada. The population was no more than 90,000 and although the first large group of settlers was Loyalists of the American Revolution, a branch of the stream of westward-moving Americans had also found their way into the province and by 1812 constituted some two-thirds of the total. They were in overwhelming majority in the area west of Burlington. What is more, the garrison of British regulars in the province numbered less than a thousand and their commander was convinced that there could be no defending the province without popular support and the enthusiastic participation of the militia. But the general population could recognize a hopeless cause when they saw it and made it clear that they would not willingly participate. It was this situation which led some members of the small conservative and largely Loyalist élite of Upper Canada to despair that the mass of the population would refuse to support any attempt to resist an American invasion,[3] and which prompted some Americans to assert that the capture of that province would involve little more than the formality of taking possession of it.[4]

Here was a situation made for propaganda: by the Upper-Canadian élite to stir up patriotism and by the Americans to maintain acquiescence and defeatism. A few people on both sides took up the challenge. The means they had for spreading their messages were meagre—word of mouth and a handful of manual flatbed presses whose limited output could be distributed only as fast as a horse could walk or a ship sail. Even at that some of the presses were destroyed during the war and supplies of paper were erratic. Nevertheless, significant propaganda was produced and a careful examination of it can help us to understand the war and the societies involved in it.

If many of those in authority in Upper-Canadian society are to be believed, American attempts to undermine their society had a history that began long before the War of 1812. Lieutenant-Governor Simcoe's policy of encouraging settlers from the United States had initially drawn little opposition in Upper Canada but as early as 1799 Richard Cartwright in Kingston began to express his fear that these settlers would not become loyal members of the structured and conservative society which he and others of the élite wished to establish in Upper Canada. Rather he suspected they would become transmitters of the corrupting democratic ideas which had helped bring on the American Revolution and were already rotting the American Republic from within. 'It is not to be expected,' he wrote to Lieutenant Governor Hunter,

> that a man will change his political principles or prejudices by crossing a River; or that an oath of allegiance is at once to check the Bias of Mind, and prevent the predilection for Maxims and Modes of estimating and conducting the concerns of the Public to which he has been trained from displaying itself, even without any sinister purpose, whenever an opportunity shall be presented.[5]

What Cartwright meant was demonstrated in a letter from a settler on Yonge Street to David Smith, the Surveyor General:

> I am sorry to find in the disposition of several of the inhabitants of Young Street, and in particular those from the Northern States, that they show a very great contempt to the Officers of our Government, both civil & Military, as it is their whole desire to have the election of all of their own officers. . . . As for Fiske and little Hide, the Schoolmasters, they use all their efforts to poison the minds of the Youth, by teaching them in republican books, in particular

the 3d part of Webster's History. . . . Youths educated in said books, by & by, will have the privilege of voting members for our Assembly, & filling the house with their own kind, & when that is the Case, what may the Governor & Council of his Province expect—trouble too much—as I had the misfortune to live in Maryland, before the rebellion in America, I was an Eyewitness to the Steps they took—makes me dread anything that may lead to any innovation in Government.[6]

As relations between Great Britain and the United States worsened, the effect of the presence of these people was more and more deplored. At the time of the *Chesapeake-Leopard* affair, Lieutenant-Governor Gore confided to Governor Craig in Quebec that he had little confidence in any of the settlers west of Kingston except those who had fought for the British during the Revolution.[7] By early 1812 the governors of both the Canadas were convinced that the United States had dispatched agents to their provinces whose task was to 'seduce the inhabitants . . . from their allegiance'.[8] Governor Sir George Prevost of Lower Canada was more fearful of the effect of these spies and secret agents than American armies and wrote in code to warn General Isaac Brock in Upper Canada. Brock discussed the matter with his executive council, who felt the matter was serious enough to warrant a proclamation warning that 'divers persons have recently come into this Province with seditious intent to disturb the tranquility thereof and to endeavour to alienate the minds of His Majesty's Subjects from His Person and Government.'[9] Brock remained convinced of the presence of American agents in Upper Canada and reported to Lord Liverpool that part of the reason for General Hull's early success in the western tip of the province was the presence of 'numerous and active' emissaries.[10]

But, despite the warnings and the fears, there is no evidence of paid American emissaries being sent to the Canadas.[11] There was no need for them. Enthusiasts for the ideas of democratic republicanism and the American cause—largely but not entirely recent immigrants from the United States—were everywhere in Upper Canada. They constituted a potent if unorganized propaganda machine which twice in 1812 frustrated Brock's attempts to get emergency war powers for his government.[12] The assembly refused to approve the necessary bills but even had they passed, wrote an astute observer, 'there is no doubt but that a rebellion would have taken place.'[13] Brock himself made a very revealing assessment of the population of the Niagara region. 'There can be no doubt,' he wrote, 'that a large portion of the population in this neighbourhood are sincere in their profusion to defend the country, but it appears likewise evident to me that the greater part are either indifferent to what is passing, or so completely American as to rejoice in the prospects of a change of governments.'[14]

Direct American propaganda of the war in Upper Canada was the product of American military men and their staffs and consisted entirely of proclamations, usually prepared on the occasion of the occupation of a portion of the province. The most famous and most important of these was that issued by General William Hull on 12 July 1812 when he took his army across the Detroit river into Upper Canada. Hull's proclamation was designed to convince Upper Canadians not to oppose his army, and its inspiration was, in part, the production of American perception of the composition and loyalty of the Upper-Canadian population. It also, though, clearly said that Upper Canada was to become a part of the United States and sought to explain the attractions of that fate. It is worth examining in some detail both for its effectiveness as a piece of propaganda and for what it conveys about American perception of themselves and their country.[15]

The most important theme of the proclamation is an invocation of the values of the American Revolution and their contrast with the situation in which Upper Canadians supposedly lived. 'I tender you,' said Hull, 'the invaluable blessings of civil, political and religious liberty.' Linked with this, though, was an appeal based on that growing prosperity in the United States which even then was being compared favorably to the situation in the Canadas: the liberties he offered them, Hull assured Canadians, carried with them as a 'necessary result', 'individual and general prosperity'.

Although it was printed in both French and English, a recognition of the character of the population of the southwestern tip of Upper Canada, the proclamation was directed at the English-speakers and appeals were made to both the Loyalists and post-Loyalist settlers. To the post-Loyalists the values of the Revolution were particularly involved: 'Many of your fathers fought for the freedom and independence we now enjoy,' and now they in turn would be 'emancipated from tyranny and oppression'. 'Raise not your hand against your brethren' was the plea. For the Loyalist and other settlers, Hull emphasized that the war was against Great Britain, not the 'peaceful, unoffending inhabitants' of Canada. 'I come to find enemies,' he declared, 'not make them.' The Canadians, in the view of the Democratic Republicans, had no reason to support Britain: 'Separated by an immense ocean and an extensive wilderness from Great Britain, you have no participation in her councils, no interest in her conduct.' The rule of Britain brought only tyranny and injustice: the Americans had come to relieve Canadians of this burden.

The gifts offered were, however, balanced by a warning. Those who took up arms with the British would be treated as enemies 'and the horrors and calamities of war will stalk before you.' Moreover, Britain was sure to employ her Indian allies in the war and that would bring even greater horrors: 'the first stroke of the tomahawk—the first attempt with the scalping knife will be the signal of one indiscriminate scene of desolation. No white man found fighting by the side of an Indian will be taken prisoner.'

Finally, it was pointed out that those who wished to join the American force would be welcome but all that was required of Canadians was that they

remain quietly at home. There their lives and their property would be preserved. 'The United States,' he concluded, 'offer you *Peace, Liberty,* and
Security—your choice lies between these and WAR, *Slavery* and *Destruction.*'

The proclamation, although it has a certain bombastic quality to modern
ears, was a skillful piece of writing which Prevost called 'artful and insidious'.[16] In the following days Canadian militia men deserted by the hundreds
to join Hull or seek his parole, the militia of Norfolk County turned out
only reluctantly and then refused to march, and many of the inhabitants of
Westminster township signed a petition inviting Hull to advance to them
and promising to join with him when he arrived. When Brock again
approached the legislature to revise the militia law and suspend *habeas corpus,*
he was again refused. 'A more decent House has not been elected since the
formation of the Province,' he asserted, but they feared reprisals.[17]

It cannot, of course, be asserted that all this was the result of Hull's proclamation; the proclamation was, after all, accompanied by an army. Nevertheless there are indications of its effect. Brock, for instance, felt it necessary
to compose a counterproclamation in which he not only asserted that he
was going to fight, which would have been all that was required if he felt
the presence of the American army had brought about the disaffection in
Upper Canada, but felt it necessary to counter the ideological arguments
which Hull made and pointed out the benevolence and generosity of Britain
and the prosperity of her subjects. He also warned that the likely fate of
Canada in the event of an American victory would be reannexation to
France.[18] There also exists a letter from an informant in Canada to General
Stephen VanRensselaer which asserts that Hull's proclamation had its effect
because it promised security for private property. The best evidence, though,
comes from one of Hull's officers, who noted in his journal that when they
landed in Upper Canada 'the inhabitants all fled in different directions from
us. The General immediately circulated his proclamation which gave great
satisfaction to the inhabitants and caused many of them to return and apply
for protection.'[19]

Had Hull followed his proclamation with military success, propaganda
might well have become a standard American weapon in the war. As it was,
however, his surrender to Brock led to public condemnation of himself and
his methods. Federalist newspapers ridiculed 'War by proclamation' and soon
carried an advertisement for the biting satire *The War of the Gulls,* the third
chapter of which showed how 'a certain doughty General of the Gulls goes
forth to play the game of Hull-Gull in Upper Canada

"And from the pinnacle of glory,
Falls headlong into purgatory." '

As a result, while there were four more proclamations or addresses to the
people of Upper Canada by American military commanders, none had the

broad propaganda content which was there in Hull's.[20] General James Wilkinson, as he began his ill-fated expedition down the St Lawrence in late 1813, informed the inhabitants of Canada that he had come to 'subdue the forces of His Britannic Majesty, not to war against his offending subjects' and promised protection for the person and property of those who remained peaceful, but left it at that.[21] Lieutenant Colonel James Preston, when he took command of the American forces at Fort Erie in late May 1813, found that there were local people anxious to join him. He quickly issued a proclamation which seemed to take the position enunciated by Hull at Detroit and General Smyth at Buffalo, that Upper Canada was to become a part of the United States. The proclamation promised the security of property and personal rights to all who voluntarily sought the protection of the United States but warned that those who 'obstinately continue inimical' were bringing on themselves 'the most rigorous and disastrous consequences'.[22] Later that same fall General George McLure, left in command on the Niagara frontier, also found it necessary to issue an address to the inhabitants. Long and rambling, it was largely a condemnation of the British for employing Indians and an assertion that 'our Free republican government' would assure the security and protection of all who remained peaceable.[23]

In contrast to the American effort, British propaganda in the War of 1812 was extensive and relatively sophisticated. Newspapers which in times of peace were usually dull compilations of advertisements, extracts from foreign newspapers about the war in Europe and local tidbits became on occasion little more than patriotic handbills, featuring editorials and prominently displayed and carefully composed letters to the editor exhorting, arguing or explaining patriotic themes. Important speeches and addresses as well as sermons which developed patriotic ideas were also featured in newspapers and sometimes printed up as handbills. This was the case in August 1812 when a carefully composed Address of the House of Assembly to its constituents, which condemned the actions of the American government and praised the system which Canadians had inherited from Britain, was ordered printed in five hundred copies and distributed about the province. Lesser numbers of a patriotic sermon by the Reverend John Strachan were ordered at the same time.[24] When the war reduced the number of newspapers in the province to one, the *Kingston Gazette*, the Upper-Canadian establishment still managed to print proclamations and addresses commenting on and giving official explanations of what was happening and distributed them through much of the province. Prevost had a reply to the proclamation of Lieutenant Colonel Preston so distributed in June 1813, and again in 1814 sent out a handbill justifying the British destruction of the settlements on the American side of the Niagara river.[25] For most settlers west of the Bay of Quinte such handbills along with army general and district orders were often the only source of news for most of the war.

Direct arguments and exhortations were not the only form of Canadian propaganda, however. The material that went into newspapers was usually very carefully managed in order to present the 'proper' view. The issue of war hotly divided Federalists and Democratic Republicans in the United States and the Upper-Canadian conservative élite was anxious that the population should understand this and its effect on the ability of that nation to wage war. Hence Upper-Canadian papers regularly republished articles from Federalist newspapers which denounced Madison's government and its war policy. The 'Old Farmer' letters originally printed in the *Boston Gazette* were regular features of the *Kingston Gazette* and prominent place was given to particularly juicy items such as Hull's and VanRensselaer's letters explaining the reasons for their failures at Detroit and Queenston and Colonel Cass's letter accusing Hull of cowardice.[26] When the declaration of war produced riots in Baltimore in which a Federalist newspaper was destroyed and several of its supporters killed or badly injured, the *Kingston Gazette* was happy to print the news under the headline 'BALTIMORE MOBS! or "Democracy Unveiled".' The same paper also explained the Federalist satire *The War of the Gulls* to its readers and even offered copies of it for sale.[27] Earlier it had placed on its front page the complete text of the address of the Massachusetts Assembly to the people of that state shortly after the declaration of war which concluded that the war was 'a wanton sacrifice of your best interests'.[28] The *York Gazette* in its issue of 24 October 1812 printed an article from a Vermont paper which reported the unwillingness of the militia of that state to have anything to do with the war.

On the other hand, important information from the Democratic Republicans was likely to be distorted. The editor of the *York Gazette* in the issue of 5 December 1812 summarized a speech made to Congress by President Madison the previous month. The summary is almost a masterpiece of distortion by subtle change, overemphasis and rearrangement. The report rendered Madison's introduction, which in the original 'invites attention to the providential favors' bestowed on the country, as 'He begins by congratulating his country and complimenting Providence on the health and abundant harvest of the year . . . ' and went on from there. After several columns he announced that 'this subject generally defeats all calm reasoning and the editor indignantly drops it.'

Clearly, also, military commanders and newspaper editors together managed the war news presented to the public in general orders and the newspapers. For instance, the official account of the battle of Stoney Creek, the only account made public during the war, not only greatly exaggerated the extent of the American defeat but neglected to mention the number of British casualties, which was high.[29] The timing of the release of news was also manipulated to produce the best effect. The American incursion, which began with the capture of Fort George on 27 May 1813, was not even noticed officially—and then only obliquely—until the general order of 28 June announcing the Canadian victory at Beaver Dams. The actual admission of the fall of Fort George was not made until 13 July when it was combined with the report of the victory at Stoney Creek. In contrast, the retaking of the fort on 12 December 1813 was the subject of a general order of 14 December, which was printed in the *Kingston Gazette* only four days later. Similar delays are found in the announcements of the fall of York and the disasters at Put-in Bay and on the Thames while the battle at Chrysler's Farm was reported within the week.

It is also possible that Canadians engaged in a bit of 'black' propaganda, that is, propaganda which attempts to conceal its source. The *York Gazette* published two letters in 1812, one in February and one in September, which seem to fit this category. The February letter purported to be a note to a friend from a Quaker recently arrived in Upper Canada. It had been brought to his attention, the editor noted, and was published because it contained worthwhile ideas 'unbiased by political or party spirit'. The second letter, addressed to 'Americans residing in Canada' and signed 'An American' was reprinted from the *Canadian Courant*. In both letters the ideas and arguments are so close to the establishment line that it is impossible to believe they are not planted.[30]

The origins of this barrage of propaganda are not too difficult to find. In part, of course, they lay in the desire to see 'truth' set up against 'falsehood' and in the very natural instinct to conceal failure and advertise success. But it is possible to go beyond that. By late 1811 developments in British-American relations made it clear that war was almost inevitable and steps were taken to prepare both of the Canadas for that eventuality. In Upper Canada Lieutenant Governor Francis Gore was sent on leave and General Isaac Brock installed as military commander and administrator of the civil government, the feeble regiment of British regulars in garrison was replaced by a well-trained and up-to-strength one, and the fortifications and stores of munitions rehabilitated and replenished. From Quebec, Prevost also sent to Upper Canada Captain Andrew Gray, an Assistant Deputy Quatermaster General. Gray's task was to make an assessment of the provincial marine establishment at Kingston and then to proceed to York. At Kingston, Gray met Richard Cartwright, the most distinguished member of the Upper-Canadian Loyalist élite. This élite had, on a number of occasions since the election of Thomas Jefferson as President of the United States, taken to the press in letters to the editor to warn Canadians of the danger to the United States and to themselves of the rising tide of democratic republicanism and Cartwright informed Gray that he had again taken up his pen; he would shortly begin publishing a series of letters under the *nom-de-plume* 'Falkland' in the *Kingston*

Gazette. A few days later Gray was in York and in the report he sent to Prevost from there he noted not only Cartwright's plans but the fact that 'We intend to let fly a drive official at them in the next *York Gazette* as the Genrl. thinks it may have a good effect on both sides.'[31] The 4 February issue of the *Gazette* contained Brock's patriotic speech on the opening of the legislature the previous day, a copy of an attack on the policy of the American government from the *Quebec Gazette*, and as a special supplement, a passionate analysis of the war addressed to the 'Inhabitants of Upper Canada' and signed 'A Loyalist'. This was the opening gun in a propaganda campaign which faltered occasionally but never entirely failed through the war years.

To the campaign a number of people contributed in important ways. Of these Brock was certainly the most significant. Not only were his speeches, proclamations and general orders important but he probably initiated the campaign and, as will be discussed shortly, he developed one whole line of propaganda himself. The Reverend John Strachan was also deeply involved in the effort. In 1810, in an attempt to arouse patriotism and loyalty (and probably also to demonstrate his own commitment), he published *A Discourse on the Character of King George the Third*, a long patriotic pamphlet which also damned the United States. When in the summer of 1812 he took up the post of rector of York and chaplain of the garrison and of the Legislative Council, he plunged immediately into the fray. He published two of his more patriotic sermons during the war and claimed to have written the 'Address of the House of Assembly to the People of Upper Canada' adopted by that body at the end of their session in August 1812 and printed and distributed throughout the province.[32] That address was both a call to patriotic duty and a strong denunciation of the United States and is particularly interesting because the assembly which adopted it had just refused to suspend *habeas corpus* and amend the militia act to punish the avoidance of duty more severely. Strachan was never one to hide his light under a bushel and he noted to a friend that, in addition to the above, he had 'many opportunities when preaching & my general knowledge of the people [sic] to preserve and increase the spirit of Loyalty which principally saved the Province during the first two years of the war.'[33]

There were, of course, others who were involved in the Canadian propaganda campaign but they remain anonymous, some because a name could not be attached to their work and others because they chose, like Richard Cartwright, to write under *noms-de-plume* such as 'A Loyalist', 'A Loyalist's Son', and 'Camillus'.

From the time of his death, Canadians regarded General Isaac Brock as a hero. That elevation was based on his military exploits but it is clear that his propaganda efforts are equally deserving of recognition. In late 1811, shortly after he arrived in the province, Brock prepared a report on his situation for his superior, General Prevost. He noted that the people were much heartened by the appointment of himself—a military man—to administer the government, and by recent additions to its military establishment. He also reported that although there were in the province 'improper characters . . . whose principles diffuse a spirit of insubordination', he had been to Niagara where he found the principal inhabitants to be firmly loyal and determined to support the government, and was assured that a large majority of the population would 'prove faithful'.[34] Over the next months, however, Brock became more and more pessimistic about the population. The first shock came in February 1812 when the Assembly, which he had confidently assumed would pass bills to suspend *habeas corpus* and amend the militia law, refused to cooperate. The reason, he felt, was 'the great influence which the vast number of settlers from the United States possess over the decisions of the Lower House'.[35] Over the next months evidence of the reluctance of large parts of the population to participate in the defence of the province continued to come in. When war was declared and Hull brought his army into Upper Canada, the worst fears came true. From all over the western part of the province reports came in of militiamen who refused to answer the call to arms or, when they did turn out, deserted at the first opportunity. The great shock, though, came from the newly elected assembly. It was called into session again to consider Brock's emergency measures but like its predecessor refused to pass them. At the end of July Brock summed up his position:

> My situation is getting each day more critical. . . . The population, although I had no great confidence in the majority, is worse than I expected to find it, and the magistrates, &c, &c, appear quite confounded and decline acting—the consequence is the most improper conduct is tolerated. The officers of militia exert no authority. Everything shows as if a certainty existed of a change taking place soon. . . .
>
> A more decent house [of assembly] has not been elected since the formation of the Province, but I perceived at once that I shall get no good of them. They, like the magistrates and others in office, evidently mean to remain passive. The repeal of *habeas corpus* will not pass and if I have recourse to the law martial I am told the whole armed force will disperse. Never was an officer placed in a more awkward predicament. The militia cannot possibly be governed by the present law—all admit that fact, yet the fear of giving offences will prevent anything effectual from being effected.[36]

Brock was sure that this situation could be cured by stationing more regular troops in Upper Canada and on numerous occasions he pleaded with Prevost for such reinforcement. This, of course, was impossible until Lower Canada itself was reinforced so Brock had to turn to other strategies. One of these was to assure the population on every possible occasion that Britain would never abandon a colony which she so highly valued and that he intended to devote all his energy to its defense.[37] Another was to ensure that good tidings were quickly disseminated. When Hull withdrew his army from Upper Canada, Brock immediately put that news into a general order, along with the first details of the capture of Michilimackinac, and directed commanding officers to ensure that it and all other general orders were read to the militia units. The general order also praised the militia and noted that 'if the Enemy is thus made to sustain severe losses at the Threshold of our Territory by a small but determined band of United Troops, what has he to expect from the whole Physical Force of the Province actuated by an ardor and Loyalty worthy of their Sires?'[38] Brock also made sure that the American prisoners of war were paraded in front of as many Upper Canadians as possible.[39]

Nor was Brock above a bit of bribery. In May 1812 he suggested to the Executive Council that permission be obtained from the home government to place on the United Empire Loyalist list the names of all militiamen, provincial mariners, and regular soldiers in Upper Canada killed, maimed or disabled in defense of the province. This would make them or their families eligible for land grants. The councillors were too jealous of Loyalist privileges to permit the dilution of the Loyalist list but they did approve of the idea of land grants and only four days later a militia general order announced the plan. This idea was further developed by John Strachan at the end of 1812 when he brought together the 'Principal Inhabitants of York and its Vicinity' to found 'The Loyal and Patriotic Society of Upper Canada'. The Society, supported by donations, announced that it would provide relief for the distressed families of militiamen and provide aid for those disabled in service. It also sought to 'reward merit, excite emulation and commemorate glorious exploits by bestowing medals or honorary marks of public approbation'.[40] Publicly Strachan stressed the benevolent aims of the society but privately he emphasized its propaganda function. Reporting in 1814 to the directors of the Society, in his capacity as treasurer, he noted that,

> . . . as it is a principal object with the Society, to nourish affection for the Government, and a determined resistance to the enemy; the committee will carefully attend to that part of the constitution, which excludes all those who have deserted their posts, or have given just cause of suspicion from participating in their bounty.[41]

General Sir Roger Sheaffe, who succeeded Brock as military commander and civil administrator in Upper Canada, thought the Society was a marvellous idea and helped to ensure that copies of the constitution were distributed, particularly into the western part of the province, as soon as possible.[42]

Brock's most subtle—and arguably his greatest—contribution not merely to the propaganda campaign but to the war itself was the public stance he maintained in the face of the widespread defeatism and disaffection he found in Upper Canada. As he became aware of its extent he could well have adopted a defeatist attitude himself and lashed out at the popular failings. The approach he took was daring and imaginative. In a letter to Prevost in December 1811 he laid it out. 'It is certain that the best policy to be pursued, should future circumstances call for active preparations,' he wrote, 'will be to act with the utmost liberality, and as if no mistrust existed.'[43] He maintained this policy even through the worst of times. Thus, although he wrote to Prevost on 20 July complaining of the poor conduct and lack of enthusiasm not only of the militia but of the population in general, when he opened the legislature a few days later he painted a very different picture in his speech:

> Our Militia have heard [the voice of loyalty] . . . and obeyed it. They have evinced by the promptitude and Loyalty of their conduct that they are worthy of the King whom they serve and the Constitution which they enjoy; and it affords me particular satisfaction that while I address you as Legislators I speak to Men, who in the day of danger, will be ready to assist not only with their Counsel but with their Arms.[44]

And although he informed the legislature that 'the disaffected . . . are few,' he gave the Executive Council a more candid report. The militia, he said, 'was in a perfect state of insubordination . . . ; had refused to march when legally commanded . . . ; had insulted their officers, and some, not immediately embodied, had manifested in many instances a treasonable spirit of Neutrality or disaffection.'[45] From the meeting of the legislature Brock hurried to Amherstburg to oppose General Hull. There the desertions from the militia were impossible to ignore but Brock merely issued a general order in which he expressed surprise at them and expressed his willingness to believe that they were motivated by a desire to return home to bring in the harvest, not by 'a predilection for the principles or Government of the United States'.[46] His treatment of the often reluctant militia of the Niagara frontier in the weeks that followed was equally gentle. Brock's successors were wise enough to carry on his policy and although there were occasional warnings to the public to beware of cowards and traitors, not until well into 1813 was there any public notice of the extent of defeatism and disaffection or any hint that the militia had not valiantly and to a man carried out its duty. By that time the British forces in the province were being reinforced and the situation in Europe gave promise of more troops being available for Canada shortly. In November the government had no hesitation in announcing the capture of 'a band of Traitors who in violation of their allegiance and of every principle of Honor and Honesty had leagued themselves with the Enemies of their country' and to try them publicly for treason at Ancaster the following year.[47]

Brock's policy was clearly the origin of the 'Militia Myth' which was for so long a part of Upper-Canadian history.[48] According to it, from the very beginning of the war the American invaders were turned back by the Upper-Canadian militia, assisted on occasion by a few hundred British regulars. The myth took hold even before the end of the war. In a letter to Dugald Stewart in 1814 John Strachan attributed the preservation of the province to the militia and in a sermon predicted that

> it will be told by the future Historian, that the Province of Upper Canada, without the assistance of men or arms, except a handful of regular troops, repelled its invaders, slew or took them all prisoners, and captured from its enemies the greater part of the arms by which it was defended.[49]

When John Clarke, a captain of militia during the war, wrote his memoirs sometime after 1837, he bragged that the declaration of war had been 'a signal for the loyal inhabitants of Canada to rush *en masse* to the frontiers of the country to repel invasion' and quoted from some of Brock's more outrageous inventions to back up his statement. By the late nineteenth century when Egerton Ryerson, in an effort to establish the place of the Loyalists as the moral founders of British Canada, wrote *The Loyalists of America and Their Times*, the myth had become the truth and he could confidently assert that Upper Canada had been saved by 'spartan bands of Canadian Loyalist volunteers, aided by a few hundred English soldiers and civilized Indians'.[50] Brock would have been pleased.

By modern standards all of the Upper-Canadian efforts still made only a very modest propaganda campaign, but given the times and the frontier and pioneer character of most of the province its extent was really quite extraordinary and is understandable only in terms of the apprehensions of the Upper Canadian élite about the willingness of the population to resist an American invasion and even about its basic loyalty. The aim of the overwhelming bulk of the propaganda which they produced was to convince Upper Canadians that they must resist an American invasion and the arguments which they used in their attempt to achieve this end are worth examining in some detail.

Some of the arguments used were simplicity itself. A number of writers, for instance, invoked the pride of the settlers in their British heritage of freedom and independence and called for a recognition of the debt they owed Britain for their generous inheritance from her in land, law, and government.[51] Combined with this, though, could be warnings and even veiled threats. Brock cautioned the assembly in a speech that without Britain's support Upper Canada, 'from its geographical position, must inevitably sink into comparative poverty and insignificance', and 'A Loyalist' suggested that although America might win some initial battles, the nation which was trouncing Napoleon on land and sea was not likely to 'suffer a parcel of peddling land jobbers to wrest from her a foot of territory'.[52]

The mainstream of the propaganda, however, had as its focus the causes of the war. The Upper-Canadian conservative élite were quite sure they knew why American relations with Britain deteriorated to the point of war. For these people, some of them victims of Patriot mob action during the American Revolution, the great illusion of the age was democracy, turning over to the mass of the people the power to choose their own governors and the course society would follow. The illusion lay in the belief that the masses were wise enough or knowledgeable enough to handle this power responsibly. The conservative élite believed that history had proved in ancient Greece and Rome and time and again since—most recently in revolutionary France—that the mass always misused its power to force conformity on minorities and itself eventually succumbed to the wiles of demagogues who soon installed themselves as tyrants. So it was that once free, happy, and prosperous societies were reduced to poverty and misery. These people did not deny that democracy had a place in society—indeed they were sure that it was an essential component of any society that aspired to liberty. They believed, rather, that democracy must be offset by responsibility and that the liberty it could bring must be a restrained and judicious liberty. In practice this meant that the leadership of society must be conceded to men of education, wealth and proven judgement who would deny the popular will when it was necessary to do so.

For the Upper-Canadian élite, avid observers of the nation to the south, the American experiment in democratic republicanism had succeeded in the 1790s because it had been led by the Federalists, whom they identified as the men of wealth and education. In the last years of the century, however, the process of decay set in, in the form of Thomas Jefferson and his followers.[53] When Jefferson was elected president in 1800 the conservative élite were sure that the decline of American society would be rapid and complete. Two things in particular condemned the Jeffersonians. First, they had split away from the Federalists and formed an opposition party, which to conservative minds of the time meant they had placed their own selfish interests ahead of the interests of the nation. Equally important, though, in the great war going on between France and England, the Jeffersonians leaned towards France while the Federalists favored England. This was no trivial distinction. In conservative eyes Britain was the champion of liberty who was devoting her treasure and the flower of her menfolk to fending off the might of Napoleonic tyranny. The 'Virginia oligarchy' demonstrated its true colors when it sided with tyranny and attacked Britain in her hour of need.[54] In the following years, particularly after the *Chesapeake-Leopard* affair, the Upper-Canadian conservative élite were sure that the Jeffersonians were becoming more tyrannical in their policies and more influenced by Napo-

leon. The tyranny was demonstrated in the trade restrictions so devastating
to the New England merchant economy and denounced by the Federalists
as 'unconstitutional, ruinous and tyrannical'.[55] The influence of Napoleon
was apparent in attitudes and policies which seemed designed to bring on
war with Britain. As the war neared and then was declared, the Canadian
propagandists repeated this analysis again and again. 'The president,' wrote
'Camillus',

> together with the majority of the members of Congress, are composed of south-
> ern epicures, whose bodies and whose minds have become enervated by idle-
> ness, intemperance, and every species of excess, and whose hearts have become
> callous to the feelings of humanity by the daily habits of tyranny and cruelty
> which they are exercising over their slaves 'who fan them when they sleep,'
> and by whose toil and sweat they are supplied with all the luxuries the palate
> of an epicure could suggest.[56]

It was these people who, once they had the power of the state in their hands,

> trampled on the rights and liberties of their constituents, destroyed their com-
> merce, ruined the merchant, disheartened the farmer, palsied every incitement
> to industry, and threw the whole nation into a kind of apathy and despair.[57]

It was these people who were the natural allies of Napoleon. In joining
the war against Britain they were following his bidding and joining 'the most
formidable conspiracy against the civilization of man that ever was con-
trived'.[58] That their motives in declaring war were not those of impressment
and the freedom of neutral trade put forward by President Madison in his
war message was made perfectly clear when the British cancellation of the
offending orders-in-council was not followed by an American peace initiative. 'The American government,' wrote Sir George Prevost in a widely
circulated general order, '. . . has proclaimed in language not to be misun-
derstood that other objects independent of those held out to the American
people as grounds of the war were originally in their contemplation.'[59] When
a copy of an address of the American General Alexander Smyth to his troops
fell into his hands, one Canadian pounced on it in a letter to the editor of
the *York Gazette*. Smyth had told the troops that they were going to 'conquer
Canada' and the writer found in that phrase the true reason for the American
declaration of war.[60]

The propagandists also went on to lay out just what Canadians could
expect from an American invasion. For 'A Canadian' it would mean joining
America in her social and political degeneration. Canadians, he said, had the
great fortune to participate in the British constitution which was protection
against such degeneration. 'We have,' he argued, 'real liberty grounded upon
the most wise and equitable laws,' protection of property, personal safety,
and prosperity, but all that would be lost 'should the enemy succeed in

persuading the Canadian people that they are come to fraternize and regenerate them, by blinding their understanding with a dose of republican Jargon'.[61] Others saw an even worse fate for Canada, reannexation to the dominion of France. That was the price of France's aid to the United States in the Revolution 'and the debt is still due'.[62] Just what that meant was made clear in a report in the *York Gazette* of 22 August 1812, which printed a list of the cargo of a French ship captured at the time of Napoleon's attempt to invade Britain. The cargo included 50,120 thumb screws, 44,201 toe vices, 25,040 pair of fetters and 479 racks. The editor commented that

> many of these instruments of torture, which were unquestionably intended to facilitate the discovery of property, had the word Liberty, at full length; and others, the initials L.E. Liberty and Equality stamped on them.

The political situation in the United States also gave the propagandists a vision of the kind of war that would be fought. Jane Errington and George Rawlyk point out in their valuable article, 'The Loyalist-Federalist Alliance of Upper Canada', that the propagandists were careful not to condemn all Americans: the war, they said, was opposed by all the best parts of American society. But that led to another conclusion: the American army would be made up of 'the refuse and scum of the earth. . . . Our fertile plains, and the fruits of our industry are no doubt temptations every way calculated to excite their avarice, and gratify their abominable and licentious passion for plunder and rapine.'[63] Richard Cartwright in one of his early 'Falkland' letters was sure that the Loyalists would be particularly singled out for ill treatment by invading American democrats.[64] When the war came, it brought opportunities for atrocity stories and they were seldom neglected.[65]

This examination of the propaganda of the War of 1812 raises a number of questions. The most obvious of these is whether or not the propaganda was intentional. Propaganda may be defined as the attempt to control people's actions by controlling their attitudes but much that could be thus defined could be unintentional; a teacher in the course of his or her work is often an unintentional propagandist. Intentional propaganda 'arises . . . from interested motives, is consciously and systematically carried on, and its primary purpose is to obtain public support for a particular idea or course of action'.[66] That this was the case with both the limited American effort and the extensive Canadian one is obvious. The intent of the various authors to persuade Upper Canadians to resist or not resist the American invasion is apparent in the content of many of the pieces, but even where it is not, other evidence exists. As already noted, Cartwright, Strachan and Brock all made clear their intentions at one time or another and Prevost established his credentials as a propagandist when he recommended to Brock, in July 1812, that the news be widely disseminated that the British government had repealed the orders-in-council. 'Although I much doubt,' he wrote,

> whether this step on the part of our government will have any effect upon that of the United States, the circulation of the paper evincing their conciliatory disposition may tend to increase & strengthen the divisions which exist among the people upon the subject of war.[67]

We can also ask if the propagandists themselves believed the ideas they put forward. There are two commonly held but erroneous ideas about propaganda, that it is essentially lies and that it is something that the bad guys engage in and which the good guys counter with 'the truth'. In reality, the chief characteristic of propaganda is that it seeks to achieve its aim not by the use of reason and balanced and objective argument but by appeals to emotion and by the use of one-sided arguments and partial information. Most commercial advertising is propaganda. The best propagandists themselves believe the ideas they put forward, but it is not their belief or lack of it which makes them propagandists—it is their methods.

With the obvious exception of such things as Brock's 'militia' campaign, it seems likely that the propagandists of the War of 1812 believed the basic ideas they propounded, for most of them can be found in peacetime settings which had no propaganda intent.[68] But it is also clear that on occasion propagandists modified or exaggerated ideas to increase their impact. Good examples of this can be found in two pieces written by the Reverend John Strachan.

In 1814 Strachan published a sermon celebrating the surrender of Napoleon. It included an account of the war and of Britain's heroic role, in the course of which he expressed directly and obliquely his very conservative views about government and society. There are, for instance, lower and superior orders of society and the latter are the natural governors; if on occasion the governors make mistakes, they should be seen as merely a failing to which all human beings are prone and not taken as a cause to incite rebellion; misery is 'inseparable from mortality', and 'no great and decided amelioration of the lower classes of society can be expected.' He also attributed the salvation of Canada to the Loyalist population and denounced the 'shortsighted and mistaken policy'—that which had opened Upper Canada to American settlers—for introducing 'traitors and false friends'.[69]

Strachan wrote the sermon in the confident expectation that British troops, freed from their European duties, would quickly bring the North American conflict to an end. Two years earlier, however, when General Hill was in Upper Canada and promising the people liberty, prosperity and happiness without end, Strachan wrote another public address, the 'Address of the House of Assembly to the People of Upper Canada'. In it he examined the war and explained the virtues of the government which Upper Canadians had been given in the Constitution of 1791. He avoided, however, discussing any of the very conservative provisions of that document, such as the clergy reserves, the powers of the governor, and the provisions for an inherited aristocracy, and never once mentioned conservative social theory. As for the many recent settlers from the United States, although they 'would naturally lean against us', their inclinations were 'in the main good'.

Finally, we can ask how effective the propaganda was. Unfortunately this question is impossible to answer with any significant degree of accuracy. Not only is there no objective evidence from which 'before' and 'after' measurements can be made but in any particular case there are always extraneous factors. General Hull's proclamation comes across as the most effective single piece of propaganda of the war, but it must be asked how much of what can be seen as its effect was in fact due to the already notorious reluctance of the Upper Canadians to resist an American invasion. As indicated earlier, there is evidence of the effectiveness of Hull's proclamation but even then it can be asked whether Upper Canadians were responding merely to Hull's promise to protect private property, as the evidence would indicate, or to the many other appeals in the proclamation as well.

The degree of success of Upper-Canadian propaganda is even more difficult to assess. On the surface it would seem to have been an exercise in futility, since the propaganda campaign which began in February 1812 could not even by August bring the agreement of a newly elected legislative assembly to Brock's emergency measures. To be sure, there was a marked decline in disaffection and defeatism in the autumn of 1812 but that could be expected as a result of the astonishing victories over the Americans at Detroit and Queenston. The fact that disaffection increased again in 1813 when the American forces achieved a series of victories would seem to clinch the case, were it not that Canadian propaganda declined markedly at that time as a result of paper shortages and the disappearance or destruction of several presses, including that at York. There are also a few pieces of evidence which indicate that the message of the Canadian propagandists did get through to some. The best of these is a letter from one Isaac Wilson, a settler in the York area and a private in the York militia, to his brother in England. He wrote as follows:

> The war is likely to prove a very disastrous one to the States. It was a foolish measure for their government. It is wholly attributed to the intrigues of the French. Many people feel they will lose their independence but how it will end no one can tell. The people in this country are very much divided in their political principles. Many of them are friendly to the States and wish the country to fall into their hands and where the Americans conquer they have no mercy on the property of the other party.[70]

Unfortunately for the historian there are not enough Wilson letters about.

There is, however, another way to appraise, although tenuously, the effectiveness of the propaganda. The basis of this is an understanding that the potential success of propaganda is limited by a number of factors. In his book *Techniques of Persuasion* J.A.C. Brown writes:

> Propaganda is limited by prevailing interests, social trends and prejudices; it is encouraged by ignorance of the acts and is more likely to succeed when it flows with the social current than when it flows against it. . . . the propagandist can accelerate or retard a trend in public opinion but he cannot reverse it.[71]

Clearly Hull's proclamation went with the flow and was correspondingly successful; had it been followed up, the outcome of the war for at least parts of Upper Canada might have been different. Canadian propagandists, on the other hand, were going against the flow and achieved correspondingly meagre results. It can be argued, though, that the military successes of the fall of 1812 did provide a base on which to build and as a result the defeatism and disaffection which reappeared in 1813 were neither as pervasive nor as threatening as in 1812.[72]

But if we cannot gauge with any degree of accuracy the effect of Upper-Canadian propaganda during the war, it is possible to speak more authoritatively of later years. As noted earlier, Brock's efforts produced the enduring 'militia myth' but it was by no means the only part of the propagandists' efforts to survive the war. Their whole interpretation of the war was passed on and lasted for more than a century. A generation after the Treaty of Ghent, Gilbert Auchinleck published in Toronto a history of the war which contained all the essentials of the Canadian propagandists' version of it. He found, for instance, that the 'reflecting portion of the community' in the United States was opposed to the war and that although Madison was not a traitor to the United States as some claimed, he was nevertheless 'entangled in the toils of French intrigue'. It was French gold, he surmised, which was behind the 'idle speculation' that Canadians were anxious to escape the tyranny of British rule. When the United States persisted in the war despite the British repeal of the offending orders-in-council, it did so 'for want of a better excuse, on the ground of the Impressment question'. He also found that while there were in Upper Canada American settlers who were 'everywhere disseminating their evil counsels', when the war came the people of Upper Canada demonstrated their loyalty to Britain. Hull's proclamation, he noted, 'failed in producing its anticipated effect'. That Auchinleck should come to such conclusions is not surprising since he quotes liberally from such propaganda pieces as Brock's proclamation, his speech to the legislature in August 1812, and Strachan's 'Address of the House of Assembly'.[73]

Although there were occasional modifications, this interpretation persisted with Canadian historians through the remainder of the nineteenth century and well into the twentieth. Not until Ernest Cruikshank began his monumental investigations into the War of 1812 was the propaganda version challenged. Cruikshank began to publish his multi-volume documentary history of the war in the last years of the nineteenth century but James Hannay's *History of the War of 1812*, published in 1905, still quoted extensively from the propagandists for its interpretation of the war. Cruikshank's 'A Study of Disaffection in Upper Canada in 1812–15' appeared in 1912 but in 1930 George Wrong could hint darkly that the issues of impressment and neutral trade were the 'ostensible' reasons for the American declaration of war and that Canada was defended by its own people with merely 'the aid' of British regulars.[74]

At the beginning of this essay it was suggested that propaganda can be revealing of the society which produced it. The very fact that propaganda was used as a weapon and the ways in which it was used are revealing but a few particular conclusions and speculations also emerge. Because there was so little American propaganda, the revelations which can be drawn from it are few and tenous. They are nevertheless interesting. For one thing it demonstrates that there were Americans who looked to the addition of Canada to the Union as an outcome of the war. This is nowhere more explicit than in an address by General Alexander Smyth to his army at Buffalo but which was immediately available across the border. In urging them to be moderate in their treatment of Canadian civilians, he wrote:

> you will enter a country that is to be one of the United States. You will arrive among a people who are to become your fellow citizens.[75]

The propaganda also demonstrates an early version of that peculiarly American conceit, that people everywhere yearn for the chance to become American citizens, and the idea from which it springs, that true liberty and the happiness and prosperity which it necessarily brings exist only in America. In just a few decades these ideas would be sanctified with the name 'Manifest Destiny'.

The Canadian propaganda is even more revealing. It demonstrates the deep conservatism of the Upper-Canadian élite and its fundamental distrust of democratic ideas because they would undermine the structured society which was at the root of social order and 'rational liberty'. It is also evidence of the shock of the élite when the war revealed how little control it had over the population. We can understand, if not sympathize with, the determination of the Family Compact in the postwar years to suppress democratic influences in general and American influences in particular, whenever they raised their heads in the province. It is also possible to see in the propaganda a basis for ideas long held in Upper Canada and subsequently Ontario. One was that the British connection was essential. The other emerges from the direction of most of the propaganda. Explicitly or implicitly it was directed at the Loyalists, and the later American settlers—who in fact comprised the majority of the population—were often ignored or at best treated as a small group who could be controlled with warnings of the price of treason. The picture that can emerge, especially when the image this can create is combined with the Militia Myth, is one of Upper Canada as a Loyalist province. When people such as Egerton Ryerson later looked back to the beginnings of the province, they could find, if they so wished, a society of Loyalist heroes created by the propagandists of 1812.

Suggestions for Further Reading

Arthur Bowler, *The War of 1812* (Toronto, 1973).

J. Mackay Hitsman, *The Incredible War of 1812: A Military History* (Toronto, 1965).

Morris Zaslow, ed., *The Defended Border: Upper Canada and the War of 1812* (Toronto, 1964).

Notes

[1] J.C.A. Stagg, *Mr. Madison's War* (Princeton: 1983), ch. 1.

[2] The *National Intelligencer*, 3 December 1811. This was one of three articles entitled *The Canadas*. All are printed as an appendix in Stagg, *Mr. Madison's War.*

[3] Isaac Brock to Sir George Prevost, 25 February 1812, printed in William Wood, *Select British Documents of the Canadian War of 1812*, 3 vols. (Toronto: Champlain Society, 1920–26), vol. 1, 169; Public Archives of Canada (PAC) C.O. 42/352, Brock to Prevost, 3 December 1811; J.B. Glegg to Thomas Talbot, 12 March 1812 reprinted in James H. Coyne (ed.), 'The Talbot Papers', *Proceedings and Transactions of the Royal Society of Canada*, Third Series, vol. 1 (1907).

[4] Ernest Cruikshank, 'A Study of Disaffection in Upper Canada in 1812–15' in Morris Zaslow, ed., *The Defended Border* (Toronto: Macmillan, 1964), 206; statements of Henry Clay and William Eustis quoted in Ferdinand Brock Tupper, *Family Records; containing the Memoirs of Major-General Isaac Brock* (Guernsey: 1835), 133.

[5] Cartwright to Hunter, 23 August 1799, Richard Cartwright Letter Books, Douglas Library, Queen's University, Kingston, Ontario.

[6] PAC, Record Group 1, Upper Canada State Papers, Major Graham to D.W. Smith, 29 March 1802.

[7] PAC, C.O. 42/136, Gore to Craig, 5 January 1808.

[8] The initiative here came from Governor Prevost who received warnings to that effect from British consuls in New York City and Philadelphia. See Thomas Barclay to Sir George Prevost, 22 January 1812 in Ernest Cruikshank, ed., *Documentary History of the Campaign on the Niagara Frontier in 1812*, part III (Welland, Ontario: n.d.), 34, and Cruikshank, 'A Study of Disaffection in Upper Canada'.

[9] A.W. Cochran to his father, 23 June 1812, quoted in Cruikshank, 'Disaffection in Upper Canada'; PAC, R.G. 1, Upper Canada Executive Council Minute Book, 18 February 1812; Proclamation published in *York Gazette*, 4 March 1812.

[10] PAC, C.O. 42/352, Brock to Liverpool, 29 August 1812.

[11]There is, however, a report by a commissioner to the Indians on the Grand River of the arrival there of Indians from the Buffalo area of New York. They were representatives of the Seneca chief Red Jacket and their purpose was to dissuade the Grand River Iroquois from joining the British in the coming war. (PAC, R.G. 1, E3, Upper Canada State Papers 79. J.B. Rousseau to Col. Claus, 7 June 1812.)

[12]In January and again in early August the assembly refused by narrow margins to pass bills which would have suspended *habeas corpus* and among other things from members of the militia demanded an oath abjuring all other loyalties.

[13]Michael Smith, *A Geographical View of the Province of Upper Canada*, 3rd ed. (Philadelphia: 1813), 83.

[14]Brock to Prevost, 25 February & 12 July 1812, in Wood, *Select British Documents*, vol. 1, 169, 352; PAC, C.O. 42/352, Brock to Liverpool, 23 March 1812.

[15]The proclamation can be found in a number of sources. It is reprinted in Arthur Bowler, *The War of 1812* (Toronto: 1983), 52 and in Wood, *Select British Documents*, vol. 1, 355. The *Kingston Gazette* printed it on 18 August 1812 and there is an original copy in PAC, C.O. 42/147.

[16]PAC, C.O. 42/147, Prevost to Liverpool, 30 July 1812.

[17]Daniel Springer to Brock, 23 July 1812, Talbot to Brock, 27 July 1812, Brock to Provost, 28 July 1812, Brock to Baynes, 29 July and 4 August 1812, Wood, *Select British Documents*, 375–6, 382, 386–7, 396, 409; PAC, R.G. 1 Upper Canada Executive Council Minute Book, Minutes of 3 August 1812; Henry Adams, *The Administration of the United States Under the Administration of James Madison* (New York: 1880), 303.

[18]*Kingston Gazette*, 31 July 1812. It is also printed in Bowler, *The War of 1812*, 53–5 and Wood, *Select British Documents*, 371–4.

[19]Cruikshank, *Documentary History*, part III, 268.

[20]It did occur to others, though. Governor Tompkins of New York felt that the very appearance of an organized American army on the Niagara frontier would end the war, especially if it were accompanied by a proclamation 'extending the hand of fellowship' to the Canadian militia, which would then revolt against Great Britain. He made the suggestion in a letter written on 12 July 1812, the day Hull issued his proclamation (Stagg, *Mr. Madison's War*, 243–4. See also p. 201).

[21]Wood, *Select British Documents*, vol. II, 441.

[22]Declaration of the American Commandant of Ft. Erie, 30 May 1813. PAC, C.O. 42/151.

[23]Cruikshank, *Documentary History*, vol. VIII, 65. Address to the Inhabitants of the Province of Upper Canada, 16 October 1813. The fourth proclamation is one mentioned by Cruikshank in his article 'A Study of Disaffection in Upper Canada' but I have not been able to find it. It was issued by General Harrison and Commodore Perry to the people of the Western District.

[24]PAC, R.G. 5, Upper Canada Sundries, p. 6532.

[25]PAC, C.O. 42/151; Cruikshank, *Documentary History*, vol. IX, 112.

[26]For the *York Gazette* see, for example, 18 March, 28 July, 29 August 1812.

[27]*Kingston Gazette*, 18 August, 19 December 1812.

[28]28 July 1812.

[29]Cruikshank, *Documentary History*, part VI, 63, General Order 8 June 1813.

[30] *York Gazette*, 26 February, 12 September 1812. The *Canadian Courant* was published in Montreal by Nahum Mower, a man noted for his enthusiastic loyalty.

[31] Cruikshank, *Documentary History*, part 3, 35–8, Gray to Prevost, 29 January 1812. Gray was killed the next year in the assault on Sackets Harbor.

[32] George W. Spragge, ed., *The John Strachan Letter Book, 1812–1834* (Toronto: 1946), 108, Strachan to Ltd. Col. Clifford, 25 April 1816.

[33] *Ibid.*

[34] PAC, C.O. 42/352, Brock to Prevost, 3 December 1811.

[35] Wood, *Select British Documents, vol.* I, 169, Brock to Prevost, 25 February 1812.

[36] Cruikshank, *Documentary History*, part III, 148, Brock to Prevost, 28 July 1812.

[37] See, for instance, *Kingston Gazette*, 18 February 1812, Brock's speech on opening the Legislature of Upper Canada; PAC, R.G. 9, Militia General Orders, 4 July 1812.

[38] Wood, *Select British Documents*, vol. I, 407–8.

[39] In bringing the prisoners from Michilimackinac and Detroit, Brock also sought, with some success, to dishearten the American forces assembling there. See Stagg, *Mr. Madison's War*, 247.

[40] Strachan published a *Report of the Loyal and Patriotic Society of Upper Canada, with an Appendix and a list of Subscribers* after the war (Montreal: 1817). The constitution was also printed in the *Kingston Gazette*, 23 February 1813.

[41] *Report of the Loyal and Patriotic Society*, 325. Although the document is undated, its position in the correspondence printed makes a date in the first half of 1814 fairly certain.

[42] Cruikshank, *Documentary History*, part V, 20, Sheaffe to W.D. Powell, 20 December 1812.

[43] Wood, *Select British Documents*, vol. I, 272, Brock to Prevost, 2 December 1811.

[44] Wood, *Select British Documents*, vol. I, 390.

[45] PAC, R.G. 1, Upper Canada State Papers 7, Brock's representation on the state of the Province & Council minutes, 3 August 1812.

[46] Wood, *Select British Documents*, vol. I, 459, District General Order, 14 August 1812.

[47] PAC, R.G. 9, Militia General Orders, 25 November 1813.

[48] C.P. Stacey, 'The War of 1812 in Canadian History' in Zaslow, *The Defended Border*, 332.

[49] Spragge, *Strachan Letter Book*, 58; Strachan, *Report of the Loyal and Patriotic Society*, 365.

[50] Egerson Ryerson, *The Loyalists of America and their Times* (Toronto, William Briggs, 1880) vol. II, 379. Ryerson printed excerpts from Clarke's memoirs in this work. This is not to deny that the militia played an important role in the war, merely that they were the essential core of the forces defending Upper Canada. The role of the militia is described in G.F.G. Stanley's 'The Contribution of the Canadian Militia to the War' in Philip Mason *et al.*, *After Tippecanoe: Some Aspects of the War of 1812* (Toronto: Ryerson, 1963).

[51] See, for instance, the 'Falkland' letters printed in the *Kingston Gazette* 18 February and 3 March 1812, Brock's proclamation in response to Hull (*Kingston Gazette*, 28 July 1812), and Strachan's 'Address of the House of Assembly to the People of Upper Canada' (*ibid.*, 5 September 1812).

[52] *York Gazette*, 4 February and 18 February 1812.

[53]See particularly the address by 'John Bull, jun.' to 'The Independent Electors of the County of Frontenac' in the *Kingston Gazette*, 26 May 1812.

[54]This paper can only touch on the complex reaction of the Upper Canadian élite to events in the United States in these years. For the full story the reader is referred to the very perceptive article by Jane Errington and George Rawlyk, 'The Loyalist-Federalist Alliance of Upper Canada' in *The American Review of Canadian Studies* XIV, 2 (Summer 1984): 157–76.

[55]*Upper Canada Gazette*, 12 January 1808, quoted in *ibid.*, 165.

[56]*Kingston Gazette*, 12 December 1812.

[57]*Ibid.*, 26 May 1812.

[58]*York Gazette*, 5 September 1812, Address of the Assembly.

[59]*Kingston Gazette*, 19 September 1812.

[60]12 December 1812. Smyth's address is reprinted in the *Kingston Gazette*, 26 December 1812.

[61]*York Gazette*, 4 February 1812. See also *Kingston Gazette*, 18 February 1812, both 'A Loyalist' and 'Falkland' letters.

[62]*York Gazette*, 28 July 1812. Brock's proclamation in reply to Hull.

[63]*York Gazette*, 4 February 1812.

[64]*Kingston Gazette*, 18 February 1812.

[65]See, for instance, *Kingston Gazette*, 26 September, 24 October 1812 and 10 August 1813. See also the handbill and proclamation printed in Cruikshank, *Documentary History*, part IV, 313 and vol. IX, 112.

[66]Philip Davidson, *Propaganda and the American Revolution, 1763–1783* (Chapel Hill: 1941), xiii. Good discussion of propaganda and propaganda techniques can also be found in Leonard W. Doob, *Propaganda; its Psychology and Technique* (New York: 1935), J.A.C. Brown, *Techniques of Persuasion* (Pelican Books: 1963), and James T. Boulton, *The Language of Politics in the Age of Fox and Burke* (London: 1963).

[67]PAC, M.G. 24, Brock Correspondence, Prevost to Brock, 12 July 1812.

[68]For instance, Admiral Berkley, British commander on the North American station noted in a letter to Lt.-Gov. Gore in 1807 that he had information of a secret agreement which provided that if Canada were captured by the United States in a war with Britain, it would be transferred to France (D. Brymer, *Report on the Canadian Archives*, 1896, Ottawa, 1896, 28).

[69]The Rev. John Strachan, D.D., *A Sermon Preached at York, Upper Canada, on the Third of June, being the Day Appointed for a General Thanksgiving* (Montreal: 1814).

[70]Ontario Archives, Isaac Wilson Diary, 5 December 1813.

[71]Pelican Books, 1963, 77.

[72]Cruikshank, 'A Study of Disaffection'; Gerald M. Craig, *Upper Canada: the Formative Years, 1784–1891* (Toronto: 1963), 77.

[73]Gilbert Auchinleck, *A History of the War Between Great Britain and the United States of America During the Years 1812, 1813 and 1814* (originally published Toronto: 1855; republished London: 1972), 42–9.

[74]Cruikshank's 'Study of Disaffection' was first published in the *Transactions* of the Royal Society of Canada, series three, section 2 (1912). Professor Wrong's 1930 work is *A History of the Canadian People* published in Toronto (see 142–3 and 151). Egerton Ryerson's *The Loyalists of America and their Times* (Toronto: 1880) carries

the propaganda interpretation in pristine form as does J.G. Bourinot's *Canada* (London: 1897). More serious works, such as William Kingsford's *History of Canada* (London: 1895, see vol. VIII) and *Canada and its Provinces* edited by Adam Shortt and Arthur Doughty (Toronto: 1913, see vol. III) managed largely to escape from the propagandists, especially when they examined the causes of the war, but even they succumbed to the militia myth.

[75]Frank Severence, 'The Case of Brigadier General Alexander Smyth,' *Publications of the Buffalo Historical Society*, vol. 18 (1914): 227–8.

16

Immigration

Elizabeth Hopkins

Between 1790 and 1860, and especially after 1815, nearly one million people from the British Isles came to the provinces of British North America. This movement was the first of several mass migrations of people into what is now Canada. They came from all parts of the British Isles—England, Ireland, Ulster, Wales, Highland and Lowland Scotland—and from all social classes. British North America had a reputation as being a 'good poor man's country', and it probably provided the most satisfactory experience for immigrants with some capital who were constricted economically at home. Immigration was especially hard, however, on the poor, those who became infirm, and on women. Among females, those from upper-middle-class (genteel) backgrounds probably experienced the greatest sense of cultural shock, and were most likely to articulate it, since they were well educated in an age when there were few other outlets for such women than 'scribbling'.

Elizabeth Hopkins discusses five British gentlewomen's descriptions of their experiences in Upper Canada in the first half of the nineteenth century. All were educated at home, and all found exposure to the isolation and lack of amenities of what Susanna Strickland Moodie called 'the bush' to be an extremely trying experience. To some extent, all five reflected as much on the difficulties of women on the frontier as on the physical and emotional hardships and deprivations of bush life, and all may have found some solace for their experiences through their writing.

Why does the author claim that these women were in some ways well prepared to adapt to the practicalities of Canadian rural life? What were they not prepared for? What does Susanna Moodie mean by describing the wilderness as 'the prisonhouse'? Would she have felt differently had she been a man? How did conditions improve for all

these women? Does the improvement suggest that discontent was
merely a stage of immigrant
experience?

This article, titled 'A Prison-House for Prosperity: the Immigrant Experience of the Nineteenth Century Upper-Class British Woman', first appeared in Jean Burnet, ed., *Looking into My Sister's Eyes: An Exploration in Women's History* (Toronto: Multicultural History Society of Canada, 1986), 7–19.

This article centres on the stories of five British gentlewomen who immigrated from Britain to Ontario in the first half of the nineteenth century. Mary Gapper O'Brien, Frances Stewart, Susanna Moodie, Catharine Parr Traill and Anne Langton all left behind written accounts of their experiences in the New World. As might be expected, these accounts have many common characteristics, but they differ from each other in ways that make the task of generalizing about the gentlewoman's adaptation to pioneering a very risky business indeed. In part this is because each of the five women clearly exposed her personal reactions to her new life and one finds oneself trying to brush aside interesting personalities—some optimistic, some pessimistic, some stoic, some enthusiastic—in order to arrive at a picture of a specific class in a specific place at a specific time in our history. So, in general, I propose to proceed on a case-by-case basis, trying to avoid my literary concerns and activate my historical and sociological reasoning as best I can to make some general observations about upper-middle-class immigration in the early nineteenth century. In the end, though, I must leave you, as Susanna Moodie says at the end of *Roughing it in the Bush*, 'to draw your own conclusions'![1]

The existence of personal, written accounts of what it was like to settle in Canada in the early 1800s is in itself a revealing matter. It means that the women who wrote these letters, diaries, journals and manuscripts were educated. They recognized the uniqueness of their own adventures and shared them in generous detail with their readers, whether distant relatives or the book-buying public. Furthermore, especially in the case of their letters and private journals, they must have raised families and written to friends who appreciated the interest and rarity of such accounts enough to preserve them through the years. The fact that the five women all had time to write, daily and lengthily, about their experiences while they lived them also shows that they were, at least to some extent, leisured—some had servants in Canada, four eventually had large families who in time were able to help run the home and thus free their mothers to write. Finally, the fragile yellow manuscripts that we can read today in the Public Archives and other collections remind us that, at the time they were written, the very materials needed to engage in writing were scarce and expensive in the backwoods. Pens, ink, paper, postage and even the artificial light from candles or lamps were luxuries not to be used frivolously in most households. Even our five gentle-women used them carefully—writing on both sides of the page, sometimes across their horizontal lines of script, writing by firelight, complaining of frozen ink and profusely thanking relatives and friends for parcels from home containing pens and paper. Thus, the very fact that we have these women's stories in their own words is a sign of their privileged backgrounds, their relative comfort in the New World and the kind of values they passed on to their children.

The education of these women deserves a little more comment than its quick mention above. In the early 1800s, with few exceptions, only the children of the well-to-do middle and upper classes received anything resembling a formal education. In the case of the sons of such families, education begun at home under a tutor would be continued at a 'public' school when the boy reached the age of eleven or twelve and finished at university if he was destined for one of the professions. For the daughters of such families, education was acquired only at home under the guidance of parents and governesses or tutors. Furthermore, the curriculum in most households was a very different matter for boys and girls. The latter were seldom exposed to mathematics or the sciences (beyond a polite smattering of nature study) and spent hours studying decorum, music, dancing, fine needlework, drawing and painting. By the 1820s the picture was beginning to change as the *nouveau riche* British middle class set up their own 'public' schools for sons and daughters. The five women in this study, however, were educated at home. The unusual feature of their schooling was the emphasis their parents and guardians placed on a well-rounded curriculum for both sons and daughters. This curriculum was one of the most valuable assets they carried to Canada as young adults. It meant that they could do more than write about their experiences; they were not helpless, unskilled or ignorant. Indeed, it clearly enabled them to survive and succeed where so many others struggled and failed.

In the Public Archives of Canada there is an unpublished memoir of her girlhood in Suffolk written by Catharine Parr Traill, sister of Susanna Moodie.[2] In it she gives a detailed account of the education their father, Thomas Strickland, devised for his six daughters and two sons. They were all taught the same subjects—reading, writing, Latin and a little Greek, history, geography, philosophy, mathematics, physics and botany. They were encouraged to read in their father's extensive library—though fiction was definitely discouraged. There were frequent walking excursions into the countryside surrounding Stowe House and Reydon Hall, their early Suffolk homes (which were also large working farms). Their father made these trips the occasion for more lessons on the care of farmland, the habits of wildlife, the art of fishing and the patterns of plant life. The only segregated part of their education came when their mother took the girls for training in small animal husbandry, the dairy, the vegetable garden and other domestic realms while their father coached the boys in farm operation. There were daily religious observances in the Strickland home, and the children were encouraged to make their own toys and games in what little leisure time they had. Needless to say, while good behaviour and polite manners were insisted upon, very little time was given to the decorative arts, though Susanna later took lessons in drawing and painting and Catharine became an accomplished embroiderer. One can hardly imagine a better education for the lives that three of the young Stricklands would one day lead.

Mr. Strickland died rather suddenly in 1818, leaving his large family in fairly restricted financial circumstances. A few years later young Samuel Strickland set out for Canada. His brother Tom joined the merchant navy, and the girls began careers as professional writers and editors while they helped their mother operate the Reydon Hall farm. After further training as a surveyor for the Canada Land Company, Samuel settled near present-day Lakefield, Ontario, and eventually prospered. Realizing that the gentleman settler's main problem was the absence of practical backwoods and farming knowledge, Samuel later established a school at Lakefield for the sons of gentlemen wishing to settle in Canada.

This digression on the education of upper-middle-class settlers helps to explain why so many of the women seemed to adapt to the practicalities of the life of a Canadian farmer's wife with relative ease. It was only when necessity forced them to help in the fields or when the isolation of the bush farm became depressing that they began to complain. In fact, most of the immigrant gentlewomen from the English and Irish countryside were much better prepared for their life in Canada than one would think. Milking cows, working in the dairy, curing and preserving meat, tending large vegetable gardens, chickens and children were tasks they approached with much more confidence than their more narrowly trained descendants could do today.

If their education made them better prepared for the life of an immigrant, however, social class and habits from the old country often threatened their new existence. Used to polite company, the sophistication of London, readily available literature, doctors, religious ministers, elegant furniture and inexpensive servants, these upper-middle-class settlers had in many ways more to learn about the New World than their less privileged fellow immigrants. Susanna Moodie's conclusion to *Roughing it in the Bush* summarizes the problem:

> I have given you a faithful picture of a life in the backwoods of Canada, and I leave you to draw your own conclusions. To the poor, industrious working man it presents many advantages; to the poor gentleman, *none*! The former works hard, puts up with coarse, scanty fare, and submits, with a good grace, to hardships that would kill a domestic animal at home. Thus he becomes independent, inasmuch as the land that he has cleared finds him the common necessaries of life; but it seldom, if ever, in remote situations, accomplishes more than this. The gentleman can neither work so hard, live so coarsely, nor endure

so many privation as his poorer but more fortunate neighbour. Unaccustomed to manual labour, his services in the field are not of a nature to secure for him a profitable return. The task is new to him, he knows not how to perform it well; and, conscious of his deficiency, he expends his little means in hiring labour, which his bush farm can never repay. Difficulties increase, debts grow upon him, he struggles in vain to extricate himself, and finally sees his family sink into hopeless ruin.

If these sketches should prove the means of deterring one family from sinking their property, and shipwrecking all their hopes, by going to reside in the backwoods of Canada, I shall consider myself amply repaid for revealing the secrets of the prisonhouse, and feel that I have not toiled and suffered in the wilderness in vain.[3]

Susanna's 'prisonhouse' was the bush near present-day Lakefield where she and her husband struggled to establish a farm for the seven heart-breaking years described in her book. She wrote these words in 1850 in the relative comfort of her stone cottage at the corner of Sinclair and Bridge streets in Belleville, Ontario. In 1839 her husband, like many British gentlemen immigrants, had been offered a government post as sheriff of Hastings County. Life in growing, bustling Belleville meant modest prosperity for the Moodies: a stone house instead of a log cabin, schools for their children, a piano from Montreal and a few servants. Although the position of sheriff carried no salary (a sheriff was expected to support himself on the proceeds of successfully prosecuted cases, and John Wedderburn Dunbar Moodie was a scrupulously honest sheriff), the Moodies managed to invest in mortgages and purchase small parcels of land as savings for their retirement. Their two daughters married 'well' — the eldest became Mrs. John Vickers, wife of the owner of the Vickers Express Company in Toronto, while her sister's second husband was Brown Chamberlin, Queen's Printer in Ottawa. Two of the three surviving Moodie sons sought their fortunes in the United States, while the youngest, Robert, built a career in the service of the Grand Trunk Railway and later in the Vickers Express Company. Although she worried constantly about money during her widowhood, when she died in Toronto one hundred years ago, Susanna left an estate of $4,700. But if her material prosperity was modest, the opportunity for social contact and literary achievement that her arrival in Belleville afforded her provided a claim to posterity.

In England Susanna Strickland had been a minor literary figure, publishing children's books, verses and sketches in Christmas gift books and such journals as *La Belle Assemblée*, and a single volume of poetry on the eve of her departure for Canada with her new husband and baby daughter. In Canada as a writer she became 'a big fish in a little pond' as the principal contributor to John Lovell's *Literary Garland*, the co-editor with her husband of the short-lived *Victoria Magazine*, and the author of *Roughing it in the Bush, Life in the Clearings, Flora Lyndsey* and half a dozen other novels. She was a figure of some notoriety in the new province, as she reports in *Life in the Clearings*, becoming known as 'that woman what writes', a person who 'tells lies and gets paid for it'.[4]

In Belleville the Moodies were members of the establishment—prominent families of the town were among their social circle and, as educated British gentlefolk, the Moodies were looked to as arbiters of social and moral standards in the community. Even the many political difficulties of Sheriff Moodie's profession did not detract from their social standing, their position as pillars of the community. When J.W.D. Moodie resigned under troubled circumstances in 1863, a local paper reprinted testimonials to his exemplary character.

For Susanna Moodie, then, the general pattern of her life in Canada was typical of immigration experiences: early years of hardship and emotional rebellion were gradually replaced by years of adaptation, acceptance and comfort, the prison-house bush gave way to the relative prosperity of Belleville.

I have started with this very brief sketch of Susanna Moodie's story because she provided the title for this paper and because *Roughing it in the Bush* is probably the account of pioneering most familiar to Canadians today. Its themes, the reasons for immigration, the high expectations for the new land, the painful separation from the old, the struggles with a hostile environment, constantly threatening poverty and emotional despair, and the final acceptance of a much-modified version of comfort and success are common to gentlefolk and poorer immigrants alike. What Susanna's background and social position did offer her was the possibility of escape from hardship and a position of influence as a writer and arbiter of social values in the new land. The stories of her sister Catharine Parr Traill, along with those of their friend Frances Stewart and the experiences of Mary O'Brien and Anne Langton, share more of these themes, but also reveal these women's differing responses to them.

Catharine Parr Traill arrived in Canada in the same year, 1832, as Susanna and for the same reason. She had married an officer of the British army, retired on half-pay after the Napoleonic Wars and suffering the ignominy of genteel poverty as the second son of Scottish landed gentry. With few respectable prospects for improving his fortunes in Britain, Thomas Traill, like hundreds of his fellow officers at the time, opted for the chance to build his own estate on the 400 acres of land granted to retired officers as inducement to settle and increase British influence in Upper Canada. In 1836 Catharine published her first account of their transatlantic voyage and early struggles in the dense cedar bush north of Peterborough. This book, *The Backwoods of Canada*,[5] takes the form of letters written home to Suffolk in which she describes her new life with enthusiasm and wonder:

> Yet I must say, for all its roughness, I love Canada, and am as happy in my humble log-house as if it were a courtly hall or bower; habit reconciles us to

many things that at first were distasteful. It has ever been my way to extract the sweet rather than the bitter in the cup of life, and surely it is best and wisest so to do. In a country where constant exertion is called for from all ages and degrees of settlers, it would be foolish to a degree to damp our energies by complaints, and cast a gloom over our homes by sitting dejectedly down to lament for all that was so dear to us in the old country. Since we are here, let us make the best of it, and bear with cheerfulness the lot we have chosen.[6]

At least in public Catharine hid her suffering, for her true story was even more heart-breaking than her sister's. Her actual, rather than her fictional, letters reveal her horror and sense of isolation in the bush, though she does her best to maintain a brave face.[7] Thomas Traill shared her shock and horror in the woods, but unlike his wife, he succumbed to long periods of serious depression in the face of back-breaking labour and constant financial worries. The growing family (they eventually had nine children) gave up the bush for a series of partially cleared farms on the Rice Lake Plains where contact with neighbours and friends was a little easier. However, they suffered endless illnesses and twice lost their homes and possessions in serious fires. Thomas never recovered from the last of these in 1856 and died a broken man in 1859. Catharine, however, with characteristic fortitude and her strong Christian faith, lived on until 1899, supporting herself with her writing and her increasingly absorbing botanical studies. Her brother Samuel Strickland built a cottage for her in Lakefield and in her long widowhood she finally achieved modest comfort and a permanent escape from the terrifying isolation of the woods. She corresponded with botanists all over the world and was eventually granted a small pension and an island as a reward for her literary and botanical efforts.

One of Catharine's closest friends was Frances Stewart, another early Peterborough region settler. The Stewarts came to Canada from Ireland in 1822—yet another case of immigration to better the sagging fortunes of the genteel but poor. Frances had grown up in the family seat of her relatives, the Beauforts. Her education was similar to the young Stricklands' and she, too, relieved the isolation of her early years in the Canadian bush by sharing the thoughts she could not speak with distant relations and friends in long letters. She was a cultured settler, an accomplished musician and water-colourist, and she and her husband brought a large library with them to Canada. This library was kept current with frequent parcels from home and was often used by Susanna Moodie and Catharine Parr Traill as a way of keeping up to date with the world of books in Britain.

In 1889 Stewart's daughter, Ellen Dunlop, edited and published her mother's letters in *Our Forest Home*.[8] The Stewarts' difficult first ten years in the bush were just beginning to be succeeded by greater comfort when the Moodies and Traills arrived in Canada, thus Frances was able to give very real emotional support and encouragement to the new settlers. She too had suffered the hardships, depressions and isolation they were just embarking upon. The Stewarts eventually achieved considerable prosperity and prominence in their new community. Thomas Stewart served as a Justice of the Peace for many years, and Frances came to be regarded as a kind of Canadian 'squire's lady'. She was noted for her efforts to maintain certain graces in her home—her silver tea service was brought all the way from Wilmont Hall in Ireland to the dense cedar bush that was to become their home, named 'Auburn' after one of the Stewart family's Irish properties.

Mary Gapper came to Canada in 1828, accompanying her mother who wanted to visit Mary's brothers, both of whom had settled on farms, north of the City of York, in what is now Thornhill. The visit stretched into a permanent immigration for young Mary who met and married an Irish gentleman settler, Edward O'Brien, in 1830. For almost ten years from the moment her ship set sail from Bristol, Mary Gapper O'Brien kept a daily journal of her life in Canada which she sent at frequent intervals to a sister who had remained in England. In 1968 Audrey Saunders Miller edited these journals for publication as *The Journals of Mary O'Brien*.[9]

The Gapper family were west country folk. They lived in yet another fine country house and were well-educated, primarily under the tutelage of their father, an Anglican clergyman. His unexpected death prompted two of his sons to immigrate to Canada. They, too, were pensioned officers—veterans of the Napoleonic Wars—and thus entitled to free grants of land. By the time Mary and their mother joined them in Thornhill, they were well-established, prominent leaders in the young community, on friendly terms with Sir John Colborne, the governor, whom they frequently visited on day trips down Yonge Street to York. Sheltered in the prosperous surroundings of her brothers' farms, introduced to their many friends and anxious to learn all about the new colony, Mary Gapper suffered none of the hardship or depression of the Moodies, Traills and Stewarts. She enthusiastically recorded her adventures and seems scarcely to have had a moment of homesickness, even when she made her decision to remain in Canada as Mrs O'Brien.

As a new bride she settled on a farm farther back from Yonge Street and more recently cleared than her brothers' properties. She joked in her journals about her first rude home, which rapidly expanded and began to fill up with fine furniture and servants. But her husband's dreams lay farther afield. He had claimed a beautiful point on Shanty Bay, Lake Simcoe, and dreamed of recreating an Irish estate out of the unbroken bush there. By 1 May 1832 the young couple, their year-old baby, servants and possessions found themselves camping in a shanty while Edward O'Brien's log mansion took shape on the rise above the bay. O'Brien himself drew up the plans for 'The Woods', as the house was called, and oversaw its construction with the help of escaped slaves who had found their way to the shores of Lake Simcoe.

Friends and acquaintances came to visit, and the O'Briens took trips down to Thornhill and York. They had congenial neighbours, help with the farm clearing and labour, and they were involved in establishing local roads, a church, the militia, a ferry service across the lake, a lending library and numerous other public endeavours. Mary, like many female settlers of her class, was particularly concerned with education for the young, teaching reading and writing to numerous girls and boys who in exchange helped her with the O'Brien babies and chores. By 1838 when Mary O'Brien's journals end, she and her husband had a large and growing family of young children and they were beginning to worry about the education of their two eldest sons. In 1845 they moved to Toronto, living at Shanty Bay only in the summer, so that the boys could attend Upper Canada College.

The O'Briens lived in Toronto and Shanty Bay until their deaths in the mid-1870s. Two of their sons became lawyers, a third, a civil engineer. Their experience seems to have had no 'prisonhouse' element, alleviated as it was by social contacts and considerably more wealth than the Lakefield settlers had brought with them. The O'Briens moved through the stage of physical discomforts quickly, and Edward saw his dream of a Canadian estate come true. Samuel Thompson in his *Reminiscences of a Canadian Pioneer* described 'The Woods' as 'a perfect gem of civilization set in the wildest of natural surroundings'.[10] Mary O'Brien took to the life of a Canadian settler with enthusiasm, humour and grace:

> June 11—Edward took me round his fields and then I went to my household work while he went to superintend the marking of the road past our lot. I went afterwards to see what they were doing and found them placing logs across a swamp to make a corduroy.
>
> I also stirred a bowl of cream into butter, in which I succeeded much to my heart's content, sitting under the verandah and reading Milton all the time. Only I found to my sorrow when my work was finished that I had ground off one of my nails.[11]

The last of the gentlewomen, whose account of a settler's life offers an interesting and cultivated analysis of her experience, is Anne Langton, the sister of John Langton who had settled on Sturgeon Lake, near the site of Fenelon Falls, in 1833. The Langtons were from yet another upper-middle-class English family who found their fortunes reduced. John came to Canada first, settling at Sturgeon Lake because it offered neighbours of his own class who shared his interests. He quickly built a log house and seemed content to enjoy a leisurely, if modest, bachelorhood looking after his needs and pursuing his reading and writing. In 1837 he was joined by his parents and sister who soon made themselves indispensable in helping with the daily tasks. Indeed, Anne, who had been deaf from an early age, never married and took it upon herself to become her brother's housekeeper until his marriage in 1845, after which she was a much-loved 'Aunt Anne' to his children, a permanent member of his household in Sturgeon Lake and later Toronto, except for long visits to England, until her death in 1893. Anne's journals from 1837–46 were edited for publication by a Langton descendant in 1950, under the title *A Gentlewoman in Upper Canada*.[12]

In addition to the usual enthusiastic responses to scenery, surprise at homestead chores and Canadian customs, Anne's journal/letters show an analytical bent that is rare in such accounts. For example, she comments on the role of gentlewomen in the New World as follows:

> I have caught myself wishing an old long-forgotten wish that I had been born of the rougher sex. Women are very dependent here, and give a great deal of trouble; we feel our weakness more than anywhere else. This, I cannot but think, has a slight tendency to sink us, it may be, into a more natural and proper sphere than the one we occupy in over-civilised life, as the thing I mean and feel, though I do not express it well, operates, I believe, as a safeguard to our feminine virtues, such virtues, I mean, as the Apostles recommended to us for I think here a woman must be respectable to meet with consideration and respect. The greatest danger, I think, we all run from our peculiar mode of life is that of becoming selfish and narrow-minded. We live so much to ourselves and mix so exclusively with one community. It is not only that the individuals are few, but the degrees and classes we come in contact with are still more limited.[13]

Anne's contemplative nature made her an excellent backwoods schoolmistress, aware of her own and her pupils' limitations under the circumstances:

> I am quite sensible that the instruction I give goes a very small way indeed towards complete education, and I have felt a misgiving lest, in some cases, the fact of a child being sent to me for two or three hours twice a week affords an excuse for neglecting it at home. I endeavour to impress it upon their friends that I by no means charge myself with the whole education, but am willing to give a little assistance such as may be in my power.[14]

Like the O'Briens, the Langtons were rather more prosperous to begin with, and certainly became more successful as their lives in Canada progressed, than the Moodies or Traills. Their motive for emigrating had not been *absolute* necessity, and Anne was able to return to England on visits from time to time. She had friends of her own class and enjoyed enough leisure to exercise her considerable talent as an artist. More importantly, the initial expectations of Mary O'Brien and Anne Langton were realistic compared with those at Lakefield. Thus the former were able to respond cheerfully when conditions improved. Neither Mary nor Anne was reduced to manual labour or suffered the threat of starvation, hence their views of their new lives are much more encouraging than those of Moodie, Traill or even Frances Stewart. What common elements might, then, be drawn from these five stories of upper-middle-class immigration?

First of all, while it was never an easy life for a woman of that period, it was a great deal more comfortable for an upper-class woman of the colonizing nation than for her poorer sister. The former crossed the Atlantic in a private cabin, not in the horrors of steerage accommodation. She was often tended by a maidservant on board ship and at least in her early years of settlement, thus allowing her some freedom to respond to her new land in aesthetic rather than purely practical ways. Despite the hardships and deprivations of bush life, the upper-class immigrant was confident in her knowledge of who she was and what her role as social and moral leader should be. Her education sometimes provided a means of earning extra income and always offered her philosophic and artistic relief from depression. While she shared homesickness and isolation with poorer female immigrants, she could write, read and eventually travel—sometimes to larger centres in Canada, sometimes even back to Britain. The lack of companionship of her own class was gradually circumvented by settlement in areas like Lakefield, Thornhill and Sturgeon Lake where other upper-middle-class settlers had preceded her. Government appointments in the militia, as a Justice of the Peace, or a county sheriff were much more likely to bless her family than that of a lower-class immigrant. In short, difficult and different though her lot in the New World was, she enjoyed class advantages that were not unlike those she might expect in the old country.

At the same time, she established a pattern of order, hard work and community service that would not have been necessary in her homeland. She was, in effect, an early version of the North American woman who, as far as she is able, does what has to be done whether or not it is woman's work. This was often a difficult lesson to learn, and was not, of course, the preserve of upper-class female immigrants alone; but for such women, with their education and expectations, it often resulted in quite remarkable achievements.

Finally, I think it is true to say that, though the reality of their lives may not have matched their hopes when they left Britain, they all did improve their family's security and material prosperity, however modest the latter. And for those who ended with modest estates there was literary and national renown.

Suggestions for Further Reading

Helen I. Cowan, *British Emigration to British North America: The First Hundred Years*, rev. ed. (Toronto, 1961).

Marion Fowler, *The Embroidered Tent: Five Gentlewomen in Early Canada: Elizabeth Simcoe, Catharine Parr Traill, Susanna Moodie, Anna Jameson, Lady Dufferin* (Toronto, 1982).

Carl Ballstadt, ed., *Roughing it in the Bush, or, Life in Canada by Susanna Moodie* (Ottawa, 1988).

Notes

[1] Susanna Moodie, *Roughing it in the Bush* (Toronto: Coles, 1980).

[2] Traill Family Collection, MG29 D81, Public Archives of Canada (PAC), Ottawa.

[3] Moodie, *Roughing it in the Bush*, 562–3.

[4] Moodie, *Life in the Clearings*, ed. Robert McDougall (Toronto: Macmillan, 1959).

[5] Catharine Parr Traill, *The Backwoods of Canada* (Toronto: Coles, 1980).

[6] *Ibid.*, 310.

[7] The majority of Mrs. Traill's extant letters are in the Traill Family Collection, MG29 D81, PAC, Ottawa.

[8] Frances Stewart, *Our Forest Home*, ed. E.S. Dunlop (Toronto: Presbyterian Printing and Publishing Co., 1889).

[9] *The Journals of Mary O'Brien, 1828–1838*, ed. Audrey Saunders Miller (Toronto: Macmillan, 1968).

[10] *Ibid.*, 118.

[11] *Ibid.*

[12] Anne Langton, *A Gentlewoman in Upper Canada*, ed. H.H. Langton (Toronto: Clarke, Irwin, 1950).

[13] *Ibid.*, 73.

[14] *Ibid.*, 134.

17

The Economy of Upper Canada

Douglas McCalla

The traditional view of Canadian economic development has always revolved around the exploitation of some 'staple' resource in the international market. In the early period these resources included fur, fish, timber, and grain—particularly wheat. According to this 'staples thesis' the relative availability of natural resources, coupled with the shortage of labour and capital, led to an emphasis on exporting these resources rather than on manufacturing products for the internal markets. Canadian economic development thus became dependent both on the land's natural resources and on the vagaries of international trade. Investment was directed into staple exploitation rather than into internal diversification, which resulted in a prosperity of sorts, but one that was inherently unstable and dependent on external forces. The economic cycle thus created tended to reflect Canada's colonial status.

A brief summary of the staple thesis, however, does not do justice either to the theory or to the host of economic factors it involves. Immigration, developments in transportation, advances in credit institutions, entrepreneurial attitudes, and above all the availability of capital play a part, and economic historians have recently been attempting to improve their understanding of these factors and fit them into the larger picture. One of the principal problems has been to discover a relation among them that accords with the known chronology of Canadian economic development.

In the following article Douglas McCalla attempts to probe the relation between wheat and economic development in Upper Canada. Most Canadians tend to associate the production of wheat with the mid-west, but it was in central Canada that the first wheat economy emerged in the first half of the nineteenth century, geared to overseas markets. In Great Britain Canadian grain (or corn, as the British called it) received favoured treatment until the 1840s. Accepting the importance of wheat as a staple product for Upper Canada, McCalla attempts to link, in a credible cause-and-effect sequence, the production of wheat to the other variables in Canadian economic development.

How do McCalla's data regarding steady economic growth in Upper Canada call into question the assumption that wheat was the basis of the province's economy? What other factors—relatively independent of the staple—might have been important? What factors would he prefer to focus on in place of the emphasis upon wheat production? To what extent does McCalla revise the staples thesis?

This article first appeared, titled 'The Wheat Staple and Upper Canadian Development', in *Canadian Historical Association Historical Papers* (1978), 34–46.

To understand the growth of the Upper Canadian economy, it is essential to understand the place in it of the wheat staple, which was 'the basis of the provincial economy in most of the settled parts of the province'.[1] Wheat remained pre-eminent even as late as 1860 when, after a decade of economic expansion and diversification, about half of the acreage cultivated in Upper Canada was still given over to wheat; of all crops grown, only wheat and barley were said to have been traded in significant amounts.[2] Earlier, wheat had been the one crop that a farmer could reasonably expect to sell each year. Not surprisingly, therefore, it has been argued that 'it was the export trade in wheat and flour that held the key to Upper Canada's development. . . . '[3]

Of the truth of this there can, in a sense, be no dispute. Yet when one tries to translate the considerable body of research that has been done on Upper Canada's wheat economy into a framework or model that explains the extent and the timing of Upper Canadian growth, one encounters difficulties. These have particularly to do with sequences of economic change and the place of wheat, especially wheat exports, in them. Moreover, if expanded wheat exports caused economic growth, what caused or permitted wheat output to increase in the first place? Could these prior factors not be more significant in explaining the process of economic expansion?[4] This paper will discuss such problems, drawing for illustration particularly upon evidence from the 1830s.

The 1830s began very favourably for the staples economy of Upper Canada, as British demand for wheat, reflected in high prices and high import volumes, increased enormously between 1829 and 1831 (Figures 1 & 2). As a result of earlier growth and despite the widely noted inadequacies of the St Lawrence transportation system, Upper Canada was able to play an important role in meeting that demand, its contribution to Canadian exports being said to have totalled about 720,000 bushels (90,000 quarters) in 1830 and about 900,000 bushels (110,000 quarters) in 1831.[5] At the same time, two major capital works, the Welland Canal and the Rideau Canal, were completed. Capital invested in these, and the reduction in transport risks and costs that they would engender on completion, must further have stimulated the economy. Drawn by the evident prosperity of at least Upper Canada, a rising volume of immigrants passed through Quebec (Figure 5).

British harvests, however, improved markedly and Britain returned, for what proved to be the last time, to a state of self-sufficiency in wheat production. As a result, British imports of wheat and the price of wheat in Britain and elsewhere fell very sharply from peak levels. In Upper Canada, prices by 1834–5 were well below minimum costs to produce and transport wheat or flour to market (Figures 1, 2, & 3). Although grain prices then revived, there were serious enough crop deficiencies in Upper Canada between 1835 and 1838 that aggregate income for many farmers may well not have increased greatly despite rising prices.[6] Thus, the entire period from 1832 to 1837 or 1838 was one of apparent difficulty for the staple-producing sector of the Upper Canadian economy.

This might have been expected, in a staples-dependent province such as Upper Canada, to have engendered a major depression and, indeed, there were some indications of depression there, especially at the lowest point in the wheat-price cycle.[7] Nevertheless, most evidence tends to belie the seriousness of any depression. Thus, until 1837, population grew at a steady rate, and the series for land under culture showed, essentially, a parallel rate of growth (Figure 4). By 1837, when the growth rate of each did slow, the price of wheat had fully recovered from its earlier decline. The note circulation of Upper Canadian banks (Figure 4) rose even more rapidly than the population and land series, and more fragmentary evidence indicates that imports to Upper Canada also rose quite steadily. Immigrant arrivals in the Canadas continued at a relatively substantial level (Figure 5). All these developments reached a climax in an intense boom in 1836.[8]

The discrepancy between trends in the grain market and those of other economic indicators poses, at first sight, something of a paradox. How could such general expansion go on when Upper Canada's basic staple faced such major problems? In some models of staples development, which begin with a stage of 'self-sufficiency' or subsistence-level farming,[9] the apparent paradox is resolved by assuming that farmers were not initially involved with or could at times withdraw completely from the market. After all, clearing a farm to begin production took time. But it also required capital to get to Upper Canada, to acquire land, to equip a farm initially, and to buy essential supplies until a surplus could be produced for sale, generally after two or three years on the land. At the normal rate at which land could be cleared, it was likely to take at least ten years to bring a farm into relatively full production.[10]

Figure 1. British imports of Canadian wheat and flour (000) quarters of wheat

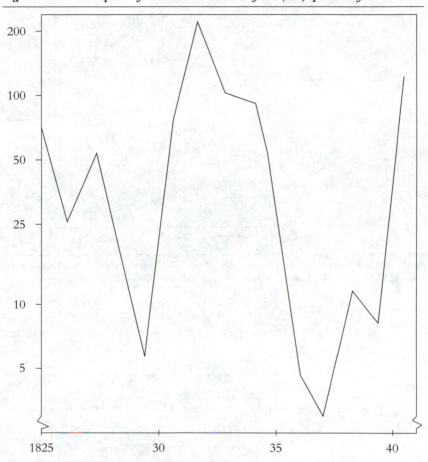

SOURCE: F.W. Burton, 'Wheat in Canadian History', *Canadian Journal of Economics and Political Science*, iii (1937), 213.

During all that time, given the improvements required or desired—for example, in buildings or tools—the farmer's need for capital must have tended to exceed his income. If in these years farmers were less involved than they might *later* be in the market, the description of the early stage as 'self-sufficient' is still inappropriate, because there can scarcely have been any new settler who did not have to draw on the market for at least some supplies on a continuing basis, whether or not he had something to sell.[11]

How could the farmer continue to buy when, first, he had no surplus or, later, he had a surplus insufficient to pay both for earlier purchases and for

Figure 2. Prices of wheat in Canada.

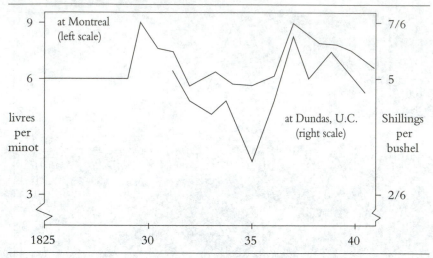

SOURCES: Dundas price (January of each year) from F.W. Burton, *op.cit.*, 215; Montreal price from F. Ouellet, *Histoire Economique et Sociale du Quebec, 1760–1850* (Montreal, 1966), 603.

Figure 3. Prices of wheat in Britain.

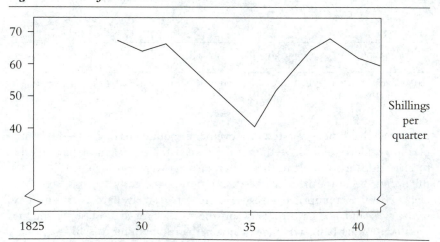

SOURCE: R.C.O. Matthews, *A Study in Trade Cycle History: Economic Fluctuations in Great Britain, 1833–1842* (Cambridge, 1954), 30.

Figure 4. Indicators of growth in Upper Canada.

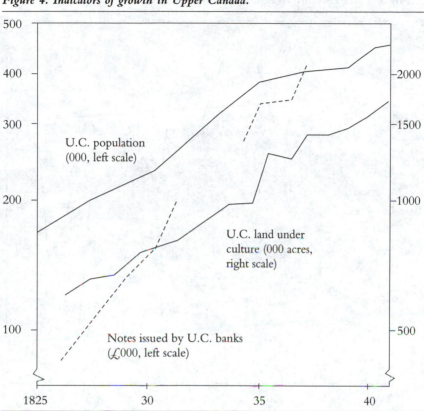

U.C. population
(000, left scale)

U.C. land under
culture (000 acres,
right scale)

Notes issued by U.C. banks
(£000, left scale)

SOURCES: Population and acreage figures from *Census of Canada, 1871*, vol. iv, 86–131; bank-note figures from R.M. Breckenridge, *The Canadian Banking System 1817–1890* (Toronto, 1894), 52, 66.

his current needs? Various expedients to raise funds might be available, but almost universally the farmer coped in part by going into debt. Despite the views of some historians, debt was not engendered by the baneful domination of the business classes nor was it an irrational choice by the farmer; rather, it was both an essential for survival and a potentially profitable investment in the future.[12] This is equally true whether debts were only for land, or, as was usual and, one suspects, more important in absolute amounts, for the stores and other goods needed to survive. Commercial credit, while nominally short term, gave the farmer time to bring his farm into production. When much of the farmer's investment in his land took the form of his own labour, the funds that sustained him, however they were advanced, were creating fixed capital. This suggests that the frequently encountered

Figure 5. Immigrant arrivals at Quebec (000)

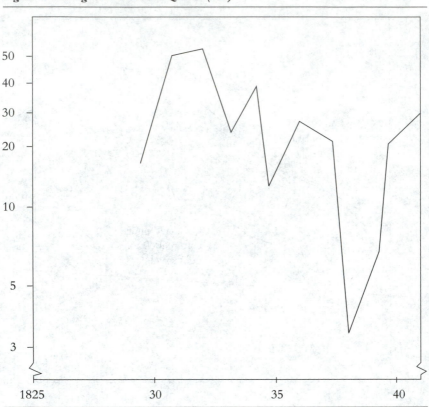

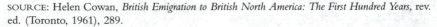

SOURCE: Helen Cowan, *British Emigration to British North America: The First Hundred Years*, rev. ed. (Toronto, 1961), 289.

distinction between long- and short-term, or fixed and circulating, capital, had at most very modest reality in the pioneer phase of the economy.[13]

To go into debt was, therefore, a reasonable investment strategy; indebtedness was further necessitated by the normal problems of fluctuating harvests and by the erratic and unpredictable course of the British grain market. Because of the time lag involved, the farmer, when he commenced the work of clearing, could not know what the market conditions would be when he at last had a surplus to bring to market.[14] Indeed, because the British market could actually be closed completely, it was possible that his crop would be virtually unsaleable, as the extremely low prices of 1834–5 revealed. Yet, once committed to the process, the farmer had little choice but to go on clearing and to increase his wheat output if he could, even in very poor market conditions—as long as he had the capital or credit to continue. In the circumstances of the wheat market in the 1830s, this implies, for the economy as a whole, an expanding credit supply.

Given the operation of the Corn Laws, the time required to begin to produce a surplus, and the illiquidity of investment in a farm, the creation of a new staple-producing wheat economy involved a degree of risk and uncertainty that was probably higher than for some other early staples and almost certainly higher than to farm in stabler and longer-established economies.[15] Such levels of risk were in part reflected in lower land prices than in more established economies, but the other real costs of beginning to farm, such as the costs of imported goods, transport costs to metropolitan markets, and any wages that had to be paid, were not variable in the same way as land costs and they were necessarily higher than in Britain. What would justify someone in paying such costs and undertaking such risks? In all likelihood, the answer lies in the prospect of relatively high returns in terms of initial investment.[16] It is here that the high prices and trade volumes of 1830–1 must come into play; by indicating the kind of profit that might be made, they could generate a new wave of investment and expansion in the economy, even if that wave did not for many years, if ever, yield the anticipated returns.

Consequent upon the market conditions of 1830–1, therefore, it was to be expected that, barring crop failures, the Upper Canadian economy would produce more wheat year by year even if the major overseas market was closed or closing. In that case, it is a problem to know what was done with the wheat. There was a local market in Upper Canada, notably among as-yet-unestablished immigrants, lumber camps, labouring gangs on such major projects as canals (although the two largest individual projects were completed just at the beginning of the slide in wheat prices), nascent urban centres, and local distilleries. Further amounts, of course, had to be held back for seed and for the farmer's own consumption. It has been estimated, however, that between 17 and 33 per cent of output was enough to meet all such demands; it has been argued that distilleries, for example, could not have taken more than 1 and lumber camps 2 per cent of Upper Canadian output.[17] There is confirming evidence of the insufficiency of local demand in that such local markets must also have required produce other than wheat; thus, if they were or could have been the pre-eminent markets for Upper Canadian farmers, agriculture there might have been expected to develop on the basis of a balanced range of market crops rather than on wheat alone. Indeed, such a balanced agriculture did exist in at least one area, the Ottawa Valley. Whether there were other such areas, and if so of what extent and significance, is less certain.

The American market, short of wheat in the years 1835–8 as a result of crop failures, took some Upper Canadian wheat, but similar harvest conditions are said to have affected Upper Canada and thus to have limited the amount it could supply.[18] More generally, Upper Canadian agricultural expansion paralleled American westward expansion, so that the two economies were more competing than complementary in most years prior to the 1850s. As a result, the American market was at best an occasional and not a reliable outlet for Upper Canadian wheat.

The primary market for Upper Canada's surplus wheat in the 1830s must, therefore, have been in Lower Canada where, as is well known, the increasingly vulnerable local wheat economy died almost completely in these years.[19] Evidently the Upper Canadian producer supplanted the Lower Canadian farmer in such markets as the cities and the lumber camps. Sales could also be made to the Lower Canadian farm market itself, but only if the Lower Canadian farmer was both willing to buy and able to find marketable alternate crops rather than, as is often argued, retreating increasingly into self-sufficiency as he was compelled to abandon wheat production. Together these various markets, plus any net increases in stocks along the mercantile pipeline, were insufficient to maintain Upper Canadian prices, but evidently they did permit each year's harvest to be sold, for some income at least, and this must have helped sustain the process of frontier expansion. A sometimes neglected cash crop, ashes, must also have been important in providing some income to farmers.[20] Because of England's long-term inability to increase wheat output as fast as population increased, of which the years from 1829 to 1831 were an indication, these years of investment and uncertainty in the 1830s ultimately paid off; as a result, the 1840s and 1850s brought further large increases in Upper Canadian population, land under culture, and wheat output.

As the 1830s indicate, it was possible for an economy to survive and grow even when faced for some years with steeply declining volumes of exports to metropolitan markets and declining prices for the basic staple export. This sequence of developments in Upper Canada illustrates in turn some of the problems in working at a detailed level with staples theory as an explanatory framework.[21] These problems include a lack of specification of both the directions and the weights of linkages amongst the economic variables and a tendency to assert, more than to demonstrate, the ways in which the leading export sector has drawn the rest of the economy forward or held it back.

It has often been argued, for example, that the wheat staple was backwardly linked to transport investments and improvements.[22] This seems to have been true of local roads, which were improved as local resources permitted,[23] but the perceived need for and the decision to undertake such larger improvements as canals or trunk roads were, it can be argued, relatively autonomous from the staple sector[24] and directly related to it only insofar as funds had *eventually* to be found in the economy to pay for such improvements. The decision to build the Rideau and Welland canals preceded, and the actual construction was at least partially independent of, the contemporaneous wheat boom of 1829–31. It is evident that élites and governments anticipated rising demand and that at some point farmers would have been able to plan in anticipation of the completion of such works, but that is not the same as saying that the improvements had direct and necessary backward links from staple expansion. If this is arguable for Canadian canals, whose capacity greatly exceeded available traffic volumes,[25] it is much more so for the railroads that were developed in the 1850s. Despite Innis, who argued that wheat 'involved railways',[26] it should not be assumed that they were necessitated by the dictates of the wheat staple rather than by the politics of interested groups, notably the élites of competing cities and towns, and by the availability of credit in Britain to these groups and the government.

Typically, economic expansion occurred in a wave-like pattern, despite the more erratic year-by-year course of exports from the staple sector. This suggests that the pioneer economy had a momentum that was not predictably, or at least simply, linked to wheat exports. Expectations contributed to this momentum but, while they were based in part on developments in the staple market, it cannot be assumed that they always led or lagged behind observable changes by definite amounts of time. Inevitably, each wave of expansion came to an end, generally when commercial crisis struck the source of colonial capital and credit, the British economy. Adjustments were then required to bring earlier expectations into line with reality, reality being indicated by the economy's ability in a liquidity crisis to maintain payments on the debts incurred during the expansion. Such adjustments were reflected in the writing away of nominal assets by businesses and in reductions in land prices from peak levels; for those farmers, tradesmen, and entrepreneurs who had borrowed more than they could now pay, they often took the more extreme form of bankruptcy and/or moving on.[27] But even failures—the result, in effect, of expectations of the future that proved incorrect—left behind real improvements that could benefit others, thus permitting the economy to carry on to renew expansion when more favourable conditions returned.

Staples theory offers a good deal of insight into the relationships of a 'mature' staple economy to a wider metropolitan setting, but arguments such as these suggest viewing at least the *development* of a staple rather as a particular example of an investment process, which need not require a special approach through staples theory. From this viewpoint, a staple export boom appears less as the cause than as the result of growth, which first involved increased imports of people, goods, and capital.[28] It is these which the historian needs first to measure and to explain. Investment did not take place in a vacuum, without cognizance of potential opportunities, including those in the export sector, but it is hard to see the export sector as such as chronologically or analytically antecedent. The economy of Upper Canada was more complex than a narrow focus on the wheat staple alone would imply,[29] and the institutions and productive activities of that more complex economy deserve investigation; they ought not to be assumed to have been simply subservient to and consequent upon the staples sector. To say this is not to deny that exports needed to be developed to pay for imports, but the imports came first. Indeed, through the commercial system, imports could, to some degree, be capitalized, so that as little as the interest on their value might need to be paid immediately, rather than their entire cost. Such capitalization could occur, for example, through the development of local banks, which could transform promises to pay into money, and through the conversion of mercantile credits into longer-term investments, as when a merchant capitalized debts owed him by a customer.[30]

These arguments suggest a need for a more detailed and explicit model into which to fit Upper Canadian development. Such a model is needed above all to account for the timing and extent of movements of factors of production into (and out of) the new territory and to elaborate upon the consequences of each such wave. Through the use of economic indicators such as those drawn upon as examples in this paper, it should be possible to describe more clearly than hitherto at least the 'extensive' growth of the Upper Canadian economy. This being established, it will also be necessary to explore the still more complex question of the economy's 'intensive' growth, that is, growth in real income and in productivity.[31] An understanding of the latter will require evidence on such matters as shifts in Upper Canada's terms of trade and on improving productivity, whether technological (as in transport), organizational (as in the emergence of more specialized and efficient economic institutions), or as a result of an increase in productive resources (including cleared land) per capita.[32]

To take an investment approach is not to ignore that in many respects the new economy was more specialized than and therefore rather different from the metropolitan one of which it was an offshoot. But the emphasis that such an approach will take is likely to vary somewhat from that of a staples approach. The latter has given special attention to the geography and technology of the staple commodity, which have sometimes been seen as virtually determining the character of the entire society that developed around the staple.[33] Geography and technology, as they were involved in the expansion of the Upper Canadian wheat staple, were, however, largely given. The interesting historical questions are what determined the timing, the extent, and the consequences of investment in the application of known technology to known resources; the focus, therefore, will be on factors which changed, rather than on factors which, however basic, remained relatively constant.

Just as with the staples approach, an investment approach will emphasize the metropolitan economy of Britain as crucial to the dynamics of Upper Canada's economic change. In the simplest version of staples theory, however, that process may be pictured as one of dependence in terms of sales of export commodities. But that is only an aspect of a more complex process involving the trans-Atlantic movement of people and capital (a good deal of the latter, it should be recalled, in the form of goods). To understand these movements, it is essential to consider conditions in the British economy ranging well beyond demand for the staple product as such. Britain supplied, through growth and industrialization, the long-term stimuli for colonial expansion; through competition, the incentive and/or necessity for some of its capitalists and some of its middle and poorer classes to seek opportunity for themselves or (sometimes through intermediaries) their funds, abroad; through its financial institutions, capital resources, and credit system, the means to develop these opportunities; through its markets, the demand for such produce as the newly opened areas eventually yielded; and through its policies and, even more, its business cycle, the controls that largely determined the trade cycle in the newly opened economy. All of these were involved in determining the character and pace of development in Upper Canada.

Of course the production and marketing of Upper Canada's wheat must be analysed, but they cannot be considered independently. For example, it does not seem possible that one could say that, given certain conditions in the wheat market, certain consequences would necessarily have followed, and in a specified time. Research must therefore proceed more broadly. Central to it will be the processes and the extent of capital migration, management, formation, and diffusion, at private and public levels. This requires an understanding both of banking and of other credit systems, public and private, that predated or supplemented the banks; in all cases, the focus needs to be less on such issues as the politics of banks and more on the actual business activities and economic implications of these credit mechanisms. Finally, fundamental to this approach is the view that to increase our understanding of economic change and growth in Upper Canada, it is necessary to develop a clearer economic chronology; a stronger, logically integrated understanding of the processes of economic change; and more satisfactory measures of the scale and intensity of the successive waves of expansion that produced the Upper Canadian economy.

Suggestions for Further Reading

W.T. Easterbrook and M.H. Watkins, eds, *Approaches to Canadian Economic History* (Toronto, 1967).

Douglas McCalla, *The Upper Canada Trade, 1834–1872: A Study of the Buchanans' Business* (Toronto, 1979).

John McCallum, *Unequal Beginnings: Agriculture and Economic Development in Quebec and Ontario until 1870* (Toronto, 1980).

Notes

[1] G.M. Craig, *Upper Canada, The Formative Years, 1784–1841* (Toronto, 1963), 146.

[2] R.L. Jones, *History of Agriculture in Ontario, 1613–1880* (Toronto, 1946), 239, 243; R.C. Harris & John Warkentin, *Canada Before Confederation* (New York, 1974), 136. In this paper, 'wheat' normally includes wheat flour as well.

[3] H.G.J. Aitken, *The Welland Canada Company* (Cambridge, Mass., 1954), 13.

[4] See H.C. Pentland, 'The Role of Capital in Canadian Economic Development before 1875', *Canadian Journal of Economics and Political Science* xvi (1950), 462.

[5] H.S. Chapman, *A Statistical Sketch of the Corn Trade of Canada* (London, 1832), 5, 33–4.

[6] R.L. Jones, *op. cit.*, 123–5.

[7] Montreal *Gazette*, 23 May 1835, quoted in H.A. Innis and A.R.M. Lower, *Select Documents in Canadian Economic History 1783–1885* (Toronto, 1933), 250.

[8] H.G.J. Aitken, *op. cit.*, 141–2; A.D. Gayer, W.W. Rostow and Anna J. Schwartz, *The Growth and Fluctuation of the British Economy 1790–1850*, 2 vols (Oxford, 1953), I, 215, 251; D.G. Creighton, *The Empire of the St. Lawrence* (Toronto, 1956), 308; R.M. Breckenridge, *The Canadian Banking System 1817–1890* (Toronto, 1894), 53–62.

[9] J. Spelt, *Urban Development in South-Central Ontario* (Toronto, 1972), 69, 71, 89, 97; Leo Johnson, *History of the Country of Ontario, 1615–1875* (Whitby, 1973), 87.

[10] K. Kelly, 'Wheat Farming in Simcoe County in the Mid-Nineteenth Century', *Canadian Geographer* xv (1971), 103–4; T.F. McIlwraith, 'The Logistical Geography of the Great Lakes Grain Trade, 1820–1850' (PhD thesis, University of Wisconsin, 1973), 70.

[11] See the classic statement of this view in V.C. Fowke, *The National Policy and the Wheat Economy* (Toronto, 1957), 11–21.

[12] See, for example, Leo Johnson, 'The Settlement of the Western District 1749–1850', in F.H. Armstrong, *et al.*, eds, *Aspects of Nineteenth-Century Ontario* (Toronto, 1974), 23; and G.W. Brown, 'The Durham Report and the Upper Canadian Scene', *Canadian Historical Review (CHR)*, xx (1939), 138.

[13] H.C. Pentland, *op. cit.*, 458, 474; T. Naylor, 'The Rise and Fall of the Third Commercial Empire of the St. Lawrence', in G. Teeple, ed., *Capitalism and the National Question in Canada* (Toronto, 1972), 6–7. Such authors argue that in Upper Canada there was a shortage specifically of long-term capital. I would argue that capital was more mutable than such analytic distinctions imply. If it is meaningful to speak of a shortage of capital at all (the term 'shortage' requires clear definition), then it was capital in all forms that was lacking.

[14] T. LeGoff, 'The Agricultural Crisis in Lower Canada, 1802–12: A Review of a Controversy', CHR, iv (1974), 5–7.

[15] J.F. Shepherd and G.M. Walton, *Shipping, Maritime Trade and the Economic Development of Colonial North America* (Cambridge, 1972), 15.

[16] *Ibid.*, 20.

[17] T.F. McIlwraith, *op. cit.*, 50–90, 334–7.

[18] R.L. Jones, *op. cit.*, 123–5.

[19] F. Ouellet, *Le Bas-Canada 1791–1840; changements structuraux et crise* (Ottawa, 1976), 175–211.

[20]T.F. McIlwraith, *op. cit.*, 44.

[21]These problems have been widely discussed. See T.J.O. Dick, 'Frontiers in Canadian Economic History', *Journal of Economic History (JEH)*, xxxvi (1976), 35; M.H. Watkins, 'A Staple Theory of Economic Growth', in W.T. Easterbrook and M.H. Watkins, eds, *Approaches to Canadian Economic History* (Toronto, 1967), 50; J.D. Gould, *Economic Growth in History, Survey and Analysis* (London, 1972), 102–5; and K. Buckley, 'The Role of Staple Industries in Canada's Economic Development', *JEH*, xviii (1958), 439–60.

[22]M.H. Watkins, *op. cit.*, 55; C.F.J. Whebell, 'Corridors: A Theory of Urban Systems', *Annals of the Association of American Geographers*, lix (1969), 8; J.M. Gilmour, *Spatial Evolution of Manufacturing: Southern Ontario 1851–1891* (Toronto, 1972), 16.

[23]T.F. McIlwraith, 'The Adequacy of Rural Roads in the Era before Railways: An Illustration from Upper Canada', *Canadian Geographer*, xiv (1970), 354.

[24]H.G.J. Aitken, 'Government and Business in Canada: An Interpretation', *Business History Review*, xxxviii (1964), 8–13.

[25]T.F. McIlwraith, 'Freight Capacity and Utilization of the Erie and Great Lakes Canals before 1850', *JEH*, xxxvi (1976), 865–75.

[26]H.A. Innis, 'An Introduction to the Economic History of Ontario from Outpost to Empire', in his *Essays in Canadian Economic History* (Toronto, 1956), 116; see also his 'Unused Capacity as a Factor in Canadian Economic History', in *ibid.*, 148, 153.

[27]This is an aspect of the more general phenomenon of 'transiency'. See M. Katz, *The People of Hamilton, Canada West* (Cambridge, Mass., 1975), *passim*; and D. Gagan and H. Mays, 'Historical Demography and Canadian Social History: Families and Land in Peel County, Ontario', *CHR*, liv (1973), 35–41.

[28]E.J. Chambers and D.F. Gordon, 'Primary Products and Economic Growth: An Empirical Measurement', *Journal of Political Economy*, lxxiv (1966), 316–17; K.H. Norrie, 'The Rate of Settlement of the Canadian Prairies, 1870–1911', *JEH*, xxxv (1975), 414.

[29]K. Buckley, *op. cit.*, 444; J.D. Gilmour, *op. cit.*, 27; D. Gagan and H. Mays, *op. cit.*, 38, 41.

[30]A.H. Imlah, *Economic Elements in the Pax Britannica; Studies in British Foreign Trade in the Nineteenth Century* (Cambridge, Mass., 1958), 70–5; B. Hammond, *Banks and Politics in America from the Revolution to the Civil War* (Princeton, 1957), vii–ix; D. McCalla, 'The Buchanan Businesses, 1834–1872: A Study in the Organization and Development of Canadian Trade' (D. Phil. thesis, Oxford University, 1972), 170–2.

[31]J.H. Dales, *The Protective Tariff in Canada's Development* (Toronto, 1966), 154–8.

[32]J.F. Shepherd and G.M. Walton, 6–26.

[32]R. Neill, *A New Theory of Value: The Canadian Economics of H.A. Innis* (Toronto, 1972), 40–4.

18

Occupational Pluralism in

British North America

Béatrice Craig

The economy of British North America in the first half of the nineteenth century may have been pre-industrial, based chiefly upon agriculture and the extraction of certain staple raw materials, but nowhere was it anything less than an extremely complex web of inter-relationships. Small manufacturing establishments employing a handful of workers—shipyards, breweries, saddleries—were widely scattered, and in only a few regions was market-oriented agriculture (usually involving grain culture) predominant. In most of the provinces of British North America, some form of subsistence agriculture was combined with staples production. One combination was farming and fishing, another farming and fur-trading, and a third, farming and lumbering. The last was most prevalent and has come to be called the 'agroforestry' system. It was practised in virtually all provinces except Newfoundland before the confederation of Canada. Agroforestry

encouraged the perpetuation of farms located on marginal (or even soil-exhausted) land and often too small to be profitable. Lumbering or timbering could exist alongside farming, since the former was essentially a winter occupation and the latter a summer one. Lumbering provided farmers winter employment and a cash income. Contemporaries thought lumbering's effect on local agriculture was disastrous, drawing farmers out of the fields into the forests, but the reality is much more complicated.

Béatrice Craig explores one of the many zones of occupational overlap in British North America, this one the agroforestry region of the Upper St John Valley in New Brunswick, sometimes known as Madawaska. She finds a regional society displaying the characteristics of both agriculture and forestry. The lumber industry made possible the growth of population, by providing economic opportunity for many who could not have survived by farming alone. But it encouraged social stratification, particularly by distinguishing successful farmers from those marginal farmers who gained their major income from cash wages and who became trapped in a cycle of impoverishment.

Did agroforestry in the Upper St John Valley prevent good farming or, alternatively, provide some sort of safety net for those who were not or could not be successful at agriculture? Why was working for wages more marginalizing than full-time farming? How would the residents of the Valley have felt about the possibility of work in the forest industry? Would they have seen this option as wage-slavery, or as an opportunity for employment that made it possible to remain close to their roots? What, on balance, were the advantages and disadvantages of agroforestry in the Upper St John Valley?

This article first appeared, titled 'Agriculture and the Lumberman's Frontier in the Upper St John Valley, 1800–70', in *Journal of Forest History*, 32 (July 1988), 125–37.

In many sections of the early nineteenth-century northeast Canadian frontier, agriculture and the lumber industry were closely interconnected.[1] We know that the interrelationships were pervasive, but we know little about the details, and as Graeme Wynn has pointed out, they defy generalization. Farmers' participation in the lumber industry varied by time, place, and the needs of the individuals involved.[2]

In some regions, an established lumber industry encouraged the creation of agricultural settlements.[3] In others, agriculture and forest industries developed simultaneously. On the Canadian shield—the Ottawa valley, Mauricie district, and Saguenay–Lac St Jean region—agriculture and the lumber industry established a symbiotic relationship. Farmers needed the supplementary income from winter work in the lumber camps, as their farms could not sell enough farm products to provide for their needs; and the lumber industry needed the cheap labor the farmers represented. The French geographer Raoul Blanchard, and more recently Norman Séguin, have dubbed this symbiotic relationship between agriculture and forestry the 'agroforestry' system.

The Canadian agroforestry system was born of the simultaneous expansion of agriculture and the lumber industry.[4] The opening of lumber camps attracted a surplus population driven from older parishes by a need for land. The roads built by the lumber operators allowed them to penetrate outlying areas but left them far enough away from major markets to preclude their integration into the larger commercial networks. The farming families therefore depended for cash income on winter work and on the sale of their commodities to the lumber camps.

Settlement in the Upper St John Valley, 1794–1870

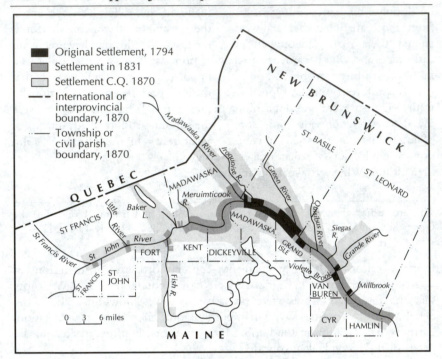

At its worst, the agroforestry system resulted in stagnant agriculture and low wages in the lumber industry. There was no incentive to increase agricultural production, and farmers had no choice but to accept the wages and conditions of work offered by the lumber companies. The latter, knowing their workers grew most of their food, kept cash wages low and viewed the money as a supplemental rather than a living wage. Under such conditions, it is not surprising that the standard of living was low and the farming population—even the land-owning families—was mobile.[5]

This model does not satisfactorily account for the development of all agricultural communities that coexisted in time and space with the forest industries. Agriculture could precede logging. What happened when an established farming community found itself in the path of the lumberman's frontier? How did the newly arrived lumber industry affect both the settlement and its individual members?

This question is pertinent because the social evolution of eighteenth- and nineteenth-century pioneer settlements in eastern Canada and New England very much reflected each community's economic base. The early years were usually characterized by a favorable ratio of resources to settlers. But sooner or later population outstripped resources. When there was no longer enough land to establish the coming generation on new farms, families either sold their holdings and moved where resources were more abundant, or each father bequeathed his farm to one son who then provided his siblings with cash settlements. In either case, some degree of social stratification and out-migration inevitably resulted. Descendants of founding families who inherited land gradually rose to the top of the social ladder, and immigrants and noninheriting children (hereafter referred to as 'nonheirs') had difficulties improving their social status and usually chose to emigrate. But if the community was able to diversify its economic resources, out-migration was slowed or even reversed, and the local social hierarchy was not always dominated by farmers.[6]

Was the lumber industry a form of economic diversification sufficient to prevent this increasing social stratification and emigration in later generations? Did it provide the additional resources necessary to support an ever-increasing population? And did the entire farming community or only a few privileged farmers directly or indirectly benefit from the forest industries?

We can try to answer these questions by examining the upper St John valley. This region now forms the boundary between Maine and New Brunswick: the south bank of the river is American; the north bank, Canadian. It was opened to settlement in 1785 by people of French Canadian and Acadian origins.[7] In its earlier days, it was also known as the 'Madawaska settlement'. In the winter of 1824, forty years after its founding, some lumbermen started operations in the vicinity, and the industry never left.[8] The lumber industry and its spinoff, pulp and paper manufacturing, joined with agriculture as the basis of the local economy. Unlike in the agroforestry system, the farming sector of the upper St John was not merely the handmaiden of the forest industry, providing lumber camps with hay and oats, teams of animals, and cheap labor. It was a viable activity that fed a fast-growing population. After the railroads reached the valley in 1869 the farms of the upper St John even began to export potatoes.

What emerged on the banks of the St John after 1825 was a dual community displaying some features found in agrarian communities and some typical of agroforestry areas. As happens in strictly agrarian communities, descendants of the founding families, in possession of the best land, soon dominated the social structure and controlled local politics. They engaged in commercial farming and benefited, often indirectly, from the presence of lumber camps. Yet the Madawaska settlement also displayed features typical of agroforestry settlements. Lumber barons and their associates controlled most of the highly capitalized business ventures: logging, lumber manufacturing, shingle and clapboard mills, and general trade. They also controlled most local wage-earning opportunities and were the major local sources of credit. At the bottom of the social ladder were poor immigrants and non-heirs, established on poorer land, working in the logging shanties in winter to make ends meet, and on the whole more footloose than the commercial farmers.

The Economic Evolution of the Upper St John Valley

The thirty-three Acadian families from the Fredericton area who first settled in the upper St John valley in 1785 were joined quickly by a slightly smaller number of families and some single people from the lower St Lawrence valley (Rivière Ouelle-Kamouraska region). By 1799 the population of the upper St John was 331, half of whom were under twelve years of age.[9] The population grew steadily afterward, thanks to a combination of natural increase and immigration from the lower St Lawrence. By 1820 the settlement had almost twelve hundred people.[10]

The local society was tightly bound by numerous kinship ties, partly as a result of intermarriage, but also because most people who moved to the upper St John had relatives already established there.[11] Until 1825, settlement and kinship networks were coterminous.

Newcomers and second-generation residents spread along the banks of the river. Settlers claimed and occupied the best sites first: intervale land, sites opposite large islands, and mill sites.[12] The residents planned ahead for future generations by reserving unimproved lots for their children.[13]

Until the opening of the lumber camps, agriculture was the sole economic base of the community. Evidence about farming in the years before 1850 is scattered: a few tithing records, some occupational mentions in the parish registers, a land-agent report for 1831, an agricultural survey taken in the winter of 1833, and some comments from visitors, journalists, and public officials.[14]

The evidence is diverse, but the picture that emerges is nonetheless coherent: established on good soil, the fast-growing community of farmers was normally able to feed, house, and clothe its members, but it was unable to integrate fully into the regional commercial networks because it was too far from potential markets. Until 1850 virtually all residents were farmers; craftsmen and millers very often farmed as well.[15] All grew wheat, potatoes, peas, hay, and oats, and raised animals. Every visitor described the land along the St John as very fertile.[16] Even today, agronomists consider the St John valley to be among the best agricultural land in Maine, New Brunswick, and eastern Quebec.[17]

One can estimate the average agricultural production per household from the tithing records for 1799 and 1804 (whole settlement), 1832 and 1841 (western section), and from the 1851 New Brunswick agricultural census, which contains aggregate figures for agricultural production (see Table 1).[18]

Table 1. Production per Household, 1799–1851

	1799	1804	1832[a]	1841[a]	1851[b]
Number of households	56	100	113	140	550
Wheat (bushels)	51	42	29	15	4
Oats (bushels)	10	11	10	22	61
Peas (bushels)	8	8	10	11	13
Potatoes (bushels)	67	75	88	123	106
Buckwheat (bushels)	1	0	0	10	59
All grains[c]	64	—[d]	—[d]	57	135

a. In these years data are only available for the western section.
b. Northern bank only.
c. Wheat, oats, buckwheat, barley, rye, Indian corn.
d. No data available.

SOURCES Tithing records for 1799, 1804, 1832 and 1841, Lettres des prêtres missionnaires; Victoria County section of the New Brunswick provincial census, 1851 (see footnotes to text for full citations).

Such quantities should have supplied the needs of the average household, which would also own a few animals, a milk cow, a garden, some meadows, and a wood-lot.[19] The figures compare favorably with the self-sufficiency threshold proposed by Bettye Hobbs-Pruitt for late eighteenth-century Massachusetts farms. She defines farms that produced fewer than thirty bushels of grain a year as not self-sufficient, and those that produced more than forty-five bushels as enjoying a comfortable surplus.[20]

Another approach would be to compare the figures above with the food rations required in 'deeds of maintenance', by which an elderly person would give his land to a younger one in exchange for maintenance until his death. The deed of maintenance very often listed in great detail everything the elderly person expected to receive. Yearly food rations usually included ten bushels of wheat or the equivalent in flour, one bushel of peas, six bushels of potatoes, one half-bushel of salt, twenty-five pounds of maple sugar, one hundred pounds of clear pork, fifty pounds of beef or mutton, some garden produce, and some store-bought items (spices, tea, brandy, rice, etc.). Buckwheat was almost never mentioned, and barley was mentioned only as a substitute for rice. The recipient of the farm also provided the donor with a plowed and manured garden lot and boarded his milk cow. Quantities of home-grown items varied very little over time or from family to family. This was not the case with store-bought items and articles of clothing, which reflected the wealth of the individual family and increased in quantity and value over the years.[21]

The average St John valley family had a diet qualitatively different from the one considered ideal by the elderly: less wheat bread, more potatoes and buckwheat pancakes. Still, food was abundant, and the average resident could eat as much food as an old farmer or farmer's wife who could afford to retire on a deed of maintenance.

The figures in Table 1 are the average per household, not per farm. They suggest that the Madawaska settlement produced enough foodstuffs globally to cover the needs of its population. They do not necessarily imply that every individual family managed to be self-sufficient. As we shall see later, a significant number of farms produced less than average at all times. Consequently some others must have produced comfortable surpluses. Such a situation is normal in subsistence-farming communities, as most of the literature demonstrates.[22]

Although agriculture provided adequately for the needs of the population in normal years, two factors slowed its development. The first was nature, which was not always cooperative. The frost-free season in the upper St John is only 108 days.[23] Untimely frosts in the spring or fall could, and did, spell disaster. Local authorities blamed the weather for the crop failures in 1816, 1817, 1828, 1829, 1833, 1840, and 1855. Provincial and state authorities, and agricultural historians, blame the failures of the wheat crop throughout the northeast (New England and Quebec) during the 1830s on the wheat midge. Whatever the reason for the failures, by 1850 farmers throughout the northeast had abandoned the cultivation of wheat.[24]

The second factor stifling agricultural development was remoteness and the resulting poor communication with urban markets. There was no local market for agricultural products before 1824, and the nearest other market at Rivière du Loup, on the St Lawrence, was seventy miles away. Travelers had to boat up the Madawaska River and Temiscouata Lake and then walk the rest of the way through the portage route, a former Indian trail. This route was adequate for people and mail, but not for bulky agricultural products. According to an 1831 report by surveyor Bouchette, the Madawaska settlers had never tried to sell products in Lower Canada.[25]

The Madawaska settlers sold their products more frequently in the more easily accessible, but far more distant, city of Fredericton, 170 miles downriver. They exported wheat there in 1825.[26] In 1831 Bouchette reported that they milled their wheat and exported 'considerable quantities' of flour to Fredericton, where it sold well at a good price.[27] In another 1831 report, American agents Deane and Kavanagh mentioned the export of large amounts of maple sugar.[28] In 1848 the St John valley sent timber, 'small quantities of wheat', fur, and maple sugar to Fredericton.[29] The exports of the Madawaska settlement, therefore, consisted mainly of high-priced grain or flour and natural products.

But ready sales and good prices did not necessarily imply a profit high enough to warrant increased production. Transportation costs were horrendous: when the provincial government had to send food relief to the settlers (corn meal and rye flour) in December 1833, transportation costs were equal to the value of the goods.[30] Bringing agricultural products to the market was inconvenient and not very profitable.[31] Remoteness both kept the Madawaska district from developing a commercial agriculture integrated into the provincial trading network and forced the Madawaskayans into a high degree of self-sufficiency.[32] The area only acquired efficient links with outside markets when the railroad finally reached the St John in the 1870s.

The upper St John boasted another natural resource that attracted considerable attention from outsiders in the second quarter of the nineteenth century: white pines. The New Brunswick forest industry had steadily pushed toward the interior of the province. Until 1820 most of the cuttings were in a broad belt that included the mid-St John valley and parts of the Miramichi and the Richibucto districts. By 1825 the major focus of activity had shifted to the northwest and included the Tobique and North Miramichi. During this period the provincial government issued the first timber licenses for the upper St John valley.[33] In the upper St John valley 4,760 tons of timber were cut in 1824–25.[34] The first sawmill directed at the export market instead of the local market was built in 1827 by the Peters and Wilmot firm, a lumber concern headquartered close to the mouth of the Tobique River on the mid-St John.[35]

The arrival of the loggers triggered an international crisis. The boundaries between northern Maine and British North America had not yet been drawn in 1825, and the upper St John was in the center of the disputed territory. Both Maine and New Brunswick were unwilling to give up the revenues that could accrue to them from the forest industry. Each party certainly did not want the other to cut what both Canadians and Americans perceived as 'their' timber. The British government decided to suspend logging in the disputed territory, and in 1826 the New Brunswick government recalled the licenses it had issued. Maine similarly prohibited logging in the disputed area.

Unfortunately for international peace, the lumber operators were unwilling to give up the opportunity to exploit the virgin pine groves of the St John and Aroostook valleys (major parts of the disputed territory), and lumbermen had a history of ignoring regulations they did not like.[36] The disputed territory was too large to be policed effectively, so the official policy was widely disregarded on both sides of the river. This outraged the state of Maine, which sent an armed posse up to the St John in 1839 to try to protect 'her' logs from lawless 'British' trespassers.[37]

The boundary conflict was settled in 1842 with the St John River becoming the international border. Americans were granted navigation rights on its waters, and lumber cut on the American side and floated down the St John was, by a clause of the treaty, considered as British timber for customs purposes. This last clause allowed operators on the American side of the St

John to benefit from imperial preference and compete in the British market on the same footing as the British North Americans.[38]

The settlement of the boundary legalized logging on the upper St John but did not result in an era of prosperity. Britain gradually reduced the tariff preference given to colonial lumber on the British market in 1842 and again in 1846, and British American merchants tried to sell large amounts of lumber in Britain before the two new laws took effect. This glutted the market and brought the industry to a standstill in 1848 and 1849.[39] Operations on the upper St John were significantly affected. The provincial authorities issued seven licenses to cut timber in the area in 1845, sixteen in 1846, seventeen in 1847, but only four in 1848 and 1849. The amount cut rose from 10,008 tons in 1845 to 32,960 in 1847, then fell to 5,990 and 2,881 in 1848 and 1849.[40]

Despite its ups and downs, the forest industry had a lasting impact upon the upper St John valley. It accelerated demographic growth and geographical expansion, created a wide range of economic opportunities for the local population, and permanently altered the local social structure.

The Lumber Industry, Demographic Growth, and Geographic Expansion

Because the Madawaska-district lumber industry attracted and retained immigrants who otherwise would have sought their fortunes elsewhere, immigration was a significant factor in local demographic growth and geographic expansion. The opening of the lumber camps coincided with the arrival of a large wave of immigrants from French Canada.[41] This wave lasted two years, from 1826 to 1827 (see Figure 1 and Table 2). The succeeding years were bleak ones for the settlement. Because of the boundary dispute, New Brunswick authorities refused to renew timber licenses, and although some cutting continued, the illegality of the industry undoubtedly slowed its growth. In addition, there were repeated crop failures. Immigration had accelerated by 1836, but this wave was also short-lived. In 1838 immigration fell to the 1826 level and continued to fall: in 1838 and 1839 war threatened in the St John valley, and in 1840 the crops failed again. After 1840 immigration increased slightly, but it dropped during the lumber bust of 1848 and 1849. During periods of stagnant immigration, the area's population shrank outright due to out-migration.

Nonetheless the population grew rapidly over the long term through the combination of immigration and natural increase. The 1,171 people of 1820 were 2,474 in 1830, 3,460 in 1840, 6,167 in 1850 and slightly more than 14,000 by 1870.[42] The newcomers and the adult children of long-established residents quickly occupied the remaining river lots. When land agent Coffin visited the settlement in 1825, the area between the Madawaska and Grand

Figure 1. Migration into and out of the Upper St John Valley, 1820–50

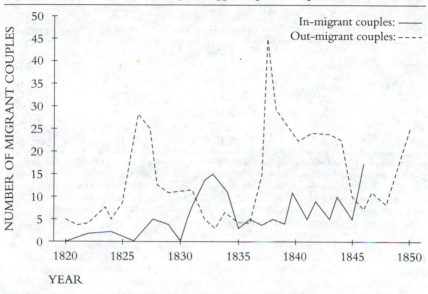

rivers was almost entirely occupied and the settlement had begun to expand upriver (see map).[43] By 1831 the occupied area had spread west as far as the Meruimticook River, creating an unbroken ribbon of farms, thirty-three miles long and two miles wide.[44] By 1845 continuous settlement extended from the east line of the state to the mouth of the St Francis River (about seventy miles). The major tributaries of the St John, especially the Madawaska River, also attracted settlers.[45] By that time some farmers, especially in the central part of the settlement, had begun to open back lots farther uphill.

On the United States side of the river, geographical and population expansion slowed in the 1860s and 1870s when the state of Maine sold most of the remaining land to large landowners who intended to exploit the timber.[46] Second, third, and even fourth tiers of settlements stacked up from the river bottoms were more common on the New Brunswick side, but geographic expansion in that direction was blocked in the 1870s when the provincial government granted large areas of the remaining uncleared uplands to the New Brunswick Railway Company.[47]

Since the birth rate among the Madawaska settlers was high and infant mortality low, the population of the Madawaska district would have increased even without immigration.[48] Immigration accelerated the growth of the district, however, and the lumber industry made immigration more attractive. This becomes clear if we compare the years between 1800 and 1825 with

Table 2. Estimated Net Migration to Madawaska, 1803–50

Date	Total population	Corrected population[a]	Natural increase[b]	Net migration
1803	456	456	—[c]	—[c]
1820	1,171	1,160	481	+ 223
1830	2,474	2,249	638	+ 451
1833	2,518	2,403	336	− 182
1834	2,272	2,170	98	− 331
1840	3,460	3,227	869	+ 188
1850[d]	6,167	5,580	1,910	+ 457

a. These figures exclude non-Catholics. These people are identified through a linkage of family reconstitution cards derived from: parish registers; the 1820, 1830, and 1850 population schedules; and the 1834 Report of the Commissioners (see note on sources). The 1834 provincial census and the 1840 US census provide only aggregate population figures. I assume the proportion of non-Catholics was the same in 1834 as in 1833, and estimate the 1840 proportion of non-Catholics by interpolation between the 1833 and 1850 figures.

b. Natural increase equals the number of births less the number of deaths.

c. The sources available do not allow such calculations for 1850–70.

d. The United States took a census of the right bank of the river in 1850; New Brunswick counted its population in 1851. The New Brunswick census also indicates the number of births and deaths during the preceding year and indicates the year immigrants arrived in the province. French Canadian immigrants all came from Canada East, a separate province. One can therefore estimate with relative accuracy the population of the left bank a year before the census was taken.

SOURCES   Parish registers of St Basile, St Bruno, and Ste Luce; Lettres des prêtres missionnaires; US censuses for 1820, 1830, 1840, and 1850; Report of the Commissioners, 1834; Papers of the Legislative Assembly relating to the Settlement of Madawaska; *Journal of the House of Assembly of New Brunswick*, 1835, appendix, PANB (see footnotes to text for full citations).

those between 1825 and 1845. In both periods immigrants sought farmland: one soon finds them clearing and planting, but the quality and/or amount of land available to the latecomers was less and less sufficient for them to live well from farming alone. Great quantities of good land were available before 1825, but the larger wave of immigrants came when the good land was almost all taken. Before 1825 immigration was numerically small (about two families, or thirteen persons, per year) and few newcomers stayed unless they had kin ties to a previous Madawaska resident (see Table 3). After 1825 immigration increased and the link between residential persistence and kinship weakened. The lumber industry may have been the key variable allowing the later migrants to do without networks of supportive relatives.

The years during which a pioneer family cleared the land were very precarious: it was difficult to raise enough food to survive, let alone find the means to stock and equip the farm. Some pioneers brought capital (stock, tools, provisions); others had relatives who would not let them starve in late spring and early summer. Those who had neither capital nor relatives were at a high risk of failing, until the lumber industry provided them with the

Table 3. Kinship and Persistence among Immigrant Couples, 1803–42

| | With kin at Madawaska | | | | | Without known kin | | | | |
| | Persisted | | Did not | | Total | Persisted | | Did not | | Total |
Period	Number	Per cent	Number	Per cent	Number	Number	Per cent	Number	Per cent	Number
1800–25	28	90	3	10	31	9	33	18	67	27
1825–29	32	80	8	20	40	18	44	23	56	43
1830–36	16	84	3	16	19	10	34	19	66	29
1837–42	35	92	3	8	38	58	67	30	34	88

SOURCES Parish registers of St Basile, St Bruno, and Ste Luce (see footnotes to text for full citations).

extra edge they needed to survive. The wages from winter work in the lumber industry supplemented the production of not-yet-profitable farms and allowed pioneer families to buy food from their neighbors.

But winter wages could not protect pioneer families from the effects of a general crop failure. When food was in short supply, the established farmers kept it for themselves. They may have shared with their children who had just started clearing, but the recent immigrants were forced to leave to escape starvation. Until 1845 out-migrant families were almost always recently arrived ones: 80 per cent of the transients had been in the community fewer than four years.[49]

By helping families survive the pioneer years, the lumber industry encouraged immigration and population growth. After 1845, when the best riparian land had been claimed and occupied, the lumber industry provided the economic alternative necessary to reduce the out-migration of newcomers and nonheirs who would otherwise have had to seek their fortunes elsewhere. But the lumber industry could not fully compensate for the shrinking supply of land. After 1845 population growth slowed down. Between 1790 and 1820 population increased by 9 to 10 per cent each year. After the lumber camps opened in the 1820s the growth rate accelerated slightly, to 11 per cent, but afterward population increases slowed—first to 8 per cent in the late 1830s, then down to 5 per cent by the 1860s.[50]

The Lumber Industry and Economic Opportunities

The impact of the lumber industry on the economy of the upper St John valley was both direct and indirect. The industry created direct opportunities for entrepreneurs, expanded the available range of wage-earning occupations, and opened a market for agricultural products. Because logging also accelerated population growth by attracting immigrants who, for a few years at least, might have difficulty living wholly off the land, the lumber industry indirectly boosted the demand for consumer goods and services. This boost may have been just enough to sustain local small-scale industries.

Between 1825 and 1870 St John valley entrepreneurs engaged in logging and lumber manufacturing, in trading wood products and general merchandise, and in milling. They seldom specialized in a single activity. Lumbermen owned stores; storekeepers and millers traded in lumber.

The wealthiest entrepreneurs devoted most of their time and energy to logging and trading timber and lumber, but it is impossible to assess the extent of their operations before 1842. Since neither Maine nor New Brunswick allowed cutting, lumbermen tried their best to keep their activities secret, playing hide-and-seek with state and provincial authorities. One of the local priests recorded an ingenious way to dodge the law: illegally cut logs were floated downriver and passed for wood legally removed from land over which New Brunswick had undisputed jurisdiction.[51]

After the boundary dispute was settled in 1842 outsiders moved to the St John valley to log, and they became the area's lumber barons. Sometimes they did not even reside in the valley permanently. A small majority of them were Americans; the others came from New Brunswick or Lower Canada. They operated on both sides of the river, and thus both in Canada and the United States. A representative family were the Glasiers from Sunbury County, New Brunswick, who logged up the St Francis River and purchased a whole township (thirty-six square miles) from the state of Maine in 1849.[52]

Large-scale logging required a large outlay of capital. Timberland was sold in large parcels (the state of Maine sold land by the quarter-township), and working that land required equipping and feeding large teams of workers and animals. In 1867, for example, the Glasiers owed their storekeeper $14,700 for provisions and equipment.[53] Activities on such a scale were beyond the reach of the locally born farmers: in 1850 the richest farmer on the American side was worth only four thousand dollars, and in 1861 the richest farmer in New Brunswick had a farm valued at ten thousand dollars.[54]

Locally born individuals were nonetheless not entirely excluded from the circle of entrepreneurs. Some managed to become small-scale lumbermen. Well-to-do farmers could afford yearly licenses, which were available for as little as two acres of New Brunswick timberland.[55] Often, small-scale logging was combined with other activities such as farming, trading, and milling. For instance, Registe Theriault, whose St Basile farm was valued at ten thousand dollars in 1861, logged regularly. He also owned a triple saw/grist/carding mill worth two thousand dollars.[56]

Unlike lumber manufacturing, which seems to have been in the hands of anglophone outsiders or immigrants, custom milling was dominated by locally born people. Custom mills were not heavily capitalized. In the period between 1860 and 1871, they were worth between four hundred dollars for a buckwheat mill and twenty-five hundred dollars for a combination mill in a prime location.[57]

On the whole, businesses that required large amounts of capital, extensive credit, and integration into extra-local commercial networks were controlled by entrepreneurs who were originally from outside the St John valley. Businesses that required smaller amounts of capital and a local market remained in the hands of the wealthier local farmers. Logging on the St John offered nonlocal entrepreneurs potentially huge profits and local farmers a chance to diversify and achieve a very comfortable standard of living.

Conventional wisdom has it that farmers in the agroforestry system needed the income of seasonal labor from logging for their economic survival. How dependent upon winter work were the Madawaska settlers?

Direct evidence about who worked in the shanties is lacking, but indirect evidence suggests that at any given time a significant number of families could not have lived from farming alone. This reflected the difficulty of colonizing and clearing the land. In 1831, 24 per cent of the lots had been in cultivation less than five years, and 18 per cent of all farms had less than five acres cleared. Clearing had not even started on 11 per cent of the lots (see Figure 2). In 1833 only 52 per cent of households had an operating farm. The others had land, but hardly any stock and little or no crops. This figure may be abnormally high because 1833 was the year of the most severe crop failure. An unusually wet summer and early frost destroyed crops. The sources also suggest the crops had been inadequate the preceding year, and many people did not have enough seeds in the spring of 1833. In 1842, 24 per cent of the lots on the American side had been taken in the previous five years. Two-thirds of these were not yet under cultivation, and the others averaged only seven cultivated acres.[58]

Evidence about farm values provided by the US census suggests the situation stayed about the same after the treaty of 1842. The 1850 US census lists the value of farms worth three hundred dollars or more, and only 40 per cent of the farms in the district qualified. Although almost all heads of households had land, and in some cases well-located land, the census-takers listed 60 per cent as 'laborers', suggesting they did not believe those people could yet make a living from their holdings.[59] Since no taxes were levied in the valley on the US side until 1869, this classification seems likely to be accurate and not to reflect the respondents' attempt to underestimate their own taxable property.

The 1870 US census lists all real estate worth more than one hundred dollars. Twenty-six per cent of all the heads of households were worth less than that amount. Some of these families were clearing, some were established on marginal land, and others had only a small amount of land to cultivate.[60] The New Brunswick census did not list the value of the farms but revealed rapid growth in their numbers: from 421 in 1851 to 943 in 1871, an increase of 124 per cent over twenty years.[61] Danhoff estimates that it took five to seven years to make a farm, so it seems likely that in a given year between 15 and 20 per cent of all the farms were not yet sufficiently cleared to support their owners.[62] These owners surely sought additional income, and after 1825 many probably worked in the woods.

Figure 2. Land Cleared on Farms in the Upper St John Valley, 1831

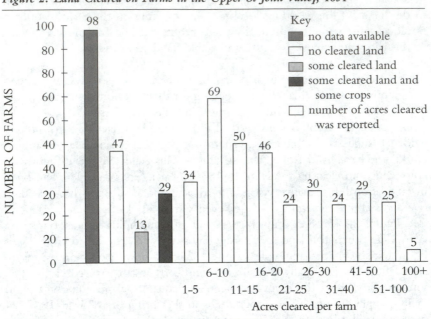

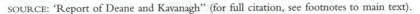

SOURCE: 'Report of Deane and Kavanagh" (for full citation, see footnotes to main text).

This could explain why cash—as opposed to agricultural products, manufactured goods, or personal labor—was the most common medium used in settling accounts in the stores.

Farmers who needed additional income were not limited to shanty work. Anyone who had a horse or a team of oxen and a sleigh—for all practical purposes, all established farmers—could earn extra money transporting supplies to the camps. General traders needed people to deliver goods first to the store and later to their customers. The rates paid by the two stores for which we have records were similar: 20 shillings ($4.86) to take a load of hay or oats from the mouth of the Madawaska to the St Francis River in winter, 35 shillings ($8.40) to Temiscouata Lake during 1845–55. This was rather good money: these same storekeepers paid general laborers 1 shilling (24 cents) a day. One of the ledgers contains a single mention of wages paid to a shanty worker: 40 shillings ($9.72) per month in 1845.[63] Carting and sleighing had some disadvantages: the work was irregular and paid in truck—in store goods rather than in cash. But it would have been an appropriate occupation for a man needing small amounts of money to purchase store goods.

Historians of the agroforestry system suggest that agriculture in these regions remained at subsistence level because of poor soil quality and poor access to markets. The farmers consumed most of what they grew, with the exception of the oats and hay they produced for the shanties. What kind of agriculture prevailed in the St John valley? And to what extent was agriculture affected by the lumber industry?

By 1850 the dominant crops in the St John valley were those usually found in agroforestry settlements: oats, hay, buckwheat, and potatoes. Wheat and potatoes had been the major crops at the beginning of the century, but a shift in crops followed the crop failures of 1828–33. Farmers gave up wheat, which they could sell but could not grow reliably in the 1840s, but this decision did not reduce the community's income by as much as it could have twenty years before. The lumber camps provided a potential substitute market for at least one of the replacement crops: oats. Nevertheless, there does not seem to be a direct cause-and-effect between the lumber industry's penetration and the crop shift. Logging had been going on for almost fifteen years before wheat was really given up (see Table 1).

Productivity was uneven. The parish of St Basile, on the New Brunswick side, was far more productive than its neighbors in 1851 and 1861, but by 1871 its production was below the valley average, which itself had dropped (see Table 4). This drop in productivity may reflect poorer soil on recently cleared farms, which would inevitably reduce mean productivity of all farms. Location, quality of the soil, acreage, and number of people able to work in the family all contributed to variations in productivity among farms.

Productivity varied not only from parish to parish, but also from individual to individual. A small number of farmers systematically produced surpluses of specific commodities. As early as 1833, a small minority (5 per cent) of the farms operating in the Madawaska district produced three to four times the average farm's totals of grain, potatoes, and hay.[64]

The same trend emerges in the 1850 US agricultural census. Paul Cyr, who had the highest-valued farm on the US side, produced five times the average quantity of oats, three times that of hay and buckwheat, and two and a half times the average amount of potatoes. Cyrille Dufour, brother to two traders, channeled his business interests into his farm. He produced 1,000 bushels of oats, when the average among the enumerated farms was only 155 bushels. He also produced more hay and buckwheat than average. The two largest amounts of hay (120 and 100 tons, six and five times the average) were cut by two anglophone farmers who had connections with the lumber industry in the western part of the settlement. Most of these people also produced very substantial quantities of other crops and had a lot of stock. They not only provided for their own needs in food, clothing, and shelter from their land; they marketed a substantial surplus as well.[65]

The number of farmers producing much more than the average of a given commodity was small, but their production was so much larger than their neighbors' that it had to have been deliberately planned. These farmers planted extra fields for a market.

Table 4. Production per Farm in Madawaska

| | 1851 | | 1861 | | 1871 | |
	St Basile	North Bank	St Basile	North Bank	St Basile	North Bank
Number of farms	103	421	120	486	215	943
Wheat	5	5	14	8	5	6
Oat	115	77	125	79	58	68
Buckwheat	128	79	76	63	59	68
All grains[a]	249	177	221	171	124	147
Peas	22	17	21	14	9	9
Potatoes	144	138	124	99	157	105
Milk cows[b]	8	6	4	4	2	2
Meat cattle	3	3	3	2	2	2
Horses	2	1	2	1	1	1
Sheep	18	12	16	10	9	7
Swine	9	6	6	4	3	3

a. Wheat, oat, barley, rye, maize, and buckwheat.
b. All figures rounded.

SOURCES   New Brunswick provincial censuses, agricultural schedules, 1851, 1861, 1871 (see footnotes to text for full citations).

But which market? The lumber camps bought oats and hay for their horses and oxen, but large-scale farmers did not limit themselves to growing more oats and hay than they needed. They also grew more grain, potatoes, and raised more animals than average. Storekeepers purchased only small quantities of agricultural products other than oats and hay from local people. John Emmerson, who supplied the Glasier camps, imported from outside the St John valley most of the foodstuffs he sold to the shanties; he bought his flour in Lower Canada, for instance.[66]

Local farmers with commodities other than oats and hay to sell must have skipped the middlemen and sold directly to their customers. The latter may have been smaller-scale lumbermen to whom they were related, or farmers with uncleared land or small holdings who went to the woods in winter. Such farmers needed supplies in the early summer, and they had money to buy them if they had worked during the winter. There was no reason for the large farmers to take their goods to the store; the customers would come and knock at their doors. Small farmers were as likely a market for local agricultural products as were lumber camps, but unfortunately it is not possible to assess the relative importance of each. We can define the range of opportunities available to farmers to earn money through nonfarming activities, and we can define the range of available marketing strategies. We cannot know, however, how individuals fit their opportunities into their economic strategies.

Nevertheless, we can draw a plausible picture of the economic impact of the lumber industry on this originally self-sufficient community of farmers. Business ventures requiring a fair amount of capital slipped into the hands of outsiders. Other economic activities, aimed mostly at providing the local population with food, shelter, and clothing, remained in local hands. Individuals who owned sizable farms and had a sufficiently large household to provide the labor they needed were self-sufficient, earned money in the winter as transporters, and raised a marketable surplus of goods. Oats and hay were sold to the lumber camps, with the local storekeeper acting as broker. Other agricultural products were sold directly to the customers, who were likely to be lumberjack-farmers. Farmers of substance had several options to provide for needs beyond mere subsistence.

But there were less fortunate farmers who could not provide for all their needs through farming alone. They had a much narrower range of options. Working in the woods during the winter may have been their only viable outside opportunity. Such farmers were vulnerable to bankruptcy and perhaps starvation in bad years, either in farming or in the lumber industry. Recessions and crop failures could force them to emigrate.

Evolution of the Social Structure

Economic and social divisions coincided. The men with capital and business contacts came from the outside. Even when they lived in the Madawaska district, they did not mingle with its other residents. Through its entire history, the St John valley population has been at least 90 per cent francophone and 95 per cent Catholic. Immigrant businessmen in the nineteenth century invariably spoke English and were Protestant. Language and religion stood in the way of full integration through intermarriage. For all their economic might and for all their money, the anglophone immigrants were not integrated into the local society and remained a force from the outside.

Some descendants of the founding families, who were all francophone and Catholic, fared very well. They inherited the best farms and the mill sites. They improved their land and diversified their activities. They not only provided for their own needs but also grew produce for market, milled, and hired servants. They married the daughters of substantial farmers and were part of an extensive network of kin.[67] They translated wealth and social capital into political power. The bulk of the state representatives, members of Parliament, justices of the peace, and other elected or nominated officials on either side of the border came from this narrow group of wealthy farmers and millers. The wealthiest farmer on the American side, Paul Cyr, was a state representative. He left all his land to his son, who was later also elected a state legislator.[68] Through a succession of well-to-do prominent fathers and sons, families that had arrived early sank permanent roots in the St John valley. Their high degree of endogamy also made them a closed and very tightly knit group.[69]

But not all farmers' sons inherited land from their fathers. Farmers were unwilling to subdivide their farms unless they had a larger-than-average amount of land or several fair-sized holdings. Even very large holdings, like Paul Cyr's, were often kept intact.[70] Holdings of the average farmer were enough to establish only one child (not necessarily a son, incidentally), or two at best.

Before 1830 this was no problem as there was still plenty of unclaimed and free intervale land. During the years of the boundary dispute neither New Brunswick nor Maine sold or granted land, but both jurisdictions turned a blind eye to squatters, and the treaty of 1842 confirmed the squatters in their possession.[71] But by 1842 all the river lots were occupied. Land was still available in the back settlements, but the soil was of uneven quality, and the lots had to be purchased from the state or the province. A nonheir in the 1840s and later therefore started life at a lower level than his parents. If an inheriting sibling bought out the nonheir, the latter would possess a small amount of capital but not enough to purchase expensive riparian land, especially as sales on credit were rare. Newly arrived immigrants faced exactly the same kind of problem: it was harder and harder for them to acquire a good farm.

In many purely farming settlements on the frontier, nonheirs and immigrants provided the bulk of the tenants and emigrants. After a few years of renting land and trying to secure 'a place to stand' in the community, they concluded that they could never purchase a farm within a reasonable time and left.[72] Tenancy was very uncommon in the St John valley. Instead of being tenants, nonheirs and immigrants bought and farmed what was often marginal land. Some squatted. Many left. The unmarried sons of farmers began leaving the settlement as early as the 1830s.[73] After 1842, when the boundary treaty was signed and free land was no longer available, some couples emigrated immediately after marriage—a phenomenon hitherto unknown.[74]

A Dual Community

The St John valley society that emerged at mid-century shared many characteristics with the upper Canadian and eighteenth-century English North American agricultural communities. But it also shared a lesser, but nonetheless important, number of traits with agroforestry settlements.

Until the arrival of the lumber camps the Madawaska district was a rather typical inland agriculture settlement. It enjoyed a favorable ratio of land to settlers but suffered from poor communication with potential markets. Left to its own devices the Madawaska population would likely have reached the limits of its growth within three generations, when the intervales and riparian land had been settled. Later generations of nonheirs would have been forced to leave if they ever wanted to establish themselves as independent farmers. In short, the Madawaska settlement would have fit the model of the agrarian community described in the introduction to this article.

The arrival of the lumber industry accelerated the rate of population growth, creating a shortage of good farmland sooner than anticipated. Farming families could not establish all their children, or even all their sons, as proprietors of farms or as self-employed craftsmen or traders. Farms were seldom divided, and though a nonheir was provided with enough personal property to give him a start in life, this was seldom sufficient to guarantee the same standard of living his parents had enjoyed.

The lumber industry created more problems than it solved for the Madawaskayans. Land shortages in agricultural settlements normally provoked the emigration and/or impoverishment of those who could not secure a decent freehold. Logging expanded the economic base of the St John valley and reduced out-migration of noninheriting children, but could not prevent their impoverishment.

The lumber industry made it possible for families established on smaller farms or marginal land to make ends meet, but it did not raise them to the standard of living enjoyed by many of the riparian farmers. Some families resigned themselves to their lower social status, but others would not accept it and emigrated. Since income from logging did not make up for the shortage of prime farmland, it was not really an adequate form of economic diversification. Even after the lumber industry was established, the land shortage still led to the emigration and/or impoverishment of noninheriting children.

Along with the economic stratification of the farm families came social stratification. Some descendants of the founding families achieved positions of social and political prominence, backed by economic power. But the farming élite had to concede economic prominence to another group, unconnected with farming or with the close kin network of the first generation of settlers. The truly rich were recently arrived timber dealers, lumber manufacturers, and merchants. The wealth of some of these individuals dwarfed even that of the better-off members of the farming élite.

For all their wealth, however, the lumber barons' control over the economic life of the upper St John was far from absolute. In other agroforestry settlements, lumber barons frequently paid their workers in truck, a form of economic control. But people in the St John valley used cash to settle the larger part of their store accounts, suggesting that cash wages were at least common, if not universal.[75] Many farms were substantial enough that their owners did not have to turn to the lumber barons for mere survival. Farmers who needed small amounts of extra income could transport goods for independent storekeepers, instead of hiring themselves out as lumberjacks. The lumber industry played a critical role in the lives of smallholders only— farmers still clearing land, those established on marginal land, and laborers.

The lumber industry cannot be blamed for stunting local agriculture in the upper St John valley. It is true that many farms operated on a subsistence level, but this was the consequence of factors largely independent of the lumber industry. The lumber industry trapped marginal farmers in an unenviable position as part-time farmers/part-time laborers, but it also directly and indirectly opened new opportunities for residents who had the required material and human assets. They began to see their farms at least partly as money-making ventures and stepping-stones to social and political power. Thus the lumber industry helped residents of the upper St John valley to integrate their community into the larger economic and political world.

Suggestions for Further Reading

Arthur M. Lower, *Great Britain's Woodyard: British America and the Timber Trade, 1763–1867* (Montreal, 1973).

René Hardy and Normand Séguin, *Forêt et société en Mauricie, 1830–1930, la formation de la région de Trois Rivières* (Montreal, 1984).

Graeme Wynn, *Timber Colony: A Historical Geography of Early Nineteenth-Century New Brunswick* (Toronto, 1981).

Notes

I would like to thank Professor Chad Gaffield and Gérard Bouchard for their help with a previous version of this paper.

[1] Percy Wells Bidwell and John Falconer, *History of Agriculture in the Northern United States, 1620–1860* (New York: Peter Smith, 1941), 79, 259; Clarence Danhoff, *Changes in Agriculture, the Northern Unites States* (Cambridge, Mass.: Harvard University Press, 1969), 119–20; Donald MacKay, 'The Canadian Logging Frontier', *Journal of Forest History* (hereafter *JFH*) 23 (January 1979), 4–17; Graeme Wynn, *Timber Colony, A Historical Geography of Early Nineteenth-Century New Brunswick* (Toronto; University of Toronto Press, 1981), 71–86.

[2] Wynn, *Timber Colony*, 86.

[3] This has been the case of the Aroostook valley, described by Richard Judd, 'Lumbering and the Farming Frontier in Aroostook County, Maine, 1840–1880', *JFH* 28 (April 1984), 56–67. Judd's article focuses on a region fifty miles south of the one analysed here.

[4]There is little overlap between *this* concept of agroforestry and the meaning of that word in recent studies of forestry and economic development, particularly in tropical countries. 'Agroforestry' in this article refers always to the relationship between forest industries and agriculture defined by Séguin and other Québec historians, and *not* to the planned growing of trees as a crop on individual farms. For the concept as used here, see: Raoul Blanchard, *L'est du Canada Français* (Montréal, Québec: Beauchemin, 1935); Normand Séguin, *La conquête du sol au 19ᵉ* (Québec: Boréal Express, 1977); Normand Séguin, 'L'économie agro-forestière: genèse du développement au Saguenay au 19ᵉ', in *Agriculture et colonisation au Québec*, ed. Normand Séguin (Montréal, Québec: Boréal Express, 1980), 159–64; René Hardy et Normand Séguin, *Forêt et société en Mauricie, 1830–1930, la formation de la région de Trois Rivières* (Montréal, Québec: Boréal Express, 1984); Claire Andrée Fortin, 'Coupe forestière et agriculture pionnière en Mauricie, le cas de St. Stanislas' (Paper presented at the 1984 meeting of the Canadian Historical Association, Guelph, Ontario); Chad Gaffield, 'Boom and Bust, the Demography and Economy of the Lower Ottawa Valley in the Nineteenth Century', Canadian Historical Association, *Historical Papers* (1982), 172–95; John Willis, 'Fraserville and its Temiscouata Hinterland, 1874–1914; Colonization and Urbanization in a Peripheral Region of the Province of Quebec', M.A. thesis, Université du Québec à Trois Rivières, 1981.

[5]Gérard Bouchard, 'Family Strategies and Geographic Mobility at Laterriere, 1851–1935', *Journal of Family History* 2 (December 1977), 365–6. Guy Trépanier, 'Sainte Flore, un exemple de mobilité dans le front pionnier mauricien de la seconde moitié du 19ᵉ siècle' (Paper presented at the 1984 meeting of the Canadian Historical Association, Guelph, Ontario).

[6]The most recent theoretical article on the socioeconomic evolution of American pioneer communities on the eastern seaboard is Darret Rutman, 'Assessing the Little Communities of Early America', *William and Mary Quarterly*, 3d series, 43 (April 1986), 163–78. Rutman, 'People in Process, the New Hampshire Towns of the Eighteenth Century', *Journal of Urban History* 1 (May 1975), 265–92; James Henretta, 'The Morphology of New England Society in the Colonial Period', *Journal of Interdisciplinary History* 2 (Autumn 1971), 380–91; Phillip Greven, *Four Generations: Population, Land and Family in Colonial Andover, Massachusetts* (Ithaca, New York: Cornell University Press, 1970); Kenneth Lockridge, 'Land, Population and the Evolution of New England Society, 1630–1790', *Past and Present* 39 (April 1968), 74–83; Charles Grant, *Democracy in the Connecticut Frontier Town of Kent* (New York: Columbia University Press, 1961) are also of interest. For Canada see Herbert Mays, 'A Place to Stand: Families, Land and Permanence in Toronto Gore Township, 1820–90', Canadian Historical Association, *Historical Papers* (1980), 185–211; David Gagan, *Hopeful Travellers: Families, Land and Social Change in Mid-Victorian Peel County, Canada* (Toronto: University of Toronto Press, 1981).

[7]Petition dated 24 February 1785, Land Petition and Application Book, Provincial Archives of New Brunswick, Fredericton, New Brunswick (hereafter PANB).

[8]Letter dated 27 March 1824, which states: 'Les effets ont assez bon cours à présent parce que des faiseurs de bois de tonnes ont ouvert cet hiver des chantiers dans nos endroits.' On the other hand, as late as November 1821 the priest was complaining

he could not sell the products collected as tithes (les effets); letter and tithing records are found in the Lettres des prêtres missionnaires du Madawaska à l'évêque de Québec, Archives de l'Archidiocèse de Québec, Québec. Wynn, *Timber Colony*, 33–53.

⁹Tithing record for 1799, Lettres des prêtres missionnaires.

¹⁰US census, 1820, M33, roll 37. Unless otherwise noted, all census materials consulted were manuscript schedules. Microfilm location numbers, provided with the first reference to each US census, refer to the population schedules for the appropriate counties of Maine, consulted on film in the National Archives, Washington, D.C. Agricultural schedules from the US censuses were consulted on film at the Maine State Archives in Augusta, Maine.

¹¹Béatrice Craig, 'Migrant Integration and Kinship Ties in a Frontier Community, Madawaska, 1785–1850', *Histoire Sociale/Social History* 38 (November 1986), 277–97.

¹²Journal of George W. Coffin, Massachussetts Land Agent, September and October 1825, Maine State Archives.

¹³W.O. Raymond, ed., 'State of the Madawaska and Aroostook Settlements in 1831, Reports of John G. Deane and Edward Kavanagh to Samuel E. Smith, Governor of the State of Maine', New Brunswick Historical Society, *Collections* 9 (1914), 453–4 (hereafter 'Reports of Deane and Kavanagh'). This source reads like a census list of individual land-owners; specific page citations are not given here if information is derived from the entire list.

¹⁴Tithing records for 1799, 1804, 1832, 1841, Lettres des prêtres missionnaires; 'Reports of Deane and Kavanagh', 366–684; Report of the Commissioners of Affairs at Madawaska, 1834, Papers of the Legislative Assembly Relating to the Settlement of Madawaska, PANB (this last is a census of people, stock, and crops taken in December 1833).

¹⁵US census, 1850, M432, roll 248; New Brunswick provincial census, 1851, PAC C996 (PANB F1591). Manuscript schedules for Canadian censuses were consulted on microfilm both at the Public Archives of Canada (PAC), in Ottawa, Ontario, and at PANB; microfilm locations are given for each archive.

¹⁶Peter Fisher, *History of New Brunswick, as Originally Published in 1825, with a Few Explanatory Notes* (St John, New Brunswick: New Brunswick Historical Society, 1921); Joseph Bouchette, *The British Dominions in North America or a Topographical and Statistical Description of the Provinces of Lower and Upper Canada, New Brunswick, Prince Edward Island, Newfoundland, Nova Scotia and Cape Breton, with a Topographical Dictionary of Lower Canada* (London, England: 1831), 104; 'Wilderness Journey, a Nineteenth-Century Journal', *Maine History News* (July 1980), 15; Edmund Ward, *An Account of the St John and Its Tributary Rivers and Lakes* (Fredericton, New Brunswick: Sentinel Office, 1841), 86; Abraham Gesner, *New Brunswick, with Notes for Emigrants* (London, England: Simmonds and Ward, 1847), 180; James F.W. Johnston, *Notes on North America* (Edinburgh, Scotland: Blackwood, 1851), 70–1.

¹⁷US Department of Agriculture, Soil Conservation Service in Cooperation with the University of Maine Agricultural Experiment Station, *Soil Survey, Aroostook County, Maine, North Eastern Part*, series 1958, no. 27, 75.

[18]Tithing records, 1799, 1804, 1832, 1841, Lettres des prêtres missionnaires; New Brunswick provincial census, 1851. The agricultural schedule of the 1850 US census only includes farms valued at three hundred dollars or more and therefore cannot be used for this purpose.

[19]According to the figures contained in the tithing records, the censuses, and the land agent reports, the mean household size varied between 6.10 and 6.7 during the 1799–1850 period.

[20]Bettye Hobbs-Pruitt, 'Self Sufficiency and the Agricultural Economy of Eighteenth-Century Massachusetts', *William and Mary Quarterly*, 3d ser., 41 (July 1984), 333–64. New England farmers grew very few potatoes in the colonial period.

[21]Carleton County Registry Office, books 1–11, 1832–50 (also on microfilm, F5024–29 at PANB); Northern Aroostook Registry of Deeds, Fort Kent, Maine, 1846–50. Before 1832 the Madawaska settlers had to travel to Fredericton to get their transactions registered, and consequently, they skipped the formality altogether. There was no American registry for this area before 1846. There were twenty-eight deeds of maintenance registered over the 1832–50 period.

[22]Hobbs-Pruitt, 'Self Sufficiency'; Christopher Clark, 'Household Economy, Market Exchange and the Rise of Capitalism in the Connecticut Valley, 1800–60', *Journal of Social History* 13 (Winter 1979), 169–89; Richard L. Bushman, 'Family Security in the Transition from Farm to City, 1750–1850', *Journal of Family History* 6 (Fall 1981), 238–43.

[23]The *Soil Survey* indicates that the last killing frost usually occurs around 30 May, and the first around 15 September, but they have been recorded as late as 28 June and as early at 28 August. For historical crop failures, see *Bangor Register* (Bangor, Maine), 10 October 1827; *Republican Journal* (Belfast, Maine), 12 August 1829; diary section of the *Journal of the House of Assembly of New Brunswick* (hereafter *Journal of the House of Assembly*) for 13, 20 February 1834 and 1, 11, 14 March 1834; *Journal of the House of Assembly*, 1840, 159–60; *Journal of the House of Assembly*, 1854–55, 106–7; Papers of the Legislative Assembly of New Brunswick relating to the Settlement of Madawaska, 1834, and Report of the Commissioners at Madawaska, 1834, both at PANB; Agriculture Crop Failures 1817–55, New Brunswick Executive Council, MG9 A1, vol. 32, 78–136, PAC.

[24]US census, 1850, agricultural schedules for Hancock, Madawaska, and Van Buren Plantations, Maine; *Journal of the House of Assembly*, 1852, appendix; J.F.W. Johnston commented in 1851 on the difficulties of growing wheat anywhere in northern New Brunswick, not only in the French settlements, *Notes on North America*, 68.

[25]Bouchette, *British Dominions*, 104.

[26]Fisher, *History of New Brunswick*, 53.

[27]Bouchette, *British Dominions*, 104.

[28]'Reports of Deane and Kavanagh', 455.

[29]Gesner, *New Brunswick*, 180.

[30]Report of the Commissioners at Madawaska, 1834.

[31]'Le journal des visites pastorales de Mgr Plessis, Evêque de Québec, en Acadie, 1811–12–15', Société Historique Acadienne, *Cahiers* 11 (mars/septembre 1980), 126.

32By self-sufficiency, I mean that the community provided almost all its needs in food, shelter, and clothing from its own natural resources; I do not imply that the upper St John valley lived in autarky, cut off from all exchange networks. Neither do I imply that each individual farmer was self-sufficient.

33Wynn, *Timber Colony*, 36–43.

34*Ibid.*, 37.

35'Reports of Deane and Kavanagh', 394; Deane and Kavanagh refer to the firm of Peters and Wilmot as the 'pioneer company to operate on the Upper St John', and describe it as 'for years, the largest lumbering business on the St John River'. It failed during the recession of 1828.

36Wynn, *Timber Colony*, 141–2; and Graeme Wynn, 'Administration in Adversity: The Deputy Surveyors and Control of the New Brunswick Crown Forest before 1844', *Acadiensis* 7 (Autumn 1977), 49–65.

37'Reports of Deane and Kavanagh', 459–60; Richard G. Wood, *A History of Lumbering in Maine, 1820–61* (Orono: University of Maine Press, 1935), 69; Charlotte Melvin-Lenentine, *Madawaska, a Chapter in Maine-New Brunswick Relations* (Madawaska, Maine: St John Valley Publishing Co., 1975).

38Howard Jones, *To the Webster-Ashburton Treaty, A Study in Anglo-American Relations, 1783–1843* (Chapel Hill: University of North Carolina Press, 1977), 33–47, and 89–90. The text of the 1842 treaty is in the appendix, 181–7.

39Wynn, *Timber Colony*, 33–53.

40Canada Disputed Territory Fund, *Journal of the House of Assembly*, 1855, appendix, cix–clix, PANB.

41I have reconstituted families from parish registers kept by the Catholic church for the 1792–1855 period. Couples who were not married locally and suddenly appear in the parish register (almost always when they bring a child to church to be baptized) are immigrants. False immigrants (local people who married in another parish and then came back) were identified using the local genealogical dictionaries and excluded from the calculations. As couples had a baby on the average every other year, I took the year preceding first mention as the year of arrival in the St. John valley. Very few non-French (and therefore non-Catholic) Canadians moved to the St John Valley at any time during the eighteenth and nineteenth century. The registers covered the parishes of: St Basile (New Brunswick), 1792–1857; St Bruno (Maine), 1838–55; and Ste Luce (Maine), 1842–58. Other sources used: Henry Langlois, *Dictionnaire généalogique du Madawaska, répertoire des mariages du diocèse d'Edmundstun, Nouveau Brunswick, et du comté d'Aroostook*, 8 vols. (St Basile, New Brunswick: Ernest Lang, 1971); Bona Arsenault, *Histoire et généalogie des Acadiens*, 7 vols. (Ottawa, Ontario: Léméac, 1978); Mgr Tanguay, *Dictionnaire généalogique des familles canadiennes*, 7 vols. (Montréal, Québec: E. Sénecal, 1871–90); *Dictionnaire national des Canadiens Français, 1608–1760*, 3 vols. (Montréal, Québec, Institut Généalogique Drouin, 1965).

42US censuses for 1820, 1830 (M19, rolls 47 and 51), 1840 (M707, roll 136), 1850, and 1870 (M593, roll 538).

43Journal of Coffin, 1825.

44'Reports of Deane and Kavanagh'.

[45]Report of the Commissioners appointed under resolve of 12 April 1854, to locate grants and determine the extent of possessory claims under the late treaty with Great Britain, Special Collection, Fogler Library, University of Maine, Orono, Maine.

[46]Northern Aroostook Registry of Deeds, books 1 and 2, 1846–52.

[47]Guy Michaud, *Brève histoire du Madawaska* (Edmundston, New Brunswick: les Editions G.R.M. 1984), 116–17.

[48]Marcella Harnish Sorg and Béatrice Craig, 'Patterns of Infant Mortality in the Upper St John Valley French Population: 1791–1838', *Human Biology* 55 (February 1983), 100–13; Completed family size averaged 11.34 children, and the infant mortality rate was 132 per thousand.

[49]Craig, 'Family, Kinship and Community Formation on the Canadian-American Border, Madawaska 1785–1842', PhD diss., University of Maine at Orono, 1983, 93.

[50]Rates based on the data contained in Table 2.

[51]Letter from Rev. Langevin to Lt. Gov. Harvey, 10 October 1837, lieutenant governor's correspondence, New Brunswick Executive Council, PAC.

[52]Northern Aroostook Registry of Deeds, books 1 and 2; *Fort Kent Centennial Brochure*, Fort Kent, Maine, 1969, 16–18 and 23–4. This section is a reprint of a brochure published in 1929 by the Northern National Bank. Northern Aroostook Registry of Deeds, book 1; Glazier File, Family History Files, PANB.

[53]John Emmerson, Inventory of Estate, 1867, Probate Court Records, Victoria County, New Brunswick, PANB.

[54]US census, 1850; New Brunswick provincial census, 1851.

[55]Crown Land Returns, *Journal of the House of Assembly*, 1841–60.

[56]US census, 1850; New Brunswick provincial census, 1861 (PAC M558, M559; PANB F1598, F1599 and F1584) and 1871 (PAC C10385, C10386; PANB F1584). The 1871 census was taken by the Dominion of Canada government; all earlier censuses were taken by the government of New Brunswick.

[57]Both sources, above.

[58]'Reports of Deane and Kavanagh'; Report of the Commissioners at Madawaska, 1834; Report of the Commissioners appointed under the resolve of 12 April 1854.

[59]US census, 1870.

[60]*Ibid*.

[61]New Brunswick provincial census, 1861 and 1871.

[62]Danhoff, *Changes in Agriculture*, 120.

[63]John Emmerson, Papers and Account Book, 1843–67, New Brunswick Museum, St John, New Brunswick; Abraham and Simon Dufour Ledger Book, 1844–48, Madawaska Historical Society, Madawaska, Maine.

[64]Report of the Commissioners at Madawaska, 1834.

[65]US census, 1850, agricultural schedule.

[66]John Emmerson, Papers and Account Books, 1849–67.

[67]Evidence derived from the family reconstitution data, based on the sources listed in footnote 41 above.

[68]Abbé Thomas Albert, *Histoire du Madawaska* (Québec: Imprimerie Franciscaine Missionnaire, 1922), 416–17.

[69]Evidence about endogamy is derived from the family reconstitution data; see footnote 41.

[70]Northern Aroostook Registry of Deeds, deed books, 1846–70; York Country Registry Office, 1785–1833, Carleton Country Registry Office, books 1–11, 1832–50, Madawaska County Registry Office, books A, B, C, 1851–70.

[71]Jones, *To the Webster-Ashburton Treaty*, 181–7.

[72]Mays, 'A Place to Stand', 198.

[73]There were 20 per cent fewer native-born males marrying at Madawaska between 1825 and 1850 than native-born females, although similar numbers of boys and girls were born in any given year, and boys did not die more frequently than girls. The 1850–51 censuses do not reveal a large pool of unmarried men either. These calculations are based on the family reconstitution data from the sources in footnote 41.

[74]Evidence provided by the family reconstitution data, sources in footnote 41. Some newlywed local residents vanish out of sight between marriage and the birth of the first child; they can be traced neither in the parish registers nor in the censuses.

[75]Dufour Ledger; Emmerson Account Book.

19

Social Order in Upper Canada

W. Thomas Matthews

One of the great conceits of Canadians is that their society today and throughout its history has been characterized by 'peace, order, and good government', a phrase which serves as the Canadian equivalent of the American 'life, liberty, and the pursuit of happiness'. Nowhere has this concept been stronger than in the ideology of Upper Canada/ Ontario, and as late as 1970 one study of Canada took the phrase 'the Peaceable Kingdom' as its subtitle. How and why Canadians came to believe in this view of their society is inextricably bound up with the desire, dating back over 200 years to the Loyalists, to distinguish the provinces that would become Canada from the United States, born in revolution and perpetuated in unbridled self-interest. Granting the existence and continuation of the belief, we may attempt to assess its implications or its accuracy. As for implications, men who believed in peace, order, and good government may well have been more

willing than their American counterparts to unleash the power of the state to control excesses. As for accuracy, one may adopt absolute or relative standards, the latter simply content to find less 'violence' in Canada than in the United States in any historic period.

In his essay on Upper Canadian society during the early Victorian period, W. Thomas Matthews alludes briefly to the creation of the myth, but he is rather more concerned to demonstrate its inaccuracy. His argument is not based on relative considerations, but on the extent of public social disorganization and 'immorality' to be found in early Victorian Canada. He concludes that Upper Canada was no model of cohesion and stability, and the maintenance of order reflects less the behaviour of the population at large than the expectations of those who governed them.

What does Matthews mean by 'the myth of the Peaceable Kingdom', and what evidence does he use to attack it? Are his arguments convincing? Does his restriction to the public arena and his avoidance of the treatment of minorities and powerless family members (women, children) weaken his argument? To what extent did the magistrates attempt to implement some notion of the 'peaceable' tradition? If they based their actions on such conceptions, was it totally a myth?

This article first appeared, titled 'The Myth of the Peaceable Kingdom: Upper Canadian Society during the Early Victorian Period', in *Queen's Quarterly* 94, 2 (Summer, 1987), 383–401.

In an address delivered to the Royal Society of Canada in 1904, Colonel George Taylor Denison, the noted military strategist, colourful Toronto magistrate and tireless champion of the Imperial cause, provided his audience with a sweeping analysis of Canadian history which among other things attributed the honest, peaceful and law-abiding nature of British North American society to the durability of the Loyalist tradition. In Denison's estimation, the United Empire Loyalists were motivated by an overriding desire to create in the backwoods of North America a more honourable, conservative and thoroughly British version of colonial society. Repelled by the liberal creed of the American rebels and its glorification of mob rule, these 'choice, picked men' who fled the Thirteen Colonies and relocated in territory still under the control of the British Crown embraced the motto 'Fear God, Honour the King' with an unbridled enthusiasm which affected virtually every aspect of their daily lives. In addition to acknowledging the importance of organized religion and a hierarchical social structure, they ensured that the law was administered honestly without favouritism or corruption and that life, property and social stability were never jeopardized by individual excesses. So profound was the legacy of our Loyalist ancestors that it left an indelible mark on the colonies which they founded. In a particularly emotional section of his address, Denison maintained that the

> result of this spirit is shown in the remarkable freedom from crime of this country in its early years. The pious, God-fearing men who had made such sacrifices for their principles, were a community almost free from crime. Murders and theft were practically unknown, and for many years the country increased in strength and population, almost without a need for legal restrictions or regulations. This tendency to avoid crime has always been more marked in Canada than in almost any other country, and has been a peculiarity of our new settlement in the Northwest Territories.

The impact of the Loyalists went far beyond this absence of crime. 'In many other ways in everyday life', he continued, 'one could point out the great advantage that we Canadians are all deriving today, from the honourable and

law-abiding example set us by our Loyalist fathers, and the influence that it
has had and continues to have upon the social life of our people.'[1]

Colonel Denison's contention that the Loyalists founded a model society
that was 'almost free from crime' typifies an influential and time-honoured
tradition in Canadian historical writing. For more than a century, scholars
have sought to downplay some of the more unpleasant aspects of the Canadian past. They have portrayed our ancestors as a peaceful, hard-working
and God-fearing people, and with few exceptions they have assumed that
British North American society was characterized by order, stability, cohesion, conciliation, and other outstanding Canadian virtues. When examining
Canada's rise from a subordinate, colonial status to a position of full nationhood within the context of a decentralized British Empire, historians writing
in the 'whig' or liberal-nationalist tradition delighted in pointing out that,
apart from the ill-fated rebellions of 1837, political change has been achieved
in Canada through peaceful means without resort to armed struggle and the
unleashing of the forces of anarchy. Evolution, not revolution, and conciliation, not confrontation, have always been, we are told, the Canadian way.[2]
Not surprisingly, the dynamics of British North American society have been
perceived in a similar light. Although the constitutional bias which pervaded
much of the traditional literature precluded serious consideration of social
issues, historians generally concluded that the communities established by the
Loyalists and their descendants experienced much less social disruption than
their counterparts in the United States. While lawlessness, violence, poverty,
immorality, and corruption reigned supreme south of the border, British
North America evolved into a cohesive enclave virtually free from violence
and crime, and untainted by dramatic socio-economic inequalities. In short,
it became what many scholars have termed the 'Peaceable Kingdom'.[3] This
characterization of British North American society has been so pervasive and
so compelling in English-Canadian historical writing that it has managed to
transcend some of the more formidable ideological barriers dividing Canadian historians into conflicting schools of interpretation. In an article examining the general pattern of violence in Canadian history, Kenneth
McNaught, one of the country's most influential labour historians, reached
the rather surprising conclusion that 'the "private" uses of violence have
been less anarchic and individualistic than in the United States.' Despite the
fact that one would expect a student of labour or working-class history to
be particularly sensitive to the importance of conflict in shaping the historical
process, McNaught further maintained that 'these differences would be consistent with the existence of a comparatively more ordered society in which,
as Sir John A. Macdonald once put it, constitutional liberty rather than
democracy was to be the guiding light.[4]

For the vast majority of Canadians, recreated pioneer villages constitute
the most accessible representation of the social implications of the myths of

the Peaceable Kingdom. With fastidious and often loving care, projects such as King's Landing Historical Settlement at Prince William, New Brunswick, and Upper Canada Village at Morrisburg, Ontario, have attempted to provide the public with an insight into the make-up of colonial society and the experiences of ordinary people during the pre-Confederation period. While recreations such as these must be applauded for fulfilling an important educational function and for their painstakingly authentic restoration of historical buildings and artifacts, they have an unfortunate tendency to seriously misrepresent important facets of the historical record. With their neat Georgian-style buildings, well-tended grounds, white picket fences, and polite guides in period costume, pioneer villages consistently present an idealized, sanitized and ultimately two-dimensional view of the past. In a very real sense, they have stripped our history of its vitality and wrapped it in the cloak of middle-class respectability. The thousands of Canadians who visit these recreations every year are left with the distinct impression that their predecessors were a prosperous, dour, and rather complacent group of people who worked from dawn to dusk six days a week and who on the seventh day went to church in order to express gratitude for their good fortune. Indeed, one searches in vain for any evidence of the escalating social tensions and class disparities which surely were just as characteristic of the social fabric as white picket fences and dignified Georgian architecture. For the most part, the many vicissitudes of colonial life are either absent or inconspicuously portrayed. Recreated pioneer villages play an essential role in acquainting the average Canadian with his or her heritage, but much more needs to be done in order to accurately depict nineteenth-century society in all of its complexity, vitality and raucousness.

What follows is an attempt to revise the so-called myth of the Peaceable Kingdom by presenting an alternative view of Upper Canadian society. Departing from the traditional approach which celebrated the virtues of the communities established by the Loyalists and their descendants, I shall argue that the colonial social fabric was anything but cohesive and stable. As John Weaver observed in a recent analysis of crime in the Gore District, 'Social disorganization was one of the most striking features of life in Upper Canada in the early Victorian period.'5 Rapid commercial expansion, fluctuations in the international economy, the commencement of large-scale public works projects, the influx of large numbers of impoverished immigrants, increased social stratification, and the emergence of bona fide urban communities combined to create a very volatile situation which many observers believed posed a potent threat to the survival of the established order. The principal manifestations of the malaise which affected Upper Canadian society were widespread poverty, immorality, crime, and class conflict. These problems reflected the forces of disruption at work on the colonial social fabric, and together, they belie the romanticized view of the past conveyed to the public in recreated pioneer villages. Despite the claims made by Colonel Denison and others, it would be erroneous to depict Upper Canada as an island of stability surrounded by a sea of anarchy. Social disorganization represented the rule rather than the exception.

Chronic poverty represented one of the most important factors undermining social stability during the early Victorian period. Although there has been a tendency for some scholars to romanticize pre-industrial society, recent studies have determined that dramatic socio-economic inequality characterized Upper Canadian society many decades before the advent of industrialization. A small minority of affluent landowners, merchants and professionals monopolized most of the wealth in the colony, while a large proportion of the population lived in a state of deprivation which for some resembled the miserable existence of the landless peasants of pre-industrial Europe. In urban communities, for example, very few people actually owned property. Focusing on Hamilton in 1860, Michael Katz discovered that a handful of residents controlled most of the assessed wealth and that approximately one quarter of the population owned all of the real estate in the city. An incredibly high rate of transiency further contributed to the insecurity created by widespread poverty. In Hamilton, as well as in other communities throughout the province, most people were rootless and propertyless, roaming from one place to another in search of greater security and a brighter future.[6] Although one might expect property ownership to have been more widespread in rural communities, David Gagan's study of Peel County reveals that structural inequality and a lack of permanence remained the inescapable facts of life whether one lived in the country or the city.[7]

The hardship endured by the poor and dispossessed was compounded during the winter months. Trade and commerce represented the life-blood of the Upper Canadian economy, and with the winter freeze-up economic activity temporarily came to a standstill. Unemployment swelled among the unskilled labourers who worked in the province's main entrepôts; large numbers of navvies who had been employed on canal and railway construction projects drifted into the urban centres. Because of the haphazard and parsimonious nature of Victorian poor relief, seasonal fluctuations in the economy were capable of precipitating disaster for many Upper Canadian families. Between November and April, the cost of essential commodities, particularly food and fuel, increased steadily, thereby contributing to an upsurge in disease and malnutrition. Furthermore, during the winter months, the competition for affordable housing became even more pronounced.[8]

The most marginalized element of the Upper Canadian population were the unskilled workers employed on public works projects. Most navvies were recent immigrants from Ireland who had not yet been drawn into the mainstream of colonial life. The product of a foreign culture and an often despised religion, they constituted a proletarian class which provided contractors with an abundant supply of cheap labour which they could shamelessly exploit. During the 1830s and 1840s, when the province's system of canals was being expanded, and during the railway construction boom of the 1850s, thousands of navvies, many of whom were accompanied by their families, lived a nomadic existence moving from one project to another in an often futile search for work. Since the labour supply usually exceeded the number of jobs available, wages remained low and unemployment was rife in their ranks. In some parts of the province, this underclass of unskilled workers represented a large proportion of the local population. In 1842, while the Welland Canal was being enlarged, there were almost as many impoverished Irish navvies and their families living in shanties along the banks of the canal as there were permanent residents in the principal towns of St Catharines and Thorold.[9] For the most part, the established population hindered, rather than helped, these recent immigrants in their struggle for survival. Fearful of the potential for public disturbances, the authorities routinely evicted poverty-stricken squatters who erected temporary shelters on vacant land, and whenever possible they prevented the navvies from establishing their camps in the vicinity of incorporated communities.[10]

Poverty had been omnipresent since the early part of the century, but the arrival of the famine Irish in the late 1840s made a bad situation even worse. Thousands of starving and diseased immigrants poured into Upper Canada, and according to all accounts the number of paupers, vagrants and beggars roaming the streets of the province's towns and cities grew tremendously. During the summer and autumn of 1847, the plight of the famine Irish in Toronto became so desperate that the city fathers feared that many of them would either starve or freeze to death with the advent of winter.[11] As Sheriff W.B. Jarvis observed in an urgent letter submitted to the mayor on 28 August 1847, the citizens of Toronto were compelled

> to witness families lying under the shelter of fences and trees, not only in the outskirts, but within the very heart of the town,—human beings begging for food, having disease and famine depicted in their countenance and without shelter to cover them.[12]

The influx of the famine Irish clearly revealed the inadequacy of municipal poor relief measures, and in Toronto it strengthened the argument of those officials who for a number of years had been advocating the expansion of the municipality's beleaguered house of industry.[13]

The year 1847 was especially difficult, but the situation did not improve appreciably over the course of the next decade. Street begging and vagrancy remained commonplace, and even with the establishment of houses of industry and similar charitable institutions, little was actually done to alleviate the suffering of the province's poorest inhabitants. Indeed, the deplorable conditions which prevailed in the institutions designed to house the indigent poor made a mockery of the high expectations which had accompanied their construction. At mid-century, for example, the squalor and overcrowding in Kingston's house of industry so offended the sensibilities of the concerned citizens who visited the institution that most of them made some reference to the plight of the inmates when they signed their names in the daily log. One gentleman noted that he 'found the inmates in a most wretched condition, destitute of food and clothing',[14] while another recorded that they 'were in a very filthy state, and the beds . . . were in a very dirty bad condition without hay or straw, decent and sufficient covering'.[15] Other visitors commented on the unpalatable soup served to the inmates, which was devoid of barley, rice, salt, vegetables, and meat, the lack of heating, the serious overcrowding, the presence of lice, rats and other vermin, and the foul state of the privy. Upon reading this litany of horrors, one is left with the distinct impression that the province's paupers may have been better off fending for themselves than they were living in the austere institutions ostensibly constructed for their benefit.

Rampant immorality aroused much more concern among the authorities than the plight of the poorest of the poor. One of the most common misconceptions associated with the early Victorian period is the notion that it was distinguished by a rigid, strait-laced, puritanical code of behaviour. In addition to ignoring the endemic nature of pre-industrial poverty, recreated pioneer villages contribute to this romanticized view of the past by suggesting that licentiousness and immorality were relegated to the periphery of Upper Canadian society. Nothing could be further from the truth. Pre-Confederation Canada was a very rough-and-ready sort of place, and in Upper Canada raucous behaviour which certain individuals deemed to be immoral constituted an integral part of popular culture. Drinking, gambling, whoring, and brawling disturbed the public peace in both urban and rural communities; attempts to establish a more stringent code of conduct were usually half-hearted and invariably doomed to failure.[16]

First and foremost, Upper Canadian society was characterized by a veritable orgy of drinking and drunkenness. The consumption of intoxicating beverages accompanied most social occasions, and even the occasional Methodist camp meeting attracted a rowdy contingent of tipplers. The proliferation of both licensed and unlicensed taverns in the decades following the province's creation generated much of the drunkenness described in contemporary accounts.[17] These establishments afforded ample opportunity to anyone intent on securing large quantities of potent drink at a reasonable cost, and they made it virtually impossible for the province's fledgeling temperance movement to inculcate more moderate drinking habits among the general population. In a report drafted in 1841, civic officials in Kingston lamented that their community was 'swarming with drunkards'.[18] More than 136 taverns operated within the confines of the town, and unfortunately the vast majority of these were 'low dram shops, the constant resort of the idle and dissolute'.[19] The authorities perceived an obvious correlation between drunkenness and crime. The profusion of 'low dram shops' was directly responsible for 'the rapid increase of crime which the last few years have exhibited', they maintained, and the 'records of the Police Magistrate will prove that in nine of ten cases which come before him, the parties either frequent or make their haunts in these fruitful nurseries of crime.'[20]

The 'lamentable effects' of widespread drunkenness were evident in many other towns and cities. In Toronto, for example, 'low dram shops' multiplied as rapidly as they did in Kingston, providing ready access to alcohol and a refuge for the undesirable elements of the city's population. According to a petition drafted by the Temperance Reformation Society in 1842, much of the 'crime and wretchedness' existing in Toronto stemmed from 'the facilities furnished for indulgence in all kinds of intoxicating drinks'. In the estimation of the petitioners, 'the character of a great majority of the Houses bearing Tavern Licenses is no less to be deplored than their numbers.' Indeed, the vast majority of these establishments

> were mere places of resort for idlers and tipplers, where vicious concerns are formed, and habits of indolence and drunkenness take root. . . . In them our youth are often initiated into all the mysteries of iniquity, and inbibe the principles of the most ruinous licentiousness. It is at these places that the poor captives of strong drink find a ready supply—for it is seldom denied to any that can pay for it. Here many spend their hard earned wages, while their families are suffering for want of the necessaries of life.[21]

Despite the zeal with which it pursued its cause, the Temperance Reformation Society represented little more than a voice crying in the wilderness. Upper Canadians stubbornly resisted all attempts to moderate their traditional drinking habits, and few politicians demonstrated a willingness to take up the cause of reform. Furthermore, in many communities local leaders compounded the problem by granting an excessive number of tavern licences and by refusing to suppress unlicensed and, therefore, illegal establishments. A combination of factors, including the need for revenue and the influence wielded by the tavern owners, shaped the response of the authorities. As one disillusioned observer contended in a newspaper article lamenting the profusion of illegal taverns in St Catharines, 'our Magistrates wink at the existence of these grog-shops, because the keepers of them turn the victory in their favour at the poll'.[22]

This fierce attachment to strong drink frustrated attempts at law enforcement. Drunkenness frequently precipitated public disturbances, ranging in severity from minor brawls and domestic disputes to full-scale riots, and drunk and disorderly conduct represented the most common transgression resulting in criminal conviction.[23] During the 1830s in Brockville, the vast majority of cases brought before the local magistrate stemmed, at least in part, from overindulgence in intoxicating beverages. On one occasion, the authorities committed a man named Owen Reynolds to the Brockville jail for causing a disturbance of the public peace while 'deranged by liquor'. According to the constable who had made the arrest, 'the Defendant . . . was drunk, and was guilty of cursings and executions, which conduct was very much to the annoyance of his neighbours.' Confirming that he 'was drunk, swore very profusely, and made much disturbance', a number of other witnesses testified that Reynolds also had attacked his wife and child compelling them to flee from the house in order to escape his abuse.[24] A similar incident concerned a well-known Brockville drunkard, Peter Tart, who according to the testimony of a blacksmith named Michael Hunter 'came to his house last night after he was asleep . . . and behaved in a most abusive manner'. Apparently, Tart had burst into Hunter's bedroom unannounced, shook his fist in the surprised man's face, and then threatened to beat him to a pulp before he was eventually convinced to leave the premises. Summarily convicting Tart of drunk and disorderly conduct, the authorities reprimanded him for causing a public disturbance and ordered him to pay a fine of twenty shillings.[25] One of the most notable cases of alcohol-induced crime contained in the records of the Brockville magistracy involved a man who was sentenced to jail for committing a long list of offences including 'drunkenness, showing his private parts, and other indecent and scandalous actions to the annoyance of the inhabitants of the Town'. The evidence presented before the court indicated that the defendant, a man named Peter Vanshank, had confronted the wife of a neighbour while he was returning home from a local tavern. Vanshank was visibly intoxicated, and he became involved in a protracted and increasingly unpleasant dispute with the woman; among a number of other insults not specified in the court record, he insisted that she was a 'french bitch'. When the woman 'rebuked him' and informed him that she was not interested in his concerns, Vanshank unceremoniously 'unbuttoned his pantaloons in front, and told her to look at his concerns (meaning his private parts)'. The offended neighbour promptly informed one of the local magistrates of Vanshank's 'scandalous actions', and the matter was taken to court for resolution.[26]

Domestic disputes and disagreements between neighbours were much less worrisome than the depredations carried out by gangs of drunken youths. Taverns and dram shops provided a focus for the rowdier elements of the colonial population; all too often drinking sprees were followed by outbreaks of brawling and vandalism. During the 1820s, for example, a series of letters printed in the *Kingston Chronicle* complained of the 'midnight frolics' of 'some spirited young fellows, who . . . are in the habit of prowling the streets at night'. Detailing the enormous amount of damage done to property by these youths, one irate resident concluded that 'there is scarcely a street in our town, but bears some marks of the wanton attacks that have been made on the houses, or property of our neighbours.'[27] Almost two decades later, Kingston was still plagued by frequent violations of the public peace and attacks on property carried out by disorderly youths who frequented the town's infamous drinking shops. 'Gangs are committing depredations upon property and disturbing the peaceable Citizens,' the committee on police declared in a report submitted to the mayor, and 'disreputable houses are kept open nearly all night for the reception of the disturbers of the peace, and to the great injury of our youth.'[28] Toronto rowdies frequented the neighbourhood adjacent to the waterfront at the foot of Yonge Street. During the late 1820s and early 1830s, the freeholders and householders residing in that part of the town petitioned the magistracy on a number of occasions complaining of 'Characters . . . whose principal object seemed to be the outraging of all order, peace and respectability.' Much to the petitioners' chagrin, however, nothing of significance was done to bring an end to these 'Lawless annihilations of the public peace'. Respectable townsfolk continued to have 'their eyes daily offended with the most violent and savage attacks' and 'their ears . . . grated with midnight yellings of beings a disgrace to human nature, of midnight marauders who stand opposed to peace, and whose only happiness seems to be confusion and desperation'.[29]

Drunkenness and its attendant problems represented only one facet of the licentiousness of Upper Canadian society. Prostitution flourished, and despite the passing of anti-prostitution by-laws and the arrest of women engaged in the trade, little progress was made during the early Victorian period in the campaign to suppress infamous houses 'where lewdness, indecencies and other immoral and scandalous actions are permitted'.[30] The general population also demonstrated a remarkable predilection for gambling. Horse races, cock and dog fights, bagatelle, and card games proved to be popular occasions for wagers, and many of these events attracted large crowds drawn from both the upper and lower echelons of society. Even though certain municipalities passed anti-gaming by-laws designed to enforce a more dignified code of behaviour, gambling continued to enjoy great popularity well into the nineteenth century.[31]

The prevalence of political corruption, pork-barrelling and voter manipulation further illustrates the absence of a strict moral code. Candidates in both provincial and municipal elections made liberal use of bribery and, if necessary, of violence and intimidation; once elected to public office, many politicians proceeded to line their pockets and the pockets of their friends and families while supposedly serving the public interest. In addition, Upper Canadian election campaigns were extremely rowdy events. Alcohol was freely dispensed to the electorate; brawls between warring factions erupted with surprising regularity. Political and ethnic rivalries were never far below the surface, and the potent combination of strong drink and excessive enthusiasm for a favoured candidate created a very volatile situation. The following ditty composed in St Catharines in honour of the 1858 municipal contest indicates that many candidates were prepared to use virtually any means at their disposal in order to secure victory at the polls. Satirizing the heavy-handed tactics of the incumbent mayor's supporters, it provides a fascinating insight into the rough and tumble of colonial politics:

I've been roaming, I've been roaming,
   Up as far as Queenston Street,
And I'm coming, and I'm coming,
   With its mud upon my feet.

I've been roaming, I've been roaming,
   'Till I scarce know what I'm at,
And I'm coming, and I'm coming,
   With a brick within my hat.

I've been roaming, I've been roaming,
   Where the boys are in a fight,
And I'm coming, and I'm coming,
   Though I think [hic] I'm rather tight.

I've been roaming, I've been roaming,
   Where each voter whisky sips,
And I'm coming, and I'm coming,
   With rum kisses on my lips.

I've been roaming, I've been roaming,
   All around, and raising Cain,
And I'm coming, and I'm coming,
   To my 'office' drunk again.[32]

A lack of respect for legal niceties characterized the political culture of the period, and scattered attempts to improve the moral tone of either provincial or municipal politics made little progress until the latter part of the century.

Despite the significance of poverty, immorality and crime, class conflict constituted the principal factor contributing to the disorderly and, often, violent nature of Upper Canadian society. Low wages and unemployment precipitated most of the strikes and riots involving disgruntled Irish navvies. Nonetheless, in order to fully understand the intensity of class conflict during the early Victorian period, one must take into account the polarization which characterized the colonial social fabric. An enormous gap separated the rich from the poor, and unskilled navvies represented the most exploited segment of the working population. Cultural alienation heightened the potential for violence created by economic exploitation. The competition between Irish and non-Irish workers for jobs, the long-standing feuds between Irish factions, the resentment of the navvies towards their affluent and almost invariably Protestant employers, the absence of effective social control mechanisms, and the scant regard given to the humanity of the workers triggered a series of violent confrontations which rocked the province with frightening regularity for more than three decades.

The focus of class conflict changed over the course of the period. As Claire Pentland noted, workers employed by the autocratic Colonel John By on the construction of the Rideau Canal went on strike at least three times during the spring of 1827 in order to protest against substandard wages.[33] Similarly, during the 1830s, the most serious disturbances occurred in the Ottawa Valley, where the so-called Shiners' War seriously tested the ability of the established authorities to enforce the rule of law. Initially a conflict between Irish and French-Canadian workers engaged in the lumber trade, the Shiners' War was transformed into a class-based struggle as the resentment of the Irish raftsmen or Shiners was increasingly directed against Bytown's affluent residents. Under the leadership of Peter Aylen, an opportunist who forcefully articulated the views of his men, the Shiners managed to seize control of the town's main streets and to terrorize the law-abiding citizenry before they were eventually dispersed by a vigilante organization established by a group of prominent townsfolk. The rioting which disrupted the Bytown area during the 1830s clearly revealed the impotence of the traditional means of law enforcement. The Justice of the Peace lacked the resources required to counter the threat posed by Aylen and his supporters, and without resort to extraordinary measures it would have been impossible to restore order and tranquillity to the battered community.[34]

The commencement of canal construction projects during the 1840s shifted the main focus of class conflict from the Ottawa Valley to the Niagara Peninsula and the south-eastern part of the province. Eager to improve the water route linking Upper Canada to the United States and the Atlantic seaboard, colonial politicians utilized the generous financial support afforded by the British government following the union of the Canadas to initiate a number of projects which demanded immense outlays of capital and a plentiful supply of cheap labour. The enlargement of the Welland Canal and the construction of a series of locks on the St Lawrence River between Cornwall and Montreal represented the most ambitious of these undertakings. Both projects were plagued by serious outbreaks of labour violence; moreover, the magistracy proved incapable of carrying out its law-enforcement responsibilities. Frightened politicians, contractors and property owners saw no other alternative than to call upon the military in order to suppress the labourers and defend their interests.[35]

The rioting which erupted in the St Catharines area during the summer of 1842, while the Welland Canal was being enlarged, attests to the serious implications of labour unrest. Angered by the decision to slash wages and offer employment to less than a third of their number, the navvies who had been attracted to the region by the promise of work decided to organize a massive strike that would compel the contractors to grant them significant concessions. After ensuring that all of the labourers in the vicinity of the canal participated in their protest, they marched *en masse* into St Catharines in order to demonstrate their solidarity and articulate their demands. None of them would work until employment was found for them all, the navvies declared in no uncertain terms, and unless they were supplied with food and other vital provisions, they would take whatever they needed by force. Several days later, when a response to their demands was not forthcoming, the angry workers made good on their threat. They proceeded to plunder the contractors' storehouse, confiscating twelve barrels of pork and two barrels of flour, and after distributing this food among the more than seventy shanties located along the banks of the canal, they paraded into St Catharines carrying a banner emblazoned with the words 'Bread or Work' on one side, and 'Peace and Union—God Save the Queen' on the other. When the authorities, led by W.H. Merritt, the canal project's most persistent proponent, ordered the crowd to disperse, the navvies replied with 'a well understood Irish shout' before pillaging much of the town including several flour mills and a schooner moored in the harbour.[36]

The most disturbing aspect of the riot was the inability of the magistracy to disperse the crowd and to effectively protect the property of law-abiding citizens. The navvies never attempted to mask their contempt for Merritt and the other justices, and for much of the summer they roamed the countryside, terrorizing the inhabitants of St Catharines and a number of nearby communities. As the immediate crisis subsided, the hostility of the local population was increasingly directed against the magistracy. While acknowledging that their efforts had been hampered by the absence of a well-armed militia, many observers concluded that the indecision and incompetence of Merritt and his colleagues had allowed the protest march to escalate into a full-scale riot. In his analysis of the disturbances, the editor of the *St Catharines Journal* no doubt echoed the concerns of many townsfolk when he chastised the justices of the peace for failing to prosecute the navvies when they first transgressed the bounds of normally accepted behaviour:

> the whole affair is disgraceful to British rule, and to those entrusted with the administration of the laws and the preservation of the peace. . . . We fearlessly aver, that a common share of the prudent and promptitude on the part of the Magistrates of this village, at the commencement of the disturbances, would have put an effectual check, if not, suppressed altogether, the shameful scenes of disorder, violence and robbery. . . . The truth is, there is no unanimity among our Magistrates, as a body: one assuming a superiority which the others will not brook, while each having a plan of his own, will yield nothing to the suggestions of another; and so, while they are wrangling about measures, the

people are rolled, churches burned, property destroyed, unoffending and quiet persons brutally beaten. . . . The inhabitants have lost all confidence in the authorities, and have become dispirited—the canallers hold them in contempt; and even our old women are beginning to cry 'Shame' upon their imbecility.[37]

Order returned to the Niagara Peninsula only after the arrival of the militia and the introduction of a state of emergency comparable to martial law.

The St Catharines riot was not an isolated incident. Equally violent disturbances erupted in a number of other communities so that the gravity of the situation eventually compelled the provincial government to institute emergency legislation designed to bolster the position of local officials. During the spring of 1845 the Governor, Sir Charles Metcalfe, gave royal assent to a bill authorizing the Executive Council to declare a state of emergency in the vicinity of any canal construction project where 'Riots and violent Outrages' were anticipated. This legislation placed stringent controls on the carrying of firearms, and it invested the authorities with sweeping powers to apprehend and hold suspected lawbreakers.[38]

Emergency measures failed to alter the pattern of violence which accompanied large-scale public works projects. During the 1850s, for example, when the province undertook a massive program of railway construction, a series of violent confrontations involving large numbers of striking Irish navvies threatened, once again, the ability of the authorities to carry out their law enforcement mandate. One of the most protracted of these disturbances occurred in Hamilton and nearby Dundas during the spring and summer of 1851, while the Great Western Railway was under construction. As he indicated in a speech delivered in the Legislative Assembly, Solicitor General Lewis Thomas Drummond was so appalled by the 'great disorders' precipitated by the workers employed on the project that he concluded that the 'experience of both Upper and Lower Canada was sufficient to show that the local authorities were far from being uniformly equal to the preservation of the public peace.' In the Dundas area, he declared, the 'officers of justice were unable to issue warrants against the rioters; and if any of the farmers interfered, their barns and property were injured or destroyed.'[39] Recognizing the need for a concerted offensive that would unite the resources of both public and private interests, Hamilton's Common Council eventually resolved to co-operate with the directors of the Great Western in creating a special police force which subsequently received instructions to suppress 'the violence of the laborers' and 'to keep order on the line of the railway'. The municipality agreed to employ twenty-seven additional constables for the duration of the troubles at a cost of more than £400.[40] Other examples could be cited, but these few are sufficient to illustrate the disruptive influence of the class conflict generated by the colony's exploitative socio-economic system. For many communities, confrontations between labour and capital represented much more than a mere annoyance. They posed a serious threat to

life and property, and most importantly, they tested the ability of the established authorities to enforce the rule of law in the area under their
jurisdiction.

The destabilizing influence of poverty, immorality, crime, and class conflict
lent a sense of urgency to the institutional innovations carried out by Upper
Canadian reformers during the first half of the nineteenth century. Although
a variety of imperatives, including the influx of moral reform ideas from
Great Britain and the United States, evangelicalism, changing perceptions of
human nature, and the need for greater economy, came into play, the crucial
link between social disruption and reform initiatives cannot be denied. All
of the reforms carried out during this period, whether they addressed the
need for public education, more efficacious law enforcement or the incar-
ceration of social deviants, were founded on a perception of colonial society
which clearly recognized the potential for disorder and disruption on an
unprecedented scale. For many reformers, institutionalism—the creation of
formal mechanisms capable of promoting social cohesion and stability—
represented the most viable alternative. Social reform ideas and specific strategies may have originated outside the boundaries of the province, but Upper
Canadian reformers embraced these new concepts with an enthusiasm comparable to that of their British and American counterparts. In addition to
bolstering the established order and facilitating both personal and social
regeneration, institutionalism promised to be the most efficient and economical way of offsetting escalating social tensions.

The move towards institutionalism at the provincial level has already been
well documented. The extensive body of literature focusing on educational
reform, for example, has indicated that the anxieties of middle-class reformers
provided a major impetus to the campaign to establish a public system of
schools accessible to all children regardless of the financial position of their
parents. Fearful of an upsurge in anti-social behaviour and convinced that
human nature was 'infinitely corruptible and society infinitely depraved',
Egerton Ryerson and his band of educational reformers perceived public
schools as a means of minimizing class conflict, uplifting the uncivilized
masses and promoting middle-class respectability.[41] While not completely dis-
counting the impact of humanitarian concerns, scholars such as Susan Houston and Alison Prentice have depicted educational reform as a well-thought-
out response to the forces of disruption at work on Upper Canadian society.[42]
A public system of schools was not the only measure of reform success. By
mid-century, the provincial penitentiary had been in operation at Kingston
for more than a decade; the provincial asylum in Toronto had recently been
completed. Both establishments reflected the faith which many reformers
placed in the transforming power of institutions, and they constituted an

important part of the move towards institutionalism which characterized the early Victorian period.[43]

A similar trend occurred at the municipal level. Indeed, the incorporation of urban communities and the subsequent creation of boards of police and common councils stemmed, in part, from a fear of social disruption and a desire to augment the security of respectable townsfolk. When it became apparent that the appointed magistracy was incapable of fulfilling many of its responsibilities, including its law enforcement mandate, the provincial government responded by revamping municipal institutions and by investing the newly created elective councils with sweeping legislative and administrative powers. Eager to utilize their full authority in order to suppress anti-social behaviour, boards of police and common councils soon initiated a barrage of public order and morality by-laws banning immoderate driving, public drunkenness, brawling, rioting, gambling, indecent exposure, vagrancy, charivaris, and prostitution. In the process, they established much stricter governmental control over the dynamics of urban life.[44]

Several other local initiatives reflected a desire to enhance social cohesion. Over the course of the 1840s and 1850s, a number of towns and cities abandoned the traditional constable-watch system in favour of professional and uniformed constabularies which resembled those already in existence in British and American cities. Informal policing may have been satisfactory in the early years following settlement, but by mid-century many urban centres required a more dependable and tightly organized, twenty-four-hour-a-day service. As Toronto's board of police commissioners maintained in 1859 in a report stressing the need for a fully professional force:

> When police service is required, it is too unsafe to entrust to any raw, unpracticed help which can be had on the sudden, for the duties of the policeman are such as demand long practice, and the exercise of many other qualities, which those unused to the discipline of the force, are very unfit to be entrusted to.[45]

By the time of Confederation, most municipalities had conceded that only a professional constabulary organized in the manner outlined in the Toronto police commissioners' report was fully equipped to satisfy their law enforcement requirements.

Workhouses and industrial farms performed a similar stabilizing function. In addition to housing the poor and providing them with sustenance, these 'charitable' institutions were expected to reform 'loose and disorderly characters' by providing 'proper training under charge of the civil authorities'.[46] During the winter of 1836, the proponents of Toronto's first house of industry were so confident in the ability of that institution to inculcate 'principles and habits of industry and moral virtue' among its inmates that they rashly predicted a speedy end to vagrancy, street begging, drunkenness, and petty crime.[47] The workhouses and industrial farms subsequently established in towns and cities throughout the province never really possessed the potential to transform the indigent poor in the manner predicted by the reformers. Nonetheless, their growing popularity and the willingness of local leaders to finance their construction provide yet another illustration of the credibility given to the reformers' public order and morality concerns. Once again, institutionalism was depicted as a panacea capable of alleviating a wide range of social problems.

Had it not been for the volatile and raucous nature of Upper Canadian society, much of the impetus behind the reform impulse would have been removed. Clearly, the need for professional constabularies, houses of industry, public order by-laws, and educational reform would have been much less pressing. Attention needs to be paid to the role of ideas and a desire for greater economy, but any analysis which fails to situate reform and the move towards institutionalism in this larger socio-economic context seriously misrepresents the historical record. Colonel Denison was mistaken when he lauded Upper Canada as a model of cohesion and stability, and subsequent historians who contributed either directly or indirectly to this romanticized view of the past were equally ill-informed. Despite the smug sense of superiority which mars much of the traditional literature, conflict, disruption and division proved to be the distinguishing characteristics of the society founded in the wake of the Loyalist influx. The fact that order was ultimately maintained attests, not to the law-abiding nature of the colonial population; but rather to the zeal and commitment of the authorities who controlled the governmental apparatus. The threat posed from both within and without was eventually countered, but only after many years of struggle.

Suggestions for Further Reading

D. Owen Carrigan, *A History of Crime and Punishment in Canada* (Toronto, 1991).
J.M.S. Careless, *The Union of the Canadas: The Growth of Canadian Institutions, 1841–1857* (Toronto, 1967).
H. Clare Pentland, *Labour and Capital in Canada, 1650–1860* (Toronto, 1981).

Notes

[1] *The United Empire Loyalists*, ed. Leslie F.S. Upton (Toronto: Copp Clark, 1967), 140.
[2] *Heritage of Canada*, ed. Hugh Durnford (Toronto: Reader's Digest, 1978), 359.
[3] One study, in particular, has incorporated this phrase into its title. See *Canada: A Guide to the Peaceable Kingdom*, ed. William Kilbourn (Toronto: Macmillan, 1970).

[4]Kenneth McNaught, 'Violence in Canadian History', in *Character and Circumstance: Essays in Honour of Donald Grant Creighton*, ed. John S. Moir (Toronto: Macmillan, 1970), 84.

[5]John Weaver, 'Crime, Public Order, and Repression: The Gore District in Upheaval 1832–1851', *Ontario History*, LXXVIII (September 1986), 177.

[6]See Michael Katz, *The People of Hamilton, Canada West* (Cambridge: Harvard Univ. Press, 1975).

[7]See David Gagan, *Hopeful Travellers* (Toronto: Univ. of Toronto Press, 1981).

[8]For a more detailed analysis of the hardship precipitated by winter, see Judith Fingard, 'The Winter's Tale: Contours of Pre-Industrial Poverty in British North America, 1815–1860', Canadian Historical Association Historical Papers, 1974.

[9]*St Catharines Journal*, 18 and 25 August 1842.

[10]Public Archives of Ontario (hereafter PAO), City of Toronto Papers (mis.), MS 385, 14 May 1834; PAO, City of Ottawa Minutes, GS 3721, 4 April 1857.

[11]City of Toronto Archives (hereafter CTA), 1847 Journal, report of the Finance Committee, 27 September 1847.

[12]PAO, City of Toronto Papers (mis.), MS 385, letter from Sheriff Jarvis to the mayor, 27 August 1847.

[13]For an excellent analysis of the British North American response to the famine Irish, see Joy Parr, 'The Welcome and the Wake: Attitudes in Canada toward the Irish Famine Migration', *Ontario History*, LXVI (June 1974).

[14]Queen's University Archives (hereafter QUA), City of Kingston Papers, House of Industry Records, Visitor's Book 1853–9, 8 February 1855.

[15]QUA, City of Kingston Papers, Kingston Report Book, report of the Special Committee to investigate the management of the House of Industry, 13 December 1852.

[16]P.B. Waite, 'Sir Oliver Mowat's Canada: Reflections on an Un-Victorian Society', in *Oliver Mowat's Ontario*, ed. Donald Swainson (Toronto: Macmillan, 1972), 12–32.

[17]For further evidence of widespread alcohol abuse, see M.A. Garland and J.J. Talman, 'Pioneer Drinking Habits and the Rise of the Temperance Agitation in Upper Canada Prior to 1840', in *Aspects of Nineteenth-Century Ontario*, ed. F.H. Armstrong (Toronto: Univ. of Toronto Press, 1974).

[18]QUA, City of Kingston Papers, Kingston Minutes, 3 May 1841.

[19]QUA, City of Kingston Papers, Kingston Report Book, draft of the communication in reply to one from the Honourable L.B. Harrison, 24 June 1842.

[20]*Ibid.*

[21]PAO, City of Toronto Papers (mis.), MS 385, petition of the Temperance Reformation Society, 11 December 1842.

[22]*St Catharines Journal*, 26 April 1849.

[23]See Weaver, 'Crime, Public Order and Repression'.

[24]Victoria Hall (hereafter VH), Brockville Minutes, Vol. I, 5 October 1832.

[25]*Ibid.*, 3 June 1834.

[26]*Ibid.*, 14 September 1835.

[27]*Kingston Chronicle*, 17 December 1824.

[28]*QUA*, Kingston Report Book, report of the Committee on Police, to April 1843.

[29]PAO, City of Toronto Papers (mis.), MS 385, petition of Robert Bead and 27 others, 20 July 1835.

[30]VH, Brockville Minutes, Vol. I, 14 July 1834.

[31]Refer to P.B. Waite, 'Sir Oliver Mowat's Canada'.

[32]*St Catharines Journal*, 23 September 1858.

[33]*Labour and Capital in Canada 1650–1860* (Toronto: James Lorimer, 1981), 190.

[34]Michael Cross, 'The Shiners' War: Social Violence in the Ottawa Valley in the 1830s', *Canadian Historical Review*, LIV (January 1973).

[35]For more detailed discussions of the class conflict associated with canal construction projects, see Pentland, *Labour and Capital in Canada*, and Ruth Bleasdale, 'Class Conflict on the Canals of Upper Canada in the 1840s', *Labour/Le Travailleur*, Spring 1981. Donald Akenson presents a somewhat different view of Irish immigration in his recent book, *The Irish in Ontario: A Study in Rural History* (Kingston and Montreal: McGill-Queen's Univ. Press, 1984).

[36]*St Catharines Journal*, 18 August 1842.

[37]*Ibid.*, 24 August 1842.

[38]*Statutes of Canada, 1844–46*, 'An Act for the better preservation of the Peace, and the prevention of Riots and violent Outrages at and near Public Works while in progress of construction', 17 March 1845.

[39]*Debates of the Legislative Assembly of Upper Canada*, ed. Elizabeth Nish, Vol. X, part II, 1505.

[40]McMaster University, Mills Library (hereafter ML), Hamilton Minutes, 11 April 1851.

[41]Alison Prentice, *The School Promoters: Education and Social Class in Mid-Nineteenth Century Upper Canada* (Toronto: McClelland and Stewart, 1977), 25.

[42]See Prentice, *The School Promoters*; Susan E. Houston, 'Politics, Schools and Social Change in Upper Canada', *Canadian Historical Review* LIII (1972); Stephen Schecter, 'Capitalism, Class and Educational Reform in Canada', in *The Canadian State: Political Economy and Political Power*, ed. Leo Panitch (Toronto: Univ. of Toronto Press, 1977).

[43]See Thomas Edward Brown, 'Living with God's Afflicted: A History of the Provincial Lunatic Asylum at Toronto, 1830–1911', Ph.D. thesis, Queen's University, 1981.

[44]For a fuller discussion of the link between local government and public order concerns refer to the author's dissertation, 'By and for the Large Propertied Interests: The Dynamics of Local Government in Six Upper Canadian Towns during the Era of Commercial Capitalism, 1832–1860', Ph.D thesis, McMaster University, 1985.

[45]CTA, 1859 Journal, report of the Board of Commissioners on Police, appendix.

[46]ML, Hamilton Minutes, 26 May 1856.

[47]PAO, City of Toronto Papers (mis.), MS 385, letter from B. Turgaard to Mayor Morrison, 28 December 1836.

20

The Rebellions of 1837/8

Fernand Ouellet

Rebellions are, of course, failed revolutions. While Canada has never experienced an upheaval that has been labelled a revolution, it has seen many uprisings of one sort or another, particularly in the provinces of Upper and Lower Canada in 1837 and 1838. Traditionally the two rebellions have been grouped together and have been viewed as responses to the failure of colonial political and constitutional institutions to respond adequately to the need for change and reform. In both provinces an entrenched oligarchy, the Family Compact in Upper Canada and the Château Clique in Lower Canada, refused to bend to new political demands from the elected houses of assembly, producing a sense of frustration that resulted in armed uprisings in both provinces against the governments in power. The rebellions were easily crushed by the local authorities with the support of the British government—less easily in Lower than in Upper Canada—but they led to an investigation of the colonial situation by Lord Durham and ultimately to responsible government. Despite a tendency to consider the rebellions together, historians have long recognized that both the problems and the responses were more intense in Lower Canada, where French Canadians constituted an embattled racial entity with cultural, linguistic, and religious differences from the remainder of British North America. The Lower Canadian Rebellion (or rebellions, for there were several uprisings divided by the visit of Lord Durham) thus constitutes a special problem of explanation. Among many questions on Lower Canada faced by historians, three inter-related ones stand out in the literature. First, were the uprisings of 1837–8 a logical outgrowth of the long-term developments within the province, or merely a response to immediate problems of the time? Second, were the uprisings produced by the dissatisfaction of a relatively few individuals within the upper ranks of Lower Canadian society, or were they a broadly based popular movement supported by large numbers of inhabitants in the province? Finally, if the Lower Canadians were responding *en masse* to longstanding grievances, what were they?

In the following article Fernand Ouellet offers a complex analysis of the rebellions of Lower Canada, one that focuses not on constitutional unrest and the nationalists but on local uprisings and their leaders. According to Ouellet there was a broadly based popular movement, led by people from the lower ranks, that was responding to deep-seated economic and social difficulties in the province and sought major change. Unfortunately, Ouellet maintains, the rebellions were defined and dominated by middle-class élites who were less interested in overturning the status quo than in gaining control of it for themselves. This élite was prepared to use

the rhetoric of French-Canadian nationalism to achieve its goal—the elimination of the *anglais* middle-class—but not to seek the genuine social reform desired by the popular movement. The result, in the last analysis, was counter-revolutionary.

Ouellet's analysis, both in its detail and in its overall interpretation, raises a number of interesting questions. Are there, for example, other possible explanations for the age differentials Ouellet detects between the popular leaders and those from the élite? What were the grievances and goals of the popular leaders and their followers? What evidence does Ouellet provide for his claim that there was an incipient class consciousness? Was popular discontent in 1837–8 (as distinct from the élite response) organized or organizable? And finally, does Ouellet make a convincing argument for a distinction between the conservatism of the élite and the radicalism of the masses?

This article first appeared in French in *Histoire Sociale/Social History* 2 (1968), 54–82.

For a long time historians focused mainly on the political aspect of the rebellions of 1837–8 in Lower Canada. That is why, despite their pathetic failure, the rebellions were seen to have their ultimate justification in the triumph of great constitutional principles that were considered eminently valuable in themselves, such as responsible government, or were regarded as essential to the survival of the French-Canadian nationality.[1] Once again the world of values had scored a striking victory over petty economic and class interests. Thus, after warning us that the movement of 1837–8 could not be reduced 'to a racial or even a class struggle without diminishing and falsifying history', Canon Groulx came to the emphatic conclusion that it was 'an episode in a political struggle for a political end'.[2] It is true that, from this point of view, the men of 1837 had committed deplorable errors: they had come to terms with 'shallow democratic ideologies'; they had surrendered to anticlericalism to the point of grave disobedience to the Church. There was much to forgive Papineau in particular. But, Canon Groulx asked, had Papineau not embodied 'the aspirations of a nationality'[3] at a highly critical moment of our national history? 'His glory', he added, 'will be recognized by more and more of us as the feeling for political independence gains ground.'[4]

This version of history, in which the political background dominates the rest, seems to me far too limited. Certainly politics has its own existence, its own standards and procedures; but it is also a setting for the fermentation and confrontation of economic interests.[5] It is no less crucial for the understanding of the phenomena we call politics to discern the manifold links between politics and society. Can political strategies be readily separated from social strategies? Behind groups and parties we usually find social groups and classes rather than isolated individuals. It could even be argued that a lengthy political crisis is one of the surest signs of fundamental social change, or of a transfer of economic and social power from one group to another, whether it be an ethnic group, a social class, or a combination of both. A resort to arms by certain elements in society would then constitute an admission, explicit or implicit, of the failure of normal political strategies. At the risk of diminishing the story of the rebellions in Lower Canada, and tarnishing some of its lustre, but in the certainty of encountering the real problems of real people, I intend to show these revolutionary events in a social light— the only light that, broadly understood, can give us an inkling of the reality of those troubled times. This perspective raises two sets of questions. To what extent, and why did ordinary people take an active part in the movement? What role did the 'élites' play and what were their relations with the common people, urban and rural? All this obviously raises the central question of what the revolutionary ideology was, and involves a close look at class consciousness.

A Popular Movement

In his book on the popular uprisings in France in the seventeenth century, Boris Porchnev throws light on a series of spontaneous mass insurrections, spread by contagion and the establishment of popular leadership. To this description Porchnev adds an observation directly relevant to my purpose:

> As long as it kept its exclusively popular character, the movement suffered from bad organization and remained blindly impulsive. When its leadership was entrusted to representatives of another social class, they distorted the movement and its essential aims. . . . They contributed to its social blindness: by confining the platform of the uprising to a fight against taxation, they prevented it from developing into a revolutionary anti-feudal, anti-absolutist movement.[6]

Reading Canon Groulx might tempt us to draw a comparison between the Lower Canadian movement and its seventeenth-century French counterpart. The former is described by Groulx as 'an improvised movement, almost spontaneous in its outbreaks of violence; beyond that, a popular movement, a fairly broad and deep rural phenomenon'.[7] Unfortunately, Groulx's reliance on the somewhat inconsistent statements made by Papineau after his defeat seems to have misled him about the social origin of the revolutionary movement. By denying any premeditation on the part of the revolutionary leaders, Papineau absolved them—and especially himself—of all responsibility, and incriminated the government against which popular anger was directed. Fair enough, perhaps; but I remain very skeptical. As Wolfred Nelson said, commenting on certain admissions of Papineau's:

> You have to fight liars, whether with their own weapons or with trickery. Frankness is a fine thing among honest men and in private life; in public, it leaves us too exposed. I am annoyed by Mr Papineau's and Mackenzie's admission that we had decided to rebel. That is to justify our opponents and to deprive us of any right to complain that we were attacked.[8]

In fact, the risings of 1837–8, just like the nationalism from which they sprang, started among the upper classes and spread downwards from them. Here is the first variation from the process outlined by Porchnev.

Since 1830 the idea of revolution had gained ground among a section of the militant Patriotes. Some leaders spoke of it as a possibility; others thought it inevitable. However, there was no systematic effort to create a revolutionary organization. It was after the Russell Resolutions in the spring of 1837, which deprived the Patriotes of all hope of success by peaceful means, that the leaders of the party felt bound to change their strategy and consider revolutionary action. It was the leaders of the Montreal region, recruited from the professional class and the merchants, who took on the task of redirecting the Patriote movement. Even though they were careful to destroy the compromising documents—Papineau admitted this himself—there is a mass of corroborative evidence showing precisely what the main lines of the revolutionary strategy were. It consisted of two stages: the first, the so-called 'legal' agitation, was aimed chiefly at forcing the government to modify its position; the second involved (in the event that the first one failed) launching a revolution 'after freeze-up'.[9] This was a compromise between the moderate and extremist elements of the party, the latter leaning more to immediate actions. Besides, how was it possible to intimidate the government without preparing the populace for a possible rebellion? The radical leaders never bothered to make this distinction. From the spring of 1837 they were openly preaching revolt. In June, Léon Charlebois, a Montreal tavern-keeper, declared 'that it was necessary to help the revolutionary party that was then in existence'.[10] At Chambly the Pacauds, who were shipowners, said they 'would be happy if the Patriotes could succeed in their plan for independence from the British government'.[11] Papineau himself did not escape the revolutionary atmosphere, which was spreading rapidly. At several meetings he even went so far as to make seditious remarks, though without refraining from ambiguity. Thus, when he warned the farmers that when the plums were ripe it was time to pick them, he was using language that was perfectly clear to them. Several witnesses testified that on the sixth of August, at a meeting at Saint-Constant, Côme Cherrier and Toussaint Peltier, two Montreal lawyers from the more moderate side of the revolutionary camp, were to make speeches 'tending to incite the local people to rebel if the English government failed to grant them what they had demanded in the Ninety-two Resolutions'.[12] These are just a few examples from a mass of evidence indicating that 'legal' opposition was more a front than a practical objective: it was a screen behind which an armed uprising could be organized—because it was illusory to think the government would yield to blackmail. If there is no doubt about the premeditation, it is also clear that the movement was not of popular origin. It germinated within the top leadership of the *parti patriote*.

The revolutionary organization, whose centre was Montreal and whose principal body was the Permanent Central Committee, relied for its support not only on the suburbs but mainly on the country districts. Members of the local élites—those who had lined up with the *parti patriote*—formed the local leadership of the movement. It was they who planned the country meetings where the 'big men from the city' appeared, held small parish meetings on Sundays after Mass, and in some cases took up collections. Not only was there large attendance at these meetings, but in some places groups of armed farmers gathered to attack local inhabitants of British origin and 'known bureaucrats'.[13] The response of the rural populace was immediate, all the more since the rebellion was the climax of over thirty years of political conflict. Throughout the summer of 1837 tension and agitation increased in the country parishes surrounding Montreal. In October Montreal acquired its own revolutionary association aimed at reorganizing the populace. The *Fils de la liberté*, with its military and civil sections (the latter a screen for the former), held meetings at which some leaders gave commentaries on books about the French and American revolutions. Thomas Storrow Brown went so far as to declare that it was time 'to arm ourselves, since the country was moving quickly along the road to independence'.[14] The *Fils de la liberté*, sometimes numbering as many as a thousand, did not hesitate to hold military exercises. For this purpose they used one of the properties, in a suburb of Montreal, of Denis-Benjamin Viger, a cousin of Papineau. This outbreak of agitation, both rural and urban, came to a head at the Six Counties rally, held at Saint-Charles on 23 October—a massive demonstration that marked a real turning point. As Nelson and Côté put it, the time for speeches was over. Papineau arrived at Saint-Charles with an armed escort of some fifteen men, though he later claimed 'to have come to this meeting only because he happened to be passing'.[15]

At the Saint-Charles rally the Patriote leaders went beyond mere violent words. They issued a declaration on the rights of man, modelled on the American declaration of 1776, and decided to get rid of all the militia officers, justices of the peace, and small-claims commissioners appointed by the government. All these officials, they declared, must be replaced by men elected by the people. This revolutionary action, openly supported by Papineau, meant the overthrow of all opponents of the movement. The Patriotes were trying to gain control of the militia and the judiciary. It was on this occasion, too, that plans for an open rebellion were again laid out by the leaders. A date was set for the beginning of December. The day after the meeting Dr Kimber, one of the leaders, would say:

> The moment the river is frozen up, we shall go with forty or fifty thousand armed men to seize Montreal; the local people are all well armed, well supplied with ammunition, and firmly resolved, and after Montreal we shall take Quebec. I was at Saint-Charles and never in any country has there been seen such a rally, so determined to rid itself of the English government.[16]

Even though Kimber could have been tipsy when he made this revelation, his statement nevertheless contained a basis of truth. A letter from Papineau to Mackenzie in February 1838 confirms this:

> If navigation had been closed down as usual about 20 November, if the election of the magistrates had taken place without violence, and only in December, as had been recommended, so that communication would be cut off between the north and south shores of the St Lawrence, the chances of success would have been better.[17]

On 23 October 1837, the day of the Saint-Charles rally, a Pointe-Claire farmer said 'that the damned *chouaguins* [cabbage-heads, or *Canadiens* who had sold out to the English] were going to be whipped now that everybody in the south and the north was armed, that there was no more law . . . and you could do what you liked—Mr Papineau knew that he had to start the revolution at this time, when no help could come from England.'[18] It is not surprising that acts of violence increased after the Saint-Charles rally. In most parishes Patriotes held 'charivaris', demanding the dismissal of militia officers and other government officials. Verbal violence reached something of a peak. A Henryville merchant, Joseph Gariépy, declared that he 'wouldn't rest until all the bureaucrats' heads were cut off'.[19] On 4 November 1837 Jacques Surprenant, innkeeper at Blairfindie, shouted at an opponent that he 'had a good mind to smash him over the head with a bottle because he, the deponent, was a bureaucrat and all bureaucrats had better get out of the country before their brains were blown out, and the said Surprenant said that he would do his utmost to help chop him into pieces.'[20]

At the beginning of November 1837 neither the government, nor members of the clergy who felt a need for strong intervention, could remain passive. Warrants were prepared for the arrest of the principal Patriote leaders. Informed by D.-B. Viger that he was in imminent danger of imprisonment, Papineau had some tense and anxious hours before he finally decided to flee Montreal. A witness to the conversation from the next room, Angélique Labadie, would later report:

> I also heard Mr Papineau say that he would never be satisfied until he was president in this country, and that he would be soon, and that if the government seized this country from him he would snatch it back. Mr Viger then told Mr Papineau that he should keep calm and wait for freeze-up and then he would just have to whistle and all the *habitants* and thousands of Americans would espouse their cause and they would soon be masters of this country.[21]

This first act of the government—the preparation of the warrants—had a magical effect. It prompted the hasty departure of the chief Montreal leaders, who took refuge in the countryside, where they prepared themselves for any emergency. Deprived of its leaders, the urban populace made no move. At Vaudreuil the situation bordered on comedy. The local leaders, fearing imprisonment, begged the people to protect them, on the grounds that they had incited them to revolt from altruistic motives.[22] Camps were formed at Saint-Denis, Saint-Charles, Saint-Mathias, Saint-Eustache, and Saint-Benoît. Intervention by government troops was then unavoidable, and between 17 November and 15 December 1837 military confrontation occurred. In short the government, sensing that matters were coming to a head, forestalled the Patriotes. Apart from this early intervention by government forces, the second rebellion, which took place during the first two weeks of November 1838, was an exact replica of the preceding one. Devised by the élite, especially refugees in the United States, it would spread to the masses through the intervention of the *Société des Frères Chasseurs*, said to have ten thousand members. Once again, lack of leadership on the spot prevented the fourteen hundred *chasseurs* in Montreal from stirring. In Quebec City, where the association was supposed to have two thousand adherents, 'they are more cautious than in Montreal',[23] according to an informed witness. On the whole, the two rebellions leave an identical impression: anarchy, disorganization, weak leadership, and paralysis. Are those not the characteristics of purely peasant uprisings, at least as Porchnev understands them? In this regard, he writes:

> These outside elements in the masses certainly left their stamp on the Nu-Pied movement. . . . There is no doubt that these elements helped the insurgents to organize, to follow a more or less systematic policy, to become a large armed

force—in a word, to overcome the movement's purely impulsive and spontaneous character.[24]

This outline is interesting, but to what extent does it apply to the Lower
Canadian movements? Several hypotheses are possible: superficiality of popular support, a marked persistence of the peasant mentality among the élite,
or—what is simpler—betrayal by the élite.

Though fomented by the élite, these uprisings nevertheless had a broadly
popular character. The rural and urban masses, which provided ninety-five
per cent of the actual revolutionaries, made up the movement's striking force.
The excuse so often put forward by the *habitants* and many others, that they
gave in to the threats of the leaders, must be largely rejected. In my view
fear is an extremely far-reaching and subtle phenomenon but it does not by
itself account for participation by the lower classes in revolutionary events.
Because its range is more general and more varied, the phenomenon of fear
is also more complex in its ramifications. On the other hand, different
excuses given by the common people merit even less attention: for example,
it is easy to assess the origin of one farmer's tale, when arrested on the road
early in the morning, that he was on his way to ask his mother (who lived
in the home of a top rebel leader) to knit him a tuque; or that of another
farmer, arrested after the battle of Saint-Eustache, who said he was about to
drive his wife to confession. Where political vows are concerned, it is so
often a matter of 'swearing with the mouth, not with the heart' that we can
delude ourselves about them.

After analysing the files on the rebels of 1837–8, I find it impossible not
to perceive a genuine popular phenomenon, widespread and deep-rooted,
prompted in large measure by specific, and different, motives than those of
the élites who controlled the movement. I reckon that, not counting the
sympathizers in Montreal, at least five thousand people were directly involved
in the first venture. The following year the number exceeded five thousand,
but the incidents took place in a much more limited area. In 1838 the
populous parishes north of Montreal made no move. Glancing at the other
regions in the province, we find an air of expectation among the people in
the Beauce, and in Kamouraska and Charlevoix. Inquiries made at Saint-
Joseph de la Beauce in the spring of 1838, after the failure of the first rebellion, revealed that 260 inhabitants were still in favour of the Patriotes. Even
if we allow for regional variations that could have a negative effect on popular
attitudes, we still find a psychological receptiveness throughout seigneurial
Lower Canada. In short, the motives that spurred farmers, craftsmen, and
labourers in the Montreal region to revolutionary action operated elsewhere
in varying degrees. The myth of the saviour was too wide-spread for the
popular response not to have had firm roots—both at the time and in the
past.

This popular movement, moreover, was almost exclusively French-Canadian. It did win over a small minority of Irish, whose motives are readily discernible. J. Coward, a Montreal merchant, declared: 'I am a rebel and I would be one as long as there would be a Scotch rascal in this town.'[25] The movement also gained some adherents among farmers of American origin who had settled in the Eastern Townships—a small minority already receptive to democratic ideas. But on the whole the revolutionary phenomenon had its principal support in French-Canadian society. However, it would be a mistake, out of a rigid idea of ethnic character or a concept of 'ethnic class', to see it as a revolt of the whole of French-Canadian society. At the popular level, wealth—which is not the privilege of the many—created a very important split. The 'bureaucrats' seem to have been drawn mainly from the comfortably-off or wealthy farmers—those who were 'fat', as the Patriotes said—while the Patriotes emerged from the most disadvantaged classes. Another observation on the scope of the movement: the distinction between farmer, craftsman, and labourer is not much use in assessing revolutionary fervour. They were attracted equally to the movement, which also appealed as much to the young as it did to older people—meaning that in rural environments economic motivations were the most decisive. Problems like the agricultural crisis and the shortage of land in the seigneuries affected all groups, but especially older people and those with large families. Setting up their children on the land was the central preoccupation for fathers, whether they were farmers, craftsmen, or labourers. The uprisings of 1837–8, then, appear to have been linked to the poverty and insecurity of the working classes, both rural and urban. In the city of Montreal fluctuations in employment were certainly a factor, but let me point out that above all the *parti patriote* brought together those who were most dependent on the land.

Another sign of a movement with a strong popular base is the ability of the rural popular classes to produce their own leadership. Such leaders were innumerable, perhaps too numerous and too unstable for the good of the revolution. I have turned up the names of 721 rural people who in various ways acted as leaders in 1837–8. It must be noted that farmers and craftsmen gained positions of leadership more readily than labourers, who made up at least thirty per cent of the rural population but provided only four per cent of the leaders. Another striking fact to note is that this popular leadership was drawn not from the young but from their elders. Of the 215 leaders whose ages I have ascertained, seventy-six per cent were over thirty and fifty-five per cent were between thirty and fifty. Between the ages of forty and sixty the proportion was forty-six per cent. Only innkeepers—who often came from peasant backgrounds—were older; half of them were between forty and sixty. Finally, fifty-one per cent of the popular leaders had more than five children.

Furthermore, these working-class leaders were far from being nonentities in the movement. A fair number had already held positions in the militia; some had even been members of the Assembly. Louis Dérigé, a Saint-Constant farmer known as Laplante, was described as 'dangerous to the British government, since in his capacity as head churchwarden, and by his influence generally, he exerts almost absolute authority over the local people.'[26] There was another group, at least as large, who saw a golden opportunity to reach the rank of 'great man'. The situation lent itself so well to overnight promotions that some of them certainly aspired to be generals. On the whole, however, their promotions stopped at the rank of captain, a level at which they proliferated, showing off with their swords. But there were some exceptions: a few were appointed—or appointed themselves—'Major' or 'Colonel', such as Joseph Dumouchelle of Beauharnois. The most famous and least authentic was undoubtedly Amury Girod, an immigrant from Switzerland, a well-educated man who called himself with pride 'cultivateur de Varennes'; at Sainte-Eustache he had no trouble in securing for himself the coveted title of 'General'. By dint of their numbers and the noise they made, and in the absence of any vigorous leadership from above, these popular leaders pervaded the movement. Another major point is that, because they were more garrulous than other country people, and probably more aware, we look to them to express the motivations, and perhaps the ideological leanings, of the masses. For we cannot accept the assumption that the masses naturally exuded class consciousness and an ideology of their own. This also needs to be explored.

The sources of rural discontent were various and of long standing. Since the beginning of the nineteenth century resentment among peasants had steadily increased. Economic troubles, especially the chronic crisis in agriculture, over-population—always more pronounced in the seigneurial lands—and increased taxation by landowners were chief causes of unrest.[27] The shortage of land as much as rural debt created deep insecurity and provoked a reaction against all forms of taxation, even the slightest, whether they were tithes, seigneurial dues, or state taxes. In 1837 the situation was aggravated by a general economic crisis. Social conflicts within the élites had helped to discredit the Establishment, especially the old seigneurial families, and even the clergy. Dissension among the clergy, notably the almost public quarrel about the creation of the bishopric of Montreal, had had an effect on the people. Finally, the clergy, because of their ideology and their attitudes to social and political reform, were out of tune with the aspirations and some of the problems of the popular classes. In some ways the clergy were remote from the people.

Under the circumstances it would have been possible to see a growing popular movement against the old social and economic regime—the seigneurial regime and the privileges of the Church. There was in fact a group within the Patriote élite that wanted to aim the blow in that direction. Dr Côté, one of the most active leaders at Napierville, had no hesitation in telling the farmers 'that they would be independent and free and pay no more revenues to the seigneurs or tithes to the priests'.[28] The Nelson brothers, Girod, and probably Chénier, belonged to this group of radicals, or rather true liberals. It is important to note that wherever this message was preached it found an echo in a section of the populace. Joseph Dumouchelle, a farmer from Sainte-Marie de Beauharnois, who had taken for himself the title of colonel, fought 'to abolish tithes and feudal dues'.[29] Not only had the farmers—somewhat guiltily—overcome clerical prohibitions and accepted the view that the clergy, through their interests, were tied to the power structure; but a fair number of them seemed inclined to take it out on the priests, whom they sometimes called 'black pigs'.[30] Jérôme Lompré, farmer, aged forty-four, with nine children, recruiting for the Saint-Eustache encampment, said to another farmer: 'Come with us; you're well armed and it's fun; it's like a wedding; we drink, we eat, we play the violin, we dance; we are free, we do what we like. Those who need leather can have it, and make themselves shoes. . . . It's our right, we don't give a damn for the king, the queen, or the priests.'[31] This quotation reveals some of the longings unleashed by hard times and the influence of liberal ideology. Hasty generalizations, however, should be avoided. It is true that the movement of 1837–8 had some of the marks of an 'anti-feudal', perhaps a democratic, struggle. All in all the rural people would have emerged with a consciousness of themselves as a class, thanks to the preachings of a small bourgeois élite, and stood up against their lifelong enemies: the monarchy, the seigneurial class, and the clergy. In short, 1837–8 would appear as an abortive attempt to achieve the democratic, bourgeois revolution so dear to the hearts of some Marxist historians. Actually, such anti-feudal and anticlerical tendencies as existed at the time were characteristic only of peasant or middle-class minorities.

In 1837 it was too late to channel popular aggressiveness into a genuinely liberal and democratic ideology. For a long time the dominant influences among the Patriotes had successfully found other outlets for popular discontent. Is this not rather a case of ideological plundering by élites concerned to use the strength of the masses for their own advantage? It would be more accurate to call it manipulation of the people by certain élites. In my opinion, between 1802 and 1838 there was no drawn-out process that could be called an affirmation of class consciousness among the French-Canadian peasants. There was, however, the arrival and the aggravation of a series of vital problems confronting the farmers—who, lacking class consciousness and sufficient political maturity, relied on the élite classes, old or new, for their ideological orientation and their political choices. It was this reliance and their psychological reactions to it that made possible the manipulation of the masses by the élite.

In actual fact the rural masses absorbed an ideology—nationalism—that had been suggested to them by the most influential elements of the *parti patriote*, by people who, though claiming to be democrats, regarded the seigneurial system and the Church as national institutions. Papineau, who would eventually break with the radicals on these issues, was their real leader. They were the ones who sought to uphold traditional economic relationships in opposition to the capitalist class. These élites had taught the common people to recognize their enemies: the government (both colonial and imperial), the capitalist, the emigrant—in a word, the *Anglais*, who, they said, were responsible for all the ills suffered by the 'poor Canadiens'. Therefore the government had to be overthrown and the *Anglais* driven out or killed. 'For a long time', declared Marcel Séné, a Saint-Césaire farmer, 'our country newspapers urged us to distrust and despise the government. Prominent people in the parish said the same thing, so we believed it.'[32] To farmers who were in debt and looking for land to settle their sons on, J.-F. Têtu, a Saint-Hyacinthe notary, said 'that before long they were going to be chased off their property by emigrants [i.e., immigrants], who would treat them like slaves and drive them out into barren country, and that poverty would hound them into the grave with no hope of protection from this government, which was set on ruining these farmers.'[33] The rural people seem to have been especially sensitive to this land issue, which would be resolved, the leaders proclaimed, by extending the seigneurial system to the whole province and by confiscating the property of the English and the French-Canadian traitors—those who, as they liked to say, had 'betrayed the sacred blood.'[34] Meunier, the notary at Saint-Damas, promised for his part that 'those who helped the friends of the region would be rewarded with the bureaucrats' property and township lands, where every house must be pulled down or burned.'[35] This central problem of land gives the best clue to the infiltration of nationalism into the rural classes. Moreover, it was not a recent phenomenon—it dated from the first decade of the century. Concerning this, William Brewster related a conversation with Christophe Laplanche, a Lacolle farmer: 'He told me that the English had no right to be here and that the country belong to the French Canadians and that there were enough of them to occupy it . . . that the country was theirs and that they wanted all the land for themselves.'[36] The attacks against, and looting of, English merchants (some of whom were seigneurs) and *chouaguins* need to be seen in this context. The farmers took advantage of these raids to destroy the account-books of these men, who were their principal creditors, for fear they would seize their lands. In November 1836 L. Lavoie, a Saint-Philippe farmer, seems to have accurately interpreted the intentions of many French-Canadian rural people: 'If they had succeeded in seizing Laprairie, they wouldn't have left a single English, Irish, or Scotch inhabitant alive—of any age or sex.'[37] This verbal violence, which is stressed in a great deal of the testimony, is certainly not without significance. The same is true of certain attacks on Protestants, who were ordered to convert or leave the country: 'we only want one religion here.'[38] The majority of rural people had no desire to see the establishment of a pluralistic society based on religious toleration, and acted on defensive instincts, notably the idea that the government 'wanted to change not only their customs but also their religion'.[39] It would be a mistake to think that there was a popular movement of religious disaffection. Even though the farmer had doubts about the conduct of the clergy and was reluctant to accept them as political leaders, he remained deeply attached to religion. In this period of anarchy and assorted temptations, his feelings are hard to gauge. But there is no justification for regarding this confusion as the sign of a rift.

Nor does it appear that the rural people were moved by democratic ideology. Once independence had been acquired, they would no doubt have favoured an authoritarian type of republic. However, several depositions indicate that the concept of a 'national monarchy', with Papineau on the throne, was closer to their way of thinking. On that score, J. Parmentier, a Nicolet shoemaker, declared: 'That he would be happy to see the crown on Mr Papineau's head, and that if he didn't behave himself as king, the Patriotes would appoint another one. That it was necessary to become independent like the American government.'[40] And this attitude, reflecting an evolution of monarchist sentiment (from monarchy by divine right to national monarchy), was not confined to the farmers. Louis Churette, a Sainte-Scholastique innkeeper, clearly expressed the kind of expectation that existed among the people after the defeat of the first uprising: 'that Papineau was no longer Papineau but was being called king and that the quarrel was going to be between two kings, that he was coming with America and Germany to fight the English . . . that Papineau was coming with fifty thousand men and fifty cannons, several of which had a range of seven leagues.'[41] J. Aubin of Sainte-Thérèse conveyed the people's hopes in the same terms: 'that we would be much better off under Mr Papineau's government, that he was expected at Montreal any evening now with fifty thousand men, twenty brass canons, and lots of others, that he was marching at the head of his army.'[42]

These uprisings, then, had quite firm roots in the masses. It was not for lack of sufficient motivation among the common people, nor for scarcity of weapons, that they failed.[43] And the clergy's attitude, although it was important, was not a crucial aspect of the successive defeats. The problem lay initially in the quality of the leadership provided by the members of the élite who supervised the insurrectionary movement.

The Élites

Who were these revolutionaries that came from the élites? From the beginning of the nineteenth century Lower Canada had undergone an economic and social transformation. The rise of the middle class had challenged the dominance of the old seigneurial families and the clergy. The tensions arising from this situation issued in a struggle for leadership. The old families, no longer representing an important element in the balance of power, were quickly ruled out. All they could do was support the more powerful groups—occasionally wavering between one dominant group and another. At the time of the rebellion their behaviour was very similar to the clergy's. The 'nobility' feared the abolition of the seigneurial regime, and saw nothing in the Patriote movement but a liberal and democratic menace. Pierre de Boucherville expressed very well the reactions of this decadent class to the perils of revolution: 'The de Boucherville family', he wrote haughtily,

> has never lacked honour. If a Seigneur de Boucherville et de Verchères joined a rebellion, he would risk losing the heritage that comes to him from his fathers. . . . If the rebellion had succeeded, he would have lost an income of four or five hundred louis a year.[44]

Aristocratic pride was still there, but dignity was gone.

The clergy, on the other hand, remained in the forefront. Having a strong economic base, able to rely on a powerful institutional network, and retaining in spite of everything considerable moral prestige, they could count on political power as well because of their connections with the State. The fact remains that the changes taking shape in society emphasized the archaic nature of their thinking and their social attitudes, and called for recasting their ideology. The status and power of the clergy were now open to challenge. Despite the efforts of Monseigneur Lartigue to reform clerical ideology and strategy under the inspiration of Ultramontanism and (up to a point) Social Catholicism, the fate of the clergy as a dominant group hung in the balance throughout the pre-rebellion period. By that I mean that the process of clericalizing society initiated by Lartigue could have failed. The explanation for the clergy's antagonistic attitude in 1837–8 lies not only in a system of beliefs and behaviour that can be called traditional, but also in the fact that the priests felt threatened by the rise of the middle classes and their ideological leanings. In this sense the clergy were defending a specific social order that was set out completely in Lartigue's *mandements* of 1837 and 1838—and in the anonymous 'Defence' of the first one, which he himself wrote. There were exceptions, of course: a few parish priests sympathized more or less openly with the Patriotes. Father Mercure, for instance, sided with them for moral reasons that had nothing directly to do with the movement. On 21 November 1837 he said from the pulpit: 'My children, I am now a Patriote like the rest of you; yesterday or the day before I went and signed up.' The effect of this avowal on the congregation was to convince them of the need to resist constituted authority.[45] But only Abbé Chartier was thoroughly committed to the movement—which didn't prevent him from running away at the critical moment.

It must be said that on the whole religious wrath was aimed at the Patriotes. The sermons of the parish priests provoked violent verbal reactions from the most confirmed militants. F.-X. Renaud reported that Édouard Moreau, a Saint-Jérôme farmer, told him at the beginning of November 1837 'that he was on the rebel Council, that he sang a revolutionary song . . . and that he said the crudest things about our Sovereign Lady the Queen . . . and if he could have found four men like himself he would have pulled Father Poirier, priest of Sainte-Anne, out of the pulpit when he preached a sermon against the revolution at Mass, and that he considered him a cur.'[46] The strangest case is that of Father Ricard, a loyalist, who declared from the pulpit 'that he had a vision telling us that in 1840'[47] the *Canadiens* would be wading ankle-deep in their enemies' blood.

As for the business class, mainly English-speaking, it drew its social prestige from its economic strength. As the principal agent of economic and social change and institutional reform, the bourgeoisie also laid claim to some control over the political structures. At the political level its leanings were conservative, because its economic future depended on the survival of certain ties between the mother country and the colonies. Like the civil servants, this English-speaking business middle class felt threatened by the assertion of French-Canadian professional classes. It was convinced that it would be ruined in an independent Lower Canada that was tied more closely than ever to subsistence farming, that had no commercial contacts, and was even more attached to the seigneury and the *Coutume de Paris*. The important businessmen were violently opposed to the Patriotes. They preferred Queen Victoria, they said, to Louis-Joseph I.

In actual fact the revolutionary phenomenon was initially an expression of the rise of the French-Canadian middle class and its need for self-assertion. Since the end of the eighteenth century the number of French Canadians active in the liberal professions and small business had been growing extremely quickly in an ever more difficult economic context. Within these groups, overcrowding soon became the rule. Even though a fair number of professionals and small businessmen came from old families fallen on hard times, or were the sons of professionals, the majority had emerged from the lower class.

When all's said and done this rise of the middle class occurred more often than not in a context of poverty, insecurity, and the necessity of really adapting to new kinds of work. These uncertainties were reflected in the numerous contradictions that shaped their aspirations. Very probably they hoped to take the place of the old seigneurial families. If so, Papineau's manorhouse at Montebello (the seigneury of *Petite Nation*) would be a good symbol of these vain endeavours. Yet the ambitions of these new social groups were not matched by their economic status or by society's opinion of their professional usefulness. Having a very exalted opinion of their own importance, these newcomers very soon aspired to the leadership of society. A class consciousness emerged that was almost spontaneously accompanied by a national consciousness. The professionals in particular identified themselves closely with what they called the '*nation canadienne*'. It must be said that they were the first to become aware of the economic inferiority of French Canadians, which they attributed to the machinations of English-speaking merchants and the discrimination practised by the colonial government. By controlling the political structures, they counted on acquiring social power, aiming indirectly at seizing economic control. From the start the professionals were no doubt opposed to the clergy, as a rival and as upholders of an ideology that was likely to frustrate their plans; but the clergy remained a secondary opponent in their eyes. The real enemies were the English merchant and his allies: the official and the immigrant. The ideology developed by this class and taken over by a political party, the *parti canadien* or the *parti patriote*, was above all directed against the English merchants who led the bureaucratic party (also called the merchant's party, the English party, or the Tory party) and who were perceived as chiefly responsible for the problems of French-Canadian society. This ideology, closely related to the increasingly hostile attitude of the masses, was destined to rally the farmers, the artisans, and the labourers to the party. This form of nationalism, the first fruit of a reaction of fear against certain economic and social changes then under way, was fundamentally conservative, on both the economic and the social level. It was, in short, opposed to any reform of the institutional apparatus that had guaranteed the survival of the old social structure. On the political level, however, these new élites were largely inspired by liberal and democratic ideologies. Despite certain authentic aspects, this liberalism and this democratic ideal served to a great extent as instruments to justify taking over political power for the sole benefit of professional people—they were actually a springboard to ultra-conservative goals. The contempt these élites displayed for economic realities was equalled only by their exaggeration of the value of political solutions. In the *parti patriote* only a small minority really wanted, as a first priority, to change society under the inspiration of the liberal ideology. A speech made by André Jobin, notary at Sainte-Geneviève, clearly shows the openly reactionary leanings of an influential section of the *parti patriote*. 'Gentlemen,' he said, 'the government wants to seize the seigneuries; you have been burned, robbed, and pillaged; they want to take away the rights of the seigneurs and the priests; it's high time you got moving because they'll come and take away your rights and your lands.'[48]

It was, then, from the professions and from small business that the 'names', the ideologists, and the principal leaders of the ideologists, and the principal leaders of the rebellions were recruited. In all, there were 190 professionals in the movement, which is to say the majority of those practising in the Montreal region. Of these, seventy-six were notaries, forty-three lawyers, sixty-seven doctors, and four surveyors. (It is surprising, on the face of it, that so few surveyors were involved. One assumes that they practised their profession mainly outside the seigneurial lands.) There were also a very few teachers, mainly foreigners. This is perhaps surprising in view of the fact that since 1836 there had been serious unemployment among teachers; but this group was dependent on the old social élite. On the other hand, the number of printers (ten) can be considered substantial. It is worth noting that the lawyers were both the most urban and the youngest group; only forty-five per cent of them were over thirty. By far the largest group in rural districts were the notaries, who were also very close to the popular leaders in age: 73 per cent of rebel notaries were over thirty. As for the doctors, 58 per cent of them were over thirty and they were the ones who figured most prominently at the top of the revolutionary hierarchy. Chenier, the Nelson brothers, Coté, and O'Callaghan are the best-known doctors.

Then came the merchants: general storekeepers, urban retailers, and inn-keepers. They were numerous in the movement and were highly motivated. I have collected 388 names, which included a high proportion of the French-Canadian merchants in the Montreal region plus a few Irishmen. They were predominantly rural rather than urban. Among them, two groups emerge. The 130 innkeepers were at the heart of the intelligence network. Though they were no help in enforcing the boycott against imported liquor, they nevertheless played a central role—for the inns were centres of discussion, where most of the various rumours came and went and where the greatest number of indiscretions were committed. None of this prevented the inn-keepers from taking part in the military events, most often as leaders. They were also the oldest group: eighty-five per cent of the lessees were over thirty. As for the other merchants, who numbered 258, they were the youngest group after the lawyers. While many innkeepers could neither read nor write, this was almost never the case with the other merchants. We can assume that a fair proportion of them had spent some time at classical colleges. The merchants ranked high in the revolutionary hierarchy and seem to have been particularly fond of the title of colonel.

The strong presence of commercial elements in the rebellions brings us back to the question of economic motivations, which were certainly signif-icant among the professionals. But this group provided a large number of candidates for government positions, since they were not doing well finan-cially. 'Dr Ainsley declared that this whole train of events had been started by Mailhiot and a few young idiots to get places.'[49] No doubt professional men were looking for economic advancement, but they seem to have been drawn even more by social prestige and political power. In business circles, however, economic motivations were central. The massive involvement in revolutionary activity of small business put it in an awkward position because most successful merchants supported the established order. J.-B. Bernard, a

merchant at Beloeil, replied to the urgings of Dr Allard: 'You have to understand that my fortunes are dependent on the English government.'[50] But
small businessmen, besides being too numerous, were the most vulnerable
to competition. They wanted to get rid of the British merchants who had
become established in country parishes. J.-N. Pacaud, a shipowner, expressed
in his own way the frustrations of small French-Canadian business operations:
'Pacaud said that the damned English had made him suffer enough, that they
hadn't been fair to him.'[51] Besides, after 1830 especially, their dependence
on the English-speaking business middle class in Montreal had increased at
the same time as wheat production was declining. Agricultural surpluses had
dwindled after 1800 and trade with the country parishes had increasingly
been based on replenishing their supplies. The supremacy the British had
acquired in the field of imports—whether of farm produce from Upper
Canada or the United States, or of goods from Great Britain or the West
Indies—helped them to control local trade. Small French-Canadian merchants in the countryside, or even in the town, seem to have wanted to
shake off the yoke. In this context their nationalism is easier to understand.
F.-X. Prieur, a Sainte-Martine merchant, shouted to the farmers under his
command: 'Fear nothing, my friends, we're going to slaughter the English.'[52]
Here again we see that this kind of nationalism initially affected the most
vulnerable elements. Those who were more secure were to be found in the
bureaucratic party.

For the farmers, for rural and urban craftsmen, labourers, most professionals, and some tradesmen, poverty during 1837–8 was certainly a strong
factor in creating a climate for revolution. That is why the people of Sainte-
Scholastique warned J. Leroux 'that he could very well be bled dry and soon
be as poor as they were.'[53] Was this the case for everyone? I have noticed,
more or less in the background, but even within the movement, the presence
of a group whose economic status was far from inferior. For instance, hov-
ering around the Banque Canadienne at Saint-Hyacinthe were comfortable
farmers, professionals, and merchants whose caginess and anxiety were obvious. It was rumoured everywhere that this institution had been set up to
finance a revolution. The same purpose was attributed to the Banque du
Peuple, which, it was said, had been founded in 1835 to serve French Canadians who had ostensibly been mistreated by the English banks. Abbé Chartier, who was in on the secrets of the rebellion to some extent, wrote: 'As
for money, was not the Banque du Peuple, which had been in existence
barely a year, universally understood to have been established for the purpose
of the revolution, and in order to help it? Is it not this motive, which the
shareholders skilfully made known, that underlay the rapid success which
came to this most patriotic establishment?' Abbé Chartier went on to say
that on the day when payments were due the 'cowardly directors' would
face a 'terrible reckoning'. D.-B. Viger told Papineau, before he left Mon-

treal, 'that their little venture would never succeed until they had toppled the government'.[54] So many trails led to the Banque du Peuple, and those in charge of it, that there had to be something suspicious about it. Édouard Fabre, one of its directors, arrived mysteriously at Saint-Denis before the battle and went away again immediately after having conferred with Papineau—which may have had no connection with the latter's flight and the final decision taken by the bank to refuse to finance the insurrection. But who knows? Some of the evidence makes me suspect that there was a small minority who had an interest in reaping profits from the revolutionary operation. Joseph Bourdon and Joseph Bertrand declared in their deposition that when victory came, the Patriotes 'would confiscate the different banks (except the Banque du Peuple) as well as the wholesale houses, to relieve the poor. That they would make John Molson pay eighty thousand pounds and make other people pay enormous sums too. . . . That Master Benjamin Hart, along with all the other Jews, must be strangled and their property confiscated.'[55] They also expected to nationalize the Lachine Canal and the Laprairie railway. As for the Banque du Peuple, it would become the government's bank. When we examine all the family ties, personal relationships, and business connections within the top leadership of the *parti patriote* and the revolutionary movement, speculation about a 'family compact'— denounced both then and later—makes more sense. Regarding this, more light needs to be shed on the role of the Vigers—D.-B. and his cousin Louis-Michel, founder and president of the Banque du Peuple. Here we touch on a world that was self-contained, closer to personal ambitions and family interests. It was also a world whose secrets were better kept.

These élites, who formed the top ranks in the uprisings, were most to blame for the collapse of the attempt to make Lower Canada independent because their function was not just to stir up the masses—it was also to provide planning, organization, and strong leadership at the crucial moment. In fact the uprisings, in 1838 as well as in 1837, presented instead a spectacle of anarchy, misdirected impulsiveness, and a sort of incapacity for effective action. The movement was dominated by fear and, except on a few occasions, had no means of overcoming it. The huge gatherings of country people, incapable of really moving of their own accord, were the result of herd instinct rather than of any genuine strategy. Some leaders, like Plamondon, a Saint-Hyacinthe merchant, declared 'that the *habitants* ought to take a look at their own cowardice, that all the confusion in the ranks in the countryside was due to their lack of courage'.[56] The farmers, on the other hand, blamed the leaders. For instance two of them related that 'Maître Ambroise Brunelle was a dangerous agitator . . . that he ran away after stirring up the common people'.[57] It seems that when it came time for action, the behaviour of the popular elements reflected the weakness of the leadership at all levels, because where leadership was strong, anarchy was overcome. Wolfred Nelson, for example, was responsible for the victory at Saint-Denis. At Saint-Eustache, in spite of Girod's sudden disappearance,[58] Colonel Chénier put up a strong resistance to the government troops. Those are exceptions, but how significant they are!

Most of the problems originated with the supreme leader, Papineau, who personified the movement—which was a sort of will to national regeneration, as it was called at the time—revelled in ambiguity and showed that he was incapable of action, hesitant, and exceedingly weak. Right from the start every serious attempt at organization was obstructed. Some local elements tried to make up for the deficiency,[59] but nobody managed to ensure any unity of action. Papineau's covert flight before the battle of Saint-Denis—which deceived no one except, perhaps, himself—caused astonishment: Lespérance declared that the locals 'were very surprised not to see him at the head of the battle'.[60] On the eve of the battle of Saint-Charles, Papineau made a speech to the local rebels urging them to be brave.[61] Then he took refuge at Saint-Hyacinthe and fled from there to the United States, where he went around under an assumed name. Meanwhile he had no doubt forgotten that he was supposed to be the negotiator in the event of a defeat. Be that as it may, his strange behaviour was a decisive factor in the failure of the rebellion.

More serious is the fact that Papineau's was not an isolated case. Even though events usually unfolded simply, without a big production, Papineau's defection had its repercussions. Michel Godet, a Saint-Hyacinthe farmer, explained his leaving Saint-Charles 'alleging as his reason that none of the big people who got them to march showed up at the camp at all.'[62] Robert Nelson and Dr Côté, who in 1837 had accused Papineau of cowardice, cut no better figure the following year.[63] In the case of T.S. Brown, lack of courage was combined with incompetence. This small merchant became famous during a street fight with members of the Doric Club. When he arrived at Saint-Charles he was appointed general by Papineau and throughout the waiting period he flitted about in a state of utter enthusiasm, certain of victory. He even refused the reinforcements Wolfred Nelson promised him and advised the thousand Patriotes gathered at Saint-Mathias to content themselves with cutting off the retreat of the troops after their defeat. Later, Brown was unable to defend himself against the charge that he had fled at the outset of the battle.[64]

There is no need to spin out the list of such defections. It would be depressingly long. Let it be enough to give one last quotation on the poverty of leadership that included too many grandstanders and too few men of action. François Darche, a Saint-Hilaire labourer, related his experience on the day of battle:

> that before the fighting began the said Captain [of the Canadian Republic] Jean Marie Tétro, called Ducharme, inspected his company and their weapons, saying to them, 'My children, be brave and pay attention: don't miss those damned villains, aim well and straight, aim at the heart, the stomach, and the head, have

no mercy and give no quarter,' . . . and that nobody saw him after that; that he supposes he ran away.[65]

The élites seem to have thought that all they had to do was egg on the people to revolt and independence would be achieved without serious risk to themselves. Going by the length of the American Revolution, some of the leaders continued to claim—even after the failure of the second uprising—that if the French Canadians would only persevere, success was bound to crown their efforts. They expected a final success to emerge from repeated abortive attempts, believing that England would ultimately, of its own accord, abandon the colony to its fate. In 1837 and 1838 the revolutionary leadership was so weak that even if there had been no serious opposition, the movement could not have succeeded. It is impossible not to detect in all this a more or less pronounced degree of bad faith, either in motives or in methods. The implausible lies told by the leaders about American aid, and its extent, illustrate this aspect. After the failure of the Québec plot—which was supposed to find expression in a rural uprising from Charlevoix to Kamouraska and a raid on the Citadel—a man called Hutton testified:

> They [the Patriotes] were determined to turn it to their advantage as all the troops would undoubtedly be informed of their danger, the habitants shall treat them with the utmost kindness on their way up and then raise a report that the English want to prejudice a strange soldary [sic] against a good and under-signing [innocent] people.[66]

Should we not also mention the treason or defection of a certain group of revolutionary leaders, specifically those who had the most interest in seizing political power and eliminating the British from commercial competition? Did a moment come when this group was afraid it saw a genuinely popular anti-feudal movement developing? The hypothesis is worth bearing in mind and investigating. It is certain that the moderates were outnumbered, especially after August 1837, by the radicals. It is significant that Abbé Chartier was later directed to curb the anticlerical and anti-feudal frenzy of the refugees in the United States.

The rebel movement, then, sprang from the élites and spread rapidly through the masses, where it had widespread support. It was the logical outcome of the nationalist crisis that had taken shape after 1800 and had continued to take root. But this movement contained the seeds of its own defeat. Instead of undertaking the task of social reconstruction and economic renewal, the liberal professions—generally speaking, and often unconsciously—stood firmly against all radical change, bending their efforts towards the preservation of the old institutional structures, raised to the rank of national values. Incapable of basing their actions on the long-term needs of society, these élites could not manage to get beyond their own group interests and ambitions. At bottom their ambition was to succeed the old seigneurial families. Montebello symbolizes this kind of attitude. It is true that a minority of genuine liberals succeeded to a certain extent in awakening a fraction of the populace to class consciousness and anti-feudal, anticlerical ideology. But the professionals on the whole worked to direct popular discontent against a particular ethnic group—the *Anglais*; one that in their eyes stood for an effort to establish a social order dominated by the commercial and industrial bourgeoisie. By doing so the professional men prevented the development of class consciousness among the populace and assured the survival of the old social order, while at the same time securing their own future. This likely explains the defection of an influential portion of the revolutionary leadership.

The deep-seated attitudes of an influential portion of the professional class, which had aspired to run society all by itself, also accounts for the continued growth of clerical power after 1840. A society that up to the end of the eighteenth century had been headed jointly by the old seigneurial families and the clergy was now succeeded by dominated by the clergy and the professionals—with the balance tipped increasingly in favour of the clergy, who were at the top of the social hierarchy. Manipulation of the masses had worked against its authors.

Ages of the Leaders
(Provisional figures)

	% Business	% Professional	% Rural	% Merchants	% Innkeepers	% Notaries	% Lawyers	% Doctors
Under 30	40	40	24	46	15	27	55	42
Over 30	60	60	76	54	85	73	45	58
30–50	44	50	55	39	62	57	37	50
40–60	36	24	46	32	50	25	22	26

Suggestions for Further Reading

Donald Creighton, *The Commercial Empire of the St Lawrence* (Toronto, 1938).
Lionel Groulx, *Histoire du Canada français depuis la découverte* 4 vols (Montreal, 1950–2), vol III.
Fernand Ouellet, *Economic and Social History of Quebec, 1760–1850* (Ottawa, 1980).

Notes

[1]My analysis is based mainly on a wealth of archival materials, preserved in 'Les Événements 1837–38' in the Archives of the Province of Quebec, and in the Public

Archives of Canada. These documents make possible an understanding of the social aspects of the movement.

[2]Lionel Groulx, *Histoire du Canada français depuis la découverte*, vol III, 235.

[3]Groulx, 'L.-J. Papineau', in *Notre maître le passé*, première série, 195.

[4]*Ibid.*, 210 ff.

[5]In my *Economic and Social History of Quebec, 1760–1850*, I believe I have demonstrated this interdependence of economics and politics.

[6]Boris Porchnev, *Les Soulèvements populaires en France de 1623 à 1648*, 325, 327. Even if one rejects Porchnev's concept of class, his study remains extremely significant.

[7]Groulx, *Histoire du Canada français*, vol III, 235.

[8]Quoted in my 'Papineau dan la révolution de 1837–38', *Canadian Historical Association Report* (CHAR) 1958, 13. This essay analyses the ambiguous behaviour of the revolutionary leader.

[9]This phrase ('la prise des glaces') recurs frequently in the documents, in reference to the plans of the rebels.

[10]Deposition of A. Brisebois, Pointe-Claire. It goes on: 'by supplying and contributing with other men of goodwill to supply all the money necessary to buy powder, balls, guns, and other things necessary to put the said rebel party in a position to set forth at the first opportunity to fight against the British government'.

[11]Deposition of J. Trudel. See also those of P. Martin and N. Berthiaume. On 18 June 1837, A. Archambault, notary's clerk of Varennes, declared 'that he was working to overthrow the government of his province to establish it as a republic and unite it to the United States or make it an independent government, whichever would be judged the more advantageous, and to have free trade with the United States and to stop trade with England'. Deposition of P. Nichols of Varennes.

[12]Deposition of H. Guérin of Laprairie. Towards the end of the summer, at Saint-Eustache, Saint-Benoît, and Sainte-Scholastique, Chénier, Girouard, and Scott spoke of arming themselves and setting up a provisional government. See the depositions of A. Dennis and E. Sabourin.

[13]Duncan McColl of Saint-Benoît related that after June 1837 the French Canadians had broken off contacts with the inhabitants of English origin. He and his brothers, one a blacksmith and the other a shopkeeper, had lost all their customers. After 3 July, the patriots had even decided to drive the British out of the parish. There are many such examples.

[14]Deposition of Weidenbacker. On 1 November 1837, R. Bélair of Montreal was said to have been present at a rally: 'that the principal object of such meeting . . . was to attack and destroy the city of Montreal.' Deposition of A. Leggo.

[15]Ouellet, 'Papineau dans la révolution de 1837–8', 20.

[16]*Ibid.*, 20.

[17]*Ibid.*, 15.

[18]Deposition of H. Macdonald.

[19]Deposition of L. Holmes. In 1838 there continued to be many such declarations. H. Lefèbvre stated his intention to 'murder all Bureaucrats as they called the English population and destroy their properties'. Deposition of T. Legrand, known as Dufresne.

20'Les Événements 1837–38', 513.

21Deposition of A. Labadie.

22Deposition of W. Kell.

23Deposition of Fratelin.

24Porchnev, 327.

25Deposition of J. Fisher.

26Deposition of M. Bruneau.

27On economic and social conditions before the rebellions, see my *Economic and Social History of Quebec, 1760–1850*.

28Deposition of J. Lécuyer.

29Deposition of M. Tremblay.

30Félix Lussier, a farmer at Varennes and son of the seigneur, said to the habitants: 'If you ask the parish priests' advice, they will certainly tell you that our wish to overthrow the government is contrary to religious principles.' L. Dumouchelle of Saint-Jérôme said that 'the Bishop of Montreal was paid a thousand louis a year by the government, that for that reason the bishop was on the government's side; that previously he had been a patriot. ... He asked the habitants if they wanted to shine the shoes of the English: that, if not, they must defend themselves.' Deposition of C.T. de Montigny.

31Depositions of J. Lévillée and Eustache Cheval.

32It is to be noted that Marcel Séné could neither read nor write. Propaganda was carried on in open-air public meetings or in the parish halls, 'where they read us *La Minerve, The Vindicator*, and *Le Populaire*. Dr Bouthillier and Father Crevier, the parish priest, read us these papers. Father Crevier told us that we ought to be Patriotes, but moderate Patriotes, that we should love our rights but also our country. He often disagreed with Dr Bouthillier.' Deposition of J. Normandin. This was a typical situation.

33Deposition of Frs Robichaud.

34See the documents on the murder of Chartrand. Deposition of G. Pinsonnault.

35Deposition of T. Gagnon. G. Lescardeau, a farmer of La Présentation, was ordered to go 'to destroy all the bureaucrats and divide up their property, not less than five hundred arpents of land to each man who would help them in the capture'.

36Deposition of W. Brewster of Lacolle.

37'Les Événements 1837–38'.

38Deposition of M. Marchesseault.

39Deposition of J. Robillard.

40Deposition of J. Parmentier in November 1837.

41Depositions of J. Martin and L. Piché.

42Deposition of A. Sanche. Gélineau, Bertrand, and Beaudin of Sainte-Martine are alleged to have said that 'Mr Papineau was a great man, a man inspired by God, and that the troubles were going to begin again sooner than anyone expected and that Mr Papineau was coming with an army.' Deposition of J.-B. Bourgogne. At Saint-Eustache, François Nadon said at the same moment, 'It's not over, Papineau is going to come and avenge all that; Canadians have been slaves too long. Damned gang of English, robbers with the whole law in their hands, you can't get at them.' Deposition of Elmire Richard.

[43]By my calculation, the Patriotes in 1837 had at least 1,600 guns at their disposal; in 1838, more than 1,800.

[44]Deposition of P. de Boucherville. Some seigneurs, as well as some parish priests, seem to have been ambivalent. It should not be forgotten that they were afraid of the Patriotes; opportunism sometimes prevailed.

[45]Deposition of A. Michon. It would be a mistake to exaggerate the effect of such a stand. J. Beauregard told of having gone to confess to Mercure: '"You're not at Saint-Charles. You must go to Saint-Charles, everybody's there and you must go there too." Seeing no obligation to comply with this advice, he decided to slip away to Granby.' This testimony, like many others, shows that the manipulation of the peasants by the parish priests or the members of the professions was possible only when they took account of the inclination and interests of the lower classes. Pure manipulation was difficult.

[46]Deposition of F.-X. Renaud, a Saint-Jérôme farmer.

[47]Deposition of E. Jones and Father Richard.

[48]Deposition of Pierre Étier.

[49]Deposition of P. Colette of Saint-Jean.

[50]Deposition of J.-B. Bernard.

[51]Deposition of J. Trudel.

[52]Deposition of N. Boyer.

[53]Deposition of J. Leroux.

[54]Deposition of A. Labadie.

[55]Deposition of J. Bourdon, J. Bertrand, and Glackmeyer. Ovide Gariépy, shopkeeper at Laprairie, for his part 'strongly advised deponent and all Canadians to retain all the bills of the Banque du Peuple they possibly could as it was a great deal better than any other bank.' Deposition of I. Lavoie.

[56]Deposition of J. Varie.

[57]Deposition of Lacoste and Morin.

[58]A. Fournier reported the flight of Girod, who had ordered him to go and meet the troops on the ice: 'We went back to the village where I saw Girod in his sleigh with another runaway; when he saw me he fired at me and the bullet hit a fence near me.' Richard Hubert in his deposition admitted that he had run away. For his part, Isaie Foisy, a blacksmith, testified that he had shod a horse for Hubert and repaired a sleigh for Girod just before the battle.

[59]See my article 'Papineau dans la révolution de 1837–38', *CHAR*, 1958, 13–14.

[60]Deposition of T. Lespérance.

[61]Deposition of O. Lussier.

[62]Deposition of Michel Godet.

[63]See the deposition of Louis Lussier and J.-B. Plante.

[64]Another example of outstanding incompetence was the capture of 150 patriots by the Indians of Sault-Saint-Louis. This had a touch of comedy.

[65]Deposition of Frs Darche *dit* L'Artifice.

[66]Deposition of Hutton.

21

Urban Poverty in Colonial British North America

Judith Fingard

While colonial British North America was in many respects a favourable 'poor man's country' and a 'land of opportunity', either good health or a decent amount of moneyed capital was absolutely essential for utilizing its advantages to the fullest; good health and capital combined together were the best arrangement. Not everyone was successful, of course, and at the bottom of colonial society were the poor. Those who through disability, incompetence, or misfortune (such as young orphans) could not look after themselves and had no one to do it for them, joined recent immigrants who arrived without capital resources and quickly settled into the ranks of the impoverished in whatever port they disembarked. Unable to accumulate enough money to move on, these newcomers often became part of the casually unemployed. Because of the seasonal nature of much Canadian pre-industrial employment, the winter saw the body of the unemployed poor greatly augmented by skilled artisans temporarily out of work, in some places by resident fishers or marginal farmers.

Judith Fingard examines poor relief in three urban centres of eastern Canada between 1815 and 1860. Such relief was not given as something to which the poor were entitled by right, but because the more prosperous had either tender consciences or social anxieties. Schemes to force the recipients of poor relief to work for their assistance were often prompted, but seldom followed up. For their part, employers usually had no compunction about laying workers off in the winter months, even if it meant throwing them to the mercy of the relief system. Fingard concludes that colonial society had failed to deal with pre-industrial poverty in any significant way, particularly in terms of providing employment, and would eventually turn to social amelioration through moral rather than economic reform.

In what ways were conditions for the urban poor probably more severe than for those in rural areas? Why did colonial society provide relief for the poor? Why did various schemes of employing the able-bodied poor fail to work adequately? What was wrong with colonial poor relief? How should it have been managed?

This article first appeared, titled 'The Relief of the Unemployed Poor in Saint John, Halifax, and St John's, 1815–1860', in *Acadiensis* v, 1 (1975), 32–53.

As the leading commercial centres in eastern British America, Saint John, Halifax, and St John's sheltered within their environs a significant proportion of the region's meagre population. This included not only the most comfortable and affluent colonists, but also three categories of poor inhabitants whose problems were never far from the minds of public-spirited citizens. Prominent among the disadvantaged were the permanent or disabled poor —a motley collection that embraced the helpless aged, the physically and mentally infirm, as well as destitute widows and orphans, those unproductive elements in the community without kith or kin to act as providers. The plight of these unfortunates aroused the greatest outward display of local sympathy, though their inescapable presence were largely taken for granted and their welfare sadly neglected. A second group consisted of immigrants who annually swelled the ranks of the poor that infested these major Atlantic ports. These included refugee blacks from the United States, settled near Halifax and Saint John after the War of 1812, who became a special class of permanent poor in town and suburb, as well as the meanest of the urban labourers. Most significant in point of numbers was the incessant flow of poverty-stricken Irish who, on arrival, crowded into the poorhouses of Saint John and Halifax and augmented the paupers of St John's.[1] Subsequently, as resident labourers, the Irish frequently re-emerged as members of the third category—the casual poor.[2] Found amongst these casual poor were individuals or families dependent on a hand-to-mouth existence, who became temporarily incapacitated through sickness or misfortune, and the seasonally unemployed, those perennial casualties who formed the most intractable problem for the commercial towns. While the majority of this latter group consisted of common labourers, they were often joined in penury by skilled journeymen thrown out of work or underpaid in wintertime. In St John's the whole operative class of resident fishermen habitually found themselves idle and destitute for seven months out of twelve, a situation which gave the colony 'a larger proportion of poor than in other British settlements'.[3] Each of these categories—permanent, immigrant, and casual poor—posed its special difficulties for the community, but as constituent elements of society, each was thought by benevolent and judicious townsmen to be entitled to some form of assistance during the period of privation. In the fluid, uncertain conditions of colonial society, prosperous inhabitants were chastened by the possibility 'that the calamities which have befallen others may soon overtake ourselves, and that their distressing lot may soon become our own'.[4]

When a conjunction of diverse circumstances, including overseas immigration and economic recession, forced urban poverty to the forefront of public attention in the period after the Napoleonic Wars, the towns of the Atlantic colonies, in contrast to those of the Canadas, could draw on a tradition of state poor relief. This government involvement took the forms of locally enacted poor laws providing for municipal assessments in Nova Scotia and New Brunswick and of executive initiative for appropriating colonial revenue in Newfoundland. The methods of dispensing these funds in Saint John, and eventually in St John's, involved a mixture of both indoor and outdoor relief, whereas in Halifax public assistance was confined to the poorhouse.[5] But the existence of facilities for public relief did not preclude individual involvement in civic welfare measures. Citizens continued to feel that they had a direct role to play both in aiding the poor and in determining the guises that public and voluntary assistance assumed. For one thing, they were well aware that the scale of public relief was inadequate to meet emergencies, a deficiency starkly demonstrated every time fires, crop failures, business recessions, heavy immigration, or ineluctable winter exacted their toll. Haligonians experienced these harsh circumstances in the decade after 1815, when large numbers of poor immigrants and unemployed labourers were thrown on the mercy of a town that had abandoned outdoor relief under public auspices and that had, therefore, to rely on voluntary efforts to ward off the threat of starvation and social disorder.[6]

Moreover, goaded by tender consciences and insistent churches, some colonists regarded benevolence as a Christian duty. Within a society that prided itself on its Christian ethos, the laws of God and humanity dictated that the poor could not be permitted to starve; the sick and aged poor must be cared for. But starvation did occur, and the numerous sick and aged poor in the towns necessitated the erection of institutions to minister to their afflictions. In the absence of this kind of large-scale capital expenditure which city councils or provincial legislatures were reluctant to undertake, privately organized dispensaries and societies for the relief of the indigent sick played a vital role in treating accidents and common illnesses.[7] For the chronically ill, however, circumstances were different. Halifax, for example, possessed no specialized institution for dealing with any category of sick poor until the opening of the lunatic asylum in 1859.[8] The failure 'to ameliorate the condition of suffering humanity' offended Christians who witnessed ample investment in facilities for transportation and commerce; the neglect of social amelioration seemed to be at odds with mid-Victorian notions of progress.[9]

In these circumstances townspeople responded sympathetically to acute destitution because they considered the existing forms of poor relief outdated and unprogressive. The purely custodial care of destitute lunatics in the temporary asylum established in St John's in 1846, for example, was said to be inconsistent with the age of improvement.[10] Citizens were particularly outspoken when their local pride was offended. To lag behind other towns in the provision of specialized facilities for the poor seemed unpatriotic as well as undesirable. The example of Saint John, where a lunatic asylum was opened in 1836 and firmly established in a permanent edifice in 1848, was constantly paraded by social critics before the lethargic citizenry of Halifax and St John's.[11] This call for imitation grew out of a search for self-esteem, since colonial towns aspired to social responsibility and an acknowledgment of their benevolence and modernity.[12]

In an age that witnessed both the heyday of the philanthropic society and in North America the 'discovery of the asylum', the custom of fostering benevolence by means of association also encouraged citizen involvement in directing local poor relief. The bewildering variety of associations, both ephemeral and permanent, that emerged for the social, physical, and moral improvement of the poor fulfilled a basic middle-class instinct for collective efforts as well as for emulating the fashionable course. While few of the large-scale societies and the asylums they sometimes sponsored could exist without some government aid to augment charitable donations, voluntary management provided communities with excellent experience in organization, fund-raising, and social investigation. At the same time, however, voluntary associative benevolence underwent a fragmentation which meant that by mid-century every church and every ethnic and interest group had its own charitable society or charitable function. This occurred despite attempts throughout the period by the most public-spirited citizens to promote the comprehensive, non-partisan relief of the urban poor, on the ground that 'we are but a part of one great human family'.[13]

Particularly significant was the bifurcation of urban society between Catholics and Protestants, which emerged most graphically in the 1840s, when Irish immigration, the introduction of unfamiliar religious orders, the ravages of epidemics, and the cry of 'papal aggression' led colonial Protestants to resent the indisputable fact that the larger proportion of poor rates and voluntary contributions went towards the relief of poor Catholics. Piqued Protestants did not tire of reminding their Roman Catholic neighbours that nine-tenths of the inmates of the poorhouse in Halifax were Catholics, or that it was the Protestant citizenry in St John's who supported the Catholic poor.[14] To such an extent did the Catholics constitute the labouring and disabled poor in the towns that the more bigoted Protestants began to pronounce publicly that the Roman Catholics were impoverished because they were Catholics.[15] Not surprisingly, a host of 'separate' charitable societies and institutions resulted. Consequently, vertical divisions in the population of the towns, not only between Catholics and Protestants, but also between Methodists and Anglicans, Irish and native-born, loyalists and non-loyalists, took precedence over the fledgling regard for the corporate well-being.

Finally, the colonist became concerned about poor relief in his capacity as a citizen of a town in which he had a vested interest, and protection of that stake demanded that the community should reflect his own particular values. When he talked therefore about subordinating the relief of the poor to the good of the community, he meant subordinating it to his own purposes. It is these underlying values, shared by contemporaries in three pre-industrial towns of Atlantic Canada, and the various schemes they spawned, that provide the focus of the ensuing discussion. Amongst the townsman's preconceptions, it was his reverence for the family, his regard for the dignity of labour, his preoccupation with good order, and his search for economy which led him to the fundamental conclusion 'That the truest charity is to find employment that will give food; and not food without employment.'[16]

Those citizens who viewed the relief of the poor within the wider context of the welfare of urban society at large undoubtedly represented the most respectable, dependable, moderately reformist, and middle-class elements in the towns. Whether they paraded as newspaper proprietors, clergymen, assemblymen, or aldermen, they were motivated by a concept of responsibility to the public, the congregation, or the electorate. They expected other men in positions of leadership and authority to take their civic duty as conscientiously as they did themselves. At the base of urban society the leadership they discerned was that of the male head of the organic unit, the family. Since the interests of the family in society received priority over those of the individual, the claims of the poor were likely to elicit a more sympathetic response if they could be fitted into the familial framework. In this respect a special sanctity was accorded the interdependent relationship between the provider and his spouse and offspring. Only sickness and unexpected unemployment were thought to constitute legitimate excuses for the failure of bread-winners to take seriously their duty as providers.[17] Drunkenness, improvidence, low wages, laziness, and fecundity were problems with which the wretched family had to contend alone, though the editor of the *Morning News* wondered whether, in cases of drunkenness as the cause of family poverty, the state should not be vested with the right to intervene and regulate employment and expenditure of wages.[18]

When it came to the vital circumstances of sickness, public health officers recognized that unless the labourer was retained in health, 'the family of the victim becomes a charge upon the town for a much longer time' than the duration of his illness.[19] When sickness of a poor or struggling head of the family led to his death, the citizenry displayed an appropriate concern for the widow and children, as it did for the orphan in the case of double bereavement.[20] Nevertheless, talk about society's responsibilities towards widows and orphans was considerably more energetic than the framing of humane measures to provide for their sustenance. Admittedly, concerted efforts for temporary assistance to widows and orphans sometimes followed severe epidemics or summers of excessive immigration, but attention to the welfare of the fatherless remnant of the family was haphazard and ephemeral.[21] In a society based on commerce, hard physical labour, and male political power, women were utterly expendable. Children, on the other hand, were exploitable as cheap labour. Orphans and foundlings were greatly in demand in the pre-industrial period as apprentices by farmers, householders, and craftsmen, apprenticeships secured by indentures that again tended to emphasize the family ambience.[22]

Society showed its greatest concerted anxiety about family welfare when large numbers of heads of families were thrown out of work. While this concern might sometimes extend to female bread-winners, it was the men as labourers and mechanics who commanded the most attention. In those instances where public measures were taken to meet the temporary emergency of seasonal unemployment, preference was given to family men. In fact the work itself, never sufficient to satisfy the demand, was usually confined to heads of families.[23] About 600 of these employed on civic works in Saint John in 1842 received from 1s. to 3s. a day according to the number of their dependents.[24] Coincident with family considerations, this preoccupation with the labouring poor stemmed from the emphasis placed by the well-to-do on the material progress of the town. As the basis of the socio-economic pyramid, the very fabric of urban society was thought to depend on the labourers' contributions, not only as hewers of wood and drawers of water, but as 'the bone and marrow of the country'.[25] When 'honest' working men faced starvation, self-interested leaders of society invariably urged the expeditious relief of 'that most indispensably useful part of the community', preferably through employment, but if necessary through relief without labour.[26]

Citizens' attitudes towards poor relief were also influenced by the need to distinguish between the honest, deserving, labouring poor and those who were undeserving, profligate, or even criminal. For the public remained anxious that the poor should not endanger the social order of the towns and that relief should preserve a properly balanced relationship between the 'haves' and the 'have-nots'. This determination to ensure that the 'haves' maintained the upper hand goes far to explain the universal abhorrence of mendicancy: begging transferred the initiative to the poor when it ought to remain with their economic betters. Mendicancy was a form of free enterprise, an activity not to be encouraged in the poor who were certain to misuse it. A successful beggar might see in crime his road to further advancement. Beggars were therefore not only an expensive nuisance,[27] but a threat to society, whose guardians through their beneficence in furnishing food and clothing might unwittingly admit to their houses imposters or thieves. Such unbecoming and potentially subversive behaviour in the poor might be avoided if the rich took it upon themselves to seek out poor families in their dwellings and investigate their degree of penury and deservedness. The efficacy of social investigation was reiterated as often as hordes of beggars descended on the towns and it became the standard practice of voluntary associations and government agencies.[28]

Despite the need for precautionary measures to safeguard the interests of the town and the welfare of the honest poor, it was often that same apprehension for the good order of society that stimulated citizens to urge generous public relief in times of severest want. In the winter of 1816–17 the first voluntary relief committee in Halifax feared that if the sufferers were 'abandoned to the horrors of starvation . . . they may be induced by despair to commit depredations'.[29] Thereafter the preference given to civic employment schemes as the most propitious form of assistance pinpointed unemployed labourers as the element in the population most likely to threaten the good order of the city. The spectre of hungry mobs of workers conjured up in the mind of the authorities frightening thoughts of uncontrollable outrage and seething insubordination. Poverty was regarded as a 'evil' which could not be allowed to reach 'that stage where it is not stopped by stone walls, or locks, bolts, or bars'.[30]

Self-interest also demanded economical relief. The search for economy encouraged attempts to eliminate some forms of poverty amongst labourers by the prevention and treatment of diseases and accidents. On its establishment in 1857 the Saint John Public Dispensary for outpatients undertook to diminish the number of inmates accommodated in the tax-supported almshouse. Its managers therefore appealed to the public not solely as a benevolent institution 'but a *money saving one to our citizens*'.[31] Similarly, the need for welfare might be reduced by the more rigorous enforcement of the board of health regulations in the city. Otherwise, the health officer argued, 'Sickness, debility, death, widowhood and orphanage, connected with pauperism, are expensive contingencies' which the town must sustain.[32] Financial considerations were also paramount in the discussion of the relative merits of indoor and outdoor relief. It was popularly but by no means universally maintained that institutional care was cheaper than outdoor measures. This assumption led to the repeated advocacy of various types of asylums which would offer both centralized and more economical relief. Enthusiasts for the erection of a poorhouse in St John's claimed that such an institution in Halifax housed more paupers than were then supported in St John's and did so at less expense.[33] Where outdoor relief was essential, the economy-minded suggested that food, fuel, and clothing should be provided at reduced rates or at cost rather than given away gratuitously to the poor. Not only would the available charitable funds then be less liable to misuse and made to go further, but those suffering from a state of temporary destitution would be retained in their constructive role as colonial consumers.[34] Interest in the poor man as a consumer also afforded a major reason why citizens preferred employment relief to charitable relief in the form of cheap food and old clothes. If he earned subsistence wages, the poor man would still continue to participate in the retail trade of the town at full market prices.[35]

A mindfulness of both economy and order led the benevolent to expect a return on their investment in alms-giving, charitable subscriptions, and poor rates. Gratuitous charity represented the worst sort of investment for an enterprising community. It precluded a productive return on welfare expenditure and did nothing to foster the virtues of thrift and self-reliance amongst the labouring poor, whereas labour extracted from the recipient of relief constituted the ideal recompense, the favoured *quid pro quo*.[36] As a correspondent to the *Acadian Recorder* explained, 'every penny given in charity to a healthy person, able to work, is a serious injury to society at large, unless that penny produces its own value by some mode of industry.'[37] The guarantee that a poor person or family relieved through charity or employment was in fact deserving formed another precautionary, money-saving consideration. Most public relief schemes or welfare services—voluntary or government sponsored—required a means test in the form of a certificate of genuine destitution from a respectable citizen or designated official.[38] Poor youths supplied their *quid pro quo* in another form. All towns and many churches within them organized clothing societies which aimed primarily at sheltering poor children against the inclemency of winter weather. But in return for free clothing, the children were expected to attend Sunday school or catechism classes where proper ideas of Christian citizenship were carefully inculcated.[39]

With their interest in economy, good order, and the wider welfare of the town, social commentators of every description urged consistently from the 1810s until the 1860s and beyond that the able-bodied poor should be relieved only in return for an equivalent in labour. Work was seen as the great panacea for the prevailing urban malaise produced by seasonal unemployment, dangerous mendicancy, and exorbitant, gratuitous aid. Effective employment relief would benefit both the poor and the town. For individual recipients, employment would supply what the majority professedly preferred—the means of obtaining the necessaries of life without sacrificing completely their independence by becoming degraded objects of charity.[40] Provision of work would eliminate reliance on charity which was both demoralizing and induced wasteful habits of idleness, intemperance, improvidence, and even worse forms of anti-social behaviour.[41] As far as the town itself was concerned, or more specifically its leading citizens, employment relief was designed to 'subserve the Public interest'.[42] In the first place, work was favoured as a security measure, the object being to avoid public mischief by keeping the labouring poor busily occupied.[43] Secondly, from the 1840s onwards, when middle-class faith in progress and improvement clearly emerged in debates on social welfare, as it did in the matter of education, relief in the shape of employment was valued as a means by which the poor could contribute significantly to the economy and development of the town and colony. The editor of the *New Brunswick Courier* aptly referred to it as a way 'in which the necessities of the labouring poor could be made to dovetail with the general interest of the whole community, so that they might be benefited by receiving work, while those who pay for it might be equally benefited by having it done.'[44] As one Halifax paper put it, 'the poor might earn a loaf and at the same time benefit the city.'[45] Such a mutually beneficial situation obtained in Saint John in 1842 when the city council spent a grant of £500 from the executive on the employment of the poor in winter. With the consequent removal of rock from the town squares, 'the City was improved and the poor people were relieved at the same time.'[46] Similarly in St John's, the editor of the *Times* applauded the insistence of the governor in 1847 that the able-bodied must work for their relief and favoured the ubiquitous resort in Newfoundland to road works as the method by which the poor could secure their subsistence while 'the country at large is benefited'.[47]

The public interest would equally be served if such employment reduced the number of those supported by government and voluntary charity. Stephen March, an assemblyman in Newfoundland, was typical of those colonists who believed that poverty was synonymous with unemployment and therefore that the availability of sufficient work would materially diminish the legislature's staggering appropriation for relief of the poor.[48] In 1829 the editor of the *New Brunswick Courier* claimed that the program of street building undoubtedly relieved Saint John of potential parish burdens.[49] This interest in economy also motivated those who were less sympathetic towards the poor, and who argued that relief for the able-bodied in the form of compulsory labour would soon send idlers and imposters scurrying to their own resources, or better still, as far as commentators in St John's were concerned, encourage them to emigrate.[50] A similarly rigorous attitude can be discerned in the workhouse ethic that emerged in the management of the almshouse in Saint John, an institution which, unlike the Halifax poorhouse, catered to the able-bodied as well as to the disabled poor.[51] Anxious to reduce the burden of the poor rate on its citizens, the grand jury of Saint John suggested in its review of the almshouse in 1842 that 'even nursing mothers should be required when in health to earn their living.'[52] Faced with overwhelming numbers of applicants, the administrators of the almshouse advocated the enforcement of labour to render the institution unattractive to the able-bodied poor. In 1849, the lieutenant-governor of New Brunswick pointed out that 'the immediate profit of the work, is not the object of main importance. The able-bodied men, as a class, may earn much less than their maintenance costs the public, but if the knowledge that hard work is required acts so as to deter others from entering the Alms House, a saving to the ratepayers will be effected, and the industry of individuals will be promoted out of its precincts.'[53]

Finally, employment relief was singularly attractive to colonial capitalists and ratepayers who relished the existence of a cheap, exploitable labour force. A report of a committee of the Newfoundland legislative council in 1849 clearly delineated how the interests of employers could be served by replacing gratuitous assistance with employment relief. It proposed that the St John's poor commissioner's office should act as a labour bureau where 'artisans and labourers might at the time be had at rates a degree lower than their ordinary rate of wages.'[54] In Saint John, a city which in contrast to St John's was keen to retain its highly mobile labourers, the inhabitants felt a particular urgency to afford employment relief for the seasonally destitute and portrayed with complacent satisfaction those 'starving for want of work' as a potentially cheap labour force.[55] For this reason, G.E. Fenety, the civic-conscious editor of the *Morning News*, proposed that the prosecution of public works should be reserved for seasons of scarcity and depression when they would not only benefit the poor by supplying work but the urban authorities would obtain the best return on the expenditure of the citizen's money in the form of useful labour, cheaply done.[56]

The range of proposals for furnishing socially useful employment for the poor was far greater than the number of schemes actually undertaken. Initially, contemporaries viewed work as a palliative for distress in a very pessimistic light. One sceptical correspondent in Saint John in 1832 urged the citizens to consider whether they had in fact any responsibility in the matter, and if so, whether such a program of work was feasible. They should determine, the correspondent suggested without expectation of a favourable response, 'Either that it is not our duty as members of a Christian community to endeavour to provide for the employment of the poor as well as their relief. Or, that it is an object which we cannot reasonably expect to attain by any united efforts in this place.'[57] Part of the trouble was that the people who took it upon themselves to advise the community on this issue tended to be men given to idle talk or theorizing, not practical men of business— newspaper editors, politicians, and bureaucrats rather than merchants, contractors, builders, and entrepreneurs. Moreover, with very few exceptions, the schemes implemented were not placed on a systematic footing, despite the necessity for regularizing employment relief advocated by the amateur political economists of the day. The projects themselves, both in conception and in practice, were of two varieties: heavy outdoor labour and indoor factory work. Public efforts were concentrated chiefly on the former because society was male-oriented and reflected the outlook of a pre-industrial age.

The most widely discussed forms of employment and the jobs most frequently organized can both be subsumed under the general heading of public
works. These differed more in time, location, and sponsorship than in form
or variety. In Halifax the urgent need for outdoor relief in the years following
the Napoleonic Wars forced citizens' committees, in the absence of government measures, to address themselves to the question of providing employment. Much to the disappointment of its energetic proponents and the
satisfaction of its critics, the Poor Man's Friend Society in the 1820s failed
in its persevering endeavours to find work for the poor, being unable to do
more than serve as a labour bureau.[58] Its successors, however, were determined to base their schemes for relieving the labouring poor on employment. Accordingly, a long tradition of outdoor relief for able-bodied men
through stone breaking for the metalling or macadamizing of the roads began
in the winter of 1830–1 and was revived for the benefit of at least 200 family
men according to need over the next three decades.[59] While the sponsorship
of this menial, degrading enterprise passed from the voluntary citizens' committees to the city corporation in the 1840s, it continued to be funded largely
by private charity with the mayor still appealing to the inhabitants for subscriptions or contributions in stone.

Meanwhile in Saint John and St John's stone breaking was also promoted,
and requests for financing it, as well as more sophisticated activities like pipe
laying and rubbish removal, were often directed to the respective executive
governments by hard-pressed civic leaders,[60] But road works remained the
ideal form of public works in St John's and the outports. Initiated principally
through the efforts of Sir Thomas Cochrane in the 1820s, road making and
repairing became a perennial resort as relief for the able-bodied and for
seasonally unemployed fishermen. To such an extent was this enterprise popularly believed to mitigate distress, that until reforms of the late 1860s the
road bill came to be associated with other appropriations for eleemosynary
aid and therefore considered as little more than a euphemism for a poor relief
bill.[61] Indeed, despite approval for the 'dovetailing' nature of this work—
that it secured 'real value to the country while reliving the necessities of the
industrious poor'—the amount of labour provided on the roads was apparently determined by the degree of distress rather than by a comprehensive
transportation policy.[62] That some contemporaries were prone to criticize
this tendency can be attributed to their preference for a systematic approach
to employment relief which would supplant the 'make work' nature of the
existing enterprise.

At the opposite extreme to such 'make work' arrangements stood the
entirely fortuitous opportunities for employment of the able-bodied poor
created by the march of progress in the Atlantic colonies. By the middle of
the century skilled and semi-skilled labourers in substantial numbers, sometimes large enough to siphon off the burdensome surplus of the towns, were
engaged on railway works in the environs of Saint John and Halifax, on road

building for the overseas telegraphic cable in Newfoundland, and on the construction of a variety of impressive civic buildings, such as the city hospital, provincial lunatic asylum, and city prison in the Halifax area.[63] For the private contractors a pool of unemployed poor supplied cheap labour at the termination of the shipping season; for the public authorities the works saved them the trouble of devising, and more important, financing an alternative employment scheme; for the community, large-scale productive labour meant a positive boon as a result of the exchange of wages for local services. As Fenety pointed out in 1858, railway construction during the depression involved 'something like a thousand pounds *distributed*, as it were, among the labouring classes every week, which in turn finds its way into the stores, and thus keeps business moving'.[64] But by its nature the work was short term and often interrupted by undercapitalization. Moreover, the climatic limitation imposed on the work when it was most needed meant that rail lines laid on frozen mud near Saint John sank in the spring thaw; that autumnal road building in Newfoundland was inefficient and could not be pursued at all in winter; and that ambitious building operations had to be halted in Halifax when frost attacked new masonry.[65] Unfortunately, such enterprises did not lay the basis of a sustained and systematic employment policy. The jobs tended to terminate with the completion of the railway, the telegraphic communications, or the public buildings concerned.

Those colonists with sufficient foresight to suggest projects that were neither wholly 'make work', nor fortuitous, nor seasonal in character, appear from a modern perspective to have had common sense to their credit.

Shrewd commentators flourished most noticeably in Saint John's, the town amongst the three which suffered most relentlessly from chronic poverty. While the distress of the inhabitants was undoubtedly complicated by the supply system practised by the merchants, contemporaries ascribed it more generally to the predominance of a single economic activity that was seasonal in nature and underdeveloped in scope. In such circumstances alternative forms of employment could be fruitfully designed to meet the demands of the local consumer market or to act as ancillary pursuits to the primary business of the fishery. Several newspaper editors and government reports recommended that both unemployment in winter and one persistent deficiency of supply in the local market might be overcome by setting the able-bodied poor to work in the woods producing lumber on a systematic basis. While many of the seasonally unemployed resorted to the woods on their own initiative, they functioned as independent, small-scale producers without the stimulus of attractive marketing facilities in town. The press suggested several times that the government ought to open a wood yard or depot in St John's on a cash basis where the poor could be sure of an equitable return for their labour and the sale of all manner of wood and primary wood products on terms advantageous both to themselves and to the public treasury.[66] A perceptive government inquiry in 1856 went a step further by advocating that the poor should be organized in supervised gangs for a more comprehensive and profitable system of employment relief in the woods.[67] Other proposals regarded employment schemes as a means of augmenting the fishery. The government report of 1856 strongly favoured the promotion of shipbuilding through tonnage bounties paid to those shipbuilders who employed a required proportion of government paupers. Not only was this a labour-intensive industry and directly related to the staple export business of the colony, but it would create many additional jobs in auxiliary areas.[68]

Alternative projects for supplementing the fishery depended on the facilities for indoor work, the other variety of employment advocated in the towns as a means of relief. The forward-looking government report of 1856, for example, claimed that publicly sponsored factories might offer employment, in lines of work suited to the country—principally the manufacture of nets and seines (imported from Britain at a cost of over £30,000 in 1860),[69] as well as small scale wooden products such as staves and shingles, the picking of oakum (25 tons of which was imported every year, according to the *Public Ledger* in 1839),[70] and the production of domestic clothing. That report, however, was published almost twenty-five years after a factory for the relief of the able-bodied had been established in St John's, an institution which had served as an inspiration for the government report and a point of departure for many other suggestions that emanated from St John's. It was a quite unique institution which in terms of longevity, popularity, non-partisanship and 'dovetailing' was the most successful of the few sustained ventures in the Atlantic towns for employing the labouring poor in this period.

The St John's factory, a non-resident and therefore non-correctional institutional, was begun in December 1832 by a group of community-conscious women who aimed primarily to teach 'carding, spinning, net making' to the children of the poor and to afford useful employment to the indigent of St John's.[71] Like any new institution, however, the managers of the factory initially encountered difficulties in obtaining appropriate raw materials to be worked into consumer goods and in raising sufficient funds to subsidize its activities.[72] Subscriptions and charity balls raised enough money to finance the construction of a permanent building in 1834 and subsequently financial assistance came from a variety of sources: bazaars, balls, benefit performances by the local theatrical group, public subscription campaigns, and fairly regular aid from the legislature.[73]

Since the factory suffered its share of vicissitudes and never achieved self-sufficiency, its community-conscious efforts were more noteworthy than its long-term accomplishments. In the first place, the factory undertook to promote industry in place of charity as a means of poor relief. This emphasis, it was popularly believed, would foster all the appropriate virtues and habits in the poor. In a community where dire poverty was endemic and the expense of poor relief crippling, the encouragement of self-reliance, independence, and self-respect amongst the poor was enthusiastically endorsed by the articulate.[74] By supplying work and useful industrial training as well as wages, the managers of the factory hoped 'to improve and elevate the mind and feeling of the poor and needy, above relying on eleemosynary aid' from other sources.[75] This was a vital consideration in St John's where the accustomed rhythm of summer fishing followed by winter distress discernibly undermined the morale and spirit of the working class and disposed them 'to lean altogether on public charity for support'.[76] The factory also undertook to supply much of its work in the slack commercial season when unemployment was at its height.[77] To those who contributed to its operations, the system pursued by the factory assured the desirable *quid pro quo* in labour. Not only did this ease the qualms of the benevolent about fostering idleness, but it stressed employment as 'the panacea for the amelioration' of the condition of the St John's poor.[78] It was also no mean consideration that the factory might reduce the burden of poor relief on the community since 'every shilling earned here is so much withdrawn from the demands on the public which pauperism engenders.'[79]

In the second place, the factory endeavoured both to employ those elements in the town population most in need of work and to extend its operations to meet emergencies that arose. Initially the institution catered to the most destitute poor of St John's, employing some 30 work people.[80] Its normal complement of workers had risen to about 60 by the severe winter of 1837–8.[81] With financial aid from the executive during the famine year of 1847–8, the factory was able to employ between 100 and 150 a day.[82] Within a few years of its foundation experience had shown that indoor employment relief was most eagerly sought by women and children, who constituted two segments of society usually neglected in the pre-industrial period but most in need of work since they comprised the majority of the year-round, as opposed to the seasonally, unemployed.[83] Its essential service as an employer of women and children was noted by the attorney general in 1856 when he asserted that 'from the effects of disease and shipwreck' St John's had more widows and orphans 'than in any other city or town of the same size'.[84] Priority of employment was given to females of every creed between the ages of 12 and 60. They laboured daily from 10 a.m. to 4 p.m. and were paid on a piece-work rate. Although the actual rate is unknown, contemporaries claimed that workers usually earned between 1s. and 1s.6d. a day, a typical relief wage. One hard-working female was reputed in 1849 to be earning as much as 12s. a week making nets. But on the basis of detailed figures for two months in 1838, the wages of the women and children averaged about 3s.6d per week, starvation wages at best. On the assumption that the adolescents were less productive and paid at a lower rate than the mature women, it is not surprising that commentators declared that it was the 'industrious' female who could earn her support at the factory. Advocates of the establishment also proudly boasted that the factory was the agency through which whole families of widows and their children could work together and earn a complete livelihood.[85] One wage packet was clearly inadequate to maintain a family.

Finally, the factory offered specialized training and concentrated on manufactures that were most needed in the community and therefore presumably guaranteed a ready, local market. Two types of manufactures were undertaken: fishing nets for the primary industry of the colony and domestic textiles required by local merchants for sale in their stores. The factory committee was proud of the quality of the nets and publicized them as being superior or at least comparable to the imported commodity.[86] Moreover, the preoccupation with net-making as an activity beneficial to the family and the community at large was frequently celebrated.

> The advantages to the colony by this branch of industry are incalculable—the women and children are taught to make nets for their husbands and fathers, and thus to employ the hitherto unprofitable season of winter—while the fisherman has only to provide the twine instead of the more expensive article, the net or seine, which latter is often beyond his means, and the want of it is not unfrequently a serious hindrance to his getting on in the world.[87]

Money otherwise sent outside the colony could thereby be kept in circulation, generating employment which would result in 'an immense saving' to the colony.[88] At the same time, the training in net-making was thought to promote 'an exceedingly useful art' in the economic circumstances of Newfoundland.[89] The needlework, always a supplementary activity, was aimed at producing necessary items of wearing apparel for local consumption. This textile branch, originally of a finishing nature, blossomed into the manufacture of textiles in 1850 when Lieutenant Governor LeMarchant provided several looms for the weaving of homespun, a fabric well suited to ordinary domestic wear and hitherto not produced in the colony. This had the advantage of adding another type of industrial training to the factory's regimen, though the institution's inability to find a qualified weaver in St John's by 1868 casts doubt on the success of the undertaking.[90]

Despite support from the legislature, endorsement by select committees, and the intermittent interest of governors, official attempts to exploit factory production as an extensive system of poor relief amounted to little more than brief enthusiasm.[91] Whatever their reasons, many prominent citizens were critical both of the management of the factory and of the quality and cost of the nets it produced. Moreover, the retail merchants of St John's did not absorb all the ready-to-wear clothing made at the factory. If the institution had been designed to employ men in winter rather than women the year round, it might have excited a more lively public concern. It is also possible that prospective workers did not always take advantage of the factory's facilities for voluntary employment. Ultimately, by the 1860s, the management of the institution came to devolve, not on a general committee of citizens as formerly, but on the Catholic St Vincent de Paul Society, a change that was accompanied by a concentration on purely hibernal operations.[92] Nonetheless, the St John's factory was the one genuine house of industry in the Atlantic region. In spite of musings about a house of industry as a palliative for poverty, Haligonians did no more than toy with the idea of providing indoor employment relief and seemed unable to devise forms of work that would fit in with the wider interests of the city and thereby appeal to the philanthropy of the townspeople.[93] After public agitation a residential house of industry for women and children was opened briefly through voluntary assistance in Saint John in 1834, but it was intended mainly as a self-supporting school of domestic industry which also trained household servants for the city.[94]

Indoor employment, therefore, did not prosper more noticeably than outdoor measures of relief. It is not difficult to discern why employment schemes foundered. For one thing, colonists believed that the conditions which caused unemployment were beyond their control and could neither be anticipated nor rectified in towns whose economies were subject to fluctuating external and international trends.[95] The sudden influxes of immigrants and erratic business depressions made the colonists feel singularly helpless. If leading townsmen felt helpless in the face of such circumstances, they would hardly be capable of helping others to help themselves. Moreover, the launching of extensive schemes for employment required capital, and no agency in the towns appeared willing to sustain a socially useful experiment in the early stages before it could become a self-supporting or even profitable operation. Despite, or perhaps because of, the amazing array of enterprises partially subsidized by government, the provincial legislatures refused to risk their revenues on long-term employment schemes or to favour leading towns at the expense of the other inhabitants in the colony.[96] For their part, the corporations of Saint John and Halifax were not wealthy enough to embark on ambitious projects and were reluctant to resort to unpopular taxation. Nor were colonists agreed how far the various levels of government should involve themselves in manipulation of the labour market. The editor of the *Newfoundland Express*, for example, pointed out that the government report of 1856 on employment for the poor 'proceeds upon an assumption which has proved a failure wherever it has been attempted to give practical effect to it—the assumption that the *organization of labour* can be effected by the state'.[97]

Left to private capitalists, however, the pauperizing patterns of unemployment were reinforced and exploited because merchants were content to employ town labourers in summer and abandon them to the mercy of government, charity, occasional public works, or sharply reduced wages in the private sector during winter.[98] With the notable exception of shipbuilders in Saint John, entrepreneurs were as yet unwilling to invest in industry and thereby ease some of the seasonal fluctuations, and this despite a general conviction by mid-century that sufficient wealth and tradition of prudence existed to sustain 'promising and well-considered commercial speculation' in local manufactures.[99] In these circumstances, voluntary, non-profit-making agencies did what they could. Such denominational societies as the St Vincent de Paul in St John's and the visiting societies attached to St Matthew's and St George's churches in Halifax went unpretentiously about the business of providing essential, if token, indoor work for women and children.[100] But more generally, associations found it easier to dispense discriminating charity without labour and thereby salve their consciences rather than campaign for effective employment relief. In fact society's inability to attack pre-industrial poverty at its source, which was unemployment, led by the 1850s to a marked preoccupation with the symptoms of poverty, especially intemperance, and a corresponding interest in social amelioration as moral rather than economic reform.[101]

Suggestions for Further Reading

T.W. Acheson, *Saint John: The Making of a Colonial Urban Community* (Toronto, 1985).
William Harris Elgee, *The Social Teachings of the Canadian Churches; Protestant: The Early Period, before 1850* (Toronto, 1964).
Judith Fingard, *The Dark Side of Life in Victorian Halifax* (Porter's Lake, N.S., 1989).

Notes

[1]Minutes, 10 November 1847, Saint John Common Clerk, MSJ, Provincial Archives of New Brunswick [hereafter PANB]; Letter from A, *Public Ledger* (St John's), 6 March 1838.

Residence Indicated for Inmates of Halifax Poorhouse, 1833–7

	Halifax*	N.S.	England	Scotland	Ireland	Nfld.	N.B.	U.S.	Other
1833	300	99	94	27	299	17	17	12	32
1834	359	79	80	27	330	27	20	22	41
1835	298	64	77	27	248	10	10	10	47
1836	280	98	71	23	243	9	12	8	62
1837	350	74	53	25	270	10	20	8	45

* With no orphanage or lying-in-hospital in Halifax more than half of the town inmates were children.
Source: *Journals of the Legislative Assembly*, Nova Scotia [hereafter *JLA*], 1834–8.

[2]Petition of JPs, Saint John, 1839, RLE/839/pe/3, No. 61, PANB.

[3]*Free Press* (Halifax), 23 December 1827.

[4]17th Annual Report of Saint Andrew's Church Female Benevolent Society, *Guardian* (Halifax), 22 January 1847.

[5]In St John's the piecemeal organization of indoor relief began in 1846 with the erection of the relief sheds or 'Camps', notorious hovels designed to house the fire victims of that year. These were not replaced until a poorhouse was opened in 1861, followed by the discontinuance of relief for the able-bodied for the first time in 1868.

[6]*Free Press*, 4, 11, 25 February, 4 March 1817; G.E. Hart, 'The Halifax Poor Man's Friend Society, 1820–27: An Early Social Experiment', *Canadian Historical Review* XXXIV (1953), 109–23. The Poor Man's Friend Society (admittedly helped by the legislature) aided as many as one-tenth of Halifax's inhabitants during the winters of the early 1820s. *Annual Reports* of the Halifax Poor Man's Friend Society. Similarly in St John's the Poor Relief Association of 1867, a voluntary organization, aided one-fifth of the inhabitants during a winter of great distress when government relief was insufficient. *Newfoundlander* (St John's), 10 May 1867.

[7]*Public Ledger*, 5 March 1847; Editorial, *Times* (St John's), 7 July 1849; 'Death from Starvation!' *Patriot* (St John's), 5 February 1853; Letter from J. Slayter, M.D., *Acadian Recorder* (Halifax), 20 January 1855; 'The Poor', *Morning Journal* (Halifax), 28 December 1855; Editorial, *Newfoundlander*, 11 February 1856; Speech by Dr Grigor, Legislative Council Debate, 3 March 1857, *Acadian Recorder*, 7 March 1857.

[8]G. Andrews, 'The Establishment of Institutional Care in Halifax in the Mid-Nineteenth Century' (honours essay, Dalhousie University, 1974).

[9]Editorial, *Christian Messenger* (Halifax), 10 January 1851; 'Lunatic Asylum and General Hospital', *Acadian Recorder*, 21 May 1853.

[10]Letter from Aqua, *Public Ledger*, 15 December 1846.

[11]J.M. Whalen, 'Social Welfare in New Brunswick, 1784–1900', *Acadiensis* II, 1, (Autumn 1972), 61; *Sun* (Halifax), 8 Janury 1851; 'New Brunswick Lunatic Asylum', *ibid.*, 15 October 1851.

[12]'Benevolent Enterprise', *Morning Post* (Halifax), 10 March 1845; 'Fancy Balls versus Hospitals and Asylums', *Presbyterian Witness* (Halifax), 16 March 1850; Speech by Dr Grigor, Legislative Council Debate, 12 March 1851, *Sun*, 17 March 1851; 'Public Hospital', *Morning News* (Saint John), 17 October 1856.

[13]Editorial, *Public Ledger*, 7 March 1837; 'The Poor—God Help Them! Let Man think of them too! Great Suffering in consequence of Scarcity of Fuel', *Morning Post*, 10 March 1846; *Morning News*, 31 July 1846; Address to the Public by the Halifax Poor Man's Friend Society, *Acadian Recorder*, 19 February 1820; Report of Indigent Sick Society, St John's, *Public Ledger*, 5 May 1840; Appeal of Committee of Ladies' Benevolent Society, Halifax, *Morning Post*, 7 October 1844.

[14]Letter from P. Power's Friend, *Guardian*, 19 March 1847; Editorials, *Public Ledger*, April 1834, 8 December 1835, 6 May 1842.

[15]'Popery in Newfoundland', *Public Ledger*, 25 September 1855.

[16]*Free Press*, 21 October 1817.

[17]Editorial, *Public Ledger*, 9 December 1828.

[18]Editorial, *Times* (St John's), 29 July 1848; Investigator, No. III, *ibid.*, 4 November 1854; 'Drunkenness, Poverty and Suffering.' *Morning News*, 11 January 1860.

[19]Board of Health, Saint John. Report for 1858, iv. New Brunswick. *JLA* (1857–58), Appendix.

[20]Letter from R.P, 'Queen's National Fund', *New Brunswick Courier* (Saint John) 13 June 1840; 'Bazaar', *Morning News*, 12 November 1855.

[21]An example is provided by the Emigrant Orphan Asylum established in Saint John in 1847. J.M. Whalen, 'New Brunswick Poor Law Policy in the Nineteenth Century' (M.A. thesis, University of New Brunswick, 1968), 32, 35–6; also the Church of England Asylum for Widows and Orphans founded in St John's after a cholera epidemic. *Times* (St John's), 27 December 1854, 20 January 1855; *Newfoundland Express* (St John's), 20 February 1858, 19 February 1859.

[22]Abstract of R.J. Uniacke's Evidence before the Select Committee of the House of Commons on Emigration, 22 March 1826, *Novascotian* (Halifax), 19 October 1826. Arranging such places for orphans was the principal aim of the Orphan Benevolent Society of Saint John which dissolved only after the city's orphanages were well established. *New Brunswick Courier*, 8 August 1840, 23 January 1858.

[23]'Stonebreaking', *Novascotian*, 20 December 1832; Matthew to Mayor, 3 January 1842 and Communication from Chamberlain upon the subject of distress of labouring poor, 3 January 1842, RLE/842/22/2, PANB. The use of the very cheap labour of British soldiers and incarcerated criminals on public works sometimes reduced the opportunities for the unemployed poor. W. Moorsom, *Letters from Nova Scotia; Comprising Sketches of a Young Country* (London 1830), 34; Letter from Clerk of the Peace to Commissioners of Streets for Halifax, Special Sessions, September 1837, RG 34, Vol. 10, Public Archives of Nova Scotia (hereafter PANS).

[24]'Employment of the Poor', *New Brunswick Courier*, 4 December 1841; 'Frightful Extent of Pauperism in the City', *ibid.*, 5 March 1842.

[25]Editorial, *Patriot*, 9 November 1839.

[26]Letter from An Inhabitant of Halifax, *Acadian Recorder*, 14 December 1816; Letter from Beneficus, ibid., 1 February 1817.

[27]Letter from A Friend to the Deserving Poor, 'Beggars', *Acadian Recorder*, 29 March 1834; 'Charity', *Novascotian*, 25 December 1844; 'Pauperism in Saint John', *Morning News*, 17 November 1847.

[28](Halifax Poor Man's Friend Society) Address to the Public, *Acadian Recorder*, 19 February 1820; (St John's Dorcas Society) Letter from Clericus, *Public Ledger*, 5 February 1833; (St John's Indigent Sick Society) *ibid.*, 27 February 1835; *Times* (Halifax), 20 December 1836; (Government relief, St John's) Resolution of the commissioners for the distribution of £300 for relief of the destitute poor, *Newfoundlander*, 27 February 1840; (St George's District Visiting Society, Halifax) *Morning Post*, 27 January 1842; (Samaritan Society, Saint John) *New Brunswick Courier*, 2 January 1847, *Morning News*, 8 March 1847; (St John's Fire Relief Committee) *Public Ledger*, 30 March 1847; (Outdoor relief, St John's) Speeches by Little and the Speaker, Assembly Debate, 22 March 1853, *Newfoundland Express*, 2 April 1853; (St Vincent de Paul Society, St John's) Editorial, *Newfoundlander*, 9 February 1854, Letter from A Clergyman, 'How the Poor may be Relieved', *ibid.*,

28 January 1858; (St Vincent de Paul Society, Saint John) *Morning Freeman* (Saint John), 22 November 1859.

29 Memorial of the Committee for distributing relief to the labouring poor in Halifax, 14 March 1817, RG 5, Series P, Vol. 80, PANS.

30 Letter from Civis, 'Feed the Hungry and the Poor—Clothe the Naked', *Morning News*, 30 November 1857; 'Employment of the Poor', *Novascotian*, 5 January 1832; Gilbert and Develier to Odell, 30 March 1842, RLE/842/22/2, PANB.

31 'St. John Public Dispensary', *New Brunswick Courier*, 4 April 1857. Similarly *Report of the Governors of Halifax Visiting Dispensary for 1860* (Halifax, 1861), 6.

32 Board of Health, Saint John, Report for 1858, iv, New Brunswick, *JLA* (1957–8), Appendix.

33 Speech by Barnes, Assembly Debate, 8 April 1845, *Times* (St John's), 12 April 1845.

34 'The Season', *Morning Post*, 19 February 1845.

35 'Relief of the Poor', *Patriot*, 30 March 1839.

36 Editorial, *Times*, (St John's), 29 September 1847.

37 Letter from Agenoria, *Acadian Recorder*, 29 November 1823.

38 *Morning News*, 11 September 1846; Notice of Commissioners for the Relief of the Poor, *Newfoundland Express*, 23 January 1861.

39 Catechistical Society, *Cross* (Halifax), 7 August 1847. The Saint John and Portland Ladies' Benevolent Society loaned clothing to the sick poor and if it was returned in good order, the party received a gift of some of the articles. *New Brunswick Courier*, 22 June 1844.

40 Editorial, *Acadian Recorder*, 6 February 1836; 'Relief of the Poor', *Patriot*, 30 March 1839; Letter from Observer, *Newfoundland*, 9 March 1848, Petition of Irish labourers (Halifax) to Sir John Harvey, 25 April 1848, RG 5, Series GP, Vol. 7, PANS; Speech by Shea, Assembly Debate, 14 December 1848; *Newfoundlander*, 21 December 1848; Speech by Hayward, Assembly Debate, 10 February 1854, *Newfoundland Express*, 18 February 1854; Speech by Surveyor General Hanrahan, Assembly Debate, 12 March 1856, *ibid.*, 31 May 1856.

41 Letter from Humanus, *New Brunswick Courier*, 2 February 1833; Editorial, *Newfoundlander*, 30 September 1847, Report of Committee of HM Council upon the expenditure on account of paupers in the district of St John's, *Public Ledger*, 3 July 1849.

42 'Employment for the Poor', *Morning News*, 29 January 1858; also *New Brunswick Courier* 30 January 1858.

43 'Employment of the Poor', and editorial comment, *Novascotian*, 12 January 1831.

44 'Winter Employment for Outdoor Labourers', *New Brunswick Courier*, 30 January 1858.

45 *Novascotian*, 11 January 1858.

46 'Employment for the Poor', *Morning News*, 29 January 1858; £500 not used in 1842 was used in 1858, Common Council, *ibid.*, 19 February, 5 March 1858; 'Employment of the Poor', *New Brunswick Courier*, 4 December 1841.

47 Editorial, *Times* (St John's), 9 October 1847.

48 Speech by March, Assembly Debate, 3 February 1853, *Patriot*, 12 February 1853.

49 *New Brunswick Courier*, 19 September 1829.

[50]*Newfoundlander*, 7 June 1855.

[51]Letter from an Inhabitant of Halifax, *Acadian Recorder*, 14 December 1816; Letter from An Old Tax Payer, 'Poor House', *Morning News*, 16 March 1842.

[52]Grand Jury Presentment, March 1842, RMU, Csj. 1/10, PANB; see also 'The Almshouse &c, &c', *Morning News*, 27 September 1850.

[53]J.R. Partelow, Provincial Secretary, to the Commissioners of the Alms House and Work House, Saint John, *New Brunswick Courier*, 29 September 1849. Work was not consistently provided, see Charges against the Alms House Commissioners, October 1860, RMU, Csj, 1/15, PANB.

[54]Report of Committee of HM Council upon the expenditure on account of paupers in the district of St John's, *Public Ledger*, 3 July 1849.

[55]Letter from The Poor Man's Friend, 'How to Employ the Poor', *Morning News*, 19 February 1858; 'Employment for the Poor', *ibid.*, 29 January 1858; Letter from Citizen, Morning Freeman, 26 March 1859.

[56]'A Word in Season—or, a Practical Lesson for the Times', *Morning News*, 3 January 1855; 'Work for Labourers', *ibid.*, 21 September 1857.

[57]Letter from Homo, 'Employment of the Poor', *New Brunswick Courier*, 14 January 1832.

[58]Editorial, *Free Press*, 5 March 1822; *Acadian Recorder*, 7 February 1824.

[59]'Employment of the Poor', *Novascotian*, 12 January 1831; 'Employment of the Poor', *Acadian Recorder*, 15 January, 31 December 1831; *Weekly Observer* (Saint John), 3 January 1832; 'Employment of the Poor', *Novascotian*, 12 January 1832; 'Stone Breaking', *ibid.*, 20 December 1832; 'The Employment of the Industrious Poor', *ibid.*, 3 January 1833; 'Stonebreaking', *ibid.*, 21 February 1833; *Guardian*, 4 January 1843; *Sun*, 4 February 1848.

[60]Letter from Homo, 'Employment of the Poor,' *New Brunswick Courier*, 14 January 1832; *ibid.*, 10 February 1838; Editorial, *Public Ledger*, 23 March 1838; Common Council resolutions, *New Brunswick Courier*, 27 November 1841, Letter from Civis, 'Feed the Hungry and the Poor—Clothe the Naked,' *Morning News*, 27 November 1857; 'Winter Employment for Outdoor Labourers,' *New Brunswick Courier*, 30 January 1858.

[61]Speech by Hogsett, Assembly Debate, 22 March 1853, *Newfoundland Express*, 2 April 1853. Speech by Hayward, Assembly Debate, 10 February 1854, *ibid.*, 18 February 1854; Speech by Hanrahan, Assembly Debate, 11 April 1854, *ibid.*, 29 April 1854; Editorial, *Public Ledger*, 24 August 1855; Speech by Prendergast, Assembly Debate, 21 January 1856, *Newfoundland Express*, 30 January 1856; Speech by Surveyor General Hanrahan, Assembly Debate, 12 March 1856, *ibid.*, 31 May 1856, Editorial, *Newfoundlander*, 12 October 1857.

[62]'State of the Poor—Its Causes', *Newfoundlander*, 10 October 1853. Moreover by the sixties road money was occasionally granted without a strict adherence to the exaction of labour on the ground that poor men 'could not, on their spare diet, be sent four or five miles out of town to work on the roads'. Assembly Debate, 22 February 1866, *ibid.*, 19 March 1866.

[63]Speeches by Parsons and Hanrahan, Assembly Debate, 11 April 1854, *Newfoundland Express*, 29 April 1854; 'Winter Work for the Industrious', *Morning Chronicle* (Halifax), 27 January 1855; 'Remember the Poor', *Morning News*, 27 November 1857;

Morning Journal, 28 April 1858; *Evening Express* (Halifax), 26 May 1858; 'Business and Prospects', *Morning News*, 29 September 1858.

64'Ship Building and Saw Mills about St John—Hard Times—The Way to Relieve Distress', *Morning News*, 10 December 1858.

65'Employment for the Poor', *Morning News*, 29 January 1858; Evidence of James Douglas before the Select Committee appointed to inquire into the Appropriation of Monies voted by the Legislature for the Relief of the Poor, *JLA*, Newfoundland, 1848–9, Appendix, p. 691; *Patriot*, 27 December 1852; Editorial, *Newfoundlander*, 12 October 1857; Speech by Surveyor General Hanrahan, Assembly Debate, 10 March 1858, *ibid.*, 18 March 1858, 'The Weather vs House Building', *Morning Journal*, 12 December 1859.

66Editorial, *Public Ledger*, 29 March 1839; 'Relief of the Poor', *Patriot*, 30 March 1839; Editorial, *Public Ledger*, 30 September 1853.

67Report of Committee of Enquiry into the State of the Poor, 26 March 1856, *Newfoundland Express*, 23 April 1856. Another winter activity which was urged in Saint John and Halifax was the ice trade. *Saint John Herald*, 10 December 1845; *Morning Journal*, 26 January 1857.

68Report of Committee of Enquiry into the State of the Poor, 26 March 1856, *Newfoundland Express*, 23 April 1856; also Speech by March, Assembly Debate, 10 December 1860, *ibid.*, 25 December 1860.

69Speech by March, Assembly Debate, 10 December 1860, *Newfoundland Express*, 25 December 1860.

70Editorial, *Public Ledger*, 29 March 1839.

71Editorial and Report of the Meeting of Committee of Ladies for establishing a Factory for the purpose of giving useful Employment to the Poor of the Town, *Newfoundlander*, 13 December 1832.

72*Public Ledger*, 26 February 1833; *Newfoundlander*, 18 April 1833; Letter from A Friend *Public Ledger*, 28 March 1834; Report of St John's Factory, *ibid.*, 27 November 1835.

73St John's Factory, *Newfoundlander*, 4 September 1834; *ibid.*, 18 September 1834; St John's Factory, *Public Ledger*, 16 January 1835, *ibid.*, 27 February 1835; Report of St John's Factory, *ibid.*, 16 August 1836; *Newfoundlander*, 23 March 1837; *ibid.*, 15 June 1837; Assembly Debate, 1 October 1838, *Patriot*, 6 October 1838, *Public Ledger*, 28 February 1840, 28 February 1851; *Newfoundland Express*, 22 October 1853; R.H. Bonnycastle, *Newfoundland in 1842* (London, 1842), Vol. 2, 232.

74Speech by Carson, Assembly Debate, 21 March 1835, *Public Ledger*, 24 March 1835; Editorial, *Newfoundlander*, 28 March 1839.

75Letter from R. Prowse, *Public Ledger*, 26 February 1847, Report of St John's Factory, *ibid.*, 16 August 1836.

76Annual Report of Committee of Factory, *Public Ledger*, 3 August 1849.

77Report of Factory Committee, *Newfoundlander*, 3 August 1837; Report of St John's Factory, *Times* (St John's), 3 August 1842.

78Editorial, *Newfoundlander*, 28 March 1839.

79Report of Committee of St John's Factory, *Newfoundlander*, 14 September 1843; Annual Report of Committee of Factory, *Public Ledger*, 3 August 1849.

80Report of St John's Factory, *Public Ledger*, 27 November 1835.

[81] Editorial, *Newfoundlander*, 5 July 1838; Report of St John's Factory Committee, *Public Ledger*, 27 July 1838.

[82] Report of St John's Factory, *Newfoundlander*, 10 August 1848; *Times* (St John's) 23 March 1849.

[83] Letter from Malthus, Poor Man's Friend Society, No. 5, 'Answer to My Opponents', *Novascotian*, 16 February 1825.

[84] Speech by Attorney General Little, Assembly Debate, 8 April 1856, *Newfoundlander* 10 April 1856.

[85] Account of persons employed at Factory, *Newfoundlander*, 5 July 1838; Letter from R. Prowse, *Public Ledger*, 26 February 1847; Editorial, *Newfoundlander* 11 March 1847; 'The Factory', *Times* (St John's), 8 September 1847, *ibid.*, 23 March 1849; Speech by Warren, Assembly Debate, 8 April 1853, *Newfoundland Express*, 28 April 1853; Speech by Prowse, Assembly Debate, 8 April 1856, *Newfoundlander*, 10 April 1856.

[86] Report of St John's Factory, *Public Ledger*, 16 August 1836; Annual Report of Committee of Factory, *ibid.*, 3 August 1849.

[87] Report of Factory Committee, *Newfoundlander*, 3 August 1837.

[88] Report of St John's Factory, *Newfoundlander*, 10 August 1848.

[89] *Times* (St John's), 23 March 1849.

[90] Editorial, *Public Ledger*, 22 January 1850; *Times* (St John's), 23 January 1850; Speech by Emerson, Assembly Debate, 22 March 1850, *Public Ledger*, 26 March 1850. See criticism voiced by Prendergast, Assembly Debate, 31 May 1852, *Newfoundland Express*, 4 June 1852, Report of Proceedings of St Vincent de Paul Society, *Newfoundlander*, 22 December 1868.

[91] Report of Committee of HM Council upon the expenditure on account of paupers in the district of St John's, *Public Ledger*, 3 July 1849, Editorial, *Newfoundland Express*, 3 May 1856.

[92] Report of Society of St Vincent de Paul, *Newfoundlander*, 20 December 1867.

[93] 'Proposal for the Establishment of a House of Industry in connexion with an Orphan Asylum'. *Novascotian*, 10 February 1836; 'An Appeal to the Public on behalf of the Establishment of a House of Industry in connexion with Orphan Asylum', *ibid.*, 28 March 1839; Letter from One of the Society, 'House of Industry, Hints to the Benevolent', *Morning Chronicle*, 11 March 1845 'House of Industry', *Guardian*, 14 March 1845; 'House of Industry', *Morning Post*, 26 March 1845; Letter from a Friend to the Poor, 'Help for the Poor', *Sun*, 19 January 1846, 'The Reclamation of Vagrants', *Morning Journal*, 22 February 1856.

[94] Letter from Homo, 'Employment of the Poor', *New Brunswick Courier*, 14 January 1832; Letter from Humanus, 'Employment of the Poor', *ibid.*, 2 February 1833; 1st Report of the House of Industry, *ibid.*, 26 July 1834; Petition of Managing Committee of Female House of Industry in City of Saint John, 2 February 1835, RLE/835/pe/4, No. 82, PANB. It also provided home employment relief for women on a piece-work basis. Report of St John Female House of Industry, *New Brunswick Courier*, 17 January 1835.

[95] Letter from a Sympathizer, 'The Present and Former Government', *Morning News*, February 1856.

[96] 'Who are the Suffering Poor?', *Morning News*, 22 February 1858.

[97]Editorial, *Newfoundland Express*, 23 April 1856; Speech by Attorney General, Assembly Debate, 21 February 1866, *Newfoundlander*, 15 March 1866; Speech by Receiver General, Assembly Debate, 6 March 1868, *ibid.*, 11 March 1868.

[98]Speech by Hogsett, Assemby Debate, 3 April 1854, *Newfoundland Express*, 11 April 1854; 'Our Trade System', *Newfoundlander*, 1 February 1855; J. Fingard, 'The Winter's Tale: The Seasonal Contours of Pre-Industrial Poverty in British North American', Canadian Historical Association, *Historical Papers* (1974), 65–94.

[99]Editorial, *Sun*, 24 December 1853.

[100]St Vincent de Paul Society, *Newfoundlander*, 2 April 1857; *Newfoundland Express*, 10 December 1861; St Matthew's Church District Society, *Guardian*, 15 November 1850; St George's Ladies' Benevolent Society, *Colonial Churchman* (Lunenburg), 15 June 1837; *Morning Post*, 15 January 1842; St George's District Visiting Society, *Church Times* (Halifax), 3 December 1853.

[101]For example, 'Providing for the Poor', *Morning News*, 18 January 1860.

22

Education in Colonial British North America

Ian E. Davey

Not so very long ago, the history of education in Canada was treated as an exercise in progressive development, ever onward and upward, from the primitive conditions of pioneer life where precious few schools existed to the modern situation where school attendance is required of every Canadian child until somewhere around the age of 16. The focus of educational history was upon the development of institutions of formal learning. Historians of education assured us that schools became a major factor in the transmission of culture and the improvement of the quality of life for all Canadians. Rapidly multiplying numbers of schools, teachers, and pupils—combined with a steadily increasing element of state control, supervision, even compulsion—were cast into a progressive tale of beneficial and beneficent educational reform.

Over recent years educational history has broadened and altered its perspective considerably. Scholars have come to realize that formalizing and institutionalizing education through schools—while perhaps the most important single development in education during the nineteenth century—was neither a simple progression nor necessarily one of automatic gains for all elements of Canadian society. New scholarship has recognized that schools do not and need not have a monopoly over education, and that the reforms of the nineteenth century were not always motivated by selfless altruism.

Ian Davey offers one critique of the progressive interpretation that emphasized the statistics of school attendance, data that he reproduces at the start of his essay. The trouble with total enrolment figures, he points out, is that they mislead by exaggerating the regularity of attendance, which for a majority of students was a part-time matter at best. Davey attempts to analyse the reasons for part-time enrolment, which he finds basically in economic privation, especially factors of mobility and poverty. Urban and rural areas had quite different patterns of irregular attendance. While parents desired education for their children, the economic needs of the family nevertheless came first and foremost.

What explanations did contemporaries offer for irregular school attendance? Why were mobility and poverty such important determi-

nants of what happened in the classroom? Despite different attendance patterns, were matters much different in the countryside than in the cities? What does Davey mean when he argues that a lack of appreciation of education was indeed 'rooted in the cultural reality of mid-nineteenth century Ontario life'?

This article first appeared, titled 'The Rhythm of Work and the Rhythm of School', in Neil McDonald and Alf Chaiton, eds, *Egerton Ryerson and His Times: Essays in the History of Education* (Toronto, Macmillan of Canada, 1979) 221–53.

> These returns present us with the painful and startling fact, of nearly one hundred thousand children of school age in Upper Canada, not attending any school. This awful fact furnishes a hundred thousand arguments to urge each friend of Canada, each friend of virtue, of knowledge and of civilization, to exert himself to his utmost until the number of children attending our schools shall equal the number of children of school age.
>
> The average attendance of pupils, compared with the whole number, is little more than half . . . I doubt not but the provision of the present Act to distribute the school fund to the several school sections according to the average attendance of pupils in each school, (and not according to the school population as heretofore), the mean attendance of summer and winter being taken, will contribute very much to increase the regular attendance at the schools and to prolong their duration.[1]

Egerton Ryerson, writing in the chief superintendent's *Annual Report* for 1850, presented the challenge to the friends of educational reform in the province. The School Act of 1850 gave legislative recognition to property assessment for school purposes, making it possible for the individual school boards to introduce free schools. If the schools were free, then there was no reason why every child of school-age should not attend them. The task was to bring the children into the schools and, just as importantly, to ensure that they attended with sufficient regularity to gain the benefits of education. The goal was regular school attendance throughout the year for all school-age children, a remote possibility in 1850 when enrolments were low and average attendance even lower.

In the succeeding years Ryerson's chronicle of the progress of the free-school movement was based largely on the increasing proportion of the province's school-age (five to sixteen) children enrolled in the schools. Every year in his annual report he compared the number of children five to sixteen years old with the number of children enrolled in the schools, commented on the narrowing gap between the two figures and deplored, as a 'public blot and disgrace', the ever diminishing residual group of unschooled children. According to this criterion, the success of the free-school movement was easily demonstrated. In the two decades prior to 1871 virtually all cities, towns, and school sections abandoned the old rate-bill system in favour of property assessment and free schools, and at the same time, registered substantial increases in the number and proportion of children who enrolled in school.

The number of five- to sixteen-year-old children reported by the local superintendents as enrolled in the common schools rose from 158,159 in 1851 to 423,033 in 1871, an increase in the proportion of the growing school-age population attending school from 61.2 per cent in 1851 to 86.4 per cent in 1871. (See Table 1.) Moreover, the increase in the common school enrolment accounted for most of the increase in attendance as the enrolment in the various private schools and academies only increased from 6,753 in 1850 to 8,562 in 1871. The increase in enrolment was more spectacular in the cities but this was only because much lower proportions of urban school-age children attended the common schools in the earlier years. In 1851 over 62 per cent of the five- to sixteen-year old children in the rural areas were enrolled in the common schools, compared to less than 38 per cent in the cities. (Of course, many city children attended private schools.) In 1871 over 85 per cent of the school-age children in both the cities and the rural areas were enrolled in the public schools of the province. Within two decades the free schools had become an accepted fact of life in Ontario and part of the experience of growing up for most children.[2]

However, the total yearly enrolment is a somewhat misleading measure of school attendance as it grossly exaggerated the number of children attending school at any one time. The figure was derived from all of those who registered in the public schools at any stage of the year. In consequence, the total enrolment included those children who were in a particular school for a week, a month, or six months, but who subsequently left. Thus, children who were working or had moved to another neighbourhood, city, town, or farming area were still counted as enrolled by the local superintendents in their annual reports to the chief superintendent.

At the same time that the total enrolment figure implied a much greater rate of attendance than actually existed, the success of the free schools was severely limited by the continuing irregularity of attendance of those enrolled. For the majority of children, schooling remained a part-time activity throughout the period. In 1856 fully 57 per cent of those who were enrolled in the common schools of the province attended for one hundred days or fewer. In 1871 the equivalent proportion was 56.5 per cent and in no intervening year did it drop below 54 per cent. (See Table 2.) The pro-

Table 1. Number of Children, 5 to 16, Attending Common Schools, 1857–71[a]

	in Ontario			in the counties			in the cities[b]		
	children	students	%	children	students	%	children	students	%
1851	258,607	158,159	61.2	227,052	141,400	62.3	13,841	5,228	37.8
1852	267,755	167,278	62.5	228,745	148,502	64.9	14,326	6,097	42.6
1853	268,957	175,422	65.2	228,776	154,185	67.4	17,272	6,812	39.4
1854	277,912	193,337	69.6	232,742	167,749	72.1	16,886	8,317	49.3
1855	297,623	211,629	71.1	257,411	184,742	71.8	26,000	11,739	45.2
1856	—	277,992	—	—	197,368	—	—	13,098	—
1857	324,888	247,434	76.2	273,836	209,754	76.6	23,524	17,136	72.4
1858	360,578	267,383	74.2	296,273	223,297	75.4	30,511	18,143	59.5
1859	362,085	279,490	77.2	298,973	233,124	78.0	26,021	18,773	72.1
1860	373,589	295,680	79.1	308,781	244,848	79.3	26,316	19,599	74.5
1861	384,980	309,895	80.5	318,499	257,994	81.0	25,811	19,526	75.6
1862	403,302	324,818	80.5	331,304	270,815	81.7	27,684	20,222	73.0
1863	412,367	339,817	82.4	340,767	280,826	82.4	25,086	21,721	86.6
1864	424,565	350,925	82.7	353,165	289,516	82.0	24,938	21,899	87.8
1865	426,757	361,617	84.7	352,166	297,335	84.4	26,955	22,823	84.7
1866	431,812	369,768	85.6	353,221	303,535	85.9	27,533	22,606	82.1
1867	447,726	380,511	85.0	365,096	311,066	85.2	27,663	22,603	81.8
1868	464,315	397,792	85.7	377,325	323,695	85.8	28,605	24,190	84.6
1869	470,400	409,184	87.0	386,190	331,917	85.9	28,780	25,581	88.9
1870	483,966	420,488	86.9	391,261	339,423	86.8	31,893	26,516	83.1
1871	489,615	423,033	86.4	392,559	337,033	85.9	32,953	28,068	85.2

[a]It should be noted that the percentages are not particularly accurate as the estimated number of children in the province was often based on guesswork by the local superintendents.
[b]The reason that there is a sharp increase in the number of children in the cities in 1855 is that from 1855 the figures for London and Ottawa were included with those of Toronto, Hamilton, and Kingston.

SOURCE: Annual reports from 1851 to 1871.

Table 2. Proportion of Common-School Students by Number of Days Attended, 1856–71

year	under 50 days			50 to 100 days			100 to 150 days			150 to 200 days			200 days and over		
	Ontario	counties	cities	Ontario	counties	cities	Ontario	counties	cities	Ontario	counties	cities	Ontario	counties	cities
1856	31.7	33.0	24.3	25.3	26.0	18.6	19.9	20.2	15.4	13.2	12.8	16.0	9.9	8.1	25.9*
1857	31.9	33.2	26.1	25.0	25.5	24.2	19.7	19.7	19.5	13.8	13.1	17.2	9.6	8.5	13.0
1858	30.2	31.3	25.0	24.5	24.9	20.8	19.6	19.8	18.9	14.9	14.4	18.6	10.8	9.6	16.6
1859	29.7	31.0	23.4	24.9	25.4	22.2	19.9	19.9	18.4	14.6	13.9	18.0	10.9	9.7	18.0
1860	30.2	31.7	22.7	25.0	25.4	23.5	19.9	19.9	20.3	14.9	14.2	17.7	10.0	8.8	15.8
1861	30.2	31.5	22.7	25.3	25.8	22.4	20.3	20.2	19.2	15.3	14.5	18.3	8.9	7.9	17.4
1862	30.7	32.1	23.5	25.8	26.2	22.8	20.1	20.1	19.3	14.8	14.0	18.6	8.6	7.5	15.9
1863	30.7	32.0	23.9	25.3	25.9	23.1	20.3	20.3	19.0	15.1	14.2	18.9	8.7	7.6	15.1
1864	31.0	32.3	23.4	25.3	25.7	22.4	20.0	20.0	19.5	15.2	14.4	19.0	8.5	7.7	15.7
1865	30.9	32.3	22.6	25.2	25.7	22.0	20.2	20.2	17.9	15.2	14.4	17.8	8.5	7.4	19.7
1866	30.7	32.3	24.0	25.9	26.3	22.2	20.5	20.3	18.4	15.0	14.1	18.3	7.9	7.1	17.1
1867	29.8	31.3	20.8	25.7	26.2	20.5	20.7	20.7	18.8	15.6	14.6	18.7	8.3	7.2	21.2
1868	29.4	31.0	19.5	25.0	25.5	19.6	20.9	20.9	19.5	15.9	14.9	21.0	8.7	7.8	20.4
1869	30.2	31.7	21.5	26.1	26.8	21.0	20.3	20.2	19.4	15.5	14.3	22.2	7.9	7.0	15.9
1870	29.9	31.6	22.4	26.1	26.5	22.7	20.5	20.4	18.7	15.6	14.5	21.1	7.8	7.0	15.0
1871	30.1	31.6	23.0	26.4	26.8	23.2	21.4	21.3	20.7	16.2	15.1	21.7	5.9	5.2	11.3

* This figure appears unrealistically high in view of the subsequent figures. It is high because 1,584 of the 3,197 students in Hamilton were recorded as attending for 200 days or more. I have found no other evidence to verify this high rate of attendance.

SOURCE: Annual reports from 1856 to 1871.

portion of children who attended for one hundred days or less was much higher in the rural areas than in the cities. In 1856 the proportion of rural students in this group was 59 per cent and in 1871, 58.4 per cent; and in the intervening years their proportion never fell below 56 per cent. The proportion who attended for a similarly short time in the cities was much less although it fluctuated considerably. In 1856 it was 42.9 per cent and in 1871, 46.2 per cent. In the intervening years the proportion attending for one hundred days or less rose as high as 50.3 per cent in 1857 and dropped as low as 39.1 per cent in 1868.

It is paradoxical that at the same time the free-school system was being adopted throughout almost all of Ontario and the proportion of children enrolled was increasing rapidly, the actual number of days most children attended remained relatively low. It became increasingly clear in the local superintendents' reports of the 1860s that the real issue was not so much non-attendance but irregularity. The structure of a permanent school system had been erected remarkably quickly; by the end of the 1860s most areas were served by schools which were free and which were open throughout the year.[3] Furthermore, as Ryerson continually pointed out, the idea of schooling had been generally accepted as the increasing enrolments demonstrated. By 1871 the actual number of children reported as not attending any school had declined to 38,535 and less than one-third of those, 12,018, were between the ages of seven and twelve, during which years attendance was made compulsory by the 1871 Act. Even though the number of non-attenders was probably larger, given the fact that the enrolment figures exaggerated the number in school, only a small group of children were not exposed to any form of schooling and most of these resided in the rural areas. In the cities, where the fear of juvenile crime was greatest, the educators had come to recognize the existence of a permanent class of poor who were beyond the reach of the public schools and for whom special institutions, such as industrial schools, were needed.[4] Once most children had been gathered into the public schools, more and more attention was focused on the ways and means of keeping them there with sufficient regularity and for a long enough time for each child to learn the lessons the schools were designed to instil.

'Irregularity of attendance,' one local superintendent declared in 1871, 'is the bane and curse of the public schools; it is a log and chain upon the progress of instruction for it blasts and withers the noblest purposes of the best of teachers.' Irregular attendance not only deprived the individual student of adequate schooling but disrupted the whole school. It made the school system inefficient as it meant that the teachers were 'unduly occupied in uncalled for repetition' thus retarding the progress of the class.[5] It also confounded attempts to grade the students by age as those who attended irregularly remained in the lower grades much longer.[6] From 1860 when

Ryerson asked each local superintendent to report the reasons for non-atten-dance, much of each report was devoted to the causes and effects of irregular attendance. By the late 1860s, the local superintendents, following Ryerson's lead, called for a measure of compulsion because it was inconsistent to have compulsory property assessment and voluntary attendance.

Opponents of the free-school system argued that the system increased irregularity of attendance because the parents did not value what they did not pay for directly. 'Where a rate-bill is charged,' one superintendent declared, 'the pupil, if present at all during the month, is sure to attend as often as possible, for the parents feel that non-attendance causes them a pecuniary loss; whereas under the free-school system any trifle is too often deemed sufficient to excuse the absence of the child.'[7] The free-school sup-porters, including most of the superintendents, were also inclined to lay the blame for continued irregular attendance on the 'criminal apathy and neg-ligence of parents' who did not appreciate the value of an education to their children.[8] Yet, clearly, the extent of irregularity of attendance was such that parental indifference could hardly be the complete explanation. Besides, it was contradicted by the rapid increase in enrolments throughout the province which, plausibly, could be considered more an expression of parental con-cern. As one superintendent put it while rebuking his colleagues in 1861, the term 'parental indifference' was used to explain poor attendance by some because it was 'a convenient way of filling up the column' in the annual report. 'Not indifference,' he continued, 'but the pressing care of providing for their bodily wants, is . . . the more general cause of non-attendance.'[9] Those other superintendents who went beyond 'convenient ways of filling up columns' agreed that material circumstance rather than criminal negli-gence was the root cause of low and irregular attendance.

> Compulsory attendance and the poverty of families, will scarcely ever harmonize. Indeed to carry out the provisions of the Free School System, we would require to furnish, either by the Legislature or the trustees, or by both combined, all the necessary books, and other things required for the school, together, with, in some, cases, even the clothes in which the children are to attend the school, or a proportion of the children, in the rural districts, as well as in the towns and cities, will be deprived of the benefits of a common school education.[10]

> When workers lost their employment—which they might do at the end of the job, of the week, of the day or even of the hour—they had nothing to fall back upon except their savings, their friendly society or trade union, their credit with local shopkeepers, their neighbours and their friends, the pawnbroker. . . . When they grew old or infirm, they were lost, unless helped by their children, for effective insurance or private pension schemes covered only a few of them. Nothing is more characteristic of Victorian working-class life, and harder for us to imagine today, than this virtually total absence of social security.[11]

The most potent determinants of attendance patterns in both urban and rural areas were the same conditions which shaped the economic and social realities of nineteenth-century Canadian life. Attendance was naturally influenced by such ubiquitous features as harsh climatic conditions, bad roads, and sickness. However, those factors which contributed to poverty and economic insecurity—trade depressions, crop failure, transient work patterns, and seasonal employment—largely determined the regularity of school attendance throughout the province.

'Two successive years of failure in the productions of husbandry, attended by a large decrease in the public revenue, and an unprecedented stagnation in every branch of business, could not fail to be seriously felt in the operation of our school system.'[12] In these words Ryerson summed up the impact of the depression of the late 1850s on Ontario. Its effect was more devastating in the larger cities which were brought to a standstill, making it difficult for them to bear the cost of the school system at the same time that attendance was more irregular. In Toronto, in fact, the superintendent of schools in 1857 and a committee of the board in 1864 advocated a return to the rate-bill schools because the free-school system was financially burdensome and had not improved either the proportional enrolment or the regularity of attendance of children in the city.[13] Depression increased the irregularity of attendance because they brought increased hardship for many people, particularly the poor who, lacking financial resources at the best of times, were often reduced to reliance on charity to survive. In Hamilton, for instance, the depression of the late 1850s brought widespread unemployment as many establishments were forced to close, and one observer reported that before 1857 'the common labourer could make almost as much in a day as he now can in a week.'[14] The Ladies Benevolent Society and the City Council distributed bread, wood, and soup in the winter months of the depression, and the ladies expressed relief that many of 'the lowest and unsatisfactory class of applicants' for aid had been forced to leave the city because it enabled them to assist 'those whose necessities are as great, but who are more diffident in making known their wants'.[15]

The effect of economic privation on school attendance during depression years was twofold. First, many children were withdrawn from school through dire necessity and scavenged for the means of keeping themselves and their families alive—stealing money, objects to sell, and coal or wood to keep them warm.[16] Second, many children were withdrawn from school when their parents were forced to leave the city in search of work. The population of Hamilton, for example, dropped rapidly during the depression of the 1850s and, as Superintendent Ormiston remarked in 1860, 'a large number of those returned as attending school only a short time, are removed from the city'.[17]

Depressed prices and bad crops had similar effects in the rural areas, reducing school expenditures and affecting the rates of attendance. As one superintendent in Haldimand County commented in 1861, 'Inferior crops and low prices for produce have caused some undertakings to be stationary and others to retrograde; but as soon as farmers are blessed with better harvests and more remunerative markets, the children will be more regular in their attendance, they will be sent longer to school, and far more attention will be given to furnishing the school-houses.'[18] Similarly, one inspector noted that the aggregate attendance was less in the first half of 1879 than in the corresponding period of 1878 while in the second half it was greater. 'It seems fair,' he concluded, 'to infer that the hard times forced people to seek help from their children, till the good harvest justified them in sending them back to school.'[19] In short, cyclical depressions and crop failures affected school attendance because in good times more parents sent more of their children to school and sent them more regularly. Yet, lower attendance during bad times resulted largely from a magnification of those factors which caused irregular attendance throughout the nineteenth century—transience and poverty.

Recent research has given us insights into the nature and extent of transience in the nineteenth century—large numbers of people in both urban and rural areas were on the move.[20] Labourers moved from farms to cities in winter and back to farms in the spring; farmers sought work in logging camps and elsewhere in the winter months; canal, railroad, and road construction workers worked their way through the countryside; skilled workers moved on when there was no more work to be found in a particular city or town; and people from all walks of life packed their bags when opportunities to better themselves seemed more probable in another neighbourhood, city, town, farming area, or county. The actual number of transients was immense. In Hamilton, for example, only about one-third of those recorded on the 1851 census were found on the 1861 census, and Katz has estimated that at least twice as many people lived in the city during a whole year as were there at any one time.[21] Those who left in the decade spanned the spectrum of Hamilton's occupational and ethnic structure, but they were less likely to be married and more likely to be young, poor, and to own no property in the city than those who stayed.[22]

The skilled workers who moved on may have drawn on past experience. Those artisans who came from England, for example, brought with them a tradition of 'tramping' which was organized to the extent that card-carrying members of particular unions moved from place to place looking for work and calling on the local branches for welfare and support. It was, as Eric Hobsbawm has pointed out, a form of unemployment relief with the numbers on the tramp much greater in depression times although younger men were likely to spend a number of years on the move.[23] Such organized tramping was not widespread in Canada in the 1850s and 1860s because the union movement was in its infancy. However, it is likely that even then itinerant workers knew where to ask for work in the various towns and cities, and numerous public houses probably acted as receiving centres as they did in England. For example, the 'Stonemason's Arms' and two or three other centrally located hotels in Hamilton were the residences of most of the city's unemployed at the time of the 1851 census. The tramping system points to a facet of artisan life also noted by Charlotte Erickson in her study of British immigrants to America.[24] Journeymen were much more likely to move around in search of work in their specific trade than to take alternative employment. Undoubtedly, many of those who left Ontario were on their way west to Detroit and beyond, but in the 1850s the lack of industry in the province may have encouraged many artisans to leave. As one contemporary observer bemoaning the lack of moneyed capital and manufacturing in Ontario put it: 'It is not true that the establishment of manufactures amongst us would detach our population from agricultural pursuits; since the first settlement of the Province, tens of thousands of citizens have passed through because they could find no employment in their trades, and tens of thousands have been deterred from coming here for the same reason.'[25]

At least the artisans had a portable skill to carry with them in their search for work. The position of the labourers was even more precarious for they had only their brute strength to sell. Much of their work such as farm and lumber work was seasonal, or else it was institutionally transient in nature like canal and railroad construction. Labourers were forced to move on when the source of work dried up, although Thernstrom concludes that those who worked in the cities only left 'when the depressed state of the local labour market made it impossible to subsist where they were'.[26] Economic conditions forced workers to move on and, in a sense, it was a vicious circle. Transience bred transience and those on the tramp were usually the last to be employed and the first to be laid off.[27] As one builder in Petrolia told the Royal Commission on Capital and Labour:

> If a tramp came along, or a man from a distance, and recommended himself to be a mechanic in want of work, and told me what he could do, and after I had given him work I found he could not perform what he had undertaken to accomplish, I would give him his money and let him go. But, if I had a man working who had been working for me for two or three months, perhaps for a year, and I knew well enough that he was not a perfect hand in certain classes of work, I would keep him on, because he would be a faithful hand.[28]

The implications for school attendance of this widespread geographic mobility were profound. On the one hand, children who enrolled in school and later left the area exaggerated the degree of irregularity in any one school by inflating the enrolment and lowering the average attendance figures. On the other, the number of children whose schooling was interrupted must have been immense. If the distance of migration was small—from neighbourhood to neighbourhood within a city or from farming community to farming community within a school district—it was possible that a child's name would appear on more than one school register in the area. One inspector of schools in the County of Middlesex, for example, pointed out that he had 'found pupils reported from a school in Metcalfe as having attended less than 100 days also reported from a school in Lobo', as the family had moved from Metcalfe to Lobo during the year. It was possible, he suggested, that they might have attended for more than 100 days if their attendance at both schools was taken together.[29] For those who moved beyond the jurisdiction of a particular school board, it was impossible to gauge how many days each year they may have attended. Certainly, school superintendents remarked on the effect of transience on poor attendance rates in their schools. The fact that Collingwood's population was 'a floating one—continually changing', was given as the reason that the average attendance was much lower than the number enrolled on the books.[30] Similarly, the failure to increase the number of students in Ottawa in 1865 was 'caused by the number of mechanics and labourers who have migrated to the U.S., in consequence of the falling off of work at the public buildings here'.[31]

Some superintendents reported that the continual movement of parents from place to place was unsettling because 'many having recently come to the place, or expecting soon to go, feel . . . indisposed to go to the expense of a set of school books, and the trouble of sending their children for the short time they may remain.'[32] The unsettled character of the population was seen to be detrimental to the progress of education. As one superintendent in the County of Prescott wrote of the French Canadian majority in his school section: 'One great impediment is . . . they do not remain long enough in one locality for their children to be benefited by the schools.'[33] It was difficult to teach transient students whose movement in and out of the schools disrupted the efficient working of the system. How efficient and settled the school system would have been if its clientele was less mobile is a moot question because, particularly in the rural areas, the teachers themselves were not immune from the transient experience. In one county, for example, 'out of one hundred and one employed on the First of January 1868, seventy-nine were not found in the same position in January 1870, and of this large number, fifty-seven had either given up teaching or had left the County.'[34]

Although geographic mobility cut across all classes in the society, as a cause of irregular attendance it was usually associated with the working class and the poor. In England, for instance, in the 1850s the president of the Department of Education noted that 'in the lower class schools the irregularity and shortness of attendance hinder the results . . . [t]heir habits are so migratory that only 35% are found in the same school for more than two years.'[35] The migratory 'habits' of the working class were perceived as part of their general want of discipline along with their unpunctuality, irregular work habits, affection for alcohol and inability to save money. And, in a sense it was true. Living in poverty or, at least, within easy reach of it, most working-class families, particularly below the skilled level, operated on a boom and bust economy. They spent their money when they had it (often in celebration of Saint Monday if they were paid weekly) and eked out an existence when they were penniless in accordance with the irregularity of their income. If, as Michael Katz has suggested, Gibbon Wakefield's evocative term 'the uneasy class' applied to Canadian entrepreneurs at mid-century, it was no less apt for artisans and labourers as economic insecurity was a fact of working-class life.[36]

Their insecurity stemmed from the practices of employing labourers by the day and journeymen irregularly throughout the year. In fact, the irregularity of employment probably contributed more to the poor economic condition of the working class than did the low wages.[37] In 1864 the editor of The Workingman's Journal, which was published in Hamilton, declared that the city's workers were likely to be on short-time amounting to five days a week for eighteen weeks in the year. He was critical of the mayor's practice of declaring general holidays 'whenever a few individuals take a fancy to have it done', and pointed out that each holiday cost the 3,000 workers in Hamilton a minimum of $3,500.[38] It was a matter of necessity for the working man to earn as much as possible in the good seasons to ward off periods of unemployment in winter and during depressions. As one moulder put it, they went on strike because 'we felt we should have more wages when we were working in order to be able to live during those portions of the year when there was nothing to do.'[39]

Moreover, it is likely that in the second half of the nineteenth century the rise of industrial capitalism brought increasing irregularity of employment for skilled workers and made their work experience much more similar to that of the unskilled labourers. As both Pentland and Langdon have demonstrated, the traditional job security of artisans was undermined by the emergence of a self-regulating capitalist labour market and 'the driving mechanization of industry'.[40] The personalized ties between master and journeymen which cushioned artisans against downturns in the economy disintegrated in the factory setting. Employers simply laid off excess workers in slack periods and rehired them when the economy rebounded.[41] At the same time, mechanization severely diluted the skills required in some trades such as tailoring, shoemaking, and printing.[42] Some artisans lost their jobs to children and 'greenhorns' who were able to operate the machines and were cheaper to employ. Those who kept their jobs were often forced to accept lower wages because of the increased competition for their jobs. The result of these processes was the weakening of the artisans' position as their hold on their employment became less secure and cyclical unemployment increased.

The plight of working people was aggravated as well by the method of wage payment. Some were paid in truck and thus forced to buy at prices set by the company store, while others who were paid monthly found themselves continually in debt to the local shopkeeper. Many workmen had 'to run monthly accounts and that puts them entirely at the mercy of the corner grocers . . . you have to take what he has got and you cannot go anywhere else . . . if a man could get his wages weekly he could run his business more on a cash basis and go where he pleased.'[43] Even those who were paid weekly found it difficult to shop economically if they were paid on a Saturday night.

> The 'hewers of wood and drawers of water', of this thriving City [Hamilton] live . . . 'from hand to mouth', and each end of the week, and we fear, in many cases the beginning, finds the dependent family, reduced to a state not very far from actual want, with no means to provide for the necessities of the Sabbath, until the week's wages is paid late on Saturday evening . . . The poor unfortunate who has, from a combination of circumstances, antagonistic to virtue, found an appetite for the maddening bowl, finds himself exhausted with the week's labour, and weary waiting around the office door for his turn to be paid. After which they too often go straight to the Recess or Tavern . . . where they remain until part or all of their earnings are spent; and when it is too late for the prudent house-wife to expend her share of her husband's hard earned money profitably, but whose necessities afford the vulturous huxter an opportunity to practise his penchant for extortion . . . Were all employers to pay any other day of the week, the poor labourer's wife could do her marketing to the best advantage and curtail very materially the year's expenditure.[44]

Plainly, the experience of most working-class families militated against the formation in their children of the virtues of orderly, regular, punctual industry. The irregularity of their work patterns made it difficult for them to commit themselves (and their children) to regular activities for any length of time. The 'lack of discipline' that middle-class observers considered to be the cause of working-class poverty was, rather, more of an accommodation to the insecurity of their economic reality. For, as Henry Mayhew shrewdly noted of the casual labourers in London:

> Regularity of habits are incompatible with irregularity of income; indeed, the very conditions necessary for the formation of any habit whatsoever are, that the act or thing to which we are to be habituated should be repeated at frequent and regular intervals. It is a moral impossibility that the class of labourers who are only occasionally employed should be either generally industrious or temperate—both industry and temperance being habits produced by constancy of employment and uniformity of income.[45]

To the list of industry and temperance observed by Mayhew, we should add the regular attendance of their children at school.

An acquaintance with irregular income and periods of poverty was not confined to the urban working class and the agricultural labourers. Many of the province's small farmers, especially those who scratched out a living from the rocky soils of the shield in the eastern and northern areas of the province, experienced the same deprivations. In one sense, the problem of irregular attendance at school was rooted in the success of the free-school program itself. It had succeeded in enrolling most of the children of the province in the schools, including most of the poor in both rural and urban areas. To expect regular and punctual attendance from them without a concomitant improvement and regulation of their life style, was to expect the impossible.

'I can say that a man with a family of two children, a son and a daughter, will find his earnings, if an ordinary workman, readily absorbed in the education of these two children, if he is so disposed . . . the moment you have any children, if even an only child, it seems to me that the earnings of an ordinary mechanic would count for very little.'[46] The ordinary workman and the small farmer had little room for manoeuvre, and if the former lost his job or the latter's crops failed, their families were often thrown into poverty until conditions improved. These not infrequent occurrences had considerable influence on school attendance patterns. The 'hard struggles of the tillers of the soil' often meant that they either required 'the actual assistance of their children, or they are unable to clothe them sufficiently well to appear in school'.[47] Some indication of the extent of hardship is provided by this latter reason, for the lack of adequate clothing and shoes was frequently given as the reason for low attendance in both rural and urban areas.[48] Moreover, those parents unable to clothe their children properly were unlikely to be able to afford the necessary books that students required for their studies. As late as 1890, one working-class journal dismissed 'free education' as 'a piece of rhetorical bombast', and declared that 'it is not to be wondered at that people, who are barely able to provide their families with bread and blankets and coal during the winter, should keep their children at home rather than incur the liability of having to find them textbooks.'[49]

Much of the poverty was associated with the seasonal rhythm of work as the harsh winter swelled the ranks of the unemployed in the cities and brought work to a standstill on the farms. Not surprisingly, this had considerable impact on attendance patterns although its manifestations were quite different in the urban and the rural areas. In the cities and towns, the coming of winter meant increased misery for large numbers of people. Those who worked outside were likely to be laid off. Labourers, carpenters and joiners, painters and decorators, bricklayers and brickmakers, and seamen lost their jobs or competed among themselves (and with the large number of agricultural labourers who came to the cities in winter) for the small number of jobs available. Those who were skilled enough, or sufficiently lucky, to keep their jobs were often forced to work for reduced wages because of competition for work and the shorter working day. Even those who worked inside were often faced with winter unemployment; the moulders, for example, were likely to be thrown onto the overcrowded labour market because most of the foundries closed down for six to eight weeks for stocktaking and retooling.[50] Winter was also the slack period in the sweated clothing trades, making it difficult for wives and daughters to supplement the family income and throwing most of the widows into the arms of the various relief agencies.[51] The plight of the urban poor was further exacerbated because of the increased price of food and fuel in the winter months. As Judith Fingard has remarked: 'winter deprived the poor of their employment at the same time as it made the necessaries of life prohibitively dear; and it endangered their health by aggravating the plight of the sick and infirm, by creating dietary problems for those at or below the subsistence level, and by causing disablement or death for others through exposure.'[52]

The effect of the harsh winter was reflected in the monthly enrolment figures in the urban areas. Without adequate clothing and nourishment, children were much more susceptible to sickness and disease in winter.' [W]hooping cough,' *The Spectator* (Hamilton) remarked in a review of the causes of death in the city in 1857, 'seems to have been exclusively fatal to the poor.'[53] In the same city in the 1880s, the number of children absent from school because of sickness in January, February, and March averaged well over 800 compared to only 306 in September.[54] Still others were kept at home because of sickness in the family or because they were needed to mind the younger children in the absence of the parents. The diaries of W.C. Wilkinson, who was the truant officer in Toronto in the 1870s, provide some insight into the depths of human suffering endured during the urban winter. Investigating the absence from school of one ten-year-old girl, he discovered that the father had recently died from typhoid and the mother was ill in bed. The widow told him 'she could not provide books for the girl to go to school nor, in fact bread for the family.' A seven-year-old boy was absent because his father was out of work and the mother was unable to get the child boots to wear.[55] Wilkinson's diaries reveal clearly that most cases of irregular attendance involved some personal catastrophe in the home, especially sickness. Few of the children were working except in exceptional circumstances such as the eight-year-old boy who, when found attending his mother's shop while she was sick in bed, admitted that he was 'guilty of truancy'.[56]

Undoubtedly, more children were able to find jobs in the summer months and contribute to the family income, but before industrialization, the commercial city did not provide large numbers of jobs for children. Some found work as messengers in the large stores, or deliverers of newspapers, girls found jobs in the sweated trades and in domestic service, and boys helped their fathers in their craft shops. Moreover, industrialization in Canada did not involve large-scale employment of young children in the factories. Only tobacco manufacturing and cotton and woolen mills provided employment for a great number of young children. Certainly, from the 1860s there was an increasing number of children working in factories and this affected school attendance. The superintendent for the village of Hespeler, for instance, complained of 'the ebb-and-flow' of attendance and suggested that: 'The irregularity is caused by the boys and girls, of almost all sizes and ages, staying out of School or going to it, according as their assistance is required or not at the factories.'[57] But the evidence suggests that most of those children who found work in industry were over the age of twelve.[58] It seems that irregular attendance in the cities and towns was not so much the result of large-scale employment of young children as of the lack or loss of jobs for their parents. In large part, irregular attendance patterns in the urban areas were the cumulative result of many personal disasters stemming from the instability of the labour market and the incidence of sickness—conditions which intersected most acutely during the winter months.

This was certainly not the case in the rural areas. The most important feature of school attendance patterns outside of the cities and towns was the pronounced seasonal variation. As the figures for 1850 to 1854 indicate, average attendance was higher in winter. (See Table 3.) Moreover, while more boys than girls attended in both summer and winter, the difference between the sexes was approximately twice as large in the winter months. That is, many more boys and fewer girls attended the rural schools in winter. This seasonal pattern is similar to that noted by Joseph Kett in rural New England for a slightly earlier period,[59] and is explained by the fact the 'the parents think the working of their farms of more importance than the education of their children.'[60] The shortage and high price of agricultural labour meant that the older children, particularly the boys, worked on the farm 'during the three-fourths of the year' and were only sent to school (or allowed to attend) in 'those months, when by the very nature of the season, the tiller of the ground is dismissed from his toil'.[61] The result, according to one of the local superintendents in York County, was that 'in summer seasons those children who are too young to labour are sent to school, and those whose labour is valuable are kept at home: in the winter this order is reversed, thus making two distinct sets of pupils in the year'.[62] The pattern of attendance, then, was determined by the seasonal demands of the farm; even the young children were called on to assist in the busiest periods and the schools were virtually emptied 'at the times of hay, wheat, oat, apple and potato harvests.'[63]

The superintendents' reports indicate that the farmers' reliance on their children's labour was almost universal, although it is likely that the practice was more prevalent in the poorer and newer farming areas. The distinctly seasonal pattern of attendance prolonged the number of years during which

Table 3. Average Attendance at Common Schools, 1850–54

year	Ontario			counties			city		
	total	boys	girls	total	boys	girls	total	boys	girls
1850—summer	76,824	41,784	35,040	70,844	37,940	32,704	2,248	1,495	753
—winter	81,469	48,308	33,161	75,215	44,385	30,830	2,163	1,375	788
1851—summer	83,390	44,647	38,743	74,438	39,541	34,897	2,581	1,423	1,158
—winter	84,981	49,060	35,921	76,389	44,076	32,313	2,376	1,377	999
1852—summer	85,161	45,409	39,752	75,762	40,253	35,509	2,730	1,482	1,248
—winter	86,756	49,867	36,889	77,656	44,620	33,036	2,580	1,448	1,132
1853—summer	90,096	48,668	41,428	78,046	41,955	36,088	4,391	2,337	2,054
—winter	90,659	52,252	37,407	78,830	45,380	33,450	3,919	2,259	1,660
1854—summer	91,880	49,475	42,405	78,682	41,359	35,823	4,368	2,615	1,753
—winter	92,925	52,696	40,229	79,306	44,694	34,612	4,441	2,670	1,771

SOURCE: Annual reports from 1850 to 1854.

rural children were in school, albeit often briefly. This is clearly borne out by the annual reports from 1871 to 1883 which included an age breakdown of those enrolled. (See Table 4.) In 1871, in the counties, 45.3 per cent of those enrolled were between five and ten years of age, 47.9 per cent between ten and sixteen, and over 6 per cent between sixteen and twenty-one. In contrast, in the cities, fully 58.5 per cent were in the younger age group of the school-age population and only 39.1 per cent were between ten and sixteen. Furthermore, the proportion of city students between sixteen and twenty-one was only 2.1 per cent. The much larger proportion of older students in the rural areas was a function of the older boys attending only for three or four months in the winter. As one superintendent remarked, 'a number of lads, who have outgrown their school-boy days, return to peruse old studies, and to make still further advancement'.[64] Fewer girls attended in winter. The younger children who attended in summer were often unable to go to school in winter because of the distance from the school and the severity of the weather. It would seem that many older girls were kept home in order to look after them.

The pattern of rural school attendance that emerges was one of age- and sex-specific seasonal absenteeism rather than irregular attendance throughout the year. This was not the case in the cities, for although the deprivations of winter resulted in some seasonal variation, the personal disasters at the heart of irregular attendance were likely to occur at any stage of the year.

The experience of all children throughout the province was also affected by the harshness of the physical conditions and the prevalence of disease. While distance from school, severe weather, and impassable roads were obvious inhibiting factors on the attendance of young children in the rural areas, they also affected children in the urban areas. The attendance of the five- and six-year-olds was so irregular in London (about 50 per cent of the time), that in 1879 the inspector of schools questioned the worth of educating them. He thought it better to concentrate on children between seven and fourteen who were 'physically more able to attend'.[65] Glazebrook has pointed out that even though the main streets in the larger centres were often paved, 'no one had to search far to find plenty of mud', especially in spring and autumn.[66] Moreover, at the same time that winter travel by sled was easier, walking any distance through the snow in bitterly cold weather was both difficult and dangerous. In consequence, any child living more than a few hundred yards from school, be it in a large city or on a farm, was often housebound because of the conditions. Wilkinson, the Toronto truant officer, found a number of children were kept at home 'owing to bad roads and want of sidewalks' and he, himself, commented that in some neighbourhoods the snow was so deep that 'it was utterly [sic] unreasonable for any child to go through.'[67]

I have already illustrated the upsurge in sickness which accompanied the arrival of winter; however, people in the mid-nineteenth century lived in

Table 4. Proportion of Public-School Students by Age Groups, 1871–83

	under 5		5 to 10		10 to 16		over 16	
	counties	*cities*	*counties*	*cities*	*counties*	*cities*	*counties*	*cities*
1871	—	—	45.3	58.5	47.9	39.1	6.2	2.1
1872	0.5	1.2	46.4	58.9	47.6	38.7	5.5	1.2
1873	0.4	0.1	46.4	61.1	47.7	38.1	5.5	0.8
1874	0.4	0.1	50.7	58.3	44.3	40.0	4.6	1.7
1875	0.4	0.1	50.9	59.3	43.8	39.5	4.9	1.1
1876	0.3	0.01	50.3	61.2	44.0	38.0	5.4	0.8

	under 5		5 to 16		over 16	
	counties	*cities*	*counties*	*cities*	*counties*	*cities*
1877	0.3	0.1		99.3	4.8	0.6
1878	0.3	0.1	94.9	99.2	4.8	0.7
1879	0.3	0.1	94.9	99.2	4.3	0.7
1880	0.3	0.1	95.4	99.6	4.3	0.3
1881	0.4	0.1	95.4	99.3	3.8	0.6
1882	0.3	0.1	95.9	99.3	3.3	0.6
1883	0.3	0.1	96.4	99.5	2.8	0.4

SOURCE: Annual reports from 1871 to 1883.

constant fear of illness and disease, and the privations of inadequate clothing, want of fuel, and insufficient food that characterized the winter months only heightened the extent of misery. Unsanitary conditions, impure water, and infected foods were a fact of life, particularly in the urban areas, and causes of infectious disease that ravaged the population.[68] Cholera, smallpox, scarlet fever, diptheria, measles, and whooping cough were among the infectious diseases which reached epidemic proportions and disrupted schools throughout the province. The concentration of children in the school was, itself, one of the causes of the spread of disease, as infected children passed them on to their classmates. In Hamilton, for example, when the scarlet fever epidemic of 1870–71 was at its peak, some suggested that the city's schools should be closed, although a subsequent investigation by the board revealed that most of the eighty deaths had occurred among children below school age.[69] It was not until the mid-1880s that provincial regulations were enacted compelling parents and teachers to report cases of infectious diseases and forbidding the infected children from attending school.[70] On a less dramatic plane, debilitating illnesses like dysentry were endemic in a society where food was stored for long periods over winter, the water was often impure, and meat was likely to become tainted in the hot summer months. As William Callowhil, an English immigrant, wrote to his parents: '[I have had] a severe bilious attack which for three or four days I thought would finish me, tho' we do not hear of anyone dying of them yet, they are so severe in this country'.[71] Epidemics could close down the schools and 'severe bilious attacks', suffered either by the child or the parent, could keep children home for days or even weeks at a time. Whatever its form or its extent, illness was a potent cause of irregular attendance in nineteenth-century Ontario.

There were other factors, outside of those related to the economic and physical conditions in the province, which affected school attendance although it is difficult to gauge their relative importance. As in the present, there were always some children who did not want to go to school and played truant. Wilkinson, the truant officer, interviewed a number of parents who were surprised (or feigned surprise) when informed that their children were absent from school and roaming the streets. Similarly, *The Spectator's* (Hamilton) warning to the aspiring horticulturists of the area must have been repeated many times throughout the province: 'as the season has now arrived when boys play truant from School, and pilfer fruit from the gardens and orchards, we would advise those concerned to keep a bright look out after the urchins.'[72] Not unnaturally, children also stayed away when local fairs or travelling shows were exhibiting in the area. As one superintendent pointed out in 1863, 'when a circus exhibited in the town, only 257 were at school out of 444 on that month's register.'[73] In fact, any break in the normal routine affected school attendance: 'The gold excitement during the first half of 1867, was the cause of many pupils in the townships of the Riding being withdrawn from the schools, and continuing so, until the excitement in some measure subsided, and business resumed somewhat of its accustomed routine during the last autumn.'[74] More commonly, some children were kept at home, or refused to go to school, because of dissatisfaction with the local teacher or classroom accommodation. Many rural superintendents, particularly in the poorer counties, complained of the poor quality of the teachers or the indifference of the local trustees as an important reason for irregular or non-attendance. As one put it, rather cryptically, 'the trustees select the teacher—the teacher makes the school.'[75]

The plethora of reasons that combined to cause continuing irregular attendance certainly went far beyond the original glib assertions of the local superintendents of 'parental indifference and negligence'. And yet, in one sense, the 'lack of appreciation of education' that they observed was rooted in the cultural reality of mid-nineteenth-century Ontario life. On the one hand, the extravagant claims of the free-school promoters regarding the benefits of education were not immediately obvious in the society. Crime and vice had not been eradicated, militant trade union organization and strikes were unlikely indications of increasing social stability, and poverty was still an ever-present problem. On the other, although it was said that 'the public is beginning to appreciate the idea that a person without education must remain during life a "hewer of wood and drawer of water",' most people probably knew someone who was a living contradiction of that same idea.[76] As one superintendent complained in 1869:

> A large proportion of our population consists of emigrants from nearly every clime and region of the earth. The majority of these came here with nothing but their sturdy thews and sinews, and their indomitable energy and perserverance. With their axes upon their shoulders, they marched boldly into the wilderness; and out of it, by stringent frugality and unremitting toil, they have carved for themselves an easy competence—a rude plenty. They have seen educated men settle around them, and decrease in wealth, whilst THEY the uneducated, have flourished and increased in it. Many of them, owing to the unavoidable force of circumstances—from sheer necessity—have been elected by those around them to situations of trust as school trustees and councillors. . . . They have waxed haughty in their grandeur, they have become inflated with their official pomp, they utterly eschew alike, education, reason and common sense.[77]

Clearly, education was not a necessary component of success in farming, unlike 'unremitting toil' in an age when mechanization was not very far advanced.

Moreover, as Harvey Graff has demonstrated, illiteracy was not a complete stumbling block to an individual's progress in the urban areas either, for though most illiterates were labourers, many held skilled jobs and some even worked in non-manual occupations.[78] In fact, in the initial stages of industrial capitalism, the new opportunities for less skilled and child labour in the mechanized factories must have made it difficult for working-class people to appreciate the benefits of schooling. This was the concern of the superintendent for Guelph when he complained in 1873 that there were fewer children in the higher grades of the public system. The children left school early because of

> the desire of parents to avail themselves at too early a period of the earnings which their children can make, and the opportunities which stores and manufacturies afford for child labour, in the disposition of employers to engage children, because of the higher wages which must be paid for the labour of grown-up persons. Account ought, also, to be made, of the course of instruction that has been prescribed and rendered imperative in our Public Schools, embracing subjects which, while valuable in themselves, are not thought necessary by parents for their children, and who, consequently, grudge the time devoted to them, and the expense that must be incurred in the purchase of text-books.[79]

If farmers and working people could not readily discern the immediate advantages of sending their children to school regularly and for sustained periods of time, the type of education offered in the common schools was not likely to improve the situation. As the superintendent for Guelph suggested, much of the curriculum seemed irrelevant or unnecessary to those engaged in the business of making a living. Although Ryerson had emphasized the importance of practical education in his 1846 report, the initial battles to get the principles of free and compulsory education accepted in the province absorbed most of his energy prior to 1871. In consequence, the curriculum of the common schools remained oriented towards the tiny minority who went on to the grammar schools and the university, and little attention was paid to more practical subjects. Thus, while the children learned how to read and write and cipher, they were unlikely to learn much of practical use to them in their working lives. Ryerson remarked in 1869 when it had become obvious that a free and compulsory education system was generally accepted: 'the tendency of the youthful mind of our country is too much in the direction of what are called the learned professions, and too little in the direction of what are termed the industrial pursuits . . . it appears to be very important, as the fundamental principles and general machinery of our School System are settled, that the subjects and teaching of the schools should be adapted to develop the resources and skilful industry of the country.'[80]

There was, then, a tension between the reality and the possibility of education as the school curriculum, grading up to the classical grammar school, bore little relation to the everyday world of most of the clientele. And this tension was exacerbated by the emergence of new industrial order in the

1860s as mechanized factory production increased economic insecurity at the same time that it devalued the importance of education. To keep children in school was to forgo the contribution of potential wage earners to the family income, a form of denial that many could not afford, particularly as much of the schooling seemed irrelevant. Adolescent labour in the factory or the sweatshop became like adolescent labour on the farm—a necessary factor in the family's struggle to make a living. For both the farmer and the working man, the family's welfare took precedence over the child's education. However, the impact on school attendance patterns was quite different. The seasonal pattern of farming meant that rural children attended school seasonally and stayed there well into their teens. In the cities, the years of attendance were more compressed, most children leaving school to go to work or help around the home after they were twelve. Thus, although from 1871 onwards the majority of children were in school, family circumstance, economic pressures, and physical conditions dictated the length of their stay and the seasonality and the regularity of their attendance.

In these circumstances it is not surprising that attendance remained irregular after 1871. The legislation for compulsory attendance, after all, had absolutely no effect upon the material conditions in which people lived. The inspector for the County of Renfrew made exactly that point in 1872:

> We must not expect to find our schools in a healthy and vigorous condition, or the claims of education properly respected, until pupils and parents learn to appreciate the importance of regular attendance . . . we cannot overlook the fact that there are, in many of our rural districts, obstacles which are simply insurmountable at present. When we take into consideration the difficulties in the way of many pupils getting to school at all; when we think of the requirements of the farm in the seasons of sowing and harvesting, in which the aid of children is indispensably necessary, we feel that these things must unavoidably interfere with School Attendance. When we take into careful consideration the claims of industry, of domestic service, and the necessary interference by sickness, we feel that considerable time must elapse before the attendance of pupils will come up to the required estimate. . . .[81]

It was not that parents did not want to send their children to school—the almost universal enrolments deny that—rather the rigour and the rhythm of work made it difficult to keep them there for sustained periods of time.

Suggestions for Further Reading

Susan E. Houston and Alison Prentice, *Schooling and Scholars in Nineteenth-Century Ontario* (Toronto, 1988).

Marcel Lajeunesse, ed., *L'education au Quebec (19ᵉ–20ᵉ siècles)* (Montreal, 1971).

Alison Prentice, *The School Promoters: Education and Social Class in Mid-Nineteenth Century Upper Canada* (Toronto, 1977).

Notes

[1] Upper Canada, Department of Public Instruction, *Annual Report of the Normal, Model, Grammar and Common Schools*, 1850, 12. (The titles of the chief superintendents' annual reports change from year to year, hereafter cited as *Annual Report* for the given year.)

[2] The increase in enrolments resulted particularly from an influx of girls into the public schools, see Ian E. Davey, 'Trends in Female School Attendance Patterns,' *Histoire Sociale/Social History*, Fall 1975, 238–54; and 'Educational Reform and the Working Class: School Attendance in Hamilton, Ontario, 1851–1891' (PhD thesis, University of Toronto, 1975) especially chapters 3 and 5. It should be noted that Ryerson's figures for those enrolled in the common schools was an aggregate of those in the public and separate schools, although in the *Annual Report*, the number attending the separate schools is also listed separately.

[3] In all but the most remote and poor areas, the schools were open throughout the year. As early as 1865, Ryerson remarked that 'the time during which schools are kept open in cities, towns and villages embraces, with scarcely an exception, the whole period required by law; and the average time . . . was 10 months and 2 days . . . about 2 months longer than the schools are kept open in any state of America.' *Annual Report* for 1856, 12.

[4] See Susan E. Houston, 'The Impetus to Reform: Urban Crime, Poverty and Ignorance in Ontario, 1850–1875' (PhD thesis, University of Toronto, 1974), Sec. III.

[5] This aspect was often referred to by the local superintendents and, after 1871, the inspectors. See, for example, *The Second Annual Report of the Inspectors of Public Schools for the City of Ottawa, 1872* (Ottawa, 1873), 14.

[6] For a discussion of this point, see Davey, 'Educational Reform', 243–5.

[7] The superintendent for the County of Durham in the *Annual Report* for 1864, Appendix A, 19.

[8] 'Parental indifference' or 'criminal neglect' or 'carelessness' were the phrases most frequently used to explain non-attendance or irregular attendance, especially in the earlier years. Perhaps an extreme example of its use (misuse?) was that of the superintendent for Bruce County in 1865 who stated regarding non-attendance: 'The common cause given in almost every report is the indifference of parents. Extreme poverty, sickness and religious convictions I would excuse, but all put together does not make one case out of ten.' *Ibid.* for 1865, Appendix A, 46.

[9] Superintendent for Wolfe Island, County of Frontenac, *ibid.* for 1861, Appendix A, 168.

[10] *Annual Report* for 1868, Appendix A, 38.

[11] Eric J. Hobsbawm, *Industry and Empire* (Harmondsworth, 1968), 155.

[12] *Annual Report* for 1858, 1.

[13] Superintendent Barber's 1857 report surveyed the progress of the Toronto free schools in the 1850s. The board passed a no-confidence motion against him in 1858 and reaffirmed the commitment to the free-school system, as they did in 1864 despite the select committee's report. During the depression years of the early 1860s and the late 1870s, the City Council tried to reduce the board's estimates because of the financial drain they represented on the city's resources. The point is that the expense of maintaining the school system was most burdensome in depression times while, at the same time, poor attendance was most obvious. For a discussion of

these reports, see Haley P. Bamman and Ian E. Davey, 'Ideology and Space in the Toronto Public School System' (paper presented to the Conference on Historical Urbanization in North America, York University, 1973).

[14]See Thomas Hutchison, *City of Hamilton Directory, 1862–63* (Hamilton, 1862), 14. For the effect of the depression on the city see 'The City of Hamilton Past, Present and Future', a letter to the editor in the *Hamilton Spectator and Journal of Commerce*, 1 January 1861.

[15]From the Hamilton Orphan Asylum and Ladies Benevolent Society, *Minutes*, Vol. 3, January 1859, Hamilton Public Library.

[16]On one day, 21 May 1859, in Hamilton two boys aged eight and thirteen were charged with stealing iron to sell, another eight-year-old was charged with stealing coal and a nine-year-old with stealing $5. The latter on conviction was fined $10 or one month's gaol. See *The Weekly Spectator*, 21 May 1859.

[17]*Annual Report* for 1860, 189.

[18]*Ibid.*, 180.

[19]Inspector for York County, North, *ibid.*, 1879, Appendix D, 66.

[20]Historians have only recently become aware of the extreme geographic mobility in the nineteenth century. See Stephan Thernstrom and Peter R. Knights, 'Men in Motion: Some Data and Speculations about Urban Population Mobility in Nineteenth Century America', *Journal of Interdisciplinary History* I (1970), 7–36. For Hamilton, see Michael B. Katz, 'The People of a Canadian City, 1851–2', *Canadian Historical Review* I, 4 (1972), 402–26; and *The People of Hamilton, Canada West: Family and Class in a Mid-Nineteenth Century City* (Cambridge, Mass., 1975), especially the chapter on transiency and social mobility; for rural Ontario, see David P. Gagan and Herbert Mays, 'Historical Demography and Canadian Social History: Families and Land in Peel County, Ontario', *Canadian Historical Review* LIV, 1 (1973), 27–47.

[21]See Katz's chapter on transiency and social mobility in *Hamilton* for an analysis of the rates of persistence in Hamilton and an analysis of the characteristics of those who stayed and those who left. It is important to note that rates for females are difficult to assess because it is hard to link those who got married in the interim period.

[22]*Ibid.*

[23]Eric J. Hobsbawm, 'The Tramping Artisan', in his *Labouring Men: Studies in the History of Labour* (London, 1964), 34–63. As he notes (40) the system was widespread in mid-nineteenth-century England among a variety of trades including compositors, lithographers, tailors, coachmakers, bookbinders, smiths, engineers, steam-engine makers, stonemasons, carpenters, ironfounders, coopers, shoemakers, boilermakers, plumbers, and bricklayers. Friendly societies also provided support for those on the move, see P.H.J.H. Gosden, *Self-Help: Voluntary Associations in Nineteenth Century Britain* (London, 1973), 47–8.

[24]Charlotte Erickson, *Invisible Immigrants* (London, 1972), 246–54.

[25]From Hon. R.B. Sullivan's address to the Hamilton Mechanics Institute on 'The Connection Between the Agriculture and Manufacture of Canada', *The Spectator*, 1 December 1847.

[26]Stephan Thernstrom, *Poverty and Progress: Social Mobility in a Nineteenth Century City* (Cambridge, Mass., 1964), 87.

[27]Erickson, *Invisible Immigrants*, 249–50.

[28] *Royal Commission on the Relations Between Capital and Labour*, Vol. 5, Ontario Evidence (Ottawa, 1889), 704.

[29] *Annual Report* for 1890, Appendix I, 182. Although this example is drawn from a later period, there must have been numerous examples of double reporting. The 600 children reported as moving from school to school in Toronto in 1852 would also have inflated the overall enrolment and lowered the average attendance.

[30] *Ibid.* for 1866, Appendix A, 60.

[31] *Ibid.* for 1865, Appendix A, 65.

[32] Superintendent for Petrolia village in *ibid.* for 1869, Appendix D, 116.

[33] *Ibid.* for 1861, Appendix A, 159.

[34] Superintendent for the County of Durham, *ibid.* for 1869, Appendix D, 69.

[35] Ryerson, in a footnote, quoting the Right Honourable W. Cowper, MP, in *ibid.* for 1857, 33.

[36] Michael B. Katz, 'The Entrepreneurial Class in a Canadian City: The Mid-Nineteenth Century,' *Journal of Social History*, Winter 1975, 1.

[37] Erickson concludes that the main grievances for most of the immigrant artisans at first 'were not low wages or long hours but irregular employment and the difficulty of securing wages in cash'. *Invisible Immigrants*, 250.

[38] *The Workingman's Journal*, 18 June 1864. This paper was published for a couple of years in the mid-1860s in Hamilton, although this is the only issue found. It is located in the Hamilton Public Library.

[39] See the evidence of Fred Walters of Hamilton in the *Royal Commission on the Relations Between Capital and Labour*, 796.

[40] H.C. Pentland, 'The Development of a Capitalistic Labour Market in Canada', *Canadian Journal of Economics and Political Science* XXV, 4 (1959), 450–61; Steven Langdon, 'The Emergence of the Canadian Working Class Movement, 1845–1875', *Journal of Canadian Studies* VIII, 2 (1973), 3, 13, and 3 (1973), 8–26.

[41] An illustration of the capitalist labour market in operation is the climax of the struggle between Wanzer & Co., the large sewing machine manufacturer in Hamilton, and its employees during the Nine-Hours Movement in 1872. The company had refused to accede to the employees demands for a nine-hour day and had locked them out. (It took the opportunity then to make repairs to its machinery.) When the company re-opened its employees stayed out on the picket line. At first the factory had only about 150 of its 400 workers on the job, but there were numerous applications for positions from other areas in Canada and the US. At least one worker was arrested for assaulting another who crossed the picket line, but, faced with losing their jobs, the employees eventually went back. See *The Spectator*, 28 May 1872.

[42] For a discussion of the relationship between the state of the craft, skill dilution, and persistence, see Clyde Griffin, 'Workers Divided: The Effects of Craft and Ethnic Differences in Poughkeepsie, New York, 1850–1880', in Stephan Thernstrom and Richard Sennett, eds, *Nineteenth Century Cities: Essays in the New Urban History* (New Haven, 1969), 49–77.

[43] Evidence of Thomas Towers, a carpenter for the Grand Trunk Railroad and Hamilton District Master of the Knights of Labor, *Royal Commission on the Relations Between Capital and Labour*, 875.

⁴⁴'Veritas, The People's Friend', letter to the editor, *The Spectator*, 27 December 1854.

⁴⁵Quoted in Eileen Yeo, 'Mayhew as a Social Investigator' in Eileen Yeo and E.P. Thompson, *The Unknown Mayhew* (New York, 1971), 83. For a superb discussion of casual labour in London in the period, see Gareth Stedman Jones, *Outcast London* (Oxford, 1971), especially 92–7; and Frederick Engels, *The Condition of the Working Class in England* (London, 1969), especially Chapter 5, 'Results'. Engels noted: 'But far more demoralizing than his poverty in its influence upon the English working-man is the insecurity of his position, the necessity of living upon wages from hand to mouth . . . ' (146). For an excellent discussion of the conflict between working-class culture and the demands of industry, see E.P. Thompson, 'Time, Work-Discipline, and Industrial Capitalism', *Past and Present* XXXVIII (1967), 56–97; for the North American experience, see Herbert G. Gutman, 'Work, Culture and Society in Industrializing America, 1819–1918', *American Historical Review* LXXVIII (1973), 531–88.

⁴⁶William Collins, a retired engineer and machinist from Burlington, in *Royal Commission on the Relations Between Capital and Labour*, 825–6.

⁴⁷Superintendent for Dereham Township, County of Oxford, in *Annual Report* for 1861, Appendix A, 184.

⁴⁸In 1865, when bad crop yields affected many areas, many superintendents attributed low attendance to inadequate clothing because of the parents' poverty. Similarly, a breakdown of the reasons for non-attendance in Toronto in 1863 showed that 216 of the 1,632 not attending reported 'want of clothes' as the reason, *ibid.* for 1863, Appendix A, 150.

⁴⁹*The Labour Advocate* I, 3 (19 December 1890).

⁵⁰The evidence in the *Royal Commission on the Relations Between Capital and Labour* is an excellent source of information on seasonal labour patterns. For the evidence of winter unemployment among moulders, see, for example, the testimony of Fred Walters of Hamilton, 794–5.

⁵¹The poverty of female-headed households is well illustrated in Michael B. Katz, 'On the Condition of Women, 1851–1861', *Canadian Social History Project*, Report No. 4 (Toronto, 1972), 16–25. For the selective benevolence of the charity workers, see Haley P. Bamman, 'The Ladies Benevolent Society of Hamilton, Ontario: Form and Function in Mid-Nineteenth Century Philanthropy', in the same report, 161–217.

⁵²Judith Fingard, 'The Winter's Tale: Contours of Pre-Industrial Poverty in British America, 1815–1860', Canadian Historical Association, *Historical Papers*, 1974, 67. It should be noted that seasonal poverty was not confined to 'pre-industrial' Canada. *The Palladium of Labour*, 1 December 1883, commented on the injustice of paying carpenters less in winter because of the shorter working day: 'Man's wants are greater in winter than at any season of the year. It costs more for fire, food and clothing and all the necessities of life, and more are consumed on account of the weather'.

⁵³*The Weekly Spectator*, 21 January 1858.

⁵⁴These figures are calculated from the monthly reports of the Internal Management Committee, Hamilton Board of Education, *Minutes*, 1882–90.

[55]Toronto Board of Education Historical Collection, W.C. Wilkinson Diaries, 1872–74, v, 23 January and 12 March 1874.

[56]*Ibid.*, III, 7 May 1873.

[57]*Annual Report* for 1874, Appendix B, 71.

[58]Davey, 'Educational Reform', Chapter 4.

[59]Joseph Kett, 'Growing Up in Rural New England', in Tamara K. Hareven, ed., *Anonymous Americans* (Englewood Cliffs, 1971), 1–14.

[60]Superintendent for South Riding, County of Hastings, in *Annual Report*, for 1861, Appendix A, 170.

[61]Superintendent for London Township, County of Middlesex, *ibid.* for 1863, Appendix A, 140.

[62]In *ibid.* for 1859, 167.

[63]Superintendent for Nelson Township, County of Halton, in *ibid.* for 1861, Appendix A, 176.

[64]Superintendent for Huron County, in *ibid.* for 1863, Appendix A, 160. This facet of winter attendance is well captured in Charles William Gordon's [Ralph Connor] *Glengarry School-Days* (Toronto, 1902). It should be noted that the figures in Table 4 indicate that in the 1870s and 1880s the trend in the rural areas was towards younger attendance.

[65]See *Annual Report* for 1879, Appendix D, 74.

[66]G.P. de T. Glazebrook, *Life in Ontario: A Social History* (Toronto, 1968), 179.

[67]Wilkinson Diaries II, 16 and 22 January 1873.

[68]For a good discussion of the governmental response to disease in Canada, see Neil Sutherland, 'To Create a Strong and Healthy Race: School Children in the Public Health Movement, 1880–1914', *History of Education Quarterly* XII, 3 (1972), 304–33.

[69]See the summary statement taken from the minutes of the board in *The History and Romance of Education*, compiled by L.T. Spalding (Hamilton, 1972), 16.

[70]Sutherland, 'To Create a Strong and Healthy Race', 307.

[71]W. Callowhil Papers, Letter, 30 September 1860, Provincial Archives of Ontario.

[72]*The Spectator*, 8 September 1847.

[73]Superintendent for Woodstock, in *Annual Report* for 1863, Appendix A, 160.

[74]Superintendent for North Riding, County of Hastings, in *ibid.* for 1867, Appendix A, 25.

[75]Superintendent for South Riding, County of Hastings, in *ibid.* for 1868, Appendix A, 14.

[76]Superintendent for Welland County, in *ibid.* for 1868, Appendix A, 25.

[77]Superintendent for Moulton Township, County of Haldimand, in *ibid.* for 1869, Appendix D, 86. The perception of the immigrants as ignorant was common in the reports, see the superintendent for Markham, County of York, in *ibid.* for 1862, Appendix A, 114, who remarked: 'The few discontented parties being ignorant persons from the old countries . . . Happily the number is few . . . and in a few years I hope it will be esteemed as great a disgrace to be ignorant as it is now considered to be intemperate. The immigrant children are growing up in ignorance, a strong contrast to our native born Canadian children, not one of whom at the age of ten years and upwards but can read, write and cipher.'

[78]Harvey J. Graff, 'Literacy and Social Structure in the Nineteenth Century', (PhD thesis, University of Toronto, 1975).

[79]*Annual Report* for 1873, Appendix B, 77–8.

[80]*Ibid.* for 1869, 24.

[81]Inspector for the County of Renfrew, in *Annual Report* for 1872, Appendix B, 30.

23

The Literary Culture of the Western Fur Trade

Michael Payne and Gregory Thomas

Another area of early Canadian history undergoing substantial re-evaluation in recent years is that of culture, partly in the anthropological sense of the sorts of assumptions people have about the way they lead their lives, but also in the sense of refinement of mind, taste, and manners, the 'intellectual' side of civilization. Earlier generations of Canadian scholars tended to dismiss the accomplishments of British North America in the latter meaning of the term, culture, arguing that colonial culture was both thin on the ground and terribly derivative and imitative of foreign models. A combination of a quest for the distinctive (for only originality would do) and an insistence on professional occupationalism (part-time 'dabblers' or 'amateurs' could hardly be taken seriously) conspired to blinker academic perceptions of any true cultural accomplishment in British North America.

As Michael Payne and Gregory Thomas point out in their study of the literary culture of the fur trade, the old perceptions will no longer suffice. At first glance no profession appeared less 'cultured' than that of the isolated fur trader spending long winter hours in a trading post. Yet it was precisely those long winter hours that made reading, good conversation, chess playing, and music making essential to the emotional and mental survival of the fur traders. Books of all kinds circulated widely throughout the fur-trading west, and the fur trade produced several important writers, including in the nineteenth century R.M. Ballantyne (a distinguished author of boys' adventure books) and Alexander Ross (author of a three-volume history of the western fur trade).

Does the availability of books and libraries necessarily suggest wide readership? Are there hints in this essay that most of those who read widely were among the 'officer class' of the fur trading companies? Why might the life of a fur trader be more conducive to literary pur- suits than that of a farmer, fisher, or lumberer?

This article first appeared, titled 'Literacy, Literature and Libraries in the Fur Trade', in *The Beaver* 63 (Spring 1983), 46–53.

In 1803 Daniel Williams Harmon, writing from the North West Company's post at Fort Alexandria in the Swan River District, lamented the fact that he would be virtually alone for the summer. 'However fortunately for me I have *dead* Friends (my Books) who will never abandon me, till I first neglect them.'

Neither Harmon's use of metaphor nor his love of books accords well with the popular image of the fur trader. From R.M. Ballantyne on, fur traders are more likely to be depicted shooting rapids or hunting polar bears than reading books or composing poetry. While it is true the fur trade could be an exciting and adventurous life, for many company officers and employees it amounted to little more than a few years' work as a trader, clerk, boatman or tinsmith. It is not surprising then, given the solitude and routine of most fur traders' careers, that many sought relaxation, self-improvement and even romance in reading, or that some would write themselves.

Very little can be said about the specific reading habits of fur traders prior to the late eighteenth century. The various fur-trade concerns required at least a core of educated employees for record-keeping and other managerial functions, and it is probable that some men must have read something besides inventories.

For the late eighteenth and early nineteenth centuries, references to reading as an aspect of fur-trade life are more frequent. It was during this period that the foundations of the various post libraries were apparently laid. These book collections at posts developed in several ways. The London Committee of the Hudson's Bay Company periodically sent out books for use at the various factories as part of their long struggle 'to Promote Virtue and Discourage Vice'. In 1778 this meant that six books of Common Prayer, one Nautical Almanac, and a copy of Dr Dodd's *Sermons* were sent to Prince of Wales's Fort. Other books the Company sent out during this period tend to mirror the contents of the 1778 list. The books were usually religious or technical volumes, and give no indication that the London Committee sought to encourage recreational reading, however virtuous the subject.

It also seems fair to suggest that books entered these collections from the private libraries of fur traders who collected for themselves. Hudson's Bay Company officer Joseph Colen claimed a personal library of 1,400 volumes at York Factory in the 1790s, and men like David Thompson, Peter Fidler and Samuel Hearne also collected personal libraries. It is somewhat ironic that Colen's penchant for book collecting very nearly resulted in the loss of the manuscript of Andrew Graham's *Observations*. Colen apparently removed a manuscript copy of the *Observations* from the Company's London head-quarters when he left England to return to York Factory. Only a specific request for its return in the General Letter of 1797 brought it back to London. Had it remained at York Factory it is unlikely that it would have survived.

Archival records indicate that these bibliophiles ordered not just technical treatises but books ranging from Ann Radcliffe's 'Gothic' novel *The Mysteries of Udolpho* to John Milton's *Paradise Lost*. These men took their reading seriously, even to the point of adopting the philosophical precepts of what they read. According to David Thompson, one Sunday after the regular religious service at Churchill, Samuel Hearne took his copy of Voltaire's Dictionary, and told Thompson and Mr Jefferson, the second in command at Churchill, that 'here is my belief, and I have no other'.

Many of the North West Company's posts also contained libraries of sorts. Forts Dunvegan, Alexandria, and Chipewyan are all mentioned by Daniel Harmon as repositories of books. Most of them, like the books at Hudson's Bay Company posts, were probably part of private collections originally, though some may have been sent out by the company itself. The collection at Fort Chipewyan, after the union of the two companies, seems to have formed the basis for the later Hudson's Bay Company library at that post, and was said to contain 'many sound books of history and general literature'. Harmon described one of these North West Company collections as being primarily 'moral and . . . religious Books', which suggests that North West Company libraries were not aimed at the recreational reader either.

No catalogues of these first libraries exist, but if the eighteenth-century materials in catalogues produced later reflect the original holdings of the fort libraries at Moose and York Factories, they included very little frivolous material. Only the odd work of poetry or comic play interrupts the list of works on astronomy, philosophy, language, medicine and other such serious subjects.

Judging by the surviving books themselves, and those archival references that have been discovered to date, it is hard to argue that prior to 1821 reading was anything else but an activity of a small élite, the chief factors and traders of the Hudson's Bay Company and the senior trading partners of the North West Company. These men, who appeared to read less for entertainment than for information, possessed the financial resources and, as important, access to means of transportation, which enabled them to assemble personal libraries. Many labourers and tradesmen, particularly the British 'servants' of the Hudson's Bay Company, were literate however. It is quite possible they carried about their own Bibles and reading material in their chests without the fact ever being noted in official correspondence, journals or inventories.

Indicative of the importance even Company servants placed on the ability to read and write is Joseph Colen's comment in 1794 that many of the most promising men for positions as inland postmasters were 'ignorant of Letters' and thus were 'fearful to undertake it [command of a post] knowing that they would expose themselves to the ridicule of there [*sic*] fellow servants'. Indeed Colen mentioned the case of one Edward Wishart, the summer master at Sipawisk House, who was unable to write his own name and was 'obliged to apply to the men to read his Letters of Introduction', much to their satisfaction.

One should not forget that in this pre-1821 era fur traders themselves wrote on a wide variety of subjects. Fur-trade companies required extensive written records, and as the Hudson's Bay Company Archives attest, some traders produced a vast record of their observations and activities. Only a tiny portion of the writings of fur traders ever achieved publication at the time, but that should not blind us to the serious intent of much of what these early residents of the Northwest wrote. Fur traders of the North West and Hudson's Bay Companies made important additions to the literature of travel and exploration; Alexander Mackenzie, Alexander Henry the Elder, and Samuel Hearne all produced outstanding examples of works in this genre that were published between 1795 and 1809. David Thompson, Henry Kelsey and Pierre Radisson kept journals that for one reason or another were not published until the twentieth century, but which clearly were intended for a larger audience when composed. Kelsey's work in particular is interesting because his travels and adventures were written at least in part in verse. Kelsey's reputation will always rest more firmly on his exploits as an explorer than on his career in letters, but it has been pointed out that he was probably the first writer of English verse in mainland Canada. Nor was his verse completely without poetic merit as the following description of a bear— presumably the grizzly—indicates.

> Another is an outgrown Bear wch, is good meat
> His skin to gett I have used all ye ways I can
> He is mans food & he makes food of man
> His hide they would not me it preserve
> But said it was a god & they should Starve

Some writers like Daniel Harmon distinguished themselves describing fur-trade manners and mores; others contributed to natural history, like Thomas Hutchins and Andrew Graham to whom Pennant's *Arctic Zoology* owes much. When one includes fur traders whose works have been published subsequently the list is even more impressive: Alexander Henry the Younger, James Isham, John Tanner and James Knight, to name a few. It is clear that the fur trader prior to 1821 was not simply an adventurer.

In the period following the union of the North West Company and the

Hudson's Bay Company the range of the reading and writing carried on in the Northwest expanded. It is also better documented. One of the most important changes was the development of formal libraries aimed at providing residents of the Northwest with reading material, and which were subject to some sort of institutional control. These libraries were distinct from the older book collections at posts, some of which remained and some of which seem to have been incorporated into the new institutions. The earliest of these was probably the Red River Library for which plans were made as early as 1816. A list of its holdings reveals that by June 1822 it contained 74 titles comprising nearly 200 volumes— soon after augmented by the personal library of HBC trader and surveyor Peter Fidler, who left his collection of 500 volumes to the Red River Settlement when he died in December 1822. The holdings of the Red River Library reflected the agricultural rather than the fur-trade base of the settlement. Although little is known about its origins, it seems to have been an organized collection, created as a reference library for the settlement.

The earliest permanent lending or subscription library at a Company post appears to have been the library set up at Fort Vancouver for the Columbia District. There had been books of a practical nature at Fort Vancouver from 1825, most of which seem to have come from a small collection at the North West Company post, Fort George. Company employees who wanted less technical reading material than handbooks on gunnery or law, however, had to look elsewhere. Dr William Tolmie, who arrived at Fort McLoughlin in December 1833 to act as a surgeon and clerk, seems to have raised the idea of a subscription library for the district. The scheme was discussed with two fellow clerks, Donald Manson and Alexander Caulfield Anderson, and Anderson in turn 'ventilated' the matter when he next reported to the Columbia depot. It was 'readily taken up' by Chief Factor McLoughlin and other officers. The actual implementation of this new library scheme is not documented, but in later years Dr Tolmie recalled that by 1836 'a circulating library of papers, magazines, and some books' was operating 'full blast'.

The collection was kept at a central location, Fort Vancouver. Subscribers met there annually, usually a week or so before the departure of the 'express canoe' on its 3,000-mile journey to York Factory. The indent for periodicals and books to be charged to the 'Columbia Library' was sent by ship from York Factory to London, where the Company's secretary placed the order with London book dealers. The following year the order was shipped back to Fort Vancouver and the 'Columbia Library' on the Company's annual supply vessel and then inland by the Company's well-established transportation network. Subscribers who were not resident at Fort Vancouver could send there for the material they wanted, returning it when convenient. This library appears to have operated into the mid-1850s, as the last reference to it in Company accounts appears in 1855.

By that time the idea of a subscription library, established at a central location, with materials circulating over an entire district to members, had taken hold. Such a library was established in the vast Mackenzie River District in the 1840s, and at York and Moose Factories in the 1850s. The Mackenzie District Library was housed at Fort Simpson. In 1849, Irish-born Company clerk Bernard Rogan Ross, a man of distinctly literary tastes, wrote to his friend William Lane, a clerk at Lower Fort Garry, describing a library at Fort Simpson that contained novels, poetry, history, biography and periodicals. Those who wished to join the library, for which Ross was librarian and treasurer, had to pay an entrance fee of £1 and an annual subscription fee of £1—rates which suggest that membership was still restricted to officers or the more affluent clerks. In return, books—'not stale old books but sterling English Editions of authors in good repute'—were circulated to Fort Resolution, Fort Good Hope and other outposts of this, the most solitary and isolated of the fur-trade districts.

In the summer of 1852 David Anderson, the first Bishop of Rupert's Land, noted that a library had recently been established at Moose Factory, though his suggestion that Moose Factory and York could profit by emulating the practice of the Fort Simpson Library, indicates that the library at Moose was intended solely for the use of residents of that post. Anderson discussed the value of libraries like those at Fort Vancouver and Fort Simpson in the following terms:

> If libraries of some extent could be established at some central posts, and the books circulated through the surrounding district, the good effect produced might be very great. It might be the means of self-improvement to young men cut off from all the advantages of society, and beguile the solitude of these retired posts.

Certainly, for the Church Missionary Society of the Church of England and the other religious denominations present in the Northwest after 1821, the development of libraries at Company posts was very much in keeping with their religious and educational mission.

A subscription library called the 'Moose Book Club' was created in due time and operated until unspecified problems caused it to be reorganized as the James Bay Library in September 1873. Minutes of the initial meeting of the new library suggest it absorbed the holdings of the old Moose Factory library since members of the original library retained borrowing privileges with the new improved subscription library. The yearly fee was ten shillings for residents of Moose Factory and eight shillings for others. Books were loaned to other posts for no more than one year, and to residents of Moose Factory for one month. Books not returned at the specified time would simply be charged to the borrower's account.

A similar library was established at Norway House in 1870, but the largest and most successful of these subscription libraries appears to have been the library at York Factory.

Given Bishop Anderson's support for libraries at fur-trade posts it is no surprise that a leading role in the establishment of the library was taken by the Reverend William Mason, the missionary at York, and that the collection at least initially contained a great deal of religious material. The initial meeting to establish the library was held on 18 February 1856 and Mason noted in his journal that 'A sufficient sum to purchase 200 vols was at once subscribed and Laws & regulations were made—Mr. Clare—Dr. Beddome—Mr. Anderson, Mr. Watson and myself were present. Mr. Mactavish gave it his approval and promised to subscribe'. The list of interested parties included most of the officers stationed at York Factory, and subsequent journal entries detailing donations and help given to the new enterprise underline the impression that initially the York Factory Library served the interests of the post's élite. Chief Factor James Hargrave, the senior Company officer, 'gave important advice respecting its management', and then a donation of 5 guineas.

From the start, however, William Mason anticipated that the library would be a great addition to life at York Factory, and that it would serve the larger post community. As his journal entry for 18 February 1856 states:

> This will be a great blessing to the Establishment when carried out upon sound principles and I sincerely hope it will succeed and prosper—The present inmates are much given to reading & I only wish I had my books which were left in Red River Settlement to lend to them.

The library commenced operations on 1 November 1856 when 'the York Factory Library was formally opened for the benefit of all classes'. The library had '133 volumes to commence with', in addition to the publications of the Religious Tract Society 'which are not only very interesting but calculated to do good'. Mason was particularly pleased to note that 'many of the servants enter their names as annual subscribers of 5s—and some 10s—. May it be a means of creating a thirst for the knowledge of eternal things.'

Mason's hopes that the library would have a beneficial impact on the religious and moral life of York Factory do not appear to have been entirely realized, but the library proved to be a great success and it retained a high degree of popularity amongst the Company servants at York Factory and environs. George Simpson McTavish, in his autobiography *Behind the Palisades*, gives a lengthy description of the library, its operations and importance to life at York Factory in 1889.

> York Factory was fortunate in having a goodly collection of books, amounting to nineteen hundred volumes when I left in 1889. . . . The duty of librarian fell to the apprentice clerk for more reasons than one, the chief however being,

that the ten shillings fee, otherwise to be paid from his first year's salary of twenty pounds, was allowed for his services, and meant much to him. The higher officers paid one pound, the clerks ten shillings and the mechanics and labourers five shillings annually, the same rate applying if I remember aught, to post managers and men in the district and adjoining ones. The books covered many fields of knowledge, selection being made from catalogues received from London by the ship, at an annual meeting, held prior to the departure of the Winter packet which carried the next year's order to England via Winnipeg. The men had a representative, but dependence was placed almost entirely on the officers, who tried to get the best, and most for the available funds.

Each year the collection of popular magazines and periodicals like *Punch* and *Chambers's Journal* was added to, and series of standard nineteenth century writers brought up to date. In addition 'tales of adventure' were purchased for the men, although 'No trash' was allowed. 'We could not afford to get worthless books.'

McTavish also noted in his memoirs that the York Factory Library provided the material not only for many social evenings but for the York Factory 'Literary Society', a social gathering where the men contributed readings, songs, recitations and even chemistry exhibits.

The library was open on Saturday nights, officially for one hour after the ringing of the post bell, but usually 'till everybody had pored around the shelves and made his week's selection'. A candle provided the only light, and as there was no fire in the library even in winter, the librarian's job could be a cold one. McTavish mentions that one evening he put the end of his pencil in his mouth 'and the graphite or lead adhered to my tongue'.

When McTavish took charge of the library it was in some disarray, as previous librarians had neglected to keep good records of its holdings or the locations of books that had been loaned to subscribers at the outposts. McTavish spent two winters taking inventory and compiling a new catalogue of the library with beneficial results for both the collection and himself:

> The overhauling and systematizing process gave me an acquaintance with the volumes under my charge, though I did not become much of a reader, till I felt the want of companionship later when located at an outpost myself. . . . That library was my best friend, and in later years I reaped the reward of my exertions, and became indebted to the founders for many happy hours.

Surviving catalogues of the fur-trade libraries suggest that McTavish's description of the books purchased for the York Factory Library is quite representative of the kinds of material to be found in the post libraries of this period. These libraries contained some reference works such as encyclopedias, dictionaries, and Bartlett's *Familiar Quotations*; large quantities of history—British, military and ancient for the most part; and some works of travel, exploration, and biography. Shakespeare's works were well represented, and poets like Byron, Burns, Longfellow, and Tennyson could be found. They also contained a fair amount of religious matter, tracts, and biographies especially, but in rather smaller quantities than William Mason had hoped. The bulk of the collections were novels, and their authors read like a who's who of nineteenth-century British letters: Scott, Dickens, Disraeli, Bulwer-Lytton, Thackeray, Trollope, Stevenson, with only the occasional title such as *Thirty Years in the Harem* by Kibizli as a change of pace. It seems the tastes of fur-trade readers differed little from those of the British public.

What is most interesting about these collections is the scarcity of books by fur traders and about the Northwest. Unlike the library at headquarters in London which contained virtually everything written about the natural history, exploration and life of the Northwest, post libraries contained little of this sort of material. Fur traders certainly read and commented on books written by or about themselves, James Isham having begun this tradition in 1748 with his critique of Henry Ellis, but such books must have been more common in personal libraries. The growth of subscription and circulating libraries in the fur-trade territory by no means put an end to private book collecting.

The nineteenth-century fur trader probably had an easier time as a book collector than his eighteenth-century counterpart. The Company did not encourage its employees to build personal collections, but it did not deny them that privilege either. Its attitude seems to have been similar to its view of the subscription libraries for which it waived transport costs on purchases. The Company could have made private book purchases all but prohibitive in expense, but it did not, and many ordered their books through the Secretary of the London Committee.

Private libraries could be assembled in a number of ways. One option for those who had the means and access to a collection was simply to purchase it outright. William Lane acquired his collection this way while at Norway House in 1847. Others interested in buying or selling books used the clerks or other officials at a major post to act as agents for them. James Hargrave, at York Factory, frequently sold or acquired books for his friends scattered throughout the interior. Hargrave, perhaps because he was such an avid reader himself, was also willing to act as conduit for book orders to be placed with the Company secretary in London. One interesting example of books acquired in this manner is the order placed for William Drever, a carpenter at York Factory in 1834. Drever requested

1 Copy Housepainter & Colourman's Guide   { By P.F.
1 Do The Varnishers Guide   { Fingay
1 Do The Cabinet Makers Do By G.A. Siddons
1 Do The Builders Practical Do   { By John Nicholson
1 Do The Millwrights Do   { Esq. Civil Engineer

1 Do The Young Mans Book of Knowledge
1 Do The Cottagers of Glenburniel
1 Do The Cottagers on the Cliff
1 Do The Sequel to Ditto

This book order is one of the very few specific references to the reading selections of anyone other than an officer of a fur-trade company, and offers a rare glimpse of the reading tastes of the Men's House. It is doubtful that Drever's book choices were typical of most Company servants—they probably indicate a greater degree of ambition and desire for improvement of technical skills than was usual—but his choice of nontechnical books is revealing. The 'cottager' novels would appear to be about the plight of Scottish crofters during the Highland Clearances, and any book about Scotland or Gaelic culture was bound to find eager readers amongst the fur traders. Sir Walter Scott's novels were particular favourites, and even a practical fur trader like Chief Factor Donald Ross could adopt a partisan position in the ongoing debate over whether or not the Gaelic poems of Ossian were in fact the creation of the Scottish poet James Macpherson.

However acquired, these private libraries were common, and indicate how important it was to fur-trade employees to be literate, informed and up-to-date. Many observers were surprised by the knowledge exhibited by fur traders, and by the sorts of reading matter one could find even in isolated posts. For example, the soldier surveyor John Henry Lefroy was astonished to find a copy of the architect John Claudius Loudon's *Cyclopedia of Villa and Farm Architecture* at Fort Simpson in 1844, only a year after it was published. J.P. Gardiner, the Anglican missionary at York Factory, in 1861 stated that the men there were 'willing to talk on any subject—science, politics—anything rather than practical Christianity'. Notwithstanding Gardiner's chagrin at their lack of interest in Christianity, it is clear fur traders of most ranks, by the mid-nineteenth century were exposed to much of what was being published during the period, and despite their apparent isolation they were far from ignorant of the ideas and news of the outside world.

Given this, it is not surprising that many turned their own hands to literary pursuits. After 1821, fur traders made fewer contributions to the literature of travel and exploration—for the most part exploration was carried out by Royal Navy expeditions, and travellers tended to be scientists like Lefroy or clerics like Bishop Anderson. Many fur traders, however, made significant scientific contributions; the relationship between fur-trade correspondents and the Smithsonian Institution and British Museum is one illustration. The nineteenth-century fur trade also produced at least one major literary figure and a few eager amateurs.

R.M. Ballantyne managed to build an undistinguished career in the fur trade at York Factory, Fort Garry, and Tadoussac into a distinguished one as a writer of boys' adventure novels. His contribution to work at York Factory was not rated highly. William Mactavish wrote with regard to his skills as a clerk: 'I think myself it would have been a better joke, since they are determined to have a farce, to have sent out, either Mr McKenzie's or Mr Finlayson's coat and trowsers stuffed with straw'. Nor were his books about the fur trade always well viewed by those he wrote about; James Anderson suggested that 'His Everyday life in Hudsons Bay was easy enough—I wish he had seen some of my everyday life for many Years . . . ' Nevertheless Ballantyne wrote several books, including *Ungava*, *The Young Fur Traders*, and *Hudson's Bay*, based rather loosely on his experiences in the fur trade. His fur-trade associates may have doubted the veracity of some of his stories, but his adoring public of Victorian school boys did not. His imperialist thinking and tendency to moralize make his books heavy going for the modern reader, but even so, he retains his reputation as one of the best and most prolific of the writers of the 'boys' own adventure' book.

Far less successful but no less interesting in certain respects are the oddities of fur-trading authors other than R.M. Ballantyne. Bernard Rogan Ross, who was to have a distinguished career as a naturalist and as a Company employee, had less success as a writer. In his youth at Fort Simpson, he produced a newspaper entitled *The Athabasca Journal and English River Inquirer*. He had quite correctly noted the desire his fellow fur traders had for news, but it appears his idea of a newspaper containing news in a light vein for the diversion of those journeying about the interior, was not a great success. He also fancied himself as a poet, and John Henry Lefroy, himself an indifferent poet, mentions that Ross 'inflicted upon me a quire of his own compositions, begging to know which I liked best. You never saw such stuff'. Lefroy's brief but caustic assessment of Ross's poetic skills might apply equally to those of Dr William Smellie, the post surgeon at York Factory from 1845 to 1849. Dr Smellie produced a volume of poetry entitled *The Sea; Sketches of a Voyage to Hudson's Bay; and Other Poems* in 1855 under the unlikely nom de plume of 'The Scald'. By his own admission the poems had 'neither the charm of romantic narrative, nor the zest of humourous description, to recommend them to the general reader'. His modesty in this regard is probably the best thing about the book of poetry. His modesty in this regard is probably the best thing about the book of poetry. His lengthy 'Sketches of a Voyage to Hudson's Bay' suggests that the muse of poetry did not embark with him, but even his dreadful poetry attests to the desire of at least some fur traders to express themselves in a literary manner.

The reading of books and the writing of books was always a part of life in the fur trade for those with literary inclinations, and if perhaps it was not as universal an experience of fur-trade life as running a set of rapids or shooting a bear or any of our other more romantic notions about life in the Northwest, that should not blind us to its importance to the fur traders themselves.

Suggestions for Further Reading

R.M. Ballantyne, *Hudson's Bay, Or, Every-day Life in the Wilds of North America during Six Years' Residence in the Territories of the Honourable Hudson's Bay Company* [1859] (Edmonton, 1972).

John S. Galbraith, *The Hudson's Bay Company as an Imperial Factor, 1821–1869* (Toronto, 1957).

Michael Payne, *The Most Respectable Place in the Territory: Everyday Life in Hudson's Bay Company Service, York Factory, 1788 to 1870* (Ottawa, 1989).

24

The Victorian Family in Colonial British North America

J.M. Bumsted and Wendy Owen

As with so many topics in social history, study of the family depends on the availability of documentation—often in short supply for Canada, and available mainly for the articulate better-off elements of society. Readings 21 and 22 suggest the families of the poor may have been structured and motivated in somewhat different ways than those of the wealthy. Two dominant themes run through the Anglo-American literature on the family. One is the patriarchal nature of the family, with the father at its head. This principle was an old one, written into law, particularly the English common law transported to colonial British North America, and probably applied to most families rich or poor. The other theme is the domesticization of the household: separating work-life and home-life, and emphasizing the role of the woman as wife, mother, and household manager. This fairly recent development began in the ranks of the rich and powerful and gradually worked its way down through society, reaching the colonial upper classes in the late eighteenth and early nineteenth centuries and the middle classes by mid-nineteenth century (see Reading 12 on Loyalist women). Domesticization was largely responsible for putting woman on the pedestal from which the later twentieth century attempted to rescue her. Its impact on the families of the poor, who could not afford to leave anyone unemployed at home if they were to survive, is perhaps problematic.

In the following essay, Wendy Owen and I explore the households and families of two articulate families from the upper reaches of society in British North America, although located in two small and relatively isolated colonies: Prince Edward Island and Red River. The Jarvises were of Connecticut Loyalist stock. The Ross family, although decidedly part of the Red River élite, was a mixed-blood family. What is striking about the two families are the similarities between them, rather than the differences. Both families, we argue, were decidedly Victorian, albeit colonial branch.

What is the relationship between 'domesticization' and 'sentimentalization' in the Victorian family?

How did patriarchy work? What were the differing expectations for the sons and the daughters? Why were these families so obsessed with a fall from respectability? How might these principles have been different in the families of working farmers? of the struggling poor?

This article first appeared, titled 'The Victorian Family in Canada in Historical Perspective: The Ross Family of Red River and the Jarvis Family of Prince Edward Island', in *Manitoba History* 13 (Spring 1987), 12–18.

While a good deal has been written in recent years about the family in nineteenth-century Britain and the United States, the study of the family as an institution is in its infancy in Canada. How were families organized, what were their preoccupations and ambitions, how did their households function? Unlike Britain and the United States, Canada had precious few self-conscious literary families in the Victorian era, and so one of the most common sources for study of the individual family—private papers assiduously collected by literary scholars—simply has not existed. At the same time, substantial bodies of personal and intimate papers of articulate Canadian families, carrying sufficient detail to enable some sort of reconstruction, do survive. Two such sets of family papers are those of the Jarvis family of Prince Edward Island and the Ross family of Red River. The Jarvis Papers are in the New Brunswick Museum in Saint John, N.B., and the Ross Papers are in the Public Archives of Manitoba. A careful reading of these geographically widely scattered documents suggests the danger of approaching them as merely local records.

Some extraordinary parallels exist between the two sets of papers and the two families, although they were separated by nearly 3,500 kilometers in two relatively isolated colonies in British North America. In terms of the study of the nineteenth-century family, what is most striking about the parallels is how well they fit into the larger patterns of recent secondary literature on the Victorian family. The Jarvises and the Rosses were not simply unique colonial families, but very much part of a transatlantic culture. Given the facts that mother Ross was an Indian and the children 'halfbreeds', the similarities between the Ross and the Jarvis families demonstrate that we must be careful not to make too much either of colonial location or of racial and cultural differences.

There was a middle-class culture in the nineteenth century which transcended many theoretically exceptionalist factors. One hesitates to limit the culture to the label 'Victorian', since it was equally powerful in the United

States and much of Europe. Those researching the family in nineteenth-century Canada ought not, we would suggest, to assume that their Canadian subjects existed in splendid isolation from general cultural developments in the western world and thus produced localized and unique patterns of behaviour. Colonial societies less often initiated than imitated, and while identifying deviations from larger patterns is crucial, one must begin with the larger patterns.

Before turning to our analysis, it might be well to introduce the two families briefly. Edward Jarvis was born in Saint John, New Brunswick, in 1789, the son of Munson Jarvis, a leading Connecticut Loyalist. Educated at King's College, Windsor, he was admitted to the New Brunswick bar in 1812 and subsequently to the bar at Inner Temple, London. He served in Malta before his appointment as Chief Justice of Prince Edward Island in 1828. In 1817 Edward married Anna Maria Boyd, the daughter of another influential Saint John family active in mercantile affairs; the Jarvis and Boyd families would intermarry frequently over the succeeding years. The couple had eight children, three of whom died in infancy and one in childhood. Those surviving to adulthood were Mary, Munson, Henry, and Amelia. Their mother—Maria, as she was known—died in 1841, and Jarvis remarried in 1843 to Elizabeth Gray of Charlottetown. This union produced three children, one of whom died in infancy. Elizabeth herself died in childbirth in 1847, and Edward a few years later in 1852. The correspondence to be discussed, mainly between members of a close-knit family writing between the Island and mainland New Brunswick, covers the period from 1828 to 1852.

Alexander Ross was born in Nairnshire, Scotland, in 1783. He emigrated to Canada as a schoolmaster, but became involved in the fur trade, joining John Jacob Astor's Astoria expedition in 1811. Ross subsequently served in the Pacific coast fur trade until his retirement to Red River in 1825. While in Oregon he had married Sarah, the daughter of an Indian chief (an Indian princess, went the family tradition) according to the 'custom of the country', and formally remarried her in Red River in 1828. The couple had at least thirteen children, of whom the important ones for our purposes are William, Henrietta, James, and Jemima. In Red River Ross became a prominent government official—sheriff, magistrate and member of the council of Assiniboia—as well as titular head of the Scots Presbyterian community. In his later years he authored three books describing his experiences in the fur trade and chronicling the development of Red River, a trio of works woefully neglected by Canadian literary scholars and students of Canadian historiography. The Ross family correspondence upon which we will concentrate in this study covers a shorter period of time than the Jarvis set, since only during the years 1852–1856, when young Jemmy Ross was studying at Knox College in Toronto, did the family correspond intimately and regularly.

Edward Jarvis and Alexander Ross were contemporaries, and both were important political and social figures in their respective communities. Their residential accommodation reflected their positions. Edward began planning his house in 1833, when he bought a farm on the outskirts of Charlottetown for 500 pounds. As he intended the house to be a family seat for 'generations yet to come', his plans called for the use of brick, an uncommon Island building material. Most of the material was imported from England, and the construction was not completed until 1835 at enormous expense—more than 'one hundred per cent upon the original estimates and contracts'. Furnishing of 'Mount Edward' was finished in 1836, and early in 1836 the Jarvises held a housewarming ball for 81 persons. We know considerably less about 'Colony Gardens', the Ross residence in the Point Douglas area of what is now Winnipeg, but it was a large and substantial frame house, a landmark in its day. On the other hand, the later (1854) construction efforts of William Ross are discussed in the correspondence. William himself enthuses, 'without boasting it is the best, the handsomest and most comfortable house on the banks of the Riviere Rouge', befitting, added his father, a 'son who had stepped into the shoes of his father'. The William Ross house still survives in Winnipeg, a museum open to the public as the oldest house yet in the city.

As paterfamilias, Edward Jarvis had a limited share in the day-to-day operations of his household. Like many nineteenth-century fathers he was often away—on circuit as the only judge of the Island's supreme court, on the mainland seeing to business matters in the summer months, and in England (for six months during the fatal illness of his first wife). At that, Jarvis was far more housebound than some of his contemporaries; the Earl of Dalhousie, when he returned to Britain from governing in Canada, had been away so long that he was totally unable to recognize his eighteen-year-old son. But absence aided the remoteness which most Victorian fathers like to maintain, and Jarvis does not appear to have been especially close to his children, especially the boys, who unlike the girls were sent away to school for much of their adolescence and brought home only under financial stringency. At the same time, Jarvis did play a key role in the upbringing of his children. Major decisions were his, and many minor ones were deferred if he were absent. Jarvis did not lose sovereignty over the household, and the family, especially the women, were expected to subordinate themselves to his needs and wishes.

The Ross papers suggest that Alexander Ross was substantially closer to his children than was Edward Jarvis. In part this attitude reflected personality, in part the fact that there was nowhere to travel in remote Red River, in part probably his wife's background. Ross did make an annual hunting expedition to Shoal Lake after the harvest, but characteristically, he turned it into a family affair which became one of the high points of the year. The Ross situation was complicated by the presence of 'mama' (both families called the mother 'mama'), who at least by the time of the correspondence of the 1850s was no longer running the household, a position assumed by the eldest unmarried daughter. Ill health was obviously a key factor in her stepping down. Nevertheless, Ross's domination of his household was typically Victorian, the family revolving around him as it did around Jarvis. While it was true that 'Ross shaped the upbringing of his half-Indian children', as Sylvia Van Kirk has emphasized, it should be noted that most middle- and upper-class Victorian fathers behaved similarly without the presence of an Indian wife. While Ross may have been less distant from his children than Jarvis, his correspondence with his absent son James demonstrated a stiffness and formality quite different from the tone of Jemmy's letters from his brothers and sisters. And like Jarvis, Ross was far more affectionate with his daughters than with his sons.

Middle-class family life in the Victorian era was characterized by two related developments. The first is generally referred to as the 'domesticization' of the household, a clear separation of work-life and home-life and the withdrawal of the various household members into the privacy of the home, which became the central social unit for 'the transmission of culture, the maintenance of social stability, and the pursuit of happiness'. This process had been completed by the Jarvis family before the opening of the surviving correspondence in 1828, and by the Ross family by the time of the intimate letters of the 1850s and indeed probably years earlier. Closely connected with domesticization was a new attitude toward human emotion usually labelled 'sentimentalization'. In its Victorian context, this attitude encouraged the effusiveness of personal feelings and sentiments on certain approved topics relating to the home and the family: love, death, marriage, and 'making it' in the outside world. Gone was the stoicism and terseness of earlier generations toward the vagaries of family life and relationships, replaced by open avowals of sentiment, often overstated. It should be emphasized that this openness was confined to approved topics and closely circumscribed by fairly clear and generally held ground rules of respectability. It is this new attitude of sentimentality, combined with the standards of respectability, that finds its closest parallels in the Jarvis and Ross papers.

In terms of the traditional milestones in the cycle of life—birth, education, marriage, and death—the Jarvis and Ross correspondence exhibit sentiment most openly and frequently on the subject of death. Indeed, nearly half of the Jarvis letters between 1828 and 1852 contain some reference to death: reporting one, responding to a report, or mourning the death of a loved one. The incidence is little different in the Ross letters. This emphasis is not surprising, since death and its aftermath were matters that often provoked a correspondent to take pen in hand. For the modern taste the sentiments expressed may border on the morbid and maudlin, but they filled a real need for those involved. Those familiar either with Victorian novels or the literature of Victorian piety will not be surprised, for example, to learn of the fascination of both our families with detailed descriptions of death-bed scenes.

We are given two eyewitness accounts of the final sufferings in 1841 of Maria. One, by her son, is of her last hours, and another, by her daughter, describes the terminal weeks. According to young Mary Jarvis, her mother had twice before the fatal day 'called us all together to bid us farewell for ever and had recovered'. A few years later Elizabeth Gray Jarvis died in childbirth, a particularly important rite of passage and a major family event, usually occurring in the home with the woman surrounded not only by the medical folk but often by friends and family as well. Spiritual preparation was important, since the risks were considerable. One gains some impression of the event and the rituals surrounding it from Munson Jarvis's description of the death of his stepmother:

> From the sudden manner of her death she must have been totally unconscious of his approach, time not even given her to bid her family farewell. Poor woman to be so suddenly summoned to appear before her Maker leaves upon us a melancholy reflection. To be promising fairly and the next moment awake in Eternity is awful. To give an idea of its suddenness, after being delivered and her little infant dandled in the arms of the nurse and kind friends around her bed and the birth announced all which took some little time, the mother called for her child and seemed most affectionately fond of it, kissing it as I was told several times, but no sooner did she resign the now Motherless babe to its nurse (but was not complaining) the Dr. was told by one in attendance that mrs. J's feet felt cold, at once the Dr. said he was so afraid she would die, and so suddenly and apparently so easily after saying she did not feel cold had her spirit taken flight, no assistance could be rendered. . . .

Obviously the doctor had not been able to help.

Within a few months in 1856 the Ross family experienced two deaths, first that of William and then that of his father Alexander. Again, there are detailed descriptions of the last hours. Alexander Ross described William's demise to James in Toronto:

> About half an hour before his last, he called me to his bedside, clasped both my hands in his, then called for his wife and Mr Black [Presbyterian minister of Kildonan and married to Henrietta Ross] and while he held my hands he offered up a most fervent and impressive prayer to God, asking forgiveness for all his sins, and resigning himself into the arms of his maker. "I know," said he in conclusion, "that my redeemer liveth and I know that I am going to be with him, Lord receive my spirit to everlasting rest, Amen." Then laying his head quietly on the pillow, soon expired without struggle or motion to the right or to the left.

The accounts of the death of Alexander himself were even more explicit. According to John Black:

About daylight he called all the family around him and we were all there but poor James and gave them his parting blessing—the most affecting sight I ever saw was when he held William's poor little orphans by their little hands altogether and spoke to and blessed them. . . . Margaret received her dying grandfather's parting kiss and blessing—Willie was at home and poor Lettie was too sick to come in. All the rest of the grandchildren were present. It was like old Jacob blessing his sons and Joseph's sons.

Further details came from Jemima:

It was 23rd before daylight he called us all around his bed one by one and shook hands with us and spoke to every one of us and blessed us and told us to be kind to one another and not feel sorry for him, though he was going away. . . . He took all their hands and held them in his for a long time that was after breakfast and at last Mr. B said that will do now you are tiring yourself; he still held them, and all the time sitting. He asked S. to say the fifth commandment, she said it, and then they went and sat down and asked for all the C. But they were not all here W. not but the baby so he asked Mr. B if he could let him have the pleasure of kissing his babe so he kissed the baby too.

These accounts all emphasize the fortitude of the sufferer and the peace with which death was faced—not hidden from view in some distant antiseptic hospital but at home, in the immediate presence of the family circle.

They also emphasize the importance of proper spiritual preparation. As the account of the death of Elizabeth Gray Jarvis suggests, the most disturbing feature here was its suddenness. The Ross correspondence makes similar points frequently. In 1852 William Ross wrote the death of 'young James Fraser' noting 'only seven days sick—what a warning for all those who are alive to prepare for death while in health for we know not the day nor the hour when the "Knock" shall be at our door'. Both Jarvis and Ross papers are full of the reminders of the constant razor-edge upon which life was balanced.

A willingness to acknowledge the trauma of the death of a loved one was also a central feature of the correspondence. The death of his first wife hit Edward Jarvis very hard, partly—one suspects—because he felt guilty about being in England for his own health while Maria was battling her fatal illness on Prince Edward Island. Daughter Mary certainly thought her father's absence, however unavoidable, contributed to her mother's demise. As Edward wrote to his wife's sister upon his return to Charlottetown late in 1841:

My own feelings have now become so nervous and sensitive that I seem to participate as much in any anxieties of my friends as if it were my own case. I cannot shake off the dreadful weight and oppression which hangs increasingly upon my spirits and the slightest exciting cause wholly overpowers me. . . . The utmost indifference to every passing event and occupation possesses me and I cannot overcome it.

Such a sense of depression was hardly surprising under the circumstances. What was different from earlier times was the openness with which Edward confessed his feelings in his correspondence for several years thereafter. Alexander Ross admitted to his son James with regard to William's death, 'The event has given a severe shaking to your mother, to myself also; but we thank God that we are able to bear with it as we do. Nevertheless our position is one of pain'. Such pain was now openly acknowledged.

If death and mourning were sentimentalized by the Victorians in words, they were also enshrined in new and more extreme ritualization. Mourning and commemoration of the dead took on new forms. Even the physical letter itself was part of the process. Munson Jarvis opened a letter to his Aunt Caroline with the words, 'You must be aware upon seeing the border of this letter that our family has been deprived of one of its members'. The first letter home of James Ross upon hearing the news of William's death was edged in black. The Jarvises were not invited to Government House on New Year evening in 1848 because 'there has been a death so recently in the family'—in this case of Edward's eldest daughter Mary.

The dead were also commemorated in ways both more ostentatious and more personal. In one letter of 1842 to his sister-in-law, Edward reported ordering from England a monument to his wife ('of white marble, of the Sarcophagus shape') and added:

> I promised you a small portion of a lock of her hair—but I find there was but a very small lock preserved—and Mary is anxious to have some of it. Your sister and I therefore concluded that it would meet with your approbation that I should send you some for your locket, only in case a little could be spared after the division with Mary. I should feel very desirous to save some for you, if possible.

Burial became a matter of considerable ritualization and a symbol of the relationships of the deceased while living. Edward's parents, after an even more protracted correspondence among the family, were disinterred and placed in a family vault in the new burying ground of Saint John. John Black reported after the death of Alexander Ross, 'On Monday 27th amid great concourse of people we laid him in the narrow house here at the Frog Plain—not alongside of William so that the graves are in a line—William lying at his father's feet'. And although the correspondence does not show it, Edward Jarvis was buried in Elm Avenue Cemetery in Charlottetown next to his first wife, while his second wife was buried elsewhere in the same cemetery along with her family.

Another important aspect of the household was the raising of children. Expectations and training were quite different for boys and girls. Both sexes were educated at home for most of their early years by both the Rosses and the Jarvises, owing as much to the scarcity of acceptable schools as to the wishes of their parents. Neither family employed governesses or tutors. The Jarvis boys were subsequently sent off Island to school, while it was hoped that a projected academy for young ladies on the Island would serve for the girls. When the academy did not appear, the girls were either taught at home or, after Maria's death, bundled off to relations on the mainland to learn the requisite skills. As for the Ross children, the younger boys all attended Red River Academy or its successor St John's College, essentially a grammar school in the British tradition established by the Church of England in Red River. For James Ross to go away to university in Toronto was a considerable step for both James and his family, although others of his contemporaries from the College attended Oxford and Cambridge. Cousin Roderick Ross, Alexander Ross reported in 1854, was off to 'Swell the list of Puseyites at degraded Oxford'. The arrival of John Black in Red River and his subsequent marriage to Henrietta Ross opened new educational opportunities in the colony, especially for the younger Ross girls. Jemima was sent off to the manse at Kildonan in 1855 to pursue her studies, learning geography, grammar, French and ciphering, and Henrietta Black herself 'got very clever' after her marriage.

As for expectations, Edward Jarvis intended his three sons to enter the professions. Munson, the eldest, was trained for the law on the Island. Second son Henry was sent to Edinburgh to medical school, and youngest son William entered the Church. According to Edward, 'I am unwilling to oppose a decided inclination in my boys for any particular profession', but it all seemed somehow to work out in fairly orthodox fashion. One suspects that Edward would have preferred the eldest to be the doctor, but Munson was not a favourite:

> Munson is very studious when required to be so and has great application, but he is very idle when there is no immediate call for his exertions, he is not inclined to volunteer hard study, but pays more attention to the young ladies and driving his tandem than to more desirous matters. . . . Henry is, on the contrary, all life, activity and industry—he greatly resembles in mind as well as countenance his beloved mother. Sir Henry Huntly told me that when he first saw Henry he thought he had never seen a countenance in which were blended so much of benevolence and intelligence.

So Henry was allowed to go to Edinburgh, where he did well professionally but disappointed his father by marrying too quickly an 'unhealthy' wife.

As for the Ross boys, the first-born son Alexander died early. William stepped smoothly into his father's shoes, as his father had obviously intended, and James was able to go to Toronto, where he prepared for the ministry, a career approved by the entire family. Upon the death of William, James hesitated, obviously debating whether to continue his studies or come home to assume his family responsibilities. His father wrote him a few weeks before his death that 'sacrifice . . . is in my opinion a better plan for all the time we expect to live to enjoy this life, than to withdraw our children from those pursuits in which their future happiness depends'. After Alexander's death, James did return to Red River and assumed leadership of the family.

For the daughters there were clearly different expectations. In one letter William Ross described the Ballenden daughters as, 'so far as we Red Riverians can judge perfectly accomplished ladies'. He continued to list the requirements:

> They can play elegantly on the Harp, guitar, piano, they sing melodiously and methodically. They can dance and waltz like true English dames, and I guess they can play the coquette too if that be any part of Ornamental Education— to tell the truth they are very nice girls.

While marriage was the ultimate goal, household management was extremely important. After the death of Maria Jarvis, Edward attempted to replace his wife as household manager with his eldest daughter. Mary escaped by marrying, after some agonizing over whether 'I make up my mind to leave my dear Papa'. Only Edward's remarriage prevented Amelia from becoming her successor. In the hiatus between Mary's marriage and his own in 1843, Edward found it difficult to continue Amelia's education, writing 'I hardly know how I can get on without her management of my household, for I shall have no one at present besides the two servant girls'. After the death of his second wife, Amelia again had the responsibility for her father, but this time she had assistance from a succession of maiden aunts.

Henrietta and Jemima Ross could easily have sympathized with the problems of Mary and Amelia Jarvis. Henrietta was running the household at the time of her marriage to John Black, and Jemima was forced to step into Henrietta's shoes. Her letters to her brother indicated her problems. 'I write to tell you', she announced in 1854, 'that I have no time to write with Hay and harvest all are busy and I am no less busy baking and cooking for those out of doors'. Mama and Isabella had gone berrying, she added. 'I wanted to go too, but I had to stop and keep house'. A few months later she wrote, 'I suppose you have heard that Hen has left me to do for myself, . . . I am now Miss Ross Master in the house'. Within a few days she commented that she was 'tired with house-keeping and all its duties, for there is no end of working'.

Brother William dealt perceptively with Jemima's dilemmas in a letter discussing family reactions to the annual excursion to Shoal Lake. 'Sister Jem', he wrote:

> only forbodes something portentous in this trip to Shoal Lake, as mama now and then gives a hint as to who is to keep house while out—poor Jem thinks she ought to go out and finds it very hard to be made to keep house before the time, but the question comes back, whose to keep house? Papa says oh I

must stay and let Jem go out, but Jem knows well that she would rather stay than her pa stay.

While Jemima was at Mr Black's pursuing her studies, her mother's health suffered, presumably because mama was forced to take over the running of the household. After a few months she was recalled to Colony Gardens. The family 'can't do rightly without her at home', William reported.

As we have been suggesting, while the household functioned around the needs of the males, it was the women who made it work. The Victorian woman's role as wife and mother ought not to obscure her onerous responsibilities as housekeeper. The role immobilized the woman and made it difficult for her to travel from the house. 'I must reluctantly stay at home', wrote Maria of a projected visit by her husband to Saint John in 1837, 'to take care of the establishment'. To see people, especially in remote colonies, women had to expect them for long housevisits, only adding to the burden. Houseguests invited by her father were coming, reported daughter Mary reluctantly in 1843, adding, 'I was very sorry for it as it will give me much more to do, . . . but I did not like to say so to Papa as he seemed to wish to have them'. Maria found herself unable to report on her housewarming ball to her sister, commenting, 'I was much too fatigued in mind and body to enjoy it and even the repetition is painful to me for I was obliged to force my spirits. . . . You will be astonished that I am alive', she concluded, proceeding to catalogue a herculean series of labours which ranged from supervising the slaughter of seven hogs to hanging the draperies in six public rooms. There is no evidence in either the Jarvis or the Ross papers of a direct act of defiance of male wishes by a female. The Ross and Jarvis women were not advanced thinkers; there was nothing in their upbringing to encourage notions of independence.

Both sexes had to beware of the great abyss for Victorians: the fall from respectability. This subject was a matter of considerable concern in both sets of correspondence, usually in terms of the peccadilloes of other people. When H. Wright married an illegitimate daughter of Sir H. Lowe, despite the fact that the girl 'lived in his family and is very well educated', her sister's concluding comment to Maria Jarvis was 'Silenzio'. A young Scotch lady in Red River was 'guilty of having made a faux pas', wrote William Ross to his brother, 'she was delivered of a boy last week'. Edward Jarvis obviously found some satisfaction when his 'old antagonist' John Stewart, after burying his wife left for England almost immediately, having 'married his servant girl, 18 years of age—he is nearly 80 himself'. Jarvis continued:

> The girl made him execute a will in her favour of all his property, which is to a large amount. He has commenced prosecutions against some of his acquaintances who interfered to prevent the marriage and alleged that he was insane.

Jarvis took equal satisfaction in recounting that a certain 'young sprig of a parson . . . with his true orthodox spectacles upon his nose', had secretly breached the canonical law by marrying his late wife's sister. This form of 'incest' remained legally forbidden in Britain, despite frequent attempts to revise the law, until well into the twentieth century. 'So you see John Gunn found out by sad experience', noted William Ross with satisfaction equal to that of Edward Jarvis, 'that instead of gaining by Slander he had lost by a good deal his former little respectability'.

Everyone well understood the implications of breaking the codes. As Edward Jarvis wrote of the Smiths, who were 'dreadfully depressed about their unfortunate brother' who had committed some unspecified offence: 'well they may be—death would be far preferable to the never-ending disgrace'. Fortunately, no Jarvis appears to have blotted the family name during the course of the correspondence.

While both families were conscious of the abyss, it gaped open much more widely for the Ross family, both because 'mama was an Indian' and because Red River was commonly perceived as a colony of semi-civilized half-breeds. The point came out quite clearly in responses to James Ross's early success as a student in Toronto. Cousin Roderick hoped to join James at university, calling for 'a mighty effort to try to make poor Red River respectable', and John Black described old Alexander's response to son-in-law George Flett at news that James had won a scholarship: 'What will they say of the Brules now, Geordie?' William was already 'in a fair way of becoming respectable', exulted his father, and James was not far behind, although extremely self-conscious about his origins.

All of the Ross family had to deal with racial hostility, even in Red River. Jemima was upset in 1854 at comments overheard at church about the number of 'blacks' in the front pews, for example. But none of the family were more sensitive than James. John Black was forced in 1855 to give James a written lecture in response to the young man's attempts to derive a complex classical etymology for the word 'halfbreed'. Black observed, 'Half breed is a simple natural homemade English term which we could have invented if we had known as little of Greek and Latin as we do of the Japanese'. Although James was extremely proud of his father's books and literary success, he protested strenuously to the old man about his treatment of half-breeds in his writings. After the death of his father, James wrote an extremely revealing and agonizing letter to his family in Red River, in which his concerns about the abyss were clearly revealed:

Remember, dear sisters, that we at present occupy a certain standing in the community. Owing to papa and to William—and to our connection with our worthy minister Mr Black—I say owing to these things, we have a certain standing and respectability, and we must keep it. . . . It seems generally the case that halfbreed families dwindle into insignificance as soon as they lose their head. But why should it be so?

James would spend the remainder of his life attempting to prove that half-breeds were as good as anyone else.

But if the abyss for James Ross (and perhaps for the remainder of his siblings) was perhaps wider and the descent into it considerably shorter, we ought not to over-emphasize the differences between the Ross and the Jarvis families. The assumptions and concerns of the two families on this and other matters were, in the last analysis, remarkably similar. Both were Victorian, colonial branch. Perhaps the Jarvises were more comfortable with their status than were the Rosses, but there was considerably more common ground than one might anticipate.

Suggestions for Further Reading

Constance Backhouse, *Petticoats and Prejudice: Women and Law in Nineteenth Century Canada* (Toronto, 1991).

Andrée Fortin et al., *Histoires de familles et de reseaux: la sociabilité au Québec d'hier à demain* (Montreal, 1987).

W. Peter Ward, *Courtship, Love and Marriage in Nineteenth-Century English Canada* (Montreal, 1990).

25

Ethnicity and Rural Discontent

Ian Ross Robertson

One of the most striking features of British North America was its extraordinary diversity—not only in its climate, natural resources, and ethnic composition of population, but even in its systems of landholding. No two jurisdictions were identical, and some were quite distinctive. Prince Edward Island, for instance, was characterized not only by its island isolation (particularly marked in winter, when the frozen sea prevented access by boat or ship), but by both its peculiar land system and the ethnic make-up of its tenantry. Until the very eve of Confederation, much of the land on Prince Edward Island was held by large proprietors who were often absentees; a great many Islanders, therefore, were tenants rather than freeholders. Here the usual generalizations about the availability of land simply did not apply. The proprietorial land system undoubtedly kept many potential settlers away from what was in many ways an attractive agricultural region, and

it encouraged a disproportionate number of less prosperous immigrants from Scotland and Ireland to settle there. The land system also had substantial political and social implications, and it was the major public issue on the Island for over a century.

In the following article Ian Robertson addresses the complex relationship between ethnicity and the land question on Prince Edward Island. As he points out, the Island was populated principally by Scots and Irish, who were divided by religious background as well as by point of origin. Political loyalties based on religious concerns were a major factor in impeding the settlement of the land question to the satisfaction of the tenantry. Though religious and ethnic tensions could occasionally break out in violence, Robertson insists that tolerance and co-operation were more usual. Nevertheless, Old World loyalties and legacies played a considerable part in the development of what was a 'relatively self-contained part of the New World'.

Why was the 'land question' such a major issue on Prince Edward Island? How did it distinguish the Island from other provinces in Brit-ish North America? If tenants were a majority of inhabitants and, after 1830, voters, why were they unable to bring about reform of the land system? How was ethnicity a polit-ical factor?

This article first appeared, entitled 'Highlanders, Irishmen, and the Land Question in Nineteenth-Century Prince Edward Island', in L.M. Cullen and T.C. Smout, eds, *Comparative Aspects of Scottish and Irish Economic and Social History 1600–1900* (Edinburgh, n.d.), 227–40.

Most studies of Scottish and Irish immigrants in North America focus upon their adaptation to a new and different environment. But in nineteenth-century Prince Edward Island these Celtic immigrants faced a problem which most had encountered previously, and which indeed had forced many of them to leave their ancestral homes: a neo-feudal system of land tenure. Their responses were no doubt conditioned by their Old World experiences, yet were complicated by the ethnic and religious mixture in their new setting. This paper examines the roles of Scottish and Irish immigrants in nineteenth-century Prince Edward Island, with particular reference to the 'land question', as it was locally known, and to their relations with each other.[1]

More than anything else, the land question was the distinguishing characteristic of colonial Prince Edward Island.[2] A leasehold system of land tenure had been established following the transfer of the island from France to Great Britain by the Treaty of Paris in 1763. The island was surveyed, and divided into 67 lots or townships of about 20,000 acres each. In 1767 a lottery was held, and each township went to a favourite or group of favourites of the crown. After the Seven Years' War, the government had been besieged by retired officers and other persons who had ingratiated themselves. They were in search of offices, titles, and land in compensation for their services, and the island land lottery was one means chosen to satisfy their appetites. There were several conditions attached to these grants. First, the grantees had to pay annual quitrents of between £20 and £60 per township to the crown. The amount varied in rough proportion to the quality of the land. Within ten years, they were to settle their estates with one person per 200 acres, or about 100 persons per township. Finally, the settlers were to be Protestants from the British Empire, the sole exception being made for Yankees who had been in North America two years or more. The penalty for non-fulfilment of these conditions was to be escheat, or reversion to the crown. Two years later, in 1769, the island was granted colonial status separate from Nova Scotia, at the behest of the landed proprietors, who wanted to be within a small political jurisdiction which they could control.[3] The expenses of the government establishment were to be paid for by the quitrents.

These were the basic elements of the Prince Edward Island land question in the eighteenth and nineteenth centuries. In essence the colony had been saddled with a neo-feudal land system. For the average settler it meant that he could not own the land he worked. He had to lease it, usually at around £5 per hundred acres, plus two, four, or six shillings in quitrents, responsibility for which was thus transferred from the landlord to the tenant. Although this sort of arrangement was not uncommon in Europe at that time, the norm in the New World was freehold tenure. Consequently, from the very beginning, settlers were disinclined to go to Prince Edward Island. Many who did go to the island colony moved on, or their sons moved on. This reluctance on the part of potential immigrants, and lack of effort by most proprietors, meant that the condition of settling 100 people on each township within ten years was not fulfilled. In fact, throughout the entire colony there were perhaps 1,300 persons after the ten-year deadline had expired;[4] there should have been at least 6,700. Of those settlers, a large proportion were Roman Catholics of Scottish or French origin, and hence should not have been there. Indeed, no proprietor fulfilled all the conditions of his grant. Since the proprietors were unable or unwilling to settle the colony, they did not take the trouble to pay quitrents.[5] Eventually, the British government had to supply money for the salaries of the governor, the chief justice, and the rest of the civil establishment. Yet the lands of the proprietors were not escheated.[6]

The effects of the leasehold system were all-pervasive. Class tensions became acute, political struggles centred on issues like escheat, and the economic development of the colony was retarded. Even more than 30 years after the lottery, there were only 4,400 inhabitants.[7] Yet, eventually, people did begin to arrive in numbers. After the Napoleonic Wars economic distress was common in the United Kingdom, especially in the Celtic fringe of southern Ireland and the Highlands of Scotland. Tens, indeed hundreds, of thousands of impoverished Celts were faced with the choice of emigration or starvation. The poorest of these often ended up on the Atlantic coast of British North America because that region was the part of the New World closest to the United Kingdom and hence the fares were the cheapest. By 1861 the population of Prince Edward Island was 81,000.[8] The vast majority of these inhabitants lived off the land, a fact which underlined the importance of the land question in the life of the colony.

As the population grew, the tenants became increasingly vocal about their very real grievances. At least 60 to 70 per cent of the occupiers of land were tenants or squatters.[9] Furthermore, it appeared as though they would have to remain tenants or squatters indefinitely, since most landlords refused to sell clear titles to tenants on terms within their capacity to pay. Cash was very scarce in rural Prince Edward Island, with the result that in their early years on the land tenants might fall far in arrears in their payments. Crop failures could have the same result. Once evicted, tenants had no legal means of obtaining compensation for improvements, such as their very houses. Yet if they tried to pay off their arrears by working hard and taking large surpluses of crops to market, that too was dangerous. If a tenant looked too prosperous, a land agent might raise the rent or evict him in order to clear the way for a new occupant at a higher rent. Thus there was little incentive to produce a visible surplus, and consequently both the tenants and the economy as a whole suffered. It was a cycle of poverty, insecurity, and oppression. Islanders frequently referred to their colony as 'the Ireland of the New World', and this unhappy situation was unlikely to change as long as the land system endured.

Those who attempted to reform or abolish the leasehold system soon discovered that they had powerful and determined foes. The proprietors, who were often absentees based in Great Britain, were backed by a local élite composed of lawyers, land agents, politicians, and public officials. Together, the proprietors and the colonial oligarchy displayed a remarkable ability either to bend lieutenant-governors to their will, or to isolate and destroy them. Between 1769 and 1824 the one governor not to be recalled in disgrace accomplished this feat of survival only through allying himself with the most powerful local faction. His successor came to grief through association with a group known as the 'Loyal Electors', which has been described as the first political society in what is now Canada. The Loyal Electors briefly gained control of the assembly (which had been established in 1773), but the proprietors exerted their influence in London to have the governor dismissed and the society ostracized as allegedly being seditious.[10]

The Loyal Electors appear to have been composed mainly of Loyalists from the old Thirteen Colonies angry at being denied the clear land titles promised to them after the American Revolution. Although their ostensible aims were to counteract the influence of speculators and to gain clear titles for themselves, they too had been interested in accumulating land. Furthermore, their strength had been largely concentrated in the area around the capital, Charlottetown, and they had thrived in a period (1806–12) when the population of the island was still minuscule. Despite the allegations of seditious intent, there had been a faintly patrician air to the Loyal Electors, patronized as they were from Government House.[11] The next significant reform movement to arise, the Escheators, would be very different in composition, and would exist in a transformed social environment.

The Escheat movement flourished in the 1830s and 1840s, after the arrival of substantial numbers of Scottish and Irish immigrants. The Escheators took their name from their advocacy of a special court of escheat, which would investigate the titles of the proprietors (or 'land claimants') to discover whether they had met their obligations. Of course none had fulfilled the conditions of the original grants. Thus, according to the Escheators' plan, the lands would be forfeited and re-granted to the farmers occupying them. Some 65 per cent of islanders were Scottish or Irish (approximately two-thirds of these being Scots, who were overwhelmingly Highlanders), and this percentage more or less coincided with the proportion of tenants within the farm population. Back in the Old World, Highlanders and Irishmen had had considerable experience with landlordism. Such tenants were not inclined to accept the system passively. The attitude of the tenant has been aptly characterized in this excerpt from a recent poem:

Ye'll get no rent for woods ye didn't cut,
Stumps dug out with a horse I had to borrow,
Land I plowed—me and my old lady
Who wasn't so old those days—me in harness
And her at the handles;

A road I made with friends and relatives;
And the wharf. When's there goin'ta be a wharf here?
Don't bother with that. We'll manage without ye
As well as we'll manage without payin' rent.[12]

Because the land agent was the most direct link of the tenant with the oppressive aspects of leasehold tenure, he was not welcome, and he was not made to feel welcome when he came calling. Means of underscoring this point ranged all the way from derision and intimidation to burning the agent's home and, at least on one occasion, murder.

The removal of civil disabilities from the large and impoverished Roman Catholic minority in 1830 combined with the low property qualification for the franchise to ensure that the strength of the Escheat movement was eventually reflected in the House of Assembly. The Escheators won a decisive victory at the polls in 1838, and they proceeded to elect as speaker of the assembly their leader, William Cooper.[13] He was a former land agent who had succeeded to that post in 1819 when his predecessor was killed by a tenant from whom he was attempting to collect rent. But by 1830 Cooper had changed sides and become a land-reform politician; he entered the assembly after a tumultuous by-election in the following year.[14] The Escheator-dominated assembly sent Cooper to London in 1839 to demand a final settlement of the land question. Yet although he had gone as a delegate of the assembly, the colonial secretary, Lord John Russell, whose sympathies were with the 'rights of property', refused to grant him an audience.[15] It was clear that the British government had no intention of permitting a court of escheat to be established. Having come to a dead end in the parliamentary process, the Escheat radicals focused their attention on continuing the struggle in the countryside. They resisted collection of rents and distraint for rents, and intimidated land agents and law-enforcement officers. Late in the winter of 1843 troops were called out to make a show of force in eastern Kings County, where the Escheat movement was strongest, and where disorders had recently taken place.[16] In a despatch, the governor, Sir Henry Vere Huntley, reported that news of the troops moving eastward had caused 'a large body of the people' to abandon a march on Charlottetown.[17] That summer a leading radical assemblyman, Duncan MacLean, was successfully prosecuted for libelling the government.[18]

While the radicals concentrated their energies on direct action in rural areas, a more moderate reform party took shape in the capital. Led by Edward Whelan, a brilliant young Irish journalist, and George Coles, a distiller who, although a well-to-do businessman, sided with the tenants for his own reasons,[19] the 'Reform' or 'Liberal' party argued that responsible government was a necessary prerequisite to solution of the land question. The Reformers, with the support of remnants of the old Escheat movement, took office in 1851, with Coles as the first premier under responsible government. In order to ameliorate and eventually liquidate the system of leasehold tenure, the Coles administration tried various expedients short of a general escheat. These were unsuccessful, and when the Reformers left office in 1859 the proportion of tenants and squatters among the occupiers of land was still between 60 and 70 per cent.[20]

The local Tory or 'family compact' party had regained office largely through dividing the tenantry along religious lines.[21] They attempted to deal with the land question through appointing a three-man commission. But when the commission reported in favour of the tenants, recommending that all tenants have the right to purchase the lands on which they lived, the proprietors successfully exerted pressure on the imperial authorities to disallow the award. The island government responded by sending a delegation to London. But Sir Samuel Cunard, the founder of the Cunard shipping empire, who owned one-sixth of the island's land mass, mobilized the proprietors to reject the proposals of the delegates.[22] These new setbacks left the tenants completely exasperated. Driven to desperation, they formed tenant leagues, organizations pledged to resist collection of rents. If a tenant were evicted, the leaguers were committed to prevent occupation of the victim's farm by anyone else; thus no rent could be collected.[23] There were public disturbances, and troops were called in from Halifax, Nova Scotia, in 1865. Although most historians have minimized the significance of the Tenant League, or dismissed its activities as futile (given the repressive measures taken against it),[24] it is certainly arguable that its willingness to resort to illegality had positive results: in 1866, after the death of Cunard, his heirs decided to sell their 213,000 acres to the government for purchase by the occupants under legislation passed by the former Coles regime. This was perhaps the major turning-point in the struggle, and it may well have been prompted by the Tenant League's organized and calculated defiance of the law. Certainly, the decisions in the mid-1860s of other, smaller proprietors to offer sale of clear titles were popularly attributed to the climate created by the Tenant League agitation.[25] The leasehold system was only completely abolished after the entry of Prince Edward Island into the Canadian confederation in 1873. One of the terms of union was support by the Dominion government for a program of compulsory purchases of estates.[26]

What were the roles played by Scottish and Irish immigrants in this story? The most obvious fact about Celtic immigrants to Prince Edward Island was their poverty. The historical geographer Andrew Hill Clark has written that

> the great majority of Highland Scots and Southern Irish . . . advanced their circumstances very slowly over the years; they were yet in the 1850s (and many of them still in the eighties) as close to the level of a European peasant tenantry as one would be likely to find in the New World. Through the middle decades of the nineteenth century, where the land was poorer, rougher, swampier, or less accessible, there Gaelic, the Acadian patois, or a distinctly Caledonian or Hibernian inflection of English was likely to be heard.[27]

This combined with the statistical fact of their numerical predominance (not to mention their Old World cultural inheritance) to ensure that the Scots and Irish played very large parts in all mass tenant movements. This was especially true of the Escheat movement, whose centre of strength was the most Scottish of the three counties, Kings. When a radical Escheat newspaper was established in 1836, it regularly included selections of Highland Gaelic poetry.[28] Although the actual leaders might often be non-Scots, such as Cooper and John LeLacheur, the rank and file were undoubtedly predominantly Scottish. Probably the most famous Escheat public meeting ever held was convened in December 1836 at Hay River in north-eastern Kings County, where a series of resolutions was adopted which provoked the majority in the assembly to commit the three Escheat members who had presided to the custody of the serjeant at arms for almost two full sessions. The official report of the meeting stated that when toasts were offered, 'An attempt was made to play God Save the King, but (we must tell the truth) our musicians are better accustomed to Highland Reels.'[29]

There were Scottish landlords as well as tenants, but ethnic kinship did not always override the antagonism inherent in the proprietor-leaseholder relationship. One of the best-known Scottish proprietary families was the McDonalds of Tracadie. In the 1770s John McDonald, known in Scotland as 'Glenaladale', settled some 210 fellow Roman Catholic Highlanders in the colony. When they realized their situation, many left for Cape Breton Island and freehold tenure.[30] McDonald's third son, a priest also named John, encountered yet more serious difficulties. After completing his education in England and France, and doing missionary work in Glasgow, he returned in 1830 with 206 Scots and Irish as tenants for lands he had inherited.[31] For several years Father John acted as both priest and landlord in the area, as well as land agent for a brother, Roderick, until local discontent led to his transfer to another part of the island, away from his estates, where a Gaelic-speaking priest was needed. Unfortunately for him, he was sent to a district adjacent to Hay River. It soon became apparent that he and his parishioners disagreed over the land question.

When in March 1843 Governor Huntley sent troops to eastern Kings County to put down disturbances on the Cunard estate, Father John, who resided nearby, gave them accommodations. The rumour spread that he had concurred in or even suggested the action of Huntley, with whom he was on friendly terms. Feelings became very tense in the parish, and after a visit in September his bishop, Bernard D. MacDonald, requested him to leave within a month. When he refused to do so, his parishioners took matters into their own hands. On 1 January 1844, led by the local Escheat assemblyman, John Macintosh (who had been censured, along with Cooper and LeLacheur, for his role at the Hay River meeting), they elected new elders and directed them to tell McDonald to leave. When he held the next Sunday mass, he refused to recognize the new elders, as these were usually chosen by the priest. Macintosh arose, demanded a hearing, and McDonald was only able to silence him by kneeling in prayer. The service then ended with the priest fleeing to the parochial house, and Macintosh angrily berating him. Contrary to the wishes of his bishop, McDonald took legal action against Macintosh and employed as his lawyers two Tory politicians. A jury acquitted the assemblyman, and the bishop ordered McDonald to leave the parish. Although much of the congregation was now boycotting his church, he would not vacate until the bishop suspended him late in 1844. Believing that the bishop and the neighbouring priests had conspired with the Escheators against him, McDonald, an island native, left the colony and spent almost all the remaining 30 years of his life in England.[32] This was an extreme case, but it indicated how deeply rooted was the resistance to leasehold tenure, when a congregation would combine against its priest on the issue, and when the local clergy, including the bishop, would feel compelled to side with the laity. Father John's elder brother Donald, another landlord (and also a legislative councillor and magistrate), had still more harrowing escapades, for at least one attempt was made to assassinate him. He himself went about, according to the governor in 1851, 'always carrying a loaded pistol in his pocket'.[33] Many buildings on his property were the target of incendiaries, and in 1865 barns belonging to his eldest son and heir, John Archibald McDonald, were destroyed by arson, almost certainly committed by tenant leaguers or their sympathizers.[34]

While Scots played very visible roles on both sides of the land question (but particularly as tenants), the part of the Irish is more difficult to trace because of their smaller numbers and more even distribution. Furthermore, aside from several politicians, few individual Irishmen reached positions of prominence in the colony. There were no Irish Roman Catholic landlords or bishops, almost no educational leaders, and even comparatively few priests in the period of the land question. However, from what is known of the voting patterns of the Irish, and from the literary evidence which survives concerning their activities at public meetings and political affrays and on other occasions, there can be no doubt that they were, as a body, strongly committed to the reform cause, and opposed to leasehold tenure.[35] The most notable Irish public figure to emerge, the journalist Edward Whelan, began his Prince Edward Island career in 1843 by emphasizing not only the parallels between the island colony and Ireland, but also the common historical problems of Highlanders and Irishmen. As well as editorials on this theme, and the latest 'repeal' news, he published poetry and fiction with a Highland slant. For a generation, Whelan stressed the centrality of the land question, and came back repeatedly to his early argument that the Scots and Irish of Prince Edward Island were facing a common and historic foe: landlordism.[36]

It is tempting to assign a leading role to Irishmen in the Tenant League disturbances of the 1860s. The league itself was a secret society, and Irishmen undoubtedly were prominent in some of the most notable actions attributed to its members.[37] Furthermore, there had been an abortive 'Tenant League of Prince Edward Island' in 1850–1, apparently supported largely by Irishmen, which counselled withholding rent (although in narrowly defined circumstances), which explicitly drew up Irish examples of how to proceed, and which planned to establish a link with the 'Irish Tenant League in Dublin'.[38] Yet there appears to have been no direct connection between it and the organization which emerged in the mid-1860s, aside from the fact that those areas which generated it tended also to support the later Tenant League, which, presumably, could thus profit from whatever lessons had been learned in 1850–1.[39]

The Tenant League of the 1860s appears to have been a more complex phenomenon than simply a carry-over from Irish agrarian radicalism. One of its most striking features was a distrust of politicians so strong that when an island-wide form of organization was adopted, MPPs and political partisanship were specifically banned.[40] According to Whelan, a crucial new element in the tenant movement of the mid-1860s was the prominent involvement of relatively prosperous tenants of English extraction who, unlike the Celtic Escheat radicals of the 1830s and 1840s, could amply afford to pay their rent.[41] As Andrew Clark has stated,

In general those of ultimate English origin (and these included descendants of people from more than half the counties of England, Loyalists, New Englanders, and disbanded soldiers) were situated where agriculture was most intensive and productive or in the best locations for ship-building or fishing. On the average they had more capital and more applicable agricultural skills.[42]

Islanders of English extraction were almost all Protestants, and tended to vote for the Tory party, which represented the interests of the overwhelmingly English and Protestant family compact. They had strongly supported the Tories at the election of 1859, when the latter had defeated the Reformers through an appeal to religious loyalties. At that time the Tories had also promised to use their close connections with the proprietors to bring about settlement of the land question; but the award of the commission they established had been disallowed. In these circumstances, they faced the distinct possibility of defeat at the next election. The Bible question of the late 1850s had ultimately been extinguished simply by giving the *status quo* a statutory basis, which amounted to an implicit admission that the Reformers had not been trying to eliminate permissive daily Bible reading in the schools, as the Tories and their allies among the evangelical clergy had alleged.[43] Given this, and the fact that the land question remained unresolved, the Tories were fortunate indeed that they were again able to discover—or manufacture— 'popish dangers' sufficiently credible that the Protestant constituencies could be persuaded to vote in a body for the government in 1863, thus maintaining them in power.[44]

From one point of view, the Protestant tenantry had once more been duped into supporting the family compact. Following the election of 1863 and its immediate aftermath (including an act to incorporate the colony's Grand Orange Lodge, which was disallowed by the Colonial Office), religious passions abated rapidly. The land question reasserted itself, and with the failure of the delegation to London in the winter of 1863–4, the Tory government proved incapable of finding a solution. It was only a few months later, in May of 1864, that the Tenant League was given its formal organization in circumstances reflecting distaste for partisan politics.[45] If Whelan's assertions about the English Protestant Tories—he even referred to them as Orangemen[46]—in the Tenant League rank and file are credited, then the apolitical bent of the society becomes more comprehensible. Given the bitter political divisions of the 1863 election, these Protestants could not accept working in an organization where George Coles, Whelan, and other Liberals would play prominent roles;[47] and given that the Tories had misled them twice in succession, with the commission and the delegation, both of which had proven fruitless, the English Protestants were willing to discard them as well. Politics had divided island tenants in the past; it would not be allowed to do so in the new organization.

Relations between Scots and Irish in Prince Edward Island were complicated by religious differences, since perhaps 70 per cent of the Scots were Calvinists of one variety or another. The bloodiest political affray in island history, the Belfast Riot of 1 March 1847, which resulted in at least three deaths, has usually been attributed to these religious differences. The occasion was a by-election in the Scottish Protestant district of Belfast, and several hundred men fought it out with cudgels.[48] While it is true that those on one side were Scottish Protestants and those on the other were Irish Roman Catholics, it is far from certain that the causes of the riot can be reduced to religion, or 'religion and nationality'. In the first place, at least in later years it was asserted by Whelan that the real issue behind the riot was 'a contest between landlord and tenant';[49] and it is a fact that the leading Tory candidate, the English-born William Douse, was the land agent for the proprietor of the area, the Earl of Selkirk. Secondly, political partisanship was certainly a factor, with Scots supporting the Tories and Irish the Reformers. Finally, it is worth noting that intimidation at elections was not uncommon at that time in Prince Edward Island. Just 16 days before the riot, Whelan had in the assembly described the turmoil at the previous controverted election in Belfast as simply 'the usual effervescence of popular will, which always will, more or less, evince itself at elections', and no more of a disturbance than regularly occurred on market days in Charlottetown. Contested elections, he continued, always require 'some degree of intimidation'.[50] A few days previously he had stated, again in the assembly, that were Irishmen told to leave their sticks at home when they went to vote, they would soon also be required to leave behind 'their wit and drollery'.[51] If such attitudes towards violence at the polls were common, it is possible that the Belfast Riot was simply a routine electoral brawl which got out of control. The facts that most of the Irish appear to have been from outside the constituency and imported to add physical force to the appeal of the Reformers, and that violence on the scale of 1 March 1847 was never repeated, would seem to lend credence to this possibility. Nonetheless, when all this is said, the further facts remain that as yet no fully satisfactory explanation for the Belfast Riot has emerged, and that the combatants *were* Irish Roman Catholics and Scottish Protestants.

In addition to the very obvious differences between Irish Roman Catholic and Scottish Protestant, there is evidence of tension between Irish and Scot within the Roman Catholic church. Although the Irish outnumbered the Scottish Catholics by a considerable proportion, the Scots monopolized the episcopal seat from the time of the first appointment of Angus B. Mac-Eachern in 1821 until the end of the century. They also tended to dominate the faculty of the diocesan college, St Dunstan's. The first rector was a Father Angus MacDonald, and the names of most of the professors in the nineteenth century were Scottish.[52] These and other considerations aroused some resentment among the Irish, and as early as 1828 an Irish priest in Charlottetown wrote to the Bishop of Quebec that MacEachern 'is well known to possess prejudice against anyone from Ireland.'[53] If this was the case, then Mac-Eachern was no different from many Scots of the day, both Protestant[54] and Roman Catholic. Furthermore, such tensions within the colonial Catholic church were certainly not unique to Prince Edward Island. One of Whelan's early mentors in Halifax had been a dynamic Irish priest, Father Richard B. O'Brien, very popular with the city's Irish population, who eventually returned to Ireland because of friction with the local Scottish bishop.[55] It would seem that the Scottish Roman Catholics of Nova Scotia and Prince Edward Island, who were themselves striving for acceptance and respectability, were sometimes none too happy to find themselves in the same congregations as the ragged Irish.

Yet there was a more positive side to the interaction of Irish and Scots in colonial Prince Edward Island. There is ample evidence of common effort in such matters as building and moving Roman Catholic churches, raising money for Irish and Scottish relief in 1847,[56] and, of course, dealing with proprietors, land agents, and sheriffs.[57] Even between Protestant and Roman Catholic there does not seem to have been much outright hostility until the late 1850s, when it became profitable for one political party to exploit religious loyalties for its own purposes. Certainly there was nothing to compare with the regular, almost ritualized violence between Irish Roman Catholics and English Protestants which disfigured Newfoundland history between the 1830s and the 1860s. The Belfast Riot should be seen as an isolated incident whose occurrence shocked both sides,[58] and lessened their disposition to resort to force. The everyday imperatives of coexistence in a small pioneer community seemed to outweigh inherited prejudices and suspicions at least to the extent of making physical violence seem counterproductive. In the final analysis, pioneer islanders wanted to live together in peace, and not be confined to ethnic and religious enclaves from which they could wander only at personal peril. Harsh words were often exchanged over the years, but the hostility remained at a verbal level even in so impassioned an election as that of 1863.

One of the striking aspects to some of the bitter arguments over the years was the extent to which the spit and fire came from Old Country natives in a colony where, by 1861, the non–native-born numbered only 22.1 per cent.[59] There were two groups in particular who tended to be prisoners of their Old World pasts when perceiving fellow-islanders. The native-Scottish Presbyterian clergymen were prone to find a scheming Jesuit behind every sign of activity on the part of the local Roman Catholic church. In contrast, the priest of this period, although trained in Quebec or on the Continent, was usually an island native, and, as the product of a pioneer community where co-operation was essential, basically pragmatic in his relations with all his fellow-colonists. His Protestant counterpart was not a colonial, but a Britisher with the problems of Puseyism and the Great Disruption on his mind—a man who associated Roman Catholicism with the traditional enemies of Britain, and an increasingly reactionary papacy.[60] On the Catholic side, Irish-born politicians insisted upon seeing local Orangemen as Old Country nightriders. Island Orangeism was a curious phenomenon, given the lack of Protestant Ulstermen in the colony. It grew slowly until the end of the 1850s, when religious loyalties became entrenched as a central factor in local politics. Whatever Orangemen were elsewhere, those in Prince Edward Island were non-violent, and in fact could best be characterized as simply farmers of Scottish and English extraction belonging to a Protestant social group. Yet when incorporation of the local Grand Orange Lodge became an issue, Whelan and other Irish-born assemblymen responded with a ferocity which owed more to memories and parental stories of Ireland than to the realities of Prince Edward Island.[61]

Such are some of the aspects of Highland and Irish heritages in Prince Edward Island in the period dominated by the land question. Many features of Celtic life were transplanted in this relatively self-contained part of the New World, which was burdened with an archaic and oppressive carry-over from the Old. Some, like the common use of Highland Gaelic and the fierce religious loyalties, remained relatively unchanged.[62] Others, such as Orangeism and the 'tenant league' tradition of Ireland, were greatly transformed by the ethnic mixture and particular circumstances of the island colony. Only one generalization can be made with certainty: that if the history of Prince Edward Island is ever to be made fully intelligible, it must be seen in the context of the heritages of the peoples who immigrated there. They did not leave their cultural backgrounds on Old Country docksides. Even a movement like Escheat, whose name owed nothing to the recent pasts of Scotland and Ireland, was clearly a hybrid of the traditions of the two countries, amalgamating the intense clan loyalties of the Highlanders with the militancy and readiness to resort to force of the Irish.

Suggestions for Further Reading

Francis W.P. Bolger, *Canada's Smallest Province: A History of P.E.I.* (Charlottetown, 1973).
Andrew Macphail, *The Master's Wife* (Montreal, 1939, rpr. Toronto, 1977).
Frank MacKinnon, *The Government of Prince Edward Island* (Toronto, 1951).

Notes

[1] I am grateful to Mr Harry Baglole of Belfast, PEI, Mr H.T. Holman of the Public Archives of PEI (PAPEI), and Prof. Joseph Levitt of the University of Ottawa for their comments on this paper in the course of its preparation. I have also benefited from reading two unpublished papers written by Mr Baglole, entitled 'A Reassess-

ment of the Role of Absentee Proprietors in Prince Edward Island History' (1970), a copy of which is in PAPEI, and 'The Origins of the Prince Edward Island Land Question: 1770–1805' (1971).

2For the legislative and political history of the land question, see Frank MacKinnon, *The Government of Prince Edward Island* (Toronto, 1951), ch. 5; and Francis W.P. Bolger, ed., *Canada's Smallest Province: A History of PEI* (Charlottetown, 1973), chs. 2, 3, 4 (by Bolger), and 5 (by W.S. MacNutt). A greater sense of immediacy is conveyed by Harry Baglole and David Weale, *The Island and Confederation: The End of an Era* (Summerside, 1973), ch. 4; and Harry Baglole, comp. and ed., *The Land Question: A Study Kit of Primary Documents* (Charlottetown, 1975). The second and third titles have been reviewed at length by I.R. Robertson in 'Recent Island History', *Acadiensis* IV, 2 (1975), 111–18, and *Canadian Historical Review* LVI (1975), 460–1.

3See MacKinnon, *The Government of Prince Edward Island*, 6–7.

4See D.C. Harvey, ed., *Journeys to the Island of St John or Prince Edward Island 1775–1832* (Toronto, 1955), 7; and Andrew Hill Clark, *Three Centuries and the Island: A Historical Geography of Settlement and Agriculture in Prince Edward Island, Canada* (Toronto, 1959), 56.

5By 1801 less than £6,500 had been collected, and £59,162/17 were owing; see Public Archives of Canada microfilm, Colonial Office (CO) 226/19, 352. In fairness, there were other factors in the non-payment: e.g., the inadequacy of the collection system, and the likelihood that any quitrents collected would be put to the private purposes of the collector.

6The only exceptions were lots 15 and 55, which were escheated by Governor C.D. Smith in 1818, and divided among the tenantry; see Bolger, ed., *Canada's Smallest Province*, 88.

7Clark, *Three Centuries and the Island*, 60–1.

8PEI House of Assembly, *Journal*, 1862, appendix A.

9See Clark, *Three Centuries and the Island*, 95, and table III, on the same page. In Clark's words, '"squatting" refers to the process by which settlers moved in and occupied land neglected or ignored by the nominal proprietors' (99).

10See D.C. Harvey, 'The Loyal Electors', Royal Society of Canada, *Proceedings and Transactions*, 3rd ser., XXIV (1930), Section II, 101–10; and Bolger, ed., *Canada's Smallest Province*, 75–84.

11Edward Palmer, the son of the Loyal Electors' leader J.B. Palmer, was absorbed into the local élite in the 1830s, and from around 1850 until the early 1860s was the leader of the Tory party of PEI.

12Milton Acorn, 'The Figure in the Landscape Made the Landscape', in *The Island Means Minago: Poems from Prince Edward Island* (Toronto, 1975), 47. For this volume of poems, many of them on the land question, Mr Acorn has received the Canadian Governor-General's Award for poetry published in 1975. An interesting elaboration upon this tenant ideology will be found in the testimony by tenant farmer James Howatt before the land commission of 1860, in *Abstract of the Proceedings before the Land Commissioners Court, held during the summer of 1860 to inquire into the differences relative to the rights of landowners and tenants in Prince Edward Island*, reporters J.D. Gordon and David Laird (Charlottetown, 1862), 84–5. As succinctly summarized by Baglole, its import is that 'when land is purchased from the proprietors the price paid—even for productive farms—should be no higher than the value of land in a wilderness state. The proprietors must not be allowed to profit from the labour of the settlers' (Baglole, comp. and ed., *The Land Question*, Section A, Document N, n.2).

[13]See Harry Baglole, 'William Cooper', *Dictionary of Canadian Biography* IX (Toronto, 1976), 155–8.

[14]PEI Assembly, *Journal*, 1832, app. A.

[15]This rebuff was in striking contrast to the easy access to the Colonial Office enjoyed by proprietors and various Tory delegations over the years.

[16]Until 1854 the governor had at his command a garrison consisting of about 100 men, whose main function was as a 'potential aid to the civil power'; J. Mackay Hitsman, 'Military Defenders of Prince Edward Island, 1775–1864', Canadian Historical Association, *Annual Report* (1964), 34, 32. According to Baglole, 'For several years it was almost impossible to find a man brave enough to serve as sheriff or constable in Kings County' (Baglole to author, 30 January 1976).

[17]CO 226/65, 133, Huntley to Lord Stanley, 21 April 1843. In the same despatch, Huntley described the militia as unreliable (135).

[18]Huntley, who had directed the prosecution, also requested that sentence be withheld, in order not to make MacLean a martyr. See *ibid.*, 190–2, 198, Huntley to Stanley, 14, 24 July 1843; and I.R. Robertson, 'Sir Henry Vere Huntley', *Dictionary of Canadian Biography* IX, 400.

[19]See I.R. Robertson, 'George Coles', *ibid.*, X (Toronto, 1972), 182–8.

[20]See *ibid.*, 185–7. Even in 1861, following the sale of the large Selkirk estate, the proportion of freeholders was only 40.4 per cent; calculation based on Clark, *Three Centuries and the Island*, 95, table III.

[21]See I.R. Robertson, 'The Bible Question in Prince Edward Island from 1856 to 1860', *Acadiensis* V, 2 (1976), 3–25.

[22]See Phyllis Blakeley, 'Sir Samuel Cunard', *Dictionary of Canadian Biography* IX, 172–86.

[23]The 'tenant's pledge' is printed in *Examiner* (Charlottetown), 30 May 1864; also see *ibid.*, 1 February 1864.

[24]See, e.g., Bolger, ed., *Canada's Smallest Province*, where the editor treats the Tenant League disturbances simply as a minor factor in the story of the island's entry into Confederation (180–1); or Clark, *Three Centuries and the Island*, who ventures the opinion that the league 'may have done more harm than good to the cause of land reform' (93), while later in the same paragraph attributing further sales of proprietors' estates to the leaguers' agitation.

[25]See, e.g., *Examiner*, 22 May, 19 June 1865, 21 October 1867.

[26]Although the resulting legislation was passed in 1875, it was another 20 years before the last estate was purchased; see MacKinnon, *The Government of Prince Edward Island*, 296–8.

[27]Clark, *Three Centuries and the Island*, 91. About one-tenth of the population was French Acadian.

[28]See *Prince Edward Island Times* (Charlottetown), e.g., 26 March 1836 (vol. I, 1).

[29] *Royal Gazette* (Charlottetown), 10 January 1837. Of course there were exceptions to this militancy among the Scottish tenants. In 1831 proprietor David Stewart, upon visiting his estate for the first time, reported that a Highlander 'thanked God, threw his bonnet up in the air and thanked God again' as an expression of joy at meeting his landlord. PAPEI, Journal of David Stewart (as excerpted in *Guardian* [Charlottetown], 16 July to 24 September 1949), entry for 28 June 1831.

[30] See anonymous [John C. Macmillan], *The Arrival of the First Scottish Catholic Emigrants to Prince Edward Island and After, 1772–1922* (Summerside, 1922), 30–1; Rosemary Hutchinson, 'Emigration from South Uist to Cape Breton', in B.D. Tennyson, ed., *Essays in Cape Breton History* (Windsor, N.S., 1973), 11; Allan F. MacDonald, 'Captain John MacDonald, "Glenalladale",' Canadian Catholic Historical Association, *Report*, 1964, 32–4; and Ada MacLeod, 'The Glenaladale Pioneers', *Dalhousie Review* XI, 1 (1931), 319.

[31] In later years one of those he took with him alleged publicly that he had deceived them as to the condition of the land to be leased, and stated that some of the immigrants had left for the United States; see testimony of John Haggarty in *Abstract of the Proceedings before the Land Commissioners' Court . . .* , 117–18.

[32] See I.R. Robertson, 'John McDonald', *Dictionary of Canadian Biography* X, 460–2. His estate was left in the care of an agent, and distraint proceedings on his behalf were a factor in the Tenant League disturbances of 1865; see PAPEI Accession 2514, James Curtis to John Morris, 14 March 1865.

[33] CO 226/79, 212, Sir Alexander Bannerman to Earl Grey, 14 August 1851 (confidential); also see *ibid.*, 214, proclamation dated 2 August 1851; *Islander* (Charlottetown), 1, 22 August 1851; *Examiner*, 10 August 1850; *Royal Gazette*, 13 August 1850. The following published account of Donald McDonald's misfortunes appears to be basically accurate: Isabella Lucy Bird, *The Englishwoman in America* (Toronto, 1966 edn), 46–7. There is evidence which suggests that McDonald had amply earned unpopularity among his tenants; see PAPEI, Palmer Family Papers, testimony of Vincent Bell in *Public Documents on Various Subjects Connected with the Interests of Prince Edward Island Ordered by the House of Assembly to be Printed, April 23d., 1841* (Charlottetown, 1841), 75–6; and Bannerman, *supra*.

[34] See *Royal Gazette*, 23, 30 July 1850, 7 June 1865; *Examiner*, 24 July 1850, 12, 19 June, 20 November 1865.

[35] For a particularly vivid account of the reception given by a group of Irish squatters in the 1860s to a surveying party led by a proprietor, Robert Bruce Stewart (the son of David Stewart), see Moncrieff Williamson, *Robert Harris 1849–1919: An Unconventional Biography* (Toronto, 1970), app. 1, 202–7. As in the Macintosh-McDonald case, a jury proved sympathetic to the popular cause in a resulting trial for 'riot and assault'.

[36] See *Palladium* (Charlottetown), 4, 7, 11, 14 September 1843; *Examiner*, 30 May 1864, 21 October 1867. When Whelan finally lost his hold on the Irish population of the colony in the mid-1860s, it was partially because of his break with the radicalism of the Tenant League; a detailed account of his deteriorating relationship with the tenant movement of later years is included in I.R. Robertson, 'Edward Whelan', *Dictionary of Canadian Biography* IX, 831–4.

[37] See PAPEI Accession 2514, Curtis to Morris, 14 March 1865; and affidavit of Bernard McKenna, dated 5 August 1865. The tenants of Donald McDonald and his son John Archibald McDonald were mostly Irish.

[38]See *Examiner*, 11 December 1850, 13 May 1851.

[39]Lots 35, 36, 37, 48 and part of 49 produced the island's first 'tenant league' and at least four of these were noted for support of the second. See *ibid.*; and Clark, *Three Centuries and the Island*, 93.

[40]See *Examiner*, 23, 30 May 1864, 19 June 1865. At this meeting (in May 1864) the name 'Tenant Union of PEI' was adopted, but the organization continued to be popularly referred to as the 'Tenant League'.

[41]See *ibid.*, 21 August 1865. Little is known about the leaders of the Tenant League, and this is not surprising, given the nature of the organization, for the emphasis was upon united mass action rather than individual leaders. One of the very few figures to emerge reasonably clearly was George F. Adams, whom the governor of the day described as 'a wild Chartist' from England. See CO 226/100, 230, George Dundas to Arthur Blackwood, 6 June 1864 (private).

[42]Clark, *Three Centuries and the Island*, 91.

[43]See Robertson, 'The Bible Question in Prince Edward Island from 1856 to 1860', *Acadiensis* V, 2 (1976), 20–5.

[44]See I.R. Robertson, 'Religion, Politics, and Education in Prince Edward Island from 1856 to 1877', McGill University MA thesis, (1968), chs. 5, 6.

[45]One of the delegates, W.H. Pope, had warned that agrarian disturbances would result from failure of the delegation; see I.R. Robertson, 'William Henry Pope', *Dictionary of Canadian Biography* X, 596.

[46]See, e.g., *Examiner*, 1 February 1864, 19 June, 7, 21 August, 4 September 1865.

[47]In fact, Whelan had played a role in the winter of 1860–1 in founding an abortive tenant movement, which was meant to become all-embracing; see *ibid.*, 23, 29 October, 31 December 1860, 7, 14 January 1861.

[48]See PEI Assembly, *Journal*, 1847, app. I; CO 226/83, 166, memorial of Dr W.H. Hobkirk to the Duke of Newcastle, 10 March 1854; and H.T. Holman, 'William Douse', *Dictionary of Canadian Biography* IX, 223. Inquests were held for two Irishmen and one Scot. Three medical doctors appear to have been involved in attending the wounded, and one claimed to have treated between 30 and 40, some of whose injuries were 'very serious'.

[49]PEI Assembly, *Debates and Proceedings*, 1864, 57.

[50]Summary report of assembly debates in *Royal Gazette*, 2 March 1847; also see the remarks of Macintosh in the same debate.

[51]Summary report of assembly debates in *ibid.*, 16 March 1847.

[52]The publicly supported college, Prince of Wales, was also dominated by Scottish professors, in this case Protestant. To a lesser extent, the same Scottish Protestant hegemony was apparent in the colony's Normal School, school visitorships, and grammar schools.

[53]Archives of the Roman Catholic Diocese of Charlottetown, Bishop Angus B. MacEachern Papers, Father Thomas Fitzgerald to Bishop Bernard Claude Panet, 28 August 1828. Access to this collection was granted by Father Faber MacDonald. For the official Roman Catholic (and Scottish) version of the differences between MacEachern and Fitzgerald, see John C. Macmillan, *Early History of the Catholic Church in Prince Edward Island* (Quebec, 1905), 227–8, 231–2, 264–5.

[54]E.g., the proprietor David Stewart appears to have taken a particularly hard line with Irish tenants, even offering them inducements to vacate; see PAPEI, Journal of David Stewart, entry for 25 June 1831.

55See Angus A. Johnston, *A History of the Catholic Church in Eastern Nova Scotia, vol. II; 1827–1880* (Antigonish, N.S., 1971), 166–7, 179–80, 215.

56There was a joint fund, which was commenced shortly after the Belfast Riot; see *Royal Gazette*, 9 March, 6 July 1847.

57It is worth emphasizing the point that, however one accounts for the Belfast Riot, over the years the land question generated far more violence than did ethnic or religious disputes.

58Shock and sorrow were the dominant sentiments expressed in the assembly debate of 12 March 1847 following Governor Huntley's message relating to the Belfast Riot; see summary report of assembly debates in *Islander*, 20 March 1847.

59Clark, *Three Centuries and the Island*, 121, table v.

60This attitude towards Catholicism was not confined to Presbyterians; one of the most contentious clergymen of these years was the Rev. David Fitzgerald, a displaced Church of Ireland priest.

61See Robertson, 'Religion, Politics, and Education in Prince Edward Island from 1856 to 1877', 39, 88–93, 130, 138–43. In fairness, it should be noted that the bill's sponsor, W.H. Pope, introduced it in an extremely provocative manner, and that he did so on St Patrick's Day.

62For an example of a Scottish Protestant community in which the way of life, religious customs, and hierarchy of values changed very little over several generations see Andrew Macphail, *The Master's Wife* (Montreal, 1939; reprint Toronto, 1977, with an introduction by I.R. Robertson); and I.R. Robertson, 'Sir Andrew Macphail as a Social Critic', University of Toronto PhD thesis, (1974), ch. 1.

26

The Beginnings of Organized Labour

Steven Langdon

Class analysis was not a central feature of Canadian historical study, particularly in the period before Confederation, until recent years. That Canadian society was divided into differing self-conscious groupings or segments has seldom been denied; but Canadian historians have tended to look to other factors (such as ethnicity or race or religion) when studying the composition of Canadian society: they have not normally seen conflict in terms of class consciousness. Nevertheless various analyses based on insights first developed by Marx and Engels have been employed by historians generally for much of this century and have recently entered Canadian scholarship. In this approach class is seen as the fundamental organizing principle of historical interpretation rather than as merely an important historical variable.

In the following selection Steven Langdon attempts to establish the necessary background for a 'class-oriented approach' to Canadian development. From his perspective, the two critical features, inextricably interconnected, are the emergence of industrial capitalism and the appearance of an organized and conscious working class. Industrial capitalism brought an element of impersonality and social dislocation that threatened job security, and especially the traditional skills of the labour force. Unskilled workers— often women, children, and immigrants from rural areas or overseas— could run the machines of the new industrialism at a lower labour cost. The result was unemployment in the traditional skilled industries and a 'collective response' towards organization by the workers, but some of them did organize within the commercial economy. The emergence of factories in the 1850s and 1860s produced new worker organizations that struggled with the industrial capitalist, although according to Langdon by the mid-1860s there was not yet a 'conscious' Canadian working class.

How does Langdon define class? If working-class consciousness is so dependent on industrial organization, which comes to Canada in the 1860s, can there be a 'class-oriented' Canadian history before that period? Why were the skilled trades so vulnerable to the new industrial system, and why were the new capitalists so hostile to labour organizations? Finally, is class conflict a sufficient organizing principle for understanding the development of Canada?

This article first appeared, titled 'The Emergence of the Canadian Working-Class Movement, 1845–1867', in *Journal of Canadian Studies* VIII (1973), 3–12.

'No important attempt has been made to base an analysis of our history on class,' says S.R. Mealing, 'nor is there any weight of research to suggest that such an analysis is possible.'[1] That statement is accurate, particularly for the time when it was published (1965).[2] But the observation is less a reflection of Canada's actual development than a serious criticism of Canadian historiography. Or so this article argues. At least for the 1845–67 period in central Canada, class was an emerging and powerful reality for many Canadians—a reality which shaped their thought and action, and influenced the future pattern of their country.

What do I mean by class? E.P. Thompson's definition is apt:[3]

> Class happens when some men, as a result of common experiences (inherited or shared), feel and articulate the identity of their interests as between themselves and as against other men whose interest are different from (and usually opposed to) theirs. The class experience is largely determined by the productive relations into which men are born—or enter involuntarily.

Thus, Thompson adds, 'class is a relationship, not a thing.' And the emphasis in understanding the relationship must be on shared, subjective feelings of common objective situation and interest—on class consciousness, that is, developed historically.

Thompson applies this definition to England in the 1780–1832 period, and finds it fits: 'Most English working people came to feel an identity of interests as between themselves, and as against their rulers and employers.'[4] A somewhat similar process of class emergence is clear among central Canadian working people, in the 1845–67 period. It represents the making of the Canadian working class—using that phrase as Thompson does: '*Making*, because it is a study in an active process, which owes as much to agency as to conditioning'.[5] Working people shaped *themselves* as a class, in interaction with a changing socioeconomic environment; and they did so without the direction of that vanguard party or intellectual élite which it is now too often the patronizing fashion to believe must carry wisdom to the workingman.

This study traces that process. It follows the gradual growth of organizational cohesion and of class consciousness among central Canadian working people from 1845 to 1867; it argues that this development had reached significant proportions by the early sixties; and it demonstrates that this rise was intimately interrelated with the emergence of an industrial capitalist political economy in the area. The importance of the process is threefold. First, at the time, it influenced Canadian development choices significantly. Second, historically, it established certain traditions and social roots which shaped today's working-class and radical movement in Canada. And third, historiographically, tracing this process of working-class emergence illustrates the basis and need for a class-oriented approach to interpreting Canadian development generally.[6]

The Industrial Capitalist Transformation

The sixties in central Canada, wrote *The People's Journal* in 1871, 'set agoing an industrial revolution . . . '.[7] From points of commercial exchange in the 1840s, dominated by merchants and oriented around trade with Britain, central Canadian cities had by the 1870s become centres of industrial capitalist production—marked by dynamic factory complexes, shaped by powerful industrialists, and inhabited by a large industrial work force. Given the leverage of these cities in patterning Canadian development,[8] this urban transformation meant central Canada had effectively become an industrial capitalist political economy.

The social process of capitalist industrialization of the first industrial revolution, in England, was thus mirrored at this later period in central Canada.[9] Large, increasingly mechanized factories rapidly expanded—especially in Montreal, Toronto, and Hamilton. In Hamilton, for instance, a significant industrial sector had already emerged by 1864 (2,300 workers were employed in 46 factories—43 per cent of these steam-mechanized—all in a city of 19,000). By 1870 this sector showed even further dramatic growth (the number of workers per factory was up 52 per cent, the percentage of steam-powered plants up 32 per cent, and so on).[10] This was the pattern across Canada. 'Factories,' wrote one 1872 observer, 'are springing up in every part of the country. . . .'[11]

Similarly, a conscious class of industrial capitalists appeared, as these factories grew. Early industrial operators in Canada were usually merchants, for whom production was a sideline; and in their political action they followed the commercial capitalist lead—as in rejecting protective tariffs for industry.[12] By the 1860s and 1870s, though, independent industrialists were organizing their own collective institutions—some for co-operation in particular sectors (like the Canadian Iron Founders Association, formed by leading stove manufacturers)—others for cohesive action throughout the whole political economy (particularly the Association for the Promotion of Canadian Industry, run by Canada's most important industrialists by 1870). These class institutions increasingly influenced public attitudes and government activities to the benefit of industrial capitalism. Macdonald's National Policy, with its high protective tariffs, was the ultimate triumph of this industrialist action.[13]

Finally, there was that most characteristic feature of industrial capitalism —the emergence of a self-regulating, impersonal labour market.[14] As Pentland shows, this institution was also developing in central Canada after mid-century.[15] The breakdown of older, personal, paternalistic employment ties is obvious in the rising strike statistics for the time; the self-regulating nature of the new market is clear in the similar wage rates, by occupation, in different Canadian cities—and in the parallel ups and downs of such wage rates city by city. By the sixties and seventies, a mature impersonal labour market was operative in the area. In fact, central Canadian working people were part of a continental labour market, marked by large-scale movement back and forth across the Canadian-American border.[16]

In England, this process of capitalist industrialization (though it also produced 'a vast movement of economic improvement') brought on an 'avalanche of social dislocation for most ordinary Englishmen'.[17] This was the case for many Canadian workers, too, in the 1860s and 1870s. The growing industrial cities were marked by grim housing conditions and serious health problems. Working conditions in the rising factory complexes were even worse. And the emergence of an impersonal labour market, especially, generated greater inequality, unemployment, and poverty in central Canada.[18]

Two interrelated trends were responsible for this. First, the rise of an impersonal labour market undermined job security. Under the old system of personalized employment ties, in the isolation of Canada, a firm had to keep its workers on the payroll, even when business suffered a cyclic decline—or else it wouldn't have enough workers to take advantage of upturns in the future. Thus the social cost of cyclic depression was fully shared by employers and employees. In an impersonal labour market, though, the employer could readily hire the workers he needed, exactly when he needed them. So in a cyclic downturn, he could simply dismiss excess workers—and be sure of getting replacements when business boomed in the future. The result was rising unemployment during cyclic declines—and increased poverty for working people. What the change amounted to was this: the social cost of the capitalist trade cycle was no longer fully shared; it was predominantly borne by employees. That helped further industrialization—because it left capitalists with more resources, to respond to business upturns when they came. But it also brought painful social dislocation to working men and women.

Second, this spreading labour market, and the driving mechanization of industry, combined to undercut the wages of employees, especially if they were skilled. The introduction of new machines meant that old craft skills were no longer as necessary in the production process. So some of those with such skills (and appropriate good wages) could be dismissed; and the labour market could provide unskilled replacements (often children or apprentices), readily able to do the routine operations on a machine, at much lower wages. This effect was reflected in the significant increases in child labour use that ongoing mechanization brought to central Canada.[19] And even where skilled workers kept their jobs, their wages ordinarily fell; machines meant there was less premium for their old skills. This process hit printers, tailors, shoemakers, cigarmakers and many others, as the material below illustrates.

So unemployment and poverty increased with industrialization. In Toronto, for instance, the number of people receiving poor relief increased by 478 per cent from 1850 to 1865.[20] Cyclic unemployment became common; by 1869 a *Globe* reporter angrily wrote that 'hundreds if not thousands of men are out of employment, families are starving, and the great cry of these men is for work. But that they cannot get.'[21]

It was in response to such social dislocation in England (says Polanyi), that 'a political and industrial working class movement sprang into being.' The purpose was to slow down and regulate change, to enforce a collective community control over it—so that economic improvement should not also mean social distress.[22] This happened in central Canada, too. The rest of this study traces how. I look at two periods, in turn, in this process of developing class cohesion and consciousness: the forties and earlier fifties, when workers' collective action was tentative, isolated, and trade-oriented; and the later fifties and earlier sixties, when trade unionism expanded, mostly in a craft context.

The Forties and Earlier Fifties

There were two significant sorts of collective action by workingmen in this period. The first involved *ad hoc* and non-institutional reaction, by workers, to particularly intolerable circumstances—without establishing a continuing organizational form after the immediate protest had either succeeded or failed. The strikes of Irish labourers, on Canada's public works, provide the best examples of this.

In 1843, for instance, workers on the Lachine and Beauharnois canal projects near Montreal struck against the further reduction of already extremely low wages, and against the way those wages were often paid—in 'Store' pay, good only at the company store. Perhaps using secret Irish societies, and certainly relying on their tight sense of ethnic community, the Lachine workers struck unanimously: 'we are all irishmen . . . ' their strike notice said. It appears that the strike was successful, too. But no continuing workingmen's organizations emerged from the event.[23]

Similarly, Irish labourers struck and rioted on the Welland canal works in 1842, protesting the fact that only 575 of 2,000 available workers had been hired for the season.[24] Irish labourers also struck, for higher wages, on the Great Western railroad near Hamilton in 1848.[25]

These strikes were all important as first signs of working people's efforts to control and regulate the impersonal labour market, which was growing around the infrastructure projects advanced by a commercial community. But they also illustrate how difficult sustained collective action was in circumstances of such shifting, seasonal, and casual employment. And without more permanent institutions of class action continuing growth of class consciousness was impossible; for it meant there was no way to assess collective actions and analyses, and improve on them in an ongoing process.

Secondly, though, there *were* some continuing workingmen's organizations that did develop in this period. Like the few trade unions that emerged in the 1820s and 1830s, however,[26] those of the forties and earlier fifties were small and confined to particular cities and particular trades. Still, there was a growing number of them: in Montreal, for example, a stonecutters' and a printers' union in the forties, and unions of shoemakers, bakers, and engineers in the early fifties;[27] in Toronto, unions of stonemasons, printers, and cordwainers (shoemakers) in the forties, and of tailors by the early fifties;[28] and in Hamilton, of printers in the forties and of tailors and shoemakers by the fifties.[29] These organizations were largely isolated from one another. There is, for instance, no mention in the Toronto Typographical Society (TTS) minutes from 1845 to 1851 of contact between the Society and any other Toronto union. And while there were some communications with Hamilton, Montreal, and Quebec typographical societies, and even with the printers' union in Rochester, these contacts were far from extensive.

Because of this localization and isolation, such unions had a tenuous existence—as the absence of records from their short lives testifies. Even the TTS (whose records do survive) experienced some very weak periods after their 1844 formation; no meetings could be held, for lack of a quorum of nine members, for six months in 1845–6. TTS members felt a sense of public hostility, too; Thomas Hill, for instance, argued against an 1845 handbill

> because the public to whom allusion is made in the statement . . . are averse to any kind of combinations among workmen, how mild soever their form or righteous their intentions.[30]

Their isolation and sense of vulnerability were a part of the reason why workingmen in their early unions were trade-oriented rather than class-oriented in their attitudes; i.e., they seem, by and large, to have expressed an identity of interest with others in their particular trade (including their employers), rather than with other tradesmen or other workers generally. The TTS, for example, had for its 'great' object 'maintaining our own position in the Trade'. Consequently, the Society stressed, the interests of employer and employee were one and the same—'one and indivisible', as the TTS President put it at an 1849 anniversary dinner for the union, at which employers were honoured guests. The union sought, it said,

> a better understanding between two parties, who are sometimes carried away with the erroneous idea that their interests are antagonistical instead of being, as they in reality are, mutual and reciprocal.[31]

Similarly, after an 1852 dispute, the Journeymen Tailors' Operative Society of Toronto sat down to celebrate the settlement with their employers in the St Lawrence Hall, over goose and cabbage.[32]

Much of this sentiment, though, was more wishful thinking than hard-held analysis. The process that was generating the early unions was placing those unions in conflict (if only occasional) with their employers; and that same process, the rise of industrial capitalism, was just as inevitably forcing workers to move beyond their trade consciousness. Consider two cases, printers and tailors.

Because newspapers were such important communication media in pre-1850 Canada, printing was one of the earliest sectors of potential large-scale production. So it was one of the earliest sectors of industrial mechanization; as early as 1844 George Brown's *Globe* introduced extensive new machinery (the first cylinder press in Upper Canada).[33] As suggested above, this undermined job security and wages for skilled printers—through the much greater use printing firms were consequently able to make of unskilled 'apprentices'. This is clearly what the TTS was reacting to in its early formation; increasing use of apprentices was an angry preoccupation of the Society right from the beginning. Thus the mechanizing Brown was strongly attacked by the TTS in 1845 for 'nearly filling his office with boys' (i.e., apprentices). The use of these men, stressed the TTS,

> would occupy the situation which regular hand otherwise be called upon to fill [sic]—and thus throw numbers of men out of employment and ultimately reduce the wages of the whole.

What the unionists opposed, of course, was not mechanization *per se*, but the use of unskilled labour on the new machinery; and their opposition grew increasingly fierce. By 1850, they were referring to 'the Monster evil—the bane and curse of every printer . . . *the indiscriminate employment of apprentices*'.[34]

Similarly, the early tailors' unions were sparked into existence by the first stages of industrial mechanization—in this case by the introduction of the steam-run sewing machine. In Toronto the struggle began in 1851–2, when workmen there, 'fearing for their craft', broke the first of these machines brought to the city and combined to prevent the introduction of others.[35] In Hamilton, the Journeymen Tailors' Protective Society reacted the same way in 1854, seeing the new machine as 'threatening extermination to the whole craft'.[36]

The significant point, though, and a further reason for the trade-consciousness of early unions, was that at first the strong solidarity of those skilled workers within the particular trade was sufficient to counter these dangers to jobs and wages. By organizing just about every skilled craftsman within a trade in any one city, and setting up a protective fund, a union's bargaining position could be strong indeed, simply because the undeveloped labour market for skilled workers meant that outside replacements for strikers were hard to find. Thus the TTS was able to defeat attempts to lower printers' wages in both 1844 and 1847, without even undertaking a strike. Even if apprentices were being more widely used, the TTS was maintaining full employment for all its members at high wages. The tailors were even more successful, effectively preventing the introduction of the sewing machine in Toronto in 1852. In these circumstances, trade consciousness was natural, because it was sufficient to defend craftsmen's positions.

But the situation couldn't last, once the labour market spread more widely, and the drive toward mechanization gathered more momentum. Employers were forced to introduce technological innovations and to try to hire the lowest-cost workers possible—or else face undercutting from competitors at home or abroad. So they had to take aggressive action against the unions that limited their freedom of action. As a result, the trade-oriented unions were forced into clear, dramatic conflicts with those employers, in which unionists had first to abandon any idea of 'one and indivisible' identity with their opponents, and then second to develop concepts of countervailing solidarity and assistance among all workingmen—across craft lines within one city, and across city lines within one craft.

This aggressive employer action was obvious by the early fifties. In 1853 and 1854, for instance, the TTS was forced into strikes to defend its pay position, and the printing firms began to find it possible to hire replacement workers. In 1854 the firms even organized themselves jointly to fight the 'secret combinations and foul threats' of their employees, hiring female typesetters as replacements for strikers.[37] In such a context, any idea of identity of interests rang hollow. By 1854, the goose dinner had also given way to court action; the firm that sought to introduce sewing machines had the executive of the Journeyman Tailors' Protective Society arrested for conspiracy.[38] As the next section shows, a new consciousness among workers developed out of such conflict; they began to draw organizational links with each other and think in similar terms.

Throughout most of this period, though, interests *did* remain trade-oriented. This led to a singular concentration by unionists on the immediate and special concerns of employment in their particular trade. Thus, between 1845 and 1851, the TTS entirely ignored social or political concerns beyond the printing trade; and on the single occasion on which there was even a hint of politics intruding (the union considered inviting Lord Elgin, then the centre of controversy over the Rebellion Losses Bill, to its 1850 anniversary dinner), the result was a serious dispute within the TTS and the president's resignation 'in consequence of the political and general ill-feeling which I have observed in several members of this Society'.[39] One exception to this apolitical pattern was an unsuccessful 1852–3 effort, supported by workers' petitions from Brantford, Hamilton, and London, to have the Legislative Assembly 'prohibit the payment to mechanics . . . of wages in goods or way of truck'.[40] But this *was* quite exceptional.

Still, the effort did preview later political action by working people. And likewise, within their city craft institutions, workers were developing a collective sense that previewed wider collective action in the future. The TTS, for instance, established mutual-benefit provisions in its constitution (which also helped keep the organization together); it committed itself to 'rescue from privation our less fortunate fellow workmen, . . . administering to the wants of others of our Profession'; and it stressed, in 1847, that:[41]

> esteeming one another as brothers of a glorious fraternity . . . we are knit together by ties that should be considered as indissoluble, being in the words of our motto, 'United to Support—not combined to Injure.'

The early stages of capitalist industrialization had generated that solidarity; and the continuing thrust of industrial capitalism would widen such feelings of common community much further.

The Later Fifties and Earlier Sixties

This was the period when factory complexes first began to develop significantly in central Canadian cities. New sectors of mechanized industry emerged, producing machines, metal goods, shoes, and tobacco particularly. In these new sectors new collective action by workers developed. At the same time, the spread of the self-regulating labour market was taking impersonal labour relations into all parts of the Canadian economy; so workers were organizing collective responses in a wide number of other sectors, too. In all these sectors the changing consciousness previewed last section was evident; workers were moving away from an identification with employers in their trade, to a greater sense of solidarity with their fellow employees, in other cities and in other trades.

The growing organizational linkages of this period were one sign of the change. The first international unions, for instance, appeared in central Canada. In the machinery sector, various locals of the Amalgamated Society of Engineers, a British-based union, organized themselves; from one local with twenty-one members (in Montreal) in 1853, the ASE had grown to include four locals and 207 members (in Montreal, Hamilton, Toronto, and Brantford) by 1867, forming a small union of highly skilled men.[42] In the metalworking sector, various local unions in Canada joined the newly formed International Molders Union (IMU) in 1859; by 1867 there were eight locals with 270 members in central Canada (mostly in Toronto and Montreal). Moulders, too, were highly skilled craftsmen.[43]

In the boot and shoe sector, union organization also moved forward quickly. During the period local unions of shoemakers were reported at various times in Montreal, Toronto, Hamilton, Oshawa, St Catharines, and London.[44] Some of these were associated with the US-based Journeymen Shoemakers of the US and Canada—which was involved in a Toronto strike in 1857–8, and had a local in Hamilton in 1858.[45] But the most dramatic sign of increasing linkages came in 1867, when shoemakers gathered in Toronto to form a Boot and Shoemakers Union of the Province of Ontario; delegates were present from eight cities.[46] Cigarmakers showed the same pattern. Local unions formed in various Ontario centres, and organized a provincial Journeymen Cigarmakers Union in 1865.[47]

Similarly, the TTS widened its contacts considerably in the late fifties and early sixties. By 1865 it was in direct communication with two British unions and at least nineteen US city typographical unions.[48] This was a prelude to the Society's decision in 1866 to affiliate with the National Typographical Union of the US. Thereafter, although the TTS was jealous of its local autonomy,[49] the Toronto printers were closely involved in affairs well beyond their own local milieu. By the end of 1867, the TTS president was a member of the International executive committee; the TTS standing committee was going office-to-office in Toronto discussing with members the proceedings of the International; and financial assistance was being granted to US strikers.[50] Contact among printers inside Canada increased as well—as shown by the encouragement the TTS sent striking Quebec printers in 1862.[51]

This pattern of organizational linkages reflected the ongoing response of workers to industrial capitalism. First, industrialization remained the key to union emergence. It brought together workers into larger collective units of production, which permitted them to form continuing organizations with some strength. And it sparked workers toward such organization by the ongoing thrust of mechanization. The new unions were as much a response to the job security and wage threats of industrial capitalist change as the printers' and tailors' unions examined above. Thus the IMU, for instance, also focused on the apprenticeship issue in its struggles; that problem, the union said in 1861, 'has given us more trouble than all others combined'.[52] William Sylvis (the IMU President) explained why on his 1863 organizing trip through Canada; he noted that in Kingston where the IMU local had collapsed, there were now 'boys without number', and moulders' wages had dropped severely.[53] That, of course, is exactly the sort of social dislocation that unregulated industrial capitalism usually generated. When employers in the US and Canada organized a grand lockout in 1866, they illustrated the importance of this unskilled-labour issue, too; one of their central objectives was to 'proceed at once to introduce into our shops all the apprentices or helpers we deem advisable . . .'.[54]

Second, industrial capitalists continued to fight the restrictions which strong unions put on their freedom to benefit from the expanding labour market. The lockout against moulders was one example of this tough employer action; shoe manufacturers also used the courts against Toronto shoemakers in 1858; while the Butler and Jackson iron foundry in Brantford warned Sylvis in 1863 it would ultimately 'break up' his union.[55] United action against the IMU was, in fact, the primary impetus toward formation of the employers' Canadian Iron Founders Association in 1865—reflecting Thompson's point, about English industrialists developing class cohesion only in the face of workingmen's collective action against them.[56]

In these circumstances, tradesmen were forced to expand their organizational horizons. Three tactical imperatives, in particular, underlay this expansion.

The critical sanction that gave workers their power in the early period of mechanization was their ability to stop strikebreakers from finding jobs if a strike were won. That is, if a worker deserted his fellows during a strike, and the strike were ultimately successful, unionists would refuse to work with the deserter, and the firm that had hired him would have to fire him if it wanted union members to come back to it. So the strikebreaker would be without a job. This sanction in favour of solidarity, however, was less effective in the transience of North America if the strikebreaker could simply move to another city without penalty. So local unions began to trade 'Ratting Registers', to enforce the ban on working with strikebreakers on a much wider basis. In 1860, for instance, TTS members in one office refused to work with a man who 'had been guilty of "Ratting" in Buffalo . . . until he shall have made ample reparation to the Buffalo Union for his offence'.[57] This tactical innovation was one factor in promoting wider union contact and co-operation.

A second imperative grew from the maturing spread of the impersonal labour market—because as a result of that spread, employers found it possible to import craftsmen from other cities during disputes. This, too, was an impetus toward cross-city union co-operation; locals began to keep each other in touch with their affairs, to discourage cross-city movements into strike-breaking situations. In 1865, for instance, the Detroit Typographical Society wrote to the TTS of an upcoming strike in that city, 'requesting that this society use its influence in preventing printers from going there at present'.[58]

Finally, as conflicts with employers became more bitter, local resources and protective funds were no longer sufficient to buttress local unions during disputes. Access to outside funds became more and more important in winning fights. This was particularly true, for example, of the four-year strike which Brantford moulders finally won against Butler and Jackson in 1864; financial aid had been given by the IMU central fund from early 1861.[59]

Wider organizational linkages developed naturally from these imperatives toward co-operation. And a correspondingly wider consciousness of common interests also developed among workers, at least in so far as the TTS provides evidence. By 1860, all the 1849 rhetoric was gone about 'one and indivisible' identity with employers; instead the TTS stressed 'the favourable opinion formed of us as a Typo body by our brethren of the craft in the US and Canada'.[60] The point of reference had shifted from employers to fellow craftsmen throughout the continent.

There were even signs of this sense of common interest spreading outside the single-craft context to encompass other craftsmen and other workers generally; unions' need to provide each other with mutual aid during disputes was a major impetus in this direction, too. Thus in 1862, local 26 of the IMU in Hamilton put its resources behind an effort by Journeymen Bakers to reduce their hours of work. The moulders resolved (and advertised to that effect in the press) that they would 'not patronize those of the master Bakers of this city, who will not comply with the request of the Journeymen Bakers . . .'. They stressed their widening sense of common interests by appealing to 'all the working class to join us in carrying out this resolution'.[61] Similarly, the TTS loaned money to the Cigarmakers' Union of Toronto in 1867.[62] A more dramatic extension of linkages came in 1863, when a city Trades Assembly was formed in Hamilton. The body seems to have had the power to sanction or forbid strikes by affiliates, and to organize contributions from fellow members to sanctioned strikes.[63] There were also signs of such co-operation (at least to the extent of organizing joint union picnics) in Toronto by 1867.[64]

These new ties reflected the maturing labour market, which left most workers in similar relationships with their employers. And as that labour market spread, so union organization spread—beyond the large cities which had industrialized earliest, beyond those large-scale sectors which had mechanized earliest (printing, metal-working, shoe manufacturing, etc.), and beyond the skilled-craft segment of the urban industrial labour force.

The first trend was clear in the wide number of smaller central Canadian cities and towns in which there were locals of the cross-city unions—the ITU, IMU, ASE, and provincial shoemakers and cigarmakers. Toronto, Hamilton, and Montreal locals were joined by those in Quebec, Brantford, Guelph, Georgetown, Stratford, London, St Catharines, Kingston, Oshawa, and Ottawa at one time or another in these unions. The second trend was clear enough, too. Carpenters' and stonecutters' unions proliferated in the fifties and early sixties. And by 1867 there were also unions of bakers, brush-makers, tinsmiths, and seamen in Hamilton; of cabinet-makers, bakers, masons, bricklayers, brushmakers, plumbers, saddlers, carriage makers, black-smiths, ship carpenters, caulkers, and tinsmiths in Montreal; and of bakers, harnessmakers, and locomotive engineers in Toronto.[65] The third trend was obvious in this range as well. Though most unions still represented skilled workers[66] (the printers, shoemakers, machinists, tailors, moulders, bricklayers, cabinet-makers, engine-drivers, harnessmakers, plumbers, and tinsmiths), semi-skilled workers were also beginning to organize (the bakers, black-smiths, carriage makers, masons, and shipwrights). There were even signs of unskilled organization (the seamen). There was other evidence of the latter, too—particularly in the rise of the Quebec Ship Labourers' Benevolent Society, a union of several thousand Irish longshoremen which had been formed in 1857, and had reached a powerful strength by 1866.[67]

So workingmen's organizations were expanding widely. The large-scale, rapidly industrializing sectors were marked by cross-boundary and intraprov-incial links among unions. These unions were recognizing and organizing their links with other working people. And these institutional developments were reflected in a consciousness that was closer to class perspectives than to trade feelings of mutual interest.

I must not exaggerate the state of central Canadian labour organization by the mid-sixties, though. Unions remained small and vulnerable, even when they had formal links with central bodies of workingmen. The IMU itself, for instance, briefly disintegrated at the International level in 1862; and var-ious of its Canadian locals had to be reorganized several times before they stayed active.[68] Even the confidence and resources of the ASE in Britain couldn't stop Brantford and Kingston ASE branches from dying several times.[69] The TTS suffered too, seeing its membership fall from 76 in 1859 to 31 by 1866, because of the 'great depression of business which prevailed throughout the larger part of the year'.[70] Society meetings lacked quorums for five months in 1863 and five months in 1865. Conditions for non-affiliated unions were even more difficult; so organizations sometimes formed, disappeared, and reformed in regular cycles of enthusiasm, difficul-ties, defeat—then resparked enthusiasm. Nor were any of the ongoing unions large at this stage; of locals for which the membership is known, none had 100 members by 1867.[71]

Nor had there been any significant movement in this period toward con-cern with wider social and political issues. Workingmen's organizations had not yet the strength, confidence, and consciousness to move outside the immediate and direct concerns of employment. And even in *those* concerns, central Canadian workers at this period seemed still to be responding, often defensively, to the continuing drives of mechanization and market adjustment in the emerging industrial capitalist economy. They had not yet reached an institutional maturity sufficient to take collective *initiatives* in society. Signs were evident, then, of the rise of a central Canadian working class during these years; but the process still had far to go by the mid-sixties.

Suggestions for Further Reading

Michael S. Cross, ed., *The Workingman in the Nineteenth Century* (Toronto, 1974).

H.C. Pentland, *Labour and Capital in Canada, 1650–1850* (Toronto, 1981).

Stanley B. Ryerson, *Unequal Union: Confederation and the Roots of Conflict in Canada 1815–1873* (Toronto, 1968).

Notes

[1] S.R. Mealing, 'The Concept of Social Class and the Interpretation of Canadian History', *Canadian Historical Review* (hereafter *CHR*) September 1965, 212.

[2] At that point, there had indeed been little weight of research presented on either the application of class analysis to Canada or, more specifically, the role of working people in Canadian history. There had, of course, been some work in the latter area—some of it cited in this study. But Forsey's judgement on much of it is justifiably brutal: 'most of the work, even the academic work, which has been done on the general history of Canadian labour simply cannot be relied on.' See E. Forsey, 'Insights into Labour History in Canada', *Industrial Relations* 20:3 (July 1965), 448. Since 1965, though, a marked increase of interest in Canadian labour history is apparent. Both as an example of the trend, and a bibliography of recent and forthcoming material, see *Committee on Canadian Labour History*, Bulletin no. 1, York University, 1971.

[3] E.P. Thompson, *The Making of the English Working Class* (Harmondsworth, 1968), 9–11.

[4] *Ibid.*, 12.

[5] *Ibid.*, 9.

[6] Such an approach should not concentrate on class *per se* as a determining factor in historical interpretation. But an emphasis on class is a useful way to interrelate so-called political, economic, and social factors of development in a *political economy* approach to analysing social change. See S. Langdon, 'The Political Economy of Capitalist Transformation: Central Canada from the 1840s to the 1870s', MA thesis, Institute of Canadian Studies, Carleton University, 1972, chap. 1.

[7] *The People's Journal*, 1 April 1871—clipping in the Buchanan Papers, Public Archives of Canada (PAC), MG 24, D 16, vol. 112.

[8] See J.M.S. Careless, 'Frontierism, Metropolitanism and Canadian History', *CHR* 1954, 1–21; also such supporting evidence for his argument as D.G. Creighton, *The Empire of the St Lawrence* (Toronto, 1956)—concentrating on Montreal's role in the earlier commercial capitalist period; D.C. Masters, *The Rise of Toronto* (Toronto, 1957); J. Spelt, *The Urban Development in South Central Ontario* (Assen, 1955)—both of which trace Toronto's dominance as it develops in southern Ontario and the rest of Canada.

[9]For description and analysis of the process in England, cf. K. Polanyi, *The Great Transformation* (Boston, 1967); E.J. Hobsbawm, *Industry and Empire* (Harmondsworth, 1969); Christopher Hill, *Reformation to Industrial Revolution* (Harmondsworth, 1969); M. Dobb, *Studies in the Development of Capitalism* (London, 1963).

[10]The statistics for 1864 are from Sessional Paper 6, 1865, 142–7. The comparisons with 1870 draw on data for the same firms from the manuscript returns of the Census of 1871, PAC, RG 31, sections 695, 705, 712–16.

[11]*Report of the Ottawa Immigration Officer*, Sessional Paper 2A, 1872, 58.

[12]W.H. Merritt, the St Catharines merchant who diversified into grain-milling and ship-building, is a good example. See J.P. Merritt, *Biography of W.H. Merritt* (St Catharines, 1875), 300 ff.

[13]See Langdon, chap. 5 and 6. The CIFA is discussed in C.B. Williams, 'Canadian-American Trade Union Relations', PhD thesis, Cornell, 1964, 92–4. The APCI is best documented in the Buchanan Papers.

[14]Polanyi explains why this market must inevitably emerge with industrial capitalism: 'Since elaborate machines are expensive, they do not pay unless large amounts of goods are produced. They can be worked without a loss only if the vent of the goods is reasonably assured and if production need not be interrupted for want of the primary goods necessary to feed the machines. . . . [That means] that all the factors involved must be on sale. . . . Unless this condition is fulfilled, production with the help of specialized machines is too risky to be undertaken.' Therefore, Polanyi continues, 'the extension of the market mechanism to the elements of industry—labour, land and money—was the inevitable consequence of the introduction of the factory system in a commercial society. The elements of industry had to be on sale.' *The Great Transformation*, 41, 75.

[15]See H.C. Pentland, 'Labour and the Development of Industrial Capitalism in Canada', PhD thesis, Toronto, 1960. A summary of part of the thesis is available in Pentland, 'The Development of a Capitalistic Labour Market in Canada', *Canadian Journal of Economics and Political Science*, 1959, 450–61.

[16]Langdon, chap. 4.

[17]Polanyi, 40.

[18]*Report of the Select Committee on Hygiene and Public Health, House of Commons Journals*, App. 8, 1873; *Report of the Commission on Mills and Factories*, Sessional Paper 42, 1882—both offer some evidence on these matters. See also Langdon, chap. 7.

[19]In Hamilton, for instance, in 32 firms for which comparable statistics are available, child labour as a percentage of employees increased from 5.9 per cent to 9.8 per cent over 1864–70—at the same time mechanization increased. Langdon, chap. 7.

[20]*Globe*, 14 November 1850; Sessional paper 10, 1866, 26. From 674 to 3,895. The latter was some 9 per cent of Toronto's 1861 population.

[21]*Globe*, 26 January 1869. This increasing poverty was reflected in the emergence of new charitable institutions, too. Langdon, chap. 7.

[22]Polanyi, 83.

[23]See H.C. Pentland, 'The Lachine Strike of 1843', *CHR* 1948, 255–77.

[24]W.H. Merritt to the Governor-General, 17 August 1842, Merritt Papers, PAC, MG 24, E 1.

[25]*Globe*, 19 January 1848.

[26]On which see Forsey, 446; C. Lipton, *The Trade Union Movement of Canada* (Montreal, 1966), 3–8.

[27]Forsey, 446–7; *Globe*, 1 May 1854; Minutes of the Toronto Typographical Society (hereafter TTS), PAC, MG 28, I 72, 2 April 1845; Canadian Labour Congress files on labour history (hereafter CLC), PAC, MG 28, I 103, vol. 247.

[28]Forsey, 446–7; TTS, 2 April 1845; *Globe*, 17 November 1847; 7 December 1852.

[29]TTS, 5 August 1846; CLC, vol. 249 (citing Hamilton *Gazette*, 16 February 1854); *Globe*, 15 June 1854.

[30]TTS, 2 July 1845.

[31]TTS, 2 April 1845; 7 March 1849.

[32]J.M. Connor, 'Trade Unions in Canada', in J.E. Middleton, *The Municipality of Toronto*, vol. 2 (Toronto, 1923), 558.

[33]J.M.S. Careless, *Brown of the Globe*, vol. 1 (Toronto, 1959), 46.

[34]TTS, 2 July 1845; 4 November 1846; 5 January 1850.

[35]*Globe*, 7 December 1852.

[36]CLC, vol. 249 (citing Hamilton *Spectator*, 10 February 1854).

[37]*Globe*, 8 June 1854; 12 June 1854.

[38]*Globe*, 13 July 1854; 17 July 1854. Note also the court action against the Toronto shoemakers' union in 1847— *Globe*, 17 November 1847; and against Hamilton shoemakers in 1854—CLC, vol. 253.

[39]TTS, 19 January 1850.

[40]*House of Commons Journal*, Index, 1852–66.

[41]TTS, 2 April 1845; 10 February 1847; 5 April 1848; February 1849.

[42]CLC, vol. 247—ASE file.

[43]Williams, 135ff; see also CLC, vol. 248—IMU file.

[44]CLC, various volumes.

[45]CLC, vol. 253.

[46]*Globe*, 20 September 1867; see also CLC, vol. 249 (citing Hamilton *Evening Times*, 21 September 1867).

[47]*Ibid*. (citing *Evening Times*, 18 November 1865). Its officers were from Toronto, Hamilton, and Brantford.

[48]TTS, 1 November 1859. Between 1859–65, the TTS was in touch with printing unions in Buffalo, Louisville, San Francisco, Boston, New York, Mobile, Montgomery, Charleston, Milwaukee, Chicago, Leavenworth, Cincinnati, Indianapolis, Albany, Cleveland, Peoria, Sacramento, Memphis, and Detroit.

[49]See the dispute over whether union locals in the ITU should have uniform constitutions—TTS, 9 October 1867; 13 November 1867.

[50]TTS, 12 December 1866; 11 September 1867; 13 November 1867.

[51]TTS, 8 January 1862.

[52]Williams, 97.

[53]*Ibid*., 115.

[54]*Ibid*., 120.

[55]*Ibid*., 114; CLC, vol. 253.

[56]Thompson, 12.

[57]TTS, 7 September 1860.

[58]TTS, 14 June 1865.

[59]Williams, 119.

[60]TTS, 17 January 1860.

[61]CLC, vol. 249 (citing Hamilton *Evening Times*, 9 September 1862).

[62]TTS, 9 January 1867.

[63]CLC, vol. 249 (citing Hamilton *Spectator*, 21 December 1863; Hamilton *Evening Times*, 1 June 1864; 10 November 1864).

[64]TTS, 10 August 1867.

[65]CLC, various volumes; *Globe*, 11 May 1854; 25 July 1867; 15 November 1967; *The Locomotive Engineers' Monthly Journal*, Department of Labour Library, Ottawa, January 1867, 12.

[66]Using, with one change, the definitions and divisions used by P.G. Goheen, *Victorian Toronto, 1850–1900* (Chicago, 1970), 229. He puts printers in the 'less-skilled' category; I place them in the 'skilled' category.

[67]J.I. Cooper, 'The Quebec Ship Labourers' Benevolent Society', *CHR* 1949, 336–43.

[68]Williams, 111, 116–18.

[69]CLC, vol. 148—ASE file.

[70]TTS, 11 January 1866.

[71]See Williams, p. 135; CLC vol. 247—ASE file; TTS, 8 January 1868. IMU local 28 (Toronto) had 96 members, Hamilton's ASE Branch 91, Montreal's ASE 77, the TTS 75 and IMU Local 26 in Hamilton 62.

27

Mid-Nineteenth-Century Quebec Agriculture

J.I. Little

While not necessarily concurring about the causes, most historians of Quebec would agree that nineteenth-century Quebec experienced a substantial agricultural crisis. That crisis involved several factors. One was a tendency for French-Canadian farmers to continue to cultivate grain, especially wheat, on land exhausted through generations of such cultivation without a corresponding restoration of fertility through improved farming practice. Ontario agriculture was likely equally slovenly, but Ontario farmers found it easier to move on to rich new land when the old became worn out, partly because of their geographical proximity to the western frontiers. Newly opened land available to farmers in what would become Quebec, such as in the Eastern Townships, was not very fertile. Because of the differences in the natural potential of the soil cultivated by French-Canadian and English-Canadian farmers in the province of united Canada, comparisons of the two groups have never been easy to make.

The extent to which farming practice was culturally determined —and which cultural factors were determinant—is problematic. In the following essay, J.I. Little examines the evolution of agriculture in two districts of the Eastern Townships populated by both French and English Canadians, the latter including a large number of Scots in one of the districts. In Compton Township, until the 1860s the French Canadians farmed in a similar fashion to the English Canadians, albeit rather less efficiently. In the 1860s, the number of French-Canadian farmers increased substantially; many were part-time farmers, not responsive to new farming opportunities. In Winslow Township, among the Scots land consolidation made possible increases in production per farmer, while French-Canadian population growth made a similar expansion of production per farmer impossible. In both townships, the

French-Canadian population grew more rapidly than the English-Canadian, and a larger proportion of French Canadians than English Canadians moved into part-time farming.

What conclusions can be inferred from the comparisons of French-Canadian and English-Canadian farming discussed by Little? Why did the French-Canadian population increase more rapidly? Why did French-Canadian farms not grow in size to the same extent as English-Canadian farms? Given the discussion of occupational plurality and agroforestry in Reading 18, what dynamic was probably at work among French Canadians in the Eastern Townships?

This article first appeared, titled 'The Social and Economic Development of Settlers in Two Quebec Townships, 1851–1870', in Donald Akenson, ed., *Canadian Papers in Rural History* I, 89–101.

The period between 1850 and Confederation was a transitional one for Quebec's agriculture. A substitute had to be found for the wheat economy, but it was with considerable hesitation that the farmers of the old seigneurial zone followed the example set by the Eastern Townships in turning to dairy production. The habitants clung to outmoded methods of farming in spite of improving markets, transportation facilities, and educational propaganda.[1] They extended their clearings as much as possible (cleared land to occupied land in Quebec increased from 44.4 per cent to 51.7 per cent between 1851 and 1870), but the majority did not increase their pasturage or improve their farming techniques.[2] The principal reason for such reluctance to improve may have been that repeated subdivisions had left many with too little land to accommodate an improved mixed type of agriculture; not only did pasture and fodder land demand a more extensive acreage than commercial crops, but field rotation and mechanization also required comparatively large units.[3] Certainly, agricultural ignorance did not prevent French-Canadian colonists from adapting quickly and relatively efficiently to the Eastern Townships landscape, where the hills and poor transportation network made a livestock economy necessary. What did hinder their progress, as we shall see, was a tendency to maintain small farms while their English-speaking neighbours consolidated their holdings.

This article traces the evolution of agriculture, over a twenty-year period, in the young township of Winslow and in the well-established township of Compton. An examination of the production of the anglophones in both townships provides a standard of comparison with the French-speaking farmers, while improving our understanding of the relationship between culture and economic development in Quebec.

Eastern Townships: counties and railroads, 1870.

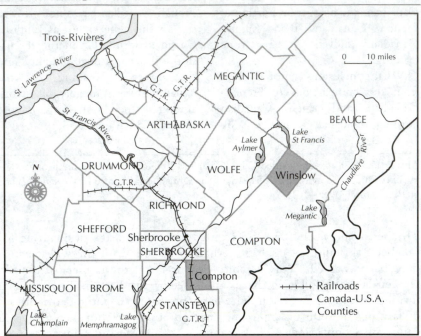

Compton Township

Because of its relatively fertile soil and its proximity to the town of Sherbrooke, Compton was one of the more prosperous of the Eastern Townships during the nineteenth century. As early as 1815 the surveyor-general, Joseph Bouchette, discovered a flourishing settlement of Americans there, with saw and grist mills, potasheries and pearlasheries, and about 700 inhabitants.[4] Subsequent progress was slow until the mid-forties when tariffs offered some protection against American competition in the province's agricultural market. Several years later the St Lawrence and Atlantic Railroad brought Upper Canadian products to the Townships for the first time, but this was offset by the proliferation of industries in Sherbrooke, and by the rapid expansion of the market south of the border.[5] By 1851 there were 2,718 inhabitants of Compton Township, 478 of whom were French Canadians.[6] In 1831 all nine French-speaking families had been farmers, but in 1851 only one-third of them were in this category.[7] As a rule, the francophones were a widely scattered, transient population, many stopping only to earn enough money to continue on their way to the United States.[8]

Most of the French-Canadian farmers operated on a very small scale; over half of them had fewer than twenty acres cleared, and nearly two-thirds owned no more than five cattle. In sharp contrast, all but 16 per cent of their English-speaking neighbours had more than twenty improved acres, and only a third of them had fewer than six cattle. On average, the English-Canadian farmer owned twice as much cleared land and almost three times as many cattle as his French-Canadian counterpart. He produced four times as much beef, and twice as much pork. Significantly, the relatively poor showing of the French-Canadian newcomers was not caused by any attempt on their part to perpetuate the grain economy of the St Lawrence homeland. Indeed, the two populations farmed similarly. Both placed an emphasis on seed crops, with oats being by far the most popular, followed by buckwheat, potatoes, and wheat.

One encouraging development for the French Canadians was their crop yields, which compared quite favourably with those of their neighbours. They might grow only half as much in total as the English Canadians, but they had only half as much land under cultivation. They were relatively more productive than the anglophones with wheat,[9] rye, and Indian corn, and they were reasonably close with barley and buckwheat. The anglophone production of oats and potatoes, which were the two major crops was, however, markedly superior as was that of animal products. Their cows averaged 48.1 pounds of butter and 17.5 pounds of cheese each, while one belonging to a francophone yielded 40.1 pounds of butter and only 1.9 pounds of cheese.[10]

More surprising, given that the French Canadians had done less land clearing (an average of 35 per cent of each of their lots was improved, compared with 52 per cent of each anglophone lot), is the fact that each of them produced only half as much maple sugar as did the average English Canadian. The reason for this seems to be that even the most advanced English-speaking farmers were reluctant to give up their precious sugar lots.[11]

It is clear, therefore, that the French-speaking farmer followed a less extensive and slightly less efficient mode of agriculture than did the English Canadian, but one which was very similar in nature. A major handicap of the French Canadians was the fact that much of their land was recently settled and of inferior quality.[12] Given their adaptability, however, there seemed to be little reason to doubt that they would make significant advances during the next decade.

Conditions continued to improve for Eastern Township agriculture during the fifties, with railroads and the 1854 Reciprocity Treaty which gave greater access to the growing American market. Compton, through which the St Lawrence and Atlantic (future Grand Trunk) Railroad passed in 1854, responded more to the American demand for cattle than to that for dairy products. Butter production increased, but cheese declined, while the number of cows remained constant. Young cattle, on the other hand, nearly doubled from 1,214 to 2,066 head. Most of them must have been sold on the hoof because dressed beef production dropped from 77,600 to 40,800 pounds. Also, Compton farmers responded more enthusiastically than most others in the Townships to the American demand for wool. Production in the fifties almost doubled, rising from 9,871 to 17,495 pounds. The fodder crops—oats, buckwheat, and turnips—all made significant gains, though hay declined. As for cash crops, competition from the West caused the production of wheat to decline, but the Compton farmers did respond to the American brewers' demand for barley, and they greatly increased their maple sugar production. Finally, potatoes made a dramatic recovery from the blight of the late forties and early fifties.

Because the major preoccupation remained cattle raising, which was less labour intensive and demanded larger agricultural units than did the earlier more self-sufficient type of agriculture, the number of Compton farmers actually declined by eighteen to a total of 340 in 1861, while improved land increased by 4,500 acres. The French Canadians were affected by this development to a greater extent than were the anglophones, for they lost fourteen from their 1851 total number of thirty-seven. They more than compensated with the increase in the number of labourers (thirty-four to fifty-seven), but this was a very transient group. Even the landholders were mobile; of the forty-two families listed in 1851, only eight were still present in 1860, and four in 1870.

Though many of the French-Canadian farmers arrived in Compton relatively late—between 1851 and 1860—they adapted very quickly to local economic conditions. Their average holding grew from seventy-three acres in 1851 to 120 acres in 1860, with sixty-two improved in 1860 as compared with twenty-six in 1851. Their cattle increased from 4.1 per farm in 1851 to 10.3 in 1860, and horses doubled from one to nearly two each. Pigs were still raised primarily for home consumption, as they averaged only one and a half per family. The most striking advance made by the francophones was in their crops. The harvest of 154.4 bushels per farmer in 1851 became 534.8 bushels ten years later. Advances were made in all the grains except wheat, but the crucial ones were oats, potatoes, and buckwheat. The French Canadians even turned to raising turnips, used for winter fodder, and modest gains were made in the harvesting of hay. In contrast to the situation in 1851 they owned almost as much land as did the English Canadians, kept almost as many cattle and sheep, and their crop yields were quite similar.[13] True, the quality of their livestock appears to have remained decidedly inferior (valued at $379.50 as against the anglophone return of $491.80 per farm), and they still produced less butter and cheese,[14] yet encouraging gains had clearly been made during the fifties.

Between 1860 and 1870 Compton continued to follow the general trend of the Eastern Townships by increasing cattle (15 per cent over the previous census), pigs (47 per cent), butter (21 per cent), hay (49 per cent), potatoes and turnips (39 per cent), and wool (9 per cent), all at the expense of cash crops. The number of horses remained constant, however, while they increased by 23 per cent in the region as a whole. Reflecting this discrepancy, oats production went down by 31 per cent between 1860 and 1870 in Compton, and only 12 per cent in the Townships region generally. Compton farmers clearly were turning more to dairying, and were shipping less live-stock to the United States, for, unlike the previous decade, the increase in milk cows was greater than that in young cattle. Butter manufacturing did not develop at a faster rate than in the fifties, but cheese factories sprang up in response to British demand in the late sixties. This was a crucial devel-opment because the American market had become much more restricted with the abrogation of the reciprocity treaty and the cessation of the Civil War in 1866.

Between 1860 and 1870, the trend towards dairy and livestock was again reflected by an expansion in the acreage of the English-speaking farmers, and by a slight decline in their numbers.[15] But, in sharp contrast to the fifties, the number of French-Canadian landowners increased dramatically (from twenty-six to sixty-three). This did not reflect an overall improvement of their status in Compton. Twelve of the twenty-six farmers in 1860 were still there in 1870, but many of the newcomers had purchased small lots. The percentage of francophones who had cleared less than ten acres was twice as high as that of the anglophones. This indicates that many of the French-Canadian landowners were not full-time farmers, and in fact only forty-three are listed as such. The number of labourers increased from fifty-seven to seventy-six, while the skilled craftsmen were up from fifteen to twenty-two.[16] The decline in the average size of the holdings (from 120.0 to 93.4 acres) and in land cleared (from 62.1 to 54.1 acres) does not therefore mean that all the French-Canadian farmers in the township were regressing. The small core of established farmers were not subdividing their holdings, as in the seigneuries, for 62 per cent of them had over thirty acres of improved land, as compared to 70 per cent of the anglophones.

The same can be said concerning cattle, for though they averaged only 5.4 per farmer, eighteen of the owners were not even listed as landholders. These people seldom owned more than one or two cows, so they make the general agricultural situation look worse than it actually was. Of course, some English Canadians were also in this part-time farming category, but not to the same degree as were the francophones. Only 44.5 per cent of the former owned fewer than five cattle as compared with 54.4 per cent of the French Canadians. This is not to argue that the French Canadians were making great progress in Compton, for they clearly were still an unstable population. However, they did include a core of reasonably progressive farmers: five had cleared more than 150 acres of land and owned between twenty-one and fifty head of cattle. Yet, overall the average productivity margin of English

Canadians over French Canadians increased.[17] The English Canadians were quicker to adopt innovations—they gave considerable attention to carrots, hops, apples, and honey for the first time, while the French Canadians tended to ignore them.

In summary, it would appear that the sixties was a decade of prosperity for the average English-speaking farmer in Compton township, but for only a limited number of the francophones. This was the price the newcomers had to pay for increasing their numerical strength in a township which had long been settled, and whose original inhabitants were reluctant to leave, for the time being at least.

Winslow Township

There were no inhabitants in the mountainous and isolated township of Winslow prior to 1848 when French Canadians and immigrants from the Hebrides took up free fifty-acre land grants offered by the government along the St Francis and Lake Megantic colonization roads. Winslow became the meeting place of two distinct population movements—French Canadians extended southward from the Stratford and Garthby colonies (in Wolfe County) fostered by Quebec City's Société de Colonisation des Townships, while Gaelic-speaking Scots moved north to avoid making payments to the British American Land Company (BAL). The Presbyterian Highlanders and the Catholic French Canadians remained remarkably aloof from each other, with each group almost totally restricted to its own municipality until late in the century when francophones began to buy farms from the departing Scots.

Winslow was further divided by a physical boundary, for a swamp two miles in width forced the settlers on the east side of the township to look for a market and supply centre in Quebec, 110 miles away, while those to the west had to travel only nine miles, albeit four of them through swamps, before reaching the BAL Company road to Sherbrooke.[18] Eventually Sherbrooke became the metropolis for the whole township once the colonization roads were completed. In comparison with the French Canadians in Compton Township, those of Winslow were not only isolated from the influence of progressive anglophone farmers but were also remote from the demands of an external market. They therefore had greater handicaps to overcome if they were to adopt the basically livestock and dairy economy of the older townships.

Many of the French-speaking settlers were young men (the average age of the landowners was only thirty) who had been neighbours in the South Shore parishes near the Bécancour River.[19] By 1851 there were eighty-four families, all Catholics, all but fourteen farmers, and all living in twenty log cabins and twenty-six 'block' houses. Forty-five of the French-Canadian colonists had claimed only the free fifty-acre lots, while ten took advantage of the additional fifty acres offered at four shillings per acre. In addition, two owned 150 acres, one owned 200, and five squatted on unsurveyed land. Two-thirds had not cleared more than ten acres in 1851, and none owned more than five cattle—in fact they averaged only one each. One sheep and one pig per farmer, and one horse per two farmers, completed the meagre livestock inventory of North Winslow. Not surprisingly, especially because 1851 was a famine year in the area, very little hay and oats were grown. Potatoes constituted almost half the eighty bushels of crops each farmer harvested. The rugged environment of Winslow effectively forced the French Canadians to suppress their strong preference for wheaten bread.[20]

The Scots arrived in Winslow about the same time as the francophones, but they were said to have better land (though swampy and subject to early frost),[21] and all but two of the twenty-six families owned at least one hundred acres. Each Scot had close to four cattle and four sheep to the French Canadian's one; consequently he produced over three times as much butter and five times as much wool. The Scots did not raise as much pork or make as much maple sugar as did the francophones, and they had only three horses among them. But they harvested 126 bushels of grain and root crops each, as compared with eighty bushels for the French Canadians. Not only did they have more land under cultivation, their crop yields, though disastrously low, nevertheless were slightly higher than those of the French Canadians.

The Scots, like the French Canadians, concentrated on growing potatoes, but barley and oats were their major secondary crops, while the French Canadians placed almost as much emphasis upon rye as they did on barley. Significantly, the Scots grew a surprising 8.5 bushels of turnips each, this being over twice as much as the wealthier English Canadian farmers in Compton township. These turnips were important in building soil fertility and may well have been used to make up for the small amount of hay they harvested. In nearly every respect, then, the Scots had a head start over the French Canadians in 1851.

By 1857, when both the St Francis and Megantic colonization roads were finally completed, North Winslow's arable land had all been settled. A visiting Catholic missionary wrote that the parish was already overcrowded.[22] There were 168 French-speaking families, twice as many as in 1851. Only eighteen family heads were listed as labourers, three were servants, and two were tradesmen. In sharp contrast to the French Canadians in Compton, over half of those who had settled in Winslow in 1851 were still there in 1860, and the age of the average landowner had increased from thirty to thirty-nine.

Most of the French Canadian homes were still log cabins, but real progress had been made. The township had four grist mills, three saw mills, and a carding mill in 1860, where there had been only one saw mill and one grist mill nine years earlier. The average French–Canadian farmer had cleared twice as much land as in 1850 and was now raising three and a half times as many cattle and sheep, and twice as many pigs. Butter production had multiplied by five in ten years, and maple sugar by two. Finally, the average harvest was over twice as large, with potatoes still in first place, followed by barley and oats. For fodder, the growth in the number of cattle was reflected primarily by the increase in hay. The improved production was due not only to an extension in acreage. Crop yields were significantly higher than in 1851.

Relative to their 1851 base, the French Canadians proportionately equalled the Scots' improvements in cattle, butter, horses, pigs, and sheep, but this did not narrow the gap between the two groups. In 1860 the average francophone's livestock was worth only $111 as compared to $160 for that of the average Scot.[23] In addition, the Scots maintained their advance over the French Canadians in grain production. Reflecting their greater interest in the raising of cattle, the Scots placed less emphasis than the francophones upon potatoes and oats, and more upon turnips and hay. As in 1851, the most startling contrast was in the commercial crops of rye and barley, for the French Canadians grew nearly all of the rye in the township, while the Scots grew most of the barley. That the Scots were beginning to specialize more in the sale of cattle and in dairying is indicated by the fact that, in contrast to the French Canadians, their wool production did not increase substantially during the fifties, and that their maple sugar and beef production actually declined. Encouraging as their progress was, the French Canadians still were less in tune than were their Scottish neighbours with the market economy of the Eastern Townships.

It would have been difficult for the French Canadians to specialize until they began to expand the size of their holdings. This of course was impossible while their population continued to grow. Even though most of the arable lots in North Winslow had been settled in the fifties, nineteen additional French-speaking families took land during the sixties. The population remained relatively stable, for 40 per cent of the landowners listed in 1860 were again there in 1870, and the average age had moved up from thirty-nine to forty-one. The vast majority of the family heads still were farmers, but the tradesmen had become more diversified; the community now included a physician, a notary, a teacher, and a curé. In fact, Winslow's struggling colonists fostered a respectable industrial growth, for there now were five grist mills, five saw mills, two wool carding establishments, and one iron forge. In comparison with 1860, the mills processed twenty times as much grain (29,550 bushels per year) and five times as much wood (103,400 feet per year), while the carding factories consumed 21,000 pounds of wool, and the forge produced $500 in iron goods.

Although growth of the francophone population had caused some reduction in the lot size, the average farmer owned ten more acres of improved land than he had ten years earlier. Sixty per cent of them now had between twenty-one and fifty cleared acres. Cattle had increased by an average of one per person, and sheep by two, while horses and pigs remained substantially the same. The average butter production was up by one third, maple sugar down by one fifth, and wool down by one half.

Granted, the Winslow francophones were responding, however falteringly, to general market conditions in the Eastern Townships where dairy products were one of the few categories to enjoy a steady demand after the Civil War and reciprocity had come to an end. This was reflected in the grain grown, with less emphasis being placed on wheat, barley, and rye, and more on the fodder crops, buckwheat, oats, and hay. The yields for the only two crops given in the census, wheat and potatoes, were slightly higher,[24] but the total harvest for each farmer had not changed since 1860.

Among the Scots, on the other hand, there was a 23 per cent increase in the grain production per farmer during the sixties. This was made possible by a consolidation of holdings among a smaller number of families. The population declined from 868 to 782 to allow the average farm to grow by thirty-seven acres. Even more significant, the expansion of improved land on the Scot's farm was double that of the French Canadian. He was therefore able to increase his herd by an average of two and a half cattle, as compared to one for the French Canadian. However, the Scots had slowed their move towards dairy production, for the ratio of milch cows to other cattle did not change, and butter production increased by only 30 per cent. Like the French Canadians, they still needed a supplementary income, but this no longer came from the cash crops, barley and rye. By 1870 the Scots had turned to wool (production multiplied five times in the 1860s). In terms of external markets, this was a regression for both groups because the American demand for barley remained high after the Civil War, while that for wool and flax had declined. In appears that the Winslow farmers could not compete against the increased Ontario production of barley,[25] so they turned to domestic industry as a new source of ready cash. The Scots' wool went towards the home weaving of cloth and flannel (multiplied five times since 1860), while the French Canadians manufactured linen (multiplied four times) from their flax.

To the French Canadians, a much more important diversion from livestock and dairying had become the timber industry.[26] For domestic consumption, each Scottish colonist chopped twenty-three cords of firewood to the francophone's twenty-seven, but for commercial purposes, he cut only five logs to the francophone's fifty-one. Almost all the square timber listed by the census was the property of two local French-Canadian entrepreneurs. Unlike the timber operators of the Saguenay-Lac St Jean region, those in the Eastern Townships did not monopolize the agricultural market, thereby forcing the colonists to work in the woods in order to survive.[27] Nonetheless, the Winslow French Canadians, without consolidating their farms by reducing their own numbers, had little choice but to sacrifice agricultural progress for subsistence farming and logging.

Conclusion

As a rule, the farmers of both Compton Township and the isolated Winslow were sensitive to external market conditions. The French Canadians within the two townships concentrated upon the same major products as the anglophones, but their crop yields usually were not as high. Whether or not this was caused by more careless agricultural practices, or simply inferior land, the primary handicap of the French Canadians was the smallness of their farms. Their failure to consolidate their holdings cannot simply be ascribed to custom acquired from generations of overcrowded conditions in the seigneurial zone because the Winslow Scots had migrated from a still more rudimentary economy where fishing and kelp-gathering were crucial adjuncts to agriculture.[28] In addition, during these early years of settlement the Scots too were isolated from the well-established English and Canadian farmers, by language as well as by geography.

The cultural identity of the French Canadians seems to have been a handicap primarily because it discouraged them from leaving Quebec, except as a last resort. Scots and English Canadians, on the other hand, did not hesitate to emigrate to greener pastures south and west. This in essence was the dilemma faced by French-Canadian nationalists who deplored the exodus from the province at a time when conditions were not ripe for large-scale industrialization. In idealizing agrarian self-sufficiency, they were making a virtue out of what they perceived to be a necessity. That this implied a static and insular society was probably more a by-product of their nationalism than a primary end in itself (though not necessarily an unwelcome one).

Suggestions for Further Reading

Jean Hamelin and Yves Roby, *Histoire Economique du Québec, 1851–1896* (Montreal, 1971).

J.I. Little, *Crofters and Habitants: Settler Society, Economy, and Culture in a Quebec Township, 1848–1881* (Montreal, 1991).

John McCallum, *Unequal Beginnings: Agriculture and Economic Development in Quebec and Ontario until 1870* (Toronto, 1980).

Notes

[1] R.L. Jones, 'The Agricultural History of Lower Canada, 1850–1867', *Agricultural History* XIX (1945), 220–2; Jean Hamelin et Yves Roby, *Histoire Economique du Québec, 1851–1896* (Montréal: Fides, 1971), 185–204.

[2] Hamelin et Roby, 193.

[3]Kenneth Kelley maintains that improved mixed farming was not adopted in Upper Canada during the first half of the nineteenth century because it was not economical on small units. K. Kelley, 'The Transfer of British Ideas on Improved Farming to Ontario during the First Half of the Nineteenth Century', *Ontario History* LXIII (1971), 110. Though many of the large French Canadian landowners of LaPrairie had no better crop yields than the smaller ones during the thirties, they were able to concentrate more upon the raising of cattle. F. Ouellet, 'Répartition de la propriété foncière et types d'exploitation agricole dans la seigneurie de Laprairie durant les années 1830', in *Elements d'histoire sociale du Bas-Canada* (Montréal: Hurtubise HMH Ltée, 1972), 144, 148–9.

[4]Joseph Bouchette, *A topographical description of the Province of Lower Canada, with remarks upon Upper Canada, and on the relative connexion of both provinces with the United States of America* (London: W. Faden, 1815), 356–7.

[5]R.L. Jones, *History of Agriculture in Ontario* (Toronto: University of Toronto Press, 1946, reprinted 1977), 133, 179–84; R.L. Jones 'French-Canadian Agriculture in the St Lawrence Valley, 1815–1850', in W.T. Easterbrook and M.H. Watkins, eds, *Approaches to Canadian Economic History* (Toronto: McClelland and Stewart, 1967), 126. See J.I. Little, 'The Peaceable Conquest. French Canadian Colonization in the Eastern Townships during the Nineteenth Century' (PhD thesis, University of Ottawa, 1976), 281–7, for Compton's economic development between 1831 and 1851.

[6]Of the 2,240 English-speaking individuals, 1,440 had been born in Canada, 562 in the United States, 336 in Great Britain, and 2 elsewhere.

[7]Unless otherwise indicated, the statistics in this article are from either the printed or manuscript census reports, which have been microfilmed by the Public Archives of Canada.

[8]Stanislas Drapeau, *Etudes sur les développements de la colonisation du Bas-Canada depuis 10 ans: (1851 à 1861)* (Québec: L. Brousseau 1863), 184.

[9]The wheat yields of twelve to fifteen bushels per acre in Compton were similar to those of the twenty-one most productive counties in Lower Canada, which averaged nine to fifteen bushels per acre. Fourteen Upper Canadian counties averaged sixteen to twenty bushels. J. Hamelin et F. Ouellet, 'Les rendements agricoles dans les seigneuries et les cantons du Québec: 1700–1850', in C. Galarneau et Elzéar Lavoie, eds, *France et Canada Français du XVIe au XXe Siècle* (Québec: Les Presses de l'Université Laval, 1966), 98.

[10]These averages compare favourably with Upper Canada where each cow produced 53.8 pounds of butter and 7.5 pounds of cheese. In Lower Canada, as a whole, the yields were only 33 pounds of butter and 1.8 pounds of cheese. *Ibid.*

[11]Until the 1880s Compton Township produced as much maple sugar as it did butter and cheese.

[12]See comments of the census taker in the 1851 manuscript census.

[13]The average crop yield for wheat and potatoes in Lower Canada in 1860 was 10.9 and 107.3 bushels per acre, respectively. Esdras Minville, *L'Agriculture*, I (Montréal: Fides, 1943), 504. Not only was Compton agriculture becoming more extensive, with expansion of improved land, but it was following the pattern of the northern United States by becoming more intensive in response to improved market conditions at mid-century. See Clarence H. Danhof, *Change in Agriculture: The Northern United States, 1820–1870* (Cambridge: Harvard University Press, 1969).

[14]The value of the cattle in an average Quebec farm in 1860 was $244 (Minville, 500). The quality of the cattle owned by Compton's French Canadians, like that of the English Canadians, was clearly improving, for the average cow owned by a francophone now produced 70.7 pounds of butter and cheese, as compared with 80.3 pounds for the anglophone. In 1851 the figures had been 42.0 and 65.6 respectively.

[15]There were fifteen fewer English-speaking farmers, but they owned 3,596 more acres and had cleared an additional 5,135 since 1860. Seven of these farmers had over 400 improved acres each.

[16]One might normally assume that this was part of the mushrooming migration to New England, but twenty-six of the families included English-speaking wives, and eleven had one or more members born in the United States.

[17]The two populations grew 9.3 and 16.8 bushels of wheat per acre, and 153 versus 232 bushels of potatoes per acre, respectively.

[18]PAC, 1851–52 manuscript census.

[19]Archives de la Chancellerie de l'Archevêché de Sherbrooke [ACAS], Papiers des paroisses, Saint-Romain de Winslow, no. 7, N. Bélanger à Mgr. Signay, 28 mars 1849.

[20]In most colonization areas the French Canadians devoted at least 10 per cent of their crop to wheat for their own use. Hamelin et Roby, 194.

[21]Remark of the census taker in PAC, 1851–52 manuscript census.

[22]ACAS, Papiers des paroisses, Saint-Romain, N. Godbout à Mgr. Cooke, 8 Sept. 1857.

[23]The butter production of the average cow owned by the French Canadians actually declined from 29.0 to 27.3 pounds between 1851 and 1860, while the Scots' increased from 25.0 to 45.5 pounds. In addition the Scots manufactured a small amount of cheese.

[24]The average yield for wheat and potatoes increased from 49.3 bushels per acre in 1860 to 62.2 in 1870. This is slightly higher than the Scots' yield of 61.7 bushels per acre in 1870.

[25]Jones, *History of Agriculture in Ontario*, 222, 239–41; 'The Agricultural History of Lower Canada', 216.

[26]The 1870 census records 6,142 cords of firewood, 7,022 logs, and 1,848,616 cubic feet of square timber.

[27]The Winslow francophones had more livestock than those in the Saguenay Valley in 1860.

	Hébertville	*Winslow*
Average holding	139.1 acres	81.2 acres
Pasture	7.6 acres	5.9 acres
Cattle	2.8	4.2
Cows	1.0	1.4
Horses	0.9	0.8
Sheep	1.6	3.3
Pigs	0.5	2.0
Butter	38 lb.	41 lb.

However, they do not seem to have been any better farmers, for they grew only 16.1 bushels of barley per acre, as compared to 13.3 for those of Hébertville, and their cows yielded only 27.3 pounds of butter each, as compared to 38.6 for those of Hébertville. Normand Séguin, 'Notre-Dame d'Hébertville, 1850–1900. Une Paroisse de colonisation au XIXe Siècle' (Thèse de doctorat, Université d'Ottawa, 1975), 13–14, 22–4, 175–6. Séguin's analysis of the exploitative relationship between the Lac St-Jean timber companies and farmers has been challenged in Gérard Bouchard, 'Introduction à l'étude de la société seguenayenne aux XIXᵉ et XXᵉ siècles, *RHAF* XXXI (1977), 13–16.

[28]Malcolm, Gray, *The Highland Economy 1750–1850* (Edinburgh: Oliver and Boyd, 1957), 144.

28

Administration of Law and Justice on the Frontier

David Ricardo Williams

Despite the fascination of generations of Canadian historians with political and constitutional questions, the development of Canadian law was until recently discussed chiefly by judges and lawyers as background context to the rendering of judicial decisions. Over the past two decades, the history of law has become one of the many flourishing specialist subfields in Canada. Yet one searches the standard historical journals and textbooks in vain for material on the development of Canadian law, which still probably suffers from a common perception of being both an arcane and an essentially dull subject.

In the goldfields of British Columbia, where hundreds of American gold miners constituted the bulk of the early population, law and the administration of justice was of serious import. David Ricardo Williams discusses the administration of justice in early British Columbia, seeing it not only as a legal question but as a political one as well. One key development for the mining community was the introduction of a quasi-judicial system copied from Australia. Another piece of legislation of potential importance was the Native Evidence Act of 1865. Williams distinguishes between the imposition of British criminal justice and civil justice, but argues that both were more easily imposed on an American population than contemporaries had anticipated.

Why was the introduction of British justice regarded as a matter of such high priority in British Columbia in the 1850s? Were the American miners 'anarchists'? Why was the Gold Fields Act so successful? To what extent did British justice succeed because it adapted itself to the needs and wishes of the miners?

This article first appeared, titled 'The Administration of Criminal and Civil Justice in the Mining Camps and Frontier Communities of British Columbia', in Louis Knafla, ed., *Law & Justice in a New Land: Essays in Western Canadian Legal History* (Toronto: 1986), 215–32.

The newly founded colony of British Columbia was populated in its early years almost entirely by American gold miners, many of whom had had experience in the California gold rush with various forms of self-government, both in respect of mining regulation and criminal justice. As a consequence, some new laws were imported into British Columbia shortly before the founding of the colony. As well, the colonial government proclaimed various statutes which made the American mining population comfortable in its new environment and willing to accept government regulation. This attitude led in turn to the peaceable settlement of British Columbia, free of civil strife. Some colonial legislation drew disapproval from London where officials looked on the measures as radical because they did not conform to traditional notions of law enforcement. But only one measure of any consequence was actually disallowed—that which purported to abolish the need for issuing commissions as a condition of holding a valid criminal assize.

Any account of the administration of justice in the colonial period must to a considerable extent be an account of Matthew Baillie Begbie, who for eight years was the only high court judge in the colony, and for another four years the only one on the mainland. Not only did he conduct trials, he also made the rules by which they were governed and drafted the most important statutes of the early colonial period which, in turn, he was frequently called upon to interpret. His judicial decisions were often unorthodox, and not at all what one would have expected from a Victorian judge; but they shaped the law, and his administrative decrees settled the framework of trial procedure.[1]

On 2 August 1858, the United Kingdom Parliament created the Colony of British Columbia. Roughly two-thirds of what is now the mainland of the province was incorporated into the new colony; the northernmost one-third, the Stikine territory, was added by further enactment in 1863. This vast area had been the preserve of the Hudson's Bay Company whose jurisdiction had straddled the 49th parallel until 1846. Queen Victoria decreed that the name of the colony should be 'British Columbia', a happy choice, as the 'British' element was to prove the determinant factor in the administrative and judicial development of the fledgling colony. Its creation was in reaction to the gold rush to the lower Fraser River in 1857 and 1858, although Edward Bulwer-Lytton, the Imperial Colonial Secretary (and novelist) who guided the new colony, was motivated as much by his aversion for the trading privileges of the Hudson's Bay Company as by a desire to preserve British North America on the Pacific coast. Nonetheless, with considerable prescience he carefully selected the apparatus of government—the administrative officials, the engineers to build roads and bridges, the police and the judiciary—all of whom were sent out post-haste from the United Kingdom to establish and maintain the British presence amongst an alien population. The native Indian population was not regarded as 'alien' (perhaps because they were not regarded at all), but the tens of thousands of miners who had flocked into the colony in 1858 were the main concern. How does a handful of colonial administrators, newly appointed, control great numbers of recently arrived settlers or transients, who themselves have had little or no experience with the forms of British government and law?

During the rule of the Hudson's Bay Company, those charged with serious offences were triable in Upper Canada, but it is not known how many persons were sent to 'Canada' for trial.[2] Civil suits were also litigable in Upper Canada, but there cannot have been many of these, if any. The Act creating the colony empowered its governor

> to make provision for the administration of justice therein and generally to make, ordain, and establish all such laws, institutions and ordinances as may be necessary for peace, order and good government[3]

James Douglas, the appointed governor, and the newly arrived Matthew Baillie Begbie, the appointed Judge of the Supreme Court of British Columbia, met at Fort Langley on the Fraser River on 19 November 1858 to pronounce various proclamations concerning the formation of the colony, one of which was the English Law Act. The latter provided that from that date the law of England both in criminal and civil matters should apply to British Columbia unless altered by specific legislation or rendered inapplicable by 'local circumstances'.[4] Thus the framework of law was established and the judicial system of British Columbia, its officials and its judiciary, were to be governed by the law of England. Gone were the arguments about jurisdiction: British Columbia courts were given cognizance of all civil suits and criminal trials with appeals only to the Privy Council in London.

The framework was soon to be tested. Miners had poured into British Columbia in 1858, estimates of their number running from 15,000 to 31,000, but most of these early arrivals did not stay long. One observer, the American agent John Nugent who had been sent to Vancouver Island in 1858 to report to the United States Congress on the treatment of American nationals by the Hudson's Bay Company, estimated the total number of arrivals by sea at 23,000 and by land from the United States at 8,000. He estimated that by the end of 1858 there were only 3,000 left.[5]

Those who did stay, joined by later arrivals, gradually worked their way into the interior of the colony seeking gold, and mining camps and settlements were established along the Fraser and Thompson rivers. New Westminster was fixed as the capital of the colony in 1859. That year and the next saw the advance eastward to Similkameen, and north to Quesnel and Barkerville in the Cariboo. At the height of gold production in 1863 about 4,000 persons lived in the Quesnel/Barkerville region. By 1864 gold seekers had established a camp at Wild Horse Creek (now the site of Fort Steele Provincial Park) which one year later grew to a population of 2,000. There was a brief flurry of mining on the upper Columbia River in 1866, and five years later, in the Omineca and Cassiar regions, formerly in the Stikine territory but by then part of British Columbia.[6]

Mining Camp Justice American Style

Although Americans formed the largest fraction of the new arrivals, the population mix was remarkably heterogeneous, many of the Americans themselves possessing varied ethnic backgrounds. Many of these Americans had been through the California gold rush, and their knowledge of mining methods and familiarity with mining regulations lent an element of stability to the shifting population. Their desire to make money at mining by lawful methods was not understood by many colonial observers, who expressed surprise at the generally peaceable nature of miners and their amenability to constituted authority.[7] The American miners were encouraged to adopt that attitude by their own countryman, John Nugent, who counselled them to show 'a decent conformity with local regulations', and to display both 'obedience to the laws' and a 'proper show of respect for the authorities by whom those laws are administered'.[8]

In each mining camp could be found hard workers and layabouts, honest men and rogues, Christians and atheists, respectable women and prostitutes. Before a camp developed into a permanent town (if it did at all), the common characteristic was the frenetic activity of the residents. The prospect of gold running out gave an urgency to all activity: one must recover what gold there was as soon as possible. One's living habits had the same urgency. Judge Begbie penned an amusing aphorism about the habits of mind of the miners:

> The miner with gold dust conceals his riches, in order to avoid plunder—the miner who has none pretends to be rich in order to obtain credit.[9]

Like all aphorisms, this one is only partly true. Many successful miners squandered their money publicly, and many failures obtained no credit and left their claims. But the attitudes of the miners, particularly the Californians, became important in the development of both civil and criminal law in the colony. The imposition of English civil law accorded fairly easily with what they had been used to in the informal regulation of mining activity. In California, in the absence of governmental statute (until 1866), self-government was the norm, and making money was dependent upon stable and just self-regulation by the miners. There, as soon as miners established themselves at a gold-bearing site, they enacted rules which were intended to have the force of law. Whether in fact they had the force of law depended upon the integrity and single-minded purpose of those chosen to administer them. The typical California experience was to elect a three-man mining committee in whose hands rested decisions over the ownership and extent of claims. Although there were differences in detail from camp to camp, there were principles recognized by all: ensuring that all claims were of uniform size, laying down the conditions of use or occupation, recording all claims, and insisting that the record was conclusive.[10]

The size of claims was governed by the levelness or steepness of the banks of a creek. Regulations were passed to dictate for what period of time a claim could be left unattended without losing entitlement, either through illness or because the claimholder had gone to the nearest town on a bender; the overt leaving of mining tools for a period of days would ensure continued title. One could stake and have recognized a 10-foot wide cross-section of an auriferous creek, but how did one determine the reference points? From where did one start? And if there were outcroppings into the bed of the creek, were they to be counted as part of the bed over which the claim extended, or should the 10 feet be extended through the workable sections of the creek to compensate for the unyielding rock intrusion?

These were problems of a civil nature, frequently leading to disputes between individuals, not only in California, but also in British Columbia. But what of behaviour dangerous to the peace of the community? The mining camps in California evolved an efficient system of criminal law which worked, generally speaking, without undue harshness, except perhaps to Indians and Chinese who were considered by the standards of the time as persons not deserving equal protection before the law. In the California mining camps, rules governing potential criminal behaviour were regarded as necessary as those relating to the regulation of mining claims, and they developed as naturally. Because they were so fundamental to the welfare of the community, the entire community, in a sense, formed the tribunal. A large camp would select a presiding judicial officer, a sheriff and a 12-man jury. A member of the camp—perhaps someone with an education—would be appointed to defend a man accused of a serious crime. In smaller camps, votes on guilt or innocence would be restricted to those living in the camp where the alleged crime occurred, unless the crime was murder, in which case members of other camps could appear and cast their vote. This vigilante system of camp criminal justice filled a vacuum. No government body existed to control crime; instead, citizens filled the breach. The phenomenon was wrongly viewed in British Columbia as a form of anarchy—'lynch law'. One reads constantly in the reports of colonial officials in British Columbia of their worry that vigilantism would come to British Columbia, by which they meant that chaos would prevail.[11]

It was worries of that kind which prompted James Douglas late in 1857 to promulgate mining regulations for the mainland over which, as Governor of Vancouver Island only, he had no jurisdiction. On payment of a licence fee of 21 shillings (1 guinea), a person could prospect for gold on the Fraser

River within a claim 12 feet square. It was a condition of the licence that the miner give 'due and proper observance of Sundays'.[12] Much more detailed regulations were enacted in 1858, which required a bond of £2,000 (a very large sum of money) and payment of a royalty of 10 per cent before a claim could be worked. The claimholder was required to employ at least 20 persons within six months of being licensed. Claims could also be larger than those authorized the year before.[13] Obviously Douglas, by these stringent measures, hoped to achieve economic stability by encouraging large-scale operations and discouraging the individual miner and riff-raff. Such an attempt, however, was futile, both because the regulations, like their predecessors, were without legal effect, and because they could not withstand the onslaught of hordes of invading miners who imposed on themselves their own regulations which, if not legal, were not demonstrably illegal and were far more practical.

Details of mining regulations in three camps in the pre-colonial period, and another in the immediate post-colonial period, have survived. Two of the former were on the Fraser at Hills Bar and Fort Yale. Each set the claim size at a 25-foot width extending backward from mid-channel to high water mark. The Hills Bar regulations required one working day in three to maintain the claim, but Fort Yale insisted on only one in five; in each case the requirement would be relaxed in cases of sickness or, as at Fort Yale, in the case of discharging 'public business'. In wintertime, however, the severity of the climate often made active work impossible, and all claims were 'laid over' until the return of spring or more clement weather. Recorders registered the claims for a nominal fee, but there were severe limitations upon the number of claims an individual could hold.

These mining regulations were fairly humdrum and were exactly what one would have expected of a Californian gold miner. What sets apart the camp regulations in British Columbia, passed by perhaps some of the same individuals or others like them in California, were those which related to criminal conduct. Theft by a white man at Hills Bar could result in forfeiture of a claim held by him (not a surprising regulation), but the same camp forbade 'molesting' of Indians and prohibited the sale of liquor to them. Punishment for the latter offence could also result in forfeiture of a claim. The camp at Fort Yale went even further: all sales of liquor, to white and Indian alike, were prohibited, and all caches of liquor were to be destroyed. Any member of the mining camp found selling or in possession of liquor would be whipped and expelled. Similarly, if any miner of the camp sold firearms to an Indian, he would be lashed and expelled. These resolutions were not, however, passed in the interest of the Indians, but 'for the better protection of life and property' of the miners themselves. Still, the regulations are illuminating as they reflect the attitudes of a law-abiding community.[14] At Rock Creek in the Similkameen area similar mining regulations were made, but there the miners—true to the California mode—forbade Chinese from holding claims.[15]

The self-imposed laws made in 1864 by American miners at Wild Horse Creek in the Rocky Mountain Trench were by far the most extensive. The mining regulations were similar to those at Fort Yale and Hills Bar, but the miners set up a system of criminal justice very much like that found in the large California camps. They elected a judge who was to be remunerated for each case. He held office 'during good behaviour' or, an interesting provision, 'until the proper civil authorities arrive'. An elected 'prosecuting attorney' was to prosecute all cases. An elected sheriff attended to the summoning of juries, the arrest of suspects and the custody of prisoners. Similarly, a clerk of the court discharged the same duties as those of present day court clerks. A treasurer collected all fines which were to be used to defray the necessary expenses of carrying out camp laws, supported in every case by proper vouchers.[16] These remarkable provisions were passed by members of a mining camp six years after the establishment of the colony, the effective jurisdiction of which had not yet extended so far eastward, and five years after passage of the first colonial legislation regulating gold mining. Not long after their passage a British Columbia Gold Commissioner, J.C. Haines, travelled to Wild Horse Creek. He did not interfere with the camp mining regulations, but exercising his authority as a Justice of the Peace, he disarmed those who carried pistols and admonished them: 'Now, boys, there must be no shooting for if there is shooting there will surely be hanging'.[17]

More remarkable still was the symbolic act of submission by American miners to British justice represented by the British Columbia Colonial Secretary, Arthur Birch, who visited the camp late in 1864. He wrote:

> I found that before the arrival of Haines [the gold commissioner] "lynch law" had been established and rules framed. . . . They [the miners] appeared to have done their work honestly and well and I was pleased when they handed me, as representing British authority, the original of the rules in force, and expressed their gratification at my having travelled so far to look after their interests and all proposed to help to their utmost the British officials.[18]

In his reference to 'lynch law', Birch expressed an attitude typical of colonial officials: because camp law was informal it was therefore dangerous. He failed to appreciate, as we now can, that precisely the opposite was the case. It was not anarchy but order.

Gold Commissioners, J.P.s, and English Courts

Mining camp administration of justice in British Columbia was, however, short-lived, because in 1859 Douglas proclaimed the Gold Fields Act.[19] The central features of the Act were the creation of Gold Commissioners and Mining Boards, which had been a feature of Australian mining laws. Of great importance also was the requirement by which only registered 'free miners' could prospect for gold, upon payment of a relatively modest licence fee.

A Gold Commissioner was responsible for recording all registrations of free miners, all mineral claims, and sources of water used in the mining process. Because mining claims were worked hydraulically, water for sluicing gold out of the paydirt was very nearly as valuable as the gold itself. Entrepreneurs constructed flumes of rough lumber hewn from trees on the adjacent hills. Water was, in effect, a public utility closely regulated by the Gold Commissioner to ensure its availability to ordinary miners. Disputes between miners and those holding 'water privileges', as they were known, were of two kinds: the fairness of distribution, and the right of a water licencee to cross one mining claim to reach others. The result was a crazy jumble of flumes, as can be seen from contemporary photographs.

In addition to their administrative duties, Gold Commissioners exercised the criminal jurisdiction of a Justice of the Peace and enjoyed limited civil jurisdiction. They heard all disputes in the first instance involving title to claims or water privileges, subject to appeals to the Supreme Court in instances where more than £20 was involved in the dispute. On such an appeal the Supreme Court could, and often did, hear the case *de novo*. Litigation not involving title to claims or water was heard in the first instance by the Supreme Court except where the amount involved was less than £50, in which case the dispute was remitted to a Gold Commissioner for hearing.

On petition of 100 free miners, a Mining Board could be constituted, consisting of at least six and no more than twelve members who had power to make by-laws to alter claim sizes and water privileges, and to regulate the filing, holding and forfeiture of claims. All decisions were to be by a majority and were not to be effective until approved by the governor. Such Mining Boards were unknown in California, although a rough equivalent existed in the camp committee. Even though the governor held a veto power and also could dissolve a board if he wished, the boards represented democracy in action and took some of the steam out of objections to colonial mining policies, and to the one-man rule of Governor Douglas (at least until 1864).

The regulations laid down by the 1859 Act dealt with matters common to mining activity both in the United States and the colony. The standard placer claim size was that set by the miners at Fort Yale and Hills Bar, a rectangle 25 feet back from mid-channel to high water mark and extending downward into the river to infinity. Groups of free miners could hold up to a claim-and-a-half per member. The three-day rule applied as at Hills Bar; failure to work in that period entailed forfeiture of the claim unless the inactivity was caused by illness. The Gold Commissioner could also order a longer period of absence to allow fresh prospecting, and of course he could allow claims to be laid over in wintertime. Similarly, on pain of forfeiture, licencees of flowing water were required to use it for mining and not to waste it. The Act and its regulations, as well as succeeding legislation, gave rise to a great volume of mining litigation in the Cariboo region, which by 1861 had become the principal centre of the colony. For example, as early as June 1863, the year of peak production of gold in the Cariboo, 60 cases (mostly involving claim jumping or abandonment) had been decided and 18 more were outstanding. The Gold Commissioner, Peter O'Reilly, frequently sat from 10:00 a.m. to 7:00 p.m. without interruption.[20]

The general framework of the 1859 Act remained intact for six years. There were changes in detail. For example, it was early recognized that rectangular claims were impractical for narrow, twisting creeks with steep banks, and thus flexibility was later permitted.[21] Claim sizes were altered, and one miner was allowed to hold two claims, one by discovery and the other by purchase.

Much, if not all, of the 1859 Act had been drafted by Begbie who, in the early years of the colony, acted as much as Attorney General as High Court Judge.[22] Not only did he pen the Act, but he also promulgated it personally by walking from New Westminster to Kamloops to hand it out, like a broadsheet, to miners and government officials alike. The 1865 Act, which was far more sophisticated and detailed than earlier legislation, was not Begbie's handiwork; but until that year, by an extraordinary anomaly, he heard a great deal of litigation involving his own creation. As it happened, the bulk of mining litigation had occurred before 1865, by which date mining had begun to decline. It can seldom have happened that the judge of a senior trial court should often hear cases calling for interpretation of major legislation which he himself had drafted. Begbie gave no indication that he was troubled by the anomaly, and none of his contemporaries ever remarked on it—not even John Robson and Amor de Cosmos, two newspaper proprietors hostile to Begbie's supposed judicial autocracy. What was the alternative? There was no one else available to Douglas to draft the Gold Fields Act, and there was no other judge.

In 1865 all earlier mining legislation was repealed by a new Act.[23] Gold Commissioners were stripped of their power to hear criminal cases, but they were given unlimited jurisdiction to decide all mining disputes, even though appeals could still be taken to the Supreme Court, which retained the power to hear cases *de novo*.

Besides proclaiming mining laws which were generally well received, and some of which were familiar to miners accustomed to practices in the United States, the colonial government also proclaimed specific Acts designed to accommodate English criminal law to local conditions. This was a sensible attempt to make the administration of criminal law in the far-flung colony both workable and acceptable to its inhabitants.

In the early days of British Columbia there was not one person qualified to practise in an English court of law and only one who could practise in the separate colony of Vancouver Island. Accordingly, Begbie decided in 1859 that American lawyers and those, curiously, from the Channel Islands or any other 'dominion' of the United Kingdom, could practise in British Columbia. (In specifically stating the Channel Islands Begbie may have been sentimentally influenced by the fact that he was schooled on Guernsey.) Lawyers from 'Canada' not qualified in the United Kingdom were excluded. Under pressure, Begbie later altered the court rules to allow even those outlandish people to practise in British Columbia.[24] The Oaths Act of 1859 allowed non-Christian witnesses to affirm (as was the case in Scotland), rather than to swear on the Bible. Similarly, Roman Catholics and Quakers were allowed to make a valid affidavit or a sworn deposition without being required to swear allegiance to the monarch if such would offend their consciences. It is probable but cannot be demonstrated that Begbie drafted this Act as well.[25]

Begbie certainly drafted the Sheriff's Act of 1860. Just as the mining camps in California could select a sheriff, so did this Act empower a court in the absence of a formally appointed officer to appoint any person to act as sheriff for one month or a renewal period. Such an *ad hoc* sheriff was given the same immunity in respect of his actions while holding office as was extended to permanent sheriffs.[26] Begbie also drafted the Jurors' Act of 1860. This sensible piece of legislation permitted non-British subjects to serve on a jury where the latter could not be found, all of whom could be summoned to jury duty on 24 hours' notice. Challenges were permitted only in cases of bias; juries were hard enough to find without losing a number of prospective jurors on peremptory challenges. The proclamation attracted the attention of the Colonial Secretary in London, who perceived that the Act ran counter to the rules of summoning juries in the United Kingdom which had been in force since the reign of Richard III. The Duke of Newcastle demurred at the legislation but did not disallow it.[27]

Sunday observance was introduced formally into British Columbia in 1862. Doubts had arisen whether the Lord's Day laws of England were effective in the colony, presumably because they might be 'inapplicable from local circumstances'. There was some basis for this reasoning since on Sundays there was more gambling, more drinking, and more activity of any kind than on any other day of the week. The proclamation could seldom have been enforced. In 1863 the colonial legislature banned hunting on the Sabbath, a rare occasion on which the authorities took leave of their common sense.[28]

The last statute of any consequence framed by Begbie was the Native Evidence Act of 1865, which resulted directly from a trial for murder he conducted the year before. Defence counsel had sought to exclude evidence from the principal Crown witness, an Indian woman, until an inquiry was held as to the basis of her religious belief. Begbie allowed her to be sworn on the oath customarily used by Christians; the accused was ultimately convicted and executed. In his usual blunt fashion, Begbie told defence counsel that the precise nature of the woman's belief would, even if she were Christian, be a hotly debated topic 'among the most learned theologians'. Moreover, he said, strict adherence to the law would result in an absurdity: a liar professing a religious belief could testify, whereas an honest atheist could not. To avoid future difficulties with native witnesses, he declared in splendid Victorian language that it would be lawful

> to receive the evidence of any Aboriginal Nature . . . of the continent of North America . . . being an uncivilized person, destitute of the knowledge of God, and of any fixed and clear belief in religion or in a future state of rewards and punishment without administering the usual form of oath. . . .

If a native declared that he would 'tell the truth, the whole truth, and nothing but the truth', then his evidence could be received, upon pain of prosecution for perjury. This was sensible though unorthodox legislation by the standards of the current common law.[29] Consistent with his attitude towards Indians, Begbie later recommended the formation of special tribunals, which were not to be governed by the ordinary rules of criminal law, to hear allegations of crime against native Indians, but no action was taken.[30]

Criminal Justice

The fact is that imposition of British criminal justice in colonial British Columbia was accomplished with little difficulty or opposition from the community. Even the Indians who did not understand the system accepted it compliantly, probably because from long experience with Hudson's Bay Company officials they respected 'King George Men' (the British), and suspected 'Boston Men' (the Americans). It is true that the enforcement of British criminal law upon an aboriginal people led to incomprehension and often sadness and tragedy, but it is also true that colonial judicial officials strove to ameliorate the natives' feeling of alienation, unlike their American counterparts in the same era.

Most crimes committed by Indian men stemmed from excessive consumption of alcohol and from resentment of the white men who debauched Indian women. In cases of drunken homicide, the law had not been sufficiently refined to permit the reduction of a charge of murder to one of manslaughter, and in such instances all Begbie could do to lighten the hand of justice within the law was to recommend executive clemency, which he frequently did. There was little more comprehension of the British forms of justice by the Chinese than by the Indians. Begbie's Bench Books reveal very little serious crime by the Chinese, but probably no statistical analysis of the crime rate among the Chinese and Indian populations is possible because we do not have full, extant records for population or criminal prosecutions.

The task of inculcating respect for the law was achieved in spite of vast distances, few constables, and woeful jails. Prisoners often escaped across the American border, but those who remained in custody long enough to stand trial generally felt justice had been done.[31] There were no lynchings in colonial British Columbia although one nearly occurred; the victim fled to the United States, pursued by a Canadian posse who hanged him on American soil.[32] In 1861, Begbie admirably summed up the condition of the colony:

> It is a continued subject of thankfulness that the amount of crime still remains very small in comparison with what might have been anticipated from the amount of population, the extent and difficulty of the country over which the population is scattered, the habits naturally induced by the unsettled and exciting life of a miner . . . looking to the state of communications and the nature of the country generally, the proximity of a long, open frontier, accessible, unfrequented passes, and the necessarily distant and scanty police force.
>
> It is clear, however, that the inhabitants almost universally respect and obey the laws, and voluntarily prefer good order and peaceful industry, to the violence and bloodshed to which other gold-mining regions have been subjected, and with such dispositions, the police force, scanty and scattered as it is, appears to have been hitherto sufficient, not only to restrain from crime those who might otherwise have committed deeds of violence, but in general to bring to justice the few persons who have been actually guilty.[33]

The conditions he described did not alter in future years, and the colony and future province remained stable and law abiding.

Civil Justice

The government, just as it did with criminal law, adapted civil justice to the unusual needs of the colony. Obviously, from the point of view of the preservation of law and order, criminal law was the more important. Still, a predictable system of administering civil law was instrumental to a developing community. The task was made easier because of there being really only one substantial commercial activity in the colony. Mining was an activity in which the Indians did not engage and from which the Chinese were discouraged; not until 1869 did Begbie record a mining dispute involving a Chinese litigant.[34] Again, pragmatism was the rule. American currency had for years freely circulated in the colony; it was more useful, in fact, than the pound sterling because there were more Americans than British. But not until 1865 did the colonial government legitimate the practice by providing that both pounds sterling and United States dollars would be legal tender. Public accounts, however, were to be kept in the decimal system and not in pounds.[35]

To discourage debtors from delaying payment of their just debts, the Legislative Council in 1864 empowered juries to award interest at the maximum rate of 12 per cent per annum on any sum awarded for damages as calculated from the time the cause of action arose. This common sense measure had vanished from the British Columbia Statutes for nearly 100 years when in 1974 it reappeared as the Prejudgement Interest Act and still flourishes as the Court Order Interest Act.

During the entire colonial period there was no court of appeal. Aggrieved litigants could appeal to the Judicial Committee of the Privy Council if more than £300 was in issue, but distance and difficulties of transportation effectively precluded appeals. Not until 20 years after the union of the colonies of Vancouver Island and British Columbia did appeals go to London. Since Begbie was the only high court judge in British Columbia until 1870, his decision was *de facto* final. As a consequence, he rather piously felt his decisions were beyond reproach.[36]

The number of lawyers grew soon after Begbie's decision to allow American attorneys to practise, and the rule was rescinded not long after its proclamation. Even so, justices, Gold Commissioners, and Begbie often tried cases of accused persons not represented by lawyers. (The same difficulty occasionally is experienced today.) Begbie frequently found himself in criminal cases conducting the prosecution as well as the defence, an extremely unorthodox state of affairs. He realized this but still claimed: 'that I have always acted absolutely correctly . . . I at least trust that I have always endeavoured impartially to elicit the truth.'[37]

There was little in the way of what we would call support staff. There were no shorthand reporters, and no court clerks on a regular basis; there were *ad hoc* sheriffs; the court registrar was more a crony of the judge than a judicial official; and there was a dual system of court levies and costs, one for the Lower Mainland and the other for the 'Upper Country' where higher tariffs obtained because of the higher cost of living. In spite of all the impediments, lack of lawyers, lack of support staff, insecure jails, *ad hoc* sheriffs, and alien juries, the colonial judiciary from the Justices of the Peace to the Supreme Court administered law in a fashion that was perceived by the disparate population as fair and reasonable. The important thing was to impress on the community and individual litigants that they should be confident that justice would be done. Begbie put his finger on it when he said in his usual trenchant manner:

> I need not point out that popular confidence in the rigidity of justice is practically of more importance than justice itself. A trial which is suspected will, though in fact strictly just, have ill effects—a trial which is reputed to be above suspicion will, though in fact not strictly just, satisfy all men.[38]

Chief Justice Begbie

British Columbia was fortunate in having pragmatic judges among its judiciary in the colonial period: persons like Peter O'Reilly and Begbie who could, as occasion required, turn a blind eye and a deaf ear to the strict forms of court practice. To those who argue that events are shaped by men and not by blind immutable forces, Begbie is a good example; by force of personality he shaped both the criminal and civil laws of the colony. A Chancery barrister from London, of good but not aristocratic family, he made unexpected decisions. In his early days in the colony, Begbie was quite able to shed his role as a newly appointed high court judge and deal with disputes informally, partly because there were no lawyers, but also because there was no settled court procedure. In a letter to Douglas about a year after his arrival in British Columbia, Begbie wrote:

> Owing to the absence of any legal practitioner, except at Fort Yale, I have been obliged on this as on other occasions, to act in cases of dispute in a very informal manner and to arrange disputes as a private friend, rather than decide them as a Judge. The list of causes formally heard therefore by no means represents the amount of litigation presented. Many questions were brought before my notice which it would have been impossible to decide judicially, but I generally found a great readiness on all sides to accept the proposals of accommodation, and to acquiesce in the views which I put forward from time to time, whether favourable or not. I hope that in this way a great deal of litigation and causes of dispute and ill feeling will have been forestalled.[39]

Begbie, on hearing an appeal from a decision of O'Reilly, was told that the successful party—the respondent in the appeal—had gone into a tavern and had boasted of 'humbugging O'Reilly'. Begbie said characteristically:

> The expression [humbugging O'Reilly] is not very lucid; but it sounds disrespectful. But I cannot allow a man to be disquieted in his title to his [mining] claim because he has been hilarious or boastful in his inn.[40]

There is common sense *par excellence*.

Three years later Begbie decided the most controversial mining case of his career. The complicated facts do not need detailing, but they involved boundaries to claims and alleged failures to work them. Because the claims were so valuable, the litigation attracted enormous interest. The trial was heard by a jury with whose verdict Begbie disagreed, saying it had arrived at a verdict contrary to law. After telling the litigants he was going to nullify the verdict on legal grounds, he offered them a choice: have a new trial, or appoint him an arbitrator and he would incorporate his decision as arbitrator into a rule of court to make it binding (only *he* made the rules of court). A new trial, of course, would have had to come before him since he was the only judge. On the grounds of expediency, the litigants opted for Begbie as arbitrator. He made a decision unpalatable to both sides, and as a result the colonial government removed the power of the Supreme Court to hear cases *de novo*, restricting it to points of law. This legislative edict coincided with the downturn in mining activity, with the result that after 1866 Begbie heard only a handful of mining cases.

Begbie turned his first murder trial early in 1859 into a showcase designed to have a 'political' effect, to achieve an object broader than that of pronouncing the guilt or innocence of the accused. Two American miners who had been drinking heavily engaged in a barroom duel with pistols. The deceased fired the first shot, missing the accused who fired back, killing him. Many people thought the accused should be acquitted, believing he had shot in self-defense. Begbie felt the man should be convicted of manslaughter but not of murder; to allow an acquittal, he thought, would encourage the use of firearms, a highly undesirable state of affairs. After Begbie charged the jury, it remained out for several hours without reaching a verdict. Begbie became concerned that it might acquit the accused. Accordingly, he sent a note into the rough jury room urging them to convict the accused of manslaughter. No response was returned. He followed this up by going personally into the jury room to speak to the jurors who, no doubt reluctantly, followed his advice. Although the normal sentence for manslaughter was life imprisonment, Begbie sentenced the man to four years' imprisonment; he was reprieved a year later. This decision, the first in a number of cases of serious crime on which Begbie acted in a most unorthodox fashion to try to secure a verdict he thought suitable, was perhaps the most justifiable. As recorded by the defence counsel, Begbie's address to the grand jury just before the trial began revealed his concern:

> [T]he use of firearms and all that can tend to attack upon the life, limb or property should be entirely discouraged—but in the early stage of society of a gold colony, life of danger, men habituated to danger, and to risk of life, do not set the same value on life. Wild sense of honour, peculiarly strong among the class of population who first open an unexplored gold [colony].[41]

According to Begbie's court clerk, the Americans on the jury voted to acquit, the British subjects to convict. Begbie persuaded the former to change their mind and convict one of their own countrymen. The signal went to the mining community that the unlawful use of weapons would not be tolerated.[42] The verdict achieved its effect.

Conclusion

The miners who came to British Columbia in its early colonial days were 'Californians' in spirit if not by actual geographical background. The term was one applied to miners who knew their business, men who did not want to shoot each other at high noon but who wanted to make money. These men brought their experience and knowledge of mining camp regulations into British Columbia. Because mining disputes formed by far the largest part of litigation during the colonial period, and because the Gold Fields Act of 1859 adopted many features of informal camp regulations inherited from California, an examination of the latter is instructive since their influence pervaded colonial laws for years. The approach by the colonial judiciary in solving legal problems, particularly in mining litigation, was not as might have been expected in the United Kingdom but was eminently practical for conditions in the new colony.

Criminal law, however, the heart and soul of law and order, was British, not American. But because of its resolute application, colonial law-enforcement officials and the judiciary had an unexpectedly easy time of imposing British justice. The American miners were, in fact, compliant, always a surprise to colonial officials. As Trimble puts it:

> [I]n British Columbia there was Law and an Executive and a Chief Justice [Begbie] and a Magistracy that expected obedience, and the mining population rendered obedience willingly.[43]

Begbie himself discussed this very subject when writing Douglas in 1860. Remarking on the population of the colony, he said:

> The nature and extent of the population is, of course, the most important consideration. But it appears that their sentiments and wishes are extremely necessary to be ascertained.
>
> A population so acute and sensitive as that of B.C. cannot be governed in a mode distasteful to its wishes. I do not think they would violently oppose any law which they disliked; they would attempt to evade it; if unsuccessful, they would leave the country. I have found the white population particularly orderly and obedient. . . . There are six justices and fourteen or fifteen constables in the entire Colony. The merit of this tranquility is therefore entirely due to the good sense of the people; and I take it as indicating an extremely valuable sort of population, scanty as it is, which has hitherto occupied the country since the first rush in the summer and autumn of 1858. That inundation contained a great many questionable elements—which all, however, subsided and drained off as rapidly as they appeared.[44]

In another respect British Columbia differed from the American experience. British Columbia had no representative government of any kind until early in 1864 when the Legislative Council held its first session; a governor and his officials autocratically imposed regulations and proclaimed laws which they felt best suited the needs of the population. This 'undemocratic' government would hardly be thought to recommend itself to Americans imbued with the notions of liberty and free expression enshrined in their Constitution, but such was the case. The Americans in a foreign land pragmatically accepted autocracy. The proclamation of such laws as the Jurors Act tended to make the alien population comfortable. The autocracy, perhaps unwittingly, adapted itself to the proletarian views of the population and by doing so secured its acquiescence to British law and order.

In 1863 the Royal Engineers completed the road up the Fraser Canyon, making the interior of the colony far more accessible and bringing it within easier reach of government. By the time the colonies of British Columbia and Vancouver Island united in 1866, gold mining had dwindled and by 1870 had virtually petered out. Civil litigation of any consequence disappeared with the decline until the commercial growth of the 1880s. Criminal activity dwindled for the same reasons, and there were few notable cases during the decade after Confederation.

The development of civil and criminal law until 1866 was not uneven or unregulated. True, there was a degree of unorthodoxy. But it was reasonable, exactly suited to exigencies of the time. There was no 'frontier justice' but British justice administered on the frontier, adapted to emergency conditions both by legislation and judicial rulings.

Suggestions for Further Reading

Jean Barman, *The West Beyond the West: A History of British Columbia* (Toronto, 1991).
Robin Fisher, *Contact and Conflict: Indian-European Relations in British Columbia, 1774–1890* (Vancouver, 1977).
David Ricardo Williams, *The Man for a New Country: Sir Matthew Baillie Begbie* (Sidney, B.C., 1977).

Notes

[1] For a full account of Begbie's life, see David R. Williams *The Man for a New Country: Sir Matthew Baillie Begbie* (Sidney, B.C., 1977). I am indebted to my colleague, Professor Hamar Foster of the Faculty of Law, University of Victoria for access during preparation of this paper to his own paper 'Law Enforcement in Nineteenth Century British Columbia: A Research Agenda', presented at the Annual Meeting of the American Society for Legal History in Baltimore, Maryland, October 1983. See his paper, 'The Kamloops Outlaws and Commissions of Assize in Nineteenth-Century British Columbia', in *Essays in the History of Canadian Law*, ed. David H. Flaherty (Toronto, 1983), II, 308–64.

[2] 1803 (43 Geo. 3, c. 138) (U.K.); 1821 (1 Geo. 4, c. 66) (U.K.). It was partly on the strength of these provisions that Louis Riel's lawyers argued that he should have been tried in Ontario rather than in the Territories.

[3] An Act to provide for the Government of British Columbia, 1858 (21 Vict., c. 99) (U.K.).

[4] 'The proclamation having the force of law to declare that English law is in force in British Columbia', 19 November 1858, *B.C. List of Proclamations*, Provincial Archives of British Columbia, Victoria (cited hereinafter as PABC).

[5]*Report to the thirty-fifth Congress, Second Session of the United States of America by John N. Nugent, a Special Agent of the United States, January 8th, 1859*, Library of Congress, Washington, D.C.

[6]For an excellent discussion of the population spread see W.J. Trimble, *The Mining Advance into the Inland Empire* (Madison, Wisc., 1909), chapter IV.

[7]See, for example, Begbie's report to the Colonial Secretary (B.C.), 19 January 1863, misc. correspondence inward, PABC file F142-F.

[8]See note 5, *supra*.

[9]Begbie, 'Report After Autumn Circuit in British Columbia', 7 November 1859, misc. correspondence inward, PABC file F142-B 17b.

[10]C.H. Shinn, *Mining Camps: A Study in American Frontier Government* (Gloucester, Mass., 1970).

[11]See, for example, Arthur Nonus Birch manuscript, Birch Family Papers, PABC, C. 4.

[12]Quoted in Kinahan Cornwallis, *The New Eldorado* (London, 1858), 401.

[13]Quoted in *Victoria Daily Gazette*, 5 August 1858.

[14]Walter N. Sage, *Sir James Douglas and British Columbia* (Toronto, 1930), 223; Cornwallis, note 12, *supra*, 402–3; Frederick W. Howay and E.O.S. Scholefield, *British Columbia From the Earliest Times to the Present* (Vancouver, 1914), II, 33–4.

[15]*Mapping the Frontier: Charles Wilson's Diary of the Survey of the Forty-Ninth Parallel, 1858–1862, while Secretary of the British Boundary Commission*, ed. George F.G. Stanley (Toronto, 1970).

[16]See note 11, *supra*.

[17]*Walla Walla Statesman*, 2 September 1864. The celebrated remark is often attributed to Peter O'Reilly (see Howay and Scholefield, note 14, *supra*, I, 670), but he did not go to Wild Horse Creek until 1865 (see his diaries at the PABC). It was undoubtedly made by Haines.

[18]See note 11, *supra*.

[19]*B.C. List of Proclamations, 1858–1864*, PABC.

[20]*The Times* (London), 26 August 1863.

[21]*B.C. List of Proclamations, 1858–1864*, PABC.

[22]Begbie to Douglas, 7 November 1859, Begbie correspondence inward, PABC, file F142-B.

[23]An Ordinance to Amend and Consolidate the Gold Mining Laws, 28 March 1865, B.C. ordinances passed by the Legislative Council of B.C.

[24]Court of British Columbia Order of Court, *B.C. List of Proclamations, 1858–1864.* In framing the repealed enactment, Begbie may have been motivated by his dislike of G.B. Walkem, a lawyer trained in Upper Canada who later became premier, and still later a member of Begbie's court.

[25]*B.C. List of Proclamations, 1858–1864*, PABC.

[26]Sheriff's Act, 1860, *B.C. List of Proclamations, 1858–1864.*

[27]Duke of Newcastle to Douglas, 22 August 1861. Colonial Secretary's correspondence, PABC, folder 327.

[28]*B.C. List of Proclamations, 1858–1864*, PABC.

[29]Begbie to Gov. Seymour, 9 November 1864, Begbie correspondence inward, PABC, file F142-F1. Native Evidence Ordinance, 26 January 1865, Legislative Council of B.C.

[30]Begbie to Colonial Secretary, 23 January 1867, Begbie correspondence outward, PABC. In 1873 he directed that Justices of the Peace leave the punishment of intoxicated and unruly Indians to their tribal chiefs. If the latter abused their authority, they could themselves be disciplined by the Justices: Begbie correspondence outward, memorandum 10 October 1873, PABC.

[31]Begbie to Colonial Secretary (B.C.), 19 January 1863, Begbie correspondence, PABC, file F142-F.

[32]Cariboo *Sentinel*, 25 July 1867.

[33]Begbie to Douglas, 30 November 1861, Begbie correspondence inward, PABC, file F142-D 21.

[34]Begbie Bench Book, V C/AB/30. 3N. 1, 13 May 1869, PABC.

[35]Decimal Currency Ordinance, 1865, Legislative Council of B.C., PABC.

[36]Begbie to Douglas, 22 December 1862, miscellaneous correspondence inward, PABC, file 142-B.

[37]Begbie to W.A.G. Young, 29 March 1861, miscellaneous correspondence inward, PABC, file 142-D7.

[38]*Ibid.*

[39]Begbie to Douglas, 7 November 1859, miscellaneous correspondence inward, PABC, file 142-B 17b.

[40]Petition for rehearing a mining case: *Re Thomas*, probably 3 August 1863, Gerald E. Wellburn papers, Victoria, B.C.

[41]Crease Coll. vol. I, folder 1; Crease's notes of trial, PABC.

[42]Begbie Bench Book, I, 10 March 1859, PABC: 'Diary of Arthur Thomas Bushby', ed. by Dorothy Blakey Smith, *B.C. Historical Quarterly* XXI; Crease correspondence, vol. 1/1, 68–80, PABC.

[43]Trimble, *Mining Advance*, note 6, *supra*, 333.

[44]Begbie to Douglas, 30 April 1860, miscellaneous correspondence inward, PABC, file F142-C6 C.

29

Indian Policy on the Pacific Slope

Robin Fisher

As in other parts of western Canada, the early history of what would become the province of British Columbia was inextricably interwoven with the fur trade and the native peoples. Until the establishment of the colony of Vancouver Island in 1849, the British government had not attempted to assert direct administrative control over the region, allowing fur-trading companies—after 1821, the Hudson's Bay Company exclusively—to exercise jurisdiction. Even after 1849, the Hudson's Bay Company remained the dominant element in the colony, although there were increasing criticisms of its government. But the fur trade was on the defensive, as it had been since American settlers began pouring into the Oregon territory in the 1830s, and the discovery of gold on the mainland in the 1850s rapidly tipped the balance from fur trade to settlement.

Until very recently Canadian historians have dealt with the settlement of new regions such as British Columbia from the perspective of the settlers. Any obstacles to rapid settlement have been treated unsympathetically, and in western Canada one of the principal targets of criticism has been the Hudson's Bay Company. Clearly the Company had a vested interest in the preservation of the fur trade, and was hardly a neutral force in the West. However, the Company's economic self-interest required it to exercise some concern for the Indians and their way of life—a concern that was not often shared by other Europeans. Historians in the past, like the settlers, tended to believe that the native inhabitants had no right to stand in the way of progress.

In the following selection Robin Fisher examines the role of the Hudson's Bay Company in British Columbia during the transitional period from fur trade to settlement. The key figure was Governor James Douglas, who was forced to confront the problem of balancing the incompatible pressures of fur trade and settlement within the context of race relations in the colony. Fisher argues that despite his fur-trader's familiarity with the Indians and his paternalistic concern for their welfare, Douglas found himself increasingly putting the future needs of settlers ahead of those of the Indians. Nevertheless, Douglas maintained a relative external tranquillity between the races which, Fisher maintains, was a positive and considerable achievement.

Is it possible to consider the confrontation between native populations and incoming European settlers in a manner that does justice to both sides? What principles and techniques did James Douglas employ to 'manage' Indians and maintain relatively peaceful relations? Was he 'pro-Indian'? On balance, is Douglas to be regarded more as a protector of Indians or as a facilitator of settlement?

This article first appeared in Robin Fisher, *Contact and Conflict: Indian-European Relations in British Columbia, 1774–1890* (Vancouver, 1977).

> The interests of the Colony, and Fur Trade will never harmonize, the former can flouish, only, through the protection of equal laws, the influence of free trade, the accession of respectable inhabitants; in short by establishing a new order of things, while the fur Trade must suffer by each innovation.[1]
>
> James Douglas, 1838

The establishment of the colony of Vancouver Island in 1849 involved a debate between the proponents of the fur trade and of settlement. Was responsibility for the development of the colony to be given to the old fur-trading company or to some new company founded specifically to foster settlement? The most plausible alternative to the responsibility being given to the Hudson's Bay Company was a scheme proposed to the Colonial Office by a clerk in the British Museum named James E. Fitzgerald. He advocated the founding of a joint-stock company to develop Vancouver Island as a settlement colony along Wakefieldian lines.[2] Some officials at the Colonial Office were, quite rightly, dubious about the efficacy of Edward Gibbon Wakefield's principles of systematic colonization, and in the end they opted for the security and the proven financial capacity of the Hudson's Bay Company. The colony of Vancouver Island was granted to the company by a Royal Charter on 13 January 1849.

In many ways the debate that had occurred in Britain prior to the founding of the colony was transferred to Vancouver Island after 1849. Fitzgerald had argued that, because its interests ran counter to those of settlement, the company would not be a vigorous promoter of colonization. Perhaps he was right, although in the end it did not matter much, for Vancouver Island held little attraction for settlers before 1858. Although the grant of the island had gone to the fur-trading company, the Colonial Office appointed Richard Blanshard, a lawyer who had no connection with the company, as the first governor. Blanshard's position was anomalous from the start. He was supposed to represent interests other than the fur trade in a colony where the fur trade was virtually the only interest. He correctly observed that the colony was really 'nothing more than a fur trading post',[3] and he soon realized that he was a governor with no one to govern. After eighteen months of fussing and frustration Blanshard left Vancouver Island, having expended his energy, money, and health in a post for which he was not suited. With Blanshard's departure the governorship passed to where the real power in the colony lay. On 16 May 1851 James Douglas, chief factor at Fort Victoria and member of the company's three-man board of management for the area west of the Rockies, reluctantly became the governor of Vancouver Island. The fur trade had temporarily reasserted its dominance. Blanshard's period of office was an interlude that, with the exception of one incident, probably went unnoticed by the Indians.

The exception was Blanshard's punishment of the Newitty, a Kwakiutl group living at the northern end of Vancouver Island, who were held responsible for the murder of three British sailors late in the summer of 1850. The company seamen had deserted in Victoria and escaped on the *Norman Morison,* probably heading for a more lucrative career in the gold mines of California. The *Norman Morison* went instead to Fort Rupert; there the men left the ship and later were reported dead, presumably killed by Indians.

It is quite possible that the Indians believed that they had been offered a reward for the capture of the deserters dead or alive. One of the servants at Fort Rupert claimed that the trader in charge, George Blenkinsop, had offered the Indians ten blankets for each of the deserters' heads. The story was in wide circulation at the time, although the company officers denied it. But Blenkinsop definitely did offer the Indians a reward for information on the whereabouts of the three men.[4] In 1850 Blenkinsop was a young man, inexperienced in leadership, and in Douglas's opinion it was an injustice to him to have to take over the responsibility for such a difficult post as Fort Rupert while William McNeill was on furlough.[5] Perhaps as a result of Blenkinsop's inexperience, the Indians gained a mistaken impression of what was being asked of them in return for the reward. It was company practice to offer the Indians rewards for bringing in deserting servants. Furthermore, from the time of first contact the Indians had assumed that ordinary seamen and, later, company labourers were slaves. Undoubtedly the Indians felt that their view was confirmed by the company's offers of rewards for deserting servants and by the punishment they received on recapture. The Indians certainly claimed that they regarded the three deserting sailors as slaves on the run.[6] In Indian society slaves had few human rights and runaway slaves had none; therefore, in their terms, killing the men was not only permissible but probably desirable. That the three men were killed by Indians was pretty well proven, but exactly which group of Indians was responsible was much less certain.

In Governor Blanshard's mind there was no doubt about where the responsibility lay. The Newitty Indians were guilty of the murders and if necessary would be held responsible as a group. In contrast to the fur traders, Blanshard lacked the ability, and probably the inclination, to delve into the subtleties of Indian motivation. He regarded the Indians as essentially irrational and could see only the need to erect safeguards against any 'sudden outburst of fury to which all savages are liable'.[7] Blanshard was ill at ease in the uncouth frontier environment of Vancouver Island, and his sense of insecurity demanded that strong measures be taken against threatening Indians. 'The Queen's name is a tower of strength', he wrote, but only 'when backed by the Queen's bayonets'.[8] The governor requested John Sebastian Helmcken, who had arrived earlier in 1850 as a company doctor, to investigate the murders. Helmcken conducted a careful, on-the-spot examination of the evidence and had to confess that he could hardly believe that the Newitty were responsible. He pointed out that the Newitty had given no previous offence to the whites and, moreover, that it was in their interest to maintain friendly relations with the traders. If Newitty killed the sailors, why, he asked, did they not murder other Europeans who were almost as vulnerable? Then there was the further possibility that the Fort Rupert Kwakiutl had implicated the Newitty in the murders out of intertribal jealousy.[9] Apparently Helmcken's reservations and unanswered questions received little attention from Blanshard.

Aided and abetted by Rear-Admiral Fairfax Moresby,[10] the governor went up the coast on HMS *Daedalus* seeking retribution. He had already asked Helmcken to tell the Indians that the 'white man's blood never dries';[11] and when the Newitty proved unwilling, or perhaps unable,[12] to surrender the murderers, their village was destroyed. The following year Blanshard went north again, this time on HMS *Daphne*, and another Newitty village was stormed and destroyed. Later a group of Newitty came alongside the company's brigantine *Mary Dare* with two bodies said, although never proven, to be two of the murderers.[13]

This brutal action came near the end of Blanshard's term of office, and soon Douglas took over. The punishment of the Newitty had been one of Blanshard's few flurries of activity, and in many ways it was misguided. The killing of the three sailors did not even remotely constitute an Indian menace of 'serious proportions', nor was the Newitty tribe particularly warlike.[14] Blanshard's reaction to the murders was exactly the one that as a fur trader Douglas had disapproved of, and under his governance fur-trading methods of dealing with the Indians were reinstituted. Still, for the Indians the destruction of the Newitty villages was a foretaste of things to come. Part of the reason for Blanshard's action was that he and Moresby considered the fur traders' methods of protecting themselves from Indian attacks inadequate.[15] The two men were representative of a new set of attitudes that were to impinge on the Indians with the advent of settlement. Methods of dealing with the Indians that the fur traders found quite satisfactory were to be inappropriate as far as settlers were concerned. In the meantime, however, the fur traders remained in control, and they had been very uneasy about Blanshard's handling of the Newitty.[16]

The appointment of Douglas as governor of Vancouver Island was largely the consequence of a recognition by the Colonial Office of the value of his long experience in dealing with the Indians. Douglas accordingly proceeded to apply many of the lessons learned as a fur trader to his new responsibilities. In fact, many critics of his administration would have argued that, because he remained a chief factor in the company until 1858, he was still more of a fur trader than a colonial governor. Douglas's dual role symbolized the transitional phase from fur trade to settlement.

Like other fur traders, Douglas was not at all happy about Blanshard's treatment of the Newitty, and as governor he considered it downright dangerous. He described the action 'as unpolitick as unjust'; poorly conceived as well as badly executed. 'In all our intercourse with the natives,' wrote Douglas, summarizing the fur traders' view, 'we have invariably acted on the principle that it is inexpedient and unjust to hold *tribes* responsible for the acts of *individuals*.' In any terms the punishment meted out to the Newitty was out of all proportion to the crime, but worse still in Douglas's mind were the possible consequences of the operation. Had the Indians made any real attempt to defend themselves, the attackers would have suffered a considerable loss of life.[17] Escalating the violence to such a level might involve the infant colony in a war with the Indians that could only be disastrous. The whites had neither the numbers nor the power to withstand any concerted assault. The fur traders recalled that the war with the Cayuse had stretched the resources of the Oregon Territory to the limit a few years earlier.[18]

Douglas's opinion that Blanshard's action had been mistaken was supported by the Colonial Office. Earl Grey, the secretary of state for the colonies, wrote to Blanshard to inform him that his superiors were by no means satisfied about the prudence of the steps that he had taken.[19] The governor was even ignominiously asked to stand the expenses of his excursion in the *Daedalus* out of his own pocket. Douglas's disagreement with Blanshard's handling of this particular affair was part of a more general difference of opinion about the need for a military presence in the colony. Blanshard believed hostile tribes should be 'speedily coerced' and thought that the colony should have a military force for the purpose. Douglas, who strongly advocated modest measures, considered troops an evil to be avoided.[20]

Douglas was convinced that in the circumstances of the colony expediency required that the old methods of disciplining the Indians be continued, and he was confident of his own ability to administer them. If not exactly a martinet, the new governor certainly believed that stern discipline should be meted out to malcontents, whether Indian or white. In March 1849 he had occasion to deal with some company sailors who had mutinied while their vessel was at Fort Langley. The unruly employees had holed up in the fore-castle, and because of the 'timidity' of the other officers Douglas had to go and root them out himself. He noted in a letter to Simpson that he thought 'a little severity would have a good effect in checking their turbulence'.[21] Douglas had the reputation for being a great hand at a flogging,[22] and he was probably originally employed by the company to act as what might euphemistically be termed a policeman. Certainly Douglas was a big, pow-erful man, quite able to acquit himself well in any activity demanding phys-ical strength. Indians, no less than Europeans, admired physical prowess, and this was undoubtedly an important reason for Douglas's much reported influ-ence over them.[23] In contrast to Blanshard, Douglas was well equipped to cope with the rough and tumble of the frontier. Confident and experienced, he saw little need to administer large doses of indiscriminate force to Indians who committed depredations against Europeans. Capture the individuals responsible and let them be dealt with as British law directs and the justice of the case requires[24]—this was Douglas's recommendation in the particular case of the Fort Rupert murders and the general course that he was to follow himself.

By treating violence as a consequence of the aberrations of individuals, Douglas tacitly denied that it had sociological causes. Those fur traders who were accustomed to co-operating with the Indians did not make the easy assumption of the settler that all Indians were hostile to all Europeans. During the fur trade violence had been on an individual and not a racial level, and Douglas presumed that this state of affairs would continue.

In 1852 there was another incident that, except for the governor's reaction, was similar to the murders near Fort Rupert. A company employee, this time a shepherd named Peter Brown, was killed by Indians in the Cowichan Valley. Apparently two Indians were involved; one was a Cowichan and the other was a member of the Nanaimo tribe. When he learned of the murder, Douglas was determined to capture the two individuals, but he was equally determined not to implicate their tribes. For reasons of 'public justice and policy' he did not want to involve all the members of the tribes in the 'guilt' of two, nor did he want to provide the closely related Cowichan and Nanaimo with a reason to form an alliance against the whites. Douglas sent messages to the tribal leaders demanding the surrender of the murderers, but when these requests produced only evasive replies, he decided that 'more active measures' were required. So in January 1853 he assembled a force made up of 130 marines from the frigate *Thetis* and a small group of militiamen who called themselves the Victoria Voltigeurs. Accompanied by this force Douglas went first to the Cowichan Valley and then to Nanaimo and was able to capture the two Indians without loss of life. But the arrests were not a simple matter. When the Cowichan charged his force as a ceremonial test of its courage, Douglas had great difficulty in restraining his men from firing a volley. The Cowichan murderer was finally surrendered by his people, but the Nanaimo Indian was a man of some prestige in his tribe and was more difficult to secure. In the end Douglas had to take him by force of arms. Once captured, the two Indians were tried and hanged before the Nanaimo people. Douglas was highly satisfied with the operation. He considered, in the case of the Cowichan, that the surrender of the killer without bloodshed 'by the most numerous and warlike of the Native Tribes in Vancouver's Island' was 'an epoch, in the history of our Indian relations'.[25]

Douglas had successfully employed the fur-trading principle of selective, rather than indiscriminate, punishment. In fact, he was of the opinion that the success of the venture owed as much to the influence of the Hudson's Bay Company as it had to the use of intimidation. In contrast to its reprimand to Blanshard, the Colonial Office considered Douglas's actions to be 'highly creditable'.[26]

Three years later, in 1856, a settler named Thomas Williams was shot and wounded by another Cowichan Indian, and Douglas treated this offence in a similar manner. With a naval force and eighteen Voltigeurs Douglas again went to the Cowichan Valley, and the attacker was captured, tried, and executed on the spot.[27] Again the Colonial Office had no hesitation in approving the proceedings, although Douglas was reminded that armed force should only be used against the Indians with great caution.[28] In response, Douglas pointed out that force had been a last resort and reiterated that, as in the earlier expedition against the Cowichan, he had operated on the principle that only the guilty were culpable. He assured the Colonial Office that the recent interracial conflict in the Oregon Territory along with Blanshard's 'fruitless expedition' against the Newitty were quite sufficient to evince the dangers and difficulties of such operations.[29] The tone of his rely indicated that Douglas had been ruffled by what he thought was a reprimand, but Herman Merivale, the permanent under-secretary at the Colonial Office, wrote to the Hudson's Bay Company explaining that no disapproval had been intended.[30]

Douglas always resented any implication that his handling of the Indians was at all ill-considered. He regarded such imputations as a slight on his years of experience as a fur trader and often cited that experience in defence of his actions. In 1859 Rear-Admiral Robert Baynes wrote to Douglas in the context of the dispute with the United States over the San Juan Islands, and among other things he expressed the belief that, in the event of conflict between the whites, the Indians would take advantage of the situation and prey on all indiscriminately. In a starchily worded reply marked 'confidential' Douglas wondered if the admiral was 'perhaps not aware of the intense hatred that exists between the Indians and the American'. He told Baynes that the Americans did not understand the Indian character, whereas his personal acquaintance with them was of many years' standing.[31]

His early years had taught Douglas the need for limiting punishment of Indians who attacked Europeans. His realization that it was inadvisable to interfere in conflicts between Indians also grew out of his familiarity with them. While he was determined to convince the Indians that the white settlements were 'sacred ground', he did not consider it prudent to interfere with the Indians' 'domestic broils'. Douglas had already told the Colonial Office that he thought it unwise to involve the government in disputes 'of which we could learn neither the merits nor the true bearings, and which probably were in accordance with the laws of natural justice'. He expounded the principle when unrest developed among the Indians of northern Vancouver Island following an 'atrocious massacre' of the Koskimo by Newitty Indians. In fact, he even went so far as to suggest that quarrels between Indians were of some benefit to the colony, since they provided an outlet for violence that might otherwise be directed against the settlers. The minutes on Douglas's letter to the Colonial Office on this subject, along with the Duke of Newcastle's reply, show that his superiors agreed with his 'discrete view' of non-interference in purely Indian matters.[32]

Policy makers at 14 Downing Street were confident enough about Douglas's knowledge of the Indians to leave much of the detail of Indian policy in the colony to his discretion. This confidence was well placed. Douglas undoubtedly did know more about the Indian way of life than any other governor of Vancouver Island or of British Columbia during the colonial period. He thought that the Indians were 'in many respects a highly interesting people' and worthy of attention.[33] In contrast to the abusive epithets that settlers often used to describe Indians, Douglas characterized the Vancouver Island Indian population as 'hospitable, and exceedingly punctilious in their mutual intercourse,—grateful for acts of kindness, and never fail to revenge an injury. Though generally dishonest, they are seldom known to violate a trust.'[34] Naturally he sometimes used harsher adjectives, but they were always tempered with a degree of sympathy. As governor, Douglas felt that one of the advantages of attempting to understand the Indians was that knowledge of their attitudes and intentions might forestall serious conflict with the settlers. Douglas said that he was prepared to make every allowance for the 'ignorance and impulsive natures' of the Indians,[35] and he was capable of settling disputes according to Indian customs. For instance, when a Stikine Indian was accidentally wounded by a sailor at Victoria, Douglas arranged for the payment of compensation to the relatives.[36] Of course, by using an

Indian method to settle the dispute Douglas also revealed that the two races did not stand equal before the law. As the Cowichan discovered, when an Indian wounded a European the statute book declared it to be an offence punishable by death. Nevertheless, Douglas did try to understand Indian society, and he had some sympathy for the predicament of the Indians faced with the encroachment of a foreign civilization.

Although Douglas's fur-trading experience influenced his Indian policy, the exigencies of the settlement frontier gradually began to press in on him. The fur traders understood that with the coming of the settlers their days would be numbered. At the time of the establishment of the colony of Vancouver Island, Ogden had assumed in a letter that Simpson would be 'fully aware that the Fur trade and Civilization can never blend together and . . . the former invariably gives way to the latter'. Douglas had also realized for a long time that settlement would bring 'a new order of things'.[37]

Unlike other colonies, Vancouver Island had not been founded for the purpose of relieving overcrowded conditions in Britain, and settlers arrived only slowly. By 1852 as few as 435 emigrants had been sent to the colony, only 11 had purchased land, and another 19 had applied for land.[38] It has often been assumed that the fur company must have been a bad colonizer because it wanted to retain Vancouver Island as a purely fur-trading pre-serve.[39] It is true that clearing land for agriculture does little to maintain the habitat of fur-bearing animals, but Vancouver Island was not very important as a source of furs by the 1850s. The company wanted to control the island to ensure the protection of the much more important region of New Cal-edonia.[40] Nor was the company's decision to charge £1 per acre for land designed to restrain settlement, as Canadian historians have tended to sup-pose. Archibald Barclay's letter to Douglas outlining the principles of colo-nization that the company intended to follow is pure Wakefield. The company secretary wrote of the desirability of transferring a cross section of British society to the colony, of disposing of land in a way that would ensure 'a just proportion of labour and capital', and of preventing the admission of paupers, squatters, and land speculators.[41] The echoes from *A Letter from Sydney* are unmistakable. The Hudson's Bay Company was thus following what many in Britain, including the Colonial Secretary, Earl Grey, thought was the last word in the theory of colonization. The experience of other colonies was to show that the theory, so promising on paper, was unworkable on the ground. The basic reason for the slow development of colonization on Vancouver Island was not the policy of the company but the few attrac-tions for agricultural settlers. Other colonies seemed to hold greater promise for the potential emigrant, and for those who came as far as the west coast of North America after 1849, California was a much more likely prospect.

It soon became evident that those colonists who did come to the island were men whose outlook on many matters differed from that of the fur traders. There was a growing group of settlers in opposition to company rule led by the Reverend Robert Staines, and these 'free settlers' expected to have 'a sore Battle to fight against the Companys'.[42] The conflicts that developed between Douglas and men like Staines may have been 'Lilliputian',[43] but they do reflect many of the attitudes of the settlers towards the fur traders. The time had come, the colonists thought, to sever the ties with Vancouver Island's fur-trading past. The British member of Parliament Charles Fitzwilliam considered that Douglas was incompetent for the post of governor because his dealings had been with Indians and not with white men.[44] This attitude was also prevalent in the colony. One of the more supercilious of the settlers wrote to her family that Douglas 'has spent all his life among the North American Indians and has got one of them for a wife so can it be expected that he can know anything at all about governing one of England's last Colonies in North America'.[45]

Annie Deans was not the only newcomer who believed that, while Douglas could handle Indians, he 'does not seem up to governing a white population at all'.[46] For many of the settlers the very quality that had recommended Douglas to the Colonial Office disqualified him as a governor. One of the jokes going round the colony was that the letters HBC actually stood for 'Here before Christ', and it was indicative of the settler opinion that the fur traders were crude and unrefined. The company men were said to be only one degree removed from the Indians. They had white skins but had been raised and educated up to Indian standards, and only with the arrival of settlers was a degree of civilization introduced to the country.[47] Some fur traders would have agreed with the description: John Tod once remarked that he saw himself as a 'half a savage'.[48] The settler was never faced with any such confusion of identity: he never got close enough to the Indian for that. While the nature of his occupation demanded that the fur trader should, to some extent, accommodate himself to Indians, settlers had no need and, therefore, no desire to be accommodating and tolerant. The settler came to re-create an alien civilization on the frontier, while the fur trader had to operate largely within the context of the indigenous culture. Although settlers arrived only in small numbers in the early 1850s, they were increasingly to influence colonial affairs in general and Indian policy in particular.

At the time that the colony of Vancouver Island was granted to the company, Douglas was asked by the management for his idea on how colonization might best be effected. He replied that he had never given the matter a moment's thought and that any attempt to discuss the subject would only reveal his own ignorance. The future governor did, however, offer some thoughts on the difficulties that colonists would face. Among them was the petty theft that the Indians would be tempted into by the careless habits of the settlers.[49] The effect of settlement on relations with the Indians was to give Douglas cause for a great deal of reflection in the next few years.

Douglas was keenly conscious of the deterioration of race relations following the advent of settlement south of the border. In 1846 the old fur-trading preserve had been divided in half by what Douglas regarded as a 'monstrous treaty'.[50] Following the Oregon Treaty the area north of the forty-ninth parallel continued to be dominated by the fur trade, while to the south settlement prevailed. Almost immediately there was racial conflict in the south. Only a year after the Americans took over, the murders at the Whitman mission and the hostilities that followed set the pattern for the next decade. As far as the fur traders were concerned there was no doubt, after the killings by the Cayuse at Waiilatpu, 'that the Americans will, in the end, glut their revenge upon the wretched Indian, although from their want of discipline and means, it will require a length of time to effect the work of destruction.'[51] The prophecy turned out to be very accurate. There was warfare with the Indians of Washington again in 1855–6, and it was accompanied by the indiscriminate slaughter of Indians by groups of volunteers. Even Phillip Sheridan, who later showed his lack of sympathy for the native American with the comment about 'the only good Indian', criticized the killing of innocent Indians in Washington for no other reason than to gratify an 'inordinate hatred' of them.[52]

Douglas usually could not empathize with the Americans at all; and he had once declared himself to be more 'suspicious of their designs, than of the wild natives of the forest'.[53] But he regarded the conflict of 1855–6 as a war of races, of civilization against barbarism,[54] and he acknowledged a moral obligation which bound Christian and civilized nations together 'in checking the inroads of the merciless savages'.[55] He therefore thought it incumbent on the colony to render some assistance to the Washington authorities, while at the same time he wanted to maintain a façade of neutrality to avoid being identified with the Americans in the mind of the Indians. So he provided the Americans with arms, ammunition, and the use of the *Beaver*, but not with any more active support.

Douglas was most anxious that violence with the Indians in the United States should not spill over the border and threaten the colony. He assumed that there must have been 'some great mismanagement' on the part of the American authorities. Nothing else made credible the antagonism of the American Indians, who had been 'softened and improved' by fifty years of commercial dealings with the Hudson's Bay Company.[56] His own Indian policies were largely designed to avoid similar mismanagement and the consequent horrors of Indian warfare. The governor also wanted to ensure that the unfamiliarity of the settlers with the Indians did not lead to major conflict on Vancouver Island. For the people in the colony to be reduced in the estimation of the Indians to the level of the Americans would, in Douglas's opinion, invite disaster.[57]

Douglas's prognostication that the carelessness of the settlers would invite depredations by the Indians was borne out from the beginning of colonization. Vancouver Island's first independent settler was Captain Walter Colquhoun Grant, who came to the colony to survey land for the company and to establish a farm. He proved to be incompetent in the first occupation and too irresponsible for the second. When he left the colony, Douglas's parting comment was that the 'unfortunate man has been an absolute plague to me ever since he came to the Island'.[58] Grant and the settlers he brought with him under his agreement with the company were apprehensive about the Indians, but Douglas was convinced that, instead of thirsting for their blood, the Indians were well disposed and willing to assist them in their labours. He impressed on the inexperienced new arrivals that it was in their own, and in the colony's, interest to cultivate the friendship of these 'children of the forest'.[59] When Grant, contrary to Douglas's advice, left his property at Sooke unattended, some articles were stolen by unknown parties, presumed to be Indians. The imprudence of the settler had elicited the expected response. Douglas knew that Grant's anxiety about Indian behaviour would become general and that the settlers would clamour for protection until a military force was sent out, a conclusion he wanted to avoid.[60]

In June 1854 a man named Thomas Greenham came rushing into Victoria from the Company's Cadboro Bay farm with a wild report that the place had been attacked and overrun by hundreds of Indians. Douglas armed some men and hastened to the spot only to find no sign of Indians and all the residents safe, except for one man who had a cut on the head. Apparently some of the labourers had fled at the sight of the Indians and completely exaggerated the seriousness of the threat. The incident set the whole settlement aflame. The Indian tribes assembled at Victoria and, from mistrust and alarm, took up arms against each other. A relatively minor event had quickly developed into an extremely critical situation. After the excitement had died down, Douglas observed that 'a labourer taken from the plough is not to be trusted in circumstances of danger, without some previous training' and that such examples of timidity destroyed the influence of the whites.[61]

During the early years of the colony there were large numbers of free-roaming cattle that were a potential source of interracial conflict. Douglas was aware that the Indians regarded cattle in much the same way as they did wild animals, recognizing none as exclusive property, and he knew that an Indian returning unsuccessful from the hunt would find the settlers' cattle irresistible.[62] To avoid offering such provocation to the Indians, Douglas wanted settlement on Vancouver Island to be confined to a specific area where settlers could protect each other. The company's practice had been to maintain sufficient men in one place to give some security, but, like settlers everywhere, those on Vancouver Island began to spread out in search of good land.

Isolated and outnumbered, the settlers felt insecure and frequently feared attacks. Douglas often received requests for protection against imagined

Indian invasions. He discounted such 'idle terrors' and was more concerned that settlers' fears might encourage the Indians to aggression. The colonists were advised to conceal their apprehensions and on all occasions to assume a 'bold countenance' with the Indians.[63] Settlers were particularly uneasy about the large numbers of northern Indians, most Haida and Tsimshian, who visited Victoria annually from 1854. The Haida particularly had a formidable reputation, and many unfounded rumours were spread about Indian plans to destroy the settlement. But Douglas recognized that the northern Indians had come to benefit from the existence of Victoria and not to end it.[64] The settlement attracted these Indians because it provided a marketplace; they came to trade and to find employment as labourers. It was settler hysteria rather than Indian hostility that produced the demands for protection, and the Indians were probably fortunate that Douglas stood between them and the settlers. In the United States public opinion had a freer rein. At Port Townsend a meeting of citizens resolved to shoot without question all northern Indians found in United States waters.[65] Settler influence was not so strong on Vancouver Island, and Douglas would never have tolerated such extremities.

By the mid–1850s, however, he had become much more conscious of the need for protecting the colony. The migrations from the north were greatly increasing the Indian population around Victoria at a time when events in the United States were raising the spectre of racial warfare. Douglas felt the Vancouver Island Indians had become 'restive and insolent' as a consequence of Indian military successes to the south.[66] Then came the news of the Cowichan attack on Thomas Williams, and Douglas began to realize that it required more coercive power to maintain a settlement frontier than the fur traders had needed. He recognized that factionalism among the Indians probably precluded any preconceived or combined attack on the settlements, but he could not discount the possibility that individual disputes could lead to a general affray. So he recommended measures to protect the colony, even if only to allay the fears of the colonists.[67] His requests for assistance from the Royal Navy and his advocacy of an armed force became more frequent.

Because of their potential power, Douglas realized that the hostility of the Indians was the worst calamity that the infant colony could face. Hence he felt it necessary to foster their good will; a duty that, according to Douglas, was often rendered difficult by the 'recklessness and imprudence' of the colonists.[68] He also recognized the potential value of the Indians as allies. In the event of conflict with the Americans over the San Juan Islands, Douglas thought he could rely on the Indians for assistance, and when the possibility of war between Britain and Russia arose, he suggested that an armed force including both Indians and whites should be raised to defend the colony. The colonists, not unexpectedly, were uneasy about the notion of arming the Indians.[69]

It has been shown that when Douglas perceived a real threat to the security of the colony he acted forcefully and decisively. Yet some settlers remained unconvinced that they were sufficiently protected from the Indians under the Hudson's Bay Company. Aware of their vulnerability, they wanted to use large doses of force to convince the Indians that they were invulnerable. There were continued requests and petitions from colonists for more defensive measures, and some who viewed their position as precarious argued that an abler man than Douglas was required as governor.[70] Many were unimpressed when he used the Indian method of paying damages to settle disputes; they thought that the Indians should be made to 'smell powder and ball, instead of perpetuating the old system of doling out blankets to them'.[71] Others dismissed such 'bribery' as perhaps appropriate to the fur trade but not to a settlement of British subjects. James Cooper, a non-company settler from 1851 to 1857, in testimony before the Select Committee on the Hudson's Bay Company, described this method of dealing with the Indians as probably humane but not judicious. However, when the patently obvious difference between race relations on the British and American sides of the border was pointed out in implied defence of the company's administration of the colony, Cooper could make no effective rejoinder.[72] Douglas often made the same point in his letters to London. He was undoubtedly aware that the contrast between the 'tragic events' taking place in the United States and his reports that on Vancouver Island the Indians continued with their 'usual quiet and friendly demeanor' reflected well on his administration.[73]

Nonetheless, the methods of dealing with the Indians that Douglas had learned as a fur trader and applied so successfully in the early years of the colony were used less and less in the later 1850s. In 1855, when the northern Indians returned to Victoria, Douglas assembled the leaders and 'spoke to them seriously' about their relations with the whites. There were no major disputes, and in cases of minor infractions of British law the Indians submitted to the decisions of magistrates. Douglas esablished a four-man police force to deal with the situation created by the continued presence of the northern Indians but noted that what was really required was a force of twenty to thirty men. Both Douglas and the Indians realized that a new relationship was being established between them. Douglas thought that the Indians were beginning to have a clearer idea of the nature and utility of British law, the object of which was to protect life and property. This awareness, wrote Douglas, 'may be considered as the first step in the progress of civilization'.[74] The Indians themselves were feeling for the first time the full impact of an alien legal system. Even internal disputes were becoming subject to European scrutiny and jurisdiction as long as the Indians remained near the settlements. Whereas earlier Douglas had been prepared to allow the 'laws of natural justice' to operate among them, gradually British notions of social control were being applied to the Indians of Vancouver Island.

Settlement impinged on Douglas's relations with the Indians in many areas besides law and order. The availability of armed force and the willingness to use it were not, in themselves, particularly significant in maintaining peaceful relations with the Indians. It has been argued that the Royal Navy provided the 'power to compel' on the northwest coast and that its presence in large part accounts for the relatively pacific nature of Indian–white relations.[75] But, as Douglas appreciated, the American example showed that the use of force could not make up for deficiencies in Indian policy.[76] Nor was the governor powerless without the navy's support. The fur traders had maintained a relatively harmonious relationship with the Indians before the navy was very active on the coast, and after 1858 Douglas was able to restrain violence between the races on the Fraser and Cariboo gold fields, areas not accessible to naval vessels. Other 'tools of statecraft' were required besides the Royal Navy,[77] for peace was not maintained by power alone.

With settlement, Europeans and Indians came into competition for the use of the land. Agricultural settlement was destructive to the Indians' methods of food gathering. In the Fort Victoria area, for example, Indian camas grounds were broken up by the plough.[78] It was true that the Indians no longer relied solely on the old methods of food gathering and that many had become accustomed to cultivating crops both for their own consumption and for sale at the forts. These groups were to come even more directly into competition with the Europeans for the best arable land. If the experience of other colonies meant anything, competition between races for land was likely to produce conflict.

In 1849 Douglas wrote to the Hudson's Bay Company drawing attention to the need for some arrangement to be made for the purchase of Indian land. In reply the company cited the report of a committee of the House of Commons set up to examine the claims of the New Zealand Company. This report argued that aborigines had only 'qualified Dominion' over their country, consisting of a right of occupancy but not title to the land. Until the 'uncivilised inhabitants' of any country established among themselves 'a settled form of government and subjugate the ground to their own uses by the cultivation of it', they could not be said to have individual property in the land. Consequently, while much was left to Douglas's discretion and knowledge of the local situation, the company authorized him to confirm the Indians in the possession of only those lands that they had cultivated or built houses on by 1846 when they came under the sovereignty of Great Britain. All other land was to be regarded as waste and therefore available for colonization.[79] In pursuance of his instructions, Douglas had eleven treaties made with the Indians of the Fort Victoria area and later two at Fort Rupert and one at Nanaimo. Because these treaties were largely based on current British opinion about the nature of aboriginal land tenure, they took little account of Indian realities. In spite of Douglas's familiarity with the Indians the treaties contained a number of 'ethnographic absurdities',[80] including the fact that only 'village sites and enclosed fields' were to be reserved: that is, areas of land of which Indian possession could be recognized in European terms. In the Saanich area Douglas found it quite impossible to sort out the real owners from the numerous claimants to the land, so an area of fifty square miles was purchased.[81]

By these treaties the Indians surrendered their lands in return for a few blankets, the reservation of a little land for their use, and the freedom to hunt on unoccupied land and to fish as before. The compensation that the Indians received for these concessions was minimal. Douglas favoured payment by annuity so that the Indians would derive a continuing benefit,[82] but apparently the Indian leaders preferred a lump sum. They were paid in goods, mostly blankets, from the Fort Victoria stores, and the value to the Indians included a markup of approximately 200 per cent over the 'department' or wholesale price. The Songhees, for instance, received goods with a retail price of £309.10.0, but the cost to the company had actually been £103.14.0.[83] With the 'small exceptions' of village sites and enclosed fields, the land had become 'the entire property of the white people for ever'.[84]

Douglas did not find these treaties easy to negotiate. He discovered that any discussion of the question of Indian rights invariably produced 'troublesome excitements'.[85] It is unlikely that the Indians comprehended the full import of the phrase 'entirely and forever'. In the pre-settlement period the Indians had no way of learning about European concepts of land ownership, and the signatories of the treaties probably thought that they were surrendering the rights to the use of the land rather than title to it. But in spite of the many inadequacies, implicit in these treaties was the notion that the aboriginal race exercised some kind of ownership over the land that ought to be extinguished by the colonizing power.

Because Douglas negotiated these treaties to facilitate settlement, he was only prepared to purchase Indian land in areas where Europeans wanted to take up land. The Cowichan Indians wanted to sell their lands in the same way as the Songhees had done, but Douglas refused their request on the grounds that settlement was not immediately moving into that area.[86] It was a decision that was to produce major problems in the future.

Once treaties were signed, however, Douglas was determined to protect Indian land from encroachment, although this rule did have one exception to prove it. Contained within the Hudson's Bay Company land around Fort Victoria was a ten-acre Indian reserve. That is, as far as everybody was concerned in 1854 it was an Indian reserve.[87] But by the end of the decade the land had been reallotted as the site of the government offices.[88] The exception is an interesting one, but generally Douglas did make every effort to protect Indian rights guaranteed by the treaties he made.

Douglas's concern for Indian welfare also found expression in areas other than land policy. His attitudes to the Indians were a mixture in which the knowledge of the fur trader was accompanied by the paternalistic concerns of the nineteenth-century humanitarian. His ideas about the need and means to 'improve' the Indians had been adumbrated as a fur trader. Now, as governor of a settlement colony, not only was the need for philanthropy greater, but there was also much more potential for action. Like those of his contemporaries who saw any hope at all for the survival of the North American Indian, his hope was expressed in terms of the Indians becoming red-skinned Europeans. Christianity, education, and agriculture—the holy trinity of British colonial policy on aborigines—were to be the means by which the Indian could achieve this new status. Consequently Douglas's intention was both to secure for the Indians sufficient land for them to develop and maintain a livelihood based on agriculture and to encourage 'schools and clergymen to superintend their moral and religious training'.[90] He believed the 'untutored reason of man' to be a contemptible thing and said that those fools who denied the ennobling influence of religion would be cured of their idle fancies by a few months' residence among the Indians.[91] So, whenever he could, Douglas gave encouragement and assistance to missionaries of all denominations who came to work among the Indians. He had his own plans for social reorganization as well. In 1860 he wrote that he had long cherished the hope that he would be able to organize the Indians into communities in which peace and the enforcement of laws would be facilitated by the appointment of Indian police officers and magistrates. As the only plan that promised to result in the moral elevation of the Indians, Douglas thought that its successful operation would 'raise an imperishable monument to the justice and philanthropy of the Government which lends it support'. He added, however, that the plan would cost money and therein lay the impediment. Douglas never found the money to put these ideas into action.[92]

Before 1849 and the arrival of the colonists there had been no need to contemplate measures for the rearrangement of Indian society. During the fur-trading period it had been unnecessary to develop policies designed to avoid hostilities with the Indians. Douglas ruled the colony autocratically; he took little advice and retained power in his own hands as much as possible, yet the settlers still influenced his policies. The mere fact of their presence demanded that new measures be taken for the regulation of race relations. Then, in spite of Douglas's predilections, the elective principle was conceded in 1856 with the establishment of a Legislative Assembly with seven members. Company men dominated the first House and the government of the colony, but their time was passing. Having established a foothold in government, the settlers were to play an increasing part in the administration of the colony. The few colonists on Vancouver Island in the 1850s were the harbingers. Besides these settlers, forerunners of a different kind also began arriving in the 1850s.

The officers of the Hudson's Bay Company were aware at least as early as 1850 that there was gold on the Queen Charlotte Islands. This kind of information could never be contained, and in 1852 gold seekers from the United States began to appear on the islands. Their presence necessitated the promulgation of laws to regulate their activities, and Douglas's responsibilities were increased when he was issued with a commission as lieutenant-governor of the Queen Charlotte Islands. The Haida were unenthusiastic about the arrival of white men come to exploit resources that the Indians regarded as theirs. Douglas knew that there was likely to be conflict, since the company had already been forced to abandon its own efforts to find gold on the Queen Charlottes because of the 'turbulent opposition' of the Indians.[93] The expectations of hostility were not to be disappointed, and American miners were driven off the islands by the Haida. The most famous incident was the capture and plunder of the *Susan Sturgis*. She carried a group of gold miners, and, according to Douglas, the captain, Matthew Rooney, disregarded all warnings about the disposition of the Indians and showed 'a lamentable want of judgement'. Fortunately, there was no loss of life. The Haida chief, Edenshaw, who had visited Victoria and presumably talked with Douglas, convinced the Indians not to take the lives of the crew of the *Susan Sturgis*.[94] But this was the kind of incident that competition between Indians and whites for resources was likely to produce, and the Queen Charlotte gold 'rush' was only a prelude to the main event.

Throughout the 1850s reports and samples indicating the existence of gold in the interior of New Caledonia had dribbled into Victoria. By the summer of 1857 it was evident that there was gold in considerable quantities along the Fraser and Thompson rivers. In November Douglas wrote to the company headquarters in London, and, in a consciously metaphorical manner, noted that the 'prospects of the district are really becoming brilliant'. Douglas also realized that, as the 'auriferous character of the country' became more apparent, an influx of 'motly adventurers' from the south was likely.[95] It was a probability that caused him concern, for gold miners arriving in large numbers would not only ferment hostilities with the Indians but also disturb the company's trading relations. The Indians of the area quickly ascertained the value of gold as a trade item and had already served notice of their opposition to intruders. A group of American miners who came north looking for gold in 1857 were forcibly ejected by the Thompson River Indians, and there were reports of another group being plundered by the Okanagans.[96]

Although he was apprehensive about the consequences of gold discoveries, the letters that Douglas wrote in the winter and spring of 1857–8 show that he still thought that the company's old relationship with the Indians would continue. While settlement was in the process of terminating the company's hegemony over Vancouver Island, Douglas assumed that the fur traders were still secure on the mainland. He obviously hoped that the arrangement that the company had with the Indians for trading furs could automatically be applied to the acquisition of gold. The Indians did not want outsiders extracting gold, and this disposition coincided exactly with the interests of the company. In fact, Douglas could not help admiring the wisdom and foresight of the Indians, who were inadvertently arranging things for the benefit of the Hudson's Bay Company. He instructed the servants to leave the Indians to work the gold themselves, on the assumption that they would bring it into the company posts as an article of trade.[97] A fort for the specific purpose of trading gold from the Indians was planned, and building was begun in April 1858 at the forks of the Fraser and Thompson rivers. It was reported in the same month that Chief Trader Donald McLean had obtained 130 ounces of gold dust over a period of eighteen days, and prospects for the future looked just as promising.[98] Even late in the spring of 1858 Douglas and the other company officers were arranging for the continuation of the same reciprocal relationship that they had always had with the Indians. They were unaware of the disruptive human deluge that was to flood into New Caledonia in the next few months: a surge of humanity that was to signal the end of the fur trade.

British colonial policy-makers had turned the administration of the colony of Vancouver Island over to the Hudson's Bay Company in 1849 and made Douglas governor for a variety of reasons. But important among those reasons was the advantage of the fur traders' 'systematic' methods of dealing with the Indians compared to the 'mere caprice of ordinary settlers'.[99] On the whole the Colonial Office was satisfied with Douglas's handling of Indian-European relations, and even some settlers were impressed with his efforts.[100] Historians, however, have been quick to criticize company rule for not fostering colonization. They have been less willing to recognize that by maintaining relatively peaceful relations with the Indians Douglas made a crucial contribution to the establishment of the settlement frontier. Douglas quite rightly pointed out that by establishing friendly relations with the Indians the company rendered the area west of the Rockies habitable for settlers.[101] Anglocentric commentators, both in the nineteenth and twentieth centuries, have evaluated the success of the company's administration according to the size of the settler population rather than by the nature of the relations with the Indians. Even in the nascent stage of settlement the Indians were becoming of secondary importance. Before many of them had realized it, settlement had established a foothold under the auspices of the old fur-trading organization that they were so used to dealing with. On Vancouver Island in the 1850s the fur-trading and settlement frontiers had merged in a way that allowed one to engender the other.

Suggestions for Further Reading

Robin Fisher, *Contact and Conflict: Indian-European Relations in British Columbia, 1774–1890* (Vancouver, 1977).

John S. Galbraith, *The Hudson's Bay Company as an Imperial Factor 1821–1869* (Berkeley and Los Angeles, 1957).

Margaret A. Ormsby, *British Columbia: A History* (Toronto, 1971).

Notes

[1] Douglas to governor, deputy governor, and committee, 18 October 1838, Rich, *McLoughlin's Letters, First Series*, 242.

[2] Fitzgerald to B. Hawes, 9 June 1847, Great Britain, Colonial Office, Original Correspondence, Vancouver Island, 1846–67, CO 305/1, University of British Columbia Library (hereafter UBCL) (hereafter cited as CO 305).

[3] Rich, *History of the H.B.C.*, 2, 761.

[4] Andrew Muir, Diary, 16 and 27 June 1850, 'Private Diary, Commencing 9 November 1848 to 5 August 1850', PABC. Muir is possibly an unreliable witness as he was currently waging a bitter feud with the company over working conditions in the Fort Rupert coal mines and would not be likely to miss an opportunity to slander his employer. Blanshard to John Sebastian Helmcken, 6 August 1850, Vancouver Island, Governor (Blanshard), Correspondence Outward, 1849–51, PABC; Helmcken to Douglas, 28 March 1851, Hudson's Bay Company Archives (hereafter HBCA), A-11/73.

[5] Douglas to Simpson, 24 February 1851, HBCA, D-5/30. A correspondent of Helmcken's concluded on the basis of the doctor's letters that Fort Rupert was 'the Lunatic Asylum of the Coast' (D.D. Wishart to Helmcken, 17 August 1850, Helmcken Papers, PABC).

[6] Beardmore's statement regarding the Fort Rupert murders [1850], HBCA, A-11/73; J.H. Pelly to Earl Grey, 14 January 1852, HBCA, A-8/6.

[7] Blanshard to Fairfax Moresby, 27 June 1851, Vancouver Island, Governor, Correspondence Outward.

[8] Blanshard to Helmcken, 6 August 1850, Vancouver Island, Governor, Correspondence Outward.

[9] Helmcken to Blanshard, 17 July 1850, Vancouver Island, Courts, Magistrate's Court, Fort Rupert, Reports to Governor Blanshard, 2 and 17 July 1850, Helmcken Papers.

[10] For Moresby's views on the question of punishment see Barry M. Gough, *The Royal Navy on the Northwest Coast of America, 1810–1914: A Study of British Maritime Ascendancy* (Vancouver: University of British Columbia Press, 1971), 92. Because of his specific concerns the author emphasizes the policy of the naval commander, but, as governor, Blanshard must bear all responsibility.

[11] Blanshard to Helmcken, 6 August 1850, Vancouver Island, Governor, Correspondence Outward.

[12] Certainly Douglas was of the opinion that the Newitty '*could* not surrender the criminals' (Douglas to Archibald Barclay, 16 April 1851, HBCA, A-11/73).

[13] Douglas to Barclay, 3 September 1851, *ibid.*

[14] Cf. Gough, *Royal Navy*, 90; and 'The Power to Compel: White-Indian Conflict in British Columbia during the Colonial Period, 1849–1871' (Paper given at the Canadian Historical Association Annual Meeting, June 1972) 10.

[15]Blanshard to Moresby, 27 June 1851, Vancouver Island, Governor, Correspondence Outward; Gough, *Royal Navy*, 92.

[16]Work to Donald Ross, 27 November 1850, Ross Papers.

[17]Douglas to Blenkinsop, 27 October and 13 November 1850, HBCA, B–226/b; Douglas to Barclay, 16 April 1851, HBCA, A–11/73.

[18]Work to Donald Ross, 27 November 1850, Ross Papers.

[19]Grey to Blanshard, 20 March 1851, Great Britain, Colonial Office, Despatches to Vancouver Island, 1849–67, PABC. In 1853 the Royal Navy established new policy guidelines for the use of force against Indians by ships' commanders (see Gough, *Royal Navy*, 92).

[20]Blanshard to Moresby, 28 June 1851, Vancouver Island, Governor, Correspondence Outward; Douglas to Barclay, 1 September 1850 and 21 March 1851, HBCA, A–11/72; Douglas to Simpson, 21 May 1851, HBCA, D–5/30.

[21]Douglas to Simpson, 12 March 1849, HBCA, D–5/24.

[22]Pelly to Grey, 14 January 1852, HBCA, A–8/6.

[23]See, for example, Admiral John Moresby, *Two Admirals: Sir Fairfax Moresby John Moresby a Record of a Hundred Years* (London: Methuen, 1913), 103; R.C. Mayne, *Four Years in British Columbia and Vancouver Island . . .* (London: J. Murray, 1862), 54; Edward Cridge, 'Characteristics of James Douglas Written for H.H. Bancroft in 1878', PABC; Charles Frederick Morison, 'Reminiscenses of the Early Days in British Columbia 1862–1876 by a Pioneer of the North West Coast', PABC, 15a; Victoria *Evening Press*, 10 March 1864.

[24]Douglas to Blenkinsop, 27 October 1850, HBCA, B–226/b.

[25]Douglas to John Pakington, 21 January 1853, CO 305/4. For other accounts of the operation see Douglas to Barclay, 20 January 1853, Douglas to Tod, 7 January 1853, HBCA, A–11/74; Douglas, Diary, 3 and 7 January 1853, James Douglas, Private Papers, 1835–77, PABC; Douglas to Augustus Kuper, 8 November 1852, Vancouver Island, Governor, Correspondence Outward, 1850–9, PABC.

[26]Douglas to Pakington, 21 January 1853, CO 305/4; Newcastle to Douglas, 12 April 1853, Great Britain, Colonial Office, Despatches to Vancouver Island.

[27]Douglas to Henry Labouchere, 6 September 1856, CO 305/7; Douglas to William Smith, 6 September 1856, HBCA, A–11/76.

[28]Labouchere to Douglas, 13 November 1856, Great Britain, Colonial Office, Despatches to Vancouver Island.

[29]Douglas to Labouchere, 24 February 1857, CO 305/8; Douglas to Smith, 18 February 1857, HBCA, A–11/76.

[30]Merivale to John Shepherd, 19 November 1856, HBCA, A–8/8.

[31]Douglas to Baynes, 17 August 1859, CO 305/11.

[32]Douglas to Newcastle, 28 July 1853, CO 305/4; Douglas to Barclay, 2 November 1853, HBCA, A–11/74; Newcastle to Douglas, 15 October 1853, Great Britain, Colonial Office, Despatches to Vancouver Island.

[33]Douglas to Grey, 31 October 1851, CO 305/3.

[34]Douglas to Labouchere, 20 October 1856, CO 305/7.

[35]Douglas to Labouchere, 13 June 1857, CO 305/8.

[36]Douglas to Captain James Prevost, 19 October 1857, Vancouver Island, Governor, Correspondence Outward.

[37]Ogden to Simpson, 10 March 1849, HBCA, D-5/24; Douglas to governor, deputy governor and committee, 18 October 1838, Rich, *McLoughlin's Letters, First Series*, 242.

[38]Andrew Colvile to Pakington, 24 November 1852, HBCA, A-8/7.

[39]Bancroft, *History of B.C.*, 206, 211; Martin Robin, *The Rush for Spoils: The Company Province 1871–1933* (Toronto: McClelland and Stewart, 1972), 14.

[40]Galbraith, *H.B.C. as an Imperial Factor*, 285.

[41]Barclay to Douglas, December 1849, Fort Victoria, Correspondence Inward, 1849–59, from the Hudson's Bay Company, London, to James Douglas, PABC.

[42]Annie Deans to her cousins, 13 August 1856, Annie Deans, Correspondence Outward, 1853–68, PABC.

[43]Victoria *Evening Express*, 10 March 1864. For details of the conflict between Staines and Douglas see Hollis G. Slater, 'Rev. Robert John Staines, Priest, Pedagogue, and Political Agitator', *British Columbia Historical Quarterly* (hereafter *BCHQ*) 14 (1950): 187–240.

[44]Great Britain, Parliament, *Hansard's Parliamentary Debates*, 3d ser., 151 (1858): 1121.

[45]Annie Deans to her brother and sister, 29 February 1854, Deans, Correspondence Outward.

[46]Charles Wilson, Diary, 8 August 1858, in George F.G. Stanley, ed., *Mapping the Frontier: Charles Wilson's Diary of the Survey of the 49th Parallel, 1858–1862* . . . (Toronto: Macmillan, 1970), 29–30; see also George Duncan Forbes MacDonald, *British Columbia and Vancouver's Island* . . . (London: Longman, Green, Longman, Roberts and Green, 1862), 271; and George Hills (bishop of Columbia), Diary, 26 December 1861, Archives of the Vancouver School of Theology.

[47]Charles Alfred Bayley, 'Early Life on Vancouver Island', PABC, 2.

[48]Tod to Edward Ermatinger, 29 June 1836, Ermatinger Papers.

[49]Douglas to Pelly, 5 December 1848, HBCA, A-11/72.

[50]Douglas and Work to governor and committee, 7 December 1846, *ibid.*

[51]Despatch from Simpson to Hudson's Bay Company, 24 June 1848, CO 305/1.

[52][P.H. Sheridan], *Personal Memoirs of P.H. Sheridan, General United States Army* (New York: C.L. Webster and Company, 1858), 1:88.

[53]Douglas to Simpson, 4 April 1845, HBCA, D-5/13.

[54]Douglas to Smith, 6 November 1855, HBCA, A-11/75.

[55]Douglas to James Tilton, 6 November 1855, Vancouver Island, Governor, Correspondence Outward.

[56]Douglas to William Molesworth, 8 November 1855, CO 305/6.

[57]Douglas to Baynes, 17 August 1859, CO 305/11.

[58]Douglas to Simpson, 24 February 1851, HBCA, D-5/30. Grant did return to the colony for a few months in 1853. For an account of his career see Willard E. Ireland, 'Captain Walter Colquhoun Grant: Vancouver Island's First Independent Settler', *BCHQ* 17 (1953), 87–121.

[59]Douglas to Barclay, 3 September 1849, HBCA, A-11/72.

[60]Douglas to Barclay, 1 September 1850 and 21 May 1851, HBCA, A-11/72 and 73.

[61]Douglas to Barclay, 15 June 1854, HBCA, A-11/75.

[62]Douglas to Grey, 15 April 1852, CO 305/3.

[63]Douglas to Tod, 7 January 1853, HBCA, A-11/74; Douglas to Labouchere, 5 May 1857, CO 305/8.

[64]Douglas to Barclay, 13 July 1854, HBCA, A-11/75; Douglas to Newcastle, 8 August 1860, CO 305/14.

[65]C.H. Mason to Douglas, 26 August 1857, CO 305/8. Apparently the Washington government also made it a capital offence for northern Indians to land on American territory (Douglas to McNeil, 21 September 1857, Fort Victoria, Correspondence Outward, 21 December 1856–25 January 1858, Letters Signed by James Douglas [Country Letterbook], PABC).

[66]Douglas to Smith, 18 February 1857, HBCA, A-11/76.

[67]Douglas to Admiral W.H. Bruce, 7 March 1856, Vancouver Island, Governor, Correspondence Outward.

[68]Douglas to Newcastle, 28 July 1853, CO 305/4.

[69]Douglas to Baynes, 17 December 1859, CO 305/11; Douglas to Newcastle, 16 May 1854, Vancouver Island, Governor, Despatches to Her Majesty's Principal Secretary of State for the Colonies, 1851–9, PABC. In instances where despatches are missing from the CO 305 records this source, which is Douglas's letterbook copies of his despatches, has been used. Margaret A. Ormsby, *British Columbia: a History* (Toronto: Macmillan, 1974), 129.

[70]Minutes of the Council of Vancouver Island, 21 June 1855, CO 305/6; Douglas to Sir George Grey, 7 March 1856, CO 305/7; Robert Swanton to Thomas Bannister, 4 January 1856, Great Britain, Colonial Office, Despatches to Vancouver Island.

[71]MacDonald, *British Columbia*, 80.

[72]Great Britain, Parliament, House of Commons, *Report of the Select Committee on the Hudson's Bay Company*, 194–5.

[73]Douglas to Smith, 11 December 1855, HBCA, A-11/75.

[74]Douglas to Lord John Russell, 21 August 1855, CO 305/6.

[75]Gough, 'The Power to Compel', *passim*.

[76]Douglas to Barclay, 22 December 1850, CO 305/3.

[77]Barry M. Gough, ' "Turbulent Frontiers" and British Expansion: Governor James Douglas, the Royal Navy, and the British Columbia Gold Rushes', *Pacific Historical Review* 41 (1972), 18. On the single occasion that navy men went up to the gold fields because of conflict between miners and Indians, the dispute was settled before they arrived (*ibid.*, 23–4).

[78]Gilbert Malcolm Sproat, *Scenes and Studies of Savage Life* (London: Smith, Elder, 1868), 55.

[79]Douglas to Barclay, 3 September 1849, HBCA, A-11/72; and Barclay to Douglas, December 1849, Fort Victoria, Correspondence Inward.

[80]An analysis of the Fort Victoria treaties in relation to what is known about Songhees ethnography has been made by Wilson Duff, 'The Fort Victoria Treaties', *BC Studies* 3 (1969), 52 and *passim*.

[81]Douglas to Barclay, 18 March 1852, HBCA, A-11/73.

[82]Douglas to Barclay, 3 September 1849, HBCA, A-11/72.

[83]The point is made by Duff, 'Fort Victoria Treaties', 24. See also Douglas to Barclay, 16 May 1850, HBCA, A-11/72. Blanshard was aware that the Indians were paid at a 200 per cent markup (Blanshard to Grey, 18 February 1851, CO 305/3).

[84]For the texts of these treaties see Hudson's Bay Company, Land Office Victoria, 'Register of Land Purchased from the Indians, 1850–1859', PABC. Edited versions are contained in British Columbia, *Papers Connected with the Indian Land Question*,

1850–1875 (Victoria: R. Wolfenden, 1875) 5–11. These papers were also published with a different pagination in British Columbia, Legislative Assembly, *Sessional Papers*, 2d Parl., 1st sess., 1876, 161–328B.

[85]Douglas to Barclay, 16 May 1853, HBCA, A-11/74.

[86]Douglas to Barclay, 16 May 1850, HBCA, A-11/72.

[87]Pemberton to Barclay, 1 September 1854, Douglas to Barclay, 26 August 1854, HBCA, A-11/75.

[88]Minutes of the Council of Vancouver Island, 25 March 1859, CO 305/10; Pearse to Colonial Secretary, 1 February 1865, British Columbia, Colonial Correspondence (Inward Correspondence to the Colonial Government), PABC, file 910 (hereafter cited as CC); Day and Son, Lithographers to the Queen, *Map of Victoria and Part of Esquimalt District* (London, 1861).

[89]In his letter to Barclay of 26 August 1854, HBCA, A-11/75, Douglas reported that the Indians had offered the ten acres to him for sale, but that he had declined the offer. The possibility remains that the land was subsequently purchased from the Songhees, although I have found no evidence of such a sale.

[90]Douglas to Lytton, 14 March 1859, Great Britain, Colonial Office, Original Correspondence, British Columbia, 1858–1871, CO 60/4, UBCL (hereafter cited as CO 60).

[91]Douglas to Hargrave, 5 February 1843, James Hargrave Collection, Series 1, Letters Addressed to James Hargrave, 1821–86, PAC.

[92]Douglas to Newcastle, 7 July 1860, CO 305/14; Douglas to Lytton, 14 March 1859, CO 60/4; Douglas to Smith, 30 October 1857, HBCA, A-11/76.

[93]Douglas to Barclay, 28 December 1851, HBCA, A-11/73.

[94]Douglas to Newcastle 8 June 1853, CO 305/4. The Haida chief had a special relationship with Governor Douglas. Edenshaw was descended from the chief named Cunneah, who had exchanged names with Captain William Douglas in the early years of the maritime fur trade. Consequently, Edenshaw and the governor of Vancouver Island shared the same name (see William Henry Hills, Journal, 23 May 1853, 'Journal on Board H.M.S. *Portland* and *Virago* 8 August 1852–8 July 1853', UBCL; and Meares, *Voyages*, 365).

[95]Douglas to Smith, 27 November 1857, HBCA, A-11/76.

[96]Douglas to Labouchere, 15 July 1857, CO 305/8; and Douglas to Smith, 26 May 1857, HBCA, A-11/76.

[97]Douglas to Simpson, 17 July 1857, HBCA, D-5/44.

[98]Douglas to Smith, 19 April 1858, HBCA, A-11/74.

[99]Minute by Frederick Peel on Douglas to Newcastle, 28 February 1853, CO 305/4.

[100]See, for example, Lytton to Douglas, 14 August 1858, Great Britain, Colonial Office, Despatches to Vancouver Island; W. Colquhoun Grant, 'Description of Vancouver Island, by its First Colonist', *Journal of the Royal Geographical Society* 27 (1857), 320.

[101]*British and American Joint Commission*, 2, 55.

30

Culture and the State

Phillip McCann

A variety of new perspectives from Europe, influenced by new critical theories of language and its relationship to society, has considerably altered and enlivened the study of culture in Canada. These 'post-modernist' interpretations, which have come to be labelled under the umbrella 'cultural studies', owe much to both psychoanalysis (Freud and his critics) and left-wing (chiefly Marxist and neo-Marxist) political theory. In general, they insist that neither language nor culture are neutral instruments, but rather are heavily freighted with a variety of meanings depending on both the user and the society in which they are found. One of the most interesting of the schools of cultural studies is that associated with E.P. Thompson, Eric Hobsbawm, and Terence Ranger. It is particularly interested in the relationship between culture and state formation, especially on the margins of the British Empire. Hobsbawm and Ranger have coined the term 'the

invention of tradition' to refer to the process by which the ruling groups and public authorities utilize and manipulate culture to create and support national identities.

In his essay on Newfoundland between 1832–1855, Phillip McCann applies the concept of the invention of tradition to the province of Newfoundland after 1832, the year in which it first received representative government. He argues that the British government quite deliberately encouraged certain organizations and symbols to support its newly reformed province. It countered expressions of Irish Catholic solidarity with a Protestant crusade, and organized a number of other institutions (an Agricultural Society, a School Society, a Natives' Society, a Mechanics' Institute) designed to create in Newfoundland a British identity with strong nativist feelings of local pride.

What does McCann mean by 'the British government'? What does he mean by 'native'? Does McCann's evidence support his assertion that the British (as opposed to the ruling authority in the province) created imperial sentiment? Were the authorities conscious that they were 'promoting cultural rituals which were moulding the consciousness of Newfoundlanders'? Does it matter whether the ruling groups fully understood and articulated what they were doing? What is important about the argument that in this period many Island traditions, rituals, and attitudes were 'invented', rather than developing naturally?

This article first appeared, titled 'Culture, State Formation and the Invention of Tradition: Newfoundland 1832–1855', in *Journal of Canadian Studies* 23, 1 & 2 (Spring/Summer 1988), 86–103.

The relationship of culture to the state or civil authority has recently begun to receive attention from historians, educationists and anthropologists. The work of Edward Thompson on cultural forms in the pre-industrial state, of Corrigan and Sayer on culture and state formation in England, of Curtis and others on education and social structure in Upper Canada, of Hobsbawm and Ranger on the invention of tradition, and of Sider on culture and class in Newfoundland[1] points the way to a widening of the concept of culture and to a more dynamic treatment of the inter-relationship of culture and society. The focus has been on both the significance of popular culture and the role of the state in the creation and maintenance of cultural hegemony, but little of this research has been concerned with the culture of colonial states, or the attempts made by imperial powers to inculcate what might be termed a colonial consciousness. Newfoundland in the mid-nineteenth century provides a particularly interesting example of a colonial state in the making, both materially and culturally. Attached to the British Crown since the sixteenth century, the island had long been used merely as a stage for the west of England fishing fleets until increasing population, the expense to Britain of direct administration, and a powerful reform movement in Newfoundland itself led to the granting of Representative Government on the Canadian maritime model in 1832.

The infant colony faced peculiar problems. Its economy was based on the infamous truck or credit system, in which the fishing population bartered the fish they caught for food and equipment with a small number of merchants. The latter were mainly Protestant; the fishing families were divided between Catholics from south-east Ireland and Protestants from south-west England. Newfoundland was regarded, together with New South Wales, as an 'anomalous society', one which lacked a sufficient number of men of property, education and loyalty to form a viable political entity.[2] Most general histories of Newfoundland have acknowledged its peculiarities, but failed to link them with either popular or state-regulated cultural activities. In these works culture has either been ignored, or interpreted merely as the arts and leisure activities, usually in an added chapter, or virtually equated with social history.[3] The growth of political culture in the sense of the encouragement of popular cultural activities by the state, with the aim of fostering social harmony among the masses, has largely been ignored.

The work of Gerald Sider has opened a new dimension, both in the meaning of culture and in its relationship to the socio-economic structure of Newfoundland. Sider argues that the family fishery, dominated by merchant capital, was the breeding ground for the main popular cultural activity—Christmas mumming—which became a means of re-ordering social and work relationships. But Sider's thesis does not encompass political structures and, in common with nearly all historians of Newfoundland, he pays insufficient attention to the fact that from 1832 onwards Newfoundland was not only dominated by merchant capital but was also a Protestant colony in the making, a 'state' which the Colonial Office and the local élite attempted to fashion on lines acceptable to the political, social and cultural norms of the mother country. In this operation, Protestant ideology played a greater role than in almost any other colony as a means of combatting the political militancy of the Catholic Irish, who formed half the population of the island.

The early attempts to construct a viable colonial community can best be examined between 1832, when Representative Government was granted, and 1855 when Responsible Government (with a Prime Minister and cabinet) was achieved. In the first years of Representative Government, the populace lacked a commitment to British colonial rule and the island was racked by political and sectarian antagonisms. It was when these tensions appeared to be making social and political integration impossible—particularly in the period 1837–41—that the British government intervened, not only instituting constitutional reform but also 'inventing tradition' by sponsoring and encouraging organizations and rituals which attempted to inculcate imperial sentiment on the basis of a 'patriotic' and nativist outlook.

The authority of ruling groups is not only maintained by economic or physical power, but is also located in cultural hegemony, 'the images of power and authority', the obverse of which are 'the popular mentalities of subordination'.[4] The ruling élite must establish or maintain the consent of the governed to the rulers' legitimacy, exact loyalty to the nation, establish conformity with 'the norms of society', and so on. The social and cultural identities of the citizens of a nation must be constructed in such a manner that the beliefs and presuppositions of the ruling élite, the strategies of authority, even the forms of economic exploitation, are accepted as normal, natural, unquestionable, and transcendant. Symbols, rituals and traditions, usually with vague or general connotations such as patriotism, loyalty, public duty, etc., are cherished, publicized or invented, that is, continuously generated, rather than transmitted. Support for the status quo usually has a national and patriotic rallying point around which unity can be formed. Conversely, groups or classes with separate or alternative identities are marginalized, or represented as outside the pale of 'normal' society.[5]

Few societies found it more necessary to attempt to construct a unified 'national' consciousness, or to denigrate those considered to be outside the mainstream, than Newfoundland after the grant of Representative Government. For centuries little more than a fishing station in which permanent settlement was discouraged, without constitutional traditions, an educational system or established civil institutions, Newfoundland in 1832 had a written constitution, in the shape of Instructions and Commission to the Governor, thrust upon it. These documents, blueprints for a settlement on the Canadian maritime model, instituted a colony with an appointed Council, an Assembly elected on virtually adult male suffrage (without which, as Lord Aberdeen pointed out later, there would have been no constituency at all),[6] and gave wide powers to the Governor. The Church of England was established as the lawful church under the aegis of the Bishop of Nova Scotia, education was to be organized according to Church principles, and the obedience of the people was enjoined.[7] The Instructions took no account of the fact that exactly half the population was Irish, nearly all of whom were immigrants by choice (in the period 1812–1830) from Tipperary, Wexford and Waterford, an economically dynamic region of farming and trade, centre of resurgent Catholicism and one of Daniel O'Connell's nationalist strongholds.[8]

The Roman Catholic Bishop, Michael Antony Fleming, an Irishman and follower of Daniel O'Connell, inspired by the new situation following the 1829 Catholic Emancipation Act, had broken with the policy of collaboration with the Protestant authorities pursued by his predecessors, the 'gentlemen-bishops' O'Donel, Lambert and Scallan. Moreover, he encouraged the political activities of his flock, backed radical-Liberal Catholic candidates for the new Assembly, and supported the establishment of publicly funded non-denominational schools established under the Education Act of 1836.[9]

During the period 1837–41 there was, in the words of Governor Prescott, 'war to the knife' between the Liberal-Catholic Assembly and the Tory-Protestant Council.[10] There were clashes over revenue bills, the supply vote, privileges, the election of officers, the administration of justice, education, and, above all, the Assembly's support for roads and agriculture, which directly threatened the merchant monopoly of the fishery in the outports. Furthermore, the Assembly, after long and bitter struggles, secured the removal of Chief Justice Boulton for maladministration and briefly imprisoned Dr Edward Kielly, the District Surgeon, and Assistant Judge Lilly for alleged breach of privilege, actions which infuriated the merchant class.[11] It was the actions of the Catholics at elections, however, which most alarmed the Protestant élite. As was common in Ireland, priests preached politics from the pulpit (there being no other channel of communication, asserted Fleming), political posters and petition tables were placed in the vicinity of the Catholic chapel, and marches with drums and banners were organized at election times to boost Catholic candidates and intimidate those who might vote for the Tories.[12]

The Catholic Irish, in the view of the ruling group, were outside the pale of 'legitimate' political and cultural expression. Governor Cochrane was amazed at the extent to which Catholicism had penetrated the civic culture of the Irish and their 'ordinary relations of life'.[13] The fact that Protestant and Catholic children were being educated side by side in the Board Schools created in 1836 on the model of the Irish National System, and that large numbers of Protestant fishermen voted for Catholic Liberal candidates,[14] further undermined the hold of the Protestant rulers on the hearts and minds of the people. In the later 1830s and early 1840s something very like a class struggle was being waged in Newfoundland. Recent research has revealed several instances of collective action by fishermen against the merchants in Conception Bay in the 1830s, and troops were called out on more than one occasion during this period.[15] R.J. Parsons, editor of the radical-Liberal *Patriot* newspaper, declared that the intervention of the priests in politics had cut the ties between merchant and fisherman; the latter, Governor Cochrane noticed, voted against merchants despite the fact they were economically dependent on them.[16] 'The politics which developed in this nascent colony,' observes historian S.J.R. Noel, 'reflected not only the traditional cleavages of ethnicity and religion but also the underlying potential of the people to realign their loyalties on the basis of economic class.'[17] The cultural underpinning of the Catholic political offensive was provided by the Benevolent Irish Society, a charitable and educational body founded in 1806, but which had come under the influence of Fleming's supporters in 1834. The St Patrick's Day festivals held under the auspices of the Society fused ethnicity and religion with a militant nationalism for all but a minority of the Newfoundland Irish.[18]

The Protestant administration could not have maintained the ideological basis for a governable state if they had allowed this situation to continue unopposed. The counter-offensive began in 1834 with an attempt to persuade Rome to discipline or remove Bishop Fleming from Newfoundland.[19] At the same time, the two Tory newspapers, the *Times* and the *Public Ledger*, joining the 'No Popery' crusade then being waged in Britain and the English-speaking world, attacked Catholicism, the Irish in general, and Bishop Fleming in particular with almost unbelievable ferocity, alleging that Catholics owed allegiance to Rome, which was directing 'enfranchised papists' to sever political, cultural and economic links with Britain and deliver Newfoundland into the hands of the Papacy.[20] The aim of isolating the Catholics and cutting the links between Catholic and Protestant fishermen was also behind an attack on the non-denominational school system. A united front of Protestants—Orthodox Anglicans, Anglican Evangelicals, Methodists and others—attacked the concept of non-denominationalism, using every device from packing school boards to keeping children from school, from attempting to force the Authorised Version of the Bible as a reading book into all Board schools to persuading the Attorney-General to reinterpret the Education Act. This campaign succeeded in making the act inoperable in many areas for seven years.[21]

The protagonists of the Protestant crusade in Newfoundland succeeded in presenting to the Colonial Office an image of the Catholic Irish as enemies of the state. The British government, seriously alarmed at what it took to be a condition bordering on anarchy, finally took action. The constitution was suspended in 1841, and a Select Committee on Newfoundland set up in the same year, which took evidence in a very partisan fashion. In 1842 the Newfoundland Act passed, which modified the franchise, joined the Council and Assembly in an amalgamated Legislature, and effectively reduced the representation of Catholic Liberals, thus satisfying the Tory Protestants who had maintained throughout the 1830s that all the ills of Newfoundland sprang from giving the franchise to 'half-civilised . . . hewers of wood and drawers of water'.[22] In September 1841 General Sir John Harvey had been appointed Governor, charged with the task of bringing harmony to the Colony and of reconstructing its political and cultural life in a manner that would prevent recurrence of the conflicts of the 1830s.

Harvey was an eminently suitable choice. A professional soldier who had won his spurs in the American War of 1812, an experienced administrator who had spent the greater part of his life attempting to keep turbulent colonies in order, Harvey had the reputation of a conciliator and peace-maker. From 1828 to 1836 he had been Inspector of Police for the Province of Leinster, before taking up his first major colonial appointment as Governor of Prince Edward Island, where he played a mediating role in a conflict of tenantry against landlordism not unlike that which he had experienced in Ireland. In 1837 he was appointed Governor of New Brunswick, where he achieved a measure of harmony by conciliatory measures and the judicious distribution of patronage among the warring factions of the colony.[23]

As Governor of Newfoundland, Harvey felt that he had been entrusted with 'a mission . . . to unite all in one common endeavour to advance the general good'.[24] He viewed the Amalgamated Assembly as 'an experiment' designed to promote practical legislation, not party interests, a forum in which 'legislative harmony' could promote 'public good'. At the same time he took practical measures to consolidate his power, persuading the Assembly to grant him the right of initiating money bills, and securing a balance of parties and the support of the officially appointed members by judicious promotions to the Council. Abjuring force and fiat, he worked to change, supplement or invent the outlooks and perceptions of his subjects. Shortly after his arrival he informed the Colonial Secretary that he had taken the first steps to unite men of all parties by inducing them to attend a meeting and send a joint address to the Queen on the birth of the Prince of Wales. In addition, he had taken the initiative in forming an Agricultural Society, becoming its patron and presiding at its first meeting.[25]

The establishment of an Agricultural Society was of great symbolic importance; Harvey persuaded both conservative merchants and Liberal Catholics to serve on its committee, thus neutralizing one of the latter's chief grievances against the mercantocracy. Harvey saw the fostering of agriculture not only in economic terms (as strengthening the fishery and thus promoting the consumption of British goods), but also as a means to the creation of a yeoman class—'brave, hardy, loyal and permanent settlers' who would form the 'Constitutional Defence' of the colony. To some extent Harvey's patronage of the Society—he attended their ploughing matches and banquets—achieved its aim, insofar as the Report of 1850 asserted that merchants were no longer hostile to agriculture, but recognized its growth to be in 'the best interests of the trade, and the moral and social condition of the people'.[26] Despite the import of cattle and seed and an increase of the area under cultivation, farming did not prosper greatly beyond St John's area, possibly because of the reluctance of merchants to capitalize the project beyond a certain point, but more probably because of the lack of viable road system. Harvey had plans for an extensive network of roads to link the capital with outlying areas and open up the country to farming and settlement, but despite increased allocation of revenue and some extension of roads around St John's, the program produced limited results.[27]

The education question was settled two years after Harvey took office by dividing the grant between the Protestant and Catholic denominations, the guerrilla warfare of the Protestant forces against the non-denominational system having prepared the way for a settlement on these lines. The Education Act of 1843 was piloted through the Assembly by Richard Barnes, whose speech on the second reading was a masterpiece of both erudition and special pleading. A member of a long-established merchant family, a deacon of the Congregational Church, and a self-educated man,[28] Barnes employed standard Protestant arguments against the concept of non-denominational education, and the bill passed easily in a House containing a minority of Liberal Catholics. Harvey, who admired Barnes but disliked 'class legislation', justified the 'deviation' (which his predecessor Prescott thought was the purchase of public instruction at too high a price) on the grounds that a 'peculiar state of society' existed in Newfoundland.[29]

The Board schools were potential generators of support for the new colonial state; but the teachers were for the most part so under-educated and the buildings so poorly equipped as to make the provision of even basic education problematic.[30] The function of 'colonial' education was, in any case, being undertaken by the Newfoundland School Society, an Evangelical missionary body founded by Newfoundland merchant Samuel Codner in London in 1823, and supported both morally and financially by the British government.[31] The Society's ideological position was based on the theory of Christian colonialism, which underwrote imperial expansion provided it was accompanied by the spread of the (Protestant) gospel. The Society's British teachers arrived in Newfoundland with the declared intention of giving Newfoundlanders 'a participation in all the religious and intellectual privileges of this pre-eminently happy land, emphatically *their* Mother Country', and the Society's Evangelical leaders in London and its teachers in Newfoundland unremittingly promoted the ideal of the British Empire and Newfoundland's place within it. In 1851 the Secretary was declaring that the Society was part of a colonizing effort, the objective of which was 'to transplant England's laws, England's language, England's children, England's Church from the mother country and give them room and opportunity to develop abroad'.[32]

Although the Newfoundland School Society's cultural imperialism did not conflict with Harvey's general aims, he had little to do with the Society, which was well-established before his arrival; he preferred to work with organizations over which he could exercise some influence. His major achievement in the campaign to modify the cultural outlook of Newfoundlanders was achieved through the support he gave to the Natives' Society. This was one of a number of ethnic societies which were founded in the late 1830s and early 1840s on the model of the Benevolent Irish Society. But whereas the British and Scottish Societies, established in 1837, and the St George's Society, founded four years later, were formed and run by expatriate merchants, partly as dining clubs fostering nostalgic memories of the homeland, partly as benefit societies for indigent compatriots,[33] the Natives' Society was a quasi-political organization dedicated to the formation of a Newfoundland consciousness in opposition to the immigrants from Britain.

The Natives' Society had been conceived as early as 1836 by Dr Edward Kielly, a 'dissident' native Catholic, as an assertion of the rights of Newfoundlanders against the policies and practices of the Liberal Catholic politicians, all Irish immigrants, and some political dinners were organized to that end.[34] Although opposition to Liberal Catholicism was evident in its early years (and warmly reciprocated),[35] the Natives' Society rapidly established itself as a third force in Newfoundland political and cultural life. Its significance was quickly recognized by Sir Richard Bonnycastle, an officer of the Royal Engineers stationed in Newfoundland and unofficial adviser to the Colonial Office, who pointed out that the Natives held the balance between the 'ultra Tory officials and merchants' and the 'Liberal middle class and people', and yielded neither to 'the absurd pre-eminence in thought, rank and puerile precedence claimed by the former, nor to the rash, ill-advised, undigested schemes of the most excited of the latter'. Bonnycastle considered the Society 'a most useful engine, if managed by skilful hands', and he hoped it would meet with every encouragement from the government.[36]

Harvey took the advice and gave the Society an unusual amount of support, attending its ball in honour of the birth of the Prince of Wales—symbolically opened by Dr Kielly dancing the quadrille with Lady Bonnycastle—and laying the foundation stone of the Natives' Hall. A procession to Government House marked the ceremony, with speeches at the site and flowery patriotic language inscribed on the stone itself.[37] But the support which Harvey gained by this action was somewhat undermined a few weeks later when appointments to the Board of Directors of St John's Academy, the Road Board, the Board of Control, and the Street Building Board were announced; of thirty-seven members, only one was a native. Immediately, sections of the press and public opinion set up a clamour against Harvey, accusing him of prejudice against those born in Newfoundland. The *Patriot* and the *Newfoundlander* (both Liberal-Catholic papers edited by natives) led the fray, the former going as far as to declare that 'the best system of Colonial Government is that which promotes the Native interest in lofty superiority to every other'. A public meeting of protest was held and controversy continued in the press throughout the summer, Harvey's supporters ridiculing the accident of birth as fitness for office.[38] Harvey defended himself by claiming that if the aggrieved parties had communicated with him they would have received a courteous explanation; the appointments had been made by him, not by the Council, and for the most part were re-appointments. He was in entire ignorance of whether or not the appointees had been born on the island, he added, but his feelings were, other things being equal, to give preference to natives.[39]

Whether or not Harvey's explanation satisfied the aggrieved natives, the incident did not appear seriously to damage his prestige or his policy, and was not subsequently held against him. In fact, the episode stimulated the native cause.[40] The Natives' Society, whose leaders were drawn from what Bonnycastle called the middle class—small merchants, agents and clerks and 'a growing, most important, and rapidly-increasing number of the sons and daughters of those respectable men who have chosen Newfoundland as the country of their children'[41]—fused nativism, patriotism and a respect for social order into a political creed. They would cooperate, asserted Dr Kielly at the first general meeting, with 'the peaceable, orderly, respectable and well-disposed inhabitants of this Island in measures of general usefulness . . . to be respectful and obedient to the laws of the land, and . . . manifest on all occasions our loyalty and attachment to our most Gracious Sovereign and Constitution under which we live'.[42]

The cutting edge of nativist criticism was turned not against the mercan-tocracy or the administration, as was Liberal policy in the 1830s, but against 'strangers' who had been 'sucking the vitals of the country' and holding the natives in 'vassalage'[43]—rhetoric which penetrated the psyche of both Prot-estant and Catholic Newfoundlanders and was to be extraordinarily effective in creating a patriotic consciousness. This patriotism subjoined Newfound-land to Britain and expressed itself in adulation of Queen Victoria and the British constitution. As Richard Barnes, treasurer of the Society and an underrated architect of the emerging Newfoundland state, pointed out, the island had little in the way of stirring history, great men or culture heroes. It was inevitable, therefore, that in seeking to forge an identity the Natives should look to 'the beloved Sovereign of the British Dominions . . . [who] reigned not only over us but in our hearts', and conceive their role as edu-cating the people in 'a knowledge of the political gifts which they enjoy'.[44]

An important role in the creation of nativist sentiment was played by ceremony and symbol; the annual dinner, with patriotic toasts, quickly became an institution.[45] In 1842, eighty members of the Carbonear Natives' Society walked in procession through the town, headed by the Society's flag; committee members carried staffs decorated with a bow of red ribbon, offi-cers wore a sash, and members a red rosette on the left breast.[46] By the 1850s the other ethnic societies were adopting similar rituals, infusing their cere-monies with tributes to the Queen and the British constitution and inviting guests from brother societies. The 1850 St Andrew's banquet was held in a hall decorated with flags 'emblematic of the union of England, Ireland and Scotland', and in 1852 the British Society marched through St John's behind the band of the Royal Newfoundland Companies 'with colours flying'.[47] It was becoming *de rigueur* for almost any group to show signs of patriotism; a Wesleyan Tea Meeting in November 1851 displayed the 'Red Cross of Eng-land', thus showing, reported the *Courier*, 'the undiminished and affectionate loyalty of the Wesleyans to the House of Brunswick'. Annual treats for school children, inaugurated in this period, were infused with a strong patriotic and moralistic content—gratitude to benefactors, dutiful obedience, and vener-ation of the Sovereign.[48]

These groups and societies were, in fact, inventing tradition, promoting cultural rituals which were moulding the consciousness of Newfoundlanders. Harvey, who knew the value of official ceremony and display in attaching people to the social order, enlarged upon the tradition inaugurated by the first civil governor, Sir Thomas Cochrane, who, believing like his contem-porary Louis XVIII of France that 'men are governed in large part by their eyes', made pageantry, love of show and a display of official dignity his guiding principles.[49] Harvey attempted to impress the populace with the public display (publicly reported) of civil and military power and lavish expenditure on soirees, banquets, balls and processions, a policy which reached its apogee on the occasion of the visit of Prince Henry of the Netherlands to Newfoundland in August 1845. 'Every honor and demonstration of public respect', vowed Harvey, 'as well as every degree of hospitable attention in my power shall be paid and offered.'[50]

'Never . . . have the deities of pleasure and festivity ruled for the time with a more undivided sway', enthused the *Newfoundlander*, 'the entire population of both sexes, of all ages, grades and distinctions . . . went forth to welcome and to greet him.'[51] Prince Henry was received under triumphal arches and proceeded to Government House through streets lined with green boughs, followed by the various societies marching in procession. During his stay he attended the races at Mount Pearl, made a cruise to Conception Bay (returning to a Royal salute and a display of fireworks), and attended a special regatta in the harbour and the Agricultural Society's annual ploughing match and dinner. He was later entertained at a soiree at Government House, a dinner given by the military, and a ball at the house of Major Robe of the Royal Engineers. Only the *Patriot*, recalling the role of the House of Orange in Ireland's history, criticized the festivities.[52]

These 'calculated occasions of popular patronage', in E.P. Thompson's phrase, simultaneously brought the different classes together and made manifest the distance between them; or as the *Courier* expressed it, with more percipience than it realized, these gala-days allowed all classes of society, normally separated by 'a visible line of distinction' to stand on 'a species of equality'.[53] The annual Regatta held at Quidi Vidi lake, and the frequent race meetings at Mount Pearl, both organized and controlled by merchant interests, had become, by the 1840s, a permanent feature of the cultural landscape.[54]

The success of Harvey's program was due in part to the lessening of the political pressure of the 1830s: Bishop Fleming concerned himself with the building of the Catholic cathedral; the Catholic Liberals, under the new constitution, could no longer command the majority they enjoyed from 1837 to 1841; the Liberal movement was temporarily in disarray following the St John's by-election of 1840; and many of the leaders had accepted positions of emolument from the government.[55] But Harvey had helped to set in motion a desire for improvement which animated not only the middle-class—small merchants, schooner owners, shopkeepers, publicans, and the upper ranks of artisans[56]—but also reached down to the common people, expressing itself not only in patriotic nativism but also in such movements as temperance and the provision of literary culture.

When the Natives' Society held their annual ball in 1844, it was organized on temperance principles. This was a significant acknowledgement of the growth of the temperance movement in the island, and a reaction against the staggering amount of alcohol consumed in Newfoundland; in 1838, 277,808 gallons of liquor of all kinds was imported for a population of

75,000.[57] Several short-lived temperance organizations had been formed in the 1830s, but the movement did not begin to flourish until the 1840s. Bishop Fleming inspired the formation of a Total Abstinence Society in 1841, which grew rapidly, attracted some Protestant support, and began to hold large public processions, replete with flags, banners with improving and patriotic motifs, ribbons, rosettes, and regalia.[58] In 1851 the Sons of Temperance, a Methodist-supported body largely patronized by 'young commercial gentlemen', held what was by this time a 'traditional' procession, with similar regalia and banners, which halted at Government House to give three cheers for the Queen—'a burst of loyal feeling', it was reported, 'emanating from hearts devoted and true to British rule'.[59]

Well aware that his support conferred 'a public and official character' upon such proceedings, Harvey bestowed some attention on the temperance movement, recognizing its role in the promotion of 'habits of industry and sobriety, strict integrity, and sound moral and religious principles' in the 'patriotic individuals' of the Colony. Temperance and nativism, he informed the Colonial Office, might seem 'trivial and unimportant' in comparison with other colonies, but in view of the peculiar situation in Newfoundland and his desire to reconcile conflicting parties and creeds, reports on such subjects might have more than ordinary interest.[60] Harvey became the Patron of the Church of England Total Abstinence Society, and addressed some of its meetings, linking temperance with Christian virtues, the maintenance of family life and the greatness of the British Empire. He attempted to give 'a less exclusive character' to the Roman Catholic Temperance procession of January 1844 by inviting Protestant congregations to join, but was too late to succeed; the procession, exhibiting 'the utmost possible order and decorum', attracted nearly 8,000 people.[61] As in Britain, the strategy of the Newfoundland temperance movement was 'moral suasion'; social ills were explained in terms of individual moral failure, and little or no attention was paid to the environmental factors which created drunkenness; nor was any attack made on the merchants whose import of liquor created the problem.[62]

If the temperance movement, in addition to reducing the consumption of spirits, exerted a widespread influence in favour of respectable patriotism—the Catholic procession of 1843 was reported to have attracted 10,000 participants, including some Protestants[63]—the establishment of libraries and reading rooms was indicative of a zeal for 'improvement' among the middle classes consonant with the mood of the times. Significantly, there were connections between opposition to drink and desire for polite literature; in 1851 commercial clerks connected with the temperance movement planned to open a temperance hotel with a reading room attached. The clerks had established a reading room in St John's as early as 1835, and provided much of the market for literary culture.[64] Their increasing numbers in the 1840s and 1850s reflected the growing centralization of commerce in St John's, described in 1845 as 'an almost entirely commercial town'. The logic of merchant capital decreed that the outports be restricted to fishing operations and that the capital should be the locus of commercial transactions. 'That "Paris is France",' observed Harvey, 'may be applied with at least equal truth to the City and District of St John's in relation to Newfoundland.'[65] Thus the clerks, educated young men sent out from England to join merchant firms, congregated in St John's; they boarded in merchants' houses but were not treated as equals, and consequently found themselves in something of a social limbo. A reading room and library, the *Patriot* thought, would provide them with suitable conversation and social recreation.[66] Under the leadership of the ubiquitous Richard Barnes, who became secretary of the institution in 1840, the Library, despite some vicissitudes, grew fairly rapidly and in 1845 received a grant from the legislature. The following year the premises were consumed in the fire and the project had to be started afresh. By 1852, no fewer than 6,201 books were being borrowed annually, or 33 volumes to each shareholder and subscriber.[67]

Sir John Harvey, ever solicitous to stimulate cultural activities, persuaded some 'leading characters' to give donations to the library, but by and large the élite did nothing to help the movement. It tended to foster literary culture of a 'useful' or 'improving' kind and to exclude publications having an 'improper or immoral tendency'. This policy, it was hoped, would form a 'correct bias' in the minds of young people 'destined to fill important positions in society'.[68] Similar considerations inspired the formation of a Mechanics' Institute in 1849, the sponsors of which hoped, by reducing fees, to attract members lower down the social scale; like similar institutions in Britain and the USA, however, the Institute was largely attended by the clerk and shopkeeper class. Two years later the Library and Institute joined forces to promote the formation of the St John's Athenaeum, but the institution did not come into being until 1861.[69]

These institutions attempted to influence the minds of young adults in the direction of sentiments favourable to the status quo, to imbue them with the idea that knowledge was primarily useful as a means of personal advancement up the social-commercial ladder, and to avoid any genuine debate upon controversial topics. The rules of the proposed literary and scientific institution in 1840 excluded religion and politics as the subjects of lectures, essays or discussion. Similar statements informed the outlook of the Debating and Elocution Society, founded in 1838 and again patronized by merchants' clerks.[70] This society remained in being until 1846, when it succumbed to the great fire of that summer which destroyed three-quarters of St John's and seriously dislocated its commercial and cultural life. However, socio-cultural activities resumed when St John's was rebuilt, and exerted an increasing influence on popular mentalities. If Newfoundland, by the time of the achievement of Responsible Government in 1855, had not become 'the brightest gem in the British colonial diadem', as Sir John Harvey had hoped,[71] it was certainly some way from the strife-torn colony which had alarmed the local administration and the British government in the later 1830s.

Harvey wished to claim much of the credit for himself; many of his later addresses to the Assembly and despatches to the Colonial Office were filled with self-justifying accounts of the success of his policies of development and conciliation. The construction of roads, the increase of educational facilities, the extension of agriculture, and improved provision for the poor he ascribed to the beneficial working of the 'experimental constitution', in whose formation he himself had played a part.[72] He viewed the Amalgamated Assembly as 'a well-contrived political machine' for raising and appropriating revenue for general improvement. More importantly, he believed that his policy had contributed to the happiness, sobriety and loyalty of the people and to the amicable relationship between the denominations, which he felt was exemplified in the laudatory address to which all members of the Assembly contributed on his departure in August 1846.[73]

Although Harvey undoubtedly had extended benevolent guidance and support, it is evident that large sections of the population were eager to participate in the ritual activities associated with the growth of patriotism, nativism and various forms of self-improvement. As meetings, processions, celebrations, and festivities became regular or annual events, a sense of stability and continuity was added to the flux of everyday life, and the mystique with which these activities were imbued exerted a powerful attraction on a people seeking a 'national' identity within the British imperial orbit. Patriotic Anglophile attitudes were perhaps most easily and securely established. The loyalty of Newfoundland to the Crown was attested in the House of Commons in 1855,[74] and the Crimean War brought an outburst of patriotic fervour hardly matched in Britain. At the beginning of 1855 a Patriotic Fund was established to raise money for the relief of widows and orphans of soldiers who had died in battle. By June subscriptions had totalled £2,118 and collections had been made in at least ten communities. It would appear that the campaign was spearheaded by substantial citizens of the Protestant faith, for few Irish names appeared in the subscription lists and no purely Irish areas sponsored a collection.[75] In St John's a public meeting of citizens was held in January to express sympathy with 'our brave troops in the Crimea'; the Governor was in the chair and the band of the Royal Newfoundland Companies opened the proceedings with the National Anthem. Again, the sponsors of the meeting were nearly all Protestant, and the resolutions identified Newfoundland with the Queen and the English nation: the people of the colony had 'the unanimous sentiments of British subjects' as to the justness of the war, felt proud that they were 'fellow subjects of Queen Victoria', and like British subjects everywhere sympathized with the death of 'our countrymen' in battle. Later in the year, when Sebastopol fell to the Allies, another public meeting was held; on this occasion the main speakers were Ambrose Shea, Lawrence O'Brien and John Kent, all leading Liberal-Catholic politicians. They composed an Address to Queen Victoria on behalf of 'Her Majesty's loyal subjects resident in St John's, Newfoundland, and deeply interested in the glory of their country'.[76]

Newfoundland was about to enter upon Responsible Government as a state in which loyalty to the concept of Empire had been achieved, particularly among the directing classes. Paradoxically, this consciousness of being British subjects resident in a colony co-existed with a strong nativist feeling. This was dramatically demonstrated in 1857, when all parties and faiths, in a great outburst of national fervour, united in successful opposition to the British government's grant of additional fishing rights to the French on the west coast of the island. Though the British and the French—to whose leaders toasts had been drunk at public dinners at the height of the war fever two years earlier[77]—were temporarily the objects of protest, little permanent damage was done to British-Newfoundland relations; but Newfoundland's sense of nationhood was greatly enhanced.

Beneath the surface, however, antagonisms of class and denomination still smouldered. Harvey had perceived that though politicians might cooperate in the Assembly, the population was still divided into virtually two classes, the merchants and the fishermen, whose interests conflicted and who were far from entertaining cordial feelings towards each other.[78] The achievement of Responsible Government in 1855, which was largely the result of a ten-year campaign led by Liberal Catholics, was excoriated by Tory Protestants as the triumph of the 'Catholic minority' over 'Protestant interests'.[79] Religious and political divisions came to the surface in 1861, when a large and angry crowd of Liberal Catholic supporters demonstrated outside the Legislative building against the Governor's dismissal of the Liberal ministry and the allegedly fraudulent Conservative election victory which followed. Troops were called out, the crowd was fired upon and a number of demonstrators were killed or wounded. This was a turning point in Newfoundland's political history, for it forced the Conservative forces to realize that they could either continue to govern by force—the 'Irish solution'—or could choose a more conciliatory path, in effect a return to the mode of administration adumbrated by Harvey. The conservative-administrative élite felt that the latter course was in their best interests and began to extend the patronage system and to 'share the spoils'—to allocate all offices of emolument and honour throughout society on a basis roughly equal to the strength of the main denominations.[80] This strategy was formally introduced into political life in 1865 when two leading Catholic Liberals, John Kent and Ambrose Shea, were invited to take office in a Conservative administration. This marked the beginning of the end of the identification of Catholicism with Liberalism and Protestantism with Conservatism and the conflicts which flowed from it.

The years 1832–55 were undoubtedly the crucial period in the formation of the state in Newfoundland. What emerged in the second half of the nineteenth century was basically a Protestant state, based largely on Protestant merchant capital and owing allegiance to a Protestant mother country. But it was also a state which was very different from that envisaged in the Instructions given to Governor Cochrane in 1832. The directing classes had not only successfully encouraged the growth of a patriotic nativism but, coming to terms with religious militancy (particularly that of the Catholic Irish) by the institutionalization of denominationalism, had also removed the underlying causes of religious conflict. The interwining of the concepts of patriotic nativism and denominational allegiance in the consciousness of the vast majority of Newfoundlanders underlay the strength of the island's social fabric in the latter part of the nineteenth century, and after. The activities which supported this outlook soon became bathed in the rosy glow of tradition, but their roots lay in Harvey's 'cultural revolution' of 1841–46. Much of what today is regarded as immemorial Newfoundland tradition, enshrined in institutions, rituals and attitudes, can be dated to the period under review.

Suggestions for Further Reading

Allan Greer and Ian Radforth, eds, *Cultural Leviathan: State Formation in Mid-Nine-teenth-Century Canada* (Toronto, 1992).
Gertrude Gunn, *The Political History of Newfoundland 1832–1864* (Toronto, 1966).
Eric Hobsbawm and Terence Ranger, eds, *The Invention of Tradition* (Cambridge, 1982).

Notes

The author is grateful to Edena Brown for research assistance on this project.

[1] E.P. Thompson, 'Patrician Society, Plebeian Culture', *Journal of Social History*, 7, 4 (1974), 382–405; P. Corrigan and D. Sayer, *The Great Arch: English State Formation as Cultural Revolution* (London: Basil Blackwell, 1985); B. Curtis, 'Preconditions of the Canadian State: Educational Reform and the Construction of a Public in Upper Canada, 1837–1846', *Studies in Political Economy*, 10 (1983); P. Corrigan, B. Curtis and R. Lanning, 'The Political Space of Schooling', in T. Wotherspoon, ed., *The Sociology of Education* (Toronto: Methuen); G.M. Sider, *Culture and Class in Anthropology and History: A Newfoundland Illustration* (Cambridge: Cambridge University Press, 1986); E. Hobsbawm and T. Ranger, *The Invention of Tradition* (Cambridge: Cambridge University Press, 1983). See also R. Samuel and G.S. Jones, eds, *Culture, Ideology and Politics* (London: Routledge and Kegan Paul, 1982).
[2] J.M. Ward, *Colonial Self-Government: The British Experience* (Toronto: University of Toronto Press, 1976), 124–6.
[3] See D.W. Prowse, *A History of Newfoundland* (London: Macmillan, 1895); C.R. Fay, *Life and Labour in Newfoundland* (Cambridge: W. Heffer and Sons, 1956); St John

Chadwick, *Newfoundland: Island into Province* (Cambridge: Cambridge University Press, 1967); F.W. Rowe, *Education and Culture in Newfoundland* (Toronto: McGraw-Hill Ryerson, 1976); F.W. Rowe, *A History of Newfoundland and Labrador* (Toronto: McGraw-Hill Ryerson, 1980); P. O'Neill, *The Story of St. John's, Newfoundland* 2 vols. (Erin, Ont.: Press Porcepic, 1975–76); K. Matthews, E.R. Kearly and P.J. Dwyer, *Our Newfoundland and Labrador Cultural Heritage* (Scarborough, Ont.: Prentice Hall, 1984).

[4]Thompson, 'Patrician Society, Plebeian Culture', 387.

[5]See Corrigan and Sayer, *The Great Arch*, 1–13, 182–208; Hobsbawm and Ranger, *Invention of Tradition*, 1–14, 263–307.

[6]Parliamentary *Debates*, 3rd ser., XLVII, 26 April 1839, 554.

[7]'Instructions to Our trusty and well-beloved Sir Thomas Cochrane, Knight, Our Governor and Commander-in-Chief of our Island of Newfoundland (July 28, 1832)', in Consolidated Statutes of Newfoundland. Third Series: 1916 (St John's, 1919), Vol. I, App.; 'Commission Appointing Captain Sir Thomas John Cochrane, Knight, Governor of the Colony of Newfoundland . . . ' (2 March 1832).

[8]Calculated from App. E, Table II, in Gertrude Gunn, *The Political History of Newfoundland 1832–1864* (Toronto: University of Toronto Press, 1966), 206; K. Whelan, 'The Irish Contribution to Newfoundland Catholicism' and 'Catholicism: The Irish Experience 1750–1900', papers read at a conference of the Newfoundland Irish Society, St John's, 19–21 March 1984.

[9]See C.J. Byrne, *Gentlemen-Bishops and Faction Fighters* (St John's: Jesperson Press, 1984). For Fleming's political activities, see P. McCann, 'Bishop Fleming and the Politicisation of the Irish Roman Catholics in Newfoundland 1830–1850', in T. Murphy and C.J. Byrne, eds., *Religion and Identity: The Experience of Irish and Scottish Catholics in Atlantic Canada* (St John's: Jesperson Press, 1987).

[10]CO 194/111, T. Prescott to Lord John Russell, 9 June 1841.

[11]Gunn, *Political History of Newfoundland*, 33 ff.

[12]CO 194/99, Prescott to Lord Glenelg, 14 October 1837, encl. 'Statement of Dr. Fleming . . .' (n.d.); McCann, 'Bishop Fleming'; see also K. Whelan, 'A Geography of Society and Culture in Ireland since 1800', PhD thesis, National University of Ireland, 1981, 13–14.

[13]CO 194/88, T. Cochrane to Lord Stanley, 2 August 1834.

[14]For the Irish National System, see D.H. Akenson, *The Irish Education Experiment* (London: Routledge and Kegan Paul, 1970), 120–1, 159–60, App. 392–402. It was estimated that 77% of the electors in Conception Bay in 1836 voted Liberal, though only 43% were Catholic. (Calculated from statistics in St John's *Patriot*, 15 October 1836.)

[15]Linda Little, 'Plebeian Collective Action in Harbour Grace and Carbonear, Newfoundland, 1830–1840', MA thesis, Memorial University of Newfoundland, 1984; Gunn, *Political History of Newfoundland*, 33–73, *passim*.

[16]*Patriot*, 2 May, 6 June 1840; Select Committee Appointed to Inquire into the State of the Colony of Newfoundland (1841), 20.

[17]S.J.R. Noel, *Politics in Newfoundland* (Toronto: University of Toronto Press, 1971), 5.

[18]*Centenary Volume: Benevolent Irish Society of St John's, Newfoundland 1806–1906* (St John's, 1906), 82–3; *Newfoundlander* (St John's), 28 February 1833; 27 February 1834; *Patriot*, 29 March 1836.

[19]See Gunn, *Political History of Newfoundland*, 27–9. Four attempts were made between 1834 and 1841.

[20]E.R. Norman, *Anti-Catholicism in Victorian England* (New York: Barnes and Noble, 1968), 13–21; G.F.A. Best, 'Popular Protestantism in Victorian Britain', in R. Robson, ed., *Ideas and Institutions of Victorian Britain* (New York: Barnes and Noble, 1967), 115–42; R.A. Billington, *The Protestant Crusade 1800–1860* (Chicago: Quandrangle Books, 1964); N.G. Smith, 'Religious Tensions in Pre-Confederation Politics', *Canadian Journal of Theology*, IX, No. 4 (1963); *Times* (St John's), *Public Ledger* (St John's), August 1838–May 1839, *passim*.

[21]P. McCann, 'The Origins of Denominational Education in Newfoundland: "No Popery" and the Education Acts, 1836–1843', in P. McCann, *Studies in the History of Education in Newfoundland 1800–1855* (forthcoming).

[22]Gunn, *Political History of Newfoundland*, 77–88; *Public Ledger*, 6 May 1836. See also *Public Ledger*, 8 January 1839.

[23]*Dictionary of Canadian Biography, Vol. VIII, 1851–1860* (Toronto: University of Toronto Press, 1985), 374–84.

[24]*Times*, 22 September 1841.

[25]CO 194/116, Harvey to Stanley, 16 January, 22 May 1843; *Royal Gazette* (St John's), 27 January 1843; CO 194/112, Harvey to Stanley, 21 December 1841.

[26]*Public Ledger*, 14 January 1842, 18 October 1844, 18 January 1850.

[27]*Morning Post*, (St John's), 20 January 1853; C.E. Hillier, 'The Problems of Newfoundland from Discovery to the Legislative Sessions of 1847', MA thesis, Acadia University, 1963, 174, 181–6, 190; P. Tocque, *Newfoundland As It Was, and As It Is In 1877* (Toronto, 1879), 434–5.

[28]*Public Ledger*, 17 March 1843; *Morning Courier* (St John's), 5 September 1846.

[29]CO 194/117, Harvey to Stanley, 25 May and 30 November 1843; A Sketch of the State of Affairs in Newfoundland. By a Late Resident of that Colony [H. Prescott], (London, 1841), 61.

[30]K.B. Hamilton (Governor) to Duke of Newcastle, cited in Colonial Church and School Society Report, 1854, 56.

[31]See P. McCann, 'The Newfoundland School Society 1823–1855: Missionary Enterprise or Cultural Imperialism?', in J.A. Mangan, ed., *Socialisation, Education and Imperialism* (Manchester: Manchester University Press, forthcoming).

[32]Proceedings of the Society for Educating the Poor of Newfoundland 1825–26 (London, 1826), 65; *Record* (London), 15 May 1851.

[33]*Times*, 22 February, 29 March, 3 January 1838; *Public Ledger*, 28 February 1837; 11 January 1839; 10 January 1840; 2 and 9 March, 16 April 1841; 15 and 28 January 1842; 9 January 1845; *Royal Gazette*, 14 January 1845.

[34]*Public Ledger*, 23 March, 29 April 1836; 12 January 1844; *Times*, 4 May 1836.

[35]*Public Ledger*, 1 September 1840; *Vindicator*, 9 October 1840; G. Budden, 'The Role of the Newfoundland Natives' Society in the Political Crisis of 1840–42', Honours Dissertation, Memorial University of Newfoundland, 1983, 15–31.

[36]CO 194/113, R. Bonnycastle to J. Stephen, 14 January 1841, encl. 'Considerations upon the Political Position and Natural Advantages of Newfoundland. St. John's 1841'.

[37]*Public Ledger*, 7 January 1842; 27 and 30 May 1845.

[38]*Newfoundlander*, 30 June–28 July 1845, *passim; Patriot*, 2 July–6 August 1845, *passim; Courier*, 21 July–8 August 1845, *passim*.

[39]Provincial Archives of Newfoundland and Labrador, GN2/2, 'Memorandum of Sir John Harvey, 19 July 1845'.

[40]*Newfoundlander*, 10 and 21 July 1845.

[41]R.H. Bonnycastle, *Newfoundland in 1842*, 2 vols. (London: Colburn, 1842), II, 120–1.

[42]*Patriot*, 15 September 1840.

[43]*Public Ledger*, 12 January 1844.

[44]*Newfoundlander*, 1 July 1841; *Morning Courier*, 12 July 1851.

[45]See *Morning Courier*, 12 July 1851.

[46]*Public Ledger*, 4 March 1842, citing *Carbonear Sentinel*, 25 January 1842.

[47]*Morning Courier*, 1 May, 3 December 1851; *Newfoundland Express* (St John's), 4 December 1851; *Morning Post*, 4 December 1850; *Public Ledger*, 2 November 1850.

[48]*Morning Courier*, 22 November 1851; *Times*, 5 July 1845, citing *Carbonear Sentinel* (n.d.); *Weekly Herald* (St John's), 2 August 1846; *Morning Post*, 31 March, 20 August 1853.

[49]A.H. McLintock, *The Establishment of Constitutional Government in Newfoundland, 1783–1832* (London, 1841), 164.

[50]CO 194/122, Harvey to Stanley, 15 July 1845.

[51]*Newfoundlander* 18 August 1845.

[52]*Newfoundlander*, 18 August, 1 September 1845; *Public Ledger*, 22 August 1845; *Patriot*, 20 and 27 August 1845.

[53]*Morning Courier*, 22 August 1845.

[54]O'Neill, *Story of St John's*, I, 318–19, 338–9; *Times*, 3 October 1838, 20 August 1845, 14 August 1843, 25 June 1845; *Newfoundlander*, 14 July, 22 September 1845.

[55]Gunn, *Political History of Newfoundland*, 66 ff, 89–109; Hillier, 'Problems of Newfoundland', 135; Budden, 'Newfoundland Natives' Society', *passim*.

[56]For a list of the self-styled 'middle-class' of St John's, see CO 194/127, LeMerchant to Grey, 24 August 1847, encl. 'The Memorial of Certain of the Middle-Class in St John's Sufferers by the "Conflagration of 9 June".'

[57]*Public Ledger*, 7 February 1844; Tocque, *Newfoundland As It Was*, 108.

[58]See *Times*, 5 February 1835, 5 August 1840; *Newfoundlander*, 12 April 1838; *St John's Total Abstinence and Benefit Society: Jubilee Volume 1858–1908* (St John's, 1908), 5–8; *Patriot*, 11 January 1843; *Public Ledger*, 5 January 1844.

[59]*Newfoundland Express*, 13 December 1851; *Banner of Temperance*, I, No. 16 (August 1851).

[60]CO 194/114, Harvey to Stanley, 14 January 1842; *Public Ledger*, 27 May 1845. Harvey was speaking to the Natives' Society. CO 194/120, Harvey to Stanley, 9 January 1844.

[61]*Times*, 2 August 1843, 21 February 1844; *Public Ledger*, 7 February 1844; CO 194/120, Harvey to Stanley, 9 January 1844.

[62]See *Banner of Temperance*, I (January–December 1851), *passim*. See also the standard work on the subject, B.H. Harrison, *Drink and the Victorians* (London: Faber and Faber, 1971), esp. 348–86.

[63]CO 194/116, Harvey to Stanley, 7 January 1843; *Patriot*, 11 January 1843.

[64]*Morning Courier*, 4 June, 26 July 1851; *Public Ledger*, 24 February 1835; *Patriot*, 10 March 1835.

[65]See S. Ryan, *Fish Out of Water: The Newfoundland Saltfish Trade 1814–1914* (St John's: Breakwater, 1986), 62; *Newfoundlander*, 18 August 1845. By law, all com-

mercial transactions had to be carried out in the capital. See S. Antler, 'The Capitalist Underdevelopment of Nineteenth Century Newfoundland', in R.J. Brym and R.J. Sacouman, *Underdevelopment and Social Movements in Atlantic Canada* (Toronto: New Hogtown Press, 1979), 192. CO 194/120, Harvey to Stanley, 9 January 1844.

[66]Tocque, *Newfoundland As It Was*, 88–9; *Patriot*, 10 March 1835.

[67]*Public Ledger*, 14 February 1837; 31 January, 7 February 1840; 9 February 1841; 27 June 1845; 12 March 1847; 10 February 1852.

[68]*Royal Gazette*, 18 February 1845; *Public Ledger*, 4 February 1842, citing 7th Annual Report of Reading Room and Library; 18 February 1845; 12 and 16 March 1847; *Morning Courier*, 12 February 1851.

[69]*Newfoundland Express*, 16 November, 13 and 16 December 1851; 16 October 1852; Louise Whiteway, 'The Athenaeum Movement: St John's Athenaeum', *Dalhousie Review*, Winter 1970–71, 542–4.

[70]*Times*, 1 and 8 April 1840; 21, 23 and 24 February 1841; *Newfoundlander*, 30 January 1845.

[71]*Banner of Temperance*, I, No. 16 (August 1851).

[72]*Royal Gazette*, 23 April 1845, 24 January 1846; CO 194/122, Harvey to Stanley, 25 October 1845; CO 194/125, 'Papers Relating to the Proposed Changes in the Constitution of Newfoundland' (5 August 1842).

[73]CO 194/122, Harvey to Stanley, 23 April 1845; CO 194/125, Harvey to W.E. Gladstone, 17 February 1846, 12 March and 22 May 1846; *Royal Gazette*, 28 April and 6 August 1846.

[74]See speech of F. Scully in a debate on the Newfoundland constitution (Parliamentary Debates, CXXXVII, 20 March 1855, 892).

[75]*Times*, 3 January 1855; *Public Ledger*, 30 January–6 November 1855, *passim*; 23 January 1855.

[76]*Times*, 3 and 6 January, 6 October 1855.

[77]Gunn, *Political History of Newfoundland*, 143–4; *Times*, 27 October, 1 December 1855.

[78]CO 194/125, Harvey to Gladstone, 12 April 1846.

[79]*Public Ledger*, 13 February 1855.

[80]Noel, *Politics in Newfoundland*, 23–4.

IV

The

Coming of

Confederation

31

The Ideological Origins of Canadian Confederation

Peter J. Smith

Historians have approached the subject of Canadian Confederation from almost every direction except that of ideology. An emphasis on the federal union of the 1860s as a product of power politics (international, imperial, and domestic) and political pragmatism characterizes the historical literature not only on Confederation, but on the politics of both the pre-national and post-national periods. An empirical suspicion of political ideology has long been characteristic of Anglo-Canadian historical writing, and the rediscovery of ideology has been one of the many major currents of modern revisionist scholarship. The term "rediscovery" is employed deliberately, since nineteenth-century politicians certainly thought that real ideological differences between Reformers and Tories existed. Whether the expressions of those ideological differences bore any necessary relationship to the realities of practical politics is another, quite separate, question. That ideology was often expressed in rhetorical terms does not necessarily disqualify it as ideology. Nor does the fact that ideology was often associated with personal self-interest, although the extent to which nineteenth-century politicians remained consistent to certain clusters of ideas throughout their careers is noteworthy.

In his essay on the ideological origins of Confederation, Peter J. Smith attempts to reintroduce ideology to early Canadian politics. He argues that Canadian union was the product of the debate, widespread across France, Britain, the United States—and British North America, between the defenders of classical republican values and the proponents of a new commercial ideology (usually associated with Tory centralism and statism). Smith sees the ideological origins of Canadian political conflict in the republican versus commercial struggles of the eighteenth century, which in British North America became translated into Reformers and Tories. In an ideological sense, he argues, Confederation was a Tory concept pressed by Tory politicians,

and (presumably) opposed by Reform ones.

What reasons could be advanced
for the refusal of Canadian historians
to see Confederation in ideological
terms? What consequences could
follow from an interpretation that
sees the British North America Act
as an essentially Tory document?
What advantages did Tory ideology
find in Confederation? Can this
ideological view be reconciled with
the mainstream view of the importance of pragmatic power politics in
the achievement of Canadian
unification?

This article first appeared, titled 'The Ideological Origins of Canadian Confederation', in *Canadian Journal of Political Science* xx, 1 (March 1987), 3–29.

This article discusses the ideological origins of Canadian Confederation. It
directly challenges a belief commonly held by Canadian political scientists
and historians that Canadian Confederation was the product of a purely
pragmatic exercise.[1] It will argue instead that the ideological origins of the
Canadian federal state may be traced to the debate that characterized eighteenth and nineteenth-century British, American and French political
culture—a debate between the defenders of classical republican values and
the proponents of a rising commerical ideology formulated during the
Enlightenment. The participants in this debate held clashing views of the
state and its role in society. Only by understanding how this debate unfolded
in nineteenth-century Canada can the particular configuration of the Canadian state that emerged triumphant in the 1860s be understood. Furthermore, an understanding of this debate also offers political scientists a broader
context for interpreting long-held Canadian attitudes toward authority, the
uses of political patronage, the public debt, capitalism, and the state and
economic development.

This insight into the ideological origins of the Canadian state has only
been made possible by the remarkable transformation that has occurred in
the interpretation of seventeenth-, eighteenth- and even nineteenth-century
trans-Atlantic political thought. New scholarship on the Whig Revolution
of 1688, the American Revolution of 1776, the Scottish Enlightenment and
the Jeffersonian era has, among other things, called into question the long-
standing perception of John Locke as the fountainhead of eighteenth-century
Anglo-American political culture. The list of contributors to this scholarly
revisionism is impressive, the most notable being John Pocock.[2] As a result
of these efforts, a richer and more complex assessment of the political and
social thought of the period is now possible. Critical to this new understanding is an appreciation of the debate between, on the one hand civic humanism, with its emphasis on civic virtue and classical citizenship (*homo politicus*)
and, on the other, a commercial ideology with its emphasis on the economic
(*homo mercator*).

One of the puzzling omissions of this intellectual renaissance is that while it has shed new light on the Anglo-American and even French political traditions, it has had little to say about Canada.[3] This is, indeed, curious given that Canada received such an influx of immigrants from both the United States and Britain in the eighteenth and nineteenth centuries. Clearly, the revised perceptions of trans-Atlantic political thought provide valuable insights into not only Canadian political culture, but also the creation of Canadian political institutions, particularly federalism. I will argue that the debate between wealth and virtue, which reached its height in the writings of the Scottish Enlightenment, is critical to comprehending the clash between Reformer and Tory in nineteenth-century Canada. I will begin by tracing the development of this debate in Britain, France and America. Special consideration is given to the conflicting views of the state held by both sides in this debate. Next, the article examines the appearance of this debate in nineteenth-century Canada stressing the radically different perspectives which Reformers and Tories had of the state, particularly the idea of union, federal and legislative. Finally, this study shows how the Tory conception of the state predominated in 1867.

The Dialectics of Wealth and Virtue

In historical terms the development of the civic humanist paradigm preceded the development of the commerical ideology—the latter responding to the former. Civic humanism had as its starting point the idea of virtue, which in turn was based on the ancient Greek and Roman notions of citizenship. Man, it was argued, was a political animal (*zōon politikon*) who fulfilled himself as a human being by participating in politics and by acting selflessly for the public good. Unfortunately, however, not everyone was fit for citizenship since citizenship required a material base, preferably land, which gave individuals the personal independence and permanent stake in their country necessary to motivate them to act on its behalf. Citizenship, moreover, had a moral as well as material aspect, for if at any time those who should be devoting themselves to citizenship were led, for whatever reason, to place their personal private interests before public virtue, then according to the strict canons of civic humanism the political community would be threatened by corruption. Corruption was an active, destructive force which, if not checked, would erode the moral commitment of citizens to participate. The result would surely be a degeneration into despotic rule and the loss of political liberty.

This depiction of the ideal citizen, which had its roots in the ancient world, had been revived in the modern era by Machiavelli and James Harrington. The meaning assigned to corruption, for example, was Machiavellian, referring to those changes which might undermine the material base and the moral and institutional superstructure of the political community.

In eighteenth-century Britain elements opposed to the ruling Whig oligarchy led by such figures as Lord Bolingbroke, John Trenchard and Thomas Gordon, known otherwise as the Country party or Country opposition, saw corruption and decay near at hand.[4] One sure sign of corruption was the emergence of new forms of property, finance and commerce, which in Country eyes injected luxury into society and brought certain decay. Greatly feared, therefore, was the financial and commercial revolution sweeping England. This had not only created a new class of moneyed men but also a vast expansion of state administration and public credit. Together they helped provide the places and pensions, the political patronage used to 'entice' members of parliament intò supporting the ministers of the Crown. Civic humanism, as it was incorporated into opposition thought, served as a powerful indictment against established or Court Whiggism and its system of corruption, credit and commerce. While in political terms the Country opposition accepted the notion of a parliamentary monarchy, it greatly feared the tendency of the Crown to centralize power and encroach on the independence of Parliament, and advocated instead some kind of separation of powers.

The most effective response to civic humanism may be found in the thought of the Scottish political economists. Although Scottish social theory provided an ideological justification for the Whig regime, one must be careful not to reduce Scottish thought to only a debate between Court and Country. By Pocock's own admission his is a 'tunnel history', the pursuit of a particular theme to its limits. Scottish thought was broader, and explored other dimensions and themes. In recent years scholars have re-examined Scottish social theory and put emphasis on yet another aspect—the importance of natural jurisprudence and the influence of Pufendorf and other natural law theorists on the Scots. These scholars, in turn, play down the centrality of the Scottish reply to civic humanism.[5]

Evidence abounds, however, of the importance of the Scottish encounter with civic humanism. In their response to civic humanism the Scots were intent on demonstrating how virtue and commerce could be reconciled. To do this it was necessary to transform the meaning of virtue by redefining it in a civil, not a civic, sense. That is, the accent on virtue was placed on the social—the economic, cultural and moral—and not on the political and military.[6] Indeed, it can be argued that the Scots had but little choice to proceed along these lines for with the Union with England in 1707, a union designed to stimulate Scotland's economic development, Scotsmen had sacrificed the institutional means by which civic virtue could be practised. As the writings of Nicholas Phillipson indicate, there arose in Edinburgh a form of Addisonian social culture with clubs and societies devoted to improving economic efficiency, manners, learning and letters. The civil virtues of politeness and enlightened taste replaced the civic humanist virtue of political participation.

The Scots, in brief, provided a sophisticated rebuttal to the charges made by opposition thinkers on the negative effects of wealth and luxury. Of all the Scots it was Hume who made the sharpest critique of opposition thought. Hume defended, for example, the system of commerce, wealth, luxury and patronage that the civic humanists saw as such a threat. Commercial societies, he believed, were those societies most conducive to the creation of wealth and luxury, which he viewed in positive terms. Hume also criticized 'men of severe morals [who] blame even the most innocent luxury and present it as the source of all the corruptions . . . incident to a civil government.'[7] Furthermore, Hume favoured the Crown's use of patronage and influence to control Parliament, so necessary, he believed, to preserving the balance of Britain's mixed constitution. Another of Scotland's literati, Adam Smith, expressed similar views on the necessity for Crown 'patronage' and 'influence'. Surveying the problems of the American colonies, Smith concluded that 'the executive power has not the means to corrupt the colonial legislatures.'[8]

What emerges, then, from the thought of the Scottish thinkers, in particular that of Hume and Smith, is the view of the state as important not so much as a means of political participation and fulfillment of political personality, but as a means of ensuring economic development. The state was charged with governing a complex market society in which, while it enlarged men's faculties and encouraged politeness, simultaneously awakened ambitions, passions and interests that were detrimental to the public good. The state therefore had to provide the framework of justice in which self-seeking individuals with their property and specialization were protected by law and authority. The purpose of government, after all, said Smith, was 'to secure wealth and defend the rich from the poor'.[9]

While Hume and Smith saw the relationship between the state and economic development as complementary—the state protecting increasing wealth, increasing wealth providing revenue for a stronger state—they had differing opinions on a variety of issues. The most important of these was the critical issue of tolerating the public debt, which along with the Bank of England, had underwritten the financial revolution that had so greatly altered the face of British political economy.[10] Hume, fearing that the public debt would lead to national bankruptcy, warned, 'either the nation must destroy public credit or public credit must destroy the nation.'[11] Adam Smith did not share Hume's dire pessimism on the public debt, although he did acknowledge that it might potentially grow too large and ruin the nation. To relieve the public debt Smith endorsed such financial instruments as the sinking fund, a special fund designed to eliminate the national debt. It was partially because the public debt was 'contracted in the defence not of Great

Britain alone, but of all the different provinces of the empire' that Smith advocated a union with Ireland and America 'to discharge the public debt'.[12] Smith's thought of union as a credit instrument to alleviate public debt and promote political stability parallels Canadian thinking, as I will indicate in the following section.

It should be stressed at this point that the debate over civic humanism was not merely an Anglo-American debate. It was a trans-Atlantic debate, keenly observed and commented on by the French, particularly Montesquieu, a figure of admiration in Great Britain and British colonies. In many ways *The Spirit of the Laws* reads as a synopsis of the debate over civic humanism, and he was proclaimed as an authority by all sides. It was in America, in particular, that the civic humanist paradigm—described by American scholars as the republican synthesis—was to be most pronounced, shaping not only the ideological justification for independence but surviving throughout the Jeffersonian era and beyond, in populist movements and in contemporary American political culture. In Bernard Bailyn's opinion, 'the effective triggering convictions that lay behind the [American] Revolution were derived not from common Lockean generalities but from the specific fears and formulations of the radical publicists and opposition politicians of early eighteenth century England.'[13] To many American colonists the English had become corrupt, and thereby lost the necessary qualities for freedom depicted in opposition thought. Americans, on the other hand, were certain that they were a virtuous people (in a civic sense), capable of sustaining a free society and a free government.

The social turmoil brought on in part by the revolution and by America's increasing social heterogeneity undermined this optimism among revolutionary leaders. James Madison, for example, came to believe that Americans no longer fully possessed the moral qualities so necessary for a virtuous people and republic. America, furthermore, was too extensive and too diverse to form a single republican state. Madison, in his attempts to address the complex relationship between representation, virtue, and extent of territory, is said to have relied heavily on David Hume's essay, 'Idea of a Perfect Commonwealth'.[14] Hume's idea of a perfect republic represented a means of avoiding the classical dilemma of choosing an appropriate form of government for a large territory. One did not have to choose between monarchy or the tumultous discord of small republics. In his essay Hume had argued:

> In a large government, which is modelled with masterly skill, there is compass and room enough to refine the democracy, from the lower people, who may be admitted into the first elections or first concoction of the commonwealth, to the higher magistrates, who direct all the movements. At the same time the parts are so distant and remote, that it is very difficult, either by intrigue, prejudice or passion, to hurry them into any measures against the public interest.[15]

In the American case, what was being refined was civic virtue, which regrettably had become mixed with local bias and self-interest. The further one was removed from the people, that is, the more refined the choice of representative, the better the chance for distilled virtue, or the ability to act for the public good. The exclusion of citizens from direct participation in decision-making was, according to Madison, one of the strengths of the new republic created in Philadelphia. Its other great advantage, in Madison's opinion, was the institutionalization of factions and parties with their self-seeking passions, ambitions, and interests into 'the necessary and ordinary operations of government'.[16]

It is evident, then, that American Federalists were edging towards (but had not arrived at) the thought of Court Whiggism. Alexander Hamilton went so far as to advocate the Court system of governing by influence, invoking Hume's name in its defence.[17] The advantages of an enlarged polity with enhanced political authority to restrain the passions and ambitions of men were now apparent. A strong central government with a powerful executive could govern a large territory and keep the states and people in check.

However much the federalism of Madison and Hamilton may have altered opposition thought, it did not signal its dénouement in America. In the 1790s Thomas Jefferson and the Republicans criticized Hamilton in much the same manner as the Country party had criticized Walpole and the Whig regime 70 years previously. At the heart of the Republican differences with Washington's government were Hamilton's policies, which included a vision of America as a great centralized commercial and military empire bound together by public credit, British investment, a healthy system of public finance including a national bank, a standing army and a powerful executive.[18] The Republican disdain for commerical capitalism and urban life became a fundamental component of the American political tradition, and was best personified in the antipathy of Thomas Jefferson towards David Hume. What Hume extolled, Jefferson denounced. While the English may have once been a wise and virtuous people,

> Commerce and a corrupt government have rotted them to the core. Every generous, nay, every just sentiment, is absorbed in the thirst for gold. I speak of their cities, which we may certainly pronounce to be ripe for despotism, and fitted for no other government. Whether the leaven of the agricultural body is sufficient to regenerate the residuary mass, and maintain it as a sound state, under any reformation of government, may well be doubted.[19]

The above discussion, I would argue, clearly indicates the extent to which the debate over civic humanism, with its emphasis on the dialectic of wealth and virtue, provides a new alternative for the study not only of eighteenth-century British and French political culture, but also of the turbulence of the revolutionary era in America and the rise of Jeffersonian democracy.

Furthermore, there is ample evidence to indicate that this debate continued into nineteenth-century America, Britain, France, and Canada as well. Admittedly it does not tell the entire story for it was to be complemented by admixtures of other belief systems, for example, those of the Dissenting religions, Cobbett radicalism, Chartism, Utilitarianism, Socialism, and Cobdenism. Yet throughout the nineteenth century the concept of corruption, with all its moral connotations, was used to attack the established order.[20] As Robert Kelly notes, in England, Canada and America,

> Tories and Republicans, as Liberal-Democrats saw the matter, ruled not simply through aristocratic élites, but through skillful use of corruption. From Jefferson's day to Cleveland few issues so obsessed the Liberal-Democratic mind as this one. . . . In nineteenth century Canadian and American politics, Liberal-Democratics were convinced that corruption was the principal danger that faced democracy and responsible government. [Alexander] McKenzie and Cleveland both believed it was the enemy's chief means for deforming the government and debasing the morals of the people at large.[21]

Land and Commerce: The Canadian Debate

It is evident, then, that in the nineteenth century fear of corruption was still widespread—its presence fed by centralization and growing executive power. Those opposed to corruption, like their predecessors in the eighteenth century, emphasized the importance of virtue, independence, political participation, decentralization of political power (in the United States and Canada at least) and the primacy of the petty producer. Furthermore, it was realized that capitalism, particularly commercial and financial capitalism, would lead to the destruction of the participatory society and towards a society and state based on privilege, influence and centralized political power.

In Canada, the quarrel between agrarian and commercial interests had its origins in the early years of the nineteenth century. According to Donald Creighton, 'the most important feature of the new age was . . . the growing antipathy between the merchants and the small rural proprietors. . . .' Commenting upon the situation in Upper Canada, Creighton notes that 'this quarrel conformed in general to a type of political conflict which was repeated regularly throughout the history of the Thirteen Colonies and the United States.'[22]

Reformist Perspectives on State and Society

This antipathy between agrarian and commercial interests was particularly marked in Upper and Lower Canada, and centred around a bitter battle over patronage—Tories believing the government possessed too little, Reformers believing it had too much. The struggle over patronage in both provinces was critical, representing, as it had in eighteenth-century England, the battle rol the civil list and public expenditure. Reformers like William Lyon ...zie perceived the Crown's influence as a threat to legislative inde-...ence. He asserted that 'the power of the Crown had increased, is increasing and ought to be diminished.'[23] Mackenzie's statement, however, was not original. He had taken it from John Dunning, an eighteenth-century British parliamentarian and supporter of the Country program, who had used the same words in support of a motion he brought before the House of Commons in April 1780.[24] Mackenzie and other members of the Upper Canadian Assembly proceeded to claim in their *Seventh Report on Grievances* that 'the almost unlimited extent of the patronage of the Crown, or rather of the Colonial Minister for the time being and his advisers here, together with the abuse of patronage are the chief causes of colonial discontent.[25]

In Lower Canada Papineau expressed similar sentiments, charging in 1831 that the provincial administration was 'corrupt in its head and in all its members' and that the 'hirelings' who administered it were 'too corrupt to be reformed and too rotten and too gangrenous to be healed'.[26] The 92 Resolutions of 1834 were to make a similar point. Crown influence, though, was just one aspect of a societal system of influence and corruption that was threatening the independence of the petit-bourgeoisie. Commercial and financial capitalism with its banks and credit system was every bit as threatening. A Reformist newspaper, *The Constitution* of Toronto, advised farmers to look upon the Bank of Upper Canada as their enemy, maintaining that 'this abominable engine of the state has been the curse of Canada. It has controlled our elections, corrupted our representatives, depreciated our currency, obliged even Governors and Colonial ministers to bow to its mandates.'[27]

Against the Tory system of centralized élite control and influence Reformers posed democracy. Democracy, to Reformers, did not simply refer to a system of government, it referred to a type of society as well. What was being argued, in Aristotelian terms, was that the social constitution of a country, its material base, very much limited the institutions that could be erected upon it. Papineau, for example, argued that the social base of Canada was democratic and he dreamed of a one-class democracy of small property owners. In 1836 he proclaimed in the House: 'The Ministers have wished to put into action and into force aristocratic principles in the Canadas[,] whose social constitution is essentially democratic, where everyone is born and dies a democrat; because everyone is a property owner; because everyone has small properties.'[28]

Democracy, moreover, required special qualities of a people. If virtuous, one political pamphlet claimed, the people 'would keep the reins of government in their hands until corruption and intrigue wrested them out.' Being a system based upon virtue democracy was the 'only form of government . . . in accordance with every feeling of an honest heart, and the happiness and prosperity of any country. Let education be encouraged, and a strict guard placed against corruption; and then democracy will be as lasting as the world.'[29]

The people, in the opinion of Reformers, French and English, represented the petty producers of Canada, particularly the farmer. One letter to the Upper Canadian *Agriculturalist and Canadian Journal* went further than most when it claimed farmers

> are the *first class*, in the noblest and best sense. The Merchants, Mechanics, Priests, Lawyers, Artists, Literati, etc., etc., are all non-producers—mere hangers-on, dependents of the husbandman. He can do without them, they cannot live without him. If you wish to see genuine virtue, true patriotism, unostentatious benevolence, sterling honesty and practical piety, go among the cultivators of the soil. Look not for these rarities in the crowded city; they will not vegetate in the tainted atmosphere that surrounds the haunts of busy, plotting rivalry, priestly intrigue, scheming political selfishness, loyal trickery, and reckless commercial gambling. Even in a country as young as Canada, with a changing, heterogeneous population, the truth of this contrast becomes every day plainer to the view. The sturdy yeoman are the true conservatives of society. They are the substratum—the foundation of the social fabric—and if that be defective, the whole building will tumble in ruins. It has been so in all past time, in all countries, it is so in ours.[30]

Because farmers formed the 'substratum' of society, it was argued that political institutions, like other social institutions, had to reflect this fact. Government, like the farmer, had to be simple, honest, independent, virtuous and close to the people. A one-class democracy of property owners demanded a more democratic government. The House of Assembly, for example, had to be independent and the principal forum of decision-making—not the executive or legislative council. What was needed was responsible government conducting public affairs with the advice of officers possessing the confidence of the people's representatives in Parliament. Government also had to be cheaper, efficient, debt-free and responsive to local concerns. Inevitably comparisons were made with state governments in the United States, which seemed to possess these features. However, only when the House of Assembly controlled public expenditures and taxation could the goal of cheap, simple government be realized.

The efforts of Reformers to construct a society and state harmonizing with their vision were delivered a severe blow by the failure of the 1837 Rebellion, which severed the links between the more radical Reform leaders (who were either exiled, imprisoned, or hanged) and their rural base. In the decade that followed, a much more moderate urban Reform leadership emerged, with Robert Baldwin, Francis Hincks and Louis Hippolyte Lafontaine becoming the primary spokesmen for responsible government. Linked intimately to the emerging notion of responsible government was the very old quarrel over patronage.[31] Baldwin and Lafontaine demanded, and eventually received, the power to control dismissals and make appointments so necessary to open the system to their supporters and build a political base. The result in Canada, like the United States, was the introduction of the spoils system into the civil service. In the decades that followed, patronage became the 'guiding principle' of civil service appointments, with scant regard for efficiency and merit. It is, indeed, highly ironic that in Canada, as in the United States under Andrew Jackson, the 'democratizing' of appointments through the spoils system did not have the salutary effect that early Reformers thought it would. Offices became the rewards of party loyalty and political patronage and corruption became entrenched more strongly than ever before.

The old Reform hostility to patronage and corruption was by no means extinguished, however. In Upper Canada in the late 1840s, the Clear Grits, reasserting the more radical agrarian element of Reformism, emerged to challenge what they perceived as the bland, moderate elitism of Baldwin. The Clear Grits were unabashed in their admiration for the American political system. As one of their supporters, the Toronto *Examiner*, put it, 'must we abjure a republican simplicity and assume the paraphernalia . . . of an aristocratical government?'[32]

While the Clear Grits became a significant political force in Upper Canadian politics, the established Reform party, now led by George Brown and an alliance of rural and urban forces dominated by Toronto business interests, rejected their platform: this had planks calling for election of officials throughout government, including the governor, the legislative council and 'public functionaries of every grade'.[33] Despite Brown's close business connections his paper, the *Globe* peppered its pages with the traditional language of Reform. The *Globe* spoke frequently of the 'intelligent and incorruptible yeomanry' of Upper Canada and never tired of attacking the corruption of the cities, the Grand Trunk and the bureaucracy.[34]

In Lower Canada the radical elements of the Reform movement never revived to the extent they did in Upper Canada. Unlike Robert Baldwin, who abandoned politics under the pressure of growing radicalism, Lafontaine, aided by his adept dispensation of patronage, managed to turn back the challenge posed by the Rouge party. Lafontaine grew steadily more conservative, strengthened by his alliance with the increasingly Ultramontane Catholic Church, which had replaced the professional petit-bourgeoisie as leader of the habitants.

The habitants, the social base of early French-Canadian Reformism, became disillusioned by the rebellion's defeat and gradually slipped into a value system which, while retaining much of its agrarian republican symbolism, became both politically and economically conservative, retreating from politics as well as commerce. This value system was combined with messianism and anti-statism and is best reflected in the popular literature of the period. Novels were filled with the image of the land and the Catholic Church as sources of economic and cultural salvation of French Canadians. The most popular was Antoine Gérin-Lajoie's *Jean Rivard*, which was widely read in French Canada in both the nineteenth and twentieth centuries. Originally printed in 1862, it enjoyed ten printings—seven alone between 1913 and 1958.[35] Gérin-Lajoie's values are captured succinctly in an abstract taken from his diary in 1849:

> I have returned to my project of going to live in the country as soon as possible. Oh, if only I were a farmer! He does not become rich by beggaring others, as lawyers, doctors, and merchants sometimes do. He draws his wealth from the earth: his is the state most natural to man. Farmers form the least egotistical and most virtuous class of the population. But this class has need of educated men who can serve its interests. The educated farmer has all the leisure necessary to do good; he can serve as a guide to his neighbours, counsel the ignorant, sustain the weak, and defend him against the rapacity of the speculator. The enlightened and virtuous farmer is to my mind the best type of man.[36]

As is clearly evident, the power of the republican idea, its disdain for commercial and city life, and its praise of agrarian pursuits, are central themes in Gérin-Lajoie's work. In *Jean Rivard* the parish, in essence, becomes a mini-republic possessing the virtuous life missing in the city. The plight of the unemployed professional and the salesman looking for jobs in business is contrasted with the rosy well-being of the farmer. Writes one of the central characters from the city to the hero: 'If you knew my friend, how much anxiety and poverty are hidden sometimes under a fashionable topcoat. One thing is certain, in the agricultural classes, with all their frugality, simplicity and apparent deprivation, there is a thousand times more happiness and I might say real wealth than in the homes of the majority of our city dwellers with their borrowed luxury and deceitful life.'[37]

There is little in this to differentiate it from other portrayals of the rural republican ideal sketched so far. What is distinctive, however, is a rejection of the political process and the willingness to accede to the hierarchy and authority of the Catholic Church. For example, in the novel, the hero, Jean Rivard, becomes a member of parliament. Not long after, he becomes disillusioned with this level of government. He finds that political parties dominate the process and nothing can be accomplished by voting as an independent. He decides to withdraw from the partisanship and turbulence of politics and return to the peace, harmony and isolation of his parish-cum-republic headed by the local priest.

In many ways *Jean Rivard* reflects the political culture of Quebec in the nineteenth and twentieth centuries. Ralph Heintzman argues that the traditional political culture of Quebec, from 1840 to 1960, was shaped by the 'dialectic of patronage'. The preoccupation of the political system with patronage and the spoils system, Heintzman claims, prompted two simulta-neous but contradictory tendencies in the French-Canadian mind—devotion to, yet suspicion of, the political process—and attempts to insulate 'govern-ment' from 'politics'.[38]

Canadian Tories and the Need for Strong Government

If Reformers, particularly those of the pre-rebellion era, displayed an aversion to centralized political power, patronage and commerce, Tories perceived matters differently. Patronage, for example, was not only a necessary check upon democracy, but a means of enhancing executive power and political stability. It was also the key to controlling public expenditures and economic development. This desire to check democracy and strengthen the executive was evident in the very creation of Upper and Lower Canada in 1791. Lord Grenville, British secretary of state at the time, felt the American colonial governments had become unbalanced in part because of weak executive authority. He believed that the defects of 'the constitution and administration of executive Government . . . had, unquestionably, a powerful operation, in producing the defection of the colonies'. One of the more glaring defects of executive government in the American colonies, one that had to be cor-rected in Canada, was the lack of influence of the colonial governors. While in the mother country the Sovereign could obtain political support by the means of 'honours, and emoluments', in the colonies the case was different —the 'rewards of the Crown were few' and 'conferred little distinction'. This would be a difficult problem to remedy, Grenville observed, in a gov-ernment 'yet in its infancy', but without due weight and influence govern-ment itself would be diminished and its duties poorly performed.[39]

Throughout the first half of the nineteenth century there were persistent calls to strengthen the executive as a counterweight to democratic assemblies. In Lower Canada Tories felt the problem was particularly pressing. David Chisholme, for example, wrote in 1829 that French Canadians, acting in a spirit of 'licentiousness, faction and envy', were threatening to swallow up all branches of government. The executive was particularly enfeebled, for 'Neither the King nor government holds any patronage in the provinces, which can create attachment and influence sufficient to counteract the rest-less arrogating spirit, which in popular assemblies, when left to itself, will never brook an authority that checks and interferes with its own.'[40] Earlier Camillus (John Henry) had made essentially the same point. Part of the problem, though, lay in the fact that too many appointments were made in England:

In Canada the Executive Government has no influence in the Commons, and very little out of it. The *PATRONAGE*, limited and comparatively insignificant as it is, does not rest exclusively with the king's representative. Many appointments to offices in Canada are made in England; and if made injudiciously—without regard to individual merit and local circumstances, have a direct tendency to diminish the influence of the Governor; on whom every office ought to feel his dependence, and with whom he ought to cooperate.[41]

In Upper Canada Tories had much the same attitude to patronage. And in Nova Scotia, Attorney-General Richard Uniacke expressed these sentiments:

> So many petty states as now exist in the colonies, having the power of legislation ill defined and as badly executed, govern'd by persons whose small salaries and emoluments are inadequate to support the dignity of the kings [sic] representatives or to uphold the authority of the mother country, together with the dependence of most of the officers of Government on the Colonial assemblies, diminishes the authority of the British Government and places those who should support it in a state of dependence.[42]

It is obvious, then, that by the third decade of the nineteenth century Canadian Tories were tired of petty provincial politics, with their factious encroaching assemblies that thwarted their dreams of economic development. They wanted an alternative, a state they could control, one capable of providing political stability, promoting economic development and serving as an outlet for the ambitions of public men.

Uniacke suggested that political union, either legislative or federal, might be the answer.[43] Many Tories agreed, and frequently proposed legislative and federal union. These proposals were hardly novel, resting as they did on similar premises as ones advanced earlier by the Loyalists. William Smith, later Chief Justice of Quebec, and Jonathan Sewell, a Massachusetts Loyalist, for example, believed that a centralized federal union of the American colonies would have prevented the American Revolution by providing a counterweight to the colonial legislatures and by enlarging the opportunities—offices—open to colonial politicians. 'Like Adam Smith', writes W.H. Nelson, 'they wanted to tame the Americans by increasing their responsibility.'[44] Nelson's insight is instructive for Smith's thoughts on union parallel those of Loyalists and Canadian Tories. Because this is the case they merit detailed consideration.

Adam Smith and Imperial Union

Smith's plan for imperial union possessed two necessary ingredients for an expanded commercial state: a strong executive and political stability, underwritten by the availability of offices—the prizes of ambition necessary to mute the spirit of faction and party; healthy public credit provided by an enlarged tax base, which also promoted political stability.

In brief, Smith's arguments went as follows: Men desire to participate in the management of government largely because of the importance it gives them. The stability and durability of free government rest on the power that leading men, 'the natural aristocracy of every country', have to defend this importance. In Smith's opinion, the 'whole play of domestic faction and ambition' in the American colonies stemmed from the attacks leading men made on one another's importance and in the defence of their own. They were most tenacious in defence of the power of local assemblies. Smith claimed that: 'Almost every individual of the governing party in America fills . . . a station superior, not only to what he had ever filled before, but to what he had ever expected to fill; and unless some new object of ambition is presented either to him or to his leaders, if he has the ordinary spirit of a man, he will die in defence of that station.' That new object of ambition, Smith suggested, should be representation in the Parliament of Great Britain. Instead of quarreling over the small local prizes of colonial faction, 'they might then hope, from the presumption which men naturally have in their own ability and good fortune, to draw some of the great prizes which some-times come from the wheel of the great state lottery of British politics.'[45]

Union would mean that the most ambitious men would be attracted to the mother Parliament. The combination of distance and skillful management of Parliament would mean that the factionalism of the colonies would sub-side. Smith believed that in all great countries under one uniform govern-ment factionalism prevailed less in remote provinces than it did in the centre of the empire. In Smith's opinion 'the distance of those provinces from the capital, from the principal seat of the great scramble of faction and ambition, makes them enter less into the views of any of the contending parties and renders them more indifferent and impartial spectators of the conduct of all.' 'The spirit of party', he noted, 'prevails less in Scotland than in England.'

The influx of American representatives to the centre could be managed and the balance of the constitution preserved only if the American colonies were taxed. Through American taxation, 'the number of people to be man-aged would increase exactly in proportion to the means of managing them; and the means of managing, to the number of people to be managed.'[46] Smith also saw union as an instrument of public credit, which would alleviate Britain's massive public debt and thereby strengthen the faith lenders had in government's ability to pay. The authority of government would thus be enhanced. Union and American taxation, then, were vital not only to the stability of the colonies but also to government at home.

Tory Proposals for Union in the Pre-Confederation Era
In the nineteenth century the extent to which Canadian Tories continued to think along these lines is evident in their pre-Confederation proposals for union, legislative and federal. Three themes emerge from these plans for union: the need to strengthen the position of the Crown in the British North American provinces; the need for outlets of ambition; and the importance of economic development.

Most Tory proposals for union in the pre-Confederation era had as their starting point the need to strengthen executive power—a need stemming from the ever-present threat of democratic excess. It was expected that as the powers of the Crown increased the influence of democratic and factious provincial legislatures would be reduced. This, at least, was the opinion of Justice Sewell of Quebec, who, in his first call for federal union in 1807, lamented the fact that 'the Crown has but little influence in the democratic branches of [the] provincial legislatures.'[47] In Sewell's mind the legislatures were factious and petty and failed to take into account the interests of the province as a whole. His proposal not unexpectedly called for a considerable reduction in the powers of the local legislatures. J.B. Robinson, attorney-general of Upper Canada, with the works of Justice Sewell before him, reflected similar concerns. Provincial legislatures were too factious and democratic; the executive branch was too often at their mercy and its independence and strength too insecure. Robinson proposed a highly centralized federal union of the provinces.[48] Bishop John Strachan repeated Robinson's diagnosis of the ills of the provinces in his observations in 1824 on the bill for uniting Upper and Lower Canada. The 'influence of the Executive is trifling', he said, and the politics of the provinces 'too agitated by local concerns and popular views.'[49] Rather than accept a legislative union, Strachan and Robinson formulated a joint proposal for a federal union of the provinces.[50]

Similar themes were to be repeated in the following decades. In the 1850s and 1860s, P.S. Hamilton of Nova Scotia, in his calls for first legislative and later federal union, expressed concern over the lack of a strong executive in the provinces. In 1864 Hamilton argued that a major cause of political instability in the colonies was the frequent change of governors general. 'We require,' he said, a 'permanent executive at home.' Hamilton's political science told him that governments without permanent executives—republics —were short-lived, and the recurring changes of governors general meant 'our political institutions are essentially republican.' Hamilton's first proposal called for a legislative union of all the provinces led by a hereditary viceroy. Such a union, he believed, would be able to transcend the pettiness, partyism and factionalism endemic to colonial legislatures. It would also ensure British ascendancy, a desire also expressed in the proposals of Sewell, Robinson, Strachan and Lord Durham. 'One great object to be obtained by the Union,' Hamilton said, 'is a complete breaking down of all local prejudices, and a fusion of races, throughout the provinces.'[51]

Of all the themes entertained by the writers just considered none is more ubiquitous than the theme of what to do with ambitious men. Most Tory advocates of union believed that the dissensions and discontent of colonial politics would be vastly ameliorated by a union of the provinces that would provide worthier offices and outlets for the ambitious few. These offices would serve as a safety valve for colonial discontent and would attract men of greater talent to political office. Once their importance was recognized, and elevated positions provided, it was argued, political passions would cool within the large union, men would become more responsible, and discontent and factionalism would virtually cease. This argument, I would point out, conforms with the lessons of eighteenth- and nineteenth-century political science which taught that the territorial size of a state and strength of executive authority were linked to political stability.

J.B. Robinson, for instance, argued that political union 'would elevate the colonies' and 'put an end to all danger and inconvenience from petty factions and local discontent'.[52] These sentiments were frequently repeated. Uniacke argued that by means of a federal union able men would find opportunities for their abilities, thus ending petty intrigues.[53] Lord Durham, in this respect, differed little from Canadian Tories. Like Adam Smith, Durham was troubled by the problem of what to do with the ambitious few who had caused so much trouble in Upper and Lower Canada. Like Smith he came to the conclusion that they could only be restrained by allowing them to assume higher offices and participate in decision-making:

> As long as personal ambition is inherent in human nature, and as long as the morality of every free and civilized community encourages its aspirations, it is one great business of a wise Government to provide for its legitimate development. . . . We must remove from these colonies the cause to which the sagacity of Adam Smith traced the alienation of the Provinces which now form the United States: We must provide some scope for what he calls 'the importance' of the leading men in the Colony beyond what he forcibly terms the present 'petty prizes of the paltry raffle of colonial faction'.[54]

For Durham either a general legislative union or a federal union of the provinces would have provided the necessary scope for the ambitious few.

Later proposals for federal and legislative union were to make similar arguments. The debates of the British American League in 1849, for example, emphasized the importance of federal union as an outlet for ambition.[55] J.W. Johnston, in 1854, continued to press the same point. He argued that the provinces were too small, too poor, too backward for the British constitutional system to work properly. Only by a larger union, in this case a legislative union, could 'an enlarged and more wholesome public opinion, a wider range for talent, and more extended scope for the aspirations of ambition, . . . be found.'[56] Finally, one finds that P.S. Hamilton made much the same argument. Hamilton felt that personal ambitions were being thwarted in British America: the result was 'A strong feeling of discontent among the more intellectual and better educated classes, and the splitting up of the whole community into small, but violent political factions.' A union of the colonies would remove the causes of discontent and smother the factious spirit of the colonists. The ambitions of the few satisfied, 'the old, narrow, partizan spirit would readily die out . . . and politicians . . . would move with a higher and nobler aim.'[57]

There were other arguments, of course, for political union besides those of political stability. In particular the problems of economic development and public debt also compelled Tories to issue calls for union. Throughout the nineteenth century they had demonstrated little fear of mounting a large public debt to finance public works. Bishop Strachan, for example, had taken David Hume directly to task for his gloomy prognostications on the public debt, arguing that they simply had not come to pass. Wrote Strachan, 'Mr Hume, in the first edition of his essays, asserted that we could not maintain our credit when our debt reached 100 millions, but he lived to see double this sum, and prudently expunged this passage in the future editions of his works observing that it was impossible to conjecture how far we might extend our credit, or what amount the debt might be raised.' In Strachan's opinion a national debt meant expensive government. This, in turn, meant high taxes. But 'enormous taxes [were] the natural consequences of the greatness of our wealth.' Furthermore, argued Strachan, 'the existence of a national debt may be perfectly consistent with the interest and prosperity of the Country, and it is only when the borrowing system has been abused, that it has become alarming.'[58] The state, in brief, was seen as a credit instrument necessary for the economic development and prosperity of the country.

The fall of John Strachan and the Family Compact with its excesses does not mean there was a disjuncture between their belief system and that of later Tories. To the contrary, claims S.F. Wise, there is an 'essential continuity of Upper Canadian with subsequent provincial history'.[59] Indeed, it is the argument here that in its essentials the nineteenth-century Tory view of the state remained much the same. From Strachan to the Confederation period, for example, Tories left no doubt that in a reorganized political union the state, with its stronger credit position, would play a more active role in the financing and building of necessary public works. In 1854, P.S. Hamilton called for a legislative union on the basis that 'political isolation hinders the provinces from carrying out any great work [for instance, railways] in which they are interested in common, and requires their joint efforts.'[60] The economic motivation underlying these plans for union has been underscored in the research of economic historians. The necessity for capital expenditures by the state was not only responsible for the act of union, argues Harold Innis, it was also responsible for Confederation and its 'expenditures on railways'.[61]

Given the attitudes of Canadian Tories it is not difficult to understand why both French-Canadian and English-Canadian Reformers displayed such an aversion to Tory calls for union, legislative and federal. Until the 1850s, the only French-Canadian proposals for a federal union came from Etienne Parent, a Reform leader. Parent's perspective on federalism was distinctly

different from the Tories, emphasizing as it did local autonomy.[62] Parent
viewed federalism not as a means of economic advancement, but as a means
of preserving the French-Canadian nation. This was to be a common refrain
of later French-Canadian discussions of federalism—would the federal state
possess adequate powers to protect the interest of the 'nation canadienne'?
Where the English commercial class tended to view federal union as an
economic venture and as a means of underwriting the cost of economic
development, French Canadians came to view it as a means of protecting
their cultural identity. Parent was merely the first to see it in this light.[63]

Similarly, it is not difficult to understand why English-Canadian Reformers were reluctant to accept the Tory idea of federal union. Not until George
Brown gave it his blessing in the late 1850s did Reformers give it active
consideration. Proposals for federations were advanced by Mackenzie and
Robert Gourlay in the 1820s, but they were so sketchy and incomplete that
it is very difficult to pass comment on them.[64] It appears that Mackenzie saw
federalism as a step towards greater control over local concerns—the post
office, bankruptcy laws, or the poor laws, for example. Unfortunately for
Mackenzie his view of the state was not reflected in the federal scheme that
emerged in 1867.

Canadian Toryism and Canadian Confederation

What finally did emerge in 1867 very much represents a fulfillment of the
historical Tory desire for a strong united commercial state. Just how the
founding of Canadian Confederation was expressive of Tory values may be
illustrated by briefly indicating the extent to which the central themes of
previous plans for unions reappear in the 1860s. These include a desire to
provide an outlet for political ambition, the importance of political stability
and the role of the state in underwriting economic development.

Canadian Confederation: The Prize of Ambition

Peter Waite has indicated that the question of ambition was a pervasive one
on the eve of Confederation. The first chapter of *The Life and Times of
Confederation* is essentially concerned with the theme of ambition, although
its ideological significance is not recognized by Waite, who (mistakenly, I
would argue) views Confederation as a 'practical' and non-theoretical exercise. Waite argues that by 1860

> There was one characteristic common to all the provinces, especially Nova
> Scotia, and one which is not easy to describe: it might be called restlessness.
> There was a pervasive feeling that colonial ambitions had reached a dead end.
> The bars of these Provincial cages were clearly too confining for Nova Scotia;
> and this same feeling was reflected in the growth of territorial ambitions in

Canada West. The little worlds of Halifax, Charlottetown, Fredericton, Quebec, perhaps even of St John's were becoming cramped for some of the politicians who made their careers there.[65]

Colonial politicians, in essence, were tiring of their 'provincial cages'. They wanted something more, they wanted greater respect from other nations and to be elevated in the eyes of the mother country.

Such sentiments were expressed by John A. Macdonald at Charlottetown in September 1864: 'For twenty long years I have been dragging myself through the dreary waste of Colonial politics. I thought there was no end, nothing worthy of ambition but now I see something which is worthy of all I have suffered.'[66] Similar statements were to be made ad nauseam throughout the Confederation Debates. D'Arcy McGee, for example, emphasized the new importance Confederation would give the colonies: 'We have given . . . to every man . . . a topic upon which he can fitly exercise his powers, no longer gnawing at a file and wasting his abilities in the poor effort of advancing the ends of some paltry faction or party.'[67] It is evident from the above that McGee, like Macdonald, thought federation a worthy object of ambition for public men and an escape from the narrowness and pettiness of provincial life.

The Need for Strong Central Government

Ambition, then, led to the desire for a larger stage for the colonists, an empire and nation of their own. A critical question at the time was, how would this nation be institutionally expressed? In the tradition established by Loyalism and Canadian Toryism, the Fathers of Confederation were concerned with extricating themselves from what they perceived to be the pettiness and perpetual deadlock of provincial politics. Only a state with strong central controlling power could bring the desired political stability. The American Revolution and Civil War had proved that. Macdonald was of the opinion that the American states had always acted as distinct and sovereign bodies with little in common. The inevitable result was civil war. 'We must', he said,

> reverse this process by strengthening the General Government and conferring on the Provincial bodies only such powers as may be required for local purposes. All sectional prejudices and interests can be legislated for by local legislatures. Thus we shall have a strong and lasting government under which we can work out constitutional liberty as opposed to democracy, and be able to protect the minority by having a powerful central government.[68]

A careful reading of Macdonald's comments confirms that he linked democracy with locality and political instability. Only a strong central government could bring stability, counteract democracy and ensure constitutional liberty. In particular it was agreed that the executive had to be strengthened to provide the central authority so desperately needed. Again American experience was to serve as a guide. The great defect of American government, claimed G.E. Cartier, 'was the absence of some respectable executive element. . . . Such a system could not produce an executive head who would command respect.'[69]

To ensure a strong central government and executive the general government was granted all the powers, mechanisms of control, and patronage that it needed to establish its supremacy within Confederation. From now on all the important 'prizes' in the raffle of Canadian politics would be in the hands of the central government. None of this was lost upon the opponents of Confederation. A.A. Dorion, for example, came to this conclusion concerning the political beliefs of Cartier and Macdonald: 'They think the hands of the Crown should be strengthened and the influence of the people, if possible, diminished—and this Constitution is a specimen of their handiwork, with a Governor-General appointed by the Crown; with local governors . . . appointed by the Crown; with [the] legislative council, . . . in the General Legislature . . . nominated by the Crown.' According to Dorion it was public knowledge that the potential promise of these positions and others was 'one of the reasons assigned for the great unanimity which prevailed in the [Quebec] Conference' of 1864.[70]

Canadian Confederation and Economic Development

While Canadian Confederation was definitely believed to be the answer to the pettiness and political instability plaguing the provinces, it was also seen as the solution to the economic problems they faced, particularly the massive public debt contracted for the creation of a transportation infrastructure. The burden of public debt eventually prompted the British to support the idea of Confederation. Donald Creighton claims this support 'might be interpreted as an effort to assist in the creation of a great holding company in which could be amalgamated all those divided and vulnerable North American interests whose protection was a burden to the British state and whose financial weakness was a grievance of British capital.'[71] In brief, Confederation was to be a credit instrument that would provide the resources necessary for the economic development of the British North American colonies.

This, at least, was the opinion of Alexander Galt. Galt believed union would provide a means of solving the problems of public debt and improving public credit. It was clear, in Galt's opinion, that 'the credit of each and all the provinces [would be] greatly advanced by a union of their resources', thus removing 'those apprehensions which have latterly affected the public credit of this country'.[72] Besides the pressure the mounting public debt put on politicians there was another important economic problem confronting the British North American provinces—the impending abrogation of the

Reciprocity Treaty with the United States. The Reciprocity Treaty had opened American markets to Canadian products and with its threatened loss Canadians had to find alternative markets that would ensure prosperity. No longer could they rely on Britain, where they had lost protected markets in the 1840s and 1850s. They had to rely on one another.

These concerns are also reflected in Alexander Galt's speech during the Confederation Debates. Union, he said, would mean that the tariffs that had impeded the free flow of goods between the provinces would be removed, thereby 'opening up . . . the markets of the provinces to the different industries of each'.[73] There is little in all of this to distinguish Galt from Adam Smith. Smith, as noted earlier, had argued for a union between Britain and its colonies for very similar reasons. In Smith's opinion a union, in this case an imperial union, would have alleviated the public debt, strengthened public credit and government, and also provided for free trade. Many others in the debates echoed Galt's arguments, particularly those concerning public debt.

Conclusion

The government that emerged conformed very closely to the image of union held by generations of Tory politicians. In many ways it could be said that John A. Macdonald obtained most of what Alexander Hamilton wanted in 1787. This included a strong central government that would possess not only the political offices that would mute political discontent and provide political stability but would, at the same time, vastly enhance public credit and provide the capital to underwrite commercial expansion across a continent. The localist attachments in Canadian political culture, particularly in French Canada and amongst English-Canadian Reformers, would have to be satisfied with the greatly inferior provincial governments they were given.

Canadian Confederation, then, was not without ideological underpinning. In nineteenth-century Canada, there were two constitutional philosophies at work, both acting in the tradition of the eighteenth-century debate between wealth and virtue, land and commerce. In the case of Canada the commercial ideology of Canadian Tories was to predominate politically in 1867. Nevertheless, the political ideology of agrarian democracy was not to be extinguished in Canada. It was to emerge as powerful as ever on the prairies in the twentieth century, giving sustenance to radical movements of both the left and the right.

Suggestions for Further Reading

Donald Creighton, *John A. Macdonald*, 2 vols (Toronto, 1952–5).
Gordon T. Stewart, *The Origins of Canadian Politics: A Comparative Approach* (Vancouver, 1986).

Peter B. Waite, ed., *The Confederation Debates in the Province of Canada, 1865* (Toronto, 1963).

Notes

Earlier versions of this article were presented in 1985 at the Tenth Anniversary Conference of the British Association for Canadian Studies in Edinburgh, Scotland, and at the annual meeting of the Canadian Political Science Association, Montreal. I am grateful not only to David V.J. Bell for his comments and suggestions at the CPSA meeting, but also for the comments of Elizabeth Smythe and of the anonymous reviewers of the *Canadian Journal of Political Science* (hereafter *CJPS*).

[1] This is a common refrain of Canadian political scientists and historians. Edwin Black, for example, argues that 'Confederation was born in pragmatism without the attendance of a readily definable philosophic rationale' (E.R. Black, *Divided Loyalities: Canadian Concepts of Federalism* [Montreal: McGill-Queen's University Press, 1975], 4). Peter Waite states that Confederation had a 'fundamentally empirical character' about it and was essentially a practical exercise (*The Life and Times of Confederation 1864–1867: Politics, Newspapers and the Union of British North America* [Toronto: University of Toronto Press, 1962], 25). Donald Smiley writes that 'Unlike Americans . . . in the eighteenth century . . . Canadians have never experienced the kind of decisive break with their political past which would have impelled them to debate and resolve fundamental political questions' (*Canada in Question: Federalism in the Eighties* [3rd ed.; Toronto: McGraw-Hill Ryerson, 1980], 285). Finally, J.K. Johnson makes the following observation on one of the leading Fathers of Confederation: 'John A. Macdonald's political "ideas" or "beliefs" have been subjected to more learned scrutiny than those of almost any other Canadian leader, a fact which is more than a little surprising, considering that the scholarly consensus has been that he was not a man of ideas at all.' Johnson also maintains that 'it is true he was essentially pragmatic, even opportunistic by nature. He did not disguise his pragmatism with political rhetoric; he positively boasted of it.' The image of 'John A.' was that of 'the plain, no-nonsense practical man of good sense' (J.K. Johnson, 'John A. Macdonald,' in J.M.S. Careless [ed.], *The Pre-Confederation Premiers: Ontario Government Leaders, 1841–1867* [Toronto: University of Toronto Press, 1980], 223–4). One of the few political scientists to take Macdonald seriously as a man of ideas is Rod Preece ('The Political Wisdom of Sir John A. Macdonald', *CJPS* 17 [1984], 459–86).

[2] Some of the more prominent contributors include John Dunn, 'The Politics of Locke in England and America in the Eighteenth Century', in John W. Yolton (ed.), *John Locke: Problems and Perspectives* (Cambridge: Cambridge University Press, 1969); Bernard Bailyn, *The Ideological Origins of the American Revolution* (Cambridge, Mass.: Belknap Press, 1969); Gordon S. Wood, *The Creation of the American Republic 1776–1787* (Chapel Hill: University of North Carolina Press, 1969); H.T. Dickinson, *Liberty and Property: Political Ideology in Eighteenth Century Britain* (London: Weidenfeld and Nicolson, 1977); Reed Browning, *Political and Constitutional Ideas of the Court Whigs* (Baton Rouge: Louisiana State University Press, 1982); Lance

Banning, *The Jeffersonian Persuasion* (Ithaca: Cornell University Press, 1978); Duncan Forbes, *Hume's Philosophical Politics* (Cambridge: Cambridge University Press, 1978); J.G.A. Pocock, *The Machiavellian Moment* (Princeton: Princeton University Press, 1975). My debt to Pocock's work is obvious in the first part of this article.

[3]The work of Janet Ajzenstat is one exception. See, for example, her 'Modern Mixed Government: A Liberal Defence of Inequality', *CJPS* 18 (1985), 119–35.

[4]The Country opposition, however, was hardly a homogeneous group. Dickinson provides a succinct overview of their internal divisions, which centred around religious matters and the question of who should enjoy active political power (*Liberty and Property*, 163–80).

[5]For a good overview on how these approaches have been applied to Scottish social thought see J.G.A. Pocock, 'Cambridge Paradigms and Scotch Philosophers: A Study of the Relations between the Civic Humanist and the Civil Jurisprudential Interpretation of Eighteenth Century Social Thought', in Istvan Hont and Michael Ignatieff (eds), *Wealth and Virtue: The Shaping of Political Economy in the Scottish Enlightenment* (Cambridge: Cambridge University Press, 1983), 235–53.

[6]This is particularly the view of Nicholas Phillipson, 'Adam Smith as Civic Moralist', *ibid.*, 179–203, and 'The Scottish Enlightenment', in R. Porter and M. Teich (eds), *The Enlightenment in National Context* (Cambridge: Cambridge University Press, 1981), 19–40.

[7]David Hume, 'Of Refinement in the Arts', *Essays Moral, Political and Literary*, Vol. 1, T.H. Green and T.H. Grose (eds), (London: Longmans, Green and Co., 1875), 300.

[8]Adam Smith, *The Wealth of Nations*, E. Canaan (ed.), (New York: Random House, 1937), bk. 14, chap. 7, 551.

[9]Adam Smith, *Lectures on Justice, Police, and Arms*, Edwin Canaan (ed.), (Oxford: Clarendon Press, 1896), as quoted in Anand C. Chitnis, *The Scottish Enlightenment* (London: Croom Helm, 1976), 104.

[10]Smith also had a more integrated and historical understanding of the relationship between the economic and the political than did Hume, believing as he did in the four stages theory of development—hunting, pastoral, agriculture and commerce. Smith was also less optimistic than Hume about the beneficial effects of commercial society. For a good overview of the intellectual differences, see John Robertson, 'Scottish Political Economy Beyond the Civic Tradition: Government and Economic Development in *The Wealth of Nations*', *History of Political Thought* 4 (1983), 451–82.

[11]David Hume, 'Of Civil Liberty', in *Essays*, 162–3.

[12]*The Wealth of Nations*, bk. 5, chap. 3, 896, 897.

[13]B. Bailyn, *The Origins of American Politics* (New York: Random House, 1972), 56–8.

[14]For more on Hume's influence see Douglas Adair, 'That Politics May Be Reduced to a Science: David Hume, James Madison and the Tenth *Federalist*', *Huntington Library Quarterly* 30 (1956–57), 343–60.

[15]David Hume, 'Idea of a Perfect Commonwealth', in *Essays*, 497.

[16]James Madison, *The Federalist Papers*, no. 10, introduction by Clinton Rossiter (New York: Mentor Books, 1961), 79. On this point see Adair, 'That Politics May Be

Reduced to a Science', and James Moore, 'Hume's Political Science and the Classical Republican Tradition', *CJPS* 10 (1977), 809–39.

[17]See Max Ferrand (ed.), *The Records of the Federal Convention of 1787* (New Haven: Yale University Press, 1966), vol. 1, 296, 376, 381.

[18]For more on this point see Banning, *The Jeffersonian Persuasion*, and Gerald Stourzh, *Alexander Hamilton and the Idea of Republican Government* (Stanford: Stanford University Press, 1970).

[19]Thomas Jefferson, 'Letter to Ogilvie, 1811', in Saul K. Padover, *Thomas Jefferson on Democracy* (New York: Mentor Books, 1939), 136.

[20]Of all the above Cobbett radicalism was sharpest in its attack upon corruption. See H.T. Dickinson, *British Radicalism and the French Revolution 1789–1815* (Oxford: Basil Blackwell, 1985), 70, 71. One of Cobbett's greatest admirers was Robert Gourlay, a radical leader in Upper Canada during the 1820s, whose views, according to his biographer, were close to 'an almost forgotten party called the Country Party which opposed court corruption' (Lois Dorroch Milani, *Robert Gourlay, Gadfly* [Thornbury, Ontario: Ampersand Press, 1971], 26).

[21]Robert Kelley, *The Transatlantic Persuasion: The Liberal-Democratic Mind in the Age of Gladstone* (New York: Knopf, 1969), 409.

[22]Donald Creighton, *The Empire of the St Lawrence* (Toronto: Macmillan, 1972), 45.

[23]*The Seventh Report from the Select Committee of the House of Assembly of Upper Canada on Grievances* (Toronto: M. Reynolds, 1832), iii.

[24]See Dickinson, *Liberty and Authority*, 208. I am grateful to James Moore for bringing this to my attention.

[25]*The Seventh Report.*

[26]L.J. Papineau, *Address to the Electors of the West Ward of Montreal* (Montreal: Fabre, Perrault and Co., 1831), 1.

[27]Toronto *Constitution*, 14 June 1837.

[28]L.J. Papineau, *La Minerve*, 17 March 1836, as quoted in F. Ouellet, *Lower Canada 1791–1840* (Toronto: McClelland and Stewart, 1980), 218.

[29]Robert Davis, *The Canadian Farmer's Travels in the United States* (Buffalo: Steel's Press, 1837), 97.

[30]Reprinted in Trevor H. Lovere and Richard A. Jarrell (eds), *A Curious Field-Book: Science and Society in Canadian History* (Toronto: Oxford University Press, 1974), 160, 161.

[31]For the relationship between patronage and responsible government see Susan Mann Trofimenkoff, *The Dream of Nation* (Toronto: Macmillan, 1982), 86–7.

[32]The *Examiner*, 19 September 1849, as quoted in J.M.S. Careless, *The Union of the Canadas* (Toronto: McClelland and Stewart, 1967), 167.

[33]*Ibid.*

[34]Frank Underhill, 'Some Aspects of Upper Canadian Radical Opinion in the Decade before Confederation', in Ramsay Cook (ed.), *Upper Canadian Politics in the 1850s* (Canadian Historical Readings; Toronto: University of Toronto Press, 1967), 2.

[35]See the introduction by Vida Bruce to Antoine Gérin-Lajoie's *Jean Rivard* (Toronto: McClelland and Stewart, 1977).

[36]Antoine Gérin-Lajoie, as quoted in Marcel Rioux, 'The Development of Ideologies in Quebec', in Richard Schultz, Orest M. Kruhlak, and John C. Terry (eds), *The Canadian Political Process* (3rd ed.; Toronto: Holt, Rinehart and Winston, 1979), 101.

[37] *Jean Rivard*, 65.

[38] Ralph Heintzman, 'The Political Culture of Quebec, 1840–1960', *CJPS* 16 (1983), 3–59.

[39] As quoted in Adam Shortt and Arthur G. Doughty, *Documents Relating to the Constitutional History of Canada*, pt. 2 (Ottawa: J. de L. Taché, King's Printer, 1918), 984.

[40] David Chisholme, *The Lower-Canada Watchman* (Kingston: James Macfarlane, 1829), 305. Chisholme (1776?–1842) was born in Scotland and emigrated to Canada in 1822, where he worked as a journalist and editor for the Montreal *Gazette*. He was also a close friend of Lord Dalhousie.

[41] Camillus (John Henry), *An Enquiry into the Evils of General Suffrage* (Montreal: Nahum Mower, 1820), as reprinted in John Hare and Jean-Pierre Wallot (eds), *Confrontations* (Trois-Rivières: Boréal Express, 1970), 100. The emphasis is Henry's. John Henry (1776–1820) was probably born in Ireland, moving to the United States at the turn of the century and then to Canada, where he became connected with the North West Company.

[42] 'Uniacke's Memorandum to Windham, 1806', in *Canadian Historical Review* 17 (1936), 35.

[43] For more on the two plans of union see B.C.U. Cuthbertson, 'The Old Attorney General, Richard John Uniacke, 1735–1830' (unpublished MA thesis, University of New Brunswick, 1970).

[44] W.H. Nelson, 'The Last Hopes of the American Loyalists', *Canadian Historical Review* 32 (1951), 23.

[45] Adam Smith, 'Essays on the Colonies', in Sir George Cornwell Lewis (ed.), *Governance of Dependencies* (London: M. Walter Dunne, 1901), 76, 77, 78. Most of Smith's essay is replicated in *Wealth of Nations*.

[46] *Wealth of Nations*, bk. 5, chap. 3, 898; bk. 4, chap. 7, 551. If Donald Winch is correct there are parallels not only with Loyalists and Tories but with Madison's thoughts on federal union. See his *Adam Smith's Politics: An Essay in Historiographic Revision* (Cambridge: Cambridge University Press, 1978), 161–2.

[47] Jonathan Sewell, Jr, 'Memoir on the Means of Promoting the Joint Interests, 1807', in J.B. Robinson, *Plan for a General Legislative Union of the British Provinces in North America* (London: W. Clowes, 1822), 7. Justice Sewell of Quebec was the son of Jonathan Sewell, Sr, of Massachusetts.

[48] J.B. Robinson, *Letter to the Right Hon. Earl Bathurst* (London: William Clowes, 1825), 31.

[49] John Strachan, *Observations on a Bill for Uniting the Legislative Councils and Assemblies* (London, 1824), in J.L.H. Henderson, *John Strachan: Documents and Opinions* (Toronto: McClelland and Stewart, 1969), 157.

[50] John Strachan (and J.B. Robinson), *Observations of the Policy of a General Union of all the British Provinces of North America* (London: William Clowes, 1824) in Henderson, *John Strachan*, 68.

[51] P.S. Hamilton, *Union of the Colonies of British North America, Being Three Papers Upon This Subject* (Montreal: John Lovell, 1864), 10, 58.

[52] J.B. Robinson, *Plan for a General Legislative Union*, 40.

[53] Cuthbertson, 'The Old Attorney General', 224.

[54] *Lord Durham's Report*, Gerald M. Craig (ed.), (Toronto: McClelland and Stewart, 1963), 162.

[55]On this point see Cephas D. Allan, 'The Genesis of the Confederation of Canada', in *Annual Report of the American Historical Association* 1 (1911).

[56]J.S. Johnston, in Edward Manning Saunders, *Three Premiers of Nova Scotia* (Toronto: William Brigges, 1909), 255.

[57]P.S. Hamilton, 'Observations Upon a Union of the Colonies, 1854–1855', in *Union of the Colonies*, 18.

[58]John Strachan, *A Discourse on the Character of King George Addressed to the Inhabitants of British America* (Montreal: Nahum Mower, 1810), 29, 30, 50.

[59]S.F. Wise, 'Upper Canada and the Conservative Tradition', in Edith G. Firth (ed.), *Profiles of a Province* (Toronto: Ontario Historical Society, 1967), 21. See also R. Whitaker, 'Images of the State in Canada', in Leo Panitch (ed.), *The Canadian State* (Toronto: University of Toronto Press, 1977), 28–71.

[60]Hamilton, 'Observations upon a Union', 20.

[61]Harold Innis, *The Fur Trade in Canada* (Toronto: University of Toronto Press, 1973), 396.

[62]See Louis Nourry, 'L'idée de fédération chez Etienne Parent, 1831–1852', *Revue d'Histoire de l'Amérique Française* 26 (1973), 533–57.

[63]See A.L. Silver, *The French-Canadian Idea of Confederation* (Toronto: University of Toronto Press, 1982).

[64]W.L. Mackenzie, 'Letter to John Neilson, 7 December 1829', in Margaret Fairly (ed.), *The Selected Writings of William Lyon Mackenzie* (Toronto: Oxford University Press, 1960); Robert Gourlay, 'To the Honourable the Commons of Upper Canada Met in Assembly, 24 December 1825', Public Archives of Canada. Co O. 42 Vol. 380.

[65]Waite, *The Life and Times of Confederation*, 93–4.

[66]Quoted by Whelan, *Union of the British Provinces*, 42, in Waite, *The Life and Times of Confederation*, 80.

[67]D'Arcy McGee, *Parliamentary Debates on the Subject of the Confederation of the British North American Provinces* (Quebec: Hunter and Rose and Co., 1865), 128 (hereinafter referred to as *Confederation Debates*).

[68]Joseph Pope (ed.), *Confederation: Being a Series of Hitherto Unpublished Documents Bearing On the British North Amercia Act* (Toronto: Carswell, 1895), 55. Minutes and notes of discussion of the Quebec Conference were kept by Hewitt Bernard.

[69]*Confederation Debates*, 62.

[70]*Ibid.*, 255, 256.

[71]D.G. Creighton, *British North America at Confederation: A Study Prepared for the Royal Commission on Dominion-Provincial Relations* (Ottawa: Queen's Printer, 1963), 9.

[72]*Confederation Debates*, 64.

[73]*Ibid.*, 64.

32

The Opponents of Confederation

Ged Martin

Perhaps no group of politicians has suffered more from the national school of Canadian historiography so prevalent before the 1970s than the Anti-Confederates, those who in the 1860s opposed the British North America Act and the establishment of the Canadian federation. Historians have charged the 'Antis' with lack of vision, parochialism, negativism, cynicism, and an absence of any real theoretical understanding of the meaning of federalism. Particular opponents, such as Joseph Howe, have been labelled political opportunists, as though those who favoured Confederation did not expect to benefit personally from its achievement. In the context of the 1860s, as well as from our present vantage point, the anti-Confederates' criticisms of the British North America Act made and make a good deal more sense than they did in the 1960s, when Centennial Year produced a plethora of historical celebrations of the achievement of Confederation. Students may find a number of interesting resonances between the situation in the 1860s and in the 1990s.

In his study of the case against Canadian Confederation, Ged Martin offers an unusually sympathetic portrayal of the opponents of union. As he observes, the central question is how Confederation seized and retained the central ground in the debates. As he also notes, many opponents claimed that they were not against the principle of unification, but only the practice of this particular scheme, which they found to be too costly, too cumbersome, and too dangerous to their existing provincial interests.

Does Martin accept his own opening speculation that the arguments against Confederation 'may give us a mirror-image of the reasons why it was actually adopted'? What difficulties does he see in any attempt to analyse rationally and historically the available material and arguments? What were the major criticisms of the opposition?

Were they consistent, and did they have to be? Martin argues that supporters of Confederation did not insist that the opponents offer rival alternatives. Why not?

This article first appeared, titled 'Painting the Other Picture: The Case against Canadian Confederation', in C.C. Eldridge, ed., *From Rebellion to Patriation: Canada and Britain in the Nineteenth and Twentieth Centuries* (Aberystwyth: Canadian Studies Group in Wales, 1989), 43–81, and in a slightly different form in Ged Martin, ed., *The Causes of Canadian Confederation* (Fredericton: Acadiensis Press, 1990), 19–49.

It was a Welshman, Robert Harris, who created one of Canada's national icons, the massive group portrait entitled *The Fathers of Confederation*. Born in the Vale of Conwy in 1849, Harris emigrated with his family to Prince Edward Island as a child, and produced his careful reproduction of the thirty-four men who attended the Quebec Conference of 1864 almost twenty years after the event. Unluckily, his main canvas was destroyed by the fire which engulfed the Parliament Buildings in Ottawa in 1916, leaving only sketches. However, in the 1960s, a Canadian insurance company commissioned a new version, which tacked on to the right of the picture three men who had not actually been present at Quebec, but who had attended the subsequent London conference in 1866, and were recognized as 'Fathers' during the sixtieth anniversary celebrations of Confederation in 1927. Thus are created the symbols of nationhood.

Harris portrayed the Fathers of Confederation as grave statesmen, formally posed in solemn conclave. From their demeanour, it would appear hard to think that any of them had ever called an opponent a liar, or promised a community a bridge to win an election. We need neither begrudge nor scorn the need which Canadians feel to weave an aura of vision around the founders of their country: in real life, the Fathers of Confederation were no more ruthless than Owen Glyndŵr, no more cynical than David Lloyd George. Our real difficulty in accepting the far-sighted wisdom of Canada's founders lies in the problem of reconciling the myth with the equally patriotic efforts of Canada's historians, who have related the saga of the coming of Confederation as if it were the inevitable outcome of the problems of the 1860s.[1] 'Only a general union, balanced with all the care and precision of a cantilever, was practical in 1864', wrote W.L. Morton a century later. If Confederation was indeed the inescapable solution in 1864, how can we attribute such superior wisdom to the Fathers? Surely they were no more than the unconscious instruments of historical inevitability? Morton implicitly confronted the issue by describing the cabinet headed by John Sandfield Macdonald, which immediately preceded the Confederation Coalition in the province of Canada, as 'provincial politicians who had failed to sense the new currents which had begun to flow in Canadian politics since 1857'.[2]

Confederation, then, was inevitable, but perspicacity and vision were needed to grasp this evident fact. By implication, those who failed to see the necessity for Confederation got it wrong.

Such an approach can hardly encourage an unprejudiced analysis of the arguments advanced between 1864 and 1867 by those who opposed the new constitutional system.[3] To understand their arguments may indirectly help to explain why Confederation was indeed adopted. The scheme drawn up at Quebec in 1864 was unpopular in the Atlantic provinces. In New Brunswick in 1865, the ministry responsible was rejected by the voters, and it is at least possible that the same would have happened in Lower Canada had there been an election there too. Thus it is at least possible to argue that Confederation was ultimately accepted in spite of the arguments against rather than because of the case made in its favour. Consideration of the arguments advanced by its opponents may enable us to decide whether Confederation really was the logical deduction from interlocking circumstances, or whether we should look to other explanations for its adoption. Was Confederation perhaps not a logical deduction from the circumstances of 1864 at all, but a panic response to what C.P. Stacey has called 'the atmosphere of crisis', in the closing phases of the American Civil War, something which was simply not susceptible to logical refutation, however detailed and effectively argued?[4] Or was Confederation, on the other hand, something which had long been seen as the ultimate destiny of the British provinces in North America, an idea whose time had come in 1864?[5] Such an interpretation would help to explain why it was that the provinces should have turned to a federal scheme in 1864, since it is hard to believe that it was possible to deduce from the circumstances of the time—a bloody war of secession to the south—that federal government was in itself an ideal system. The pre-existence of a mental 'blueprint' for the union of the provinces would also help explain inconsistencies in the pro-Confederation case: for instance, that a scheme intended to contribute to a long-term continental balance of power should abruptly be put forward as part of an immediate defence package against the United States, that the Intercolonial Railway, which physically could not be constructed quickly and politically was unlikely to be agreed immediately, should be embraced as a device to deter or resist an American invasion which might come within weeks or months. Some colour is lent this line of interpretation by the fact that some politicians argued whether or not Confederation was an entirely new idea,[6] while others concentrated not on whether it was a desirable outcome in itself, but on proving that it was premature. The arguments against Confederation, then, may give us a mirror-image of the reasons why it was actually adopted.

There is a second, longer-term reason for examining the arguments of the critics of Confederation. When the Confederate States were overwhelmed in 1865, the Southern fire-eater Edmund Ruffin wrapped himself in the

Stars and Bars flag and blew his brains out. By contrast, the critics of Canadian Confederation proved to be embarrassingly good losers. Sandfield Macdonald became Sir John A. Macdonald's Ontario lieutenant in 1867, Joseph Howe joined his cabinet in 1868, Christopher Dunkin followed the next year. This may prove only that they were hypocritical in their opposition to the new system, but it is probably fairer to conclude that in coming aboard, they helped in practice to shape it to meet their concerns. In contrast to countries in which major constitutional change left a long-lasting legacy of bitterness, the distinction between those who had argued for or against Confederation quickly blurred. In the 1870s, the admittedly unimpressive cabinet of Alexander Mackenzie was largely composed of Anti-Confederates. In the 1880s, the provincial campaign to roll back the frontiers of central control was led by Oliver Mowat, himself a Father of Confederation, while the author of one of the most scornful and spirited dismissals of the case for Confederation quoted in this paper was to be prime minister of Canada from 1896 to 1911.[7] In the longer term, the 'Antis' were to prove Fathers of the Canada that we know today.

There are basic difficulties in assessing the validity of the debates and petitons on Confederation. How far were they designed to convince, and how far merely to mobilise? The historian seizes, if with perhaps muted enthusiasm, on the thousand pages of the published *Confederation Debates* of 1865 in the Canadian provincial parliament in the spirit within which historians operate—that of logical discussion.[8] Yet this may not be faithful to the spirit of the original. 1867 was the year not only of the British North America Act, but of Britain's Second Reform Act, which Maurice Cowling portrays as a classic exercise in 'high politics'—the exploitation of a major issue not in its own terms, but as part of the manoeuvrings for alliances and offices among a key group of political leaders.[9] Confederation is more than susceptible to a similar analysis. Viewed from the patriotic point of view of Canadian nation-building, George Brown's coalition with Macdonald and Cartier in June 1864 was a remarkably magnanimous departure from old feuds. Seen through the less rosy spectacles of factional politics, Confederation offered a sufficiently lofty reason for old enemies to get into bed—and, more importantly, office. On what other issue could Brownite Reformers have coalesced with Macdonald Conservatives and Bleus?[10] The problem with putting together a majority on such an overarching issue was that too rapid a delivery of the goods would remove its unifying purpose: the Cartier-Macdonald government had used the aim of federation to win Galt in 1858–59,[11] and could hope to repeat the exercise with Brown in 1864. Two years later, minus Brown but still backed by a significant slice of his former followers, the Canadian cabinet showed itself so lacking in zeal to get to Britain and tie the knot with the Maritimes that the governor-general hinted at resignation.[12] In other provinces, a similar case can be made. Arthur Gordon, lieutenant-governor of New Brunswick, can be dismissed as a sardonic observer, but he may well have been right in reporting in December 1864 that there was 'an indisposition to believe that change is seriously meditated and an inclination to regard the plan as intended to produce by its agitation some immediate effect on the condition of political parties than as designed to inaugurate a new Constitutional system'.[13] From Newfoundland, Ambrose Shea assured Galt that 'the question will break up our local parties' adding, 'if even for no other reason I should hail its introduction on this account'.[14] Perhaps the best example of personal rivalries was that between Howe and 'that d——d Tupper', which prompted the former to disavow his earlier rhodomontades in favour of British North American union.[15]

A 'high politics' view of Confederation would lead us to question the value of the actual arguments put forward against Confederation, since the root reason for opposition in many cases could be assumed to be resentment at not being taken aboard. At the very least, the prospect of loaves and fishes could soften the opposition of some critics of Confederation. Members of Albert J. Smith's New Brunswick ministry were prepared to take up the question in 1866, despite having been elected in 1865 to oppose it.[16] In Nova Scotia, the spectacular bolt to change sides in April 1866 was alleged to have been touched off by the suspicious decision of two Anti-Confederates that others would rat first, and 'we . . . had better get into line or we should be left out in the cold and lose all chance of obtaining good positions'.[17]

The two major sources on which this paper is based are the *Confederation Debates* of 1865 in the province of Canada, and the Nova Scotia petitions of 1866 in the *British Parliamentary Papers*. The Canadian parliament had not previously printed its debates, and we may echo the lament of Dr Joseph Blanchet, four weeks and 545 pages after discussion began on 3 February 1865 that the decision 'to have the speeches of this House printed in official form certainly did no good service to the country'.[18] Yet vast as was the eventual volume, it does not necessarily do justice to the opposition case. In the early phases of the debate, there was a tendency to demand further information—for the Quebec plan required much fleshing-out of practical details on which the ministers were unforthcoming—and it was tempting to debunk the visionary orations of Macdonald and McGee by trumpeting that there was no case to answer. Luther Holton replied to the first great onslaught of explanations with the flourish that if the government's speeches 'contain all that can be said in favour of this scheme, we have no fear of letting them go unanswered'.[19] As the debate was getting into its stride, so news arrived of Tilley's defeat in New Brunswick which, as Dorion said, caused the issue 'to lose much of its interest'.[20] Much of the debate was taken up with members taunting each other with inconsistency, which usually provoked elaborate apologetics. Some speeches were intended to drag matters out while petitions were circulated:[21] Cartier embarrassed Eric Dorion, by reading into the record a circular letter he had sent to supporters requesting them to have anti-Confederation petitions 'signed as soon as possible by men, women and children'.[22] Similar devices were used to produce petitions in Nova Scotia, as the governor-general, Lord Monck, and a former lieutenant-governor, the Marquess of Normanby, assured the House of Lords in 1867.[23] It is certainly hard to believe that the 210 inhabitants of the district of Port Medway who signed their names to a massive, two-thousand word petition against Confederation were entirely unprompted,[24] and it may be doubted if any of the petitions emerged from the sober atmosphere of a political science seminar. At Yarmouth, Joseph Howe preceded a two-hour assault on Confederation with 'an eloquent eulogy on the character of Her Majesty Queen Victoria, as a child, a wife and mother, a queen and a widow' which was much cheered.[25] It is not surprising that opposition to Confederation came in Nova Scotia what modern American politics would term a 'motherhood' issue.

There are other difficulties in accommodating the available material to the logical approach of the historian. A sound historical analysis would seek to balance arguments for and arguments against, coming to a fair and reasonable conclusion. The arguments *for* Confederation, which we normally equate with the reasons for its adoption, are clear enough and are capable of neat presentation. The arguments *against* offend our sense of order. Cartier was able to have fun playing off opposites: the Montreal *Witness* warned that Protestantism in Lower Canada would be doomed by Confederation, while its deadly rival, the *True Witness* saw it as the destruction of French Canada.[26] The easy but fallacious assumption behind such debating devices is that the two strands of argument cancel each other out, whereas in reality one or the other—perhaps even both, but for different reasons—might well be entirely valid. Perhaps the real task of explanation is not to explain *why* Confederation was accepted, but *how* it managed to seize the central ground and divide the opposition to right and left.

'I do not know of anyone opposed to union in the abstract', said New Brunswick's Timothy Warren Anglin, 'but my impression is that the time has not arrived for any kind of union, and I will oppose it to the last'.[27] This was a common theme among the critics: intercolonial union in principle, union one day, but not this union, not now.[28] As Edward Whelan put it, the critics accepted the principle of ploughing the field, but objected to destroying the daisies and field mice.[29] How sincere were these protestations—by some, but by no means all the critics of Confederation—in favour of an eventual British North American union? Perhaps they were gestures of open-mindedness merely to win over waverers: David Reesor found it 'extraordinary' that so many members of the Legislative Council spoke 'strongly and emphatically against many of the resolutions', while declaring their reluctant intention to vote for the package.[30] Yet even Dorian, who went to some lengths to clear his name of the slander of ever having spoken favourably of the idea, could leave open a faint and distant possibility. 'Population may extend over the wilderness that now lies between the Maritime Provinces and ourselves, and commercial intercourse may increase sufficiently to render Confederation desirable'.[31] As late as 1864, admittedly at a social occasion, Joseph Howe proclaimed: 'I have always been in favour of uniting any two, three, four, or the whole five of the provinces'.[32] It is not necessary to follow McGee in the full flight of his oratory, but it may well be that the idea of Confederation had become an autonomous cause of its own happening. 'If we have dreamed a dream of union . . . it is at least worth remarking that a dream which has been dreamed by such wise and good men, may, for aught we know or you know, have been a sort of vision—a vision foreshadowing forthcoming natural events in a clear intelligence.'[33]

If some of the opponents subscribed to the idea of an eventual interco-lonial union, most of the critics in the province of Canada argued that Con-federation was not a solution to present difficulties, and it would itself require a far greater degree of political wisdom than was necessary to rescue the existing system. Henri Joly felt that the various provinces would meet in a confederated parliament 'as on a field of battle'.[34] Christopher Dunkin referred to the airy dismissals of such warnings by ministerial supporters: 'Oh! there won't be any trouble; men are in the main sensible, and won't try to make trouble'. If public men were so reasonable as to be able to work the new system, why then had the province of Canada had 'four crises in two years'?[35] In any case, even if it were accepted that Upper and Lower Canada were not living together in harmony, the answer was surely for them to work out a new system of government and not to claim that only through a wider union could they get along. Dunkin noted that in the years between the lapsing of Galt's federation initiative in 1859 and the formation of the Grand Coalition of June 1864, 'we quarrelled and fought about almost eve-rything, but did not waste a thought or a word upon this gigantic question of the Confederation of these Provinces.'[36] 'Surely', Thomas Scatcherd argued, 'if parties could unite as they did in June last, they could have united to prevent the difficulty complained of . . . without entering upon a scheme to subvert the Constitution'.[37]

While some critics of Confederation admitted that the Canadian Union had its problems, others felt them to have been exaggerated. Henri Joly contrasted Taché's claim that 'the country was bordering on civil strife', with the ministry's throne speech, which thanked 'a beneficent Providence for the general contentment of the people of this province'.[38] Joseph Perrault asked 'have we not reason to be proud of our growth since 1840, and of the fact that within the past twenty-five years, our progress, both social and material, has kept pace with that of the first nations in the world?'[39] Some Lower Canada members were suspicious of the motives behind the agitation for 'representation by population' in Upper Canada, dismissing it—in Joly's words—as 'one of those political clap-traps which ambitious men, who can catch them in no other way, set to catch the heedless multitude'. Both Joly and Perrault argued that hypocrisy was proved by the alacrity with which Upper Canada Reformers entered the Macdonald-Sicotte administration of 1862, which was bound not to press the issue—proof that 'Upper Canada is much more indifferent, and its leaders much less sincere touching this question of the representation, than they would have us believe'.[40] Perrault, however, went much further. In a speech presumably aimed at stoking every French Canadian fear of assimilation—it ranged from the Acadian deportation, via the history of Mauritius to the francophobia of Lord Durham's Report—Perrault denied that Upper Canada had more people than Lower Canada at all. The 'true total' of the population of Upper Canada had been 'greatly exaggerated. . . . Did not all their journals declare that the census of 1861 *must* indicate a very large total population in favour of Upper Canada over Lower Canada?' The prophecy had been self-fulfilling, 'the number of the living increased and the number of the dead diminished', a fraud revealed when it was noticed that the population under the age of one year exceeded the live births of the previous twelve months by eight thousand. The census had also under-counted the population of Lower Canada, for 'our farmers have always stood in dread of the census, because they have a suspicion that it is taken with the sole object of imposing some tax, or of making some draft of men for the defence of the country'. Confusingly, he also contended that even if Upper Canada's population did exceed that of Lower Canada, it was no more than a temporary blip, caused by Irish famine migration, which had now ceased. So too had the outward flow of French Canadians to New England, with the result that within ten years, the higher birth-rate of Lower Canada would bring the two provinces back to equality of population.[41]

The core of the case against Confederation was that there was no crisis sufficient to justify so large a change. Consequently, critics largely refused to enter the trap of offering alternative solutions. 'We are asked, "what are you going to do? You must do something. Are you going to fall back into our old state of dead-lock?" ', Dunkin reported, adding that whenever he heard the argument 'that something must be done, I suspect that there is a plan on foot to get something very bad done'.[42] Henri Joly took the same line. 'I am asked: "If you have nothing to do with Confederation, what will you have?" I answer, we would remain as we are.'[43] 'Now my proposition is very simple', Joseph Howe told the people of Nova Scotia. 'It is to let well enough alone.'[44] Not surprisingly, the opponents of Confederation indignantly rejected the argument that they were—wittingly or otherwise—working for annexation to the United States. They replied that the campaign for Confederation itself contained the germ of an annexationist threat. Matthew Cameron, one of the few prominent Upper Canada Conservatives to oppose the scheme, warned that the delusive arguments of material gain from Confederation with the tiny Maritimes 'are arguments tenfold stronger in favour of union with the United States'.[45] Nor did the danger lie simply in encouraging hopes of greater prosperity, as was shown when a moderate Lower Canadian journal could proclaim 'qu'à tous les points du vue, nos institutions, notre langue, et nos lois seront mieux protégées avec la confédération américain qu'avec le projet de confédération de l'Amérique du Nord'.[46] 'Once destroy public confidence in our institutions', warned T.C. Wallbridge, 'and it is impossible to predict what extremes may be resorted to.'[47] Joseph Howe predicted that the imposition of Confederation on unwilling provinces would lead to 'undying hatreds and ultimate annexation'.[48]

At first sight, it may seem surprising that the opponents of Confederation were able to escape the tactical trap of a challenge for alternative solutions to intercolonial problems. Christopher Dunkin and Joseph Howe were on insecure ground in offering the far more ambitious idea of imperial federation,[49] while Tupper found that Maritime Union had no friends at all when he attempted the ploy of reviving it in 1865.[50] The truth was that in the province of Canada, the demand for an alternative would have been dangerous indeed for the cause of Confederation after its defeat in the New Brunswick election of 1865. The coalition government had been built around an ambiguous policy, which seemed to make a federation of the two Canadas the fall-back position if wider union could not be achieved—a federation which, as Dorion put it, 'might hereafter extend so as to embrace other territories either west or east'.[51] For John A. Macdonald, such a solution could offer little comfort: as a Conservative, he had been dependent since 1857 upon Bleu support for his periods of office. Anything which strengthened Upper Canada and its Reform party against Lower Canada could only sell opposition to the Conservative party. Once New Brunswick had apparently dropped out, the pressure was on Brown and his Upper Canada Reform colleagues to deliver the small print of the coalition bargain. 'The Administration could not give a pledge that they would carry the Confederation of all the provinces', Dorion reminded his former allies, 'but they could pledge and did pledge themselves to bring in, in the event of the failure of that scheme, a measure for the federation of Upper and Lower Canada.'[52]

Consequently, supporters of Confederation had little motive in demanding that its opponents come up with rival schemes, but rather preferred to present the Quebec scheme as an immutable package, agreed behind locked doors as a balanced intercolonial treaty. Critics objected to being faced with the resolutions as a package. 'What is the use of considering them if we cannot come to our conclusions and give them effect in the shape of amendments?', asked James Atkins.[53] At Quebec, Dunkin pointed out, twenty-three men had sat for seventeen working days to produce 'a scheme of a Constitution which they vaunt as being altogether better than that of the model republic of the United States, and even than that of the model kingdom of Great Britain'.[54] William Annand thought that a scheme 'matured in a few weeks, amid exhaustive festivities' could not be the best constitution possible.[55] Joseph Howe noted that the inflexibility of the Quebec scheme would be carried forward to the future. 'No means are provided by which the people, should it be found defective, can improve it from time to time. Whenever a change is required they must come back to the Imperial Parliament.'[56] Let it never be said that Joseph Howe lacked vision for the future.

Coupled with resentment at the rejection of any possibility of amendment was anger at the total refusal of a popular vote on so major a constitutional change. As a Hamilton paper put it, if there was to be no general election on Confederation, the polling booths 'may as well be turned into pigpens, and the voters lists cut up into pipe-lighters'.[57] In Nova Scotia, where petition after petition dwelt on the province's long tradition of representative and responsible government, the people of Shelburne put the issue in more fundamental and sober terms: 'whilst Your Majesty's petitioners freely admit the right of their representatives in Provincial Parliament to legislate for them within reasonable limits, they cannot admit the right of such representatives to effect sudden changes, amounting to an entire subversion of the constitution, without the deliberate sanction of the people expressed at the polls.'[58] As Joseph Howe put it in more succinct and homely terms, the local legislature had 'no right to violate a trust only reposed in them for four years, or in fact to sell the fee simple of a mansion of which they have but a limited lease'.[59] If the scheme were beneficial, which the people of Queen's County flatly doubted, 'the means employed to force it upon the country without an appeal to the people, and with full knowledge of their intense dislike of the measure' were enough to discredit it.[60]

Both in Canada and the Altantic provinces, opponents of Confederation attacked the scheme as 'very costly, for the money is scattered on all sides in handfuls'.[61] Simply listing the promised commitments left critics breathless with horror. Joseph Howe recounted that with a debt of $75,000,000, 'the public men of Canada propose to purchase the territories of the Hudson's Bay Company, larger than half Europe', take over British Columbia and Vancouver Island, 'provinces divided from them by an interminable wilderness', as well as absorb the Atlantic provinces '—countries severally as large as Switzerland, Sardinia, Greece, and Great Britain'.[62] Dunkin similarly warned that with 'a promise of everything for everybody', the scheme could only 'be ambiguous, unsubstantial and unreal'.[63] Others feared not disappointment but jobbery. 'The proposed Constitution framed by arch jobbers is so devised as to provide for the very maximum of jobbing and corruption', Arthur Gordon assured Gladstone.[64] Unfortunately, responses to the threat of corruption depended on assessments by individuals of whether they would be victims or gainers from it. 'Are the people of Nova Scotia prepared to yield up their flourishing customs revenue to a federal treasury in Canada, there to be squandered in jobbery and corruption?', asked the Yarmouth *Tribune*.[65] The people might indeed balk at the idea, but their elected representatives were open to persuasion: as Joseph Howe lamented, when John A. Macdonald 'opened his confederation mousetrap he did not bait it with toasted cheese'.[66] None of this could bode well for the future. Christopher Dunkin warned that the representatives of each province would seek popularity back home by inching up federal subsidies or taking special arrangements for one province as a benchmark and precedent for comparable arrangements. They would prove to be 'pretty good daughters of the horse-leech, and their cry will be found to be pretty often and pretty successfully —"Give, give, give!" '.[67]

Related to the general question of cost were various predictions about the effect of Confederation on tariffs. James Currie predicted that Canada's tariff would have to rise by fifty per cent to produce the necessary revenue to pay for Confederation.[68] Other Canadian critics recognised that the province's existing tariff, which leaned towards protectionism, would have to be cut in order to meet the free-trading Maritimers half-way. This would reduce revenue at a time when more, not less, money was needed to meet increased costs. Lettelier de St Just predicted that 'the deficit which that reduction of our revenue will produce will have to be filled up by the agriculture and industry of Canada'[69], and Dunkin thought it 'rather strange' that a government should propose to cut its tariff income and 'at the same time, so to change our whole system as to involve ourselves in the enormous extravagances here contemplated'. Dunkin felt that no plan of direct taxation could possibly meet the cost, and that the only alternative was a reckless policy of borrowing, except that 'we cannot even borrow to any large amount unless under false pretences'.[70]

If Canadian critics feared the consequences of lowering the tariff at the dictation of the lower provinces, Maritimers feared even the compromise increase that Confederation seemed to imply. 'Unless Canada consents to economize and curtail its expense to a very considerable degree, which is not likely to happen', explained the Fredericton *Headquarters*, 'the Lower Provinces will have to raise their tariffs to that standard, as they will require a greater revenue to meet the expenses of government under the new confederation.'[71] Whereas the Canadian tariff was intended to protect industry, Nova Scotia's commercial policy was aimed at fostering the province's carrying trade:[72] consequently raising the tariff would destroy trade rather than increase revenue—pointing to direct taxation, which Ambrose Shea warned from Newfoundland was 'a point on which it is easy to alarm the masses everywhere'. It certainly had that effect on Prince Edward Island, where the despairing Edward Whelan reported that it scared 'the asses of country people, who can't see an inch beyond their noses'.[73] A British journalist who visited Charlottetown in 1865 reported that taxation was regarded as 'an evil which not only the Prince Edward Islanders, but the British colonies generally throughout North America, seem to consider as the greatest which can befall a community'.[74]

Textbook explanations of the coming of Confederation assume that Confederation was necessary for the construction of the Intercolonial Railway, and that the Intercolonial was necessary both for defence and to give Canada a winter outlet, freeing its trade from the twin strangleholds of a frozen St Lawrence and a capriciously hostile United States. Opponents accepted neither argument and indeed found much to object to in the whole scheme. First, the railway project was actually written into the Quebec resolutions, and would thus form part of the British legislation and the constitution of the Confederation—'a novelty, perhaps, that might not be found in the constitution of any country'[75] and one which, to say the least, gave an unusual status to a mere railway line, the more so as the line had yet to be surveyed, let alone built. Arthur Gordon argued forcefully that to include such a provision in an Act of the British parliament would 'be either unnecessary or unjust'—unnecessary if, as everyone assumed, the federal legislature proceeded with the scheme, 'unjust if it were to have the effect of forcing on the people of British America the execution of a work which their representatives in Parliament may consider it inexpedient to undertake'. In any case, such a provision 'would be impossible to enforce, as no penalty could be inflicted after the passage of the Act, in the event of the subsequent neglect of its provisions by the Federal Government and Legislature'.[76]

As might be expected, provincial politicians were less concerned by the constitutional impropriety of giving a railway the same constitutional status as peace, order and good government as by the fact that it gave the Intercolonial an advantage over their own preferred projects, especially Upper Canadian hopes for a communications link to the Red River.[77] Suspicions were further fuelled by ministerial reluctance to say where it would run or how much it would cost, thus prompting the prediction that 'it will be a piece of corruption from the time of turning the first shovelful of earth'.[78] It was widely appreciated that the reason for the vagueness lay in the local politics of New Brunswick, where military security pointed to a direct route along the thinly populated North Shore, but political expediency hinted at the possibility of a longer line up the Saint John valley, never far from the

American border. Tilley attempted to offer all routes to all men, prompting the only durable piece of doggerel from the Confederation controversy:

Mr Tilley will you stop your puffing and blowing
And tell us which way the railway is going?[79]

The question of the cost of the Intercolonial was a sore point to Upper Canada critics of the Confederation. In 1862, the Macdonald–Sicotte ministry had withrawn, abruptly and in an unedifying manner, from an inter-provincial agreement backed by an imperial loan guarantee, by which the province of Canada undertook to pay five-twelfths of the cost of the line— which, as Henri Joly pointed out, meant that the railway could be built if required without an accompanying political union.[80] Now Canada, with three-quarters of the population, was accepting a *pro rata* obligation to shoulder double that share. 'This will involve five to seven millions of dollars of an expense more than we had any occasion for incurring', complained David Reesor, 'for the other provinces were all [sic] willing to have been responsible for the rest, and there is very good reason why they should.'[81] Ironically, Canada's sudden outburst of generosity aroused counter-suspicions in the Maritimes, where the alleged bad faith of 1862 had left a deep mark. In New Brunswick, Albert J. Smith argued darkly that Canada must have some hidden motive for increasing the very offer it had so often dishonoured.[82]

Fundamentally, opponents argued that the Intercolonial was no more attractive a project in 1865 than it had been when rejected in 1862. 'I have not heard any reason why we should pledge our credit and resources to the construction of the Intercolonial Railway, even previous to any estimate of its cost being made, that was not urged in 1862 when the question was before the country', Dorion asserted.[83] William McMaster, one of Toronto's leading merchants, challenged the argument that the Intercolonial was 'an indispensable necessity in order to secure an independent outlet to the sea-board'.[84] Rather than use the existing railways to American ports, Upper Canada merchants and millers preferred to pay warehousing, insurance and interest charges to keep wheat and flour in store through the winter months, 'until the opening of the navigation'. They were even less likely to use a railway to Halifax, which would be double the distance to the US winter ports. Henri Joly also doubted whether the Intercolonial could be used to transport flour to the Maritimes, for 'the cost of transport over five hundred miles of railway would be too great'.[85]

The critics did not merely doubt whether trade could profitably flow along the Intercolonial; they also wondered whether Canada and the Maritimes were likely to have any trade at all. 'Let us not . . . be lulled with fancies of the great commercial advantages we shall derive from a Confederation of these provinces', intoned Eric Dorion. 'We have wood, they produce it; we produce potash, and so do they.'[86] 'With regard to timber', said

Henri Joly, 'the Gulf Provinces have no more need of ours than we of theirs.'
Canada imported its coal direct from Britain, as ballast on returning timber
ships. If that supply should ever fail, 'Upper Canada will probably get its coal
from the Pennsylvania mines, which are in direct communication with Lake
Erie.'[87] Yet at the same time, the critics could argue that free trade with the
Maritimes could be achieved without 'this mock Federal union', just as the
provinces had enjoyed a decade of closer economic relations with the United
States through the Reciprocity Treaty.[88] Equally, too, it was alleged that some
Halifax merchants were 'strenuous opponents of union because union in
their estimation means more businessmen, greater competition, less profits,
more trouble'.[89]

The critics were no more convinced by the argument that the Intercolonial was necessary for the defence of the provinces. Dorion argued that 'a
railway lying in some places not more than fifteen or twenty miles from the
frontier, will be of no use whatsoever. . . . An enemy could destroy miles of
it before it would be possible to resist him, and in time of difficulty it would
be a mere trap for the troops passing along it, unless we had almost an army
to keep it open'.[90] Another speaker, encountering a disbelieving heckler
when he made the same point, retorted that if 'the country to be traversed
by the Intercolonial Railway is of such a nature that no one could get
through to it, the sooner we cease saying anything further about it the better'.[91] In fact, however far the Intercolonial snaked away from the American
border, there was an existing stretch of the Grand Trunk 'at places within
twenty-six miles of the boundary of Maine',[92] and thus easily vulnerable to
American attack. Far from transporting large numbers of troops, the Intercolonial would need large forces simply to guard it. 'Unless with a very
strong force to defend it, in a military point of view, it would be no use at
all.'[93] In summary, the Intercolonial, centrepiece of so many textbook explanations of the causes of Confederation, was comprehensively dismissed by
James L. Biggar:

> Looking at it from a military point of view, it is well known that part of the
> proposed line would run within twenty-six miles of the American frontier, and
> that the communication could be cut off at any moment by an American army;
> and that as a commercial undertaking it could never compete with the water
> route during the season of navigation; and in winter it would be comparatively
> useless on account of the depth of snow.[94]

In fact, the opponents of Confederation were entirely unconvinced that
the political union of the provinces would strengthen their defence in any
way. 'We do not need Confederation to give us that unity which is indispensable in all military operations—unity of headship. A commander-in-
chief will direct the defence of all our provinces', argued Henri Joly.[95]
Defence had remained outside the orbit of colonial self-government until
very recent times, and the provinces' record on militia reform was hardly

impressive. Consequently, the argument that unity meant strength is one which appeals more to the twentieth-century observer than it did to contemporaries, especially when the unity proposed involved such tiny provinces. John S. Sanborn was simply bewildered. 'How the people of New Brunswick could be expected to come up to Canada to defend us, and leave their own frontier unprotected, he could not comprehend.'[96] Conversely, Matthew Cameron asked why Canada should be taxed to build fortifications in the Maritimes. 'Fortifications in St John, New Brunswick, would not protect us from the foe, if the foe were to come here.'[97] Sanborn argued that if there were indeed a war with the USA, each province would be attacked from a neighbouring state. 'Under these circumstances, each section of the Confederation would have enough to do to attend to its own affairs.'[98] Except, contended Dorion, that New Brunswick could not defend itself, since the province's population of a quarter of a million was only one-third that of the adjoining state of Maine. 'Those 250,000 Canada will have to defend, and it will have to pledge its resources for the purpose of providing means of defence along that extended line.'[99]

In the Atlantic colonies, the arguments were inverted. Petitioners from Digby County were ready to rally to 'the defence of their country and their flag' but were 'not disposed to adopt, as a means of ensuring their more efficient defence, a union with a Province which in 1862 refused to sanction a measure involving increased outlay for the better and more elaborate organization of their militia.'[100] Joseph Howe deftly alluded to Canadian complicity in border raids by Southern sympathisers, and the resulting threats of Northern retaliation, proclaiming: 'let those who provoke these controversies fight them out.'[101] He objected to a system under which Nova Scotia's militia 'may be ordered away to any point of the Canadian frontier'.[102] Prince Edward Islanders feared that they would be 'marched away to the frontiers of Upper Canada' or—as John Hamilton Gray put it with vivid bitterness, 'drafted for slaughter'.[103] In Newfoundland, the outspoken Charles Fox Bennett spoke of the island's young men 'leaving their bones to bleach in a foreign land', a phrase which he was to refine in the 1869 election into the celebrated reference to 'the desert sands of Canada'.[104]

In three of the four Atlantic provinces, insularity was a physical as well as a mental factor. 'We are surrounded by the sea', proclaimed Joseph Howe and—what was more to the point—'within ten days' sail of the fleets and armies of England'.[105] J.C. Pope of Prince Edward Island echoed Canadian critics in predicting that an American attack would make it 'necessary to retain all available strength in each of the provinces for the defence of their respective territories'. His emphasis differed in his confidence that local efforts would be powerfully seconded by the British navy and army.[106]

Many critics argued that Confederation would either make no difference to the defence of the provinces, or would actually make it more difficult. Henri Joly argued that there was 'no need' of political union to warn 'our neighbours' not to pick on a single province. The Americans were 'sufficiently sharp-witted to discover, without being told it, that if they content themselves with attacking us at a single point at a time, of course they will have to meet all our strength'. Perhaps they could be persuaded to 'enter into a contract, binding them to attack us at a single point only at one time—say Quebec?' They might be given free use of the Grand Trunk to move their troops.[107] More seriously, L.A. Olivier warned that if Confederation was thrust upon an unwilling population, they could not be expected to rally to the defence of their homeland with the full enthusiasm shown in past conflicts.[108]

'With Confederation, neither the number of men in the several provinces, nor the pecuniary resources now at their disposal, will be increased.'[109] The kernel of the opposition case on defense was that Confederation involved too much territory and no additional manpower. 'Can you alter the geographical position of the country?', asked Benjamin Seymour. 'Will you have any more people or means?'[110] 'If nature were to make the necessary effort and move their territory up alongside us, and thus make a compact mass of people, I would at once agree that it would strengthen us in a military point of view', Phillip Moore ironically conceded. In reality, however, Confederation 'will weaken instead of strengthen us' since 'the union will give an extension of territory far greater in proportion to the number of the population than [sic] now exists in Canada'.[111] The planned massive extension of empty and inaccessible territory westward to the Pacific struck Dorion as 'a burlesque' in terms of defence.[112] In short, critics found the defence argument literally laughable. 'If we could attach the territory possessed by the moon to these provinces, and obtain the assistance for our joint defence of the man who is popularly supposed to inhabit that luminary, we might derive strength from Confederation.'[113]

Critics were equally impressed by ringing talk of a 'new nationality' in British North America. 'I cannot see that the Federation of these provinces has anything of a national phase in it', commented Thomas Scatcherd. 'When you speak of national existence, you speak of independence; and so long as we are colonists of Great Britain we can have no national existence.'[114] Some Nova Scotian petitions protested that Canada was 'incapable of forming a new nationality',[115] but the loyal people of Barrington township had an each-way bet in wanting no part of 'new nationalities too feeble to stand alone, yet difficult to be controlled'.[116] Their governor, Sir Richard Mac-Donnell, was

> unable to see in what way England would be less vulnerable through Canada or Canada less vulnerable through England when a confederated Parliament meets at Ottawa than now. There is not a foot of territory in all these hundreds of thousands of square miles which would thereby become less English than now, so long as the Queen's Representative is head of the Federation; nor is

there any obligation in regard to these Provinces which now devolves upon Britain that would be diminished by their being thus huddled into one heterogeneous assemblage.[117]

In fact, critics feared that Confederation would actually provoke Americans into hostilities. Howe warned: 'let this guy of "new nationality" be set up . . . and every young fellow who has had a taste of camp life in the United States will be tempted to have a fling at it.'[118] Christopher Dunkin even expressed alarm at the tone of the Confederation debates, asking 'how is the temper of the United States going to be affected . . . by the policy here urged on us, of what I may call hostile independent effort—effort made on our part, with the avowed object of setting ourselves up as a formidable power against them [?]'[119] The Northern States, Dorion pointed out, had put into the field an army of 2,300,000—'as many armed men as we have men, women and children in the two Canadas'. Military expenditure on any large scale would be useless and 'we are not bound to ruin ourselves in anticipation of a supposed invasion which we cannot repel'. Public opinion should force the Canadian press to cease its anti-American outbursts: 'The best thing that Canada can do is to keep quiet, and to give no cause for the war.'[120] Joseph Howe agreed that British North America could never stand alone militarily against the United States, but took the argument a stage further. 'Inevitably it must succumb to the growing power of the republic. A treaty offensive and defensive with the United States, involving ultimate participation in a war with England, would be the hard terms of its recognition as a separate but not independent state.'[121]

Given the overwhelming rejection of the case for Confederation as a defence measure, it is hardly surprising that this aspect of the scheme produced some of the most colourful imagery among critics. Joining with the Maritimes, said James Currie, 'was like tying a small twine at the end of a long rope and saying it strengthened the whole line'.[122] Incorporating the vast Hudson's Bay Territories, said Henri Joly, would create 'the outward form of a giant, but with the strength of a child'.[123] John Macdonald, member for Toronto West, thought 'the casting of the burden of defence upon this country is like investing a sovereign with all the outward semblance of royalty, giving him a dollar per day to keep up the dignity of his court.' Macdonald has been overshadowed by his namesake to the point of invisibility, but he had a homely touch in his comments, telling the legislators as they met for the last year in Quebec City that Confederation was like taking the engine from the Lévis ferry and using it 'to propel the *Great Eastern* across the Atlantic'.[124] In a far smaller town, an angry young Rouge editor denounced Confederation in a less whimsical imagery. As a defence against the United States it was like being 'armed with an egg-shell to stop a bullet . . . a wisp of straw in the way of a giant'.[125] The writer's name was Wilfrid Laurier.

Opposition to Confederation within the individual provinces has been studied in some detail, and tended to concentrate on the risks and practical disadvantages of Confederation to each community.[126] However, while the objections made on behalf of each province were naturally contradictory, they fell into a common pattern. John Simpson denied that seventeen additional MPs would be of any use to Upper Canada,[127] while Matthew Cameron argued that if the eighty-two Upper Canadians proposed to develop the North-West, they would be outvoted by 'sixty-five members from Lower Canada and forty-seven from the Lower Provinces, whose interests will be united against us'.[128] By contrast, Joseph Howe warned that New Brunswick and Nova Scotia 'must be a prey to the spoiler' for 'having but forty-seven representatives, all told, it is apparent that the Government of the confederacy will always rest upon the overwhelming majority of 147 and that, even when close divisions and ministerial crises occur, the minority can easily be split up and played off against each other for purely Canadian purposes'.[129] French Canadians challenged that assumption of a unity of purpose, doubting that 'all the members from Lower Canada would make common cause on any question'.[130] Although the province was guaranteed sixty-five M.P.s in perpetuity, they would not all be francophones. 'We shall have forty-eight members in the Federal Parliament against one hundred and forty of English origin; in other words, we shall be in a proportion of one to four. What could so weak a minority do to obtain justice?'[131] Joseph Howe obviously felt that French Canadians possessed a greater measure of political skill than Maritimers, for he warned that 'as the English will split and divide, as they always do, the French members will in nine cases out of ten, be masters of the situation.'[132] Dorion agreed that they 'would go as a body to the Legislature, voting as one man, and caring for nothing else but the protection of their beloved institutions and law, and making government all but impossible', but he felt this 'a deplorable state of things'.[133]

It is a commonplace that there was little direct contact between Canada and the lower provinces prior to Confederation, and therefore perhaps surprising to discover the extent of their mutual antipathy.[134] The 'plain meaning' of the Canadian ministry's desire to force through the Quebec resolutions without amendment was 'that the Lower Provinces have made out a Constitution for us and we are to adopt it', said Dorion.[135] Voting at the Quebec conference had been by provinces, which 'made Prince Edward Island equal to Upper Canada',[136] and it was the tiny Gulf community which aroused the angry contempt of Canadian critics. Dorion complained of 'the humiliation of seeing the Government going on its knees and begging the little island of Prince Edward to come into this union'.[137] Maritimers returned the hostility. James Dingwell of Prince Edward Island thought 'Canadians had not been able to manage the business of their country as we have been able to manage ours; and why should we trust the management of our own affairs to people who have never been able to manage their own with any satisfaction?'[138] With colourful exaggeration, Joseph Howe claimed that Canadians were 'always in trouble of some sort, and two or three times in open rebellion'.[139]

Despite Howe's suspicions that Lower Canadian solidarity in the Federal parliament would entrench French power, hostility to Confederation in the Atlantic provinces seems to have been directed against the whole of what later became the monster of 'central Canada' and was relatively free of explicit francophobia. There was a hint of it in an open letter to Lord Carnarvon in January 1867, when a recitation of Nova Scotia's loyal service to the empire in wars against France was followed by the waspish comment: 'We are now asked to surrender it to Monsieur Cartier.'[140] Possibly francophobia was so endemic that it was not necessary to articulate it, but there may have been other reasons for the muted tone. Inter-communal flashpoints in the mid-nineteenth century were more likely to concern sectarian education than the politics of language: to raise fears of French power in the Maritimes might have been to conjure counterproductive prospects of Irish advantage. In any case, Acadians were as suspicious of Confederation as their anglophone neighbours, and it suited Howe to portray them as one of the contented minorities—along with Micmac and Blacks—who had flourished under the benign institutions of an autonomous Nova Scotia.[141]

In each province, critics argued that their constituents had got the worst of the bargain. That their arguments were contradictory did not much matter, since by definition they were directed to parochial minds, to those whose 'mental vision', as an impatient Halifax newspaper put it of local doubters, 'is bounded by Dartmouth on the one side, and Citadel Hill on the other'.[142] However, claims in each province of a bad deal provoked supporters of Confederation into refutations which were seized upon by critics elsewhere as confirmation of their fears. One of the earliest public expositions of the Quebec scheme came in a major speech by Galt in November 1864. Tupper admired it, but mildly complained that it was 'a little too much from the Canadian point of view to suit this meridian'. From Prince Edward Island, Edward Whelan similarly warned that 'in the Lower Provinces a view of the Confederation question with a very decided Canadian colouring is apt to lessen confidence in it as we barbarians down in these lower regions are terribly doubtful and suspicious of Canadian intentions.'[143] Within a few months, desperately hard-pressed Confederates in the Maritimes had turned the balance to the advantage of critics of Canada. David Reesor read into the record extracts from Tilley's election speeches to show that the politicians in the Maritimes 'see the great advantage they have gained over Canada, and are not slow to set them [sic] before the people'.[144] Dorion similarly quoted Tilley and Whelan, and pictured them 'chuckling over the good bargains they have made at the expense of Canada'.[145]

Behind these mutual suspicions, there surely lay something deeper than the cussedness which we normally dismiss as parochialism. Even in the super-heated provincial politics of the mid-nineteenth century, it seems exaggerated that Cartier could have been accused of 'la lâcheté la plus insigne dans la trahison la plus noire', merely for forming a coalition with George Brown, or that Prince Edward Island representatives at the Charlottetown conference were pointed out in the street as 'the men who would sell their country'.[146] The fact that such remarks were made suggests that the different provinces felt themselves to possess distinct social and political cultures. This was most obvious in Lower Canada, with its minority language and religion. 'Confederation is in fact a Legislative union, because upon the Federal Government is conferred the right of legislating upon those subjects which Lower Canada holds most dear.'[147] The complication in Lower Canada was the existence of a minority-within-a-minority, equally suspicious of those aspects of the new constitution which guaranteed provincial autonomy and consequently a local francophone majority. Principal Dawson of McGill thought that 'scarcely anyone among the English of Lower Canada desires Confederation, except perhaps as an alternative to simple dissolution of the Union.'[148] This was a case where clashing objections had a reinforcing effect, for every reassurance offered to the Lower Canada English was a confirmation of French Canadian fears.[149]

French Canada's claims to be considered as a distinct society are obvious. What is less obvious is that in other provinces there was a sense of identity just as distinct from that of the province of Canada as that which modern Canadians would today feel separates them from the United States. True, Joseph Howe could welcome the Canadian delegates, fresh from Charlottetown, with the sentiment: 'I am not one of those who thank God that I am a Nova Scotian merely, for I am a Canadian as well.'[150] Yet the picture which emerges from his subsequent anti-Confederation campaign is of a province not simply resentful of losing its autonomy, but fearful of being subordinated to the capricious and unattractive values of 'those who live above the tide', 'the administration of strangers'.[151] A recurrent theme of Nova Scotian opposition was loss of its historic self-government. Behind the issue of high principle, there lay practical and local fears. The petitioners of Digby County pointed out that 'while that portion of this country which borders on the sea is thickly inhabited and rapidly increasing in population and wealth, there still are considerable districts but lately reclaimed from the primaeval forest', which required grants of public money for the development of roads and bridges. They regarded 'with dismay' the transfer of control over public expenditure 'to a Government by which they would necessarily all be expended for widely different purposes'.[152] Canada was associated with inflationary paper money and high interest rates. 'Every post-master and every way office keeper is to be appointed and controlled by the Canadians.'[153]

Canada was as distant from Nova Scotia as Austria from Britain.[154] 'You cannot . . . invest a village on the Ottawa with the historic interest and associations that cluster around London.'[155] To the modern mind, Joseph Howe was descending to the darkest depths of petty parochialism when he proclaimed that travellers 'can scarcely ride five miles in Upper Canada without being stopped by a toll bar or a toll bridge. There are but two toll-bridges in Nova Scotia and all the roads are free.'[156] Yet Howe's complaint was really very little different in spirit from modern Canadian concern to defend medicare and welfare programs against American allegations of unfair wage subsidies.[157] The two island colonies possessed an equally sharp sense of a distinct local culture. In this context, New Brunswick—torn between the two pulls of its Laurentian and New England axes, and comprising the sharply different loyalties of its Acadian, Loyalist and Irish populations—may have been the exception. In 1862, Arthur Gordon had concluded that there was

> very little *Provincial* feeling, which might lead to the formation of parties founded on the differences of political principle. The different counties hated each other & they all unite in hating & abusing Halifax, but it does not appear to me that they have any strong feeling of independance [sic] as New Brunswickers.[158]

Obviously, the advantages of the Intercolonial and the dangers of American invasion would both be arguments which would have more impact on New Brunswick than upon its neighbours, but it is hard to imagine anyone telling the legislature in Fredericton, as Cornelius Howatt did in Charlottetown, that Confederation 'was a question of "self or no self" '.[159]

A further theme common to the critics, whatever their regional loyalty, was rejection of both the proposed provincial governments and the confederate upper house as safeguards for their rights. 'Ce n'est donc pas une confédération qui nous est proposée, mais tout simplement une Union Législative déguisée sous le nom de confédération', argued Dorion.[160] George Coles predicted that under Confederation, the legislature of Prince Edward Island 'would be the laughing stock of the world', left 'to legislate about dog taxes, and the running at large of swine'.[161] Such critics concluded that the whole plan of union should be abandoned. Others, however, argued from similar premises, but thought rather that the union should be strengthened. The Halifax *Citizen* agreed that the Quebec scheme 'has given these local legislatures very little to do', and predicted that they would occupy themselves in mischief, preserving local loyalties which would prevent 'the fusion of the British American population in one actual indivisible nationality'.[162] 'One of the worst features of the Union plan proposed by Canada is, that it will leave our local legislature still in existence', lamented the Saint John *Globe*, which would have preferred to see it scrapped.[163] Even the fervent

Anti-Confederate T.W. Anglin, writing in the rival *Freeman*, agreed that if they had to have Confederation, 'it would be better to abolish the local Legislatures at once in appearance as well as in reality.'[164]

The critics similarly criticised the central appointment of both the lieutenant-governors and members of the upper house. The prospect of lieutenant-governors drawn from provincial politics aroused no enthusiasm. 'Let any one of our dozen or twenty most prominent Canadian politicians be named Lieutenant-Governor of Upper or of Lower Canada, would not a large and powerful class of the community . . . be very likely to resent the nomination as an insult?' asked Christopher Dunkin.[165] In Canada, where the Legislative Council had become elective in 1856—with life-members retaining their seats—there was resentment at the re-introduction of nomination, 'because the Maritime Provinces are opposed to an elective Chamber, and hence we in Canada—the largest community and the most influential—must give way to them'.[166] There was also resentment at the provision in the Quebec resolutions by which the first confederate legislative councillors would be appointed from the existing Legislative Councils (except in Prince Edward Island)—a transparent bribe to curb the upper houses in discharging the very task of disinterested second thoughts for which they were supposed to exist. Worse still, the first upper house under Confederation was to be appointed, for life, on the nomination of the existing provincial governments, most of which, as Dorion pointed out, happened to be Conservative. 'For all time to come, as far as this generation and the next are concerned, you will find the Legislative Council controlled by the influence of the present government.'[167] Future appointment by the central government aroused no more enthusiasm. It might be, Dunkin suggested, that a government would be formed in which an entire province 'either is not represented, or is represented otherwise than it would wish to be'. How would such a province, 'out in the cold', be served when vacancies in the upper house came to be filled?[168] From the point of view of hindsight, we must surely agree that the opponents of Confederation had a strong argument.

The arguments of the critics of Confederation must be conceded to have been at least plausible. Why then did they fail to prevent the passage of the British North America Act in 1867? First, we should note that their arguments did not pass unchallenged. Just as conventional studies of the causes of Confederation tend to underplay the opposition case, so a study of the critics necessarily distorts the debate in their favour.[169] In any case, arguments which high-minded posterity may find irrefutable could perhaps have produced diametrically opposite responses among contemporaries: Upper Canadian critics, in damning the Intercolonial as an irresponsible waste of money, might convince Lower Canadians of its value as a regional development scheme.[170]

In any case, historians have misled in presenting too neat and interlocking an explanation for Confederation. Even if the opposition against the Inter-colonial railway was overwhelming, Confederation might still be supported on general grounds as the highest common factor of solution to a range of problems. The Confederation package mattered more than the interlocking detail, and not everybody bothered with those details. Bishop Laflèche did not allow ignorance of the latter to inhibit him from pronouncing on the former. 'Le projet de Confédération est tellement vaste et complexe en lui-même et dans ses détails qu'il est bien difficile de l'aborder sans en avoir auparavant fair une étude spéciale; et c'est que je n'ai point fait.' What Laflèche saw was a province in which the legislative process was paralysed, where political opponents confronted each other almost like enemy camps, a state of affairs which could only end disastrously for Lower Canadians— either in 'la guerre civile ou la domination du Haut-Canada dans l'Union Législative'.[171] The bishop was probably wrong, but could anyone be sure? In any case, even if the argument were won inside the provinces, there remained that 'atmosphere of crisis' over the North American continent. 'Look around you to the valley of Virginia', McGee challenged those who wanted to know why Confederation was necessary, 'look around you to the mountains of Georgia, and you will find reasons as thick as blackberries.'[172] Perhaps the fundamental mistake of the opponents of Confederation was to ask people to react logically to the activities of Macdonald and Cartier in the conference chamber rather than to the operations of Grant and Sherman on the battlefield. The question for explanation then becomes why it should have been intercolonial union—rather than, say, neutrality or annexation— which met the psychological need for a dramatic response to continental crisis. The answer can only be that the idea had been around for a long time, an answer looking for a question. 'Everybody admits that Union must take place sometime', said John A. Macdonald. 'I say now is the time.'[173]

In seeking to account for the adoption of so vast a scheme as Canadian Confederation, historians have naturally turned to the arguments put forward by its supporters, and have been tempted to conclude that the arguments put forward *for* Canadian Confederation equal the reason *why* Canadian Con-federation came about. Certainly hindsight finds it easy to draw neat lines of causation linking argument to outcome, a circular process which identifies the winners of history as—in Morton's terms—those who sensed the cur-rents of events. Yet we should not forget that the case against Confederation was argued as tenaciously, eloquently and—we must assume—sincerely as the case in its favour; hindsight may conclude that while the Antis lost the battle, they won at least some of the arguments. There are indeed historians who sternly conclude that posterity is not entitled to second-guess past con-troversies, that a century later we cannot award points to individual argu-ments, for or against, since we cannot make ourselves fully part of the atmosphere of the time. Yet such an attitude is tantamount to an uncritical abdication of our own judgement to each and every claim made by those who were on the winning side perhaps for reasons other than the simply intellectual. 'La raison du plus fort, c'est toujours la meilleure' is not the most appropriate strategy for the historian to adopt. And even if we conclude that those who carried Confederation had the better of the debate, we should still not forget those who were firmly and comprehensively opposed to the scheme because—in the words of Matthew Cameron—they believe that 'politically, commercially, and defensively, as a matter of economy or sectional benefit, it will not be one tittle of service to this country, but on the contrary will inflict on it a vast and lasting injury.'[174] If the critics of Confederation were even partly justified in their objections, then we must look beyond the narrowly logical for an explanation for their defeat.

Suggestions for Further Reading

D.G. Creighton, *The Road to Confederation: The Emergence of Canada 1863–1867* (Toronto, 1964).

W.L. Morton, *The Critical Years: The Union of British North America 1857–1873* (Toronto, 1964).

P.B. Waite, *The Life and Times of Confederation 1864–1867: Politics, Newspapers, and the Union of British North America* (Toronto, 1962).

Notes

[1]The major accounts of the coming of Confederation remain D.G. Creighton, *The Road to Confederation: The Emergence of Canada 1863–1867* (Toronto, 1964) which expands the account given in his *John A. Macdonald: The Young Politician* (Toronto, 1952), chs 12–15. W.L. Morton, *The Critical Years: The Union of British North America 1857–1873* (Toronto, 1964) and P.B. Waite, *The Life and Times of Confederation 1864–1867: Politics, Newspapers, and the Union of British North America* (Toronto, 1962). My debt to Waite's study of press sources is obvious from the footnotes below, in which the book is cited as *Life and Times*. There is a useful overview of writing on Confederation in D.A. Muise, ed., *A Reader's Guide to Canadian History: I, Beginnings to Confederation* (Toronto, 1982), 237–48.

[2]W.L. Morton, *The Kingdom of Canada: A General History from Earliest Times* (2nd ed., Toronto, 1969), 317, 314–5. Possibly the view of Confederation as a logical response to the common challenge facing the provinces owes something to the spirit of the 1960s, when English-Canadians were faced with an increasing need to identify with national symbols independent of traditional imperial ties at a time when the reforms of the Lesage government in Quebec opened the threat that Canada itself might break up.

John Sandfield Macdonald was premier of the province of Canada, 1862–64. Curiously, despite being labelled as a complete failure by most historians, he re-emerged as John A. Macdonald's choice for premier of the new province of Ontario in 1867.

[3]Opposition to Confederation in individual provinces and sections has been widely studied, paradoxically, given the relative lack of general overviews, conveying the impression that parochialism predominated. *Life and Times*, chs 9–14 covers Upper and Lower Canada (modern Ontario and Quebec), which formed a united (if intermittently quarrelsome) province between 1841 and 1867, and the four 'Lower Provinces' of Newfoundland and the three Maritime provinces, Prince Edward Island, Nova Scotia and New Brunswick. The key province of New Brunswick has been studied in two articles by A.G. Bailey, 'Railways and the Confederation Issue in New Brunswick', *Canadian Historical Review* (hereafter, *CHR*) xxi (1940), 367–83 and 'The Basis and Persistence of Opposition to Confederation in New Brunswick', *CHR* xxiii (1942), 374–97 and widely reprinted, and more recently by Carl Wallace, 'Albert Smith, Confederation and Reaction in New Brunswick: 1852–1882', *CHR* xliv (1963), 285–312. See also W.S. MacNutt, *New Brunswick: A History 1784–1867* (Toronto, 1963), ch. 16. For Nova Scotia, see Kenneth G. Pryke, *Nova Scotia and Confederation 1864–74* (Toronto, 1979) and his 'The Making of a Province: Nova Scotia and Confederation', *Canadian Historical Association Annual Report* (1968), 35–48. Dr James Sturgis kindly allowed me to consult his work-in-progress paper, 'Opposition to Confederation in Nova Scotia, 1864–1870'. For Prince Edward Island, Francis W.P. Bolger, ed., *Canada's Smallest Province: A History of P.E.I.* (Charlottestown, 1973) chs 6 and 7 (by Bolger) replaces the older article by D.C. Harvey, 'Confederation in Prince Edward Island', *CHR* xiv (1933), 143–160. The debate in Lower Canada is discussed by A.I. Silver, *The French Canadian Idea of Confederation, 1864–1900* (Toronto, 1982), chs 2–3. Silver (27) points out that Joseph Perrault, one of the bitterest critics of Confederation, was in fact defeated in 1867. However, it is not clear how far Confederation was an electoral issue once the British North America Act had been passed, and Perrault's constituents might have felt that so notable an opponent of the new system was less than qualified to win their riding a share of its proffered benefits.

Biographies of some leading critics supplement our knowledge of the opposition campaign, but in some cases patriotic Canadian biographers have been reluctant to speak ill of the dead.

[4]C.P. Stacey, 'Confederation: The Atmosphere of Crisis' in Edith G. Firth, ed., *Profiles of a Province: Studies in the History of Ontario* (Toronto, 1967), 73–9. J.L. Finlay and D.N. Sprague take a similar line in *The Structure of Canadian History* (2nd ed., Scarborough, Ontario, 1984), 179: 'Were it not for two external factors, Great Britain and the United States, the cause of the confederates would have remained becalmed indefinitely.'

[5]Ged Martin, 'An Imperial Idea and its Friends: Canadian Confederation and the British' in G. Martel, ed., *Studies in British Imperial History: Essays in Honour of A.P. Thornton* (London, 1986), 49–94.

[6]Critics argued that the idea of British North American union had barely been a public issue in recent years; supporters that they had 'forgotten that the question of Confederation was discussed both in Parliament and in the country in 1859, and that since then the Legislature and the press have occupied themselves with it often enough.' Compare Joseph Armand (209) and Dr Joseph Blanchet (545) with Philip H. Moore (226) and Christopher Dunkin (484) in *Parliamentary Debates on the Subject of the Confederation of the British North American Provinces* (3rd Session, 8th Provincial Parliament of Canada, Quebec 1865).

[7]John A. Macdonald (1815–91) was leader of the Upper Canada Conservatives who dominated Canadian politics for over forty years. The two-volume biography by D.G. Creighton (1952–55) is one of the classics of Canadian history.

Joseph Howe (1804–73), Nova Scotia orator and former Liberal leader, who had himself conjured visions of British American union in previous years. He accepted an imperial appointment as fisheries commissioner in 1863, but re-entered politics in 1865 to attack the Quebec scheme. A major two-volume biography by J. Murray Beck was published in 1982–3.

Oliver Mowat (1820–1903) followed the Reform leader, George Brown, into the coalition in June 1864, but accepted a judicial appointment in November. He returned to active politics in 1872 to become premier of Ontario, holding office until 1896.

For Christopher Dunkin, see n.35 below.

[8]The published Confederation Debates (full citation in note 6 above) began on 3 February 1865 and ended at 4:15 a.m. on 11 March. The atmosphere is well described by P.B. Waite in his introduction to the abridged version, *The Confederation Debates in the province of Canada 1865* (Toronto, 1963), i–xviii. References below are to the complete edition, cited as CD, with the name of the speaker where appropriate but dates omitted.

[9]Maurice Cowling, *1867: Disraeli, Gladstone and Revolution* (Cambridge, 1967).

[10]J.M.S. Careless, *Brown of the Globe: II, The Statesman of Confederation 1860–1880* (Toronto, 1963), chs 3–6.

George Brown (1818–80), proprietor of the Toronto *Globe*, was the leader of the Upper Canada Reformers. His attempt to form a ministry in 1858 lasted only two days.

[11]Morton, *Critical Years*, ch.4; Creighton, *Macdonald: Young Politician*, ch.11; O.D. Skelton, *Life and Times of Sir Alexander Tilloch Galt* (Toronto, 1966), chs 7, 8.

Alexander Tilloch Galt (1817–1893), spokesman for Lower Canada Protestants, broke with the Reform party in 1857. His calls for British North American federation led him to join the reconstructed Cartier-Macdonald ministry in 1858.

[12]Ottawa, Public Archives Canada, *Macdonald Papers*, Vol. 50, Memorandum by Monck, 6 June 1866, fos 19827–33, printed in J. Pope, *Memoirs of the Right Honourable Sir John Alexander Macdonald* (Toronto, 1894), 710–11, and Monck to Macdonald, confidential, 21 June 1866, *ibid.*, 316–18.

[13]London, Public Record Office [cited as PRO], CO 188/141, Gordon to Cardwell, no.93, 5 December 1864, fos. 395–96. For his attitude to Confederation, see J.K. Chapman, *The Career of Arthur Hamilton Gordon: First Lord Stanmore 1829–1912* (Toronto, 1964) ch. 2 and his 'Arthur Gordon and Confederation', *CHR* xxxvii (1956), 142–57.

[14]Shea to Galt, 15 December 1864, in W.G. Ormsby 'Letters to Galt Concerning the Maritime Provinces and Confederation', *CHR* xxxiv (1953), 167–8.

Ambrose Shea (1815–1905) was leader of the Liberal opposition in Newfoundland, and duly used the Confederation issue to join a coalition government in 1865.

[15]Quoted in E.M. Saunders, *Three Premiers of Nova Scotia* (Toronto, 1909), 371. Ironically, one of the most widely publicised antecedent calls for intercolonial union had been Howe's 1854 oration published as *Speech of the Hon. Joseph Howe of Nova Scotia, in Favour of the Union of the North American Provinces* (London, 1855).

Charles Tupper (1821–1915) abandoned medicine to enter politics in 1855, defeating Howe and rising to leadership of the provincial Conservatives. He was briefly prime minister of Canada in 1896. Arthur Gordon waspishly described him in 1863 as 'a man possessed of but very moderate abilities, considerable obstinacy and a large share of vanity'. PRO, CO 188/139, Gordon to Newcastle, most confidential, 28 September 1863, fos 58–63.

[16]Cf. Bailey, 'Basis and Persistence' and Wallace, *loc. cit.*

Albert J. Smith (1822–1883) was a Liberal who led an anti-Confederation ministry in New Brunswick in 1865–66.

[17]G. Patterson, 'An unexplained incident of Confederation in Nova Scotia', *Dalhousie Review* vii (1927), 442–6. One of the two, William Miller, was likened to John Wilkes Booth, the murderer of Abraham Lincoln. Sturgis, *loc. cit.*, 18.

[18]CD, 545. Joseph-Godric Blanchet (1829–90) was a Liberal-Conservative MPP for Lévis.

[19]CD, 147. Luther Hamilton Holton (1817–80) was a leading anglophone Liberal from Lower Canada, who had served as finance minister under Sandfield Macdonald in 1863–64. He was MPP for Châteauguay.

[20]CD, 682.

[21]*Life and Times*, 154.

[22]Not reported in CD, but see Waite, ed., *Confederation Debates*, xv–xvi.

[23]*Hansard's Parliamentary Debates* (3rd series), clxxxv, 19 February 1867, cols. 579–80, 577.

[24]*British Parliamentary Papers* [cited as BPP], 1867, xlviii, Correspondence Respecting the Proposed Union of the British North American Provinces, 75–7.

[25]*Ibid.*, 68. Howe's tour is described in J.M. Beck, *Joseph Howe:* II, *The Briton Becomes Canadian 1848–1873* (Kingston, 1983), 201.

[26]CD, 61.

[27]Speech of 7 April 1866, quoted in William M. Baker, *Timothy Warren Anglin 1822–1896: Irish Catholic Canadian* (Toronto, 1977), 103, and see also 58. Anglin was editor of the Saint John *Morning Freeman*. According to Creighton, Anglin was 'an unsubdued ex-rebel' who 'flung the full force of his abusive and mendacious journalism against Confederation' (*Road to Confederation*, 251 and see also 247). It is unlikely that Anglin took part in the Irish rising of 1848 and no reason to think that his journalism was unusually mendacious or abusive by contemporary standards, which were admittedly low. Thus have critics of Confederation been dismissed.

[28]Similar views were expressed in the Canadian Legislative Council by James G. Currie, Billa Flint and David Reesor and in the Assembly by Christopher Dunkin, Joseph Perrault, Thomas Scatcherd and T.C. Wallbridge. CD, 46, 164, 319, 483, 585, 749, 660.

[29]Charlottetown *Examiner*, 30 January 1865, quoted in *Life and Times*, 186.

[30]CD, 328.

[31]CD, 248.

[32]Speech in Halifax, 13 August 1864, in J.A. Chisholm, ed., *The Speeches and Public Letters of Joseph Howe* (2 vols, Halifax, 1909), II 433. A Nova Scotian critic, John Locke (MLA for Shelburne) discounted the fact that 'at different times various politicians have . . . made grand speeches in favour of Union' because 'it was well understood at that time, that nothing was to come of it.' Quoted by Sturgis,

'Opposition to Confederation in Nova Scotia', 7. However, the statements quoted in this section were all made after the Charlottetown meeting.

[33]CD, 126.

[34]CD, 352. Henri-Gustave Joly (1829–1908) was an unusual figure. A Protestant, born in France, he represented Lotbinière, which was also the family seigneurie. In 1888, he formally added 'de Lotbinière' to his surname.

[35]CD, 508. A Conservative, the MPP for Brome, Christopher Dunkin (1812–81) opposed Confederation, delivering the longest speech of the debates, which stretched over two evenings and lasted for eight hours, despite ill health. As Waite observes, it was 'a criticism of the Quebec Resolutions that towers over all others', *Life and Times*, 153. His dry and aloof manner may have undermined the effectiveness of his criticisms. McGee commented: 'we ought to aim at perfection, but who has ever attained it, except perhaps the hon. member for Brome'. CD, 136. Despite his stand, he joined Macdonald's cabinet in 1869.

[36]CD, 485.

[37]CD, 747. Thomas Scatcherd (1823–76), a Reformer, was MPP for Middlesex West.

[38]CD, 357. Etienne-Paschal Taché (1795–1865) was a Bleu who had retired from active politics in 1858, but was persuaded to return in 1864, and presided over the coalition ministry. On his death, John A. Macdonald called him 'as sincere and truly honorable a gentleman as ever moved in public or private life'. Quoted, *Life and Times*, 152.

[39]CD, 586. Joseph-François (also known as Joseph Xavier) Perrault (1838–1905) was MPP for Richelieu. A Rouge, he delivered a five-hour attack on the Quebec scheme in the Confederation debates.

[40]CD, 357 (Joly) and cf. 591 (Perrault).

[41]CD, 593–5, 625–6.

[42]CD, 543.

[43]CD, 356–7.

[44]Open letter, 10 April 1866, in Chisholm, ed., *Speeches and Public Letters of Joseph Howe*, II, 463.

[45]CD, 456.

[46]*L'Ordre*, 7 June 1865, quoted *Life and Times*, 147.

[47]CD, 659. Thomas Cambell Wallbridge was Clear Grit MPP for Hastings North.

[48]Howe to Isaac Buchanan, 20 June 1866, in Chisholm, ed., *op. cit.*, II, 464. In his 1866 pamphlet, *Confederation Considered in Relation to the Interests of the Empire*, Howe complained that in the New Brunswick election that year, 'one half of an an entirely loyal population were taught to brand the other half as disloyal'. Quoted in Chisholm, ed., *op. cit.*, II, 484.

[49]Dunkin spoke about imperial federation in CD, 545, and was criticised by Frederick Haultain, MPP for Peterborough, 646. Howe's longstanding enthusiasm for the organic union of the empire culminated in his 1866 pamphlet, *The Organ of the Empire*, Chisholm, ed., *op. cit.*, II, 492–506. Tupper savagely exploited the logical contradictions in Howe's position: within an imperial federation, Nova Scotians would be in a far more insignificant minority within Confederation, liable to fight in bloody wars in all corners of the world, a scheme 'as useless as it would be unjust and repressive'. Letter in Halifax *British Colonist*, 13 December 1866, in E.M. Saunders, ed., *Life and Letters of Sir Charles Tupper* (2 vols, London, 1916) I, 139–40.

[50]Creighton, *Road to Confederation*, 266–7.

[51]In negotiations for the formation of the Canadian coalition in June 1864, Macdonald and Brown had agreed to 'address themselves, in the most earnest manner, to the negotiation for a confederation of all the British North American Provinces' but that 'failing a successful issue to such negotiations, they are prepared to pledge themselves to legislation during the next session of Parliament for the purpose of remedying existing difficulties by introducing the federal principle for Canada alone', with provision for subsequent expansion. Pope, ed., *op. cit.*, 684, and quoted by Dorion, CD, 654. See also CD, 248.

[52]CD, 657. Dorion's challenge came on 6 March 1865; on 23 March the coalition came close to breaking up over Brown's insistence on invoking the fall-back position. Careless, *op. cit.*, II, 191–2. Brown pressed the issue again in negotiations for the succession to Taché in August 1865. Pope, *op. cit.*, 700–6.

[53]CD, 155, 158. James Aikins (1823–1904) was MLC for the Home District. A former Clear Grit, he joined Macdonald's government in 1867.

[54]CD, 487.

[55]Halifax *Morning Chronicle*, 24 January 1866, quoted in *Life and Times*, 221. Annand used the argument, not to reject Confederation, but as a device to suggest an alternative approach.

[56]BPP 1867, xlviii, Howe, Annand and McDonald to Carnarvon, 19 January 1867, 13.

[57]Hamilton *Times*, November 1864, quoted in *Life and Times*, 122. See also Bruce W. Hodgins, 'Democracy and the Ontario Fathers of Confederation', in Bruce Hodgins and Robert Page, eds, *Canadian History Since Confederation: Essays and Interpretations* (2nd ed., Georgetown, Ontario, 1979), 19–28.

[58]Shelburne Petition, June 1866, in BPP 1867, xlviii, Correspondence, 70.

[59]BPP 1867, xlviii, Howe *et al.* to Carnavon, 19 January 1867, 18.

[60]BPP 1867, xlviii, Correspondence, 75.

[61]CD, 179 (L.A. Olivier, MLC for De Lanaudière).

[62]*Confederation*, quoted Chisholm, ed., *op. cit.,* II, 473.

[63]CD, 490.

[64]Gordon to Gladstone, private, 27 February 1865, in Paul Knaplund, ed., *Gladstone-Gordon Correspondence, 1851–1896, Transactions of the American Philosophical Society*, ns., 1i, pt 4 (1961), 46.

[65]Yarmouth *Tribune*, 9 November 1864, quoted *Life and Times*, 202.

[66]Speech at Dartmouth, NS, 22 May 1867, quoted Chisholm, ed., *op. cit.*, II, 514.

[67]CD, 520.

[68]CD, 50. James Currie was MLC for Niagara.

[69]CD, 188. Luc Letellier de Saint-Just (1820–81) was MLC for Grandville and served in the Sandfield Macdonald ministry. In 1876, he became lieutenant-governor of Quebec and in two years controversially dismissed the province's Conservative government and installed the Liberals under Henri Joly.

[70]CD, 524.

[71]Fredericton *Headquarters*, 19 October 1864, quoted in Bailey, 'Basis and Persistence', 375.

[72]'We have the trade of the world now open to us on nearly equal terms, and why should we allow Canada to hamper us?' Yarmouth *Herald*, 15 December 1864, quoted in *Life and Times*, 202.

[73]Shea to Galt, 15 December 1864 and Whelan to Galt, 17 December 1864, in Ormsby, *loc. cit.*, 167, 168.

The Atlantic colonies in particular depended on customs duties for their revenue. In 1863, while the province of Canada derived 35.95% of its revenue from customs, New Brunswick derived 66.12%, Nova Scotia 81.09%, Prince Edward Island 74.66% and Newfoundland 86.08%. However, in per capita yield, Canadians paid roughly double Maritimers. The figures for 1863 customs revenues (with year of population in parentheses) were: Canada (1865) £1.04; New Brunswick (1861) £0.46; Nova Scotia (1861) £0.52; Prince Edward Island (1863) £0.36; Newfoundland (1857) £0.79. (Calculated from BPP 1966, lxxiii, Colonial Trade Statistics, 126, 148–9, 160–1, 168, 174). Estimated wage rates (*ibid.*, 159, 173, 181) for tradesmen in 1863 were between £0.3 and £0.4 per diem in Newfoundland, and £0.25 and £0.4 in New Brunswick, but the Prince Edward Island figure (£40 per annum) suggests that tradesmen were employed for only 100 to 160 days each year. Thus for a tradesman on Prince Edward Island supporting a wife and four children, a rise in per capita tariff yield to Canadian levels would have cost over £4 a year, or about five weeks wages.

[74]Charles Mackay, 'A Week in Prince Edward Island', *Fortnightly Review*, v (1865), 147.

[75]CD, 17 (Holton).

[76]PRO, CO 188/143, Gordon to Cardwell, no. 23, 27 February 1865, fos 181–85, printed in BPP 1867, xlviii, Correspondence, 88–9. Cf. his letter of the same date of Gladstone, cited in n.64 above.

[77]Article 69 of the Quebec Resolutions offered only that improved communications to the Red River 'shall be prosecuted at the earliest possible period that the state of the Finances would permit'. According to T.C. Wallbridge, this meant 'that the North-West is hermetically sealed'. CD, 453 and cf. Matthew Cameron, 423–53. L.A. Olivier objected that a North Shore railway was far more important as a defence route. CD, 176.

[78]CD, 759 (Scatcherd).

[79]Fredericton *Headquarters*, 1 February 1865, quoted by Bailey, 'Basis and Persistence', 379.

[80]CD, 356.

[81]CD, 164. The 1862 agreement involved only the two provinces of New Brunswick and Nova Scotia. Contrasting the 1862 terms with the Confederation bargain, Galt had told Maritimers at a banquet at Halifax, on 12 September 1864, 'you will get the best of the bargain'. Edward Whelan (comp.), *The Union of the British Provinces* (Charlottetown, 1865), 48.

[82]Wallace, *loc. cit.*, 289. The Nova Scotian deputation to London in 1867 could 'scarcely bring themselves to discuss' the Intercolonial, 'so selfish and unfair at all times has been the conduct of the public men of Canada in regard to it'. BPP 1867, xlviii, Howe *et al.* to Carnarvon, 19 January 1867, 8.

[83]CD, 263.

[84]CD, 230. William McMaster (1811–87), MLC for Midland, was a Liberal. He was enthusiastic about Confederation, perhaps because his banking and business interests in Toronto involved him in rivalry with Montreal. He was benefactor of Toronto Baptist College, which later became McMaster University.

[85]CD, 356.

[86]CD, 863. In 1863, Canada took 1.11% of its imports from the other British North American territories, and sent them 2.2% of its exports. New Brunswick took 2.3% of its imports from Canada, to which it sent 0.87% of its exports. Prince Edward Island took 2.1% of its imports from Canada, to which it sent 0.6% of its exports. Newfoundland took 3.9% of its imports from Canada, to which it sent 0.68% of its exports. (Calculated from BPP 1866, lxiii, Colonial Trade Statistics, 132, 152, 170, 177). Nova Scotia figures are less helpful, but in 1866 the province took 5.5% of its imports from Canada, and sent 7.15% of its exports (1865 figures being 3.5% and 4.96%). (Calculated from BPP 1867–68, lxxi, Colonial Trade Statistics, 144.)

[87]CD, 355.

[88]CD, 356 (Joly) and 528 (Dorion).

[89]Halifax *Evening Reporter*, 10 December 1864, quoted in *Life and Times*, 208.

[90]CD, 257.

[91]CD, 321. The speaker was Billa Flint (1805–94), Clear Grit MLC for Trent.

[92]CD, 750 (Scatcherd).

[93]CD, 521 (Dorion).

[94]CD, 883. James L. Biggar was MPP for North Northumberland.

[95]CD, 355.

[96]CD, 123. John S. Sanborn (1819–77), MLC for Wellington, was a Reformer, born in Vermont and with an annexationist background.

[97]CD, 456.

[98]CD, 124.

[99]CD, 256.

[100]BPP 1867, xlviii, Correspondence, 69–70.

[101]Halifax, *Morning Chronicle*, 11 January 1865, quoted in Chisholm, ed., *op. cit.*, II, 435 (the first of the celebrated 'Botheration Scheme' letters).

[102]Speech at Dartmouth, 22 May 1867, quoted, *ibid.*, II, 512.

[103]*Islander*, 6 January 1865 and J.H. Gray to Tupper, 7 January 1865, quoted in *Life and Times*, 186, 183.

John Hamilton Gray (1811–87), Conservative premier of Prince Edward Island who chaired the Charlottetown meeting but was forced out of office over the Confederation issue in December 1864.

[104]*Newfoundlander*, 12 January 1865, quoted in *Life and Times*, 167.

It was alleged that in the 1869 election, Newfoundlanders were told 'that their young children would be rammed into guns' by Canadians. James Hiller, 'Confederation Defeated: The Newfoundland Election of 1869', in J. Hiller and P. Neary, eds, *Newfoundland in the Nineteenth and Twentieth Centuries: Essays in Reinterpretation* (Toronto, 1980), 83.

Charles Fox Bennett (1793–1883) put together in Anti-Confederation party and led it to victory in the 1869 election, serving as premier until 1874. He was one of the few Newfoundland merchants to have invested in industrial and mining interests in the island.

[105]Quoted in Chisholm, ed., *op. cit.*, II, 435–6.

[106]Quoted in Bolger, ed., *Canada's Smallest Province*, 175–6.

James Colledge Pope (1826–85) disagreed with his brother, William Henry Pope, over Confederation, and became premier in January 1865.

[107]CD, 354.

[108]CD, 180. Joseph Howe similarly warned that if the rights of Nova Scotians were 'overridden by an arbitrary Act of Parliament, very few of them will march to defend Canada'. BPP 1867, xlviii, Howe *et al.* to Carnarvon, 19 January 1867, 7.

[109]CD, 176 (Olivier).

[110]CD, 203.

[111]CD, 229. Philip Henry Moore (1799–1880) was one of the remaining life members of the Canadian Legislative Council, to which he had been appointed in 1841. He was independent, concerned mainly with the interests of the Eastern Townships.

[112]CD, 263.

[113]CD, 234 (John Simpson, MLC for Queen's). The Halifax *Citizen* alleged that Tupper was perfectly capable of campaigning for federation with the Moon if he thought it would divert public attention. Quoted *Life and Times*, 200.

[114]CD, 748. Critics dismissed appeals to Italian and German unity as proving that the spirit of the times pointed to wider unions. Henri Joly gave a list of federations which had failed (CD, 346–8), while the imperially minded Howe likened Confederation to a handful of small states withdrawing from the North German Confederation, or 'a few offshoots from Italian unity' attempting to form 'an inferior confederation'. BPP 1867, xlviii, Howe *et al.* to Carnarvon, 19 January 1867, 21.

[115]E.g., Petition from King's, BPP 1867, xlviii, Correspondence, 67.

[116]*Ibid.*, 71.

[117]PRO, CO 217/235, MacDonnell to Cardwell, 22 November 1864, fos 187–212.

[118]Quoted, Chisholm, ed., *op. cit.*, II, 487.

[119]CD, 529.

[120]CD, 257.

[121]Quoted, Chisholm, ed., *op. cit.*, II, 489.

[122]CD, 46.

[123]CD, 353. Henri Joly doubted comparisons between the Hudson's Bay Territories and European Russia, doubting that the West could ever support a large population. It may be noted that he ended his public career by serving as lieutenant-governor of British Columbia, 1900–1906. John A. Macdonald believed in 1865 that the prairies were 'of no present value to Canada' which had 'unoccupied land enough to absorb the immigration for many years'. To open Saskatchewan would be to 'drain away our youth and strength', Macdonald to E.W. Watkin, 27 March 1865, in Pope, *op. cit.*, 397–8.

[124]CD, 753. John Macdonald (1824–90), MPP for Toronto West, was a wealthy dry good merchant and independent Reformer.

[125]Quoted J. Schull, *Laurier: The First Canadian* (Toronto, 1966), 57.

[126]See n.2 above. Localism could also be harnessed to Confederation, influencing the kind of scheme which emerged. Elwood H. Jones, 'Localism and Federalism in Upper Canada to 1865', in Bruce W. Hodgins, D. Wright and W.H. Heick, eds, *Federalism in Canada and Australia: The Early Years* (Waterloo, Ontario, 1978), 19–41.

[127]CD, 232. John Simpson (1812–85) was Liberal MLC for Queen's.

[128]CD, 452–3.

[129]Quoted, Chisholm, ed., *op. cit.*, II, 490.

¹³⁰CD, 191 (J.O. Bureau, Rough MLC for De Lorimier).

¹³¹CD, 624 (Perrault). McGee argued that in addition up to seven members from the Lower Provinces would represent largely francophone ridings. CD, 137.

¹³²Halifax *Morning Chronicle*, 13 January 1865, quoted *Life and Times*, 212.

¹³³CD, 264.

¹³⁴T. Heath Haviland of Prince Edward Island recalled that when he visited Montreal in 1860, he had encountered 'the utmost difficulty' in finding so much newspaper from the Lower Provinces'. Speech at Montreal, 28 October 1864, in Whelan (comp.), *Union*, 115.

¹³⁵CD, 252.

¹³⁶CD, 47.

¹³⁷CD, 656. There was suspicion of a provision in the Quebec Resolutions guaranteeing Newfoundland an annual payment of $150,000 in perpetuity in exchange for its mineral rights. L.A. Olivier wondered whether the island possessed any minerals. Taché insisted that it was 'a well-ascertained fact that there are mines in the island of Newfoundland of great value'. Canada's official geologist, Sir William Logan, appeared to assume that since the interior of Newfoundland was useless for agriculture, it would be rich in mineral ores. Olivier continued to describe the payment as 'compensation for mines which perhaps do not exist'. (CD, 175–6, 179). The provision is an example of the way in which what posterity may view as an apparent incentive could rebound. C.F. Bennett, the owner of the Tilt Cove mine, was a fervent anti-Confederate. A century and a quarter later, most of the interior of Newfoundland remains untouched by mining.

¹³⁸Quoted, Bolger, ed., *op. cit.*, 177.

¹³⁹Howe to Earl Russell, 19 January 1865, quoted in Chisholm, ed., *op. cit.* II, 437.

¹⁴⁰BPP 1867, xlviii, Howe *et al.* to Carnarvon, 19 January 1867, 16. See also *ibid.*, 12 for an unsubtle reference to the Hundred Years' War.

¹⁴¹*Ibid.*, 17. Cf Léon Thériault, 'L' Acadie, 1753–1978: Synthèse Historique' in Jean Daigle, ed., *Les Acadians des Maritimes: Etudes Thématiques* (Moncton, 1980), 63–8.

¹⁴²*Morning Chronicle*, 23 December 1864, in *Life and Times*, 208.

¹⁴³Tupper to Galt, 13 December 1864 and Whelan to Galt, 17 December 1864, in Ormsby, *loc. cit.*, 166, 168.

¹⁴⁴CD, 329.

¹⁴⁵CD, 261.

¹⁴⁶*Le Pays*, 27 June 1864, in Creighton, *Road to Confederation*, 78, and *ibid.*, 122.

¹⁴⁷CD, 174, and cf. 192 (Bureau) and 350 (Joly). An emotive example cited was the central control of divorce proceedings.

¹⁴⁸Dawson to Howe, 15 November 1866, quoted in *Life and Times*, 135.

¹⁴⁹CD, 351 (Joly).

¹⁵⁰Speech, 13 August 1864, in Chisholm, ed., *op. cit.*, II, 433. Howe rose to speak at ten minutes to midnight. 'Who ever heard of a public man being bound by a speech delivered on such an occasion as that?', he asked three years later. Beck, *op. cit.*, II, 182.

¹⁵¹Speech at Dartmouth, 22 May 1867, in Chisholm, ed., *op. cit.*, II, 511.

¹⁵²BPP 1867, xlviii, Correspondence, 69–70.

[153]Dartmouth speech, Chisholm, ed., *op. cit.*, II, 512, 511.

[154]Port Medway petition, BPP 1867, xlviii, Correspondence, 76; Howe *et al.* to Carnarvon, 19 January 1867, 7.

[155]BPP 1867, xlviii, Howe *et al.* to Carnarvon, 19 January 1867, 15. At Bridgetown in 1867, Howe proclaimed: 'we prefer London under the dominion of John Bull, to Ottawa under the dominion of Jack Frost'. J.W. Longley, *Joseph Howe* (Toronto, 1906), 202, and cf. Beck, *op. cit.*, II, 202. The reference to 'a village' was, of course, unfair, but Dunkin was concerned that the federal capital was to remain 'within the jurisdiction of a subordinate province'. CD, 507.

[156]BPP 1867, xlviii, Howe *et al.* to Carnarvon, 19 January 1867, 17 and cf. Dartmouth speech, 22 May 1867, in Chisholm, ed., *op. cit.*, II, 517.

[157]The Nova Scotian press, it was alleged, emphasised the less attractive aspects of Canadian life, just as modern Canadians often reflect a cataclysmic view of the United States. 'Not a fight occurs, not a train runs off the track and kills one or two persons in that Province but it is blazoned forth in that press.' Speech by Dr Hamilton, 1865, quoted in Sturgis, *loc. cit.*, 19.

[158]University of New Brunswick, *Stanmore Papers*, reel 3, Gordon to Monck, copy, 8 May 1862.

[159]Quoted in Bolger, ed., *op. cit.*, 182.

[160]Dorion's anti-Confederation manifesto was widely published in 1864. Quoted in *Life and Times*, 142.

[161]Quoted in Bolger, ed., *op. cit.*, 174. George Coles (1810–75) represented PEI both at Charlottetown and at Quebec, but came out against the terms of the union.

[162]Halifax *Citizen*, 19 November 1864, quoted *Life and Times*, 203. The lieutenant-governor, Sir Richard McDonnell, used the same argument a few days later in a dispatch: 'I do not believe that so long as the boundaries of the different Provinces are maintained and their Local Legislatures and petty politics fostered, the Confederation can rise to that status, and that dignity of national feeling, which creates and maintains a national military spirit and self-reliance.' PRO, CO 217/235, MacDonnell to Cardwell, 22 November 1864, fols 187–212.

[163]Saint John *Daily Evening Globe*, 17 October 1864, quoted *Life and Times*, 136.

[164]Saint John *Freeman*, 3 November 1864, quoted in Baker, *Anglin*, 65. Joseph Howe also condemned the duplication of legislatures as 'cumbrous and expensive'. Howe to Earl Russell, 19 January 1865, in Chisholm, ed., *op. cit.*, II, 437.

[165]CD, 504. Perrault alleged that some politicians were influenced by hopes of 'being governor of one of the Federated Provinces', as did Letellier, who subsequently became a lieutenant-governor himself. CD, 626, 188.

[166]CD, 157 (Aikins).

[167]CD, 253.

[168]CD, 494–5. The fear was a real one for French Canadians. Cf. CD, 174 (Olivier).

[169]James Skead (1817–94), Conservative MLC for Rideau, claimed he had decided to support Confederation after listening to the debate. CD, 242.

[170]Since historians tend to treat the motives of mid-Victorian colonial politicians with some cynicism, it is well to record the dilemma of J.B. Pouliot, MPP for Témiscouata, who opposed Confederation as a threat to French Canada, but regretted

that his allies had impugned that excellent project, the Intercolonial Railway, which would traverse his riding.

[171]Laflèche to Boucher de Niverville, 2 March 1864, quoted in Walter Ullman, 'The Quebec Bishops and Confederation', xlviii (1963), 218.

[172]Speech at Montreal, 29 October 1864, in Whelan (comp.), *op. cit.*, 122–3.

[173]Speech at Halifax, 12 September 1864, *ibid.*, 46.

[174]CD, 463.

33

Confederation and Quebec

A.I. Silver

French Canada was in many ways pivotal and critical throughout the achievement of Confederation, as it has been ever since. The anglophones of the Province of Canada were the chief architects of unification, while Nova Scotia and New Brunswick almost had to be coerced into the scheme to make the new nation credible. But French Canadians had been in large measure responsible for the political stalemate that led English Canada to seek new terms of reference as well as French Canada's acceptance of the new plan. This included a separate province encompassing the traditional homeland of French Canadians and certain constitutional protections for matters that were of peculiar importance to them. Unlike the Americans in 1789, British North America did not submit the scheme for Confederation to popular ratification, partly because to do so would not have been within British constitutional traditions, and partly because such a submission

might have been rejected. Nonetheless there was much public debate over Confederation, and a good deal of special pleading on the part of the spokesmen for union. Most of those critical of the plan foresaw the emergence of a strong—too strong —central government. Those most active in drafting the final arrangements intended that the proposed federal state should hold the preponderance of power.

As Arthur Silver points out in the following selection, what was important to French Canadians was whether or not their nationality would find adequate protection in the new Canada. According to the proponents of Confederation, this protection was built into the scheme, chiefly in the provision for a separate province and in several constitutional guarantees. Those French Canadians who defended Confederation did so by interpreting the union and particularly the autonomy of the provincial assemblies—making it much more absolute than English-Canadian leaders had intended—in ways most favourable to the concerns of French Canada. Complete independence for Quebec was impossible, argued the Confederationists, for economic and military reasons, and what had been achieved met all the requirements for autonomy with none of the disadvantages. Here was the origin of the theory that Confederation was a compact among the involved provinces guaranteeing local autonomy, a view that was to become increasingly influential.

Consider the way in which the British North America Act was explained to French Canadians by those among them who supported Confederation. In what respects were French Canadians misled? Is such political special pleading legitimate? Is it wise? Perhaps more significantly, how did the debate over Confederation in French Canada anticipate the problems that would be faced by the new nation that came into being on 1 July 1867?

This article first appeared in A.I. Silver, *The French-Canadian Idea of Confederation 1864–1900* (Toronto, 1982), 33–50.

When French Lower Canadians were called on to judge the proposed confederation of British North American provinces, the first thing they wanted to know was what effect it would have on their own nationality. Before deciding whether or not they approved, they wanted to hear 'what guarantees will be offered for the future of the French-Canadian nationality, to which we are attached above all else'.[1] From Richelieu's Rouge MPP to Quebec's Catholic-Conservative *Courrier du Canada*, everyone promised to judge the work of the Great Coalition according to the same criterion.[2] Even Montreal's *La Minerve*, known to be George-Etienne Cartier's own organ, promised to make its judgement from a national point of view:

> If the plan seems to us to safeguard Lower Canada's special interests, its religion and its nationality, we'll give it our support; if not, we'll fight it with all our strength.[3]

But this quotation reminds us that concern for the French-Canadian nationality had geographical implications, that Canadians in the 1860s generally considered French Canada and Lower Canada to be equivalent. When French Canadians spoke of their *patrie*, their homeland, they were invariably referring to Quebec. Even the word *Canada*, as they used it, usually referred to the lower province, or, even more specifically, to the valley of the St Lawrence, that ancient home of French civilization in America, whose special status went back to the seventeenth century. Thus, when Cartier sang 'O Canada! mon pays! mes amours!' he was referring to the 'majestic source of the Saint-Laurent';[4] and Cartier's protégé, Benjamin Sulte, versifying like his patron, also found French Canada's 'Patrie . . . on the banks of the Saint-Laurent'.[5]

Throughout the discussion of Confederation, between 1864 and 1867, there ran the assumption that French Canada was a geographical as well as an ethnic entity, forming, as the *Revue canadienne* pointed out optimistically, 'the most considerable, the most homogeneous, and the most regularly constituted population group' in the whole Confederation.[6] *La Minerve*, which, as has been seen, characterized Lower Canada by a religion and a nationality, referred also to a 'Franco-Canadian nationality, which really exists today on the banks of the St Lawrence, and which has affirmed itself more than once'.[7] Nor was the equation of Lower Canada with French Canada only a pro-Confederationist notion. The editors of the *Union nationale* also maintained that the way to defend the French-Canadian nationality was to defend the rights of Lower Canada.[8]

It followed from this equation that provincial autonomy was to be sought in the proposed constitution as a key safeguard of the interests of French Canada. 'We must never forget,' asserted the *Gazette de Sorel*, 'that French Canadians need more reassurance than the other provinces for their civil and religious immunities. . . .' But since French Canada was a province, its immunities were to be protected by provincial autonomy; hence, 'this point is important above all for Lower Canada. . .'.[9]

On this key issue, French Canadians felt themselves to have different interests from those of other British North Americans. Thus, Cartier's organ:

> The English . . . have nothing to fear from the central government, and their first concern is to ensure its proper functioning. This is what they base their hopes upon, and the need for strong local governments only takes second place in their minds.
>
> The French press, on the contrary, feels that guarantees for the particular autonomy of our nationality must come before all else in the federal constitution. It sees the whole system as based on these very guarantees.[10]

Le Courrier de St-Hyacinthe agreed that 'we do not have the same ideas as our compatriots of British origin concerning the powers which are to be given to the central government. . . . We cannot consent to the loss of our national autonomy. . . .'[11] The Rouges also saw opposition between French- and English-Canadian interests. It was because of this opposition, they commented pessimistically, that George Brown had been able to reveal details of the Quebec Resolutions in Toronto, to the evident satisfaction of Upper Canadians, while in Lower Canada the ministers refused to make any information public.[12]

New Brunswick's governor, A.H. Gordon, in whose house Cartier had been a guest after the Charlottetown Conference, also saw an opposition between English- and French-Canadian aspirations. He reported to the

Colonial Secretary that while the former seemed to expect a very centralized union, ' "federal union" in the mouth of a Lower Canadian means the independence of his Province from all English or Protestant influences. . . .'[13]

This was, indeed, what it seemed to mean to the French-Canadian press. Thus:

> We want a confederation in which the federal principle will be applied in its fullest sense—one which will give the central power control only over general questions in no way affecting the interests of each separate section, while leaving to the local legislatures everything which concerns our particular interests.[14]

A confederation would be a fine thing, but only 'if it limited as much as possible the rights of the federal government, to general matters, and left complete independence to the local governments'.[15] As early as 1858, French-Canadian advocates of a British North American confederation had argued that 'it would certainly be necessary to give the separate [provincial] legislatures the greatest possible share of power', and even that the federal government should only have its powers 'by virtue of a perpetual but limited concession from the different provinces'.[16]

While most papers did not go so far as to support the provincial sovereignty which that last implied,[17] they did opt for co-ordinate sovereignty:

> The federal power will be sovereign, no doubt, but it will have power only over certain general questions clearly defined by the constitution.
> This is the only plan of confederation which Lower Canada can accept. . . .
> The two levels of government must both be sovereign, each within its jurisdiction as clearly defined by the constitution.[18]

What, after all, could be simpler than that each power, federal or provincial, should have complete control of its own field?

> Isn't that perfectly possible without having the local legislatures derive their powers from the central legislature or vice versa? Isn't it possible for each of these bodies to have perfect independence within the scope of its own jurisdiction, neither one being able to invade the jurisdiction of the other?[19]

To be sure, the fathers of Confederation were aware that French Canadians would reject complete centralization. John A. Macdonald told the Assembly that though he would have preferred a legislative union, he realized it would be unacceptable to French Canadians. Nevertheless, he felt the Quebec Resolutions did not provide for a real federalism, but would 'give to the General Government the strength of a legislative and administrative union'. They represented 'the happy medium' between a legislative and a federal union, which, while providing guarantees for those who feared the former, would also give 'us the strength of a Legislative union'.[20] In short, he appeared to understand the Quebec scheme to provide for the closest thing possible to a legislative union, saving certain guarantees for the French Canadians' 'language, nationality and religion'.

This interpretation was hotly rejected by French Canadians of both parties, including those who spoke for Macdonald's partner, Cartier:

> Whatever guarantees may be offered here, Lower Canada will never consent to allowing its particular interests to be regulated by the inhabitants of the other provinces. . . . We want a solid constitution . . . but we demand above all perfect freedom and authority for the provinces to run their own internal affairs.[21]

Let there be no mistake about it: anything close to a legislative union 'cannot and will not be accepted by the French-Canadian population'. A centralized union would be fatal to the French-Canadian nationality.[22] The *Courrier de St-Hyacinthe*, in fact, summed up the whole French-Canadian position when it said:

> But whatever guarantees they decide to offer us, we cannot accept any union other than a federal union based on the well-understood principles of confederations.[23]

In taking this view, French Canadians were led to reject another position adopted by John A. Macdonald: that the United States example provided the necessity of a strong central government. He argued that the Civil War had occurred there because the individual states had too much power under the American constitution—power which had given the federation too much centrifugal thrust. To avoid this, British North America must have a dominant central authority.[24]

In French Canada, even *La Minerve* considered Macdonald's reasoning to be nonsensical. 'We believe that this is a specious argument. The United States have a strongly centralized government, which is even capable of acting despotically, as we can see every day.' If you gave a central government too much power over too many localities, it would inevitably antagonize some of them.

> This is precisely what happened in the United States, where the war was caused not by the excessive power of the local governments, but by the central government, whose tyrannical actions came into direct opposition to the particular interests of a considerable part of the confederation.[25]

Le Journal de Québec agreed wholeheartedly. The causes of the American Civil War were to be sought, not in the powers of the states, but in 'the awful tyranny which the central government of the United States imposes on the state authorities, by taking them over and stealing their most inalienable powers. . .'.[26]

There was agreement between Bleus and Rouges that the autonomy of a French-Canadian Lower Canada was the chief thing to be sought in any new constitution. Accordingly, the Confederation discussion revolved around whether or not the Quebec plan achieved that aim. As far as the opposition was concerned, it did not. The Rouges maintained that this was an 'anglicizing bill',[27] the latest in a line of attempts to bring about the 'annihilation of the French race in Canada', and thus realize Lord Durham's wicked plans.[28] And it would achieve this goal because it was not really a confederation at all, but a legislative union in disguise, a mere extension of the Union of 1840.[29] 'It is in vain,' cried C.-S. Cherrier at a Rouge-sponsored rally, 'that they try to disguise it under the name of confederation. . . . This *quasi* legislative union is just a step toward a complete and absolute legislative union.'[30]

The evidence of Confederation's wickedness could be seen by its opponents on every hand. Did it not involve representation by population—the dreaded 'Rep by Pop' which French Canadians had resisted so vigorously till now?[31] And were not English Canadians proclaiming that centralization was to be the chief characteristic of the new regime? The Canadian legislature had even ordered the translation and publication of Alpheus Todd's essay on the provincial governments—an essay which included the remark that these would be 'subject to the legal power of the federal parliament'.[32] Indeed, argued the Rouges, it was hardly worthwhile for Quebec to have such an elaborate, two-chamber parliament as was proposed, since, as Todd made clear, the federal legislature 'will be able to quash and annul all its decisions'.[33]

The Quebec Resolutions themselves indicated that Todd was right, that the provincial powers would be scarcely more than a mirage:

> Mind you, according to everything we hear from Quebec, the prevailing idea in the conference is to give the central government the widest powers and to leave the local governments only a sort of municipal jurisdiction. . . .[34]

Le Pays had been afraid of this from the time the Great Coalition had announced its program. 'Without finances, without power to undertake major public works, the local legislature will hardly be anything other than a big municipal council where only petty matters will be discussed.'[35] When the Quebec Conference had ended, opposition papers still had the same impression: 'In short, the general parliament will have supreme control over the local legislatures.'[36] Even provincial control of education was an illusion, since the governor-general at Ottawa could veto any provincial legislation in the field.[37]

Finally, English-Canadian talk of creating a new nationality only strengthened Rouge fears that Confederation meant centralization and assimilation. When the legislature refused to pass A.-A. Dorion's resolution of January, 1865, that Canadians neither desired nor sought to create a new nationality, his brother's newspaper became convinced that it was all over for Lower Canada and its French-Canadian nationality.[38]

In answering all these opposition arguments, the Bleus certainly did not attempt to defend the notion of a strong or dominant central government. But, they maintained, that was not at all what British North America was going to get. Lower Canada, liberated from the forced Union of 1840, would become a distinct and autonomous province in a loose and decentralized Confederation—that was the real truth of the matter.

The defenders of Confederation refuted the opposition's arguments one after another. Did the Rouges speak of Rep by Pop? Why, any schoolboy ought to see the difference between Rep by Pop, which the Bleus had opposed as long as the legislative union remained, and a 'confederation which would give us, first of all, local legislatures for the protection of our sectional interests, and then a federal legislature in which the most populous province would have a majority *only in the lower house*'.[39] As long as there was only a single legislature for the two Canadas, Rep by Pop would have put 'our civil law and religious institutions at the mercy of the fanatics'. But Confederation would eliminate that danger by creating a separate province of Quebec with its own distinct government:

> We have a system of government which puts under the exclusive control of Lower Canada those questions which we did not want the fanatical partisans of Mr Brown to deal with. . . .
>
> Since we have this guarantee, what difference does it make to us whether or not Upper Canada has more representatives than we in the Commons? Since the Commons will be concerned only with general questions of interest to all provinces and not at all with the particular affairs of Lower Canada, it's all the same to us, as a nationality, whether or not Upper Canada has more representation.[40]

This was central to the Bleu picture of Confederation: all questions affecting the French-Canadian nationality as such would be dealt with at Quebec City, and Ottawa would be 'powerless, if it should want to invade the territory reserved for the administration of the local governments'.[41] As for the questions to be dealt with at Ottawa, they might divide men as Liberals and Conservatives, but not as French and English Canadians. 'In the [federal] Parliament,' said Hector Langevin, 'there will be no questions of race, nationality, religion or locality, as this Legislature will only be charged with the settlement of the great general questions which will interest alike the whole Confederacy and not one locality only.'[42] Cartier made the same point when he said that 'in the questions which will be submitted to the Federal parliament, there will be no more danger to the rights and privileges of the French Canadians than to those of the Scotch, English or Irish.'[43] Or, as his organ, *La Minerve*, put it, Ottawa would have jurisdiction only over those matters 'in which the interests of everyone, French Canadians, English, or Scotch, are identical'.[44] For the rest—for everything which concerned the French Canadians *as* French Canadians—for the protection and promotion of their national interests and institutions, they would have their own province with their own parliament and their own government.

And what a parliament! and what a government! Why, the very fact that Quebec was to have a bicameral legislature was proof of the importance they were to have. 'In giving ourselves a complete government,' argued the Bleus, 'we affirm the fact of our existence as a separate nationality, as a complete society, endowed with a perfect system of organization.'[45] Indeed, the very fact that Ontario's legislature was to have only one house while Quebec's had two served to underline the distinctiveness, the separateness, and the autonomy of the French-Canadian province:

> It is very much in our interests for our local legislature to have enough impor-
> tance and dignity to gain respect for its decision. . . . For us, French Canadians,
> who are only entering Confederation on the condition of having our own
> legislature as a guarantee of our autonomy, it is vital for that legislature not to
> be just a simple council whose deliberations won't carry any weight. . . .
>
> The deeper we can make the demarcation line between ourselves and the
> other provinces, the more guarantee we'll have for the conservation of our
> special character as a people.[46]

Here was the very heart and essence of the pro-Confederation argument in French Lower Canada: the Union of the Canadas was to be broken up, and the French Canadians were to take possession of a province of their own—a province with an enormous degree of autonomy. In fact, *separation* (from Upper Canada) and *independence* (of Quebec within its jurisdictions) were the main themes of Bleu propaganda. 'As a distinct and separate nation-ality,' said *La Minerve*, 'we form a state within the state. We enjoy the full exercise of our rights and the formal recognition of our national independence.'[47]

The provinces, in this view, were to be political manifestations of distinct nationalities. This was the line taken in 1858 by J.-C. Taché, when he wrote that in the provincial institutions, 'the national and religious elements will be able to develop their societies freely, and the separate populations realize . . . their aspirations and their dispositions.' And it was widely understood that Taché had played a vital role in influencing the course of the Quebec Conference.[48] Cartier himself had told that conference that a federal rather than a unitary system was necessary, 'because these provinces are peopled by different nations and by peoples of different religions'.[49] It was in this light that *La Minerve* saw the Quebec program as establishing 'distinctly that all questions having to do with our religion or our nationality will be under the jurisdiction of our local legislature'.[50] All the pro-Confederation propa-gandists were agreed that 'the future of our race, the preservation of every-thing which makes up our national character, will depend directly on the local legislature.'[51] It was the Lower Canadian ministers who had insisted, at the Quebec Conference, that education, civil and religious institutions should be under provincial jurisdiction, in order that Quebec should have the power to take charge of the French-Canadian national future.[52] Indeed, that power extended well beyond civil and religious institutions. It included 'the ownership and control of all their lands, mines, and minerals; the control of all their municipal affairs'[53]—everything 'which is dearest and most precious to us'[54]—all power, in fact, necessary to promote the national life of French Canada.

All these powers were to be entrusted to the government of a province in which French Canadians would form 'almost the whole' of the population, and in which everyone would have to speak French to take part in public life.[55] Yes, Confederation, by breaking up the union of the two Canadas, would make the French Canadians a majority in their own land,[56] so that 'our beautiful French language will be the only one spoken in the Parliament of the Province of Quebec. . . .'[57]

What was more, the control which French Canadians would exercise over their wide fields of jurisdiction would be an absolute control, and 'all right of interference in these matters is formally denied to the federal government.'[58] The Bleus, in fact, claimed to have succeeded in obtaining a system of co-ordinate sovereignty. 'Each of these governments,' they explained, 'will be given absolute powers for the questions within its jurisdiction, and each will be equally sovereign in its own sphere of action.'[59] Some over-enthusiastic advocates of the new régime even claimed that the provinces alone would be sovereign, 'the powers of the federal government being considered only as a concession of specifically designated rights.'[60] But even the moderate majority was firm in maintaining that the provinces would be in no way inferior or subordinate to the federal government, that they would be at least its equal, and that each government would be sovereign and untouchable in its own sphere of action:

> In the plan of the Quebec conference there is no delegation of power either from above or from below, because the provinces, not being independent states, receive their powers, as does the federal authority, from the imperial parliament.[61]

Politicians and journalists expressed this same view, in the legislature as well as in print. Thus, Joseph Blanchet told the Assembly: 'I consider that under the present plan of confederation the local legislatures are sovereign with regard to the powers accorded to them, that is to say in local affairs.'[62]

It may be that French-Canadian Confederationists went farther than they ought to have done in interpreting the Quebec Resolutions the way they did. Part of the reason for this may have been ignorance. A Bleu backbencher like C.B. de Niverville of Trois-Rivières could admit in the legislative debates that he had not read the resolutions, and what's more, that his ignorance of the English language had prevented him from following much of the debate. In this very situation he saw—or thought he saw—an argument for Confederation. For as he understood it, the new arrangement would remove French-Canadian affairs from an arena where men such as he were at a disadvantage, and place them before a group of French-speaking legislators:

> Indeed, what sort of liberty do we have, we who do not understand the English language? We have the liberty to keep quiet, to listen, and to try to understand! (Hear! hear! and prolonged laughter.) Under Confederation, the Upper Canadians will speak their language and the Lower Canadians will speak theirs, just as today; only, when a man finds that his compatriots form the great majority in the assembly in which he sits, he'll have more hope of hearing his language spoken, and as they do today, members will speak the language of the majority.[63]

Such an argument seems virtually to have ignored the very existence of the federal parliament, or at least of the authority it would have over French Canadians.

The case of de Niverville may have been extreme, but it was certainly not the only case of Bleus interpreting the Confederation plan in such a way as to maximize the powers of the provinces and minimize those of Ottawa far beyond anything we have been accustomed to. The federal power to raise taxes 'by any mode or system of taxation' was interpreted so as to exclude the right of direct taxation.[64] The federal veto power was represented not as a right to interfere with provincial legislation, but only as an obligation upon Ottawa to act as 'guardian of the constitution' by keeping clear the distinction between federal and provincial jurisdictions.[65]

But more important than any of these *specific* arguments was the wide-ranging exuberance of pro–Confederation propaganda. Here was a source of rhetoric that seemed to be promising that Confederation would give French Canadians virtual independence. Quebec was 'completely separated from Upper Canada and has a complete governmental organization to administer *all its local affairs* on its own.'[66] In the legislative council, E.-P. Taché interrupted his English-language speech on Confederation to tell his French-Canadian followers in French: 'If a Federal Union were obtained, it would be tantamount to a separation of the provinces, and Lower Canada would thereby preserve its autonomy together with all the institutions it held so dear.'[67] This could not be too often repeated: 'The first, and one of the principal clauses of the constitution is the one that brings about the repeal of the Union, so long requested by the Rouges, and separates Lower Canada from Upper Canada.'[68] What patriotic French Canadian could fail to be moved by what the fathers of Confederation had achieved?

> We've been separated from Upper Canada, we're called the Province of Quebec, we have a French-Canadian governor ... we're going to have our own government and our own legislature, where everything will be done by and for French Canadians, and in French. You'd have to be a renegade ... not to be moved to tears, not to feel your heart pound with an indescribable joy and a

deserved pride at the thought of these glorious results of the patriotism and unquenchable energy of our statesmen, of our political leaders, who . . . have turned us over into our own hands, who have restored to us our complete autonomy and entrusted the sacred heritage of our national traditions to a government chosen from among us and composed of our own people.[69]

This sort of exaggerated rhetoric invited an obvious response from the opposition. If you really are serious about separation from Upper Canada, they asked, if you really do want to obtain autonomy for French Lower Canada, then why not go the whole way? Why not break up the old union altogether, instead of joining this confederation? 'Everyone is agreed that only the repeal of the union would give us the independence of action needed for the future of Lower Canadians.'[70] If necessary, some sort of commercial association would be sufficient to satisfy Upper Canada in return for political separation.[71]

The Confederationists answered this, not by saying that Quebec's independence was an undesirable goal, not by saying that French Canadians wanted to join together with English Canadians to form a Canadian nation, but by claiming that complete independence was simply not practicable:

> The idea of making Lower Canada an independent State . . . has appealed to all of us as schoolboys; but we don't believe that any serious adult has taken it up so far. . . . We simply cannot do everything on our own. . . .[72]

This was, perhaps, a temporary condition, and it was to be hoped that one day Quebec *would* be in a position to make good her independence. Yes, French Canada 'can and must one day aspire to become a nation';[73] for the moment, however, 'we are too young for absolute independence.'[74] Of course, whoever says 'we are too young' implies that one day we shall be old enough—and Confederation, in the meanwhile, would preserve and prepare French Quebec for that day of destiny.[75]

One obvious reason why complete independence was not a realistic goal for the present was that Lower Canada was still part of the British Empire, and imperial approval, without which no constitutional change was possible, could not be obtained in the face of intense English-Canadian opposition.[76] But beyond that, it should be clear that an independent Quebec would inevitably be gobbled up by the United States. 'We would be on our own, and our obvious weakness would put us at the mercy of a stronger neighbour.'[77] French Canadians must understand, therefore, that 'unless we hurry up and head with all sails set toward Confederation, the current will carry us rapidly toward annexation.'[78]

The weakness of an independent Quebec would be both military and economic. The first of these weaknesses could hardly be more apparent to Quebeckers than it was in the mid-1860s, for just as the Anglo-American frictions created by the Civil War were impressing upon them the dangers arising from American hostility, the desire of British politicians to disengage themselves from colonial defence responsibilities was causing Canadians to think as never before of their own defences. Intercolonial co-operation seemed a natural response to the situation:

> No-one could deny that the annexation of the British colonies, either by their consent or by force, is intended and desired by the northern states; it is a no less evident truth that, as things stand today, we could resist their armies with help from Europe; but that on their own, without a political union, without a strong common organization, the colonies could, in the foreseeable future, sustain such a combat—that is something which no-one would dare to maintain. . . .[79]

It was in these circumstances that the Confederation project presented itself. Only weeks after the end of the Quebec Conference, the St Alban's raid brought the fear of imminent war with the United States. Yet at the same time, recent British military reports on colonial defence made Quebeckers wonder how much help they could expect if war broke out. 'We must not place unlimited hopes on the support of the mother-country in case of war with our neighbours. Circumstances more powerful than the will of men could render such confidence illusory.'[80] Yet the prospect for the separate British North American colonies without British support was bleak: 'separate from each other, we'd be sure to be invaded and crushed one after the other.'[81] Not only would Confederation give Quebec the advantage of a joint defence organization with the other colonies, but also, by this very fact, it would make Britain willing to give more help in case of war than she would have been willing to give to the isolated and inefficient defence effort of a separate Quebec.[82]

Quebec's economic weakness could be seen already in the flood of emigration directed toward the United States. Clearly, French Lower Canada's economy was not able, on its own, to support all its population. To keep her people at home, the province must co-operate with others to create opportunities. As French Canadians went to seek manufacturing jobs in New England, manufacturing must be established in Lower Canada;[83] by 1867, Quebec papers were appealing to outside capital to set up mills in the province.[84] Long before, Hector Langevin, in a prize-winning essay, had looked to the development of the St Lawrence transportation system to check emigration by providing jobs in commercial enterprises.[85] But the St Lawrence was an interprovincial organization—even more in the era of railroads than in that of the canal.[86]

Thus, the need for economic viability dictated some form of central authority and prevented Quebec's independence from being complete:

> The more provinces there are gathered together, the greater will be the revenues, the more major works and improvements will be undertaken and con-

sequently, the more prosperity there will be. What Lower Canada was unable to do on its own, we have done together with Upper Canada; and what the two Canadas have been unable to do together will be done by the confederation, because it will have markets and sea ports which we have not had.[87]

The British North American provinces had been endowed with resources enough. If they worked together to develop them, they could enjoy abundance, material progress, and even economic power.[88] But if they failed to co-operate, if they remained separate and isolated, then their economies would be weak, and inevitably they would become dependent on the United States, the prosperous neighbour to the south. 'But we know that where there is economic dependence there will also be political dependence. . . .'[89]

There were strong reasons, then, why Quebec's independence could not be complete, why the nationalist longing for separateness had to compromise with the practical need for viability. But if some form of association with the rest of British North America was necessary, the degree of unification must be the minimum required to make Quebec viable. In the spring of 1867, on his way home from London, where he had helped write the BNA Act, Cartier told a welcoming crowd at a station-stop in the Eastern Townships that his main pre-occupation had always been to protect the French-Canadian nationality, language, and institutions. 'That is why I was careful to make sure that the federal government would receive only that amount of power which was strictly necessary to serve the general interests of the Confederation.'[90] This meant, as E.-P. Taché had explained in 1864, that Ottawa would have enough power 'to do away with some of the internal hindrances to trade, and to unite the Provinces for mutual defence', but that the provinces would remain the agencies to which the 'majority of the people' would look for the protection of their 'rights and privileges' and 'liberties'.[91]

Perhaps this arrangement was not *ideal*; perhaps, even, Confederation was only 'the least bad thing in a very bad world'.[92] The French-Canadian leaders, after all, had not been alone at the constitutional conferences, and French Canada's own needs and aspirations had had to be reconciled with 'our condition of colonial dependence and the heterogeneous elements which make up our population'.[93]

Nevertheless, it had to be admitted that, despite Rouge protestations to the contrary, the old union could not have continued longer,[94] that the only alternative to Confederation would have been Rep by Pop,[95] and that, whatever degree of central authority there might be in the confederation, the patriotism of French-Canadian leaders could be relied on to promote the interests of their nationality, just as their patriotism had already won so much for French Canada in the making of the confederation.[96]

And what, then, in the final analysis, had they won? According to Bleu propaganda, Confederation was to be seen as an 'alliance' or 'association' of nations, each in its own autonomous province, and co-operating for the common welfare.[97] And this 'alliance with your neighbours',[98] this *'federal alliance among several peoples'*,[99] was to be regulated by the terms of a treaty or pact drawn up freely among them. Even the imperial authorities, according to Cartier, in preparing and passing the British North America Act, had accepted that they were only giving the official stamp of approval to an interprovincial compact. 'They understood . . . that the Quebec plan was an agreement among the colonies, which had to be respected, and they respected it.'[100] Confederation had, thus, been achieved because four separate colonies had formed 'a pact' among themselves.[101]

And in the federal alliance thus formed, Quebec was to be the French-Canadian country, working together with the others on common projects, but always autonomous in the promotion and embodiment of the French-Canadian nationality. 'Our ambitions,' wrote a Bleu editor, 'will not centre on the federal government, but will have their natural focus in our local legislature; this we regard as fundamental for ourselves.'[102] This was, no doubt, an exaggerated position, like the statement of de Niverville in the Canadian legislature, but what it exaggerated was the general tendency of the Confederationist propaganda. It underlined the Quebec-centredness of French Canada's approach to Confederation, and the degree to which French Quebec's separateness and autonomy were central to French-Canadian acceptance of the new régime.

Suggestions for Further Reading

Donald G. Creighton, *The Road to Confederation, 1864–1867* (Toronto, 1967).
A.I. Silver, *The French-Canadian Idea of Confederation 1864–1900* (Toronto, 1982).
P.B. Waite, *The Life and Times of Confederation* (Toronto, 1961).

Notes

[1] *La Gazette de Sorel*, 23 June 1864.
[2] Perrault quoted in the *Gazette de Sorel*, 3 September 1864; *Le Courrier du Canada*, 24 June 1864.
[3] *La Minerve*, 9 September 1864. After the Quebec Resolutions were known, journalists, politicians, and clergy still claimed to judge them by the same criterion. See, e.g., *Le Journal de Québec*, 24 December 1864. Joseph Cauchon, *L'Union des provinces de l'Amérique britannique du Nord* (Quebec, 1865), 19, 41; *Nouvelle Constitution du Canada* (Ottawa, 1867), 59.
[4] Most relevantly quoted in Auguste Achintre and J.B. Labelle, *Cantate: La Confédération* (n.p., n.d.), 4. Cartier, indeed, saw French Canada as geographically defined. J.-C. Bonenfant claims that while he fought for the French Canadians, 'seuls à ses yeux comptent ceux qui habitent le Bas-Canada.' See Bonenfant's article, 'Le Canada et les hommes politiques de 1867', in the *RHAF*, XXI, 3a (1967), 579–

80. At the 1855 funeral of Ludger Duvernay, the founder of the Saint-Jean-Baptiste Society, Cartier had warned that every nationality, including French Canada, must possess an 'élément territorial' in order to survive. See Joseph Tassé, ed., *Discours de Sir George Cartier* (Montreal, 1893), 95. Cartier also used the very expression 'French Canada' in a geographical sense, meaning Lower Canada. See, e.g., Tassé, 83.

[5] *La Revue canadienne*, I (1864), 696.

[6] *Ibid.*, IV (1867), 477.

[7] *La Minerve*, 25 September 1865.

[8] *L'Union nationale*, 3 September 1864. All of these quotations, of course, are merely variations of Louis-François Laflèche's statement (in *Quelques Considérations sur les rapports de la société civile avec la religion et la famille* [Trois Rivières, 1866], 43), 'Les Canadiens-français sont réellement une nation; la vallée du St-Laurent est leur patrie.'

[9] *La Gazette de Sorel*, 14 January 1865. Also, *La Minerve*, 10 and 14 September 1864.

[10] *La Minerve*, 14 September 1864.

[11] *Le Courrier de St-Hyacinthe*, 23 September 1864. Also, *Le Journal de Québec*, 4 July 1867.

[12] *Le Pays*, 8 November 1864.

[13] In G.P. Browne, ed., *Documents on the Confederation of British North America* (Toronto, 1969), 42–3. Also, 47, 49, 168 for Gordon's other assertions on the matter.

[14] *Le Courrier de St-Hyacinthe*, 2 September 1864.

[15] *La Gazette de Sorel*, 30 July 1864.

[16] J.-C. Taché, *Des Provinces de l'amérique du nord et d'une union fédérale* (Québec, 1858), 147, 148.

[17] Some did support provincial sovereignty, however—at least at times. See, e.g., *La Gazette de Sorel*, 27 August 1864.

[18] *Le Courrier de St-Hyacinthe*, 2 September 1864. Also, 28 October 1864.

[19] *Le Journal de Québec*, 1 September 1864. Also, 6 September 1864; *Le Courrier du Canada*, 30 September 1864, and 10 October 1864.

[20] In P.B. Waite, ed., *The Confederation Debates in the Province of Canada, 1865* (Toronto, 1963), 40, 41, 43. Macdonald's belief that he had obtained something more centralized than a federation is dramatically expressed in his well-known letter of 19 December 1864 to M.C. Cameron (PAC, Macdonald papers), in which he predicts that within a lifetime, 'both local Parliaments and Governments [will be] absorbed in the General power'.

[21] *La Minerve*, 15 October 1864. See also *Le Courrier de St-Hyacinthe*, 2 September 1864.

[22] *Le Courrier du Canada*, 16 September 1864.

[23] *Le Courrier de St-Hyacinthe*, 18 October 1864. See also *Le Pays*, 13 October 1864; *L'Ordre*, 14 October 1864; *Contre-poison: la Confédération c'est le salut du Bas-Canada* (Montreal, 1867), 9.

[24] The argument is stated clearly and briefly in the letter to M.C. Cameron mentioned above, note 20. See also Donald Creighton, *John A. Macdonald* (2 vols.; Toronto, 1966), I, 369, 375–6, 378–80; P.B. Waite, 'The Quebec Resolutions and the *Courrier du Canada*, 1864–1865', in the CHR, XL, 4 (December, 1959), 294; etc., etc.

[25] *La Minerve*, 15 October 1864.

[26] *Le Journal de Québec*, 27 August 1864. See also Joseph Cauchon, *L'Union des provinces*, 39. *Le Courrier du Canada*, far from seeing the US constitution as embodying the error of excessive decentralization, found it an apt model for the Quebec Conference to follow. See J.-C. Bonenfant, 'L'Idée que les Canadiens-français de 1864 pouvaient avoir du fédéralisme', in *Culture*, XXV (1964), 316. Some Rouges, notably Médéric Lanctôt in *L'Union nationale*, went so far as to maintain that it would be more desirable for Lower Canada to join the US than the British North American Union, precisely because it would have more autonomy as an American state.

[27] *Le Pays*, 27 March 1867.

[28] *Ibid.*, 2 April 1867. Also, 23 July 1864; and *La Confédération couronnement de dix années de mauvaise administration* (Montréal, 1867), 5.

[29] *La Confédération couronnement*, 5, 8; *Le Pays*, 12 November 1864, 9 February 1865, 2 April 1867.

[30] C.-S. Cherrier, *et al.*, *Discours sur la Confédération* (Montreal, 1865), 13.

[31] *Le Pays*, 23 and 28 June, 14 July, 8 November 1864; *L'Ordre*, 27 June 1864; *L'Union nationale*, 8 November 1864; *Confédération couronnement*, 13.

[32] Alpheus Todd, *Quelques Considérations sur la formation des Gouvernements locaux du Haut et du Bas-Canada* . . . (Ottawa, 1866), 5.

[33] *Le Pays*, 28 July 1866. Also, 27 September 1864, and 19 July 1866.

[34] *Le Pays*, 25 October 1864.

[35] *Ibid.*, 23 July 1864. Also, *L'Ordre*, 22 July 1864.

[36] *L'Union nationale*, 11 November 1864. Also, 3 September 1864; *Le Pays*, 14 and 23 July 1864.

[37] *L'Ordre*, 14 November 1864.

[38] *Le Défricheur*, 25 January 1865. All these fears which inspired the opposition also provoked doubts in the minds of some people who were otherwise supporters of the government. 'Nous avons toujours dit,' remarked *Le Canadien*, on 3 August 1866, 'que dans le plan de confédération actuel, on n'avait pas laissé assez de pouvoir aux gouvernements locaux et trop au gouvernement général.' See also, e.g., 3 February 1865.

[39] *Le Journal de Québec*, 5 July 1864.

[40] *Réponses aux censeurs de la Confédération* (St-Hyacinthe: Le Courrier, 1867), 47–9.

[41] *La Minerve*, 20 September 1864. Also, *Le Courrier du Canada*, 11 July 1864.

[42] *Parliamentary Debates on the Subject of the Confederation of the British North American Provinces* (Ottawa 1865), 368.

[43] *Ibid.*, 54–5.

[44] *La Minerve*, 15 October 1864.

[45] *Ibid.*, 17 July 1866.

[46] *Le Journal des Trois-Rivières*, 24 July 1866. Also, *Le Courrier de St-Hyacinthe*, 10 July 1866.

[47] *La Minerve*, 1 July 1867. Also, 2 July 1867: '[Comme] nation dans la nation, nous devons veiller à notre autonomie propre. . . .'

[48] Taché, *Des Provinces*, 151: 'Les éléments nationaux et religieux pourront à l'aise opérer leurs mouvements de civilisation, et les populations séparées donner cours . . . à leurs aspirations et à leurs tendances.' During the Confederation Debates, Joseph Blanchet claimed that the Quebec Resolutions were, essentially, the very

scheme which Taché had presented in his 1858 pamphlet (457 of the Ottawa edition of the debates). Joseph Tassé asserted in 1885 that Taché had acted as special adviser to the Canadian ministers at the Quebec Conference. (See J.-C. Bonenfant, 'L'Idée que les Canadiens-français de 1864', 314.) And Taché's son told an interviewer in 1935 that his father (whose uncle, Sir E.-P. Taché, had repeatedly recommended the nephew's scheme to the conference) had several times been called into the sessions, 'vraisemblablement pour donner des explications sur son projet.' See Louis Taché, 'Sir Etienne-Pascal Taché et la Confédération canadienne', in the *Revue de l'Université d'Ottawa*, v (1935), 24.

[49] In Browne, *Documents*, 128.

[50] *La Minerve*, 30 December 1864. See also *Le Journal de Québec*, 24 December 1864.

[51] *Le Courrier de St-Hyacinthe*, 28 October 1864. Also, 23 September and 22 November 1864.

[52] *Le Courrier du Canada*, 7 November 1864. See also 11 November 1864.

[53] *Le Courrier du Canada*, 13 March 1867. Also, 28 June 1867.

[54] *La Minerve*, 1 July 1867. Also, 2 July 1867; and the speech of Sir Narcisse Belleau in the *Confederation Debates* (Waite edition), 29.

[55] *Le Courrier de St-Hyacinthe*, 10 July 1866.

[56] Cauchon, *L'Union*, 45.

[57] *Contre-poison*, 20. See also *Réponses aux censeurs*, 48.

[58] *Contre-poison*, 20. Also, *Le Journal de Québec*, 15 November 1864, and 24 December 1864; Cauchon, *L'Union*, 45–6; *L'Union des Cantons de l'Est* (Arthabaskaville), 4 July 1867; Governor Gordon in Brown, *Documents*, 75; Bishop Larocque in *Nouvelle Constitution*, 75.

[59] *Le Courrier de St-Hyacinthe*, 28 October 1864.

[60] E.-P. Taché, quoted in Bonenfant, 'L'Idée que les Canadiens', 315.

[61] Joseph Cauchon, *Discours . . . sur la question de la Confédération* (n.p., n.d.), 8: 'les provinces, n'étant pas des états indépendants, reçoivent, avec l'autorité supérieure, leurs organisations politiques du Parlement de l'Empire. Il n'y a que des attributs distincts pour l'une et pour les autres.' See also Cauchon's *L'Union*, 40, 52; *Le Courrier du Canada*, 7 November 1864, and in Waite's 'The Quebec Resolutions and', 299–300.

[62] Joseph Blanchet in *Débats parlementaires sur la question de la Confédération des provinces de l'Amérique Britannique du Nord* (Ottawa, 1865), 551.

[63] *Ibid.*, 949.

[64] *L'Union des Cantons de l'Est*, 12 September 1867. This argument about direct taxation will not be as unfamiliar to historians as to other payers of federal income tax.

[65] *La Minerve*, 3 December 1864. Also, 11 November 1864; *Le Courrier de St-Hyacinthe*, 22 November 1864; *Le Courrier du Canada*, 7 November 1864.

[66] *Contre-poison*, 13.

[67] *Confederation Debates* (Waite edition), 22.

[68] *Contre-poison*, 11. Episcopal statements recommended Confederation on the same basis. Bishop Baillargeon of Tloa, who administered the diocese of Quebec, noted in his pastoral letter that, although there would be a central government, Confederation would, nevertheless, comprise four distinct provinces. 'C'est ainsi que le

Bas-Canada, désormais séparé du Haut, formera sous le nouveau régime une province séparée qui sera nommé "la Province de Québec" ' (in *Nouvelle Constitution*, 53).

[69]*Contre-poison*, 3.

[70]*L'Union nationale*, 3 September 1864. Also, *Confédération couronnement*, 5.

[71]*L'Union nationale*, 7 November 1864. Even the pro-Conservative *Gazette de Sorel* admitted, on 23 June 1864, that it had always preferred a straightforward breakup of the union as the best solution for French Canada. Also, 30 July 1864.

[72]*La Minerve*, 5 January 1865.

[73]*Le Journal de Québec*, 17 December 1864.

[74]*Le Pionnier de Sherbrooke*, 9 March 1867.

[75]See Cauchon, *L'Union*, 29.

[76]*La Minerve*, 28 September 1864.

[77]*Le Courrier de St-Hyacinthe*, 25 November 1864. Also, *Le Courrier du Canada*, 10 October 1864.

[78]Cauchon, *L'Union*, 25. Cartier put the same alternative to the legislative assembly, when he said: 'The matter resolved itself into this, either we must obtain British American Confederation or be absorbed in an American Confederation.' (*Confederation Debates*, Waite edition, 50.) See also *La Minerve*, 13 January 1865; and *Nouvelle Constitution*, 60, 66–7, 78ff.; *La Revue canadienne*, II (1865), 116, on Confederation as an alternative to 'le gouffre et le néant de la république voisine'.

[79]*La Revue canadienne*, II (1865), 159.

[80]*La Minerve*, 7 December 1864. The danger of war with the US was announced not only by *La Minerve* in December 1864, but also by *Le Courrier du Canada*, 26 November 1866, and *La Gazette de Sorel*, 19 November 1864, while the need to prepare for British disengagement was urged by the *Journal de Québec*, 17 December 1864, and *Le Courrier du Canada*, 5 October 1864.

[81]Cauchon, *L'Union*, 32. See also Jules Fournier, *Le Canada: Son présent et son avenir* (Montreal: *La Minerve*, 1865), 4.

[82]*Contre-poison*, 8.

[83]*L'Union nationale*, 19 July 1866.

[84]*L'Union des Cantons de l'Est*, 3 January 1867.

[85]Hector Langevin, *Le Canada, ses institutions, ressources, produits, manufactures, etc., etc., etc.* (Quebec, 1855), 96.

[86]*L'Union des Cantons de l'Est*, 8 August 1867.

[87]*Contre-poison*, 48–9.

[88]Taché, *Des provinces*, 10–11; *Le Courrier de St-Hyacinthe*, 23 July 1867; *Réponses aux censeurs*, 3–4; Achintre and Labelle, *Cantate*, 2–3, 8; Cauchon, *L'Union*, 3; Henry Lacroix, *Opuscule sur le présent et l'avenir du Canada* (Montreal, 1867).

[89]*La Revue canadienne*, II (1865), 103. See also Fournier, 2–3, who argued that as long as Canada was economically dependent on overseas trade, she would be politically at the mercy of the US, unless she had her own all-British rail link with an ice-free port in New Brunswick or Nova Scotia. See also Cauchon, *L'Union*, 34–5.

[90]*L'Union des Cantons de l'Est*, 23 May 1867.

[91]Taché was speaking at the Quebec Conference. In Browne, 127–8.

[92] Quoted in Waite, 'The Quebec Resolutions and', 297. See *Le Courrier du Canada*, 11 November 1864.

[93] *Le Courrier de St-Hyacinthe*, 22 November 1864. The opposition tried to stress the weakness and isolation of the French-Canadian delegates to the constitutional conferences as a reproach to them. E.g., *Le Pays*, 13 October 1864. But Confederationists thought it only reasonable to take realities into account. E.g., *La Minerve*, 25 February 1865; *La Gazette de Sorel*, 1 September 1866.

[94] *La Gazette de Sorel*, 23 June and 23 July 1864, 14 January 1865; *Le Courrier du Canada* 24 June 1864; *Le Courrier de St-Hyacinthe*, 8 November 1864; *L'Union des Cantons de l'Est*, 4 April 1864; *La Minerve*, 9 September and 30 December 1864; *Le Journal de Québec*, 15 December 1864; Cauchon, *L'Union*, 19; *Contre-poison*, 7; the pastoral letters of Bishops Cooke and Larocque, in *Nouvelle constitution*, 58–9, 68.

[95] *La Minerve*, 28 December 1864; *La Gazette de Sorel*, 30 July 1864; Louis-François Laflèche and Bishop Baillargeon, quoted in Walter Ullmann, 'The Quebec Bishops and Confederation', in CHR, XLIV, 3 (September 1963), reprinted in G.R. Cook, ed., *Confederation* (Toronto, 1967), 53, 56, 66.

[96] *La Courrier du Canada*, 22 June 1864; Bishops Baillargeon and Cooke in *Nouvelle Constitution*, 54–5, 60; E.C. Parent to J.I. Tarte, Ottawa, 4 September 1866, in PAC, Tarte papers (MG 27, II, D16). Just as they had promoted French-Canadian interests at the constitutional conferences, Quebec's sixty-five MPs would watch over French Quebec's interests at Ottawa. For they would be sent to Ottawa as representatives of Quebec, the French-Canadian province, and their responsibility would be toward that province and its autonomy. See Bonenfant, 'L'Idée que les Canadiens français,' 317; *Le Courrier de St-Hyacinthe*, 22 July 1864.

[97] *La Gazette de Sorel*, 25 February 1865; *La Minerve*, 1 July 1867. It was perfectly clear, of course, what Quebec's nationality was considered to be. It was French-Canadian. But what nationalities were to be attributed to the other provinces was never certain. French Canadians were aware of distinctions among the English, Scottish, and Irish nationalities, and they may have seen the other provinces as having unique national characters determined by their respective blends of these various elements. But they were always vague on this point. Cartier, however, did suggest a similar distribution of religious characteristics when he said (in the legislative debate on the Quebec resolutions) that Ontario would be Protestant, Quebec Catholic, and the Maritimes pretty evenly divided between the two denominations (e.g., in Tassé, 422).

[98] *L'Union des Cantons de l'Est*, 4 July 1867.

[99] *Contre-poison*, 8. Also, 10.

[100] *L'Union des Cantons de l'Est*, 23 May 1867.

[101] *Le Journal de Québec*, 4 July 1867. See also the Bishop of St-Hyacinthe, in *Nouvelle Constitution*, 65. J.-C. Taché had assumed, in 1858, that a confederation would necessarily be brought about by an intercolonial pact. See his *Des provinces*, 139.

[102] *Le Courrier de St-Hyacinthe*, 10 July 1866. We shall find this point of view adopted not infrequently by French-Quebec journalists in the first decades after Confederation.

34

The International Context of Confederation

The Confederation of British North America was no simple achievement, for it was brought about only after a number of internal and external obstacles were overcome. The basic internal problem was that most of the prospective member provinces had no compelling sense of the advantages of unification. The British Empire had provided a secure base for most provinces from which they could attempt to deal with new economic pressures and the vast and powerful American republic to the south. In 1861 the United States began a civil war, and this titanic struggle provided a backdrop against which the drive for Confederation was played out. In addition to its colonial status, British North America was a part of a larger international community and subject to forces beyond its control. Whatever its people wanted as a future would require both the active support of the British government and the tacit acceptance of the Americans.

W.L. Morton looks at Confederation in the context of the entire North American continent—a larger perspective than is traditionally employed. He discusses the responses to international economic pressures of three 'essentially dependent societies'—Mexico, the southern American states, and the provinces of British North America—arguing that they shared common problems and ideological characteristics and that their fate was shaped in large measure by the American Civil War. The breakdown of stability on the continent in the early 1860s helped contribute to the emergence of a united Canada, for British policy pushed two recalcitrant provinces into Confederation, while at the same time it was also supporting American hemispheric power.

Are the parallels Morton draws among Mexico, the American South, and British North America convincingly portrayed? Did British policy triumph (as Morton suggests) or make the best of a bad situation?

Why is the *Trent* affair regarded by Morton as such an important turning point? Finally, to what extent does Morton's continental perspec- tive by portraying Canada as a pawn in larger struggles for power underrate internal pressures for reform?

This article first appeared, titled 'British North America and a Continent in Dissolution 1861–1871', in *History*, n.s., XLVII (1962), 139–56.

The Continental Crisis, 1861

The American Civil War was not only an American struggle. It was also the central and decisive feature of a crisis that disturbed the whole continent of North America in 1861. Not only did the disruption of the American Union greatly affect Mexico and the British North American colonies; they were themselves undergoing, the former a civil war, the latter a prolonged malaise, which were, it may be supposed, parts of a general crisis in continental affairs. That crisis arose, it would seem, from the reaction of the politically independent but economically dependent societies of North America to the impact of European industrial capitalism. Staple exports of cotton, wheat, and timber, foreign loans and investment, railway and factory construction, large-scale imports of manufactured goods, and the resistance of domestic industries to the competition of European products, these were the symptoms of an economic maladjustment underlying the political crisis. A social war in Mexico, the secession of the plantation society of the South from the American Union, and the first full-scale attempt to overcome an obdurate provincial regionalism and form a colonial union in British North America, all were the social and political movements in which the economic pressures manifested themselves.

The three local variations of the crisis of course differed in many respects. In Mexico the 'clericals' and the conservative landlords revolted against a semi-popular and republican government in the name of social stability. In British North America a politically conservative but economically liberal set of politicians combined to overcome the limitations and backwardness of small and isolated communities. They sought to achieve a political union and larger field of economic enterprise by imperial action and, as it proved, without direct popular ratification. This, as in Mexico, was a 'revolt of the right', but it was essentially a liberal movement. In the United States the conservative-agrarian society of the South had been under pressure for a generation. In the Civil War it struck out against a constriction that it believed would be fatal to it, the opposition of the free, soil states to the spread of slavery into the territories. In seceding, it defied a coalition of conservative commercial and industrial capitalists of the North-east with agrarian democrats of the North-west, and began the armed struggle of a

Southern nationalism against a capitalist and democratic imperialism of the North. The Civil War was thus neither a social war, despite ideological overtones, nor an attempt to overcome regional limitations, despite strong sectional features. It was a struggle between two fully constituted societies, a war of two nations in which the immediate aim of the South was independence, of the North the preservation of the Union,[1] with all that it implied.

Despite these differences, the three crises shared two related ideological conflicts—the antagonism of democratic republicanism, discredited a decade before in Europe, to the monarchical ideal of a permanent executive, and the opposition of the concept of social hierarchy to that of social equality. In Mexico the conflict of ideologies was open and avowed. The war began as an attempt to destroy the republic, went on to the establishment of an imperial monarchy with French help, and ended in the restoration of the republic with the help of the United States. In British North America the adoption of responsible government has softened the contrast of republic and monarchy, and the actual republicans had retired from politics. But the ruling liberal-conservative politicians were strongly monarchical in opinion, meaning by that term the constitutional and parliamentary monarchy of Victorian England, and they were strenuously anti-republican and anti-democratic in sentiment.[2]

In the United States the South was not, of course, monarchical, but it was conservative and it stood by implication for a society organized in a social hierarchy of great planter and poor white, and founded on the racial supremacy of the whites. Northern society was, in the main, a union of commercial and industrial capitalists with small farmers and industrial workers. It was this social union which explains the identification, not logically necessary, of the preservation of the Union with the advance of democracy. The interests of the capitalists required that the Union be maintained. Sentiment for the democratic cause took the form of the desire for free land and of opposition to the hated stereotype of European monarch and landlord (easily converted to southern planter). It made those—whether they were native American, Irish, or German immigrant—who wanted a 'Red Republic', as the Duke of Newcastle warned,[3] the enthusiastic and convinced allies of the great merchants and manufacturers of the North-east. These for their part wished to hold the markets and shipping of the South, the Caribbean, and the West, and exclude their British rivals from them. It was this alliance which explains why there emerged from the Civil War a democracy as nationalist, as conservative, and at bottom as imperialist as any society known to history.

In addition to the general economic impact and ⸴ conflict, the three North American communities sh⸴ means equal or identical, concern with the issue ⸴

outcome of that struggle would be of decisive and equal importance to all three. If the American Union were to be permanently disrupted and the Confederacy established as an independent nation, then the supremacy of the United States in North America, not admitted but also not challenged since 1823, would be conclusively ended. With its end would come the renewal of the balance of power in America and of the intervention of the great powers in the relations of the American states. The disruption of the Union would be, moreover, a great setback for the cause of democratic government, and a great vindication for those who held that any considerable society required a strong and permanent executive and a stable social structure. In short, the issue was whether the American system under the hegemony of the United States was to be confirmed, and with it the superiority of republican democracy, or whether the American states, like those of Europe, were to regulate their relations and maintain their identities by means of alliances and the balance of power within and beyond the Americas, and to maintain social order by strong government not necessarily resting on popular and periodic assent. The general crisis of the Americas would be resolved either by the victory of the democratic or the monarchical principle, and by either the victory of national independence, along European lines, or by the re-assertion of the American hegemony. In the latter event, all remaining imperial and monarchical powers would withdraw from the Americas before the victorious republic and all other sovereignties in the Americas would be conditioned by, and in the last resort would be subordinate to, the American hegemony. Independence and sovereignty in the Americas would, in effect, be juridical rather than political concepts, more matters of law than of power.

It is possible, then, to agree with Lincoln that the Civil War was one to maintain democracy by maintaining the Union. But it is necessary to insist that it was also one to maintain American supremacy in the Americas by maintaining the Union. The struggle on the part of the North was, as Lord John Russell declared, one 'for empire', for the government of the Union by a majority and for the domination of the Americas by the United States. It therefore followed that the Republic of Mexico, if restored, and the Union of British North America, if carried out, would either have to form alliances with one or other of the Federal or the Confederate unions, or to reconcile their independence and their form of government and society with the fact of the supremacy of a reunited United States.

British North America in 1861

The chief characteristic of the British North American provinces, one common to them all, was provincialism. The provinces and 'the provincials', as ˜mericans called them, were provincial in spirit as well as in status. And the general provincialism of colonial society broke down into an intense particularism in each region of British North America, and an obdurate parochialism in each colony. It was this ingrained colonial localism which had insisted on responsible government, and which responsible self-government in turn had intensified. And self-government was so developed by 1861 as almost to make the colonies independent states.[4]

The particularism of the British North American colonies had grown out of the physical separation of the provinces and their regions, and the racial and religious differences of their peoples. By 1861, however, the railroad had made it materially possible to overcome the separation of the Atlantic provinces from Canada, and to an increasing degree the separation of the Atlantic provinces from one another. Such a union had been discussed from time to time, and by 1861 considerable and even urgent interests were to be served by union, especially in the Canadas, but also in the Atlantic provinces. Even to the imperial government, deeply concerned since the Crimean War and the development of the steam-propelled and ironclad warship with problems of home defence, such a union was desirable, if it made the British American colonies capable of assuming responsibility for their own defence.

All the elements of union, all the impulses which made for it, had been already present when in 1858-9 the Canadian government proposed to the other colonies and the imperial government a union of all the British American provinces. By an unfortunate set of accidents and misunderstandings, the project did not receive the imperial support it merited, and which it required, since colonial particularism made union by colonial action alone impossible.[5]

In this situation, what the American Civil War did, and particularly the Trent affair, was to make the defence of British North America so great a danger to Great Britain as to ensure imperial support for the next colonial attempt at union. The military hazards implicit in the British connection with the colonies were such that some honourable and dignified way of disengagement had to be found. The best available was that of colonial union. Union would enable the colonies to assume responsibility for their local defence. It would put them in a position, not so much to resist attack by the United States, as to avert encroachment by appealing for respect as a new North American nation, one not hostile to the American system, though not wholly part of it. Such was the situation in British North America when the American Civil War began, and first shook the provinces in the *Trent* affair of November 1861.

The Canadian Declaration of Independence, 1861

The *Trent* affair was a decisive event in British American history,[6] because it made imperial policy an active element in British American union. But it was decisive because it also checked a drift towards continentalism which had been going on imperceptibly since 1846. The end of the old commercial empire in the abolition of the Corn Laws and the Laws of Trade and Navigation, and the release of the British colonies to continental influences by the grant of self-government, had naturally brought the provinces into closer relations with the states. The provinces came to feel more independent of the metropolis and more American in interest and outlook. This many people in the colonies, as did many in the United Kingdom and the United States, thought might be the prelude to union with the United States.

Relations between the American neighbours had been good for over a decade except for the flare-up of 1856 over recruiting for the Crimean War. The boundary had at last been settled in 1846. American expansion now seemed to threaten only the Caribbean. The northern merchants of the United States had obtained the routes and bases they wanted for trade with Latin America and the Far East.[7] The seizure of San Juan island in 1859 had been only a footnote to the nature of American imperialism, an occupation of bases rather than of territory. Only the growing trade of St Paul with Red River and of San Francisco with British Columbia seemed to threaten new encroachments, as Canadian claimants of the Hudson Bay Company territories realized. But these were not too pressing dangers, and British Americans in general took good relations with the United States for normal, if not for granted, in 1860.

Under the growing friendliness with the continental neighbour, however, was a steady hardening of colonial resolution to maintain, against either British or American intervention, the practical independence which responsible government had begun. The interference, as it was considered, of the Court of Queen's Bench at Westminster, with the disposition by the Canadian courts of the case of the fugitive slave, Anderson, produced a strong feeling of resentment in all Canada.[8] And not only did Canadian and Maritime agricultural and industrial interests require protection from American competition, the great majority of British Americans deliberately preferred self-government under British institutions within the liberal Victorian empire to independence within the democratic republic of the United States. It was a choice that the events of 1861 to 1865 were to make more definite still.

British North America, then, at the time of the secession of the Southern states, was closely bound to the United States by trade and was responding to the continental affinities of the two Americas. It was nevertheless pursuing its own destiny and holding to its own institutions and manners, especially in a preference for a parliamentary government and a conservative social order. It is not surprising, therefore, that the initial reaction of the provinces to the secession of the cotton states, as of the United Kingdom, was on the whole sympathetic to the maintenance of the Union of the States when its dissolution was first attempted. French Canadians, it is true, were from the first pro-Southern in feeling.[9] But most English–Canadian sympathy was with the North, because it was thought to be anti-slavery. The British Americans prided themselves on their early abolition of slavery and their reception of fugitives from the slave states after 1850.[10]

This general sympathy with the preservation of the peace and union of a neighbouring community and with the anti-slavery cause did not, however, prevent British Americans from early perceiving the fundamental issues raised by the disruption of the American union. These were the prospect of a continent subject to the balance of power and the intervention of non-American states. Such would be a continent in which small communities might defend a real, if precarious, independence by judicious alliance within and without the Americas. It would, moreover, be a continent not necessarily committed to the spread or maintenance of republican democracy. In such a continent British American independence and parliamentary monarchy might perhaps have their best opportunity for survival.

Some English-speaking conservatives, such as the young Toronto swashbuckler, George T. Denison, saw this, and pursued it as a goal to be desired for the next four years.[11] Some liberals saw it also, such as George Brown of the Toronto *Globe*, and Thomas D'Arcy McGee, leader of the Canadian Irish of Lower Canada, and rejected it explicitly and firmly.[12] So in effect did the majority of English-speaking British Americans. Much as their sympathies were to alter, they never came to the point of consciously desiring, still less of actively seeking, the permanent dissolution of the American Union and the return of the balance of power to the Americas. Some English conservatives, and French Canadians in the majority, would have welcomed the defeat of the North; very few were prepared to raise a finger to bring about that result.

Policy, as distinguished from sentiment and opinion, was of course determined by the imperial government. It adopted a policy of neutrality on 13 May 1861, and maintained it, not without errors and acts of negligence, but always without deliberate departure from the main line of policy. British neutrality bound the provinces, and they accepted it without dissent, as a policy they would themselves have adopted had they been independent. The quarrel was not of their making, and its settlement was not in their hands. Indeed, the abstention of the provincials from the war is very striking. A few thousand fought for pay, or because they had been crimped;[13] the few idealists who fought for a cause almost to a man fought for the North. But even its ideological implications, emphasized as they were after 1862, stirred few pulses to fight for or against democracy, a striking example of how superficial were the ideological affinities of provincials and Americans.

British neutrality, however, incurred much Northern resentment, as its refusal to recognize the Confederacy aroused much Southern. The North regarded British neutrality as designed to help the South. As that resentment was expressed in the Northern press in the second half of 1861, coupled with the threats to retaliate by seizing the colonies, it was met by the rise of anti-Northern sentiment in the provincial press. The British Americans, annoyed by the threat of attack, were puzzled and disillusioned by Lincoln's insistence that the war was a war only to preserve the Union, and not a war to free the slaves. It was the 'only' which was objected to, not the preservation of the Union. The question of the border states, the vast material issues involved in emancipation, the Northern identification of the preservation of the Union with the advance of democracy, these were considerations which, though not unappreciated, did not come home to most provincials.

The continuation of the war of course raised the possibility of the provinces being involved in the struggle. Palmerston insisted despite doubts among his cabinet colleagues on the despatch of some reinforcements before winter.[14] This, however, was done quietly, except for the unfortunate publicity attending the use of the new *Great Eastern* as a transport. The reform of the militia was pushed harder in the provinces. But no great apprehension was felt in either the United Kingdom or the colonies until, in November 1861, Captain Charles Wilkes seized the Confederate commissioners, James M. Mason and John Slidell, on board the British mailship SS *Trent*. This manifest violation of neutral rights left the United Kingdom no option but to demand release of the prisoners and some suitable expression of regret. Even so, the tone of the British note was moderate, and the British Minister, Lord Lyons, was instructed to leave the American government 'every opportunity for a graceful retreat'.[15] What made the situation dangerous was that Northern resentment at British neutrality led to an outcry in the press against any release of the prisoners, which made it difficult for Lincoln and his cabinet to accede to the British demand.

There was thus a real prospect of popular anger in the Northern States forcing the American government to refuse release, so making a British declaration of war unavoidable. For the United Kingdom, while it had refrained from presenting the United States with an ultimatum, was quite clear that if release and apology were refused, it must go to war. And such was the outcome anticipated in England. 'I fear war is upon us,' wrote Newcastle to Monck in mid-December[16] at the height of the crisis. Eleven thousand troops, including two battalions of the Guards, committed to the grip of the Canadian winter and of the spring break-up, when no reinforcement was possible, were earnest of what the government expected.

Had there been war, there can be no doubt that, whatever it would have meant to British America, it would have resulted in the independence of the Confederacy and the permanent disruption of the Union, with all that implied for the Americas. Had the United Kingdom indeed been looking for a *casus belli*, it could have made the *Trent* affair one with a turn of phrase.

Nothing demonstrates more clearly the deliberate decision of Great Britain, adhered to under provocation great for the day, not to exploit the secession of the Confederacy in order to destroy the supremacy of the United States in America. It was a decision accepted by every responsible body of opinion in the colonies, even by those against whose sympathies it ran.[17]

The American government was, of course, inclined to peace; Lincoln and the presidential powers were assurance of that. But it had to wait until the mood of angry defiance passed, until, as Lincoln said in the presence of the Canadian cabinet minister, Alexander Galt, the time had come that he could 'fix it'.[18] And even if the American government had desired war, it would have been madness to have incurred it. The firmness of France in support of England, backed as both powers were by the united opinion of Europe, made war impossible for the North. In short, Britain not only had a clear case; it for once had a free hand.[19] Had it cared to exploit the disruption of the Union, it could have done so with less immediate risk than in any of the four years to follow. This fact further underlines the moderation with which Palmerston and Russell handled the *Trent* affair, and still more the rocklike quality of the decision implicit in the policy of neutrality, not to seek to confirm the break-up if the Union and, as a result, to accept the supremacy of the United States in the Americas.

That decision was of course the outcome of widely differing views within the British cabinet and British public opinion. Differences in public opinion ranged all the way from Bright's and Cobden's all-out defence of the North and American unity to J.A. Roebuck's demand for the recognition of Southern independence.[20] Within the cabinet the differences extended from Palmerston's probable readiness to welcome the break-up of the Union[21] to Argyll's wholehearted support of the North.[22] Gladstone, despite his notorious Newcastle speech, had expressed and generally held the view that the preservation of the Union was in the interest of England.[23]

But both halves of the spectrum of opinion favoured a policy of neutrality, if for opposite reasons. Those like Palmerston and *The Times*, who were unsympathetic to the North, thought until late 1864 that the South could not be conquered.[24] More liberal observers were impressed by the stability and toughness of Southern society under the strain of war; no servile insurrection, no defection of poor whites challenged the leadership of the great planters. This is what Gladstone meant when he spoke in the Newcastle speech of Jefferson Davis making a nation. The Union, other liberals held, could only be restored by the destruction of the Southern nationality, and a union so restored would not be the Union as it was. Thus many liberal humanitarians were for neutrality and even mediation in order to end a struggle which seemed pointless. Had they thought a Northern victory possible, most of them would have been with the outright supporters of the North, like Bright, who favoured neutrality only because they thought neutrality favoured the North.

Thus, while it is true that large and important sections of British and still more of colonial opinion desired the victory of the South and the permanent disruption of the Union, no one was prepared to go to war to bring about those results. They hoped for Southern victory, but did nothing to ensure it. In effect, therefore, they accepted the possibility of the preservation of the Union and of the reassertion of American supremacy in the Americas. To say that they willed such a result would be absurd; their refusal to take the measures necessary to avert it, however, constituted a covert assent to its realization. The consequence was a practical and decisive policy of neutrality.

Beause of the British resolution to remain neutral and at peace, the Trent affair was one event contributing to the restoration of the Union and the reaffirmation of American supremacy. It also had other results, of subordinate but still great importance.

The first was that it set before British North America two clear alternative outcomes of the war, alternatives already seen by thoughtful men.[25] One was that the South might be victorious in defending its independence, and the North seek compensation in the conquest of British America. The other was that a victorious and militarily powerful North might attack the provinces in order to employ war-hardened troops, to complete the work of Manifest Destiny and to relieve the resentment at what was considered the hostile policy of the United Kingdom and the provinces. Whichever alternative occurred, British America must be prepared to defend itself. Thus the question of imperial and British American defence became one of immediate urgency, an urgency underlined by the improvisations of the *Trent* crisis and the retention of the eleven thousand reinforcements in America until the summer of 1864. In this necessity of imperial policy the sufficient pressure, the fusing heat, required to overcome British American particularism came into being.

The second subordinate effect of the *Trent* affair was therefore to make firm and final the already forming British decision to withdraw from all military commitments within the American continent, once the provinces were put in the way of defending themselves by the improvement of their own forces and by political union. Behind the groupings of military policy was the hard-headed determination of Gladstone as Chancellor of the Exchequer from 1859 to 1865 to economize in all expenditure for defence, and particularly for colonial defence. It was henceforth certain that when the provinces took up the question of union in anything like agreement, the Colonial Office and the British cabinet would push the work to completion. As they alone could overcome the particularism of the provinces, this was a matter of first signifiance to British America. Not again could a British government hope to have the firm support of the shifty Napoleon III, or the aid of the cool-hearted Lincoln to save it from a major war in America, when its metropolitan security demanded that it be able to concentrate its forces in Europe. Schleswig-Holstein, Sadowa, Sedan and the ending of the Black Sea clauses of the Treaty of Paris were to drive the point home before 1871.[26]

The final effect of the *Trent* affair was to make British Americans realize, and Americans also realize, that the colonies would fight for their independence.[27] Provincial and dependent societies are always somewhat unrealistic, for they do not themselves have to make all the choices affecting their lives. In the *Trent* affair British America had its moment of truth. It emerged as a community with its own will and destiny. The unanimity of French and English, of Protestant and Catholic Irish, of governments and people, surprised the provincials themselves. It delighted the British government and press, and it took aback the press and people of the North, who were astonished and wounded to see their Northern neighbours spring to arms against them.[28] The hectic early winter days when the steamers were racing for the St Lawrence before the ice closed the river; and when the Guards and the line battalions, muffled like Russians, were being drawn in sleighs through the forests of New Brunswick, were days of decision in British America. The provincials were American, it was true, but they would be American in their own way, British American. The *Trent* affair, the foolish act of an ambitious officer, was the Canadian Lexington and Concord, the definite initiation of Canadian independence.

The Two Years Doubly Indecisive, 1862 and 1863

The Trent crisis was the first turning point of the war; it decided that the war would remain a civil war and not become, like the War of Independence, a world war of great powers. There remained, however, the possibility of a Southern victory, and with its approach, intervention by the European powers to mediate between the belligerents and to recognize the independence of the South. The course of the war would decide whether or not there would be such intervention.

Meantime, in Mexico the continuance of the Civil War led to events which underlined the issues and implications of the Civil War in the American states. The republican regime of Benito Juàrez has stopped payment of interest on bonds by his opponents. This provoked intervention by Spain, France, and England to enforce payment. Spain, still mistress of Cuba and Puerto Rico, had already intervened in Santo Domingo and seemed on the verge of attempting to extend its power in the Caribbean. Louis Napoleon, despite general opposition in France, was moved to intervene by clerical pressure and by his own vague dream of France as world power and of himself as the champion of a strong but popular government. The man who had already revived French ties with Canada[29] would make France once more a power in America. England, however, had no motive except to ensure the servicing of the loans, and the Treaty of London of 1 October 1861 bound all three powers to that limited purpose. By April of 1862 the military and naval intervention of the three powers had assured the resumption of payments, and England withdrew its ships and marines. Spain followed. Provoked by a defeat suffered by his troops in May, Louis Napoleon, however, now decided to intervene further on behalf of the rebels in order to set up a monarchy in Mexico. The French conquest of Mexico followed, involving an ever heavier commitment of troops and money. Eventually in 1864, Maximilian of Habsburg was to become Emperor of Mexico, nominally by vote of the Mexican people, but actually as a dependent of the French. For the moment it is enough to point out that no such adventure could have been attempted had it not been for the American Civil War.

In British America the two years 1862 and 1863 told a very different story. The things which ought to have been done were a vigorous reorganization of the militia, the immediate undertaking of the Intercolonial Railway between Canada and the Atlantic provinces, and an urgent campaign to unite the provinces. But the second two were attempted only to fail; the first was not even attempted. On the contrary, affairs fell into a state of indecision and deadlock suggesting that which prevailed in the struggle to the South. Just as the improvised armies of the North and South lacked the skill and experience to achieve and exploit victory, so the weak and sundered provinces floundered in their poverty and their parochial concerns, no longer driven, as in the Trent affair, by the impetus of the continental convulsion, to achieve the union necessary to survival.

This paralysis was not caused by the *Trent* affair being forgotten, or because the Civil War did not continue to affect the life of the province, as it did daily. It was clear, all the two years, that whatever the outcome of the war, the union of the provinces was necessary to their survival. British American opinion was still hotly engaged in the war; it became steadily more anti-Northern in reaction to the attacks in the Northern press and the intermittent talk of the need to conquer Canada. But the provincial governments enforced the policy of neutrality and most British Americans were content to keep out of the war. Only the *Globe* of Toronto and some liberals staunchly supported the North.

It was not any change of sentiment or outlook, then, which explained the failure of the provinces to respond as needed to the demands of the situation created by the war. The explanation was in fact the dislocation of the provincial revenues by the over-building of railways, especially the Grand Trunk, and the depression of private business and government revenues during the first years of the war. This financial stringency in large part explains the failure of Canada to respond to the situation revealed by the *Trent* affair. When the Cartier-Macdonald government accepted the report of a commission on defence and brought in a Bill to provide a militia force of 100,000 men at a cost of $5,000,000 a year, it was defeated and resigned. The reasons for the rejection of the Bill have been debated ever since. Probably the chief one was that a majority of members simply thought the cost beyond the resources of the country.[30] A second was that a considerable number of Canadians, English and French, firmly believed that the defence of Canada was primarily an imperial responsibility because Canada could be attacked only by the United States and would be attacked only as part of the British Empire. In such an event the Canadian militia should co-operate with the imperial forces, but in a secondary capacity and without previous cost and training. This outlook was absurdly provincial and isolationist, but it came from a belief deeply engrained and obstinately held. To what extent that belief was a rationalization of the firm colonial refusal to pay direct taxes for any purpose not strictly local can only be a matter of speculation.

The Canadian ministries which followed that of Cartier-Macdonald were accordingly committed to policies of retrenchment, and applied them in the great issues of militia reform, construction of the Intercolonial Railway, and the opening of communications with the Pacific coast. As a result, little was accomplished in the years 1862 and 1863 in these matters, and nothing whatever in the greatest matter of all, the union of the provinces. And meanwhile dissatisfaction with the Union of the two Canadas and the growing difficulty of working the parliamentary system threatened to bring Canadian administration to a halt in political deadlock.

In the war below the border a parallel military stalemate occurred during these years. The victories of the North early in 1862 were offset by the Southern success at Second Manassas. Then the Southern offensive into Maryland was turned back at Antietam, as it was to be again and finally at Gettysburg in July 1863. Because the military contest was deadlocked also, the floundering provincials to the North did not have to pay the penalty of their weakness, particularism, and indecision. They did, indeed, frankly count on the valour of the South to keep the North engaged.[31]

At the same time, the stalemate almost produced the intervention of the European powers so dreaded by the North, with the almost certain consequence of the recognition of the independence of the South. Convinced that the North could not conquer the South and that humanity bade that an attempt be made to stay a useless slaughter, Palmerston and Russell decided in September 1862 that the time had come to offer mediation. They agreed that France and Russia be asked to co-operate, and that the offer be made only if the Northern reverses should continue.[32] The cabinet when consulted, was divided, but which side would carry the verdict would itself be determined by the outcome of the engagements of the late summer.[33] Then the North prevailed sufficiently at Antietam to make it clear that it need accept no offer of mediation, the announcement of an emancipation proclamation strengthened the pro-Northern party in the cabinet, and on

23 October the decision was taken to postpone the offer to mediate.[34] It was in fact a decision not to intervene, as was shown when in November the British government declined a French proposal to offer mediation.[35] This meant that the war would be ended only by the action of the two belligerents. The second international crisis of the war, potentially as dangerous to the North as the *Trent* affair, had passed.[36] The war would now be fought to a finish and this almost certainly meant a Northern victory.

From that date on British policy was to accept, without further attempt in any way to intervene or influence the decision, the restoration of the Union by force of arms and the re-assertion of American supremacy. In British America there was no questioning of this policy, but sentiment, if anything, became more anti-Northern as the war went on.[37] This perhaps was the result of a growing realization that a victorious North and a restored union would now have to be faced in a year or two.

The Resolution of the Continental Crisis, 1864–7

Certainly in 1863 the pace and temper of events became urgent and revolutionary. The war was at last organized and became a war of mass and material. The American economy was industrialized, thus completing the transformation begun by the impact of British industrialism. The attack on slavery, the first blow at the structure of the old agrarian society of the South, had begun.[38] And it became increasingly apparent that the Union when restored would not be the Union as it was. The South, it was taken for granted, would be a South socially and perhaps politically reconstructed. In Mexico the great adventure moved to its well-meant but unconvincing climax, the proclamation of the Empire, which promised a stable social order to a devastated country and challenged with a resurgent monarchy the dawning republican victory of the North. And in Canada opinion began to move against the petty and penurious politicians who had done nothing to prepare the provinces to meet the crisis which would follow the victory of the North. The first result of this movement was to end the political division of English Canada, and put the expansionist force of Upper Canada behind Canadian Union.

In June 1864, George Brown carried the majority of his Upper Canadian liberal following into a coalition with Macdonald's and Cartier's conservatives and thus formed an alliance of commercial and agrarian interests, much like the early Republican party, to carry a union of all British America. At the same time the Atlantic provinces of Nova Scotia, New Brunswick, and Prince Edward Island prepared to discuss a local union. The colonial governors, the business interests, all that was enlightened and conservative in Canada and the Maritimes, combined to meet the situation which would arise when republican democracy was vindicated and the United States restored to continental supremacy, with no internal check imposed by the South, and no external check by any counter-balance in America.

Clearly, if Canadian expansion were to be safeguarded and parliamentary monarchy preserved, a union of the provinces must be formed while Britain was yet disposed to lend its imperial prestige to the project. British America therefore began to move, like Mexico, but quietly and without challenge, towards a parliamentary and monarchical union, one not founded on popular assent, but ratified by the colonial assemblies and the imperial parliament, and one not won by colonial arms but fostered by British power. While there was yet time, the last residue of British power in America was to be used to preserve a colonial nationality and British institutions against the pressure of the triumphant and irritated American democracy.

Here at last was the pressure urgent enough to overcome the obstacles which had defeated the attempt at union in 1858. It was fortunate for British America that the determination of the Americans to re-establish republican hegemony was now matched by the British determination to withdraw its military forces from Canada.[39] The putting of the colonies in a state to resist American pressure was the preliminary to the evacuation of the continental garrisons. The British provinces were therefore face to face with reality at last. They had to unite or be annexed; scarcely anyone doubted that by 1864.[40]

There followed the rapid coalescence of the project for union of the Atlantic provinces with the Canadian project of a general union, the quick elaboration of a scheme of union at Quebec, 1864, and its acceptance by the imperial cabinet the following month. When early in the following year New Brunswick rejected the scheme, a precious year was lost, but in 1866 the recalcitrant province was quietly brought into compliance by imperial pressure and Canadian election funds. A growing movement of opposition in Nova Scotia, and the refusal of Newfoundland and Prince Edward Island to come in, were ignored. Fenian attacks on Canada and New Brunswick from American soil stiffened the colonial resolve to unite. In 1867 the imperial parliament brought the provinces together in the Dominion of Canada.

The Consolidation of the New Order, 1867–71

It remained to be seen how the United States would accept this unobtrusive but definite denial of Manifest Destiny and American supremacy. The new Dominion had to face a United States still angry with British policy and attitudes during the Civil War and insistent on reparation for the damages done by the *Alabama*. Around this powerful and irritable power the continent was once more crystallizing. The Mexican empire, abandoned by France to mend its fences on the Rhine, fell before the Mexican republicans, and American hegemony once more prevailed in the Americas, with only the vestiges of Spanish and British empire to be removed at a later date. In the north Russia liquidated its American empire by the sale of Alaska to the United States.

In the United States itself the agrarian republic had perished. The war to preserve the Union had not preserved the contractual democracy of ante-bellum days, for the Union no longer rested on consent of its members, but on the coercion and the forcible reconstruction of one-third of its society. The old South had not only been defeated, it had been destroyed in one of the most ruthless of all modern conquests. American democracy had used the sword not only to chastise rebellion, but also to recreate a dissident society in its own image. And with the death of the first republic came the beginning of the American empire of the second, the heir of all the empires in America.[41]

In the face of such a power, the formation of the British American union was a work of great nerve and infinite tact. The sure touch and unruffled calm of the great Whig liberals, Palmerston, Russell, Clarendon, and Granville, yielded neither to the sapping of Bright in Westminster, nor to the pressure of Seward and Fish from Washington. The United States, for its part, accepted the Dominion, an outcome in the North so different from that in the South, because it was war-weary and involved in reconstruction, because it had the trans-Mississippi West to develop unimpeded, because it had the profits of the new industrial order to absorb, and because it did not expect the ramshackle structure to endure. Manifest Destiny for the moment had no allure, as the reluctance to purchase Alaska revealed.

But the Republic accepted the Dominion also because of compromises with American power and prejudice written into the creation of the new North American nation. Constitutionally a monarchy, it was called a Dominion to spare American susceptibilities. In military alliance with the United Kingdom, there was an understanding that it would not be a military power in its own right, that no defence would be its best defence. A semi-sovereign power, its sovereignty was limited not only by the British connection but still more by the concession to the United States of American claims to temporary rights in its fisheries and by the right to navigate the St Lawrence in perpetuity granted in the Treaty of Washington of 1871. Finally, the United States held the strategic controls on the Pacific—Alaska and San Juan—and on the Atlantic might hope to obtain Newfoundland. Canada was no threat to the integrity of the Union, or to American supremacy in North America.

The establishment of the Dominion of Canada, then, between the Quebec Conference of 1864 and the Treaty of Washington in 1871, was a miracle of political management by the colonial politicians and of unobtrusive pressure on the Atlantic provinces and unhurried negotiation with the United States by the imperial secretaries of state. Nor was the miracle wholly of

British working. Seward and Johnson, Fish and Grant, might have pushed their local advantage much harder than they did. One must indeed ask why the government which had acted and was acting so ruthlessly to destroy a society in the South should have dealt so moderately with the feeble and alien community to the North.

The answer is obviously manifold. Apart from internal factors, such as war-weariness, reconstruction, and the chances of expansion in the West, British steadiness in the great withdrawal from the re-ordered continent was beyond doubt a major element. The respect inherent in the American char-acter and tradition for the self-determination of genuine nationalities played its part, despite much scepticism concerning the validity of Canadian nation-ality. But the main factor was that Canada, because of the British withdrawal, was neither an actual nor a potential threat to the supremacy of the United States in the Americas.[42]

Behind the suavity of the Washington Conference of 1871, then, and between the lines of the Treaty, the fundamentals of the new situation stand out clearly. By British and Canadian acquiescence, as well as by its own imperial will and civil agony, the United States possessed the empire of the Americas. In power and authority it was the sole heir of Spain and France, of Britain and Russia in the Americas, and to the territory of all four north of the Rio Grande and south of the Great Lakes.

The inheritance of the continent, however, was shared north of the Rio Grande with a second American nation, Canada, a nation reared not at all in the American tradition but still American, a country continental in extent if hemmed in by American outposts, an independent state if more with a legal than a political sovereignty, a sovereignty conditioned by the supremacy of the United States.[43]

At the same time, however, and conversely, the empire of the United States in the Americas, the new power system of the hemisphere, was itself con-ditioned by the erection of the British colonies into an independent nation-ality. As it were by a tacit compact, the United States accepted the independence of Canada, provided it were not such as to imperil the con-tinental power system, as Canada acquiesced in the supremacy of the United States in the faith that it would not infringe Canadian independence under the American supremacy.

The dissolution of the continent in 1861, then, had resulted by 1871 in a Mexican revolution made free to continue with American support, if in fact only to stagnate in irrelevant American forms. It had led to the second American republic, the affirmation of the democratic imperialism and national centralization which were, with industrialization, the dynamics of Lincoln's America. And it brought about the British American union, a vindication of the liberal imperialism and strategic caution of Victorian Eng-land. In total the terrible anarchy of 1861 to 1865 had recrystallized in a system of power of which the significance, and the interest, lie in the attempt, so far surprisingly successful, to combine in a working order the undoubted supremacy of one great power with the actual independence of many lesser ones.

Suggestions for Further Reading

Helen Macdonald, *Canadian Opinion in the American Civil War* (New York, 1926).
W.L. Morton, *The Critical Years: The Union of British North America* (Toronto, 1964).
Robin Winks, *Canada and the United States: The Civil War Years* (New York, 1960).

Notes

[1] The remoter consequences of these immediate aims were, for the South, supremacy in the Caribbean, for the North, the reaffirmation of the supremacy of the United States in the Americas. It was because of these remoter aspects of the struggle that Lord John Russell, in his speech at Newcastle-on-Tyne, 14 October 1861, said the North and South were not fighting over slavery or tariffs, but 'the one for empire, the other for power'. *The Times*, 15 October 1861. Leading Northerners, like Charles Summer, bitterly resented this *real-politik* view; the North, he told John Bright, was 'fighting the battle of Civilization'. British Museum, Add. 43390, Bright Papers, Summer to Bright, 15 October 1861. It is no doubt all but impossible to make a just and accurate statement of the circumstances at the beginning of the war. The best attempt remains that of Goldwin Smith, *The United States* (New York, 1893), 247–9.

[2] Expression was first given to their views by Thomas D'Arcy McGee in *The Crown and the Confederation* (Montreal, 1864), and by 'A Colonist' in *A Northern Kingdom* (Montreal, 1864).

[3] University of Nottingham Library, Newcastle Papers, 134, Newcastle to Sir Edmund Head, 5 June 1861.

[4] The practical independence of the colonies was frequently remarked; see, for example, *Archives des Affaires Etrangères, Angleterre, Québec, Correspondance Politique* (hereafter, AAE) 35(4), G. Boilleau to Walevski, 21 January 1860, 'Le Canada est indépendant du fait'.

[5] As has been set out by D.G. Creighton in 'The United States and Canadian Confederation', *Canadian Historical Review* (hereafter, *CHR*) XXXIX (1958), 209–27.

[6] The *Trent* affair has of course been variously viewed. The Canadian historian, F.W. Landon, saw it only as a farcical incident, despite its manifest perils. 'The *Trent* Affair of 1861', *CHR* III (1922), 48–58. It was, however, perhaps the most perilous moment of the war for all concerned, as Allan Nevins suggests: *The War for the Union, i, The Improvised War, 1861–1862* (New York, 1959), 394. For the effect of the French stand on the *Trent* affair, see the recent article by Lynn M. Case, 'La France et l'affaire du "Trent" ', *Revue historique*, juillet-septembre, 1961, 57–86.

[7] See Norman A. Graebner, *Empire on the Pacific: A Study of American Continental Expansion* (New York, 1955).

[8]AAE, 35(31), Boilleau to Thouvenel, 5 February 1861: *ibid.*, 35(39), Boilleau to Thouvenel, 22 May 1861: Newcastle Papers, 11, 348a, Head to Newcastle, 18 February 1861.

[9]AAE, 35(39), Boilleau to Thouvenel, 22 May 1861: 35(41), Boilleau to Thouvenel, 14 June 1861.

[10]See Helen Macdonald, *Canadian Public Opinion on the American Civil War* (New York, 1926) and Robin W. Winks, *Canada and the United States: the Civil War* (New York, 1960), ch. 2.

[11]Winks, *Canada and the United States*, 237–8, 308–34.

[12]See particularly McGee's speech, of 26 September 1861, on 'Canada's Interest in the American Civil War' published in Chas. Murphy (ed.), *D'Arcy McGee, 1825–1868, Speeches and Addresses* (Toronto, 1937), 168–90.

[13]See Winks, *Canada and the United States*, ch. 10.

[14]Russell Papers, Palmerston to Russell, 31 May 1861, 25 June 1861; G.F. Lewis (ed.), *The Letters of Rt. Hon. Sir George Cornwall to Various Friends* (London, 1870), 398, Lewis to Head, 24 June 1861; British Museum, Add. MS. 44099, Gladstone Papers, Argyll to Gladstone, 13 September 1861. This paper had been completed before Kenneth Bourne's 'British Preparations for War with the North, 1861–1862', *English Historical Review*, October 1961, 600–32, appeared. That article presents with clarity and detail the mixture of reluctance and resolution with which British statesmen faced the prospect of war with the North in December 1861.

[15]A. Nevins, *The War for the Union, i: The Improvised War*, 392.

[16]Newcastle Papers, 10, 856, Newcastle to Monck, 14 December 1861; also 15 December 1861: 'War is too likely to be the result.'

[17]It must be said, on the other side, that one factor in the acceptance of neutrality was the widespread belief, which persisted down to 1863 and even 1864, that the South could not be conquered. British memories of the War of Independence, of Napoleon's fate in Russia, even of the war of 1812 and 1814, lay behind this belief.

[18]Newcastle Papers, 11, 390, Monck to Newcastle, 20 December 1861.

[19]H.C. Bell, *Lord Palmerston*, ii, 295; Palmerston wrote to the queen that Great Britain was 'in a better state than at any former time to inflict a severe blow upon and to read a severe lesson to the United States'.

[20]British Mueseum, Add. MS. 43384, Bright Papers, Bright to Cobden, 6 February 1861. 'I agree with you as to the grandeur of the free states, free from political brotherhood with the South. Still it was a noble prospect to see a great continent under one central Republican Govt.—I cannot help hoping it may yet be realized.' *The Times*, 12 August 1862.

[21]H.W.V. Temperley and L.M. Penson, *Foundations of British Foreign Policy from Pitt to Salisbury, 1792–1902*, 296; Gladstone wrote of an independent Southern confederacy, July 1896, 'Lord Palmerston desired this severance as the diminution of a dangerous power, but prudently held his tongue. . . . '

[22]British Museum, Add. MS 44099. Gladstone Papers, Argyll to Gladstone, 13 September 1861, 13 May 1862.

[23]*The Times*, 13 January 1862, Gladstone at Leith; *United Kingdom Debates*, H. of C., 171, 1800, 30 June 1863; quoted in Morley, *Life of Gladstone*, II, 86.

[24]E.g., *The Times*, 9 May 1861, 13 January 1862, 22 July 1862.

[25]Newcastle Papers, 11, 357, Head to Newcastle, 26 April 1861; Special Correspondent [John Rose], *The Times*, 16 January 1862. W.H. Russell, *My Diary North and South*, III, 85, 201.

[26]L. Wolf, *Life of the First Marquis of Ripon* (London, 1921), I, 238–9.

[27]*The Times*, Special Correspondent, 16 January 1862.

[28]*The Times*, From a Correspondent, 8 January 1862; Special Correspondent, 16 January 1862; Own Correspondent (probably W.H. Russell), 21 January 1862. AAE, 35(53) Boilleau to Thouvenel, 27 December 1862.

[29]By the visit of the *Capricieuse* in 1855 and the appointment of a French consul to Quebec in 1858.

[30]AAE, 35(63), Boilleau to Thouvenel, 22 May 1862, emphasizes French-Canadian objection to the cost, which would result in increased taxation; *The Times*, 5 June 1862, letter to Editor by 'P', from Quebec, declared the Bill a bad one, and government sure to have been defeated; defeat of Bill not to be blamed on French.

[31]AAE, 36(82), Boilleau to De Lhuys, 1 May 1863: 'Le Canada met principalement sa confiance dans les ressources des états confédérés, le courage de leurs soldats et l'habileté de leurs chefs.' At no point in the war did any military action by the imperial or colonial authorities lead the Northern government to divert first-line troops to the provincial frontier. I owe this information to Dr Robin W. Winks.

[32]Public Record Office, Russell Papers, Palmerston to Russell, 14 September 1862; Russell to Palmerston, 17 September 1862; British Museum, Gladstone Papers, Gladstone to Palmerston, 25 September 1852.

[33]Public Record Office, Granville Papers, 18, Granville to 'dear Ben', 1 October 1862.

[34]*Ibid.*, Palmerston to Russell, 21, 24 October 1862; Bell, *Palmerston*, II, 326.

[35]*Ibid.*, 328; Russell Papers, Palmerston to Russell, 2 November 1862.

[36]Nevins, *The War for the Union*, II, 242.

[37]Macdonald, *op. cit.*, 114; Winks, *op. cit.*, ch. 11; AAE, 36(87), Boilleau to De Lhuys, 10 July 1863, on bitter disappointment in French Canada on the Receipt of the news of Gettysburg; *ibid.*, 36(91), Boilleau to De Lhuys, 17 September 1863, on loss of confidence in South's capacity to hold out.

[38]Nevins, *The War for the Union*, II, 241.

[39]Not, of course, from the naval base at Halifax.

[40]AAE, 37(5), Gauthier to the Minister, 24 October 1864, reporting what he had learned of the Quebec Conference then in progress.

[41]R.W. Van Alstyne, *The Rising American Empire* (Oxford, 1960), 121–3.

[42]*Library of Congress, MSS. Div.*, Diary of Hamilton Fish, no. 2, vol. I, 173–4, 9 November 1869, a report of a discussion in cabinet in which President Grant said that if England got out of Canada, the United States would be satisfied with actual damages in the *Alabama* case, and the settlement of the law of maritime neutrality. Grant favoured the acquisition of Canada.

[43]*Cf. Westminster Review*, New Series, vol. 27, January–April 1865, 'The Canadian Confederacy', 552. 'For British America there is no absolute independence.' That is, the colonies had to continue the British connection to avoid absorption in the United States. But the reverse was equally true, that to avoid absorption, they had to qualify their independence of American control.